The SAGE
Handbook of

The Philosophy of
Social Sciences

Edited by
Ian C. Jarvie
and Jesús Zamora-Bonilla

Los Angeles | London | New Delhi
Singapore | Washington DC

SAGE Publications Ltd
1 Oliver's Yard
55 City Road
London EC1Y 1SP

SAGE Publications Inc.
2455 Teller Road
Thousand Oaks, California 91320

SAGE Publications India Pvt Ltd
B 1/I 1 Mohan Cooperative Industrial Area
Mathura Road
New Delhi 110 044

SAGE Publications Asia-Pacific Pte Ltd
33 Pekin Street #02-01
Far East Square
Singapore 048763

Library of Congress Control Number: 2010932337

British Library Cataloguing in Publication data

A catalogue record for this book is available from the
British Library

ISBN: 978-1-84787-400-9

Typeset by Glyph International
Printed in Great Britain by MPG Books Group, Bodmin, Cornwall
Printed on paper from sustainable resources

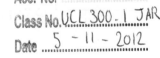

MIX
Paper from
responsible sources
FSC
www.fsc.org
FSC® C018575

Contents

List of Contributors

Joseph Agassi, FRSC, studied in a rabbinical school, in the Hebrew University of Jerusalem (MSc., physics) and in the University of London, where he was an assistant to Karl Popper. He is currently Professor Emeritus in Tel Aviv University and in York University, Toronto. He has edited about ten books, authored twenty plus and has about 500 contributions to the learned press. Among his books are *Towards a Rational Philosophical Anthropology* (The Hague, 1977), *Philosophy from a Skeptical Perspective* (with Abraham Meida; Cambridge University Press, 2008) and *A Critical Rationalist Aesthetics* (with Ian C. Jarvie; Amsterdam, Rodopi, 2008).

Patrick Baert is Reader in Social Theory at the University of Cambridge and a Fellow of Selwyn College, Cambridge. He is interested in social theory, philosophy of the social sciences and the sociology and history of intellectuals. He has written extensively on the implications of neo-pragmatist philosophy for a reflexive notion of the social sciences. Amongst his recent publications are, for instance, *Social Theory in the Twentieth Century and Beyond* (co-written, 2010), *Philosophy of the Social Sciences: Towards Pragmatism* (2005), *Conflict, Citizenship and Society* (co-edited, 2010) and *Pragmatism and European Social Theory* (co-edited, 2007).

Antoinette Baujard is an Associate Professor of Economics at the University of Caen Basse-Normandie since 2004. She has done her PhD under the supervision of Professor Maurice Salles on individual welfare. She works on the definition of welfarism, as well as on the compatibility of utility and freedom in economic contexts. Besides, she has notably organized the quasi-field experiment of new voting rules during the French Presidential elections in 2007.

Anne Beaulieu is Senior Research Fellow at the Virtual Knowledge Studio for the Humanities and Social Sciences (VKS) of the Royal Academy of Arts and Sciences in Amsterdam. Her research follows two main lines: the study of the use of databases and networks in knowledge creation, and the development of new ethnographic approaches to cultural and social phenomena in mediated settings. Together with Sarah de Rijcke (VKS), she is currently pursuing an ethnographic study of knowledge production around databases of images on the web entitled *Network Realism*.

Gregor Betz is Junior Professor of Philosophy of Science at the Karlsruhe Institute of Technology, Germany. He graduated and obtained his PhD at Freie Universität Berlin, before he held positions at the Potsdam Institute of Climate Impact Research, Freie Universität Berlin and Universität Stuttgart. Besides economic forecasting, his main interests in philosophy of science pertain to the methodology of climate science and the role of scientific policy advice in democratic societies. Moreover, he has published a book on argumentation theory (*Theorie dialektischer Strukturen*, Klostermann 2010), and developed the argument-mapping software Argunet (www.argunet.org).

Giacomo Bonanno obtained his PhD in Economics from the London School of Economics in 1985, he spent two years as a Research Fellow at Nuffield College, Oxford and has been at the University of California, Davis since 1987. He is editor of the journal *Economics and Philosophy* and Associate Editor of *Knowledge, Rationality and Action* and *Bulletin of Economics Research*. He is also editor for the Logic and Games section of the *Journal of Logic and Computation* and Advisory Board Member for the book series *Texts in Logic and Games*. He has organized several conferences and workshops, in particular eight of the nine interdisciplinary LOFT conferences. He is the author of more than 60 journal articles and has edited a dozen books and special issues of journals. His web page is at http://www.econ.ucdavis.edu/faculty/bonanno.

Alban Bouvier is currently Senior Fellow at the Institut Jean Nicod (Ecole Normale Superieure of Paris and Ecole des Hautes Etudes en Sciences Sociales, Paris) and Professor at the University of Aix-Marseille I at the Department of Sociology (also affiliated at the Departments of Philosophy and Economics). He obtained his PhD from Sorbonne in 1991. He taught previously at the Sorbonne. He was educated first in philosophy and then in sociology. The main areas of his teaching are the philosophy of social sciences, the philosophy of social phenomena, theoretical sociology, social epistemology and cognitive sociology. His areas of specialization are argumentation theory and its links to rational choice theory, on the one hand, and to social epistemology and cognitive sociology on the other. His publications include *Philosophie des Sciences Sociales*, (ed.) *Pareto aujourd'hui* and *L'argumentation philosophique. Etude de sociologie cognitive*.

Jeroen Van Bouwel is a Postdoctoral Fellow of the Research Foundation (FWO) Flanders, and a member of the Centre for Logic and Philosophy of Science at Ghent University. His research deals with topics in philosophy of the social sciences, social epistemology and general philosophy of science, especially the conundrum of scientific pluralism. His articles have appeared in journals such as *Economics and Philosophy*, *Philosophy of the Social Sciences*, *Foundations of Science, Philosophical Explorations, History and Theory* and *Journal for the Theory of Social Behaviour*, and he is the editor of *The Social Sciences and Democracy* (Palgrave, 2009).

Sun-Ki Chai is Associate Professor at the Department of Sociology, University of Hawaii. He has a BS in Mathematical Sciences, MS in Computer Science and a PhD in Political Science, all from Stanford University. His main theoretical interests are the study of formal models of culture and their integration with choice-theoretic models of action and network models of structure, and finally their implementation in software systems. More recently, he has been doing work on a specialized web crawler that uses social science theories and methods to identify and analyze virtual communities, and to provide better means for locating salient information. He is the author of *Choosing an Identity: A General Model of Preference and Belief Formation* (University of Michigan Press, 2001) and co-editor of *Culture and Social Theory* (Transaction Publishers, 1998) and *Advances in Social Computing* (Springer, 2010). Elsewhere, he has published papers in journals and edited volumes in disciplines ranging from sociology, political science, economics and computer science.

Fred D'Agostino was educated at Amherst College (BA, 1968), Princeton University (MA, 1973) and the London School of Economics (PhD, 1978). He was Research Fellow in Philosophy at the Australian National University from 1978 to 1984, and worked at the University of New England from 1984 to 2004, where he was Associate Dean of Arts, Head of the School of Social Science and Member of the University Council. He is now Professor of Humanities and Associate Dean (Academic) in the Faculty of Arts at The University of Queensland. He has edited the *Australasian Journal of Philosophy,* is currently editing *Politics, Philosophy and Economics* and has published four books – *Chomsky's System of Ideas* (Clarendon Press, 1986), *Free Public Reason* (OUP, 1996), *Incommensurability and Commensuration* (Ashgate, 2003) and *Naturalizing Epistemology* (Palgrave, 2010). He recently completed work on an ARC Discovery Grant project in social epistemology, and on an Australian Learning and Teaching Institute grant for educational leadership development, and is a fellow of the Australian Academy of the Humanities.

Alex Dennis is Lecturer in the Sociology of Deviance at the University of Salford. He wrote *Making Decisions About People: The Organisational Contingencies of Illness* (Ashgate, 2001) and co-edited *Human Agents and Social Structures* with Peter J. Martin (Manchester University Press, 2010). He has written on social theory, ethnomethodology and symbolic interactionism, and his research interests include petty crime, non-criminal deviance, workplace studies and the interactional development and maintenance of knowledge and opinion.

Maarten Derksen is Assistant Professor of Theory and History of Psychology at the University of Groningen, The Netherlands. He has written on the popularisation and demarcation of psychology, on the history of clinical psychology in Great Britain, and on the concept of culture in evolutionary psychology. Boundaries - between nature and culture, psychology and common sense, people and machines - are a recurrent theme in all his work, including that on social technology.

Heather Douglas is Associate Professor in the Department of Philosophy at the University of Tennessee. She received her PhD from the history and philosophy of science department at the University of Pittsburgh in 1998. Her book, *Science, Policy, and the Value-Free Ideal*, was published in 2009 by University of Pittsburgh Press. Her work has been supported by the National Science Foundation, and she is currently a visiting fellow at the Center for Philosophy of Science at the University of Pittsburgh. She has served on the Governing Board of the Philosophy of Science Association, on the steering committee of the International Society for the History of Philosophy of Science, and the Section L committee for the American Association for the Advancement of Science.

Steve Fuller is Professor of Sociology at the University of Warwick. He obtained his PhD from Pittsburgh in 1985. Originally trained in history and philosophy of science, he is best known for his work in the field of 'social epistemology', which addresses normative philosophical questions about organized knowledge by historical and social scientific means. 'Social epistemology' is also the name of a quarterly journal he founded in 1987 and the first of his eighteen books. His most recently published books are *The Sociology of Intellectual Life: The Career of the Mind in and around the Academy* (SAGE, 2009), *Science: The Art of Living* (Acumen, 2010) and *Humanity 2.0: Foundations for 21st Century Social Thought* (Palgrave Macmillan, 2011). In 2007, Fuller was awarded a 'higher doctorate' (DLitt) by Warwick for long-term major contributions to scholarship.

Till Grüne-Yanoff is a Fellow of the Collegium of Advanced Study at the University of Helsinki. Before that he held appointments at the Royal Institute of Technology, Stockholm and the London School of Economics. His research focuses on the methodology of economic modelling, on decision and game theory, and on the notion of preference in the social sciences.

He has published in Journals like *Synthese, Erkenntnis, Theoria, Journal of Economic Methodology*, amongst others, and has edited (together with Sven Ove Hansson) a book on *Modelling Preference Change* (Springer, 2009).

Francesco Guala is Associate Professor in the Department of Economics at the University of Milan. He was previously Associate Professor of Philosophy at the University of Exeter. He is the author of *The Methodology of Experimental Economics* (Cambridge, 2005) and co-editor with Dan Steel of *The Philosophy of Social Science Reader* (Routledge, 2010). His articles on methodology and ontology have appeared in many social science and philosophy journals.

Stephan Hartmann is Chair of Epistemology and Philosophy of Science at Tilburg University and founding director of the Tilburg Center for Logic and Philosophy of Science (since 2007). He obtained his PhD in Philosophy from the University of Giessen in 1995. He has been publishing extensively on various topics from philosophy of science and formal epistemology.

Peter Hedström is an Official Fellow of Nuffield College, a Professor of Sociology at the University of Oxford and a well-known authority in the field of analytical sociology. He is particularly interested in the analysis of diffusion processes and complex social networks, as well as the methodology of the social sciences.

Frank Hindriks is Assistant Professor at the Department of Philosophy of the University of Groningen. His research interests include social ontology, political philosophy, economic methodology, philosophy of action and ethics. He was awarded a research grant by the Netherlands Organization for Scientific Research for his project Normativity in Action: A New Theory of Moral Responsibility. He has published in journals such as *Economics and Philosophy Erkenntnis, Philosophical Quarterly and Philosophical Studies*.

Geoffrey Hodgson is a Research Professor at the University of Hertfordshire and Editor-in-Chief of the *Journal of Institutional Economics*. Among his publications are *Darwin's Conjecture: The Search for General Principles of Social and Economic Evolution* (2010, with Thorbjørn Knudsen), *The Evolution of Institutional Economics* (2004), *How Economics Forgot History* (2001), *Economics and Evolution* (1993) and over 120 academic journal articles.

Ian Jarvie is Distinguished Research Professor Emeritus at York University, Toronto. He is Managing Editor of the SAGE journal *Philosophy of the Social Sciences*. His most recent books are *The Republic of Science: The Emergence of Popper's Social View of Science 1935–1945* (Rodopi, 2001) and (with Joseph Agassi) *A Critical Rationalist Aesthetics* (Rodopi, 2008). Besides ongoing research into social science methods, he hopes one day to complete his sociological study *Mass Media Pornography*.

María Jiménez-Buedo is a Research Fellow at the Department of Logic, History and Philosophy of Science at UNED in Madrid. She holds a PhD in Social and Political Science from the European University Institute and an MSc in Philosophy of the Social Sciences from the London School of Economics. She has worked in the fields of political economy, science policy and philosophy of the social sciences, with an emphasis on methodological issues. Some of her recent work has been published in the *International Journal of Comparative Sociology*, the *American Journal of Economics and Sociology* and *Theoria*.

Laurence Kaufmann is currently Professor of Sociology at the University of Lausanne, Switzerland, after several years of research in France and in the United States. Her publications are primarily concerned with the ontology of social facts, from a historical and sociological point of view (how institutions emerge and change over time) as well as from a philosophical and psychological perspective (what abilities human beings need to build to maintain the strange "entities" the institutions are). She has recently edited, with D.Trom, a collection of essays titled *Qu'est-ce qu'un collectif? Du commun au politique*, Paris, EHESS, 2010.

Anthony King is a Professor of Sociology at Exeter University, UK. He has written widely on football, social theory and the armed forces, including his book on overcoming structure and agency, *The Structure of Social Theory* (Routledge, 2004). He has just finished a book on the military called, *The Transformation of Europe's Armed Forces: from the Rhine to Afghanistan* (Cambridge, 2010).

Tarja Knuuttila is a Senior Research Associate in Philosophy at the University of Helsinki. She holds degrees in philosophy (MA and PhD, University of Helsinki) and economics and business administration (MSc, Helsinki School of Economics). The main themes of her work have been modelling and scientific representation, the methodology of economics as well as the commodification of science. She has published on these themes in numerous edited books and in many journals, including *Erkenntnis, Philosophy of Science, Science, Technology and Human Values, Science Studies, Semiotica, Studies in History and Philosophy of Science* and *Forum: Qualitative Social Research*.

Hans-Herbert Kögler is Professor and Chair at the Department of Philosophy at the University of North Florida, Jacksonville. He obtained his PhD from the Goethe University of Frankfurt in 1991, graduate studies at Northwestern University, the New School and Berkeley, teaching since 1991 in the US. He is a frequent guest professor at the Alpe-Adria University, Klagenfurt/ Austria and the Czech Academy of Social Sciences, Prague. Research interests cover social philosophy, the philosophy of the social sciences, hermeneutics, accounts of agency and power, intercultural understanding and conditions of cosmopolitanism. Major publications include *The Power of Dialogue: Critical Hermeneutics after Gadamer and Foucault*, (German 1992, American 1996, 1999); *Michel Foucault* (2nd edition, 2004), *Kultura, kritika, dialog* (Prague, 2006) and the co-edited volume *Empathy and Agency: The Problem of Understanding in the Human Sciences* (2000). Participation in special journal issues concerning 'New Directions in the Sociology of Knowledge' (Social Epistemology, 1997, based on Kögler's target article), 'Human Agency and Development' (New Ideas in Psychology, 2010), and 'Rational Agency as Ethical Life' (Inquiry, 2010).

Jaakko Kuorikoski is a Post-doc Researcher at the University of Helsinki. His work is centred on the themes of explanation and modelling, mainly in economics and the other social sciences. He has published on topics such as comparing and relating explanations, different concepts of mechanism, the ontology and epistemology of models and the conceptualization of understanding in the context of simulation in journals such as *The British Journal for the Philosophy of Science, Erkenntnis, International Studies in the Philosophy of Science, Philosophical Studies, Philosophy of Science* and *Philosophy of the Social Sciences*.

Daniel Little is Chancellor of the University of Michigan-Dearborn. He serves as Professor of Philosophy at UM-Dearborn and Professor of Sociology at the University of Michigan-Ann Arbor. His research interests lie within the philosophy and methodology of the social sciences.

He is the author or editor of eight books, including most recently *The Paradox of Wealth and Poverty: Mapping the Ethical Dilemmas of Global Development* (Westview Press, 2003), *The Future of Diversity* (Palgrave, 2010, edited with Satya Mohanty) and *New Contributions to the Philosophy of History* (Springer, 2010). He serves as a book review editor for the *Journal of Asian Studies* and is a regular participant in the Social Science History Association. His academic blog can be found at understandingsociety.blogspot.com.

C. Mantzavinos holds the Chair of Economics and Philosophy at Witten/Herdecke University, Germany. He is the author of *Wettbewerbstheorie* (Berlin: Duncker & Humblot, 1994), *Individuals, Institutions, and Markets* (Cambridge: Cambridge University Press, 2001) and *Naturalistic Hermeneutics* (Cambridge: Cambridge University Press, 2005) and the editor of *Philosophy of the Social Sciences* (Cambridge: Cambridge University Press, 2009). He has published numerous articles in scholarly journals in four languages, notably 'Learning, Institutions, and Economic Performance' in *Perspectives on Politics*, 2004 (with Douglass North and Syed Shariq). He has taught at Freiburg, Bayreuth and Stanford, was a Senior Research Fellow at the Max Planck Institute and served as a Visiting Scholar at Harvard (twice) and at Maison des Sciences de l'Homme, Paris (twice). He holds two PhDs, one in Economics and one in Philosophy, both from the University of Tübingen, Germany.

Joan de Martí is an Assistant Professor at Universitat Pompeu Fabra. His research interests include: game theory, social networks, organization theory and economics of identity. His research has been published in journals such as the *American Economic Review* and the *Journal of the European Economic Association*.

Martin Morris teaches the Social and Political Theory of Communication at Wilfrid Laurier University in Ontario, Canada. His research interests include critical theory, communication and justice, democratic theory, cultural political theory and 'embodied' cognition. He is currently working on a book project entitled *Communicative Power: Body, Mind, and the Political*.

Véronique Mottier is Fellow and Director of Studies in Social and Political Sciences at Jesus College, Cambridge as well as part-time Professor in Sociology at the University of Lausanne. Her research interests are in the areas of discourse theory, French social theory and politics of sexuality and gender. Her books include *Sexuality* (Sterling, 2010), *Sexuality: A Very Short Introduction* (Oxford University Press, 2008) and the co-edited *Pflege, Stigmatisierung und Eugenik* (2007), *Genre et politique* (Gallimard, 2000) and *Politics of Sexuality: Identity, Gender, Citizenship* (Routledge,1998).

Cédric Paternotte obtained his PhD in Cooperation and Collective Actions from IHPST/ Université Paris 1, Sorbonne and is currently a Postdoctoral student within the Evolution, Cooperation and Rationality project, Department of Philosophy, University of Bristol.

Fabienne Peter is an Associate Professor of Philosophy at the University of Warwick. She specializes in political philosophy and in issues at the intersection of economics and philosophy. She is the author of *Democratic Legitimacy* (Routledge, 2008). Her articles have appeared in journals such as *Economics and Philosophy*, *Episteme*, and *Politics, Philosophy, and Economics*. She has co-edited a volume on public health ethics with Sudhir Anand and Amartya Sen (*Public Health, Ethics, and Equity*, OUP 2004), and a volume on *Rationality and Commitment* (with Hans Bernhard Schmid, OUP 2007).

Andreas Pickel is Professor of Global Politics and Director of the Centre for the Critical Study of Global Power and Politics at Trent University in Canada. Over the past two decades he has published on problems in the philosophy of the social sciences, postcommunist transformations, nationalism and global order. His current work focuses on developing systemism and mechanisms-based explanation as a framework and approach in the social and cultural sciences.

Angel Díaz de Rada holds tenure in the Department of Social and Cultural Anthropology at the UNED, Spain. As ethnographer, he has worked on scholastic institutions and education, expressive culture and ethnic processes, in several urban and rural places in Spain and north Norway. A line of work, parallel to these ones, has been methodology and epistemology of ethnography. He has authored *Los primeros de la clase y los últimos románticos. Una etnografía para la crítica de la visión instrumental de la enseñanza* (1996); and coauthored, among other books, *La lógica de la investigación etnográfica* (1997, with Prof. Honorio Velasco) and *La sonrisa de la institución. Confianza y riesgo en sistemas expertos* (2006). In English, he has contributed with Prof. Francisco Cruces to volumes edited by Jeremy Boissevain (*Revitalizing European Rituals*, 1992), Kirsten Hastrup and Peter Hervik (*Social Experience and Anthropological Knowledge*, 1994) and Åsa Boholm (*Political Ritual*, 1996). His article "School Bureaucracy, Ethnography and Culture: Conceptual Obstacles to Doing Ethnography in Schools" (*Social Anthropology*, 15, 2, 2007) is the access door to the elaboration of the concept of culture which is presented in this volume and in his last book *Cultura, antropología y otras tonterías* (2010).

Julian Reiss has taught at several European universities and is currently Associate Professor in the Philosophy Department of Erasmus University Rotterdam. He received his degree from the University of St. Gallen, Switzerland, and his PhD from the London School of Economics. He specialises in philosophy of economics and general philosophy of science and is the author of *Error in Economics: Towards a More Evidence-Based Methodology* (Routledge, 2008), *Causality Between Metaphysics and Methodology* (forthcoming with Routledge), 'Causation in the Social Sciences: Evidence, Inference, and Purpose', *Philosophy of the Social Sciences* 39(1): 2009, 'Counterfactuals, Thought Experiments and Singular Causal Analysis in History', *Philosophy of Science* 76(5): 2009, 'The Philosophy of Simulation: Hot New Topic or Same Old Stew?' (with Roman Frigg), *Synthese* 169(3): 2009.

Don Ross is Professor of Economics and Dean of Commerce at the University of Cape Town, and Research Fellow at the Center for Economic Analysis of Risk at Georgia State University. Until 2010 he was also Professor of Philosophy at the University of Alabama at Birmingham. He is the author of several books and numerous articles on the foundations of economics, interrelationships among the behavioral and social sciences, the experimental economics and neuroeconomics of impulsive consumption and trade and industry policy in Africa.

Paul Roth is a Professor in the Department of Philosophy at UC-Santa Cruz. His research and publications focus on problems of explanation in the natural and social sciences, especially historical explanation. He also works on topics related to Quine, naturalized epistemology and the theory of meaning. For information regarding recent publications, see his web page at: http://philosophy.ucsc.edu/directory/details.php?id=10.

Maurice Salles is Professor of Economics Emeritus at the University of Caen-Basse-Normandie, Honorary Research Associate at the Center for Philosophy of the Natural and Social Science at the London School of Economics, and member of the Murat Sertel Center at

Bilgi University in Istanbul. He is Coordinating Editor of 'Social Choice and Welfare' and President-elect of the 'Society for Social Choice and Welfare'.

Kai Spiekermann is a Lecturer in Political Philosophy at the London School of Economics. Among his areas of interest are political philosophy, ethics, decision theory and philosophy of science. His research focuses on social norms, cooperation, social epistemology and issues arising from environmental change.

Jan Sprenger is Assistant Professor of Philosophy at Tilburg University (since 2008). He obtained his PhD in Philosophy from the University of Bonn in 2008. Jan's work focuses on philosophy of statistics, philosophy of probability, decision theory and formal modelling in social epistemology.

Daniel Steel is an Associate Professor of Philosophy at Michigan State University. His research interests are in the philosophy of science, with a particular emphasis on issues relating to causation and inductive inference that arise in social and biological sciences. His work has appeared in such journals as *Philosophy of the Social Sciences*, *British Journal for the Philosophy of Science*, *Biology and Philosophy*, *Philosophy of Science* as well as in a book titled, *Across the Boundaries: Extrapolation in Biology and Social Science* (Oxford, 2008).

David Teira is Associate Professor in the Department of Logic, History and Philosophy of Science at Universidad Nacional de Educacion a Distancia, Madrid, Research Associate of the Urrutia Elejalde Foundation and Deputy Editor of Theoria. An International Journal for Theory, History and Foundations of Science. He works on the history and philosophy of statistics, analysing how it is used in economics and medicine. Recent publications include 'The Politics of Positivism: Disinterested Predictions from interested agents' [in U. Mäki, ed., The Methodology of Positive Economics, Cambridge U.P., 2009)] and 'Frequentist versus Bayesian Clinical Trials' [in Fred Gifford, ed., Philosophy of Medicine (Handbook of Philosophy of Science, vol. 16), Elsevier, 2010].

Erik Weber is Professor in Philosophy of Science at Ghent University (UGent). Most of his research relates to general theories of causation and explanation, or to problems relating to causation and explanation in specific scientific disciplines (mathematics, psychology and the social sciences). He also works on the application of non-classical logics in the philosophy of science. His articles have appeared in journals such as *Analysis*, *Economics and Philosophy*, *International Studies in the Philosophy of Science*, *History and Theory*, *Logique et Analyse*, *Philosophy of the Social Sciences* and *Synthese*.

Darin Weinberg is University Senior Lecturer in the Department of Sociology, Cambridge University and a Fellow of King's College, Cambridge. His research focuses primarily on the practical purposes to which concepts of addiction, mental disorder and learning disability are applied in various historical and contemporary contexts. He is particularly interested in how these concepts figure in state-sponsored campaigns of social welfare and social control, and in what their uses reveal about how and why people distinguish the social and natural forces held to govern human behaviour. His books include *Of Others Inside: Insanity, Addiction, and Belonging in America* (2005), *Talk and Interaction in Social Research Methods* (edited with Paul Drew and Geoffrey Raymond, 2006) and *Qualitative Research Methods* (edited, 2002).

Petri Ylikoski is an Academy Research Fellow at University of Helsinki. His specialities are philosophy of social sciences, philosophy of biology and science studies. He is particularly interested in issues related to explanation, evidence and disciplinary relations.

Jesús Zamora-Bonilla is Professor of Philosophy of Science in the Department of Logic, History, and Philosophy of Science of the National Open University of Spain (U.N.E.D.), Madrid, and holds a PhD in both Philosophy and Economics. His research has centered on scientific realism and on the application of rational choice theory to philosophy of science. Some of his recent papers in international journals are 'An economic model of scientific rules' (*Economics and Philosophy*, 2006, with J.L. Ferreira), 'Rhetoric, induction, and the free speech dilemma' (*Philosophy of Science*, 2006), 'Optimal judgment aggregation' (*Philosophy of Science*, 2007), 'Credibility, idealization, and model building: an inferential approach' (*Erkenntnis*, 2009, with X. Donato) and 'What games do scientists play?' (*EPSA: Epistemology and Methodology of Science*, 2010). He has authored several books in Spanish.

Yves Zenou is Professor of Economics at Stockholm University and Senior Research Fellow at the Research Institute of Industrial Economics. His research interests include: Social interactions and network theory, urban economics, segregation and discrimination of ethnic minorities, criminality and education. He is currently the Editor of *Regional Science and Urban Economics*, and Associate Editor of the *Journal of Public Economic Theory*, the *Journal of Urban Economics*, the *Journal of Urban Management*, the *Scandinavian Journal of Economics* and *Annals of Economics and Statistics*.

Acknowledgements

The present project is as an outcome of the Summer School on 'New Philosophy of the Social Sciences' that editor Jesús Zamora-Bonilla organised at the University of the Basque Country (San Sebastian, Spain, July 2006), under the patronage of the Urrutia Elejalde Foundation. Many of the participants in that exceptional meeting have contributed original chapters to *The SAGE Handbook of The Philosophy of Social Sciences*. However, the project soon expanded far beyond the limits of that Summer School, comprising a systematic and up-to-date survey of topics and a truly international team of authors. We want to thank in the first place all the contributors, for the quality of their work and their patience with the editors' requirements. We also thank the members of the advisory board for their help and support. We further thank Miranda del Corral, María Jiménez-Buedo, Ana María Rodríguez Fernández and David Teira for their invaluable assistance in carrying out the project.

Special thanks are given to the Urrutia Elejalde Foundation and to the Spanish Government's research project 'Towards a new foundation of the social sciences' (FFI2008-03607/FISO), for their financial and institutional help.

The editors

Advisory Board

Introduction

Philosophical Problems of the Social Sciences: Paradigms, Methodology and Ontology

Ian Jarvie

We are not students of some subject matter but students of problems. And problems may cut right across the borders of any subject matter or discipline.

Popper (1952: 67)[1]

'Philosophy of the social sciences' designates a set of problems that repeatedly emerges from, and within, the social sciences. This is akin to the way philosophy of science is a set of problems that emerges from, and at times even within, science in general and natural science in particular. It is also an intellectualist characterisation of the subject of this handbook. Such a characterisation needs to be complemented: any academic subject is also a social institution that has developed its own traditions (Fuller, Chapter 35). Subjects are institutionalised within the commonwealth of learning as disciplines and these days also in the modern university as departments or sub-departments. The social sciences entered academe as intellectual concerns and rose to become academic departments, in some places achieving the status of a faculty. The philosophy of the social sciences emerged within the social sciences in much the same manner that philosophy of science emerged within science. Philosophy of the social sciences is taught as a field or subject both in certain social science and in some philosophy programmes. Like the philosophy of science its earliest literature is written by social scientists themselves.

As a set of problems, the philosophy of the social sciences is wide-ranging, untidy, interdisciplinary and constantly being reconfigured in response to new problems thrown up by developments in the social sciences; in short, disorderly. As an institutionalised discipline, by contrast, philosophy of the social sciences emerged from the academic division of labour that fosters specialisation and professionalisation, that is, order and discipline. There is always a tension between the unruliness of intellectual inquiry and the urge towards order and discipline. The imposition of order and discipline is useful for textbook design or for surveys, for example, this handbook. But we need to avoid excessive emphasis on bureaucratic or technical matters if we are not to thwart inquiry. Intellectual tidiness is a scholastic rather than scientific virtue.

Although the field was from the start an amorphous cluster of problems, there was perhaps one question that was formative: should inquiry into the problems of society proceed in the same way as inquiry into the problems of nature? The modern background was this. One view of the difference between the American and French Revolutions was that the latter, but not the former, had attempted to remake society from top to bottom. All of society was to be rationally reconstituted. The impulse was to rectify the social order under the dictates of reason. Critics charged that applying reason to society led directly to the Terror (launched against the enemies of reason). Such criticism assumed that pre-existing social restraints were not rational (authority, religion, monarchy). Their overthrow and replacement in the name of reason and order resulted in catastrophe. A rational approach to improving society could easily make things worse, perhaps much worse. Hence, it was said, a purely rational (viz. scientific) approach to society and its defects rested on a dangerous misunderstanding. Conclusion: the rational experimental approach should be confined to nature (Guala, Chapter 30). This line of reasoning stimulated a debate between two parties who have been labelled the 'anti-naturalists' and the 'pro-naturalists'. The former argued that thinking about society in the same way as we think about the experimental exploration of nature was an error. The latter rejected the claim that rational scientific thought was a cause of the Terror, arguing instead that reason remained the greatest hope of humanity for enlightenment and emancipation. The Terror was an unintended and unwanted consequence of the actions of individuals who could, and definitely should, have avoided it. Their error does not discredit reason as applied to society

as such; it does not warrant giving up the rational approach to society and its deficiencies.[2] Underlying the controversy was a first-order problem, how rational are humans and their society? This problem links to another: How best can we grow our knowledge of human social life?

Traditionalists tend to be anti-naturalists and so they are inclined to the view that knowledge of society is practical and built into its operations. Anti-naturalists are inclined to deny, and pro-naturalists to affirm, that folk knowledge of society is just as riddled with error as folk knowledge of nature. On the pro-naturalistic view, growing our knowledge of the social consists mostly of refutations of folk knowledge and of other pre-scientific ideas. The social science that replaces them is often counter-intuitive. The professionalising of the social sciences in the twentieth century entrenched the dominance of the pro-naturalists, but philosophical balance requires registering and assessing extant anti-naturalist arguments. Overcoming those arguments often shaped the programmes of the naturalists.

A 'handbook', originally a manual of practicalities, has taken on an expanded meaning in scholarship, where it is expected to include concise reference material covering a given field.[3] The metaphor of a 'field' means firstly a division of the facts of the world. Examples of social science fields would be economics, sociology and history.[4] The field metaphor begins to crack when practitioners of these subjects assert imperial claims to be *the* comprehensive or master social science. In the twentieth century, historiography and historical explanation played a role in the emergence of philosophy of the social sciences (Gardiner, 1959).[5] History is the field concerned with the past, including economic and social facts, hence economic history and historical sociology. What then to make of the oxymoronic field of 'contemporary history'? When history is construed narrowly as political history, then 'contemporary history' is recent political history. More widely construed, history may be the history of any field. In that case to explain what 'contemporary history' means we need to turn to another meaning of 'field': contemporary history claims to apply the *methods* of history to the study of contemporaneous facts. 'Methods' or 'methodology' need spelling out. They can refer to sheer technique, for example statistical regression analysis; or to an overall approach, a rational or a scientific one, for example, rational reconstruction. Considered as sheer technique, the philosophy of the social sciences is a set of technical and conceptual nuts and bolts. Such a tight focus would make this volume a handbook in the original sense. A broader understanding would attach such *technicalia* to their long tail of history and of problematics. To the present editors this latter alternative seems the more useful to the student and researcher; it also offers a longer shelf-life. Moreover, the field is a hybrid and only parts of it would be captured by the narrower approach.[6] In our view methodological issues in the field are easier to grasp and are better grasped if presented with some indications of their historical lineage and problematics, both first-order and philosophical. Hence in designing this handbook we have included some chapters that look at the way the subject has been built up and we have given all authors the option to include such material in their guides to contemporary sub-divisions of the field. We acknowledge that our choice reveals our own metaphysical and methodological bias towards situating technical matters in their original context so as to render them more understandable, while recognising that their significance lies in their having acquired broader domains of application.

We have divided the handbook into three parts: ontology, paradigms and methods. 'Ontology' addresses the entities and processes of the social world (and whether they can/should be distinguished from those of the natural world). 'Paradigms' looks at the main approaches to social science, their strengths and their weaknesses. 'Methods' encompasses the variegated methodologies that have been used in the social sciences and the problems that have been identified with them. Such a division is already highly contentious. Naturalists would tend not to place ontology first, as a prior philosophy, since they would expect ontological questions to be deferred to science: we look to science to tell us what there is. Those interested in causal explanation divide between those who think it is somehow a matter of metaphysics and those who think it is strictly a matter of method. (Not to mention those who think metaphysics and method come in package deals.) Consider also the placement of the issue of objectivity: the word appears both in the title of Chapter 14, listed under ontology, and Chapter 28, under methodology and assessment. There being no perfect solution to the matter of organisation, it behooves this Introduction to try to put ours into context. The reader will not always find perfect agreement between the presentation of issues in this Introduction and their presentation in the individual chapters. This is, perhaps, as it should be. Philosophy is a field of contestation. The hope is always that debate and argument throws some light on the matters at hand.

ON ACADEMIC DISCIPLINES IN GENERAL AND PHILOSOPHY OF THE SOCIAL SCIENCES IN PARTICULAR

We begin with the emergence of the philosophy of the social sciences as an arena of thought and as a set of social institutions. The two characterisations overlap but are not congruent.

Academic disciplines are social institutions. Before venturing further, let me sketch my broad understanding of social institutions. My view is that institutions are all those social entities that organise action: they link acting individuals into social structures. There are various kinds of institutions. Hegelians and Marxists emphasise universal institutions such as the family, rituals, governance, economy and the military. These are mostly institutions that just grew. Perhaps in some imaginary beginning of time they spontaneously appeared. In their present incarnations, however, they are very much the product of conscious attempts to mould and plan them. We have family law, established and disestablished churches, constitutions and laws, including those governing the economy and the military. Institutions deriving from statute, like joint-stock companies are formal by contrast with informal ones such as friendships. There are some institutions that come in both informal and formal variants, as well as in mixed ones. Consider the fact that the stock exchange and the black market are both market institutions, one formal one not. Consider further that there are many features of the work of the stock exchange that rely on informal, non-codifiable agreements, not least the language used for communication. To be precise, mixtures are the norm: if we are tempted to think of a university as created by statute from whole cloth we make an error. The idea of a university has a known history, where it crystallises out of earlier institutions serving different purposes some enacted (medical training; the need to train clergymen), some spontaneous (students' need to find crammers). From constitutions at the top to by-laws near the bottom we are always adding to, or tinkering with, earlier institutions, the grown and the designed are intertwined.

It is usual in social thought to treat culture and tradition as different from, although alongside, institutions. The view taken here is different. Culture and tradition are sub-sets of institutions analytically isolated for explanatory or expository purposes. Some social scientists have taken all institutions, even purely local ones, to be entities that satisfy basic human needs – under local conditions (Malinowski). Others differed and declared any structure of reciprocal roles and norms an institution. Most of these differences are differences of emphasis rather than disagreements. Let us straddle all these versions and present institutions very generally (like Agassi) as structures that serve to coordinate the actions of individuals.[7] Institutions themselves then have no aims or purpose other than those given to them by actors or used by actors to explain them (Agassi, 1960, 1975; Popper, 1945: Chapter 7, n23).

Language is the formative institution for social life and for science (Hindriks, Chapter 5). Both formal and informal language is involved, naturally grown or designed. (Language is all of these to varying degrees.) Languages are paradigms of institutions or, from another perspective, nested sets of institutions. Syntax, semantics, lexicon and alphabet/character-set are all institutions within the larger institutional framework of a written language. Natural languages are typical examples of what Ferguson called 'the result of human action, but not the execution of any human design' (Ferguson, 1767: Part 3, Section2; see Hayek, 1967); reformed natural languages and artificial languages introduce design into their modifications or refinements of natural language. Above all, languages are paradigms of institutional tools that function to coordinate.

The moment of articulation in language marks a threshold between *thoughts and beliefs* that are more on the private side and *assertions* that are more on the public side, especially rituals, decrees and public proclamations. Assertions take the values of true and false, of adequate or not to the problems that they are intended to solve. Sciences, natural and social, are sets of public assertions together with attempts to assess their truth or falsity, their adequacy to the problems they address. This claim is quite radical: science is not belief in any shape or form. Sciences (other than psychology) need not concern themselves with what goes on in scientists' heads or with what they or the public 'believes'. Sciences offer public claims than can be tested. What people choose to believe is a separate and private matter.

So 'philosophy of the social sciences' is the name both of a set of linked social institutions and of a vaguely demarcated arena of thought. The social institutions include courses, journals, readers, text-books, library classifications,[8] conferences, sub-departments and special subjects. At play in the resultant arena of thought are many sub-institutions: problems, ideas, schools of thought and debates. The lists in the previous two sentences are all social institutions (Jarvie, 1972, 2001). Perhaps we had better distinguish those institutions that comprise the content of the subject from those institutions that house that content. Philosophers of the social sciences devote most of their attention to content and especially its methodological and ontological aspects. Its institutional aspects are also important. Institutional housing is inescapable, no doubt, but the current trend towards professionalisation and specialisation is vulnerable to the criticism that it allows the originating problems to be buried and the clarifying debates to be forgotten.

As an institutionalised speciality, the philosophy of the social sciences is a relatively recent arrival. One criterion of achieving institutionalisation is a specialised literature. The first two social sciences to emerge in the modern period – history and economics – discussed ontological and methodological questions as part and parcel of their specialist literature. Their methods and their relations to one another fuelled the first great debate about method (the *Methodenstreit* – of the late 1880s and early 1890s). Gradually there began to appear institutions housing non-discipline specific discussion of the methodological and philosophical issues thrown up by social science research. The first dedicated English-language journal was *Studies in Philosophy and Social Science* which lasted from 1939 to 1941.[9] English-language work appeared in the cognate journals of general philosophy of science *Philosophy of Science* (founded 1934) and *The British Journal for the Philosophy of Science* (founded 1951).[10] More specialised journals followed: *Inquiry* (founded 1958), *Theory and Decision* (founded 1970), *Philosophy of the Social*

Sciences (founded 1971), *Journal for the Theory of Social Behavior* (founded 1971) and *Economics and Philosophy* (founded 1985). The present handbook is a self-exemplifying case. Given publication pressure, these journals created incentives for research in this field. Earlier, classic papers appeared in first-order social science research journals and also turned up in journals of general philosophy. Two formative examples: Ernest Gellner's seminal 'Time and theory in social anthropology' appeared in *Mind* in 1958 and Peter Winch's much-discussed 'Understanding a primitive society' appeared in *American Philosophical Quarterly* in 1964. Despite the present existence of specialised organs in the philosophy of the social sciences, the literature in it is still scattered and the diligent researcher needs to cast a wide net especially as regards multi-authored volumes which still sometimes elude search engines and their associated databases.

The field is already big enough to be fragmented. Three rough divisions would be: literatures deriving from economics and politics; from psychology and from sociology, anthropology and history. Those interested in economics lay much stress on testability, methodological individualism and rational calculation, including games and choice. By contrast the latter group is much given to discussing causation in history and society, the nature of social wholes, problems of meaning and the social construction of reality. Psychology is an area where much of the discussion we might think of as philosophy of the social sciences is carried out in the pages of its own journals.[11]

Compounding the scattered character of the article literature, the book-length monograph remains a favoured format. Examples of important monographs include the German-language literature of the first *Methodenstreit* by Dilthey, Rickert and Windelband, out of which came Weber's commentaries, especially his *Roscher and Knies: the Logical Problems of Historical Economics* (1903) and *Critique of Stammler* (1907), as well as his other works. Georg Simmel's more or less unclassifiable work comes from this milieu. Durkheim's *Rules of Sociological Method* (1895) emerged from a different problematic and there was a flurry of material published during the second world war, Hayek's 'Scientism and the study of society' (1942–1944, book version 1952), Neurath's *Foundations of the Social* Sciences (1944), Popper's 'The poverty of historicism' (1944–1945, book version 1957) and Kaufmann's *The Methodology of the Social Sciences* (1944 developed from a German original of 1936). Alfred Schutz merits mention here too, not least because he was once a collaborator of Kaufmann's. Unlike Kaufmann, however, he continued to work within a Husserlian framework. For English-language scholars there were huge gaps of untranslated material in German and French that only began to be filled in the post-World War II period. Schutz's 1932 book was only published in translation in 1967, like his collected papers, appearing only posthumously (1962–1966). The appearance of such translations was another mark that philosophy and methodology of the social sciences was becoming an active field of research in its own right, as was the publication of works clearly designed for undergraduate teaching.

The first teaching instruments were readers or anthologies, viz. Feigl and Brodbeck (1953), which included an influential section on 'philosophy of the social sciences'. It was followed by Gardiner (1959) and Brodbeck (1968), both showing by their bulk just how much the literature had burgeoned since 1953 and how the range of problems was expanding. There was enough material for a volume rather than a section of a volume. The popularity of these works indicates a demand, explicable by reference to a growing list of problems (see Table 1). Those that the Feigl and Brodbeck anthology covered were classical (i.e. versions of problems considered by Mill): whether the complexity of social phenomena made them intractable to science (Morris Cohen), whether social science can be value-free (J.A. Passmore), whether the role of *Verstehen* (comprehension)

weakens the claim to scientific status (Theodore Abel), whether the logic of historical explanation can be assimilated to the model intended for explanations in the natural sciences (Ernest Nagel), whether 'dialectic' can contribute to knowledge (Sidney Hook), whether there are laws of history (Edgar Zilsel), whether Weber's ideal types are explanatorily effective and sufficiently individualistic (J.W.N Watkins), and what are the scope and method of economics (Oscar Lange).

Gardner's volume covered historical explanation, social laws, ideal types and the holism/individualism dispute. The expanded problem-set in Brodbeck's anthology (1968) was: what is the explanation of human action; can the social sciences be *wertfrei*; what is the logic of functional explanation (King, Chapter 21); are social facts to be explained by means of social laws (Hedström and Ylikoski, Chapter 18); are explanation and prediction two sides of the same logical coin (Betz, Chapter 34); what are social theories; how do the social sciences use models and measurement (Knuuttila and Kuorikoski, Chapter 28); and is there a conflict between free will theories and determinism? Between the publication of these two readers had come the sceptical monograph of Winch (1958) *The Idea of a Social Science* to be discussed in the next section. Subsequently, both Quentin Gibson (1960) and the present writer published pro-naturalistic monographs (1964, 1972), as did Richard Rudner (1966). Maurice Natanson edited a reader with catholic selection criteria in 1963, David Braybrooke a slim analytic one in 1965. In the flurry of publishing activity from this period we should not overlook Borger and Cioffi's anthology of original contributions, *Explanation in the Behavioural Sciences* (1970), and the highly influential anthology of previously published contributions edited by Bryan Wilson as *Rationality* (1970). For a longer list see Table I.2.

Feigl and Brodbeck were philosophers aligned with logical empiricism and so their anthology unabashedly promoted the

Table 1.1[1] Principal Problems in Philosophy of the Social Sciences

What sorts of entities and processes populate the social world
and what knowledge do we have of them?

Are or can social studies be sciences?
- on Bacon's criteria for science;
- on Whewell's criteria for science;
- on Duhem's criteria for science;
- on the Logical Positivist criteria for science;
- on Popper's criteria for science;
- on Kuhn's criteria for science

If so, do social studies aim to explain or understand (in the sense of *Verstehen*) social phenomena, or both?
How (if at all) can understanding (in the sense of *Verstehen*) be explanatory?

What is the logic and role of
- causal explanation in social studies?
- functional explanation there?
- historical explanation there?
- rational explanation there?

What difference do the following peculiarities of social studies make?
- their complexity;
- their self-fulfilling (Oedipus) effect;
- their use of *Verstehen* or empathy;
- their reliance on the rationality principle;
- their value-impregnated status;

How, if at all, do *Verstehen,* the rationality principle and value-saturation differ?

Are there universal social laws?

Are there historical laws or law-like trends?
Is there such a thing as the spirit of the age? Of the nation?

Is there a master or fundamental social science (like physics in the natural sciences)?
If so, is it economics, psychology, social anthropology or some other field?

What role do (statistical) modelling and (Weberian) ideal-types play in social studies?

How do postulating ideal types differ from the mere use of the rationality principle?

Can all social studies be reduced to one, for example psychology or sociology?

Can all social studies be reduced to natural science, for example sociobiology?

Do social studies endorse cognitive and value-relativism?

What are the merits and demerits of the theories of:
- Structural-Functionalism
- Marxism
- Hermeneutics
- Critical theory
- Game theory
- Decision theory
- Ethnomethodology
- Strong Programme
- Systems theory

Table 1.2   Problematics in 14 Selected Anthologies

	1953	1959	1963	1965	1966	1968	1969	1970	1977	1988	1994	1994	2005	2007
Unity of method	•		•	•	•		•	•		•	•	•	•	•
Scientific explanation	•				•	•	•	•		•	•	•		•
Historical explanation	•	•					•					•	•	
Functional explanation	•				•	•				•	•	•		
Are there social laws?	•	•			•	•	•			•	•			
Free will and determinism	•					•	•							•
Weber's Ideal Types	•	•	•		•		•			•		•		
Explaining action	•			•			•			•	•			
Economics	•		•	•						•	•			•
Value freedom	•	•					•			•	•			•
Social theories		•					•			•				
Models and measurement							•							
Rational choice										•	•			•
Holism vs. individualism	•	•								•	•			•
Critical realism													•	
Critical theory													•	•
Reduction						•		•				•		•
Ideology							•							
How is society possible?				•	•		•	•	•					
Social policy					•									•
Objectivity					•		•					•		•
Social science exceptionalism					•		•							
Rationality												•		•

pro-naturalistic view. This dictated their choice of problems. Not surprisingly, then, as a reaction, anti-naturalistic work began to get into anthologies. Natanson's (1963) *Philosophy of the Social Sciences – a Reader*, already mentioned, Krimerman's (1969) *The Nature and Scope of Social Science: A Critical Anthology* and Dallmayr and McCarthy's (1977) *Understanding and Social Inquiry* are examples of anthologies with an anti-naturalist tendency. Some time later Martin and McIntyre (1994) also tried in their selections to bridge both camps. As distinct from anthologies, the first teaching monograph was Richard Rudner's (1966) slim *Philosophy of the Social Sciences*, in the *Foundations of Philosophy* series edited by Elizabeth and Monroe Beardsley. When Alan Ryan published his monograph in 1970 it was clearly for use in a lecture course, as was Emmett and MacIntyre's slim companion anthology (1970). The latter was in competition with David Braybrooke (1965) and Stuart Brown (1979). Ryan's book has been the model for a number of subsequent volumes by authors such as Vernon Pratt (1978), David Papineau (1979), Wisdom (1987), David Braybrooke (1987), Alexander Rosenberg (1988), Michael Root (1993), Martin Hollis (1994), Ted Benton and Ian Craib (2001), Patrick Baert (2005) and Robert Bishop (2007). Mantzavinos (2009) is a conference volume that focuses on basic problems of sociality, laws, and explanation, and on how philosophy and the social sciences can enrich one another. Since 1998 three enterprising philosophers of social science, Paul A. Roth, Alison Wylie and James Bohman have organised an annual Roundtable that meets each Spring for the presentation of current philosophy of the social sciences research. A selection of the papers is then published the following March in *Philosophy of the Social Sciences*.

It is noteworthy that most of Feigl and Brodbeck's original problem set was clearly derivative from the programme of Logical Positivism rather than from the full range of philosophical problems thrown up by actual social science work.[13] Anything smacking of metaphysics, for example, was minimal. The measure of scientific character, for another, was to be natural science, that is, physics. As the list of problems treated under the rubric lengthened, as shown in Table 1.2, a wider range of problems was embraced, drawing both on other philosophical approaches and on the work of social scientists themselves. My sense is that in those formative decades few of the philosophers engaging with social science were actually fans of it, that is were scholars some substantial part of whose programme of reading was first-order social

science. There are honourable and excellent exceptions, of course, but one could wish that these exceptions were the rule.[14]

Alongside teaching materials, a discipline also crystallises in the bureaucratic arrangements that house those carrying on its discourse. Under this aspect would be included courses in 'philosophy of the social sciences' and its variants, scholarly societies or caucuses, conferences and seminars, journals and monographs, specialised research and degrees. In the mid-twentieth century the London School of Economics was perhaps the leading institution in the emerging field having at that time on its staff Robbins, Hayek, Popper, Hutchison, Gellner, Wisdom and Watkins. Agassi and the present author were doctoral students in those days. There is no single world centre any more, but the subject can be intensively studied at a number of venues in Europe, North America, Japan and elsewhere. It has arrived!

Turning back from institutionalisation to intellectual content, what we now call *philosophy of the social sciences* brought together strands from extant fields: should economics inform history, and vice versa? (One result was 'economic history'.) What is the role of the assumption of rationality in the social sciences? What is the logic of explanation? (see Table 1.1)[15] Vigorous debate ensued. That a new discipline emerged from all this presumably has to do with the advantages of intellectual division of labour: specialisation and focus. But the discipline is not perfectly organised. As mentioned, lots of work referred to by philosophers of the social sciences is still embedded in the literature of the social sciences themselves and in philosophy simpliciter. For the foreseeable future, specialists in this field will have to keep up on those adjacent areas of intellectual endeavour and vice versa. To put it more positively, the problems of the speciality, with its own journals, centres of research strength, major and influential thinkers, dedicated panels, sections, conferences and all the other accoutrements of a distinct field, depends upon problems generated by

first-order research. The second-order philosophical results feed back into research,
usually generating new problems in a continuing dialectic interaction. Such an ongoing intellectual process is better presented
in the raw than tidied up. At the end of
this chapter we shall look at the example of
anthropology, an area of research almost
destroyed by arguments drawn from philosophy of the social sciences. These arguments
were taken to demolish scientific anthropology. This demolition job rested on utterly
invalid inferences.

Journals receive submissions that stem
from social scientists wanting to take account
of, to use, the latest results in philosophy
to improve their investigations. First it was
Logical Postivism, then Popper, then language philosophy, then Kuhn, then Foucault,
then deconstruction. The social scientists
seemed to think that the latest philosophical
talking points might be imported to their
discipline and applied to solve some conundrum or other. The debate over falsification
in economics is a case in point (see Klappholz and Agassi, 1959; Agassi, 1971; Boland,
1989). There are innumerable problems with
this way of seeing things. For one, philosophy not being science, all ideas, new and old,
are contested: they are seldom 'results' that
ought now to be applied (where results are
positions that more-or-less won in a fair
contest).[16] Hence importing the latest thing
from philosophy was to import only the latest
fashion. Logical Positivism was losing
ground to philosophy just as it came to the
fore in the social sciences.[17] For another,
importing and 'applying' a new philosophical gimmick was a formula for the generation
of PhD theses and journal articles, but this
formula seldom led to any contribution to
knowledge.

The spine of the field – of any field – is
problems and controversies over them.
A problem is sometimes equated with a question. A richer conception of a problem is a
contradiction within our putative knowledge,
such as between theory and observation or
between theory and theory. Social sciences
emerge from contradiction within folk social
thought or between it and some observations.
New theories or better observations can
resolve such contradictions. Thus do we
improve folk social thought? Is such learning
a form of science, social science? Here lies
the transcendent controversy of the field
under discussion: whether there is or even
whether there can be sciences of the social
(Ross, Chapter 4). Anti-naturalists answer
both parts of the question in the negative.
If anti-naturalism is correct, then the tasks of
philosophy of the social sciences are to show
why this is so and to explain the alternative,
that is, what sort of endeavour learning about
the social amounts to. Parallel to the question
of the possibility of social science is the
problem of the possibility of social philosophy (Agassi, Chapter 1; Derksen and
Beaulieu, Chapter 37). Here was a task for
the analytic school: to show that although
Wittgenstein was right and philosophy is
dead, Wittgenstein-style social philosophy
thrives. This was important for analytic
philosophers, as they were tired of repeating
the claim that philosophy is impossible and
wanted to contribute something to philosophy without contradicting the Master. It is on
this quest that Peter Winch is an important
pioneer of the emerging discipline. At the
heart of philosophy of the social sciences lies
a vigorously defended and equally vigorously attacked claim to the effect that there is
no such thing, even that there can be no such
thing (Hutchinson et al., 2008). Although
long ago presaged in methodological discussions about history and society that go back
to Hegel and Marx, it was most vigorously
propounded as the discipline was crystallis-
ing by Peter Winch and Charles Taylor (see
later sections), Winch from the analytic
Wittgensteinian viewpoint and Taylor from
his curious blend of analytic philosophy,
Marxist radicalism and ultra-conservative
Catholicism. To argue that there can be no
sciences of the social amounts to a social
philosophy of sorts, namely unreflective
endorsement of the status quo (Gellner 1975;
Agassi, Chapter 1 this handbook).

The main problem for twentieth-century anti-naturalists is the plain contradiction between their scepticism about a science of the social and the stock of empirical knowledge resulting from studies that see themselves as scientific. It is presumptuous to deny these results scientific status *en gros*. Not every anti-naturalist is convinced or deterred by this elephant in the room, as we shall see. What explains the rise of such social studies? The most general answer is that they are a response to modernity. Modern society can be conceived of as the successor to traditional society (all such discussions make use of Max Weber's idea of the ideal type). Modern society is rationalised and legitimated by defensible principles. By contrast, traditional society reproduces itself with only minimum alterations as *per necessitam* and legitimises itself by reference to some such formula as 'this is the way it is done, this is the way it has always been done'. Various scenarios can disrupt traditional social stability. A society conquered or dominated by another cannot use traditional legitimation for its current form. Natural disaster can have a similarly disruptive effect. So can the introduction of new ideas such as nationalism or democracy or fascism along with their normative legitimation. Sustained social change, however, brought about or embraced, tests the limits of traditional legitimation. Traditional understandings are problematised, so that legitimations require revision and these may be criticised and defended. The status quo no longer being self-legitimating, the structure of society comes up for consideration and alternatives are opened up: modernism – revolution, rebellion and reform – as well as the traditionalist reaction to modernism, of course. On this account social science replaces tradition because tradition is not much help during times of rapid social change – unless defended by a reactionary demand to return to some remote past. So the counter to the view that there is and can be no 'science' of the social is that there is and has to be if we are to take command of social change rather than simply be its creatures.

The connection posited between the rise of the social sciences and the problems of legitimation under modernity does not sit well with the known antiquity of social thought. This is a strong refutation. It suggests that we be careful to see social science as a particular variation or extension of social thought, one that aspires to scientific status comparable to that of natural science. Thought about nature is also ancient but this does not rule out the idea of a sea change in it that we call the Scientific Revolution. From Plato to J. M. Keynes, the attempt at rational social thought was a response to social change, a response that morphs over time from speculation to empirically testable theories. (Unchanging societies invite explanation as much as changing ones; but in times of change the need to explain is felt with great force.)

To repeat, an academic field or discipline is a socially constructed institution *par excellence*. It is a classification created by academics and academic librarians, who aim to organise the storage, transmission and growth of knowledge. Philosophers sometimes write as though academic fields corresponded in some natural way, one to one, with divisions in nature itself.[18] There are plentiful arguments to refute that view, no matter how intuitively convincing it seems. One of the most general refutations is this. All academic fields have borderlines with other fields, borders that have to be drawn under arbitrary constraints. Philosophical argument is often used to emphasise the artificiality of such borders in an effort to break them down and legitimise what is called interdisciplinary research. Interdisciplinary research is testimony to the artificiality, the constructedness of disciplines. They have a tendency to become rigid and to police their boundaries. (How often do we face futile discussions about whether or not some line of argument is or is not 'really' philosophy? Whether social 'science' is 'really' science?) Only a problem-oriented approach can make sense of this. Problems are oblivious to bureaucratic boundaries.

Philosophy of the social sciences is an exemplar, even a paradigm, of an interdisciplinary field. Its literature, both classical and current, is mostly the work of scholars whose speciality is cognate: social scientists, philosophers, philosophers of science, natural scientists. Although by the end of the twentieth century the field began to display the stigmata of professionalisation, there remains some way to go before it will achieve full recognition as a field. A principal reason is that it is a home to those who challenge the legitimacy of the entire enterprise of social science. *Ergo*, philosophy of the social sciences is partly about deconstructing the pretensions of social 'science' to be science proper. Another reason, stated earlier, is that some of its problematic is set by progress in the social sciences. There is a tension between the unruliness of both its deconstructors and its nurturers on the one hand, and any hopes for disciplinary neatness and tidiness on the other.

THE TRANSCENDENTAL CHALLENGE TO NATURALISM

In this section we look at the main attempts, during the formative period of the subject, to articulate the transcendental challenge to the very project of sciences of the social. Peter Winch and Charles Taylor are placed front and centre.

It would seem trivial that there could be no philosophy *of* the social sciences unless there were some social sciences. This is not so, and, indeed, both the philosophy of science and the philosophy of the social sciences preceded their being named as such. So a constituting problem of the philosophy of the social sciences is less whether there *are* social sciences but whether there *can possibly be* social sciences.[19] Again, it would seem that if the social sciences already exist then the answer to whether they are possible

must be affirmative: they exist, therefore they are possible. This inference is invalid. The claimants that the social sciences exist usually presuppose that there are unproblematic criteria for recognising science. There are not; this is contested ground (Roth, Chapter 3).

Do the social sciences exist? Any answer will be a social construction, a convention, depending on one's choice of criterion.[20] Take a few examples. Wilhelm Dilthey classified as science any organized body of thought.[21] (Paul Feyerabend's notorious refutation of Kuhn by nominating safecracking as a paradigm-dominated science holds equally against Dilthey.) Compare three of Herbert Feigl's five criteria for science in the essay 'The scientific outlook: Naturalism and humanism': Intersubjective testability, reliability and comprehensiveness.[22] Feigl and Brodbeck included this essay in the Introductory material to their 1953 anthology already mentioned, *Readings in the Philosophy of Science*. The counterattack of 1971 by Charles Taylor will be discussed in the next section. He says flatly:

> We can not measure such sciences against the requirements of a science of verification: we cannot judge them by their predictive capacity. We have to accept that they are founded on intuitions which all do not share … These sciences cannot be "*wertfrei*"… Finally, their successful prosecution requires a high degree of self-knowledge, a freedom from illusion, in the sense of error which is rooted and expressed in one's way of life; for our incapacity to understand is rooted in our own self-definitions, hence in what we are. To say this is not to say anything new: Aristotle makes a similar point in Book I of the *Ethics*. But it is still radically shocking and unassimilable to the mainstream of modern science. (Taylor, 1971: 51)

Social thought is at least as old as ancient cuneiform and hieroglyphic writings, or at least as Hebrew and Greek writings. Plato and Aristotle were brilliant social thinkers, so brilliant that some of their ideas are part of the body of current social scientific knowledge whereas almost all of their attempts at natural science have been utterly superseded.[23] If such a long time-line is granted to social thought, then clearly Bernard Mandeville, Charles de Montesquieu, Adam Smith and his Scottish Enlightenment colleagues (Broadie, 2003), David Ricardo, Alexis de Tocqueville, Karl Marx, J. S. Mill, Léon Walras, Alfred Marshall, Vilfredo Pareto, Georg Simmel, Max Weber, Emile Durkheim, Franz Boas, J. M. Keynes, Bronislaw Malinowski, just as much as C. Northcote Parkinson are among those who have contributed to it. Somewhere in that list it is reasonable to claim that social thought became comparable to natural scientific thought. We might call the work of each of these social thinkers exemplars or paradigms of emerging and emerged social science.[24]

Viewing social science as a real and accomplished research project having a long time-line may seem easy to do. It is also easy to criticise. Such criticism comes from natural scientists and analytic philosophers as much as from those influenced by the Hegelian tradition of Dilthey and Schutz, not to mention Wittgenstein. For example, in 1908 the physicist Henri Poincaré already wrote, 'nearly every sociological thesis proposes a new method, which, however, its author is very careful not to apply, so that sociology is the science with the greatest number of methods and the least results' (Poincaré, 1908: 19–20).

Fifty years later the historian of science Thomas Kuhn wrote:

> To a very great extent the term 'science' is reserved for fields that do progress in obvious ways. Nowhere does this show more clearly than in the recurrent debates about whether one or another of the contemporary social sciences is really a science. These debates have parallels in the pre-paradigm periods of fields that are today unhesitatingly labeled science. (1962: 160)

And less than two decades ago the analytic philosopher Raimo Tuomela wrote of: 'the fairly primitive and undeveloped state of the social sciences' (Tuomela, 1991: 250n).

These scientific critics may have been condescending, but at least they granted that the social sciences exist, albeit in primitive form. The attacks with the most heft in our subject did not hold out such hope for development, they were transcendental: bringing us to Peter Winch (1958, 1964) and Charles Taylor (1971).[25] Winch argued thus: philosophy of the social sciences *is* social science: the sociological concepts with which we try to understand social life are themselves social. The concepts we employ are also employed by the social actors and so affect their behaviour in a way that the concept of gravity in no way affects the behaviour of inert matter. Human behaviour is intelligible because it is rule-following behaviour so the notion of what it is to follow a rule is a basic matter for the social sciences. The analysis of following a rule is fundamental to both social science and its philosophy. 'The notion of human society involves a scheme of concepts which is logically incompatible with the kinds of explanation offered in the natural sciences' (p. 72). 'Whereas the man learns to understand the rule the dog just learns to react in a certain way ... the concept of understanding is rooted in a social context in which the dog does not participate as does the man' (p. 74).[26] So different is the study of the social from the material, that Winch speaks of it less as explanatory and more as aiming at 'rendering intelligible', or, simply, understanding.

The underlying problem that beset Winch, as it happens, was far from any social study. It was: what is the message of the later Wittgenstein? He took it for granted that Wittgenstein had one and that it is important. He found a reading of the later Wittgenstein that satisfied him and it presupposed a view of society. In the name of Wittgenstein he offered the hypothesis that, philosophy leaves everything as it was. (This is what Wittgenstein said as a variant of his idea that there are no meaningful philosophical statements. Following Durkheim on this point Gellner said, even meaningless incantations have ritual significance and so they do signify. There is more to it: as sociological, the Wittgenstein–Winch claim is perhaps the most spectacularly refuted hypothesis in the field, with the American, French and

Russian revolutions as the counterexamples to it.) When Winch published his book the Wittgenstein industry was just getting under way. Winch had not just provided a new set of arguments for anti-naturalism, for a new and different demarcation between natural and social science; he also gave the impression of being very avant-garde. He referred to Wittgenstein's (then) unpublished *Nachlass*. In due course other true believers would charge him with getting it wrong.[27]

Besides being a transcendental challenge to sciences of the social as such, and, *inter alia*, a challenge to naturalism, Winch's intervention had two further fallouts for philosophy of the social sciences. It challenged the self-understanding of the field as it emerged in the backwash of Logical Positivism (or logical empiricism). Philosophy of the social sciences had originally been presented as a special case of philosophy of science, a combination of descriptive analysis of the methods of the social sciences with some prescriptive offerings where special problems arise (Van Bouwel and Weber, Chapter 33). By contrast, Winch's view was that philosophy concerns the understanding of reality. Hence, such sub-fields of philosophy as the philosophy of religion, the philosophy of science, the philosophy of politics, etc., attempt to explicate what sort of understanding of reality is provided by religion, science, political theory, etc. Winch also made the intriguing claim that some kind of empathy is essential if behaviourism is to be avoided. Thus, a philosopher of religion with no feeling for religion, for example, was crippled/disabled in the project of rendering intelligible the understanding of reality provided by religion, or the religious way of life.

An obvious difficulty was lying in ambush for Winch's view that 'philosophies of' were explications of the understandings of reality provided by the specific variables religion, science, politics, etc. How are we to apply it to philosophy of the social sciences? Social science research was clearly a social practice, however small the numbers of its practitioners, however disputed the scientific status of their work, and, clearly, social science conveys certain understandings of social reality. For example, from psychology to economics, social science tends to suggest that reality need not be what it seems: that actor understandings and folk understandings are oftentimes inadequate to explain repeatedly observed features of life in society. An example would be Durkheim on suicide. He was not at all concerned to convey actors' understandings of the reality of their lives that led them to suicide. He undertook the study expressly in the opposite direction, trying to avoid all that is anchored in the individual and the psychological; he focused instead on rates of suicide in different societies. He found it interesting that there are substantial differences. He tried to explain suicide rates as a function of (i.e. varying with) certain organisational features of society.[28] This way Durkheim exemplified a social practice that was followed by the whole *L'Anneé sociologique* school of sociologists and all of those who trace their work from them. How would Winch handle this? We shall see.

THE TRANSCENDENTAL TRILEMMA

The main challenge to the anti-naturalists is the very existence of social studies that view themselves as sciences and whose practices and successes have to be accounted for. The favoured explanations are that 'social science' is a misnomer or a disguise for social/political intervention. As a counter, pro-naturalists embraced a liberal criterion of science. However, the Logical Positivism on which this criterion rested collapsed. Pro-naturalism can be salvaged, however, by substituting Popper's even more liberal criterion for science.

The anti-naturalist challenge creates a transcendental trilemma: in the face of a community of practicing social scientists and their paradigmatic work there are three options, all unsatisfactory for one reason or another, to one degree or another.

'Social science' is a misnomer

The transcendental anti-naturalist simply discounts all this work, all these people, this community of practices, this form of life and insists that no social *science* is possible. What goes under that name is something else or alternatively the phrase is vacuous. These alternatives are not the same but both are used, and not only by anti-naturalists. The condescension of Poincaré, Kuhn and Tuomela is a variant of the misnomer option, albeit a pro-naturalistic one.

Social science comprises flimsily disguised attempts at social control

By reinterpreting the long time-line and its community of practices as a form of false consciousness, failed self-understanding, social science can be seen as construing itself as science when what it amounts to are proposals for changing or rationalising society. For example, sociology = socialism.

The unity of science

This was the name of a programme of Otto Neurath and his followers among the Vienna Circle of Logical Positivists. It accepted that the long time-line of attempts to build sciences of the social had yielded success by criteria similar to those used for the natural sciences. An immediate problem arises: just how and when did thinking and talking about society become science? Popper proposed a minimal criterion for the natural sciences that obviously applies to both natural and social science: falsifiability – we have many falsifiable theories in both the natural and the social sciences. Kuhn proposed a paradigm criterion: a discipline becomes scientific when it adopts a unifying paradigm; by

Kuhn's criterion, the social sciences were 'pre-paradigm', that is, in the stage of preliminary deliberations, and so not there yet.[29] Kuhn's book was the final published volume of Neurath's *International Encyclopedia of Unified Science*. Yet Kuhn's condescension was not in the spirit of Logical Positivist aspirations; Popper's ideas fit that programme much better. Let me now expand on these three prongs of the trilemma.

'Social science' is a misnomer

The key question here is not to whether the social sciences are hermeneutic – concerned with meanings; or to put it another way, that they offer understanding rather than explanation (Kögler, Chapter 22). Pro-naturalism is not threatened by such claims, which have their parallels in natural science. The key question is how to view the work that stands in what I have called 'the long time-line'. Both Winch and Taylor were quite clear. Look at the work, show that it cannot possibly amount to what is claimed for it, then reinterpret it in a way that discards some and retains other parts of it. Winch looked at Durkheim, Pareto and Weber; he castigated especially the first two. Looking a little closer, however, one finds that Winch looked not at their sociology, but at their philosophising. He did not quote and discuss *Suicide* and tell us what he made of the reasoning and explanations that he found there. Was he searching for the view of reality embodied in the way of life of social research? No: he viewed Durkheim's *Rules of Sociological Method* as a view of reality and rejected it as such. Why challenge him on this reading? Answer: it is commonplace in the philosophy of science that the 'philosophical' bits in scientific work may not be congruent with how the work was done (this was Poincaré's point). Also, it is commonplace in the social sciences that what people do, what they say or think they do and what they say they do or say or think are all quite distinct and need to be separated, since they often differ

(Malinowski), so that they are better examined as independent claims. This goes equally for people acting as social scientists just as much as it goes for the informants on whom social scientists rely. Winch nowhere asks whether Durkheim's accounts and claims correspond to what he did as a sociologist. To do that he needed to examine *Suicide, The Division of Labour in Society*, and *Elementary forms of the Religious Life*.

This is not to say that Durkheim is unreliable (although his handling of statistics was challenged; see Turner, 1996); it is to say that his evidence like all other evidence invites critical scrutiny (including using empirical evidence).[30] As it happens, the passage Winch quotes and declares 'incompatible' with a proper conceptual grasp of human social life, does chime well with the practice of *Suicide*. Durkheim says there that actor explanations are not sociological explanations. To put it more bluntly, both actors' behaviour and actors' explanations of their behaviour invite sociological explanation. Does this apply to the behavior of Durkheim the scientist too? This question Durkheim left open (Durkheim and Mauss 1903: conclusion). Why is that? The answer was formulated most clearly by Hayek, although he was only summarising discourse of the Austrian school: social scientists are not engaged in explaining individual human action; they are engaged in explaining its unintended consequences. The individual suicide has no notion of contributing to the comparative rates of suicide that interested Durkheim. Similarly, Durkheim has no (sociological) interest in the particular account of a particular case of suicide. What interested him are broad categories regarding suicide: sex, age, religion, social class, profession, nationality and especially certain features of the society in which it took place. If the comparative rates vary in systematic ways with these or with even more abstract social variables (integration/anomie, egoism, etc.) then the sociologist can attempt to offer an explanation of the differential rates of suicide that depends not on individual characteristics but on social ones.

It was perhaps in response to this kind of objection that Winch in his 1964 paper chose to engage with one of the Durkheimian classics of twentieth century anthropology: *Witchcraft, Oracles, and Magic Among the Azande* by Evans-Pritchard. So far from budging Winch from his position, this engagement led to an attack on Evans-Pritchard and to assertions by Winch that are difficult if not impossible to differentiate from epistemological relativism. Instead of going into that (which I have criticised elsewhere, 1970, 1984; see also Phillips, 2007), I return to Durkheim.[31] Both Winch and Taylor (see below) would counter-claim that the actions Durkheim deems acts of suicide are suicide only if within the conceptual scheme of the actors they are suicide. There is no conceptually neutral description of suicide that resembles the neutral description of inert matter in natural science. Actors and the meanings of their actions are necessarily part of any account of suicide. To this, as it happens, Durkheim had a ready reply. It wasn't he who classed the deaths as suicide but the medical and clerical bureaucrats who determined the cause of death and recorded it as suicide. These were the given 'social facts' he was considering. They were constructed, of course, and of course he knew it. Nonetheless, they were social facts, as was their construction. The objectors would say that there were no such facts and that therefore Durkheimian social science is focused on an artifact. (This comes perilously close to the philosopher of the social sciences telling the social scientist their business, as Winch did in 1964.[32]) It is easy to counter this point: description, like interpretation, is open to discussion and correction. It is hard to know if Durkheim would agree, but were he told that it holds for the natural sciences too, then he might have waived any objection to it that he might have held during his lifetime. The fallibility of all descriptions never concerned Winch, however, and on this he was plainly in error by his own lights (not to mention Wittgenstein's lights).

Another argument to the same effect is that sometimes the ideas of social scientists enter the discourse of actors *as a part of their action*. Social class is a good example. Social class is possibly almost as old as human society, yet it enters into social science thinking mainly from Marx, who thought it had great explanatory power, and is then seen as radically different from traditional categories such as rank, estate, caste, etc. By the mid-twentieth century sociologists were still wrestling with this complexity. Moreover, in *Social Mobility in Industrial Society* (Lipset and Bendix, 1959) rates of mobility were found to be smaller than expected, but it is also reported there that most people classify themselves as middle class – which defeats the whole exercise of using class to explain. In this situation social scientists had little other option than to treat actors' explanations as problematic and in need of explanation. For an update see (Little, Chapter 12).

In Taylor we find only slight variation from Winch's thrust. Taylor concentrates mostly on political science. Taylor:

> The realities here are practices [his examples are, entering into negotiations, breaking off negotiations, offering to negotiate, negotiating in good faith, concluding negotiations, making a new offer] and these cannot be identified in abstraction from the language we use to describe them, or invoke them, or carry them out … this range of practices couldn't exist without the prevalence of this or some related vocabulary … what this points up is the artificiality of the distinction between social reality and the language of description of that social reality. The language is constitutive of the reality, is essential to its being the kind of reality it is. To separate the two and distinguish them as we quite rightly distinguish the heavens from our theories about them is forever to miss the point. (Taylor, 1971: 24)[33]

'[T]he point' is the anti-naturalism that Taylor is strenuously advocating. To put it another way, he is claiming that armchair philosophers are in as good or a better position to produce understanding of human behaviour than are those who 'miss the point' and see the human sphere as amenable to the same approach as we take to the explanation of the heavenly spheres. We might see this as the Winch–Taylor axis, or perhaps even the Dilthey–Weber–Schutz–Winch–Taylor axis of anti-naturalism: allies in their anti-naturalism if not much else. It is an extension of the argument from the unavoidable lack of objectivity of humans studying humans taken to the point of claiming there is an unavoidable lack of intelligibility without actors' conceptual schemes and self-understandings. All forms of actor error, from delusion through self-deception to honest mistake are ruled out. They are also ruled in, for the student of society must be free of them, as in the quotation above from Taylor (p. 51).

The argument is a Wittgenstein-style linguistic philosophy version of the Observer from Mars argument, much discussed in the first half of the twentieth century, although its origin is uncertain.[34] Allegedly, some positivist or empiricist social scientists envisaged their task as to view human society from a detached perspective, as would a Martian observer studying earth through a powerful telescope. The objection lodged was not conceptual, it was that social science stems from what human beings find problematic in their society, a perspective obviously closed to the hypothetical Martian. The Martian might explain observable repeatable events, but could hardly *see* social problems such as suicide, mental illness, witchcraft, the trade cycle, to cite a few obvious examples. For that the Martian would presumably have to communicate with humans. (Hence, the supposition behind the metaphor is the inductivist myth that science makes no conjectures, only observations.) It is what humans find problematic that is hidden to the Martian: how they conceive reality or the nature of their 'conceptual scheme' may also be hidden but is hardly the issue. The most fundamental error behind the idea of the observer from Mars is the supposition that observers of social events should be as utterly objective as natural scientists allegedly are. It is an impossible demand. No observer is utterly objective and all observations and their articulation in descriptions are subject to critical scrutiny.

Taylor continues with a critique of Dahl (1963) and of Lipset (1963) on political legitimacy, and a short case study on the integration of the new industrial working class into British society in the early-nineteenth century. The gist of the argument is that:

> the great interdependent matrix of labor is not just a set of ideas in people's heads but is an important aspect of the reality which we live in modern society. And at the same time, these ideas are embedded in this matrix in that they are constitutive of it; that is, we wouldn't be able to live in this type of society unless we were imbued with these ideas or some others which could call forth the discipline and voluntary co-ordination needed to operate this kind of economy. (Taylor, 1971: 39)

Translating this out of the hybrid language of Hegel and Wittgenstein that Taylor employs, it says that actors voluntarily coordinate because they have internalised the necessary imperatives and dispositions for acting in modern industrial society. This seems quite trivially true. The imperatives and dispositions in question are co-coordinating social institutions that had to be invented, elaborated, distilled and instilled. To take a concrete instance: the factory system imposed a very different way of measuring time from that of the pre-existing farming system. Workers had to live by the factory clock and divide their time into 'work time' and the rest. Failing to do work in 'work time' would lead to no work getting done, hence no livelihood. The measurement of time is a created social institution that shapes the lives of those within it. The way time is spoken of, the meaning it has, is constitutive of the way of life of the factory worker, indeed of industrial society as a whole. Nonetheless, time is not a social construction; time is one of the four dimensions of the physical world which encompasses all social life. Measurement of time and building time measurement into the factory system are social constructions. Of any such social construction it can be asked, could it be improved?

Taylor's voluntaristic language obfuscates. To view the factory system as he does is already to stand outside the 'matrix of labour', that is, the constituting set of concepts required to operate it. In fact the institutional set-up for factory work is describable in many ways, including ways that make it possible to assess it along such parameters as whether it is well designed, how it could be improved, where it has unintended consequences of a negative kind, and the like (Agassi and Heycock, 1989). Both Winch and Taylor find the idea of such thinking-through unintelligible because it seems to stand outside one system of concepts in order to assess it. Their move has the effect of cutting off discussion of ways of improving the factory work system on grounds that it makes no sense to do so. Yet they have to admit that it does make sense, as it is operative. They fail to notice that their own discourse is both external and intelligible. Just as the factory system was devised, it is constantly scrutinised and improved. Such external description and assessment goes on in all social institutions: economic, political, educational, religious, legal, familial and so on. In fact, description and assessment is part of the folk theories that Winch and Taylor endorse. What these philosophers declare impossible individuals accomplish by their regular actions.[35]

The kind of reasoning that Winch and Taylor offer is agreeable to analytic or linguistic philosophers, it seems, including those who took up the cudgels against them on this or that detail. Interestingly, both labour the language dependence, or rather conceptual dependence, of social life. All science begins from description and there are no limits to the correct descriptions we can impose on nature and society. Why can there not be accurate descriptions of human behaviour that describe it differently from the way actors describe it? Were we to lump Winch and Taylor's own religious practices into a general study of ritual we could be doing violence to their sense of the reality of their religion. But we can acknowledge that sense and nevertheless offer explanation of why their sense of that reality is as it is. That too may ignore their own conceptions, although bridging to them might be possible.[36]

Social science = Socialism

The politics of the dispute between the anti- and the pro-naturalists is complicated because all political persuasions are to be found on both sides. What was said earlier about the general project of legitimation in modern society shows the association of social science with change, with conscious assessment of society and its arrangements, to be fair enough. That there are also conservative, even reactionary, social scientists, from Plato to Leo Strauss, is no news either. Their agenda is to halt change, perhaps even to go back to a better stage. Thus they can be as radical as any *gauchiste*. Those who spurn social science and mythologise the *status quo ante* are rejecting rational control. It is true that the formal or institutionalised social science they oppose has long had a close association with social and political radicalism: it sought 'progressive' social change. This is an elective affinity since the opposing viewpoint, traditionalism, tends to the policy of 'let's leave well alone', or 'if it ain't broke don't fix it'. The best way to leave well alone is to avoid (rational) thinking about society as such and to denounce those who indulge in it (as Oakeshott (1962) did). Yet progressive reformists need not claim anything in society is broken: it is sufficient for their purposes to claim that current social arrangements can be improved and so should be thought about and even that they should be thought about if only to prevent some future mishap.

The political colouring of Logical Positivism and of its first hero, Russell, was gauchiste. By contrast, as David Pole and Ernest Gellner argued, Wittgenstein's later philosophy translated into a conservative, traditionalist and quietist social philosophy. And few would doubt that Hegelian philosophy tends to favour the traditionalists and, more latterly, some 'communitarian' thinkers, of whom Taylor emerged as a leading figure.[37]

It is true, then, that social scientists are not *wertfrei*:[38] they treat society and its institutions as mechanisms that can be assessed and tampered with, not as a sacred womb that must be adored. One can see why traditionalists shudder. But is that shudder is reasonable? Everybody engages in thinking about some aspects of their society in objectifying ways: When they book a movie ticket online; when they purchase something; when they vote in a referendum; when they enroll their child in a school or when they take some responsibility in an organization. The fact that they simultaneously participate, and help, constitute the entities they are objectifying (viz. the audience; the sale; the political decision; schooling; the organization's goal) does not present a problem in practice. Hence their behaviour is both reasonable and intelligible and without their objectifying detachment nothing would get done.

Moreover, the principle 'if it ain't broke, don't fix it' involves thinking about society in a detached and rational way. We might reverse the argument and say that accusing progressive social scientists of brutal rationalism is a smoke screen to distract from an equally brutal endorsement of the status quo. Yet even the status quo invites correction: do not mend it, but do overhaul it as the need arises.

All Science is One: Methodology and Ontology

The idea of the unity of science and hence of the scientific status of social inquiry comes in many variants. We can truncate the long time-line and focus on the aftermath of the Scientific Revolution. Just before the Scientific Revolution, Bacon argued that what is and is not science ('the mark of knowledge', Bacon, 1620: II, Aph. x) should be decided operationally. Science is an approach to gaining knowledge that radically departs from authority, tradition and intuition and relies on some kind of public process of observation. Bacon is associated with induction, but he was a better inductivist than most of those who invoked him, since he articulated almost all the problems of any naïve inductive approach.[39] Hume articulated the remainder. Bacon's successors such as Herschel and Mill were less subtle than he. Mill (1843) is important because unlike Bacon and Herschel he specifically addressed the problem of applying the methodology of the natural sciences to the social sciences. Himself an economist and social reformer, he was well acquainted with the social sciences extant in his time: namely history, economics, sociology, politics and psychology. Despite Hume's arguments, he offered Bacon's inductive model as he understood and modified it for both natural and social sciences. He treated psychology as the fundamental social science while elsewhere in London, Karl Marx was working on the supposition that social conditions explain psychology and not vice versa.

There was a gap in English-speaking debates over the social sciences after Mill. He was taken for a long time as having had the last word. By contrast, in Germany fierce *Methodenstreit* broke out in the fields of history and economics. The works of Weber, Dilthey, Rickert, Menger and Hayek all take some stimulus from it.[40] But as I have noted, as long as these materials remained untranslated they were not much discussed in English-speaking philosophical circles.

It was the Logical Positivists who were the stimulus to the post-Mill revival of these issues in English-language philosophy. The unity of science was a central tenet of the Vienna Circle manifesto and the difference between science and non-science was Manichean: the difference between light and dark, knowledge and ignorance. Hence the stakes were high. The *International Encyclopedia of Unified Science* was always planned to have volumes on the special sciences, some of which were social or human.

The Logical Positivist paradigm for science was the mathematical physics of the nineteenth and twentieth centuries and they looked for criteria of the scientific that could extend over the whole corpus of scientific knowledge. The logic they relied on was that of Frege and Russell, which made Mill's logic seem quaint and antiquated. All that was missing for their goals was an inductive logic that they hoped would be achieved overnight by developing a proper approach to probabilities.

The pro-naturalists who take the view that there are ways to study the social that warrant the honorific 'science' all agree that from the philosophical point of view the social sciences differ in some specific ways from the natural sciences. The lines of controversy fall between the different efforts to spell out the difference. Logical Positivist ideas were put forward forcefully in 1936 in German and later in revised form in 1944 by Felix Kaufmann's *The Methodology of the Social Sciences*. In the same year Otto Neurath published his contribution to the *International Encyclopedia*. It is surprisingly conciliatory. In 50 pages he focuses mostly on language. Science is formulated in statements; facts are statements that confront theories, which are other statements. Vocabularies are shifting and hard to systematise and fix. Hence an empiricist approach is fraught with difficulties. Although he is a realist and an empiricist he is suspicious of the old metaphysical terms 'true' and 'false'. He abandons a key component of Comte's programme when he argues that all the sciences interpenetrate one another and so cannot be arranged in a hierarchy. His case rests on how human labour alters geological facts and hence the trajectory of parts of the earth. Perhaps most striking are its final pages where Neurath, conceding a lot to the hemeneuts, laments the lack of sociological reflexivity.[41] He also brings in the relevance of sociology to how people wish to live their lives and the impact of the scientific outlook replacing the religious outlook. To those wanting crisp formulas he offers no comfort.

He more or less explicitly repudiates evangelism, envisaging rather 'a tolerant world community [where] empiricists and non-empiricists may live together peacefully' (p. 46).

Kaufmann does not even mention Dilthey. He mentions Hegel only as the subject of Marx's critique. Kaufmann has nothing substantial to say about Durkheim and Simmel. He focuses, like Winch, on the elusive Max Weber. Kaufmann seems most at home in economics, especially marginal utility theory. As an Austrian he is perhaps immersed in the controversies of the *Methodenstreit*, Austrian economics and the planning debates initiated by Von Mises and Hayek (the latter nowhere mentioned).[42] Summarising Kaufmann's methodological views in a review of the posthumous edition Agassi wrote that:

> ...the author advocates two methodological rules, both of which are by now widely accepted among economists, one concerning science in general and the other concerning the social sciences. The general rule is: State explicitly explanatory hypotheses and try to refute them. The specific rule is: Incorporate in hypotheses concerning social phenomena the rationality principle; explain as that which is most adequate to given aims under given circumstances. These two rules cover almost the whole ground; what is missing is the problem of how to treat social institutions. (Agassi, 1961: 100)

Kaufmann held that

> the logic of scientific procedure is identical in all provinces of human inquiry; and though he stressed important differences between the subject matters of the natural and social sciences, he saw no warrant for the claim that these differences require the adoption of different standards of validity in inquiries into human affairs. (Nagel, 1950)

Ernest Nagel could have been writing *in propria persona* rather than summarising someone else. When Nagel published his major treatise on *The Structure of Science* in 1961 he rebutted all claims that there were insuperable barriers to modelling social science method on natural science method.

The criterion for science favoured by the Logical Positivists was empirical verifiability.

This, they insisted requires absolute conceptual clarity. They added – stealthily – the demand for a systematic approach. They took for granted basic modern logic (Kaufmann, 1944: Chapter IV). The verification programme of the Logical Positivists was refuted for science in general by the combined guns of Church (who refuted the verifiability theory of meaning 1949), of Popper (who showed the verification criterion to be both too narrow and too wide 1935, 1963) and by Quine, who drove a truck over the analytic/synthetic distinction and who showed that the Vienna Circle philosophy entails a phenomenological (idealist) ontology, no less (Quine, 1951). That left clarity and a systematic approach, criteria that would have warmed the heart of Descartes.

Popper viewed clarity and systematisation as relative values – relative to the problem situation and the kind of precision and order minimally necessary. In his 1935 book *Logik der Forschung* he had suggested instead a demarcation of empirical science as those theories that can be formulated in such a way that some possible empirical observation could refute them. Like the positivists, Popper intended his demarcation for physics, and like them he saw no reason to restrict his criterion to natural science. Historians used documentary evidence to refute, economists used statistics to refute, sociologists and psychologists used their observations to refute. Not all science was empirical science, however. Popper did not deny that mathematics was science; but it certainly was not empirical. Because he was a deductivist, he viewed the detection of inconsistencies, in, say mathematical physics or mathematical economics as also part of scientific criticism. Popper's was a very different approach to the strong criteria of the positivists, even those of the author of the final volume of the *International Encyclopedia of Unified Science*, Thomas Kuhn. Popper's criterion of science was minimal and might be equated with any rational inquiry; rational inquiry checked by empirical arguments was then a subset we call empirical science. The value of empirical test was that it kept us in touch with the real: only empirical test bumped our theories against the observable world.

When Popper turned from problems of natural science method to make a contribution to intellectual history and political science in his *The Open Society and Its Enemies* (1945) he mixed the empirical with the logical as part of rational and scientific inquiry. He marshalled facts to refute some of Marx. He also marshalled logical arguments to point up lacunae and inconsistencies. Thus he was engaged in an unacknowledged project: generalising and loosening his falsifiability criterion for the status of being science. Historically he was at one with the tendency in German academic circles to consider everything from art history to legal theory a kind of *Wissenschaft*. Popper had come to think the rational approach to inquiry was more fundamental than the subset of rational inquiry that achieved empirical falsifiability. He valourised critical rational inquiry as the high road to science, empirical criticism as its crowning achievement. This way he solved another problem: how did empirical science evolve out of the pre-scientific, mythical way of thinking? We shall come to this presently.

When the present writer began his studies in the 1950s the phrase 'philosophy of the social sciences' was novel: the field was called 'methodology of the social sciences'.[43] The underlying problem of the field is that scientific status claims are contested. The value of science is contested, who shall be classed 'scientist' is contested, its ubiquity is contested and its boundaries are contested too. There can be no problematic called philosophy of the social sciences until there is, or might be, modern social science – proper or in pretension – and there can be no modern social science until there is modern science – proper or in pretension. Conventionally, modern science is dated from the Scientific Revolution of the mid-seventeenth century. Popper, however, thinking of science minimally, as an approach to the growth of knowledge, traced it back at least to the Presocratics, a long time-line indeed (1958).

The crucial social institution Popper put into play was that of the school, the philosophical school. He characterised this as an institution devised and sustained with the aims of preserving and teaching a philosophical doctrine in its purity. He was alluding to the Pythagorean school, the Stoics, the Sophists, etc., to say nothing of religious schools, and he proposed that there was continuity with the tradition of (Western) science. The continuity is something historians are fairly agreed upon. Popper gave their studies its philosophical rationale, one that invites reconsideration and a more detailed indication of the threads of the scientific tradition.[44]

Popper offers the following historical conjecture about science. One Presocratic school is unique, the Milesian School of Thales and his pupils Anaximander and Anaximenes. The uniqueness of this School is that on the fundamental cosmological question of the shape of the earth and its stability the school preserves the doctrine of Thales ('the earth is supported by water on which it rides like a ship, and when we say that there is an earthquake, then the earth is being shaken by the movement of the water' (Popper, 1963: 138)), and the doctrines of his two students that are incompatible with it, as well as with each other. Anaximander theorised that 'The earth ... is held up by nothing, but remains stationary owing to the fact that it is equally distant from all things. Its shape is ... like that of a drum ... We walk on one of its flat surfaces, while the other is on the opposite side' (Popper, 1963: 138). Anaximenes was, according to Popper an eclectic, a systematiser, an empiricist, a man of common sense uncomfortable with Anaximander's bold conjecture. Anaximenes reinstates Thales structure, only now the flat earth rides on air as the lid of a pot may ride on steam, or a ship on water.

Three revered leaders, three answers to a basic question, all preserved with no effort at a compromise or any other reconciliation. How could a school be structured like this? It might have been expected that the pupils would each have founded their own schools.

Instead, their ideas are preserved alongside their teacher's. Popper conjectured that Thales had institutionalised a new attitude: here is a problem; here is my solution; I challenge you to criticise my solution; if you can, suggest a better one; let us keep them distinct and discuss them. Thales' school institutionalised the rationality of discussion, which is the high road to science.

Certainly Popper was both conjecturing and idealising. Nonetheless, no historian contests that the tradition Popper delineates was critical; his innovation was the idea that this characteristic should suffice. And he had his finger on something. Ernest Gellner remarks

> Newtonian physics … was revered by many thinkers as the very paradigm of well-established, permanent truth. It is interesting to note when Newtonian physics was tumbled from this pedestal, virtually no tremors were noticed in the rest of the social fabric. Little or no entrenchment had in fact taken place, contrary to what philosophers had supposed. (Gellner, 1974: 167)

Gellner could have taken the story further, and considered the revolutions of Einstein and Bohr and their similar failures to initiate changes in society. (Darwin was another matter.) A Milesian-type school of natural science, if we may call it that, remains stable while within it there are factions backing these and those persons and ideas. Popper is not claiming anything like *wertfrei* status, but he is claiming that matters can be debated without the debate leading to too much social strife. This renders his idealisation smaller than others'. It contrasts sharply the critical scientific tradition with dogmatic schools such as those of the major monotheisms, all of which allow their internal and their external disputes to lead to segregation, purge and violence.

Popper thus provides a way of unifying all rational inquiry under one approach, one that even makes space for transcendental critique, provided it is logical, scholarly and responds to rational argument. Rational inquiry also, crucially, depends on sociality and cooperation. As I have indicated above, the overwhelming rational argument, towards which the anti-naturalists have no coherent strategy, is the real presence of social science and its accomplishments

ONTOLOGY, METHOD AND METAPHYSICS

Do individuals exist? Do only individuals exist? Questions framed thus smack of Aristotle's *Metaphysics* of substance and essence. Pro-naturalists are reluctant to say what there is, as opposed to saying clearly what there is not, that is, the supernatural. They defer ontological questions to science. Fair enough, as long as the ontological hence metaphysical presuppositions of science are not denied. Popper's critical method suggests placing them front and centre. We have to start somewhere. The best place to start is myth or folk knowledge or common sense. Science consists in the first instance of criticism of those starting points. The inertia of folk knowledge is such that components of it may continue to be held despite telling criticism. Hence the body of what is supposed and presupposed is logically untidy.

Philosophy of science has seen much discussion about 'occult entities'[45] assumed in natural science. If empirical observation was *de rigeur*, as both the Logical Positivists and Popper agreed, what was to be made of atoms, sub-atomic particles, physical forces, chemical bonds, double helixes and the like? All of these were postulated of the submicroscopic level, and so theories about them could be empirical only in a sense different from the sense that any inductivist philosophy could suggest. In the social sciences there was a similar problem, already present in the observer from Mars discussion: many of the institutions, structures, traditions imputed to, and explanatory of, the social order are interpretations of empirical data. The debate often turned around Durkheim's notion of 'social fact' and his insistence that social facts were observable. (Records of suicide are empirical but imputed intent is not.) No-one quite knew what to make of this other than to see it as an affirmation of his positivist insistence that empirical science must be observational.

Traditional empiricism conflicts with commonsense ontology: are the entities assumed in common discourse to be endorsed by science, and what is the status of entities assumed by science that are unknown to common discourse and possibly counter-intuitive to common understanding? Examples of entities widely assumed in common discourse would be demons, race, conspiracy, character (national and gender and individual), individual selves, hierarchies of all sorts, money (liquid and assets) and so on. Some of these have been dropped from the explanans of social science. Entities found in social science but not in common discourse would be the perfect market, rationality, marginal utility, the trade cycle, liquidity preference, the forces and relations of production, the movement of history, social structure, organic solidarity and so on. (Some of these enter common discourse, such as human rights, pension rights and social mobility.) Perhaps the most positivist solution to the problem of ontology would be total deference to science: those things exist which science finds it fruitful to employ in its explanations (Quine). Some entities in the explananda will be in the explanans, others will be explained away.

Ontological questions are metaphysical. Popper said that every scientific theory includes assertions that, taken by themselves, are metaphysical. The Logical Positivists vehemently denied that. Metaphysics was anathema to them. Their way forward was the linguistic turn, translating substantial questions into questions about language and meaning, viz. unverifiable statements are meaningless. They originally hoped to construct a language for science in which metaphysical claims could not be formulated. Another way of minimising metaphysical discussion and maximising empirical science was to translate metaphysical questions into procedural or methodological form. (Russell; Popper uses this tactic in *Logik der Forschung* on causation and truth.) This tactic shifts interest from a claim like 'only individuals exist' to a different one that contains no existential assertion: 'consider unsatisfactory any social explanation that does not in principle reach to the level of the typical acting individual'.

The principal ontological/methodological problems in early philosophy of science were the status of the invisible world, the status of laws, and whether science was exploring the real world or simply providing useful equations and calculations for prediction and control of it. Many of the entities, processes, relations postulated in the major natural sciences of physics, chemistry and biology are invisible. If invisible they are hardly observational or empirical. If they are claimed to be indirectly observable, through cloud-chambers, accelerators, electron microscopy- and so on, then clearly they are objects subject to interpretations, not 'simple' or 'direct' observations, however specified. (Bacon had meant observations to be theory-independent, so as to avoid all bias when relying on them.)

This preamble brings us to one of the longest standing ontological debates in philosophy of the social sciences, that over methodological individualism (MI) (Bouvier, Chapter 8). The question is, if only individuals exist, what to make of social institutions? Can we explain social events without reference to them? Emerging from Weber and the Austrian school before there was a philosophy of the social sciences, this in a way was the founding debate of the subject in the 1950s. Watkins, Goldstein, etc., in the Feigl and Brodbeck anthology debated the claim of Von Mises, Hayek and Popper that MI was the most fruitful method in social science.[46] Unlike Von Mises and Hayek, Popper went to some lengths to be clear that to be methodological proper MI should not be ontological: so it need not be reductionist (we need not deny the reality of social wholes or explain them away), need not be, should not be, psychologistic, and it was not the same as political individualism. Following the Logical Positivists, Popper tried to minimise ontology, that is, metaphysics, but on the understanding that this avoidance cannot – need not – be successful all the way. So he would not reject outright the holistic method, à la Hegel and Marx. He brought arguments instead to show that in its extreme versions it was not fruitful, but in common sense versions it is observable whenever structures are observed. The difference between him and the positivists was striking. His argument was that the explanatory social whole was not self-explanatory. He did not reject holism but showed that it invited further explanation. An individualist method was fruitful, but only if we do *not* conclude that social wholes are unreal. Wholes are, rather, part of what we might describe as the initial conditions of individual social action, 'the situation'. He also did not freight the notion of the individual with traits, dispositions, intentions or the like, since the scientific focus was necessarily on the typical and repeatable, not the particular. The goal-directedness of action was to be read off from its appearance and the circumstances in which it appears. The emphasis was on repeatable events (which is essential for testability and) which meant that the analysis was general, not particular, and that the descriptions of the circumstances should guarantee repeatability.

A fascinating attempt to mediate between social wholes and individuals is the systematism of Bunge and others (Pickel, Chapter 10). This view has the beauty that it unifies the natural and the social sciences. Systems are seen as a universal feature of the world. The identification of systems (of which individuals are nodes) and their workings is methodologically fundamental. To this observer mechanisms, which have now a considerable literature (Hedström and Ylikoski, Chapter 18; Steel, Chapter 13) or a sub-set of systems.

A sub-debate of MI turned on rationality – a crucial idea in economics, strongly championed by Von Mises. *Homo economicus* acts rationally as a utility maximiser (D'Agostino, Chapter 7). He can only maximise in a perfect market situation. Simplifying this idea, Popper argued that rationality was relative to goals and situation. He suggested that the assumption of actor rationality was a so-called zero method, by which he meant that the social sciences modelled the typical in the typified situation and them compared actual outcomes with predicted outcomes. While economists were looking at markets and firms anthropologists were looking at magic and witchcraft which were, to the Enlightenment, paradigms of irrationality. If, however, they were dominant traits of some simpler societies, the issue arose of how to explain viability. That could be called the debate over the rationality of magic.

Methodological individualism in its most aggressive form is called 'rational choice theory'(Bauhard and Salles, Chapter 17; Chai, Chapter 25). To put it in a nutshell, rational choice theory created artificial or ideal-type situations, set up a limited number of options and modelled the utility-maximising behaviour of the actors. Its main interest was its ability to model unintended consequences, especially in the prisoner's dilemma and the free rider problem. Arrow had already shown the impossibility of certain kinds of desirable outcome for systems of at least two choosers and three options (Arrrow, 1951). These sorts of results seemed to mathematise a claim that Hayek had made long before regarding the price system. It was, he argued, a form of diffuse knowledge and a mechanism for taking account of that knowledge. Yet it was not knowledge that could be accumulated and be held in one place by one body, say, a planning board. These sorts of difficulties and impossibilities showed how methodological individualism could be fruitful.

The last quarter of the twentieth century saw some excited discussion of collective intentions and collective attitudes (Gilbert, 1989; Tuomela, 1991; Searle, 1995, 2005). It is not apparent where this fits in. Gilbert in particular and Searle to a lesser extent seem to suggest that because we sometimes talk as though speaking for more than one person, explanation must be sought in intentions somehow collectively affirmed or at least collectively reached. No doubt there are such cases: soldiers swearing an oath of loyalty in public, for example. But generalising this amounts to the doctrine of the social contract in a mythical multiple versions. And on any version this doctrine is scientifically super-fluous even if philosophically desirable (Wittgenstein may have preferred[47] group intention to institutions as they avoid the problem of the existence of institutions by avoiding mention of them), as quite generally the social sciences are not concerned with actor intentions.[48] They are concerned with the unintended consequences of actions. The actions used to explain the unintended conse-quences are generalised and typified and are modelled as rationally oriented to achieving an aim or goal. An aim or goal is seldom read off from what is said; usually it requires a careful and inventive analysis of how people act. It is here that interpretation is needed, interpretation that may be out of reach of the observer from Mars. Collective intentions look a lot like an attempt to sustain method-ological individualism without acknowledg-ing the separate reality of institutions. If so, then it is a form of psychologism, heir to the insuperable difficulties of that position (Popper, 1945: Chapter 14). If not, it is incumbent on the authors of these theories to explain their underlying problematic as it relates to the descriptions and explanations of social science.

Traditional individualism and psycholo-gism are rooted in both the traditional ver-sion of empiricism that takes theories as resting on individual observations and in the idea that individual people are moral centres whereas social institutions are not. These ideas treat social science as concerned with concrete people and institutions. A most interesting, even exciting, metaphysical idea of Popper that has been little discussed, even by him, is the opposite, what he calls the abstract character of much of social life. By this he means that in a modern as opposed to a face-to-face society we carry out much of our social interaction at a distance, via medi-ated communication and through a screen of roles. As noted above, we objectify to some extent people who are in certain role rela-tions to us, including siblings. We do so much more often and much more systemati-cally, and even the whole way, with such anonymous people as the bank clerk, shop assistant, policeman and so on, whose ano-nymity is a condition that is pervasive in the modern world. We approach them and inter-act with them (and they with us) not as people we know, but rather as people who are the sum of their role performance (Banton, 1965). We expect a bank clerk to be polite, numerate and efficient; we expect a shop assistant to be pleasant, helpful and yet not intrusive. We expect them to smile even when they grieve, which has added the charge of hypocrisy to the charge of alien-ation that modern society imposes on its members. The hope that the policeman will be professional, matter-of-fact and reason-able is not one we impose on friends, family members, strangers chatted to on aeroplanes. They too are playing roles, necessarily, but the roles are not nearly as purely instrumen-tal as in what Popper calls the abstract soci-ety. Our ability to play abstract roles and also to shift back and forth between abstract and concrete social interactions has been a preoc-cupation of some social scientists, such as the symbolic interactionists and the *sui gen-eris* Erving Goffman (Dennis, Chapter 23).

As the vigour of the MI debate waned a new and more general one appeared.[49] Traditionally there had been three schools of thought about science: realists, idealists and instrumentalists. The first and last were dom-inant. Realists thought that the (physical or social) world was real and explanations of its features should strive to use true premises. Instrumentalists wanted to avoid the real/ unreal question and insisted instead that the main criterion of explanation was effective-ness or usefulness. Idealists were *rara avis*. This was to change radically. The reason seems to be simple: instrumentalism leaves open the metaphysical question of reality, whereas realism ascribes reality to whatever entity a well tested (natural or social) theory postulates. Instrumentalism assumes too little, realism too much.[50] Instead, idealism was revived, even though (perhaps because) those doing so did not realise it.

The trend began in 1966, when Peter Berger and Thomas Luckmann, both sociologists, published the influential philosophical treatise *The Social Construction of Reality* (compare Segerstedt, 1966; Holzner, 1968; Wisdom, 1973; Baert et al., Chapter 24). Their bold thesis was that the world of concrete social interaction was nothing of the sort: what was real and unreal was socially constructed. That is, behaviour is routinised, then institutionalised, simultaneously infused with meaning and also with solidity, with reality. The givens of social life are not inevitable and are sustained only by the constant reinforcement of them in social interaction. Families and schools were brought into existence and are sustained by their constant construction in our interactions. Similarly, racial prejudice is not a response to differences in the real world, differences between races, but a construction part of which is the construction of the category of race itself.

Berger and Luckmann were more Durkheimians than Durkheim in their sociological approach and less conservative than he was in social philosophy. Like many provocative ideas, theirs was at once obvious (taken with a pinch of salt) and absurd (taken literally). Restricted to social ontology it had a point. The actual form of the family differs from society to society and only vague and general characterisations can claim necessity (e.g. the human infant cannot survive without prolonged adult nurturing; viable societies have to have institutions to accomplish that). But when their ideas were generalised from the reality of the social world to the reality of the world *tout court*, the absurdity became obvious, not to mention offensive.[51] In all description using language there are elements of convention, no doubt. But the quest for true description is not thereby rendered futile.

The reality of the Holocaust, to use an emotionally charged example, was of a large social process of real things that were done to real people, extinguishing most of them. It is not an option to say that its reality is nothing more than something we construct and then sustain, even though there is an element of obvious truth in that. Similarly, it trivialises environmental damage from nuclear tests to claim that such reality as it has is a social construction. In short, the value of the idea of Berger and Luckmann is that it sharpens our perceptions and raises new problems, some of which are interesting.

The reason that some of these problems are not interesting is the metaphor of construction. 'Construction' evokes a picture like that of an empty piece of land where workers and machines are assembled and where in due course there is a building. The workers and the machines withdraw, but the building remains. If the social constructionists had emphasised the staying power of the institutions they would seem more sensible and less offensive. The fact seems to be that once we have institutionalised some social interactions or other they have an inertia sufficient not only to sustain themselves, but to resist conscious and deliberate attempts to dismantle them and even to reorganise them. One thinks, of course, of the classic studies of bureaucracy and its resistance to reform. The social constructionist reply, fully developed in ethnomethodology, is that the construction of society has to be continuously sustained in social interaction. The institutionalist reply in turn would be that our sustaining activities are themselves sustained by social structures which must be, to some extent, more than our sustaining activities, which they foster and circumscribe.

The metaphysics behind all this is one of the oldest: the contrast between truths by nature and truths by convention. It was always held that a truth by nature, such as the phases of the moon, or the succession of the seasons, gave us true knowledge of unchanging reality. Truths by convention, by contrast, were local and thus mere opinion (*doxa*). If a group believes that a storm at sea is a manifestation of the anger of Poseidon that is, as our students say, their point of view, one we cannot and should not gainsay. A different group may view it as the gods at play, or as due to the swaying of the earth. None of these is privileged. None of these is a truth by nature.

The dichotomy between truth by nature and truth by convention does not hold. All language is in part convention, in part natural, a mixture. But if language is a mixture then perhaps the most important institution of human society – language – is not reducible either to nature or to convention. The very institution that makes science and philosophy possible embodies a pragmatic refutation of such reduction.

The dichotomy between truth by nature and truth by convention includes the theory of substance that is too vague to be of any use (Russell, 1927: 253ff; 1946: 210–211). It also categorises all that is not substantial as convention, even when it is hardly conventional in the conventional sense. Institutions, for example, are sometimes enshrined in buildings, but they are not buildings; like markets, they usually have many people interacting in them, but not always, since words, ideas, and laws are all institutions that shape people but do not consist of them.

The view that there are only truths by nature might be called naturalistic fundamentalism. A moderate naturalism not only allows for truth by convention, it also views human social interaction as best explained by statements that mix truths by nature and truths by convention. Like all sets of philosophical problems, the field of philosophy of the social sciences is at times subject to the pull of idealism, we might call another fundamentalism. In the twentieth century it developed new names, 'the social construction of reality', 'discourse theory', 'postmodernism', 'deconstruction', 'theory' and others. Its critics call it 'linguistic idealism'. Philosophers as different as Husserl, the later Wittgenstein, Foucault and Derrida have been its inspiration. Mostly this idealism has

had little impact on empirical social science except in one rather negative way. Idealism is sufficiently repugnant to the empirically inclined that they would rather retreat into instrumentalism than engage in idle philosophical dispute. Without this fall-back idealism can undermine the confidence of empirical social scientists that they are making scientific progress.

The prevailing direction of flow in philosophy of the social sciences goes from first-order social science to philosophy of the social sciences. But there is feedback. The problem is that sometimes the feedback is destructive. A case in point is anthropology, which Winch explicitly criticised in his 1964 article. Winch held, to cut a long story short, that Evans-Pritchard was in no position to say that Azande witchcraft was unreal, since that treated witchcraft as though it made an empirical claim about the world. In fact, Winch held, witchcraft was part and parcel of the Azande outlook (as Evans-Pritchard held), their way of doings things (as everybody agrees), their culture (ditto) and that they could not think their culture was wrong (oh dear), since what was wrong and what was right was a distinction drawn within that culture. Azande culture endorsed witches and witchcraft therefore witches and witchcraft were real for the Azande. The question of whether they were real *tout court* could not be asked. At the time Winch was writing social anthropology was flourishing and bid fair to be the master social science. Winch's ideas were stoutly rebutted and his fame faded. But it seems that idealism in one form or another was eating away at the confidence of anthropologists, who were also beset by the moral and political assault of post-colonial studies. By the new millennium the game was over and the idealists were dominant. Not so much the particular idealism Winch was advocating, but another idealism, 'post-modernism', had come to dominate anthropology. Its guru was Clifford Geertz and his more radical offspring, and the entire claim to a universal science of human kind was repudiated (Gellner, 1992;

Yoshida, 2007). The post-modernists replaced it with a particularism that was sheepishly self-conscious and, often enough, inextricably politicised. Anthropology is an extreme case of a subject auto-destructing under the impact of idealist arguments from the philosophy of the social sciences. It is a case showing that this particular 'philosophy of' is not parasitic or merely descriptive (*pace* Winch). It shows that philosophy of the social sciences 'dialectically' interacts with first order scientific endeavour. It is to be hoped that we will have no further casualties of philosophical idealism.[52]

CONCLUSION

Presenting the philosophy of the social sciences through the lenses of ideas and of institutions I have tried to throw light on why there is such a subject and why it has the double tendency to unruliness and to discipline. Although I have alluded to some worries about the institutional entrenchment of specialisation and technicality, these seem to me less dangerous when weighed against the power of ideas. Hopefully, the social sciences are part of the great project of modern science, bringing knowledge and enlightenment. If they are, then they bring the same hope that natural science brings, namely, that we can better come to terms with the world with the aid of better knowledge of it. The social sciences can help us come to terms with social life and its problems by showing which can be solved and how, and which have eluded us and need to be pursued.

Just as knowledge of nature has a sorcerer's apprentice side to it, so does knowledge of society. We can learn enough to know how to destroy individuals and societies. Our explorations also have unintended consequences. It is doubtful whether the mentors of idealism meant to undermine the self-confidence of anthropology and effectively destroy the subject (Diaz de Rada, Chapter 11). That is what happened, however. It is also doubtful whether they saw themselves as promoting relativistic nihilism. On the contrary, they thought of themselves as promoting tolerance and understanding (Jarvie, 2007). The road to hell is paved with good intentions. Knowledge is power, whether social or natural, and even sceptical questioning has power, and power needs to be used wisely. Philosophy of the social sciences is a subject that challenges the way things are sometimes done in both the social sciences and philosophy. Even as it flourishes, gets more specialised and, sometimes, more technical, it behooves us to attend both to its origins in the real problems of the social and to the effects it has on the social sciences themselves.

NOTES

1 'The belief that there is such a thing as physics, or biology, or archaeology and that these "studies" or "disciplines" are distinguishable by the subject matter which they investigate, appears to me to be a residue from the time when one believed that a theory had to proceed from a definition of its own subject matter. But a subject matter, or kinds of things, do not, I hold, constitute a basis for distinguishing disciplines. Disciplines are distinguished partly for historical reasons and reasons of administrative convenience (such as the organization of teaching and of appointments), and partly because the theories which we construct to solve our problems have a tendency to grow into unified systems' (Popper, 1952). Popper is putting his finger on the methodological essentialism that undergirds our academic institutions, one that was shown by Galileo to be the arch-enemy of scientific progress. This conflict is the main reason why interdisciplinary programmes emerge and also why new departments and divisions get created.

2 Yet it should be noted that, as late as the middle of the twentieth century, advocates of revolution in the name of reason could contemplate violence and terror with equanimity, if not relish. See Judt (1992) which makes a depressing read.

3 An early usage of this kind in social science is Isaac Schapera's (1938) A Handbook of Tswana Law and Custom. Commissioned by the then Bechuanaland Protectorate Administration for the use of its officers, anthropological tradition has it that it was also consulted by Tswana chiefs and judges. Its catalogue of laws and customs is embedded in a sophisticated

anthropological framework that was, characteristically of its author, left unstated.

4 There are many more: geography, psychology, demography, political science, media and cultural studies, economic history, criminology and so on.

5 The leading anti-naturalist Hegel considered all human studies a part of history, asserting that only humans, not sticks and stones, have history. This argument was answered by Heinrich Rickert, Henri Poincaré and others: both social and natural studies have universal and historical parts.

6 Sheer technique would not capture meta-methodological issues; metaphysical issues; boundary issues; unity of science issues, and more.

7 This formulation differs somewhat from the view of many philosophers writing in the wake of the late Wittgenstein. Note in this volume Peter and Spiekermann (Chapter 9) and Mantzavinos (Chapter 19). Mantazavinos writes of institutions as 'normative social rules'. While some institutions have rules, formal and tacit, 'grown' institutions like families are hardly captured by such a characterisation. (Tolstoy oversimplified: both happy and unhappy families vary widely.) The use of 'rules' implies the possibility of articulation, has a nuance of orderliness and system, with overtones of coercion or at least pressure on individuals to conform. To avoid these implications, I prefer to use the idea of structure. 'Structure' suggests permanent or slowly changing features that aid individuals to navigate in the first instance and which they subsequently learn to exploit. It seems to me that it is minimal structural resemblances that make families rather than normative social rules. Both are present, but the former is necessary. No matter how unruly a family is we can still identify it as one by its structure.

8 Most of the volumes mentioned below will be found at H61 in the Library of Congress classification. Nonetheless, the scatter pattern to be discussed is apparent in that works emphasising economics are moved into HB, those emphasising sociology into HM and those impinging on anthropology to GN. Oddly, Popper's *Poverty of Historicism* is with historiographical works at D16. Anything on Marxism moves to HX and if the cataloguer judges philosophy to be predominant the work will be in B. It is instructive to look at the catalogue assignments of the relevant works of Elster, Hayek and of various contributors to social studies of science. Of the journals to be mentioned, only *Theory and Decision* is in H61. The underlying metaphysics behind cataloguing is no more transparent than that behind supermarket shelving systems.

9 It was an official continuation of the Frankfurt School's journal *Zietschrift für Sozialforschung*.

10 The pioneers Feigl and Brodbeck (1953) drew one piece from each, others from an economics journal, a sociology journal, a scientific monthly and monographs. Feigl followed the logical positivist lore

that denies the possibility of philosophical problems. So did many others of the writers cited below. Yet his anthology, as well as the later works, revolve round problems as the Tables illustrate.

11 The very large social sciences, history, economics and psychology have many philosophically inclined authors who mainly engage with fellow practitioners by publishing in the trade press of their discipline.

12 Tables I.1 and I.2 are related as follows. Table I.1is an attempt to list the problems in some kind of logical order; Table I.2 proceeds book by book, listing the problems covered in each and extending the list as more books are covered. Neither attempt at tidying up the subject succeeds.

13 A dismaying aspect of this was that since Logical Positivists denied that philosophical problems exist their choice of problems was not stated openly, much less chosen according to a criterion – unless we allow a vague naturalism to be a criterion.

14 Popper (1952) said that philosophical problems arise out of science; when they do not philosophy becomes as barren as the Positivists feared it was.

15 It should go without saying that this table can never be complete. As argued, the problem-set of philosophy of the social sciences is always changing. Add to this that the focus of scholarly interest also changes in independent ways and we can see why any such table is partial, preliminary and *pro tem*.

16 The most resolute pro-naturalists would deny this. They can point to logic where the revolution in logic of the late-nineteenth and early-twentieth centuries completely changed the subject. By contrast, from Bacon's *Novum Organum* (1620) to Ryle et al.'s *The Revolution in Philosophy* (1956) to Foucault's *Archaeology of Knowledge* (1969), these new beginnings more typically fizzle out. Sometimes, but only sometimes, there are reasonably conclusive refutations of some philosophical claim. (The central tenets of Logical Postivism clearly suffered this fate.) Most of the time, however, the claim to have superseded previous views is a combination of bluff and of the reification of shifts of fashion into progress. Other times, as in utter refusal to accept that induction, say, is a non-starter, it is cargo-cult style wishful thinking.

17 One thinks of the heyday of the behaviourist revolution of the 1950s in political science, although it could also trace its roots back to Merriam in the 1920s.

18 See note 1.

19 One way to read the following from Hegel is to see him saying that social science is impossible because there is no social scientific prediction: 'Only one word more concerning the desire to teach the world what it ought to be. For such a purpose philosophy at least always comes too late. Philosophy, as the thought of the world, does not appear until reality has completed its formative process, and

made itself ready. History thus corroborates the teaching of the conception that only in the maturity of reality does the ideal appear as counterpart to the real, apprehends the real world in its substance, and shapes it into an intellectual kingdom. When philosophy paints its grey in grey, one form of life has become old, and by means of grey it cannot be rejuvenated, but only known. The owl of Minerva, takes its flight only when the shades of night are gathering.' (Hegel, *Philosophy of Right* 1820, Preface, using the Dyde translation.)

20 'Why is progress a prerequisite reserved almost exclusively for the activities we call science?' asks Kuhn (1962, final chapter, opening paragraph), and he adds (second paragraph), 'Notice immediately that part of the question is entirely semantic. ... the term 'science' is reserved for fields that do progress in obvious ways.' Does art not progress in some ways?

21 See his *Introduction to the Human Sciences*, Book I, chapter 2, p. 57 of the 1989 English translation.

22 Of these three criteria, only intersubjective testability is clear in that there is consensus about some tests. What degree of reliability counts is moot, and comprehensiveness, taken literally, was never achieved, whereas taken as the universality of its assertion is achievable all too easily (by near-tautologies so-called).

23 Scientific knowledge is distinct from common sense or folk knowledge in that much of the latter the former declares false. Both natural scientific and social scientific ideas found in Plato and Aristotle are found in contemporary folk knowledge, for example, the idea that male and female are parts of an original whole that yearns for reunion. Other ideas in these philosophers, such as that slaves are naturally inferior, and that women are in many senses inferior to men, linger in folk knowledge despite refutations in natural and in social science. By contradistinction, the scientific ideas of Archimedes are not commonsense and they are among the oldest to appear in the contemporary science textbook.

24 This was immediately pointed out to Kuhn. It is not so much that the social sciences have not found their Galileo, but that they have found several. Of course, the strict Kuhnian reading is that multiple paradigms are a sign of a pre-scientific stage.

25 For an alternative Wittgensteinian approach, equally anti-naturalistic, see Louch (1966).

26 See Dilthey (1883): 'The real categories ... are nowhere the same in the sciences of the Spirit as they are in the sciences of Nature' ['Die realen Kategorian sind aber in den Geisteswissenschaften nirgands dieselben als in den Naturwissenschaften'], *Gesammelte Schriften*, vol. VII, *Der Aufbander Geschichtlichen Welt in Den Geisteswissenschaften, III Plan der Fortsetzung zum Aufbau des Geschichtlichen Welt in Der Geisteswissenschaften, 3, Der Zusammenhang des Lebens*, para 3, p. 197.

27 Gellner said, Winch got Wittgenstein right and Wittgenstein was manifestly mistaken. The attacks on Winch were thus for not obfuscating Wittgenstein's doctrine sufficiently to immunise it against falsification. Wittgensteinians preferred obscurity to interesting falsity (Gellner, 1964, 1968, 1975, 1984).

28 This is not to endorse Durkheim's study of suicide: the variables that he found most relevant to suicide are high levels of integration or of *anomie*, neither of which is free of psychology; rather they are socially dependent psychological traits.

29 Kuhn seems not to have realised that his criterion could be easily satisfied by designating work under each paradigm a separate subject, paradigm dominated, hence scientific. Think of social psychology, physiological psychology, sociology, social anthropology, cultural anthropology, historical linguistics, social history, economic history and so on.

30 Winch offers his view as not empirical. Is it an *a priori* valid truth?

31 Winch is alive and well in his defenders, see Gunnell's (2009) review of Hutchinson et al. (2008).

32 The relation of philosophy of science and of the social sciences to first-order science is contested. Those who demand value freedom and those who conceive of philosophy as utterly a priori agree that there can be no normative import to philosophising. To those who take a more interactive view of problems, ideas and criticisms passing back and forth the normative import is inescapable. In the latter case the danger is presumption, which is curbed by intellectual humility.

33 In 1958 when Taylor reviewed *The Poverty of Historicism* for *Universities and Left Review*, he aligned himself with Marxist historicism, which amusingly he both affirmed (Marx's philosophy was not historicist) and denied (historicism is a straw man of Popper's creation). He subsequently published a book, *The Explanation of Behaviour* (1964), which is a critique of behaviourism. This seems to have been a turning point. The social or human sciences are about human behaviour and behaviourism is unable to identify and describe it, much less to explain it, just because it aims at describing it externally with no reference to purpose (and thus not as behaviour proper). (This was also Chomsky's critique of Skinner's behaviourist theory of language (Chomsky 1959).) Perhaps then all external descriptions and vocabularies are distorting. So far the argument is valid. The invalid inference takes place at the next step. It is a conclusion that is essential for Taylor's case. He notices this when he qualifies in the quotation above with 'or some related vocabulary', thus rendering the actors' vocabulary not necessary after all. The argument from distortion or bias or unintelligibility in principle is simply too strong. It obviates all social science and leaves philosophy in the absurd position of viewing Durkheim, Weber, Pareto and

Evans-Pritchard as the ones who do not know what they are talking about and who do not know what they are doing. Much worse, the same holds for the natural scientists too. This overreaching occurs because of a confused sense that social scientists are not necessarily talking about what the philosophers want to talk about.

34 At the London School of Economics (LSE) in the 1950s people pointed to Sidney and Beatrice Webb as formulating this idea. I have not found it asserted in their writings although the corresponding attitude certainly informs them sometimes. See also Edman (1926).

35 Part of the trouble comes from focusing on concepts and systems of concepts as though they were closed. Another part comes from failure to utilise the powerful notion of the metalanguage. Natural languages permit their own discussion by shifting to a metalanguage. Strangely, linguistic philosophy presupposes the idea of the metalanguage yet simultaneously engages in pragmatic contradiction by seeing conceptual systems as closed. It will be unable to get free of this mess without acknowledging that Wittgenstein denied the metalanguage all meaning and that he was in dire error.

36 In *Remarks on Frazer's* The Golden Bough, Wittgenstein says, Frazer just does not get the hang of ritual activity. It is not goal-directed or instrumental but self-sufficient: we do it and are satisfied. Suppose this is true. Is that a reason that the social scientist should be satisfied? Suicides kill themselves and are dead. Is that the end of the matter for the social scientist? What Wittgenstein wanted is to show that we need not explain the roles of rituals; yet we do just that, since they serve diverse roles (they are not self-sufficient); they spread joy during weddings and grief during funerals. Sometimes we are satisfied and sometimes we are not. Rituals are, in short, *problematic*. That there are no philosophical problems is a constant in Wittgenstein's thought, early and late.

37 Just how conservative and traditional has emerged in the works of Taylor's old age (see especially 2007).

38 Ludwig von Mises stressed (1957) that social theories should be value-free, not social thinkers: value-free thinking is liberal.

39 Bacon's theory of science was of the prepared mind. Science was a struggle against bad mental habits (the famous idols). The well prepared mind is filled with the facts and has used these to safeguard itself against prejudices, that is, anticipations (conjectures). If all prejudice is shot down then true axioms and generalisations will directly emerge from the facts. Being a political conservative he did not recommend the scientific study of society (of the law) but only of nature. His disciples never accepted this restriction.

40 Hacohen (2000) argues there was an impact upon Popper too, although Popper obscured it. Hacohen is not sure why. The reason is that tradition requires acknowledgements for discoveries of facts and for new ideas, not for debates, even when these are enlightening.

41 Driving this home he writes 'altering our scientific language is cohesive with altering our social and private life. There is no extraterritoriality for sociologists, or for other scientists, and this is not always sufficiently acknowledged' (1944: 46). In his final paragraph he sketches the metaphor of human beings as sailors far out to sea trying to reconstruct their vessel from materials to hand and drifting by, changing their plans as they go along, and already reconsidering them before they are finished. 'But they cannot put the ship in dock in order to start from scratch' (1944: 47). It is intriguing to ask whether Oakeshott's variation (1962) on the same metaphor was a conscious or an unconscious one.

42 Politics at work again, perhaps. As the *Methodenstreit* continued into the period between the wars, the Planning Debate became part of it and of course planning was a wedge issue for the socialists of the Vienna Circle. Popper's work showed that the planning issue is separable and invites different and commonsense considerations.

43 The OED credits the first usage of the phrase 'philosophy of the social sciences' to Hans Reichenbach in his book *The Rise of Scientific Philosophy* (first edition 1951). This would suggest it was in the air among the positivist diaspora in the 1940s.

44 For an interesting sketch of such threads surrounding evolution see Fuller (2008). See also Hodgson, Chapter 20.

45 Galileo objected to the postulate of forces (of William Gilbert) as occult. The scientific revolution rejected all occult qualities out of hand. Some objected to Newton's force of gravity as occult. He took offence and argued against the charge. Berkeley repeated the charge.

46 I have gisted the formative first part of the debate (i.e. before rational choice came to dominate it) in an appendix to Jarvie (1972).

47 It is hard to divine Wittgenstein's intentions, but at least his having condemned explanation as such makes the Gilbert–Searle position more admissible than if we want to explain concerted intentions. Such explanations refer to institutional arrangements (as is in the case of taking the oath in public).

48 The exceptions are certain branches of psychology and of history. Perhaps we should label the rest of the social sciences, economics, sociology, anthropology, political science as the sciences of social institutions and unintended consequences – *tout court*.

49 *The Stanford Encyclopedia of Philosophy* entry on methodological individualism postulates a whole

second phase initiated by Elster, or rather, by rational choice theory upon which Elster rides (Elster, 1982, 1989). As the author, Joseph Heath, notes, Elster took a step backwards. For Hayek and Popper the individual is a cypher in a situation that invites rational reconstruction. Elster wants a psychologically enriched individual. Elster also muddied the waters by suggesting high-handedly that the best of Marx is compatible with MI (Elster, 1982, 1985); Popper had already shown that some of the best of Marx's analyses were situational, and that he did not develop the general theory of it. Heath's interesting entry fails to list the three best papers that emerged from the (first) debate: Agassi (1960, 1975) and Wisdom (1970). Udehn's coverage is better (2001).

50 This difficulty for realists disappears if realism is modified, and rather than being the view of theories as (literally) true, it becomes the view of theories as (literally) true-or-false. It then fits well with most modern philosophies of science, but only Popper laid stress on it.

51 It is the sociological version of what is called in natural science the anthropic principle. In both versions it needs careful handling if idealism, even solipsism is not to be the fallout.

52 It goes without saying that anthropological research continues (sometimes heavily camouflaged), as do departments and professorships of anthropology. We are, as the man said, students of problems and not of subject matters. Problems outlive the shifting morale of practitioners.

REFERENCES

Agassi, Joseph (1960) 'Methodological individualism', *British Journal of Sociology* 11: 244–70.

Agassi, Joseph (1961) 'Review of Felix Kaufmann, *The Methodology of the Social Sciences*', *Econometrica*, 29: 100–101.

Agassi, Joseph (1971) 'Tautology and testability in economics', *Philosophy of the Social Sciences*, 1(1): 49–63.

Agassi, Joseph (1975) 'Institutional individualism', *British Journal of Sociology*, 26: 144–155.

Agassi, Judith Buber and Stephen Heycock (eds) (1989) *The Redesign of Working Time: Promise or Threat?* Berlin: Edition Sigma.

Arrow, Kenneth J. (1951) *Social Choice and Individual Values.* New York: Wiley.

Bacon, Sir Francis (1620) *Novum Organum.* London: Apud Joannem Billium. Collected works edited by James Spedding, Robert Leslie Ellis and Douglas Heath, London: Longmans 1862–1901.

Baert, Patrick (2005) *Philosophy of the Social Sciences: Towards Pragmatism.* Cambridge: Polity.

Banton, Michael (1965) *Roles: An Introduction to the Study of Social Relations.* London: Tavistock Publications.

Benton, Ted and Ian Craib (2001) *Philosophy of Social Science: The Philosophical Foundations of Social Thought.* New York: Palgrave.

Bishop, Robert (2007) *The Philosophy of the Social Sciences.* London: Continuum International Publishing Group.

Berger, Peter and Thomas Luckmann (1966) *The Social Construction of Reality: A Treatise in the Sociology of Knowledge.* Garden City, NY: Doubleday.

Boland, Lawrence A. (1989) *The Methodology of Economic Model Building.* London: Routledge.

Borger, Robert and Frank Cioffi (eds) (1970) *Explanation in the Behavioural Sciences.* Cambridge: Cambridge University Press.

Braybrooke, David (ed.) (1965) *Philosophical Problems of the Social Sciences.* New York: Macmillan.

Braybrooke, David (1987) *Philosophy of Social Science.* Englewood Cliffs, NJ: Prentice Hall.

Broadie, Alexander (ed.) (2003) *The Cambridge Companion to the Scottish Enlightenment.* Cambridge: Cambridge University Press.

Brodbeck, May (1968) *Readings in the Philosophy of Social Science.* New York: Macmillan.

Brown, Stuart C. (ed.) (1979) *Philosophical Disputes in the Social Sciences.* Brighton: Harvester.

Church, Alonzo (1949) 'Review of A. J. Ayer, *Language, Truth and Logic*, 2nd edition', *Journal of Symbolic Logic*, 14(1): 52–53.

Chomsky, Noam (1959) 'Review of Skinner's *Verbal Behavior*', *Language*, 35: 26–58.

Dahl, Robert (1963) *Modern Political Analysis.* Englewood Cliffs, NJ: Prentice-Hall.

Dallmayr, Fred R. and Thomas A. McCarthy (eds) (1977) *Understanding and Social Inquiry.* Notre Dame, IN: University of Notre Dame Press.

Dilthey, Wilhelm (1883) *Introduction to the Human Sciences.* Volume I of the *Selected Works*, Rudolf A. Makkreel and Frithjof Rodi (eds), Princeton: Princeton University Press, 1989.

Durkheim, Émile (1897) *Suicide: A Study in Sociology.* Translated by John A. Spaulding and George Simpson, Glencoe, IL: Free Press, 1951.

Durkheim, Émile (1895) *The Rules of Sociological Method.* Translated by Sarah A. Solovay and John H. Mueller and edited by George E. G. Catlin, Chicago: University of Chicago Press, 1938.

Durkheim, Émile and Marcel Mauss (1903) *On Primitive Classification.* Translated by Rodney Needham, London: Cohen and West, 1963.

Edman, Irwin (1926) 'Adam, the baby, and the man from Mars', *Journal of Philosophy*, 23(14): 449–459.

Elster, Jon (1982) 'The case for methodological individualism', *Theory and Society*, 11: 453–482.

Elster, Jon (1985) *Making Sense of Marx*. Cambridge: Cambridge University Press.

Elster, Jon (1989) *Nuts and Bolts for the Social Sciences*. Cambridge: Cambridge University Press.

Emmett, Dorothy and Alasdair MacIntyre (eds) (1970), *Sociological Theory and Philosophical Analysis*. London: Macmillan.

Evans-Pritchard, Edward E. (1937) *Witchcraft, Oracles and Magic among the Azande* Oxford: Clarendon Press.

Feigl, Herbert and May Brodbeck (1953) *Readings in the Philosophy of Science*. New York: Appleton-Century-Crofts.

Ferguson, Adam (1767) *An Essay on the History of Civil Society*. Edinburgh: Printed for A. Millar & T. Caddel in the Strand, London, and A. Kincaid & J. Bell, Edinburgh.

Foucault, Michel (1969) *The Archaeology of Knowledge*. London: Tavistock Publications, 1972.

Fuller, Steve (2008) *Dissent over Descent: Intelligent Design's Challenge to Darwinism*. Cambridge, UK: Icon Books.

Gardiner, Patrick ed. (1959) *Theories of History: readings from classical and contemporary sources* Glencoe, IL: Free Press.

Gellner, Ernest (1958) 'Time and theory in social anthropology', *Mind*, 67(2): 182–202.

Gellner, Ernest (1964) *Thought and Change*. London: Weidenfeld and Nicholson.

Gellner, Ernest (1968) 'The new idealism – cause and meaning in the social sciences', in I. C. Jarvie and J. Agassi, (eds), *Cause and Meaning in the Social Sciences*. London: Routledge, 1973, pp. 50–77. (This volume was reprinted as *The Concept of Kinship*, Oxford: Blackwell 1987, and again as volume I of *Selected Philosophical Themes* by Routledge once more in 2003. The original appeared in I. Lakatos and A. Musgrave, (eds), *Problems in the Philosophy of Science*. Amsterdam: North-Holland Pub. Co. 1968. pp. 377–406.)

Gellner, Ernest (1974) *Legitimation of Belief*. Cambridge: Cambridge University Press.

Gellner, Ernest (1975) 'A Wittgensteinian philosophy of (or against) the social sciences', *Philosophy of the Social Sciences*, 5(2): 173–199.

Gellner, Ernest (1984) 'The Gospel according to Saint Ludwig', *American Scholar*, 53(2): 243–263. (Reprinted with small changes as Chapter 7 in *Relativism and the Social Sciences*, Cambridge: Cambridge University Press, 1985.)

Gellner, Ernest (1992) *Postmodernism, Reason and Religion*. London: Routledge.

Gibson, Quentin (1960) *The Logic of Social Inquiry*. London: Routledge.

Gilbert, Margaret (1989) *On Social Facts*. London: Routledge.

Gunnell, John G. (2009) 'Review of Hutchinson et al., 2008', *Philosophy of the Social Sciences*, 39(4): 595–621.

Hacohen, Malachi (2000) *Karl Popper: The Formative Years 1902–1945*. Cambridge: Cambridge University Press.

Hayek, F. A. von (1952) *The Counter-Revolution of Science: Studies in the Abuse of Reason*. Glencoe IL: The Free Press.

Hayek, F. A. von (1967) 'The results of human action but not of human design', in his *Studies in Philosophy, Politics and Economics*. London: Routledge & Kegan Paul, pp. 96–105.

Hegel, G. W. F. (1820) *Hegel's Philosophy of Right*. Translated by S. W. Dyde, London: G. Bell. 1896.

Hollis, Martin (1994) *The Philosophy of Social Science: An Introduction*. Cambridge: Cambridge University Press.

Holzner, Burkart (1968) *Reality Construction in Society*. Cambridge, MA: Sheckmann.

Hutchinson, Phil, Rupert Read and Wes Sharrock (2008) *There is no Such Thing as a Social Science. A Defence of Peter Winch*. Aldershot: Ashgate.

Jarvie, I. C. (1964) *The Revolution in Anthropology*. London: Routledge and Kegan Paul.

Jarvie, I. C. (1970) 'Understanding and explanation in sociology and social anthropology', in Robert Borger and Frank Cioffi (eds) *Explanation in the Behavioural Sciences*. Cambridge: Cambridge University Press. pp. 231–245. Expanded as Chapter 2 of Jarvie 1972.

Jarvie, I. C. (1972) *Concepts and Society*. London: Routledge.

Jarvie, I. C. (1984) *Rationality and Relativism* London: Routledge.

Jarvie, I. C. (2001) *The Republic of Science. The Emergence of Popper's Social View of Science, 1935–1945*. Amsterdam: Rodopi.

Jarvie, I. C. (2007) 'Relativism and historicism', in Stephen Turner and Mark Risjord, (eds), *Handbook of the Philosophy of Science. Philosophy of Anthropology and Sociology*. Amsterdam: Elsevier, pp. 553–589.

Judt, Tony (1992) *Past Imperfect: French Intellectuals, 1944–1956*. Berkeley and Los Angeles: University of California Press.

Kaufmann, Felix (1944) *Methodology of the Social Sciences* New York: Oxford University Press.

Klappholz, Kurt and Joseph Agassi (1959) 'Methodological prescriptions in economics', *Economica*, 26(101): 60–74.

Krimerman, Leonard (1969) *The Nature and Scope of Social Science: A Critical Anthology*. New York: Appleton-Century-Crofts.

Kuhn, Thomas S. (1962) *The Structure of Scientific Revolutions*. Chicago: University of Chicago Press.

Lipset, S. M. (1960) *Political Man: The Social Bases of Politics*. Garden City, NY: Doubleday.

Lipset, Seymour Martin and Reinhard Bendix (1959) *Social Mobility in Industrial Society*. Berkeley and Los Angeles: University of California Press.

Louch, A. R. (1966) *Explanation and Human Action* Berkeley and Los Angeles, CA: University of California Press.

Mantzavinos, C. (2009) *Philosophy of the Social Sciences. Philosophical Theory and Scientific Practice*. Cambridge: Cambridge University Press.

Martin, Michael and Lee C. McIntyre (eds) (1994) *Readings in the Philosophy of Social Science*. Cambridge, MA: MIT Press.

Mill, John Stuart (1843) A system of logic, ratiocinative and inductive : being a connected view of the principles of evidence and the methods of scientific investigation London: John W. Parker, West Strand.

Nagel, Ernest (1950) 'Memorial address for Felix Kaufmann', *Philosophy and Phenomenological Research*, 10(3): 464–469.

Nagel, Ernest (1961) *The Structure of Science: Problems in the Logic of Scientific Explanation*. New York: Harcourt, Brace, and World.

Natanson, Maurice (ed.) (1963) *Philosophy of the Social Sciences: A Reader*. New York: Random House.

Neurath, Otto (1944) *Foundations of the Social Sciences*. (*International Encyclopedia of Unified Science*, Volume II, Number 1.) Chicago, IL: University of Chicago Press.

Oakeshott, Michael (1962) *Rationalism in Politics and Other Essays*. London: Methuen.

Papineau, David (1979) *For Science in the Social Sciences*. New York: St. Martin's.

Phillips, Patrick J. J. (2007) *The Challenge of Relativism. Its Nature and Limits*. London: Continuum.

Poincaré, Henri (1908) *Science and Method*. Translated by Francis Maitland, Edinburgh: Nelson (Dover Reprint 1958).

Pole, David (1958) *The Later Philosophy of Wittgenstein*, London: Athlone Press.

Popper, Karl R. (1935) *Logik der Forschung. Zur Erkenntnistheorie der Mordernen Wissenschaft*, Wien: Julius Springer. Translated by the author as *The Logic of Scientific Discovery*, London: Hutchinson 1959.

Popper, Karl R. (1945) *The Open Society and Its Enemies*. London: George Routlege & Sons.

Popper, Karl R. (1952) 'The nature of philosophical problems and their roots in science', reprinted as chapter 2 of *Conjectures and Refutations*, London: Routledge and Kegan Paul 1963.

Popper, Karl R. (1957) *The Poverty of Historicism*. London: Routledge and Kegan Paul.

Popper, Karl R. (1958) 'Back to the Presocratics', *Proceedings of the Aristotelian Society*, 59: 1–24; reprinted as Chapter 5 of *Conjectures and Refutations*, London: Routledge and Kegan Paul 1963.

Popper, Karl R. (1963) 'The demarcation between science and metaphysics', Chapter 11 of *Conjectures and Refutations*, London: Routledge and Kegan Paul 1963.

Pratt, Vernon (1978) *The Philosophy of the Social Sciences*. London: Methuen.

Quine, W. V. O. (1951) 'Two dogmas of empiricism', *Philosophical Review*, 60: 20–43, reprinted in his *From a Logical Point of View*, Cambridge, MA: Harvard University Press 1953.

Reichenbach, Hans (1951) *The Rise of Scientific Philosophy*. Berkeley and Los Angeles: University of California Press.

Root, Michael (1993) *Philosophy of Social Science: The Methods, Ideals, and Politics of Social Inquiry*. Cambridge, MA: Blackwell.

Rosenberg, Alexander (1988) *Philosophy of Social Science*. Boulder, CO: Westview.

Rudner, Richard (1966) *Philosophy of Social Science*. Englewood Cliffs, NJ: Prentice-Hall.

Russell, Bertrand (1927) *An Outline of Philosophy*. London: Allen and Unwin.

Russell, Bertrand (1946) *History of Western Philosophy*. London: Allen and Unwin.

Ryan, Alan (1970) *The Philosophy of the Social Sciences*. London: Macmillan.

Ryle, Gilbert ed. (1956) *The Revolution in Philosophy*. London: Macmillan.

Schapera, Isaac (1938) *A Handbook of Tswana Law and Custom: Compiled for the Bechuanaland Protectorate Administration*. London: for the International Institute of African Languages and Cultures by Oxford University Press.

Schutz, Alfred (1962–66) *Collected Papers*, 3 volumes, The Hague: Nijhoff.

Schutz, Alfred (1967) *The Phenomenology of the Social World*. Translated George Walsh and Frederick Lehnert, Evanston, IL: Northwestern University Press.

Searle, John, R. (1995) *The Construction of Social Reality*. New York: Free Press.

Searle, John, R. (2005) 'What is an institution?', *Journal of Institutional Economics*, 1: 1–22.

Segerstedt, T. T. (1966) *The Nature of Social Reality*. Totowa, NJ: Bedminster.

Taylor, Charles (1958) 'The poverty of *The Poverty of Historicism*', *Universities and Left Review* 4(Summer):77–78.

Taylor, Charles (1964) *Explanation in the Behavioural Sciences,*. London: Routledge.

Taylor, Charles (1971) 'Interpretation and the sciences of man', *Review of Metaphysics*, 25(1): 3–51.

Taylor, Charles (2007) *A Secular Age*. Cambridge, MA: Harvard University Press.

Tuomela, Raimo (1991) 'We will do it: An analysis of group intentions', *Philosophy and Phenomenological Research*, 51: 249–277.

Turner, Stephen (1996) 'Durkheim among the statisticians', *Journal of the History of the Behavioral Sciences*, 32(4): 354–378.

Udehn, Lars (2001) *Methodological Individualism: Background, History and Meaning*. London: Routledge.

Von Mises, Ludwig (1957) *Theory and History: An Interpretation of Social and Economic Evolution*. New Haven, CT: Yale University Press.

Weber, Max (1903) *Roscher and Knies: The Logical Problems of Historical Economics*. New York: Free Press 1975.

Weber, Max (1907) *Critique of Stammler*. New York: Collier Macmillan, 1977.

Wilson, Bryan (ed.) (1970) *Rationality*. Oxford: Blackwell.

Winch, Peter (1958) *The Idea of a Social Science*. London: Routledge.

Winch, Peter (1964) 'Understanding a primitive society', *American Philosophical Quarterly*, 1: 307–324.

Wisdom, J. O. (1970) 'Situational individualism' in Borger, Robert and Frank Cioffi (eds) (1970) *Explanation in the Behavioural Sciences*. Cambridge: Cambridge University Press. pp. 167–217.

Wisdom, J. O. (1973) 'The phenomenological approach to the sociology of knowledge', *Philosophy of the Social Sciences*, 3(3): 257–266.

Wisdom, J. O. (1987) *Philosophy of the Social Sciences*. Aldershot: Avebury.

Wittgenstein, Ludwig (1979) *Remarks on Frazer's Golden Bough*. Retford, UK: Brynmill.

Yoshida, Kei (2007) 'Defending scientific study of the social: Against Clifford Geertz (and his critics)', *Philosophy of the Social Sciences*, 37(3): 289–314.

PART 1

The Development of the Philosophy of Social Science

The Philosophy of Social Science from Mandeville to Mannheim

Joseph Agassi

THE METHODOLOGY OF THE SOCIAL SCIENCES DEPENDS ON SOCIAL PHILOSOPHY

Discussions of methodology in general usually center on the natural sciences, with attention to the social sciences absent or merely thrown in for good measure. Discussion of the methodology of the social sciences looks less to the point than discussions on the methodology of the natural sciences for a reason. Methodology (from the Greek 'hodos', meaning way), the study of the ways to acquire knowledge, relates to epistemology (from the Greek 'epistēmē', meaning knowledge) as means to an end. It seldom refers to details from science, and then either as illustrations or as items to explain. It is usually empiricist, and, under the influence of traditional positivism (= negative attitude towards speculations), it seldom refers to natural philosophy, since tradition considers it a part of speculative metaphysics. Not so the methodology of the social sciences: traditionally its stronger link is not to epistemology but to social philosophy proper (or to what it should or might be). Oddly, this has traditionally the blessing of positivism. (We will come to the reasons for this later and learn that these reasons are poor. Hence, positivism is flawed, not to say inconsistent.)

A document from the later stages of the methodology of the social sciences covered in this chapter may illustrate this dependence of the methodology of the social sciences on social philosophy. It expresses a major point: Durkheim viewed his methodology as 'distinctive' since it is 'entirely independent of philosophy' (Durkheim, 1895: 141, opening of the Conclusion), in obvious conflict with what he said a little earlier (p. 124): 'if ... we say that social life is natural, our reason is not that we find its source in the nature of the individual. It is natural rather because it springs directly from the collective being which is, itself, a being in its own right'. Durkheim's methodology of the social sciences is thus part-and-parcel of his collectivist social philosophy, and so in conflict with his positivism. For another instance, Karl Mannheim made a famous contribution to the methodology of the social sciences; it is known as the sociology of knowledge.[1] It is a methodological suggestion to 'seek to comprehend thought in the concrete setting of an historical situation' (Mannheim, 1936: 3). It is a theory of thoughts as generated by social situations (and hence explained by reference to them). This leads invariably to the question, does this idea apply to historians and sociologists and to their results? Does this idea apply to itself with no trouble? All thinkers who shared the view of knowledge as socially generated took this question as basic, yet they hedged their answers. Durkheim, for a very conspicuous example, raised it and left it open (Durkheim and Mauss, 1903: 86–7). Mannheim answered it in the negative: some 'unattached intellectuals' (Mannheim, 1936: Chapter 3, §4) are 'free-floating' spirits, exempt from bondage to their social environment. All this leaves open many questions (especially that of how we are to explain their conduct and its impact), yet it unites diverse thinkers, from Karl Marx to Thomas S. Kuhn, in the proposal to study the social and intellectual background of thinking, with a bias towards the view that researchers owe to their background more than to their inventiveness (more to luck than wit). Whether this is so or not, it is an instance of a supposition that profoundly influences versions of methodology and of research practices.[2]

Both these instances were collectivist. As an individualist instance, we may consider an assertion of Ludwig von Mises about methodological individualism (Mises, 1957: Introduction *et passim*). The proposal to explain conduct and to do so while referring to the philosophy of the actors under study is not philosophical indifference, he said; it is the time honored liberal philosophy. Right or wrong, again we see a social philosophy in action as a major component in the methodology of the social sciences. Indeed, as the present discussion will show, liberalism is the major motivating force for the rise and growth of the social sciences as they are today.

This is no surprise. The methodology of the natural sciences developed in efforts to keep the researcher out of the picture as much as possible in the name of objectivity, to focus study on efforts to grasp a true picture of the natural world. Social researchers can hardly avoid asking at each stage of their studies, how their assertions apply to themselves, how the social situation of researchers and their social philosophy influence their researches and vice versa. It is amusing to see how much is said that is false just because it is said.[3] The rubber-stamp example for such an assertion is the inconsistent assertion, 'every assertion is false'. A socially more important example is any offer (including that of Mannheim) to set us free of all prejudice. And yet the basis of the philosophy of the Enlightenment Movement (including its liberalism) is the following idea that Francis Bacon pronounced with great assurance early in the seventeenth century: good will suffices as means for overcoming all prejudice.

This idea of Bacon allows for the possibility of a society free of prejudice, namely, founded on perfectly rational or fully scientific principles; it was thus (rightly) taken as the invitation to design such a society once science is sufficiently advanced. This is the Utopianism of the Enlightenment Movement of the Age of Reason. Its methodology, we shall see, was liberal and led to liberal social sciences, mainly politics and economics, and not by accident.

This way, unlike the methodology of the natural sciences, the methodology of the social sciences was initially tied to liberal social philosophy and thus to the rise of liberalism and to the reaction against its failed effort to establish Utopia. These efforts began with the French Revolution, continued in the Utopian colonies that sprang up in the early-nineteenth century, and they more-or-less ended with the recent folding of the Soviet macro-Utopianism and the Kibbutz Movement's micro-Utopianism.

Are failed Utopian experiments refutations of Utopian theories? It is a common error to answer this question before articulating a theory and a refuting observation. Once this is done, it is not hard to check whether the conjunction of the theory and the observation is consistent. Many technological experiments are offered to the public not as clear-cut applications of clear-cut theories; and when they fail, we do not know if their failures are refutation of any specific scientific theory. This lack of specificity wastes the intellectual value of Utopian experiments. Utopianism in general is irrefutable in any case, of course, even if it is limited to this or that view of human nature (unless that view itself is refutable). The most famous Utopia, Plato's *Politeia*, was not designed as a thought experiment in the sense in which the term is used in the natural sciences, where a thought experiment often comes to illustrate a theoretical idea. Thus, Galileo's famous thought experiment about gravity illustrated the inconsistency of the theory of gravity that he wished to replace. Carnot's famous thought experiment is a deduction of his law of maximal efficiency of heat-engines from the second law of thermodynamics. It is a thought experiment, since it is an idealization that comes to eliminate inefficiencies that possibly may be eliminated. Its aim is to show what inefficiency cannot be fully eliminated because heat tends to dissipate. Einstein's famous thought experiment regarding the speed of light is different: it is a device of merely heuristic value (= conducive to discovery) that helps to introduce the Lorenz transformation equations; it is a mere step in the development of an idea (relativistic kinematics). Possibly, all thought experiments in the natural sciences are mere devices that illustrate the strength or weakness of a theory, unless it is heuristic; either way, they are inessential.[4]

Not so Utopian thought experiments: they are ideas of the best society spelled out (including some inessential details). This is true of Plato, Sir Thomas Moore and Tomasso Campanella. It is not true of Mandeville. He wanted to illustrate his view that a society comprised of totally virtuous individuals must break down; he was criticizing and rejecting one of the most popular social philosophies of all time, namely, that virtue is essential for the smooth running of society. And his argument is a thought experiment: *The Fable of the Bees* (1714). It is no refutation, not even when the view that virtue is essential for the smooth running of society is supplemented with an explicit specification of all the virtues that are allegedly required. He was simply rejecting the prevalent social philosophy without refuting it and advocating liberalism in its stead. Thus, in the methodology of the social sciences thought experiment plays a totally different role to the one it plays in the methodology of the natural sciences: it has its honorable place in natural science and in social philosophy but not in social science. What the failure of the Kibbutz experience proves, for example, is unclear, and is open to debate. The same goes for the collapse of the Soviet Union, to take an example that is much harder but also much more significant. Participants to these debates could benefit from the recognition that what we can learn from such failures is not as clear-cut as what we can learn from the failure of a scientific experiment proper. For this, before the experiment begins the theory should be specified well enough to indicate what kind of observation would refute it and what would corroborate it.[5]

The story is odd, since initially liberalism, as Mandeville presented it, is the idea that 'Private Vices by the dextrous Management of a skilful Politician may be turned into Publick Benefits' plus the recommendation, of course, to manage society this way.[6] It then became liberal Utopianism, a theory of governments that do not impose on their subjects, and thus are more or less anarchistic.[7] Its translation into a theory of deductive explanation of social affairs – methodology – came as a result of efforts to employ it in practice, as a theory of minimal legislation[8] (Russell, 1946: 744) that follows a political theory (Russell, 1946: 614) that rests on a theory of human nature. The value of thought experiments, especially the thought experiment of Mandeville, is generally recognized. The point of the present introductory discussion is an interesting and scarcely noted characteristic of the social sciences that this fact displays: unlike the methodology of the natural sciences, the methodology of the social sciences is intertwined with social (including political) philosophy.

TRADITIONAL AND MODERN VIEWS ON THE METHODOLOGY OF THE SOCIAL SCIENCES DIFFER GREATLY

Ancient theories of society are irrelevant to current research since, like almost all known cultures, it took for granted the view that the individual and society are in conflict. This view received backing from traditional metaphysics and from traditional methodology: human nature is anti-social, and society is prior to individuals: students of human affairs should study individuals as parts of the wholes to which they belong, and to which they should submit. Plato reinforced this tradition, and his works on social studies stayed within it, focusing on the central traditional problem: how should rulers control their subjects in addition to policing and to similar state controls? Traditions, particularly Western, used religion and its threats of hellfire and brimstone as weighty means for reinforcement as well as legitimation of policing and of state controls. As modern views became largely liberal, traditional philosophy increasingly opposed political traditions, *a priori,* until the rise of the Reaction. The foundations of modern methodology are found in the works of liberal critics of political traditions, including Machiavelli, Hobbes, Spinoza, Mandeville, Hume and Smith. They left behind the traditional demand for measures to control the common people. This demand stems from the traditional view that common people cannot control themselves and the traditional defense of tyranny by reference to people's alleged anti-social tendencies. Tyranny of one sort or another was the traditional remedy to the alleged weakness of common people. The liberal critics of traditional politics wanted law and order to satisfy the prevalent wish to cooperate for personal benefit. The metaphysical basis for this assumption was individualism: societies are

mere aggregates of individuals: people are real; societies are constructs. The methodological basis for this assumption was also individualism: scientific theory rests on observations and we observe individuals not societies.

As long as the major task for those who care for humanity was to maintain social stability, and as long as the only means known for that task was controlling the population and preventing too much anti-social conduct, any method of keeping people in check seemed right as long as it was politically practicable. Whatever happens to work was thus deemed proper.[9] The only possible difference between the known different methods was a matter of efficiency. But the question of which method is most efficient was seldom asked and is very difficult to answer anyway. The thinker who first asked the question openly was St. Augustine of Hippo (d. 430), and he answered it clearly. He declared that the received method was useless and offered an alternative. Ironically, the received method was relatively new and his alternative was a revamped version of the prevalent, old method. He called the useless method The City of Man and the alternative to it The City of God. The City of Man was the Roman Empire with all its military might. Its army was well organized with a clear-cut hierarchy, but it became increasingly corrupt. So Rome instituted a spy system to control its armies. When soldiers and spies colluded, the Empire slowly collapsed. St. Augustine saw the beginning of the collapse in the periphery, where he was raised. The City of Man places people to control people, he observed, and the controllers needed to be controlled. This is his criticism of the Platonic system that relies on an élite: élites too are only human. (This powerful criticism of élitism echoed through the ages.[10]) In The City of God, the sense of guilt incapacitates individuals and tames them. This solution to the problem of social control worked well enough; it even eased up during the Renaissance, when liberalism appeared on the horizon. It demanded a new social philosophy.

Machiavelli was demonized because he dared to say that Moses had invented religion as a means of social control and was a ruthless prince to boot. His was a powerful, if tacit, critique of the existing illiberal system. He offered new ideas and thus inaugurated a public debate spun out over centuries. The demand for critical study of society came in the wake of the new liberal ideas: detailed views on society had implications for how to implement liberalism. Such critical study, in its turn, was but a step from empirical science, a step that scholars took up in the seventeenth and eighteenth centuries.

Liberalism is a social philosophy par excellence. The methodological parallel to it is individualism, the (moral and intellectual) concern with individuals and as prior to the concern for society. This will not do, of course, as the survival of individuals depends on the survival of their societies, so that it is in their supreme interest. This justifies wars of defense that sacrifice individual soldiers for the sake of survival in relative freedom. The opposite of individualist methodology is collectivism, and this is both a methodology and a social philosophy – so much so that both have the same name. But then collectivism will not do either, as life in an intolerable society is intolerable. This brought Georg Simmel, around 1900, to the idea that concern for society is as indispensable as concern for individuals. This idea, obvious as it surely is, did not please those whose task it was to harmonize the two – scarcely possible without placing the interests of one or the other as dominant. Simmel noted this and boldly took the contrary view: he rejected almost all social theories as presenting too harmonious a picture and thus idealizing excessively, Utopian indeed (Simmel, 1922/1955: 71).

It is thus not surprising that during the Age of Reason two concerns were central and opened the road to the development of theories that are empirical to some extent, in politics and in economics.

In politics the central problem was, and still is, what demarcates a good government from a bad one? The standard answer was contractualism: a good government is in accord with its citizens. Put differently, what right has a government to impose on its citizens? The standard answer was contractualism: the imposition rests on agreement, on the readiness to accept it. Of course, this assumption does not imply the existence of an explicit contract; the contractualist idea is that a good government has the right to impose on its citizens since its power rests on consent of sorts. This idea failed to solve the problem. The evidence for the presence of a contract of sorts was that people who do not consent could leave. Of course, serfs cannot leave, and this makes the government of a country that allows serfdom illegitimate. This is the strength of the theory. Its weakness is that it legitimizes every regime that has open borders on the supposition that staying within the state's border amounts to consent. This supposition was the target of an objection that Hume and Smith voiced: even if a citizen is free to leave, they observed, emigration is too taxing to be practicable. This argument has some force, yet the fact that some people tried to flee communist countries at risk to life and limb shows that contractualism is valid up to a point. The fact that most citizens cannot emigrate does not matter so much: waves of emigration testify to poor government, and ideal government is impossible anyway. In other words, if we do not take liberalism to be ideal, if we replace it with a scale or even scales of liberty, then a reasonable version of contractualism may appear in the near future.

Contractualism explains why Machiavelli and Hobbes were once considered liberal: they justified the ruthlessness of rulers by the consent of their populations, thereby raising the powerful question, how much ruthlessness is really necessary? This raises the question, necessary for what? Discussions of these questions often verge on empirical examinations of diverse answers to them. This is how empirical discourse on government developed.

The title of first empirical political economist is usually reserved for Adam Smith, since his book uses theoretical and quasi-empirical arguments against mercantilism – chiefly his classical argument that import duties reduce total national wealth. Yet a major aspect of his economic theory is its liberalism, taken as commonsense rather than as an empirical finding. How empirical is Smith's theory? This question remains open. The greatest critic of Smith's ideas was the Reverend Thomas Malthus, who showed that Smith had tacitly assumed that natural resources are unlimited and tried to refute him. Malthus thus criticized the theory of progress. He was endlessly maligned for it. Smith had evidently taken progress in his stride.

Smith's vision was a rationalist Utopia rather than a descriptive study: he said the only place that somehow comes close to his idea is the Hanseatic League (Smith, 1776/1937: III, 3.9), perhaps also the Republic of Berne and Holland.[11] Smith appeared late on the scene and without problem orientation. It is not easy to see how his economic theory differs from earlier liberal economic theories, beginning with Locke. The problem that economists first faced was how to raise productivity? The answer was, get rid of parasites. This is the answer of the physiocrats, and they viewed both the upper classes and the traders as parasites. Mercantilism was a critique of this theory: the economy needs an organization that should manage goods and services. Smith answered this by the theory of the market as self-regulating. He managed this by refuting the idea that commerce is useless, making the claim that free commerce rests on expectation of gain – an expectation that repeated satisfaction reinforces. He thus shifted the problem: whence the profit from commerce? His answer is the key: specialization. It increases productivity and has some sort of commerce or another as its unintended but utterly unavoidable consequence. His book begins by declaring that he will not discuss slave economies since it does not stand to reason that putting people in chains gives an incentive to work. To show that this is no

empirical claim, suffice it to examine the options open to a slave-owner: under what conditions is it economically more advisable to free them than to keep them. Admittedly, some slave-owners freed their slaves, and others worked for reform of the law; but the drive for these actions was not the profit motive. And yet there is a strong empirical aspect to Smith's theory. The problem that the physiocrats had defiantly raised was what is the good of commerce? The mercantilists answered it. Smith criticized their answer empirically or quasi-empirically, went to basics and declared trade the unintended consequence of the division of labor. This made economic theory center on one basic problem, that of the allocation of resources: what is the best division of labor? In each situation, the market makes the profit motive generate the best answer to this question, he said. In many situations, such as rapid change of tastes,[12] this mechanism breaks down. Clearly, Smith assumed some sort of social stability. The preference for equilibrium conditions in all extant versions of neo-classical economics is a matter of methodological convenience masked as an empirical hypothesis. The best and most up-to-date versions of classical economics are variants of the theory of dynamic equilibrium of Léon Walras (Friedman, 1955; Walker, 1983: Chapter 8), and they are all so excessively idealized that it is hard to say how they comply with the demand for empirical scrutiny. A most famous essay on the subject by Milton Friedman (Friedman, 1953), late doyen of contemporary neo-classical economic theory, denied the need for such scrutiny, claiming that the predictive success of the theory suffices. Yet this very claim for success sorely invites the kind of empirical scrutiny that is still sorely missing.

This discussion may provoke annoyance: it is clear that some of the theories of the Age of Reason, political as well as economic, are very enlightening and rest somehow on some individualist assumption or other; they also rest to some extent on commonsense observations (or rather on observations that became part-and-parcel of the stock of common sense) and to some extent on careful reasoning. All are open to critical scrutiny, such as they received from Marx, Keynes and others; what does it matter whether they are labeled empirical or not?

Such expressions of annoyance are quite apt. Traditionally, when ideas had to be demonstrated or declared contraband (Kant, *Critique of Pure Reason*, Preface to first edition, 1781), the stark choices forced thinkers to check their proofs. Barring that, how much empirical content a theory possesses matters little, except insofar as it does or does not possess empirically testable observational consequences that it explains or that are to be tested. Yet our historical concerns obviate this cavalier attitude, since tradition identified rationality with proof (or proof surrogate). The rise of modern science took place in a radical mood: we must eschew all traditional thought. This was not quite the whole story, of course: Euclidean geometry, Archimedes' laws, and even Aristarchus' astronomy, were not eschewed. Nor was all ancient methodology: if not all of ancient dialectics was embraced, at least its variant in Aristotle's theory of induction won steady respect. And to examine the situation *vis-à-vis* the social sciences we have to examine ancient methodology and ancient social theory. As to methodology, there is dialectic, if it qualifies as such, and, to the extent that it does, it is a fixture of all rational discourse: abiding by it is a minimal requirement. Even though Descartes and Spinoza, for example, claimed that their theories are certain, they invited criticism. What more ancient methodology had to offer is under dispute and so it is wise to sidestep it in the present context as much as possible. Yet mention of Aristotle's theory of definition – a science is a set of definitions placed hierarchically – is not to be avoided, as it is still exceedingly popular. Here is another basic difference between the natural and the social sciences: the natural science avoid discussing definitions (under the influence of Galileo and Boyle), whereas a large portion of the social sciences is devoted to definitions. As modern logic has ruthlessly discredited Aristotle's theory of definition, however, we need not discuss it here, especially since we may nevertheless continue any debate on any definition that comprises a significant part of a significant text – by considering it a hypothesis. This incurs no loss of its content (Popper, 1945: ii, Chapter 11, Section 2 and notes there.).

Before delving into ancient social theory, let me say a word about classical methodology. We may ignore here the most widespread idea about the acquisition of knowledge, even though it is a central item in the philosophies of Plato, Aristotle and most mediaeval philosophers, as well as in the philosophies of most mystics – ancient and modern the world all over. It is that knowledge is attained through proper inspiration during a trance, so that the main problem of methodology is, what sparks the trance off. (There is also the problem, raised by William James, of discrimination between real and fake trance. It was hardly ever studied. Russell said [Russell, 1917], it does not matter what the source of an idea is, only whether it is open to critical examination. Popper agreed with him, saying, the sources of ideas are often unsavory, but this does not matter at all as long as they are open to critical examination.) We are left, then, with the empirical method. What is it? There are at least four options here, and regrettably the literature merges them regularly. First, the method of generalization or of induction by enumeration usually ascribed to Aristotle. We see a white swan and we conclude that all swans are white. Perhaps, better, all the swans we see are white, and so we conclude etc. The second method is Sir Francis Bacon's: collect as many observations as possible, and the right theory will emerge from that collection – like wine out of grapes, he said. This method, he stressed, works only if we avoid the making of any hypothesis. Worse, we have learned some hypotheses in school and these despoil the pressing. In antiquity, the dialectic was supposed to be the correction. Bacon distrusted dialectic, since we can always save a hypothesis from refutation and regrettably we usually do. So he recommended the suspension of all judgment as a token of good will. The third method is dialectical: it is the famous hypothetico-deductive method. Assuming that the first, or at least the second method works, how is it applicable to the social domain? We cannot observe societies, only individuals. Hence, the initial statement of this method (assuming it is applicable) is that individuals exist; societies, then, are theoretical constructs. The method is reductionist: all social science rests on individuals and their psychology. This conclusion strongly illustrates the difference between ancient and modern social thinking: inductivists frown at premature ideas whereas dialecticians take them as grist for their mills. The fourth and final method is that of developing theories dialectically and then declaring their axioms true by convention. This idea is very important in the philosophy of the natural sciences. It has played no role in the social sciences except in one case, Milton Friedman's apologetic defense of neo-classical economic theory (Friedman, 1953). (In the present context we may ignore the once-popular idea that the social sciences have the status of geometry and so they are certain but not on empirical grounds. The only thinker who has advocated it is Spinoza, unless the leading twentieth-century economist Ludwig von Mises counts too (Boettke and Leeson, 2005: Introduction).

Nor is that the end of this methodological discussion. The same idea that depicts the social sciences as reducible to psychology necessitates also depicting psychology as reducible to physics. This reductionism has a very extreme version. It proposes that research on humans should start by making do with the assumption that they are physical objects. This proposal is known as the adoption of the viewpoint of the Martian observer: that observer has no human prejudices and studies humans purely inductively: by observing their overt conduct. This was never tried, of course, for want of tools. It borrowed

terms from physics, such as 'drives' and 'motives' for ends and wishes and such, 'power' for control and such, and 'mechanism' for patterns of mental dispositions. This way, even psychological characteristics like memory should not be described beyond viewing them as written pages. Already Descartes viewed memory banks as physical. Toys devised in the eighteenth century that could write a few words came to illustrate the possibility of this idea. Nevertheless, it was a blind alley until the mid-twentieth century, when attempts were made to view minds as full-fledged computers. It led to no discovery despite the efforts of behaviorists, yet it was popular, allegedly as methodologically sound, since it ignored the inner world that purely physical objects lack. Now the assumption that the inner world exists is undeniable; the assumption that behaviorists advocated was that the inner world could wait its turn, since it is not observable and so its very existence must rest on observations that must engage the attention of researchers first. The only research tool that behaviorism allows is the conditioned reflex, or to be more faithful to the behaviorist program, a few stimulus-response patterns that they declared observable. Pavlov's dogs salivating at the signal or a meal appeared as the novelty that shows the significance of his allegedly new method. They do not, as dogs have an inner world too. A more appropriate instance is conditioning the kidney to secrete urine upon a cue.[13] Yet this turned to be a blind alley. The rise of cybernetics rekindled the hope to find such cases and so new ways to reduce psychology to physics and with it all social science. This was the artificial intelligence project whose early designers gave it up – perhaps only pro tem (Agassi, 2003: 279).

Ancient theories of society are mostly irrelevant to all this as well to other current researches. It is obviously impossible to ignore them as parts of the study of human conduct, since they helped shape it: conduct is greatly influenced by the theories extant in its environment. Yet no matter how important ancient theories of society were at the time and even throughout the ages, considering them reasonable today is not serious. Compare this with the current state of affairs in physics, where the value of some superseded theories is acknowledged; progress from an old theory to its contemporary replacement scarcely reduces its value. Thus, Newton's theory still holds a very central position, obsolete though it surely is. Even some older theories in physics are still valued. Of the ancient theories, to repeat, physics recognizes almost none. Biological or social theory has evolved much less than physical theory: allegedly, social science hardly has an Archimedes or even a Copernicus.[14] The reason is that ancient social theories were primitive; even today, most popular theories are primitive. Much debate has revolved around the label 'primitive', incidentally, as its meaning is usually pejorative, hence politically incorrect. But the politically incorrect meaning is derivative; excluding it, we have not only primitive societies and cultures but also primitive conditions and factors and even terms. What drives us to characterize a culture as primitive is a concern with myth and magic. Commentators usually lump these two together and they often suggest or at least imply that modern society is (relatively) free of myth and magic. They do so largely because they hold myth and magic in contempt. (Contempt, alas, is still often respected; only its explicit expression is banned as politically incorrect.) Finding myth and magic too foolish to take seriously, they refuse to ascribe belief in them even to primitive people and instead they view them as make believe. Now make believe, myth as well as magic do indeed go together, but this view abolishes the difference between primitive and modern societies. This difference refuses to vanish; refusing to view primitive societies as ridden with myth and magic, some commentators deem them pre-scientific. This small and innocuous term may conceal three huge assumptions: first, that the pre-scientific need not be ridden with myth and magic; second, that all societies

are destined to go through the same historical process, and sooner or later open up to progress; and third, that progress is necessarily scientific. Since these assumptions are huge and questionable and currently less popular than in the nineteenth century (see below), the meaning of the word 'primitive' is significantly narrowed down, and primitive societies are now characterized as those devoid of science, perhaps also of literacy. This view rests on scientism,[15] on the contempt for any idea not endorsed by science, on taking all non-science as superstition and prejudice. Scientism stems from the works of Sir Francis Bacon (in a possibly simplistic reading); today it is itself a superstition; it amounts to no more than the lumping of myth and magic together with theology and other sorts of non-science. The initial intent to avoid advocating the view of primitive societies as ridden with myth and magic thus reappears in a scientistic guise (Jarvie, 1984: 117).

Are myths necessarily superstitious? This is a popular question. It is politically correct yet it is distinctly unfriendly. We may at times find it necessary to be unfriendly, of course. It is advisable at least to try to be as friendly as we can, and thus see what we must reject. As the social sciences began in a scientistic atmosphere,[16] their followers deemed practically all societies superstitious and advocated science-run societies. As all or most societies are not, scientism rendered social studies Utopian. The early-nineteenth century reaction to the French Revolution offered a new kind of social studies – more realistic but alas quite anti-scientific. What we can salvage from this movement is the idea that the avoidance of Utopianism and the study of real societies in a friendlier attitude to non-science (or folk-science, as it is often called). It is friendlier to replace the question, are myths necessarily superstitious? The new question is, are myths necessarily unscientific? Scientism makes these two questions one, as it is inherently unfriendly to non-science; avoiding it when possible should be the default option. Ignoring scientism, then, we may discuss myths anew, beginning with the most obvious ones: creation stories. These can be viewed as explanatory. They persist in the absence of efforts – characteristic of science – to examine general ideas, and to offer new ones as their replacements or supplements. This is the critical attitude that, everyone acknowledges, science must possess. Given the critical attitude, Karl Popper said (Popper, 1963: 136ff), there is no need for the repeated demand to drive myths out: under the pressure of criticism we may improve them and thereby enrich science or else they wane by themselves. This is not the end of the story: scientific theories are mostly general theories and rarely stories; but let us leave this for now and turn to magic.

Magic is a mix of myth and rite. Rites, according to Frazer, are technologies of sorts. Because they are ineffective, he deemed them pseudo-scientific. Others, notably R. G. Collingwood, deemed the same rites merely theatrical activities, a sort of make-believe. They shared – as a matter of course – the refusal to ascribe to people straightforward endorsement of magical ideas. Both deemed magic too silly to assume that some sane people take it seriously. Liberalism requires the acceptance of people and their beliefs as they are.[17] Yet in the name of liberalism, they self-righteously refuse to admit that people believe in the magic ideas that they say they do. This is improper despite the support that it receives from great souls like Frazer and Collingwood. As Ernest Gellner has observed, many people find it hard to attribute unscientific ideas only to members of alien cultures and not to members of their own culture. This, in his view, shows the difficulty rooted in plain ethnocentrism (Gellner, 1987: 49).

Rectifying this will not render traditional theories of society relevant to the contemporary study of humans. Their irrelevance rests on neither myth nor magic, even though traditions are drenched in them. Otherwise, the various maneuvers that are at hand to de-fang myth and magic would help revive ancient social theories. Indeed, it is easy to render

myths innocuous and endorse them while stripping them of their mythical character, taking them as allegorical, as many anthropologists suggest. Already in the Age of Reason some thinkers who had opposed myths in general endorsed some as allegories. A conspicuous example is the myth of Prometheus. Freud did the same with the myth of Oedipus. It is easy, likewise, to endorse magic rites while stripping them of their supernatural character. This we do when we cross fingers, knock on wood or anoint a king – perhaps in line with Collingwood's idea of rites as theatrical. What makes traditional theories of society irrelevant to contemporary social studies is an idea that is ubiquitous and that has met with no opposition except in the Greek tradition and in the scientific tradition that owes its very existence to Greece. This ubiquitous idea is the view of Man as inherently evil, the myth of the Beast in Man. It may well characterize primitive society best; it goes deeper than many myths. Thus, the great Moses Maimonides, immensely influential on medieval thought, was as hostile to myth and magic as could be, yet he could not break away from the fetters of magic. In order to check the Beast in Man he endorsed all the magic rites of his society, including the reciting of ancient myths, although he offered as allegorical a reading of as much of them as he could.

What makes primitive theories of society irrelevant to current social studies, then, is the idea that human nature is anti-social. And this idea all primitive societies take for granted: 'for the imagination of man's heart is evil from his youth' (*Genesis*, 8: 21).[18] There are worse things to be found in the literature: conflict between individual and society is often tragic but always inevitable: Romeo and Juliet must die, their innocence notwithstanding. Shakespeare signals the advent of liberalism: his play differs from the myriads of variants of their story in that it and it alone ends with the noble demand for reform so as to prevent the recurrence of this intolerable tragedy.[19] Everywhere else, the judgment is that the conflict between individual and society is inevitable and that invariably the individual must lose.[20] This idea has a stronger grip than any myth and magic,[21] as we may conclude from the fact that so much magic in modern society is innocuous and does not disparage science – perhaps because science often plays the role of a new kind of super-magic, thus allowing for magic to pose as scientific. Indeed, myth and magic address the conflict between the individual and society and the need to yield to taboo simply because they operate within the taboo system (Evans-Pritchard, 1946). The idea that only individuals are real, clashes forcefully with the idea that they must die for society. The clash is in evidence in many ways and in many discussions. It blocks much straight social scientific thinking.

The alleged priority of society over individual appears regularly as the contrast of the ability of society to survive the death of the innocent lovers with the inability of any single individual to grow up as human in the absence of a social environment. Many thinkers through the ages endorsed the conclusion from this that society is more important than any individual, at least in the sense that the lives of the many have priority over the lives of the few. This conclusion directs methodology to guide research to society in the first instance and to individuals only as subordinate parts of it. This is the social significance of the thesis that society is primary and the individual is derivative. Our present society is so individualist that we tend to dismiss this priority as barbarian. But consider the presuppositions of sending our youth to die on the battlefield for the good of their society. True, current civilized societies are reluctant to send their youth to die on the battlefield and demand, at least in principle, that governments try to avoid this whenever possible. Yet primitive societies are usually not very different on this. The exception is human sacrifice. We condemn it (and dismiss faith in Moloch as superstitious). To show that this makes a real difference, we portray Nazi commanders – presumably in truth – as willing to kill innocent soldiers under their command when these happen to stand in their way. How much this differs from the present practice of sending soldiers on dangerous but presumably vital missions is hard to say, yet this is where modern Western thinking claims to be different from older traditions – rightly or not. Can this difference, be it true or imaginary, explain other peculiarities of the modern world, including science and technology and art and the modern liberal democratic nation-state? We would all like to think so. We should therefore give it a try. But we should also remain critically-minded and ready to test seriously our ideas, no matter how noble they are. Modern experimentalist methodology encourages this.

The claim for the unavoidable victory of society over the individual is quite general, East and West. Two alleged arguments in favor of this verdict repeatedly appear everywhere. First, man to man is a wolf. Second, people helplessly follow their desires that conflict with the needs of reasonably stable society. These two arguments may be one, if people fight simply because they desire exclusive rights for whatever they fancy, but not if they put added value on antagonism (as de Sade insisted). This, however, is a fine point. Even if they do not wish to antagonize each other, the alleged desire for each other's property suffices to secure perpetual conflict. The conflict is not only between individuals but, and more importantly, also between every individual and society, as well as between societies.

Current methodology of the social sciences takes it as a legitimate challenge to explain the lifestyle and conduct of samurai or of saints, regardless of their being exceptional and scarcely relevant to the central problem of social philosophy. Not so traditional methodology of the social sciences that discusses chiefly the task of maintaining social stability. Traditional folk psychology is unflattering: people are irrational, petty and misanthropic. Folk psychology scants the desire for love and friendship, curiosity for its own sake and love for truth and of justice. Tradition promotes noble qualities, but it takes for granted that these, and more so self-sacrifice, are and must remain too rare to count as significant social and political factors (except for education, as according to folk wisdom education aims at the highest values although these are unattainable). Folk psychology takes it for granted that people are so lazy, that too few will till the soil: without coercion we will all starve. This is amply refuted. Even simians, it turns out, cannot tolerate idleness for long and they seek out challenge (Day, 2007: 31). And members of simple and subsistence cultures take work for granted. Indeed, according to modern psychiatry chronic laziness is a symptom of depression with private or social causes, such as the reluctance to perform work of poor quality and the inability to find better work (Argyle, 1992: 88–9). The improvement of the quality of working life, experience shows, is better incentive for work than preaching and social pressure.

Primitive societies are not as misanthropic as ancient culture. Plato reinforced the traditional view of humanity as misanthropic and this had a tremendous influence over the millennia, tempting the spiritual and intellectual leadership to side with nasty traditions. Under the influence of his teachings, Western governments used policing as well as religion. Policing included torture and terrible incarcerations and burning at the stake. Religion included threats of hell-fire and brimstone. Both were powerful tools for the reinforcement of state control and the reinforcement of the legitimacy of the state, of the status quo, of social and political stagnation. The stagnation did not last. The causes of the deviation from accepted norms, whatever these were, were partly the circumstances, such as the Crusades or rather whatever made the Pope (Urban II, 1095) declare them (presumably out of fear of social instability, be it population pressure, economic changes, threat of Muslim expansion or a combination of these) and partly the

awakening of the spirit in the yearning for the ancient world.

The first recognizably modern thinker on Western social affairs is Machiavelli. His influence was second only to the ancients. He dreamt of the revival of antiquity, or rather of the glory of ancient Rome. He conceived of a ruthless, hyper-ambitious ruler who could bring this about and in his notorious *The Prince*[22] he counseled him in the art of gaining power by any means. Spinoza understood the title to refer to Scripture: 'Put not your trust in princes' (*Psalms*, 146:3); he ascribed to Machiavelli the liberalism expressed in his *Discourses on the First Ten Books of Livy*, a better characterization of his worldview than the cynicism of *The Prince*. The link between these two books is in the conclusion of *The Prince* that teaches the ruler that *in his own interest* he should show benevolence towards his subjects.[23] So is Machiavelli's recommendation of a national militia instead of the traditional preaching to the professional army to desist from its 'cruelty and avarice' (*Prince*, Chapter 19).[24] Whatever the message of *The Prince* is, the message of Machiavelli's other works is distinctly liberal: lower moral standards in order to make probable, if not certain, the attainment of the right or desirable social order, or in order to conquer chance. This is in line with a very simplistic view of Socratic *eudemonia*: immorality conflicts with self-interest. Machiavelli wanted the interest of the citizens adjusted so as to promote law-abidance. To that end, laws should be friendly to the common citizen. Today this is an accepted major principle of liberal legislation, especially of the secularization of government. Secularization is best achieved by the separation of religious and secular powers as Machiavelli and Montesquieu recommended, and as the United States and France enacted. Alternatively, it is achievable by instituting a state religion as Hobbes and Spinoza recommended, and as England, Denmark and Sweden enacted.

These proposals took account of the criticism launched against traditional political theory – of the traditional demand for moral, religious, social and political control of common people. They thus also took account of the elitist view of common people as unable to think for themselves. The most important elitist assumption that these proposals took account of is this: common people cannot control themselves; they are therefore given to their whims: these incline them to act in anti-social manners. The long and the short of this is that common people are in need of guidance – by religious and political leaders. This is how élitism justifies tyranny. Hence it is erroneous on all counts, especially politically. There was thus a need for a particularly strong resistance to overcome it. The resistance was that of a battery of great thinkers: Machiavelli, Hobbes, Spinoza, Mandeville, Hume, Smith and others. The most important of these was the central principle of liberal legislation: laws can be framed so as to direct human conduct into channels that are of benefit to society. Mandeville invented the slogan, 'private vices, public virtues' that serves as the subtitle to his *Fable of the Bees*. The advantage of this move is that it ignores private aspects of conduct. It is thus independent of Locke's theory of human natural goodness. And although liberal thinkers often did rely on Locke's view, behind all classical liberal theories is the different idea that all human interests can be in harmony (Adam Smith's celebrated 'invisible hand'[25]): no matter how much given individual interests may be in conflict, their rational resolution is possible and advantageous for all (Thomas Paine, Ben Franklin[26]).

The *prima facie* refutations of this expectation of harmony abound. The Marquis de Sade presented some and gained this way the status of a significant philosopher. His argument is that people enjoy hurting others. It was not new. Liberal thinkers developed a policy towards all such allegations. They tried to show that alleged vices are socially beneficial (greed was the paradigm here); otherwise, they viewed them as perversions: normal people love their neighbors. In immunizing liberalism this way against refutation, it was rendered irrefutable.

Although classical liberalism is irrefutable, in the advanced parts of the world every specific implementation of it was carefully tested empirically and in stages. Hence, refutations of its refutable versions were hardly ever as harmful as they might have been: in cases in which legislation rested on error, it was rescinded. Popper called this procedure piecemeal social-engineering (where piecemeal is not a matter of scale but of the avoidance of wholesale Utopian engineering, of making the whole system hostage to the experiment with no lines of retreat in the case of bumping into serious error; Popper (1945: Chapter 3, §IV)). Also, when liberal piecemeal experiments failed, their liberal advocates would often blame the low level of general education and would demand educational reforms. Hence, refutable or not, liberalism was almost always beneficial. The obvious counter-instances to this general observation are wholesale (Utopian) implementations of liberal regimes. The failure of such all-out liberal legislation has been serious and harmful. It first occurred perhaps in the Puritan Revolution, perhaps in the French Revolution, possibly also in the Russian Revolution, as well as in quite a few post-colonial situations in the post-World War II world. The liberal world may tolerate the resultant tyrannies on the ground that at least they affirm liberalism. (The paradigm case of such toleration was the outrageous willingness, unqualified and qualified, to defend Stalin's regime and find excuses for its deliberate barbarism.)

Despite the attribution of the failure of the French Revolution to liberalism (to Enlightenment itself, some say), liberals refused to acknowledge the general shortcomings of liberalism before World War II. The suggestion is still irresistible that the law should be designed to give incentive to ordinary people to cooperate (with each other as well as with the state) for personal profit. The recognition is increasing that this is not as easy to implement as was classically taken for granted, yet the idea remains that the combination of egoism and altruism makes for a good society. In systems where this liberal idea is not operative, the liberal political question is, what changes of these systems will make it operative, and what is the best way to implement these changes?[27]

THE MODERN VIEWS FOCUS ON THE INDIVIDUALIST VERSION OF SOCIAL PHILOSOPHY AND SCIENCE

Stable political systems use self-interest as the incentive for law abidance. Spinoza tried to legitimate this method by developing the Socratic theory of eudaimony: all enlightened selfishness is good. Locke tried to legitimate this same method by developing the theory of human natural goodness. (The difference between Spinoza and Locke, if it exists, is very subtle and politically barely significant for either research or reform.) To repeat, the individualist method raised the new problem of *scientific* explanation of human conduct. Enlightenment optimism faced the question, whence human evil? Its task then was to explain the ubiquity of evil conduct. Both the Spinozist theory of enlightened self-interest and the Lockean theory of human natural goodness declare all social evils unintended consequences of action from good intentions undertaken in ignorance. This idea is still a part of our liberal heritage and is an integral part of the social and political philosophies of Russell and of Popper.[28] This is the great difference between classical and modern liberal political philosophy *and* methodology: the former took the unintended consequences of actions to be public benefits, whereas the modern one takes them to be a mixed bag that requires correction, usually by legislation but also through education and government intervention in the economy, be it monetary, fiscal or any other.[29]

All this explains the profound changes that the heuristic regarding the unintended consequences of actions underwent in the twentieth century. Dismissing institutions as harboring traditional prejudices and advocating legislation as expressions of rationality, the traditional liberal heuristic led to the search for liberalizing legislation that would alter incentives and thereby reduce the conflict between the interest of society and of individual – of the state and of its citizens. The same heuristic promoted the further study of human affairs. Its method rested not on the assumption that individual citizens possess adequate knowledge but on the assumption that they are autonomous and willing to learn. The resultant theories thus did not aim at explaining current affairs, except marginally, on occasions that won the approval of liberal students of human affairs – simply because most conduct was, and regrettably still is, not very other-regarding. Explanations of illiberal conduct in the liberal vein developed in the mid-nineteenth century, as liberal thinkers endorsed some historicist methodology (in Popper's sense of historical inevitability) and thus some versions of historicist theory, despite its manifest[30] illiberal features.

The liberal political guide-rule for legislation is simple: in order to enlist cooperation of its subjects, the political system should be such that (practically) all enlightened self-interest should be conducive to law-abidance. This sounds unobjectionable and thus it heralds the victory of liberal philosophy. This is an illusion, as enlightened self-interest seldom operates. Thus, liberal regimes allow for actions in accord with strong obsessions, even though such actions obviously preclude rational deliberation. To be effective, then, the law should help people overcome weaknesses and develop their ability to recognize their interests and to act on them. The law, then, should educate and enhance individual autonomy.[31] Is this task feasible? This is a very difficult question. Immanuel Kant spoke of it as the education of humanity. He took it for granted that the best system is perfectly liberal. But he had no idea how this desirable system was achievable, if at all, and until then he deemed it is necessary to act in accord with strict moral principles.

The flaw of his mock-liberalism[32] highlights Mandeville's wisdom.

Since ignorance of self-interest is common, liberals may perhaps suggest that legislators should think this out and impose laws that should make people behave in accord with it. This important idea is paternalism, the opposite of liberalism. The paternalist slogan is, the state should impose guidelines on its subjects for their own good. Paternalists take for granted that the supreme interest of every citizen is that the state should function well – even when its interest and the immediate interest of the citizen diverge. Your own good becomes then identified with the good of the state, the nation, the collective or whatever else the citizen's social environment happens to be. This means that the supreme interest of every citizen is the same as that of the authorities. Paternalism has a saving grace: it is a liberal version of traditional political philosophy, since it does not depend on the traditional misanthropic supposition about human nature being inherently evil: it allows for the view that the root of all misconduct is ignorance, not selfishness. Hence, the very possibility of paternalism proves conclusively that the classical liberal view of humans as inherently good (or at least as not hopelessly sinful) is an insufficient guide for liberal legislation, perhaps also unnecessary. At best, then, liberal legislation must be viewed as a protracted process that involves education for toleration and enlightenment – for individual autonomy. Moreover, since, obviously, the survival of society is in the supreme interest of every citizen, liberalism is possible only when the state is not under constant threat. The illiberal say this is impossible: threat is permanent.[33]

This is not how things stood traditionally, because traditionally discussion over the principles of legislation rested on discussion that governed all social and political philosophy: it concerned the deepest principle as it revolved around views of human nature, no less. This is how things stood until Popper proposed to eliminate the need to appeal to something as problematic as human nature.[34]

Ignorant about human nature though we are, we know enough about it to consider the two traditional views of it as simply too extreme. The classical liberal view is too flattering. It is the principle that following enlightened self-interest should suffice. It is too ideal: it makes parliamentary democracy unnecessary.[35] The traditional view of human nature is too disparaging; it makes society depend on the few wise and dedicated individuals in charge, and explains fluctuations in the quality of the life of citizens as largely due to the differences in the qualities of those who happen to be in charge.[36] In particular, as tradition ignores the mechanisms of appointments to positions of power, it prevents discussion of the causes of these fluctuations. Plato's claim that the appointment of the best for the position of autocrat assures social stability is thus vain. And any suggestion to institute political machinery that should regulate the appointment of rulers, said Popper, shows the poverty of Plato's idea that the best should rule, and then it suffices to open the road to the institution of some machinery for the selection of rulers and thus to open the road to democracy (Popper, 1945: i, 122).

Locke tried to legitimate liberal legislation by developing a theory of natural human goodness. The image of humanity as good looks more convincing when developed in detail than when asserted in the abstract (in isolation) as a mere conviction. Yet the advantage of a detailed picture lies in that it offers the opportunity to examine it critically. Now, suppose the detailed picture collapses under criticism. This is not the disaster that it may seem, since it may take liberals back to the drawing board in efforts to remedy the situation and improve upon Locke in detail while remaining faithful to his principles. However, this way of efforts to remedy his liberalism might easily be dogmatic; liberals do not usually approve of tinkering with an idea instead of replacing it; so why should they approve of it when it comes to the liberal principles? This question seldom appears explicitly in the literature, yet it was central;

competing answers to it have led thinkers to explore the situation in different directions. The default answer is, liberalism is self-evident. This answer is no longer a serious contender, no less so because the paradigm of self-evidence, Euclidean geometry, turned out to be insufficient and Einstein replaced it with a much more detailed, much more sophisticated alternative far from self-evident. Another reason for the default answer not having a serious contender any longer is that it makes the details superfluous. The next obvious answer is, we must start somewhere. This answer is a version of fideism (the idea that since a philosophy free of supposition is impossible, it must rest on an arbitrary axiom). It is dangerous, as it gives equal weight not only to liberalism and paternalism, but also to the most pernicious theories. Moreover, it likewise makes the details superfluous. And so the next obvious answer to our question is, liberalism is the most moral of all the extant alternative starting points. This moralistic view is question begging unless it comes with a detailed examination of the moral impact of the diverse alternatives on societies that tried them out. (This requires a developed social science.) Which point brings us back to the position that imposed the question at hand: why prefer liberalism to paternalism? The least question begging answer is, of course, we need not favor liberalism: we may examine each of the extant alternatives, see each at work in its diverse ramifications, and see how much it agrees with available data. This is the scientific attitude and the demand for the effort to develop social science. The same holds for competitors to liberalism: we may develop liberalism, paternalism and each reasonable alternative to them, and keep examining all and each of them. Query: is this attitude partial to liberalism in any way, or is it impartial? If it is impartial, should legislation be liberal or paternalist, depending on whether the one or the other offers a better social science?

Max Weber presented the situation this way around 1900. He advocated the use of the classical liberal method for the study of non-liberal societies – and even of anti-liberal ones. This was so welcome that the limitations of Weber's method were barely noticed. Surprisingly, they are commonplace. First is his insistence on certitude for his theories. Second is his inability to explain liberal reforms. As to certitude, the classical liberal thinkers were able to sustain a semblance of it because their psychologism was overt: they took the siblinghood of humanity as obvious on the ground that all discrimination is baseless, and they ascribed to the individual only such characteristics as they deemed very obvious, perhaps only the will to survive. This is an error, of course, yet it was taken for granted in the Age of Reason. Ernest Gellner said, be the siblinghood of humanity true or not, taking it as self-evident is astonishing (Gellner, 1979: 234). As to Weber's inability to cope with liberal reform, whereas others could take it for granted, he had declared his major aim to explain social change, and he could not do that. Talcott Parsons, a leading sociologist of the next generation, at first followed Weber, and then, disappointed at Weber's inability to explain social change, switched allegiance to Durkheim (whose views will be discussed below). Weber allowed for – not explained – only one kind of social change, the rise of a charismatic leader who establishes a bureaucracy that creates a social system *ex nihilo*. His famous lecture, 'Politics as a Vocation' (Gerth and Wright Mills, 1948), refers to membership in legislatures as distinct from public administration. He did advocate democracy, but merely as means for electing strong leaders. These, then, may effect change, but only in the specific way that he described, not democratically. Although Weber advocated democratic reform of his country, since he was an extreme German nationalist who placed state power above all other social and political factors, it is far from clear what precisely his liberal creed was. This is still a favorite question for historians of social and political thought, especially in Germany.

It is easy to sidestep this discussion by observing the most obvious aspect of Weber's methodology at least as understood somewhat anachronistically in the light of Popper's methodology. First, this methodology exhibits a readiness to scrutinize diverse options; this is liberal. A theory that a researcher examines need not be liberal, but the conduct of the researcher as a researcher is and must be. Why? Popper said, liberalism is the most becoming social philosophy for the ignorant, and we all are ignorant. This idea is contrary to Weber's faith in certainty. His famous lecture, 'Science as a Vocation' (Gerth and Wright Mills, 1948) says, 'Whoever lacks the capacity to … come up to the idea that the fate of his soul depends on whether or not he makes the correct conjecture … may well stay away from science.'

So it is not clear what makes Weber's methodology liberal. We can ignore him for the moment and continue with the idea (Russell, 1928: Chapter 14) that it becomes the ignorant to be liberal: 'If we certainly knew the truth', said Bertrand Russell, 'there would be something to be said for teaching it'. This, our ignorance of society, is what raises the problem of scientific explanation of human conduct, especially of evil conduct. Explanation is thus essential for liberal politics: evil consequences of our actions are unintended or at least avoidable only under conditions that we do not know as yet. This is a point on which modern liberalism is superior to classical liberalism: the older version seeks total coherence between individual and society, whereas the newer version seeks coherence as good as current knowledge of how to implement it allows – in the hope for improvement, of course. The assumption is no longer that people act in their own best interest but that they do so as best they can, given their inner constitution and state of knowledge in addition to their familiarity with their physical and social circumstances.

Now ignorance serves as a strong argument for paternalism. The liberal response to the paternalists is dual: paternalism is doubly erroneous: the knowledge of the rulers is seldom superior to that of the ruled, and their intent is seldom pure. Now commonsense says that experts are better informed than common people are, and so paternalists suggest that decisions should pass to their hands. And so we may take elections away from the public and leave to it only the democratic checking of the conduct of the expert rulers.

This response forces the liberals to alter their response to paternalism. The strongest response is one that Hume and Smith stated: people can be trusted best to act in their own interests (as best they know them). Is this true? Classical liberal thinkers left this question open, we remember, allowing people to seek what they wish, as this is a matter of personal taste. As liberals respect people's tastes, whatever they are, they need not scrutinize them.

This tolerance of people's tastes is possible, to repeat, only on the (tacit or explicit) understanding that sadistic tastes are not too common: a taste for violence, torture, child cruelty, etc., not to mention the taste for crime as such ('stolen water is sweet', *Proverbs*, 9:17). Liberals cannot possibly respect these tastes. Liberalism then requires a prior principle or consensus about the boundaries or extremities of taste. This is notoriously impossible to achieve. Moreover, it is obvious that tastes are open to examination since they follow fashions, since the market can manipulate fashions, and since the vagaries of fashion raise challenges for the suppliers who cater for them. Thus, briefly, there is no escape from the scrutiny of assertions about tastes, although it is better to conduct it within the liberal viewpoint.[37]

Liberal accounts of crime were always problematic. The prime liberal response to crime is anarchism: crime is the product of laws: since crime is lawbreaking, the absence of laws makes crime logically impossible. This is true but to no avail. As anarchy has no proscription, it allows immoral conduct like sadism. (Absolutist regimes place supreme rulers above the law, and they are often sadists.) Anarchists may say, better allow immoral conduct than impose draconian laws. If so, then anarchists assume that all laws are draconic. Admittedly, they often are; this is why legal reform is at the heart of all liberal democratic political philosophy. Anarchism goes further, however: it is the view that all legislation is redundant at best. Even were this true, anarchists may have to agree that the quality of laws (and more so of legal systems) is variable. Anarchists are impatient with this claim; hence, their doctrine rests on a specific view of human nature: the natural goodness of humans is so forceful that it devalues even the difference between the best and the worst legal systems. And erroneous as anarchism is, repeatedly extreme liberals find themselves attracted to positions as near to it as their reason permits: anarchism is the loveliest Utopia: it is the liberal brand of Utopianism or the Utopian brand of liberalism: it envisages totally perfect, harmonious society, one with no crimes. And so the general critique of Utopianism is the strongest criticism of all brands of anarchism. What is wrong with anarchism is its impatience. Considering it – or any other Utopianism – a mere distant ideal is a different matter altogether as Jarvie has suggested (Jarvie, 1987). We may then consider anarchism the regulative idea of both liberal thought and liberal conduct – especially legislative. This may be the best wording of liberalism to date. Its influence on social scientific research should be more than obvious: it places theories of liberalization high on its agenda in the hope of reducing the crime rate.[38] It also recommends taking people as they come and explaining their conduct, which is the rationality principle applied to real situations (John Stuart Mill, 1843;1848) not to ideal ones (Adam Smith, 1776). And, of course, these two items, theories of liberalization and explanatory theories, may easily conflict with each other, as for example, the liberal legislator's view that education for toleration is of supreme value may clash with the liberal readiness to take people as they come, on their intolerance and all.[39]

There is room for caution here. The wish to approach anarchy is traditional and many opponents of anarchism gladly share it, from Maimonides through Spinoza to Marx and his myriad fans. Much as we may share it, much as we wish to approach anarchy, it is never to be fully implemented, and for the following reasons. We need laws for two basic reasons. First, we need laws that should protect the weak against the strong even if the strong have no wish to harm the weak (as it is the right of the weak not to depend on the good will of the strong). Second, we need laws as means of coordination for our activities that depend on activities of others. The paradigm case is the law of the road: it matters little whether people drive their cars on the right or on the left as long as the law imposes the same option on all.[40] Also, deviations from such laws may be tolerated if they do not disturb the peace or if they come to prevent worse offenses. Kant proved his idea that laws must hold universally unconditionally by reference to the fact that a law is void if everyone is to break it. (For example, if we all steal, then there will be no property to steal and thus no theft. Also, if we all lie, then we will lose all credibility.) This makes sense if we read this to say, even occasional deviations from the law of the road are intolerable as they are dangerous. Yet there is a limit to this too. Hence, the severity of Kant's position renders it downright impractical and hence absurd. Following it rigorously should give way to following it as the default option. Moreover, the consensus that Kant spoke of is between all rational beings. The consensus about the law of the road to drive is arbitrary, and so, by Kant's book it is no moral imperative.[41] Yet it is a valuable imperative and laws have to regulate its being the default option. And so, quite generally, the very need for consensus conduct depends on laws that regulate normal conduct; these laws are liberal if and only if obeying them conspicuously helps people to advance their aims; and this is possible only for a relatively educated public, and even then only if tastes are not too frequently too sadistic or otherwise contrary to the public interest.[42]

Economists speak of tastes as given, as exogenous, as not dependent on the consensus. This is agreeable only if economic theory is satisfactorily explanatory. Is it? Do economists explain phenomena that relate to the diverse aims of diverse individuals? Two answers to this question are available in the literature. One is that tastes are the same everywhere.[43] This is a doubtful supposition. It invites speculations on human nature and so it dangerously leads the discussion astray. Nor is it necessary. The market translates all demands to their current expressions in their market prices. Liberals suggested that as long as the market is free, satisfaction is optimal. This is under dispute, but, right or wrong, it is not the answer to all economic problems. As even the most liberal economists allow for some government intervention in the market, if only by regulating the flow of money by diverse means, this raises many problems, such as, what is the best way for governments to intervene? Rather than discuss the problems that liberal economists raise and struggle with, it is better to notice that we have digressed here from the wish to explain to the wish to apply liberal principles properly. Economic theory as classical economists envisaged it explains, if at all, only the perfectly rational conduct in perfect markets. Adam Smith, to repeat, said he ignored the practice of slavery, because, evidently, putting people in chains is no inducement to raise efficiency. Still worse, the same holds for any action under irrational constraints and the absence of irrational constraints is Utopian: as Utopia does not exist, liberal economic theory explains practically nothing. The most developed model of this idea is the theory of dynamic equilibrium of Léon Walras of around 1900, and it is frankly Utopian (Jaffé and Walker, 1983). Walras ignores even the fact that borrowing incurs interest, let alone all the social ills that borrowing notoriously incurs, not to mention the bubbles that can bring the market almost to a halt. How are liberals to approach these problems? How do they square economic theory with the classical liberal theory of human natural goodness?

Suppose Utopia is possible. What will bring it about? Is it possible that all slave-owners will agree to free their slaves and legislate against slavery? Will this bring about a Utopian regime with no transition period? The problem of transition to Utopia appeared first in the works of Marx. He was not concerned about slavery but about what he called wage slavery. And he said his prediction that this regime will come to an ending was certain. But that ending will not guarantee the advent of a Utopia, he admitted: a strong government ('a dictatorship of the proletariat') will then be necessary to prevent a regression to the old regime. And this strong government will give up its power, he promised, because there will be no room to exercise it: plenty will eliminate all political problems and so government will wither away. This indicates how poor his theory of government and of its role was.

Freeing one's slaves need not be rational despite the justice of Smith's condemnation of slavery as irrational. Freeing one's slaves is noble, and so in a deep sense it is most rational, but not in the simple liberal sense of wedding the right with the desirable: in a slave society, owning slaves is useful; hence, freeing them is a sacrifice.[44] (Here we see again that Kant's a-historical, abstract version of liberalism impedes intellectual progress.) It is a small concession to say that the application of liberal principles to a slave society is restricted: the main application of liberalism to that case is to struggle for the abolition of slavery, as de Tocqueville noted (de Tocqueville, 1835: Chapter 18). Furthermore, liberal economic theory is valuable, and not only as an expression of the wish to approach anarchy; has it also helped assess the degree to which this wish is implemented. To that extent, it also explains economic facts. The situation is methodologically identical with that of the ideal gas law (in physics and physical chemistry). As there are no ideal gases, that law explains nothing. But together[45] with the assertion that diverse gases (beginning with hydrogen) approach the ideal, the gas law is informative and explanatory and testable (and refuted and replaced by van der Waals' law). This renders liberalism applicable and explanatory to this or that degree, depending on its constitution.

How much then, if at all, does such a consideration apply to the theory of natural goodness? Can we render testable the theory of the ideal society the way the theory of the ideal gas was tested (and refuted and improved)? If this is a reasonable expectation, then we may view anarchy as the supreme ideal of political rationality[46] and explain misconduct as deviation from rationality due to error, ignorance, carelessness, and neglect, perhaps also perversion. This will expand the already popular idea that the ill effects of human conduct are unintended consequences of actions from good intentions undertaken in ignorance. It is doubtful. Improvement of knowledge about nutrition, for example, is known to have reduced, not to have eliminated, the suffering that the system of food supply has caused. Certain foodstuffs cause damage and knowledge of this fact reduces but does not eliminate their use. Many suggestions of nutritionists go unheeded and many poisons are still in the market on sale. Moreover, sadism exposes as naïve the idea that all social evils are unintended. Ill will, the desire to harm and to spoil, is much more common than mere sadism, especially during war, more so in the systematic employment of scorched-earth tactics. Yet in war this tactic may be eminently rational. (Remember the burning of Moscow that broke the back of Napoleon's campaign; remember Sherman's march to the sea – the beginning of the end for the Confederacy.)

To what extent, then, does rationality determine patterns of conduct? And how is not fully rational human conduct at all open to explanation? In particular, since no government is fully liberal, all government limits the rationality both of its members and of its subjects – even under the best available conditions and in accord with the best intentions. How then is human conduct explicable? The received opinion is that human

conduct is explicable by reference to individual rational action, yet governments are not individuals and no individual is quite rational. Can we nevertheless explain human affairs by appeal to individual rationality? We can see how the ideal gas law is applicable as we can easily describe a near-ideal gas; we can see how the perfect market model is applicable as we can describe small deviations from it. But we know too little about what happens in markets outside the liberal sphere – in societies with hardly any free market – and about what happens in traditional non-liberal societies in general.

The heuristic meant to help efforts in this direction is, search every society[47] for harmonization of private and public interests. It usually misfires, amounting to little more than the suggestion to be less descriptive and more prescriptive. Although beneficial, it can easily develop in dangerous directions, all of them known under the blanket label of populism. Indeed, populism is but a vulgar version of classical rationalism, the doctrine of enlightened self-interest. Whereas classical rationalists considered enlightenment a challenge and a perpetual task, populists find it self-understood[48] and conclude that political decisions must be unanimous, that prior to collective action on an idea, its truth as truth (political, as it happens) should be sufficiently understandable to command unanimous assent. Populism is obviously false: significant truths are seldom self-understood. It is also dangerous, as it invites demagogues to whip up self-deception.[49] Here the liberal efforts at explanation meet a truly awesome obstruction, since, it is no news, self-deception seriously impedes enlightenment, and in populism it is as systematic as in neuroses. Freud has explained the rise and the persistence of neuroses as the outcomes of misguided but rational actions and patterns of conduct (under stress) that are hard to reverse (and are thus in need of psychotherapy). Nothing like this happens in politics: pathological conduct of governments has provoked much discussion, politico-pathology has provoked none and politico-therapy much less.

Government misconduct is worse than riots and similar mob violence: these are rational in extreme situations of mass catastrophe, usually caused by government folly. How then, if at all, can pathological political conduct be rationally explained?

This is a particularly difficult question. Classical liberalism rested on the assumption that individuals are autonomous. Autonomous individuals are not supposed to display mob violence or behave along the lines of populism or chauvinism or worse. Taking people as they come, liberals should also take governments as they come.[50] Of course, this does not preclude efforts to improve both individuals and their governments. But how can liberals explain the systematic folly of governments?

The first to raise this question and to face it squarely were the liberal thinkers of the nineteenth century, especially Alexis de Tocqueville, Auguste Comte and John Stuart Mill. These three found their political views similar; so we can treat them together to some extent.[51] De Tocqueville naïvely distinguished both prescriptions from descriptions and observations from their explanations. Comte, however, was less successful, as he apprenticed to the philosophy of Henri Saint-Simon. This philosophy must have been a great novelty, as it shook the world, but the novelty is hard to spell out. Like many of his predecessors, especially Rousseau and Condorcet, Saint-Simon took it for granted that history shows steady progress towards freedom. He wanted social science akin to natural science – inductively based on facts, explanatory and reliably predictive. Comte focused on the assertion that there is no logical difference between explanation and prediction. Mill was greatly influenced by Comte, but found this view of explanation in the social sciences wanting, especially his way of explaining past social success.

Mill's theory of explanation in the social sciences is his most lasting contribution, despite the great significance of his other work – in philosophy, economics and political

thought, as well as his political activities. His *Logic* is important because of its part on the logic of the moral (i.e. social) sciences. Accepting Saint-Simon's view that the method of the social sciences is the same as that of the natural sciences, he concluded that they are all consequences of psychological assertions about human nature (allegedly inductively extracted from observations). Accepting Comte's view that science must be predictive, he allowed sociology and politics to be somewhat free from psychology at the cost of losing some of its certitude. Loss of certitude is compensated by the addition of the historical method, to wit, the prevalent view of the inevitability of progress. Out of all this came his idea, in line with economic theory more than anything else: social explanations should rest on human nature as much as possible, and so take individual actions as central to explanations. This individualism is loose, as it allows explanatory efforts to rest on descriptions of the circumstances of a given action, not only the observable surroundings but also abstract items like social institutions. He took these to be shorthand for psychological factors, on the assumption that social factors are aggregates of individual ones. This assumption was supposed to free social explanation for attributing any success to past social settings, allegedly in dissent from Comte's view. Whether this is fair to Comte or not is less important than whether is it is acceptable. As it happened, it invited and received criticism.

It is hard to go over the criticism of Mill, as his view is these days assimilated into that of Max Weber. Without going into exegesis we can ask, did Weber's get things right? This question is still under dispute, but on the whole his views are losing ground. Efforts to explain human affairs as due to individual rational conduct seem pretty hopeless. Even before Weber appeared on the scene, such considerations led to efforts to supplement the individualist idea of explanation of human affairs by reference to factors more social than psychological, such as historical trends. He added to this the observation that some individuals are much more influential than others, such as charismatic leaders. This idea is quaint, as it lies on the borderline between psychology and social science proper. Yet it is the most obvious case for individual actions (under the charm of the Leader) accumulating into a social factor proper (mobilization, say, to fight a holy war).

NINETEENTH-CENTURY INDIVIDUALIST METHODOLOGY FUSES HISTORICISM INTO EXPLANATION

Autonomy poses a challenge to the social order, but it also offers incentives for the study of human nature – on the assumption that autonomy is a part of it. This assumption can be useful for enlightened legislation. Only modern legal systems and their social aspects were the remit of the social sciences, with the study of canon law left to the churches and the study of non-modern secular laws consigned to social and political history. The crowning outcomes were studies of the spectacular American and French legal systems that celebrate the secular state (McManners, 1965). These were cast in the frameworks of large-scale theories of the history of human affairs as the history of progress. They served as historical explanations of the American and French Revolutions and thus as their moral, philosophical and historical justifications.

To repeat, liberalism emerged in several forms: as a legislative strategy, a policy for legislation and legislation proper, as well as a metaphysical framework. As such, it does not apply to systems that have no legislative apparatus: legislation is impossible in a closed society (in Popper's sense of the term), since closed societies consider their laws (or customs) divine and thus immutable. This does not mean that liberal legislatures are democratic or vice versa. Our paradigm is the Western-style liberal-democratic nation-state, which we take almost unawares.

We then take for granted and forget that certain liberties are safeguarded there and certain discriminations are prevented there at least *pro forma*. As India and Israel officially practice religious discrimination, they are not Western-style liberal-democratic nation-states, yet they do possess active, democratically elected legislatures. Nation-states proper secure their citizens' freedom of conscience; India and Israel do not. Yet they are democratic in the sense that their legislation is piecemeal, and so their failures can undergo amendments. This, strangely, applies even to pre-civil-war United States of America. For many possible failings the regime of a country can fall short of the current paradigm of Western-style liberal-democratic nation-state. But if legislators are liberal, then their first order of business will be to rectify the laws that provoke lawless conduct. For this the freedom of conscience is essential, and maintaining it is oddly the key to all liberal reforms and thus to liberalization.

Liberalism is thus a theory, a vision, large-scale-Utopian and quasi-anarchist. The application of such a theory is always revolutionary, and to the extent that its revolutions were successful, it was because they gave rise to its piecemeal, democratic, practical variants of themselves.[52] The piecemeal version enjoys the success that is the alliance of Western-style liberal-democratic nation-states: these comprise the advanced part of today's world (advanced in many senses). After all, much of the input for this success was due to the Utopian version of liberalism that cannot but end in failure, even to its unsuccessful French Revolution that began as liberal and ended in terror and in the Napoleonic wars. The large-scale-Utopian, theoretical version of liberalism was also not intended to explain the sorry state of the human race.

The explanatory uses of liberalism came as an afterthought, accompanying the vision of having the social and the natural sciences on a par and effort to make it so. Attempts at explanations of social and political phenomena immediately became an essential aspect of this effort (with de Tocqueville, Comte and Mill, we remember). The identification of liberalism with individualist explanations is very common now. It persists despite the non-explanatory liberalism and liberal non-individualist explanations – pre-nineteenth century liberalism and historicist and functionalist explanations. (Historicism and functionalism have scientific-liberal versions as well as anti-scientific-anti-liberal ones.[53]) if any discussion heralded the intellectual revolution that explanatory liberalism is, then it is the discussion of the scientific character of liberalism. Initially, this discussion was part-and-parcel of the reactionary critique of liberalism, of its radical, Utopian character, beginning with Edmund Burke's classical *Reflections on the Revolution in France* (1790) that boldly declared liberalism radical and radicalism unscientific and so a prejudice, no less! The reason for the tremendous change in liberal thought, then, is that in the West liberalism was almost exclusively rationalist, and rationalism requires scrutiny, and scrutiny requires explanation.[54]

Strangely, the fathers of the explanatory trend in liberalism, Comte and Mille, presented explanatory social science and liberal thinking as one, and they did so in the name of rationality.[55] This move demands scrutiny. The nineteenth-century version of liberalism advocated the version of positivism that is still taught in economics courses under the label of positive (!) economics. Positivism is the rejection of all that is unscientific as harmful superstition.[56] Its first casualty is ethics. Positivists wanted to replace ethics with science-based prescriptions: instead of advising people to abide by the law and avoid criminal conduct, they declared scientific the assertion that criminals hurt themselves: crime does not pay. They were in obvious error: very regrettably, all too often crime does pay and even handsomely. Criminals get away with murder more often than not. (This is ironic, since the positivism with which economists defend positive economics

is the claim that science is descriptive, not prescriptive. And a descriptive theory need not be explanatory. Indeed, the standard version of positive economics, the neo-classical theory, is Utopian, and it leaves scarcely any room for explanatory theories.[57]) Positivism is thus liberal; the liberal assertion that crime does not pay should read not as descriptive but as prescriptive: wise legislation should render crime unprofitable. Of course, they meant not only legislation conducive to a life of honesty, but other actions that would further that end, chiefly education and social security, for which the rubberstamp example is the recommendation to replace the traditional condemnation of prostitution with incentives for the adoption of a better way of life – by the institution of a welfare system that eliminates ignorance and poverty.[58]

Positivism is thus hardly anything more than a sophisticated effort to proscribe preaching (Heine, 1833/1986: 65) and smuggle liberalism into social thinking in evasion of scrutiny although it behooves rationalists. In particular, positivists took for granted the desirability of the autonomy of the individual and thus of as much equality as is possible. This is admirable. Coupling it with the idea that prescription should give way to description made us all autonomous free of charge. This is nothing short of theft – for a good cause, of course. (It is also inconsistent as it is a prescription to avoid prescription.[59] But criticism of this sort is always answerable by careful reformulation.[60])

Autonomy is still too scarce: the most autonomous are still more dependent on received opinion than strict reason allows, and it is very hard to try to increase autonomy by criticizing ever-greater parts of received opinion. The example that is pertinent here is Weber's view that the rise of capitalism has much to thank frugality for, and that this frugality has much to thank (some version of) Protestantism for. His claim is shaky since industrialism undergirds capitalism, and frugality is needed, if at all,[61] for mercantile or manufacturing capitalism, and these forms of capitalism preceded the Reformation: Protestants took the praise of frugality over from Catholicism. Similarly, Weber himself, a devoted anti-religious positivist, advocated frugality as rational: it is deferred gratification. The doctrine of deferred gratification is easy to refute. (It was amply refuted by specific experiments, although commonsense suffices.) It is obviously more autonomous and more rational to seize the day than to postpone enjoyment of what life offers.

The demand for autonomy was always a challenge rather than an observation of facts, and it was usually understood this way. Hence, it led to the study of human nature as going deeper than the empirically observed facts that show people as in possession of only partial autonomy at best. And easily available empirical information shows that people are motivated not only by their self-interests, much less by its enlightened version. Nevertheless, positivists and empiricists of all sorts fully ignored this claim and all of its empirical support. Yet in another context they had to struggle with this very claim, and they did, as it caused much political damage: it supported paternalism and entrenched the view that autonomy for common people is undesirable as it causes political instability.[62]

The positivism that is concerned more with empirical science than with human nature awaited the invention of new ideas by which to overcome the limitation of traditional liberalism. The first effort at such a new brand of positivism is of Benjamin Constant and Madame Germaine de Staël of the early-nineteenth century. They attempted to enrich classical liberalism by adding to its view of human nature factors that they hoped would raise the empirical relevance of reference to human nature. To that end they added to human nature social dispositions and the sense of history that (they averred) dwell in each individual soul. For, the reaction to radicalism demanded that social studies should be historical, namely, that they should expound the laws not of human nature but of history (Winegarten, 2008: 288–95). Their aim was thus to compromise the old and the

new. Regrettably, they did so in a manner that was hardly self-critical or comprehensive. They were important all the same, as they initiated conservative liberalism as a corrective to classical liberalism that is radical. This was the reason for their hope to render social studies less Utopian and more empirical. Heine thought poorly of them – he called her doctrinaire (Heine, 1833/1986: end of preface to the first French edition) – since they did not grapple with the challenge to their views that the clash between autonomy and historical necessity pose: can historical law permit individual autonomy? How? The idea that human conduct is subject to the torrents of history, revived by Burke and amplified[63] by his Continental followers, was a collectivist doctrine, and it transferred autonomy from individual to nation (as the nation's right for self-determination[64]). As the idea of individual autonomy was traditionally part-and-parcel of the ideas of the scientific ethos, Hegel revived and intensified the idea of historical law as precluding scientific prediction of human conduct so as to cut human studies away from the grip of science: he replaced the egalitarian attitude of science with the idea that every epoch has its supreme nation and its supreme heroes. Saint-Simon and Marx turned around this historicist idea: with the discovery of historical law, they declared, historical prediction became available as the basis for scientific history, and the future that they predicted was Utopian. Thus, while rejecting Hegel's claim that social science is impossible, they demanded the endorsement of his historicism and thus the postponement[65] of a liberal regime to the rosy future. Liberal legislation dropped out of the theory (with the blessings of Hegel and Marx, who put down the law of the land as merely formal – Hegel preferring custom over law and Marx preferring inexorable economic forces). Ironically, this made Marxism anti-political.

The naïve combination of autonomy and historical law that Heine viewed as too shallow remained problematic and unresolved. The classical rationalists took autonomy to be total and free of all tradition and thus yielding the Utopia that the commonwealth of learning should soon be. The Reaction rejected autonomy and Utopianism, and by implication social science too. Hegel dismissed all autonomy, even of people who follow their own desires. They only feel that they act on their wishes, Hegel declared, but in truth they serve History.[66] The desires that he spoke of were not self-interest but the lust for fame and glory that characterizes Great Men, those who make History. For, History, too, he viewed as the rise and fall of empires:[67] he saw the powerful as also the most cultural, as he identified Reason with History, thus achieving in one stroke a reversal of social studies from ultra-radical rationalism to ultra-conservative irrationalism. He declared in that vein that the victory of Reason is real, namely, military: God reveals Himself on the battlefield.[68] Marx did not share Hegel's fascination with glory. He accepted Hegel's gloomy view of humanity, but as adequate for the past, not for the necessarily rosy future: industry must follow the law of the free market, so that participants in it have to yield to the profit motive that brings about quite unintentionally but with historical necessity the concentration of wealth and thus socialism. Full autonomy will then replace historical necessity; Marx answered Heine's criticism of historicism: freedom and necessity do not clash as they divide History between them. The weakest aspect of the philosophy of Marx, said his follower Bernard Shaw, is his denial of the very possibility[69] of effective legislation that limits the freedom of the market: while Marx described the impossibility of effective social legislation, it took place under his nose (Shaw, 1984: §50).

Shaw's criticism is easy to generalize. As autonomy can be a useful assumption and it can be a noble aim for effective enlightened legislation, the theory of historical necessity is useless: it discourages democratic societies from deciding on priorities and on the best way to implement them by enlightened legislation. Reactionary thinkers understandably dislike reform, and they discuss change only as part of the course of history.

Why then did democratic legislation play such a marginal role in the explanation of rational behavior? The answer is different for the conduct of rationalist social thinkers before and after the rise of reactionary thinking in the early-nineteenth century. Explanations of social events were either historicist in oblivion to autonomy or they were adequate to given individual aims in given circumstances. Researchers in the Age of Reason ignored the social settings of conduct. (This is why the crowning glory of their researches was economic theory that considered free trade institution-free and political theory that based government on abstract accord between individuals.) Later, under the impact of the Reaction, the social settings of conduct were included in its circumstances, and on the authority of Mill, who allowed these as a mere stopgap. Understandably, whereas classical (radical) liberals of the Age of Reason considered the social a result of the individual and so they spoke of individuals in given circumstances that include physical conditions and other individuals but not to any society, reactionary collectivists considered the individual a mere part of the social, a vehicle of social forces. So they ignored individual action, including legislation and centered on social forces – in indifference to the difference between legal systems and lawless tyrannies.[70] Individualists naturally took over from the reactionaries whatever they found useful, including the idea of historical necessity. And so, concern with explanation made legal reform fall by the wayside. Explanation fell short of covering past legal reforms, not to mention the rise of new legal systems (revolutions). Weber attempted to do this and failed, we remember.

Reactionary collectivists discussed autonomy. How much and what kind of it do social forces allow? Their concern was the same as all traditional social thought: the preservation of social stability. Yet they allowed for changes, and even[71] for progress and for autonomy – but as limited to exceptional individuals, as it is above the ability of ordinary flesh-and-blood. It thus became the privilege of Great Men. Since every citizen may want to be great, and since this threatens all social stability, the Great Man must pass tests or ordeals like mediaeval knights and also attain success, even if only posthumously.

Unlike the Utopian social thought of the Age of Reason, the Reaction allowed historians of the law to defend it as rational and their justification of their specific legal systems was on the presumption that they approximate the presumed ideal natural law.[72] As it is traditional to identify rationality with justification, this is understandable. But it is too problematic and too remote from practice and even from genuine philosophical controversy. The odd fact remains, observes Benjamin Akzin: legislators justified their conduct by reference to human nature thus implying that their proposed reform is perfect. How many times, he asked (Akzin, 1968), can one propose a change as final and still get away with it?

Even the far-fetched suggestion that the diverse modern European legal systems are replicas[73] of the natural law would not do, since the older ones are obviously traditionalist and so they were judged irrational and so contrary to natural law. Studies of legal systems and of their social aspects were then limited to the study of modern European systems, with the study of canon law left to the churches and the study of non-modern secular laws left to social and political historians. (A possible exception is the essentials of Roman law that are allegedly liberal and comprise the root of much liberal legislation, especially the presumption of innocence that runs contrary to the presumption of guilt that characterizes the inquisition and the modern totalitarian states. As Roman Law was deemed liberal, it was allowed to serve as foundation of all European Law, so that its Republican principles were deemed proper subject for study. All this could be ignored with the establishment of the idea that individualist methodology is explanatory.) It is understandable that the evidential basis of modern legal studies is limited to extant documents, yet this excludes most societies, as these are preliterate. The study of law in preliterate cultures is limited of necessity to extant primitive societies. To bridge this gap Lewis Henry Morgan proposed in the mid-nineteenth century the progressivist-historicist hypothesis that all societies evolve on the same evolutionary track, that the same measure of progress applies to all aspects of society, including technology, culture and politics, so that the distance from contemporary primitive society to ancient society is very small (Morgan, 1877: 261 *et seq.*). (Even the distance between the most advanced and the most primitive societies he saw as merely a difference in timing: societies that have evolved faster are the more advanced.) He viewed even Homeric Greece as democratic, so he declared that the Aztec kingdom was at a lower level of progress than Greece. (His program was of little help to classical studies: he wanted to assist with the suggestion that the ancient Greeks resembled some living primitive societies, but he ended up saying that the Greeks were backward only in physical and biological technologies, not in social and political ones.) Primitive societies have hardly any legislation, their law being identical with custom, in contradistinction to literate society where law and custom may differ. Yet primitive custom too alters over time, largely because custom has its own customary courts that adjudicate in cases of conflict. Unfortunately, most anthropologists were functionalists and thus they saw the primitive societies that they studied in a romantic light as harmonious, and so they glossed over conflicts and social change (Gellner, 1958; Jarvie, 1973).

The chief difference, then, between preliterate and literate societies concerns open legal reform. Indeed, even the faithful recording of customs/laws is already a major legal reform and the need to alter the fixed laws creates a diversity of legal methodologies that culminate with courts developing rules of precedents and democratic legislatures writing laws freely. All this owes its existence to Solon and more so to Cleisthenes who invented vast legal reforms and who was almost entirely ignored until after World War II (Snodgrass, 1980: Introduction). As conflict is the leaven of social change, it is beyond the ability of any court of any system to resolve conflicts embedded in that system. This is the rationale of the institution of legislatures: systematic and significant failure of any system may cause political upheavals, and legislation came to prevent this. Of course, conflicts are not naturally given and changed views of rights and wrongs may be a major cause of the new conflicts that courts may be unable to handle. Thus, new ideas, especially new religions, are the most significant and forceful factors behind the demand for legal change. Such situations call for swift legislation and these may happen within the system. When change is tardy, a revolution or disintegration is in the offing. All this is very obvious yet not seen due to its being obviously not historicist and obviously not sufficiently rational: efforts at achieving rational system and at explaining them rationally do not go together, since rational explanation justifies and so excludes any reason for change.

The delay in the combined study of explanation of situations and of changes still is odd. After all, the crowning outcomes of rationalist social studies were the spectacular American and French Revolutions and the rise of the secular state. But even the students' revolution in the late 1960s, especially in France, is of the same ilk. Thus, legislation and revolution may be subject to similar analyses and explanations. As legislation was so neglected by explanatory social science, attention centered on revolutions, namely, on rapid large-scale changes (peaceful or not). The very large scale of phenomena seems to suggest explaining them along historicist lines. The very need to correct a system repeatedly, however, is the recognition of the imperfection of the system and of the individual aspect of efforts at reform. This is why there was a gulf between legal histories and social explanations of them. Perhaps the very

introduction of social history (Trevelyan, 1944) was so revolutionary because it sidestepped the problems that constrained traditional studies. Indeed, late-nineteenth-century European political reformers were thinkers who felt strong need for information about social conditions, and that testifies to the backwardness of the social sciences of the time (Simey, 1960: 89). So does the fact that rapid large-scale changes were viewed in the light of large-scale theories of the history of human affairs such as theories of history as the history of progress and the history of progress as manifestation of historical inevitability. They were hardly explanations in the sense of inferences with the items to explain appearing as conclusions in them; they were mock historical explanations of the revolutions as their justifications.[74]

Thus, it should not surprise us that liberals are unwilling to share this view of history and that they prefer, instead, to study relatively stable social situations. Yet this is a drawback that reinforces the Reaction. Liberalism rightly suggests that some rapid changes are to the good and others not, especially the bloody ones. They insist that bloody revolutions are due to failures to prevent them, and so, regardless of their being progressive or regressive, regardless of rights or wrongs, bloody revolutions are not as successful as efforts to prevent them by wise legislation could be. This is the central idea of de Tocqueville, who admired the British just because they managed to avoid the bloody revolution that France had to suffer. Thus, in the light of the possibility of removing obstacles to progress by peaceful means, we must consider bloody revolutions as failures even if they successfully remove obstacles to progress. All this, again, is fairly obvious, yet the limitation of traditional methodology made it hard to see.

This also explains the recent popularity of the preposterous view of Herbert Marcuse that peaceful reforms do not suffice, so that blood must be spilled for the cause of progress, that therefore reforms only worsen this situation by prolonging the birth pangs of the revolution. The argument in favor of his line of reasoning is obvious: a revolution is an expression of utter dissatisfaction with the current regime, whereas liberalism aims at making the system accommodating. Talcott Parsons, to repeat, began his career as a follower of Weber, and when he found Weber's view of social change inadequate, he disappointedly switched allegiance to the collectivist and functionalist sociology of Durkheim. It is hard to believe it possible to push conflict-ridden modern society on to a Procrustean bed of social harmony so tight that each item in the division of labor is optimal and deviation from it disastrous. Yet this is what Durkheim claimed; he also claimed that criminals contribute to harmony (Dunman, 2003). His explanation for this must be thin, since in the interest of harmony crime and conflict are better minimized. No argument can gloss over the fact that some characteristics of society are desirable, some not; Durkheim was fully aware of this, of course; his claim then was that even the undesirable is not utterly undesirable. This is trivially true. It is no surprise that in the turbulent days of the race riots, students' revolt and the rise of the new women's movement, the shares of Durkheim plummeted. The surprise is that they were once so high.

THE METHODOLOGY OF THE REACTION TO THE MODERN VIEWS RESTS ON HISTORICIST COLLECTIVISM

The transition of fashion from rationalism to the Reaction is marked by the American and French Revolutions. The French Revolution had a greater impact on social philosophy and methodology than the American one, just because it was a failure. Politicians may have feared the success of the revolutions in establishing equality; intellectuals feared its failure. It led them to realize that classical rationalism is Utopian and that Utopianism led to bloody upheavals. This is the nineteenth-century background to both the Reaction and the tempered liberalism.

Prior to World War II, European social and political thinkers ignored the success of the USA.[75] This despite the tremendous success of de Tocqueville's study (1835) of democracy in America. Things changed after Hiroshima. The older significant historical fact about the U.S. – as well as about the Republic of France – is that they recognized human rights and citizen rights that are independent of origin or creed, a recognition that included the idea of equality before the law, later built in to the United Nations Declarations and Charter, but earlier viewed by aristocratic Continent of Europe differently. Now equality is troublesome.[76] The abolition of inequality due to origin and creed already meant much, but economic inequality is troublesome, as not everyone wants the complete elimination of economic inequality that socialism requires. Fighting poverty, the welfare state reduces – not eliminates – the worst aspects of economic inequality. Matters of equality, however, are only a part of the non-liberal critique of the standard modern liberal democratic nation-state; the upheavals that France suffered during the nineteenth century comprise a much more severe critique of liberalism, not to mention the collapse of the liberal Weimar Republic that gave rise to the most atrocious regime ever. All this does not apply to the U.S., despite the Civil War there that was an even greater an internal upheaval than what France ever witnessed: it is generally agreed that despite this disaster, the U.S. showed tremendous social stability and, judged from the liberal viewpoint, it is on the whole a success story. This, it seems, is one reason why European scholars ignored the U.S. After World War I, it was hardly possible to ignore it to that extent, yet many scholars began to notice it only after World War II, when they had some severe (and often just) criticism of American foreign politics. Its internal politics has still not received from political European thinkers the attention, not to mention the praise, that they deserve.

The fear of the spread of the ideals of the French Revolution that bred reactionary social and political philosophy brought about new studies, mainly historical, and much of this is of great interest even if it was a sort of propaganda for collectivist social and political philosophy. The most conspicuous instance is the tremendous growth of philology, yet this growth encouraged racism (as it explained the migration of languages by the – empirically refuted – assumption that the migration of tribes had caused it). Another conspicuous instance is the rise of the study of local folk culture, the study that began with the Grimm fairytale collection and that later, in the twentieth century, includes studies by Béla Bartók and Zoltan Kodaly as well as by Martin Buber. The earlier contributions were meant to support collectivism and collectivist politics, the later not in the least. Conspicuous as these cases are, the most significant ones were the political histories of the nineteenth century, mostly revealing the influence of Hegel. They often presented religion as a part of culture and politics as conferring culture its significance.

The arsenal of reactionary social and political philosophy included some alluring romantic ideas: anti-science historicism; the notion that only exceptional individuals are autonomous; the notion that the test for autonomy is (not good breeding but) success, that real success follows the laws of history, and that treating these laws comprises a better alternative to the Enlightenment search for natural laws. Next, Saint-Simon and Marx declared historical laws scientific because they provide historical predictions. This was a pro-science version of historicism that aspires to develop theories that should explain and predict large-scale (political) changes (Jarvie, 1982).

The appeal of hostility to science lies in its offer to combat the perceived threat that scientific ideas and science-based technology bring about a new world. Some thinkers and their followers looked forward to this new world; others loathed it.[77] This raised a most important and interesting question: can

reason adjudicate on such preferences? The appeal of the reactionary philosophy was here: the reliance on gut feelings is preferable to the reliance on reason, as the deepest feelings you have are independent, and so they are right. (If your feelings lead you astray, then you should dig deeper inside yourself. Hence, this idea is irrefutable. This will appeal to romantics, not to rationalists.) What the deepest gut feelings are is not so important; the important thing is to be authentic, as plain honesty requires. This idea became more central in the twentieth century, when not only philosophers like Heidegger advocated it, but also scientists like Konrad Lorenz: you must admit that you are carnivorous and so not too merciful; and you must admit that you are at times moved by envy and other aggressive feelings. Liberals, I think, must take this attitude seriously, as they preach taking people as they are, on all of their weaknesses; but liberals need not and should not endorse the Romantic indulgence towards vices, much less consider them virtues. The rational is civilized and the civilized should be honest about their aggression towards the other and control it in the light of reason: the civilized acquire the ability to tolerate the other as much as possible. The question that liberalism faced is, what is the place of toleration in the scheme of things and how does social science account for different attitudes towards it?

It is not clear if the liberal response to weaknesses sits well with the (eudaemonist) idea that we should follow our inclinations rationally. Here, oddly, reactionary thinkers speak in favor of enlightened self-interest disregarding the interest of other members of the collective, on the supposition that we share the real interest – to support our collectives. And we need not mind the other collective or its members: our duty is to our own. This confused appeal to the duty to be selfish is the doctrine of Friedrich Nietzsche, for example, who continues to win praise for his extremist individualism despite its blatant brutality over which he put a very cultural face and very perceptive remarks that go down well in parlor conversation. He was very critically minded, though, and whatever we take his ideas to be, we should not overlook his criticism and challenges that at times raised levels of discussions.

The important question then is: how do we test our ideas? The reactionary answer is, we have to yield to the judgment of history. This is how, behind the doctrine of authenticity, stands the doctrine of historical necessity. The idea that only exceptional individuals can be autonomous was the sole innovation in the reactionary-romantic ideology and the sole concession it made to classical rationalism. The concession turns out to be both greater than it seems and less dangerous to traditionalism than it seems. It is less dangerous as it poses an impossible challenge to every aspirant for autonomy, describing the autonomous, as it does, as free of all obligations and as utterly lonely and utterly original: the autonomous goes to the desert to develop somehow super-human strength; you do not qualify; you must submit to authority. It is a big concession, nevertheless, and quite counter-intentionally, since it allows or even demands of the autonomous that they initiate revolutions. This idea Weber employed (in a version that he developed under the influence of Nietzsche) in his theory of social change: all change is due to charismatic heroes. The idea of the hero as autonomous and as moving mountains had great appeal as it looks more realistic than the rationalist idea that everyone is potentially a mover and shaker. (This was the excuse that the intelligent, worldly-wise Bernard Shaw gave repeatedly for his puerile hero worship.) It is, primarily, an expression of contempt for common people. (This shows that Shaw's rationale is an excuse: he repeatedly denied that he held common people in contempt.[78]) It is also a version of success worship, since it leaves to the judgment of History the decision as to who is a genuine hero (Shaw, 1889: Prefaces). Romantics show contempt for common ambition as slavish, and view the test for autonomy as large-scale success. Such success follows the laws of History;

this allegedly comprises an improvement over the Enlightenment idea of natural laws. Yet its seeming explanatory power is betting on a horse after the race is over.

To repeat, Saint-Simon and Marx developed a pro-science version of the romantic and anti-scientific idea of historical necessity, aspiring to develop theories that should both predict correctly large-scale changes and explain human affairs. The question arises, can autonomous conduct be predicted? This question is still under dispute. Under Hegel's influence, Marx answered it, saying that historical predictions are of large-scale progress that permits individual freedom on a small scale. He viewed the progress that history shows as dependent on technological progress, and this is largely due to scientific progress and other expressions of individual ingenuity. This reasoning is erroneous, observed Popper, and for the following reason. Marx saw the rise of efficiency under capitalism as the cause of the accumulation of capital and the polarization of class society, factors that render the socialist revolution both easy and inevitable. The reason for that is the centrality of steam engines in nineteenth-century industry. For, their efficiency significantly increases with size. Once the electric dynamo entered the market, observed Popper, considerations of efficiency altered and the middle class proliferated. Authors who allegedly represent Marxism (Goldthorpe et al., 1976; Marcuse, 1964), incidentally, view the workers as traitors. Farewell to historical inevitability.

This is not to deny that certain considerations may lead to some large-scale predictions. Yet they may be false and they may indicate changes but leave much open. For example, Bertrand and Dora Russell noted (Russell and Russell, 1923) that industrialization will continue for quite some time, proliferate the division of labor and thereby increase the interconnectedness of different parts of society (most people's food comes from sources that they are ignorant of and unable to control). This interconnectedness, they further observed, requires coordination, and in the last resort the coordinator is the state, so that state power will be on the increase. One may have the impression that this is the very opposite of the view advocated by most economists according to which the best means for this orchestration is the free market, and that all government intervention in market activity is harmful. This impression is false. Even had governments avoided intervening in the market, they would remain most important in coordinating the diverse aspects of life, especially in control over security and the currency.[79] Industrialization makes them ever stronger. The Russells feared that this rendered modern society illiberal and undemocratic. By contradistinction, Popper viewed the same facts as raising both the need for democratic control and the importance for liberalism of devising, enhancing and empowering of such controls. Popper's is the most basic way to link liberal legislation with the liberal-democratic way of life.[80] And, of course, there is no disagreement between the Russells and Popper: their forecast is more in the nature of a warning than a scientific prediction.

INSTITUTIONAL INDIVIDUALISM IS THE LATEST BUT NOT THE LAST WORD ON THE TOPIC

All the alternative ideas about human nature developed more-or-less in parallel: the descriptive, the prescriptive and the mixed versions of the theories of human affairs, as well as their Romantic, more blatantly historicist versions. This forced the individualists to develop a competing system of explanation; at first, we remember, this was historicist too. This gave way in stages to methodological individualism that led to the rise of institutionalist–individualist explanations in the social sciences that eschew discussion of human nature and of institutions and takes for granted instead the existence and the modifiability of social and political institutions. What is peculiar to

institutionalist individualism then is that it denies entities aims of their own (Popper, 1945: Chapter 7, n. 23; Popper, 1963: 350), so that only individuals are actors[81] and their strongest means of influencing others is by effecting institutional reforms (Russell, 1916: 19, 27, 32, 52, 93, 161, 163), intended and more often unintended[82] (Hayek, 1960: 59).

Liberal social thinkers tried hard to avoid prescription in line with their toleration and utilitarianism.[83] They said, science could only provide descriptions of the consequences of actions, not recommend any. Yet they were deeply convinced that since peace and harmony are in everybody's interest, of necessity their tolerant, utilitarian social and political philosophy, especially its application to legislation, would bring about peace and harmony. This amounts to a historicist theory of progress, of course. Already Condorcet said (Condorcet, 1795), since reasonable people will emulate successful conduct, the future would assuredly be rosy if only people will act rationally. Will they? Here views of human nature, benevolent prescriptions and blind faith in progress, have tipped the scale: the commonwealth of learning became increasingly optimistic until the outbreak of the Great War that strangely surprised everyone.

The mood altered after Hiroshima and Auschwitz.[84] Spokespeople for the commonwealth of learning said, scientific technology is a tool, and tools are morally neutral. The tragedy is that this change was quite surreptitious and raised no public protest. That instruments are neutral is obvious, yet the question is whether their introduction is beneficial. We may say it is inevitable, since if one side of any conflict did not develop some weapon – especially nuclear weapon – the other side would. This is technological determinism. It is a new version of historicism, and it is rampant. It was adumbrated already in the writings of Karl Mannheim, before the discovery of nuclear weapons. (These were scarcely needed for the argument in question, since weapons of mass destruction were available already in

World War I.) The attraction of Mannheim's version is that it squares with all alternative ideas about human nature, and the descriptive, prescriptive and mixed versions of the theories of human affairs. It also squares with the classical and the Romantic views of rationality by his historicist version of the theory of knowledge, known as his sociology of knowledge, that seemed very scientific as it observed common knowledge without discussing its validity, thereby sidestepping the major difference, the difference that is between declaring folk views superstitious and taking them as expressions of the spirit of the collective. He did this by his specific use of the (obviously true) observations that all knowledge is in part a social product (as all human products are created in society that makes them possible and signify only if they are not forgotten as soon as they die) and that knowledge helps individuals to adjust to society (which is obviously true only of some knowledge; other knowledge, such as of abstract set theory, is socially neutral, and still other knowledge, such as of Bible criticism, is socially disruptive in the societies that teach the dependence of social stability on faith in the Bible). Mannheim noted that these observations invite exceptions. He called exceptional individuals free spirits and allowed them to engage in what Popper called socio-therapy in parallel to psychotherapy (Popper, 1945: ii, 215–16). This conduct may be understood as liberal legislation, and it was so understood by many of his disciples. Popper said, Mannheim's view of human nature as malleable was not liberal; whereas Utopians sought a society that is fit for humans, Mannheim wanted humans to become fit for society (Popper, 1957: 70). Of course, Mannheim's abstention from discussing human nature as a part of any political program undermines the whole of his project.[85] Whether human nature is malleable or not matters little; that human conduct is malleable remains very important: reasonable liberal legislation renders people tolerant. What liberal legislation is reasonable, then?

Any detailed answer to this question, and any discussion of it, will force individualists to develop competing explanatory systems. This is, indeed, what has happened. At first, the explanations were hardly satisfactory, as they were historicist. This gave way in stages to Weber's methodological individualism, to his idea that the explained situations refer to individuals with different philosophies, individualism being one of them, so that the individualism that researchers abide by is limited to their research methods, without attributing it to the individuals under study. It was important to Weber that the question, do collectives exist, is not a question of method. He recommended sidestepping it, and he declared that this was a methodological step rather than ambivalence about a metaphysical matter. This sidestepping, it turns out, is too limiting, as all sorts of factual questions constantly come up and depend on answers to the factual question that he wished sidestepped. In particular, we remember, it is hard to sidestep the liberalizing force that Weber ascribed to explanations and recommendations regarding legislation.[86] More elementary questions then surfaced. For example, to what extent is the ancient analogy valid between individual and collective. Collectivism often drew force from this analogy. How far does it go?

Efforts to answer this question gave rise to institutionalist explanations in the social sciences that culminated in institutional individualism that eschews discussion of human nature and takes for granted the existence and modifiability of social and political institutions. It allows for all analogies between individual and collective, general or specific, tame or wild, on the single proviso that they be put to test. The only exception to this, to repeat Popper's point,[87] is that only individuals, not collectives, can make decisions and consider having made them or refrained from having made them responsible or irresponsible. Otherwise, we may try to ascribe to society any individual traits (and vice versa) as we want and put the ascription to test.

To conclude, a society may display to some extent a given social philosophy. Methodological Individualism easily tends to ascribe to individuals the social philosophies inherent in their societies. This is an error that has far-reaching consequences.[88] People can see the philosophy that their societies embed only to the extent to which they are familiar with these ideas. Thus, Athens was seen as a direct democracy until the idea of participatory democracy developed (together with the idea of pluralism) and then it came to the notice of historians – much to their surprise (opening of Snodgrass, 1981) – that Athenian society had a large portion of its citizens participate actively in the daily work of the government (Snodgrass, 1981: 199, 204, 206). Earlier, commentators saw the peculiarity of Greek democracy as its being direct, which of course no modern democracy can emulate, not in its being participatory, which, of course, is an advantage that every democracy may beneficially adopt. Participatory democracy has its practical advantages, its administrative advantages and its legislative ones. Its theoretical advantage is that it refutes Weber's theory of the bureaucracy as a privileged social class (not of society as the embodiment of a socio-political philosophy). Participatory democracy need not be pluralist, although the size of modern nation-states makes pluralism practically inevitable, so that the two ideas appeared together after World War II. Contrary to Plato's and Mannheim's theories that require fitting individual to society, it is possible to fit society to diverse kinds of individuals (Popper, 1957: 70). This very possibility renders liberal philosophy the default option: all other options should be seen as deviations from it. This is the thrust of the philosophy presented in Spinoza's unfinished *Political Treatise*.

ACKNOWLEDGEMENT

Ian C. Jarvie has my gratitude for his significant input to this chapter.

NOTES

1 The sociology of knowledge of Max Scheler preceded that of Mannheim, yet as it is a contribution to Husserl-style phenomenology rather than to social philosophy (Schilpp, 1927), it does not belong here.

2 Consider the notorious Marxist (or pseudo-Marxist) explanation that Boris Hessen offered for the very appearance of Newton's theory of universal gravity. The way the literature treats it (Freudenthal, 2005; Graham, 1985) despite much public derision is quite indicative.

3 Amusingly, Ludwig Wittgenstein's view of all self-reference as meaningless, led him to admit (Wittgenstein, 1922: end of preface) that his work (that significantly, scarcely noticed the social sciences) is meaningless. It is not: it is inconsistent (Popper, 1945: ii, Chapter 24, note 8).

4 Refutations are usually observation reports. By convention, the default option is that they oust the theories that they conflict with (Boyle, 1661; Popper, 1959/1935: §30). Some refutations happen to be so imposing that they need no performance. (A case in point is Davy's melting ice in a vacuum by friction.) Taking these thought experiments as making real ones redundant renders them not redundant. Whether geometrical counterexamples (Lakatos, 1976) belong to physics or mathematics is hard to say, since their being constructible makes them physics but their role as refutations of mathematical theorems renders them mathematical.

5 This is the lesson that William Whewell drew from the refutation of the allegedly confirmed Newtonian optics (Whewell, 1857: Bk. IX, Ch. X). He said it was never properly confirmed. The rigorous procedure of confirmation, he explained, involves proper tests: writing down the expected result of observation before and after it was made, and comparing the two reports, of the expected and of the perceived results. This way most theories are refuted and forgotten, he added, and few are confirmed and they enter the stock of knowledge. Einstein and Popper agreed with him about test procedures and viewed their assessments differently. They said, refuted theories signify, as they stay as approximations and special cases of their successors.

6 In this wording, liberalism is refutable, together with its alternative that promotes law-and-order. Yet, as variants of both philosophies are available, this is far from settling matters.

7 It is never too much to repeat that anarchy is no government, not disorder; it is thus the absence not of coordination but of aggressive imposition (of it). See note 8.

8 'The essence of liberalism is an attempt to secure a social order not based on irrational dogma, and insuring stability without involving more restraints

than are necessary for the preservation of the community' (Russell, 1946: end of preface). Thus, anarchism is the most extreme form of liberalism – the one that denies the need for restraint.

9 Methodology justified the taboo that anthropologists placed on 'survivals', that is, on explanations of the survival of societies by reference to past events: such explanations are untestable for societies with no written records. Consequently, the ability to function today justifies survival today. Thus, functionalism is highly traditionalist (Gellner, 1958; Jarvie, 1964: 34; 1972: 13, 32–3, 67, 102, 105, 122, 235).

10 The Roman poet Juvenal asked (in a misogynist context), 'But who shall guard the guardians?' (*Satires*, 347); Karl Marx echoed this in political context in (Marx, 1842: 24): 'if we are all prisoners, who will be the prison warden?' He also remarked (posthumous Theses on Feuerbach, Third Thesis) on the need to educate educators. A hybrid of these two remarks is a forceful, popular slogan frequently attributed to him: 'who will educate the educators?'

11 Spinoza supported taxation, observing that despite heavy taxes Amsterdam is popular among traders, thus echoing a lively contemporaneous debate (Feuer, 1958: esp. 163).

12 The role of tastes in economic theory is the concern of a famous paper (Stigler and Becker, 1977) that finds the variety of tastes theoretically insignificant. My proposal is to dismiss the whole theory of tastes – of consumers' behaviour – since consumption enters the picture only as aggregate. That consumption aggregates is an added assumption: the whole is the sum of its components. This added assumption is redundant and erroneous: it is refuted by aping, such as in fashions, especially in those that change so rapidly as to destabilize markets. The added assumption is sociological yet it belongs to economic methodology, thus illustrating again the difference between the methodology of the natural and the social sciences. The better alternative to consumers' behaviour theory is to view the price system as an institution (Boland, 1982: 50).

13 Russell's account of behaviorism (Russell, 1946: 741) is probably the best and most succinct. He uses the example of the kidney there. It echoes the old observation (Cabanis, 1802: vol. 1, 4th Memoir, 196), popularized in 1846 by the notorious Carl Vogt: 'thought stands in the same relation to the brain as … urine does to the kidney' (Harrington, 1996: 12).

14 This allegation is hard to discuss rationally. It may rest on the unwise awe that the inability to read texts in the natural sciences inspires. Anyway, what makes one question this allegation is the recent sharp increase of the quality of life of common people in contemporary rich countries.

15 The *Oxford English Dictionary* defines 'scientism' as the characteristic of scientists and as 'excessive belief in the power of scientific knowledge and

techniques'. (The excess is contempt for non-science and scientific imperialism.) The *Webster Dictionary* makes do with the opaque definition: methods and attitudes typical of or attributed to the natural scientist. *Dictionary of the Social Sciences* of Julius Gould and William Kolb, Art. Scientism, elaborates on to the *OED* but adds nothing to it. It has no item on superstition and limits its discussion of prejudice to ethnic and psychopathological phenomena. Strange.

16 The Royal Society of London for the Improvement of Natural Knowledge, was so labeled to exclude discussions of the supernatural. The most conspicuous case of insistence on this in the early days of the Society was its refusal to accept Joseph Glanville to its ranks until he rewrote a book of essays of his to expurgate it of supernaturalism (Jones, 1961/1982: 335, 337, 341–2).

17 Liberalism comprises a version of the paradox of freedom (Popper, 1945: i, 123): people whom we take as they come, all too often refuse to take people as they come. Liberalism fits only some crowds and none fully: it is thus an educational program. Opposing Locke, Russell said, we are born with wild dispositions that require taming. Opposing both, advocates of authenticity said, we should be true to our dispositions. The surprise is not that Nazis like Martin Heidegger advocated authenticity but that the humanists like Sartre do. He alarmingly declared frank Nazis morally superior to habitual self-deceivers, forgetting that the superiority of self-awareness is that it yields hope for self-improvement (Guignon, 2004: Preface).

18 This is quoted from the King James translation. It perhaps softens the original idea that seems more primitive: it is better translated as referring to inclination rather than to imagination. The *Vulgate*, incidentally, refers to the evil in the human heart as *cogitatio*, which is possibly more damning than either evil inclination or evil imagination.

19 Contrast Shakespeare's *Romeo and Juliet* with Plato's *Politeia*. The tragic character of the former is obvious and much commented on; that the same holds for the latter should be obvious, as it subordinates love to the good of the polis. Yet commentators seldom refer to this aspect of this work, and they even suggest, with straight face, that it is Utopian. Not so Plato: the serenity of the style of his *Politeia* clashes powerfully with its tragic anti-individualism and thus bespeaks resignation. Plato the artist is much praised – but only as a servant of Plato the philosopher; his literary criticism is much discussed; yet his output is hardly discussed as literary masterpieces. Even his most powerful literary work, *Symposium*, is discussed as philosophy, as literary criticism, as history, etc., hardly ever as art. The only possible exception is Popper's (1945/1966) *The Open Society and Its Enemies* that expresses both insightful admiration and harsh criticism.

20 Madame Bovary and Anna Karenina are conspicuous examples of literary classics that endorse this verdict. Even the allegedly scientific novel/play *Thérèse Raquin* of the leading liberal Émile Zola, approvingly consigns its heroine to a tragic end (her conscience punishes her) for the same illiberal rationale. Censure of useless sacrifices of oddballs, dissenters and minorities fills a vast literature (novels, ballades, plays or movies), liberal or socialist, artistically and socio-politically impressive or unimpressive, of the genre of social criticism, with sub-genres such as social and anti-war protest, semi-documentaries and even philosophical novels and science fiction.

21 The phenomenon here noticed, of the fusing of science with magic, is the unintended consequence of the valuable deflation of élitism, boosted by the popularity of instrumentalist philosophy of science that identifies theoretical science with applied mathematics: rejecting all scientific explanation, it dooms the success of science to remain inexplicable and thus magical. This explains the new sense of urgency of the old problem of the demarcation of science.

22 *The Prince* is thus a Machiavellian manipulation pushing some power-hungry adventurer to restore Rome.

23 This runs contrary to Rousseau's reading of *The Prince* as a cunning warning against tyranny.

24 H. G. Wells deemed Machiavelli the initiator of the idea, usually ascribed to Hobbes: rulers should be above the law (Wells, 1921: 752–3), and as the foundation of liberalism. (This has little to do with Machiavellism since the ruthless need no theory. Similarly, Wells did not link him to imperialism (pp. 1011, 1015, 1027–8)). He saw the roots of nationalism in Machiavelli's advocacy of a citizens' militia and of the separation of state and church. Mandeville was considered a follower of Hobbes, in sharp contrast to the liberals of the next generation, David Hume and Adam Smith. All this has to do with a number of factors, including the understanding of the very idea of the ruler being above the law. Thus, whereas Jonathan Swift complained (Swift, 1708: Section II, paragraph that begins with 'But though a Church of England man thinks every species of government equally lawful') that he was living in an unbearable tyranny, Hume viewed the Britain of his time 'as near republican as possible' (Hume, 1741, 'Whether the British government inclines more to absolute monarchy, or to a republic'), and they both assumed that monarchy was petering out.

25 Smith goes beyond Mandeville in that his 'invisible hand' maximizes efficiency. Mandeville goes beyond Smith in that he advocated taking people as they come quite unconditionally. He contrasted liberalism with moralizing and left it at that. (All he said about political economy is that the accumulation of wealth requires 'a mild government'.) This is often overlooked. Cropsey's comparison of the two (Cropsey, 1977) contrasts their views ethics (p. 54). Contrary to tradition, both said, greed deserves approbation, yet only Mandeville denied greed its distinction as a vice – thus ingeniously curtailing futile debate. (This is the point of the title of his initial poem, 'The Grumbling Hive: or, Knaves Turn'd Honest' as well as of his book: *The Fable of the Bees, or: Private Vices, Publick Benefits*.) This renders liberalism independent of ethics, establishing it as commonsense. Smith agreed, yet, regarding ethics proper he found Mandeville's aloofness 'licentious' (p. 75). He disagreed on ethics with everyone in sight – Hume included. The utilitarianism of (Spinoza and) Hume identifies virtue with benefit. Smith rejected this as not empirical (p. 78) and as reductionist (p. 86). Mandeville expressed no view on it and for this he won Smith's censure. Being abstract this way, his idea is still unpopular. So is Popper's 'Public Opinion and Liberal Principles' (Popper, 1963: 347–54): his defense of public opinion is not popular as it is abstract, namely, independent of whether public opinion is right or wrong. (For more on political economy as ethics, see Sassower, 1993: 91–5.)

26 The admirable commonsense of Paine and Franklin illustrates (as does that of Mandeville) the advantage of the avoidance of deep philosophical discourse when it is possible. Whether altruism is reducible to egoism or not, it is the mix of the two that makes for stable interpersonal cooperation. And, indeed, the two are never fully separate. This is important and reductionists ignore it to their loss – even on the suggestion that ultimately reductionism is true (Hume, Essay on Principles of Government).

27 Marx considered Smith's analysis a true description of the extant economic system and took trade cycles as evidence against Smith's view of this system as best: it is efficient only in the short run as it enhances competition, not in the long run, as it enhances class conflict. Hence, only a fundamental change will create harmony. This is Marx's Utopianism. He opposed Utopianism in the sense of offering a social blueprint, yet he advocated utopianism in the sense of promising total harmony. That such utopianism leaves no room for reconsideration in a case of failure is known as the adage, 'The revolution like Saturn devours its own children' of Georg Büchner (*Dantons Tod*).

28 As traditional rationalists ignored institutions as folly, they referred only to individual folly, stressing that institutions rest on individual foolish endorsement of them. Hence, all folly requires the same treatment: the renunciation of prejudice. This is Enlightenment Utopianism. As Russell and Popper disagreed with it, they referred to private and to public folly separately (Popper, 1963, final three chapters; Russell, 1918/1995; 1954).

29 Amusingly, since economists disagree as to what government intervention is less harmful, monetary or fiscal, they scarcely notice other interventions.

This is so chiefly because, perhaps under the tremendous influence of Arthur M. Okun, the concern with the influence of taxation on economics was with equity rather than with government intervention. Also, in a pinch, changing tax rates is deemed a part of monetary intervention. This is too cavalier.

30 Even if History progresses and progress liberalizes, the idea of historical necessity opposes the traditional liberal spirit, as it plays down human action (Popper, 1945: ii, 208).

31 Averroes, Avicenna, Maimonides, Spinoza and Russell envisaged the law this way. Spinoza is the first among them to have meant it in broad, anti-élitist liberalism. Russell fully concurred.

32 Kant managed to conceal his arbitrariness and appear logical. He proved his moral principle yet declared it valid only until the completion of the education of humanity. His moral principle was rigid (Schiller ridiculed it), yet it should yield to the enlightened self-interest that will then steer the future virtuous, educated humanity (Pitte, 1971: 13, 25).

33 Popper quotes Plato's observation that the need for unity in war times entices tyrants to maintain permanent war (Popper, 1945: i, Ch 6, §vii). Hence, the task of liberal governments is to cater for their citizens' security and tranquility.

34 Popper could make do without reference to human nature due to his having generally eliminated the demand for epistemic justification, replacing it with the demand to proceed directly to urgent problems of the day and to encourage public criticism. This should not exclude some long-range deliberations, however (Jarvie, 1987).

35 Contemporary economic theory is the closest to classical liberalism. Its advocates viewing democracy with suspicion as ever expanding, parasitic and tyrannical bureaucracy: all government is necessary evil. Hence the additional demand to limit legislation to the barest minimum, and particularly the demand to avoid interference with the market. These ideas usually appear in the economic literature as one.

36 Fluctuations in the quality of rulers may influence the quality of any regime, democracy included. But usually this influence is marginal there. For, the rule of law should reduce the dependence of the regime on any individual, and thus the ability of the wrong people in authority to do too much harm. This requires provisions for a smooth transition between different rulers. Institutional design is thus supposed to limit personal differences (and even differences of political opinions) to some sort of non-disruptively narrow band. Such limitations are often subject to criticism and modifications.

37 Liberals apply the maxim that people can be trusted best to take care of their own interests. Both obsessive conduct and self-sacrifice refute it. The default suggestion is that irrational conduct is better ignored (in accord with Smith's *Wealth of Nations*). It renders liberalism Utopian – even where

obsession is sufficiently rare to be negligible. Self-sacrifice is indisputably more serious. Hume discusses it at the very end of his *An Enquiry Concerning the Principles of Morals* and dismisses it as conduct in self-interest, that interest being the desire to maintain peace of mind. This argument is poor, since that desire in question is to live up to the right morality. To dismiss this objection is to declare moral conduct irrational. Hume deemed tastes given, non-rational, but he also deemed following them the only rational conduct, so that following morality is not. This way he allowed for social passions, especially the concern with justice. This too is erroneous on his part, as justice is no matter of taste. See also note 44.

38 That the absence of crime is desirable goes without saying. As to harmony, if it renders coercion minimal, then it is desirable; if it banishes politics, then it is not (Crick, 1962: Chapter 7).

39 The need for toleration limits liberalism: a society ridden with (religious) intolerance cannot be liberal. To further liberalism in such societies may require illiberal moves. The nearest to liberalism then is the paternalist effort to implement liberal education (Popper. 1945: ii, 276). It is then hard to say where the limit of toleration is to be drawn (Jarvie, 1986: 61).

40 Do citizens have the right for welfare? Hayek (and President Ronald Reagan) viewed dispensing welfare as the task of non-government organizations. He rejected the idea of welfare rights on the strength of a simple criterion: such rights do not boost individual liberty (Hayek, 1960: Index, Art Rights *et passim*). He ignored the fact that lovely as this criterion is, it is Utopian and does not apply to rules that comprise decent means of coordination.

41 Kant's moral theory is full of holes (Mérö et al., 1948: Chapter 4). For example, he considered obvious the difference between categorical and conditional imperatives. Consider his ban on lying even in the case of lying to save a life. It follows from the view that this ban is categorical. Hence, this case proves that this ban is conditional. *We do not know what imperative is categorical*; hence, his proof of its existence is empty.

42 See note 31.

43 See note 12.

44 J. O. Urmson and Joel Feinberg criticize traditional moral philosophy for its leaving no room for the supererogatory (Feinberg, 1970: Chapter 1). They regrettably do not touch upon the noble, supererogatory abstention from engaging in legal-but-immoral acts.

45 Popper, Einstein and Russell said, obviously, testability is a quality of a theory, not in every single sentence in it. This is traditional. It would be taken for granted but for Wittgenstein's and Carnap's contrary view. They declared it the peak of modern logic yet it was nothing of the sort.

46 Popper made a bolder abstraction as he took the principle of rationality itself as ideal akin to that of the ideal gas (Miller, 2007).

47 Much of the functionalist literature followed this heuristic. Strangely, the recent literature on economic anthropology is (pseudo-)Marxist and centers on the (valuable) works of Karl Polanyi. Raymond Firth had more advanced ideas (Firth, 1967: opening essay, esp. first few pages, as well as page 65 there). For a funny philosophical debate on the matter, see the exchange between Dalton and Ortiz in *American Anthropologist* (1971).

48 An older vulgar variant of classical rationalist optimism replaces its challenge with quietism (Wiley, 1940: 44).

49 There is always room for efforts to forestall factors conducive to demagoguery. The obvious instance for such a factor is the clinging to a refuted doctrine. The populist view of the truth as easily discoverable invites efforts to explain refutations away. One ready explanation is that some individuals conspire to subvert or hide the truth. Populism grew strong in the United States as it explained the relaxation of the gold standard known as bimetallism – by reference to a conspiracy of anonymous owners of silver mines. The anonymity of conspirators facilitates dreaming up all sorts of assumptions about them (Hofstadter, 1965).

50 The great difference between Spinoza's 1670 *Tractatus Theologico-Politicus* and its unfinished, posthumous replacement, his 1675/76 *Tractatus Politicus,* is just this: only in the corrected version does he take governments as they come and tries to show how to improve them, that is, liberalize them.

51 Amplifying the difference between Comte and Mill, Scharff claims that Mill misunderstood Comte (Scharff, 2002: Chapter 2).

52 The major lesson of Popper regarding wholesale political engineering is this. Due to human fallibility it cannot be error-free, yet unlike piecemeal social engineering, it has no contingency plan, thus opting for what he has called 'unplanned planning' (Popper, 1957: 69). This way, the wish to create heaven on earth creates hell (Popper, 1945: i, 165, ii, 237, 333, 358).

53 Anti-scientific philosophies are usually but not exclusively anti-liberal. As after Hiroshima science won the day, the distinction between pro-scientific and anti-scientific versions of historicism soon faded away. Refreshing its memory was then a great help (Jarvie, 1982).

54 Criticism is not limited to scientific explanation, of course, as is evident in the criticism of some non-explanatory theories, such as metaphysical ones. Still, explanatory theories are obviously more open to criticism than any metaphysical ones, and more systematically so.

55 Comte's theory of the hierarchy of the sciences is a variant on tradition, from Bacon to Ampère. Its novelty was in its introduction of the idea of explanatory social science. Mill praised it. Mill's own theory of explanation likewise echoes the traditional view from Descartes to Laplace (if not since Antiquity), but as applicable to social phenomena too. This innovative aspect of it was soon forgotten. Some commentators discovered it a century later simply out of ignorance of the long history of the theory of scientific explanation as hypothetico-deductive.

56 This disdain of superstition that scientism and positivism share renders them synonymous. Yet they occur in somewhat different contexts, since scientism denounces mainly widespread superstitions and positivism denounces mainly scholarly ones.

57 The leading advocate of neo-classical economics is Milton Friedman, whose view (1953) was, perhaps still is, most influential. His argument is instrumentalist, and thus he inadvertently forwent any claim for explanatory power. (As instrumentalism denies that scientific theories are true or false it deprives them of explanatory power.)

58 To the extent that this liberal idea has worked, it renders liberalism morally commendable; its inability to succeed fully even in the most advanced welfare states empirically refutes it and the variant of liberalism to which it belongs. Here then is an example in social technology of a very useful refuted theory – in line with most physical technology.

59 Wittgenstein's assertion that ethics is meaningless (1922: §6.42) demolishes the idea that it is inconsistent due to self-application. This excited his followers: it allegedly restored ethics – as meaningless! This is a remarkably highly sophisticated form of cheap self-deception.

60 Twentieth-century 'logical' positivism rests on the claim that it uses sophisticated up-to-date methods and simple, horse common sense. It is, however, merely Europocentrism run wild.

61 Veblen and Keynes refuted the idea that frugality is a virtue with the aid of the same received economic theory that Weber relied on when recommending frugality. When hire-purchase was facilitated in Britain in the late fifties of the twentieth century as measures against recession, it met with public moral criticism. Government economists then argued that recession is morally worse than waste, even of borrowed money. Yet Weber's mistake is still very popular.

62 That autonomy posed a challenge to the social order is obvious: the autonomous is less submissive. The search for ways to reconcile autonomy and stability was politically important in modern times. From the days of Al-Farabi and Maimonides to Machiavelli, if not to the days of universal suffrage, tradition sustained stability by elitism, by the view of the educated, not the common people (the masses) as autonomous. Machiavelli implicitly rejected this. Spinoza understood him that way and to further it he

used the idea of Maimonides that the law should educate to argue that liberal laws train people for autonomy. Liberal education is a profound aspect of all of his teachings: he took it as the challenge that paternalist education refuses. Taking the challenge seriously, however, allows skipping the discussion of human nature. Russell noted that adding to human nature a will to power (à la Nietzsche) is inherently undemocratic (Russell, 1938: final chapters), yet he added it and stuck to democracy nonetheless. Popper made a similar move (Popper, 1945: ii. 276).

63 The most interesting amplification of collectivism was Quetelet's statistics that later Durkheim tried to use, taking as self-evident that it is distinctly collectivist.

64 Advocates of the right of individuals for self-determination always presented it as unqualified and unproblematic with no reference to any empirical information. The nation's parallel right was always posed with a practical question: when is a group cohesive enough to qualify for this right? This is the question of the definition of the nation that occupied the German idealists and all their followers up to and including Joseph Stalin. The received *desideratum* from the definition was that the Jews should not count. This forced European Jews to view themselves as a separate nation. This led to the rise of the Jewish national movement (Agassi, 1999: 106–10).

65 This led Popper to his astute observation that the inner logic of historicism vitiated Marx' initial liberalism (Popper, 1945: ii, Chapter 21).

66 Hegel had two significant ideas. First, he said whenever two people meet they struggle for power. This is the idea of pecking order that was later discovered in barn hens and in cows. Egalitarianism refutes it, yet it is still deemed empirical and profound (e.g. Kain, 2005: 150–1). The other idea is that we are all tools of History that plays with our passions: the leaders are thus even more infantile than the led (Hegel, 1810/1902: 409).

67 Samuel Huntington's theory of the clash of civilizations (Huntington, 1996) looks like a variant of Hegel's. It is hard to know, as Hegel identified civilizations with empires and Huntington did not.

68 This is the thesis of Hegel's philosophy of history (1810/1902): he viewed war as 'an absolutely necessary phenomenon in the course of the World Spirit's unfolding in history', as one enthusiast has put it (Germino, 1969: 906). 'The history of the world is the world's court of justice', he said. Hence, the Shoah is proof of the truth of anti-Semitism.

69 Marx said, were reform of capitalism possible, it would not be desirable, as it is only a partial cure that postpones the revolution that is a cure-all. He once (Preface to the second edition to *Kapital*) wrote otherwise.

70 As Russell and Popper have noted, Hegel's *Elements of the Philosophy of Law* (*Grundlinien der Philosophie des Rechts*) (1821), backs the Prussian absolute monarchy of his day.

71 Hostility to rationalism naturally led the Reaction to pessimist (Popper, 1945: ii, 75). Nevertheless, it recognized progress, especially in the rise of reactionary philosophy, of course.

72 The dichotomy between truth by nature and truth by convention forced all legal philosophers and historians into a dilemma. Only the extreme, consistent conventionalism of Devlin forced Hart to choose a gradualist middle ground (Agassi, 1978). The dichotomy was imposing as it identified truth with justified truth. And so the explicit idea of approximation to the truth had to wait another century or so.

73 Claude Lévi-Strauss said all myths are replicas of the Ideal Myth. To reconstruct it he wished to superimpose all extant myths. This is more of a metaphor than of a research program.

74 Around the turn of the twentieth century, a few thinkers asserted that the idea of a historical law is confused. Among them were Poincaré and Rickert. Popper expanded on it in the middle of the twentieth century, and even then some leading commentators still misunderstood it.

75 Admittedly, European public opinion and European politics repeatedly display both admiration for the United States and efforts to imitate it (often in cargo-cult style). Mixed with much envy, the admiration often produces hatred. Jules Verne's *From the Earth to the Moon* (1865) presents the United States as a near Utopia; hostility to America, began early in the day, won prominence after World War II, beginning with the 1948 short satirical novel *The Loved One: An Anglo-American Tragedy* by Evelyn Waugh and became gigantic in the mass media. European intellectuals fell in and expressed hostility to the USA, the mass media and the masses – in political elitism (Shils, 1962). During the Cold War, the Cominform (Communist Information Bureau) personified the USA as Coca-Cola-and-blue-jeans. Mock-Marxist mock-progressivism thus met élitism with vulgar anti-American slogans. American anti-Americanism took the lead – due to the American leadership in the media, in culture in general and in the political tradition that begun as the fathers of the nation were wary of democracy and even wanted to proscribe political parties the way they proscribed lobbies. Although American tradition is of democratic rugged individualism, American political philosophy repeatedly swayed between anti-political liberalism and anti-democratic populism; it sticks to democracy only during serious stocktaking. Fortunately, this suffices to keep the USA democratic.

76 Anatole France put this in a slogan: 'The law, in its majestic equality, forbids the rich as well as the

poor to sleep under bridges, to beg in the streets, and to steal bread' (1894: Chapter 7).

77 There are more intermediate positions, such as that of Martin Heidegger, who loathed all technology except the weapon industry in the service of the Third Reich (Rickey, 2002: 138–41).

78 This may be an error on my part, as Shaw praised the aristocracy and the working class as autonomous by disparaging the middle class (e.g. *Fanny's First Play; Major Barbara*). Yet his praise for the working class seems to me insincere.

79 The neo-classical preference for monetary over fiscal intervention will fade away if the Russells were right. Hence, their view is testable.

80 Possibly, the very rise of the modern nation-state as liberal-democratic and industrial is a combined process due to conscious efforts (Gellner, 1983).

81 The Hegelian idea of the cunning of History ascribes to collective aims but allows them to act only through individual agents.

82 The novelty of Hayek's idea, too, is unclear, given that Smith's invisible hand is a metaphor for market efficiency as an unintended consequence of individual trade. The novelty of Hayek's idea is that institutional reforms too are largely unintended. In 1960, when his book appeared, the part in it that drew public attention most was the chapter on social security legislation. He said there, its outcome is different from what its initiators had in mind and it will surprise them more.

83 Both Heine and Russell said, utilitarianism was popular only because it served a non-moral basis for the moral demand for toleration (Heine, 1833/1986: 65; Russell, 1934/1962: 91).

84 Needless to say, the bombing of Hiroshima – and of Dresden, for that matter – was regrettable but legal; placing it here together with the Auschwitz genocide has a very limited scope: they are here put together only as refutations of Enlightenment optimism that had shattering effects.

85 Marxists such as Marcuse and Goldthorpe accused workers for not behaving in accord with the predictions of Karl Marx. Their accusation was non-specific and understood as the ascription of greed, indifference to social problems and such. Their refusal to discuss human nature opened their texts to all vulgar readings extant.

86 As Weber preferred strong rulers to democratic governments, he wanted liberalism to raise democracy and lead to the rule of fitting strong men. Hence, he viewed liberalism as educational means towards his final end. His appeal to strong men is due to the influence of Nietzsche. Shaw, also under the influence of Nietzsche, wanted a democracy of supermen (Shaw, 1965: 179).

87 As John Maynard Smith and Mario Bunge repeatedly stress, the supposition holds for all animals: only individuals have aims, not species and not nucleic acids. This supposition is benign: it leaves unchanged the informative content and testability of theories.

88 The existence of significant ideas that no one advocates, such as laws that are on the books and that a spirited lawyer can discover and apply, are examples of what Popper called objective knowledge. Obviously, individual scientists contribute to the fund of knowledge that no single person can encompass; what is this fund of knowledge? This question upsets many a scientist.

REFERENCES

Agassi, Joseph (1978) 'Liberal forensic medicine', *The Journal of Medicine and Philosophy*, 3: 226–241.

Agassi, Joseph (1999) *Liberal Nationalism for Israel*. New York: Gefen.

Agassi, Joseph (2003) *Science and Culture, Boston Studies in the Philosophy of Science*. vol. 231, Dordrecht: Kluwer.

Akzin, Benjamin (1968) 'Legislation and Natural Law', in David L. Sills (ed.), *International Encyclopedia of the Social Sciences*, New York: Macmillan, 2nd edition, 9: 230–231.

Argyle, Michael (1992) *The Social Psychology of Everyday Life*. London: Routledge.

Boettke Peter and Peter Leeson (eds) (2005) *The Legacy of Ludwig von Mises: Theory and History*, 2 volumes. Aldershot, UK: Edward Elgar.

Boland, Lawrence A. (1982) *The Foundations of Economic Method*. London: Allen and Unwin.

Boyle, Robert (1661) 'Proëmial essay', *Certain Physiological Essays*.

Cabanis, Pierre Jean George (1802) *Rapports du Physique et du Moral de l'Homme*. Paris.

Condorcet, Marie Jean, marquis de (1795) *Sketch for a Historical Picture of the Progress of the Human Mind*, trans. June Barraclough. London: Weidenfeld and Nicolson, 1955. http://www.fordham.edu/halsall/mod/condorcet-progress.html.

Crick, Bernard (1962) *In Defence of Politics*. London: Weidenfeld and Nicolson.

Cropsey, Joseph (1977) *Political Philosophy and Issues of Politics*. Chicago: University of Chicago Press.

Dalton, George (1971) 'Comment on Ortiz's review of Economic Anthropology', *American Anthropologist*, 73: 986–989.

Day, Clarence Jr. (2007) *This Simian World*. Charleston SC: BiblioBazaar.

de Tocqueville, Alexis (1835/1840) *Democracy in America*, Book 1.

Dunman, L. Joe (2003) *The Émile Durkhem Archive.* http://durkheim.itgo.com/crime.html.

Durkheim, Émile (1895) *The Rules of Sociological Method.* Eighth edition, translated by Sarah A. Solovay and John H. Mueller and edited by George Catlin. Glencoe IL: Free Press 1964.

Durkheim, Émile and Marcel Mauss (1903) *Primitive Classification.* Translation and Introduction by Rodney Needham. London: Routledge, 1963.

Evans-Pritchard, Sir Edward (1946) 'Applied Anthropology', *Africa.* Reprinted in his *Social Anthropology and Other Essays.* Glencoe IL: Free Press, 1962.

Feinberg, Joel (1970) *Doing and Deserving: Essays in the Theory of Responsibility.* Princeton NJ: Princeton University Press.

Feuer, Lewis S. (1958/1964) *Spinoza and the Rise of Liberalism.* Boston: Beacon.

Firth, Raymond (1967) *Themes in Economic Anthropology.* London: Tavistock.

France, Anatole ([1894] 1908) *The Red Lily.* Boston MA: Indypublish.com.

Freudenthal, Gideon (2005) 'The Hessen-Grossman thesis: An attempt at rehabilitation', *Perspectives on Science*, 13: 166–193.

Friedman, Milton (1953) 'The methodology of positive economics' in Milton Friedman (ed.) *Essays in Positive Economics.* Chicago: University of Chicago Press. pp. 3–43.

Friedman, Milton (1955) 'Leon Walras and his economic system', *The American Economic Review*, 45: 900–909.

Gellner, Ernest (1958) 'Time and theory in social anthropology', *Mind*, 67: 182–202.

Gellner, Ernest (1979) *Spectacles and Predicaments.* Cambridge: Cambridge University Press.

Gellner, Ernest (1983) *Nations and Nationalism.* Ithaca NY: Cornell University Press

Gellner, Ernest (1987) *Plough, Sword, and Book: The Structure of Human History.* London: Routledge.

Germino, Dante (1969) 'Hegel as a political theorist', *The Journal of Politics*, 31: 885–912.

Gerth, Hans H. and Charles Wright Mills (eds) (1948) *From Max Weber: Essays in Sociology.* London: Routledge.

Goldthorpe, John H., David Lockwood, Frank Bechhofer and Jennifer Platt (1968) 'The affluent worker and the thesis of "embourgeoisement"', in Joseph A. Kahl (ed.) *Comparative Perspectives on Stratification: Mexico. Great Britain, Japan.* Boston: Little, Brown. pp. 115–137.

Graham, Loren R. (1985) 'The socio-political roots of Boris Hessen: Soviet Marxism and the history of science', *Social Studies of Science*, 15: 705–722.

Guignon, Charles (2004). *On Being Authentic.* New York: Routledge.

Harrington, Anne (1996) *Reenchanted Science.* Princeton NJ: Princeton University Press.

Hayek, Friedrich von (1960) *The Constitution of Liberty.* London: Routledge.

Hegel, Georg Wilhelm Ffriedrich (1810) *Philosophy of History.* NY: Collier 1902. http://www. marxists.org/reference/archive/hegel/works/hi/ lectures.htm.

Heine, Heinrich (1833) *Religion and Philosophy in Germany.* Albany NY: SUNY Press 1986.

Hofstadter, Richard (1965) *The Paranoid Style in American Politics, and Other Essays.* New York: Knopf.

Hume, David (1741) *Essays, Moral, Political and Literary.*

Huntington, Samuel (1996) *The Clash of Civilizations and the Remaking of World Order.* New York: Simon and Schuster.

Jaffé, William and Donald A. Walker (eds) (1983) *Essays on Walras.* Cambridge: Cambridge University Press.

Jarvie, Ian C. (1964) *The Revolution in Anthropology.* London: Routledge and Kegan Paul

Jarvie, Ian C. (1972) *Concepts and Society.* London, Routledge and Kegan Paul.

Jarvie, Ian C. (1973) *Functionalism.* Minneapolis MN: Burgess.

Jarvie, Ian C. (1982) 'Popper on the difference between the natural and the social sciences', in Paul Levinson, (ed.) *In Pursuit of Truth.* Atlantic Highlands, NJ: Humanities. pp. 83–107.

Jarvie, Ian C. (1984) *Rationality and Relativism: In Search of a Philosophy and History of Anthropology.* London: Routledge.

Jarvie, Ian C. (1986) *Thinking about Society: Theory and Practice. Boston Studies in the Philosophy of Science*, 93. Dordrecht: D. Reidel.

Jarvie, Ian C. (1987) 'Utopia and the architect', in Joseph Agassi and Ian C. Jarvie (eds) *Rationality: The Critical View.* Dordrecht: Kluwer. pp. 227–243.

Jones, Richard Foster (1961/1982) *Ancients and Moderns.* New York: Dover.

Kain, Philip J. (2005) *Hegel and the Other: A Study of the Phenomenology of Spirit.* Albany NY: SUNY Press.

Lakatos, Imre (1976) *Proofs and Refutations.* Cambridge: Cambridge University Press.

Marcuse, Herbert (1964) *One-Dimensional Man. Studies in the Ideology of Advanced Industrial Society*. Boston: Beacon Press.

McManners, John (1965) *The New Cambridge Modern History*, Volume 8, *The American and French Revolutions, 1763–93*. Chapter XXII: The historiography of the French revolution. New York: Cambridge University Press.

Mandeville, Bernard (1714) *The Fable of the Bees: or, Private Vices, Publick Benefits*.

Mannheim, Karl (1929) *Ideology and Utopia*. London: Routledge, 1936.

Marx, Karl (1842) *Articles from the Rheinische Zeitung*. http://www.scribd.com/doc/4353606/Marx-Rheinishe-Zeitung

Mérö, Lászlo, Anna C. Gosi-Greguss and David Kramer (1998) *Moral Calculations: Game Theory, Logic, and Human Frailty*. New York: Springer.

Miller, Boaz (2007) *Popperian Idealization: A Fresh Look at Popper's Rationality Principle*. http://individual.utoronto.ca/boaz/handout-hapsat-miller-popper.pdf

Mises, Ludwig von (1957) *Theory and History and Interpretation of Social and Economic Evolution*. New Haven: Yale University Press.

Morgan, Lewis Henry (1877) *Ancient Society*. New York: Henry Holt.

Ortiz, Sutti (1971) 'Reply to Dalton', *American Anthropologist*, 73: 989–992.

Pitte, Frederick van der (1971) *Kant as a Philosophical Anthropologist*. The Hague: Nijhoff.

Popper, Sir Karl (1935). *The Logic of Scientific Discovery*. London: Hutchinson, 1959.

Popper, Sir Karl (1945/1966) *The Open Society and Its Enemies*. Fifth edition. London: Routledge.

Popper, Sir Karl (1957) *The Poverty of Historicism*. London: Routledge.

Popper, Sir Karl (1963) *Conjectures and Refutations*, London: Routledge.

Rickey, Christopher (2002) *Revolutionary Saints: Heidegger, National Socialism, and Antinomian Politics*. University Park PA: Penn State University Press.

Russell, Bertrand (1916/1977) *The Principles of Social Reconstruction*. London: Routledge.

Russell, Bertrand (1917) 'Mysticism and Logic', in his *Mysticism and Logic*. London: Allen and Unwin.

Russell, Bertrand (1918/1995) 'Human character and social institutions', in Richard A. Rempel (ed.) with the assistance of Bernd Frohmann, Mark Lippincott, Albert C. Lewis, Margaret Moran. *The Collected Papers of Bertrand Russell*. London: Routledge, 14: 419–25.

Russell, Bertrand (1928) *Sceptical Essays*. London: Allen and Unwin.

Russell, Bertrand (1934/62) *Freedom versus Organization: 1814–1914*. New York: Norton.

Russell, Bertrand (1938) *Power: A New Social Analysis*. London: Allen and Unwin.

Russell, Bertrand (1946/1971) *A History of Western Philosophy*. London: Unwin.

Russell, Bertrand (1954/1962) 'Zahatopolk', in Bertrand Russell (ed.) *Nightmares of Eminent Persons and Other Stories*. Harmondsworth: Penguin. pp. 81–127.

Russell Bertrand and Dora Russell (1923) *The Prospects of Industrial Civilization*. New York: Century.

Sassower, Raphael (1993) *Knowledge without Expertise*. Albany NY: SUNY Press.

Scharff, Robert C. (2002) *Comte after Positivism*. Cambridge: Cambridge University Press.

Schilpp, Paul Arthur (1927) 'The "formal problems" of Scheler's sociology of knowledge', *The Philosophical Review*, 36: 101–120.

Shaw, Bernard George (ed.) (1889/1891/2006). *Fabian Essays in Socialism*. New York: Cosimo.

Shaw, Bernard George (1927/1984) *The Intelligent Woman's Guide to Socialism and Capitalism*. New Brubswick NJ: Transaction.

Shaw, Bernard George (1965) *The Complete Prefaces of Bernard Shaw*. London: Hamlyn.

Shils, Edward (1962) 'The theory of mass society', *Diogenes*, 39: 45–66.

Simey, Thomas Spensley (1960). *Charles Booth, Social Scientist*. Oxford: Oxford University Press.

Simmel, Georg (1922) *Conflict and the Web of Group Affiliations*, translated and edited by Kurt Wolff, Glencoe IL: Free Press, 1955.

Smith, Adam (1776/1937) *An Inquiry into the Nature and Causes of the Wealth of Nations*. Edwin Cannan (ed.). New York: The Modern Library.

Snodgrass, Anthony (1980) *Archaic Greece: The Age of Experiment*. Berkeley CA: The University of California Press.

Stigler, George J. and Gary S. Becker (1977) 'De Gustibus Non Est Disputandum', *The American Economic Review*, 67: 76–90.

Swift, Jonathan (1708/1898) *The Sentiments of a Church of England Man, with Respect to Religion and Government. Swift's Writings on Religion and the Church*, vol. I. London: Temple Scott.

Trevelyan, George M. (1944) *English Social History: A Survey of Six Centuries from Chaucer to Queen Victoria*. London: Longmans.

Walker, Donald Anthony (1983) *William Jaffé's Essays on Walras*. Cambridge: Cambridge University Press.

Wells, H. G. (1921) *The Outline of History*. Third edition, New York: Macmillan.

Whewell, William (1857) *History of the Inductive Sciences*, 3 vols. London: Longmans.

Wiley, Basil (1940) *The Eighteenth Century Background, Studies on the Idea of Nature in the Thought of the Period*. London: Chatto and Windus.

Winegarten, Renee (2008) *Germaine de Staël and Benjamin Constant: A Dual Biography*. New Haven CT: Yale University Press,

Wittgenstein, Ludwig (1922) *Tractatus Logico-Philosophicus*. C. K. Ogden (trans.), London: Routledge & Kegan Paul.

2

Continental Philosophies of the Social Sciences

David Teira

INTRODUCTION

In my view, there is no such thing as a continental philosophy of the social sciences. There is, at least, no consensual definition of what is precisely *continental* in any philosophical approach.[1] Besides, there are many approaches in the philosophy of the social sciences that are often qualified as continental, but there is no obvious connection between them. The most systematic attempt so far to find one is Yvonne Sherratt's (2006) monograph, where continental approaches would be appraised as different branches of the Humanist tradition. According to Sherratt, philosophers in this tradition draw on the ideas and arguments of the ancient Greek and Roman thinkers, since they understand philosophy as an accumulative endeavour, where the past is a continuous source of wisdom. Unlike empiricist philosophers in the analytic tradition, humanists see the world as an intrinsically purpose-laden, ethically, aesthetically and spiritually valuable entity. However, once you adopt such a broad definition in order to encompass such different thinkers as Marx, Nietzsche, Heidegger or Foucault, it seems difficult not to see humanist traits in analytic philosophers as well.

Moreover, when it comes to the philosophical study of actual social sciences, it is not clear whether adopting a humanist stance makes, as such, any difference in the analysis: as we will see below, the arguments of the continental philosophers discussed here do not presuppose a particular commitment with, for example, ideas from classical antiquity.

Certain Greeks named those who did not speak their language *Barbarians*, but it was never clear who counted as a proper speaker of Greek. Similarly, there is no clear empirical division differentiating *continental* authors from philosophers of any other kind. I will, therefore, focus on a few paradigmatic instances of continental philosophies of the social sciences, discussing each one separately without any attempt to find a common thread. The following three sections will deal, in this order, with Marxism, phenomenology and, more briefly, Foucault. I have chosen these three approaches for just one reason: they have had a real influence on how social research has been conducted throughout the twentieth century.[2] There have been Marxist, phenomenological and Foucauldian social scientists and they can claim that their research methods are effectively grounded in philosophical principles that analytically-oriented social scientists do not share. Next, I will focus on positive guidelines implemented in current social sciences rather than on principled philosophical discussions about how they should be cultivated. In the case of Marxism, this implies an assessment of major contributions in several fields, whereas phenomenologists or Foucauldians have so far been a dissenting minority with minor professional impact. I follow the (mostly) analytically-minded habit of working with case studies where methodologies are actually implemented. The aim of this chapter is to show the relevance of continental ideas for certain research agendas, focusing more on their efficacy in actual scientific practices than on their internal philosophical merits. This judgment is admittedly analytically inspired, but I hope not entirely unfair to the continental accomplishments.

My own understanding of continental philosophy is partial and biased or, if you prefer, situated. I was exposed to these philosophies when I studied philosophy as an undergraduate in Spain and I do not have original views on any of the authors I will deal with: I draw on standard interpretations, which are not always consensual and I will make my sources explicit at every step.[3] The first section is, then, about Marxism. It surveys its typical explanatory patterns (functionalism and methodological individualism) on particular issues in economics (value theory) and history (the connection between productive forces and relations of production). I will also discuss value judgments in the Marxist tradition, with a brief overview of the positivism dispute. In the second section, on phenomenology, I will present Husserl's views on the connection between philosophy and the social sciences of his time, discussing their implications for the assessment of cultural anthropology. I will also deal with Schütz's contributions to sociology and how they contributed to the articulation of ethnomethodology, the most accomplished phenomenological research paradigm so far. A quick discussion of the embodied approach

to cognitive science closes the section. In the third and final section, I will explore Foucault's initial appraisal of the social sciences that I take to generalize his experience with psychology. I also consider his more mature views on *governmentality*, trying to explain the success of this concept in current research across several fields. Each section can be read independently.

To many, my final conclusion will probably state the obvious. Marxism is of more interest today for philosophers than for social scientists – which is probably not a good thing for the former, since this usually implies neglecting the latter's more recent contributions. So far, phenomenology has only achieved success in actual social research today at the cost of dispensing with many of its central assumptions. Foucauldian-inspired research, finally, influential as it is, is based on minimal philosophical presuppositions, but these presuppositions are restrictive enough to limit the kind of analyses that are acceptable. By its own construction, it cannot aspire to become a mainstream paradigm. Obviously, none of this partial conclusion precludes that some other continental philosopher may succeed in inspiring social scientists in the near future, but I personally would not bet on anybody's success at this point.

MARXISM

It is impossible to cover in just one section the many issues of interest for the philosophy of the social sciences arising within the Marxist tradition.[4] To a great extent, this tradition hinges on the interpretation of the works of Marx and Engels, but there is no agreement about how we should read them. The circumstances in which they were published or edited have significantly complicated (almost up to today) our understanding of many central points in Marxian thought. In addition, interpretative and political disagreement often came hand in hand: communist parties all over the world have justified their strategies in terms of fidelity to the 'true' thoughts of Marx and Engels, generating a self-serving literature, still virtually inexhaustible.[5]

Nonetheless, its practical relevance certainly helps to explain the impact of Marxism in the social sciences of the twentieth century. In the USSR, and then in many other communist regimes, Marxism was enforced among the social scientists by the ruling party, according to their interpretation of choice. In the Western world, Marxism could be adopted by a social scientist for purely intellectual considerations, but a certain degree of commitment with one or another communist party was not rare – and if there was none, this circumstance was often denigrated.[6] We may well wonder how relevant Marxian thought would have been, had there been no USSR. Perhaps, Marx's intellectual influence would have been more like, say, Comte's or Spencer's and, regarding politics, no greater than any other utopian socialist of his times. But, in point of fact, Marxism was either the dominant approach or one of the main contenders in many social sciences during the second half of the twentieth century, playing a major role in the methodological literature of those disciplines.[7] By the same token, after the fall of the USSR, the philosophical discussion of Marxist social science has become increasingly rare, at least in mainstream philosophy journals in the English-speaking world.

The aim of this section is to survey the main issues in the methodological discussion around Marxian social sciences, comparing the Marxist approach, broadly conceived, with the mainstream methodological tenets in analytical social science. We owe this comparison mostly to Gerald Cohen, John Roemer, Jon Elster and the work of the September group in the 1980s and early 1990s, when the discussion stalled, with no major developments since then.[8] We will then briefly consider the functional explanation, the controversy around the Marxian theory of value (in economics), methodological

individualism, the central tenets of historical materialism and, to conclude, the treatment of normative issues in the Marxist tradition.

According to Elster (1985: 4), the main Marxist contribution to the methodology of the social sciences (analytically reconstructed) would have been the causal explanation of aggregate phenomena in terms of the individual actions that go into them: pursuing their individual goals, the actors bring about an unintended outcome, namely by making erroneous assumptions about one another. These unintended consequences could be beneficial (or not) to the actors. In Elster's view, Marx often considered these benefits as an explanation of the actions that brought them about. Hempel, Nagel and other philosophers of scientific explanation usually consider such a *functional* approach to explanation faulty if no *causal connection* is shown between the actions and their consequences. Otherwise, it would be difficult to understand how an event in the future (the benefits) can generate an individual action without the actor anticipating it. This is the standard appraisal of Marxian functional explanations among analytical philosophers of the social sciences.

However, Marx was part of a broad philosophical tradition in which teleological explanations of social processes were considered acceptable.[9] For German idealists from Kant onwards, History could only be appraised through conceptual analysis, where concepts were somehow objectively inscribed in the social processes under discussion. Such concepts had a logic of their own: Marx took his own version from Hegel and this was *dialectics*. It presided over social aggregates (e.g. classes), guiding their development independently of the intentions of their individual members, who nonetheless benefitted from (or suffered) the consequences. Despite numerous attempts, there is still no consensual elucidation of Marxian dialectics, at least in the philosophy of the social sciences.[10] At most, the style of conceptual analysis cultivated by Marx in his economic writings has been somewhat clarified in terms of *abstraction* and *idealization*, but without much impact on actual social research.[11]

Indeed, many methodological debates in the Marxist social sciences can be interpreted in the light of the philosophical inspiration (roughly speaking, *analytic* or *continental*) of each side. One prominent example is the controversy about the Marxian theory of value, which has been going on for more than a century now.[12] Broadly speaking, the value of an economic good is the amount of *homogenized socially necessary labour time* it takes to produce it in a given social setting. For Marx, the value of a good would *explain* its exchange price. Yet, in Marxian economics this explanation may take different forms, deserving more or less attention depending on the philosophical taste of the reader. In many of his economic writings, Marx articulates the discussion of value drawing on Aristotelian (e.g. *form/substance*) and Hegelian (e.g. *essence/appearance*) categories, whose correct interpretation requires a certain degree of competence in the History of Greek and German philosophy.[13] Through these categories Marx would have articulated a general view of social life hinging on productive activities, for example, Gould (1980). Value theory would illuminate how production is truly organized in capitalist societies and the explanation of market prices it yields allowed Marx to establish a conceptual connection between such disparate phenomena as, for example, economic exploitation, class division or the future collapse of capitalism. The philosophical categories articulating this worldview are no longer part of the standard vocabulary of most social sciences, but many Marxian philosophers appraising economics in the continental tradition (e.g. Negri, Žižek) still rely on their own version of these concepts. Here, philosophy and the social sciences parted ways several decades ago.

But Marx's theory of value also owed a great deal to classical political economy, which sought to establish a concrete explanatory relation between values and prices. Marx tried to show that, in capitalist markets, commodities tend to be exchanged in a certain proportion to the labour time they 'embody'. Marx's key insight is that the profit earned by the owner of the means of production when she sells the good in a market arise from the unpaid labour of the worker who produced the good. This surplus value measured the exploitation of the worker, independently of her own intentional economic choices. Marx attempted to state this proportion in algebraic terms, giving rise to the so-called *transformation problem*: it has been argued (Roemer, 2008) that Marx's equations are either unnecessary for calculating prices or internally contradictory.

The transformation problem created a methodological dilemma among economists. Some argued that the labour theory of value should be abandoned for some other economic approach to price calculation (usually, neoclassical demand theory). At this point, this seems to be the choice of the majority within the profession. Others have tried to reform the equations, preserving the concept of value while arguing that its main role within the theory is the analysis of exploitation rather than exchange prices. More recently, John Roemer has restated the key Marxian normative insights about exploitation, using standard analytic tools in neoclassical economics that is modeling the agents' interaction in a way that makes their individual choices explicit, that is their microfoundations.[14]

Philosophers of the social sciences have appraised the dilemma created by the transformation problem from various perspectives. To name just a couple within the analytic tradition, on one hand, we find a number of set-theoretic (*structuralist*) reconstructions of the Marxian theory of value.[15] Here the concept of value is either epistemically justified in terms of the role it plays in the architecture of the theory or, alternatively, grounded in formal analyses of the measurement conditions of Marxian value. However, these reconstructions show that it is possible to clarify, in certain respects, the conceptual articulation of the theory, despite the transformation problem, but they do not provide substantive reasons to accept it. Analytical Marxists, such as Roemer or Elster argue instead that there are, rather, positive reasons to reject it: whatever its aim, in most formulations, the concept of value is methodologically obscure, because it does not involve any consideration of the individual choices of the economic agents. For instance, it has been argued that Marx was interested in 'abstract' labour time, rather than in imputing 'concrete' labour time to different commodities. But shouldn't the 'abstract' be the aggregate of 'concrete' instances? Once you incorporate micro-foundations into Marxian economics, you can either analyze exploitation or calculate prices without Marxian values.[16]

The point of contention illustrated by this case is whether the social sciences should adhere to methodological individualism or not, in Elster's minimal characterization: whether collective actions should be explained in terms of the desires and beliefs that enter into the motivation of the individuals participating in them. Marxists and other continental philosophers of the social sciences usually question such an assumption, whereas neoclassical economists and analytically oriented philosophers usually defend it.[17] Notice that this is more a conceptual than an empirical issue. The analysis of prices in neoclassical economics relies on individual choices as explained by utility theory. But for many decades this latter was accepted with hardly any positive experimental evidence, just as Marxian values were.

Again, the debate on methodological individualism can be appraised at two different levels. On one hand, it can be conducted as a conceptual discussion about social ontology: should we take individuals or, rather, groups of individuals (classes, for Marx) as the basic units of social analysis? Originally, this was mostly a controversy on the realism of the assumptions of each theory: on the neoclassical side, did utility theory represent any individual psychological process? On the Marxist side, how could class analysis account for

individual choices? The debate was initiated by the Austrian school in the late nineteenth century and was somehow closed in the 1960s with the gradual turn to instrumentalist justifications of utility theory by neoclassical economists: as long as any economic theory provides good statistical predictions, we can dispense with the realism of its assumptions.[18] Whether neoclassical theories ever yielded such a good prediction remains a controversial issue, but their supporters were, at least, more eager to adopt econometric techniques than Marxian economics. For many Marxists, statistical analyses reduced social entities to aggregates of individual data, which was considered to be contradictory to the reality of classes.[19] This is, perhaps, why Marxism never really competed against neoclassical economics with predictions. However, most varieties of Marxism remained firmly committed to realism and resisted individualistic reductions of social aggregates.[20]

On the other hand, it can be posed as a reflection on the explanatory virtues of the analytical tools applied by neoclassical economics, namely decision and game theory. In these latter, it seems possible to interpret expected utility as a combined expression of the beliefs of the agents about the probability of the alternatives considered and their desires, that is, the utility resulting from each of these alternatives. Hence, we may explain in principle the aggregated effects of individual decisions on intentional grounds. However, such an interpretation is often challenged on various grounds: first, expected utility theory can be applied to group agents, where there is a less clear intentional basis, and second, explanatory reductions to individual decisions are often theoretically unreachable and, even in game theory, the analyses of individual choices may depend on macro-features. Despite various attempts at a more precise definition of methodological individualism, there is no consensus yet and it is mostly defended on *heuristic* grounds: the formal analysis of individual decisions has led to fruitful theoretical results in many different social domains. However, holism in the Marxist tradition is no less difficult to define and, as of today, there are no consensual formal results providing a general framework for social analysis.[21]

History and economics were the two main disciplines in the Marxist social sciences. The central claim of the methodology of historical materialism is the connection between productive forces and relations of production, which we shall explore here following Gerald Cohen's (2000) reconstruction – once again, the best bridge, so far, between the analytical and the continental Marx. In Cohen's interpretation, the productive forces are, namely, the means of production (tools, raw materials, etc.) and labour-power. In turn, the relations of production are defined namely in terms of the property relations of the producers with regard to the means of production and their own labour-power (e.g. a capitalist worker owns the latter, but not the former), with some additional provisos. Marx's major claim is that, throughout history, the relations of production first 'correspond' to the productive forces and then enter into a 'contradiction' with them. The interpretation of this claim is controversial. In Cohen's view, the correspondence means that certain relations of production are optimal for the development of certain productive forces and this is why the former appear and take hold. When they are no longer optimal, the relations of production change. Hence, there is a functional connection by which the development of the productive forces explain the relations of production. For Marx, this functional link allows us to explain the transition between the different modes of production that feature in human history. Historical materialism thus affirms the (explanatory) primacy of the productive forces.

However, as we already mentioned regarding mechanisms, Marxian analyses usually do not provide all the necessary details for a coherent functional interpretation along the lines suggested by Cohen. Nonetheless, throughout the twentieth century, Marxist historians applied this approach without much regard for explanatory patterns as such. The main point of contention was, instead, how to assess the autonomy of individuals in a materialist perspective. For instance, the so-called *structural* accounts of Marx prevailing in the 1960s granted them little autonomy, putting all the explanatory weight on the teleological connection between productive forces and relations of productions. This line was widely contested (e.g. the Althusser–Thompson–Anderson debate: Lewis, 2005), but Marxist historiography never reached a clear methodological consensus about the role of individual choices in explanation.[22] It is interesting to note that a somewhat clearer view of functional explanations was developed by an intellectual offspring of Marxism in anthropology, the cultural materialism school (Bueno, 1978). Marvin Harris (1999) argued, for instance, that individuals select infrastructural innovations depending on their estimations of the costs and benefits for them, making the collective adoption of those novelties that increase the efficiency of their productive and reproductive processes more likely. This principle seems particularly plausible in the analysis of populations constrained in well-defined ecological niches, where the effects of certain cultural traits on the production and consumption of calories can somehow be measured. In these niches, individual choices about these traits can result in the niches either sustaining or exhausting their carrying capacity, thus explaining why such traits survive or disappear. Even the best examples of such anthropological analyses are, nonetheless, controversial (e.g. Dawson, 2002), but there is at least an explicit principle linking infrastructural changes and their cultural effects through individual behaviour.

An implicit question in this methodological dispute is how autonomous individuals were in making their choices. This was a normative issue of foremost relevance,[23] and it often appeared in the debate on the practical implications of Marxist theories – or the *unity of theory and praxis*, to use a more traditional statement of the problem among Western

Marxists. Marx was, indeed, as much an activist as a theorist and it often seems as if his arguments aimed to both describe and transform capitalist societies. How his arguments would achieve such a transformation was, again, open to dispute. Those who more explicitly denied their normative dimension (e.g. Lenin and the Soviet tradition) usually assumed that communist activists were just acting in accordance to the laws of history. Marxian theories would provide communist parties with the tools to properly interpret these laws and act accordingly. In this approach, Marxists would act instrumentally: given that communism is the objective end of history, and they want it to arrive, their political activity should just find the proper means to bring it about sooner than later. However, there have been Marxists, even if only a minority, who defended a more explicitly normative version of communist politics (e.g. Rosa Luxemburg or Antonio Gramsci). The most philosophically influential among them come from the Frankfurt School, namely Adorno and Horkheimer, on one hand, and Jürgen Habermas, still active today. Unlike other Marxists, they not only confronted their own tradition, but presented their case in open dialogue with Anglo-American philosophers. A good case in point, regarding the philosophy of the social sciences, is the so-called *positivism dispute* in the 1960s (Adorno, 1976), bringing the Frankfurt school face to face with Popper and other critical rationalists. We will shortly consider here two crucial points in this debate, presenting Habermas' current stance regarding both.

The positivism in dispute in this controversy can be traced to the definition of economics presented by Lionel Robbins in *An Essay on the Nature and Significance of Economic Science* (1932): the unity of subject of the discipline lay in the 'forms assumed by human behaviour in disposing of scarce means'. If the means are scarce and the agent must choose a particular combination of them in order to achieve her goals, the economist can provide a mathematical analysis of the degree of achievement (say, satisfaction) reported by each combination. It will be (instrumentally) rational for the agent to choose the combination of means that maximizes the achievement of her goals. About the ends as such, Robbins adopted a skeptic stance: these were value judgments and, in case of ultimate disagreement about them, we can only fight to solve the conflict. In *The Poverty of Historicism* (1957), Popper added a corollary about what sort of political intervention the economist could advise to this view. For instance, the statistical analysis of demand theory could just ground what Popper called *piecemeal social engineering*. Testing how much a model deviates from empirical data predictions provides guidance for policy-makers, inspiring their reforms in the model. But since the model deals with just a few variables, usually complicated to isolate and measure, its application can only yield partial reforms. Popper claimed, against Marxism, that there were no general laws in history and any global transformation of society based on such laws was utopian.

In sum, for the positivist social scientist, the social scientists are neither morally committed to the transformation of society (or to any other normative position) as a result of their research. His theoretical contribution to this enterprise is necessarily restricted to the analysis of means for partial reforms. This instrumental view of science and rationality was widely contested in Frankfurt, with a view to criticize the theoretical approaches to society developed both in the 'capitalist' and the 'communist' world. Up until the 1970s, Horkheimer and Adorno's *Dialectic of Enlightenment* (1972) provided the most influential statement of this position. But nowadays the discussion hinges, rather, on Jürgen Habermas' restatement, perhaps because Habermas' view has been elaborated incorporating many insights from analytic philosophy.[24]

For Habermas, the pragmatics of linguistic communication reveals a use of language that is irreducible to instrumental rationality: speech acts commit the speakers to achieve mutual understanding, evaluating the epistemic claims that each of them undertake through their utterances. Communication requires the speaker to justify those claims for the sake of mutual understanding, creating a web of inferential commitments where words acquire their meaning. Social norms would be grounded on such communicative demand for mutual accountability, constituting publicly shared reasons for action. Instrumental rationality would only appear derivatively, against a background of shared meanings and social norms.

In Habermas' view, the social sciences should accept this irreducibly moral setting of our social life and appraise individual interactions taking their communicative dimension into account. Marx would have missed this in making the instrumental rationality of labour the key to any social analysis. The normative mission of the social sciences would be to contribute to the critical elucidation of the communicative practices that sustain our social life, as psychoanalysis did, paradigmatically. The social scientist should be morally committed to the advancement of democracy, understood as the regime that best promotes such communicative practices. It is open to discussion whether there is much left of Marx in Habermas, leaving aside the intellectual genealogy. Nonetheless, today Habermas provides the more articulated philosophical account of the connection between facts and values in the social sciences, a connection that the Marxist tradition struggled for decades to make (against positivism) without much intellectual success.

What is left, then, of Marxism for the philosopher of the social sciences? In 1986, Jon Elster closed *An Introduction to Karl Marx* with a chapter entitled 'What is living and what is dead in the philosophy of Marx?' He listed six items that were still worth considering: dialectics and the theories of alienation; exploitation; class consciousness; ideology and technical change. In the last two decades, none of these topics has received major attention as such, in any social science, at least if we judge according to informal searches conducted in the Social Sciences Citation Index

(SSCI). Nonetheless, this does not imply that Marxism, either in its traditional guise or in its analytical reconstruction, lacks interesting developments: for example, class analysis is certainly alive (Wright, 2005) and there are very good Marxist historians still at work (e.g. Perry Anderson or Robert Brenner). The moral issues involved in exploitation and alienation are still discussed in philosophy, but, as happens with Habermas, dissociated from most claims traditionally linked to Marx and the Marxist tradition. Among the topics that Elster considered dead were all those discussed in this brief review, namely: scientific socialism, functionalism, Marxist economics and the theory of productive forces and relations of production. Another informal look at the SSCI provides evidence that none of these items are being widely discussed. Philosophers re-reading Marx today are motivated more by his moral intuitions than by the scientific cogency of the concepts he used to elaborate them. For these approaches, current debates in the mainstream social sciences apparently do not seem very relevant.[25] Habermas went further than anyone within the Marxian tradition in keeping the connection between social research and philosophy up to date, but only until the 1970s: the theories he discussed, for example, in sociology or psychology, are not cutting-edge research paradigms anymore. Marx and Marxism will always be relevant for the philosopher who cares for the development of the social sciences and the Marxian tradition contributed to articulate many of our ongoing debates (e.g. explanation) in the field. However, if we want the philosophy of the social sciences to be driven by actual research in the target disciplines, it seems as if Marxism will not be a progressive research program to be considered in the twenty-first century.[26]

PHENOMENOLOGY

Phenomenology is one of the major philosophical trends of the twentieth century, with an impact only second to Marxism or analytic philosophy.[27] There is a phenomenological approach to most topics in philosophy and the social sciences are no exception: there is indeed, a phenomenology of the social sciences, with its own conferences and journals.[28] However, it seems as if the impact of this approach on actual research is minor, at least insofar as the Social Citation Index can capture it. And, so far, there has been no major debate confronting phenomenology with other philosophical accounts of social research.[29] In my view, this can be (partially) explained by considering, on one hand, Husserl's normative position regarding the social sciences. And, on the other hand, by how phenomenological claims are, so to speak, diluted when social scientists incorporate them into their theorizing. Let me first summarily present how Husserl introduced phenomenology in opposition to certain trends in the *Geisteswisseschaften* of his time.[30] I will then discuss the most accomplished attempt so far to transform phenomenology into an actual philosophy of the social realm, namely Alfred Schütz's attempt, and the impact of his ideas on ethnomethodology – as of today, the most successful phenomenological venture in the social sciences. I will quickly address an emerging interdisciplinary paradigm that vindicates part of the phenomenological legacy, the so-called *embodied* cognitive sciences. A brief recapitulative discussion will close this section.[31]

In his landmark 'Philosophy as Rigorous Science' (Husserl, 1965), Husserl articulated phenomenology in opposition to a couple of alternative paradigms in philosophy emerging from positive research in psychology and history.[32] Experimental psychophysiology, as developed by W. Wundt, aimed at establishing a natural science of consciousness, in which mental phenomena would stem from physical events accessible in the laboratory. Historical research in multiple domains accumulated more and more evidence about the particularity of each manifestation of our social life. Historicism would make sense of such empirical diversity with classifications aimed at understanding their particularity, without normative considerations about their validity. According to Husserl, both naturalism and historicism promoted epistemic relativism, since there are no absolute grounds for scientific knowledge in any of them, just the particular psychological or social facts established by positive research on either our epistemic capabilities or what a concrete group called 'science'. Husserl constructed his phenomenology in contrast to such kinds of relativism.

Let us briefly examine the case he made in the Second Book of his *Ideas Pertaining to a Pure Phenomenology* (Husserl, 1989). Husserl argued here that positive science presupposed a particular connection between mind and world that philosophy should elucidate. What scientists take as purely external events, for the sake of their own research, are always intentionally appraised, that is, they appear in a particular aspect of our consciousness (they are perceived, remembered, expected …). Once we appraise the world in its connection with our subjectivity, we can discern an invariable and universal element in these multiple presentations of an object. Following Husserl, we can isolate and classify these elements according to their internal relations. Our world can thus be divided into different regions according to these universal and invariable structures. The sciences will study their empirical manifestations.

Husserl explained our access to these *a priori* structures through a set of concepts such as *eidetic reduction*, *epoché*, etc., whose precise interpretation is still debated by the different schools of phenomenology.[33] Putting aside here how we access the *a priori*, we should notice that Husserl distinguished three different types of *a priori* structures, depending on how the object appears in our consciousness. Each type corresponds to a particular mode of scientific inquiry. The natural sciences deal with the first type, where objects appear individuated by their temporal and spatial characteristics together with causal links to other entities, that is, as *material things*. Psychology deals with the second type of *a priori* essences, those that appear in animal bodies exhibiting some sort of subjectivity, a kind of embodied first person perspective that is irreducible to psychophysical connections. Husserl was ambiguous enough to capture both human and non-human traits, again another issue of contention in the phenomenological tradition. The third type of *a priori* refers to our social world and is captured by the *Geisteswissenschaften*. Items in this domain (be they groups, institutions, traditions, tools or works of art) present some sort of *motivational* connection (*Motivationsbeziehung*) to our consciousness: we appraise them acknowledging their intentional creation and we operate with them according to the intentions we discern. For Husserl, this intentional dimension can only be understood by reconstructing the particular *history* of each entity, which can never be explained in a naturalistic fashion.

The social sciences, therefore, have their own irreducible ontological realm. However, this created quite a thorny problem. On one hand, the natural and the social sciences each have their own types of *a priori* structures. But, on the other hand, the intentional dimension comes first in our appraisal of any object, whatever its ontological realm. How can we access, say, the universal laws of physics from our folk understanding of physical objects, whose *a priori* structure is always particular and culturally situated? Husserl tried to solve this apparent dilemma by articulating his concept of *Lebenswelt* (usually translated as *lifeworld*). This concept refers to our primary apprehension of the world, balancing its universal and particular dimensions. According to Husserl, even in a culturally situated setting, we are able to grasp universal structures, namely by drawing on perception. But Husserl never fully clarified how this transition from particular appraisals to universal structures takes place.

My colleague Jesús Díaz has defended an interpretation based on Husserl's text on the origins of geometry.[34] Ancient mathematical statements are expressed in a way entirely conditioned by their cultural context, but nonetheless we are able to grasp their ideal content, which is potentially universal. In order to grasp this content, we only need to master the argumentational skills that Ancient Greek philosophers first studied, which are preserved in the European tradition to this day. These argumentational skills allow us to discern universal structures not only in science, but also in art and other domains of our *lifeworld*. Despite the relative success of this concept among philosophers,[35] Husserl's stance is in contradiction to every form of particularism in social research.

For instance, phenomenologists like San Martín (2009) have been extremely critical of cultural relativism in anthropology, taking it to be a result of anthropological theory's inability to deal with the distinctions introduced above and account for the objectivity of, among other things, science.[36] In other words, from this phenomenological standpoint, anthropologists would be theoretically misguided in their appraisal of the particularity or universality of certain cultural items. Right or wrong, such an *a priori* approach is certainly at odds with the philosophical tastes exhibited by professional anthropologists throughout the twentieth century, which is probably why phenomenology does not count as a major influence in their methodological debates, despite its influence on philosophers.

There have been less principled attempts at hybridizing phenomenology and social theory. Among these, the most accomplished social phenomenology is still that of Alfred Schütz. Schütz (1899–1959), a Viennese lawyer with a background in Austrian economics and interpretative sociology, spent part of his career in the United States and introduced phenomenology to American social scientists through his writings and personal exchanges.[37] Schütz's main contribution was to develop a phenomenological philosophy of the social sciences, namely by reinterpreting Max Weber's theory of action through Husserl's approach.

Instead of taking the subjective meaning of individual actions as a primitive category, like Weber, Schütz analyzed its phenomenological grounds.[38] His goal was to go beyond a merely commonsensical understanding of subjective meanings, isolating their *a priori* sources and explaining the emergence of a shared *Lebenswelt*. The operations of our consciousness analyzed by Husserl would also generate, for Schütz, the shared *structures of meaning* allowing us to understand each other's action. Each individual would appraise the social world from a particular perspective. Social agents would then make abstractions from these individual appraisals (here-and-now experiences), generating ideal types in order to grasp wider regions of the social world, temporally and spatially, gradually more and more distant from the *hic et nunc* self. Communication of increasingly abstract types generated inter-subjective meanings. The social sciences should account for this shared understanding of reality. Any purportedly objective concept they may construct (e.g. statistical aggregates) should always be interpretable from the point of view of these shared meanings, since, ultimately, they constitute the social world they intend to capture.

However, for Schütz, Husserl's approach had failed to solve the problem of transcendental intersubjectivity, which was necessary to deal with this relational dimension of the social world. He claimed instead that the social scientists should proceed from the natural understanding of the subjects under study, without paying so much attention to their transcendental foundations. Stimulated by American pragmatism, Schütz focused on the problem of why we take anything social as real. For him, our appraisal of the social world is structured according to the relevance we discern in any of its features – whether because these are externally imposed as relevant or due to their connection with our own purposes. We use different cognitive styles to deal with these relevant features, depending on the operations we perform on them. Together, these cognitive styles and the

systems of relevance define meaning-contexts in the social world and each of them can be considered a reality of its own. Our sense of 'paramount reality' arises, for Schütz, in the 'world of working', our bodily interactions with relevant physical objects. We grasp the reality of other realms as variations on these basic experiences. However, we live through all these meaning-contexts, without presupposing any unified sense of reality: switching between realms may come as a shock for an individual. Any self is, in this respect, divided to some extent, depending on the variety of her world experiences. In this framework, the understanding of individual actions requires an analysis of how the agent articulates the different systems of relevance operating in her particular *Lebenswelt* (Hermida, 2009) in a personal life plan. Despite being a scientifically reconstructed *ideal type*, this abstract plan should be understandable to the agent whose action is under analysis.

Schütz's philosophy of the social sciences is as much an ontology of the social world as a methodology for its investigation. However, this ontology stems to a great extent from categories already in use, at least in sociology, and Schütz's phenomenological twist was never completely at odds with the sociological mainstream. Nonetheless, up to the present day, there has never been a mainstream Schützian social science, if we judge it, at least, by the content of the various compilations on the topic.[39] We may guess that Schütz never succeeded in bringing phenomenology closer to standard approaches in social theorizing. And the problem may, again, have been that the flavour of Schütz major categories was still aprioristic. The most successful research program stemming from Schütz's legacy is ethnomethodology, which, however, loses the phenomenological aspiration to objectivity and universality.

Originating in the 1960s with Harold Garfinkel's seminal contributions (followed promptly by Harvey Sacks and Aaron Cicourel, among others), ethnomethodology constitutes a broad and reasonably well-established research program in sociology.[40] However, the possibility of finding some sort of methodological or genealogical unity in this program is widely contested by its own practitioners, making it scientifically questionable for analytical philosophers of the social sciences. Since ethnomethodologists themselves question the idea of science promoted by these latter figures, this is not a debate in which progress can be expected. Even from a phenomenological standpoint, ethnomethodology may seem too radical, despite the debt Garfinkel acknowledged he had to Husserl, Schütz and Gurwitsch, challenging at the same time their misunderstanding of actual scientific practice.

Ethnomethodology is usually presented as the study of any kind of ordinary practice, trying to capture its *order* as it emerges from the activities of the participants. However, this ethnomethodological *lifeworld* cannot be more different from Husserl's or Schütz's: the aim is not to discern general eidetic or meaning structures, but rather to grasp the here-and-now arrangements the agents generate in their everyday activities. In ethnomethodology, action is not understood from abstract ideal types. The sense of reality that the participants 'naturally' share can be questioned in order to apprehend it (e.g. in the famous disruption experiments conducted by Garfinkel), but this does not lead to a superior phenomenological appraisal of its foundations. Ethnomethodology deals with 'haecceities', not with *ideal* structures.

Equally diverse, though perhaps less successful among social scientists than ethnomethodology, and also partially inspired by phenomenology is the *embodied* approach to cognitive sciences advocated in such diverse fields as ecological psychology, behaviour-based Artificial Intelligence or dynamic systems theory, to name just a few.[41] Whereas in the mainstream approach models of cognitive activities involve some sort of computational manipulation of representational inner states, as if it were a game of chess, embodied models of cognition treat them more like a game of pool, in which you

need to take into account real-time physical interactions. In the case of human decisions, models should consider our sensorimotor interaction with a given environment plus our social interaction with other agents. All this is conceived of as a continuous process that should be modeled (and explained) as such: that is, describing the range of changes that the agent-cum-environment system experiences over real time. In principle, there is no need to invoke standard mental representations or a global plan of action. This certainly departs from standard intentional explanations in the analytical social sciences, where beliefs and desires alone account for decisions via expected utility theory.

Perhaps the most significant phenomenological trait in this literature lies in the claim that perception, rather than a passive reception of external information, is an enactive process inseparable from action.[42] When applied to action, Shane Gallagher (2005) has argued for an embodied alternative to standard theories of mind, in which we would not need belief or desire attribution to understand each other's actions. This understanding would often be primary, originating in body expressions that we would apprehend directly through perception without mental representations (as in the standard theories of mind).

However, we should note that the success stories of this emerging paradigm come mostly from studies of the lower levels of cognitive activity, whereas at higher levels (e.g. semantics or social interaction), empirical evidence is less compelling or, at least, it is open to a more traditional interpretation. Ultimately the question whether it is possible to exhaustively identify an agent's experience and the underlying sensorimotor exercise, as a fully embodied approach would require, remains a moot point. And it remains to be seen how coherent this is with the phenomenological view.

In conclusion, in phenomenology we find a conception of subjectivity that goes beyond the belief-desire analysis of intentionality prevailing in mainstream social science. For Husserl, we are able to grasp in our consciousness essential structures defining the social world, despite its cultural particularities. These structures also support, in Schütz's view, the meaning of our actions, providing patterns for their analysis. A substantial minority of social scientists has found inspiration here for their approaches. Nonetheless, phenomenology is philosophically built up on *a priori* grounds that are often in conflict with the empiricist vein most common in social research, as we saw with San Martín's indictments against relativism as a sort of professional philosophy of cultural anthropologists. We have equally seen how the success of ethnomethodology owes much to the nominalistic deflation of phenomenological *a priori*. As of today, the phenomenology of the social sciences should still strike a balance between Husserl's original normative project and the actual practices of scientists that it should engage with.

FOUCAULT

It is an open question whether Michel Foucault was more a philosopher or a social scientist/theorist (e.g. O'Farrell, 1989).[43] Historians were probably the first to appreciate that his work involved a new approach to their discipline.[44] And, indeed, Foucault's claims are grounded more on compelling accounts of the most diverse episodes of the past than on purely conceptual arguments which are often confined to short, sometimes occasional, pieces. Hence, Foucault has no explicit philosophy of the social sciences but, nonetheless, we find a philosophical history of several psychological and economic ideas in his works. Even if historians of these disciplines usually do not find such narratives consensual, their conceptual articulation has provided inspiration for research in a number of social disciplines. In this brief section, I will try to present Foucault's key ideas on the social sciences as they appear in two of his major works, trying to separate the influential parts from a number of claims that already seem outdated.

Foucault's earliest appraisal of what we would today call social science took place in the 1940s:[45] in 1949, he obtained a degree in psychology, then taught it at the *École Normale* and even acquired some clinical practice. The psychology that Foucault learnt was a mixture of psychoanalysis, phenomenology and some experiments and tests. Despite this initial interest, Foucault proved to be sensitive to the arguments questioning the scientific status of psychology that proliferated in the 1950s in Paris.[46] A common thread in these critiques was the *conceptual confusion* of psychology, as judged by comparison either with *true* sciences or *good* philosophy. For example, at this point Foucault showed sympathy for the approach of George Politzer, for whom Marxism provided a standard for science and philosophy alike. For Politzer, psychologists did not know how to articulate the physiological basis of mental disorders with their social roots and only a Marxist analysis of the articulation of these two dimensions would provide the grounds for a truly scientific psychology. Gaston Bachelard or even Maurice Merleau-Ponty adopted different epistemic standards but argued against psychology along the same lines. Over the 1950s and the early 1960s, Foucault was equally critical of the theoretical confusion of psychology in a series of minor (and a few major) pieces on psychology. Gradually, he lost interest in adopting a positive philosophical position about what psychology should be and opted instead for exploring the origins of its (ill-founded) concepts.

In 1966, in *The Order of Things* (1970) Foucault generalized this skepticism to the *human* sciences (*sciences humaines*), including here 'some admixture of psychoanalysis and ethnography, certain kinds of literary analysis and various reflections of a Marxist origin' (Hacking, 2002: 78). All these disciplines would analyze the representations we unconsciously live by, beyond our natural constraints. Focusing on representations was just a consequence of Foucault's main thesis about knowledge: namely, that it depends on our understanding of the nature of signs (particularly linguistic signs) used to formulate truths of each moment of history. *The Order of Things* is a general exploration of how signs were understood in several disciplines throughout history. According to Foucault, philosophy had traditionally dealt with conscious representations, but by the late eighteenth century, we came to accept that we were using representations that we could not access consciously. The human sciences emerged to study these, importing concepts and quantitative approaches from the natural sciences and restating traditional philosophical topics in purportedly positive terms. Foucault claimed that such an epistemic enterprise was bound to fail: the human sciences could never be real sciences, because it was impossible to turn every unconscious representation into a conscious one.[47]

Again, Foucault's skepticism was not based on an explicit analysis of the performance of their theories or methods, that is, a philosophy of science. He opted instead for a genealogical theory of knowledge, aimed at exploring the representational standards underlying these theories and methods as they had emerged historically. For Foucault, these standards would be part of a system of conceptual possibilities (an *episteme*), that each discipline (and each approach within each discipline) exploits for its own purposes. This system would constitute a kind of 'historical a priori' implicitly assumed by all the proto-social scientists studied in *The Order of Things*. Foucault did not take sides with any of the epistemic alternatives they explored, but rather documented the difficulties all these disciplines found in defining their conceptual categories. In his interpretation, such difficulties would stem from the very articulation of our modern *episteme*: unlike in previous ages, we assume that human beings create every representation, but since the creator cannot be totally included in any of them, there is always something left out. Representations, as studied by the social sciences, are thus intrinsically limited and, as long as the modern *episteme* holds,

social research will remain scientifically unaccomplished.

This part of Foucault's approach to the social sciences never gained wide philosophical currency, even among Foucauldian scholars: on one hand, reconstructing entire *epistemes* along Foucault's lines might have seemed excessively demanding to many;[48] on the other hand, the analyses of particular disciplines presented in *The Order of Things* failed to convince the competent scholars of their cogency, partly because of Foucault's exclusive emphasis on representations.[49] As Hacking put it (2002: 77), it might have been the first and last masterpiece of its kind.

However, Foucault's method, his so-called *archaeology of knowledge*, inspired many analyses of various social disciplines. In order to reconstruct these shared epistemes, Foucault focused not only on the masterpieces in each discipline, but on all sorts of minor works and *grey literature* used in actual practices. His assumption, again, is that epistemes emerge from the interaction of entire communities, rather than from the contribution of any outstanding individual. The participants in these interactions are not intentionally promoting any part of the episteme: unaware of its very existence, they unconsciously play by its rules. The reconstruction of the episteme, then, should not pay attention to the intentional meaning of any statement: there might well be no coherent view in any particular individual. The archaeologist of knowledge should try to extract it from multiple sources as it literally emerges in them in the historical process. Citing Hacking again (2002: 83), 'Foucault propounds an extreme nominalism: nothing, not even the ways I can describe myself, is either this or that but history made it so'. Such a nominalistic approach to historical records prevails today among many historians of science, preventing them from making the generalizations philosophers would expect.

Another influential part of Foucault's legacy is the political consequences of this nominalism. History makes things the way they are through relations of power operating in the very interaction of individuals, rather than imposed from above. It does not arise from the plans of particular agents or groups, since they are 'made' in the same process. These agents use the social sciences to pursue their goals, giving rise, collectively and unintentionally, to relations of power: people extend and legitimize their grip on other people through scientific discourses that can be mobilized according to different strategies; but science can also help to resist somcone else's impositions. Again, we will not find in Foucault a cognitive account of such discursive grips, skeptical as he was of psychology, but a thorough and compelling documentation of these power-plays in the most diverse context. Foucault adopted a positive tone in his analyses; personally, he was quite critical of a number of disciplinary institutions (e.g. prisons), but he did not advocate for a particular alternative.[50] Once again with Hacking, once you establish there is no human nature, there is no salvation to promote: each practice creates its own dangers and the archaeologist of knowledge can only make their origin explicit.

In addition to this methodology for the historical study of the social sciences, there is another Foucauldian contribution that we should consider here. Namely, his concept of *governmentality*, paradigmatically presented in his 1978–1979 lectures in the Collège de France on *The Birth of Biopolitics*, edited only 25 years later (Foucault, 2008).[51] With this concept, Foucault tried to capture the way a body of knowledge allows actual government, that is, the articulation of the *episteme* shared by practitioners and theoreticians, from which ideologies, political agendas, discourses, social engineering techniques, etc., stem. Despite such a broad definition, the concept of *governmentality* is gaining increasing currency among scholars studying politics in various fields, perhaps because it pointed in a novel way to the interplay of theory and practice. As Francesco Guala (2006) once noticed, Foucault was probably trying to capture (although not exclusively)

what we now call, after Donald MacKenzie, the *performativity* of the social sciences, that is, the different roles they play when they become part of the social process they intend to analyze. Sometimes the participants in these processes use concepts from a given theory (*generic performativity*) in their discourse. *Effective performativity* occurs when, as a result of that use, something happens in the process they are involved in. Finally, what MacKenzie calls *Barnesian performativity* refers to those instances in which practical use of an aspect of a given theory makes the process under analysis more like its theoretical depiction.[52]

In *The Birth of Biopolitics* Foucault explored how certain varieties of economic theory came to articulate the *neoliberal art of government*, namely governing through markets. Unlike classical liberalism, neoliberal economists understood that market competition required government intervention, to monitor and maintain it. They constructed theoretical arguments in order to justify this intervention, appealing mostly to its efficiency as compared to other forms of social organization. Foucault documented the emergence of some of these arguments and their practical uses, suggesting (rather than showing) their performative effects: neoliberal government of actual markets made them come closer to the theoretical models of neoliberal economists. Foucault thus posed a dilemma for the philosopher of economics: we can only discuss the truthfulness of an economic model once reality starts being reformed to match it.

I think it is fair to conclude that Foucault certainly succeeded in pointing out a number of philosophically interesting issues in the history of the social sciences, documenting them in detail. His studies provide paradigms that have been widely imitated and will probably continue to be imitated.[53] It is open to discussion, though, whether his nominalism can be further articulated into a more systematic philosophical or historiographical approach. In its present form, it has not attracted much attention among mainstream philosophers of science, but, with further developments, this may well change in the future.

CONCLUDING REMARKS

The history of the social sciences shows that there is a certain continuity with philosophy. Analytical philosophers of the social sciences usually draw on the achievements of certain methods, usually mathematical approaches originating in economics. But, so far, their success has never been so outstanding as to close, once and for all, the philosophical debate about the scientific status of social research. Even if there is a mainstream in most disciplines, we often find alternative research agendas as well. Continental philosophies of the social sciences are usually tied to these alternatives, showing that it is possible to defend them on many different conceptual grounds. I guess that if continental philosophies seem attractive to many social scientists, it is because they offer the prospect of a somewhat radical reconstruction of current research practices, satisfying demands that they apparently leave unanswered. By way of conclusion, I would suggest that even if this reconstruction happens, it will probably be less radical than we would now expect from reading continental authors.

The case of Marxism, examined in the second section, illustrates this claim well. Though at some point in the late-nineteenth century Marxism might have appeared as a contender to better established theories, it became as big as a social science could then be within a few decades. And it collapsed equally quickly. The most promising approaches to Marxism consist either of incorporating it (both philosophically and methodologically) into the analytical canon or reinterpreting its philosophical foundations, usually from a post-modern stance – implemented, if at all, in emerging fields such as cultural studies (see Dworkin, 1997).

Independently of our assessment of any of these prospects, if they succeed, Marxism will be substantially transformed in a way that Marx himself would have never expected.

This has already occurred with phenomenology. Here, there has never been the illusion of an orthodoxy (or the means to sustain it), as there was with Marxism: Husserl never made a direct impact on the social scientists. It has been claimed that most qualitative or hermeneutical approaches can be traced back, genealogically, to Husserl, making phenomenology something closer to the mainstream in social research. Were this true, it would prove that phenomenology is something philosophically less substantive than we would expect it to be. Ethnomethodology illustrates how far from Husserl's idea of science a phenomenologically inspired sociologist can go. With Foucault, philosophy does not come first, but rather emerges from rich case studies, where particular philosophical points seem to be exemplified. The possibility of generalizing them into a general paradigm for the social sciences is still under discussion. And if a fully fledged nominalist approach is ever articulated, it might be Foucauldian, but we certainly will not find it in Foucault.

Paradigms in the social sciences have been coming and going relatively quickly and, skeptical as I am now, I have no final argument to exclude continental philosophies from coming to prevail in the elucidation of the success of the social sciences. But the evidence so far suggests that, even if they do, the sort of paradigm they will account for will probably be something different than what continental philosophers would want it to be now.

ACKNOWLEDGEMENTS

I have received comments and suggestions from competent scholars on each part of the paper, which I have acknowledged at the beginning of each section. I am also grateful to Luis Arenas, Francesco Guala, Eric Schliesser, William Outhwaite and Jesús Zamora for their observations on the entire piece. Bruno Maltras provided much help in the analysis of the Social Sciences Citation Index.

NOTES

1 Nonetheless, there have been several attempts at defining this dichotomy: for a sample, see D'Agostini (1997), Sáez Rueda (2002) and Piercey (2009).

2 In my view, other authors such as Pierre Bourdieu or Clifford Geertz would have equally deserved a section in this survey, even if philosophers have not paid them much attention so far. Gender-oriented research has had an impact on the social sciences (e.g. feminist economics), but the underlying philosophy is not necessarily continental. Given the usual time constraints, I have opted for the three approaches that seem to be at least equally popular among philosophers and social scientists. For a more extensive consideration of other 'continental' approaches, see the papers of Kögler, on the one hand, and Baert, Weinberg and Mottier in this volume; see also Turner and Risjord (2007).

3 I avoid discussing primary sources, for the sake of brevity. The secondary literature I cite is never exhaustive, but rather, at most, introductory. Following these leads, I hope the interested reader will easily find more complete information.

4 I am grateful to Andy Denis, Adolfo García de la Sierra, Andrew Levine, Daniel Little and Félix Ovejero for their comments on this section. They made their disagreement explicit at many points, so the responsibility here (more than in any other section) remains mine.

5 My own understanding of the Marxist tradition owes much to Kolakowski (2005). Among Spanish Marxists, I am indebted to Sacristán (1983) and Bueno (1991). Walker and Gray (2007) and Glaser and Walker (2007) provide updated overviews. Carver (2003) and Little (2007) provide insightful presentations of this section's topic.

6 For example, the so-called professorial socialists (*Kathedersozialisten*) affiliated with the *German Verein für Socialpolitik* in the late nineteenth century.

7 A good overview is provided by the entries indexed under Marxism in the 1968 edition of the *International Encyclopedia of the Social Sciences* (Sills and Merton, 1968) and the 2001 *International Encyclopedia of the Social and Behavioral Sciences* (Smelser and Baltes, 2001).

8 A quick overview and a basic reference list is provided in van Parijs (2001). I am clearly aware that taking sides with analytical Marxism, as I do in this section, is clearly questionable for most other Marxists, so the reader should be warned of my partiality. Certainly, it is historically misleading to present the Marxist tradition solely from the standpoint of its analytical reconstruction, which is only 30-years-old and never played a significant role in Marxism as a social movement. Nonetheless, for most philosophers of the social sciences, analytical Marxism seems to be the standard approach to the discussion of Marx. Critical assessments of analytical Marxism can be found in Roberts (1996), Levine (2003), Tarrit (2006) and Veneziani (2008).

9 On the sources of teleological explanations in social research, see Turner (2003). The connection between Marx and Hegel regarding this point was widely discussed in the 1960s, mostly around the works of Althusser: Lewis (2005) provides an introduction to these debates, even if it is partial to Althusser.

10 For an overview, see Wilde (1991). Philosophical discussions of the role of dialectics in Marxian methodology in the light of contemporary philosophy of science are presented in Little (1986) and Walker (2001).

11 On idealization and Marxian economics, see Nowak (1980), De Marchi and Hamminga (1994) and García de la Sierra (2007).

12 Two overviews from a different perspective can be found in the latest edition of *The New Palgrave*: Foley and Dumenil haskar and Callinicos (2003).

13 Kincaid (2008) provides a quick overview. For a more extensive analysis, see Turner and Risjord (2007: 213–395).

14 For a recent sympathetic overview of Marxist historiography, see Blackledge (2006).

15 But take into account that the dichotomy between facts and values was rarely acknowledged as such within Marxism: see Wood (1991) and Cohen (1996) about the controversial status of moral philosophy within Marxism. The standard study of Marxian ethics is Kamenka and Marx (1969).

16 For the purpose of this analysis, I will mostly follow Heath (2001). I have taken some insights about Habermas' view of the social sciences from Bouchindomme (2002). Key references for the reassessment of Marxism by Habermas are his works of 1971, 1976 and 1988.

17 This is, at least, how I read Carver (1998).

18 Obviously, some think otherwise (see Gamble et al., 1999). Again, this section hinges on a particular approach to the philosophy of the social sciences, but there are alternative accounts in which Marxism fares somewhat better: see, for instance, Little (2003: 196–203).

19 I am grateful to Havi Carel, Jesús Díaz, Lester Embree, Pablo Hermida and Javier San Martín for their comments on this section.

20 For a short hisstory of *The Society for Phenomenology and the Human Sciences* (and its journal *Human Studies*) see http://pages.slu.edu/faculty/harriss3/SPHS/aboutSPHS.html (accessed on 7 January 2010). For a short overview of the phenomenological philosophy of the social sciences with an introductory bibliography, see Embree (1997), or for more extensive analyses, Fay (2003) and Outhwaite (2007).

21 Nonetheless, there have been significant exchanges that did not attract the attention of either philosophers or social scientists, for example, between Schütz and Talcott Parsons on social action, as documented in Schütz, Parsons & Grathoff (1978).

22 Lester Embree (personal communication) reminded me that the *Geisteswissenschaften* (*human sciences*), going back to Dilthey, included the historical sciences and were, thus, broader than the social sciences. Whereas Husserl was concerned with the former, Schütz would focus instead on the latter.

23 Not being a phenomenologist myself, my understanding of this tradition is strongly influenced by my colleagues Javier San Martín and Jesús Díaz who, together with Carmen López, run an active research group in phenomenology of the social world at my home university. See San Martín (2005) for an overview of this Spanish approach to phenomenology. Much to my regret, I can only provide a very incomplete picture of phenomenology, focusing on the thread that goes from Husserl to ethnomethodology through Schütz. For a more thorough analysis and a different assessment see the paper by Hans-Herbert Kögler in this volume.

24 I owe this interpretation of Husserl to Díaz Álvarez (2003).

25 My own understanding of Husserl's transcendental phenomenology is based on San Martín (1986).

26 See Derrida (1978) for the English text with a commentary. I here follow the interpretation of Díaz Álvarez (2003: 259–298).

27 Mostly thanks to Jürgen Habermas, who made this concept part of his *The Theory of Communicative Action* (1984).

28 A more phenomenologically oriented anthropology, for San Martín, would be Cancian (2009).

29 Like other German-speaking social scientists, Schütz emigrated to the United States fearing the ascent of the Nazis, condemning 'Jewish phenomenology' (Wagner, 1983).

30 I owe my interpretation of Schütz to P. Hermida's unpublished doctoral dissertation (Hermida Lazcano, 2001), conducted under the supervision of J. San Martín at the UNED, as part of San Martín's research project on the phenomenology of the social world. For a general overview with an updated bibliography, including the English editions of Schütz's major texts, see Barber (2010).

31 See, for instance, Embree (1999) or Psathas (2004). Perhaps the most successful Schutzian approach was Berger and Luckmann (1966).

32 There are many surveys on ethnomethodology. Here, I have used Atkinson (1988), Maynard and Clayman (1991) and Lynch (1999, 2007). On the connection between phenomenology and ethnomethodology, see Psathas (1999) and, for a witness account, Garfinkel and Liberman (2007) and Garfinkel (2007).

33 For a recent overview, see Calvo and Gomila (2008). One already classical contribution is Hubert Dreyfus (1972, 1992) phenomenologically inspired critique of artificial intelligence: see Kenaw (2008) for an updated presentation.

34 Classical phenomenologists provide various conceptual foundations for this claim: see Gallagher (2005) for a review.

35 I am grateful to Thibault Le Teixier, José Luis Moreno Pestaña, Christopher Payne and Iara Vigo de Lima Onate for their comments on this section.

36 See, for instance, Veyne (1996) and Potte-Bonneville (2004).

37 In this paragraph, I follow the sociological reconstruction of Moreno Pestaña (2006).

38 It is tempting to apply here the same principles that Kusch used to reconstruct the German debates on psychologism in the late nineteenth century, namely as a defensive professional reaction on the part of philosophers: see Kusch (1995).

39 I owe my understanding of *The Order of Things* to pieces compiled in Hacking (2002) and, more systematically, to Gutting (1989).

40 For a general discussion of a Foucauldian approach to science studies, see Kusch (1991).

41 See Leary (1976) for an early review essay. My assessment is based mainly on the fate of Foucault's approach in economics (paradoxically, not a proper human science in *The Order of Things*): see Lallement (1984), Amariglio (1988), Birken (1990); see also Vigo de Lima Onate (2010) for a general assessment. Tribe (1978) is usually considered as the best example of Foucauldian analysis in this field.

42 Foucault often changed sides in politics throughout his career and, despite the widespread image of a philosophical rebel, the precise nature of his own political commitments—that were many, particularly in the 1970s—is still under discussion: see Moreno Pestaña (forthcoming).

43 More precisely, Foucault discussed the concept of governmentality in a number of places (e.g. Foucault et al., 2007) but for the sake of simplicity I will just focus on Foucault (2008). For a general discussion on the implications of this work for the social sciences, see Cohen (2006). On Foucault's general view of the history of liberal and neoliberal economics at this point, see Grenier and Orlean (2007) and Steiner (2008). A wonderful Foucauldian study of British neoliberalism is Payne (2010).

44 For the definitions, see MacKenzie (1996: 16–14). For an alternative approach to the same phenomena, more directly connected to Foucault's approach, see Hacking (1999).

45 A sample of recent Foucauldian monographs on various disciplines could include: Berns (2009), McKinlay and Starkey (1998), Miller and Rose (2008), Napoli (2003) and Rose (2006).

46 It is tempting to apply here the same principles that Kusch used to reconstruct the German debates on psychologism in the late nineteenth century, namely as a defensive professional reaction on the part of philosophers: see Kusch (1995).

47 I owe my understanding of *The Order of Things* to pieces compiled in Hacking (2002) and, more systematically, to Gutting (1989).

48 For a general discussion of a Foucauldian approach to science studies, see Kusch (1991).

49 See Leary (1976) for an early review essay. My assessment is based mainly on the fate of Foucault's approach in economics (paradoxically, not a proper human science in *The Order of Things*): see Lallement (1984), Amariglio (1988), Birken (1990); see also Vigo de Lima Onate (2010) for a general assessment. Tribe (1978) is usually considered as the best example of Foucauldian analysis in this field.

50 Foucault often changed sides in politics throughout his career and, despite the widespread image of a philosophical rebel, the precise nature of his own political commitments—that were many, particularly in the 1970s—is still under discussion: see Moreno Pestaña (forthcoming).

51 More precisely, Foucault discussed the concept of governmentality in a number of places (e.g. Foucault et al., 2007) but for the sake of simplicity I will just focus on Foucault (2008). For a general discussion on the implications of this work for the social sciences, see Cohen (2010). On Foucault's general view of the history of liberal and neoliberal economics at this point, see Grenier and Orlean (2007) and Steiner (2008). A wonderful Foucauldian study of British neoliberalism is Payne (2010).

52 For the definitions, see MacKenzie (1996: 16–14). For an alternative approach to the same phenomena, more directly connected to Foucault's approach, see Hacking (1999).

53 A sample of recent Foucauldian monographs on various disciplines could include: Berns (2009), McKinlay and Starkey (1998), Miller and Rose (2008), Napoli (2003) and Rose (2006).

REFERENCES

Adorno, T. (1976) *The Positivist Dispute in German Sociology*. New York: Harper & Row.

Álvarez, J. (1991) 'Valor y explotación', *Arbor*, CXL(550): 71–92.

Amariglio, J. (1988) 'The body, economic discourse, and power: An economist's introduction to Foucault', *History of Political Economy*, 20(4): 583–615.

Armstrong, P. (1994) 'The influence of Michel Foucault on accounting research', *Critical Perspectives on Accounting*, 5(1): 25–55.

Arteta, A. (1993) *Marx: Valor, Forma Social Alienación*. Madrid: Libertarias.

Atkinson, P. (1988) 'Ethnomethodology: A critical review', *Annual Review of Sociology*, 14(1): 441–465.

Barber, M. (2010) 'Alfred Schütz'. In E. Zalta (ed.), *The Stanford Encyclopedia of Philosophy (Spring 2010 Edition)*. http://plato.stanford.edu/archives/spr2010/entries/schutz/.

Berger, P. and Luckmann, T. (1966) *The Social Construction of Reality: A Treatise in the Sociology of Knowledge*. Garden City, NY: Doubleday.

Berns, T. (2009) *Gouverner sans Gouverner une Archéologie Politique de la Statistique*. Paris: Presses universitaires de France.

Bhaskar, R. (1998) *The Possibility of Naturalism: A Philosophical Critique of the Contemporary Human Sciences*. London; New York: Routledge.

Bhaskar, R. and Callinicos, A. (2003) 'Marxism and critical realism: A debate', *Journal of Critical Realism*, 1(2): 89–114.

Birken, L. (1990) 'Foucault, marginalism, and the history of economic thought', *History of Political Economy*, 22(3): 557–569.

Blackledge, P. (2006) *Reflections on the Marxist Theory of History*. Manchester: Manchester University Press.

Bouchindomme, C. (2002) 'Une querelle de famille I. Aux sources de la controverse entre Apel et Habermas', in R. Rochlitz (ed.), *Habermas. L'usage Public de la Raison*. Paris: PUF. pp. 31–65.

Bueno, G. (1978) 'Determinismo cultural y materialismo histórico', *El Basilisco*, 4: 4–28.

Bueno, G. (1991) *Primer Ensayo Sobre las Categorías de las 'Ciencias Políticas'*. Logroño: Cultural Rioja.

Calvo, P. and Gomila, A. (2008) *Handbook of Cognitive Science: An Embodied Approach*. Oxford: Elsevier.

Cancian, F. (2009) *What Are Norms? A Study of Beliefs and Action in a Maya Community*. Cambridge: Cambridge University Press.

Carver, T. (1998) *The Postmodern Marx*. University Park, PA.: Pennsylvania State University Press.

Carver, T. (2003) 'Marx and Marxism', in T. Porter and D. Ross (eds), *Cambridge History of Sciences: The Modern Social Sciences* (vol. 7). Cambridge, NY: Cambridge University Press. pp. 183–201.

Cohen, G. (1996) 'History, ethics, and Marxism', *Iyyun: The Jerusalem Philosophical Quarterly*, 96(45): 71–83.

Cohen, G. (2000) *Karl Marx's Theory of History: A Defence*. Princeton, NJ: Princeton University Press.

Cohen, Y. 'Foucault déplace les sciences sociales: la gouvernementalité et l'histoire du XXe siècle', in F. Audren et al. (eds), *Les Sciences Camérales*. Paris: PUF.

D'Agostini, F. (1997) *Analitici e continentali: guida alla filosofia degli ultimi trent'anni*. Milano: R. Cortina.

Davis, J. (2003) *The Theory of the Individual in Economics: Identity and Value*. London; New York: Routledge.

Dawson, D. (2002) 'The marriage of Marx and Darwin?' *History and Theory: Studies in the Philosophy of History*, 41(February): 43–59.

De Marchi, N. and Hamminga, B. (1994) *Idealization VI: Idealization in Economics*. Amsterdam-Atlanta: Rodopi.

Derrida, J. (1978) *Edmund Husserl's Origin of Geometry, An Introduction*. Stony Brook, NY; Boulder, CO: N. Hays.

Díaz Álvarez, J. (2003) *Husserl y la historia : hacia la función practica de la fenomenología*. Madrid: UNED.

Dreyfus, H. (1972) *What Computers Can't Do: A Critique of Artificial Reason*. New York: Harper & Row.

Dreyfus, H. (1992) *What Computers Still Can't Do: A Critique of Artificial Reason*. Cambridge, MA: MIT Press.

Dworkin, D. (1997) *Cultural Marxism in Postwar Britain: History, The New Left, and The Origins of Cultural Studies*. Durham, NC: Duke University Press.

Elster, J. (1985) *Making sense of Marx*. Cambridge, UK; New York; Paris: Cambridge University Press.

Elster, J. (1986) *An Introduction to Karl Marx*. Cambridge UK; New York: Cambridge University Press.

Embree, L. (1997) *Encyclopedia of Phenomenology*. Dordrecht; Boston: Kluwer Academic Publishers.

Embree, L. (1999) *Schutzian Social Science*. Dordrecht, Netherlands; Boston: Kluwer Academic. Fay, B. (2003) 'Phenomenology and social inquiry: From consciousness to culture and critique', in S. Turner and A. Roth (eds), *The Blackwell Guide to the Philosophy of the Social Sciences*. Malden, MA: Blackwell Publishing. pp. 42–64.

Foley, D. and Duménil, G. (2008) 'Marxian transformation problem', in S. Durlauf and L. Blume (eds), *The New Palgrave Dictionary of Economics*. Basingstoke: Palgrave Macmillan.

Foucault, M. (1970) *The Order of Things: An Archaeology of the Human Sciences*. London: Tavistock Publications.

Foucault, M. (2008) *The Birth of Biopolitics. Lectures at the Collége de France, 1978–79*. Basingstoke, UK; New York: Palgrave Macmillan.

Foucault, M., Senellart, M. and Davidson, A. (2007) *Security, Territory, Population. Lectures at the College de France, 1977–1978*. Houndmills, Basingstoke, Hampshire; New York: Palgrave Macmillan.

Gallagher, S. (2005) *How the Body Shapes the Mind*. Oxford; New York: Clarendon Press.

Gamble, A., Marsh, D. and Tant, T. (1999) *Marxism and Social Science*. Urbana: University of Illinois Press.

García de la Sienra, A. (1992) *The Logical Foundations of the Marxian Theory of Value*. Dordrecht; Boston: Kluwer Academic.

García de la Sienra, A. (2007) 'Idealization in the labor theory of value', in J. Brzezinski (ed.), *The Courage of Doing Philosophy: Essays Presented to Leszek Nowak*. Amsterdam: Rodopi. pp. 59–115.

García-Bermejo, J. (2006) 'Sobre el individualismo metodológico', *Éndoxa*, 21: 313–346.

Garfinkel, H. (2007) 'Lebenswelt origins of the sciences: Working out Durkheim's aphorism', *Human Studies*, 30(1): 9–56.

Garfinkel, H. and Liberman, K. (2007) 'Introduction: The Lebenswelt origins of the sciences', *Human Studies*, 30(1): 3–7.

Glaser, D. and Walker, D. (2007) *Twentieth-Century Marxism: A Global Introduction*. London; New York: Routledge.

Gould, C. (1980) *Marx's Social Ontology: Individuality and Community in Marx's Theory of Social Reality*. Cambridge, MA: MIT Press.

Grenier, J. and Orléan, A. (2007) 'Michel Foucault, l'économie politique et le libéralisme', *Annales. Histoire, Sciences Sociales*, 62(5): 1155–1182.

Guala, F. (2006) 'Critical notice: M. Foucault, naissance de la biopolitique', *Economics and Philosophy*, 22(3): 429–439.

Gutting, G. (1989) *Michel Foucault's Archaeology of Scientific Reason*. Cambridge: Cambridge University Press.

Habermas, J. (1971) *Knowledge and Human Interests*. Boston: Beacon Press.

Habermas, J. (1976) *Zur Rekonstruktion des Historischen Materialismus*. Frankfurt am Main: Suhrkamp.

Habermas, J. (1984) *The Theory of Communicative Action*. Boston: Beacon Press.

Habermas, J. (1988) *On the Logic of the Social Sciences*. Cambridge, UK: Polity Press.

Hacking, I. (1999) *The Social Construction of What?* Cambridge, MA: Harvard University Press.

Hacking, I. (2002) *Historical Ontology*. Cambridge MA; London: Harvard University Press.

Harris, M. (1999) *Theories of Culture in Postmodern Times*. Walnut Creek, CA: AltaMira Press.

Heath, J. (2001) *Communicative Action and Rational Choice.* Cambridge, MA: MIT Press.

Hermida Lazcano, P. (2001) *Para una filosofía de la cultura. Alfred Schütz: relevancias y planes de vida en el mundo sociocultural.* Madrid: UNED.

Hermida Lazcano, P. (2009) 'Relevancias y planes de vida en el mundo sociocultural', in *Schutzian Research: A Yearbook of Worldly Phenomenology and Qualitative Social Science, 1.* Romania: Zeta Books.

Hertz, S. (2000) 'Statistique de l'État et statistique mathématique. Un texte remarquable d'Emil Julius Gumbel: "Statistique et lutte de classes" (1928)', in T. Martin (ed.), *Mathématiques et Action Politique.* Paris: INED. pp. 163–187.

Horkheimer, M. and Adorno, T. (1972) *Dialectic of Enlightenment.* New York: Seabury Press.

Husserl, E. (1965) *Phenomenology and the Crisis of Philosophy: Philosophy as a Rigorous Science, and Philosophy and the Crisis of European Man.* New York: Harper & Row.

Husserl, E. (1989) *Studies in the Phenomenology of Constitution.* Dordrecht; Boston: Kluwer Academic.

Kamenka, E. and Marx, K. (1969) *Marxism and Ethics.* London: Macmillan.

Kenaw, S. (2008) 'Hubert L. Dreyfus's critique of classical AI and its rationalist assumptions', *Minds and Machines*, 18(2): 227–238.

Kincaid, H. (2008) 'Individualism versus holism', in S. Durlauf and L. Blume (eds), *The New Palgrave Dictionary of Economics.* Basingstoke: Palgrave Macmillan.

Kolakowski, L. (2005) *Main Currents of Marxism: The Founders, The Golden Age, The Breakdown.* New York: W.W. Norton.

Kusch, M. (1991) *Foucault's Strata and Fields: An Investigation into Archaeological and Genealogical Science Studies.* Dordrecht: Kluwer Academic.

Kusch, M. (1995) *Psychologism: A Case Study in The Sociology of Philosophical Knowledge.* London: Routledge.

Lallement, J. (1984) 'Histoire de la pensée économique ou archéologie du savoir', *Oeconomica*, 2: 61–92.

Lawson, T. (2003) *Reorienting Economics.* London: Routledge.

Leary, D. (1976) 'Michel Foucault, an historian of the sciences humaines', *Journal of the History of Behavioural Sciences*, 12(3): 286–293.

Levine, A. (2003) *A Future for Marxism?: Althusser, The Analytical Turn, and The Revival of Socialist Theory.* London; Sterling, VA: Pluto.

Lewis, W. (2005) *Louis Althusser and the Traditions of French Marxism.* Lanham, MD: Lexington Books.

Little, D. (1986) *The Scientific Marx.* Minneapolis: University of Minnesota Press.

Little, D. (2007) 'Marxism and method', in D. Glaser and D. Walker (eds), *Twentieth-Century Marxism: A Global Introduction.* London; New York: Routledge. pp. 230–245.

López Sáenz, M. (1994) *Investigaciones fenomenológicas sobre el origen del mundo social.* Zaragoza: Universidad de Zaragoza.

Lynch, M. (1999) 'Silence in context: Ethnomethodology and social theory', *Human Studies*, 22(2): 211–233.

Lynch, M. (2007) 'The origins of ethnomethodology', in S. Turner and M. Risjord (eds), *Philosophy of Anthropology and Sociology.* Amsterdam; Boston: Elsevier. pp. 485–515.

MacKenzie, D. (2006) *An Engine, Not a Camera: How Financial Models Shape Markets.* Cambridge, MA: MIT Press.

Mäki, U. (2009) *The Methodology of Positive Economics: Reflections on the Milton Friedman Legacy.* Cambridge, UK; New York: Cambridge University Press.

Maynard, D. and Clayman, S. (1991) 'The diversity of ethnomethodology', *Annual Review of Sociology*, 17(1): 385–418.

McKinlay, A. and Starkey, K. (1998) *Foucault, Management and Organization Theory: From Panopticon to Technologies of Self.* London; Thousand Oaks, CA: Sage Publications.

Mespoulet, M. (2008) *Construire le socialisme par les chiffres enquêtes et recensements en URSS de 1917 à 1991.* Paris: INED.

Miller, P. and Rose, N. (2008) *Governing the Present.* Cambridge: Polity Press.

Moreno Pestaña, J. L. (forthcoming). *Foucault, la gauche, le néolibéralisme.* Paris: Textuel.

Moreno Pestaña, J. (2006) *En devenant Foucault. Sociogenèse d'un grand philosophe.* Bellecombe-en-Bauges: Éd. du Croquant.

Napoli, P. (2003) *Naissance de la police moderne. Pouvoir, normes, société.* Paris: La Découverte.

Nowak, L. (1980) *The Structure of Idealization: Towards a Systematic Interpretation of the Marxian Idea of Science.* Dordrecht; Boston: D. Reidel.

O'Farrell, C. (1989) *Foucault: Historian or Philosopher?* New York: St. Martin's Press.

Outhwaite, W. (2007) 'Hermeneutic and phenomenological approaches', in S. Turner and M. Risjord (eds), *Philosophy of Anthropology and Sociology.* Amsterdam; Boston: Elsevier. pp. 460–483.

Payne, C. (2010) *The Consumer and Debt: Governing the British Economy.* London: LSEEditor.

Piercey, R. (2009) *The Crisis in Continental Philosophy: History, Truth and the Hegelian Legacy.* London; New York: Continuum.

Popper, K. (1957) *The Poverty of Historicism.* Boston: Beacon Press.

Potte-Bonneville, M. (2004) *Michel Foucault, l'inquiétude de l'histoire.* Paris: Presses universitaires de France.

Psathas, G. (1999) 'On the study of human action: Schutz and Garfinkel on social science', in L. Embree (ed.), *Schutzian Social Science.* Dordrecht, Netherlands; Boston: Kluwer Academic. pp. 47–68.

Psathas, G. (2004) 'Alfred Schutz's influence on American sociologists and sociology', *Human Studies,* 27: 1–35.

Robbins, L. (1932) *An Essay on the Nature and Significance of Economic Science.* London: Macmillan.

Roberts, M. (1996) *Analytical Marxism: A Critique.* London; New York: Verso.

Rockmore, T. (2002) *Marx after Marxism: The Philosophy of Karl Marx.* Oxford; Malden, MA: Blackwell Publishers.

Roemer, J. (1981) *Analytical Foundations of Marxian Economic Theory.* Cambridge; New York: Cambridge University Press.

Roemer, J. (1982) *A General Theory of Exploitation and Class.* Cambridge, MA: Harvard University Press.

Roemer, J. (2008) 'Marxian value analysis', in S. Durlauf and L. Blume (eds), *The New Palgrave Dictionary of Economics.* Basingstoke: Palgrave Macmillan.

Rose, N. (2006) *The Politics of Life Itself: Biomedicine, Power, and Subjectivity in the Twenty-First Century.* Princeton, NJ: Princeton University Press.

Sacristán, M. (1983) *Sobre Marx y marxismo.* Barcelona: Icaria.

Sáez Rueda, L. (2002) *El conflicto entre continentales y analíticos.* Barcelona: Crítica.

San Martín, J. (1986) *La estructura del método fenomenológico.* Madrid: UNED.

San Martín, J. (2005) *Phänomenologie in Spanien.* Würzburg: Kœnigshausen and Neumann.

San Martín, J. (2009) *Para una superación del relativismo cultural.* Madrid: Tecnos.

Schmidt, A. (1981) *History and Structure: An Essay on Hegelian-Marxist and Structuralist Theories of History.* Cambridge, MA: MIT Press.

Schütz, A., Parsons, T. and Grathoff, R. (1978) *The Theory of Social Action: The Correspondence of Alfred Schütz and Talcott Parsons.* Bloomington: Indiana University Press.

Sherratt, Y. (2006) *Continental Philosophy of Social Science: Hermeneutics, Genealogy, Critical Theory.* Cambridge; New York: Cambridge University Press.

Sills, D. and Merton, R. (1968) *International Encyclopedia of the Social Sciences.* New York: Macmillan.

Smelser, N. and Baltes, P. (2001) *International Encyclopedia of the Social and Behavioral Sciences.* Amsterdam; New York: Elsevier.

Steiner, P. (2008) 'Foucault, Weber, and the history of the economic subject', *The European Journal of the History of Economic Thought,* 15(3): 503–527.

Tarrit, F. (2006) 'A brief history, scope, and peculiarities of "Analytical Marxism"', *Review of Radical Political Economics,* 38(4): 595–618.

Tribe, K. (1978) *Land, Labour and Economic Discourse.* London: Routledge and Kegan Paul.

Turner, S. (2003) 'Cause, the persistence of teleology, and the origins of the philosophy of social science', in S. Turner and A. Roth (eds), *The Blackwell Guide to the Philosophy of the Social Sciences.* Malden MA: Blackwell Publishing. pp. 21–41.

Turner, S. and Risjord, M. (2007) *Philosophy of Anthropology and Sociology.* Amsterdam; Boston: Elsevier.

van Parijs, P. (2001) 'Analytical Marxism', in N. Smelser and P. Baltes (eds), *International Encyclopedia of the Social and Behavioral Sciences.* Amsterdam; New York: Elsevier. pp. 484–486.

Veneziani, R. (2008) 'Review essay: A future for (analytical) Marxism?', *Philosophy of the Social Sciences,* 38(3): 388–399.

Veyne, P. (1996) *Comment on écrit l'histoire.* Paris: Ed. du Seuil.

Vigo de Lima Onate, I. (2010) *Foucault's Archaeology of Political Economy.* Basingstoke: Palgrave Macmillan.

Wagner, H. (1983) *Alfred Schutz: An Intellectual Biography.* Chicago: University of Chicago Press.

Walker, D. (2001) *Marx, Methodology, and Science: Marx's Science of Politics.* Aldershot, Hampshire, England; Burlington, VT: Ashgate.

Walker, D. and Gray, D. (2007) *Historical Dictionary of Marxism.* Lanham, MD: Scarecrow Press.

Wilde, L. (1991) 'Logic: Dialectic and contradiction', in T. Carver (ed.), *The Cambridge Companion to Marx.* Cambridge, UK; New York: Cambridge University Press. pp. 275–295.

Wood, A. (1991) 'Marx against Morality', in P. Singer (ed.), *A Companion to Ethics.* Cambridge: Blackwell. pp. 511–524.

Wood, A. (1993) 'Hegel and Marxism', in F. Beiser (ed.), *The Cambridge Companion to Hegel.* New York: Cambridge University Press. pp. 414–444.

Wright, E. (2005) *Approaches to Class Analysis.* Cambridge, UK; New York: Cambridge University Press.

3

The Philosophy of Social Science in the Twentieth Century: Analytic Traditions: Reflections on the Rationalitätstreit

Paul Roth

My point is that if we are intelligibly to attribute attitudes and beliefs, or usefully to describe motions as behaviour, then we are committed to finding, in the pattern of behaviour, belief, and desire, a large degree of rationality and consistency … .The limit thus placed on the social sciences is set not by nature, but by us when we decide to view men as rational agents with goals and purposes, and as subject to moral evaluation.
> (Donald Davidson (1980)
> 'Psychology as Philosophy')

I wish to say: nothing shows our kinship to those savages better than the fact that Frazer has at hand a word as familiar to us a 'ghost' or 'shade' to describe the way these people look at things. … A whole mythology is deposited in our language.
> (Ludwig Wittgenstein (1979) *Remarks on Frazer's Golden Bough*)

Broadly speaking, questions of how to explain human action can be answered in one of two conflicting ways, each of which argues for its priority over the other. On the one hand, the epigraphs by Davidson and Wittgenstein each incorporates, in its own way, a common and powerful argument that maintains that any accounting of purposive behavior requires rationalizing it. Rationalizing explanations must in turn proceed by domesticating actions via translation into an intentional or evaluative idiom familiar to the "translator"/explainer. Rationalizing actions just means *inter alia* providing *good* reasons, that is, reasons that motivate individuals to act as observed. What makes an explanation of action *social*, moreover, will involve how people's reasons take into account the doings of others. This argument forges together the notions of action explanation and of agent rationality. The former cannot be had without the latter.

Yet the grip exercised by a requirement that a normatively inflected vocabulary must be employed when explaining social actions only serves to anchor one part of a fundamental philosophical dilemma. For, on the other hand, insofar as the notion of a social *science* exerts a hold, explanations will be bound to a requirement to discern law-like regularities that can be exploited for purposes of prediction and control. But statements incorporating normative idioms have not proven amenable to being regimented in this fashion.

The relevant notion of scientific rationality thus proves antithetical to what makes ordinary action explanations rational – providing good reasons in an agent's sense. This creates the dilemma: if of the social, then explanations cannot satisfy the standard that scientific rationality requires; and if of a science, then explanations cannot incorporate what the rationalizing of social action requires – the use of an intentional or evaluative vocabulary relevant to agency. The *Rationalitätstreit* arises from this dilemma. What counts as rational by way of ordinary explanation of social action cannot satisfy what counts as rational by way of scientific explanation.

This dilemma continues to haunt philosophical discussions of the social sciences. Yet, surprisingly little discussion tracks how an altered philosophical understanding of science comports with the dilemma as formulated. And especially within the analytic tradition, much has changed with regard to how to understand the term "science," and so what this implies with regard to related explanatory endeavors.

Does the dilemma still obtain? By exposing and examining those philosophical premises used to legitimate and so perpetuate the conceptual divide, reasons for rejecting these assumptions can be recalled. This will allow for dissolution of the dilemma. For as formulated, the dilemma in the context of the philosophy of social science imposes a forced choice of explanatory strategies or vocabularies. But what anchors each end of the dilemma depends, or so I shall argue, on a particular metaphysics about the objects of knowledge and notions of rationality and explanation tailored to the respective metaphysics. Put another way, once the underlying metaphysics goes, so goes any claim for there being a preferred meta-method or explanatory strategy. Philosophical reasons

for mandating a forced choice of explanatory strategies disappear.

The core dilemma noted above has bedeviled analytic philosophy of social sciences from its inception. A review of the history and origins of this debate, at least as it has developed over the last century, suggests a type of rational reconstruction of analytic philosophy of social science in terms of this particular issue. Seeing it from the perspective of how the debate originates in the late-nineteenth century reveals that differing explications of rationality map onto incongruent conceptions of what I shall term "the objects of understanding." (Roth, 2000) Assumptions about these objects of understanding constitute the traditional metaphysics of knowledge that weighs like a nightmare on the philosophy of social science.

A distinction emerges late in the nineteenth century between nomothetic as opposed to idiographic accounts of human behavior. A nomothetic view presumes that laws characteristic of explanation in the natural sciences also must serve as the engines of explanations in the social sciences as well. (As discussed below, logical positivism provides what becomes for all intents and purposes the canonical account of the logic of explanation. See Salmon (1989) for an excellent overview.) An idiographic account of human actions insists that the human sciences account for meaningful behavior in terms of what humans could recognize as good reasons for that behavior. What determines the goodness of reasons depends, in turn, on citing factors specific to the time and place as explanatory of that action. But such contextualized reasons preclude generalization because they are context specific.

The appeal to "good reasons" or motivations connects idiographic accounts, moreover, directly to a precursor of the dilemma that concerns us, viz., the venerable Humean dichotomy between descriptive and evaluative statements. This dichotomy configures the problem as the analytic tradition inherits it. As enshrined in the philosophical literature, the Humean is/ought distinction maps onto the view that scientific regularities can only traffic in relations of fact. But any evaluative statement transcends what a description of mere facts provides. Since no evaluative statement can be derived from descriptive ones alone, *a fortiori* no account of "good reasons" can be derived from any bare recounting of facts.

Put another way, any sense of cause that "good reasons" supply people for their actions cannot be a type of cause that a science could harness. For reason–action connections so described cannot translate *under that description* into some parallel regularity between successive physical states of an object. Thus the hoary distinction between the nomothetic and the idiographic lingers on, seemingly intrinsic (as the opening quote from Davidson insists) to any effort to explain human action.

Interestingly and importantly (since the analytic tradition reproduces this part of the original debate as well), contextualization was not for historicists such as Dilthey any bar to objective knowledge of historically specific situations (see Apel, 1984: 3–6). When desiring to learn how those not like them understood their natural environment and social relations, historicists and their heirs also assumed that there exists a determinate object of understanding at which their inquiry aims. This object consists of a stable, shared set of meanings about that social sphere, a "Rankean reality" knowable *wie es eigentlich gewesen* (Iggers, 1983: 133–40). The fact that people successfully communicate seemingly establishes the *prima facie* legitimacy of assumptions regarding shared and stable meanings. Because languages alter and vary across times and cultures, there exists as well a need to contextualize assessments of such shared meanings.

Each approach – the nomothetic and the idiographic – claims to be a science. Each styles itself as a source of objective knowledge and as possessing its own distinct associated method of systematic inquiry. Each has its own specific object in view, and a method tailored to investigating and so

learning truths about its object. The "objects of understanding" for each realm (the natural and the social) rationalize the methods of inquiry specific to that realm. The fit of method to object and the claim to deliver truths about the realm under investigation entitles each to claim the title of a science, overt differences of form notwithstanding.

The analytic tradition puts its own mark going forward, however, on the form that the older debate takes. On the one hand, the Humean line just rehearsed incorporates a view that runs from Bertrand Russell through logical positivism and out to contemporary philosophies of science and epistemologies that claim to be forms of naturalism. For in this tradition, natural science sets the standard for explanation, and intentional idioms receive respect only insofar as they abet or conform to programs of regimenting experience to scientific standards. Programs here run the gamut from reductionist approaches to evaluative idioms through to those that hold that such seemingly intractable idioms have their own (tractable) theoretical structure.

On the other hand, the analytic tradition also remains heir to thinkers such as G.E. Moore, J.L. Austin, and various thinkers who claim the legacy of the later Wittgenstein. This second strain within the analytic tradition takes seriously accounts of action that invest with *prima facie* significance ordinary language talk of reasons as causes. For thinkers in this branch of the analytic tradition, ordinary intentional talk must be respected, not purged, when it comes to action explanations. This carries forward to contemporary debates concerning, for example, collective intentionality, and its role in explanations of social behavior (influential works here include Gilbert, 1989; Searle, 1995). The competing camps within the analytic tradition – friends of naturalism versus friends of ordinary language – only recapitulate the traditional divide in somewhat different dress.

These dual lines of descent further help perpetuate seemingly irresolvable disputes regarding what an explanation of the social requires. Put another way, debates in analytic philosophy of social science regarding rationality tie to questions of how a posited object of inquiry rationalizes and so legitimizes particular forms or vocabularies of explanations. In these respects at least – the differing logics of scientific explanation and of purposive explanation as well as the associated metaphysics of objects of knowledge for each – the analytic tradition in the philosophy of social science inherits nineteenth century philosophical presuppositions. These underlie distinctions made between the *Geisteswissenschaften* and the *Naturwissenschaften*. Each engenders competing and incompatible explications of terms such as "rationality" and "explanation." They also continue to fuel the *Rationalitätstreit* into the twenty-first century. With the advantages of hindsight, competing views about rationality can be reconstructed as competing views regarding the object of explanation.

The rise of logical positivism and their calls for a "unity of method" made a profound mark on the social sciences through the early 1960s in part because of the absence of any methodological consensus on the interpretative side (Novick, 1988). Problems that attended Dilthey's neo-Kantian effort to mount a "critique of historical reason" have been told well by others (see Apel, 1984; Iggers, 1983). For present purposes, it suffices to note that a core problem remains through many iterations and variations on the interpretative position. In order to preserve their distinctive "space of reasons," the space so imagined must not exist as any proper part within some realm of physical facts. For then such facts would simply be ones to which some natural scientific method applies. But by removing the space of reasons to a realm of non-physical facts, a slippery slope to radical relativism or historicism invariably ensues. For protestations of determinacy notwithstanding, nothing emerges in the process of inquiry on which to anchor attributions of meaning in a space so imagined.

Ultimately, historicism preserves the sphere of understanding at the price of sacrificing claims to being a science. When confronted with a philosophical theory such as logical positivism that spoke with authority regarding what "real" science requires, interpretivists were not convinced. But they did not possess any plausible alternative account of their own method that had the precision and the clarity of the criteria promoted by logical positivism.

Especially in the context of post-World War II social science in the United States, an image of logical positivism could be identified as influential and important because it provided a characterization of the fundamental desiderata of scientific theorizing. "[First,] its deductive-nomological account of explanation and concomitant modified Humean interpretation of 'cause'; second, its belief in a neutral observation language as the proper foundation of knowledge; third, its value-free ideal of scientific knowledge; and fourth, its belief in the methodological unity of the sciences" (Fay, 1975: 13). The unity of method thesis counted against, for example, incorporating terms or concepts into a science that could not ultimately be reconciled with the framework of physics.

Hempel notes that Otto Neurath, the member of the Vienna Circle to write most extensively on the social sciences, "put mentalistic terms such as 'mind' and 'motive' on his *Index* [of proscribed terms] on the grounds that they tended to be construed as standing for immaterial agencies and that this kind of reification gave rise to much stultifying perplexity concerning the relation of those mental agencies to the physical world" (Hempel, 1969: 169). Hempel goes on to remark that, in this respect at least, Neurath's position prefigures later philosophical efforts such as Gilbert Ryle's (1949) influential *The Concept of Mind*. Indeed, Hempel himself insists that

all branches of empirical science test and support their statements in basically the same manner, namely by deriving from them implications that can be checked intersubjectively and by performing for those implications the appropriate experimental or observational tests. This, the unity of method thesis holds, is true also of psychology and the social and historical sciences.

(Hempel, 1969: 191)

Hempel's own reflection on the methodological unity thesis thus too explicitly rejects, even through this late formulation of the position, all appeals to introspection or empathy. Yet as Hempel also observes, Neurath softened over time regarding how to interpret the demand for "unity of method," moving from a doctrinaire physicalism to a more pragmatic and instrumentalist view. This easing did not signal some new found appreciation of the scientific legitimacy of the intentional. Rather, as difficulties arose from strict demands for a reduction to some form of observational base for concepts even in the natural sciences, other bases were recognized for legitimating theoretical entities whose foundation in observation could not be readily established.

As American social science imbibes the unity of method thesis, this results in what Bernstein terms a form of naturalism, one most notable for proscribing any evaluative conclusions from its scientific work. Contrary to Marx's famous injunction, a social scientist's job *qua* social scientist "is to interpret the world not to change it; he interprets it by offering and testing theoretical explanations. He knows … that if one is seriously interested in 'changing the world,' this can best be accomplished through scientific knowledge" (Bernstein, 1978: 44).

In this context where the political and methodological agendas of social science meet, the import and influence of Sir Karl Popper's work demands mention (particularly Popper, 1957). An interesting, influential, and certainly at the time important controversy closely related to topics discussed in this essay can be found in (Adorno, 1976). For unlike the discussions sketched below that emanate from the work of Peter Winch, the so-called *Methodenstreit* explicitly features both methodological and political agendas. On the one hand, Popper's falsificationist approach made an important and enduring

impact on conceptions of scientific method contained in the social scientific literature. On the other hand, however, Popper's key methodological precept of falsificationism fades in significance in the philosophy of science literature. It met the same fate that verificationism did at the hands of (Kuhn, 1996). Neither provides the desired key by which to rationalize actual processes of theory acceptance and theory change.

Upon examination, debates surrounding Popper's works turned out to have less to do with disputes about scientific rationality *per se* and instead become connected to controversies regarding the types of social arrangements that promote open or free inquiry (exemplary here is Horton, 1970). In particular, Popper opposes social scientific approaches that would license large-scale social engineering. Certain philosophers who drew initial inspiration from Popper such as Paul Feyerabend greatly radicalize this thesis by worrying the issue that a petrified notion of scientific method itself will hamper criticism and the growth of knowledge.

Neither the logical positivists nor those inspired to a science of the social under their banner were wedded to any doctrines of political quiescence. The value neutrality of science would be rather exactly what allowed social science, in the view of Carnap, Neurath, and others, to serve political purposes. For, once the facts were in, policy makers could then debate with some objective assurance.

[Carnap and Morris] also shared, with Dewey and Neurath, a progressive political agenda. They saw a political role for a scientific philosophy that helped with the internationalist and progressive project of unifying scientific knowledge in support of social needs. Indeed, Morris and Carnap both felt that their scientific attitude was inseparable from a politically responsible philosophy.

(Richardson, 2003: 11)

Popper maintains that the demands of scientific rationality mandate a limited policy role for social science; Carnap et al. hoped that the scientific status of social inquiry would prove an aid to designing progressive policies. (See discussion in Richardson 2003.) But the critical point that emerges in these discussions concerns not the political agendas of positivists or others, but the inability of social science to reasonably approximate in its research and results the level of logical rigor or production of generalizations demanded by the unity of method thesis.

Although this story of positivism's rise and demise has been told well (Bernstein, 1976: especially Part I; Hempel, 1969), certain aspects related to this story bear emphasis and repeating. Particular note needs to be made with regard to the ways in which Kuhn's work eclipses that of logical positivism as an accepted account of theory acceptance or rejection. Pre-Kuhn, philosophical tradition had it that when taking the object of understanding to be the natural world, scientific method constitutes the rational method of inquiry. Following the logic of scientific inquiry provides a prescriptive procedure by which to obtain knowledge (truths) about the objects in that realm. Post-Kuhn, the philosophical community came to accept the implied irony of Kuhn's title; scientific revolutions had no logical structure.

On the philosophical side, the most decisive criticisms emanate from the positivists themselves. In this regard, Hempel's "The empiricist criteria of cognitive significance: problems and changes" (Hempel, 1965) still proves instructive as to how positivism fails to succeed on its own terms. Hempel details with clarity and precision the logical shortcomings of proposed criteria of meaningfulness in terms of empirical verification. In particular, formulations of the criterion of cognitive significance either regularly exclude statements that would be scientifically acceptable or can be teased into admitting statements that lack empirical significance. Ironically, the very clarity of the logical positivist criteria ultimately made possible the counter-examples that defeat them.

Further, reasons emerge for believing that such a criterion of meaningfulness cannot in principle be formulated. A key point made

by (Hempel, 1965), publishing on this matter only a year before Quine's (1953) "Two Dogmas of Empiricism" appears, concerns the fact that statements of a theory cannot be evaluated individually, in isolation from one another. In order to test the truth of any single statement, many statements in that language/theory must be held or assumed true. Within the next few years as well, Sellars develops his critique of the "myth of the given," (Sellars, 1956) arguing in parallel fashion to Quine that the supposed sensory substrata on which the most basic attributions of knowledge supposedly rely also presuppose prior theoretical framing. Thus, the twin pillars on which the autonomy of scientific knowledge supposedly rested – the logical structure that made plain the true conditions of individual statements and the unvarnished news of the senses (Quine's phrase) that provides the incorrigible evidence – proved to be unable to bear the weight of these claims.

Yet another important underlying assumption here concerns a belief in the cumulative view of scientific knowledge, that is, that changes in theory preserve or add to truths about the *same* objects. However, the arguments that challenged the rationality of theory acceptance and change also challenged the growth of knowledge assumption as well. For as theories change, so do its posits. But with different posits, there turns out to be no way to connect successive theories as theories about the same objects, and so as part of some narrative of accumulation of truths. Absent an account of how truths accumulate despite changes in theory, nothing rationalizes a belief in a generic scientific method. Instead, methods of inquiry and norms of explanation must be tailored to the specifics of the theory they serve (on Kuhn's impact, see Ball, 1976; Stephens, 1973). This defeats expectations that philosophers could hope to identify and explicate generic notions that constitute some core account of scientific rationality, an expectation that motivates much of the attention that logical positivism gives to the workings of scientific practice. Indeed, absent a stable object of inquiry, nothing remains to legitimate a belief even in a generic characterization of the notion of a science (Shapere, 1969: 122–3).

The disappointment on the social science side of this account of scientific rationality proves no less fundamental. Most importantly, what most fueled the sense that positivism constituted a failed program were that attempts to corral the social by means of what were taken to be the methods of science never yielded the results expected in terms of either laws of social behavior or predictable results. First and foremost, in short, was "the tremendous disparity between the insistence on what theory is and the failure to actually produce it" (Bernstein, 1978: 52). For example, various theoretical failures to establish the reducibility of non-observables to observables undercut commitments to any strict form of behaviorism or physicalism. The compelling influence of a model of scientific rationality such as logical positivism formulates resided in the thought that adherence to science so outlined explains both the instrumental success and apparent growth of scientific knowledge (Bernstein, 1978: 24). Yet the repeated failures of empirical theory in the positivist mode to deliver on the theoretical promises finally only reinforced arguments in the philosophy of social science to the effect that the study of what made behavior social could not, in principle, be characterized by an empirical science.

But it would be a mistake to conclude on the basis of such disagreements that debates regarding the role of rationality in the social sciences reduces to tired aporias between a hermeneutically grounded *Geisteswissenshaften* and nomologically oriented sciences of the social (see Apel, 1984: Habermas, 1988). What needs fuller appreciation concerns how just these changes regarding a generic logic of science alter the possibility space for a philosophy of social science. This returns us again to considering the parallels between the nineteenth century debates and debates post-positivism on the notion of rationality in analytic philosophy of social science.

The important question to ask, I suggest, is this: once logical positivism falls from philosophical favor as a unifying account of scientific rationality, why does *any* analog to the nineteenth century debate remain? In tracking how the nineteenth century debate comes to be perpetuated post-positivism, Peter Winch's classic work (1958, 1964) represents the most significant guise that it assumes. Winch initiates debate on the implications that understanding the social as "rule governed behavior" has not only for the possibility of a science of the social, but also for how the notion of rationality can plausibly be construed. Ironically, from a study of Winch's work the answer that emerges indicates that it is interpretivists who insist upon and perpetuate the old dichotomy. They do so in order to preserve a particular metaphysical entity, their own unique object of understanding.

With the waning of logical empiricism and the rise of post-Kuhnian philosophy of science, in other words, it becomes too easy to miss a key motivating factor in the earlier debates. Debates about rationality were fueled by thought that some special link existed between, on the one hand, the method of science and, on the other hand, the growth or success of scientific knowledge (see for example Suppe, 1977: especially 659–705). This presumed attunement of objects and methods that can access them highlights an important assumption shared by those who believe, whether in the manner of Hempel or of Winch, that knowledge of the social is possible. For with respect to the terms in which Winch frames the debates and in which those who support or oppose him continue it, no question exists regarding the object of understanding. A methodology of inquiry attuned to that object should yield an accumulation of truths about it.

It comes as no surprise to note that logical positivism presumes its favored notion of rationality to be grounded in and validated by its established utility in fostering the growth of knowledge. More surprising is that this assumption underlies positions that otherwise appear adamantly opposed to the positivist account of scientific rationality as appropriate to the human sciences. But both the methodological unity thesis and the methodological duality thesis emanate from this assumption. For just as Hempel assumes the stability of the objects of explanation in formulating his logic of explanation, so too Winch assumes the stability of the species of internal relations as the objects of social inquiry. Winch explicitly holds that "social relations are expressions of ideas about reality" (Winch, 1958: 23). The study of social behavior, according to Winch, consists in learning the rules by which people constitute social reality. Since rules constitute the social, they must be shared *qua* rules. But since rules do the work of making the social "appear" to people, the study of the social can only be the study of the idea of the social—the concepts applied so that the social has being at all.

A remark by Habermas (on Weber) succinctly voices a still common view and gives good evidence of the persistence of the traditional view noted at the outset. "Social action belongs to the class of intentional actions, which we grasp by reconstructing their meaning. Social facts can be understood in terms of motivations. ... Through understanding, I may interpolate a rationally pursued goal as sufficient motivation for an observed behavior." (Habermas, 1988: 11). Philosophers outside the analytic tradition writing on the philosophy of social science, for example, Charles Taylor, also simply do not challenge the alleged adequacy of a logical positivist model of rationality as appropriate to the *natural* sciences. Taylor just insists on inapplicability of these models to the social sciences. And when writing on themes from Winch more than two decades after Winch reinitiates this debate in the analytic tradition, Taylor approvingly asserts, "In the end, there is no way to finesse understanding if we are to give a convincing account of the explanatory significance of our theory." (Taylor, 1981: 196–7). Investing explanations of the social with meaning requires

positing some systematic link between what motivates social actors and a method for determining these motivations and so use of the intentional idiom. The "realm of understanding" constitutes a space in which facts of meaning can be discovered. (On this point, see the exchange between Rorty, Dreyfus, and Taylor (Rorty, 1980a, 1980b). For an important work that anticipates the need to move beyond the dilemma, see Turner (1980).

Winch's writings also prove important to extending the older debate because they contain significant even if unintended parallels to more mainstream philosophical criticisms of logical positivism. For example, although he nowhere cites Hempel's worries as broached in "The empiricist criteria of cognitive significance," Winch makes closely related points. What people take science to be and what they take to be reality cannot be prised apart. The conceptions prove mutually defining. Beliefs cannot be examined one at a time for their scientific goodness, for science does not exist as some neutral criteria for the goodness of belief. Rather it helps shape what people in the first instance take as candidates for belief. The two notions prove mutually influencing and influenced.

Moreover, beliefs do not (as Hempel ruefully acknowledges) stand or fall individually, but their very intelligibility relies on holding true many background beliefs as well. As noted above, Hempel's essay appears in the same time frame as the more critical essays by Quine and Sellars. Their work, of course, turns out to be much more generally influential because each provides an important philosophical critique of foundational accounts of rationality and knowledge within the analytic tradition. Winch's work easily assimilates into debates in "analytic philosophy" because it connects readily to closely related criticisms from within the analytic mainstream.

Importantly, Winch never challenges logical positivism as a model of natural scientific reasoning. And like the historicist tradition linked to Dilthey, he defends a *sui generis* notion of social knowledge. Each sphere – the natural and the social – has its object and its associated method. "On my view then, the philosophy of science will be concerned with the kind of understanding sought and conveyed by the scientist; the philosophy of religion will be concerned with the way in which religion attempts to present an intelligible picture of the world; and so on" (Winch, 1958: 19). Winch offers no hints with regard to how to identify to which sphere any bit of discourse belongs. But that each bit clearly belongs to some sphere he never questions.

For Winch, what disqualifies the social from being studied in the manner of the natural world concerns not the lack of an object, but that the object of social inquiry just has a different ontological status than those studied by the natural sciences. But this ontological difference does not make them less real or preclude having knowledge of about them. In this respect, to learn how rules apply is to learn what normative standards people in a particular society employ.

The Humean dichotomy once again intrudes to hive off the study of the social from the study of the natural. That is, Winch extends the conceptual account of the social developed in (Winch, 1958) to argue in (Winch, 1964) that different societies possess different ways of constituting social reality as well as different ways of licensing inference from within their shared categories. In his influential paper, "Understanding a primitive society," (Winch, 1964), Winch makes his primary target the view that there exists a generic logic of science, and that this logic equates to what it means to be rational. He challenges this generic conception because he maintains that it distorts action explanations. A generic notion of scientific rationality distorts such explanations because it misses (or wrongly dismisses) perfectly good rationales people give for their actions. That is, Winch worries that what people take as good reasons for actions will be rejected as explanations of their own actions when viewed from the standpoint of scientific rationality.

Since irrational reasoning cannot explain, this seemingly precludes the possibility that people whose beliefs do not measure up to our standard of logical consistency must be incapable of rationally accounting for their own actions. Winch took this conclusion to be unacceptable, and argues instead for taking each people's reasons for action as rational by construing standards of rationality as a contextual matter. Winch's position was taken to restrict judgments regarding the rationality of actions to a perspective internal to each group or society.

"Understanding a primitive society" ties in neatly with other criticisms of positivism that precede it by just a few years. Its arguments also participate in key aspects some key considerations broached in *The Structure of Scientific Revolutions*. Although Winch never mentions Kuhn's epochal work (the first edition of *Structure* appears in 1962), Kuhn's discussion of paradigm shifts and revolutions makes common issues with (Winch, 1964), especially with regard to its attribution of incommensurable (a term that Winch never uses) standards of rationality to different groups. Kuhn too has an interest in preserving the rationality of pre-modern scientific reasoning.

Winch attempts to garb a type of cultural relativism in Wittgenstein's authority. But his argument also redoes the historicist debate from the late-nineteenth century – rationality of actions construed as a culturally specific matter. Recovering reasons required recovering ways of thinking either lost or alien to us (or both). Because historically specific, such reasoning did not allow for generalizing in the manner of scientific laws. But since it was putatively based on shared internalized rules, it constituted an object that could be systematically studied, something with its own reality. (For an interesting and informed updating of some of these matters, see Lloyd (2007)).

The debate plays out in the terms that Winch casts it for several decades. A classic manifestation of its earliest form is Wilson (1970). However, most of the essays in

Wilson (1970) still reflect a lingering philosophical faith in the belief that the requisite notion of scientific rationality could be cashed out in a way that transcended the vagaries of time and place. Debate at least through the 1980s rehashes the rationality issue in the local versus universal terms in which Winch casts it. (See Hollis and Lukes, 1982, for a good representative sample of the post-Winchian debate.)

The rise of post-Mertonian sociology of science in the late 1970s played upon this inferential gap that Kuhn brings into view between when scientists shift theoretical allegiance and the absence of logically compelling reasons for doing so. The self-described "relativism" of some sociologists of science (see for example the essay by Barnes and Bloor, 1982) consists of no more than the insistence that theory change in science, if it's to be explained, must be explained in terms of contextual factors. Since purely logical factors (abstractly characterized) cannot suffice to account for the historical timing of shifts in theoretical allegiances in the sciences, their argument goes, contextual and contingent factors must count into the decision-making of scientists. As Rorty aptly put it,

> Reflection on the method of science has become increasingly thinner since Kant. If there's any upshot of that part of modern philosophy, it's that the scientists didn't have a secret. There isn't something there that's either effable or ineffable. To understand how they do what they do is pretty much like understanding how any other bunch of skilled craftsmen do what they do. Kuhn's reduction of philosophy of science to sociology of science doesn't point to an ineffable secret of success; it leaves us without the notion of the secret of success. (Rorty, 1980b: 55)

Scientists, like Azande, thus come to be studied not because they have insight into some special form of rationality that transcends cultural bounds, but rather because of their role as gatekeepers to what receives designation as "knowledge." The gatekeepers too turn out to be creatures of their time and place, reasoning from parochial concerns.

Yet Kuhn's way of telling the history and the philosophical work on which Kuhn explicitly draws from Quine essentially changed the terms in which this rationality debate could be cast. For as became evident from reactions even to the first edition of Kuhn's book, the work was understood to pose a direct and not obviously answerable challenge to any hope for some meta-justification of a generic notion of rational inquiry (see, for example, Shapere, 1969: 122–3). Philosophical critics of inductive inference from Hume to Goodman emphasize that reasoning from evidence rests for all intents and purposes on non-logical notions such as "custom and habit" or "entrenchment." Quine and Kuhn add two key considerations to this mix. First, they argue that categorization and inferential connections do not undergo evaluation in an isolated, piecemeal fashion, but always against and embedded in a more general set of assumptions about the nature of things. Second, even the best accounts of how the world works – those represented by received theories in the natural sciences – change historically in ways that make it impossible to demonstrate that different theories represent logical successors to their predecessors.

The notion of scientific rationality thus breaks down as a result in at least two decisive ways. But one has been better noticed than the other. Better noticed has been how any ahistorical account of scientific rationality fails to prove plausible when viewing a history of science through Kuhnian lenses. For methods, on Kuhn's telling of the tale, stay tied to specific theories or their related experimental paradigms. Shifts in theories, typically as driven by shifts in experimental paradigms, alter the conception of accepted method as well. What was rational by way of inquiry under one theory is not so for its successors. (See Zammito, 2004 for an excellent and philosophically well-informed intellectual history of debate on this topic.)

Less noticed, I maintain, has been the extent to which previous aporias in this area made certain metaphysical assumptions about the object of understanding. So, for example, under pressure from post-Kuhnian, historicized accounts of natural science, philosophers have surrendered any notion of a generic scientific method that can be applied to carve the natural world at its joints (Dupré, 1993; Galison and Stump, 1996). Moreover, the case for there being a stable object of knowledge – natural or social – interconnects with some conception of the growth of knowledge. For only on the assumption that theories theorize the same world of objects can knowledge be quantified across changes of theories.

Quine's *Word and Object* (1960) appears two years before Kuhn's *Structure*. Quine rejects as philosophically untenable a conception of truth that Kuhn was to show historically untenable. He forcefully rejects not only the idea that appeal to a method of inquiry or the facts suffices to settle questions of truth, but also denies that some single, stable notion of truth can be salvaged.

Peirce had attempted to define truth outright in terms of scientific method, as the ideal theory which is approached as a limit when the (supposed) canons of scientific method are used unceasingly on continuing experience. But there is a lot wrong with Peirce's notion, besides its assumption of a final organon of scientific method and its appeal to an infinite process.

For ... we have no reason to suppose that man's surface irritations even unto eternity admit of any one systematization that is scientifically better or simpler than all possible others. ... Scientific method is the way to truth, but it affords even in principle no unique definition of truth. Any so-called pragmatic definition of truth is doomed to failure equally. (Quine, 1960: 23)

Putting the points together, even if there were a viable notion of scientific method, it would not yield a unique characterization of truth. But there does not exist, in any case, any such organon of science, and post-Kuhn no reason to believe that there will be one. Finally, absent any unique account of truth, then the assumption that there exists some stable object of knowledge about which to collect truths cannot be justified

either. Accepted theories license certain statements, and these we call its truths. Nothing more metaphysically robust can be warranted.

That scientific knowledge had increased over time was, pre-Kuhn, an unchallenged dogma of the history and philosophy of science. But once Kuhn raises the specter of incommensurability between paradigms, no cogent account of the growth of knowledge could then be formulated. Kuhn's history ruptures progressive narratives regarding the growth of scientific knowledge. This removes as well another philosophical prop relied upon to support a notion of scientific method as representing rational inquiry *überhaupt*. The objects of science do not remain stable as theories change. Consequently, trans-theoretical claims to the accumulation of knowledge cannot then be warranted. And, lest one forget, Kuhn stigmatizes the social sciences as pre-paradigmatic: "it remains an open question what parts of social science have yet acquired such paradigms at all" (Kuhn, 1996: 15). Without a paradigmatic frame, not even progress in normal scientific terms can be charted.

But the primary point to now emphasize concerns how this break in the growth of knowledge narrative negatively impacts the Winchian side of the problematic as well, that is, the alleged connection between a method for studying the idea of the social and its putative object. Kuhn cites Quine's challenge to the analytic/synthetic distinction as motivating him to construe theory commitments in science as interrelated (Kuhn, 1996: vi). But this point applies, *mutatis mutandis*, to rules and their putative interrelationships as well. That is, just as scientific theorizing supposedly proves constitutive of beliefs about what there is, so too rules supposedly constitute shared conceptions of the social.

What does not get taken seriously enough, I am suggesting, finds early expression in Wittgenstein's remark on Frazer. For this intimates that any attempt at such a "translation" of actions – finding our words for another's reasons – brings with it willy-nilly a translator's heritage of myth-making. On this view, translators never escape from a "hermeneutic circle." Translation requires initial choices, including choices about what even to count as evidence for meaning. Every choice in turn patterns and limits subsequent efforts in this regard. The Humean dichotomy links with those of the hermeneutic circle to create what Quine calls the "indeterminacy of translation."

> The problem is not one of hidden facts, such as might be uncovered by learning more about the brain physiology of thought processes. To expect a distinctive physical mechanism behind every genuinely distinct mental state is one thing; to expect a distinctive mechanism for every purported distinction that can be phrased in traditional mentalistic language is another. The question whether … the foreigner really believes A or believes rather B, is a question whose very significance I would put in doubt. This is what I am getting at in arguing the indeterminacy of translation. (Quine, 1970: 180–1)

There does not appear to be, in Quine's (much disputed) formulation, any fact of the matter by which to arbitrate between imputations of incompatible interpretations (Roth, 2003). And incompatible attributions can be too easily found.

Fixing a realm of facts for the natural sciences will not (indeed, cannot) fix the translational options. For the latter necessarily incorporate intentional and evaluative statements that cannot be caught in any scientific image. Any realm of meaning still remains unsettled even after the realm of physical facts has been fixed. Thus, Quine's remarks about indeterminacy indicate that interpretivists still assume the burden of establishing that there exists their putative realm of facts, their alleged particular "object of understanding." If a realm of facts about meaning exists, the nature of facts in this realm remains quite mysterious (for an important critique, see Turner (2010)).

As Kripke (1982) has made the philosophical community appreciate, specifying what rules a person internalizes proves to

be an impossible task. Thus the underlying legitimating assumption that mere communication among people suffices to establish the existence of a shared and stable meaning structures cannot, it now turns out, license that belief after all. More plausibly, to use Quine's topiary metaphor, one has individuals trimmed into outward conformity, but the underlying structures turn out, on examination, to be radically different. This proves true whether one studies the physiology of human nerve endings, and tries to account for "sameness" in that way, or if one empirically investigates the associations that individuals have to specific terms. The case for uniformity cannot be made by empirical investigation, and it cannot be validated by conceptual inquiry.

In sum, under pressure from Quine, Kuhn, and Kripke, neither principled nor empirical arguments can be mounted that there even exists anything that answers to the objects of knowledge that interpretivists seek. This consideration proves *additional* to those considerations that argue for the severing of any link between a method of inquiry and the growth of knowledge.

What Davidson adds to this story, although he sometimes puts the point as if it were anti-Kuhnian, consists of a demonstration that meaning-making involves how rationalizing others consists in part of the *imposition* of a structure of belief on others. If translatable at all, others will in key respects turn out to believe much of what their translators do. If they did not turn out this way, Davidson argues, their language would be literally untranslatable. Indeed, the question would arise as to whether or not they spoke a language at all.

> It would be wrong to summarize by saying we have shown how communication is possible between people who have different schemes, a way that works without need of what there cannot be, namely a neutral ground, or a common coordinate system. For we have found no intelligible basis on which it can be said that schemes are different. It would be equally wrong to announce the glorious news that all mankind – all speakers of language, at least – share a common

scheme and ontology. For if we cannot intelligibly say that schemes are different, neither can we intelligibly say that they are one.

(Davidson, 1973–4: 20)

All that can reasonably be asserted, Davidson maintains, is the success of translation. But success comes at the price of making others into believers like us.

To return one last time to the epigraph from Wittgenstein with which the essay begins, note how it can be read as anticipating Davidson's now famous view on conceptual schemes. Wittgenstein's remark suggests that insofar as attribution of meaning consists of a form of interpretation of what people say or do, interpreters have no choice but to make others like themselves. No interpretation without conceptual assimilation.

The thesis that reasons ought to be part of any explanation of actions remains extremely tendentious. On the one hand, it appears to rule out without argument explanations of actions that require no appeal to reasons as causes, for example, biological explanations of behavior. (For a polemical statement of this view, see Rosenberg (1980)). More recent and sophisticated attempts to incorporate frameworks native to the natural science as part of a scheme to explain macro-social phenomena also make no reference to reasons in the explanations offered of behavior (see, for example, Diamond, 1999). In such cases, it need not be the case that causes reduce to blind biological imperatives. Rather, reason operates "behind the back" of the individuals involved, as can be found in rational choice explanations of, for example, the location of trading centers.

On the other hand, the notion of rationality to which reason explanations appeal has proven notoriously elusive and difficult to specify, and runs a gamut from extremely contextualized historicist notions to historical formalizations of principles of rational decision making. (For an array of current views on this matter, see Little (1990) as well as the exchange between Henderson (2005), Risjord (2005), Stueber (2005), and Roth (2005)). If accounts of rationality can

be "thin" (require little specific context, as in game theoretic models), then formal models and their mathematical expressions of principles of rationality should do the needed work. This would preserve attributions of rationality without any loss of generality. If accounts of the social require "thick" conceptions of rationality (i.e. ones rich in specifics of time and place), then a science of the social appears unlikely. The weight of contextual detail does not allow the account to rise to the level of useful generalizations about behavior. (See, for example, Obeyesekere, 1992 and Sahlins, 1995 for how these competing "thin" and "thick" views of rationality play out in a specific interpretive dispute.) But this debate too threatens only to replay the presumed divide between explanation (thin accounts) and understanding (thick accounts). Moreover, with regard to reasons specific to historical situations, no consensus can be identified regarding a method to access this or to provide an uncontroversial mark of correctness of an historical reconstruction (see Novick, 1988).

But once the respective objects have been thrown into question as determinate and stable, it deprives a basis for meta-debates about methods of rationality, at least in those terms that the debate has traditionally been cast. Likewise, but even less appreciated, taking to heart the implied consequences of interpretation as assimilation makes moot disputes about reconstructing how any individual or group "really" thinks about things. But once metaphysical assumptions regarding perduring stable objects of inquiry go – the "real" world or "real" meanings – so goes notions of fixed methods for accessing these objects and determinate ways of rationalizing alleged findings. In this context, a more pluralistic, purpose-tied account of how inquiry proceeds emerges.

Barry Barnes proposes an account of what he terms "natural rationality," which he stipulates as "cognitive propensities" that make inductive inferences happen more or less automatically (Barnes, 1976: 115). On this account, to treat rationality, understood as the process of inferring inductively in ways that one's social group finds licit and acceptable (hence "rational") naturalistically just means to treat it as itself an *empirical* phenomenon, that is, one learned by studying what people actually do in specific situations. In Barnes's pejorative use of "philosophers," philosophers insist on characterizing the notion of rationality in an *a priori* fashion. Barnes quite plausibly maintains that this has proven to be a failed project. (Barnes betrays no evidence of having read in 1976 either Davidson on conceptual schemes or Quine on naturalism.) But that point should not be taken as critical. Rather, whatever people accept, from poison oracles to theorem proving on Barnes's view, constitutes grist for a naturalist's mill. No matter what a group accepts as knowledge "does not mean that its emergence, acceptance, and persistence are not empirical phenomena. Acts of validation and assertions of validity are themselves empirical phenomena, and as such are available for sociological investigation." (Barnes, 1991: 321). Barnes ultimately comes to recognize and acknowledge Quine's account of "epistemology naturalized" and Kripke's account of rules as intellectually akin (Barnes, 1991: 334). Barnes's discussion of how to study and understand the notion of rationality thus has many important features in common with Quine and Davidson.

We began with the question of whether or not rationalizing behavior can be made compatible with explaining that behavior, where the term "explanation" implies placing that behavior in a scheme of causes and related causal laws. This led to a dilemma, a dilemma fostered I have argued by a number of problematic philosophical assumptions, all tied in one way or another on the account given to a particular metaphysics of knowledge. Debates about rationality assume this metaphysics of objects and a related epistemology. Yet neither the metaphysics nor the epistemology has proven philosophically viable. The conclusion urged has been that the nineteenth century debate no longer

should be credible. Nothing remains by which to engineer its philosophical divide.

Thus, despite the continuation of a nineteenth century debate about rationality through the present day, by the late 1970s the philosophical tide had turned. The notion of rationality with regard to inferences about matters of fact long ago lost any claim to *a priori* status. In addition, accounts of scientific rationality could not vindicate a specific method as linking the process of inquiry and the growth of knowledge. But once the notion of how our beliefs themselves faced the "tribunal of experience" changed from having them adjudged one-by-one to having them operate in concert with one another, the question of how to validate beliefs took on a radically different philosophical aspect. That process comes to be understood as internal to the beliefs that support particular practices of inference making. Finally, with the work of Kripke and Davidson in hand, the study of the constitutive rules by which shared meanings become possible, and so the social, itself stands revealed as an artifact of being imposed on the subjects of study (Bernstein, 1978: 92–3).

Ironically, disconnecting discussions of rationality from an implausible metaphysics of knowledge proves enabling rather than paralyzing. For it allows for what might be termed a methodological pluralism in the social sciences at least. (Whether, in Paul Feyerabend's infamous phrase, one should also adopt a stance of being "against method" in the natural sciences is left for others to debate.) Absent assumptions about a determinate logic of science or a specific theory of meaning, debate in the analytic tradition in philosophy of social science permanently transmutes. It no longer needs to obsess about what counts as a *science* of the social because there now exists no fixed or determinate meta-notions of science, explanation, rationality, or understanding.

Methodological pluralism, in this case, does not deny systematic processes of inquiry that ties a notion of rationality to the ends of inquiry. (This is a guiding theme of Turner and Roth (2003), both with regard to their joint essay and the volume as a whole.) This helps fill out what sense to make of appeals to "methodological pluralism" and "pragmatism." (See Rorty (1980a) for prescient remarks on this matter.) The issue of rationality becomes pragmatic at least in the sense of 'pragmatic' that ties to the ends of inquiry, and what methods abet attainment of those ends. The ghost of a nineteenth century philosophical dispute about rationality should at last finally be exorcised, and the dead hand of tradition made to release its grip on the philosophy of social science.

ACKNOWLEDGMENTS

I wish to thank Jay Peters, Mark Risjord, and Stephen Turner for their comments on an earlier draft of this essay. Responsibility for what appears remains mine.

REFERENCES

Adorno, T., H. Albert, R. Dahrendorf, J. Habermas, H. Polot and K. Popper (1976) *The Positivist Dispute in German Sociology*. New York : Harper Torchbooks

Apel, K.-O (1984) *Understanding and Explanation*. Cambridge, MA: MIT.

Ball, T. (1976) 'From paradigms to research programs: Toward a post-Kuhnian political science', *American Journal of Political Science*, 20: 151–177.

Barnes, S.B. (1976) 'Natural rationality: A neglected concept in the social sciences', *Philosophy of the Social Sciences*, 6: 115–126.

Barnes, S.B. (1991) 'How not to do the sociology of knowledge', *Annals of Scholarship*, 8: 321–335.

Barnes, B. and D. Bloor (1982) 'Relativism, rationalism and the sociology of knowledge'.(Hollis and Lukes 1982), 21–47.

Bernstein, R.J. (1978) *The Restructuring of Social and Political Theory*. Philadelphia: The University of Pennsylvania Press.

Davidson, D. (1973–1974) 'On the very idea of a conceptual scheme', *Proceedings and Addresses of the American Philosophical Association*, 47: 5–20.

Davidson, D. (1980) 'Psychology as Philosophy'. *Essays on Actions and Events*. New York: Oxford University Press.

Diamond, J. (1999) *Guns, Germs, and Steel: The Fates of Human Societies*. New York: Norton.

Dupré, J. (1993) *The Disorder of Things*. Cambridge, MA: Harvard University Press.

Fay, B. (1975) *Social Theory and Political Practice*. London: Allan & Unwin.

Galison, P. and D. Stump (ed.) (1996) *The Disunity of Science*. Stanford, CA: Stanford University Press.

Gilbert, M. (1989) *On Social Facts*. New York: Routledge.

Habermas, J. (1988) *On the Logic of the Social Sciences*. Cambridge, MA: MIT Press.

Hempel, C.G. (1965) *Aspects of Scientific Explanation*. New York: Free Press.

Hempel, C.G. (1969) 'Logical positivism and the social sciences', in P. Achinstein and S. Barker (eds) *The Legacy of Logical Positivism*. Baltimore: The Johns Hopkins Press. pp. 163–194.

Henderson, D. (2005) 'Norms, invariance, and explanatory relevance', *Philosophy of the Social Sciences*, 35: 324–338.

Hollis, M. and S. Lukes (eds) (1982) *Rationality and Relativism*. Cambridge, MA: MIT Press.

Horton, R. (1970) 'African traditional thought and Western science', in B. Wilson (ed.) *Rationality*. Oxford: Blackwell. pp. 131–171.

Iggers, G. ([1968]1983) *The German Conception of History*. Revised edition. Middletown, CT: Wesleyan University Press.

Kitcher, P. (1985) *Vaulting Ambition: Sociobiology and the Quest for Human Nature*. Cambridge, MA: MIT.

Kripke, S. (1982) *Wittgenstein on Rules and Private Language*. Cambridge, MA: Harvard University Press.

Kuhn, T. ([1962] 1996) *The Structure of Scientific Revolutions*, 3rd edn. Chicago: University of Chicago Press.

Little, D. (1990) *Varieties of Social Explanation*. Boulder, CO: Westview.

Lloyd, G.E.R. (2007) *Cognitive Variations: Reflections on the Unity and Diversity of the Human Mind*. New York: Oxford University Press.

Novick, P. (1988) *That Noble Dream: The 'Objectivity Question' and the American Historical Profession*. Cambridge: Cambridge University Press.

Obeyesekere, G. (1992) *The Apotheosis of Captain Cook*. Princeton, NJ: Princeton University Press.

Popper, K. (1957) *The Poverty of Historicism*. Boston, MA: Beacon.

Quine, W.V.O. (1953) 'Two dogmas of empiricism', in W.V. Quine (ed.) *From a Logical Point of View.* Cambridge, MA: Harvard University Press. pp. 20–46.

Quine, W.V.O. (1960) *Word and Object.* Cambridge, MA: MIT.

Quine, W.V.O. (1969) 'Epistemology naturalized', in W.V. Quine (ed.) *Ontological Relativity and Other Essays.* New York: Columbia University Press. pp. 69–90.

Quine, W.V.O. (1970) 'On the reasons for the indeterminacy of translation', *The Journal of Philosophy*, 67: 178–183.

Richardson, A.W. (2003) 'Logical empiricism, American pragmatism, and the fate of scientific philosophy in North America', in G. Hardcastle and A.W. Richardson (eds) *Logical Empiricism in North America.* Minneapolis, MN: University of Minnesota Press. pp. 1–24.

Risjord, M. (2005) 'Reasons, causes, and action explanations', *Philosophy of the Social Sciences*, 35: 294–306.

Rorty, R. (1980a) 'A reply to Dreyfus and Taylor', *Review of Metaphysics*, 34: 39–46.

Rorty, R. (1980b) 'A discussion', *Review of Metaphysics*, 34: 47–55.

Rosenberg, A. (1980) *Sociobiology and The Preemption of Social Science,* Baltimore: Johns Hopkins University Press.

Roth, P.A. (2000) 'The object of understanding', in B. Kögler, (ed.) *Empathy and Agency.* K. Stueber & Boulder, CO: Westview pp. 243–269.

Roth, P.A. (2003) 'Why there is nothing rather than something: Quine on behaviorism, meaning, and indeterminacy', in D. Jacquette (ed.) *Philosophy, Psychology, and Psychologism: Critical and Historical Readings on the Psychological Turn in Philosophy.* Kluwer Academic. pp. 263–287.

Roth, P.A. (2005) 'Three grades of normative involvement', *Philosophy of the Social Sciences*, 35: 339–352.

Ryle, G. (1949) *The Concept of Mind.* New York: Barnes & Noble.

Sahlins, M. (1995) *How 'Natives' Think: About Captain Cook, For Example.* Chicago, IL: University of Chicago Press.

Salmon, W.C. (1989) *Four Decades of Scientific Explanation.* Minneapolis, MN: University of Minnesota Press.

Searle, J. (1995) *The Construction of Social Reality.* New York: Free Press.

Sellars, W. (1956) 'Empiricism and the philosophy of mind,' in H. Feigl and M. Scriven (eds) *Minnesota Studies in the Philosophy of Science, Volume I.* Minneapolis, MN: University of Minnesota Press. pp. 253–329.

Shapere, D. (1969) 'Towards a post-positivist interpretation of science', in P. Achinstein and S. Barker (eds) *The Legacy of Logical Positivism.* Baltimore, MD: The Johns Hopkins Press. pp. 115–160.

Stephens, J. (1973) 'The Kuhnian paradigm and political inquiry', *American Journal of Political Science*, 17: 467–488.

Stueber, K.R. (2005) 'How to think about rules and rule following', *Philosophy of the Social Sciences*, 35: 307–323.

Suppe, F. (ed.) (1977) *The Structure of Scientific Theories,* 2nd ed. Urbana, IL: University of Illinois Press.

Taylor, C. (1981) 'Understanding and explanation in the *Geisteswissenschaften*' in S. Holtzman and C. Leich (eds) (1981) *Wittgenstein: To Follow a Rule.* New York: Routledge.

Turner, S. (1980) *Sociological Explanation as Translation.* Cambridge, MA: Cambridge University Press.

Turner, S. (1994) *The Social Theory of Practices: Tradition, Tacit Knowledge, and Presuppositions.* Chicago, IL: University of Chicago Press.

Turner, S. (2010) *Explaining the Normative.* Malden, MA: Polity

Turner, S. and P. Roth (2003) 'Ghosts and the machine: Philosophy of social science in contemporary perspective', in S. Turner and P. Roth (eds) *The Blackwell Guide to the Philosophy of the Social Sciences.* Malden, MA: Blackwell. pp. 1–17.

Wilson, B. (ed.) (1970) *Rationality.* Oxford: Blackwell.

Winch, P. (1958) *The Idea of a Social Science and its Relation to Philosophy,* Second edition. Atlantic Highlands, NJ: Humanities Press.

Winch, P. (1964) 'Understanding a Primitive Society,' reprinted in (Wilson, 1970).

Wittgenstein, L. (1979) *Remarks on Frazer's Golden Bough.* Atlantic Highlands, NJ: Humanities.

Zammito, J.H. (2004) *A Nice Derangement of Epistemes: Post-Positivism in The Study of Science From Quine to Latour.* Chicago, IL: University of Chicago Press.

PART 2

Central Issues
in Social Ontology

4

Naturalism: The Place of Society in Nature

Don Ross

INTRODUCTION

'Naturalism' about the ontology of society can most blandly be characterised as the belief that socialphenomena are among the class of natural phenomena. Contemporary scholars are apt to regard this thesis as bland because its denial seems quaint at best, if not outright unhinged, after a century and a half of development in the social sciences. There has, however, been a powerful tradition in Western culture that has understood the 'artificial' as a primary contrast class with the 'natural', and which has interpreted the social as a creation of human beings that stands over and against the natural realm. Often this understanding has incorporated a normative component, sometimes positive and sometimes negative. To many enlightenment thinkers, society in its 'civilised' form represented transcendence of anarchic, dangerous and amoral nature. By exact contrast, the romantic temperament has frequently conceived society as a tyrannical obstacle to human realisation of a 'natural' and more harmonious style of being. This polarisation of perspectives is by no means a merely historical phenomenon; it continues to resonate in popular culture. Film plots, for example, abound with 'noble savages'[1] who achieve authenticity and moral realisation by rebelling against 'unnatural' social conventions and oppressive norms, as well as with cool-headed heroes who use reason, inventiveness and clever technology to rescue life, limb and good order from rampaging sharks, bears, earthquakes – and impulsive savages.

The pervasiveness of the idea that the social is not natural is, arguably but plausibly, an inheritance of doctrines associated with the great Middle Eastern religions. St. Augustine maintained that the city on earth should aspire to approximate the City of God, that is to say, to transcendence of the natural order. The idea that human willpower, rather than contingent causal regularities, might be or might become the dominant regulator of social relationships has been a recurrent feature of transformative political ideologies, of both left and right. For this reason, ideologues have tended to be particularly hostile to economics, the social science that is least optimistic about the deliberate engineering of large-scale social structures. Hegel argued that society evolves in the direction of an ideal, becoming progressively more rational and self-aware. On the other side, continuing to (mordantly) exploit the romantic theme, Sartre's version of existentialism held the network of interlocked social expectations to be the principal barrier to individual achievements of 'authenticity' – 'Hell is other people', as he famously put it.

However, the opposing view of the social as natural has never been absent from leading quarters of Western philosophy. For Aristotle society in the form of the city state is simultaneously the ideal and the natural context of life for people; as in his philosophy generally, the principal aim of his political and social thought is the reconciliation of *telos* and nature. In the early modern period, Hobbes was a thoroughgoing naturalist, notwithstanding his contrast between a 'state of nature' and the state established by a social contract. The animating idea of *Leviathan* (Hobbes, 1651/2010) is that it is natural for people to value their security and well being and to create regulatory institutions in service of them. Hume, whose game-theoretic intuitions were astonishingly well developed in their completeness, clarity and reliability, repeatedly explained moral rules governing social conduct as explicit regimentations of what we now recognise as equilibrium behaviour in coordination games and other collective action problems. This deepened the foundations of Hobbesian naturalism, since it grounded the social order in 'natural' evolution rather than 'artificial' normative construction.

Inspired partly by the development of game theory, and partly by the turn to evolutionary foundations in recent psychology and anthropology, the Humean project of naturalising regulatory institutions (including moral codes) by identifying them as equilibria of evolutionary games is among the most flourishing enterprises in the social sciences and in social philosophy. (For exemplary instances from among a very large set of possible citations, see Bicchieri, 2005; Binmore, 1994, 1998, 2005; Skyrms, 1996, 2003; Joyce, 2006.) Gintis (2004) argues that evolutionary game theory unifies the social and behavioural sciences. By this he means

not only that it provides them with a shared method of analysis, but, more importantly, that it connects them with biology. This programme, if fully carried through, would amount to naturalisation in operational terms, as opposed to merely endorsing an assertion to the effect that the social does not stand outside of or against the natural.

Popular ambivalence notwithstanding, let us take it as given that social phenomena are natural in the sense of not transcending the contingent regularities studied by science. Because this merely denies a thesis that no contemporary scientist takes seriously, it implies almost nothing in the way of a positive thesis about the ontological status of society and sociality. In particular, it is silent on the extent to which an account of the psychological and biological foundations of the social might or might not *eliminate* the social as a distinctive kind by reducing it to properties of individuals. That is, it leaves open the question of whether efforts to operationally naturalise the social might turn out to vindicate reductive individualism, and thereby explain the social in naturalistic terms by explaining it away. It was such reductive individualism that Margaret Thatcher had in mind when she famously asserted that there is no such thing as society. In the philosophy of the past half century, this has been the main source of challenge to the idea that sociality has a distinctive place in the account of the natural world (Kincaid, 1997).

I will not concentrate attention on reductive individualism *within* social sciences (as opposed to in their general foundations), partly because this is the subject of another chapter (Chapter 9) of the present handbook. It is often asserted that neoclassical economics presupposes individualism, and in this respect denies a foundational assumption of sociology. I have argued elsewhere (Ross, forthcoming) that where economics is concerned this is a myth, notwithstanding the large number of economists who assent to it. In fact, individualism does no interesting work in economic theory, which treats any entity that consistently pursues goals as an agent, is untroubled by the possibility that such an agent might be an aggregation of other agents, and allows the possibility that the aggregate agent's properties might not factor neatly into properties of the agents from which it is aggregated. (For example, the aggregate agent's utility function might not be the utility function of any of the disaggregated agents, particularly if the former results from strategic interactions among the latter.) Even economists who continue to take preferences as 'given' are methodologically free to suppose that what 'gives' them are processes of social learning and adaptation. It is true that utility functions may not take one another as arguments, but this is a purely technical requirement that does not prevent an economist from describing relations of interdependency as complex as a particular case warrants. It is also true that many leading economists have been normative individualists, in the sense of holding that social welfare decomposes without residue into the aggregate welfare of individuals. But normative and descriptive individualism are independent theses.

The fact that no social science presupposes individualism, however, does not imply that the biological foundations of sociality might not turn out to be individualistic. Consider, for example, the dominant research tradition in ecology and ethology that aims at explaining grouping behaviour in animals. As reviewed in Krause and Ruxton (2002), this literature rigorously follows the paradigm of explaining the existence, size, stability, composition and geometric arrangement of herds, flocks, schools and other aggregations by reference to impacts of these variables on fitnesses of individual organisms. For example, animals in groups may be more likely to find food patches they can exploit, but suffer from competition with conspecifics in harvesting their discoveries. The ecology of grouping explores conditions under which one of these selection pressures trumps the other. Similarly, animals in groups may be less vulnerable to predators once spotted, but easier to locate in the first place. They may suffer fewer bites from flying parasites that

encounter more hosts across which to distribute attention, but be more vulnerable to parasites that breed in the tissues, cavities or fluids of fellow group members. The research attempting to tease apart such competing evolutionary influences takes grouping to be something individual animals, whose individuality is determined exogenously to the models, do or don't do for their own benefit. In this tradition, although there can be no group unless several organisms adopt grouping behaviour at the same time, the properties that explain properties of groups are all properties of individuals.

A main methodological bias that makes this approach to the study of grouping inherently individualistic is that it ignores the possibility of group, or multi-level, selection (Okasha, 2007; Sober and Wilson, 1998). The possibility of such selection was rejected by biologists for many years on grounds that it conflicted with individual fitness maximisation; less fit individuals that improve their prospects by sheltering within groups, or that sacrifice their own fitness for the advantage of their colleagues, should be out-competed by more fit invaders who have no greater reliance on the group than does the average individual from the population. Thus, if there are advantages to grouping for members of a given species, it should be irrelevant to expected fitness which group an individual finds itself in, and a disposition to herd or flock should be modelled as an individual trait like any other. However, Sober and Wilson (1998) caused a resurgence of interest in group selection by demonstrating the theoretical possibility that some group might have a *group-level property* that increases the relative fitness of its members so long as they enjoy the effects of the property by remaining affiliated. Suppose, for example, that members of one human group are culturally prepared to coordinate their activities so as to jointly plant, harvest and defend a crop, and this behaviour increases each member's fitness relative to that of members of a hunter-gatherer society even while the fitness of the hunter-gatherers is greater than the fitness of the farmers would be if the farmers were removed from their group. Suppose furthermore that the individual hunter-gatherers have characteristics that impede or block their incorporation into the agricultural community. In models of such processes, groups are selected in consequence of the way in which group-level properties affect individual-level fitness, so the tension identified by critics of earlier conceptions of group selection dissolves.

Group selection allows for the possibility that social properties irreducible to properties of individual organisms play a necessary role in empirically adequate models of evolutionary trajectories. As the example above suggests, this principle seems especially well motivated in application to cultural evolution. It is familiar from human history that individuals in the grip of a functionally inferior practice in one area might annihilate or genetically swamp people with functionally superior beliefs in that area if, in addition, the former live in a group that has evolved infrastructure to collectively manufacture and deploy deadlier weapons (Diamond, 1997).

In wondering about the natural foundations of sociality, we should be interested in the question of how much of the work individual-level selection can do. In real evolutionary processes on Earth (as opposed to processes in models and simulations) is the cognitive capacity for culture a necessary prior condition for the operation of group selection? If so, one aspect of individualism would be vindicated: recognisably human individuals, we would conclude, had to arise first and then these smart creatures constructed groups whose fates were influenced by group-level properties. The opposing alternative idea would be that group selection produced groups of organisms that could evolve, thanks to the social properties of their groups, into recognisably human individuals. Defenses of this increasingly popular idea are given by Donald (1991), Boyd and Richerson (1985), Tomasello (1999),

Sterelny (2003), Richerson and Boyd (2004) and Ross (2006).

Krause and Ruxton (2002) are aware of controversies arising from the new model of group selection. However, they avoid appeal to such models in accounting for grouping behaviour in non-human animals for two reasons. First, they say, 'the evidence supporting group selectionist theory remains scarce, and in part anecdotal' (p. 121). Second, they add, 'multi-level selection models are not simply wrong, they are just another way of looking at aspects of natural selection that are less controversial when described in other ways. They are not describing a fundamentally different process of evolution, just a different way of representing the theory we already accept' (p. 121). What Krause and Ruxton allude to here is an earlier suggestion of theirs that so-called group selection is merely frequency-dependent selection. It is difficult to understand how both of these alleged objections to group selection – that it might not actually occur, and that it is merely common-and-garden selection re-labelled – could be thought to apply at the same time.

Regardless of its justification, Krause and Ruxton's skepticism would encourage us to suppose that irreducible social processes, if there are any, remain *sui generis* in nature, arising when and only when humans developed culture. This would be one way in which proponents of the old hostility to naturalistic accounts of society might win the substance of the argument, even if they granted that society is natural in the sense of not being *super*natural. If it is concluded that people construct society in something like the way in which they construct explicit institutions, then there is a *sense* in which the view of society as artificial would be vindicated.

In the remainder of this chapter I will review the basis for a radically different perspective. According to this view, sociality is pervasive throughout the biological realm. Within the framework I will review, there is no need to ask whether this or that modeling approach unifies the social sciences with the biological ones, because most of biology is a kind of social science to begin with.

SOCIALISATION AS AN EVOLUTIONARY PHASE SHIFT #1: MULTICELLULARITY

For most humans, the paradigmatic instances of individual organisms are, like humans themselves, large multicellular organisms. This is somewhat ironic, since on the conception of community that we readily and uncontroversially apply to groups of people, large multicellular organisms are also communities.

Multicellularity involves more than mere grouping of cells, in the sense of grouping reviewed by Krause and Ruxton as discussed above. It crucially requires specialisation of function, in consequence of which most cells in the multicellular organism could not live independently. Szathmáry and Wolpert (2003) operationalise multicellularity as follows: 'If at least some parts of the metabolism or the information processing of the cells (confined to a single cell in unicellular organisms) are shared in a coordinated manner by all cells of the colony, we are dealing with a multicellular organism' (p. 272). Their review of current literature finds uncertainty as to when such organisms first arose; it might have been as long ago as 1.2 billion years, or as recently as 850 million years. However, it is clear that the conquest of the global ecology by multicellular assemblages of eukaryotes occurred at the beginning of the Cambrian period. Though they have co-evolved ever since with continuing trajectories of successful prokaryotes and unicellular eukaryotes, their development brought natural selection into operation at entirely new scales, both temporal and spatial. (It should not be supposed, however, that evolution necessarily follows a trajectory that reliably works up from simplicity towards complexity; there is evidence, for example, that unicellular yeast had multicellular ancestors.)

Identification of some organisms as multicellular implies, as a matter of logical priority, a basis for distinguishing cells. Cells are differentiated by varying sequences of active genes; the basis of cellular individuality is variation in biochemical expression and response. Hence at the level of organismic sociality the analogy to the familiar reduction of human social processes to individual behaviour would be reduction of biology to biochemistry. However, though all biological processes have crucial biochemical aspects, such reduction does not comprehensively describe the direction of biological research. (See Rosenberg, 2006 for a dissenting view, and Dupré, 2007 for a rejoinder to Rosenberg. See also Kincaid, 1997.)

How did multicellularity arise, and which main obstacles did it need to overcome in order to stabilise? This has been a subject of intense interest in recent evolutionary theory. Buss (1987) argues that a crucial evolutionary wedge was provided by organisms in which the germ line was open to genetic variation arising during ontogeny; such variations were then accumulated into sophisticated, replicable epigenetic programmes. This raises the same question at the level of fundamental phylogeny as has been addressed with respect to cultural evolution in the debate over human group selection. How did variants that favour *both* the proliferation of the cell lineage and the fitness of the multicellular organism win out against selfish variants that favour the replication of the cell lineage *at the expense of* the cellular society? Buss describes a long period of neglect of this question in the history of biology, for which he identifies August Weismann as having been significantly responsible. During the development of the grand evolutionary synthesis, Buss maintains, Weismann and his followers introduced a fundamental bias in favour of taking complex organisms for granted. This mainly resulted from lack of emphasis on the fact that the germ-soma barrier had to be constructed by natural selection. Correcting for this, Buss develops a model that represents patterns in embryonic cleavage, gastrulation, mosaicism, induction and competence as built from conflict between the evolutionary interests of cells and those of multicellular organisms, expressing the thesis that heterochrony (variations in the timing of developmental events) is the principal basis for evolutionary change in complex organisms.

Szathmáry and Wolpert (2003) ask whether the transition to multicellularity was 'difficult' (p. 287). Their first answer is 'not at all', on grounds that multicellularity has evolved more than twenty times (Bonner, 2000). What this in itself shows, however, is only that there is some recurrent advantage to sociality among cells, so that it constitutes a strong basin of attraction for natural selection. However, most such evolutionary developments stalled at the stage of simple aggregates, such as slime moulds. Such colonies do not develop from eggs that implement Buss's epigenetic programmes, and therefore do not give rise to the complex patterns of heterochrony he identifies. As Szathmáry and Wolpert (2003) go on to say 'there are only three lineages that produced complex organisms: plants, animals and fungi. Three hits in 3.5 billion years are not that many. So one is left with the feeling of some extrinsic or intrinsic difficulties'. The primary extrinsic difficulty they hypothesise (following Maynard Smith and Szathmáry, 1995) is a shortage of oxygen before the large-scale development of plants. In addition they suggest two main intrinsic obstacles. The first is the problem of suppressing cell division across an increasing array of cell types. 'As Szent-Gregory once remarked, the fact that cancer cells divide like hell is not a miracle; the fact that most cells of the organism do not is amazing, however' (p. 287). The second intrinsic problem 'may be the complexity of development as such' (p. 288). By this they mean just what Buss does: 'What is required for a complex organism … is complex development, which in turn requires complex regulation in the network of genes'.

In wondering, then, whether nature 'sees' sociality as a fundamental kind of process, we may be led towards an affirmative answer by recognising a deep qualitative difference between aggregative processes that build 'herds' of cells (e.g. slime moulds) and processes of transcription-translation separation that lead to richly variant, epigenetically controlled heterochrony. The latter, but not the former, introduces a phase-shift into an evolutionary process, in the sense that selection thereafter occurs at scales that were not previously possible as platforms. So far as the history of life is concerned, the Cambrian explosion was not just 'more of the same'.

Why, after it finally arose, was multicellularity promoted by selection? Lachmann et al. (2003: 344–345) review several advantages it offers. These include various benefits of size: larger organisms can disperse more widely, and so gain insurance against local environmental changes; they enjoy reduced ratio of surface area to volume, which allows for slower exchanges with their external environments (e.g. protection from heat loss and maintaining higher osmotic pressure); they are usually better equipped to escape from predation by smaller organisms and to consume larger, more nutritious prey; they are subject to less random motion in watery solutions and windy conditions; and they have internal cavities they can use as warehouses for storing nutrients. Another class of advantages derives from changes in temporal scales: multicellular organisms can reduce their effective mutation rate relative to the total number of cell divisions by controlling the rate of division of somatic versus germ cells. A third general class of benefits follows from specialisation and information-processing redundancy: cells in multicellular coalitions can concentrate on efficient processing of particular chemical resources to the exclusion of others, and can devote attention to specific information from the environment that they then pool with the reports of other specialists, yielding collective wealth for the reasons made familiar by economics.

We can summarise all of these advantages as deriving from scale shifts. At the most abstract level, the payoffs to such shifts need not simply be conceptualised in terms of getting larger, less volatile and more physically powerful. Changing scale allows for exploitation of whole niches – that is, classes of resources – that are not available for harvesting by processes and organisms on other scales. This explains both why evolution broadly trends in the direction of simplicity to complexity, and why this general trajectory is sometimes reversible. On the one hand, the basic thermodynamic asymmetry in our part of the universe precluded a phylogenetic pattern of starting with large, slow creatures and then shrinking and speeding some of them up to exploit small-scale niches. On the other hand, larger-scale niches can become more crowded over time, or locally unproductive, and shed capacity for tenants to micro-scales; thus yeast cells, to cite an earlier example, apparently abandoned the multicellular strategy at some point, while following ecological disasters such as the K-T impact the very largest organisms tended to downsize (though most did not scale back in complexity while doing so).

Development of multicellularity required the evolution of mechanisms to mediate conflict among units. Cells are in principle interchangeable, so can be predicted to compete with one another. Even specialists will often be under pressure to adopt the strategies of others that earn higher individual returns. Sexual reproduction, which improves adaptiveness at the collective level, implies that lineages can change partners between generations, and therefore have imperfectly aligned interests. The very germline-soma distinction that facilitated multicellularity generates asymmetric transmission and strength of kinship association among types of cells. Replication rates and mutational spaces may be less than perfectly coordinated.

Michod (2003) and Lachmann et al. (2003) review widespread mechanisms of conflict mediation to contain these pressures. Specialisation is plausibly the most crucial such mechanism: lineages of somatic cells devoted to vegetative functions, for example, typically have no evolutionary future if they defect from service to the community.

Most multicellular organisms begin life through a unicellular bottleneck, increasing kinship. This imposes the cost of an upper bound on propagule size, which presumably pays for itself in limitation of scope for conflict. Germ lines are sequestered early in the process of cell division; this reduces threats of deleterious mutations at the cost of fewer cells available for wider ranges of somatic function. Germ line cells are protected from metabolic influences to limit mutation frequencies. Organism size is often strictly capped by epigenetic programmes (though less in some species, such as crocodiles, than in others), which reduces the potential advantage to cells of engaging in selfish growth races. A specialised police force – the immune system – attacks cancerous cells, though in the context of dynamic arms races that yield no possibility of ultimate victory. Finally, processes of programmed cell death confine many cells to limited-term service, which favours their pitching in to contribute to current organismal projects – probably at the very significant general cost of the ultimate senescence and death of the individual community as a whole.

Blackstone and Kirkwood (2003) suggest that there may be a direct relationship among programmed cell death, the origin of multicellularity in the biochemistry of the eukaryotic cell, and the relationship between mitochondria and host cells. They summarise their hypothesis as follows:

> Given the crucial role of programmed cell death in regulating cell-level conflicts, implication of mitochondria in this process provides the tantalizing suggestion that the evolutionary dynamics of the simple-to-complex cell transition may subsequently have influenced the unicellular-to-multicellular transition. Likely, as groups of bacteria were evolving into complex eukaryotic cells, these emerging groups were simultaneously evolving into multicellular communities and kin groups. The evolution of these highest-level communities may have been facilitated by the recruitment of lower-level (i.e. mitochondrial) pathways for the regulation of the intermediate level (i.e. the individual cell). In other words, mechanisms of conflict resolution within the eukaryotic cell may have been immediately co-opted into mechanisms of conflict resolution between eukaryotic cells within larger

communities ... Tri-level evolutionary dynamics may have enhanced the tendency of eukaryotes to form multicellular groups and ultimately contributed to the emergence of the crown groups: plants, fungi, and animals.

(Blackstone and Kirkwood, 2003: 322)

This hypothesis reminds us that the emergence of new scales for evolutionary competition did not always proceed gradually from stage to stage, with dynamics at one scale consolidated before another arose. Compare recent views of the history of human communities and social intelligence – the subject of the next section – which suggest that as new human communication conventions were called forth by agricultural lifestyles, they were immediately co-opted to regulate much larger societies than had previously been possible, thus deepening social and economic interdependence on multiple scales.

Another crucial dimension to the evolution of multicellularity was the refinement of new mechanisms of intercellular signaling necessary for coordination. Szathmáry and Wolpert (2003: 275–278) argue that most of these had their basis in pre-multicellular lineages, indeed sometimes in prokaryotic ones, but that 'concomitant with the origin of multicellularity, these signaling systems have undergone radical evolution toward increased complexity' (p. 278). Principal pre-adaptations for signaling include various proteins and protein kinases that are the basis for pheromones and other information that is transduced across cell membranes. The example given by the authors of radical evolution for complexity is a comparison of two fully sequenced species of cyanobacteria. The unicellular *Synechocystis* has 3200 expressed proteins, while the multicellular *Nostoc* has 7400. As we will review in the next section, such explosions in information-processing capacity are hallmarks of the emergence of sociality at all scales.

Multicellularity not only involves the integration of a general community of cells to constitute the whole complex organism. In plants and animals with specialised parts, sub-communities can be distinguished

following the principles of Chandebois's (1983) 'cell sociology'. (For discussions of her principles in the context of contemporary cell biology, see Bolker, 2000 and Gass and Hall, 2007). This theory of collective cell behaviour focuses on what she calls 'autonomous progression', in which developing cell structures can continue to grow when explanted and cultured in vitro, but only if the integrity of the cell group is maintained. In contrast to the standard interpretation of embryonic induction, Chandebois interpreted such processes as indicating that some cell groups have collective properties that are not simply aggregates of properties of the individual cells. Cell groups with such properties are referred to as 'modules' by Bolker (2000) and Gass and Hall (2007). Their collective properties are based on intercellular signalling of a type that Chandebois called 'homotypic interactions'. According to Maclean and Hall (1987), the mechanisms for such signalling include paracrine signalling, cytoplasmic connections (in animal cells) and plasmodesmata (in plant cells).

The various phenomena just reviewed as associated with the evolution and maintenance of multicellularity – coalition formation, intergroup conflict, regulation and policing of outlaws and signalling for coordination – are the daily preoccupation of all social sciences, but are also ubiquitous throughout the life sciences generally. This justifies the idea that sociality is a basic kind of natural process, at least on Earth, and that it vastly pre-dates human culture. Sociality is a scale shift in the dynamics of a selection process; moreover, it is almost the *only* mechanism for shifts in the upward direction, given the myopia of natural selection that must make the best of the platforms from which it engineers novelties.

SOCIALISATION AS A BIOLOGICAL PHASE SHIFT #2: INTELLIGENCE

Let us adopt the following operational stipulation for what shall be meant by 'sociality' in a population of distinct organisms. A group of organisms constitutes a *society* when

1   the expected individual fitness of each organism is partly a function of the differential fitness of the group;
2   individuals are to some extent restricted, by factors going beyond geographical proximity or physical barriers, in their ability to switch groups;
3   most group members are associated with some other members, aside from mates, direct ancestors and direct descendants, in ways that influence their expected fitness, and;
4   random re-permutations of the individuals figuring in these within-group associations would produce wide variations in fitness distributions after sex and age differences were controlled for.

This stipulation is not intended as an analysis of the concept of sociality. The point of it is simply to achieve approximate reference to prototypical instances of the networks of social relations we find among organisms. It should not be expected to neatly sort all sets of animals into social and asocial, without borderline cases; natural selection by its nature almost never produces such crisp boundaries.

Where property 4 describes a group, the explanation for this fact must to some extent appeal to socially relevant distinctions among individuals. Lest sociality reduce to mere herding, the phenomenon reviewed by Krause and Ruxton, it must involve radiation and stabilisation of non-identical social roles. In social insects, the roles in question are built on distinctions of caste, for example, between workers and soldiers. In social birds and mammals, they may be distinctions with respect to dominance status, personality or history of remembered reciprocity.

One form of sociality that evolution has produced multiple times – in many species of hymenoptera, in termites, and in two species of mole rat – is eusociality based on sterile castes, members of which promote their inclusive fitness by promoting the direct fitness of their siblings (Wilson and Hölldobler, 2006). This ecological pattern seems to be encouraged by haplodiploid sex determination, in consequence of which sterile sisters have more genes in common than they would with hypothetical sexually produced offspring. However, haplodiploidy is neither necessary nor sufficient for eusociality, since most hymenoptera are not eusocial and neither termites nor mole rats are haplodiploid.

To the extent that eusociality is explained entirely by reference to kin selection, which in some traditional models reduces erstwhile group properties to fitness maximisation by individual genes (e.g. Wilson, 2005), it may be wondered whether it is fundamentally different from the kind of aggregative grouping reviewed by Krause and Ruxton. An older but still vigorous tradition in biology (Lumsden, 1982; Queller and Strassman, 2002; Wheeler, 1911) models eusocial colonies as single organisms, to which the component members stand in a relationship analogous to that between cells and multicellular individuals. As Ratnieks and Reeve (1992) and Yang (2007) argue, to the extent that this perspective is useful for predicting and explaining aspects of eusocial ethology, the same pressures for regulation of internal conflict arise as were reviewed in the previous section with respect to dynamics among members of multicellular coalitions. And indeed we find instances of most of the same generic regulatory mechanisms. In addition, Yang (2007) surveys evidence of wide variation among eusocial structures within species that have their origins in path-dependent colony development interacting with environmental contingencies. Thus there is no persuasive basis for denying that eusociality is genuine manifestation of sociality, and one which constitutes a recurrent basin of attraction for selection.

Induction on the distribution of complex sociality in animals by species indicates that if sacrifice of direct reproduction by specialised castes is one principal evolutionary path to it, the other is coevolution of distinctive social roles and intelligence. To see this, let us assemble, on a casual observational basis, two lists of vertebrate species. In the first list include animals that are known to typically be capable of relatively rapid learning of specially tailored adaptive responses to novel contingencies – that is, animals that demonstrate qualitatively enhanced cognitive plasticity, both in the wild and in ethological experiments. This list (making no serious effort at comprehensiveness)[2] might include apes, monkeys, canines, toothed whales, pinnepeds (especially walruses), elephants, hyenas, rats, raccoons, pigs, corvids and parrots. In the second list include animals that engage in social interactions that transcend herding, satisfying to a marked extent the operationalisation of sociality offered at the beginning of the present section. The two lists would be more or less exactly coextensional. Note that both lists would exclude some animals closely related to others on the lists, indicating that selection has produced coevolution of high cognitive capacity and complex sociality on several occasions.

The so-called 'Machiavellian intelligence' hypothesis (Byrne and Whiten, 1988; Dunbar, 1998; Whiten and Byrne, 1997) has gained wide currency as an explanation for high intelligence based on the demands of social life. According to this hypothesis, the main selection pressure that gave rise to advanced cognitive facility in various species was the value to individuals of remembering particular social colleagues' identities, along with their varying track records of reciprocal cooperation and tendencies to engage in conflict over mates, food, status and other resources. In its basic form, the Machiavellian model takes the existence of social relations as exogenous and explains the evolution of intelligence as a response to it. More sophisticated versions are explicitly coevolutionary. The efficiency advantages of learned specialisation within groups – as contrasted, for present purposes, with herds of generalists, rather than with epigenetically controlled specialists as in ants and bees – have been explored in rich detail by economists. The capacity to learn specialised roles plausibly depends on a capacity to learn contingent relations in general. Then as individuals become reliant on special knowledge or talents of others – for example, as elephants that must cross deserts take to following those who have reliably located water on previous treks – the selective value of memory resources that can support reciprocity is encouraged. If group selection is operative, and if groups that find cooperative equilibria in repeated games fare better than groups that are more prone to coordination failure, the result may be selection pressure for facility at social learning. Furthermore, such dynamics will tend to amplify the operation of group selection. An elephant who can remember who in her group is a reliable guide to water has an extra advantage in staying with *that* group, which might trump factors that favour her switching to another group. (This of course entails no denial that inclusive fitness considerations may *also* furnish key support for group stability.) Essentially, this form of speculative account consolidates Machiavellian intelligence with the Baldwin Effect (see Dennett, 1995; Weber and Depew, 2003).

Eusociality is inherently limited in the range of complementary specialists it can generate within a species, because each caste requires natural selection to produce a distinct epigenetic programme. By contrast, specialisation based on cognitive plasticity is in principle unlimited. In practice, however, it is bounded by the fact that complementary specialists only realise gains from trade efficiently if their expectations are coordinated. A novel specialist whose potential contributions can't be anticipated by other members of society will in general neither find nor profit from social relations. As will be discussed in the next section, in humans this constraint is relaxed to a unique degree by cultural structures made possible by the human signaling system. Before turning to the strange ecology of *H. sapiens*, however, let us say a bit more about the relationship between social stability and role specialisation in animals that achieve sociality by means of cognitive plasticity.

There has recently been a wave of interest among ethologists in the distribution of distinct types of *personality* in non-human animals. The personality construct refers to a particular animal's matrix of response dispositions with respect to the social emotions (e.g. rage, fear, lust, care, panic, play).[3] It maps expected ranges of intensities-of-response across a set of social emotion types to social situations (which are so far not, in the animal personality research literature, organised by any systematic theory). On the basis of such mappings, animal personalities are assigned as scalars on some or all independent dimensions of a five-factor model derived from human social psychology. The dimensions are neuroticism vs. emotional stability, agreeableness vs. antagonism, extraversion vs. introversion, openness vs. closedness (to new experiences) and conscientiousness vs. impulsiveness (Gosling and John, 1999).[4] While these constructs perform tolerably well in tests of criterion validity (Gosling and Vazire, 2002), they obviously represent compressions of more fine-grained underlying differences across ranges of behavioural dispositions. For this reason, most researchers have been reluctant to regard them as individually adaptive. It has heretofore been more common for personalities to be treated as non-adaptive variations within adaptive ranges of population-average behaviour. On this interpretation personality distributions are epiphenomena – stochastic products of development of underlying dispositions that stabilise at some point in an organism's maturation – so far as the explanation of sociality in terms of role specialisation is concerned.

Indications are emerging, however, of more interesting connections. Dall et al. (2004) argue that personalities may represent frequency-dependent equilibrium strategies in within-species evolutionary games that have polymorphic equilibria. It is premature to empirically evaluate this suggestion. To do so ethologists would need to design ranges of game-theoretic models of intraspecific dynamics, predict personality distributions within populations on the basis of these models, and then test the predictions.

Dall et al. (2004) describe no such tests as having yet been performed, though Dall (2004) interprets a field study by Dingemanse et al. (2004) of differential survival among great tit personality types under different levels of seasonal severity as evidence of matching of personality distributions to shifts in selection pressures. Investigation of this hypothesis is suggested as a promising road to greater understanding of sociality that transcends eusociality but falls qualitatively short of the complexity that is manifest in patterns and structures of human social interaction.

SOCIALISATION AS A BIOLOGICAL PHASE SHIFT #3: SOCIAL APES CONQUER THE WORLD

Humans are very unusual animals from an ecological point of view. The main respects in which this is so are obvious: they have penetrated every geographical niche type on earth except the bottom of the ocean; they integrate a range of tools into their behavioural repertoire to an extent that vastly outstrips that of any other animal; they massively transform their physical habitats to accommodate and amplify their security, comfort and access to resources; and their basic habits of feeding, mating and child-rearing vary much more than what is observed for any other species. All of these peculiarities complement and amplify one another in multifarious ways. They also all fundamentally rely on social cooperation based on division of labour. By contrast, an isolated human – say, one stranded on an island – is hardly ecologically unusual among mammals at all, except for his relative lack of competence at survival even given ample supplies of food and water and moderate climate.

It is of course for just this reason that so many people have distinguished the social from the natural, and that they have wondered only about the naturalness of *human* sociality. (No one has ever suggested, as far as I know, that dolphin or raven sociality is unnatural.) One other human property, also obviously social in its main function, has featured at least as large in the reasons people have given for setting themselves apart. This is the human signalling system, which has generally been regarded by both popular opinion and scholarly tradition as qualitatively unique in both its main properties and its range of applications and consequences. One should distinguish, however, between two different versions of the claim that language is a main basis for human specialness. According to one version, human brains first evolved the capacity for language, and this enabled their special social ecology to develop. The alternative hypothesis is that the human signalling system is not in itself sharply different from those used by other animals, but the human social niche allows it to be put to unique uses, particularly long-term storage of information, and meta-representation that allows humans to be self-conscious about their own participation in culture. A comprehensive and rigorous defense of the first thesis is given by Bickerton (1990). The second perspective is becoming increasingly popular. Arguments in its favour can be found in Ross (2007) and Tomesello (2008), among other sources. The relevance of this issue to the present topic is that the second perspective takes sociality to be fundamental to the nature of humans in a way that the first does not.

Defenders of both theses can agree, however, that the human capacity to store and widely share records of experience and examples for others to follow is fundamental to the species' prodigious recent accomplishments. Inventions and discoveries can be preserved and improved upon from generation to generation. More fundamentally, as philosophers have recently emphasised (Clark, 1997, 2004; Sterelny, 2003), cultural representations of the social, natural and technological order structure an individual human's thought itself, in several ways. First, individual people can use the cultural storehouse to expand both their long-term and their working memories. Without the standard algorithm for doing long number division on paper, for example, most people would not have been able to do long division at all in the days before electronic calculators. Second, the cultural record coordinates social agreement on what kinds of objects and processes there are, over and above those that evolution of perceptual judgment biases has settled for humans such as animals and water. Thus language canalises human options on what to think about, and prevents what would otherwise be continuous comedies of cross-reference in communication. Third, humans learn to use public linguistic structures to talk to themselves, and thereby cue the parallel processing association engines between their ears to simulate the kind of serial computation that makes abstract, orderly, logic-governed thought possible; this is in turn a prerequisite for the development of complex technology. This perspective corrects the venerable atomistic tradition in Western culture that imagines individually clever people rationally contracting to join forces and thereby giving rise to ('artificial') society. It is instead society that enables the distinctive forms of human cleverness.

The division of roles among humans goes far beyond mere variation in epigenetically developed personalities. Humans in addition vary, both between and within their cultural networks, with respect to kinds of preferences, styles of self-description, and sensitivity to different bases for forming beliefs. These are the basic dimensions of human *self-hood*, which are of overwhelming importance to people and are the basis for widespread normative individualism. People generally bond closely with particular others not just as representatives of personality types (or as instances of genetic relatives), but as distinctive selves. (Thus, for example, a person whose mate has lost their self to trauma or disease will not be consoled if the mate's personality type has remained constant.) Many, if not most, people will risk and even willingly embrace death in defence of the integrity of their self, with its distinctive record of associations, experiences, accomplishments, mistakes and ethical and ideological commitments. It is difficult – and rather pointless – to try to imagine how different human social organisation would be without this dimension of variation.

There is a hint of irony in this, because the basic rationale for humans' tendency to fiercely defend their self-integrity is that stability of the self is essential for coordination with others. Ross (2004, 2005, 2008) models the social role of the self as follows. By virtue of the complexity of human institutions, the range of games humans can encounter is open-ended and unpredictable. Furthermore, humans, but not other animals, can construct and circulate detailed records of their own games and the games of others throughout their societies. As a result, the lives of humans are dominated by repeated rather than one-shot games – to the point where, as indicated by a range of evidence from behavioral economics, when experimental human subjects are set into one-shot games they initially mistake them for repeated games and play accordingly for some time until learning corrects the error (Binmore et al., 1995; Ledyard, 1995; Sally, 1995). Humans therefore face not only a huge variety of game forms, but mainly play games in which the so-called 'folk theorem' applies, giving rise to multiple equilibria. In such circumstances, knowledge of ranges of distribution of personality types, and even knowledge mapping personality types onto specific individuals, will generally offer insufficient guidance for shared perceptions of game forms and then for finding equilibrium strategies once games are determined. A social species whose members cannot find equilibrium strategies in games with one another must either evolve away from sociality or face extinction. Thus, since social cooperation is fitness-promoting for people, natural selection has incentivised them to cultivate devices that help them jointly determine game structures and identify equilibria (though there is often conflict over which identified equilibria it would be best to play).

People therefore tend to avoid playing games with individuals whose selves they cannot model. A person with whom others will not play games is a person in a desperate predicament. (She is also a biological entity with a low fitness coefficient, though this in itself might not matter to her as a person.) This explains the overwhelming importance people attach to their selves. Selves are necessary devices for playing successful coordination games among people, and coordination games are the basic ecological tasks facing people.

According to an increasingly prevalent *narrative theory* of selfhood (see Bruner, 1992, 2002; Ross, 2005; Dennett, 1991), selves are social constructions of a special sort, which probably have no counterparts among other animals (except, perhaps, some socialised by people, such as Alex the Parrot in Pepperberg (1999)). A self is a narrative construct similar to a character in a novel,[5] a virtual object 'spun' in public discourse and stabilised by the network of social expectations to which it gives rise. Humans begin to tell simple stories with themselves as objects when they are children, picking up on cues suggested first by parents and later, and more influentially, by peers (Harris, 2007). The child's contributions to these stories are (unless the child is neglected) enthusiastically reinforced when the contributions are narratively consistent with what has already been developed, and with prevailing social norms. Within the limits of such norms, distinctiveness is typically encouraged, though there is wide cultural variation on the domains in which distinctiveness is allowed. Early in a self-narration, many possibilities remain open; but as people get older consistency requirements cause the possibility space to become narrower. This reduced space *is* the self; the reduction is what enables others, along with the subject herself, to predict what the person will do across a range of situations and to thereby enter into cooperative projects and exchanges that exploit division of labour, and build the cultural artifacts with which *H sapiens* has conquered the planet.

Since the human cycle of invention, cultural representation and reinvention exploded in very recent evolutionary history, selection for dimensions of sociality has operated on multiple, entirely novel scales. This continues a pattern which, I have suggested here, has characterised the natural development of sociality since some eukaryotic cells formed into teams of specialists. New possibilities for complementarity in resource harvesting open new niches for the operation of selection. This in turn begets new forms of sociality. Thus one reasonable organising principle from which the narrative of the natural history of life on earth can be written is that of the extension and increasing complexity of the social. It should not be concluded that this process is bound to go on indefinitely; humans may bring about their own extinction (Rees, 2003), and if they do so, it will be sociality itself that will have turned out to be unstable at a certain scale. Churchland (1988) offers the interesting speculation that perhaps the reason we've found no trace of other intelligent life in our galaxy is that intelligence capable of technological progress is inherently unstable and tends to flicker only briefly before self-extinguishing. If there should happen to be such a limit, however, it would be entirely appropriate to regard it as natural.

NOTES

1 Contemporary noble savages generally live modern urban lifestyles. Often they work for police forces, or as private detectives. Both their nobility and their savagery consist in their disposition to break the rules, in service of 'basic', uncorrupted, moral values. The popularity of this trope has been remarkably enduring since the 1930s, and it seems to be found in every culture that produces entertainment in modern media.

2 For a compendium of the sort of research that will gradually produce a less casual basis for comparison, see de Waal and Tyack (2003).

3 This list is taken from Panksepp (2001). There is not yet complete consensus among behavioural scientists as to how the social emotions should be categorised. My use of Panksepp's list should be taken as merely exemplary.

4 Most animals do not admit of measurable variation on the last dimension.

5 Though Dennett (1991) appeals to this analogy because he assumes his readers will have thought about where characters in novels come from more than they will have thought about where selves come from, in one sense it reverses figure and ground. People are able to understand the idea of a character in a novel because they already understand the idea of the self, even if they have never thought explicitly or theoretically about it.

REFERENCES

Bicchieri, C. (2005) *The Grammar of Society.* Cambridge: Cambridge University Press.

Bickerton, D. (1990) *Language and Species.* Chicago: University of Chicago Press.

Binmore, K. (1994) *Game Theory and the Social Contract, Volume One: Playing Fair.* Cambridge, MA: MIT Press.

Binmore, K. (1998) *Game Theory and the Social Contract, Volume Two: Just Playing.* Cambridge, MA: MIT Press.

Binmore, K. (2005) *Natural Justice.* Oxford: Oxford University Press.

Binmore, K., Gale, J. and Samuelson, L. (1995) 'Learning to be perfect: The ultimatum game', *Games and Economic Behavior,* 8: 56–90.

Blackstone, N. and Kirkwood, T. (2003) 'Mitochondria and programmed cell death: "Slave revolt" or community homeostasis?', in P. Hammerstein (ed.) *Genetic and Cultural Evolution of Cooperation.* Cambridge, MA: MIT Press. pp. 309–325.

Bolker, J. (2000) 'Modularity in development and why it matters to evo-devo', *American Zoologist,* 70: 770–776.

Bonner, J. (2000) *First Signals: The Evolution of Multicellular Development.* Princeton: Princeton University Press.

Boyd, R. and Richerson, P. (1985) *Culture and the Evolutionary Process.* Chicago: University of Chicago Press.

Bruner, J. (1992) *Acts of Meaning.* Cambridge, MA: Harvard University Press.

Bruner, J. (2002) *Making Stories: Law, Literature, Life.* New York: Farrar, Strauss and Giroux.

Buss, L. (1987) *The Evolution of Individuality.* Princeton: Princeton University Press.

Byrne, R. and Whiten, A. (eds) (1988). *Machiavellian Intelligence: Social Expertise and the Evolution of Intellect in Monkeys, Apes and Humans.* Oxford: Oxford University Press.

Chandebois, R. (1983) *Automation in Animal Development: A New Theory Derived From the Concept of Cell Sociology.* J. Faber trans. Basil: Karger.

Churchland, P. (1988) *Matter and Consciousness.* 2nd edition. Cambridge, MA: MIT Press.

Clark, A. (1997) *Being There.* Cambridge, MA: MIT Press.

Clark, A. (2004) *Natural Born Cyborgs.* Oxford: Oxford University Press.

Dall, S. (2004) 'Behavioral biology: Fortune favours bold *and* shy personalities', *Current Biology*, 14: R470–R472.

Dall, S., Houston, A. and McNamara, J. (2004) 'The behavioural ecology of personality: Consistent individual differences from an adaptive perspective', *Ecology Letters*, 8: 734–739.

de Waal, F. and Tyack, P. (eds) (2003) *Animal Social Complexity.* Cambridge, MA: Harvard University Press.

Dennett, D. (1991) *Consciousness Explained.* Boston: Little Brown.

Dennett, D. (1995) *Darwin's Dangerous Idea.* New York: Simon and Schuster.

Diamond, J. (1997) *Guns. Germs and Steel.* New York: W. W. Norton.

Dingemanse, N., Both, C., Drent, P. and Tinbergen, J. (2004) 'Fitness consequences of avian personalities in a fluctuating environment', *Proceedings of the Royal Society of London B: Biological Sciences*, 271: 847–852.

Donald, M. (1991) *The Origins of the Modern Mind.* Cambridge, MA: Harvard University Press.

Dunbar, R. (1998) *Grooming, Gossip and the Evolution of Language.* Cambridge, MA: Harvard University Press.

Dupré, J. (2007) 'Is biology reducible to the laws of physics? Review of Alexander Rosenberg', *Darwinian Reductionism: Or, How to Stop Worrying and Love Molecular Biology. American Scientist*, 95: 274–276.

Gass, G. and Hall, B. (2007) 'Collectivity in context: Modularity, cell sociology and the neural crest', *Biological Theory*, 2: 349–359.

Gintis, H. (2004) 'Towards the unity of the human behavioral sciences', *Politics, and Economics*, 3: 37–57.

Gosling, S. and John, O. (1999) 'Personality dimensions in nonhuman animals: A cross-species review', *Current Directions in Psychological Science*, 8: 69–75.

Gosling, S. and Vazire, S. (2002) 'Are we barking up the right tree? Evaluating a comparative approach to personality', *Journal of Research in Personality*, 36: 607–614.

Harris, J. (2007) *No Two Alike.* New York: Norton.

Hobbes, T. (1651/2010). *Leviathan*, ed. I. Shapiro. New Haven: Yale University Press.

Joyce, R. (2006) *The Evolution of Morality.* Cambridge, MA: MIT Press.

Kincaid, H. (1997) *Individualism and the Unity of Science.* Lanham, MD: Rowman and Littlefield.

Krause, J. and Ruxton, G. (2002) *Living in Groups.* Oxford: Oxford University Press.

Lachmann, M., Blackstone, N., Haig, D., Kowald, A., Michod, R., Szathmáry, E., Werren, J. and Wolpert, L. (2003) 'Group report: Cooperation and conflict in the evolution of genomes, cells, and multicellular organisms', in P. Hammerstein (ed.) *Genetic and Cultural Evolution of Cooperation.* Cambridge, MA: MIT Press. pp. 327–356.

Ledyard, J. (1995) 'Public goods: A survey of experimental research', in J. Kagel and A. Roth (eds) *The Handbook of Experimental Economics.* Princeton: Princeton University Press. pp. 111–194.

Lumsden, C. (1982) 'The social regulation of physical castes: The superorganism revived', *Journal of Theoretical Biology*, 95: 749–781.

Maclean, N. and Hall, B. (1987) *Cell Commitment and Differentiation.* Cambridge: Cambridge University Press.

Maynard Smith, J. and Szathmáry, E. (1995) *The Major Transitions in Evolution.* Oxford: W.H. Freeman.

Michod, R. (2003) 'Conflict mediation in multicellular organisms', in P. Hammerstein (ed.) *Genetic and Cultural Evolution of Cooperation.* Cambridge, MA: MIT Press. pp. 291–307.

Okasha, S. (2007) *Evolution and the Levels of Selection.* Oxford: Oxford University Press.

Panksepp, J. (2001) 'The neuro-evolutionary cusp between emotions and cognitions', *Evolution and Cognition*, 7: 141–161.

Pepperberg, I. (1999) *The Alex Studies: Cognitive and Communicative Abilities of Grey Parrots.* Cambridge, MA: Harvard University Press.

Queller, D. and Strassman, J. (2002) 'The many selves of social insects', *Science*, 296: 311–313.

Ratnieks, F. and Reeve, H. (1992) 'Conflict in single-queen hymenopteran societies: The structure of conflict and processes that reduce actual conflict', *Journal of Theoretical Biology*, 158: 33–65.

Rees, M. (2003) *Our Final Hour.* New York: Basic Books.

Richerson, P. and Boyd, R. (2004) *Not By Genes Alone.* Chicago: University of Chicago Press.

Rosenberg, A. (2006) *Darwinian Reductionism: Or, How to Stop Worrying and Love Molecular Biology.* Chicago: University of Chicago Press.

Ross, D. (2004) 'Meta-linguistic signaling for coordination amongst social agents', *Language Sciences*, 26: 621–642.

Ross, D. (2005) *Economic Theory and Cognitive Science: Microexplanation.* Cambridge, MA: MIT Press.

Ross, D. (2006) 'The economics and evolution of selves', *Journal of Cognitive Systems Research*, 7: 246–258.

Ross, D. (2007) '*H sapiens* as ecologically special: What does language contribute?', *Language Sciences*, 29: 710–731.

Ross, D. (2008) 'Classical game theory, socialization and the rationalization of conventions', *Topoi*, 27: 57–72.

Ross, D. (forthcoming) 'The economic agent: not human, but important', in U. Mäki (ed.) *Handbook of the Philosophy of Science*, vol. 13: *Economics.* Amsterdam: Elsevier.

Sally, D. (1995) 'Conversation and cooperation in social dilemmas: A meta-analysis of experiments from 1958 to 1992', *Rationality and Society*, 7: 58–92.

Skyrms, B. (1996) *Evolution of the Social Contract.* Cambridge: Cambridge University Press.

Skyrms, B. (2003) *The Stag Hunt and the Evolution of Social Structure.* Cambridge: Cambridge University Press.

Sober, E. and Wilson, D. S. (1998) *Unto Others.* Cambridge, MA: Harvard University Press.

Sterelny, K. (2003) *Thought in a Hostile World.* Oxford: Blackwell.

Szathmáry, E. and Wolpert, L. (2003) 'The transition from single cells to multicellularity', in P. Hammerstein (ed.) *Genetic and Cultural Evolution of Cooperation.* Cambridge, MA: MIT Press. pp. 271–290.

Tomasello, M. (1999) *The Cultural Origins of Human Cognition.* Cambridge, MA: Harvard University Press.

Tomasello, M. (2008) *Origins of Human Communication.* Cambridge, MA: MIT Press.

Weber, B. and Depew, D. (eds) (2003) *Evolution and Learning: The Baldwin Effect Reconsidered.* Cambridge, MA: MIT Press.

Wheeler, W. (1911) 'The ant-colony as an organism', *Journal of Morphology*, 22: 307–325.

Whiten, A. and Byrne, R. (1997) *Machiavellian Intelligence II.* Cambridge: Cambridge University Press.

Wilson, E. (2005) 'Kin selection as the key to altruism: Its rise and fall', *Social Research*, 72: 159–168.

Wilson, E. and Hölldobler, B. (2006) 'Eusociality: Origin and consequences', *Proceedings of the National Academy of Sciences*, 102: 13367–13371.

Yang, A. (2007) 'Thinking outside the embryo: The superorganism as a model for evodevo studies', *Biological Theory*, 2: 398–408.

5

Language and Society

Frank Hindriks

Society is socially constructed. There can be little doubt about this. How it is constructed and by what means is less obvious. Some believe that language plays an essential role in the social construction of society. In this chapter, I ask whether this is indeed the case. It is clear that language plays a crucial role in many social phenomena. Uniting two people in holy matrimony, arresting a criminal, and adjourning a meeting are done at least in part by means of words. Given the prevailing conventions they could not be done in other ways. Outside of particular conventional contexts it is imaginable that words would not be used. Nevertheless, it seems that some publicly understood signal or symbol has to be used. It is, for instance, conceivable that two people get married by both of them receiving the same otherwise unique stamp in their passports. For the purposes of this chapter language can be understood broadly so as to include conventional symbols of all kinds. Given such a broad use of the term "language" the imagined procedure for getting married would involve language after all. The question of this chapter can then be reformulated as the question whether public or conventional symbols are essential for the existence of society. Even though they are in fact crucial for many social phenomena as these are shaped in particular contexts, it is far from obvious that conventional symbols are prerequisites in some deep(er) sense for all things social.

In the first section, I say more about what social construction might be and about the idea that all social phenomena might be constructed at least partly by means of language. The notion of linguistic constructivism is introduced. Both hermeneutical and Wittgensteinian versions of this position are briefly discussed. In the second section, I consider the question whether institutions require language for their existence. There I criticize John Searle's defense of this claim. My discussion of Searle's view is preceded by an introduction of the Standard Model of Social Ontology (Guala, 2007). The third section concerns the status that language and language use have in society. Language is commonly taken to be an institution. But what about the speech acts we perform? Are they institutional actions? So I start by providing a general introduction to the role that language might play in the construction of society. I then go on to criticize Searle's position on this issue. And I end by considering how speech acts fit into an ontology of society.

THOUGHT, LANGUAGE, AND REALITY

Language can have causal effects on social phenomena. A reason why hate speech is so controversial is that it might cause harm, for instance by inciting people to riot. The relation between language and social phenomena can also be non-causal. A marriage is in part constituted by the words uttered during the relevant ceremony. Views differ as to what exactly causal and constitutive relations are. Causal but not constitutive relations are usually assumed to involve time.[1] Billiard balls can enter into causal relations with one another. A statue and the piece of marble of which it consists cannot. The statue is instead constituted by the piece of marble. As the examples given above reveal, it is possible for language to enter into both causal and constitutive relations to some social phenomena. The extent to which language has a causal impact on social phenomena is a contingent matter that is in principle open to empirical research. Most of those who defend the idea that language is constitutive of some part of reality hold that this is necessarily the case. The distinction between causal and constitutive relations provides the basis for drawing a distinction between two kinds of social construction, causal and constitutive construction (see Haslanger, 1995; Kukla, 2000; Mallon, 2008).

The strongest thesis one might seek to defend about language and reality is that all of reality is constituted by language. This thesis is known as the Linguistic Relativity Hypothesis (which is a descendant of the Sapir–Whorf thesis; see Swoyer, 2003). The underlying idea is that languages differ from one another in important ways and that the structure and/or vocabulary of a language systematically influence perception and conceptualization in such a way that people who employ different languages inhabit different worlds. Now this (version of the) hypothesis is rather extreme and has few adherents. First of all, although claims to the effect that different people really do inhabit different worlds can readily be found, on closer inspection the claim actually defended often turns out to be that the people involved have very different systems of belief about the world. Second, language plays only a relatively minor role in many versions of constitutive constructivism, and some theories that at first sight seem to be versions of constitutive linguistic constructivism are in fact versions of causal linguistic constructivism.[2] Finally, some versions of constructivism concern only part of reality rather than all of it.

These last two qualifications are particularly important for the purposes of this chapter. I am concerned with the construction of society or social reality, rather than the world as such. Insofar as the social world is concerned, there is and can be less of a gap between reality and beliefs about reality, because the social world depends in some way on those beliefs (Ruben, 1989). This implies that the first qualification is less pertinent. At the same time, it makes salient the question whether society is constructed by means of language or thought. For dialectical purposes I shall forcefully push the idea that (certain) social phenomena are constructed by thought rather than by language. In other words, what I shall call "linguistic constructivism" is on trial, and the charge is that conceptual constructivism is to be preferred to it.

Linguistic constructivism comes in many guises, and the distinction between causal and constitutive versions is a distinction among many others that could be made. Another important division is between approaches that are hermeneutical and those that are not. Charles Taylor (1994 [1971]) defends a version of hermeneutical constructivism. He is explicitly concerned with the domain of the social only, or, as he puts it, with "the sciences of man." He argues that these sciences must be hermeneutical, by which he means that the primary goal be interpretation. He goes on to note that the issue is an epistemological one, but that "it is inextricable from an ontological one" (p. 182), because it concerns the meanings that situations actually have for particular subjects. Some of the things he writes suggest that he defends a version of constitutive linguistic constructivism. This is supported in particular by his discussion of practices of negotiation, which involve actions such as making offers, negotiating, and breaking off negotiations. He compares Western societies to the Japanese society in which consensus plays a very important role. Taylor argues that the difference between these societies is not adequately expressed by saying that "we have a vocabulary to describe negotiation which they lack" (p. 193). Instead, the difference is not "just a difference of vocabulary, but also one of social reality" (p. 193). Furthermore, he goes on to defend the idea that "[t]he language is constitutive of the reality, is essential to its being the kind of reality it is" (p. 194). In other words, Taylor holds that insofar as social reality is concerned language does not simply represent the way the world is but partly determines it.

Two qualifications should be added to this interpretation of Taylor both of which provide reasons for doubting that he is a constitutive linguistic constructivist. First of all Taylor emphasizes that the kind of meaning that he is concerned with when he argues for the need for an interpretative approach to the social sciences differs from linguistic meaning. He calls it "experiential meaning." Both linguistic and experiential meanings involve a subject for whom something has meaning. Furthermore, meanings of both kinds are relational in the sense that something can only be meaningful in relation to other things that are meaningful (Taylor, 1994 [1971]: 186). The difference is that linguistic meaning involves words or other symbols, whereas this need not be the case for experiential meaning, or, as Taylor formulates it, that linguistic meaning "is the meaning of signifiers and … is about a world of referents" (p. 186). Experiential meaning concerns the goals people pursue

in their actions, and the desires, feelings, and emotions that explain those actions. This first observation puts into doubt the idea that Taylor is a linguistic constructivist. It appears that actions, goals, desires, feelings, and emotions involve thought rather than language.

At some point Taylor explicitly discusses the relation between linguistic and experiential meaning. Even though this discussion suggests that language plays a rather important role in Taylor's hermeneutics after all, it provides reason for doubting that he is a constitutive constructivist rather than a causal constructivist. The following passage reveals that on Taylor's view experiential meaning is not independent from linguistic meaning: "The range of human desires, feelings, emotions, and hence meanings is bound up with the level and type of culture, which in turn is inseparable from the distinctions and categories marked by the language people speak" (p. 188). Taylor goes on to argue that the relationship between the two kinds of meanings is not a simple one. He rejects both the idea that the vocabulary people use merely describes pre-existing feelings, and the thought that thinking about feelings in certain terms makes them what they are. When constitution is thought of as a determination relation or as a relation of (one-way) dependence, as it usually is, this implies that language does not play a constitutive role. Instead, Taylor must have in mind some kind of mutual influence. This reading is confirmed by Taylor's claim that a social scientific explanation can provide an interpretation that is clearer "than the lived interpretation," and can be "internalized by the agent as his self-interpretation" (p. 189). The upshot is that Taylor has a dynamic conception of the role that language plays in interpretation, which means that we would not do justice to him if we were to interpret him (only) as a constitutive linguistic constructivist.

Another strand within philosophy in which linguistic constructivism plays a significant role is practice theory. Theories within this tradition, a line of social ontological inquiry substantially influenced by Ludwig Wittgenstein, hold that practices form the fundamental component of social life. David Bloor's theory of institutions belongs to this tradition. Bloor is clearly a committed constitutive linguistic constructivist. Bloor defines an institution as "a collective pattern of self-referring activity" (1997: 33).[3] Bloor analyzes the reflexive or self-referring character of institutions in linguistic terms. In relation to the institution of money he contends that "metal discs *are* coins because they are *called* 'coins'" (p. 29). He goes on to note that "speaking of a thing as a coin isn't meant to refer to a purely verbal act, but to the whole pattern of behaviour into which such explicit verbalisations are woven" (p. 29). So in addition to the use of a certain vocabulary, ways of thinking about things and ways of treating them are involved in institutions. This qualification makes it a bit fuzzy how essential language really is for Bloor. The fact that Bloor calls the position he defends with respect to social reality "linguistic idealism" supports my interpretation of him as a constitutive linguistic constructivist (he takes the term from Elisabeth Anscombe). The following passage elucidates what this involves in his case: "A 'social object', by contrast, is constituted by the descriptions actors and participants give it. It has no existence independent of their beliefs and utterances about it; hence it cannot be described 'more closely' by, as it were, getting behind these descriptions" (p. 35). The upshot is that on Bloor's view institutions are what they are both due to certain ways of thinking and due to particular uses of words.

Language plays a significantly less important role in the Wittgensteinian theory of practices and institutions that Theodore Schatzki has proposed. Schatzki defends a version of practice theory according to which understanding orders or structures social reality and intelligibility articulates it (1996: 12–13). He explicitly states, however, that

language plays a relatively minor role in his theory: "[I]n speaking of the articulation of intelligibility, I do not imply any particular significance for language therein" (p. 13). On Schatzki's view non-verbal behavior plays a more important role than verbal behavior insofar as practices are concerned. He denies that "social existence reduces to language in some fundamental way" (p. 13). It seems safe to conclude that in Schatzki's view it is not constituted by language either.

Schatzki employs a non-linguistic notion of meaning in much the same way as Taylor does. He also believes that language does play an important role in it. He distinguishes his own position from Taylor's by making explicit that in his view intelligibility cannot be fully captured by means of language (pp. 127–128; the same holds for understanding, (p. 13)). Schatzki does not believe that the vocabulary someone employs constrains their thinking. Whereas most defenders of the Linguistic Relativity Hypothesis will hold that the richness of a language determines the richness of someone's thought, Schatzki seems to hold that the expressive power of language fails to capture all aspects of our thinking (and acting). All in all Schatzki resists what he calls an "overlinguistified" conception of intelligibility" (p. 111).

What is striking about the positions discussed thus far is that the considerations put forward in favor of these positions or against rival positions are far from compelling. Argumentation is often suggestive at best and stipulative at worst. It is not easy to see how this situation could be improved for theories that fall within the traditions discussed. Some of Swoyer's (2003) observations and suggestions are instructive in this respect. He considers methods of testing instances of the Linguistic Relativity Hypothesis, and observes:

Often the *only* evidence cited in favor of such hypotheses is to point to a difference between two languages and assert that it adds up to a difference in modes of thought. But this simply assumes what needs to be shown, namely that such differences *give rise to* cognitive differences. (Swoyer, 2003: 7)

He goes on to discuss empirical evidence that counts against strong versions of the hypothesis. It is not obvious, however, that theses such as these are (wholly) empirical (cf. Davidson, 1984 [1974]). Hence it is difficult to say anything with a reasonable amount of confidence about the plausibility of the positions discussed.[4] The conclusion that Swoyer (2003: 1) draws about the dialectical situation regarding linguistic relativism can be readily transposed to linguistic constructivism in general: the conviction and passion of partisans on both sides of the issue far outrun the available evidence. Recall that in the context of this chapter, linguistic constructivism has to prove that it is more attractive than conceptual constructivism. Against the background of this dialectic it is safe to conclude that we have thus far not found sufficient reason to abandon the idea that social phenomena such as institutions depend primarily on thought rather than language.

In the next section, I turn to the collective acceptance account of institutions in general and the version of it that has been proposed by John Searle in particular. Searle rejects the notion of experiential meaning. Furthermore, he holds that language is partly constitutive of institutions. In his case there can be little doubt about him being a constitutive linguistic constructivist. Finally, he puts forward a relatively well circumscribed argument in favor of this position. For these reasons an extensive investigation of his view is warranted. Before turning to his view and the tradition of which it is part, I should emphasize that the discussion of positions in this paper is by no means exhaustive. I have not mentioned, for instance, Ian Hacking's ideas about the construction of mental illness and about human kinds more generally.[5] A discussion of the constructivist views about race and gender categories would not have been out of place here either.[6] Another set of theories that is worth mentioning here concerns the notion of rule following as it has been articulated within the Wittgensteinian tradition. The main question here is whether thought and language as such are social phenomena. Thought and language involve the following of rules and the very phenomenon of rule following might be (necessarily) social. The key consideration adduced in favor of this view is that the possibility of making mistakes, or the normativity of rule-following cannot be made sense of other than in social terms, in particular in terms of people "criticizing" or "negotiating" with one another. Some of these ideas are discussed elsewhere in this handbook (see Chapters 6, 7, and 9).[7]

INSTITUTIONS AND LANGUAGE

A major difficulty in answering the question whether society as such is constituted by language is that society is an amorphous entity. The term "society" is used for collections of people ranging from the inhabitants of a state to social groups much smaller than that; think, for instance, of the Aristotelian Society. Societies that have the size of states are composite entities that encompass a wide range of social groups and institutions. It may be that language plays an important role in some of these but it is unlikely that it does so in all. There does not appear to be an intuitive pre-theoretic division between social phenomena that do essentially depend on language, and social phenomena for which this does not hold. A more promising route is to turn to theory. Over roughly the past two decades a consensus has emerged within social ontology as it is practiced in analytical philosophy as to which are the key notions required for analyzing the social world. Francesco Guala (2007) refers to this set of key notions as the Standard Model of Social Ontology (SMOSO). After introducing this model, I shall use it to present a specific proposal about the relation between language and society, the one that has been proposed and defended by John Searle.

The Standard Model of Social Ontology

The three notions that make up SMOSO are collective intentionality, performativity, and reflexivity.[8] The key idea underlying SMOSO is that beliefs, intentions, and other intentional attitudes play a crucial role in the constitution of social reality. Joint actions and social groups, for instance, are taken to depend crucially on *collective beliefs and intentions*. What exactly such collective intentional states are is a contentious issue. Michael Bratman (1999), for instance, has argued that people who perform a joint action have intentions that mutually depend on one another in the sense that one person has the intention to share in an action because the other does so and vice versa. Furthermore, he argues that the people engaged in a joint action have meshing subplans and will mutually adjust their actions. Margaret Gilbert (1989) maintains that joint actions are performed by people who have jointly committed themselves to doing so. She defends the strong claim that any joint action involves a mutual obligation on the part of the members of the group that performs it, which provides the basis for criticizing people who do not do what they have committed themselves to. In addition to this, she holds that people who have jointly committed themselves to perform a particular joint action, form a collective agent or – in her own terminology – "a plural subject." What these views have in common is that collective intentionality is a basic building block of social reality in general, and joint actions and social groups in particular.

Ever since John Austin (1962) it has been commonplace that we can do things with words. Austin focused on the performative role that language often plays, for instance, when a chairperson opens a meeting, or when a new ship is baptized. Baptisms form particular vivid examples of the performative role of language, as in their case the link between the use of language and what is achieved by it is very direct and conspicuous.

Nowadays the term *performativity* is used also to indicate the effects that our beliefs and other intentional attitudes have on the way things are, given that we often act on the basis of those attitudes. This holds in particular for beliefs concerning social practices and institutions, as in the case of such social constructs those beliefs contribute to their very existence. Certain pieces of paper are money, for instance, because they are collectively accepted as money. This enables us to use them in market exchanges. The notion of *reflexivity* is used to capture the idea that intentional attitudes are (also) necessary (rather than merely sufficient) for the existence of many social entities. The fact that Valentine's Day is in many Western countries the traditional day on which lovers express their love by sending cards, presenting flowers, or offering confectionery allows us to infer that this is collectively accepted in those countries.

These three notions can be used for drawing a distinction between two kinds of facts within the social world, social facts, and institutional facts.[9] Social facts involve collective intentional states. The existence of a joint intention or of a social group is a social fact. In addition to depending on collective intentional states, institutional facts are characterized by performativity and reflexivity. The existence of Valentine's Day and the existence of euro banknotes and coins are institutional facts. In the characterization of performativity and reflexivity I have already used the notion of collective acceptance, which is the technical term for human agreement. Facts that essentially depend on collective acceptance are institutional facts. Now, it may be that within a certain community it is collectively accepted that the earth is flat. It will, however, be recognized that the shape of the earth as such is not an issue that is settled by our opinion. This means that facts concerning the shape of the earth do not essentially depend on collective acceptance. Genuine institutional facts, such as which kind of object constitutes money within a particular context, do essentially depend on collective acceptance.

Language and Institutional Facts

SMOSO as such is not committed to language playing an important role in the social world. It can, however, be used to circumscribe a position that does. John Searle maintains that institutional facts essentially involve language. He does not hold that all institutional facts involve an event akin to a baptism in which words are explicitly used for bringing it about (although his recent use of the confusing term "Status Function Declaration" could easily be (mis)taken to imply this; see Searle (2008: 50)). There are too many counterexamples to this for it to have any initial plausibility. On his view, instead, an adequate explication of the way in which institutional facts depend on collective acceptance must refer to language. Let me review the exact claim Searle makes and the argument he gives for it.

Searle maintains that "language is essentially constitutive of institutional reality" (1995: 59). This can mean various things. One of these is that you cannot have institutions other than language in a certain context if no language is used within that context. Searle endorses this idea. He claims that "the institution of language is logically prior to other institutions" and regards language as "the basic social institution in the sense that all others presuppose language, but language does not presuppose the others: you can have language without money and marriage, but not the converse" (p. 60). It can also mean that language is involved in each particular institutional fact. Presumably this would mean that sentences reporting institutional facts would then have to include one or more words specific to the institutional fact at issue. Searle stops short from supporting this claim, as is apparent from the following passage:

> Money is only money if people think that it is money; a game is only a game if people think that

it is a game. But it is impossible for us to have these thoughts without a certain sort of vocabulary. *It is not necessary to have the actual word money or some synonym of it, but there has to be a vocabulary appropriate for buying, selling, and exchange generally* for us to be able to manifest the collective intentionality which invokes the constitutive rules of private property and the exchange of property in return for money. (1991: 342–43; emphasis added)

Searle does, however, defend a view that comes close to this. He holds that "each institution requires linguistic elements of the facts within that very institution" (Searle, 1995: 60). Presumably each institution comprises several institutional facts. Although not each institutional fact involves language that is peculiar to it, each institution does.

So each institution involves some kind of linguistic representation. What Searle has in mind exactly can best be understood in terms of the counts-as locution that he uses for explicating the ontology of institutions. This locution is "X counts as Y in circumstances C." Instances of this locution are "Certain pieces of paper issued by the European Central Bank count as money in the Eurozone," or "Barack Obama counts as the 44th president of the United States." The phrase "counts as" is indicative of the role of collective acceptance. Barack Obama is the president of the United States exactly because this is collectively accepted to be the case by the American people (because they accept a system of rules of which this is a consequence). Terms and concepts that can take the position of the Y term in the counts-as locution are institutional or status terms and concepts. Searle maintains that collectively accepting something as having a certain institutional status necessarily involves symbolization or linguistic representation. This in turn means that such collective acceptance requires a conventional and public device used for representing an institutional status (Searle, 1995: 61).

What is Searle's argument for this view? Searle takes institutional statuses to be status functions, which he characterizes in two ways. First, in contrast to the functions of technical artifacts, status functions go beyond the physical features of the entities that have them. Whereas the physical features of a screwdriver usually suffice for the performance of its function, this does not hold for the physical features of objects that are used as money, traffic signs, or wedding rings. Second, status functions require agreement or collective acceptance for their imposition and performance. These two features of status functions provide support for the requirement of language on Searle's view, as is revealed in the following passage:

> [T]here can be no prelinguistic way to represent the Y element because there is nothing there prelinguistically that one can perceive or otherwise attend to in addition to the X element, and there is nothing there prelinguistically to be the target of desire or inclination in addition to the X element. (Searle, 1995: 68)

The idea seems to be that because institutional statuses exist only in virtue of collective acceptance we need some way of representing them, and language is the only means available for this purpose. Further support for this reading is provided a page later:

> Because the Y level of the shift from X to Y in the creation of institutional facts has no existence apart from its representation, we need some way of representing it, because the Y element has no natural prelinguistic features in addition to the X element that would provide the means of representation. So we have to have words or other symbolic means to perform the shift from the X to the Y status. (Searle, 1995: 69–70)

Now, it is one thing to say that we need to have some way of representing an institutional status if we are to collectively accept that it exists, but it is quite another to say that the representation needs to be a linguistic one. Searle is well aware of the difference, which he explains in the following passage: "It is a sufficient condition for a *fact* to be language dependent that two conditions be met. First, mental representations, such as thoughts, must be partly constitutive of the fact; and second, the representations in question must be language dependent" (p. 62).

That institutions involve thoughts follows from the role that collective acceptance plays in their constitution. This leaves us with the question why these thoughts have to be language dependent. As is suggested by the preceding discussion, the answer to this question "must come from an understanding of the nature of status-functions" (p. 63). In a nutshell, Searle's answer is that "the move from X to Y is *eo ipso* a linguistic move, even in cases that apparently have nothing to do with language" (p. 63).

I do not find this answer very convincing. The ways in which Searle characterizes status functions is not substantial enough to warrant this conclusion. The second characterization concerns the requirement of collective acceptance, but this establishes only the need for some form of representation, and does not imply that nonlinguistic mental representations cannot do the job. What about the first characterization? This is at bottom a negative characterization. The physical features of the entities on which they are imposed do not suffice for the performance of status functions. It is not terribly clear what this means. A positive characterization of status functions is needed in order to make a convincing case for the claim at issue. As it happens, a positive characterization can be found in Searle's work. He holds that most if not all status functions involve deontic powers. Searle does not really give an analysis of what deontic powers are. He maintains that they "regulate relations between people" (p. 100). In addition to this, he provides a list of examples: deontic powers encompass "rights, responsibilities, obligations, duties, privileges, entitlements, penalties, authorizations, permissions" (p. 100). All this fits nicely with the widely accepted view that institutions are somehow normative, or have a normative dimension. And this insight can help us to make some progress with the issue at hand.

Searle in fact claims that deontic powers require language: "Institutional facts ... involve a deontic component, and with that deontic component comes the requirement of language." (2003: 304) However, it is not clear at all why this would be so. It appears that an institution can exist in virtue of some norm being collectively accepted to be in force. Such a norm can, but need not, involve special institutional vocabulary. The rule that one has to drive on the right- or left-hand side of the road does not appear to involve any special kind of vocabulary, but its acceptance constitutes an institution all the same. Of course, one can develop this institution and restrict the rule to public roads, and the distinction between public and private roads is itself an institutional phenomenon. This, however, does not deter from the fact that one can conceive of a simple system of traffic rules that does not employ institutional terms at all.

As another example, consider a prototype of our institution of property, property* (the asterisks indicate that the term is a technical or specially defined term) (cf. Lewis, 1969). This institution pertains to land use only, and stipulates who has the right to exclusive usage of the relevant pieces of land. In the proto-society I imagine, the only condition one has to meet in order to possess a piece of land is that one be the first to occupy it, for instance, by building a fence around it. All it takes for this institution of property* to work is that the following norm be collectively accepted: If one is the first to occupy a piece of land, one has the right to its exclusive use. In the situation I am imagining those who participate in the institution do not use terms such as "property*," or "owner*." It is we, as theoreticians, who might introduce such special terms for convenience, but the participants may not find a need for doing so. Of course, they could do so. They could accept a rule according to which in the relevant circumstances a piece of land is someone's property* exactly if s/he is (was) the first to occupy it. Along with this rule, they could accept another rule with the following content: Whoever's property* a piece of land is has the right of its exclusive use. These rules employ the institutional term "property*." It appears, however, that the institution and the actions in which its participants engage in is

hardly, if at all, affected by whether or not special terms are or have been introduced.[10]

Many alternative conceptions of institutions are available in which language plays no role at all. Consider for instance the conception of institutions as game theoretic equilibria that goes back to David Lewis (1969) and Thomas Schelling (1960).[11] Preferences and expectations about behavior form the key ingredients of analyses of conventions and institutions in this tradition. Although such analyses can, and sometimes are, applied to language, language plays no special role in them, and there is no reason to deem them inadequate because of this. An advantage that Searle's analysis has over these is that his ontology is better equipped to deal with institutional entities other than actions, in particular institutional objects. Objects play a marginal role at best in the Schelling–Lewis tradition. Another advantage that Searle's analysis has is that it does justice to the normative dimension of institutions. Lewis, for instance, treats the normativity of conventions as purely incidental. It is rather unattractive to conceive of the normativity of institutions as an add-on.[12] But there is little reason to believe that it cannot be done justice at all within a game-theoretic framework. A step that has already been made in that direction is to employ some notion of normative expectation (see, for instance, Bicchieri, 2006). This provides a means for bringing normativity to the core of the analysis. So even though the adequacy of analyses of institutions within the Schelling–Lewis tradition is up for debate, this is not because language fails to play an essential role in them. The intentional attitudes requisite for institutions must somehow capture their normativity, but no special linguistic representations are needed for this.

I have tried to explicate what exactly Searle means when he claims that institutions essentially involve language, and I have considered his argument in favor of this claim. Neither the notion of a status function nor that of deontic power, however, provides an adequate basis for it. I conclude that the argument is unconvincing. As his argument is developed in relatively great detail, and certainly is the most prominent one currently available, I am rather pessimistic about the idea that a convincing case has been made for the claim. It appears that mental representations can do the job just as well as linguistic representations. Language may play an important role in communication about institutions, perhaps in creating convergent expectations, but it is not essentially constitutive of institutional reality.

SPEECH ACTS AND INSTITUTIONS

Language is itself an institution. Sentence and word meaning are public and conventional. Depending on the theory you favor, they depend on things such as preferences and expectations concerning behavior, or perhaps on collective acceptance of sound waves or marks on paper having a certain status. In order for communication between people to be successful certain institutions have to be in place. Lewis (1969) argues that the main institution that facilitates communication is the convention of truthfulness. Kent Bach and Robert Harnish (1979) argue that communication is guided by the communicative presumption. According to this convention, there is a mutual belief in a linguistic community that whenever a member says something to another member, she is doing so with some recognizable intention (p. 7). It is uncontroversial that institutions are implicated in meaning and communication in one way or another. Rather than elaborating on these widely accepted ideas, I want to focus on a more contentious issue. The question I pursue in this section is whether speech acts are institutional actions.

The notion of a speech act goes back to Austin, the philosopher that I already mentioned when introducing the notion of performativity. In a time when it was still commonplace to focus exclusively on representation as the function of language, Austin explored what else we do with words other than representing states of affairs. We tell people what to do, we ask questions, and we make promises. These are all examples of speech acts. Austin observed that only a relatively small part of communication is devoted to making assertions. Furthermore, a fair number of the things we do with words concern institutions. Think of a priest who unites two people in holy matrimony, of a judge who pronounces a prison sentence, or of a university that confers a degree on a student. It appears that these last three examples are speech acts that are also institutional actions. So it may well be that some speech acts are institutional actions. In addition to this claim, I investigate the stronger claim that receives support from philosophers such as Austin, Searle, and Timothy Williamson that all speech acts are conventional or institutional actions.[13] Here I shall again focus on Searle's defense of this view. The contours of his conception of institutional actions have already been introduced. Another reason that makes focusing on his view attractive is that he has spelled out the idea in some detail, and has thereby provided a suitable basis for scrutinizing it.

The main hypothesis of Searle's book *Speech Acts* is that "speaking a language is performing acts according to rules" (1969: 36–37). More specifically, (the early) Searle defends the following claim:[T]he semantic structure of a language may be regarded as a conventional realization of a series of sets of underlying constitutive rules, and [...] speech acts are acts characteristically performed by uttering expressions in accordance with these sets of constitutive rules (p. 37). This passage implies that there is an intimate relation between speech acts and constitutive rules. Constitutive rules are rules that have the structure of the counts-as locution discussed above ("*X* counts as *Y* in *C*").

Somewhat confusingly Searle also refers to the rules he takes to be constitutive of speech acts as "essential rules."[14] An essential rule, he explains, pertains to what a speaker does or attempts to do in performing a speech act of a certain kind. In performing a speech act the agent expresses an attitude, and, at least in the usual case, achieves some end by doing so. To assert something, for instance, is to express a belief and thereby to undertake that the content of the belief represents an actual state of affairs (pp. 65–66). Similarly, to make a request is, on Searle's view, to express a wish or desire and thereby to attempt to get the person to whom the act is directed to do something (pp. 65–66). As a final cxample, to make a promise is to express an intention and thereby to undertake an obligation to act on the intention (pp. 62–65).

Let us look at some examples of essential rules. Searle formulates the essential rule of promising as follows: "The utterance of Pr [a sentence that can be used for making a promise] counts as the undertaking of an obligation to do A" (p. 63). In line with this, Searle argues that "promising is, by definition, an act of placing oneself under an obligation" and writes: "the constitutive rule that to make a promise is to undertake an obligation" (Searle, 1964: 45 and 56). The overview of types of speech acts that Searle presents suggests these formulations of the essential rules for assertions and requests: "To assert p counts as an undertaking to the effect that p represents an actual state of affairs"; "To request H to do A counts as an attempt to get H to do A" (1969: 66; see 1999: 147 for similar formulations).

At first sight it makes a lot of sense to regard essential rules as constitutive rules, as Searle does. After all, Searle employs the phrase "counts as" in his formulations of essential rules. If essential rules are indeed genuine constitutive rules, Searle has provided a powerful defense of the idea that speech acts are institutional actions. It would follow that an act is an instance of a particular kind of speech act exactly if it meets certain collectively accepted conditions. A closer investigation of essential rules, however, provides reasons for doubting they are genuine constitutive rules. In spite of the fact that Searle uses it in his formulations of them, the

phrase "counts as" is not doing any work in essential rules. Its occurrence in essential rules is deceptive.

Consider the essential rule for making a request: "To request H to do A counts as an attempt to get H to do A." The occurrence of the phrase 'counts as' in this rule sounds somewhat odd. One might react by saying that to request something does not (only) count as an attempt to get someone to do something, it really is such an attempt. Now, as was suggested above, the phrase "counts as" stands for the idea that an X is a Y because we collectively accept it as a Y. This implies that the fact that something counts as something else is perfectly consistent with the fact that it really is that something else. In spite of this, the feeling that the occurrence of the phrase in the rule is odd does not go away. The reason for this, I suggest, is that the fact that a request is an attempt to get someone to do something does not derive from its being collectively accepted. This is simply what a request is. Now, if this does not depend on collective acceptance, the phrase "counts as" is not doing any work in the essential rule of requesting. This is evidenced by the fact that the rule could be rephrased in terms of "is" rather than "counts as" without any loss (which results in: a request is an attempt to get someone to do something). William Alston makes the same point as follows: "What my utterance was an attempt to do is a psychological fact about my motivation, and no rule could make the utterance "count as" an attempt at one thing rather than another" (2000: 102).[15]

There are other disanalogies between the essential rule for making a request and constitutive rules. In the counts-as locution the Y term marks an institutional status. The X term need not do so. The essential rule for making a request has a different form, because the position of the X term is taken by the act that is characterized by the rule. Furthermore, the Y term of a constitutive rule marks something that involves deontic powers (Searle, 1969) employs the term "normative consequences"). This does not hold of the essential rule for making a request. These are further reasons for doubting that making a request should be analyzed in terms of constitutive rules, and hence for doubting that this speech act is an institutional action. Similar considerations can be adduced against the idea that assertion is an institutional action.[16]

It may still be, however, that some, or even many speech acts are institutional actions. In light of some of the examples given at the beginning of this section, this is in fact rather plausible. The ends that are characteristically achieved by speech acts such as promising, adjourning a meeting, or commanding are institutional phenomena. It is, however, not obvious that the speech acts involved in the achievement of these ends are themselves institutional actions. Consider commanding someone to do something. The end that is characteristically served by this action is to obligate someone to do something. In order for this end to be achieved successfully, an institutional background has to be in place. The agent performing the action needs to have the requisite authority. Although this establishes that the speech act of commanding is intimately related to institutional phenomena, it falls short from establishing that it is itself an institutional action. It also reveals that one can command someone to do something, but fail to obligate him because one is not in the position to do so. In other words, one can command someone to do something without the appropriate institutional background being in place and without thereby achieving the end. In such cases it seems strange to say that an institutional act has been performed, and it is much more plausible to say that the act is merely a social one – directed at someone else, involving an institution only indirectly.[17]

Following this line of thought Alston (2000) and Bach and Harnish (1979: 289n4) propose to separate conventional, or institutional matters (or moral ones for that matter) from semantic ones. In the case of commissive speech acts such as promising, and directive speech acts such as authorizing, they leave the obtaining of a right, entitlement, or

obligation out of the analysis. Alston develops this idea further by suggesting that in performing such acts we *purport* to achieve the relevant end. In order for us to do so successfully, the relevant social norms or institutions have to be in place. Furthermore, the conditions set by these norms or institutions have to be met (think of the requisite authority relation in the case of commanding).

In the case of promising, to give another example, this means that if we perform the speech act of promising we purport to obligate ourselves (Alston, 2000: 96). This falls short of actually obligating ourselves. That effect is due to extralinguistic conventions. Alston does not deny that performing the speech act is sufficient for the creation of the obligation in our society, but he argues that this is because "society 'allows' a speaker to take on an obligation *just by saying something*" (Alston, 2000). The upshot is that, even though in practice all promises generate obligations, one can still usefully distinguish the obtaining of an obligation from the performance of the speech act. If this is correct, the achieving of the institutional ends can and should be left out of the analysis of commissives (such as promising) and directives (such as commanding).[18]

Alston argues that we should separate the conventional or institutional from the semantic in the case of declarative speech acts such as adjourning a meeting and joining a couple in holy matrimony as well. The problem that he has to confront is that most declarative verbs involve the obtaining of the relevant conventional effect. Whereas one can fail to obligate someone if one commands that person to do something, one cannot adjourn a meeting and fail to stop it. In spite of this, he maintains that we should distinguish between the semantic act of performing a declarative and the act of achieving the related institutional end. Bach and Harnish (1979) take a different line. On their view, it is part of the nature of such acts that the ends are achieved by performing them. As long as one does not appeal to the distinction (later) introduced by Alston between, for instance, adjourning and purporting to adjourn, this is of course correct. It is hard to think of a reason for siding with one or the other on this issue. A consideration that counts in favor of going along with Alston is that accommodating the idea of purporting to do something in the analyses of all types of speech acts enhances their symmetry. However, it is not very clear how much weight should be put on this consideration. In light of this, I do not wish to claim to have established that no speech acts are institutional actions. Instead, I have made a case for the idea that, in spite of Searle's view to the contrary, far from all speech acts are institutional actions.

CONCLUSION

Language plays an important role in social reality in general and institutional reality in particular. How important exactly is a controversial issue? It surely plays a causal role and in some cases language is partly constitutive of institutional facts or events. Searle's argument for the claim that this is true for all of institutional reality has been found wanting. In the first section, we saw that other versions of linguistic constructivism have their own share of problems.

Language itself is an institution. In order to really get to grips with the relation between language and society, we also need to understand the social and institutional dimensions of linguistic phenomena. Because of this the third section addressed the question whether all speech actions are institutional actions. It was argued that many speech acts are social rather than institutional actions.

NOTES

1 The marriage example might appear to be an immediate counterexample. Note, however, that a marriage is effectuated at the very moment that the relevant official utters the appropriate words. So the event of getting married is partly constituted by the uttering of those words. The state of being married depends on this event having taken place in the past. Although there is a time gap involved here the fact that the events mentioned stand in a constitution relation to one another provides reason for regarding the dependence relation involved in the state of being married as a non-causal relation as well.

2 Consider Berger and Luckmann's (1966) classic *The Social Construction of Reality*. The title of their book suggests they are concerned with the construction of reality itself. However, they claim instead to be concerned with "whatever passes for 'knowledge'" (Berger and Luckmann, 1966: 3, cf. 185). It appears, then, that their work addresses beliefs about reality rather than reality itself. Furthermore, language plays an important role in their work, but less so than one might expect. They maintain that human experiences are in fact transmitted by means of language, but that they could theoretically be transmitted through common activity rather than a sign system (p. 68). These claims suggest first, that language is not essential, and second that Berger and Luckmann are (primarily) concerned with the causal role that language in fact plays in the transmission of human experiences rather than with the constitutive role it might be taken to have.

3 Barnes (1983) emphasizes the importance of self-reference or reflexivity for social entities. His work has had a significant impact on Bloor, as has Winch's classic, *The Idea of a Social Science and its Relation to Philosophy* (1958).

4 This is not to say that many of the criticisms voiced against particular versions are unwarranted. It has, for instance, been argued that assigning a significant role to interpretation in explanation need not be inconsistent with taking explanation to be causal. Another sensible point of critique that has been put forward is that to insist that all explanation within the social sciences must employ hermeneutic methods is overly restrictive. See part III of Martin and McIntyre (1994) for these and other criticisms.

5 A good place to start exploring Hacking's work is his, *The Social Construction of What?* (1999).

6 See for instance Haslanger (2000, 2005).

7 Many of those who defend a Wittgensteinian theory of institutions also have a closely related theory of rule following. Bloor, for instance, combines his claim that institutions are "collective processes having a self-referring or performative character" with the claims that "a rule is a social institution," and that "following a rule is participating in a social institution" (1997: 134). Such a view is by no means compulsory. Pettit (1993) defends the idea that rule following is a social phenomenon, but maintains a clear distinction between institutions on the one hand and the kinds of rules involved in thought on the other (see Pettit (2000) for a

discussion how these two notions relate in Winch (1958)). The view that rule following is social has most prominently been defended by Kripke (1982). It is criticized, among others, in Blackburn (1984) and Hindriks (2004). See Haukioja (2005) for a criticism of Hindriks (2004).

8 These three notions play a particularly prominent role in Searle (1995) and Tuomela (2002).

9 The term "social fact" can be traced back to Durkheim (1994). John Searle (1964) uses the term "institutional fact." His usage is inspired by a distinction Anscombe (1981 [1958]) draws between brute and non-brute facts. Searle distinguishes between social and institutional facts along the lines laid out in the main text. Similar distinctions between (merely) social and conventional or institutional phenomena can be found in Gilbert (1989), and Tuomela (2002). Note that even though the distinction is often drawn in terms of facts, fact-talk is not essential to it. An analogous distinction can be drawn between social and institutional phenomena or entities or properties depending on the kind of ontology one favors.

10 An in depth treatment of these issues would have to engage with the distinction between regulative and constitutive rules, which plays an important role in Searle's social ontology. This, however, lies beyond the scope of the current paper. Let me note here that Warnock (1971) and Ruben (1997) argue that the distinction is only a linguistic one. In Hindriks (2009) I argue that, in spite of what I have just argued for in the main text, the notion of a constitutive rule does have ontological significance.

11 See also Ullmann-Margalit (1977), Schotter (1981), Sugden (1986), Young (1998), and Bicchieri (2006).

12 An escape route that is available to Lewis is that he is concerned with conventions rather than institutions. Even though it is rather natural to conceive of conventions as a kind of institutions, this view is by no means mandatory.

13 This view is known as "force conventionalism" (Green, 2007). The thought that Williamson supports this claim has the following background. Williamson (1996, 2000) argues that assertion is necessarily governed by the knowledge rule, according to which the person who makes the assertion should know that which he asserts, and he suggests that similar rules can be formulated for other kinds of speech acts. He maintains that the knowledge rule is the constitutive rule of assertion. He likens constitutive rules to the rules of games. The notion of a constitutive rule is primarily invoked in relation to institutions, and the analogy with the rules of games is rather common in that context as well. Because of the link between constitutive rules and institutions on the one hand and the connection Williamson hypothesizes between speech acts and constitutive rules on the other, it is reasonable to conclude that he regards speech acts as institutional actions. See Hindriks (2007) for a critique of Williamson's proposal.

14 Presumably this is because his analyses of speech act kinds involve several kinds of rules, including a sincerity rule and a prepositional content rule, and essential rules capture the essence of those acts.

15 Another way of making the point would be to observe that the phrase "counts as" has a merely classificatory use in addition to the kind of use that indicates dependence on collective acceptance (Grossi et al., 2006). On this line of thought the claim that essential rules are constitutive rules would be due to a fallacy of equivocation.

16 Not all of these considerations apply to the essential rule of promising. As we saw above, Searle formulates this rule as follows: "The utterance of *Pr* counts as the undertaking of an obligation to do *A*." This rule does not have the speech act verb in the position of the *X* term. Oddly enough, however, the speech act verb does not appear in it at all. Searle also writes that "the utterance of such and such expressions under certain conditions counts as the making of a promise" (p. 37). This formulation does have the structure of the counts-as locution. I return to the case of promising below.

17 Pagin (2004) argues that the speech act of assertion is not even a social act, but merely a psychological one.

18 These speech acts could be linked to their characteristic institutional ends by social norms such as "If one purports to obligate oneself to do *A*, one (obligates oneself and hence one) ought to do *A*" (for the case of promising), and "If someone purports to obligate *H* to do *A* and the appropriate circumstances obtain, *H* (is obliged and hence) ought to do *A*" (for the case of commanding).

REFERENCES

Alston, W.P. (2000) *Illocutionary Acts and Sentence Meaning*. Ithaca: Cornell University Press.

Anscombe, G.E.M. (1981/1958) 'On brute facts', in *The Collected Papers of G.E.M. Anscombe*, vol. 3. Oxford: Basil Blackwell. pp. 22–25.

Austin, J.L. (1962) *How to Do Things with Words*. Cambridge, MA: Harvard University Press.

Bach, K. and R.M. Harnish (1979) *Linguistic Communication and Speech Acts*. Cambridge (MA), MIT Press.

Barnes, B. (1983) 'Social life as bootstrapped induction', *Sociology*, 4: 524–545.

Berger, P.L. and T. Luckmann (1966) *The Social Construction of Reality. A Treatise in the Sociology of Knowledge*. New York: Doubleday & Company.

Bicchieri, C. (2006) *The Grammar of Society: The Nature and Dynamics of Social Norms*. Cambridge: Cambridge University Press.

Blackburn, S. (1984) 'The individual strikes back', *Synthese*, 58: 281–301.

Bloor, D. (1997) *Wittgenstein, Rules and Institutions*. London: Routledge.

Bratman, M.E. (1999) *Faces of Intention*. Cambridge: Cambridge University Press.

Davidson, D. (1984 [1974]) 'On the very idea of a conceptual scheme', in *Inquiries into Truth & Interpretation*. Oxford: Clarendon Press. pp. 183–198.

Durkheim, E. (1994) 'Social facts', in M. Martin and L.C. McIntyre (eds) *Readings in the Philosophy of Social Science*. Cambridge (MA): MIT Press. pp. 433–440.

Gilbert, M. (1989) *On Social Facts*. London: Routledge.

Green, M. (2007) 'Speech acts', in Edward N. Zalta (ed.) *The Stanford Encyclopedia of Philosophy (Fall 2007 Edition)*, <http://plato.stanford.edu/archives/fall2007/entries/speech-acts/>.

Grossi, D., J.-J.Ch. Meyer, and F. Dignum (2006) 'Classificatory aspects of counts-as: An analysis in modal logic', *Journal of Logic and Computation*, 16: 613–643.

Guala, F. (2007) 'The philosophy of social science: Metaphysical *and* empirical', *Philosophy Compass*, 2: 954–980.

Hacking, I. (1999) *The Social Construction of What?* Cambridge (MA): Harvard University Press.

Haslanger, S. (1995) 'Ontology and social construction', *Philosophical Topics*, 23: 95–125.

Haslanger, S. (2000) 'Gender and race: (What) are they? (What) do we want them to be?' *Nous*, 38: 644–673.

Haslanger, S. (2005) 'What are we talking about? The semantics and politics of social kinds', *Hypatia*, 20: 10–26.

Haukioja, J. (2005) 'Hindriks on rule-following', *Philosophical Studies*, 126: 219–239.

Hindriks, F. (2004) 'A modest solution to the problem of rule-following', *Philosophical Studies*, 121: 65–98.

Hindriks, F. (2007) 'The status of the knowledge account of assertion', *Linguistics and Philosophy*, 30: 393–406.

Hindriks, F. (2009) 'Constitutive rules, language, and ontology', *Erkenntnis,* 71: 253–75.

Kripke, S. (1982) *Wittgenstein on Rules and Private Language*. Cambridge (MA): Harvard University Press.

Kukla, A. (2000) *Social Constructivism and the Philosophy of Science*. London: Routledge.

Lewis, D. (1969) *Convention: A Philosophical Study*. Cambridge (MA): Harvard University Press.

Mallon, R. (2008) 'Naturalistic approaches to social construction', in Edward N. Zalta (ed.) *The Stanford Encyclopedia of Philosophy (Winter 2008 Edition)*, <http://plato.stanford.edu/archives/win2008/entries/social-construction-naturalistic/>.

Martin, M. and L.C. McIntyre (eds) (1994) *Readings in the Philosophy of Social Science*. Cambridge (MA): MIT Press.

Pagin, P. (2004) 'Is assertion social?', *Journal of Pragmatics*, 36: 833–859.

Pettit, P. (1993) *The Common Mind. An Essay on Philosophy, Psychology, and Politics*. Oxford: Oxford University Press.

Pettit, P. (2000) 'Winch's double-edged idea of a social science', *History of the Human Sciences*, 13: 63–77.

Ruben, D.H. (1989) 'Realism and the social sciences', in H. Lawson, and L. Appignanesi (eds) *Dismantling Truth*. London: Weidenfeld. pp. 58–75.

Ruben, D.H. (1997) 'John Searle's *The Construction of Social Reality*', *Philosophy and Phenomenological Research*, 57: 443–447.

Schatzki, T.R. (1996) *Social Practices: A Wittgensteinian Approach to Human Activity and the Social*. Cambridge: Cambridge University Press.

Schelling, T. (1960) *The Strategy of Conflict*. Cambridge (MA): Harvard University Press.

Schotter, A. (1981) *The Economic Theory of Social Institutions*. Cambridge: Cambridge University Press.

Searle, J.R. (1964) 'How to derive "ought" from "is"', *Philosophical Review*, 73: 43–58.

Searle, J.R. (1969) *Speech Acts: An Essay in the Philosophy of Language*. Cambridge: Cambridge University Press.

Searle, J. R. (1991) 'Intentionalistic Explanations in the Social Sciences' *Philosophy of the Social Sciences* 21: 332–344.

Searle, J.R. (1995) *The Construction of Social Reality*. New York: The Free Press.

Searle, J. R. (1999) *Mind, Language and Society* London: Weidenfeld and Nicolson.

Searle, J. R. (2003) 'Reply to Barry Smith', *American Journal of Economics and Sociology,* 62: 299–309.

Searle, J. R. (2008) *Philosophy in a New Century: Selected Essays*. Cambridge: Cambridge University Press.

Sugden, R. (1986) *The Economics of Rights, Co-operation, and Welfare*. Oxford: Basil Blackwell.

Swoyer, C. (2003) 'The linguistic relativity hypothesis', in Edward N. Zalta (ed.) *The Stanford Encyclopedia of Philosophy (Winter 2008 Edition)*, <http://plato.stanford.edu/archives/win2008/entries/relativism/supplement2.html>.

Taylor, C. (1994 [1971]) 'Interpretation and the sciences of man', in M. Martin and L.C. McIntyre (eds) *Readings in the Philosophy of Social Science*. Cambridge (MA): MIT Press. pp. 181–212.

Tuomela, R. (2002) *The Philosophy of Social Practices: A Collective Acceptance View*. Cambridge: Cambridge University Press.

Ullmann-Margalit, E. (1977) *The Emergence of Norms*. Oxford: The Clarendon Press.

Warnock, G.J. (1971) *The Object of Morality*. London: Methuen & Co.

Williamson, T. (1996) 'Knowing and asserting', *Philosophical Review*, 105(4): 489–523.

Williamson, T. (2000) *Knowledge and Its Limits*. Oxford: Oxford University Press.

Winch, P. (1958) *The Idea of a Social Science and its Relation to Philosophy*. London: Routledge & Kegan Paul.

Young, P.H. (1998) *Individual Strategy and Social Structure: An Evolutionary Theory of Institutions*. Princeton: Princeton University Press.

6

Social Minds

Laurence Kaufmann

INTRODUCTION

Broadly speaking, the concept of mind refers to a whole variety of mental phenomena: perception, attention, consciousness, intentionality, belief, memory, representation and so on. For social theorists, the issue at stake is to specify the way and degree to which these different mental states can be said to be social. Whereas holistic approaches tend to limit the individual mind to the functional role of a 'society bearer', thereby providing society with the minimal amount of cognition and agency that society needs to be produced and maintained, individualist approaches tend to reduce society to the coordination effect of self-contained minds. The prevailing views of the mind have thus been tendentiously polarised in the ever-lasting opposition between a 'top-down', 'society-shapes-mind' model and a 'bottom-up', 'mind-shapes-society' model.

But even in the most extreme versions of those reductionisms, downward or upward, there remains a tension between mind and society that is never completely resolved. Mind and society tend to be seen as two opposite forces between which individuals are tossed back and forth, exempted from selfhood to be better enslaved by society and vice versa. So the very expression 'social mind' can be misleading – it suggests that the conciliation has been successful, whether theoretically or empirically. Now, it is precisely because such conciliation has not yet occurred in the social sciences that social theorists need to consider to what extent the mind might be social mind is social. The conceptual construct 'social mind' itself manifests both the *interdependency* of mind and society and the necessity, intellectual and political, of the possible *separation* of the individual from the social unit to which he belongs (Valsiner and Van Der Veer, 2000). Although the concept of 'social mind' appears only, as such, in the intellectual matrix proper to the scientific field of the nineteenth century, the epistemic and political conditions of the *mind–society* gap that this concept encapsulates are anterior. Actually, the very issue of the 'social mind' arises from the contractualist view, typically *modern*, of the 'society of individuals' that imposes itself, at the end of the eighteenth century, with the rise of democracy and the establishment of the unalienable rights of the citizen in modern national governments (Kaufmann, 2003). This ideological shift from community to society is the beginning of a never-ending political and intellectual inquiry into the kind of social cement that would be able to glue together the collection of independent minds that constitute the building blocks of modern societies.

This inquiry has given rise to different theoretical attempts to bridge the gap between mind and society – attempts that diverge as regards the heaviness and depth of the 'social load' that they are inclined to impose on the individual mind and, by way of implication, on individual behaviour. Roughly, five prevailing attempts to account for the 'socialness' of the mind can be distinguished.

1 The *individualist approaches to the social* – whether individualist or infra-individualist, tend to see the social as a matter of mental contents, either conscious or unconscious, which result from the translation of the social world *around* the mind *into* representations. On these views, the boundaries of the mind are so to speak naturally given, either by the physical limits of the brain or by the first-person monopoly of phenomenal sensations and rational decisions.

2 In contrast to these (infra) individualistic views, the *social approaches to the mind* emphasise the social dimension of any perceptions, expectations, categorisations, emotions and representations that furnish, in a more or less explicit way, the human mind. Subjective minds are nothing but the holders of the common meanings and impersonal rules that constitute the objective mind of a given community. As such, the mind has no boundaries: it takes place in the space between people, that is, in a social, communal world of shared experience and public language.

3 The *approaches to the extended mind* also call into question the demarcations of skin and skull, and the current assumption that what is outside the body is also outside the mind. From an externalist point of view, indeed, the mind has not the prerogative of cognition; cultural products such as language or artefacts lie beyond the skin but they partake in human cognition in the same way as the neuronal workings of the brain do.

4 Some *analytical approaches to collective intentionality* also advocate the view that minds are not 'in the head'. Here, the extension of the mind to its environment takes the form of an additional 'mind bearer', that is, groups. Whereas advocates of methodological individualism admit only individual human beings as the repositories of the intentionality, whether individual or collective, that enables joint coordination and

action, others see group agency as carried out by a 'group mind' that is not reducible to the we-intentions and shared beliefs of group-members.

5 The *approaches to the 'social brain'* draw from developmental, comparative and evolutionary psychology the hypothesis according to which social species are endowed with *pre-wired* well-adapted cognitive devices to process specific ontological domains, in this case the social domain. Such perspective potentially reconciles the infra-individualist focus on cognitive micro-mechanisms with an ontology of social facts as 'things-like', objective phenomena that evolved minds are prepared to grasp.

As shown by this short preview, the different approaches addressing the connection between mind and society are all concerned with the question as to whether the mind, once assumed to be social, goes *beyond and over* the individual, and even beyond the bounds of the brain and the body. Each of those approaches tries to find a way to solve what could be called, by analogy with the well-known *mind–body* problem, the *mind–society* problem. Just as the distinctiveness of both body and mind is central to the philosophy of mind, the ontological (in)dependency of mind and society is critical to the philosophy of the social sciences. It is the overview, of course not exhaustive, of the different solutions to this problem that this chapter means to provide.

INDIVIDUALIST APPROACHES TO THE SOCIAL

The rational mind[1]

As the intellectual counterpart of the modern, political view of the society of individuals, the different versions of *methodological individualism* tend to portray society not as an a priori community of minds but as a 'collective a posteriori' that derives from the temporary, fragile convergence of individual interests, goals and actions.

Actually, the main assumption of methodological individualism is that collective phenomena must be treated solely as the outcomes and modes of organisation of individual acts and thoughts. If society exerts a force on individual minds, it is on the condition that it has been translated into subjective, conscious and meaningful representations. According to one of the most esteemed advocates of methodological individualism, the sociologist Max Weber (1968), only one kind of action deserves the qualifier 'social', that is, the intended action, which takes into account the behaviour of others, whether present or absent, known or unknown. To effectively orient individual behaviour, social facts must take the representational form of *reasons for acting*, which permit the bridging of the gap between minds and society 'from the inside'. Admittedly, agents often act without a clear awareness of their means and goals, in part shaped by historical, social and economical configurations. But methodological individualists must proceed *as if* the activity of individuals really was directed by their intended meaning and really was rational enough to be understood by any observer (Weber, 1949). Although social theorists, just like ordinary social perceivers, do not have direct access to the agent's underlying subjective reason for acting, they can have *interpretive access* to it thanks to their own capacity of enactment or simulation. This capacity is made easier by *the assumption of rationality*, which postulates that anyone, interchangeable as a rational being, would have performed the same action in the same circumstances. This rational typification allows social scientists to bypass the empirical singularity of actors and to reintroduce necessity within a theoretical system, which otherwise, with the proliferation of singular descriptions, might lead to mere indeterminacy. Therefore, the object of such a version of methodological individualism is not the complex psychic forces effectively at work in social life, describable as such by psychology; it is the action itself – an action that triggers by definition an 'action-theoretic' level of comprehension and explanation (Heath, 2001).

In more recent versions of methodological individualism, such as the sociological 'theory of cognitive rationality' (Boudon, 1991), the 'rationalising' typification that, for Weber, made the interpretation and explanation complementary, is turned into an empirical assimilation; in other words, the subjective motivation that allowed the analyst to rationalise a given behaviour is turned into the effective *cause* of the action. In Boudon's chain of determination, which goes from individual motives and beliefs to the collective 'aggregates' and their unintended effects to which social facts tend to be reduced, mental events such as reasons for acting are endowed with causal properties. Turning methodological assumption into ontological causation, interpretation into explanation, Boudon's extended model of rationality reifies the model of the rational mind: any decision making is assumed to be rational, in a somewhat unfalsifiable manner (Boudon, 1996). Thus, in a given situation, social conformism can be seen as rational because it avoids the psychological cost that disagreement with peers represents, but acting according to one's own set of preferences can also be seen as rational.

This just goes to show that, according to this view, reasons for acting are not reducible to the maximisation of personal interests and private motivations that are at the centre of the model of utilitarian rationality. Rationality can also be 'axiological' so that reasons for acting include tradition, beliefs and values. Above all, reasons for acting have a public and normative dimension: they are 'good reasons' for acting and if they are good reasons, this is because they are considered as good by most of the people in a given context and within their cognitive limitations (Boudon, 1995, 2010). It is the 'shareness' of reasons for acting that makes the individual mind potentially transparent, not only for the actors, who always know the reason of their actions, but for the interpreters, who can reconstitute the rational logic of the behaviour that they observe.

In a way, the mind depicted by the analytical philosopher John Searle (2001) is not far away from Boudon's view of a transparent

Self. But there is an essential difference between both approaches. Whereas Boudon insists on the public dimension of reasons for acting, Searle establishes his interesting distinction between 'desire-independent reasons' and 'desire-dependent reasons' for acting from the point of view of an idiosyncratic self. Unlike desire-dependent reasons that refer to things that the agent wants to do, desire-independent reasons refer to things, such as obligations, commitments, responsibilities or requirements, that agents have to do whether they want to or not. In Searle's model, desire-independent reasons do not jeopardise individual agency and freedom because they are fully dependent upon the good will of the self. Indeed, the binding force of commitments and obligations depends upon the willing self-involvement on the part of the agent, who decides to bind his will in the future (e.g. I promise to come to your party), as well as upon their ulterior recognition, still by the agent, as valid reasons for acting (e.g. I accept the desire-independent reason to come to your party) (Searle, 2001). Thanks to the two irreducible mental 'gaps' that separate reasons from the final action, that is, a gap between reasons and decision-making, and a gap between the decision and its execution, reasons for acting are never causes. This is the somewhat mysterious figure of the Self that is in charge of the final selection of the reason for acting. In short, in Searle's approach, it is up to the agent to subjectively consider certain facts, for instance, the fact that a woman is in trouble, as a good reason for acting, in this case, for helping her (Kaufmann, 2005). Thus Searle's individualism falls into what Philip Pettit (1996) calls 'atomism': reasons for acting are defined from the solipsist point of view of a totally isolated individual agent, whose thoughts and behaviours are completely independent from the interaction with others.

Beyond their divergences, those different versions of methodological individualism have an important common denominator. The rational portrait of the mind that they defend leads them to discard the motivations, dispositions or inclinations that cannot take the shape of mental sentences, intrinsically propositional, duly summoned before the tribunal of consciousness. The social world, unless it is to be duly translated into reasons for acting, is *around* the mind but not *in* it. Thus, social behaviours that may be *unconsciously* brought about by rule-following, conformism, tradition or emotions (Elster, 1989), fall beyond the scope of rational analysis, thereby dramatically reducing the range of actions worthy of inquiry. By making the infra-individual incentives that glue individuals together literally incomprehensible, such versions of methodological individualism tend to depict a 'straw mind' that lacks descriptive thickness and psychological plausibility. Moreover, they conceive of the state of society as a fragile and precarious equilibrium. Indeed, individuals must consciously – and rationally – have social referents in mind, whether it be another person, a rule or a value, so that their actions can be deemed social, which strangely excludes from inquiry social phenomena such as unintended imitation or mass behaviour. The state of society ultimately depends on the conscious, reflexive states of mind of its members, who seem to always enjoy the possibility of 'beating a retreat' and refusing to play the social game.

The infra-individual mind

It is precisely the definition of the mind as a matter of propositional contents and the work of conscious reasons for acting as gap-bridging between mind and society that infra-individualist approaches call into question. Far from taking up the level of individuation that the rational models of the mind take for granted and that they want to save at any cost, these approaches break the supposedly unitary mind into a myriad of micro-psychological facts. Within these intra-psychological approaches of the social, the elementary ontological unit is neither a rational actor, nor a conscious sovereign self, but an *organism*, conceived as the site of the production, conflict and coalition of mostly unconscious cognitive representations and micro-mechanisms (Sperber, 1997).

Thus, for Gabriel Tarde, in his ground-breaking and somewhat unacknowledged work in the early-twentieth century, 'social quantities' such as money, custom or fashion are nothing but the propagation, the repetition and the opposition of two essential 'psychological quantities', desires and beliefs, which circulate between individuals through imitative flows (Tarde, 1899). For Tarde, what characterises society is the mode of transmission and the law of repetition it is based upon: whereas the physical world is characterised by repetition through vibration, and the organic life by repetition through heredity, the social life is characterised by repetition through imitation. Society is nothing but the similarity of desires and beliefs in a given population, justifying thereby an individualist epistemology that explains the large by the small, the big by the detail (Tarde, 1962). This being so, the Tardean model of the mind is not psychological but sociological: even if mental states ultimately cause social behaviours, most of those mental states come from the outside, via the other individuals whose ideas and goals have been imitated (Karsenti, 2002).

Thus, in Tarde's model, the social bond is a matter of *mental similarity*, the society a matter of flows of imitation and the subject in society is a 'hypnotised' individual who takes over the ideas of others without even knowing it. In this framework, social facts have a very distinctive ontology: they depend exclusively on the 'communion of minds' and on the hypnotic states that this communion makes possible. 'United people believe to see or to hear things that they no longer see or hear when they are isolated' (Tarde, 1989: 67). But this somnambulist-like stance does not lead to the individual lapsing, without proper judgment, into a floating magma of social illusions. In spite of their unconscious, unintentional tendency to mimicry, human beings are potentially able to assess the truth or falsity of contagious thoughts, mainly thanks to the biological boundaries and the cognitive capacities for survival that characterise them as organic beings (Schmid, 2004).

Most of Tarde's insights are present in the recent naturalistic approach to culture proper to the 'epidemiology of representations' (Sperber, 1996). In this materialist and evolutionary framework, society or culture is said to be reducible to a chain of 'mental representations, which are born, live and die within individuals skulls, and public representations which are plain material phenomena – sound waves, light patterns, etc. – in the environment of individuals' (Sperber, 1990: 28). But this causal chain of mental and public representations, which are 'ontologically correct' thanks to their observable materiality, cannot be compared, as in Tarde's model, to viral contagion (Clément, 2006). Unlike memetics, which sees cultural transmission as a replication mechanism (Dawkins, 1976), the 'epidemiology' of representations sees each episode of transmission as bringing new cognitive variations and communicative interpretations.

Within the 'intra-cerebral' framework of epidemiology, in its old version as in its contemporary cognitivist version, it is when a 'psychological quantity', to take up Tarde's expression, is widespread that it wins over its status of social representation and thereby becomes a 'social quantity'. As Sperber (1996) put it, mental representations are made social *via* their distribution: social or cultural representations, such as myths, narratives or tales, are defined as complex representations, widespread, enduring and constantly repeated, which are the object of a multiplicity of individual interpretations or 'mental versions' among a given population. To achieve cultural success, a representation that cannot 'naturally' impose itself on the human mind thanks to its intrinsic epistemic validity must have other cognitive properties, such as counter-intuitiveness, which enhance its probability of being replicated and entertained by human minds (Atran, 2002; Boyer, 2001; Sperber, 1975).

Despite their epidemiological success, cultural representations are endowed with a specific cognitive status: they are bracketed between circumspect 'quotation marks', which prevent their direct implication in inferences and actions linked to the tangible, indubitable reality of the natural world. In other words, individuals do not necessarily believe what cultural institutions instruct them to believe and subjective minds do not necessarily merge with the 'objective mind' of their society (Veyne, 1988). On the contrary, the innate ability of individuals to distance themselves from the cultural world allows them to draw an impervious boundary between basic-level experiences, which enjoy a cognitive primacy, and well controlled situated cultural evocations.

In summary, in infra-individual approaches, the subject loses its sovereignty not because of social forces exerted from above but because of uncontrolled, unintentional rays of imitation (Tarde) or adaptive cognitive micro-mechanisms (Sperber). But the degree of socialness of the mind is not the same in both approaches. Whereas the hypnotic 'state of society' can go down to the deepest level of the Tardean imitative mind, the Sperberian two-layer, 'split mind' keeps cultural representations at the surface of the cognitive architecture with a 'for-evocation-only' status that can hardly account for the ontological commitments that ideology, politics or religion can foster.

The social as quantity

By conceiving the individual as the ultimate source of action and meaning, *methodological* individualism and infra-individualism are never far away from their *ontological* counterparts, which would claim that the ultimate constituents of the social world are only individual or sub-individual minds. Beyond their divergences, these approaches have several characteristics in common. First, the boundaries of the mind are, so to speak, naturally given. For the infra-individualists, who

emphasise unconscious cognitive processing, the mind is confined within the physical limits of the brain and is fully dependent of its neuronal underpinnings. For the individualists, it is less the natural counterpart than the first-person point of view that is the main criterion for limiting the mental to its corporeal boundaries: here, the mind is assimilated to the self as the sole agent for either phenomenal sensations or rational decisions. Second, individual minds become social only temporarily and *a posteriori*, in function of the nature of the representations that furnish it. Far from being a latent variable that suffuses all aspects of belief, intention and collective life (DiMaggio, 1997), society or culture are facultative options. Third, since society is a collection or an association of beings, the 'cement of society', to take up Elster's (1989) expression, is not a matter of quality, for instance normativity or constraint; it is essentially a matter of *quantity*, similarity or convergence, sometimes intended, often unexpected, between either representational contents or individual actions. All those approaches thus face the difficult task of explaining how a minimum of similarities and commonalities, necessary for 'doing society', is possible for a collection of minds which are a priori isolated and independent from one another.

SOCIAL APPROACHES TO THE MIND

For the *social approaches to the mind,* the community of minds is not that problematic. From their holistic standpoint, the 'doing society' puzzle that (infra)individualist approaches are confronted with is artificially created by the striking absence of *institutions*, in the restricted sense of constraining, enforceable legal and political obligations, as well as in the extended sense of customary practices and ordinary ways of thinking and acting. Mental commonalities are ensured from early infancy by the enculturation or socialisation process, inherent to any community membership, which renders the separation between minds and society merely fictional. Thanks to this logical and ontological predominance, more or less determinative, the individual minds or their sub-intentional workings are relieved of the hard duty to hold society together.

But above all, in these views, the social bond is less a matter of psychological sameness than a matter of *social interdependency*, shared meanings and structural differentiation. In these views, social phenomena are not individuated, discrete 'items' that human minds can adopt, believe, share or imitate with different levels of awareness and adherence. They consist, instead, of public reasons for acting, role bearing and institutional practices whose *first-person plural ontology* is irreducible to the mental representations, conscious or infra-conscious, which furnish the narrow, opaque context of a particular mind (Kaufmann, 1999).

Given their 'We-ontology', common meanings, concepts and rules do not need the spatial location that physical and psychological definitions of the mind require. They belong to a collective mind whose nature is *semantic*. Far from the individualist mind 'cooking up in its internal kitchen' a decision and using only 'the ingredients that it has allowed through the door' (Dennett, 2003: 123), the semantic mind lies by definition *outside*, above, beyond or between people, in the public realm of shared meanings and institutions. In other words, the subjective mind is necessarily part of the 'objective spirit', that is, the 'institutions of meanings', the norms of conduct, thought-forms and religious, juridical and philosophical representations that make intelligible any mental and physical activities (Descombes, 1996; Taylor, 1994). In these holistic approaches, the expression 'social mind' is, so to speak, a *pleonasm*. Mind and society are two different parts of the same whole structure, two levels of instantiation of the same object, which is conveniently called 'society' (Elias, 1991). As such, the mind has no boundaries: it takes place in the space between people, that is, in a social, communal world of shared experience and public language (Vygotsky, 1978).

The mind as society bearer

Holistic views of the mind as the bearer of social rules and institutions emphasise, each in its own way, the shared 'subjective' counterpart of the objective social world, whether it be called habitus (Bourdieu, 1979), typifications (Schutz, 1962), member competence (Garfinkel, 1967) or category thinking (Macrae and Bodenhausen, 2001). Learned through socialisation, this subjective counterpart is subjective only in the technical, internal sense of 'known from within': it is composed of commonsense patterns and skills, embodied anticipations, and background expectancies, common to a given community, which permit one to divide the social world into graspable, predictable categories, to respond appropriately to the situated requirements of social settings and to anticipate in a practical, unreflexive way the socio-logical chain of actions. Thanks to the practical expectations and tacit knowledge that result from the long-term, pre-reflexive adaptation of individuals to their socio-cultural environment, institutions do not need to resort to violence to ensure their binding force. The social mind is a mind sufficiently educated and routinised to take social reality for granted and to thereby forget the arbitrary, artificial nature of the world that it has been handed down.

Although holistic accounts of the mind agree that the collective is the ultimate source of meaning, they disagree over the part of the mind, if any, that might remain individual-specific. So in Durkheim's version of holism, there are two levels of the description of reality: a *social level*, which consists of social emergent properties and laws that can explain macro phenomena such as the suicidal rate, and a *psychological level*, which consists of individual-dependent reasons for committing suicide (Durkheim, 1995, 1912). An up-to-date analogy between the relationship of *brain/mind* and *individual/society* allows Durkheim to justify the coexistence and autonomy of those two levels: just like the high-level mental properties of the mind emerge and are liberated from the low-level configuration of the neurons in the brain, norms and institutions have collective properties that emerge from the interactions between minds and are irreducible to mental properties (Durkheim, 1996: 34; Sawyer, 2002). Exclusively social emergent properties, which might take the form of collective representations, institutional rules or regular practices, have an inner consistency and interdependency that makes them irreducible to any psychological phenomenon. For Durkheim, however, the ontological autonomy of social facts and thereby also the epistemological independency of sociology do not entail the rejection of individual representations and biological instincts; on the contrary, those individual-level phenomena can only be accounted for by psychology or biology (Berton, 2008; Guillo, 2006).[2]

This being so, the tensions induced by the 'dual consciousness' that turns every individual, as Durkheim (1996) put it, into an 'homo duplex', are mostly theoretical. Practically, such tensions are mostly defused by the internal harmonisation between social obligations and individual desires, if not biological instinct, which morality brings into play. Although mostly identified by their capacity to impose external constraints on the individual, social facts tend to take a moral form that makes them, if not desirable, at least intrinsically valuable, thereby facilitating their translation into internal motivations. Thanks to this internal translation, the society is a 'supra-individual' reality but 'given in the experience' so that the distinction between individual and collective representations is often hard to maintain (Durkheim, 1995).

If Durkheim admits the possibility of individual-dependent thoughts and representations, for others, like Bourdieu (1997), assuming a potential dissociation between individual and collective representations does not make any sense: individual representations directly *derive* from the collective certainties, shared categorisations and relational commonalties that constitute the symbolic armature of a community. In this radical version of holism, the parts can be fully explained by the whole, the individual choices and preferences by the social order, so that there is no room left for psychology. The Bourdieusian mind, totally opaque to its 'owner', is an accomplice in the reproduction of social structures that are 'out there'. So in Bourdieu's theory, social structures exist, so to speak, twice: at the level of the first-order objectivity proper to objective structures, and at the level of the second-order objectivity proper to a system of dispositions, the *habitus*, which is the product of the internalisation, from an early age, of structural conditions and social necessities (Bourdieu, 1992).

Thanks to this twofold existence of the social, individuals can appropriately play the social game, without following explicit rules or manipulating mental representations: the 'knowing-how' proper to the 'logic of practice' enables the practical, un-reflexive anticipation of 'what must be done' in such-and-such situation (Bourdieu, 1980). Society is thus implemented, in the head or rather in the body, through a long-term process of 'implicit pedagogy' that ensures the social reproduction of the established order: dominant representations are in fact the representations of the dominating agents that have succeeded in turning the arbitrariness of their viewpoints into taken for granted values and beliefs. In this framework, social theorists must avoid taking up the superficial, self-satisfying rationalisations that overshadow the effective causes and unconscious strategies of the behaviour. They have to construe the expression 'taking one's stand' literally: the statements and mental states of the agent or, rather, of the *patient*, are the direct manifestations of the position that she or he occupies in the field of social forces that defines the social world.

While taking up Bourdieu's emphasis on the importance of dispositions and habits, socio-genetically constructed, some scholars have criticised the unidimensionality and invariability of the habitus (Corcuff, 1999). In the contemporary world, more than ever, the perfect adjustment between objective possibilities of action and subjective dispositions is rendered impossible by the plurality of socialisation spaces in which individuals are immersed from an early age. The disparity of roles, preferences and dispositions that coexist in the same mind (e.g. to be simultaneously a manager, a football fan, a husband, an ecologist, etc.) and the difficulty of reconciling them (e.g. to be both a great mother and an efficient scientist) leads individuals to behave in a partly unpredictable way (Lahire, 1998). But if agents are necessarily 'plural', they are nevertheless irreducibly singular: the singular 'folds' that characterise them are nothing but the individual-level effect of composition of social plurality, the particular form that the social takes 'locally' and that only a 'psychological sociology' can track down (Lahire, 1999). Such psychological sociology is both dispositionalist and contextualist: it situates the individual at the junction of the long-term, multifaceted incorporation of social regularities and norms and the short-term attunement to the situated requirements of particular situations.

Attentional commonalities

While also emphasizing the socialness of human minds, some approaches, mainly in cognitive sociology, ecological psychology and social psychology, insist on the attentional *commonalities* that mediate the perception, qualification and recognition of salience, define what information is relevant in which situation, and offer opportunities for action. Thus, the cognitive sociology proposed by Zerubavel (1993) shows how 'optical socialisation' teaches us how to 'look' at things in a conventional way, whether it be the beauty of a landscape, the similarity of sexes instead of differences, the relevance of the lions in the zoo instead of the fences, etc. Since those 'optical' norms are internalised

enough to become an 'ossified mental cage', deviations are rare and specially risky: optical deviants who maintain a view of the world that is at odds with the one commonly shared by others around them risks cognitive – and social – excommunication (Zerubavel, 1997). Interestingly, studies in ecological psychology confirm the importance of the socialisation of perception and attention. Agents who are socially competent have learnt how to 'be affected' by the world around them through the education of attention and have received the incentive to recognise some social 'affordances', that is, shared, public opportunities for action and perception, as worthy of being acted upon (Loveland, 1991; Sanders, 1997; Schmidt, 2007).

The culture-dependency of the 'attentional bias' that frames and shapes cognitive processing in a largely non-conscious manner is strikingly revealed in *cross-cultural* and *cross-social* experimental studies on logical inference, perception, categorisation and causal analysis (Choi et al., 1999; Nisbett, 2003). For instance, Easterners give priority to relationship processing, background elements and holistic explanations, whereas Westerners focus on individual properties, mentalistic attributions and analytic thinking (Nisbett and Masuda, 2003). Along the same lines, both farming and fishing communities, which emphasise harmonious social interdependence, exhibit greater holistic cognitive tendencies in attention, categorisation and reasoning than herding community, even if the three types of communities belong to the same national, geographic, ethnic and linguistic regions (Uskul et al., 2008). Cultural and social variations in apparent universal, automatic processes of perception and cognition show that the mind, far from being 'society-proof', is the product of the 'schematizing power of institutions' (Bruner, 1990: 58).

The mind as a 'society of me'

While also emphasising the socialness of cognitive and perceptual processes, the work of the social psychologist George Herbert Mead specifies the way in which society enters the mind: the social pathway to the individual mind goes through the normative expectations associated with role-taking and generalised expectations about other's responses to one's own actions (Cefaï and Quéré, 2006; Mead, 1967). Actually, the mind and in particular the so-called self, simultaneously subject and object, *I* and *me*, is by definition social: it emerges from the never-ending and imperfect alignment between the first-person view of the subject (*I*), which consists of unorganised flows of experience and impulses and the third-person perspective of the other (*Me*), which results from seeing one's own behaviour from others' standpoints. Through the process of role taking, actors respond to their own oncoming behaviour in the same way as others would, and then use the anticipated response to guide their own lines of conduct. The process of having others in mind appears very early in the ontogenetic development of the mind: mainly thanks to their exposure to mirrors and other self-reflecting devices, infants as young as two years of age begin to see themselves with the eyes of someone else, to simulate the public outlook to evaluate their own conduct and appearance; in short, to exist 'through' in addition to 'with' others (Rochat, 2003). Progressively, infants detach themselves from the particular expectations of their 'close others', that is, specific persons-in-contexts, (e.g. *my* mother is angry because I spilled the soup now), and anticipate the normative expectations of the 'Generalised Other' (e.g. *one* does not spill the soup) (Berger and Luckman, 1966; Mead, 1967).

Although most pragmatic approaches agree over the definition of the mind as a society of 'me', that is, as a bundle of social roles, they do not necessarily agree over the link capable of binding those 'me' together. Thus, less unified, coherent and serene than the Meadian mind, the mind that William James (1981) portrays encompasses many social selves, most often in conflict, whether it be the 'me-of-yesterday' and the 'me-of-tomorrow' or the 'me-as-philosopher' and the 'me-as-lady-killer', etc. Thus the Jamesian mind appears mostly as a battlefield in which each self tries to win over its rivals. Other more dialogical approaches see the self as polyphonic, if not democratic, by nature: the *I*-position moves among characters or selves, even to weaker ones, so that each can express its own view in the first person, and can comment on, and evaluate, the various points-of-view of other selves (Barresi, 2002). But beyond these divergences, pragmatic views raise the same issue: is this society of selves reconciled by a meta-process of unification or does it remain irremediably a composite aggregate whose 'members' pop up in the service of inner deliberations or external solicitations? If every mind constitutes a micro-society on its own, how can it meet the social expectations of 'entitativity' associated with subjecthood, mainly stability and unity? Whereas, for James, the somewhat mysterious *I* is put in charge of this unifying process, other approaches have more convincing hypotheses. Roughly speaking, the 'multiple personality disorder' that characterises every single mind can be overcome thanks to two different, but potentially complementary, processes of totalisation: one of these processes can be called *dramaturgical*, the other *narrativist*.

In the *dramaturgical* view, the social mind is a mind on stage, gifted enough to convince the public of the reality of the coherent, unitary self that that public normatively expects to encounter (Goffman, 1969). While endorsing the virtual selves that social roles constitute, individuals repeat public displays of self-mockery or half-commitment in order to distance themselves from their current self-in-role on the stage. By maintaining a distance between self-as-performer and self-as-character, role bearers hold out the possibility of the existence, backstage, of an alleged genuine self. In this dramaturgical model, the self is a self by default, a 'negational self' that refuses to be reduced to role bearing and rule compliance: 'I am not what

I do', 'I am not a stubborn bureaucrat', etc. (Chriss, 1999). In the radical version of role distanciation that Piette (1998) proposes, social actors are able to gain, thanks to the 'minor mode' of their self-involvement in role bearing, a 'supplement of being'. Mental distance from role requirements, withdrawal from official situational stakes – in short, inattention and distraction – are the privileged means, for people that Piette (2009) portrays as *Homo Minimalis*, to indicate that they are unique and hence irreducible to the typicality of role requirements, social practices and collective beliefs.

In the *narrativist* view, individuals have at their disposal another 'material' of self-construction, less 'negational' and more enduring than dramaturgical performances: *narratives*. As Bruner (1986) put it, narratives are the 'cultural scaffoldings', the 'prosthetic devices' by which human beings can weave together life events and create an identity invariant over time. Narratives turn the situated sense of oneself into a permanent, persisting self by organising personal experiences into a recognisable, conventional story and by instantiating social and personal identities that culture affords. So the narrative production and maintenance of selfhood is not an individual performance, but a more or less asymmetrical social and political achievement. Families can be indeed seen as micro-'Panopticons' whose narrative elicitations, expectations, evaluations and prohibitions force the 'self-in-construction' to lay out one's actions, thoughts and feelings and to structure them into tellable, culturally acceptable stories (Ochs and Capps, 2001). In fact, narrative is both restrictive and 'enabling': the narrative-mediated path of access to ones' own personal experiences obliges and enables people to join a culturally and socially organised world of common experiences and emotions (Miller et al., 1990).

Reflections on the dramaturgical performances and canonical narratives that, far from expressing the private, pre-existing reality of a unitary self, sustain the normative ideal of selfhood, are driven to extremity in what could be called the grammatical approaches of the mind. Such approaches shift the focus of the inquiry from the real mind-as-matter, even when penetrated by the social to the deepest level of representations, to *the grammar of mental concepts* that enable the members of a given community of practice and language to make sense of their behaviours (Ryle, 1949; Wittgenstein, 1981).

The third-person grammar of the mind

For the heterogeneous proponents of a *Wittgensteinian approach to the mind*, the mind is not an enclosed substance, an opaque entity; it is said to be fully observable, in the quality of orientedness of public actions as well as in the thick description of behaviours that the mastery of mentalistic accounts of action makes possible (Crane, 1998; Quéré, 1996; Winch, 1958). So mental states are no longer a *resource* of explanation but a *theme* of investigation for social theorists, who have to be agnostic, if not unrealistic, as to the very existence of those mental states and, of course, as to the causal power that those hypothetical mental states could exert over behaviour (Coulter, 1989; MacIntyre, 1986). In short, the grammatical inquiry focuses on what *counts as* mental in which community.

According to these views, mental states are not an extra-linguistic reality whose psychological matter would be independent of the concepts used to describe it (Bouveresse, 1996). On the contrary, mental states are said to be determined by a 'language game', whether called the semantics of action, the intentional stance or the theory of mind, which accounts for behaviours in terms of mental states, such as intentions, desires and beliefs (Dennett, 1987; Ricoeur, 1994; Sharrock and Coulter, 2004). Far from being an instrumental tool, necessary to translate private, inner states, into public expressions, the semantic repertoire of mental concepts is *constitutive*. Thanks to the identifying features that such a repertoire provides, an a priori shapeless, vague flow of sensations and feelings can be recognised as the normal, typical exemplar of a 'registered' state of mind (e.g. complaint, pain, doubt, etc.). Along the same lines, reasons for acting are not mental events, independent of the actions that they motivate; rather, they are encapsulated in the action itself, which is made intelligible thanks to the standard, typical 'vocabulary of motives' that goes with it (Mills, 1940; Von Wright, 1983). For instance, learning to vote entails learning good, justifying reasons for voting, such as satisfying citizenship duty, showing concern for matters of general interest, etc.

Thus, the semantics of the mind has a *normative* dimension; it indicates what mental states people *should* have within a shared normative context, underpinned by the mutual expectations, commitments and obligations at work in a given community of interpreters. Mental attributions, whether they be self- or hetero-attributions, are made on the basis of what people are doing and what they are supposed to do in some circumstances; as such, they presuppose the use of a public language that responds to *appropriateness and correctness criteria* (Baker and Hacker, 1984; Strawson, 1959). For instance, 'suffering' is an attribution that can be used only in some conditions; the attitude of an adult who claims 'to suffer' because he cannot have sweets does not satisfy the criterion of correctness that governs the 'good use' of the mental verb 'suffering' and risks being considered as irrelevant and invalid, if not pathological.

Far from having the status of primitive, private entities, mental states thus have the status of mental *predicates*, that is, pre-defined, publicly available categories that anyone can understand independently of the empirical occurrences that are susceptible to instantiate them. Within this semantic framework, mental states can be literally taken as the furniture of the mind: just like

the 'furniture of a material room', they can be described by an *external third-person stance* that totally disregards its singular owner (Wittgenstein, 1981). Once the vagaries of individual psychologies are left aside in favour of their public mode of description, the apparent referential opacity that characterises mental states when they are confined within the oblique context of the individual mind disappears and, with it, the well-known 'problem of other minds' (Descombes, 1996). Actually, other minds are no longer opaque since the access to mental states is perfectly *symmetrical* for ego and alter, for the actor and the interpreter. From the side of the actor, individuals lose their alleged first-person privileges, mainly the alleged transparency and infallibility of the knowledge of their own mental states, accessible through introspection. As confirmed by experimental research with children (Gopnik, 1993) or adults (Nisbett and Wilson, 1977), when people give reasons for their beliefs, preferences or behaviours, they do not go into their memory to read out mental contents; rather, they make up a 'plausibility judgment'; they exercise inferential, theory-like reasoning that results from them turning their interpretative skills upon themselves. From the side of the interpreter, the public availability of the common, impersonal semantics, which establishes a rule-governed link between psychological attributions and the 'entities' that are supposed to satisfy them, entitles the observer to call into question the mastery of a mental concept that the agent uses, even regarding his own feelings (Kripke, 1982). Thus, the third-person interpretation of a public behaviour, such as breaking a chair, leads one to attribute to the agent the emotional state normally associated with this behaviour, in this case the state of anger, even if the agent in question denies being angry (Bedford, 1986). Just as reasons for acting must meet the 'standards of reasonable behaviour current in society' (Winch, 1958), emotions must meet the standards of emotional behaviour.

A recent version of the grammatical account of the mind as a public set of common resources of intelligibility and justification is found in the French approach called *pragmatic sociology*. Actually, the so-called model of 'economies of worth' shifts social determinants, traditionally placed within the individual minds, towards the hierarchy of worth and the principles of evaluation and justification that allow the closure of what can be envisaged or not in a given situation (Boltanski and Thévenot, 2006). For instance, the worth of selfish interest is constitutive of the 'grammar' of economical exchange but not of love life; the denunciation of a political scandal grammatically involves a feeling of indignation and the appeal to a 'regime of justice' in which there is necessarily a victim and a culprit (Boltanski, 1990; Thévenot, 1990). In this framework, the mind is thus endowed with the 'grammatical' competence necessary to navigate the interweaving multiple orders of worth (e.g. inspirational, domestic, civic, recognitional, industrial and commercial), to switch from a regime of action to another (e.g. familiarity to justification), to resort to reflexive accounts, and to maintain with others the pursuit of a 'common good', either material (e.g. the purchase of a house) or ideal (e.g. equality) (Bénatouï, 1999; Boltanski and Thévenot, 2006).

Three important, and potentially problematic, characteristics that are common to these different grammatical approaches are worth noticing. First, grammatical enterprises assume that ordinary agents are endowed with the universal, generic member competence that the status of 'being in society' requires (Button, 1991; Cicourel, 1974; Garfinkel, 1967). Such competence is the abstract, singular, indefinite common denominator of social living and is, as such, neither socially distributed, nor culturally dependent. Second, grammatical investigations, which are of a *descriptive* nature, must lay out the public resources of inference and action that are brought into play by the actors themselves. This descriptive ambition prevents social grammarians from resorting to 'beings' and values, such as class membership, social force or symbolic violence, that these very actors do not deem relevant. Last but not least, the third-person status of the grammar of the mind ensures a *semantic* symmetry between oneself and others that dismisses the leading role of the self in the determination of one's own mental states and actions. Every competent community member is entitled to evaluate the likelihood of, and to possibly put right, the agent's psychological accounts. But if individuals lose their first-person privileges, how can they nevertheless enjoy an authority about their own thoughts and sensations – an authority that is the very condition of a moral, responsible being that takes up a stance and answers for what he/she is doing? How is 'doing subject' possible for agents who are ensnared by an impersonal social grammar that calls into question their first-person authority and responsibility? It is only on this third issue, central to the *mind–society* problem, which the next section dwells on.

The return of the asymmetry: the process of doing subject

The Wittgensteinian solution to this first-person authority puzzle lies in the pragmatic emphasis on the constitutive power of self-ascriptions. Actually, the normative expectations of accountability and justifiability proper to the grammar of intentional concepts (e.g. actions, reasons for acting, beliefs, etc.) consecrate the point of view of the agent as their ultimate mode of validation (Baynes, 2001; Davidson, 1984; Strawson, 1959). Now, from a *pragmatic* standpoint, those normative assumptions do not remain at the level of an objectifying 'process of individuation', which merely responds to the semantic question 'of whom this action is' or 'to whom is happening' (Descombes, 1991). Such assumptions give rise to a 'process of individualisation',

fundamentally self-implicative and subjec-
tifying, which is both moral and practical:
I do not *report* a promise that would be pre-
established in the inner space of my mind,
I am *making* one at the same time as I express
it (Sluga, 1996). Such a self-binding component turns the semantic symmetry between
self and other into a pragmatic asymmetry
in the absence of which the very concept of
the subject would not make any sense.

But this final pragmatic asymmetry does
not recreate an asocial mind. In the *long-
term,* 'self-ascriptions' are the ultimate results
of a social chain of interpretative presumptions and normative hetero-ascriptions
of responsibility and freedom from other
people, authorities and institutions (Harré,
1983; Martin and Sugarman, 1999). In
other words, Meadian in inspiration, the
first-person stance adopted by the individual who claims responsibility for his
actions derives from the third-person stance
taken by others towards him (Strawson,
1959; Kaufmann, 1999). In the *short-term*,
the status of the subject is never acquired
once and for all; paying tribute to the self
is the never-ending work of the first-person
enunciations, judgments, or actions that
allow the agent to win over a privileged
stance, although contextual and temporary.
As Benveniste (1966) put it, the subject
is nothing but a discursive position, a linguistic enactment that allows, through the
use of 'I', the maintenance of the fragile
asymmetry between the first-person and the
third-person. In other words, an individual
counts as a subject when he performs an act
that allows him to present and to commit
himself as a responsible subject. In this
view, the self is 'not a noun but a verb', that
is, an achievement made only possible by
the skill of reflexively 'self-referring' (Fay,
1996: 39). Of course, this achievement is
not solitary; on the contrary, it depends
upon the interpellation scene where the 'I'
faces a 'You' who *recognises* the right of
this 'I' to speak and act 'as an I', to speak
of oneself in terms of thoughts, actions and
intentions; in short, to take the position of a
subject in the interlocution process (Butler,
2001; Honneth, 1996).

The mind as social quality

On condition that the criterion for having a
mind is not phenomenological consciousness
and minimal self-awareness (the 'what is it
like' of mental life) but rather mental states
and capacity for acting, holistic and grammatical approaches of the mind agree over
the status of the conceptual furniture of the
mind. Far from idiosyncratic contents, mental
'entities' are said to derive from public reasons for acting, prevailing frames and normative categorisations that characterise a given
community. In these views, the mind and
its mental endowments are so fully dependent upon the social, cultural and historical
environments that speaking of an 'individual
mind' is almost an oxymoron. Not only is the
mind by definition a 'society in miniature'
(Douglas, 1986), but also the dualist issue of
the external link between mind and society
assumes a division point that has no reason
to exist. Subjective minds are nothing but
the holders of the public representations and
common meanings that constitute the objective mind of a given community.

This being so, one of the properties of those
public representations and common meanings
is to portray, at least in modern societies, the
individual as a mind-minded, autonomous
and responsible self. Now by dint of talking
and acting *as if* a self was 'in there', individuals, whether they be virtuoso actors or
talented novelists, contribute to making this
canonical narrative come true. So holistic
and grammatical approaches of the mind are
not necessarily stuck with a public theatre,
very different from the well known private
Cartesian theatre of the mind, in which the
actor would make his public believe, thanks to
his dramaturgical and narrative performance,
in the existence of his fictional self. Even as
a mere 'centre of narrative gravity', such a
fictional self has real effects: it prompts the
persons who endorse it to act accordingly,

mainly by holding themselves accountable for what they are doing and feeling (Dennett, 1992). In short, the self is a social institution, but a social institution powerful enough to trigger a genuine ontological commitment from those who are exposed to it.

Roughly put, holistic and grammatical approaches have attacked the sovereignty of the individual, self-enclosed mind on two 'fronts': one attack, carried out from above, consists in immersing the individual mind in a public system of meanings and inter-dependencies; the other attack, from below, inserts the social into the deepest layers of the mind, via a socio-genetic system of dispositions, perceptual schemas and abilities. But there is another important way of emphasising the contribution of the outside world to the constitution of mental states. In *externalist approaches*, very influential in analytical philosophy, the contribution of the social world to the mind is *logical* rather than *socio-genetical*. Indeed, their line of argument concerns less the vertical subordination of the mind to social systems, either *bottom-up* or *top-down* and more the horizontal boundary between the inner mind and the outer word (*in-out*).

EXTENDING THE MIND'S BOUNDARIES

Social deference

Against the internalist reduction of the mind to a narrow inner circuit, externalists argue that the external world contributes to the individuation of any mental content, except for phenomenal sensations, objectless hallucinations and vague memories. Since mental states are characterised by the intentional property of *aboutness* whose nature is by definition *relational*, they cannot turn without gripping real elements of the outer world (Chisholm, 1972). On the contrary, their representational content necessarily emerges from the encounter with an element of the environment, which thereby becomes an integral part of their conditions of satisfaction (e.g. the belief that I have a frog in front of me is true only if there is really a frog).

Whereas *natural externalism* emphasises the causal link between an intentional state and the external, physical properties of the natural entity it is about, for instance water or gold (Putnam, 1975), *social externalism* insists on the fact that mental contents are not only dependent on the nature of the entities they are about, but also on the conceptual and linguistic way in which the community refers to those very entities (Voltolini, 2005). Individuals can meaningfully use concepts, such as arthritis, elm or synecdoche, that they do not really master or even understand because they tacitly defer to the public language, fixed by the linguistic community and passed on by authoritative experts, which establishes what counts as arthritis, elm or synecdoche (Burge, 1979, 1986). From this social externalist view, the mere use of certain concepts and words enrol the individual *de facto* in a deferential chain of communication that relates him or her to the empirical referents in an indirect, oblique way. In other words, most conceptual and linguistic usages, if not all, are characterised by their 'social indexicality': contrary to appearances, the person who speaks of 'arthritis' refers not to the arthritis itself but to what 'physicians call arthritis', thereby deferring the ultimate determination of the reference to the competent agent for the conventions in force in the public language (Récanati, 2000, 2001).

Beyond skin and skull

According to those externalist views, mental states are only the internal counterpart of intentions, representations, beliefs and desires whose natural, social or historical external constituents are partly out of reach of the individual mind. Whereas this kind of externalism does not call into question the distinction between the mind, 'brainbound' and neurally realised, and the outer world, the thesis of the 'extended mind' claims that there is no reason to a priori bind the mind by skin and skull (Clark and Chalmers, 1998). In this thesis, the mind has not the prerogative of cognition; cultural products, such as language or artefacts, lie beyond the skin but they partake in human cognition in the same way as the neuronal workings of the brain do. According to the so-called 'Parity Principle', which is a principle of functional equivalence, all cognitive 'bearers', whether it be mental states (desires, beliefs, knowledge) or external supports (notebooks, tattoos, tools, artefacts, etc.), which actively contribute to our long-term knowledge, dispositional beliefs and current behaviours, must be accepted as part of the cognitive process (Clark and Chalmers, 1998; Clark, 2010). Thus, the beliefs stored in a notebook of an Alzheimer's patient, on the condition that the content of the notebook is automatically endorsed and easily accessible, should be seen as functionally akin to the memories stored in the biological memory of a non-disabled person's brain (Clark and Chalmers, 1998).

In this joint cognitive venture, the external, immediate environment does not make do with providing representational contents or informational inputs; the constitutive role that it plays in the determination of the behaviour is just as causally relevant as typical internal features of the brain. Writing, pen, paper, computer and the like are more than tools; they are cognitive extensions that have moulded our brain from birth (Goody, 1977). Without those external contributions and improvements, human cognitive and behavioural competence will drop, just as it would if we removed parts of the brain (Clark and Chalmers, 1998). Far from being mere instruments, social organisation and cultural scaffolding such as language, technological artefacts or external computing resources are parts of the cognitive 'body-and world- involving cycles' that 'supersize the mind' (Clark, 2008).

Along the same lines, the model of 'distributed cognition' shows that the performance and experience of a supposedly single mind are in fact made possible by situated, fine-tuned coordination with other people as well as by access to artefacts or tools (e.g. cockpit, blackboard, writing, etc.) that encapsulate the information necessary for carrying out a given course of action (Salomon, 1993). Contrary to artificial cognition, experimentally isolated from its material and social context, 'cognition in the wild' is a collective process, distributed across the members of a social group, which relies heavily on a cognitive and social division of labour (Hutchins, 1995). So cognitive properties, which have been mistakenly attributed to the individual mind, must be given back to that which they belong, that is, complex socio-cultural systems and collectives of agents.

Models of 'embodied cognition' also call into question the 'Classical Sandwich Model' of cognition as a system of representations and operations stuck, in the *head* of isolated individuals, between the moment of perception (perceptual inputs) and the moment of action (motor outputs) (Hurley, 2001). It is the whole *body* rather than the mere brain that is seen as the central mediation of any engagement with the world. Instead of a 'spectatorial', distant manipulation of symbols, cognitive activity is an enactive, mostly infra-conscious anticipation of the action to perform (Gallagher, 2006). Mind is embodied, that is, shaped by sensorimotor experiences that resonate with the properties of a physical and social environment which is essentially a field of practice, a 'taskcape' (Ingold, 2001). The 'structural coupling' between the behavioural and cognitive capacities of a given organism and the objective properties of its environment is a mutually constitutive relation. Far from an immanent cognitive structure, and far from an abstract disengaged 'ego-pole', the mind is geared to its encounter with the world (Cermolacce et al., 2007; Varela et al., 1991). Such coupling is illustrated by the paradigm of colour: colour is neither a pre-given fact in the world, nor a subjective representation in the head: it is 'interactional' (Lakoff and Johnson, 1999).

Beyond their divergences, these different approaches call into question the current assumption that what is outside the head is also outside the mind. In the absence of an enabling web of bodily, social, cultural and technological scaffolding, the individual mind would be literally *insignificant*.

COLLECTIVE MINDS

The issue of collective ascriptions

Giving up on the idea that the mind is bounded by skin and bones removes a major barrier to the idea of *collective minds* (Tollefsen, 2006). In analytical philosophy, recent debates over collective intentionality and group minds also discuss whether the right of admission within the mental realm can be extended beyond the individual head. But here the issue is whether the extension of the mind to its environment can take the form of an additional 'mind bearer', that is, groups. Can the commonsense use of *collective* predicates, such as 'the Army destroys its enemies' or 'the football team loses hope', be reduced to a linguistic shortcut, a convenient way of speaking; in short, a fictional abstraction? Can and must those collective predicates be replaced with individual predicates, deemed ontologically correct, which would be equally distributable among a *collection* of state, army or football team members?

In fact, such nominalist reduction seems only to be applicable to collective assertions that are obviously of a distributive nature: '*we went to France*' can be translated into 'I went' or 'each of us went to France'. Other collective predications are of an ambiguous nature (e.g. we have voted for the first candidate) and can be the object of either a distributive reading (e.g. each of us have voted for the first candidate) or a collective reading (e.g. we as a group have voted for the first candidate). Along the same ambiguous lines, subjects of collective statements can be construed in two main ways (Jones, 2005; Sacks, 2005). As 'set-names', they are reducible to a list of single empirical members who must, all and without exception, satisfy the common predicate that has allowed to establish the list in question (e.g. coin collectors always search for new coins). But as a stereotype-based, membership category, such collective statements concern an unlimited population (women, Black, home buyers, etc.) and are 'protected against induction': so the category-bound statement 'women are fickle' is not dismissed by the fact that Mary, who is a woman, is not fickle (Sacks, 2005). Last but not least, an important number of collective attributions cannot be distributed at all: it is indeed a mistake to infer from a statement such as 'we have won the war' the statement 'I have won the war'. Accounting for this kind of attribution is precisely the main issue in the controversial debates over the status of collective beliefs, group minds and collective intentionality that actually prevail in social ontology.

The first account of non-distributive collective attributions can be called *instrumentalist:* the attribution of collective predicates to groups is fully justified, not because groups satisfy the metaphysical criteria for existence, mainly that of exerting a causal power, but because such attribution fulfils explanatory, interpretative and predictive needs. Endorsing the intentional stance to interpret a collection of individuals *as if* they were a unique agent, motivated by a unique set of beliefs and intentions, is as heuristic as endorsing it to construe individual behaviours (Dennett, 1990). At the individual scale, just as at the collective scale, the intentional stance allows one to consider subunits, whether it be people or cells, as thinking and behaving as if they were a unitary, rational and purposive agent (Jones, 2001). In both cases, the intentional stance does not necessarily involve any ontological commitment; it is above all a good tool for making a priori opaque preferences and behaviours intelligible and predictable. For instance, collective agency assumed in a statement such as 'France declares war' allows one to predict the logical subsequent course of action (e.g. military attacks, strategical moves, etc.).

However, by emphasising pragmatic convenience instead of metaphysical necessity, this instrumentalist view does not determine precisely enough the criterion that permits

distinguishing groups which can be legitimately considered as a valid locus of authority
and responsibility from the arbitrary bundles
of people that are abusively treated as homogeneous and reified into groups (Brubaker
and Cooper, 2000). It is precisely such a
criterion that the 'we-ness' or the 'jointness'
proper to the approaches in terms of collective intentionality provides.

Collective intentionality

Approaches in terms of *collective intentionality*, which is, so to speak, the subjective
counterpart of groupness, allow one to distinguish a real group from a nominal category
of individuals, established by hetero-categor-
isation and based on a supposedly common
property (e.g. home buyers, race or ethnicity,
etc.). In these views, collective attitudes are
both the *theoretical glue* that ensures the
conceptual transversality between micro- and
macro-scale collectives (e.g. stroll, orchestra,
nation, etc.) and *the social glue* that allows
one to transform an aggregate, for instance
two people sitting accidentally in a bus near
each other, into a genuine collective, that is,
two people sitting *together.*

The first view of collective intentionality is clearly *individualist*: joint intentions
are considered as a specific, complex 'species' of individual mental states. This allows
one to maintain the individualistic premise according to which intention, belief or
action can only have one individual, brainbound bearer. But whereas Bratman (1993)
admits only a difference in content between
individual and so-called shared intentions,
Searle (1990) considers 'we-intentions' as
sui-generis intentions whose specific 'psychological mode' makes them irreducible to
a summation of singular intentions. Taking
up Weber's argument for differentiating
social actions from individual actions, Searle
distinguishes collective intentionality, which
occurs whenever people take into account
the action of others to determine their own
action (e.g. playing a symphony), from the

contingent similarity between uncoordinated
but objectively convergent individual movements (e.g. running to a common shelter in
order to escape from rain) (Searle, 1990).
In the shelter case, the common goal (e.g.
to escape from rain) can be reduced to a set
of *I*-intentions, possibly supplemented with
mutual beliefs about the intentions of others;
in contrast, in the symphony case, collective
intentionality rests on the complementarity
and interdependency of individual assignments, each contributing in its own way to
the realisation of the overall collective goal
(e.g. if *We* play in a symphonic orchestra,
then *I* have to play the piano score) (Searle,
1990). This view, extremely influential in the
debate about social ontology, raises two main
issues. The first issue is that, since the reposi-
tory of intentionality, whether collective or
individual, is the individual head, one single
delusional person or even 'a brain in a vat'
could mistakenly entertain a *We*-intention
(Searle, 1990: 407). This odd conclusion
turns Searle's methodological solipsism into
'ontological individualism', which overlooks
the objective, external consistency proper to
the mutual, binding commitment between
participating individuals in a We-relation
(Meijers, 2003). The second issue raised by
Searle's model is that it only addresses a specific kind of collective intentionality, namely
the ordinary, explicit and voluntary sense of
'intending to do'. By leaving aside the broad
sense of intentionality, that is, the property
of 'aboutness' of mental states that externalist approaches have well emphasised, such
a view cannot account for collective beliefs
as well as for the contribution of the physical and social world to their production and
maintenance (e.g. we believe in God).

It is precisely those two issues that the
model of a 'plural subject' proposed by
Margaret Gilbert (1989) allows one to solve.
First, the plural subject, that is, the *We*
formed by several individuals, cannot be an
illusion confined in one single head since
it is composed of different individuals who
mutually commit themselves to joint actions
and collective beliefs and readily endorse the

deontic rights and obligations linked to this commitment. For Gilbert (1990), the paradigmatic social fact, which offers a model for society at large, is 'walking together': the walkers jointly agree to form a 'We', duly unified by the common goal of walking together in the company of each other, and have the consciousness of constituting a unity with the others. Those veridical clauses of mutuality and awareness, which make 'other-orientedness' depend upon the real presence of other individuals, avoids the Searlian solipsist view of primitive we-intentions as well as the atomist reduction of collectives to non-mutual *I*-intentions and I-beliefs. Second, intentionality in the sense of aboutness is central in Gilbert's model, in which a collective belief is not a largely shared belief, but a particular case of joint commitment by which individuals give up their full authority over their own action to the group, believe as a single mind and act as 'a single body' (Gilbert, 2002). What makes a given belief collective, then, is the *normativity* and the conformity expectations associated with it: group members are supposed to accept and publicly endorse the official beliefs of their group and if they do not, they can be blamed for not fulfilling their obligations.

Thus, Gilbert's collective belief, partly inspired by Durkheim's 'dual consciousness', is close to what Tuomela (1995) calls 'positional belief' or 'we-mode belief', that is, a belief that an individual endorses as a group member, but does not necessarily endorse as a private person. For instance, members of a literary circle can 'We-believe' that Shakespeare is the best poet of all times without privately endorsing the correspondent 'I-mode belief' (Tuomela and Tuomela, 2003).

Supra-individual organisations

The main issue raised by the model of plural subject is that it mainly applies to a particular kind of group, namely the small-scale informal group, which can reach shared intentions by means of joint commitments,

personal communication and mutual agreement (Jansen, 2004). Such a model cannot account for institutions that are not based on mutual agreement, such as the actions of corporations (e.g. a nation declaring war or a government taking legal action against a public company) or for informal consensus and normative expectations (e.g. we are used to raising our hat to newcomers). This is because corporation actions fall less within the province of a collective 'We-stance', still characterised by the subjective, deliberate allegiance of the multiple 'I-stances' that constitute it, than within the province of an impersonal 'One'. As an anonymous, agentless force, the 'One', deprived of the 'index of subject' reserved for *I*, *You* and *We*, operates as a 'non-person' (Benveniste, 1966). Such 'non-persons' are grounded in a certain *type of organisation*, which is less sustained by we-attitudes and collective intersubjectivity than by what Latour (1994) calls an 'interobjectivity', that is, a whole system of objects that frame interactions and stabilise institutions (e.g. chalice, chair, flag, speaking grill, administrative form, etc.).

Once the analytical focus is on the type of organisation rather than on collective intentionality per se, it becomes easier to see how purposive collectives can develop a mind of their own, mimicking or simulating the performance of an individual agent and imposing the discipline of reason at the collective rather than at the individual level (Pettit and Schweikard, 2006). There is a group mind when individuals act jointly to set up common goals and to establish a *rational* procedure and body of judgments for guiding the pursuit of those ends (Pettit, 2003). Thus, a parliament can bring forward a certain motion only if it obeys certain formalities, regulated in the constitution. The main characteristic of group minds, such as co-authorships, partnerships, civic associations, commercial companies, churches or courts, is that they are starkly discontinuous with the mentality of their members and that their place in social life parallels that of individual persons: they own property and enter contracts, they are responsible for their commitments, and they are treated as agencies with which it is possible to reason, just as one person may reason with another (Pettit, 2003; Tollefsen, 2002).

In this line of argument, the mark of the social is less the 'togetherness' effect that emerges from many intersubjectivities than the heaviness of the organisational architecture and the inertia of the structural interdependency that ultimately characterise social reality. As Descombes (2000) put it, society is not only made of groups and collective actions; it is also made of 'concrete totalities' (e.g. team, nation, family), defined by the internal relationships that relate their parts, as well as by the specific kinds of actions they can carry out. So, contrary to what Gilbert's model suggests, genuine social actions cannot be performed either by several persons or by a single one (e.g. to go for a walk); they can only be achieved by a plurality of individuals or under the name of this plurality (e.g. to ratify a peace treaty with France) (Descombes, 1996). Such plurality is organised into a *structural system*, which allocates complementary and interdependent roles to its 'bearers'. For instance, economical exchange structurally entails a triadic relationship involving two complementary roles, in this case the salesman and the buyer, and an overall market rule (Descombes, 1996). Those structural systems are characterised by relational properties that are, as such, neither group-level, nor individual-level properties. By definition, indeed, relational properties cannot be grounded in individuals, whether they be singular or collective, for the good reason that they are *constitutive of both* (Descombes, 1995; Kaufmann, 2010).

THE SOCIAL BRAIN

The mind's aptitude for sociality

A final, fascinating approach to the social mind that is worth mentioning sheds light,

thanks to advances in developmental, comparative and evolutionary psychology, on the essentially social nature of the *brain*. The minds of evolved organisms, just like their physiology, are assumed to be the well adapted result of long-term adaptation to their physical and social environment (Cosmides and Tooby 1994; Hirschfeld and Gelman, 1994; Sperber et al., 1995). Thus, according to the 'social intelligence' (Humphrey, 1976) or the 'social brain' hypothesis (Brothers, 1997; Dunbar, 2003), selection has favoured larger brains and more complex cognitive capacities that increase fitness advantages in an environment in which social coalitions and alliances are imperative for survival. On this view, the term 'social' refers to a specific ontological domain that pre-wired specific mechanisms enable one to grasp. The mind is thus said to be social because it is endowed with a 'faculty of social cognition', which is not the result of an ontogenetic progressive moulding, but rather the product of phylogenetic selective pressures (Jackendoff, 1992).

The mainstream view of social cognition as domain-specific sees social information processing as *mindreading*, that is, the capacity to explain others' behaviour in terms of mental states such as knowledge, desires and beliefs. This fundamental ability, called 'Theory of mind', is one of the main preoccupations of *social neurosciences*, which try to pinpoint, thanks to functional magnetic resonance imaging study (fMRI), the regions of the brain activated by tasks requiring mindreading (Gallagher et al., 2000; Völlm et al., 2006). More precisely, theory of mind, which is said to be at the heart of the functioning of the social brain, would be underlain by two main neural mechanisms (Frith & Wolpert, 2003; Frith, 2008). A low-level 'mirror mechanism', which would enable the direct understanding of the meaning of the actions and emotions of others by internally replicating or simulating them, and a high-level mentalizing mechanism, which would give rise to conceptual reasoning about other people's minds (Adolphs, 1999). Since the activity of the mirror system, first discovered in the brain of non-human primates, provides an observer with the understanding of a perceived action by means of the motor simulation of the agent's observed movements, it has been largely construed as the motor building block of social cognition, empathy and even morality. Direct simulation of the witnessed behavior is said to bridge, at a very low level, the motor gap but also the social and moral gap between self and other, inducing immediate understanding of conspecifics (Rizzolatti et al., 2001; Gallese et al., 2004). Along with other levels of brain activations, such as biological motion and agency detection, the mirror neuron system is thus usually construed as the neural building block of theory of mind: it would reveal the brain's capacity to resonate with the actions and emotions of others, to imitate them, in short to empathize with one's fellows (Grezes & Decety 2001). Neural mirroring would thus solve the 'problem of other minds', that is, how we can access and understand the minds of others, and make intersubjectivity possible, thus facilitating social behavior (Iacoboni, 2009).

It is worth noticing, however, that the social scope of the mirror system actually raises controversies (Southgate et al., 2008). After all, the fact that some brain areas light up both when perceiving an action and when performing one, which was said to induce a direct matching between self and others, is essentially a matter of *motor* simulation, based upon the observer's ability to match an agent's perceived action. But motor simulation is very different from the understanding of other's social actions and intentions: a lot of social behaviors do not require the matching of observed movements, for instance in response to the perception of a threat, it might be more adaptive to flee, not to simulate the threatening agent's observed movements! (Jacob & Jeannerod, 2005). But if specific neural circuits involved in more sophisticated theory of mind inferences are still controversial, most scholars generally agree that the ability to 'mind read' is central to social understanding and that it is the product of the expansion of the primate brain, especially the

neocortex and limbic system, including the amygdala (Emery & Perrett, 2000).

The hypothesis of a 'social brain', that is, of the existence of specific cognitive mechanisms devoted to social information processing, is also found in evolutionary and developmental psychologists, cognitive scientists and primatologists. Thus, in primatology, the social brain refers to the abilities that enable evolved primates to cope with the complexities of social living, mainly by deceiving others, tracking down potential deception, calculating the balance of advantage and loss; in short, by serving whatever is susceptible to promoting reproductive success (Premack and Woodruff, 1978; Whiten et al., 1991). From this perspective, social cognition tends to be assimilated to the partial, shaky and rudimentary knowledge of others' mental states that primates, as 'goods psychologists', would master (Cheney and Seyfarth, 2007). In developmental psychology, theory of mind is also seen as the main, if not the only, crux of social cognition, whether it refers to the 'cold cognition' proper to 'belief-desire psychology' (Wellman, 1990) or to the 'hot cognition' proper to inferences about others' affective states (Hobson, 1994). In these different approaches, the cornerstone of the social mind is assumed to be the ability to understand others' psychology, thereby fostering the assimilation of social interactions to the '*interaction of minds*, which can be properly understood only when one takes into account what people think about other people's thoughts' (Perner and Wimmer, 1985: 438).

Countering the reduction of social cognition to a set of mechanisms enabling social beings to enter, conceptually and/or phenomenologically, the private worlds hidden in the minds of others, some scholars have argued for another conception of the domain-specificity of the social brain, based upon social and yet non-mentalistic predictions and inferences. One of the specificities of the social brain, neglected by the under-socialised view of society assumed by mainstream theory of mind advocates, would be the capacity to rapidly detect *affiliations, relationships and memberships* (Fiske, 1992; Jackendoff, 1992). The hypothesis is that the identification of out-group members whose behaviour is potentially predatory was so critical for survival that it generated patterns of exclusively social inferences and expectations dedicated to group affiliation and social categories (Hirschfeld, 1995, 2001). While also insisting on the sorting of conspecifics into inductively rich group categories, some researchers consider that the conceptual primitive of non-mentalistic social cognition is less group membership or social relationships than *deontic rules* which indicate what one may, must, or must not do in a given set of circumstances (Cheng and Holyoak, 1985; Cosmides and Tooby, 2005; Cummins, 1998).

Beyond their important divergences, studies on coalition recognition and deontic reasoning agree over the existence of an elaborate social accounting system, that is, an 'aptitude for sociality' that enables one to monitor the relationships of kinship, group membership and dominance, and to keep track of the network of rights and obligations underlying them (Conein, 2006; Jackendoff 1999). In this non-mentalistic version of social cognition, the social mind is endowed with innate abilities that allow it to see not what conspecifics are *thinking* but what they are *doing*, to prioritise inputs according to their degree of relevance, and to use impersonal commonalities to determine one's own behaviour as well as to anticipate what others will do. Those competences, not only intentional but also *attentional*, permit one to engage in shared topologies of salience, to recognise the sameness of rule-governed situations, to draw a conceptual family resemblance between unknown and known situations; in short, to identify social *Gestalts* (Kaufmann and Clément, 2007; Klin et al., 2004). The absence of such attentional abilities, manifest in pathologies such as autism or schizophrenia, deprives individuals, as Collins (1998) put it, of 'the capacity to attain social fluency'.

Mindminded paths to culture

Interestingly, in the different views of the social brain, mindedness and socialness are no longer inversely proportional. On the contrary, the mind becomes genuinely *social* when it gains *cognitive* capacities for sociality and for culture (Herrmann et al., 2007). Actually, it is thanks to their cognitive ability to escape from the reality principle that humans can endorse and sustain cultural facts, that is, symbolic commonalities and common intangibles that are not perceptible or non-existent – whether absent people (expatriate friend), future or hypothetical events (the invitation of next Saturday), fictional entities (Sherlock Holmes, Mickey Mouse), institutional facts (the United States, God), or counterfactual goals (scientific inquiry, political project) (Harris, 2000; Tomasello et al., 2005). This sophisticated human-specific ability to endorse, by a stretch of the imagination, a group-level order of reality that departs from the actual state of affairs, and to entertain joint attention to unobservable entities, generates, as Simmel (1983) put it, a 'supplement of society'. Indeed, there is 'society' when reciprocal action and communication give rise to an enduring entityå or persisting form that relates individuals via their common, mediated relationship to a third entity, whether it be a supra-individual entity (God, State) or a collective whole (nation, couple, family) (Simmel, 1999). Cognitive capacity for bringing into existence socio-political forms and entities, whose apparent exteriority imposes itself on the very same individuals who have contributed to its emergence, is, therefore, essential to the process of 'doing society' and holding it together. It just goes to show that the supplement of society requires a *supplement of mind*, not its lessening or, worse, its elimination.

CONCLUSION: THE MODERN MIND

Even if 'doing society' and 'doing subject' are not two inverse, incompatible processes, most approaches have difficulty in integrating this fact into their framework. All approaches addressing the connection between mind and society tend implicitly to assume their separateness. Their main issue is whether the mind goes *beyond and over* the individual, and even beyond the bounds of the brain and the body, to reach in some way or another the social world. Most of the time, the mediations necessary for ensuring this reach and thereby for bridging the gap between mind and society are passed over in silence. So radical *individualist* accounts tend to see the social mind as a kind of *oxymoron*: mental states and reasons for acting are seen as the exclusive property of a sovereign, if not solipsistic, self which tends to be both irresponsible and asocial. Radical *holistic accounts* tend to see the social mind as a *pleonasm*: the mind, stuck at the intersection point of two determining forces, one from above (social structures), the other from below (dispositions), has less the status of an actor than that of a patient whose first-person authority is essentially a social illusion.

But even the utmost radical versions of those approaches remain resolutely marked by the *modern* shift from community to society – an intellectual shift that is also a political conquest. Indeed the invention of democracy in the eighteenth century and the contractualist view of society that goes with it are grounded in the political consecration of the potential tension between minds and society, private interests and general interest, subjective preferences and public order. The distance between the individual and the city, the 'multitude and the one', is the very object of the *politics* in the noble, emancipatory sense of the term (Castoriadis, 1991; Foucault, 1986). So social scientists face an unusual task: even if they think that, *de facto*, the individual mind is by definition social, they must maintain, at any cost, the political distance between mind and society – a distance which is the normative *ideal* of modern politics.

This normative ideal is also, although only partially, a social reality. In modern contemporary society, individual recognition is less based upon pre-established, consistent roles or inherited social status than upon 'just-in-time' negotiations and demands over a supposedly extra-social self (Taylor, 1991). Moreover, the diversification of socialisation spaces, which decreases the taken-for-granted character of social experience, often prevents the 'modern mind' from maintaining the intentionality without intention, the acting without thinking about it that characterises the 'traditional mind'. The modern mind is rendered more distant and reflexive by the 'obdurate resistance' that the social world offers to its thoughts and actions, *via* expectation breaches or conflicting versions of the situation (Franks, 1985). Coming up against the mind-independent reality of the world generates a 'feelings of effort' and an 'experience of resistance' that foster individual reflexivity, mindedness and self-awareness (Cassam, 1997). In other words, the resistance and partial unpredictability of the modern world enhance the more or less painful process of 'doing subject'.

This being so, it is worth mentioning that variations in the process of 'doing subject' do not only depend on historical macro-contexts such as modernity. Capacities for selfhood and claims for first-person authority are heterogeneously distributed over the social space. There is an implicit hierarchy, to take up Goldstein's (2005) expression, between the *selved* and the *unselved*, between those who have access to the process of individualisation and those who do not. So individuals with low socio-economical status are too taken up with the maintenance of local, interdependent networks of solidarity and attention to relationships to develop self-concern; by contrast, middle and upper social classes are marked by the culture of independence, authenticity and self-expression (Knight and Nisbett, 2007; Pasquier, 2005). Along the same social lines, dominant groups appear and present themselves as a 'collection of individuals', in which everyone stands out, such as a pearl, thanks to its unicity, whereas subordinate groups are perceived and perceive themselves as a homogeneous collective whose members are interchangeable and equivalent (Lorenzi-Cioldi, 1998). In short, as Dewey (1927) put it, the political and social possibility of going from the state of a 'lost individual', subjected to systemic interdependencies and external forces that are beyond her reach, to the state of an 'individualized' agent who masters the conditions and the consequences of one's action is not accessible to everyone, even in liberal democracies.

Of course, these normative, political and social concerns need further research. Hopefully, such research would lead to a model of mind that would have plausible correlates in the actual mental processes described by psychologists and cognitive scientists. For the moment, indeed, meta-theoretical assumptions on the social nature of the human mind are rarely translated into an *empirical* enquiry. Such empirical investigation, which has to cut across the interdisciplinary boundaries separating philosophy, sociology, psychology and neurosciences, would allow one to falsify some unfounded postulates and to force social theorists to be, at last, realistic about the mental.

NOTES

1 Since three chapters of this handbook dwell specifically on the issues of individualism and rationality, that is, 'Rational choice and its alternatives', 'Rational agency' and 'Individualism, collective agency and the micro-macro relation', this section will only address a number of sociological versions of methodological individualism.
2 In a way, the Durkheimian mind, like the Sperberian one, is also split into two layers, one individual and the other collective. But, whereas the Sperberian split mind is supposed to be the object of one single naturalistic approach, the Durkheimian's is the object of two epistemologically autonomous disciplines.

REFERENCES

Aboulafia, M. (2001) *The Cosmopolitan Self: George Herbert Mead and Continental Philosophy*. Illinois: University of Illinois Press.

Adolphs, R. (1999) 'Social cognition and the human brain', *Trends in Cognitive Sciences*, 2: 469–479.

Atran, S. (2002) *In Gods We Trust. The Evolutionary Landscape of Religion*. Oxford: Oxford University Press.

Baker, G.P. and Hacker, P.M.S. (1984) *Scepticism, Rules and Language*. Oxford: Blackwell.

Barresi, J. (2002) 'From "the thought is the thinker" to "the voice is the speaker": William James and the dialogical Self', *Theory & Psychology*, 12: 237–250.

Baynes, K. (2001) 'Practical reason, the space of reasons and public reason', in W. Rehg and J. Bohman (eds) *Pluralism and the Pragmatic Turn: The Transformation of Critical Theory*. Cambridge, MA: MIT Press. pp. 53–85.

Bedford, E. (1986) 'Emotions and statements about them', in R. Harré (ed.) *The Social Construction of Emotions*. Oxford: Basil Blackwell. pp.15–31.

Bénatouï, T. (1999) 'A tale of two sociologies: The critical and the pragmatic stance in contemporary French sociology', *European Journal of Social Theory*, 2(3): 379–396.

Benveniste, E. (1966) *Problèmes de Linguistique Générale 1*. Paris: Gallimard.

Berger, P. and Luckman, T. (1966) *The Social Construction of Reality*. NY: Doubleday.

Berton, R.M. (2008) 'Holisme durkheimien et holisme bourdieusien. Étude sur la polysémie d'un mot', *L'Année Sociologique*, 58(2): 299–318.

Boltanski, L. (1990) *L'amour et la justice comme compétences. Trois essais de sociologie de l'action*. Paris: Métaillé.

Boltanski, L. and Thévenot, L. (2006) *On Justification. The Economies of Worth*. Princeton: Princeton University Press.

Boudon, R. (1991) 'Weber's notion of rationality and the theory of rationality in contemporary social sciences', in H.J. Helle (ed.) *Verstehen and Pragmatism. Essays in Interpretative Sociology*. Frankfurt: Peter Lang. pp. 33–46.

Boudon, R. (1995) *Le Juste et le Vrai. Etudes sur l'Objectivité des Valeurs et de la Connaissance*. Paris: Fayard.

Boudon, R. (1996) 'The "cognitivist model". A generalized rational-choice model', *Rationality and Society*, 82: 123–150.

Boudon, R. (2010) 'La théorie générale de la rationalité, base de la sociologie cognitive', in F. Clément and L. Kaufmann (eds) (forthcoming) *La Sociologie Cognitive*. Paris: Orphys.

Bourdieu, P. (1979) *La distinction. Critique sociale du jugement*. Paris: Minuit.

Bourdieu, P. (1980) *Le Sens Pratique*. Paris: Minuit.

Bourdieu, P. (1992) *Réponses*. Paris: Minuit.

Bourdieu, P. (1997) *Méditations Pascaliennes*. Paris: Seuil.

Bouveresse, J. (1996) *Wittgenstein Reads Freud: The Myth of interiority*. Princeton: Princeton University Press.

Boyer, P. (2001) *Religion Explained. The Evolutionary Origins of Religious Thought*. New York: Basic Books.

Bratman, M.E. (1993) 'Shared Intention', *Ethics* 104(1): 97–113.

Brothers, L. (1997) *Friday's Footprint: How Society Shapes the Human Mind*. Oxford: Oxford University Press.

Brubaker, R. and Cooper, F. (2000) 'Beyond "Identity"', *Theory and Society*, 291: 1–47.

Bruner, J. (1986) *Actual Minds, Possible Worlds*. Cambridge, MA/London: Harvard University Press.

Bruner, J. (1990) *Acts of Meaning*. Cambridge, MA: Harvard University Press.

Burge, T. (1979) 'Individualism and the mental', *Midwest Studies in Philosophy*, IV: 73–121.

Burge, T. (1986) 'Individualism and Psychology', *Philosophical Review*, 95: 3–45.

Butler, J. (2001) 'Giving an Account of Oneself', *Diacritics*, 31(4): 22–40.

Button, G. (ed.) (1991) *Ethnomethodology and the Human Sciences*. Cambridge: Cambridge University Press.

Cassam, Q. (1997) *Self and World*. Oxford: Oxford University Press.

Castoriadis, C. (1991) *Philosophy, Politics, Autonomy. Essays in Political Philosophy*. Oxford: Oxford University Press.

Céfaï, D. and Quéré, L. (1934/2006) 'Introduction', in G.H. Mead (1934/2006) (ed.) *L'Esprit, le Soi, et la Société*. Paris: PUF.

Cermolacce, M, Naudin J and Parnas, J. (2007) 'The "minimal self" in psychopathology: re-examining the self-disorders in the schizophrenia spectrum', *Conscious Cogn*. 16(3): 703–14.

Cheney, D. L. and Seyfarth, R. M. S. (2007) *Baboon metaphysics. The Evolution of a Social Mind*. Chicago: Chicago University Press.

Cheng, P. and Holyoak, K. (1985) 'Pragmatic reasoning schemas', *Cognitive Psychology*, 17: 392–416.

Chisholm, R. (1972) 'Intentionality', *The Encyclopedia of Philosophy*. New York: Macmillan. pp. 201–204.

Choi, I., Nisbett, R.E., and Norenzayan, A, (1999) 'Causal attribution across cultures variation and universality', *Psychological Bulletin*, 125(1): 47–63.

Chriss, J.J. (1999) 'Role distance and the negational self', in G. Smith (ed.) *Goffman and Social Organization. Studies in a Sociological Legacy*. London: Routledge. pp. 64–80.

Cicourel, A. (1974) *Cognitive Sociology. Language and Meaning in Social Interaction*. New York: The Free Press.

Clark, A. (2004) 'Memento's revenge: the extended mind revisited', in R. Menary (ed.) *The Extended Mind*.

Clark, A. (2008) *Supersizing the Mind: Embodiment, Action, and Cognitive Extension*. Oxford: Oxford University Press.

Clark, A. (2010) 'Memento's revenge: the extended mind revisited', in R. Menary (ed.) *The Extended Mind*. Cambridge: MIT Press. pp. 43–66.

Clark, A. and Chalmers, D.J. (1998) 'The extended mind', *Analysis*, 58: 10–23.

Clément, F. (2006) *Les mécanismes de la crédulité*. Genève: Droz.

Collins, H. (1998) 'Socialness and the undersocialized conception of society', *Science, Technology and Human Values*, 23(4): 494–516.

Conein, B. (2006) *Les Sens Sociaux, Trois Essais de Sociologie Cognitive*. Paris: Economica.

Corcuff, P. (1999) 'Le collectif au défi du singulier: en partant de l'habitus', in *Le Travail Sociologique de Pierre Bourdieu; Dettes et Critiques*. Paris: La Découverte. pp. 95–120.

Cosmides, L. and Tooby, J. (1994) 'Origins of domain specificity: The evolution of functional organization', in A. Hirschfeld and S.A. Gelman (eds) *Mapping the Mind. Domain Specificity in Cognition and Culture*. Cambridge: Cambridge University Press. pp. 85–116.

Cosmides, L. and Tooby, J. (2005) 'Neurocognitive adaptations designed for social exchange', in D.M. Buss (ed.) *The Handbook of Evolutionary Psychology*. Hoboken, NJ: Wiley. pp. 584–627.

Coulter, J. (1989) *Mind in Action*. London: Polity Press.

Crane, T. (1998) 'Intentionality as the mark of the mental', in A. O'Hear (ed.) *Contemporary Issues in the Philosophy of Mind*. Cambridge: Cambridge University Press. pp. 229–251.

Cummins, D.D. (1998) 'Social norms and other minds', in D.D. Cummins and C. Allen (eds) *The Evolution of Mind*. Oxford: Oxford University Press. pp. 30–50.

Davidson, D. (1984) 'First person authority', *Dialectica*, 38(2–3): 101–111.

Dawkins, R. (1976) *The Selfish Gene*. Oxford: Oxford University Press.

Dennett, D. C. (1987) *The Intentional Stance*. Cambridge: MIT Press.

Dennett, D. C. (1992) 'The self as a center of narrative gravity', in F. Kessel, P. Cole and D. Johnson (eds)

Self and Consciousness: Multiple Perspectives. Hillsdale, NJ: Erlbaum. pp. 103–115.

Dennett, D. (2003) *Freedom evolves.* New York: Viking Press.

Descombes, V. (1991) 'Le pouvoir d'être soi', *Critique*, pp. 529–530; 545–576.

Descombes, V. (1995) *La denrée mentale.* Paris: Minuit.

Descombes, V. (1996) *Les institutions du sens.* Paris: Minuit.

Descombes, V. (2000) 'The philosophy of collective representations', *History of the Human Sciences*, 13(1): 37–49.

Dewey, J. (1927) *The Public and its Problems.* New York: Holt.

DiMaggio, P. (1997) 'Culture and cognition', *Annual Review of Sociology*, 23: 263–288.

Douglas, M. (1986) *How institutions think.* New York: Syracuse University Press.

Dunbar, R.I.M. (2003) 'Evolution of the social brain', *Science*, 302(5648): 1160–1161.

Durkheim, E. (1912/1995) *The Elementary Forms of Religious Life.* New York: Free Press.

Durkheim, E. (1924/1996) *Sociologie et Philosophie.* Paris: PUF.

Elias, N. (1970/1991) *Qu'est-ce que la sociologie?* Paris: Agora Pocket.

Elster, J. (1989) *The Cement of Society: A Study of Social Order.* Cambridge: Cambridge University Press.

Emery, N. and Perrett, D. (2000) 'How can studies of the monkey brain help us understand "theory of mind" and autism in humans?', in S. Baron-Cohen, Tager-Flusberg, S. and Cohen, D. (ed.) *Understanding other minds: perspectives from developmental cognitive neuroscience.* Oxford: Oxford University Press, pp. 274–305.

Fay, B. (1996) *Contemporary Philosophy of Social Science. A Multicultural Approach.* Oxford: Blackwell.

Fiske, A.P. (1992) 'The four elementary forms of sociality. Framework for a unified theory of social relations', *Psychological Review*, 99(4): 689–723.

Foucault, M. (1986) 'Omnes et singulatim: vers une critique de la raison politique', *Le Débat*, 41: 5–35.

Franks, D.D. (1985) 'The self in evolutionary perspective', *Studies in Symbolic Interaction*, 1: 29–61.

Frith, C. (2008) *Making up the Mind. How the Brain Creates our Mental World.* Oxford: Blackwell.

Frith, C. and Wolpert, D. (2003) *The Neuroscience of Social interaction.* Oxford: Oxford University Press.

Gallagher, H.L. et al. (2000) 'Reading the mind in cartoons and stories: an fMRI study of "theory of mind"

in verbal and nonverbal tasks', *Neuropsychologia*, 38(1): 11–21.

Gallagher, S. (2006) 'Logical and phenomenological arguments against simulation theory', in D. Hutto and M. Ratcliffe (ed.) *Minding our Practice: Folk Psychology Re-assessed.* New York: Springer Publishers, pp. 63–78.

Gallese V. et al. (2004) 'A unifying view of the basis of social cognition', *Trends in Cognitive Sciences*, 8(9): 396–403.

Garfinkel, H. (1967) *Studies in Ethnomethodology.* Englewood Cliffs, NJ: Prentice-Hall.

Gilbert, M. (1989) *On Social Facts.* London: Routledge.

Gilbert, M. (1990) 'Walking together: A paradigmatic social phenomenon', *Midwest Studies in Philosophy*, XV: 1–14.

Gilbert, M. (2002) 'Belief and acceptance as features of groups', *Protosociology*, 16: 35–69.

Goffman, E. (1969) *The Presentation of Self in Everyday Life.* Harmondsworth: Penguin Press.

Goldstein, J. (2005) *The Post-Revolutionary Self: Politics and Psyche in France, 1750–1850.* Cambridge, MA: Harvard University Press

Goody, J. (1977) *The Domestication of the Savage Mind.* Cambridge: Cambridge University Press.

Gopnik, A. (1993) 'How we read our own minds: The illusion of first-person knowledge of intentionality', *Behavioral and Brain Sciences*, 16: 1–14.

Grezes, J. and Decety, J. (2001) 'Functional anatomy of execution, mental simulation, observation, and verb generation of actions: a meta-analysis', *Hum Brain Mapp*, 12(1): 1–19.

Guillo, D. (2006) 'La place de la biologie dans les premiers textes de Durkheim: Un paradigme oublié?', *Revue Française de Sociologie*, 47(3): 507–535.

Harré, R. (1983) *Personal Being.* Cambridge, MA: Harvard University Press.

Harris, P.L. (2000) *The Work of the Imagination.* Oxford: Blackwell.

Heath, J. (2001) *Communicative Action and Rational Choice.* Cambridge, MA: MIT Press.

Herrmann, E., Call, J, Hernàndez-Lloreda, MV., Hare, B. and Tomasello, M. (2007) 'Humans have evolved specialized skills of social cognition: The cultural intelligence hypothesis', *Science*, 317(5843): 1360–1366.

Hirschfeld, L.A. (1995) 'Do children have a theory of race?', *Cognition*, 54: 209–252.

Hirschfeld, L.A. (2001) 'On a folk theory of society: Children, evolution, and mental representations of social groups', *Personality and Social Psychology Review*, 5(2): 107–117.

Hirschfeld, L.A. and Gelman, S.A. (1994) *Mapping the Mind. Domain Specificity in Cognition and Culture.* Cambridge: Cambridge University Press.

Hobson, P. (1994) 'Perceiving Attitudes, Conceiving minds', in C. Lewis and P. Mitchell (ed.) *Children's Early Understanding of Mind: Origins and Development.* East Sussex, UK: Lawrence Erlbaum, pp. 70–93.

Honneth, A. (1996) *The Struggle for Recognition. The Moral Grammar of Social Conflicts.* Cambridge: MIT Press.

Humphrey, N.K. (1976) 'The social function of intellect', in P.P.G. Bateson and R.A. Hinde (eds) *Growing Points in Ethology.* Cambridge: Cambridge University Press. pp. 303–317.

Hurley, S. (2001) 'Perception and Action: Alternative Views', Synthese, 129 : 3–40.

Hutchins, E. (1991) 'The social organization of distributed cognition', in L. Resnick, J. Levine and S. Teasley (eds) *Perspectives on socially shared cognition.* Washington, DC: American Psychological Association. pp. 283–307.

Hutchins, E. (1995) *Cognition in the Wild.* Cambridge: MIT Press.

Iacoboni, M. (2009) 'Imitation, Empathy, and Mirror Neurons', *Annual Review of Psychology*, 60: 653–670.

Ingold, T. (2001) 'From the Transmission of Representations to the Education of Attention', in H. Whitehouse (ed.) *The Debated Mind.* New York: Berg, pp. 113–153.

Jacob, P. and Jeannerod, M. (2005) 'The motor theory of social cognition: a critique', *Trends in Cognitive Sciences*, 9(1): 21–25.

Jackendoff, R. (1992) *Languages of the Mind: Essays on Mental Representation.* Cambridge: MIT Press.

Jackendoff, R. (1999) 'The natural logic of rights and obligations', in R. Jackendoff and P. Bloom (eds) *Language, Logic, and Concepts: Essays in Memory of John Macnamara.* Cambridge, MA: The MIT Press. pp. 67–95.

James, W. (1890/1981). *Principles of Psychology.* Cambridge, MA: Harvard University Press.

Jansen, L. (2004) 'Who has got our group-intentions?', in J.C. Marek and M.E. Reicher (eds) *Erfahrung und Analyse. Beiträge des 27. Internationalen Wittgenstein Symposiums.* Kirchberg am Wechsel: ILWG.

Jones, T. (2001) 'What CBS wants. How groups can have difficulty to uncover intentions', *Philosophical Forum*, XXXII(3): 221–252.

Jones, T. (2005) 'How many New Yorkers need to like bagels before you can say "New Yorkers like bagels"? Understanding collective ascription', *Philosophical Forum*, 36(3): 279–306.

Karsenti, B. (2002) 'L'imitation. Retour sur le débat entre Durkheim et Tarde', *Raisons Pratiques*, 183–215.

Kaufmann, L. (1999) 'Esprit, es-tu là? Le sociologue et l'autorité de la première personne', *Information sur les Sciences Sociales*, 38(2): 203–248.

Kaufmann, L. (2003) 'Le dieu social. Vers une sociologie du nominalisme en révolution', *Raisons Pratiques*, 14: 123–161.

Kaufmann, L. (2005) 'Self-in-a-Vat. On Searle's Ontology of Reasons for Acting', *Philosophy of the Social Sciences*, 35(4): 447–479.

Kaufmann, L. (2010) Faire collectif: de la constitution à la maintenance. *Raisons pratiques*, 20: 331–372.

Kaufmann, L. and Clément, F. (2007) 'How culture comes to mind: From social affordances to cultural analogies', *Intellectica*, 46/47: 221–250.

Klin, A. et al. (2004) 'The inactive mind, or from actions to cognition: lessons from autism', in U. Frith and E. Hill (eds) *Autism: Mind and Brain.* Oxford: Oxford University Press. pp. 127–159.

Knight, N. and Nisbett, R.E. (2007) 'Culture, class and cognition: Evidence from Italy', *Journal of Cognition and Culture*, 7: 283–291.

Kripke, S. (1982) *Wittgenstein on Rules and Private Language.* Cambridge, MA: Harvard University Press.

Lahire, B. (1998) *L'Homme Pluriel. Les Ressorts de l'Action.* Paris: Nathan.

Lahire, B. (1999) 'De la théorie de l'habitus à une sociologie psychologique', in B. Lahire (ed.) *Le travail sociologique de Pierre Bourdieu; dettes et critiques.* Paris: La Découverte. pp. 121–152.

Lakoff, G. and Johnson, M. (1999) *Philosophy in the Flesh: The Embodied Mind and its Challenge to Western Thought.* New York: Basic Books.

Latour, B. (1994) 'Une sociologie sans objet? Remarques sur l'interobjectivité', *Sociologie du Travail*, 4: 587–607.

List, C. and Pettit, P. (2006) 'Group agency and supervenience', *The Southern Journal of Philosophy*, 44: 85–105.

Lorenzi-Cioldi, F. (1998) *Individus Dominants et Groupes Dominés.* Grenoble: PUG.

Loveland, K. A. (1991) 'Social Affordances and Interaction II: Autism and the Affordances of the Human Environment', *Ecological Psychology*, 3(2): 99–119.

MacIntyre, A. (1986) 'The intelligibility of action', in J. Margolis et al. (eds) *Rationality, Relativism and the Human Sciences.* Dordrecht: Martinus Nijhoff Publishers. pp. 63–80.

Macrae, C. N. and Bodenhausen, G.V. (2001) 'Social Cognition: Categorical person perception', *British Journal of Psychology*, 92: 239–255.

Martin, J. and Sugarman, J. (1999) 'Is the Self a kind of understanding?', *Journal for the Theory of Social Behaviour*, 31(1): 103–114.

Mead, G.H. (1934/1967). *Mind, Self and Society.* Chicago: University of Chicago.

Meijers, A.W. (2003) 'Can collective intentionality be individualized?', *American Journal of Economics and Sociology*, 62(1): 167–183.

Miller, P.J., R. Potts, R., Fung, H., Hoogstra, L. and Mintz, J. (1990) 'Narrative practices and the social construction of Self in childhood', *American Ethnologist*, 17(2): 292–311.

Mills, W.C. (1940) 'Situated actions and vocabularies of motive', *American Sociological Review*, 5: 904–913.

Nisbett, R. and Wilson, T. (1977) 'Telling more than we can know: Verbal reports on mental processes', *Psychological Review*, 84(3): 231–259.

Nisbett, R.E. (2003) *The Geography of Thought: How Asians and Westerners think differently…and Why.* New York: Free Press.

Nisbett, R.E. and Masuda, T. (2003) 'Culture and point of view', *Proceedings of the National Academy of Sciences of the United States of America*, 100: 11163–11175.

Ochs, E. and Capps, L. (2001) *Living Narrative.* Cambridge, MA: Harvard University Press.

Pasquier, D. (2005) *Cultures Lycéennes : la Tyrannie de la Majorité.* Paris: Autrement.

Perner, J. and Wimmer, H. (1985) 'John thinks that Mary thinks that…": Attribution of second-order beliefs by 5- to 10-year old children, *Journal of Experimental Child Psychology*, 39: 437–471.

Pettit, P. (1996) *The Common Mind: An Essay on Psychology, Society, and Politics.* Oxford: Oxford University Press.

Pettit, P. (2003) 'Groups with minds of their own', in F. Schmitt (ed.) *Socializing Metaphysics.* Lanham, Maryland: Rowman and Littlefield. pp. 167–193.

Pettit, P. and Schweikard D. (2006) 'Joint actions and group agents', *Philosophy of the Social Sciences*, 36(1): 18–39.

Piette, A. (1998) 'De la distance au rôle au mode mineur de la réalité. Contribution à la sociologie de l'inter-action', *Social Science Information*, 372: 275–329.

Piette, A. (2009) *L'Acte d'Exister. Une Phénoménographie de la Présence.* Socrate Éditions Promarex.

Popper, K. (1944) 'The poverty of historicism I', *Economica*, 11: 86–103.

Premack, D. and Woodruff, G. (1978) 'Does the chimpanzee have a theory of mind?', *Behavioral and Brain Sciences*, 1: 515–526.

Putnam, H. (1975) 'The meaning of meaning', in *Mind, Language and Reality*, II. Cambridge: Cambridge University Press. pp. 215–271.

Quéré, L. (1996) 'Cognition in practice', *Concepts and Transformation*, 1(1): 79–110.

Récanati, F. (2000) 'Deferential concepts: A response to Woodfield', *Mind and Language*, 15(4): 452–464.

Récanati, F. (2001) 'Modes of presentation: Perceptual v. deferential', in A. Newen, U. Nortmann and R. Stuhlmann-Laeisz (eds) *Building on Frege: New Essays on Sense, Content, and Concept.* Stanford: CSLI Publications. pp. 197–208.

Ricoeur, P. (1994) *Oneself as Another.* Chicago: University of Chicago Press.

Rizzolatti, G., Fogassi, L. and Gallese, V. (2001) 'Neurophysiological mechanisms underlying the understanding and imitation of action', *Nature Review Neuroscience*, 2: 661–670.

Rochat, P. (2003) 'Five-levels of self-awareness as they unfold early in life', *Consciousness and Cognition*, 12: 717–731.

Ryle, G. (1949) *The Concept of Mind.* London: Hutchinson.

Sacks, H. (2005) *Lectures on Conversation 1.* Oxford: Blackwell.

Salomon, G. (ed.) (1993) *Distributed Cognitions: Psychological and Educational Considerations.* Cambridge: Cambridge University Press.

Sanders, J.T. (1997) 'An ontology of affordances', *Ecological Psychology*, 9(1): 97–112.

Sawyer, R.K. (2002) 'Durkheim's dilemma: Toward a sociology of emergence', *Sociological Theory*, 20(2): 227–247.

Schmid, H.B. (2004) 'Evolution by imitation Gabriel Tarde and the limits of memetics', *Distinction. Scandinavian Journal for Social Theory*, 9: 103–118.

Schmidt, R.S. (2007) 'Scaffolds for Social Meaning', *Ecological Psychology*, 19(2): 137–151.

Schutz, A. (1962) *Collected Papers I: The Problem of Social Reality*, edited by M. Natanson. The Hague: Martinus Nijhoff.

Searle, J. (1990) 'Collective intentions and actions', in P. Cohen et al. (eds) *Intentions in Communication.* Cambridge: MIT Press. pp. 401–415.

Searle, J. (2001) *Rationality in Action.* Cambridge, MA: MIT Press.

Sharrock, W. and Button, G. (1991) 'The social actor: social action in real time', in G. Button (ed.) *Ethnomethodology and the Human Sciences.* Cambridge: Cambridge University Press. pp. 137–175.

Sharrock, W. and Coulter, J. (2004). 'TOM: A critical commentary', *Theory and Psychology*, 14(5): 579–600.

Simmel, G. (1890/1983) *Sociologie et épistémologie.* Paris: PUF.

Simmel, G. (1908/1999) *Sociologie. Etudes sur les formes de la socialisation.* Paris: PUF.

Sluga, H. (1996) '"Whose house is that?" Wittgenstein on the self', in H. Sluga and D.G. Stern (eds) *The Cambridge Companion to Wittgenstein.* Cambridge: Cambridge University Press. pp. 320–353.

Southgate, V., Gergely, G. and Csibra, G. (2008) 'Does the mirror neuron system and its impairment explain human imitation and autism?', in J. A. Pineda (ed.) *Mirror Neuron Systems: The Role of Mirroring Processes in Social Cognition.* New York: Humana Press, pp. 331–354.

Sperber, D. (1975) *Rethinking Symbolism.* Cambridge/New York: Cambridge University Press.

Sperber, D. (1990) 'The epidemiology of beliefs', in C. Fraser and G. Gaskell (eds) *The Social Psychological Study of Widespread Beliefs.* Oxford: Clarendon Press. pp. 25–44.

Sperber, D. (1996) *Explaining Culture: A Naturalistic Approach.* Oxford: Blackwell.

Sperber, D. (1997) 'Individualisme méthodologique et cognitivisme', in R. Boudon, F. Chazel and A. Bouvier (eds) *Cognition et Sciences Sociales.* Paris: PUF.

Sperber, D., Premack, D. and Premack, A.J. (eds) (1995) *Causal Cognition: A Multidisciplinary Debate.* New York: Oxford University Press.

Strawson, P. (1959) *Individuals: An Essay in Descriptive Metaphysics.* London: Methuen Mills.

Tarde, G. (1890/1962). *The Laws of Imitation.* Mass: Gloucester.

Tarde, G. (1899) *Social Laws: An Outline of Sociology.* New York: Macmillan.

Tarde, G. (1901/1989). *L'Opinion et la Foule.* Paris: PUF.

Taylor, C. (1991) *Le Malaise de la Modernité.* Paris: Cerf.

Taylor, C. (1994) 'Interpretation and the sciences of Man', In M. Martin and L.C. McIntyre (eds) *Readings in the Philosophy of Social Science.* Cambridge: MIT Press. pp. 181–211.

Thévenot, L. (1990) 'L'action qui convient', *Raisons Pratiques*, 1: 39–69.

Tollefsen, D.P. (2006) 'From extended mind to collective mind', *Cognitive Systems Research*, 7: 140–150.

Tomasello, M., Carpenter, M., Call, J., Behne, T. and Moll, H. (2005) 'Understanding and sharing intentions: The origins of cultural cognition', *Behavioral and Brain Sciences*, 28: 675–691.

Tuomela, R. (1995) *The Importance of Us. A Philosophical Study of Basic Social Notions.* Stanford: Stanford University Press.

Tuomela, R. and Tuomela, M. (2003) 'Acting as a group member and collective commitment', *Protosociology*, 18–19: 7–66.

Uskul, A.K., Kitayama, S. and Nisbett, R.E. (2008) 'Ecocultural basis of cognition: Farmers and fishermen are more holistic than herders', *Proceedings of the National Academy of Sciences of the United States of America*, 24(10525): 8552–8556.

Valsiner, J. and Van Der Veer, R. (2000) *The Social Mind. Construction of the Idea.* Cambridge: Cambridge University Press.

Varela, F., Thompson, E. and Rosch, E. (1991) *The Embodied Mind.* Cambridge: MIT Press.

Veyne, P. (1983/1988) *Did the Greeks Believe in Their Myths? An Essay on the Constitutive Imagination.* Chicago: University of Chicago Press.

Völlm, B.A. et al. (2006) 'Neuronal correlates of theory of mind and empathy: A functional magnetic resonance imaging study in a nonverbal task', *NeuroImage*, 29(1): 90–98.

Voltolini, A. (2005) 'On the metaphysics of internalism and externalism', *Disputatio*, 18: 127–150.

Von Wright, G.H. (1983) *Practical Reason.* New York: Cornell University Press.

Wacquant, L. (1992) 'Introduction', in P. Bourdieu (ed.) *Réponses.* Paris: Seuil.

Weber, M. (1949) *The Methodology of the Social Sciences.* Glencoe: Free Press.

Weber, M. (1968) *Economy and Society.* Berkeley: University of California Press.

Wellman, H. M. (1990) *The child's theory of mind.* Cambridge: MIT Press.

Whiten, A. (ed.) (1991) *Natural Theories of Mind. Evolution, Development and Simulation of Everyday Mindreading.* Oxford, UK: Basil Blackwell.

Winch, P. (1958) *The Idea of a Social Science and its Relation to Philosophy.* Atlantic Highlands, NJ: Humanities Press.

Wittgenstein, L. (1953/1981) *Philosophical Investigations.* Oxford: Blackwell.

Zerubavel, E. (1993) *The Fine Line.* Chicago: University of Chicago Press.

Zerubavel, E. (1997) *Social Mindscapes. An Invitation to Cognitive Sociology.* Cambridge: Harvard University Press.

7

Rational Agency

Fred D'Agostino

INTRODUCTION

The idea of rational agency plays an important role, especially in relation to autonomy, in philosophy of action and ethical and political theory. It plays a crucial role, too, in Dennett's ideas about the intentional stance and Davidson's account of radical interpretation. Within the social sciences per se it is subjected to analysis by Weber in his metasociology and is shown as an effect rather than a primitive in his *The Protestant Ethic and the Spirit of Capitalism* (1976). Within philosophy of social science, the notion plays a crucial role in methodological individualism, in the school of Popper. Within economics and those forms of political science and legal studies influenced by economics, rational agency appears as a posit of theorizing, specifically in the form of *homo economicus* and in the model of rational decision theory. Ironically, Hayek, like Weber, sees rational agency as an effect not a presupposition of the market and of other forms of instrumentally rational behavior and looks to social evolutionary processes to explain its presence and distribution. The *homo economicus* model is problematized by Simon's analysis of bounded rationality and, perhaps more radically, by the observation that some

preferences are adaptations to rather than given orientations towards a particular social environment. Value pluralism and the possibility of value incommensurability problematize the idea that there must, in any given situation, be a determinate best thing to do according to the dictates of reason and form part of the background to the recent development of constructed preference theory. Recently, the individualistic, atemporal, and disembodied elements of classical rational agency models have been challenged by the situationist approach of Suchman, Clark, and Hutchins, which is resonant with earlier work in a different tradition by Oakeshott, who had already pointed to an approach to rational agency that sited both reason and agency in tradition and practice.

RATIONAL AGENCY IN GENERAL PHILOSOPHY

In general philosophy, the notion of rational agency is associated especially with the philosophy of Kant, according to whom (Kant, 1996): "man is subject only to his own, yet universal, legislation"; insofar as he acts in accordance with such legislation, he achieves rational agency, on this account (see Chapter 10). Rational agency in this sense depends upon an individual's capacity to assess reasons for action and to be guided only by those reasons which can be formulated as maxims which are free-standing in relation to empirical contingencies – that is, could be affirmed independently of the particularities of a specific individual's circumstances. When we behave in conformity with such maxims, we are self-governing and hence free in a morally significant sense; we do not find ourselves at the mercy of the commands of others or of motives which cannot withstand critical scrutiny. Since the maxims which we give ourselves in this way must, on Kant's account, pass certain tests that reason sets (specifically, universalizability), they will provide a sound basis for collective life, implicitly defining a system of mutual respect or a "kingdom of ends." Crudely, to pass the test of universalizability, a maxim must be affirmable from every perspective. But, if it is, then, from every perspective, it will define a basis for action that can be affirmed from that perspective and, accordingly, it will harmonize the actions taken from these perspectives on this basis.

In philosophy of action (see, for example, Goldman, 1970), the notion of rational agency enables us to distinguish between actions properly speaking and things that happen to people or, more specifically, between action and (mere) behavior. Indeed, of two behaviorally indistinguishable events, we may say that one was an action and the other a mere happening insofar as one was, and the other was not, an expression of rational agency, or, more specifically, was rationally intended by the individual and occurred on account of that intention's being realized. It is important, in considering behaviorism – as a psychological, more broadly social scientific, methodology – that two events might be behavioristically indistinguishable while differing in kind in their fundamental qualities – one an action undertaken intentionally, the other a tic or an undeliberated habitual performance.

In ethical and political theory, rational agency sometimes serves as a foundation for the justification or assessment of actions, practices, and institutional arrangements. This is most conspicuous, perhaps, in contractarian thinking where the rational agency of the individual contractors, be they hypothetical or otherwise, is a crucial argumentative premise. Crudely, unless the contractors exercise rational agency in agreeing that such-and-such an institution or practice is to be endorsed, then their endorsement is not normatively significant. This closely follows everyday thinking about contract in the legal sense, where mere agreement does not suffice to bind the contractors. The agreement reached by ordinary contractors must also reflect their rational agency, at least in the sense of being undeceived, uncoerced, and reflectively endorsed (as is evidenced in some contractual domains by the institution of a cooling-off period). In applied ethics, the notion of free and informed consent has a clear resonance with the more general idea of rational agency and with the ideas we see at work in relation to ordinary contracts. Typically, a person's participation as a medical patient or experimental subject must be grounded in their free (i.e., uncoerced) and informed (i.e., undeceived) consent. That person must deliberate about their participation and must arrive at a decision that exhibits their own rational agency (see, for example, National Commission, 1979).

At the interface between general philosophy and philosophy of social science narrowly construed, we have two important (and related) ideas: the idea of "the intentional stance," enunciated by Dennett, and that of "radical interpretation," as developed by Davidson (trading on earlier work by Quine) (see Chapter 6).

According to Dennett, it is typically, though defeasibly, sensible to adopt towards our fellow human beings (and others), as a strategy for understanding their behavior, a specifically intentional stance, which treats them as if their behavior can be understood, explained, and predicted as that of a rational agent. Their being rational agents is, as it were, a presupposition of their intelligibility to us (though not, of course, of the predictability of their behavior, which might be secured by a strictly causal analysis of the kind undertaken by natural scientists). Dennett (1987: 17) provides a concise summary:

> Here is how it works: first you decide to treat the object whose behavior is to be predicted as a rational agent; then you figure out what beliefs that agent ought to have, given its place in the world and its purpose. Then you figure out what desires it ought to have, on the same considerations, and finally you predict that this rational agent will act to further its goals in the light of its beliefs. A little practical reasoning from the chosen set of beliefs and desires will in most instances yield a decision about what the agent ought to do; that is what you predict the agent will do. Dennett (1987: 17)

Davidson's widely discussed principle of charity advises that it is a condition of the intelligibility of another being as a subject that his beliefs, desires, actions be those that we could attribute to a rational agent and, in particular, that they cohere in certain ways. As LePore and Ludwig put it (2005: 210):

> One of the most important constraints Davidson imposes on a theory of interpretation is that its interpretations of sentences and corresponding assignments of beliefs and other attitudes make speakers out to be *rational agents*. ... Thus, speakers' beliefs must be made out, on the whole, to be consistent, and their preferences sensible, and, more particularly, their beliefs and preferences must, on the whole, be rational in the sense of conforming to the axioms of decision theory.

Charity and the intentional stance clearly play, and have been seen to play, a role in all interpretive social science but, of course, especially in anthropology, where the tension between making sense of informants in their own terms and making sense of them in *our* own terms has provoked a lively and protracted discussion (see, for example, Hollis and Lukes, 1982).

Related to ideas about "the intentional stance" is a debate, prosecuted very vigorously in the 1960s and 1970s about the relation between reason and cause. On some understandings, explanation is always "deductive-nomological" in the sense that it derives the explanandum (e.g., the description of an action performed) from a causal law (or set of laws) as an instance of that law (or laws) in particular circumstances. On other understandings, an action as such must be understood in terms of the particular reasons which warrant its performance, for example, in the form of the beliefs and desires of the agent whose action it is. There is, on some accounts, tension between these two approaches, summarized by the question: Are reasons causes? Winch (1958) and Davidson (2001) are key figures in the debate, which mirrors, in some ways, a tension in the sociological meta-theory of Max Weber, who looked both to causal and interpretational approaches for a proper grasp of human behavior and action.

Also anticipated by Weber is a distinction between procedural and substantive rational agency, on which see Hooker and Streumer (2004). On the proceduralist account, an agent is rational, *ceteris paribus*, if she acts on reasons which it is appropriate for her to have given her situation. On the substantivist account, more is required and, in fact, an agent's actions are rationally grounded only if they are based in reasons which are, putting it crudely, the right reasons to have (whether or not they are the reasons it is appropriate, *given the circumstances*, to have). This is related, in a general way, to Weber's distinction between formal and substantive rationality and to internalism and externalism in the philosophies of mind and of language.

RATIONAL AGENCY IN WEBER

One of the profoundest and most influential theorists of rational agency, Weber, is also one of the most obscure and complicated (see Chapter 1). In particular, in attempting to understand Weber's contributions, we need to distinguish (and trace the connections among) at least the following ideas: instrumental rationality, value rationality, formal rationality, substantive rationality, and rationalization as an historical process (see, generally, Weber, 1968).

Instrumentally rational (*zweckrational*) action is action which is conditioned by expectations about the situation and reflects an appropriate adjustment, in light of these expectations, of the action to the goals or ends for which it is undertaken. This is the kind of rational agency which Dennett's intentional stance allocates, by default, and also anticipates Davidson's project of radical interpretation and the assumptions underpinning the *homo economicus* model (see fourth section below). Value-rational (*wertrational*) action is undertaken, on the other hand, to express some overriding commitment and without any special reference to its possibilities of success. There are echoes here, perhaps, of the Kantian deontology of universalizable maxims and of the account of commitment rationality given by Benn and Gaus (1986) and, in a different context, by Harsanyi (1986). On this account, a person exhibits value rationality in, say, being truthful, insofar as her truthful behavior reflects her conformity with a universizable maxim of, or a principled commitment to, truth-telling and without reference to the contribution, positive or negative, that the action might make to the achievement of the agent's contingent goals. The same behavior would be instrumentally rational if it were undertaken to achieve some goal, for example, to curry favor with a potential business partner (and, of course, if it were well-adapted to that objective).

Whereas both instrumental and value rationality are characteristics associated with the individual agent, and hence directly relevant to our concerns here, formal and substantive rationality are characteristics of social situations or institutions. Formal rationality shows itself typically in bureaucratic organizations and characterizes a social setting wherein individual action is subject to general rules. (The general rules in question are not necessarily universizable maxims in the sense associated with Kantian agency.)

Efficient use of means for the realization of ends, transparency, and consistency in the application of general rules to specific cases are hallmarks of formally rational activities. (It is clear, then, that formal rationality may either encompass or promote both value-rational behavior (as with the application of general rules) and instrumentally rational behavior (as with the application of efficient means to ends)). Substantive rationality shows itself when an institution functions effectively to meet its publicly defined objectives.

Rationalization, finally, is a historical process in which any given human activity or institution is rendered more efficient through the systematic analysis of its fundamental processes according to criteria of efficiency and effectiveness. Rationalization is sometimes understood in contrast to traditional, customary, and habitual forms of conduct. Taylorization (Taylor, 1915) in manufacturing processes is an example of rationalization in this sense (see also Shenhav, 2002). As we will see, the distinction between rational and traditional is put under some pressure by the idea of selected rationality; see below.

One way in which these ideas are related is evident in Weber's best-known work, *The Protestant Ethic and the Spirit of Capitalism* (Weber, 1976). Crudely, the argument there, often obscured by concrete detail, is that a capacity and disposition for instrumental rationality is more widespread in modern than traditional societies because of a specific historical development, involving the influence of Calvinist religious ideas. The wider diffusion of formal rationality, especially in commercial and manufacturing contexts, is likewise an effect of this historical development. Perhaps most importantly for our purposes, Weber by implication makes rational agency an *explanandum*, rather than a given, or even a starting-point of social inquiry, as it is in other theoretical contexts. In this, he anticipates other theorists, such as Hayek, who see the maximizing behavior of the economic agent not as a precondition of the market as an institution, but, rather, as a potential product of that institution (see fourth section below). The sociologist Ritzer has updated this analysis in his amusing, but acute recent (2004) book *The McDonaldization of Society.*

RATIONAL AGENCY AND METHODOLOGICAL INDIVIDUALISM

Methodological individualism has its roots in the methodological pronouncements of Weber (1968), enters sociology through the action frame of reference articulated by Parsons (1949), and plays a prominent role in Austrian economics (on which see for example Boettke, 1994). It appears as a distinctive issue in philosophy of the social sciences through mid-century debates which involved, *inter alia*, Watkins and Gellner (on which see Udehn, 2002; see O'Neill, 1973 for some of the key papers; see also Chapter 9). It is disputed whether methodological individualism presupposes a rational agency model of the individuals on whose attitudes, behaviors, and interactions social facts are supposed to depend. Some thinkers assimilate methodological individualism to a more general ontological thesis which gives explanatory priority to individuals considered as such, but independently of their rationality or agency. (For example, the generative social science of Epstein (2006) and others is explicitly individualist without emphasizing full rational agency, depending, rather, on simple rules that orient to locally observable signals.) Nevertheless, methodological individualism, especially as it is manifested in economics, and in those sectors of sociology and political science which adopt economistic models, does typically incorporate rational agency models of the individual into its fundamental explanatory schemata. In its Weberian versions, this follows from Weber's commitment to the *verstehen* principle, according to which explanation presupposes interpretability (and, hence, rational intentionality).

Notwithstanding these complexities, methodological individualism, as an explanatory heuristic, enjoins us to look for explanations of large-scale social phenomena, for example, changes in the values of macroeconomic indicators, in terms of the intelligible behavior of individual human beings. (The work of Epstein (2006) and others, already mentioned, provides a vivid illustration of the way in which this program can be facilitated via computer simulation (see Chapter 32)). Hayek added an important, indeed crucial, caveat to this approach by insisting that the large-scale change may be a result of intentional actions but not always of actions intended to produce that particular change. This is developed, in a striking manner, in Hayek's discussion (1942) of the way in which individuals, without coordinating their actions, and without any of them intending the outcome, might beat a path through a forest. We can explain the gradual improvement of the path in terms of the intelligible actions of individuals, but we need not and probably should not explain this process in terms of any particular individual's intentions, or, a fortiori, in terms of a collective decision to produce this outcome. (The idea of unanticipated consequences appears strikingly in Smith's *The Wealth of Nations* (1776) and enters contemporary discussions both through Hayek's work and through the work of Merton (1936).

HOMO ECONOMICUS

Within economics and those forms of sociology (Hechter and Kanazawa, 1997), political science (Alt and Shepsle, 1990), and legal studies influenced by economics, rational agency appears as a posit of theorizing, specifically in the form of *homo economicus* and in the model of rational decision theory (Bacharach and Hurley, 1991).

In characterizing the *homo economicus* model, it is more than usually difficult to avoid oversimplification and anachronism. As with methodological individualism, there are different ideas about what is unavoidably a part of the model and what is not. The basic ideas are nevertheless reasonably familiar.

According to the *homo economicus* model, the rational agent chooses among courses of action by considering, for each course of action open to her, what the pay-off would be of taking that course of action if it is successful and, crucially, what the probability is of that course of action being successful if she takes it. According to the model, rational agents discount the absolute value of an outcome by the probability of its being attained and then choose that course of action which promises the best outcome (in respect of probability-discounted absolute value). So far, this is just standard-issue instrumental rationality. As Gaus has pointed out (2008: sec. 1.3), however, *homo economicus* models add some specific elements to the more general account. First of all, outcomes for *homo economicus* are characterized by diminishing marginal value, so that, while *homo economicus* always prefers more to less (other things being equal), she typically does not value the $n + 1$-th unit as much as she values the n-th unit of some factor which is valuable to her. This is true, in part, because of the opportunity costs of accepting the additional unit, in the form of foregone opportunities to substitute for it some quantity of another factor which is also, though differently, of value to her. Finally, *homo economicus* is non-tuistic, in the sense that it is her values which she seeks to advance, rather than those of others (except insofar as she has herself internalized the values of others). Another assumption, implicit in the notion of opportunity costs, is that *homo economicus* is capable of reducing all values to a common denominator, or, in other words, of pricing out non-monetized values, as cost-benefit theorists put it (see, for example, Sugden and Williams, 1978). This assumption appears, in mainstream economic theory, in the so-called axiom of continuity, on which see for instance Dyke (1981).

On this model, the rational agent is a well-informed maximizer of value, subject, in particular, to the discipline of opportunity costs. Such a model presupposes a number of capacities on the part of the rational agent. In particular, the model assumes that rational agents are well informed about (a) options, (b) the values of these options, and (c) the likelihood that an action will realize an option. Each of these assumptions has been challenged, as have other features of the *homo economicus* model of rational agency (see fifth and sixth sections below).

One of the most interesting developments in recent social and political thinking has been the adoption in other academic domains of the *homo economicus* model of rational agency, understood in this more specific way. A particularly important example is the movement known as the economic analysis of law (Posner, 1992), where developments in legal institutions and thinking are analyzed on the assumption that judges, lawyers, clients, and others have the outlook of *homo economicus* and are concerned with maximizing value construed in non-tuistic or monetary terms. The influence of the model is much more widely felt, however, with Becker (1978) explaining family relations, crime, and other phenomena more usually associated with sociological or psychological modes of explanation, in terms of *homo economicus* modeling, and Dunleavy (1991), following Downs (1957) applying this sort of rational agency model to politics.

The degree to which a *homo economicus* model is committed to a narrow understanding of human values, whether specifically all value is value as it might be conceived by an entrepreneur is a lively but unedifying dispute. Certainly, the formal apparatus of rational decision theory does not mark out some sorts of values as privileged and others as inadmissible. Indeed, there is recognition, within *homo economicus* modeling, of the potential diversity of values which a rational decision-maker would need to take account of (see, for example, Bell et al., 1977 and sixth section below).

One of the most interesting contributions to *homo economicus* modeling is due to Hayek and in particular to his insight that the market does not presuppose but rather produces rational agents in the *homo economicus* sense. As he puts it (Hayek, 1973–6: vol. III, p. 76): "it is therefore in general not rationality which is required to make competition work, but competition, or traditions which allow competition, which will produce rational behaviour....Competition is as much a method for breeding certain types of minds as anything else ...." Again, like Weber earlier, Hayek makes rational agency (though now in a narrower sense than Kant or Weber had in mind) an *explanandum* rather than an axiomatically introduced *explanans*. On his account, it is market competition that puts a premium on, and thus fosters the wider uptake of specifically instrumentally rational capacities and dispositions (see twelfth section below). As Dean reminds us, this is Foucault's strategy too in relation to rational agency. As he puts it:

> One way of characterising the most general object of Foucault's genealogies would be the analysis of the historically specific modalities within which diverse practices of self-formation take place ... Such an analysis is concerned with displacing notions of the founding rational subject by way of an analysis of the means which seek to establish and promote particular human capacities – including those we might wish to regard as "reasoning" – within bodies of knowledge and types of rationality, forms of power and government, and ethical practices. (Dean, 1994: 63)

BOUNDED RATIONALITY

Simon (1992) is widely thought to have put the *homo economicus* model under pressure by his observations, beginning in the 1950s, on the ways in which putatively rational agents actually make decisions and about their infirmities relative to the idealizations implicit in the *homo economicus* model. (In Pluralism and Incommensurability, we consider another way in which this model has been put under pressure.) In particular, Simon pointed out that individuals were unavoidably ill-informed about precisely the

matters about which the *homo economicus* model characterized them as well informed – that is, what their options are, how those options are valued, and what the probabilities are of attaining these options – and that they lacked the time, resources, and computational capacities to perform the sorts of maximization that the *homo economicus* model was based on. Accordingly, whatever the model might imply, rational agents make decisions in a different way – typically, according to Simon, by satisficing – that is, by setting an aspiration level and then exploring the options until one is found that is adequate relative to the aspiration level. Rational agents are not, on this account, maximizers of value (or even of expected value); rather, they try, perhaps using decisional heuristics, to identify outcomes which are good enough and then implement that action which leads to these outcomes. (March and others have explored different alternatives to maximizing calculations, in particular the use of rules and routines, especially in organizational settings. See for example March (2002) and, the *locus classicus*, March and Olsen (1976).

Some theorists working within the *homo economicus* tradition (e.g., Stiglitz, 2000) responded to Simon's analysis by developing the idea of information costs and by pointing out that we might, under certain circumstances, know how to calculate, using the *homo economicus* machinery, the optimal amount of information to collect and analyse and that we might, in this way, retain contact with the underlying ideas of the *homo economicus* model. Other scholars (e.g., Gigerenzer, 2000) proposed an even more radical resort to heuristic short-cuts than Simon himself had advocated.

While Simon pointed to the difficulties of calculating maximum values, other scholars have identified a family of other difficulties under which the aspiring rational agent has, perforce, to work. Dequech (2001) refers to fundamental uncertainty, which shows itself especially clearly in two ways. First of all, insofar as rational agents are to identify all the outcomes, they may be hampered by the fact that, at some particular time, some of the outcomes that may well follow from available actions may not be visible to them or may indeed be unconceivable. (This is stronger than the point, in section Homo economicus above, that some actions may have unintended consequences.) This will certainly be true with long-term planning in societies which exhibit rapid and radical technological or cultural change. Second, insofar as rational agents are required to discount values by likelihoods, they will be hampered in this by the impossibility of estimating likelihoods in these same situations of rapid change.

One of the things which become evident at this point is that two or more rational agents may have quite different patterns of choice and behavior, even if they share the same values and understanding of the options for action. For one thing, some agents may set high and others low aspiration levels. This may be related to their different risk aversion, which may, in turn, reflect their differing capital endowments, where capital may include non-monetary elements (see, for example, Friedman and Savage, 1948). Second, because a boundedly rational agent does not complete (or even attempt) a comprehensive search of the options, which options come to the attention of otherwise similar boundedly rational agents may differ from agent to agent. The identification of an option as meeting the satisficing requirements will therefore often be path dependent (see, for example, Arthur, 1994). (Since the search is not comprehensive, one agent, following a certain path through the option-space, may reach a satisfactory option that is not even considered by another agent who follows a different path through that space to reach a different option that is nevertheless satisfactory by her criteria. Which option each reaches is dependent, in other words, on the path taken.) Both of these are reasons why two agents sharing the same values may nevertheless reach different conclusions about what to choose or to do. At this point we need to talk about rational agency in the plural, rather than, as with Kant, in the singular or general.

PLURALISM AND INCOMMENSURABILITY

Discussion of bounded rationality has already shown that two rational agents might arrive at different conclusions about what option to pursue. This discussion does not itself, aside from the fundamental uncertainty analyzed by Dequech, undermine the idea, central to unreconstructed *homo economicus* theory, that there *is* a unique best option. But it is precisely that idea that is put under pressure, and without invoking fundamental uncertainty about what the options are, by the notion of incommensurability (on which see Chang, 1997; D'Agostino, 2003).

That there might be a number of distinct choices that a given individual could make in a given situation without failing to be a rational agent is either obvious or self-contradictory. It is self-contradictory if we assume that, equally ranked best options aside, there is always a *uniquely* best alternative, a uniquely maximally valuable option. This idea is challenged, even in the absence of the sorts of infirmities by which Simon's original work was inspired, by forms of evaluative pluralism, such as that associated with Berlin (1969) and, in particular, by the idea that some values may be incommensurable in the sense that they do not trade off against one another in the way presupposed by the idea that there is always a uniquely best alternative. (The idea of incommensurability stands at odds, in particular, with those versions of *homo economicus* theory which are narrowly economistic in reducing all values to a common, monetary, denominator. It therefore also puts pressure on cost–benefit approaches to public policy, which seek to effect this reduction by considering the willingness to pay of stakeholders and using these data to define a system of pricing out that applies to values that are not already monetized. It stands in direct contradiction to the axiom of continuity, mentioned earlier as a key premise in economic thinking.)

Consider three options and three values against which these options might be assessed. We may easily have a situation where each option is best according to one evaluative criterion, worst according to another criterion, and middling according to the third criterion. (This analysis borrows from, and extends, the fundamental insights of Arrow (1963). In this case, we may have it that the options are incommensurable unless there is some way in which we can reduce the three evaluative criteria to a common denominator, for example, through establishing a coherent system of trade-offs in such a way that we obtain a well behaved overall ordering of the options. And when the options *are* incommensurable, it is not guaranteed that every rational agent will, even if she evaluates the options using these and only these criteria, reach the same conclusion about which option is to be preferred or chosen.

A plurality of evaluative criteria creates another difficulty for the specifically *homo economicus* model, even in the absence of incommensurability. When we consider how a rational agent might, in deliberation, search a space of options for the best option, we are confronted with the fact that she may encounter a space whose systematic exploration is difficult and unrewarding. Insofar as the multiple evaluative criteria are interdependent (so that, for example, an improvement along one dimension may lead to a deterioration along another dimension), the deliberator will encounter a space where there are multiple peaks of overall value, with little to distinguish one from the other, and with little to guide a systematic search that will reliably identify the uniquely best point on that space (see for example Frenken, 2006, and notice that this analysis presupposes commensurability).

For this reason and for the reasons identified by Simon, it may not be appropriate to refer to *the* rational agent as if all individual variations in the behavior of rational agents were due to differences in their values or correctable infirmities in their deliberations. Rather, we may have a family of rational agents, characterized by different schedules of trade-offs among competing values, different search strategies in relation to options, and different aspiration levels.

CONSTRUCTED AND ADAPTIVE PREFERENCES

Elementary presentations of instrumental rationality, and hence of rational agency insofar as it encompasses instrumental rationality, often presuppose, if only by implication, that an individual's values are given and, accordingly, that her deliberations involve considering whatever options she does consider in relation to these values, which exist prior to and ground her particular deliberations and, *a fortiori*, the particular actions she undertakes as result of these deliberations. Two recent discussions complicate this picture.

March (1986) drew attention to several ways in which the concrete empirical agent differs from the idealized agent of *homo economicus* theory. In particular, according to March (1986: 589), "[r]ational choice involves two kinds of guesses: guesses about future consequences of current actions and guesses about future preferences for those consequences" and, as March puts it, "[n]either guess is necessarily easy." Indeed, as March argues, both guesses may be little more than just that, guesses, rather than empirically grounded predictions of future attitudes. And, more importantly, our guess about future preferences (in our terms, values) may be quite misbegotten, at least insofar as the word "guess" suggests that there is something fixed that may be discoverable (or at least guessable). Instead, as March observes (March, 1986, emphasis added), "preferences appear to change over time, at least in part *as a consequence of actions taken.*" With this (inadvertently?) ambiguous utterance, March in effect alludes to two ideas of considerable subsequent significance for our understanding of agency.

On the one hand, March seems here to, and later unequivocally does, draw attention to the idea that preferences are not given prior to and hence are not available to serve to ground our decisions and actions, but, rather, are themselves discovered through (experimental) action in pursuit of vaguer or more ambiguous (or maybe just multi-faceted) goals. Payne et al. (1999) provide a succinct account. In particular, they distinguish between two philosophies – of basic and articulated values. According to the latter approach, individuals bring to a decision problem an articulated system of values which maps directly onto the options being evaluated. According to the former notion, however, "people lack well-differentiated values for all but the most familiar evaluation tasks" and, instead, have to construct them as they decide. Deciding, then, is not a matter of considering how the options measure up to existing well defined values, but, rather, involves a reciprocal cycle of deliberation in which an individual's "basic values" become articulated to the point where they can guide decision-making precisely by being experimentally deployed in deliberated action-taking. As Payne et al. put it (1999), we "could view the construction of a preference as a process by which a decision maker comes to 'learn' his or her value for an object." They add: "… However, the contingencies of decision making make clear that the learning of preferences can be highly path-dependent, i.e., what is learned can depend on initial anchor values." There will, accordingly, be multiple pathways for otherwise similar agents and, as before, a family of rational agents (with the same basic values).

That our values are constructed through rather than grounding the decision process is one idea which we owe to March. That our values might be adaptations to our choices or, more likely and more significantly, to our unchosen circumstances, is also implicit in what March said and has been developed, influentially, by Elster (1983) who considers, especially, the ways in which our values

might be adjusted to our circumstances, for example, through mechanisms identified by cognitive dissonance theory (Festinger, 1959) and having, of course, considerable ethical and political significance, as Sen (1999), for example, has pointed out. In particular, if our values are shaped by our circumstances, then the fact that those values may be realized or realizable in those circumstances may not be as significant as might have been thought in validation or moral evaluation of those circumstances. More specifically, we cannot conclude from the fact that an agent finds his values reflected in his circumstances, that he has good reason to endorse those circumstances. The slave who has internalized the values of the slave master is not free because of the alignment of his values with those that are realized in his environment. The idea that some values are adaptations to, rather than, through our actions, shapers of our circumstances is another way, then, in which rational agency can be seen as an *explanandum* rather than *explanans*.

MINIMAL RATIONALITY

The unreconstructed *homo economicus* model is defined in terms of superlatives. We consider *all* the options, and we identify the one which is *best* according to *all* the criteria, and in relation to *all* the information about likelihoods. What Simon in effect pointed out is that *all* may be inaccessible in many concrete empirical situations and that if this is what rational agency consists of, then there isn't very much of it around, even in places where we pre-theoretically might think it exists. This point is taken up, in a systematic fashion, by Cherniak (1986) who developed an account of rational agency which is more modest in its demands. Cherniak builds such an account around the notion (1986: 8) of "the *finitary predicament*," which, as he says, affects all potential agents in that they "do not have infinite memory and computing time." In particular, he draws on complexity theory to argue (1986: 80) that the individual's deliberative powers encounter, in many ordinary situations, "the very large and important class of 'nondeterministic polynomial time' (NP) problems, which … are generally regarded as computationally intractable," and which, accordingly, cannot actually be solved by those confronting them, who therefore cannot be rational agents if solving such problems is a precondition of that status.

Having said that those facing the finitary predicament cannot be held to account against the standards of a theory of rational agency which requires more of them than any finite individual could in fact do, Cherniak offers, instead, a minimalist theory of rational agency which is perhaps less demanding than it needs to be simply in order to correct the deficiencies of the overly demanding approach whose idealizations he rightly rejects. For where the *homo economicus* model is defined by all-statements, Cherniak's model is defined, instead, merely by some-statements, which require less of the agent than is ordinarily thought necessary for rational agency. While it is unreasonable to demand for rational agency that a person consider all the data or draw all the inferences that might be relevant to her decision, it is surely not demanding enough merely to require that she consider some data or draw some inferences. What she needs to do is to consider the data and draw the inferences that it would be reasonable to draw, given her circumstances. Unfortunately, there is probably very little to be said about where the line is to be drawn. Surely, though, it ought to be drawn at some higher level than "some."

STRATEGIC RATIONALITY

One of the most important and influential refinements in technical modeling of rational agency is associated with game theory, as developed, originally, by von Neumann and Morgenstern (1953), who examined situations in which individuals, attempting to max-imize the value of outcomes of their actions, were faced with other individuals on whose behavior their own outcomes would depend (see Chapter 16). Some game situations are cooperative, in the sense that every player benefits from an agreed joint action. Other game situations are competitive, so that what one player gains, other players lose. In either situation, however, as Hargreaves Heap et al. put it (1992: 94), "the basic method of game theory is to argue that individuals try to predict what others will do in reply to their own actions, and then optimize on the understanding that others are thinking in the same way." Such a situation is called a strategic one to recognize the dependence of outcomes on the understanding that individuals have of each others' strategies for optimization.

One of the most widely discussed issues of all in formal social science was thrown up relatively early in game-theoretical modeling of rational agency. This is the prisoners' dilemma game situation, in which each individual, acting to optimize given her understanding of what the other individual is likely to do, chooses a course of action that, combined with the course of action chosen by the other individual, produces an outcome that is, from the point of view of both individuals, inferior to the best potentially available (see for example Poundstone, 1993).

What the prisoners' dilemma situation appears to show is that there is a valid procedure, basically that of instrumental rationality, for deciding how to act that, in the strategic situation of a competitive game, leads to an outcome which is not the best outcome theoretically available – and not, as with other situations we have considered, because of any infirmities of knowledge or of deliberative powers on the part of the participants. The best outcome is not the result of the right choice, at least when values and options are arranged as they are in prisoners' dilemma situations, as, indeed, they often are in concrete empirical situations, and, of course, at least when choices are made according to the canons of instrumental rationality.

The most promising solution of the prisoners' dilemma is via the notion of multiple iterations of this game situation through which players learn, by being rewarded for behavior which is jointly optimizing and punished otherwise, to make the choices that will lead to the optimal outcome (see for example Axelrod, 1984). Insofar as such a strategy itself can unravel if agents examine the underlying bases for their behavior, hard-wiring good strategies, for example, via the evolution of a disposition to use them in prisoners' dilemma situations, may be necessary. As Epstein (2006: Chapter 9) shows, winning strategies can emerge and endure in situations where individuals can pair-off with other individuals of the same disposition. Skyrms (1996) shows, in a related development, that evolutionary mechanisms are able to select strategies which optimize outcomes even when these are not the strategies which, in another sense, it would be rational for agents to adopt (see Chapter 17).

Perhaps most importantly, game theory introduces into our understanding of rational agency a strategic perspective, where this means, specifically, that the outcome to a rational agent depends not only on his actions but also on the actions of others.

FAILURES OF RATIONALITY

The notion of rational agency is uneasily poised between normative and descriptive interests. On the one hand, we might take the notion as presenting a normative account of how an individual being ought to behave in order to exhibit rational agency. On the other hand, we might take the notion as presenting a descriptive account of how individual, presumptively rational agents, do actually behave. This, if you like, is the relevance of the issues about boundedness, incommensurability, and so on. The descriptive account appears to be put under pressure by the fact that many agents, not otherwise grossly disqualified as putatively rational (and agentic),

could not actually fully conform to the normative model given the finitary predicament.

Further pressure is put on the use of normative models as themselves (typically) descriptive by a series of developments, beginning in the 1950s, that have come to be associated with the work of Kahneman and Tversky (and their colleagues). (For influential contributions, see the collection Kahneman and Tversky, 2000.) What these studies seem to show is that, independently of the limitations associated with the finitary predicament, individuals fail systematically and typically to satisfy the requirements of rational agency as these have been understood, especially in relation to instrumental rationality.

Using a model pioneered by Allais (for discussion see Allais and Hagen, 1979), Kahneman and Tversky conducted a series of psychologically rigorous experiments which appeared to show that individuals systematically misapprehend the significance of likelihoods in identifying a best action or choice. Among the alleged misapprehensions they identified are:

1 The non-linearity of likelihoods in relation to values calculations. In particular, likelihoods are weightier in individuals' evaluative calculations at certain tipping points, for example, between zero likelihood and any positive likelihood and between any finite likelihood and certainty.
2 Errors in calculating compound likelihoods.
3 A failure to take account of base rates when estimating the significance of certain possible outcomes.
4 Framing effects, so that the same system of options, values and likelihoods is understood differently by agents when it is differently represented.
5 An overemphasis on vivid information (and consequent neglect of how it fits with already established data relevant to the choice situation).
6 The use of a heuristic which trades on stereotypes and ignores, once again, base-rates in a population as a whole.

These results pose a dilemma, according to Stich. On the one hand, if the Davidson/

Dennett account of intentionality and, more generally, rational agency, is correct, then "it is simply incoherent to suggest that people reason in ways that depart seriously and systematically from what is rational or normatively appropriate ... [and accordingly] psychologists who claim to have evidence for extensive irrationality ... must be mistaken" (Stich, 1990: 11). On the other hand "[p]hilosophy has a long history of trying to issue a priori ultimatums to science ... [a]nd those a priori decrees have a dismal track record." Leaving aside Stich's more metaphysical concerns, we are still left with a serious problem. How, in the face of the Kahneman/Tversky results, and others of their kind, are we to understand the modality of our models of rational agency? Are they normative or are they descriptive? If they are descriptive, then they would appear to be false. If they are normative, the Kahneman/Tversky results are, perhaps, less significant than the argumentation associated with the bounded rationality literature. After all, the mistakes made by subjects in these experiments are correctable, even for agents beset by the finitary predicament, whereas the infirmities associated with NP (nondeterministic polynomial) computational problems or with fundamental uncertainty are intractable in relation to any finite being and thus pose a more serious problem for accounts of rational agency that are incompatible with their recognition.

AKRASIA

Whether it is even possible to fail in rational agency is an issue also in play in the literature associated with the notion of weakness-of-will, or akrasia. Akrasia is manifested, on standard definitions, when an individual performs an action which is not, by her own lights, the best action to perform in the relevant situation. Such an individual is an agent in cases where the action actually performed is performed intentionally – that

is, is willed and is performed because it is willed. But where the action intentionally performed by the agent is not the one which is best by her lights, her agency is not rational agency. The primary protagonists in the debate about akrasia are Hare (1952) and Davidson (2001). According to Hare, it is conceptually impossible that we perform an action which we ourselves do not consider the best action to perform. Accordingly, any action performed by a rational agent is necessarily the action that agent considers the best action for him. The reasoning behind Hare's position is derived from his meta-ethical analysis of evaluative judgments. According to Davidson, on the other hand, there is no, as it were, metaphysical impediment to our performing, intentionally, an action other than the one we consider it best to perform. Indeed, we might actually do so when we refuse to move from the judgment that a particular action is best all things considered to the conclusion that it is best "all out." While such a movement of thought is a natural one, according to Davidson, it is not definitional of agency per se. On his account, then, it is possible, though rare, for agents to knowingly behave sub-optimally (by their own lights).

Indeed, MacIntyre (1990) goes further, suggesting that, because of a potential gap between what it is objectively best to do and what it is all-things-considered best to do (from the agent's point of view), some akratic actions may even be rational, at least in the sense of being better adapted to the agent's actual circumstances than the action he deliberatively identifies as the best. One possibility, though it is not one emphasized by MacIntyre himself, is that an agent's intuitions or habits are, through some mechanism or another (see below) better aligned to her interests than are at least some courses of her deliberative analyses of outcomes and likelihoods. When her deliberative judgments are overcome by an intuitive or habitual counterweight, this may indeed sometimes initiate an (objectively) appropriate (and hence, in some sense, rational) course of action.

SELECTED RATIONALITY

One of the profoundest contributions to our understanding of rational agency in fact draws habit and tradition – traditionally (!) portrayed as at odds with rational agency (e.g., in Weber) – into the network of ideas surrounding rational agency (see Chapter 17). This adjustment to our understanding was essayed, usefully, by March (1986), who distinguished various forms of calculated rationality involving deliberation and action on the basis of deliberative processes from, *inter alia*, what he called "selected rationality," which he described as follows (March, 1986, p. 149):

> Ideas of *selected rationality* emphasize the process of selection among individuals or organizations through survival or growth. Rules of behavior achieve intelligence not by virtue of conscious calculation of their rationality by current role players but by virtue of the survival and growth of social institutions in which such rules are followed and such roles are performed.

With this account, we return, of course, to Hayek's idea (see fourth section above) that the capacity and disposition to deliberate (e.g., in a maximizing way) might itself be a product, rather than a presupposition of, social circumstances. Indeed, March's idea of selected rationality is, in effect, an instance of Hayek's more general thesis (1973–6: vol. I, p. 11) that, rather than rational agent, in the classical sense associated, for example, with the *homo economicus* model,

> [m]an is … a rule-following animal … [a]nd he is successful not because he knows why he ought to observe the rules which he does observe, … but because his thinking and acting are governed by rules which have by a process of selection been evolved in the society in which he lives ….

Here we see a striking convergence between traditions which seem to be largely unaware of one another – Hayek doesn't cite Simon, from whose thinking March's ideas descend, and March doesn't cite Hayek. This convergence is even more notable when Hayek mentions (Hayek, 1973–6) "[t]he permanent limitations of our factual knowledge," thus seconding (or, really, anticipating (see for example Hayek, 1945)) Simon and March's preoccupations with what Cherniak calls the finitary predicament.

Human beings, on this account, act largely on routines, rules, habits, and traditions and what they do is rational (in the sense of being well adapted to their situations) because or insofar as the routines, rules, and so on have been selected for in a quasi-evolutionary fashion. With this convergence of ideas, we entirely abandon what Gellner, for instance, called (1992: 13) the "programme for man's liberation from culture." We embrace, instead, an account of rational agency that is at once Oakeshottian and Darwinian. The account echoes Oakeshott's in accepting his fundamental premise (Oakeshott, 1962) that "[a]ll actual conduct … springs up within an already existing idiom of activity … [i.e.] a knowledge of how to behave appropriately in the circumstances." The account is Darwinian or at least quasi-Darwinian in its reliance, to explain how habits could be well-adapted to people's interests, on the idea that, in a population which exhibits variety in the aptitudes and dispositions of its members, those aptitudes and dispositions will gradually come to predominate, at subsequent generations, which do indeed provide an idiom of activity that caters for individuals' needs and interests (and does so without making extravagant demands on their informational or deliberative capacities) (see for example Witt, 1993). Indeed, this account potentially pulls apart rationality and intentionality, especially insofar as routines, habits, and the like may lie beyond the boundaries of what is ordinarily understood as intentional behavior.

SITUATED AND COLLECTIVE RATIONAL AGENCY

According to Hayek, rational agency is an effect rather than a precondition of particular cultural settings. According to March (and Oakeshott) rational agency may be manifested not through deliberation but, rather, through intuition or habit that has been adaptively shaped by cultural and other circumstances. These themes and others, involving the materiality of the circumstances in which rational agency might be exhibited have usefully (and influentially) been explored recently by scholars working on so-called situated rationality, who emphasize, as Hutchins (1996: xvi) puts it, that "the environments of human thinking are not 'natural' environments." He continues: "They are artificial through and through. Humans create their cognitive powers by creating the environments in which they exercise those powers." On this account, which is developed also in the work of Suchman (1987) and Clark (1997), rational agency consists, not primarily of deliberation to plan action intended to achieve outcomes, but, rather, of a flexible engagement with an environment which provides (and in some situations has been constructed so that it will provide) cues to successful action. This approach plays an important role in the design of environments, as, for instance, in the work of Norman (1998).

If Hutchins, Suchman, Clark, and Norman, for example, emphasize the situatedness and materiality of rational agency, other theorists look at the dynamic facilitators and inhibitors of collective forms of rational agency, especially in relation to knowledge. For a summary, see D'Agostino (2008).

REFERENCES

Allais, M. and Hagen, O. (1979) *Expected Utility Hypotheses and the Allais' Paradox; Contemporary Discussions and Rational Decisions under Uncertainty with Allais' Rejoinder.* Dordrecht: Reidel.

Alt, J.E. and Shepsle, K.A. (1990) *Perspectives on Positive Political Economy.* Cambridge: Cambridge University Press.

Arrow, K. (1963) *Social Choice and Individual Values.* New Haven: Yale University Press.

Arthur, W.B. (1994) *Increasing Returns and Path Dependence in the Economy.* Ann Arbor: University of Michigan Press.

Axelrod, R. (1984) *The Evolution of Cooperation.* New York: Basic Books.

Bacharach, M. and Hurley, S.L. (1991) *Foundations of Decision Theory: Issues and Advances.* Oxford: Basil Blackwell.

Becker, G. (1978) *The Economic Approach to Human Behavior.* Chicago: University of Chicago Press.

Bell, D., Keeney, R. and Raiffa, H. (1977) *Conflicting Objectives in Decisions.* Chichester: Wiley.

Benn, S. and Gaus, G.F. (1986) 'Practical rationality and commitment', *American Philosophical Quarterly,* 23: 255–266.

Berlin, I. (1969) *Four Essays on Liberty.* London: Oxford University Press.

Boettke, P.J. (1994) *The Elgar Companion to Austrian Economics.* Aldershot: Edward Elgar.

Chang, R. (1997) *Incommensurability, Incomparability, and Practical Reason.* Cambridge, MA: Harvard University Press.

Cherniak, C. (1986) *Minimal Rationality.* Cambridge, MA: MIT Press.

Clark, A. (1997) *Being There: Putting Brain, Body, and World Together Again.* Cambridge, MA: MIT Press.

D'Agostino, F. (2003) *Incommensurability and Commensuration: The Common Denominator.* Aldershot: Ashgate.

D'Agostino, F. (2008) 'Naturalizing the essential tension', *Synthese,* 162: 275–308.

Davidson, D. (2001) *Essays on Actions and Events.* Oxford: Clarendon Press.

Dean, M. (1994) *Critical and Effective Histories: Foucault's Methods and Historical Sociology.* London: Routledge.

Dennett, D.C. (1987) *The Intentional Stance.* Cambridge, MA: MIT Press.

Dequech, D. (2001) 'Bounded rationality, institutions, and uncertainty', *Journal of Economic Issues,* 35: 911–935.

Downs, A. (1957) *An Economic Theory of Democracy.* New York: Harper & Row.

Dunleavy, P. (1991) *Democracy, Bureaucracy and Public Choice: Economic Models in Political Science.* London: Pearson.

Dyke, C. (1981) *Philosophy of Economics.* Englewood Cliffs, NJ: Prentice-Hall.

Elster, J. (1983) *Sour Grapes: Studies in the Subversion of Rationality.* Cambridge: Cambridge University Press.

Elster, J. (1986) *Rational Choice.* New York: New York University Press.

Epstein, J. (2006) *Generative Social Science.* Princeton: Princeton University Press.

Festinger, L. (1959) *A Theory of Cognitive Dissonance.* London: Tavistock.

Frenken, K. (2006) *Innovation, Evolution and Complexity Theory*. Cheltenham: Edward Elgar.

Friedman, M. and Savage, L.P. (1948) 'The utility analysis of choices involving risk', *Journal of Political Economy*, 56: 279–304.

Gaus, G.F. (2008) *On Philosophy, Politics, and Economics*. Belmont, CA: Thomson Higher Education.

Gellner, E. (1992) *Reason and Culture: The Historic Role af Rationality and Rationalism*. Oxford: Blackwell.

Gigerenzer, G. (2000) *Adaptive Thinking: Rationality in the Real World*. Oxford: Oxford University Press.

Goldman, A. (1970) *A Theory of Human Action*. Englewood Cliffs, NJ: Prentice-Hall.

Hare, R.M. (1952) *The Language of Morals*. Oxford: Clarendon Press.

Hargreaves Heap, S., Hollis, M., Lyons, B., Sugden, R. and Weale, A. (1992) *The Theory of Choice: A Critical Guide*. Oxford: Blackwell.

Harsanyi, J. (1986) 'Advances in understanding rational behavior', in J. Elster (ed.) *Rational Choice*. Oxford: Basil Blackwell, pp. 82–107.

Hayek, F.A. (1942) 'Scientism and the study of Man I', *Economica*, 9: 267–291.

Hayek, F.A. (1945) 'The use of knowledge in society', *The American Economic Review*, 35: 519–530.

Hayek, F.A. (1973–6) *Law, Legislation and Liberty*. Chicago: University of Chicago Press.

Hechter, M. and Kanazawa, S. (1997) 'Sociological rational choice theory', *Annual Review of Sociology*, 23: 191–213.

Hollis, M. and Lukes, S. (1982) *Rationality and Relativism*. Cambridge, MA: MIT Press.

Hooker, B. and Streumer, B. (2004) 'Procedural and substantive practical rationality', in A. Mele and P. Rawling (eds) *The Oxford Handbook of Rationality*. Oxford: Oxford University Press, pp. 57–74.

Hutchins, E. (1996) *Cognition in the Wild*. Cambridge, MA: MIT Press.

Kahneman, D. and Tversky, A. (2000) *Choices, Values, and Frames*. Cambridge: Cambridge University Press.

Kant, I. (1996) *Practical Philosophy*. M.J. Gregor (ed.). Cambridge: Cambridge University Press.

LePore, E. and Ludwig, K. (2005) *Donald Davidson Meaning, Truth, Language, and Reality*. Oxford: Clarendon Press.

March, J. (1986) 'Bounded rationality, ambiguity, and the engineering of choice', in J. Elster (ed.) *Rational Choice*. Oxford: Basil Blackwell. pp. 142–170.

March, J. (2002) 'Understanding how decisions happen in organizations', in Z. Shapira (ed.) *Organizational Decision Making*. Cambridge: Cambridge University Press, pp. 9–33.

March, J. and Olsen, J.P. (1976) *Ambiguity and Choice in Organizations*. Bergen: Universitetsforlaget.

McIntyre, A. (1990) 'Is akratic action always irrational?', in O. Flanagan, and A. O. Rorty (eds) *Identity, Character, and Morality*. Cambridge, MA: MIT Press, pp. 379–400.

Mele, A.R. (2004) *The Oxford Handbook of Rationality*. Oxford: Oxford University Press.

Merton, R. (1936) 'The unanticipated consequences of purposive social action', *American Sociological Review*, 1: 894–904.

National Commission for the Protection of Human Subjects of Biomedical and Behavioral Research (1979) *The Belmont Report: Ethical Principles and Guidelines for the Protection of Human Subjects of Research*. Department of Health, Education, and Welfare, Washington, DC.

Norman, D. (1998) *The Design of Everyday Things*. London: MIT Press.

O'Neill, J. (1973) *Modes of Individualism and Collectivism*. London: Heinemann Educational Books.

Oakeshott, M.J. (1962) *Rationalism in Politics, and Other Essays*. London: Methuen.

Parsons, T. (1949) *The Structure of Social Action: A Study in Social Theory with Special Reference to a Group of Recent European Writers*. Glencoe, IL: The Free Press of Glencoe.

Payne, J., Bettman, J. and Schkade, D. (1999) 'Measuring constructed preferences: Towards a building code', *Journal of Risk and Uncertainty*, 19: 243–270.

Posner, R. (1992) *The Economic Analysis of Law*. Boston: Little, Brown.

Poundstone, W. (1993) *Prisoner's Dilemma*. New York: Anchor Books.

Ritzer, G. (2004) *The McDonaldization of Society*. Thousand Oaks, CA: Pine Forge Press.

Sen, A.K. (1999) *Commodities and Capabilities*. New York: Oxford University Press.

Shenhav, Y.A. (2002) *Manufacturing Rationality: The Engineering Foundations of The Managerial Revolution*. Oxford: Oxford University Press.

Simon, H.A. (1992) *Economics, Bounded Rationality and the Cognitive Revolution*. Aldershot: Edward Elgar.

Skryms, B. (1996) *Evolution of the Social Contract*. Cambridge: Cambridge University Press.

Smith, A. (1776) *An Inquiry into the Nature and Causes of the Wealth Of Nations*. Printed for A. Strahan and T. Cadell, in the Strand, London.

Stich, S.P. (1990) *The Fragmentation of Reason: Preface to a Pragmatic Theory of Cognitive Evaluation*. Cambridge, MA: MIT Press.

Stiglitz, J. (2000) 'The contributions of the economics of information to twentieth century economics', *Quarterly Journal of Economics*, 115: 1441–1478.

Suchman, L. (1987) *Plans and Situated Actions*. Cambridge: Cambridge University Press.

Sugden, R. and Williams, A.H. (1978) *The Principles of Practical Cost-Benefit Analysis*. Oxford: Oxford University Press.

Taylor, F.W. (1915) *The Principles of Scientific Management*. London: Harper & Brothers.

Udehn, L. (2002) *Methodological Individualism: Background, History and Meaning*. London: Routledge.

Van den Berg, A. and Meadwell, H. (2004) *The Social Sciences and Rationality: Promise, Limits, and Problems*. New Brunswick, NJ: Transaction Publishers.

Von Neumann, J. and Morgenstern, O. (1953) *Theory of Games and Economic Behavior*. Princeton: Princeton University Press.

Weber, M. (1968) *Economy and Society: An Outline of Interpretive Sociology*. New York: Bedminster Press.

Weber, M. (1976) *The Protestant Ethic and the Spirit of Capitalism*. New York: Scribner's.

Winch, P. (1958) *The Idea of a Social Science and its Relation to Philosophy*. London: Routledge & Kegan Paul.

Witt, U. (1993) *Evolutionary Economics*. Aldershot: Edward Elgar.

8

Individualism, Collective Agency and The "Micro–Macro Relation"

Alban Bouvier

The significance of methodological individualism (MI) in social science is one of the most classical issues in the philosophy of social science and nowadays it is customary to set it in opposition to methodological holism, although this expression (introduced by Watkins, 1957 is much less common than "holism," which might be much more appropriate. This has replaced the notion of "collectivism," which was sometimes used in the middle of the twentieth century (O'Neill, 1973); but this notion was still much more misleading. Not only did it carry a possible political meaning but also because political concerns were really core elements of certain viewpoints (notably Hayek, 1988; Popper, 1945), despite there being no logical link between the epistemological and the political issues.[1] I shall, however, leave aside here this political dimension.

I claim that what is at stake, generally speaking, when one speaks of "holism" is a complex and confused intuition that might not still have been completely exhausted by advocates of analytic methods, more than a specific methodology, but such that its specificity is constantly reduced as analytic methods are becoming more and more integrative.[2] Certain important issues are currently tackled without specific reference to the notion of holism (*a fortiori* collectivism), such as many debates on collective behavior, collective action, collective agency, collective intentionality, etc. However the main issues are basically the same: *to what extent is collective action proper understood not only (that means: is not reducible to) a mere sum of individual actions*? And how can collective action properly understood result or emerge from these individual actions? In this specific context, discussions are focused just on action and the dynamic aspects of social life more than discussions about holism are (those notably include an analysis of collective beliefs not specifically oriented towards action). In other words, the question is to know whether there is an *ontological* specificity of a certain kind of collective action compared to individual action, such that its account would require a proper concept: the concept of collective agency.

The treatment of this question has always been complicated by interferences with other (sometimes subtle) methodological and theoretical issues. For example, more and more frequently, one speaks of "micro–macro mechanisms" (Hedström and Swedberg, 1998) to refer to the processes leading from individual to collective phenomena (in the various senses of "collective") as if one was dealing with processes from micro-phenomena to macro-phenomena. Thus, in this context, "micro" and "macro" are implicitly identified respectively with "individual" and "collective." But there is much confusion about the relation between individual and collective agency, on the one hand, and the notion of micro-macro relation, on the other. This latter opposition has also other, very different meanings. Thus, if two people are enough to constitute an elementary group (Simmel, 1971), dancing a tango is already a "collective action" (Gilbert, 1989) and could be said therefore, according to the previous criterion, to be a "macro-phenomenon" compared to a pure individual action, which would be a "micro-phenomenon." In many cases, however, the distinction between micro and macro refers to a quite different criterion and only means a *difference of scale* between two objects, events, or processes, so that, according to this new criterion, dancing the tango with one's partner or repainting one's flat with her (Bratman's favorite example, Bratman, 1999) would be micro-phenomena compared to macro-phenomena such as a riot (or a revolution) or the entire reconstruction of a town (or of a country) after a war. Similarly, when the branch of a company and a State act in a coherent way, their acts can be described as individual actions (as if they were indivisible), compared to the acts of a company or the acts of allied States (Coleman, 1990), described therefore as micro-phenomena according to the first criterion, although they are evident macro-phenomena according to the second. In a relation between objects of different scales, some

of them may also be parts of others (a branch of a company/a company), but may also not be, as in cases when what is compared is a small-scale event (e.g., the assassination of the heir to the Austro–Hungarian throne at Sarajevo in 1914), with its possible large scale consequences (e.g., the First World War). Following this (difference of scale) criterion, it is sometimes useful to introduce (relative) intermediate levels of scales, notably when one deals at the same time with the relations between parts and whole. Thus, in a sociological case study on gangs in a city, it can be useful to distinguish between the town scale (macro), the gang scale (meso) and the gangsters scale (micro).This second distinction (micro/macro as a scale difference) is a priori very trivial but often not only interferes with the previous one (individual/collective), as in the latter example, but also is confused with it.

There is still a much more important difference between these first two conceptual distinctions and a third one. I shall focus here on the difference between the first and the third. Actually, in social science one often distinguishes, with good reason, between *different levels of data*: the macro-level of statistical (aggregate) data (e.g., suicide rates), and the micro-level of individual behaviors (e.g., case studies of suicides). And one of the main issues in social science is to construct a bridge between these levels. Thus collective behaviors themselves (macro-phenomena according to the first criterion) can be investigated either at the macro-level (e.g., statistics on the frequency of "macro-phenomena" such as riots in a modern city) or at the micro-level (e.g., case studies of certain riots, therefore still "macro-phenomena," according to the same criteria).[3] Reciprocally, all the aggregate or macro-level data (statistics) do not deal with collective or macro-phenomena; thus, most suicides are individual and not collective: the macro-level data regarding suicides deals mainly with micro-phenomena regarding the first criterion, so that there is also a "micro–macro relation" issue (or a "macro–micro relation" issue, depending on the path of investigation chosen) between levels of data. And this issue, regarding the relation between levels of data, unlike the previous ones (namely, the relation between individual behaviors and collective behaviors, on the one hand, and between different scales on the other), is not ontological but only epistemic: a "collection" of suicides distributed in a region, as statistics can display, has exactly the same extension as the mere addition of all the suicides in this region and it is not a collective suicide in any sense; and the statistical collection of all Protestants distributed in the Europe compared to other affiliation collections is just the addition of all these Protestants, not a Protestant community.

As I said, however, these three meanings are very often confused when one speaks of MI, especially the first and the third.[4] It happened, I contend, primarily because, as Little (1994) said, the debate for a long time has been held in places far away from what social sciences actually do, by importation from issues coming from the philosophy of language, philosophy of logic or metaphysics (and not even from the philosophy of physics and biology, which anyway have been dominated by these domains for a long time also). On the contrary, I shall try to remain as close as possible to the discussions internal to the social sciences, covering work that runs the gamut from the historical to the contemporary. To summarize the main point of this introduction: is MI a way of taking account of collective agency by coming down to its individual components, a way of explaining certain large-scale phenomena by coming down to smaller scale phenomena, or a way of taking account of macro-level data by coming down to micro-level phenomena? Actually, it should be all three if it is true that *the sole distinctive principle of MI is to systematically pursue the collective concepts and clarify their use (therefore hunt out their misuses)* to avoid the introduction of pseudo-entities in the explanation of social facts.

In this chapter, I shall analyze very progressively and in succession the different meanings of the concept of "micro–macro"

relation and shall restrict as much as possible the content of the concept of collective agency properly understood, which I shall reach at the very end of this chapter, introducing intermediate comments on related issues (such as the notion of macro-macro relation or the notion of distributive agency). I shall argue that collective agency properly understood requires collective intentionality (itself understood in a specific sense).

DIFFERENT LEVELS OF DATA: MICRO-LEVEL AND MACRO-LEVEL

The simplest starting point is the very basic fact that the social sciences, generally speaking, deal with data of different levels. Some data are relative to individuals in the logical sense of the term ("particulars") through questionnaires, interviews, empirical inquiries, including investigating registry offices, historical enquiries, and case studies etc., others to "aggregates" of individuals, through statistical data. One often calls the level of individuals the "micro-level" and the level of aggregates the "macro-level."

Hayek (1952a, 1988) is one of the rare social scientists to have really focused attention on the difference between this issue and the issue of the "emergence" (in a weak or in a strong sense, see below) of certain large-scale social facts from other smaller scale facts. But Hayek quickly dismissed the former issue because, according to him, it dealt mainly with demography and sociology but not so much with economics, which was his sole topic. Actually, Hayek's assessment leads economists to minimize macro-economics (and consequently macro-sociology) and also a certain orientation of MI, which Weber favors on the contrary. Nevertheless, unlike Hayek, I shall carry on first with this issue, which is close to Weber's concerns and which lets us compare MI with one of the main representatives of the so-called holistic tradition, Durkheim.

Let us take some examples. Statistics show that more Protestants commit suicide than Catholics (Durkheim, 1897/1952). There are, of course, many other regular correlations regarding suicide, for example between the suicide rate and the fact of being married or not married, of having children or not. These specific correlations, established by Durkheim (1897/1952) in *Suicide*, have been confirmed both for his time and nowadays (while others have been refuted). But statistics coming from other sources show that there is also a significant correlation between religious affiliations and the fact of being an executive in a company in the eighteenth century in Europe. These latter correlations are the starting point of Weber's *Protestant Ethic and the Spirit of Capitalism* (Weber 1904/2002).The most striking difference here between Durkheim's and Weber's methodology, very often bluntly opposed, is that Durkheim is much more careful (and therefore exact) than Weber in the analysis of statistical data and much more precise (analytical) in his characterizations of what is correlated, but both take their starting point in the macro-level. In economic life, one observes as well correlations at a comparable aggregate level, between, for example, the inflation rate and the unemployment rate, to take the most famous example in this respect.

It is useful to notice that natural sciences meet the same duality of data (individual level, aggregate level). Physiology, for example, is based on an addition of observations at the level of human individuals practiced by physicians and biologists and these particular observations let appear regular correlations at the aggregate level, and only at this level, between, for example, smoker rates and lung cancer rates, fruit consumption rates, and absence of colon cancer rates and so on. Besides, on the one hand, physiology also deals with data of various dimensions or scales, regarding whole bodies as well as specific organs or blood components, hormones and bacteria, etc. On the other hand, in these matters, the issue of the (functional) relation between the different organs of a body and the body itself as a relation between parts and the whole is also at stake.

MACRO–MACRO CORRELATIONS

In order to understand not only the nature of research programs focused on micro–macro relations (meaning relations between data of different levels), but also the real significance of such programs within general social science, it is necessary to compare them to other programs, namely the programs devoted to the analysis of macro–macro correlations (for which holism is often mistook). Consequently this will provide a more complete view of the relations between entities (objects, humans, events, processes, etc.) to which the statistical macro-data, which we have started to consider, refer.

It is reasonable to envisage that there might be causal relations between statistically correlated phenomena. But it is sometimes difficult to prove that such causal relations exist and, if so, what their direction is. The direction of the possible causality relation is sometimes just truism (e.g., between being married or not married and committing suicide, since the other direction is just non-sense). But it is also sometimes impossible to decide which direction it is in considering the sole macro-level; evidence might have to be found at the micro-level. Besides, the correlation is often enigmatic in itself.

Thus, a regular correlation between the number of Protestants in a country and the number of suicides suggests that the kind of affiliation may play a role but does not say which role. The fact that there is also a regular correlation between the day of the week and the number of suicides could suggest that there is also a causal link between these two facts; but this correlation is at least as much enigmatic as the previous. Similarly, a regular correlation between the rate of Protestants in a country and the number of industrial companies suggest that there might be a causal relation between these two phenomena but not which nor why. Regular correlations in economic life raise the same kind of question.

A very much debated methodological question inside the social sciences has to do with the issue of the legitimacy of autonomy for macro-level (or macro–macro) analysis; that is, the legitimacy of considering it as a self-standing domain. According to the autonomy thesis, it would not be required at all in social science to search for the micro-foundations of the macro-macro correlations. On the contrary, such a macro-micro program might even be illegitimate if what is at stake is really science and that science is only finding regularities and subsuming them under mathematical laws (as Kepler did in astronomy). Even if one does not uphold such a narrow positivist viewpoint, we may argue that the research of statistical regularities and correlations is the main basis of any science (even within a globally nomological-deductive conception of science, Hempel, 1962, 1965), so that moving on to the investigation of the micro-bases of macro-data eventually leads to neglecting the macro–macro level too much and therefore to losing the opportunities of discovering significant correlations. One can guess that it is for similar reasons that certain positivists, in economics, in sociology, and in demography have spontaneously but deeply shown reluctance about extending their invest to this level.

This debate has been particularly intense in economics for specific reasons. Actually macro–macro programs can induce a specific form of economic policy: thus, governments can try to influence macro-data (e.g., unemployment rate) by intervening in other macro-phenomena (e.g., inflation rate) through regulation; in other words, it favors an interventionist conception of States, such as that enunciated by Keynes, while liberals would uphold that States have only to hunt out the obstacles to the free choices of producers and consumers (free market). The domain of economics that restrains

itself to this macro-level is sometimes called "macro-economics," however ambiguous this phrasing is.[5]

In sociology, the consequences regarding social policy are not as clear. The reasons for this are two: first, sociology covers a much larger domain than economics (which is, strictly speaking, the science of market exchanges) and, second, it still has not succeeded in finding as many quantifiable regularities as economics. But there are also research programs that remain at this sole level. These programs are often called "quantitative analysis" because one of their main concerns is to give a statistical format to the much vaguer statements, which are so numerous in folk sociology (see Goldthorpe, 2000). Demography, till recently, remained at this sole level (comparing, for example, fecundity rates and economic growth levels in different countries).

We can also see a similarity here with the natural sciences, where the legitimacy of research programs located at the sole macro-level is not controversial. Thus, in biology, it is useful to know that lung cancer is regularly associated with smoking so that a causal relation is plausible. It lets physicians advise patients not to smoke in order to prevent lung cancer, even if it is not known more precisely why it is so. The main difference between social science and natural science here is that the sociological or economical "laws" are based on regularities that are not so strong as most regularities in physics or in biology; but even in these domains, the notion of law, taken in its logical sense, which implies an absolutely constant correlation to allow the physicist to say that this relation is necessary (and so satisfies Hempel's nomological-deductive model, Hempel, 1965), is too strong (Cartwright, 1983). One should only think of statistical regularities (which even Hempel may have recognized).

This sort of (macro–macro) program was given much consideration by Durkheim himself. His famous statement that "social facts have to be explained by other social facts" is often understood (wrongly) as having only that meaning. But one must notice that *de facto* Durkheim did not restrict his scope to the analysis of macro-macro correlations. As Durkheim already did, and most economists now do, few sociologists nowadays consider that social science must restrict its investigation to this domain. Goldthorpe (2000) himself, formerly one of the UK's leading figures of macro–macro analysis opened the path towards micro-foundational programs. And biology (just to take this example in the natural sciences) clearly requires other models of explanation than Hempel's (Cartwright, 1983; Darden, 2007). It is this topic that I shall now investigate in detail.

SEARCHING FOR THE MICRO–MICRO PROCESSES EXPLAINING MACRO–MACRO CORRELATIONS

Whether the previous level can be legitimately autonomized or not and whether it is necessary or not to seek the micro-foundations of the correlations observed at the macro-level, it is at least anyway possible to do it.[6] And if one wants to have a fuller understanding of the social phenomena, this is required. It is because the "causal" macro-relationships (between entities or processes to which statistical data refer) often remain enigmatic (see above), that one can be led to look for their micro-"foundations" in order to give a more complete explanation. It would mean to evidently go beyond Hempel's criterion of explanation (the subsumption of particular empirical statements under universal laws).

Thus, Weber examined (by investigating historical cases) which psychological process might have occurred in the mind of Protestants that contributed to them becoming the actors of the capitalist world more often than others. This process was roughly the following: because the Protestant Ethic, on the one hand, enjoins to consider any professional activity as equally pleasing God, and therefore does not encourage at all

people to have contempt for commercial and bank activity (unlike Catholics) and, on the other hand, urges on people to work as much as they can and to devote as little money as possible to material well-being. Protestants tend to become heads of companies or bankers and to accumulate money much more than members of any other religious affiliation. If they invest their earnings and are successful, they will even increase their capital. Furthermore, companies' and banks' Protestant employees will also work as much as they can, again just to please God. And finally, if belief decreases, the habit of working hard without spending one's money will remain: it will become what Weber calls an "ethos."

Similarly, to quote Heath (2005),

> one might notice a constant correlation between the date of the first frost and fluctuations in the price of wheat. But we do not really understand the phenomenon until it has been explained in terms of the rational actions of economic agents: an early frost reduces yields, leading to less intense price competition among suppliers, more among consumers, etc.

Durkheim, contrary to a wide-spread misconception, which always opposes him with Weber, again proceeds in a comparable way (see above about the macro-relations), looking for processes at the micro-level of individuals that could explain the hypothetic causal macro-correlations (between, for example, being Protestant and committing suicide). Unlike Weber, however, Durkheim does not try to discover the complex and diverse psychological mechanisms that lead certain people to commit suicide, for example, investigating either *numerous* individuals or *typical* individual (particular) historical cases. Instead, Durkheim just reconstructs a few plausible simpler psychological mechanisms, and tries to take account of the numerous data at the macro-level by using this simple explanatory model. One of these mechanisms (and the only one that contemporary social science has kept after further conceptual analysis and empirical tests) is that people need to feel integrated, need to have strong ties to feel well. If these ties are missing, people are more inclined to commit suicide. This psychological hypothesis accounts correctly for all the macro-level data. Then Durkheim focuses attention on the different kinds of social ties that protect from suicide (being married, having children, being affiliated with an integrative religion, etc.). Moreover, another significant difference between Weber and Durkheim is that the latter is not cautious at all about using collective concepts or, more generally, concepts implicitly implying superfluous entities, such as the concept of "pathogenic flows" (*courants suicidogènes*), which make explanations confusing (but actually do not play any effective role in the explanations).

Many contemporary sociological and economic investigations searching for the micro-foundations of statistical macro-correlations use a method of *reconstruction* very much similar to Durkheim's, as opposed to a method based on historical investigations that was employed by Weber in *The Protestant Ethic* (see Coleman, 1966; Boudon, 1973). Actually, what the social scientists are supposed to do when they deal with macro-data is just to find a *plausible* psychological functioning shared by most people. So even though the hypothesis deals with psychological processes, social scientists are *not* doing psychology properly understood and do not deserve the very frequent accusation of psychologism (see Udehn, 2001, for example). The point is that, in these kinds of investigation, they do not search for an empirical validation at the (micro) psychological level while trying to account for macro-data; on the contrary, the validation is searched for only at this macro-data level (does the plausible micro-process explain the macro-correlation?).[7]

Among the current reconstructions of plausible motivations of individuals, most are based not on psychological hypotheses close to Durkheim's (motivations like the need to be integrated), which are anyway epistemologically quite acceptable, but on the psychological hypothesis that individuals are *purposive* (or intentional) (Boudon, 1973, 1979/1981; Coleman, 1990). Most of the times methodological individualism is identified with this *very specific* micro-foundational program aimed at finding the processes at the basis of macro-correlations and restricting these processes to intentional actions.

Many contemporary advocates of MI still add, in their models of explanation, that the purpose of individuals is their self-interest, however broad this notion might be understood. What is often called Rational Choice Theory is even a narrower version of this general paradigm. But economists and sociologists sometimes, such as Sen (1977, 1999), Coleman (1990), and Boudon (2005), use a much broader version in which the purpose is not necessarily one's own material self-interest but may be, for example, other-interest instead (see below).

Even Weber did not explain the birth of capitalism with the assumption that the sole micro-foundational hypothesis should be that the social actors act intentionally: when the religious belief had disappeared, that which urged ex-Protestants on to work as hard as they could without enjoying their life and spending money was no longer intentional; it has become just an *ethos* or an *habitus*. Consequently, it is similarly wrong bluntly to oppose Bourdieu's method and micro-foundational programs. The opposition is rather with intentionalist programs (and restricted conceptions of MI). On the other hand, what is not satisfying logically speaking in many of Bourdieu's statements is that Bourdieu (Bourdieu and Passeron, 1990) often seems to implicitly consider that the real actors of social life are not human individuals but the social structure itself (incorporated in *habitus*), which seems quite unintelligible if one considers that which is at stake is only a trivial request: recognizing that human individuals are the only active source of social facts (as, generally speaking, living animals are in their own environment).

The reason that there has been such a focus on intentional or purposive model of actors is because a large part of social science has been oriented towards a specific kind of policy-making (more or less opposed to policy-making based on macro-economics), which requires that individuals act intentionally and were as much as possible aware of the plausible consequences of their acts (including the "by-products," which can be both unintended and *expected*, such as the death of civilians during a war). So, the reasons are excellent but they are not scientifically constraining. A better reason, methodologically speaking, to a priori favor the mechanisms of purposive action when testing hypotheses, is that these mechanisms seem simpler than mechanisms such as *habitus* or *ethos*.

What is at stake in the search for the micro-micro processes explaining the macro-macro correlations, is the confirmation (or refutation) of the hypothesis of causal links suggested by these correlations, which is a very general method that one encounters even in natural science. Thus, in biology, the proof of the absence of a "causal" relation between excess gastric acidity and gastric ulcer, however regularly observed this phenomenon is at the macro-level of aggregate data, is presence, at the micro-level, of processes involving the role of the bacterium *Helicobacter pylori* in the deterioration of gastric tissues, and correlatively, the recovery of the ulcer patient after antibiotic therapy. These micro-processes prove that gastric acidity is neither the cause nor even the main cause of gastric ulcers (although statistically correlated).

One major underlying epistemological issue here is, of course, that macro–macro programs and macro–micro programs illustrate two conceptions of explanation: first, to explain is to subsume under a necessary general law, which is roughly Hempel's conception (cf. above); and, second, to explain is to find the "cause" of a fact, to discover the mechanism (or the process) that leads from one state to another, which is roughly Cartwright's (1983) conception in physics, Darden's (2007) in biology and Elster's (2007) in social science.

Finally, it must be clear, first, that it would not make any sense to say that the statistical data (macro-level) are the *effects* (in any sense) of the individual human acts observable at the micro-level. The data at the macro-level only *express* some characteristics of the data at the micro-level in another logical form. Similarly, if there is a hypothetic "causal" relation between macro-data, this causal relation just *expresses* a hypothetic causal relation at the micro-level, which in social science means a (psychological) process. Thus, what is sometimes called here a micro-macro relation is just a *relation of expression*. It is evident that the "collection" of individual acts that constitute the source of macro-data about suicides, Protestantism, Capitalism and so on does not require any concept of collective agency; the concept of individual agency in its different aspects (intentional or not, egoistically rational or not) is sufficient. And if Weber deserves to be recognized as having explained certain features of the "emergence" of capitalism, it is only because he accounted for the process by which *individual* intentions could transform themselves into *individual* ethos.

UNINTENDED AND UNEXPECTED COMPLEX LARGE SCALE SOCIAL PHENOMENA. DISTRIBUTIVE AGENCY

The previous issue is often confused, as anticipated in the introduction of this chapter, with a different issue which deals with the "emergence," in a weak or in a strong sense, of *new phenomena* resulting from involuntary interactions between interdependent individuals.[8] As these new phenomena have a bigger *scale* than the actions or behaviors that produced them, it is often more or less implicitly thought that this issue deals with the micro-macro relation issue in one sense or another. One of the simplest examples is a traffic jam (I shall speak of weak emergence in this case).[9] More complex still, is the free fish market in a harbor (possibly strong emergence). A still more complex and on a larger scale is the free-market system, generally speaking, or capitalism (possibly strong emergence). I shall concentrate in this heading on phenomena that are emergent in a weak sense and not in the strong and most proper sense (see next heading).

At first, it may be useful to be aware clearly of a possible bias originating in the history of social sciences. Actually, many trends in current social science often refer both to Carl Menger (who inspired Hayek deeply) and to Max Weber as the founders of MI as if they shared the same conception of social science. But Menger and Weber met essentially on the criticisms of collective concepts in social science (such as "capitalism," "state," and so on), in a context in which ideas close to Hegel's were re-emerging, mainly through Gustav Schmoller's work, one of the leading figures of a historical approach of economics and Weber's former teacher.[10] Both considered that such concepts were deceptive because they can induce the implicit belief that there is something else than human individuals related to each other in various ways under these concepts. But there were major differences of viewpoint between Weber and the Austrian School members, particularly Hayek, regarding the issues at stake here. Thus, unlike both Weber and Durkheim, Hayek focuses straightly on micro-level data.

Hayek's way of thinking can be seen in many contemporary works and I guess it is more pedagogical here to take one's starting point in a very basic example borrowed from Thomas Schelling (1978). A traffic jam is a collective behavior in the sense that many individuals are involved and also in the sense that the jam is the result of the interactions of drivers whose behaviors are closely interdependent (e.g., if a driver goes ahead at a red traffic light, he might block the way of other drivers). Interaction and interdependence are essential here. It makes sense to say that a traffic jam is a larger scale phenomenon than its causes, namely each driver's individual

behavior, and that this larger scale and more complex phenomenon is the *effect* of composition of these smaller and simple events.

Traffic jams are a very good model of other (natural or social) phenomena. Traffic jams are similar to natural "bottlenecks" phenomena, which happen when solids or liquids cannot pass through the same passage at the same time or when people are crushed in a panic because of a narrow exit. But much more complex phenomena like the student revolts in the late 1960s in the Western universities can be explained partially as "bottleneck"-like phenomena: there had been a "baby boom" after the Second World War and a democratization of universities, so that many more students entered into universities, most of them hoping to have a job similar to the qualified students of the previous generations. But as the number of attractive jobs did not increase at all at the same time, students (often too late) realized that the expectations of many of them would not be satisfied, therefore, they felt deeply fooled. The bottleneck situation is an effect resulting from the interactions between student expectations (similar to the molecules of water in a bottle) and the social or occupational structure of their country (similar to the bottleneck of a bottle). One major feature of this complex phenomenon is that the carriers of students are interdependent (as the movement of molecules in a closed space): if a student finds a job on the job market, a space will be missing for the others (Boudon, 1981).

The most striking aspect of the outcomes in the previous examples is that they were unintended and often even unexpected (Merton, 1968), although many of them were the products of intentions. Besides, each of the drivers who causes a traffic jam probably has reasons that seem subjectively good to him or her, but the result of similar interdependent behaviors is not only different from what each one wanted but also is exactly the opposite (the result is worse than if they had waited). Much more large-scale (and historically significant) facts can be explained in this way, such as diplomatic relations leading to a war although no State really wanted it. The First World War is often described in this way, the Sarajevo assassination being only the triggering event of a series of events depending on a huge network of interdependent interactions, which were often "blind" interactions (in the sense that each other's relevant intentions were not known).

The unintended outcomes of these blind interactions between interdependent actors are often disadvantageous for all or most people, as the previous examples show. But they also can be beneficial to certain people and disadvantageous to some others. A fruit seller can decide to decrease the price of his cherries to attract customers and then earn more money. But if every fruit seller does the same at the same time, the customers will keep on going to the same seller, the competition will not have the result that was looked for and the sellers will finally lose money while the customers will benefit. In this case, there is an (unintended) counter-result for the sellers and an unintended positive result for the customers, therefore a sort of *social disorder* if one considers that social order requires a kind of functional unity.[11]

All these previous cases display a situation that is different from Weber's history of capitalism. It is surely not only an arithmetic addition of behaviors that leads to the outcome in the previous examples and moreover, each time the result is really a new phenomenon, different from the phenomena that were at the origin of the process. However, if a certain "collection" of individual actions produces this result, it would be hard to speak of collective action in a strong and proper sense, since the outcome did not result at all from collective intentionality between the individuals (which requires a communication of intentions at least). The "whole" is here just what logicians sometimes call a "distributive" whole – which is not a collective whole properly understood, if one agrees to reserve this phrasing for something very specific, involving collective intentionality. Consequently, the concept of *distributive agency*, which

results from the "blind" interactions between interdependent individuals, suffices, although one could surely say that the action is collective in a weak (and everyday) sense of the term.[12]

EMERGENT SOCIAL PHENOMENA. DISTRIBUTIVE AGENCY AND SOCIAL ORDER. SOCIAL STRUCTURES AND INSTITUTIONS

The investigation of interdependent interactions has to be carried on. It seems that on certain occasions, blind interactions (in the sense of interactions without linguistic communication of intentions) between interdependent actors can be advantageous for *everybody*: one may observe a sort of harmony that any planned action could have plausibly reached, so that he or she could be entitled to speak of a "spontaneous order" (Hayek, 1948) and of strong emergence.[13] One of the best examples of an emergent order, according to some social scientists (Hayek, 1948, 1988), is a free market though, strictly speaking, no existing free market is completely free (there are always regulations). The emergence of languages is another example of an emergent order (Hayek, 1948, 1988). Both are based on numerous reciprocal inter-individual adjustments, which are all the more remarkable since they do not proceed from any will attempting deliberately to impose an order. On the contrary, an order emerges when there is no voluntary intervention.

Let us again take an example. If customers want to get cherries during winter, there will surely be sellers who will try to find them for these customers; and they will do it not because they are altruistic (or because they look for harmony, that is "order," in the social world,) but just because they want to earn money. On the other hand, if customers do not want cherries any longer in the winter, because, for example, they find them not tasty enough, then the suppliers will be led to sell something that is a better fit with their new demands in order to turn a profit. Austrian economists, such as Menger, von Mises, or Hayek, other economists such as Walras and Pareto, and before them, Adam Smith and Mandeville, have shown that, in economic exchanges, there should be a tendency to equilibrium between supply and demands as long as exchanges are free and production and consumption are not hampered, given the well-spread propensity of most people to search for their material self-interest.

Hayek (1952b) used the same model to account for the emergence of a "spontaneous order" in biological and physiological or more precisely neuro-physiological domains, where the model is convincing since the proof of the functionality of a biological system is that it lives if it works and it dies if it does not. But this model is not entirely convincing in economic matters: many social scientists from Ferguson (1995) to Pareto (1916/1935) to Hirschman (1977) have proved that there might be people who suffer in a completely free market, even if the whole (the society) is beneficial.

But Hayek's analysis is convincing on a related issue, important for our concerns. Actually, Hayek demonstrates how prices (e.g., the prices of the cherries in the market) are just the result or the *aggregation of interdependent interactions* (between sellers and sellers, customers and customers, sellers and customers). Evidently this kind of aggregation (between particular acts at the micro-level, producing particular events such as the price of cherries) does not have at all the same meaning as the *aggregation of data* from the micro-level to the macro-level (cf. Weber's or Durkheim's analyses), which the use of the same concept of aggregation may veil.[14] According to this research program, an analysis of social facts similar to Weber's investigation of the birth of capitalism just *misses the point* of the explanation required: capitalism would not have been possible with actors just individually working as hard as they could and investing money as

much as they could; heads of companies necessarily could not have been only worried about their virtue or have just expressed their addiction to work; they had to focus attention on the (possibly changing) needs of the consumers in order to invest in the specific goods that could satisfy consumers' (possibly changing) preferences and not just anywhere. The birth and development of capitalism *cannot* be understood but as the result (if not the emergent result in a strong sense) of interdependent interactions.

If such a spontaneous, harmonious order does not emerge from the social interdependent interactions as evidently as Hayek contends, it is nevertheless true that many disadvantageous consequences, such as the bottleneck situations, are partially the effect of certain *pre-existing structures* (advantageous to everyone or not, therefore "emergent" in a strong sense or not) produced by previous interactions. There are traffic jams because the streets are too narrow, there are unemployed qualified students finishing schooling because the social structure offers too few positions, and so on. On the one hand, the social structures are not the sole cause (other causes are the decisions of people within this framework), so that speaking of structures as entirely "determining" individual actions, as French structuralists (e.g., Bourdieu) have sometimes upheld, does not mean anything significant. On the other hand, these structures are themselves the outcome of previous individual acts so that what is at stake is just a *feed-back* from the institutions to the individuals. Nevertheless, noticing this does not require assuming the autonomous existence of structures (in a strong sense of existence involving that these structures are real actors).[15] But there is no difficulty in accepting Popper's very inoffensive idea of a "world 3" (including social institutions) (Popper, 1972) as far as this just means that there is a difference between, for example, a country where *there is* a certain kind of job, a certain kind of politeness conventions, etc. and another one where *there is not*.

Again the situation is comparable to certain natural facts: although a hive's alveoli are the result of the interactions between the interdependent behaviors of bees, when alveoli have been built, they constrain the subsequent behavior of the same bees (and of others). On the other hand, they also represent opportunities for storing honey and nursing larvae (see Jarvie, 1972: XIII; Popper, 1994: 167). Similarly, when professional positions, for example, have been created (more or less voluntarily), they constitute both opportunities and constraints. Coleman's (1974, 1990)[16] and Boudon's (1973) works are exemplary of what can be called structural analysis or "structural individualism" (Udehn, 2001).[17] In a comment on *The Protestant Ethic*, Coleman even implicitly adds to Weber's analysis the idea that Protestantism, when instituted, became both a constraint and an opportunity structure for people (Coleman, 1990).

Popper's *situational analysis* is another version, just more substantial (the previous, more formal one, retains only the structure or certain structural aspects of the situation), of the same idea, namely, that choices are always made within a particular context.[18] Agassi (1975) and Jarvie (1972, 2001) have elaborated on the same vein of ideas in introducing the notion of *institutional individualism*.

Thus, contrary to what some scholars have contended (e.g., Udehn, 2001), there is no logical contradiction or oxymoron in structural and institutional individualisms. Each expresses a specific research program in which the idea that structures and institutions are just the result of individual actions (so that they cannot be introduced as effective actors in an explanation) is *taken for granted*. The focus, within these programs, is to investigate the role of social situations and social structure (both as opportunities and as constraints) in the choice of individuals and the outcome of their choices.

As these structures are either not intentional or only partially intentional, speaking of collective agency properly understood

again does not seem legitimate whereas speaking of (possibly spontaneously ordered) distributive agency would be relevant.

INTENDED PHENOMENA. PARADOXES OF COLLECTIVE ACTION

It is a truism that institutions, generally speaking, are not completely unintended. But the role of intentions is still much more significant in specific institutions, such as in Law and in Politics, and still more so in more concrete institutions (such as schools, hospitals, companies, churches, Trade Unions, and also various informal associations of people sharing any common interest). In these cases, given that social order (even if it does exist) does not spontaneously emerge in all the aspects of social life, anyway, there may be procedures (such as voting, negotiation, or argumentation in which intentions are at least partially revealed) to arrive at deliberate collective decisions where one of the main goals is to avoid the unintended *undesirable* effects of intentional or unintentional individual actions.[19]

But a vexing issue has been tackled by many sociologists and economists within the framework of this empirically fruitful although narrow version of MI, namely Rational Choice Theory. It methodologically restricts the model of explanation to the idea of individuals rationally seeking their self-interest, more specifically their material self-interest, and raises the issue: to what extent individuals who have interest to act together *effectively* do act together? Karl Marx, who however tried to elaborate on the conditions of a revolution, therefore at least a partially deliberate collective action, seems to have entirely missed this specific point (Elster, 1985). Marx seems to implicitly think that when people have common interest to act together, they automatically do so. Thus collective action would result or emerge straight from the awareness of shared goals. According to Marx and most Marxists, if workers do not act together it is either because they do not clearly perceive that they have common goals (they are deceived by ideology) or they misrepresent their genuine goals (yet because of ideology) or they minimize their opportunities. What communists have to do is – and mainly – is to make workers aware of their genuine common goals and of the means at their disposal for reaching these goals.

But observation proves that this analysis does not take into account a very striking fact: that very often people who share common interests, who know that they share these common interests, and who are pretty well-informed of the reasonable chances of success, *do not* act together. Mancur Olson (1965) has brilliantly displayed numerous cases of this kind, explaining them by the fact that if actors are looking out for their material self-interest, participating in the collective action is not worth the time and energy since anyway they will benefit from the result as much as those who participated. So calculators should encourage the other people to join trade unions and to go on strike while they do *not*.

Exerting external pressure on individuals (threat of penalty, effective penalties) in order to favor collective action is surely in principle a way of increasing the effective participation of individuals in the collective search of the common good, whatever it is. But it is also empirically well known that what is done only under pressure is usually done badly. Amartya Sen's view is not so far from Max Weber's when Weber said that capitalism would not have been possible if heads of companies and employees had not worked as much and *as best* as they could (Weber's account is not precise enough; he does not distinguish between hard work and careful work). Sen (1977, 1999) expresses more specifically the necessity of a *sense of duty* or of everybody's *commitment* to the common good of the company in order for this to succeed. Other social scientists, such Hirschman (1970), have noticed the

necessity of what they call (reciprocal) *loyalty* between employees and heads of companies or more generally between superiors and subordinates, any violation of these implicit contracts leading either to "exit" (when it is possible) or to "voice."[20]

COLLECTIVE INTENTIONALITY AND COLLECTIVE AGENCY PROPERLY UNDERSTOOD

Amartya Sen has introduced the concept of commitment to account for the construction of what can be genuine collective action or a kind of action close to genuine collective action. But, in his very famous paper, before introducing this concept, Amartya Sen (1977) first had examined the relevance of another notion, the notion of identification (with others' interests), introduced by Adam Smith (1759/2002) to equilibrate self-interest (or self-love) as core motivations of human actions. Adam Smith's suggestion has also been re-examined by many other contemporary authors and in various ways (notably by James Coleman, 1990, and Russell Hardin, 1995) to account for certain kinds of collective actions. One can envision identification of people with a common goal, or with a representative oriented towards this common goal, or with the community to which they belong.

But the concept of identification is very complex (the identification with a community is, for example, related to Durkheim's concept of the need for integration) and seems to encompass many kinds of different situations. So that, here as elsewhere, the right methodology might be first to try to investigate the relevance of simpler concepts, such as the concept of intentional or purposive action (which anyway does not exclude infra-intentional processes such as identification). Besides, as the dominant MI framework is currently focused on the model of an intentional or purposive action (cf. above), it is not astonishing that a lot of analyses have been recently elaborated on the nature of collective intentionality.

Thus, von Mises wrote that "it is always single individuals who say *We*; even if they say it in chorus, it yet remains an utterance of single individuals" (von Mises, 1949: 44), thereby clearly taking an individualist stance, he did not elaborate further on this point. John Searle (1995), on the contrary, coming from a philosophy of language perspective and assuming holistic intuitions, has offered an elaboration of this issue. As Bratman (1999) summarizes: "A we-intention, for Searle, is a distinctive attitude of an individual – an irreducible addition to the kinds of attitudes of which we are capable. On the tack I am taking, my intention that we J and my intention to play my part in our J-ing are both intentions – they are both instances of the same attitude; but they are intentions that differ in their content" (Bratman, 1999: 115, n16). Searle takes the example of a violinist in a concert as well. *My* intention as a violinist to play my part in a symphony depends on *our* collective intention to play a symphony and not the reverse. But, although my participation *qua* symphony violinist in a concert depends on the existence of a (transitory or permanent) symphony group, the existence of this group depends on the will of each participant *qua* individual violinist. Be that as it may, Searle does not explain the production (or "emergence") of collective intentionality.

Tuomela (1995, 2002) suggested making a distinction between two modes of willing to do a collective task: the "I-mode" and the "We-mode." One can participate in a collective action (in a broad sense) in the I-mode, which means that everybody is looking out for their own goals, by adjusting them to the goals of others in order more surely to attain their own, which can turn out to provide satisfaction for everybody (as in Hayek's model of reciprocal adjustments between sellers and consumers). But one also can act in the we-mode, which means that everybody is searching for a common goal or attempting to achieve a "joint action." According to Tuomela, joint action would be

the core of collective agency, but he did not explain the content of this "joint action" in detail. Tuomela's analyses, focused on the search for formal models, are very much disconnected from empirical studies (just as Bratman's). Therefore their relevance is hard to assess, although Tuomela tackles exactly the same issues as social scientists such as Hardin, namely, how to understand situations described by slogans like "one for all and all for one"? (see Hardin, 1995).

Gilbert's analyses are more explicitly connected to issues in the social sciences and hence have a clear empirical significance. She tries to interpret certain intuitions of Durkheim in a more analytical way (Gilbert, 1994). Gilbert's main idea is that sociality is based principally on tacit "joint commitments," that is the sort of implicit contracts such that everyone feels committed to do something if and only if others feel committed to do the same (which supposes sort of a *common knowledge* of every personal commitment). It is sort of an extension of Rousseau's and Hobbes's contractualist models to situations in which there is no explicit contract. But, unlike Sen's concept of commitment, Gilbert's concept of commitment does not have any moral significance, although it clearly has a normative significance (1989, 1996).[21] Joint commitments can evidently also occur not only in a collective action as charming as a tango or as ethical as anti-apartheid activism but also in collective actions as cruel as those that Russell Hardin (1982, 1995) discusses, namely, deliberate genocides.

The most problematic issue with Gilbert's viewpoint, according to the concerns of this chapter, is that she does not avoid ambiguity in her assumption of "holism." Strictly speaking, she would need only to say that individuals jointly committed feel *as if* they were members of an autonomous *plural subject* (Gilbert's concept, 1989), so that the subject of a collective action properly understood would be individuals (*feeling* as members of a plural subject) but not an objective plural subject. In other words,

Gilbert could – and even should – have clearly upheld just a "subjective" holism, without assuming the objective existence of these plural subjects. Sometimes, however, Gilbert seems contrarily to assume the existence of such "wholes," that is, supporting objective holism, which is impossible to accept if "existence" is taken in its strong and proper sense. Human beings, like animals, exist in a perfectly understandable meaning of "to exist" (Popper's "World 1" or material world); this is not the case with a plural subject. Or plural subjects exist just as elements of what Popper would have called the "World 2" (consciousness), which is subjective. In other words, Gilbert claims that a genuine collective action requires a plural subject. I claim that it only requires joint commitments (at least most of the times).[22]

CONCLUSION

The notion of "collective action" is often used in social sciences in a very broad sense. One of the main concerns for social scientists and philosophers is always to try to account for collective action as distinct from a mere sum of individual actions. Most of the recent, often very subtle, analyses proposed by philosophers of social phenomena, have been elaborated within the framework of intentionalist models, and done both by proponents of a strict individualist stance and advocates of more holistic-style intuitions. But, if these debates are currently more and more closely related to discussions inside the social sciences themselves, there is still a large gap not only between purely conceptual analyses and empirical case studies but also between philosophical analysis and the proper concerns of social scientists, whereas there is sometimes yet weak interest from social science for subtle philosophical analyses.

The main gap, however, might be between these conceptual analyses of collective agency as requiring collective intentionality and the much broader conceptual domain of social science, in which the construction of collective action (strictly understood) as a micro-macro mechanism turns out to be only one problem among the many problems raised by the so-called "micro-macro link problem." The philosophy of social science, especially when included within the still broader field of the general philosophy of science, can surely here still offer further precious clarifications, especially if it remains closely related to the actual making of the social sciences.

NOTES

1 See, for example, Lukes (1973).
2 See Udehn (2002). I only refer to common uses of the term "holism," not to very specific ones, such as Pettit's (1993).
3 I use "collective behavior" in a more general and neutral sense than its usual sense in sociology (Blumer, 1952), restricted to *not planned* social processes such as riots.
4 Watkins (1957) typically does not care for these distinctions. As Watkins was often considered as expanding Popper's views on MI and as comments on Watkins have fueled a considerable literature (see, for example, Lukes, 1968, also very influential), a large amount of the further debate is biased, especially the issue of "reducibility" of macro-explanations (in which sense?) to micro-explanations (in which sense?).
5 When one speaks of macro-economics, one can first think of a domain in which significant correlations are searched for at the statistical macro-level of economic life, whatever the scale of the social entities. But most times statistics considered by macro-economics are *national* statistics (such as national unemployment, national inflation, national income, national output, national consumption, etc.), that is statistics at a specific scale, the scale of a state.
6 One must be aware that what many authors call the "micro-foundations" issue in social science generally does not mean specifically this problem or this problem only (see above about the entanglement of several issues). See, for example, Little (1994). So there is only a "family resemblance" with the comment given by Little on Jon Elster's methodology in this passage: "Note the ambiguity [...] between 'social processes can only be explained in terms of individuals' and 'It is possible to explain social processes in terms that only refer to individuals'" (Little, 1994: footnote 2, p. 493). See also Udehn (2001: 216).

7 It is the well known issue of the *bridge-principles* between scientific statements and data (Hempel, 1965). Lukes (1968) misses this point when he supposes that MI might mean that "in the social world only individuals are observable" and refers to individuals' intentions as examples of alledgedly observable facts, in order to demonstrate how irrelevant such a methodology is (p. 453).

8 There is a huge literature on emergence. Regarding social science, see Sawyer (2005) for a useful comparative synthesis. I shall consider here that *weak emergence* requires the apparition of a new phenomenon resulting from the interaction of smaller scale phenomena and having, for that reason, a higher complexity than its sources, even possibly a structure. If this structure displays a functional unity (which is often disputable) and only in this case, I would speak of *strong emergence* or *emergence properly understood*. I have chosen this definition among many possible others because it fits with genuine interrogations on various social facts.

9 See Note 8.

10 The inverted comas used by Weber in the title *The Protestant Ethic and the 'Spirit' of Capitalism* were a mark of irony clearly directed towards Hegel's notion of the "spirit of peoples."

11 See Note 10.

12 Hayek (1988) also used the concept of distributive agency, but in a significantly different (stronger) sense. See farther.

13 See Note 8

14 Of course, one can also calculate the *statistical* price of cherries in a country (or in a market)

15 Coleman's diagram (Coleman, 1990) or what Bunge (1996) calls the "Boudon–Coleman diagram" accounts for this feedback of social structures on individual actions. See also Lukes (1971) and Udehn (2002).

16 See also Colemanet (1966).

17 See also Wippler (1978) for a comparable viewpoint, more focused on the structural effect of social networks.

18 Boudon (2005) also uses situational analysis. Winch's (1958) and Lukes's (1968) objections to Popper do not take situational analysis into account. See Jarvie (1972).

19 Pettit's recent work accounts for collective intentional subjects characteristic of these contractualist situations (2003). But this account again (although unconventionally called "holist") does not require more than individuals.

20 See also Stewart on loyalty (1994).

21 Michael Bratman (1999) has contested that (joint) commitment was necessary for collective intentionality, but recognizes that this is a much less frequent case. Bratman elaborates on the notion of interpersonal adjustment (but, unlike Hayek or Tuomela, towards a common goal).

22 See Note 21.

REFERENCES

Agassi, J. (1975) 'Institutional individualism', *The British Journal of Sociology* 26(2): 144–155.

Blumer, H. (1952) 'Collective behavior', in A. M. Lee (ed.) *Principles of Sociology*. New York: Barnes & Noble. pp. 67–121.

Boudon, R. (1973) *Education, Equality and Social Opportunity*. New York: Wiley.

Boudon R. (1981) *The Logic of Social Action. An Introduction to Sociological Analysis.* London: Routledge & Kegan Paul (Original work published 1979).

Boudon, R. (2005) *The Poverty of Relativism*. Oxford: Bardwell Press.

Bourdieu, P. and J.Cl. Passeron (1990) *Reproduction in Education, Society and Culture.* (Richard Nice. Trans.) London: Sage Publications.

Bratman, M.E. (1999) *Faces of Intention*. Cambridge: Cambridge University Press.

Bunge, M. (1996) *Finding Philosophy in Social Science.* New Haven: Yale University Press.

Cartwright, N. (1983) *How the Laws of Physics Lie.* Oxford: Oxford University Press.

Coleman, J.S. (1966) *Equality of Educational Opportunity*. Washington, DC: US Department of Health, Education and Welfare.

Coleman, J.S. (1974) *Power and Structure of Society.* New York: Norton.

Coleman, J.S. (1990) *Foundations of Social Theory.* Cambridge: Harvard University Press.

Darden, L. (2007) 'Mechanisms and models', in D. Hull and M. Ruse (eds) *The Philosophy of Biology, The Cambridge Companion of Biology.* Cambridge: Cambridge University Press. pp. 139–159.

Durkheim, E. (1915) *The Elementary Forms of the Religious Life* (J.W. Swain, Trans.). London: George Allen and Unwin Ltd. (Original work published 1912).

Durkheim, E. (1952) *Suicide* (J. A. Spaulding and G. Simpson, Trans.). London: Routledge & Kegan Paul (Original work published 1897).

Elster, J. (1985) *Making Sense of Marx.* Cambridge: Cambridge University Press.

Elster, J. (2007) *Explaining Social Mechanisms.* Cambridge: Cambridge University Press.

Ferguson, A. (1995) *An Essay on the History of Civil Society.* London: Transaction Publishers. (Original work published 1767).

Gilbert, M. (1994) 'Durkheim and social facts' in W. Pickering and H. Martins (eds) *Debating Durkheim.* pp. 86–109, London: Routledge.

Gilbert, M. (1989) *On Social Facts.* Princeton: Princeton University Press.

Gilbert, M. (1996) *Living Together. Rationality, Sociality and Obligation.* London: Rowman & Littlefield.

Goldthorpe, J. (2000) *On Sociology.* Oxford: Oxford University Press.

Hardin, R. (1982) *Collective Action.* Baltimore: Johns Hopkins University Press.

Hardin, R. (1995) *One For All. The Logic of Group Conflict.* Princeton: Princeton Universty Press.

von Hayek, F. (1948) *Individualism and Economic Order.* Chicago: University of Chicago Press.

von Hayek, F.A. (1952a) *Scientism and the Study of Society.* Glencoe, Il: The Free Press.

von Hayek, F. (1952b) *The Sensory Order. An Inquiry into the Foundations of Theoretical Psychology.* London: Routledge & Kegan Paul.

von Hayek, F. (1988) *The Fatal Conceit. The Errors of Socialism.* London and New York: Routledge.

Heath, J. (2005) 'Methodological individualism', *Stanford Encyclopedia of Philosophy.* (On line;. http://plato.stanford.edu/entries/methodological-individualism/)

Hedström, P. and R. Swedberg (eds) (1998) *Social Mechanisms. An Analytical Approach to Social Theory.* Cambridge: Cambridge University Press.

Hempel, C. (1962) 'Explanation in science and in history', in Robert G. Colodny (ed.) *Frontiers of Science and Philosophy.* Pittsburgh: University of Pittsburgh Press. pp. 9–32. Reprinted in Curd M. and J.A. Cover (1998), *Philosophy of Science. The Central Issues.* New York and London: W.W. Norton and Company.

Hempel, C. (1965) *Aspects of Scientific Explanation.* New York: Free Press.

Hirschman, A. (1970) *Exit, Voice, and Loyalty: Responses to Decline in Firms, Organizations, and States.* Cambridge, MA: Harvard University Press.

Hirschman, A. (1977) *The Passions and the Interests: Political Arguments For Capitalism Before Its Triumph.* Princeton, NJ: Princeton University Press.

Jarvie, I. (1972) *Concepts and Society.* London: Routledge & Kegan Paul.

Jarvie, I. (2001) *The Republic of Science: The Emergence of Popper's Social View of Science 1935–1945.* Amsterdam and Atlanta: Ripodi.

Little, D. (1994) 'Microfoundations of Marxism', in M.Martin and L.McIntyre (eds) *Readings in the Philosophy of Social Science.* Cambridge: MIT Press. pp. 479–496.

Lukes, S. (1968) 'Methodological individualism reconsidered', *British Journal of Sociology,* 19: 119–129, Reprinted in M. Martin and L. McIntyre (eds) (1994) *Readings in the Philosophy of Social Science.* Cambridge: MIT Press. pp. 451–458.

Lukes, S. (1973) *Individualism,* New York: Harper & Row.

Merton, R.K. (1968) *Social Theory and Social Structure.* New York: Free Press. (Original work published 1949).

von Mises, L. (1949) *Human Action: A Treatise on Economics.* New Haven: Yale University Press.

Olson, M. (1965) *The Logic of Collective Action: Public Goods and the Theory of Groups.* Cambridge: Cambridge University Press.

O'Neill, J. (1973) *Modes of Individualism and Collectivism:* London: Heinemann.

Pareto, V. (1935) *The Mind and Society.* Harcourt, Brace. (Original work published in 1916.)

Pettit, Ph. (1993) *The Common Mind.* Oxford: Oxford University Press.

Pettit, Ph. (2003) 'Groups with minds of their own', in F. Schmitt (ed.) *Socializing Metaphysics.* Lanham: Rowman and Littlefield. pp. 167–93.

Popper, K. (1945) *The Open Society and Its Enemies.* London: Routledge.

Popper, K. (1972) *Objective Knowledge: An Evolutionary Approach,* London: Oxford University Press.

Popper, K. (1994) *The Myth of the Framework: In Defence of Science and Rationality.* London: Routledge.

Sawyer, K.R. (2005) *Social Emergence: Societies as Complex Systems.* Cambridge University Press.

Schelling, Th. (1978) *Micromotives and Macrobehavior.* Newton: W. W. Norton and Company.

Sen, A.K. (1977) 'Rational fools: A Critique of the Behavioral Foundations of Economic Theory' in *Philosophy and Public Affairs.,* 6(4): 317–344.

Sen, A. (1999) *Reason before Identity: The Romanes Lecture.* Oxford: Oxford University Press.

Searle, J. (1995) *The Construction of Social Reality.* New York: Free Press.

Simmel, G. (1971) *On Individuality and Social Forms: Selected Writings, edited and with an introduction by D. Levine.* Chicago: University of Chicago Press.

Smith, A. (2002) *The Theory of Moral Sentiments.* Cambridge University Press (Original work published 1759).

Stewart, F. (1994) *Honor.* Chicago: University of Chicago Press

Tuomela, R. (1995) *The Importance of U : A Philosophical Study of Basic Social Notions.* Stanford: Stanford University Press.

Tuomela, R. (2002) *The Philosophy of Social Pratices. A Collective Acceptance View.* Cambridge: Cambridge University Press.

Udehn, L. (2001) *Methodological Individualism. Background, History and Meaning.* London: Routledge.

Udehn, L. (2002) 'The changing face of methodological individualism', *Annual Review of Sociology*, 28: 479–507.

Watkins, J. (1957) 'Historical explanations in the social sciences', *British Journal for the Philosophy of Science*, 9: 104–117. Reprinted in M. Martin and L. McIntyre (eds) *Readings in the Philosophy of Social Science*. Cambridge: MIT Press. pp. 441–450.

Weber, M. (2002) *The Protestant Ethic and 'The Spirit of Capitalism'*. London: Penguin Books (Peter Baehr and Gordon C. Wells, Trans.) (Original work published 1904).

Winch, P. (1958) *The Idea of a Social Science and its Relation to Philosophy*. London: Routledge.

Wippler, R. (1978) 'The structural-individualistic approach in Dutch sociology', *Netherlands Journal of Sociology*, 4: 135–155.

9

Rules, Norms and Commitments

Fabienne Peter
and Kai Spiekermann

INTRODUCTION

In Christopher Nolan's film *The Dark Knight* (Warner Bros. Pictures, 2008), the character of the Joker claims that 'the only sensible way to live in this world is without rules'. The Joker is portrayed as a powerful and malicious figure, determined to sow chaos by defying all those rules which influence and direct the lives of the people he interacts with. The Joker breaks the conventions of daily city life, mocks the mafia's code of honour and defies moral principles such as the principle that one should not harm innocents. As a result of the destructive force of the Joker's conduct, the social structure as it is defined by a multitude of rules, and normally upheld by those whose actions follow these rules, starts to falter. The film suggests that this produces an outcome that is considerably worse than the previous stalemate between organised crime and those seeking to enforce the law. The film thus contradicts the Joker and seems to endorse the widely held view that while not all rules are beneficial, some rules are necessary for, and perhaps even constitutive of, social life. On this widely held view, rules and rule-based behaviour are ubiquitous and following rules makes sense.

Even if this broad view is accepted, there is still a range of challenging questions to be faced by philosophers of social science. First, what are rules? Are rules primarily solutions to coordination or cooperation problems, or is there more to them? Some have argued that rules do not just regulate existing behaviour, but help create new social facts. Others insist that rules are necessary for any meaningful action. Second, what motives do individuals have to follow rules? Is rule-following itself, not just the avoidance of sanctions, in the individual's self-interest? Do individuals follow rules for reasons other than self-interest, perhaps for reasons that relate to the normativity of certain rules? And, finally, how do rules emerge and what determines their stability? Pointing to the fact – functionalistically – that a rule would have a beneficial effect if followed by all individuals does not explain how rules come into being in the first place, and how they can persist.

This chapter looks at different approaches to answering these questions. In the next section, we provide an overview from a historical perspective. In subsequent sections, we discuss in some more detail three approaches which dominate contemporary debates about rules and rule-following: rational choice theory, including classical game theory, evolutionary theories, including evolutionary game theory, and approaches based on collective intentions.

THE ONTOLOGY OF RULES AND RULE-FOLLOWING

Terminological Issues

As we shall use the term, the concept of a rule includes the possibility of making mistakes, of failing to conform to a rule (Winch, 1958: 32; Coleman, 1990: 242; Pettit, 1993: 82). In this weak sense, the concept of a rule is necessarily prescriptive. It involves expectations that oneself and other people might have towards one's behaviour. We use the term rule to cover both conventions and social and moral norms. Following David Lewis' influential approach, conventions may be understood as solving coordination problems by fixing expectations about people's behaviour. Their content is relatively arbitrary from a normative point of view and it is in everyone's best interest to follow the convention. An example is the convention to drive on one particular side of the road.

For social and moral norms there is currently no clear standard for how they should be understood. Norms tend to be seen as more prescriptive than conventions. H. L. A. Hart's influential account of norms captures this feature by defining them as rules of obligation (Hart, 1961: 84–85). As rules of obligation, social norms come with a normative expectation to conform, and there are sanctions against those who deviate. Norms are also deemed more important – more socially beneficial – than other rules. A third feature of norms understood as rules of obligations is that acting in conformity with them may often be in conflict with what narrow self-interest dictates. According to Raimo Tuomela (1995: 16), norms in this sense typically have the form 'an agent of kind F ought to perform task T in situation S'. Such norms (he calls them 'ought to do norms') may be grounded in agreement or in

mutual belief, and there is some social pressure to conform.[1]

What motives do people have to follow norms? One possibility is the desire to avoid sanctions. But norm-following may also be the result of commitment. We call commitment the willingness to make a particular rule the motive for one's action. In the case of social and moral norms, commitment responds to the 'ought' contained in these norms. The rules in question may, however, also refer to conventions or to personal plans. Examples are 'always drive on the left side of the road', or 'exercise every day'.

It is widely accepted that rules have two main functions. There are rules which regulate existing forms of behaviour and there are rules which create the very possibility of some forms of behaviour. John Searle (1995: 27) calls the former 'regulative rules' and the latter 'constitutive rules'.[2] An example for a regulative rule is the convention to drive on one particular side of the road. This convention does not create the possibility of driving, and driving does not depend on the existence of such a rule. The rule merely solves some problems that might arise with driving. The rules that define the game of chess, by contrast, enable a form of behaviour that does not exist without these rules. The general form of constitutive rules, in Searle's distinction, is 'X counts as Y' or 'X counts as Y in context C' (Searle, 1995: 28). That is to say, a constitutive rule identifies for some object X, at least in some contexts, some particular properties Y which are not reducible to its physical properties. Searle's favourite example is how certain pieces of paper count as money in a particular country. In the context of chess, the set of rules specifies how a particular set of moves of figures on a chequered board count as a board game.

It may not always be possible to sharply distinguish between the two types of rules. Anthony Giddens (1984: 19ff), for example, has argued that constitutive rules, such as the rules of chess, tend to involve regulative elements too, and, conversely, regulative rules tend to contain constitutive elements.

An example is the convention to keep offices open from nine to five, which may be part of what constitutes 'work', as opposed to 'leisure'. But the distinction is nevertheless helpful to shed light on different approaches to the question of what rules are and what their significance is. Approaches prominent in sociology – functionalism, structuralism and interpretivism – have tended to focus on constitutive rules (or on the constitutive element in regulative rules) in their explorations of 'social' as opposed to 'natural' facts. Rational choice theory, by contrast, has tended to highlight regulative rules (or the regulative element in constitutive rules).

Ontological Issues

The early days of sociology were marked by the struggle for an independent discipline devoted to the study of social phenomena – as distinct from biological, psychological or economic phenomena. Emile Durkheim (1895) famously argued that there are independent social facts, and that it is sociology's task to study these facts. Rules such as family norms or dress codes are important examples of social facts. These social rules, exist because of the function they fulfil for society as a whole. According to Durkheim, such social rules exist externally to individuals and have coercive power over them. In this view, the regularities observed in individuals' behaviour, and even the individuals' subjective desires to conform to social rules, must be explained as produced by social rules, and not as the result of individuals' subjective wills. Durkheim (1895: 96) discusses the example of norms of blame and punishment to illustrate this effect of social rules. He argues that such norms exist because of their contribution to maintain social order. Instead of seeing these norms as the result of 'the intensity of the collective sentiments which the crime offends', he argues that these sentiments are necessary to sustain the punishment of crime, and should be seen as produced by these norms.

Max Weber defended the opposite view. He takes the subjective meaning individuals attach to their actions as starting-point, not objective social structures. Weber distinguishes action ('Handeln') from behaviour ('Verhalten'); the former is behaviour to which the agent attaches subjective meaning. According to Weber, it is the study of 'social action' – meaningful behaviour that 'takes account of the behaviour of others and is thereby oriented in its course' (Weber, 1922: 88) – that should define the core of the discipline. As Weber (1947: 88) puts it: '[s]ociology ... is a science which attempts the interpretative understanding of social action in order thereby to arrive at a causal explanation of its course and effects'.

Weber gave much room to social action that results from a commitment to social rules. But he was also adamant that not all observed behavioural regularities derive from the commitment towards social rules. He stressed how action can be oriented by social rules by being directed against them; actions can thus be rule-oriented without being determined by them. In addition, in a move that foreshadowed rational choice theory, Weber argued that people's self-interested action, including action that settled on some conventional course of action, could also bring about social regularities (Weber, 1922: 120ff).

Many followed Weber's view that the concept of 'social action' defines the subject matter of social science. Some, however, argued that because of Weber's emphasis on subjective meaning, his theory cannot capture the causal impact of social structures, including social rules, on individual action. According to Talcott Parsons, sociology has to overcome the 'utilitarian dilemma' which affects individualist theories of action (Parsons, 1937: 64). As James Bohman puts it, this dilemma is the following: '*either* the actor is independent in choosing his or her end, in which case the ends are random rather than rational; *or*, the actor is not independent, in which case the causes are external rather than voluntary' (Bohman, 1993: 33, his emphasis), for example determined by biological factors. Parsons sought a theory of action that avoided both horns of the dilemma.

He did so by combining insights from Weber and Durkheim. Parsons argued that 'Weber ... missed the important distinction ... between motivation considered as a real process in time and atemporal complexes of meanings as such' (Parsons, 1937: 636). The former refers to the actual subjective meaning an agent attaches to his or her actions and captures a particular relation between ends, means and conditions. The latter sense of meaning, however, can be detached from the motivations of the particular agent, and refers to systems of ideas and the value frames embodied in social structures. It is a property of objective social structures and accounts for their normative force. According to Parsons' structural-functionalist theory, all actions take place in a 'frame of reference' (Parsons, 1937: 733) that logically connects 'ends, means, conditions and norms'. As a result, individual actions, while endowed with subjective meaning, are not random. Nor are they directly determined by social norms. But by defining the frame of reference, social structures give individual actions a normative orientation: 'action is ... the process of alteration of the conditional elements in the direction of conformity with norms' (1937: 732). In his later work, when pressed to explain how the norms that are part of the action frame of reference remain not merely external to the motivation of individuals but actually come to influence individual action, Parsons added the idea that individuals internalise norms in the process of social action.

Many have objected to Parsons' version of structural-functionalism that it leans too far to the objectivist side and neglects the role of rational agents. Rational agents are able to give an account of their reasons for acting in a particular way. They are aware how rules constrain their actions, and there are different ways in which they might factor in these constraints in their instrumental or ends-oriented deliberations. Parsons' theory of social action fails to take into account the role individual agency plays in the production and reproduction of social structures and social rules.[3] There is a tendency in Parsons'

theory of social action to treat individual agents as '"judgmental dopes" who passively assimilate the rules and roles they are socialised into and merely act out the value orientations of their culture and its institutions' (Bohman, 1993: 37). As such, it rests on an implausibly strong and rigid notion of individual commitment to social norms.

The opposite stance is taken by defenders of rational choice theory (RCT; see: Rational Choice Theory). The standard version of the theory shifts the emphasis away from Weber's concept of social action to individual action when explaining social phenomena. It also brackets the influence the normative content of rules might have on individual action. Rational choice theorists embrace the first horn of Parsons' utilitarian dilemma. They deal with the problem of randomness that troubled Parsons by using a stripped-down conception of rationality. According to this conception, rationality demands that individual preferences are well-ordered and that individual actions are describable as an attempt to best satisfy such well-ordered preferences. Following Savage's (1954) seminal work, if an agent's preferences meet certain axioms of consistency, then the preferences can be represented as utilities over consequences and subjective probabilities over states. A rational agent in Savage's sense acts as if maximising expected utility. While Savage developed his theory for parametric decisions of a single agent, game theory has drawn on his decision theory to develop theories of strategic interactions between agents (see Game Theories), which form an important part of RCT. Rational choice theorists explain observed behavioural regularities as being the result of such utility maximising behaviour. Applied to rule-following behaviour, RCT implies that a convention or a social norm is observed because the action that the rule recommends happens to be the one that maximises individual utility. Game theory in particular has made much headway in answering the question whether complying with a rule is individually rational.

RCT's success comes at a price, however. The standard model of RCT highlights how certain rules are compatible with individual rational action. This perspective does not have much room for rule-following behaviour as such. Because the standard model identifies the content of individual preferences by whatever the individual subjectively values, it is particularly affected by the following dilemma (McClennen, 2004: 223). Suppose that a particular rule requires an individual to do A in circumstances C. If there is a better alternative B, then B is the rational choice – not following the rule. If there is no better alternative in C, then A should be chosen. But again, the recommendation is not to follow the rule, but to do A because it best satisfies individual preferences. As Amartya Sen (1977) famously put it, the standard model of rational choice theory neglects the possibility of individuals acting from commitment to particular rules. If a convention merely helps individuals to coordinate by identifying one among several alternative courses of actions judged equally good, this seems not much of a problem. In most cases of rule-following, however, there is something at stake if one rather than another rule is followed. In addition, rule-following behaviour – as opposed to behaviour that is merely in accordance with a rule – seems ubiquitous. Neglecting commitment is thus not satisfactory.

The contemporary literature is marked by three responses to this problem. The first, adopted by many rational choice theorists, is to explore the possibility of extending the standard model to incorporate rule-following (see the third and fifth sections). Evolutionary game theorists adopt a second response (see the fourth section). They model individual actions as based on strategies and study the survival chances of different strategies. Social norms are interpreted as strategies and models of evolutionary game theory aim to analyse the emergence and evolutionary stability of different strategies or norms. Finally, there are also some philosophers who are not convinced that revising rational choice theory

or moving to evolutionary game theory will solve the problem. These philosophers advocate alternative theories of practical reason (e.g. Anderson, 2000; 2001; see the fifth section).

A rather different perspective on rules and rule-following is taken by those defending an interpretative approach to the social sciences. Interpretivism does not endeavour to link rules to the explanation of regularities in people's observed behaviour. What makes social rules important, according to this approach, is how they relate to what counts as meaningful action. The most influential account of this kind has been given by Peter Winch (1958).[4]

Winch, like Parsons, starts with Weber's concept of social action and treats it as the fundamental concept for the social sciences. In a first step, Winch focuses on the question of what constitutes meaning. He claims that all meaningful action is action that follows a rule. Winch (1958: 50) argues that meaningful action is committed action, in the following sense. It commits the agent to act in a similar way in a similar situation in the future. And committed action, thus interpreted, is rule-bound: 'I can only be committed in the future by what I do now if my present act is the *application of a rule*' (1958: 50; his emphasis). One of his examples is the norm of promise-keeping. But his broad conception of commitment is not limited to that; one can also be committed to private actions, Winch argues, such as when one places a bookmark with the intention to continue reading at the marked passage.

In a second step, Winch links this account of meaningful action to Wittgenstein's insights about language and rule-following. Winch claims that because rule-following is a social concept, all meaningful action is social. His argument is, briefly, the following. The concept of rule-following is related to the concept of making mistakes. Without the possibility of failure, the idea of following a rule does not make sense. This makes rule-following an evaluative concept and links our actions to the actions and expectations of other people

(Winch, 1958: 32). Drawing on Wittgenstein's private language argument, Winch argues that although it is possible to formulate and follow rules that apply only to one's own behaviour, the very concept of rule-following as something that qualifies appropriate behaviour relies on the possibility of external checks – on other people being able to recognise one's behaviour as following rules and evaluate its appropriateness. Individuals can only develop a sense of rules that apply to their private behaviour if they have experienced behaviour governed by established social rules, Winch claims. It is for this reason that rules point to a social setting. Winch concludes that Weber was wrong to distinguish between meaningful behaviour and meaningful behaviour that is social: 'all meaningful behaviour must be social, since it can be meaningful only if governed by rules, and rules presuppose a social setting' (1958: 116). This amounts to an anti-individualist view, according to which individuals non-causally depend on each other (Pettit, 2000: 70).

Anticipating objections to his interpretation of the concept of social action, Winch stresses that such rule-following behaviour need not be conscious. It is present whenever it makes sense to distinguish between a right and a wrong way of doing things (Winch, 1958: 58). In addition, Winch insists that rule-following behaviour needs to be interpreted broadly. An example that he discusses is the anarchist. Even the anarchist can act meaningfully; the relevant rule in this case may be 'break all rules'. This distinguishes the anarchist from the 'berserk lunatic', whose behaviour is indeed pointless and thus does not qualify as social action (Winch, 1958: 53). The Joker in the *Dark Knight* vividly illustrates the difference between the two.

Yet, some important objections to this approach to rules and rule-following remain. A first objection is that Winch's broad conception of commitment includes too much. There can be meaningful behaviour that does not rest on a distinction between doing things correctly or incorrectly and hence does not

follow a rule. The objection can be stated in terms of Weber's account of meaningful behaviour: there is subjectively meaningful behaviour that is not influenced by customs or the social order. Climbing a particular mountain, for no other reason than one has at some point formed the desire to climb that mountain, is an example. In defence of Winch it can be argued that all meaningful behaviour – action done for a reason – involves concept possession. Insofar as concept possession covers the correct and incorrect usage of the concept, Winch is right that all meaningful behaviour is rule-based in this sense (Gilbert, 1989: 71; Pettit, 2000).

The problem with this defence is that it leads to a very thin interpretation of rule-following. Hence even if Winch can be defended along this line, there is a further main objection against Winch which states that his broad conception of commitment demands too little. Winch fails to explain the special influence that some social rules have on human behaviour – some social or moral norms, for example. The commitment to such norms does not follow from mere concept possession. So the question remains why people are deeply committed to some rules, both with regard to their own behaviour but also with regard to the behaviour of other people, while quite indifferent about others. Winch's argument only shows that meaning is something that must be shareable, but not why and how groups of people establish certain rules of obligation that orient the actions of their members (Gilbert, 1989: 93 and 400; see also the fifth section below).

Philip Pettit (1993; 2002) proposes to combine elements of rational choice theory and sociological approaches in order to get to an answer to the question as to what gives certain rules, such as social norms, their resilience (see also Elster, 1989). As Pettit puts the question (2002: 309): 'what ensures that in suitable circumstances those norms can be relied on to emerge and persist?' His answer to this question draws on the following two ontological claims. The first concerns the effect of structural regularities on individual agency. The kind of collectivism that Durkheim endorses implies that there are social regularities such as particular cultural norms or the incidence of suicide which are not causally or logically continuous with regularities in the intentional actions of individuals (Durkheim, 1897). Such 'socio-structural' regularities, as Pettit calls them, have the power to 'override' individual agency in Durkheim's theory. Pettit's more moderate claim, compatible with ontological individualism, is that while it can often make sense to invoke structural regularities in explaining social phenomena, such regularities need not be seen as undermining the status of individual intentional agents. The second claim concerns the relation between individual agents. Pettit rejects the atomist ideal, endorsed in the standard model of rational choice theory. According to atomism, the actions of individual intentional agents may be causally affected by the actions of other agents, but their status as agent does not depend on others. Instead of atomism, Pettit endorses the holist view that individual intentional agents non-causally depend on their relations with other agents, for example in their capacity to think, or to be rational. In defending this view, Pettit, like Winch, relies on the link between meaningful action and rule-following, and agrees with Winch that meaning, thus interpreted, is social (Pettit, 2000).

With the help of these two claims, Pettit (2002: 308ff.) develops the following answer to the question of what accounts for the resilience of social norms. Pettit identifies three requirements for a rule to be a social norm: (i) it is a regularity with which people generally conform; (ii) conformity with the regularity attracts widespread approval and deviation attracts widespread disapproval, and (iii) the fact of approval and disapproval helps ensure that people generally conform to the norm. The third requirement is key for Pettit's approach, as it ties the first two requirements together.

Pettit defends this approach as an extension of rational choice theory. It starts, not from the question which course of action is rational, but from the question what attitudes rational individuals should adopt. Such an attitude-based derivation of social norms, Pettit claims, can 'show that a certain sort of behaviour is bound to attract approval, its absence disapproval, and that such sanctions ought to elicit the behaviour required, thus establishing norms' (Pettit, 2002: 323). He gives the example of a norm against over-grazing in a 'tragedy of the commons' situation. In this situation, standard rational choice theory predicts that free-riding will prevail. However, since avoiding overgrazing is better for all than an attitude which favours over-grazing, it is likely that there is approval of behaviour that avoids overgrazing and disapproval of other behaviour. The presence of disapproval, then, makes overgrazing more costly, and hence supports the norm. What Pettit argues, in sum, is that there is a social rationality which brings about attitudes that facilitate the emergence and persistence of this regulative rule. Note that this amounts to an exact reversal of Durkheim's claim, mentioned earlier, that it is the structural regularity or rule which produces the attitudes (sentiments) necessary to sustain it.

RATIONAL CHOICE THEORY

RCT comes in different versions. In its most stripped-down version it only assumes that agents act consistently according to Savage's axioms, without making any assumption as to how and on which grounds agents form preferences. However, when RCT is applied in the social sciences, it is usually assumed that agents maximise their own welfare (Hechter and Kanazawa, 1997), presupposing a specific motivation that determines preferences.[5] We call this the standard model of RCT. The idealised agent of these rational choice models is often called a 'homo economicus' to underline the focus on personal welfare and on the maximisation of payoffs. Over the years, the standard model has been changed or extended in many ways to incorporate social phenomena that are difficult to capture with the assumption of personal welfare maximisation.

An important charge against the standard model of RCT is that it fails to model rules, norms, and commitments in an adequate way. We assess this charge from several perspectives and look at proposals to extend RCT to address this problem. First, there are inherent problems in game theory to explain how agents coordinate actions. These problems are addressed by introducing the notion of conventions. Second, game theory predicts the breakdown of cooperation in one shot mixed motive games such as the prisoner's dilemma (PD). Since cooperation problems are often solved through norms of cooperation, we look into recent attempts to extend the game-theoretical analysis to model such norms. Third, we examine whether committed action is necessarily outside of the explanatory reach of RCT, or whether the standard model of RCT can be extended to incorporate it.

Rational Choice Theory and Sanctions

Standard rational choice explanations of norms focus on how it may be rational for a homo economicus to act in accordance with social norms. Such explanations must take into account that acting in accordance with norms often poses a dilemma of cooperation: it is attractive to free-ride while others comply. The dilemma of cooperation may take the form of a public good problem: mutual compliance is a public good, but it is difficult to provide the public good because self-interested agents find it more attractive not to comply and benefit from whatever level of compliance is reached by other agents.

Rational choice theorists argue that sanctions can change agents' payoffs such that acting in accordance with norms is in their rational self-interest (Hausman and McPherson, 2006: 72–76, 80–85; pace Elster, 1989: Chapter 3). Sanctions decrease the utility attached to some outcomes, and the subject of the sanction is supposed to change preferences and behaviour in anticipation of these sanctions. One can distinguish between formal and informal sanctions. Threat of bodily harm or death, imprisonment, unpaid work, etc., are formal sanctions typically applied to enforce legal norms. Formal sanctions may also play a role for the enforcement of social norms in violent societies or subcultures (think of enforcement of social norms in the mafia or street gangs). However, most of the time social norms are not enforced with formal sanctions, but in more subtle, informal ways. Individuals do not only care for their bodily integrity, their freedom and their money, but also for less measurable goods such as social contacts, approval, recognition and reputation. Informal sanctions are based on these desires.

Ostracism is one example of an informal sanction. For instance, in laboratory experiments where participants could choose their level of contribution in a public good game, contributions were significantly higher when participants were able to exclude low contributors for the next rounds (e.g. Cinyabuguma et al., 2005). The option to deprive agents of cooperation gains from future interactions is a strong incentive to cooperate or comply with norms.[6] Another informal sanction is withdrawal of social approval in reaction to norm violations. Social approval can be intrinsically or instrumentally valuable. If it is intrinsically valuable, agents care for social approval as such. If agents care for social approval instrumentally, they consider their reputation and how a good or bad reputation will influence future interactions with other agents.

Sanctions are important to enforce social norms. However, a second-order question emerges: since meting out sanctions is costly in terms of time and effort, how do groups solve the collective action problem of sanctioning? Some claim that humans are biologically disposed to punish those who do not cooperate (Gintis, 2000). Others maintain that some of the most effective sanctions are costless. For instance, Brennan and Pettit (2004) argue that we reward and sanction people by holding them in esteem or disesteem, which is costless for the person supplying or withholding esteem. This is part of Pettit's proposal to extend standard RCT by incorporating attitudes, as mentioned above.

These considerations show that RCT in its standard form or with some extensions can offer explanations why it may be instrumentally rational for people to comply with norms. We now address problems arising within the game-theoretical foundations of RCT and will later return to the question whether RCT and its focus on sanctions give an adequate motivational account as to why people comply with norms.

Conventions

We start with a discussion of conventions as solutions to coordination problems. Game theory struggles to explain seemingly innocuous solutions to coordination problems between two or more people. To understand the coordination problems at hand, consider an example. Ann and Bob drive towards each other on a road. Both drivers can either drive on the left or on the right. The two cars can pass each other if they drive on different lanes (i.e. both drivers drive on their left or right side), but they will crash if they both try to use the same lane. Table 9.1 shows the associated coordination game. The numbers in this table (and all Tables below) are utility indices, and all agents maximise expected utility.

There are two pure strategy, strict Nash equilibria in this game: (left, left) and (right, right). In these two equilibria, Ann and Bob choose the best strategy available, conditional on the strategy of the other player: if Ann drives on the left, it is best for Bob to drive on the left, and vice versa. If Ann drives on the right, then it is best for Bob to drive on the right, and vice versa.[7]

A standard assumption in game theory is that players have common knowledge of the

Table 9.1   Driving Game

		Bob	
		left	right
Ann	left	1, 1	0, 0
	right	0, 0	1, 1

structure of the game and their respective perfect rationality. Ann's and Bob's rationality is common knowledge if Ann knows that Bob is rational, and Bob knows that Ann is rational. Also, Ann knows that Bob knows that she is rational, and Bob knows that Ann knows that he is rational, and so on. Rational players should end up in one of the two pure strategy equilibria, but the game-theoretic rationality does not tell us in which. Ann reasons that she should use the same strategy as Bob. She knows that Bob reasons that he should use the same strategy as Ann. This leads to an infinite regress: Ann knows that Bob knows that Ann knows…. No equilibrium can be selected on grounds of rationality.

One might think that the problem of equilibrium selection occurs only in symmetrical games, where the players are indifferent between both equilibria. But this is not the case. Consider the 'Hi-Lo' game in Table 9.2. Ann and Bob cannot communicate, but they have common knowledge of their rationality and the game. According to common sense, Ann should play top and Bob should play left, thereby realising the Pareto-optimal outcome. But this does not follow from the assumptions of rationality and common knowledge of rationality. There are still two strict, pure strategy Nash equilibria: (top, left) and (bottom, right). The Pareto-inferior

Table 9.2   Hi–Lo Game

		Bob	
		left	right
Ann	top	2,2	0,0
	bottom	0,0	1,1

(bottom, right) is a Nash equilibrium because Ann and Bob each play their best strategy, given the opponent's strategy. If Ann expects Bob to play left, she should rationally play top, if she expects Bob to play right, she should rationally play bottom, and vice versa for Bob. The problem is that, within standard game theory, there is no reason to expect one equilibrium or the other. Both Nash equilibria are the result of rational play, and the result is underdetermined (Bacharach 2006: Chapter 1).

Lewis (1969) argues that coordination problems like the driving game and the Hi-Lo game are solved by *conventions* (see also Cubitt and Sugden, 2003). His work is probably the first formal analysis of conventions. However, it has roots in David Hume's (1740) notion of a convention as a rule that emerges in repeated interactions, and draws on Thomas Schelling's (1960) work on coordination games. Schelling finds that most individuals have no difficulty to coordinate on one equilibrium in practice, despite the game-theoretical problems described. For instance, when asking persons what they would do to meet a person in New York if they had not agreed on a time and a place, most suggest 'noon, central station'. Schelling calls these intuitive equilibria 'focal points'.[8]

Game theory informs us about the Nash equilibria, but it does not tell us which equilibrium the agents should aim for, and therefore the agents may fail to coordinate. A convention creates expectations as to which equilibrium is preferred. Conventions can emerge spontaneously by relying on precedence (Lewis) or focal points (Schelling). The driving game is usually solved by precedence: Ann and Bob have seen many drivers (in the UK) driving on the left, and they have reasons to believe that their counterpart has seen them, too, and therefore knows of and follows the convention to drive on the left. The Hi-Lo game, by contrast, is more likely to be solved by identifying outcome (top, left) as the focal point. Both players realise that (top, left) is Pareto-optimal. Even though they have never played this game before, they expect the opponent to play top (or left). Real players usually succeed to coordinate on (top, left) immediately.

According to Cristina Bicchieri, a convention is a behavioural rule for a coordination game.[9] The convention exists if (a) there is a sufficiently large number of agents in the population who know of the rule and know that it applies to coordination games in certain situations; (b) a sufficiently large number of agents prefer to conform to the rule in the coordination game if they expect sufficiently many other agents to conform with the rule in the coordination game; and (c) a sufficient number of agents believe that enough other agents will conform with the rule and therefore they prefer to conform with the rule (Bicchieri, 2006: 31–38; compare Lewis, 1969: 78). Conventions are thus conditional rules: if we expect enough other people to aim for one equilibrium, then we also prefer to aim for this equilibrium. An important feature of this analysis of conventions is that it is arbitrary which equilibrium is primed by the convention, it only matters that the convention creates expectations to coordinate on one of them. This feature can also be used to distinguish conventions from social norms. Norms create not just empirical expectations but normative expectations as well.

Social Norms

Problems of cooperation, which must be distinguished from problems of coordination, may be solved by social norms.[10] Consider a two person PD as in Table 9.3 (we focus on two person games for the sake of simplicity,

Table 9.3   Prisoner's Dilemma

		Bob	
		cooperate	defect
Ann	cooperate	2,2	0,3
	defect	3,0	1,1

but the argument can be extended to multi person games).

The PD has only one strict Nash equilibrium, (defect, defect), because the strategy 'cooperate' is dominated by 'defect', that is no matter what the opponent plays, defection is always preferred over cooperation. The 'dilemma' in the PD is that rational players are unable to achieve mutual cooperation, even though both prefer it over mutual defection. In experiments where subjects face payoffs in the structure of a PD, subjects cooperate much more frequently than the game theoretical analysis suggests. Either these cooperating agents are irrational, or they perceive the situation differently, that is have different utilities attached to the outcomes. Interestingly, communication before the game increases the level of cooperation, suggesting that subjects may be able to agree on or remind each other of norms of cooperation and commit themselves to cooperate, often successfully (for a meta-analysis see Sally, 1995).

Bicchieri (2006: 3) argues that social norms transform mixed motive games such as the PD into coordination games. If both players endorse a social norm of cooperation, it changes the players' utilities such that they prefer to cooperate as long as their opponent cooperates. Thus, if both players expect to play against someone who also endorses the social norm, they play a coordination game in the form shown in Table 9.4, as argued by Bicchieri (2006).[11]

Endorsing a social norm means that an agent knows that the norm applies to specific situations and that the agent has a conditional preference for cooperation: the agent prefers to comply, conditional on the agent's

empirical expectations that enough others comply, and on the normative expectation that enough others expect the agent to comply, and may sanction non-compliance (Bicchieri, 2006: 11). These expectations transform the cooperation problem into a coordination game.[12]

Note that a coordination game does not lead to cooperation by default. The coordination game has two pure strategy Nash equilibria: (cooperate, cooperate) and (defect, defect). This also implies that the norm can exist without being followed: it might be the case that all relevant agents know the norm, and have conditional preferences for norm-following, but do not expect others to comply, and consequently do not comply themselves.

Bicchieri's analysis shows that game theoretical concepts can be used to analyse norm compliance in an extended rational choice framework. A key ingredient is the formation of expectations about other players in an environment of private information. However, it remains an open question what motivates the transformation of the mixed motive game into a coordination game. Sanctions are one possible cause, but Bicchieri thinks that normative expectations alone can also give reasons to comply. The issue of normative reasons will resurface in the analysis of commitment in the next section.

Commitment

Sen criticises standard RCT for advocating a view of human agents as 'rational fools' (Sen 1977). As we have seen, the standard model of RCT assumes that agents always act to maximise their personal welfare. Sen thinks that this view is too simplistic. By introducing the notion of commitment and contrasting it with the notion of sympathy, he shows how personal choice and personal welfare come apart.

If an agent is motivated by *sympathy*, she cares for another agent because seeing the other agent suffer decreases her welfare. In the case of sympathy, welfare and personal

Table 9.4 Coordination Game

		Bob	
		cooperate	defect
Ann	cooperate	3,3	0,1
	defect	1,0	2,2

choice are aligned. By contrast, if an agent is *committed* to help another agent, she provides help even though it does not increase her own welfare, and may well reduce it. Welfare and personal choice come apart. Sen asserts that committed agents are rational, and that rationality is therefore not equivalent to the maximisation of one's own welfare. More controversially, Sen also claims that a committed agent may not even act to pursue her own goals and still be rational. He offers an example (2007:348): you have the window seat on a plane. Your neighbour, playing a (in your opinion) silly video game, asks you to draw the window blind so that he can see his screen. You oblige, even though you would have preferred to see the sun, and even though you disapprove of your neighbour wasting his time with silly video games. Sen claims that you show 'socially normed behaviour' (p. 349). The social norm prescribes not to frustrate the goals of other people unnecessarily. You, by shutting the window blind, do not maximise your own welfare, nor are you following your own goals. However, even though you helped your neighbour to pursue his goal, it would be wrong to say that his goal has become your goal: you would rather see him read the New York Times than play video games. But you are willing to restrain the pursuit of your own goals because you are committed to a social norm of tolerance and helpfulness.

Sen gives many examples of committed action, among them voting, contributing to public goods, activities to protect the environment, cooperating in a game with the payoffs of a PD, and many instances of moral action. If Sen is right, almost all norm-guided behaviour, and in particular moral behaviour, is motivated by commitment, not self-interest. This is why standard RCT fails where social or moral norms matter, that is in most areas of human interaction, with the possible exception of some economic interactions. The standard model of RCT, with its limitation to the self-interested homo economicus, fails to address important factors of human behaviour, in particular being motivated by

social and moral norms. The failure is both descriptive and normative: on the descriptive side, RCT is unable to explain and predict committed behaviour. On the normative side, RCT recommends an impoverished notion of rationality.

It is important to distinguish Sen's notion of commitment from other uses of the term. Schelling (1960) and Elster (1979) talk about *causal commitment devices*. Elster uses Homer's famous example of causal commitment. Ulysses is sailing home to Ithaca. En route his ship will pass the Sirens' island. Ulysses knows that once he and his sailors hear the song of the Sirens, they will not want to stay their course, lured away by their voices. To prevent this, Ulysses stops the ears of his sailors with wax and has himself tied to the mast. This ensures that Ulysses's ship sails on to Ithaca. In this example, Ulysses physically restricts his set of options in the future, taking the option to change course off the table. Similar causal commitments can be achieved if the subject can change future preferences such that it leads to the preferred future action.

Schelling's and Elster's notion of causal commitment is easy to model in a decision theoretic framework: this is a sequential decision where the agent first decides whether she chooses to use the commitment device, and the future decision nodes are changed accordingly, that is options are unavailable or payoffs differ (see Güth and Kliemt, 2007). There are two differences between causal commitment and Sen's notion of commitment. First, causal commitment renders some future actions impossible, while Sen's notion of commitment does not remove the option, but draws on normative reasons to refrain from choosing that option. Second, causal commitment is typically used to maximise welfare from an ex ante point of view, while Sen's notion invokes normative reasons that may well demand welfare reducing actions. Sen's notion of commitment can therefore not adequately be modelled in a single all-things-considered preference ranking. Including the effects of commitment into the agent's preferences, such that the preferences reflect the choices after the consideration of commitments, would not account for the conflict between self-interest and commitment.

In his 1977 paper, Sen proposes to add more structure to agents' preferences. Each agent should have several preference orderings, and these orderings should be ordered in a meta-ordering. Following Sen, an agent may have an ordering of alternatives according to his narrow self-interest, a second ordering based on sympathy for others and a third ordering that respects relevant norms and commitments. In addition, the agent also ranks these different preference orderings according to which ordering is most preferable to act upon. While this added structure allows the modeller to capture commitment, it has an important drawback: it sacrifices the notion of unified, all-things-considered, action-guiding preferences (Hausman, 2007). Sen's richer model leaves it open as to how agents derive choices from their richer preference structures, while the standard model has a clear answer to that question: agents do what they prefer most according to their preferences.

The issues raised by Sen have been taken up in debates on dynamic choice and the rationality of plans. Edward McClennen (1990), David Gauthier (1986, 1997) and Michael Bratman (1987) argue that acting according to plans is a core feature of human rationality, and they attempt to revise RCT to accommodate for plans. McClennen (1990, 2004) proposes a theory of 'resolute choice' to accommodate planning and rationality. Resolute choice is a mode of deliberation that allows agents to make plans and stick to them, even if it requires rejecting alternatives that are preferred while the agent follows the plan. This means that agents can plan a certain course of actions over time and stick to this plan in future choice situations; even though they may prefer to abandon the plan once they face the choice. Gauthier develops related ideas regarding interpersonal choices in his 'Morals by Agreement' (1986) and

discusses intrapersonal resolute choice in subsequent work (e.g. Gauthier, 1997).

One interesting question is which psychological mechanisms could allow agents to stick to plans and commitments. First, there is the option to develop dispositions and to internalise norms. Second, agents may be boundedly rational and stick to plans simply because a constant recalculation of utilities is too demanding. Bratman (1987) discusses this mechanism among others. Bounded rationality is a good explanation for the rationality of planning in some cases, but fares less well when explaining commitments that are usually honoured not because agents are cognitively limited, but because they feel *obliged* to do so. This leads to the third mechanism: agents may stick to plans, and in particular commitments, because they have normative reasons to do so. Bicchieri endorses normative reasons as a motivation to comply with norms when she writes that a 'reason for compliance with a norm is that one accepts others' normative expectations as well founded' (Bicchieri, 2006: 23). Such normative reasons go beyond the instrumental rationality of RCT, but appear indispensable for a complete picture of human rationality (Sugden, 1991; Hollis and Sugden, 1993; Hausman and McPherson, 2006: 85–95; Verbeek, 2007, see Rational Agency). Following Sen, the failure of RCT is to either ignore normative reasons, or to trivialise them by subsuming them under one single preference ranking for each agent. The characterisation of normative reasons for committed action leads to difficult psychological and philosophical questions. Allan Gibbard (1990: 30) remarks that 'the relevant psychology [of norms] is not sitting neatly arranged on library shelves'. The question how norms motivate also leads to intricate problems with regard to practical reasoning and metaethics, which are beyond the scope of this review (see Wallace, 2008 for a survey). The tension between the focus on the individual rational agent on the one hand, and the desire to incorporate normative reasoning to aim for a richer, social notion of human rationality on the other, is a contemporary version of the earlier debates in sociology regarding the relation between the individual and the social, as examined above. We return to this question in the section on collective intentions.

EVOLUTION AND COOPERATION

We have seen that one explanation of why social norms are beneficial is that they transform mixed-motive games into more cooperative games. However, showing that a rule is beneficial is not sufficient to explain the existence of a rule. One also needs to show how the rule came into being and how it was able to persist. Answers to the questions as to how norms evolve and how they are maintained can be addressed with tools borrowed from theoretical biology, in particular evolutionary game theory. Models that were originally developed to analyse the biological evolution of organisms are applied to related questions in the social sciences, leading to evolutionary models of cooperation and culture. This transfer raises difficult questions, but it has also sparked off an interesting and productive research literature on the evolution of human cooperation and norms (see Evolutionary Approaches). We focus on a few models that aim to explain the evolution of norms and give one example as to how theoretical and empirical research from biological evolution, in particular evolutionary psychology, can matter for these models.

Evolutionary Game Theory

Martin A. Nowak succinctly summarises the approach taken in evolutionary game theory:

> Evolutionary game theory does not rely on rationality. Instead it considers a population of players interacting in a game. Individuals have fixed strategies. They interact randomly with other individuals. The payoffs of all these encounters are added up. Payoff is interpreted as fitness, and

success in the game is translated into reproductive success. Strategies that do well reproduce faster. Strategies that do poorly are outcompeted. (Nowak, 2006: 46)

This approach is applicable to both biological and social contexts. Following Daniel Dennett (2006: 341), evolution is 'substrate neutral' and 'will occur whenever and wherever three conditions are met:

1 replication
2 variation (mutation)
3 differential fitness (competition)'

In biological evolution, a gene replicates through the offspring of its organism, variation is provided by recombination and mutation of genes, and differential fitness is the relative success to replicate compared to other genes, which in turn depends on the success of the organism to survive and replicate. Roughly speaking, genes of more successful organisms (where success means replicating the gene as often as possible) are selected for. For the social sciences, by contrast, the most likely unit of selection are patterns of behaviour (called strategies) and evolution happens through learning (Young, 1998). The behavioural pattern is replicated if individuals learn a behavioural pattern from other individuals; variation is caused by mistakes (or learners trying something new), and differential fitness is given by the competition between different patterns of behaviour.

One important (but by far not the only) question that can be addressed with evolutionary game theory is whether and under what conditions cooperative strategies can evolve. We briefly discuss two attempts to answer this question: Robert Axelrod's 'Evolution of Cooperation'[13] and models of cooperation based on indirect reciprocity and assortation.

To explain the emergence of cooperation, it is useful to focus on repeated games. Axelrod (1984) conducted computer tournaments of different strategies for iterated PDs. Axelrod invited researchers to submit small computer programs that had to play 200 PDs against each other in a round-robin tournament. The programs had to decide between 'cooperate' or 'defect' in every PD and could use the outcome of previous games as input to decide on the next move. In Axelrod's tournaments, 'TIT-FOR-TAT' emerged as the most successful strategy. TIT-FOR-TAT cooperates in the first round, and copies the last move of the opponent in all subsequent rounds. If two agents play TIT-FOR-TAT against each other, they cooperate in all rounds. If a player with TIT-FOR-TAT strategy plays against an opponent who defects in all rounds, he only gets exploited in the first round, but not in any further round. However, TIT-FOR-TAT is not the only successful or even the best strategy in iterated PDs.[14] The important insight from Axelrod's work is not the focus on TIT-FOR-TAT, but the fact that cooperation can emerge in iterated settings, and that successful cooperative strategies should be cooperative in a conditional way, that is they should 'reward' cooperation and 'punish' defection. In Axelrod's view, TIT-FOR-TAT is a rudimentary norm of reciprocity. For instance, Axelrod argues that a TIT-FOR-TAT norm evolved between French and German troops in trench warfare. Axelrod's computational results tie in with the game-theoretical analysis of iterated games. The folk theorem (e.g. Osborne and Rubinstein 1994: 143–149) shows that mutual cooperation is one of many Nash equilibria in the infinitely repeated two-person PD, if the discount rate for future payoffs is low.

Axelrod's analysis is restricted to the prolonged and potentially infinite interaction between two individuals. However, regarding norms it is more fitting to consider repeated interactions between different people. We consider two approaches to explain cooperation in these settings: indirect reciprocity and assortation. Firstly, *indirect reciprocity* works if there is a public track record of how individuals behaved in the past (see Nowak and Sigmund, 2005 for a review). Given this track record, non-cooperative behaviour can be reciprocated (this could be interpreted

as 'retaliation'), even though victim and reciprocator do not have to be identical. Apart from reciprocating non-cooperative behaviour, it is also possible, secondly, to exclude defectors and work towards an *assortation* of cooperators and defectors. The internet auction platform EBay is a good example for indirect reciprocity and assortation. It invites its customers to rate the behaviour of their trading partners. Having a good track record of previous trades is essential for doing business on EBay, and this creates an incentive to comply with the relevant social and legal norms of trading. Even though it would be beneficial for a rogue trader to cheat if he considered only the current round, it will damage the reputation of the trader in all future rounds, and will result in fewer trades, or even in reciprocal, retaliatory cheating by future trading partners.

Brian Skyrms's influential 'Evolution of the Social Contract' (1996) has popularised evolutionary models of norm emergence. The idea is that norms can be universal replicators in Dennett's sense: norms replicate through learning, mutation happens by mistakes in the transmission (or attempts to try something new), and differential fitness is given by the relative success or failure of a norm to spread through a society. The idea is that some norms are more easily learned or transmitted than others. This is particularly plausible if some norms create more utility for agents than other norms, such that individuals learn to follow the 'high-utility norm'.

While these models are highly simplified, they can give indications as to how certain norms may have evolved and how stable they are. Models of cultural evolution are most easily applied to rules of prudence and technological know how (Sterelny, 2006). For instance, Henrich and McElreath (2003) describe how Australian Aborigines have developed elaborate techniques to gather and process food to survive in a scarce environment. These rules of prudence ('this is how you hunt a fish', 'this is how *nardoo* seeds are processed') are successfully passed on between members of these societies and from generation to generation because they are useful for the agent who knows these rules. The evolutionary perspective is apt because the rate of replication (i.e. transmission) for rules of prudence is likely to be positively correlated with how useful the rule is. In the case of social norms it is less clear how the content of a norm relates to the rate of its replication. Skyrms (1996), Dennett (2006), Binmore (2005) and Alexander (2007) develop explanatory evolutionary models of normative content with regard to norms of distributive justice, mutual aid and even religion. Research in this area is still at an early stage and it is unlikely that evolutionary game theory can fully capture the rich processes involved in the emergence of norms. Alexander (2003: Section 4.2) offers a sceptical outlook:

> Although an evolutionary game theoretic model may exclude certain historical sequences as possible histories (since one may be able to show that the cultural evolutionary dynamics preclude one sequence from generating the phenomenon in question), it seems unlikely that an evolutionary game theoretic model would indicate a unique historical sequence [that] suffices to bring about the phenomenon.

Apart from explanatory underdetermination, there are at least three further conceptual problems. First, we currently have a very limited understanding as to what makes one norm 'fitter' than another. Second, it is unclear whether the unit of selection should be norms, systems of norms, or perhaps even societies applying norms. Third, if evolutionary models are applied to norms, it is difficult to disentangle genetic and cultural effects. Recent movements towards multilevel selection and gene-culture co-evolution try to address these difficulties (Richerson, Boyd and Henrich, 2006).

Evolutionary Models and Empirical Support

There are many links between evolutionary theory and human behaviour in general (Laland and Brown, 2002). While evolutionary

game theory is a primarily theoretical undertaking, other approaches take a more empirical route. One important field within biological evolutionary theory relevant for the analysis of cooperation and norms is *evolutionary psychology*. Briefly put, evolutionary psychology assumes that human minds have evolved in an environment of evolutionary adaptedness (primarily hunter-and-gatherer societies of the Pleistocene); that evolution has therefore created adapted brain 'mechanisms' or 'modules' to solve certain groups of problems (thereby rejecting the claim that the brain has evolved as a general all-purpose reasoning device); and that these modules still influence human cognition and behaviour today, such that testable predictions can be made (Barkow, Cosmides and Tooby, 1992). One example for a potentially evolved mechanism is *cheater detection*. Since our ancestors in the environment of evolutionary adaptedness frequently encountered dilemmas of cooperation, and since these dilemmas can be solved more efficiently if it is possible to identify cheaters, evolutionary psychologists argue that one can expect such an evolved mechanism for cheater detection. There is some evidence for the existence of such a module: experiments show that people are much better at solving cognitive tasks when these tasks are framed in the form of a cheater detection problem, compared to a logically equivalent task framed in different ways (Cosmides and Tooby, 1992).[15] In a related body of work, the economist Robert Frank (1988: Chapter 3) argues that human *emotions* function as commitment devices to avoid cheating. He argues that cooperators and defectors send out different emotional signals. By picking up these emotional signals cooperators can recognise each other and cooperate with their own kind, while defecting against defectors. Theoretical and empirical studies support the claim that emotions facilitate cooperation in dilemma situations (Sally, 2000) and that even short ex ante interactions allow agents to predict with better-than-random probability whether their opponents will cooperate or defect in a PD (Frank et al. 1993). From an evolutionary point of view, being able to commit through emotions can increase fitness because cooperation gains can be accrued. However, Frank notes that 'mimicry' results in even higher fitness: an agent who can pretend to be committed is able to defect and exploit the other committed agents, underlining the need for cheater detection.

The models and approaches discussed can only give a glimpse of manifold attempts to link evolutionary thinking with the social sciences. Such models can be of help to explain the emergence and stability of norms. Attempts to link theoretical models with empirical work (such as the psychological experiments to corroborate theories of evolutionary psychology) seem particularly promising because they provide empirical micro-foundations for an otherwise theoretical and frequently speculative literature.

COLLECTIVE INTENTIONS

The rational choice approaches discussed in the third section shed only limited light on the social processes that lead to the emergence and sustenance of social rules, especially of social norms. Many have argued that this limitation is a result of restricting the analysis to the consequences of individual intentions. At the same time, many are reluctant to give up the ontological commitment to individualism and to embrace a Durkheimian collectivism. Some have started thus to explore the question whether there is a form of intentional analysis which could complement the analysis based on individual intentions. What these scholars suggest is that social rules are, at least in part, the result of collective intentions (Gilbert, 1989, 2007; Tuomela, 1984, 2000; Hollis and Sugden, 1993; Searle 1995; Bratman 1999). Their focus is on non-summative accounts of collective intentions, or 'we-intentions'. On the summative account, collective intentions are simply the sum of individual intentions, plus a common knowledge assumption. Such an account is both too weak and too strong. It is too strong, because it demands that all members of a collective have a particular intention for there to be a collective intention. But an utterance such as 'the University is committed to a high standard of excellence in research' may be meaningful without it being true that all of its members are individually so committed. And it is too weak, because it assumes that intentions are necessarily 'I-intentions' and neglects the possibility of intentions at the collective level.

Collective Intentions and Social Rules

Collective intentions can be seen as underlying the creation of social facts. The claim is that social groups create social facts which are not explicable in terms of individual intentions. Consider the following simple example (Sugden, 2000). You are a member of a group of friends, who originally organised regular trips to explore new pubs and sample little-known beers. While the main activities of the group may have shifted over time, it is quite possible that, when they are out as a group, beer remains the preferred drink, even if, individually, they all prefer wine over beer. Searle defends the more general claim that the creation and sustenance of all those facts which are not brute facts, that is facts which do not exist independently of human institutions, depend on collective intentions. His argument links collective intentions to constitutive rules ('X counts as Y in context C'). In the first instance, collective intentions assign functions to things that have nothing to do with their physical properties. An example is to use the shadow of a tree as a classroom. Another of Searle's examples, as already mentioned, is a piece of paper that gets assigned the function of money. Beyond this initial assignment of function, collective intentions formulate and support constitutive rules. As such, they ensure that these functions gain permanence and help create social institutions.[16]

Some authors connect collective intentions to the creation of normativity, that is to the explanation of how certain social rules acquire binding force. The most prominent advocate of this line of reasoning is Margaret Gilbert (1989; 2006). According to Gilbert, collective intentions are the product of social groups. She calls such groups 'plural subjects' (Gilbert, 1989: 18). A group of individuals 'constitute a plural subject ... if and only if they are jointly committed to doing something as a body' (Gilbert, 2006: 145). The idea of a 'joint commitment' of all group members, which is necessary for collective intentions in her sense, also entails an account of how social rules acquire normative status and become action-guiding. As she puts it:

> Being a group member takes work. ... In order to enter a group ... one must give over one's will to a sum or pool of wills which is itself dedicated to some cause... This entails taking on or accepting a new set of constraints on one's behaviour. (One also accepts certain new entitlements.) (Gilbert, 1989: 411)

According to her, social rules are 'of the fiat form'; they are 'rules which we as group members prescribe for ourselves' (Gilbert, 1989: 387). 'The fiat forms is ... the expected form for rules whose force is seen as deriving from judgment or will' (1989: 400). Her point is that this 'fiat form' of rules created by collective intentions constitutes a source of obligations which is different from moral obligations and prudential recommendations. Because it includes an explanation for the special normative force of social norms, Gilbert's account differs not just from Searle's take on collective intentions and their relationship to social rules, but also from Lewis' account of conventions, or other accounts based on game theory. She objects to these accounts that they capture mere regularities. Her account, she argues, focuses on the binding rules that social groups impose on themselves and can thus explain how these rules become action-guiding.

The persuasiveness of arguments for the importance of collective intentions for the explanation of social norms and norm-following behaviour depends on how plausible the concept itself is. How should one make sense of the very concept? David Velleman (1997) has a particularly clear presentation of the problem. Take Bratman's (1984) distinction between intentions as goals and intentions as plans as a starting-point. An agent may have two mutually exclusive goals and let the world decide between them. This is not possible in the narrower sense of intentions as plans. Interpreted as plans, intentions refer to things that are up to the agent. An agent cannot rationally plan to pursue two mutually exclusive outcomes. Intentions interpreted in this narrower sense raise the following challenge for theories of collective intentions:

> how can I frame the intention that 'we' are going to act, if I simultaneously regard the matter as being partly up to you? And how can I continue to regard the matter as partly up to you, if I have already decided that we really are going to act? The model seems to require the exercise of more discretion than there is to go around (Velleman, 1997: 35)

If collective intentions are interpreted in the narrow sense of plans, this implies that there has to be one token intention.

This interpretation of collective intentions rules out summative accounts of collective intentions and points to the need of a non-summative account. But it also rules out some non-summative accounts, such as the one put forward by Searle (e.g. Searle, 1995). Searle takes 'we-intentions' to be a biologically primitive phenomenon, located in individual brains. Individuals are thus capable of forming two types of intentions: one type takes the form 'I intend' and the other 'we intend', and neither is reducible to the other. On a view of this sort, there is collective action based on collective intentions if each individual member of the collective forms the corresponding we-intention in his or her brain. That is to say, each individual holds the same token we-intention, but there is no single token intention at the collective level.

Gilbert's 'plural subject theory', by contrast, is compatible with the interpretation of intentions as plans. Gilbert, as discussed, insists on the obligation-generating force of collective intentions. In Searle's account, the coordination and cooperation that is necessary to create and sustain social rules happen as long as the we-intentions of different individuals happen to coincide. Such individuals can thus not 'think as a team' (Schmid, 2003). In Gilbert's account, once different group members have expressed the joint commitment that constitutes a 'plural subject', they are bound to perform their part of the collective action until they jointly rescind their commitments (Gilbert, 2006: 141ff.).[17]

Collective Intentions and Commitment

An analysis based on collective intentions may help shed light on individuals' motivations to follow norms and conventions. Such an analysis shifts the perspective from the question 'what should *I* do?' to the question 'what should *we* do?' As such, the analysis contrasts with rational choice approaches to conventions and norms, as discussed in the third section. Both the standard model of rational choice theory and extensions such as Bicchieri's only invoke I-intentions. The advantage of moving to the analysis of collective intentions is that the question 'what should we do?' suggests natural solutions to coordination problems such as the Hi-Lo game or cooperation problems such as the PD that are not available to those who merely ask 'what should I do?' More generally speaking, it suggests that committing to rules may be the rational thing to do in many social situations.

Does this shift of perspective necessarily imply that an analysis of social rules based on collective intentions is in conflict with rational choice theory – and perhaps provides an alternative to it – or can the two be integrated?

The answer depends, again, on how collective intentions are interpreted. In the following we want to briefly discuss two opposing answers to this question. Elizabeth Anderson (2001) argues that Gilbert's account provides a strategy for overcoming the limitations of standard rational choice theory and points the way towards an alternative theory of rational action. Robert Sugden (2000), meanwhile, rejecting Gilbert's idea that collective intentions generate obligations, argues that collective intentions can be incorporated in rational choice theory.[18]

Anderson's starting-point is Sen's concept of commitment. She tries to show that the perspective of we-intentions allows for an account of what makes committed action rational: 'committed action turns out to be action on principles (reasons) that it is rational for *us* to adopt, and thus that it is rational for any individual who identifies as a member of that group to act on' (Anderson, 2001: 24). In a first step, she argues that the recommendations of standard rational choice theory, which focus on what is rational for an isolated individual, must be rejected when individuals identify as members of a group. Individuals who do identify as members of a group should reason in terms of strategies which make sense for them as a group. Next, she combines this with Gilbert's interpretation of collective intentions as obligations-generating. This yields an explanation for why individuals who reason in this way end up being rationally committed to conform to a social norm such as 'reciprocate favours'. Finally, Anderson stresses that this model of practical reasoning is compatible with the Kantian idea that moral action is continuous with rational action. This is not to say that all principles that members of a group might regard as rational to adopt for them amount to moral norms. There is thus still a difference between social and moral norms. But those principles that are rationally adopted from a universal perspective are moral norms: 'If it would be rational for a collective to encompassing all of humanity to adopt a certain principle of committed action, then action on that principle is morally right'. (Anderson, 2001: 24f; italics omitted).

Let us grant that the 'we-perspective' provides a helpful answer to the question as to what might motivate individuals to act according to principles in coordination or cooperation games which, if they look at the situation from an isolated perspective, they will not be inclined to adopt. But does that indeed necessitate a radical departure from rational choice theory, as Anderson suggests? Sugden (2000) argues that this is not the case. His theory of 'team agency', he claims, is compatible with a generalised version of rational choice theory. That is to say, the received interpretation, which focuses on the reasoning of isolated individuals, is just the special case of a team that only includes one member.

Sugden rejects Gilbert's normative take on collective intentions. He argues, instead, that both the existence of a 'team' and its objectives are empirical issues.[19] His theory of team reasoning starts with individuals who take themselves as members of a team – for example, members of a football team, or members of a family. If all individuals have some confidence that the team actually exists, Sugden claims, they will be prepared to engage in 'team-directed reasoning'. In a coordination game such as the Hi-Lo game, for example, team-directed reasoning assigns a single team utility index to each outcome, as opposed to separate utility indices for each individual. Individuals thus do not approach the game by asking what is rational for them, individually, to do, but what it is rational for them, as a team, to do. As such, team-directed reasoning escapes the infinite regress that individual-directed preferences may generate for coordination games.[20] Team reasoning and team agency, then, become possible if each member of a team engages in such team-directed reasoning, and each is confident that the team exists and that each member will do his or her part. Under these conditions, what individuals are motivated to do derives from team preferences and team reasoning. This approach, too, has thus an answer to the question why individuals might be ready to commit to conform to social norms. But it rejects the idea that such a commitment may be binding.

NOTES

1 For this account, see also Ullman-Margalit (1979), Tuomela (1984), Miller (2001) and Gilbert (2006), among others. Note that there is some disagreement in the literature about how to define rules, norms, and conventions. One alternative approach invokes a stronger criterion of prescriptiveness and maintains that conventions are not prescriptive and hence not rules (e.g. Gilbert, 1989; Searle, 1995). Verbeek (2008) does not distinguish between norms and conventions as we do here, but interprets norms as conventions in Lewis' sense.

2 For related distinctions, see Rawls (1955) and Giddens (1984). Giddens distinguishes between 'constraining' and 'enabling' rules.

3 It neglects, in other words, what Giddens (1984: 191) calls 'structuration' – the interplay between individual agency and social structures; see also Coleman (1990).

4 Other important contributors to this tradition include, for example, Taylor (1971) and Habermas (1981).

5 More precisely, the claim is that in many situations agents act *as if* they were maximising their welfare. Therefore, RCT is not refuted by showing that agents do not always actually maximise welfare.

6 See also Spiekermann (2007) for a formal model.

7 There is also one mixed strategy Nash equilibrium available: both players randomise their choice with probability 0.5. It is a Nash equilibrium because both players have no better response, given the other player's strategy. But it is a Pareto-inferior, unstable equilibrium, and hardly ever found in reality, so we leave the mixed strategy equilibrium aside.

8 Schelling's focal points are an informal explanation of how conventions come into being. In the driving case, there are also legal norms and enforcement mechanisms to ensure driving on the right side of the road. But the convention would work even without these, as long as all people have non-crazy preferences over the avoidance of car crashes.

9 Bicchieri rules out games with nonstrict Nash equilibria because this would imply that one or more players would not prefer to coordinate on one equilibrium, but are indifferent between two or more actions.

10 Verbeek (2008) presents an alternative approach, which uses Lewis conventions as a framework to analyse moral and social norms.

11 Vanderschraaf (2006), in contrast, thinks that a norm can turn the game into an 'assurance game' (Sen, 1967), also called a 'stag hunt' (Skyrms, 2004, referring to Rousseau, 1984).

12 Herbert Gintis (2009: 243–245) proposes a related framework for social norms. He claims that social norms can induce 'correlated equilibria' (Aumann, 1987). According to this view, a social norm functions like a 'choreographer' who simultaneously instructs the players to perform actions such that all actions are best responses to each other. Obeying the 'choreographer', that is the social norm, is therefore a Nash equilibrium.

13 Strictly speaking, Axelrod's original computer tournament does not apply evolutionary game theory in Nowak's sense, but it is inspired by concepts derived from evolutionary game theory.

14 There are strategies that systematically outperform TIT-FOR-TAT (Nowak and Sigmund, 1993). Also, TIT-FOR-TAT is very sensitive to trembling and mistakes: A single mistake can lock two TIT-FOR-TAT players into a vicious circle of retaliation (Fudenberg and Maskin, 1990).

15 Whether the evidence supports the conclusions drawn by evolutionary psychologists is contested. See Buller (2005) for critique, Cosmides et al. (2005) for a reply, and Buller et al. (2005) for a counter-reply.

16 For a related argument, see Tuomela (1995).

17 There are important objections to Gilbert's theory, most importantly that it is circular, as the concept of quasi-readiness already invokes some form of we-intentions. See Tuomela (1984, 1995), Velleman (1997), Bratman (1999) for discussions and alternative accounts.

18 For a comprehensive discussion which covers a range of approaches, see also Gold and Sugden (2007).

19 Susan Hurley (1989), by contrast, argues that rationality decides what the appropriate unit of agency should be.

20 See also Hollis and Sugden (1993) and Gold and Sugden (2007).

REFERENCES

Alexander, J. M. (2003) Evolutionary Game Theory. In E. N. Zalta (ed.), *Stanford Encyclopedia of Philosophy* (Summer 2003 edition).http://plato.stanford.edu/archives/sum2003/entries/game-evolutionary/.

Alexander, J. M. (2007) *The Structural Evolution of Morality.* Cambridge: Cambridge University Press.

Anderson, E. (2000) Beyond Homo Economicus: New Developments in Theories of Social Norms. *Philosophy and Public Affairs*, 29: 170–200.

Anderson, E. (2001) Unstrapping the Straitjacket of 'Preference': on Amartya Sen's Contributions to Philosophy and Economics. *Economics and Philosophy*, 17: 21–38.

Aumann, R. J. (1987) Correlated Equilibrium as an Expression of Bayesian Rationality. *Econometrica*, 55: 1–19.

Axelrod, R. M. (1984) *The evolution of cooperation.* New York: Basic Books.

Bacharach, M. (2006) *Beyond Individual Choice. Teams and Frames in Game Theory.* N. Gold and R. Sugden (eds). Princeton and Oxford: Princeton University Press.

Barkow, J. H., Cosmides, L. and Tooby, J. (eds) (1992) *The Adapted Mind: Evolutionary Psychology and the Generation of Culture.* New York and Oxford: Oxford University Press.

Bicchieri, C. (2006) *The Grammar of Society. The Nature and Dynamics of Social Norms.* Cambridge: Cambridge University Press.

Binmore, K. (2005) *Natural Justice.* Oxford: Oxford University Press.

Bohman, J. (1993) *New Philosophy of Social Science.* Cambridge, MA: MIT Press.

Bratman, M. (1987) *Intentions, Plans, and Practical Reason.* Cambridge, MA: Harvard University Press.

Bratman, M. (1999) *Faces of Intention.* Cambridge: Cambridge University Press.

Brennan, G. and Pettit, P. (2004) *The Economy of Esteem: An Essay on Civil and Political Society.* Oxford: Oxford University Press.

Buller, D. J. (2005) Evolutionary Psychology: The Emperor's New Paradigm. *Trends in Cognitive Science*, 9: 277–283.

Buller, D. J. Fodor, J. and Crume, T. L. (2005) The Emperor is Still Underdressed. *Trends in Cognitive Science*, 9: 508–510.

Cinyabuguma, M., Page, T. and Putterman, L. (2005). Cooperation under the threat of expulsion in a public goods experiment. *Journal of Public Economics,* 89: 1421–1435.

Coleman, J. S. (1990) *Foundations of Social Theory.* Cambridge: Harvard University Press.

Cosmides, L. and Tooby, R. (1992) Cognitive Adaptations for Social Exchange. In J. H. Barkow, L. Cosmides and J. Tooby (eds). *The Adapted Mind: Evolutionary Psychology and the Generation of Culture*, pp. 163–228. New York & Oxford: Oxford University Press.

Cosmides, L., Tooby, J., Fiddick, L. and Bryan, G. A. (2005) Detecting Cheaters. *Trends in Cognitive Science*, 9: 505–506.

Cubitt, R. P. and Sugden, R. (2003). Common Knowlegde, Salience and Convention: A Reconstruction of David Lewis' Game Theory. *Economics and Philosophy,* 19: 175–210.

Dennett, D. (2006) *Breaking the Spell: Religion as a Natural Phenomenon.* London: Penguin.

Durkheim, E. (1895) *The Rules of Sociological Method.* Ed. S. Lukes, trans. W. D. Halls (1982). London: Macmillan.

Durkheim, E. (1897) *Suicide.* Trans. J. A. Spaulding and G. Simpson (1951). New York: The Free Press.

Elster, J. (1979) *Ulysses and the Sirens.* Cambridge: Cambridge University Press.

Elster, J. (1989) *The Cement of Society.* Cambridge: Cambridge University Press.

Elster, J. (2000) *Ulysses Unbound.* Cambridge: Cambridge University Press.

Frank, R. H. (1988) *Passions within Reason: The Strategic Role of the Emotions.* New York & London: Norton.

Frank, R. H., Gilovich, T. and Regan, D. T. (1993) The Evolution of One-Shot Cooperation: An Experiment. *Ethology and Sociobiology,* 14: 247–256.

Fudenberg, D. and Maskin, E. (1990) Evolution and Cooperation in Noisy Repeated Games. *The American Economic Review,* 80: 274–279.

Gauthier, D. (1986) *Morals by Agreement.* Oxford: Clarendon.

Gauthier, D. (1997) Resolute Choice and Rational Deliberation: A Critique and a Defense. *Noûs,* 31: 1–25.

Gibbard, A. (1990) *Wise Choices, Apt Feelings: A Theory of Normative Judgment.* Oxford: Clarendon Press.

Giddens, A. (1984) *The Constitution of Society. Outline of the Theory of Structuration.* Cambridge: Polity Press.

Gilbert, M. (1989). *On Social Facts.* Princeton: Princeton University Press.

Gilbert, M. (2006) *A Theory of Political Obligations.* Oxford: Oxford University Press.

Gintis, H. (2000) Strong Reciprocity and Human Sociality. *Journal of Theoretical Biology,* 206: 169–179.

Gintis, H. (2009) *The Bounds of Reason: Theory and Unification of the Behavioral Sciences.* Princeton: Princeton University Press.

Gold, N. and Sugden, R. (2007) Theories of Team Agency. In Peter, F. and Schmid, H. B. (eds), *Rationality and Commitment,* pp. 280–312. Oxford: Oxford University Press..

Güth, W. & Kliemt, H. (2007) The Rationality of Rational Fools: The Role of Commitments, Persons, and Agents in Rational Choice Modelling. In F. Peter and H. B. Schmid (eds), *Rationality and Commitment,* pp. 124–149. Oxford: Oxford University Press.

Habermas, J. (1981) *The Theory of Communicative Action. Volume 1.* Trans. T. McCarthy (1984). Boston: Beacon Press.

Hart, H.L.A. (1961) *The Concept of Law.* Oxford: Oxford University Press.

Hausman, D. and McPherson, M. S. (2006) *Economic Analysis, Moral Philosophy, and Public Policy.* 2nd edition. Cambridge: Cambridge University Press.

Hausman, D. (2007) Sympathy, Commitment, and Preference. In F. Peter and H. B. Schmid (eds), *Rationality and Commitment,* pp. 49–69. Oxford: Oxford University Press.

Hechter, M. and Kanazawa, S. (1997) Sociological Rational Choice Theory. *Annual Review of Sociology,* 23: 191–214.

Henrich, J. and McElreath, R. (2003) The evolution of cultural evolution. *Evolutionary Anthropology: Issues, News, and Reviews,* 12(3): 123–135.

Hollis, M. and Sugden, R. (1993) Rationality in Action. *Mind,* 102(405): 1–35.

Hume, D. (1740) *A Treatise of Human Nature,* Ed. L. A. Selby-Bigge (1978), 2nd edition, Oxford: Clarendon.

Hurley, S. (1989) *Natural Reasons.* Cambridge: Harvard University Press.

Laland, K. N. and Brown, G. R. (2002) *Sense & Nonsense: Evolutionary Perspectives on Human Behaviour.* Oxford: Oxford University Press.

Lewis, D. (1969) *Convention. A Philosophical Study.* Cambridge, MA: Harvard University Press.

McClennen, E. (1990) *Rationality and Dynamic Choice: Foundational Explorations.* Cambridge: Cambridge University Press.

McClennen, E. F. (2004) The Rationality of Being Guided by Rules. In A. R. Mele and P. Rawling (eds), *The Oxford Handbook of Rationality.* pp. 222–239. Oxford: Oxford University Press.

Miller, S. (2001) *Social Action: A Teleological Account.* Cambridge: Cambridge University Press.

Nowak, M. A. (2006) *Evolutionary Dynamics: Exploring the Equations of Life.* Cambridge, MA: Belknap Press.

Nowak, M. and Sigmund, K. (1993) A strategy of win-stay, lose-shift that outperforms tit-for-tat in the Prisoner's Dilemma game. *Nature,* 364: 56–58.

Nowak, M. A. and Sigmund, K. (2005) Evolution of indirect reciprocity. *Nature,* 437 (7063): 1291–1298.

Osborne, M. J. and Rubinstein, A. (1994) *A Course in Game Theory.* Cambridge, MA and London: MIT Press.

Parsons, T. (1937) *The Structure of Social Action.* New York: Free Press.

Pettit, P. (1993) *The Common Mind.* Oxford: Oxford University Press.

Pettit, P. (2000) Winch's Double-Edged Idea of a Social Science. *History of the Human Sciences,* 13(1): 63–77.

Pettit, P. (2002) *Rules, Reasons, and Norms.* Oxford: Oxford University Press.

Rawls, J. (1955) Two Concepts of Rules. *Philosophical Review,* 64: 3–32.

Richerson, P. J., Boyd, R. T. and Henrich, J. (2006) Cultural Evolution of Human Cooperation. In P. Hammerstein (ed.), *Genetic and Cultural Evolution of Cooperation,* pp. 357–388. Cambridge, MA: MIT Press.

Rousseau, J.-J. (1984) *A discourse on inequality.* Trans. M. Cranston. Harmondsworth: Penguin.

Sally, D. (1995) Conversation and Cooperation in Social Dilemmas: A Meta-Analysis of Experiments from 1958 to 1992. *Rationality and Society,* 7: 58–92.

Sally, D. (2000). A general theory of sympathy, mind-reading, and social interaction, with an application to the Prisoners' Dilemma. *Social Science Information,* 39: 567–634.

Savage, L. J. (1954) *The Foundations of Statistics.* New York: John Wiley.

Schelling, T. C. (1960) *The Strategy of Conflict.* Cambridge, MA: Harvard University Press.

Schmid, H. B. (2003) Can Brains in Vats Think as a Team? *Philosophical Explorations,* 6(3): 201–217.

Searle, J. R. (1995) *The Construction of Social Reality.* New York: Free Press.

Sen, A. (1977) Rational Fools: A Critique of the Behavioral Foundations of Economic Theory. *Philosophy and Public Affairs,* 6: 317–344.

Sen, A. (2007) Rational Choice: Discipline, Brand Name, and Substance. In F. Peter and H. B. Schmid (eds), *Rationality and Commitment,* pp. 339–361. Oxford: Oxford University Press.

Skyrms, B. (1996) *Evolution of the Social Contract.* Cambridge: Cambridge University Press.

Skyrms, B. (2004) *The Stag Hunt and the Evolution of Social Structure.* Cambridge: Cambridge University Press.

Spiekermann, K. (2007) Integrity, Translucency and Information Pooling: Groups Solve Social Dilemmas. *Politics, Philosophy & Economics,* 6(3): 285–306.

Sterelny, K. (2006) Memes Revisited. *British Journal for the Philosophy of Science,* 57: 145–165.

Sugden, R. (1991) Rational Choice: A Survey of Contributions from Economics and Philosophy. *The Economic Journal,* 101: 751–785.

Sugden, R. (2000) Team Preferences. *Economics and Philosophy,* 16: 175–204.

Taylor, C. (1971) Interpretation and the Sciences of Man. *Review of Metaphysics* 25: 3–51.

Tuomela, R. (1984) *A Theory of Social Action.* Dordrecht: Kluwer.

Tuomela, R. (1995) *The Importance of Us: A Philosophical Study of Basic Social Notions.* Palo Alto: Stanford University Press.

Ullmann-Margalit, E. (1979) *The Emergence of Norms.* Oxford: Clarendon.

Vanderschraaf, P. (2006) War or Peace? A Dynamical Analysis of Anarchy. *Economics and Philosophy,* 22: 243–279.

Velleman, D. (1997) How to Share an Intention. *Philosophy and Phenomenological Research,* 57: 29–50.

Verbeek, B. (2007) Rational Self-Commitment. In F. Peter and H. B. Schmid (eds), *Rationality and Commitment,* pp. 150–174. Oxford: Oxford University Press.

Verbeek, B. (2008) Conventions and Moral Norms: The Legacy of Lewis. *Topoi,* 27: 73–86.

Wallace, R. J. (2008) Practical Reason. In E. N. Zalta (ed.), *The Stanford Encyclopedia of Philosophy* (Fall 2008 Edition). http://plato.stanford.edu/archives/fall2008/entries/practical-reason/.

Weber, M. (1922) *The Theory of Social and Economic Organization.* Edited by T. Parsons, trans. by A. M. Henderson and T. Parsons (1947). New York: Free Press.

Winch, P. (1958) *The Idea of a Social Science and its Relation to Philosophy.* 2nd edition. London: Routledge.

Young, H.P. (1998) *Individual Strategy and Social Structure: An Evolutionary Theory of Institutions.* Princeton: Princeton University Press.

10

Systems Theory

Andreas Pickel

Systems theory has played a significant role in science, philosophy of science, the major social science disciplines as well as many applied fields from engineering to management since the 1930s. It had its heyday from the 1940s to the 1960s as a paradigm and candidate for universal scientific theory and practice. It lost its prominence in the 1970s in the face of both theoretical and political criticisms from which, in the core social sciences it has never fully recovered. However, it has re-emerged in a number of new guises in the biosocial and social sciences over the last three decades under names such as: dynamic systems theory, complexity theory, chaos theory, autopoietic (or self-organizing) systems theory, and emergentism. An important analytical distinction is between systems theory as philosophy of (social) science, paradigm, or heuristic, on the one hand, and systems theory in the narrower sense of substantive explanatory theory, on the other. Classical or general systems theory in the mid-twentieth century had both sorts of ambitions, with the specifically theoretical claims subsequently by and large abandoned. Systems theory qua ontology, paradigm, or analytical framework – henceforth referred to as systemism – has always been embraced by

many scholars, whether explicitly or implicitly. The question of the status of system thinking and its implications for the social sciences has only recently been addressed again in an explicit fashion by a small but growing number of scholars. This chapter provides a philosophical, historical, and political contextualization of systems theory, an overview of "new" systems theories, and a programmatic restatement of systemism.

PREHISTORY

Systems thinking has a long philosophical tradition going back to the pre-Socratics. Systems were synonymous with the natural order about which knowledge was sought. Natural order traditionally referred to the real properties and structures of the world, rather than a perspective imposed on the world by the human observer. Whether systems exist independently of the observer, as realism holds, or whether systems are a construction of the human mind, as nominalism maintains, remains a controversial issue in debates about systems in the social sciences. Philosophers from Aristotle to Hegel proposed comprehensive metaphysical systems designed to explain the world as a whole. None has survived the onslaught of modern science since the nineteenth century in anything but a fragmentary fashion. Philosophers have had to become philosophers of science to the extent that they remained interested in making serious claims about reality at all. Attempts at constructing universal or encompassing ontologies as a result were largely abandoned. Systems theory of the mid-twentieth century, in contrast, was an attempt to reconstruct a scientific ontology with the capacity to reunite the increasingly differentiated and unconnected disciplines in the burgeoning natural and social sciences. In the philosophy of the social sciences today, systemism as a worldview or cosmology does not enjoy much popularity, though it is defended by some philosophers of science in strong terms, as we will see in more detail below. As the most eloquent of them, Mario Bunge (2003b: 286), writes:

> [Unlike most other cosmologies] systemism is not committed to any hypothesis concerning the stuff systems are 'made' of: it is essentially a structural (though not structuralist) view. Hence systemism is consistent with idealism as well as with materialism, and it can be adopted by religious believers as well as unbelievers. Therefore it is an incomplete cosmology, one that can be used as a scaffold for building alternative cosmologies.

Systemism as an "incomplete cosmology" is present as a basic philosophical building block in the classical sociological theories. This does not make them into systems theories proper, but further underlines the fact that systemic thinking was not invented by the mid-twentieth century systems theorists. Society, a concept that has been fundamental in social thought since the nineteenth century, is usually equated with the social systems corresponding to the modern nation-state (in anthropology the concept also refers to premodern or preindustrial collectivities that are linguistically and/or ethnically defined). This view of society as a real, concrete entity accounts for its traditional

status as the single most important general unit of analysis in the social sciences, the problematic character of which is routinely exposed in the contemporary globalization debate. We can distinguish three basic types of systems in early sociology. First, a historicist conception of social systems for theories seeking to explain the forms and dynamics of rapid social change. Comte's positivism, Marx's historical materialism, and Spencer's evolutionary historicism attempted to capture social reality in terms of distinct historical systems following a progressive, law-governed trajectory. Second, a structural-functionalist conception of social systems originating in anthropology for explaining the functioning and reproduction of existing social systems. The strict functionalisms of Radcliffe-Brown and Malinowski, Merton's refined functionalism for complex societies, and Levi-Strauss's structuralism based on communications systems are prominent examples of this second kind of underlying systems philosophy. Third, action-oriented theories seeking to explain social phenomena in terms of the action of individuals or collectives and their intended and unintended systemic results. Examples are neoclassical economics which postulates a general state of equilibrium in economic systems and the hermeneutic approaches in which the motivations and choices of individuals provide the key to explaining social systems. Of course, the term system is not always used, and in the case of methodological individualists is avoided, but it is clear that systemic assumptions abound.

GENERAL SYSTEMS THEORY

The key figure in mid-twentieth century systems theory is Ludwig von Bertalanffy, a biologist and philosopher who starting in the 1920s advocated an organismic conception of biology in opposition to the "mechanistic, one-way causal paradigm of classical science." Situated in the problem context of theoretical biology, Bertalanffy developed the distinctions and vocabulary used in systems theory and beyond to this day: distinctions between closed and open systems, between causality and functional complexity, and a generalized concept of entropy (Müller, 1996: 64). In *General System Theory* (1969), published near the end of his career, Bertalanffy declared confidently that a "'new science" has become a "reality." (p. xvii). This grand view seems to have been shared at the time also by some of its opponents. Thus even the bona fides anti-scientific philosopher Martin Heidegger was convinced that cybernetics was about to take the place of philosophy, even if he himself could not bring himself to consider systems theory as genuine philosophy.[1] Bertalanffy's final statement of general systems theory, published at a time when systems theory in the social sciences had already passed its zenith, is useful for determining in what respects "new" systems approaches in the social sciences in the early twenty-first century are breaking new ground or are unfruitful attempts at reviving what became widely considered a failed research program.

"'The system problem," wrote Bertalanffy (1969, 18), "is essentially the problem of the limitations of analytical procedures in science." Their applicability depends on two conditions: (1) that there be no significant interactions between parts of a larger whole; and (2) that the behavior of parts can be described in a linear fashion. These conditions do not apply to entities called systems consisting of parts in interaction. A system, or "organized complexity," is characterized by strong interactions between parts that are non-trivial and therefore non-linear. Biosocial systems tend to be of this kind.

General System Theory (GST) is composed of three parts: "systems science," "systems technology," and "systems philosophy." Systems science was conceived as scientific exploration and theory of systems in the various sciences, "[a] doctrine of principles applying to all systems." Its underlying assumptions were the wholeness and irreducibility of systems, isomorphism of laws common to all systems, and parallelism of general cognitive principles in different fields. *Systems technology* referred to all applied fields of science, in particular systems engineering, operational research, linear and non-linear programming, assuming generally applicable principles and models, such as isomorphic feedback models. GST, according to one of its champions, was leading a "cooperative research effort involving an ever-widening spectrum of scientific and engineering disciplines. We are participating in what is probably the most comprehensive effort to attain a synthesis of scientific knowledge yet made" (Ackoff, 1959, quoted in von Bertalanffy, 1969: 9). While Bertalanffy shared this ambition, he was aware that the optimistic view of GST as the "positive expansion of knowledge and beneficent control of environment and society" could be matched by an equally plausible, pessimistic view that saw in the systems movement "the arrival of *Brave New World* and *1984*" (von Bertalanffy, 1969: 10).

Systems philosophy was the new scientific paradigm designed to transcend analytical philosophy of science. The new philosophy of science contained a *systems ontology* postulating a distinction between real systems existing independently of the observer and conceptual systems constructed by the observer, such as religion and science. Bertalanffy admitted that making this analytical distinction in scientific practice could often be difficult. The new paradigm also contained a *systems epistemology* that was considered "profoundly different from the epistemology of logical positivism or empiricism" (p. xxii). Systems epistemology rejected the analytical procedure of classical science as insufficient for the investigation of organized wholes on account of its built-in reductionism and linear causality. New analytical categories such as interaction, transaction, organization, teleology, etc. were proposed. Systems epistemology was critical of the empiricist view that perception is a reflection of "real things" and knowledge an approximation to truth or reality. Instead, it emphasized the interaction between knower and known that depended on a variety of biological, psychological, cultural and linguistic factors. As such, it stressed GST's humanistic dimension and central concern with normative questions and values.

The hope for a systems science, the first component of GST, proved beyond the reach especially of the social sciences. A theory that would apply to concrete systems in general did work, albeit only for certain kinds of systems. These "hard" systems theories are mathematically-based and technology-oriented. They include automata theory, control theory (cybernetics), statistical information theory, linear systems theory, and synergetics. "Soft" systems theories, on the other hand, boiled down to what was discussed above as systems philosophy, that is, basically an ontological, epistemological, and methodological framework for analysis. In his *General System Theory*, Bertalanffy had already prepared the ground for saving other elements of systems theory by invoking Kuhn's notion of paradigm (p. 18). But when the GST ship sank, systems science took systems philosophy down with it. It might be useful at this point to list the approaches Bertalanffy (1969: 19–24) considered to fall in the category of systems theories, since most of them have survived the decline of GST:

- Classical system theory[2]
- Computerization and simulation
- Compartment theory
- Set theory
- Graph theory
- Net theory
- Cybernetics: theory of control systems
- Information theory
- Theory of automata
- Game theory
- Decision theory
- Queuing theory
- Verbal models

The decline of GST as a paradigm started in the mid-1960s and needs to be accounted for in philosophical, theoretical, and political terms. Philosophically, GST had not been able to unseat the analytical tradition. Systemic ontology was dismissed as metaphysical, though it is not without irony that, like systems theory, posivitist philosophy of science was itself marginalized by the same forces that elevated Kuhn ("paradigms") and Feyerabend ("anything goes") as the new authorities in the philosophy of science. The post-behaviorist and post-modernist backlash in the social sciences and humanities that shaped the remainder of the century was by and large not interested in philosophy of science. Salvageable elements of GST, such as in its systemic epistemology – anti-reductionism, complexity, interaction between knower and known – had to be rediscovered, often via lengthy detours through various non- or anti-scientifically oriented philosophies.

Theoretically, the GST movement had produced some notable results in the social sciences by the late 1960s: Talcott Parsons, *Societies* (1966), and *The System of Modern Societies* (1971); David Easton, *A Systems Analysis of Political Life* (1965), and Karl Deutsch, *The Analysis of International Relations* (1968) were the mature works of three of the most influential authors in systems theory, but their reception was already much less enthusiastic than that of their earlier, less developed works in the 1950s (Müller, 1996: 312). Based on his interdisciplinary general theory of action, Parsons became the single most influential systems theorist, carrying the system concept into psychology, psychoanalysis, economics, and political science. Yet like Bertalanffy, Parsons admitted that he had not been able to develop a *theory* of social systems. "The crucial characteristic of structural-functional theory is its use of the concept system *without a complete knowledge of the laws which determine processes within the system* … What we have presented is a paradigm and *not a theory*" (Parsons, 1951: 483).

As Klaus Müller (1996: 309) has shown, the fundamental problems of GST are reflected in Parsons' sociology: a structurally conservative concept of system; failure to bridge the gap between individual and collective or structural levels; an ambivalent system concept vascillating between epistemology, logic, and empirical science. Yet it was probably not Parson's theoretical shortcomings that account for the decline of systems theory in the social sciences. His fate as well as that of other systems theorists was intimately connected with the decline of systems theory as a public philosophy whose influence had been felt not only in the sciences, but also in the area of social and political technologies of planning and public administration.

Politically, the GST movement became synonymous with scientific optimism and rational social engineering in the post-World War II era of rapidly expanding modern states. The crisis decade of the 1970s undermined public faith in science and politics. Systems theories seemed to have a strong bias towards stabilizing existing social structures at a time when economic systems encountered profound crises and political systems proved increasingly unable to offer solutions. With the rise of critical social science in the late 1960s, existing systems were fundamentally called into question theoretically, with systems theory seen as unable to explain, let alone guide, social change. It is worth noting that a major theoretical source for critical social science was Marxist thought, which itself is based on a systems philosophy (see above). The cultural revolution of the late 1960s demanded social relevance and an activist political orientation from the social sciences. The 1970s also produced another political and economic revolution, though with very different, revisionist content and goals. The neoconservative political revolution (Reagan, Thatcher) and the neoliberal economic revolution of the 1980s were part of a major backlash against the radical ideas of the 1960s cultural revolution and the practice of post-World War II Keynesianism and state intervention in the economy. The theorists providing intellectual guidance to the neoconservative/neoliberal movement and governments were market fundamen-

talists such as Friedrich von Hayek and Milton Friedman who preached their own version of a systemic doctrine according to which free market systems have immense self-organizing powers that as a rule are negatively affected by government intervention and regulation.

Neither neoliberal ideologues nor their critics were interested in systems theory. The social sciences since the 1980s seemed equally uninterested in the major scientific movement of the mid-twentieth century. In one sense, GST has left its mark on academic discourse, above all in the generalized use of the term system and related concepts. But as a movement and scientific ideology, systems theory for the time being was finished.

SYSTEMIC APPROACHES IN THE SOCIAL SCIENCES TODAY

If the 1970s was the decade of the decline of general systems theory, it was not the end of systems concepts; and more or less new systems theories were about to re-emerge in the social sciences under different names. Let us begin with a few examples of system concepts that show the continued influence of systems thinking.[3] As the section on systems in early sociology argued, even the strongly individualistically oriented social sciences, above all neoclassical economics, have an implicit systems theory. Take the key systems concept of equilibrium. While its use has precipitously declined since 1980 in psychology, it has increased somewhat in sociology and political science, and positively surged in economics, especially in the 2000s. The related concept of homeostasis has surged in psychology, but not in the other three core social sciences. The key systems concepts of positive and negative feedback, infrequently used in the 1980s have been used increasingly since the 1990s and especially in the 2000s. The same trend can be observed for the concepts of isomorphism and self-organization in all four basic disciplines. "Dynamic systems" has surged in psychology over the last two decades, reflecting the rise of dynamic systems theory in that discipline. Sociology and political science, on the other hand, have not embraced the concept nearly as enthusiastically, probably owing to a more deep-seated post-Parsonian aversion to the very term "systems" in those disciplines.

Reference to "system(s) theory" in general has recovered in all four disciplines over the last two decades. The more specific "general system(s) theory" and "cybernetics," on the other hand, directly associated with the Bertalanffyian and Parsonian era, have steadily declined since the 1980s. "Game theory" and "decision theory," less directly associated with this tradition, have stayed at roughly the same level since the 1980s. It is a different story for the "new" systems theories, which are appearing under different labels. Only one, "dynamic systems theory," even has the term system in its name, and its influence is almost completely confined to psychology. The systems theories that have found increasing resonance since the 1980s in economics, sociology, and political science are called "complexity theory," "network theory," "chaos theory," and "autopoiesis." Finally, looking at the relevance of specific authors, with the exception of a notable increase in the 2000s in psychology, Bertalanffy is very rarely mentioned (keyword) or referenced (bibliography) in the social sciences. Parsons, on the other hand, except in sociology is mentioned with increased frequency in psychology, economics, and political science. Luhmann (1995), with his autopoietic systems theory who began his rise in the 1980s, is the shooting star of the systems revival in the social sciences in all but economics. The "new" systems theories, with the exception of Luhmann, are difficult to pin down as distinct, elaborated approaches. For this reason, a few words on Luhmann's systems theory, followed by a list of major principles stressed by the other new approaches.

In Luhmann's strongly idealist approach, the fundamental units of social systems are communicative events. His approach, moreover, is strongly holist (rather than individualist) in that the central theory of autopoiesis denies the influence of lower level properties on the behavior of higher level properties. This contrasts sharply with the assumption of other "new" systems approaches according to which specific properties of higher levels emerge from the interaction of lower level components. Finally, rather than causal explanation, Luhmann is primarily interested in the problem of discursive self-reference which calls for the analysis of the meaning of communications (for further on this see Elder-Vass, 2007).[4]

Luhmann is thus a special case among new systems approaches most of which have a materialist and causal explanatory orientation. New systems theories such as dynamic systems theory, chaos theory, and complexity theory share a number of core principles, which may be considered "new" with respect to GST or at least significantly reformulated, include the following (some are overlapping):

1 multideterminism/non-additive determinism/ reciprocal determinism;
2 biopsychosocial development as a dynamic system;
3 multiple levels of analysis at multiple time-scales;
4 multicausality, nested time scales and self-organization;
5 concepts and models of non-linear dynamic systems;
6 self-organization and emergence: systems generating novelty through their own activity;
7 hierarchical ontological levels, but no single level or element with causal primacy;
8 considerable indeterminacy within processes that have globally similar outcomes: random processes at one level appear as causal processes at another;
9 small differences in beginning states can have a large impact on subsequent outcomes: initial conditions, path dependency.

Principles, postulates, or axioms of this sort are to apply to biosocial systems in general. Yet perhaps the most fundamental characteristic of "new" systems theory is a recognition that concrete biosocial systems at various levels of reality, on different time scales, and in different environments may differ in their basic properties, structures, and mechanisms to such an extent that a range of distinct systems theories will be required to explain how they work.[5] Take, for example, the political economy literature on varieties of capitalism.[6] While there is agreement that Anglo-Saxon, European continental, and East Asian economic systems are part of a global capitalist economy, there are different types of capitalist systems at regional and national levels whose working cannot be adequately captured by one and the same systemic model (such as the neoclassical model).

It is beyond the scope of this chapter to look at recent theoretical work informed by systems approaches in any systematic fashion.[7] The reader may keep in mind, however, that some approaches that would seem to use a systemic framework do not necessarily employ systemic terminology for historical and political reasons discussed earlier.[8] Other approaches that do use systems terminology today, on the other hand, may repeat some of the basic weaknesses of classic systems theory. Take, for example, world systems theory, which is not merely a description of the world in terms of systems but rather aims to explain how fundamental social, economic, and political changes everywhere are driven by a global historical dynamic, in a theory that assigns causal primacy to top-down processes from the world system to all lower systems. Similarly, autopoietic systems theory is more than a set of descriptions of various social systems with an emphasis on their communication systems. Rather it makes the theoretical claim that the core dynamics of modern societies should be sought in the workings of discrete communications systems that self-organize corresponding, more or less autonomous societal subsystems such as politics, the mass media, education, arts, and law. This holistic explanatory logic is at odds with some of the basic principles of "new" systems theory enumerated above. A systemic philosophy that hopes to be up to the needs of twenty-first century social science has to offer ways of dealing with fundamental problems of this sort more successfully than other philosophies and research programs. The clearest and most systematic philosophy of systems available today can be found in the work of Mario Bunge (2003a, 2003b, 1998a, 1998b, 1996, 1977). The final section presents some fundamentals of Bunge's systemism.

BEYOND INDIVIDUALISM AND HOLISM: SYSTEMISM AS A PHILOSOPHY FOR A NEW GENERATION OF SYSTEMS THEORIES

Individualism sees the trees but misses the forest, whereas holism sees the forest but overlooks the trees. Only the systemic approach facilitates our noticing both the trees (and their components) and the forest (and its larger environment) (Bunge, 2003a: 75).

Methodological individualists have always been suspicious about any claim about the systemic properties of wholes – whether by structural-functionalists, Marxists, or idealists. They have maintained, rightly, that holist approaches refuse or are unable to account for individual actors as effective agents not reducible to a particular structural logic. And that any social wholes have to be explained, or be explainable in principle, in terms of the structural outcomes of individual actions. Clearly, any new systems approach has to take a position in the individualism vs. holism debate in the social sciences. More than that, such a position should be a step forward, offering a clear response to the legitimate claims of both positions. Traditional systems theories are holist, but systemic thinking does not have to be, as Mario Bunge (2004: 190–1) explains:

Systemism is the alternative to both individualism and holism (Bunge 1979a, 1979b; Sztompka 1979).

Presumably, it is the alternative that the historical sociologist Norbert Elias ([1939] 2000) was looking for in the late 1930s, when he felt dissatisfied with the conceptions of the person as the self-contained *homo clausus*, and of society as a black box beyond individuals. Arguably, systemism is the approach adopted by anyone who endeavors to explain the formation, maintenance, repair, or dismantling of a concrete complex thing of any kind. Notice that I use the expression "systemic approach," not "systems theory." There are two reasons for this. One is that there are nearly as many systems theories as systems theorists. The other is that the "systems theory" that became popular in the 1970s (e.g., Laszlo 1972) was another name for old holism and got discredited because it stressed stasis at the expense of change and claimed to solve all particular problems without empirical research or serious theorizing. Systemism is just as comprehensive as holism, but unlike the latter, it invites us to analyze wholes into their constituents, and consequently it rejects the intuitionist epistemology inherent in holism.

It also satisfies the central concern of methodological individualists that the actions of individuals – that is, the prime constitutents of social systems – not be reduced to a structural or systemic logic, but indeed individual actors be treated as the producers of any social wholes. Systemism takes this concern aboard, but considers it only one among other basic elements in a comprehensive ontology and methodology. The other, equally basic elements that make any social system, indeed any concrete system, work are the relations between its constituents (the system's architecture or structure) and the relations with other natural and social systems (the system's environment). In clear contrast to methodological individualism, any system has characteristics that are the result of its structure and environment (emergent properties), which is why we can speak of a system as a separate entity in the first place. In further contrast to methodological individualists, the constituents of all systems in the universe are systems themselves – in the case of human individuals they are biopsychosocial systems (Pickel, 2005). Most important, in contrast to both methodological individualism and holism,

entities emerge, exist, and submerge as a result of key processes (mechanisms, dynamics) in a system.

> The twin concepts of system and mechanism are so central in modern science, whether natural, social, or biosocial, that their use has spawned a whole ontology, which I have called systemism. According to this view, every thing in the universe is, was, or will be a system or a component of one. For instance, the electron that has just been knocked off an atom on the tip of my nose is about to be captured by a molecule in the air. Likewise, the prisoner who just escaped from the county jail is about to be either recaptured or absorbed by a family or a gang. There are no permanent strays or isolates.
> (Bunge 2004: 190)

What is a system?

> A system is a complex object whose parts or components are held together by bonds of some kind. These bonds are logical in the case of a conceptual system, such as a theory; they are material in the case of a concrete system, such as an atom, cell, immune system, family, or hospital. The collection of all such relations among a system's constituents is its structure (or organization, or architecture).
> (Bunge 2004: 188)

What are concrete or material systems?

> Depending on the system's constituents and the bonds among them, a concrete or material system (see Figure 10.1) may belong in either of the following levels: physical, chemical, biological, social, and technological. The semiotic systems, such as texts and diagrams, are hybrid, for they are composed of material signs or signals, some of which convey semantic meanings to their potential users.
> (Bunge 2004: 188)

Concrete social systems such as multinational corporations, universities or hospitals, not to mention entire societies and civilizations, are exceedingly complex entities. In the most basic terms, they can be modeled as having components, structures, mechanisms and environments. In the systemic view, concrete systems are real, but of course they

Ontology	Systems	Bonds	Mechanisms
Conceptual	Kinds of systems	Logical	[none]
Semiotic	Symbolic systems	Cultural	Communication
Material	Concrete systems	Social	Biosocial, economic, political

Figure 10.1   Systems and mechanisms.

can be conceived, described, and explained only in conceptual terms, that is, through models and theories. While people experience (being part of) social systems directly, they identify and understand social systems through symbolic, in particular semiotic systems, such as shared social representations. Such actors' models are a central part of any human social system and play a central role in the mechanisms that make the system work. In contrast to a concrete system, which is in constant flux, a model of this system is a snapshot in time and space. The basic ontological and methodological assumptions of systemism as a general framework can be summed up in the following way:

A Ontology
1   Systems are the basic entities of the natural and social world.
2   Systems are real entities.
3   There are material, mixed, and non-material systems.
4   Each concrete system is directly or indirectly related to all other systems which form their proximate or distal environment.
5   While some systems are nested and ordered hierarchically, others are non-nested and overlap.
6   Systems have a different spatial and temporal reach.
7   In addition to a system's components, their relations with each other (organization or structure), and the system's environment, there are key processes (dynamics or mechanisms) that make it work.
8   In addition to linear or proportionate causal effects, there are non-linear or disproportionate causal effects.

B Methodology
1   The conception of system is basic to and relates all sciences and disciplines. Individual humans are both systems and components of systems.
2   Systems exist independent of the models, conceptualizations, or theories through which we try to understand and explain them.
3   Materialist and idealist reductionisms in the social sciences are inadequate.
4   Conceptualizations in terms of "part-whole" or "base-superstructure" are too rigid to capture the complexity of real social systems.
5   Instead, conceptualizations have to remain open to more complex orderings.
6   Time and space are crucial in accounting for social systems.
7   While the concept of system as entity may suggest stasis, the mechanisms or dynamics of any system are central in explaining emergence, persistence, and dissolution of concrete systems.
8   Causal relationships cannot be inferred from linear correlations.

These basic assumptions of systemism pose a challenge to social scientists content to leave questions of ontology aside, while at the same time implicitly speaking of real social entities, employing quasi-systemic concepts such as structure, social relations, network, field, actor constellation, institutional configuration, regime, discourse, etc. As one proponent of "new" systems theory, concludes: "It is time for a paradigm change in sociological theory, in the sense intended by Kuhn and Lakatos. The old concept of system is widely discredited. The attempt to build social theory without (at least implicitly) using the concept of system has failed." (Walby, 2007: 450)

NOTES

1 Heidegger's response in 1966 to an interview question by Spiegel editor R. Augstein: "What will come after Philosophy?" – "Cybernetics. But this will not be Philosophy anymore" (quoted in Kornwachs, 2004).

2 Applying classical mathematics (e.g., generalized principles of kinetics, diffusion).

3 The generalizations and trend reports in this and the following paragraph are based on a systematic evaluation of keyword and reference citations by the author, using four indexes: PsycINFO, EconLit, Sociological Abstracts, and Worldwide Political Science Abstracts, made in September 2008.

4 Luhmann's systems theory is highly controversial. The theory has had most influence in Germany. For a brief overview, see Osterberg (2000); critically: Bluhdorn (2000); Elder-Vass (2007); and Wagner (1997). As Walby (2007: 457) concludes: "Luhmann is perhaps at best an uninspiring ambassador of complexity theory for much contemporary Sociology; at worst, a distraction that slowed the utilisation of the toolkit of complexity thinking within social theory and discouraged wider engagement in the rethinking of the concept of social system."

5 The following are recent examples of "new" systems theory from various literatures: general works: Capra (2005), Nowotny (2005), Pickel (2004), Sawyer (2005), Turner (2001), Wadsworth (2008); linguistics: de Bot et al. (2005); cultural studies: Chao and Moon (2005), Erez and Gati (2004); psychology: Lewis (2005), Smith and Thelen (2003); economics: Stahel (2005); ecology: Folke et al. (2005); social neuroscience: Cacioppo (2002), Boyer et al. (2005); sociology: Archer (1995), Burns (2006), Mingers (2004), Watts (2004); organization studies: Schneider and Somers (2006); political economy: Jessop (2001); global studies: Pickel (2006); Urry (2005); European integration: Pollack (2005).

6 Authors following this approach usually do not describe their work as "systems theory," but in the revised view presented here it clearly qualifies. For a similar perspective on the varieties of capitalism literature, see Becker (2007).

7 For a number of exemplary attempts at "rethinking systems theory," see the contributions to a special issue of *Philosophy of the Social Sciences* (37(4) December 2007) under that title by: Elder-Vass on Luhmann and emergentism; Hofkirchner with a critical social systems view of the internet, Summers-Effler on social systems as turbulent flows, and Walby on systems theory and multiple intersecting social inequalities.

8 I would include, among others, historical sociologists like Mann (1993), Sassen (2006), and Tilly (2005) in this category.

REFERENCES

Archer, M.S. (1995) *Realist Social Theory: The Morphogenetic Approach*. Cambridge; New York: Cambridge University Press.

Becker, U. (2007) "Open systemness and contested reference frames and change. A reformulation of the varieties of capitalism theory," *Socio-Economic Review*, 5(2): 261–286.

Bluhdorn, I. (2000) "An offer one might prefer to refuse: The systems theoretical legacy of Niklas Luhmann," *European Journal of Social Theory*, 3(3): 339–354.

Boyer, P., Robbins, P. and Jack, A.I. (2005) "Varieties of self-systems worth having," *Consciousness and Cognition: An International Journal. Special Issue: The Brain and its Self*, 14(4): 647–660.

Bunge, M. (1977) *Ontology*. Dordrecht; Boston: Reidel.

Bunge, M. (1979a) "A systems concept of society: Beyond individualism and holism," *Theory and Decision*, 10: 13–30.

Bunge, M. (1979b) *Treatise on Basic Philosophy, vol. 4: A World of Systems*. Dordrecht: Kluwer/Reidel.

Bunge, M. (1996) *Finding Philosophy in Social Science*. New Haven, CT: Yale University Press.

Bunge, M. (1998b) *Philosophy of Social Science*. New Brunswick, NJ: Transaction.

Bunge, M. (1998a) *Social Science Under Debate: A Philosophical Perspective*. Toronto: University of Toronto Press.

Bunge, M. (2003a) *Emergence and Convergence: Qualitative Novelty and the Unity of Knowledge*. Toronto; Buffalo: University of Toronto Press.

Bunge, M. (2003b) *Philosophical Dictionary* (Enl. ed.). Amherst, NY: Prometheus Books.

Bunge, M. (2004) 'How does it work? The search for explanatory mechanisms', *Philosophy of the Social Sciences*, 34(2): 182–210.

Burns, T.R. (2006) 'The sociology of complex systems: An overview of actor-system-dynamics theory', *World Futures*, 62(6): 411–440.

Cacioppo, J.T. (2002) 'Social neuroscience: Understanding the pieces fosters understanding the whole and vice versa', *American Psychologist*, 57(11): 819–831.

Capra, F. (2005) 'Complexity and life', *Theory, Culture and Society*, 22(5): 33–44.

Chao, G.T. and Moon, H. (2005) 'The cultural mosaic: A metatheory for understanding the complexity of culture', *Journal of Applied Psychology. Special Section: Theoretical Models and Conceptual Analyses – Second Installment*, 90(6): 1128–1140.

de Bot, K., Verspoor, M. and Lowie, W. (2005) 'Dynamic systems theory and applied linguistics: The ultimate "so what"?', *International Journal of Applied Linguistics*, 15(1): 116–118.

Deutsch, K.W. (1968) *The Analysis of International Relations*. Englewood Cliffs, NJ: Prentice-Hall.

Easton, D. (1965) *A Systems Analysis of Political Life*. New York: Wiley.

Elder-Vass, D. (2007) 'Luhmann and emergentism', *Philosophy of the Social Sciences*, 37(4): 408–432.

Erez, M. and Gati, E. (2004) 'A dynamic, multi-level model of culture: From the micro level of the individual to the macro level of a global culture', *Applied Psychology: An International Review*, 53(4): 583–598.

Folke, C., Hahn, T., Olsson, P. and Norberg, J. (2005) 'Adaptive governance of social-ecological systems', *Annual Review of Environment and Resources*, 30(1): 441–473.

Hofkirchner, W. (2007) 'A critical social systems view of the internet', *Philosophy of the Social Sciences*, 37(4): 471–500.

Jessop, B. (2001) 'Regulationist and autopoieticist reflections on Polanyi's account of market economies and the market society', *New Political Economy*, 6(2): 213–232.

Kornwachs, K. (2004) 'System ontology and descriptionism – Bertalanffy's view and new developments', *TripleC*, 2(1): 47–62.

Lewis, M.D. (2005) 'Bridging emotion theory and neurobiology through dynamic systems modeling', *Behavioral and Brain Sciences*, 28(2): 169–245.

Luhmann, N. (1995) *Social Systems* [Soziale Systeme]. Stanford, CA: Stanford University Press.

Mann, M. (1993) *Sources of Social Power. The Rise of Classes and Nation-States 1760–1914*. Cambridge: Cambridge University Press.

Mingers, J. (2004) 'Can social systems be autopoietic? Bhaskar's and Giddens' social theories', *Journal for the Theory of Social Behaviour*, 34(4): 403–427.

Müller, K. (1996). *Allgemeine Systemtheorie: Geschichte, Methodologie und sozialwissenschaftliche Heuristik eines Wissenschaftsprogramms*. Opladen: Westdeutscher Verlag.

Nowotny, H. (2005) 'The increase of complexity and its reduction: Emergent interfaces between the natural sciences, humanities and social sciences', *Theory, Culture and Society*, 22(5): 15–31.

Osterberg, D. (2000) 'Luhmann's general sociology', *Acta Sociologica*, 43(1): 15.

Parsons, T. (1951) *The Social System*. Glencoe, IL: Free Press.

Parsons, T. (1971) *The System of Modern Societies*. Englewood Cliffs, NJ: Prentice-Hall.

Parsons, T. (1966) *Societies*. Englewood Cliffs, NJ: Prentice-Hall.

Pickel, A. (ed.) (2004) 'Systems and mechanisms: A symposium on Mario Bunge's philosophy of social science', *Philosophy of the Social Sciences*, 34(2–3).

Pickel, A. (2005) 'The habitus process: A biopsychosocial conception', *Journal for the Theory of Social Behaviour*, 35(4): 437–461.

Pickel, A. (2006) *The Problem of Order in the Global Age: Systems and Mechanisms*. New York: Palgrave Macmillan.

Pickel, A. (2007) 'Rethinking systems theory', *Philosophy of the Social Sciences*, 37(4): 391–407.

Pollack, M.A. (2005) 'Theorizing the European Union: International organization, domestic polity, or experiment in new governance?', *Annual Review of Political Science*, 8: 357–398.

Sassen, S. (2006) *Territory, Authority, Rights: From Medieval to Global Assemblages*. Princeton, NJ: Princeton University Press.

Sawyer, R.K. (2005) *Social Emergence: Societies as Complex Systems*. Cambridge; New York: Cambridge University Press.

Schneider, M. and Somers, M. (2006) 'Organizations as complex adaptive systems: Implications of complexity theory for leadership research', *The Leadership Quarterly*, 17(4): 351–365.

Smith, L.B. and Thelen, E. (2003) 'Development as a dynamic system', *Trends in Cognitive Sciences*, 7(8): 343–348.

Stahel, A.W. (2005) 'Value from a complex dynamic system's perspective', *Ecological Economics*, 54(4): 370–381.

Summers-Effler, E. (2007) 'Vortexes of involvement', *Philosophy of the Social Sciences*, 37(4): 433–448.

Tilly, C. (2005) *Identities, Boundaries, and Social Ties*. Boulder, CO: Paradigm Publishers.

Turner, B.S. (2001) 'Social systems and complexity theory', in A. J. Treviño (ed.), *Talcott Parsons Today: His Theory and Legacy in Contemporary Sociology*. Lanham, MD: Rowman and Littlefield Publishers. pp. 85–100.

Urry, J. (2005) 'The complexities of the global', *Theory, Culture and Society*, 22(5): 235–254.

von Bertalanffy, L. (1969) *General System Theory; Foundations, Development, Applications*. New York: G. Braziller.

Wadsworth, Y. (2008) 'Is it safe to talk about systems again yet? Self-organising processes for complex living systems and the dynamics of human inquiry', *Systemic Practice and Action Research*, 21(2): 153–170.

Wagner, G. (1997) 'The end of Luhmann's social systems theory', *Philosophy of the Social Sciences*, 27(4): 387–410.

Walby, S. (2007) 'Complexity theory, systems theory, and multiple intersecting social inequalities', *Philosophy of the Social Sciences*, 37(4): 449–470.

Watts, D.J. (2004) 'The "new" science of networks', *Annual Review of Sociology*, 30: 243–270.

11

The Concept of Culture as an Ontological Paradox

Angel Díaz de Rada[1]

THE CONCEPT OF CULTURE AND THE ANTHROPOLOGICAL ENTERPRISE

The word *culture* has already had a long life in the social sciences, and its importance in the development of social and cultural anthropology can hardly be disputed. To show the initial relevance of this word in the development of anthropology, Edward B. Tylor's definition, first published in 1871 in his work *Primitive Culture* (Tylor, 1920), is often mentioned. A taxative statement made by Robert Lowie in his 1917 work *Culture and Ethnology* (Lowie, 2008) is another definition that is usually pointed out: culture, he says, is the main subject of ethnology (cf. Kuper, 2000). Today, few anthropologists would embrace such a conclusive definition of the discipline. However, the concept of culture continues to be a fundamental pretext to debate the meaning of the practice of anthropology (Abu-Lughod, 1991; Brightman, 1995; Fabian, 2001; Gupta and Ferguson, 1992; Kuper, 2000; Rapport, 2003; Rapport and Overing, 2000; Stolcke, 1995; Weiner, 1995). This is not surprising, as the concept of culture has been a powerful lens for viewing what is encompassed in the expression

"human reality." Just like the concept of society, the concept of culture has been and still is a fundamental ontological tool.

Like the majority of words that make up the analytic vocabulary of the social sciences, the word *culture* already had a long semantic history before it turned up in the writings of sociologists, historians, and anthropologists. This history has been told to quite diverse ends and with very different nuances (Kroeber and Kluckhohn, 1963: 11–73; Kuper, 2000; Markus, 1993; Williams, 1976). Similarly, like most of the words in the vocabulary of the social sciences, the word *culture* has been invested with multiple meanings, in researchers' professional practice and outside of it, and it has been handled daily as a euphemistic version of all kinds of ideological fundamentalisms (Stolcke, 1995).

I am going to focus on exploring the analytic profiles of the concept of culture, particularly in social and cultural anthropology. In recent decades, there have been anthropologists who have suggested that the concept of culture be abandoned, arguing that its overextension in anthropology and the abuses that it has suffered outside of the discipline have turned it into a concept with no analytic value (Hann, 2001; and, particularly, Kuper, 2000). I will refute these positions here. In order to do this, I will first show that the concept of culture is, in its professional uses, much more precise than it might seem from reading these authors. The truth is that it is a very encompassing concept but, contrary to Adam Kuper's opinion, I maintain that the concept of culture cannot be substituted by concepts such as "knowledge, or belief, or art, or technology, or tradition, or even [...] idcology..." (Kuper, 2000: x). Each of these terms mentions types of cultural action, but none of them includes the more abstract meaning of the concept of culture. As for the idea of abandoning the concept of culture in anthropology because of the abuses it has suffered upon entering ordinary language, it is absurd. After all, I would not expect physicists to abandon their concept of energy even if I hear charlatans and soothsayers use it; so, as an anthropologist, I see no reason to give up the concept of culture unless, of course, there are powerful analytic reasons to do so. And I do not think that there are. On the other hand, it is necessary to critically acknowledge the weight of reification, essentialization, and exotization that the concept of culture has carried within anthropological discourse, particularly in connection with the predicates of otherness in a context of colonial relations (Abu-Lughod, 1991; Fabian, 2001; Stolcke, 1995). But a concept of culture that is restored from the consciousness of these limitations also requires us to consider that these contemporary criticisms may have derived "their cogency and persuasiveness from a strategic and selective retrospective reconstruction of the meaning of the concept in earlier conditions of anthropology" (Brightman, 1995: 510).

The discipline that has worked on the concept of culture with greatest intensity and historical continuity is social and cultural anthropology. However, it is a cliché that definitions of the concept have proliferated in anthropology, and that these definitions do not coincide (Jones, 2007: 365). Consequently, venturing into the ontological

dimensions of the word *culture* does not seem very promising, unless we first delimit as clearly as possible what we want to say with this word. In this chapter, I will follow the strategy of formulating these dimensions after offering a sequence of seven definitions. In presenting this sequence, I am not attempting to offer an exhaustive historical recapitulation, although I am convinced that this sequence of definitions connects, from the first definition ("way of life") to the seventh ("discourse of conventions"), two extremes of a clear scientific progression. That is, I believe that this seventh definition, in relation to the first, is more logically consistent and more empirically adequate, in addition to being later in historical time. By formulating these seven definitions, and coordinating them with a certain amount of bibliography, I only aspire to cover a minimum common denominator of the anthropological concepts of culture, based on a language that is precise and, therefore, easy to challenge. It would be too ambitious to attempt to instigate any universal agreement regarding these definitions, but by formulating them as precisely as possible, I hope at least to offer a corpus of notions that will allow (a) a clear expression of the disagreements, and (b) the construction of a clear position regarding the kind of ontological assumptions the word *culture* contains.

The concept of culture is, historically, at the nucleus of anthropological reflection. That is why it has suffered the essential tensions of the discipline. In 1992, George W. Stocking proclaimed the tension that, in my opinion, has been the most important one: anthropology has been struggling, since its very genesis, in the tension between the *anthropos* and the *ethnos* (Stocking, 1992). That is, it has struggled in the tension between producing knowledge about the human species, *Homo Sapiens*, as the universal *anthropos*, and producing knowledge about each of the local *ethnic* varieties of the species. In parallel, the concept of culture has developed at the very heart of this tension, as a concept that describes the species as a unit, and as a concept that describes each of its social manifestations differentially. Anthropology's commitment to scientific universalism has thus been affected by a kind of ontological pluralism: what describes the human *being* is diversity in the *ways of being* (one of which is, of course, being a social scientist).

DEFINITION 1: CULTURE IS A FORM OF SOCIAL LIFE

In his semantic review of the word culture, Raymond Williams formulated this definition, among others: "a particular way of life, whether of a people, a period or a group, from Herder and [XIXth Century]" (Williams, 1976: 80). This definition is a good starting point, because analysts coincide in pointing to Herder and his romantic emphasis on the diversity of ways of human life as a fundamental precedent in the kind of empirical inquiry that would later take the canonical shape of anthropological field work (Caisson, 1991; Kroeber and Kluckhohn, 1963; Markus, 1993; Williams, 1976).

By attributing culture to "a people [...] or a group," Raymond Williams offers a very exact image of the kind of logical use that the word has had, and continues to have, in the social sciences and, of course, of the use that Herder himself wanted to give it. As a way of life, culture is, in this sense, a *property* of a social subject. As we advance in the successive definitions in this essay, I will show that this notion of culture is empirically untenable and analytically sterile. If the entire meaning of the notion of culture were contained in this idea of "a particular way of life, whether of a people, a period or a group," then we would do well to follow the suggestion of authors like Kuper or Hann: get rid of such a concept definitively.

The main problem of this meaning of the word *culture* stems from the assumption that human beings live in societies that have, each and every one of them, *one* way of life. Thus, the concept of culture constitutes a potent

metaphor of social order. This metaphor holds all the traps that the anthropological emphasis on diversity specifically attempts to get around. This concept of culture (a) reifies a social subject, which it (b) interprets as a unit that is isolated from the rest of the social subjects, (c) positing an identity for this social subject that (d) is the identity of all the lesser units that make it up. By involving a concept of society that underlines the substantive dimension as a society of subjects and not the active, processual dimension as socialization among agents (Ramírez Goicoechea, 2007), this concept of culture is reifying, isolating, and homogenizing.

DEFINITION 2: CULTURE IS THE CONVENTIONAL FORM OF HUMAN ACTION

Nevertheless, there is a notion in this first definition that is, in fact, empirically and analytically fertile: the notion of form ("way"). Human action takes on conventional forms.[2] These conventional forms of greeting, speaking, kissing, thinking, eating, working, etc., constitute a broad sphere of our activity as human beings, and the analytic concept of culture points to these forms. It is immediately clear that this concept of conventional form does not necessarily go hand-in-hand with "*one* people, *one* group." Human actions have conventional forms even if these forms are diverse or are carried out by social subjects that are not part of *one* people.

Because the concept of convention is central to my entire line of argument, it would be a good idea to address it here first. Steven Mailloux has offered the following definition, discussing a set of classic contributions: "Conventions refer to shared pratices" (Culler, 1981; Lewis, 2002; Mailloux, 2003: 399; cf. Mailloux, 1982; Putnam, 1981).[3] Since the word *shared* is always problematic, Mailloux has underlined the analytic difference between the traditional and prescriptive aspects of human conventions and the constituent aspects, that is, conventions as shared exercises for determining the form *in the course* of an action, text, or situation (Mailloux, 2003: 399). As for the way I use the concept of convention in this text, I will highlight two points of emphasis: (a) conventions are generated in communicational practices, and they can be stabilized objectively (be objectified), by intertwining with one another in a diversity of productions: laws, furniture, dialogue, urban planning, roads or air routes, and musical scores. When agents put conventions into practice on a stage of coordinated action (Lewis, 2002), (b) they make use of semiotic resources, such as representations, rules, codes, interpretants, etc., whose existence is embodied in human institutions that are relatively stabilized in social time (Searle, 1997).

Alfred Kroeber and Clyde Kluckhohn were the ones who, in their conceptual review in 1952, emphasized the notion of a conventional form for characterizing the concept of culture: "In the operation of definition [of the concept of culture] one may see in microcosm the essence of the cultural process: the imposition of a conventional form upon the flux of experience" (Kroeber and Kluckhohn, 1963: 78). This concept of culture as a conventional form of action presents a double ontological status, also to be found at the root of the way the concept of *practice* developed over the last century. A practice presents an experiential moment that we could call subjective and, when it is carried out, it also presents an objectified moment: the practice produces effects in the world because it intervenes in the world (Bourdieu, 1988, 1990; cf. Turner, 1994). The same thing happens with the concept of culture: culture is the conventional form of action and also the conventional form of the product of this action, that is, of its objectifications, with a meaning close to that given by Franz Boas in this passage in 1916.

An inexperienced basket-maker who does not control the movements of her hands will produce an uneven fabric, the stitches of which will for this reason possess an irregular surface. On the other hand, the expert basket-weaver will have such control over her movements that all the various operations will be performed in an automatic manner; so that the intensity of pull and the manner of twisting that are necessary in these operations will be performed with even intensity. For this reason the stitches will be absolutely regular, and the regularity itself will produce an esthetic effect. (Boas, 1982: 535; see also Stocking, 1996)

DEFINITION 3: CULTURE IS A SET OF CONVENTIONS BY MEANS OF WHICH PEOPLE SHAPE THEIR SOCIAL RELATIONS

Conventional form implies social relation. By means of the concept of convention, the concept of culture makes it possible to distinguish between the objects of the world that are produced without the mediation of social institutions, and the objects of the world that owe their existence to some social institution. This is the difference that the archaeologist perceives between a *geo*fact produced by tectonic pressure, for example, and an *arti*fact, produced by action resulting from social learning: between a stone from a mountain and a piece of pottery.

In order to extract all the analytic potential that this definition holds, we must be mindful of certain nuances and difficulties.

First of all, the very notion of form can operate with different meanings. Kroeber and Kluckhohn, when they referred to this notion in English, used a varied set of words: *form, way, mode, pattern*.

The word 'mode' or 'way' can imply (a) common or shared patterns; (b) sanctions for failure to follow the rules; (c) a manner, a 'how' of behaving; and (d) social 'blueprints' for action. (Kroeber and Kluckhohn, 1963: 98)

One of the variants preferred by Alfred Kroeber should be added to these: *configuration* (see, for example, Kroeber, 1951), a word that he and his colleagues used with a meaning very close to that of the German term *Bildung*, as in the following expression from Max Weber: "Bis in die frühesten politischen *Bildungen* zurück, finden wir ..." [When we go back to the earliest political *configurations*, we find...] (Weber, 1992: 164, emphasis added). This idea of form – a complex way the agents arrange themselves in institutions, and the way the institutions arrange themselves with respect to one another– allowed Weber to talk about ideal institutional types, defined by their properties concerning the configuration of the social relations produced in them.

In this last sense, culture is a set of conventions by means of which people shape their social relations, objectifying them, to some degree, institutionally.

Second, the word "convention," applied to the form of social relations, requires a reflection on the problem of compulsion. Otherwise, all of the problems of reification, insularity, and homogeneity that we tried to clear away earlier come right back. In the social sciences, the tension between compulsion and agency that the concept of convention contains constitutes, without a doubt, a Gordian knot. This knot ties up all the loose ends of the classic dualisms: structure and agency, or structure and structuration (Durkheim, 1982; Giddens, 1984, 1993; Kockelman, 2007).

If the concept of convention is taken to the extreme of understanding it as a *norm* or *rule* of action that is completely shared by a community as a whole, the resulting notion of culture is misleading, because it is homogenizing; but if this concept of convention disappears completely, then describing the majority of human behavior becomes impracticable (Searle, 1997). Anthropologists like Roger Keesing (1982) and social philosophers like Stephen Turner (1994) have alerted us to the inconsistencies derived from the notion of rule in its most compulsive versions. In the analysis of social life, it is as important to highlight the idea that human beings communicate by means of sets of conventions through which they

establish their links, as it is to acknowledge that these conventions are highly variable regarding their degree of compulsion. Thus, conventions can work like traffic rules, like a set of norms dictated by a legislative organism and written down, allowing behavior to be subjected to strict sanctions; but they can also consist of loose orientations for mutual understanding, like turn-taking when people converse (Silverman, 1998), which, by carrying them out, produce a more or less finished community of understanding or, to use a more flexible terminology, a habitat of meaning (Bauman, 1992; Hannerz, 1998: 40).

In this third definition, the expression "a set of conventions" introduces an additional nuance regarding the order or coherence that these conventions maintain among themselves. When I write *set* instead of *system* or *structure*, I am trying to avoid the insular vision of a social whole closed upon itself, in a perfectly structured systematic or systemic order. When he used the word *system*, Clifford Geertz was obliged to add the following explanation: "Systems need not be exhaustively interconnected to the systems. They may be densely interconnected or poorly, but which they are – how rightly integrated they are – is an empirical matter" (Geertz, 1975a: 407). On the other hand, the word *set* is not contradictory with respect to the traditional holism of the concept of culture; and it specifically endows the concept of culture with an entity that we cannot reduce to the most elementary concept of convention: human conventions form complex, irregularly interconnected meshes – cultures. Conventions do not work one by one, but in relation to one another. However, the word *set* really is incompatible with the idea of a completely prefigured whole in social life previous to any analytic purpose. In order to be operative, a holistic concept of culture must deal with an analytically constructed whole, starting out from concrete research problems: a whole that is relative to a universe of problems (Díaz de Rada, 2003).

DEFINITION 4: CULTURE IS A SET OF CONVENTIONS BY MEANS OF WHICH PEOPLE SHAPE THEIR ACTION

Given that social relations must be produced by means of concrete actions and interactions, this fourth definition is just a logical extension of the previous one. Any human action is a process in time. And, although this category of time is not independent of the very way social life is conventionally constructed (Fabian, 1996), we can tentatively accept it as a universal condition of experience: the condition that describes experience as a stream, a continuity in which we still capture discontinuities (Handler, 1984). Any human action is produced in relation to a more static pole, the pole of the *repertories* of conventions at the agent's disposal in his surroundings, and to a more dynamic pole, the pole of the specific implementation of these repertories, in action itself (Cohen, 1982). The metaphor of culture as language is pertinent here. Language, with its dimensions of competence and performance, has often been considered a good analogy for culture (see, for example, Goodenough, 1981). The analogy is, in reality, a synechdochy because, as a special form of human action, the use of language is nothing but a part of the whole of the action (Durbin, 1972).

A frequent error regarding the notion of culture is contained in the idea of causation, as if the repertories of relatively objectified conventions were the causes of human beings' concrete actions. Thus, the conclusion that culture causes or even determines human behavior has been reached (*contra* Keesing, 1982). The idea is, in itself, crude because it does not contemplate the different possible variants of the concept of cause; and, when taken to the extreme of stating that culture is the only cause of behavior, it turns into the kind of reductionism that we call *culturalism*. In logical terms, the problem is quite simple: how can the *form* of a concrete behavior, a property that can be posited about it, *cause* that concrete behavior?

In order to avoid this sterile mess, the fourth definition that I am offering here is explicit regarding the genesis of social action: people are the ones who give shape to their action using culture (that is, the repertory of conventional forms available in their environment). People, not culture, produce action. Endowing culture with the capacity to act is only possible at the cost of personifying culture. It is essential to dismantle this figure of speech in order to eliminate cultural fundamentalism (Rapport, 2003). This kind of fundamentalism can lead us to exonerate a specific person of responsibility for the commission of an act, appealing to the causative force of her culture. That is why it is necessary to repeat: culture does not do anything, it is people who, in every case, do things using culture, intentionally or not.[4] Analogously, language is not what writes this text; I – Ángel – write it, using repertories of communicational and linguistic conventions.

The debate on cultural fundamentalism has become rather lively recently (Rapport, 2003; Stolcke, 1995), but the idea contained in this fourth definition was formulated very precisely as early as 1952, by Alfred Kroeber and Clyde Kluckhohn, when they criticized Talcott Parsons' culturalism: "[…] Culture is obviously not only a way of behavior, but also a product of human beings. Its cause in the modern sense of the word, equivalent to the Aristotelian efficient cause, is the actions of men – human behavior, in contemporary phraseology (Kroeber and Kluckhohn, 1963: 265)." By writing this text referring to old Aristotle, they were using one of Alfred Kroeber's earlier lines of argument: "In the case of a house the 'material cause' would be its wood; the 'formal,' the plan or design of the building; the 'efficient,' the carpenter; the 'final,' the goal of shelter." (Kroeber, 1948: 410).

If there is any causal relationship between culture and behavior, this relationship – noted Kroeber – would be a formal causality, not an efficient causality. Culture as a set of conventions makes it possible to carry out actions with a form, a design, a plan;

but it is a human being who carries out the actions, following this design or plan more or less in practice (Sperber, 1996: 62–63). This approach leads me to acknowledge, with Todd Jones, that the psychological level is fundamental to comprehending causation in the social sciences (Jones, 2007: 373), but with the warning that agents act in institutional surroundings. This means that the units that shape the analytic language of psychology (motives, rewards, perceptions, memories, individuals) are generally interwoven in spaces of social relationship and in sets of conventions (Harris, 1989; Harré, 1992).[5]

Indicating that "people, not culture, produce action" does not mean that the concept of culture is incompatible with the concept of cause. It is compatible, as I have pointed out, if the concept of cause is understood in its *formal* meaning. Regarding its *efficient* meaning, all that is included in this formula is that the concept of culture cannot be wholly identified with a concept of cause that is independent from the action of concrete human beings. Understood as the conventional form *of* action, the concept of culture is subsidiary to the concept of action. Naturally, the conventional form of a social agent's behavior can be an integral part of the constellation of efficient causes that cause or motivate the behavior of *another* person (or the *later* behavior of that very same person). Nevertheless, these forms of action only come into existence through these actions, never independently from them. Besides, these actions happen in social scenarios, so that "The locus of agency may often rest not in the individuals but rather in their ongoing interactions and the institutions that enable these" (Kockelman, 2007: 382)[6].

THE LIMITS OF CONVENTION

We must admit that authors with anthropological training are tempted toward culturalist reductionism, with Kroeber himself being a militant enthusiast 30 years before he wrote these texts, in a classic piece titled "The superorganic" (Kroeber, 1917). But we must also reflect critically on the predominance of the instrumental paradigm in our vision of the world (Sahlins, 1976; Velasco and Díaz de Rada, 1997; Díaz de Rada, 2007a). This paradigm's first move is to lead us to believe that all knowledge, in order to be valid, must be formulated in causal terms; its second move leads us to reduce all forms of causality to efficient causality. We would not be doing much of a favor to the criticism of culturalist reductionism if we used instrumental reductionism as a tool of epistemological criticism.

This same nuance in formulating the relationship of culture to behavior was highlighted by Clifford Geertz, when he indicated that the concept of culture points toward a form of logical-significant integration, at the heart of which the conventions arrange themselves like a semiotic framework whose coherence does not depend, at least not exclusively, on a causal-functional order (Geertz, 1957: 34; Habermas, 1988).

On the other hand, admitting that culture is a set of conventions by means of which people shape their action requires us to determine the conditions in which human behavior can be described using conventions. In this sense, culture is a partial property of human behavior. The concept of culture helps to describe human behavior in its conventional dimension, but only with the assumption that this conventional dimension does not cover the totality of behavior. Otherwise, the concept of culture imposes a new form of fundamentalism: an outlook that reduces everything that human action contains to a description based on conventions. This consideration of culture as a partial dimension is useful for escaping the traps that have, in recent decades, characterized the radical textualization of action and have been examined under the label – which is, at any rate, not very precise – of *postmodern anthropology* (see, for example, Tyler, 1986, 1992). In addition, considering culture to be a partial dimension of behavior can help us to reflect on the formation of human conventions on planes of description and analysis that involve elements such as semiotic processes that are not based on conventions (cf. Kockelman, 2007) or neurophysiological processes (Sperber, 1996), among others.

First of all, it is necessary to acknowledge that the communicative and expressive character of human convention, and its arbitrary consistency, cannot be considered sufficient features for describing action in its totality. There are many other features of human action that are not generated from these same constitutive principles. Human action develops in plexuses of symbols, messages, and rules (all of them conventional forms), but also in plexuses of contingencies, regularities, and efficient causes, which are not conventional. Human behavior is built on a gradual semiosis (Eco, 1979; Kockelman, 2007). Some behavior, such as the chaotic movement of a body dizzy with a glucose overload, are located at the lowest threshold of semiosis. This lower threshhold of semiosis, which presents an evident limit to the cultural interpretation of behavior, shows up when we deal with human processes and products which, like the processes and products of technology, must respond to phenomena in which orders of instrumental causality intervene: just try eating soup with a convex spoon. So it is particularly reasonable to understand culture as a set of conventions that mediate, with more or less functional success, between human action and these orders of instrumental causation (Keesing, 1974). Other behavior, such as a psychoanalyst's psychosomatic interpretation of this dizzy person's behavior, are located at the maximum threshold of semiosis, sometimes due to an erroneous overinterpretation (Eco, 1979, 1994).

This reasoning can also be applied to the strength with which human conventions are codified. Within a purely semiotic interpretation of action, it is one thing to adopt a perspective directed by the concept of the *code*, which tends to underline the most statically structural pole, inscribed in the linguistic system (Saussure, 1985); it is another thing to adopt a perspective directed by the concept of the *interpretant*, which underlines the most dynamically structuring pole and which opens up from the linguistic system as a code of rules to follow toward the general system of action (linguistic and non-linguistic), as a pragmatics of conventions and other semiotic processes being shaped (Peirce, in Hoopes, 1991; Eco, 1979; Kockelman, 2007).[7]

In second place, it is necessary to acknowledge the gradual character of the concept of arbitrariness. Cultural productions establish frameworks which, even though they are conventional, are not therefore entirely modifiable following the free will of each social interpreter. Some of these conventions, such as legal codes, constitute environments of interpretation that frequently operate as empirical limits to agency. Besides, a concrete agent's possibilities of action can become effectively constricted by the complex confluence of different environments of this kind which, taken separately, would not produce this same coercive effect. Based on human conventions, the legal codes that regulate economic transactions are established in complex frameworks of this sort (tax regimes, labor agreements, tariff frameworks, etc.), whose confluence in each specific case of action can regularly provoke movements of capital that do not depend, either solely or fundamentally, on the agents' free acts of interpretation, or even on their immediate knowledge of the situation.

These problems point toward an issue that is of the greatest interest for experts on culture: How can the sets of conventions by means of which the agents give their actions a specific shape be related to plexuses of contingencies and regularities that do not strictly depend on the conventional processing of action (Sperber, 1996: 9)? In a 1974 text, "Theories of culture," Roger Keesing offered some keys for putting together a concept of culture capable of integrating multiple levels of description: adaptive, cognitive, structural, and symbolic description.

DEFINITION 5: CULTURE IS A *DESCRIPTION* OF THE SET OF CONVENTIONS BY MEANS OF WHICH PEOPLE SHAPE THEIR ACTION

The concept of culture refers to a double reality, and in this aspect it is also analogous to the concept of language. On one hand, "culture" refers to the sets of conventions that social agents use in their life world (*lebenswelt*, Schütz and Luckmann, 1989); on the other hand, "culture" refers to the textual description that the ethnographer carries out when he interprets, from the outside, this life world. And also, as happens in the case of linguistic studies, the relationship between both concepts of culture is complex, because no external interpreter is so external that his capacity to interpret is totally limited, and no internal agent is so internal that her reflexivity about her forms of action is completely limited. Every ethnographer must, to some extent, be native (a "marginal native," in the classic formulation by Freilich, (1970)), and every native is, to some extent, an ethnomethodologist (Garfinkel, 1984).

This double reference of the concept of culture in reality includes a relativist warning. The ethnographer, too, as a human being, lives in his own life world, in which the conventions of interpretaton that he selects as an analytic framework make sense. What this double reference encloses, then, is a criticism of the assumption – both naturalist[8] and positivist – that the natives' cultural reality is there, to be merely transcribed by a cognitively and morally neutral ethnographer (Hammersley and Atkinson, 1989). This warning does not mean that ethnographers' interpretative description inevitably talks about inexistent realities, as Dan Sperber (1996) suggests. It is simply a warning against ingenuous realism. The objects that are *out there*, the webs of conventions

and institutions that social agents produce, end up *represented* in ethnography through an analytic interpretation whose validity is always, as with any scientific reflection, an object of debate.

This double reference of the concept of culture contains, in addition, another problem: what should we understand an internal or native perspective of the culture to mean? Without a proper reflective examination, the idea of native perspective can take us right back to a concept of culture that is excessively intellectual, a reduction of culture to a set of ideal and conscious norms that the social agents apply to their own lived world. When we do not reflexively think about what we want to say by native perspective or native point of view, we run the risk of offering an idealistic reduction of culture. However, this idealistic reduction is not necessary at all in the concept of culture that I am working out here.

We anthropologists have traditionally understood this problem through the categories *emic* and *etic*, taken from the linguist Kenneth Pike (1967). However, we have not always really agreed with him. Emic refers to the internal point of view from which a linguistic system is constructed as a practical system, a system of speech (pho*nemics*). Etic refers to the point of view that an external observer (e.g., a linguist) has of this speech system, using his own listening capabilities or certain instruments for capturing and analyzing sound (phon*etics*). Using phonetic analysis, the linguist can notice sound differences that the native speaker does not consider relevant from the classificatory (phonemic) model of sounds he uses to produce his speech.

The concept *etic* contains little ambiguity regarding the propositional character of analytic knowledge.[9] A linguist works basically with her own conscious reflexivity, she works creating ideas, ideas which are usually formulated as verbal propositions. The problems appear when we project this same conscious reflexivity onto the native speakers of the language. Making use of this projection,

Marvin Harris went so far as to maintain that the emic perspective is the ideal perspective that the natives have of their own culture. The debate between Pike and Harris can be found in an excellent edition organized by Thomas N. Headland in 1990: *Emics and Etics. The Insider/Outsider Debate*. In my opinion, Kenneth Pike always maintained an unequivocal position on the issue, which he reiterated clearly in Headland's edition:

> An emic unit, in my view, is a *physical or mental* item or system *treated* by insiders as relevant to their system of behavior and as the same emic unit in spite of etic variability. (Pike, 1990: 28, emphasis added)

The order of reality of the *emic* plane is not, then, exclusively a mental order, and much less an ideal propositional order in Pike's view, but rather a practical order (Bourdieu, 1990). And this is the order of reality of culture, if we hold with all the definitions I have offered here, except for this definition 5. It is not that cultural agents consciously consider a unit of behavior to be relevant, but that they "treat it" as if it were. This is also the meaning that Clifford Geertz gave to the expression "from the native's point of view" (Geertz, 1983). Culture, in its first meaning with reference to the native world, is not necessarily a set of conventions already translated as ideas and verbal propositions about the world, but rather a set of conventions put into practice by living in the world.

This concept of culture does not, on its own, impose any kind of idealist reductionism.

DEFINITION 6: CULTURE IS A SET OF CONVENTIONS BY MEANS OF WHICH PEOPLE SHAPE THE RELATIONS THEY MAINTAIN WITH THE CONVENTIONS IN CONCRETE SITUATIONS

When people act in concrete situations, they bring into play a particular form of convention that we can call metaconventions.

These metaconventions operate as markers, by means of which the agents in this situation shape their relationship with the more basic set of conventions that constitutes the tissue of action and of social relation. These second-order conventions can operate as metarules (see, for example, Mailloux, 2003: 403) that allow the connotation of the way the rules can be understood in context, meta-signs (Hodge and Kress, 1988: 262), or any other conventional formats of communication, meaning, and signification.

A young employee, impeccably dressed facing his boss, blandishing his line of argument with certainty and conviction, is doing something more than using his wardrobe or talking in English. He is also expressing, with these markers, a particular relationship to authority and perhaps to the company. When we examine the concept of culture, it is necessary to reflect upon this new dimension, which indicates the evaluative component of any cultural action. In the words of Jean-Claude Passeron: "A culture is as much a system of relationships to the rules as a system of rules" (Passeron, 1983: 22).

Culture operates here as a tool for producing social difference and this difference often translates into hierarchy through additional metaconventional markers. In each social action, the agents ratify or deny the social positions that they occupy in relation to one another, in a specific field of practice. So they formulate and reformulate, in a generally unequal game, the criteria of social distinction when they make their capitals and competencies count in the sphere of differences in capital (cf. Bourdieu, 2007, Díaz de Rada, 2007b).

Here, also, culture offers its two faces of repertory and practice (competency and performance). In its most static, objectified pole, this set of metaconventions comes before concrete action, it frames and labels it (Bateson, 2000), evoking fields of power over which the agents have no direct influential capacity. Concrete social agents in concrete situations already start out from differential positions as far as power goes, that is, as far as their capacity to produce legitimate social reality that is accepted by others as *reality*. In its most dynamic and situational pole, the agents play at reshaping these positions, with relative success and generally in a very limited way. Because of this, in order to detect the keys to any situational power game, it is necessary to include the frameworks of relation and the markers of relation to the conventions in the analysis, frameworks and markers which tend to be produced somewhere outside of the concrete situation of the game. This is why a microethnography of culture, based solely on the examination of concrete interaction, can hardly reveal the structuring process of social relations in the field of power, or will do so in a deceptive way, if what we are trying to do is to interpret the more stable structural positions that have been objectified for a long time (Bourdieu and Wacquant, 1992; Giddens, 1984; Ogbu, 1981). But, on the other hand, we should consider that these objectified frameworks of conventions that (like written legal laws) limit cultural practice in concrete situations, are also necessarily produced in some concrete situation. Otherwise, we are doomed to a mystification of culture, that is, to the illusion that the forms of culture sanctioned by the existing structures of authority and legitimacy have arisen *ex nihilo*. In any of its dimensions, the comprehension of cultural conventions leads us, rationally, to examine the practices of cultural production, not only to study the ways culture is reproduced (De Certeau, 1979; Willis, 1981a, 1981b).

This metaconventional dimension of culture, because it is made up of conventions that are relatively stabilized biographically or historically, presents itself to us as an order that is more real than the order of the first level conventions (definitions 3 and 4) (Berger and Luckmann, 1966). This has had important consequences for the concept of culture. In fact, this legitimate (or, more correctly, legitimated) culture has often received and often still receives today, the general denomination of *culture*: culture in the singular form, the culture which represents the

artistic, intellectual, school, and political elite, as well as, following another direction, the culture that represents the customs of a people, revealed in the texts of these same elite groups (Burke, 1994; Velasco, 1990). Similarly, in the work of Pierre Bourdieu, culture has been systematically understood to be *cultural capital* accumulated in the objectifications legitimized by political authority or by the property registry, school certificates, or cultural goods (Bourdieu, 1993, 2007; cf. Grignon and Passeron, 1982).

The concept of culture that I present here is not reduced to this culture in the singular form. This concept takes any set of human conventions as its reference. Every human being is an agent of cultural conventions in any of the meanings that I am offering here, with or without school, with or without property to declare.

DEFINITION 7: CULTURE IS A DISCOURSE OF CONVENTIONS CARRIED OUT IN SOCIAL TIME

In his book *The Structure of Social Action*, Talcott Parsons wrote:

> The culture systems are distinguished from both the others [nature systems and action systems] in that they are *both* non-spatial and atemporal. They consist, as Professor Whitehead says, of *eternal* objects, in the strict sense of the term eternal, of objects not of indefinite duration but to which the category of time is not applicable. They are not involved in "process." (Parsons, 1968: Vol. II, p. 763)

In this text, originally published in 1937, Parsons evokes the superorganic definition of "culture" offered by Kroeber in 1917. In successive reissues of his work, Parsons maintained this point of view and thus ignored all the practical, processual, historical, and dynamic development that the concept of culture was undergoing before his eyes (cf. Kroeber and Kluckhohn, 1963 [1952]). With his selective comprehension of the concept, Parsons detemporalized the notion of culture, isolating it from the empirical processes of action.

However, social action takes on a conventional shape when it is put into practice by flesh-and-blood social agents. Today, the concept of culture is unthinkable, at least for anthropologists, outside of time and process, outside of the course of action (Comaroff and Comaroff, 1992; Fabian, 1983, 1996).

> We have thus progressed from a reified through a processual to a discursive understanding of culture. (Baumann, 1999: 139)

Talcott Parsons' vision remains in force to a great extent, however, in the uses given to the concept outside of the sphere of social and cultural anthropology, and it carries with it a powerful argument in favor of reification, with important political consequences. Culture thus becomes a set of conventions (or rather, here, a system or structure), generally ideas, that characterize a society as a whole "eternally." This does away with the work of theoretical reduction that the analyst practices in order to reach this integrated conception of social order (definition 5), and the dissent and, possibly, the conflicts that all human social action entails become clouded. From this perspective, the most consensual profile of the concept of convention is underlined.

Re-situating culture in action means interpreting it as a discourse of conventions in social, biographical, or historical time, in concrete action situations and in concrete contexts of interpretation.[10] We can then detect that, in fact, what is shared in culture is, in any case, a horizon of understanding among social agents, or an assumption that responds to concrete frameworks of legitimacy (Jackman, 1999: 303[11]; Mailloux, 1983). In practice, all social discourse is, to a certain point, dissensual, because all social agents are interpreters of conventions, interpreters equipped to a certain point with the capacity to shape their actions and their social relations. Just like musical discourse, cultural discourse is a series of interpretations that never quite converge. What is

shared is, at its minimum limit, this general metaconvention of coexistence, as well as, in many cases, the general competencies of interpretation, but not necessarily the concrete forms of performance.

> If there is one thing that is true, it is that the truth of the social world is a framework of struggles [...]. The representation of the world is not a datum or its equivalent, a recording, a reflection, but rather the fruit of innumerable actions of *construction* that are always already done and that always need to be redone. (Bourdieu, 2002: 249)

ONTOLOGICAL PARADOX

Because the concept of culture broken down into its parts in these definitions highlights the conventional form of any kind of human action, we may be tempted to conclude that nothing in human reality escapes from culture. This is why the suggestion to unite the words *ontology* and *culture* is not new (Feibleman, 1951; Sperber, 1996; and the recent debate held in Manchester and summarized by Rollason (2008)[12]). However, if it is to have analytic value, the concept of culture requires precision. Culture is a property that we find, in one way or another, in each human action; but, at the same time, it is a very specific property: its conventional form.

The concept of culture incorporates an inevitable ontological paradox: no culture can transcend its own institutional, artificial reality. As human beings, we cannot stop interpreting reality, constructing it, by means of conventional forms, but we can only expand the horizon of our knowledge about the world by acknowledging the limitations that these tissues woven by conventions impose upon us. There are, basically, two kinds of these limitations: the kind of objects susceptible to being posited by culture (the movements of the stars do not incorporate culture, although they do partially incorporate our descriptions of them), and the kind of ways and methods we use to construct our knowledge.

Beyond any anthropocentric illusion, we cannot gain access to all kinds of phenomena through the concept of culture, not even to all kinds of social phenomena, but only to those that are founded on acts of convention. Which does not mean, naturally, that we cannot gain access to these other phenomena by doing without the concept of culture, even only partially or gradually.

In relation to a general concept of ontology, the concept of culture can be useful in several ways, all of them, as has been said, partial.

1   From the native, emic perspective (definition 5), and most especially at the most ideological and conscious pole of human reflexivity, culture tends to give meaning to human experience. This means that it helps human beings, in their concrete life situations, to articulate their experience of conventional order with the experience of everything that transcends that order (Geertz, 1975b, 1975c; Lévi-Strauss, 1985: Chapter I).

2   From the analytic, etic perspective (definition 5), the concept of culture can help us to:

2.1   Better understand the contribution of human conventions (and of the human capacity to create conventions) to forming links, social plots, and sociality, understood as a formative process (Carrithers, 1992; Ramírez Goicoechea, 2005, 2007).

2.2   Better understand that, at least insofar as social life is concerned, there are multiple forms of existence (definitions 3 and 4) and multiple reflexive interpretations of these forms (definition 6). We can also manage to better understand that these multiple forms of existence, and these multiple ontologies (Feibleman, 1951), when they come into communicative contact on the social scene, do so as struggles, if not collisions (definition 7); so they are discourses committed to the power of defining reality and to the fight for legitimacy.

Beyond these limits, it is, of course, possible to take on, along with Dan Sperber, an ontological commitment that, by bringing us closer to the way the knowledge of natural sciences is constructed, will lead us to overcome the interpretational indetermination of the *real* existence of cultural objects

(Sperber, 1996), or, expressed in his own terms, its presence in the "furniture of the world":

> ... if I am right in claiming that the anthropological vocabulary is interpretive, then anthropological accounts are wonderfully free of ontological commitments. Just as the appropriate use of 'goblin' by an anthropologist tells us nothing regarding the existence of goblins, the appropriate use of 'marriage,' 'sacrifice,' or 'chiefship' does not tell us whether marriages, sacrifices or chiefships are part of the furniture of the world. (Sperber, 1996: 18)

At any rate, Sperber's attempt entails several limitations that it would be worth spelling out and that, as we shall see, take us back once again to the ontological paradox that I stated.

In the first place, Sperber chooses for his attempt a variant of the concept of reality that we must not take for granted. Sperber does not seem satisfied with the possibility that *matrimony*, *sacrifice*, or *chieftainship* are part of the "furniture of the world" specifically as conventional facts, institutional facts (the same way, for example, that the English language is part of this "furniture," to the point that I, Ángel, consider the possibility of being translated into it). Defending the idea that the kind of reality of things such as marriage, sacrifice, chieftainship, or the English language is a conventional kind, in the category of institutional acts (Searle, 1997), does not mean that anthropologists' analytic discourse is destined to talk about unreal things or about things that only come into existence in the "native point of view." It does, however, mean that anthropologists, when dealing with these things, should take into account the relatively local nature of their practical uses and also, to a certain extent, the natives' understanding of these uses. The concept of culture that I am defending here has an explicitly external reference and an explicitly realistic meaning. It is, therefore, a concept that allows empirical and analytic falsation of the descriptions, explanations, and interpretations that anthropologists provide. Culture is *observable* as a set of conventions that are produced by agents in the course of their action.

The variant of the concept of reality that Sperber chooses is important, and it is no doubt fruitful for the progress of our knowledge about culture, but does not lack additional limitations. Sperber prefers a causal analysis to an interpretative one:

> One might choose as a topic of study these causal chains made up of mental and public representations, and try to explain how the mental states of human organisms may cause them to modify their environment, in particular by producing signs, and how such modifications of their environment may cause a modification of the mental states of other human organisms. (Sperber, 1996: 26)

At the center of his causal system the representations (or, as in the previous text, the signs) can be found. This leads to the second and third limitations.

We can, of course, focus on these representations, but that does not automatically lead to the naturalist vision of culture that the approach promises.[13] It will not do this unless we decide to overlook the important detail that the representation itself, and most especially the sign, is an act of convention whose essential connection, the connection of the significant with what is signified, is not causal, as Sperber himself demonstrated splendidly in his book *Rethinking Symbolism*, making use of the tradition of semiotic studies (Sperber, 1975).

The third limitation of Sperber's approach affects the very concept of representation as the fundamental element of his ontological commitment. It is not only that the kinds of examples of representation that he himself acknowledges having selected – concepts, beliefs, narratives – refer to a form of appropriation that is characteristically individual and not necessarily social (Sperber, 1996: 75); rather, there is another much more relevant problem. All of these kinds of representation refer to a kind of referential reflexivity that circulates fundamentally in a verbal medium. Outside of these kinds of representation, there are all the practical

conventions that, within language and outside of it, are neither verbal nor referential (Díaz de Rada and Cruces, 1994). *Representation*, in the verbal-referential meaning that Sperber gives to this word, is nothing but a special, limited case of the concept of convention (Lewis, 2002: Chapter IV)[14].

Sperber's proposal presents a fourth limitation that already has a long history as a subject of discussion in social and cultural anthropology. His ontological commitment boils down to a project about an epidemiology of cultural representations that makes it possible to construct a map where causal chains can be detected. Distributional models of culture, segmented in sets of characteristics, are nothing new; on the contrary, they are famous. And that is why it is surprising that they are not even mentioned in the bibliography of *Explaining Culture* (Schwartz, 1978 and, above all, Murdock, 1963, 1967). These models have been very fruitful, as Sperber's proposal can be, when the goal is to offer distributions and, based on the distributions, causal hypotheses (although these hypotheses can also be reached by interpretative paths). But the correlational logic (Murdock, 1937) that is at the root of any epidemiological distributional model does not include the magic wand of causation. A distributional language, taken on its own, continues to be a descriptive language. Even so, this is not the fundamental limitation of these models.

The fundamental limitation is that the features of any culture, for example, the representations, are relevant for human action in contextual configurations, tissues of conventions (definition 3). Thus, the model involved in the word *epidemiology* offers an additional limitation to the one Sperber acknowledges:

> Whereas pathogenic agents such as viruses and bacteria reproduce in the process of transmission and undergo a mutation only occasionally, representations are transformed almost every time they are transmitted, and remain stable only in certain limiting cases. (Sperber, 1996: 25–26)

I agree. But in addition – and this is where a good part of the dilemmas that lead to the ontological paradox I have formulated are to be found – in contrast to a bacteria or a virus, which is individually aggregated to others that are functionally equivalent, a representation (or any other kind of human convention) is what it is precisely because of its relationship to other representations that are not functionally equivalent, in a concrete configuration. When I communicate this text, I use rhetorical, semantic, syntactic, and other conventions along with the person who is reading it. This situation would become even more complicated if the communicational scenario of this text were oral and in person, with the intervention of institutions (i.e., conventional forms) that regulate and constitute this interaction. The relations between all of these conventions (some of which are representations) can hardly be reduced to an elementary aggregation. These conventions are not relevant to anthropological analysis because they go together, but because they adopt certain *forms* together. Of course, we can extract the representations from their configurations, and deal with them individually to distributional or comparative ends, but when we do this we must not ignore the special methodologically provoked mutation that these representations suffer at the very moment when we amputate them from their context (Cruces and Díaz de Rada, 1991; Strathern, 1987, 1992, 2004).

IDENTITY IS NOT *CULTURE*

With the exception of definition 1, the other six definitions of the concept of culture that I have given in this chapter lead to an important corollary: *culture is a property, an attribute of human action, not of social agents. Culture* must be posited about an action, not about a subject. Because of this, *identity* is not a logical equivalent of *culture*. In light of the definitions that I have presented, the expression *being cultured* would, when applied to

people, vaguely indicate having learned a set of competencies for using conventions in concrete social situations. This concept of culture does not territorialize a group of subjects enclosed in the interior of a symbolic frontier, but rather puts them into communication with one antoher or coordinates them in their social environments (Gibson, 1984). These environments would need to have their boundaries marked, in each case, according to concrete theoretical interests (Díaz de Rada, 2003).

We ethnographers and anthropologists have contumaciously denied this concept of culture, by constructing a discourse that is constantly saturated with ethnonyms: the *Nuer*, the *Inuit*, the *Sámit*, the *Maya*; it is not by chance that, for the colonized populations, this imitates the way sociologists characteristically describe subjects in relation to the colonizing nation states: *Spaniards*, the *English*, the *French*, etcetera (Díaz de Rada, 2008). This reifying, essentializing language of social identities took its first serious blow from Fredrik Barth's book *Ethnic Groups and Boundaries* (1998 [1969]), in which the concept of ethnic group was constructed as a relational concept, not a territorial one. There had, of course, been previous blows, such as Clyde Mitchell's, in 1956:

> It is impossible to generalize about the operation of these principles [of human asssociation in "tribes"], without reference to the specific social situation in which the interaction takes place. (Mitchell, 1956: 43)

And there were other later blows such as the one given by Ronald Cohen in 1978: "Ethnicity has no existence apart from interethnic relations" (Cohen, 1978: 389).

But, above all, it is the empirical evidence of a world characterized by an unprecedented territorial mobility that has led social anthropologists to a growing realization that, if we need to stay faithful to an identity (and generally territorial) concept of culture, then we had better theorize "beyond culture" (Gupta and Ferguson, 1992).

Starting with definition 2, I have offered a set of definitions of the concept of culture that, remaining faithful to the theoretically productive aspects of the anthropological tradition, is completely independent of the concepts of identity and territoriality. I have done it this way because I feel that the onto-logical status of the concept of culture must in no way be confused with the ontological status of the notion of identity, if we are to move in the essential tension of the *anthro-pos* and the *ethnos*. There is no use clinging stubbornly to the use of the word *identity* using attributes such as *multiple*, *fragmen-tary*, and *fluid* because, as Brubaker and Cooper have indicated:

> It is not clear why what is routinely characterized as multiple, fragmented, and fluid should be con-ceptualized as 'identity' at all. (Brubaker and Cooper, 2000: 6)

A concept of culture such as the one I have set forth in these pages, focused on the conventional aspects of human action, on human action as social discourse, is the most adequate vehicle for acquiring ontological commitments "beyond identity" (Brubaker and Cooper, 2000); although these com-mitments, being paradoxical, may not fully satisfy the desire to achieve a totalizing knowledge.

NOTES

1 This text was translated into English by Nancy Konvalinka. I would like to thank Eugenia Ramírez-Goicoechea, Fernando Monge, and Nancy Konvalinka for their useful comments. The main argument of this chapter is extended in Díaz de Rada (2010), though I have used here a more precise language.

2 The concept of culture that I will discuss here is, on the other hand, compatible with the behavior of other species, at least regarding definitions 2, 3, and 4 (Sapolsky, 2006).

3 This definition only points toward a category of practices that, in the words of Todd Jones, is ambig-uous and polysemic, and that he himself, following Lakoff (1987), interprets as a 'radial structure, with a prototypical core meaning': 'What is done' in concrete situations (Jones, 2007: 389 and *passim*).

4 This idea, however, does not resolve the problem of judgment that the legal doctrine of

imputability involves. Culture does not exonerate anyone of responsibility for the commission of their actions, but these actions will need to be interpreted, when necessary, in a context or configuration of events and conventions.

5 This same warning always appears whenever the *autonomous speaker* is mentioned in the area of linguistic conventions (Jackman, 1999; cf. Lewis, 2002).

6 Paul Kockelman (2007) has broken down the components of the concept of agency analytically, taking Peirce's semiotic theory as his reference.

7 For an analogous reflection related to the notions of sign and symbol, see Sperber (1975).

8 Regarding this concept of naturalism, see Note 13.

9 For a detailed reflection on the ambiguities of the etic/emic pair of concepts, both in Kenneth Pike and in Marvin Harris, see Aurora González Echevarría, (2009).

10 The concept of *discourse* can incorporate the risk of an excessive textualization or verbal compre-hension of culture. This is not the meaning Baumann uses in the preceding quote, nor is it the meaning that I am using here. 'Discourse' should be under-stood a *course over time*, as a *course* of action, whether occurring on the verbal level or on any other type of enactive level. By using the word 'discourse,' we simply seek to highlight that culture is produced in a *process* of social action.

11 Any adequate examination of a cultural kind, starting with linguistics, must be sensitive to the metaconventional dimension involved in human institutions (definition 6): it is not practice alone that shapes convention, but the political relationship that the agents maintain with the convention, even after they acknowledge its arbitrary nature (cf. Jackman, 1999: 308).

12 When preparing this text, I only had the sum-mary provided by William Rollason. This summary, which includes sketches of the contributions by Michael Carrithers, Matei Candea, Karen Sykes, and Martin Holbraad, has been a source of inspiration to me.

13 In this text, I am using two different concepts of naturalism: the one that Hammersley and Atkinson (1989) use, mentioned in definition 5, and the one Sperber uses here. The first one involves an episte-mological attitude that tends to take the natives' (emic) descriptions of reality as valid in ethnographic texts. The second concept involves an epistemologi-cal attitude that seeks to incorporate the analytic language of the natural sciences into the analytic language of the cultural sciences.

14 Paul Kockelman also shows, analytically, that the verbal-propositional variant is a specific form of the set of semiotic processes and, within this set, of the processes of forming conventions. Regarding this, see his distinction between the

concepts 'residential agency' and 'propositional agency' (Kockelman, 2007).

REFERENCES

Abu-Lughod, Lila (1991) 'Writing against Culture', in Richard G. Fox (ed.) *Recapturing Anthropology: Working in The Present.* Santa Fe: School of American Research Press. pp. 137–162.

Barth, Fredrik (1998 [1969]) *Ethnic Groups and Boundaries. The Social Organization of Culture Difference.* Long Grove: Waveland Press.

Bateson, Gregory (2000 [1971]) *Steps to An Ecology of Mind: Collected Essays in Anthropology, Psychiatry, Evolution, and Epistemology.* Chicago: University of Chicago Press.

Bauman, Zygmunt (1992) *Intimations of Postmodernity.* London: Routledge.

Baumann, Gerd (1999) *The Multicultural Riddle: Rethinking National, Ethnic and Religious Identities.* London: Routledge.

Berger, Peter L. and Thomas Luckmann (1966) *The Social Construction of Reality: A Treatise in The Sociology of Knowledge.* New York: Doubleday.

Boas, Franz (1982 [1916]) 'Representative Art of Primitive People', in *Race, Language and Culture.* Chicago: The University of Chicago Press. pp. 535–540.

Bourdieu, Pierre (1988 [1986]) 'Espacio social y poder simbólico', in *Cosas Dichas.* Barcelona: Gedisa. pp. 127–142.

Bourdieu, Pierre (1990 [1980]) *The Logic of Practice.* Stanford: Stanford University Press.

Bourdieu, Pierre (1993) *The Field of Cultural Production. Essays on Art and Literature.* Cambridge: Polity Press.

Bourdieu, Pierre (2002) *Le bal des célibataires. Crise de la société paysanne en Béarn.* Paris: Seuil.

Bourdieu, Pierre (2007 [1979]) *Distinction: A Social Critique of The Judgement of Taste.* Harvard: Harvard University Press.

Bourdieu, Pierre and Loïc, J. D. Wacquant (1992) 'La pratique de l'anthropologie réflexive', in *Réponses. Pour une anthropologie réflexive.* París: Seuil. pp. 187–231.

Brightman, Robert (1995) 'Forget Culture: Replacement, Transcendence, Relexification', *Cultural Anthropology*, 10(4): 509–546.

Brubaker, Roger and Frederick Cooper (2000) 'Beyond "Identity"', *Theory and Society*, 29: 1–47.

Burke, Peter (1994) *Popular Culture in Early Modern Europe.* Hampshire: Ashgate Publishing.

Caisson, Max (1991) 'Lumière de Herder', *Terrain*, 17: 17–28.

Carrithers, Michael (1992) *Why Humans Have Cultures: Explaining Anthropology and Social Diversity.* Oxford: Oxford University Press.

Cohen, Anthony P. (1982) 'A Sense of Time, a Sense of Place: The Meaning of Close Social Association in Whalsay, Shetland', in *Belonging. Identity and Social Organization in British Rural Cultures.* Manchester: Manchester University Press. pp. 21–49.

Cohen, Ronald (1978) 'Ethnicity: Problem and Focus in Anthropology', *Annual Review of Anthropology*, 7: 379–403.

Comaroff, John and Jean Comaroff (1992) *Ethnography and Historical Imagination.* Oxford: Westview.

Cruces, Francisco and Ángel Díaz de Rada (1991) 'Traducción y derivación. Una reflexión sobre el lenguaje conceptual de la antropología', *Antropología. Revista de pensamiento antropológico y estudios etnográficos*, 1: 85–106.

Culler, Jonathan (1981) 'Convention and Meaning: Derrida and Austin', *New Literary History*, 13(1): 15–30.

De Certeau, Michel (1979) *L'Invention du quotidien, I: Arts de faire.* Paris: Union Générale d'éditions.

Díaz de Rada, Ángel (2003) 'Las formas del holismo. La construcción teórica de la totalidad en etnografía', *Revista de dialectología y tradiciones populares*, LVIII(1): 237–262.

Díaz de Rada, Ángel (2007a) 'School Bureaucracy, Ethnography and Culture: Conceptual Obstacles to Doing Ethnography in Schools', *Social Anthropology*, 15(2): 205–222.

Díaz de Rada, Ángel (2007b) 'Valer y valor. Una exhumación de la teoría el valor para reflexionar sobre la desigualdad y la diferencia en relación con la escuela', *Revista de antropología social*, 16(7): 117–158.

Díaz de Rada, Ángel (2008) '¿Dónde está la frontera? Prejuicios de campo y problemas de escala en la estructuración étnica en Sápmi', *Revista de Dialectología y tradiciones populares*. LXIII(1): 187–235.

Díaz de Rada, Ángel (2010) *Cultura, antropologia y otras tonterías.* Madrid: Trotta.

Díaz de Rada, Ángel and Francisco Cruces (1994) '"The Mysteries of Incarnation". Some Problems to Do with The Analytic Language of Practice', in Kirsten Hastrup and Peter Hervik (eds) *Social Experience and Anthropological Knowledge.* London: Routledge. pp. 101–120.

Durbin, Mridula A. (1972) 'Linguistic Models in Anthropology', *Annual Review of Anthropology*, 1: 383–410.

Durkheim, Émile (1982 [1895]) *The Rules of Sociological Method and Selected Texts on Sociology and Its Method.* New York: The Free Press.

Eco, Umberto (1979 [1976]) *Theory of Semiotics.* Bloomington: Indiana University Press.

Eco, Umberto (1994 [1990]) *The Limits of Interpretation.* Bloomington: Indiana University Press.

Fabian, Johannes (1983) *Time and The Other.* New York: Columbia University Press.

Fabian, Johannes (1996 [1991]) *Time and The Work of Anthropology. Critical Essays 1971–1991.* Amsterdam: Harwood.

Fabian, Johannes (2001) 'Culture with An Attitude', in *Anthropology with An Attitude. Critical Essays.* Stanford: Stanford University Press. pp. 87–100.

Feibleman, James K. (1951) 'Culture as Applied Ontology', *The Philosophical Quarterly*, 1(5): 416–422.

Freilich, Morris (ed.) (1970) *Marginal Natives: Anthropologists at Work.* New York: Harper & Row.

Garfinkel, Harold (1984 [1967]) *Studies in Ethnomethodology.* Cambridge: Polity Press.

Geertz, Clifford (1957) 'Ritual and Social Change: A Javanese Example', *American Anthropologist*, 59(1): 32–54.

Geertz, Clifford (1975a) 'Person, Time, and Conduct in Bali', in *The Interpretation of Cultures.* London: Hutchinson. pp. 360–409.

Geertz, Clifford (1975b) 'Religion as A Cultural System', in *The Interpretation of Cultures.* London: Hutchinson. pp. 87–125.

Geertz, Clifford (1975c) 'Ideology as A Cultural System', in *The Interpretation of Cultures.* London: Hutchinson. pp. 193–233.

Geertz, Clifford (1983) '"From The Native's Point of View": On the nature of anthropological understanding', in *Local Knowledge. Further Essays in Interpretive Anthropology.* New York: Basic Books. pp. 55–69.

Gibson, Margaret A. (1984) 'Approaches to multicultural education in the United States. Some concepts and assumptions', *Anthropology and Education Quarterly*, 15(1): 94–120.

Giddens, Anthony (1984) *The Constitution of Society. Outline of the Theory of Structuration.* Cambridge: Polity Press.

Giddens, Anthony (1993 [1976]) *New Rules of Sociological Method.* Stanford: Stanford University Press.

González Echevarría, Aurora (2009) *La dcotomía Emic/Etic. Historia de una confusión.* Barcelona: Anthropos.

Goodenough, Ward H. (1981) *Culture, Language and Society.* Menlo Park: Benjamin/Cumming.

Grignon, Jean-Claude and Jean-Claude Passeron (1982) *Sociologie de la culture et sociologie des cultures populaires.* Paris: Gides.

Gupta, Akhil and James Ferguson (1992) 'Beyond "Culture": Space, Identity, and The Politics of Difference', *Cultural Anthropology*, 7(1): 6–23.

Habermas, Jürgen (1988) 'Discusión con Niklas Luhmann (1971): ¿Teoría sistémica de la sociedad o teoría crítica de la sociedad?', in *La Lógica de las Ciencias Sociales.* Madrid: Tecnos. pp. 309–419.

Hammersley, Martyn and Paul Atkinson (1989 [1983]) *Ethnography: Principles in Practice.* London: Routledge.

Handler, Richard (1984) 'On Sociocultural Discontinuity: Nationalism and Cultural Objectification in Quebec', *Current Anthropology*, 25(1): 55–69.

Hann, Chris (2001) 'From *Volkgeist* to Radical Humanism: Culture and Value in Economic Anthropology', *Reviews in Anthropology*, 30: 1–30.

Hannerz, Ulf (1998) *Conexiones transnacionales. cultura, gente, lugares.* Valencia: Frónesis.

Harré, Rom (1992) 'The Discursive Creation of Human Psychology', *Symbolic Interaction*, 15(4): 515–527.

Harris, Grace G. (1989) 'Concepts of Individual, Self, and Person in Description and Analysis', *American Anthropologist*, 91: 599–612.

Headland, Thomas N., Kenneth L. Pike and Marvin Harris (eds) (1990) *Emics and Etics. The Insider/Outsider Debate.* London: Sage.

Hodge, Robert and Gunther Kress (1988) *Social Semiotics.* Cambridge: Polity Press.

Hoopes, James (ed.) (1991 [1867–1908]) *Peirce on Signs. Writings on Semiotic by Charles S. Peirce.* Chapel Hill: North Carolina Press.

Jackman, Henry (1999) 'Convention and Language', *Synthese*, 117: 295–312.

Jones, Todd (2007) 'What's Done Here – Explaining Behavior in Terms of Customs and Norms', *The Southern Journal of Philosophy*, XLV: 363–393.

Keesing, Roger M. (1974) 'Theories of Culture', *Annual Review of Anthropology*, 3: 73–97.

Keesing, Roger M. (1982) 'Cultural Rules. Methodological Doubts and Epistemological Paradoxes', *Canberra Anthropology*, 5(1): 37–46.

Kockelman, Paul (2007) 'Agency. The Relation between Meaning, Power, and knowledge', *Current Anthropology*, 48(3): 375–401.

Kroeber, Alfred L. (1917) 'The Superorganic', *American Anthropologist*, 19: 163–213.

Kroeber, Alfred L. (1948) 'White's View of Culture', *American Anthropologist*, 50(3): 405–415.

Kroeber, Alfred L. (1951) 'Configurations, Causes, and St. Augustine', *American Anthropologist*, 53(2): 279–284.

Kroeber, Alfred, L. and Clyde Kluckhohn (1963 [1952]) *Culture: A Critical Review of Concepts and Definitions.* Cambridge: Peabody Museum of Anthropology.

Kuper, Adam (2000 [1999]) *Culture. The Anthropologists' Account.* Harvard: Harvard University Press.

Lakoff, George (1987) *Women, Fire, and Dangerous Things. What Categories Reveal about the Mind.* Chicago: University of Chicago Press.

Lévi-Strauss, Claude (1985 [1949]) *Las estructuras elementales del parentesco.* Barcelona: Planeta-Agostini. 2 Vols.

Lewis, David (2002 [1969]) *Convention. A Philosophical Study.* Oxford: Blackwell.

Lowie, Robert H. (2008 [1917]) *Culture and Ethnology.* Whitefish, MT: Kessinger Publishing.

Mailloux, Steven (1982) *Interpretive Conventions: The Reader in The Study of American Fiction.* New York: Cornell University Press.

Mailloux, Steven (2003) 'Convention and context', *New Literary History*, 14(2): 399–407.

Markus, George (1993) 'Culture: The Making and The Make-Up of A Concept (An Essay in Historical Semantics)', *Dialectical Anthropology*, 18: 3–29.

Mitchell, J. Clyde (1956) *The Kalela Dance. Aspects of Social Relationships among Urban Africans in Northern Rhodesia.* Manchester: Manchester University Press – The Rhodes-Livingstone Papers (XXVII).

Murdock, George P. (1937) *Statistical Correlations in The Science of Society.* New Haven: Yale University Press.

Murdock, George P. (1963) *Outline of World Cultures.* New Haven: Human Relations Area Files.

Murdock, George P. (1967) *Ethnographic Atlas.* Pittsburgh: University of Pittsburgh Press.

Ogbu, John U. (1981) 'School ethnography: A Multilevel Approach', *Anthropology and Education Quarterly*, XII(1): 3–29.

Parsons, Talcott (1968 [1937]) *The Structure of Social Action.* New York: The Free Press. 2 Vols.

Passeron, Jean-Claude (1983) 'La inflación de los títulos escolares en el mercado de trabajo y el mercado de los bienes simbólicos', *Educación y Sociedad*, 1: 5–27.

Pike, Kenneth L. (1967 [1954]) *Language in Relation to a Unified Theory of The Structure of Human Behavior.* The Hague: Mouton.

Pike, Kenneth L. (1990) 'On The Emics and The Etics of Pike and Harris', in Thomas N. Headland, Kenneth L. Pike and Marvin Harris (eds) *Emics and Etics. The Insider/Outsider Debate.* London: Sage. pp. 28–47.

Putnam, Hilary (1991) 'Convention: A Theme in Philosophy', *New Literary History*, 13(1): 1–14, 253.

Ramírez Goicoechea, Eugenia (2005) *Evolución, cultura y complejidad. La humanidad que se hace a sí misma.* Madrid: Editorial Universitaria Ramón Areces.

Ramírez Goicoechea, Eugenia (2007) *Etnicidad, identidad y migraciones. Teorías, conceptos y experiencias.* Madrid: Editorial Universitaria Ramón Areces.

Rapport, Nigel (2003) '"Culture is No Excuse." Critiquing Multicultural Essentialism and Identifying The Anthropological Concrete', *Social Anthropology*, 11(3): 373–384.

Rapport, Nigel and Joanna Overing (2000) 'Culture', in *Social and Cultural Anthropology. The Key Concepts.* London: Routledge. pp. 109–120.

Rollason, William (2008) 'Ontology – Just Another Word for Culture?', *Anthropology Today*, 24(3): 28–31.

Sahlins, Marshall (1976) *Culture and Practical Reason.* Chicago: Chicago University Press.

Sapolsky, Robert M. (2006) 'Social Cultures among Nonhuman Primates', *Current Anthropology*, 47(4): 641–656.

Saussure, Ferdinand de (1985 [1916]) *Curso de lingüística general.* Barcelona: Planeta-Agostini.

Schwartz, Theodore (1978) 'Where is The Culture? Personality As The Distributive Locus of Culture', in George D. Spindler (ed.), *The Making of Psychological Anthropology.* Berkeley: University of California Press. pp. 419–441.

Schütz, Alfred and Thomas Luckmann (1989 [1979]) *The Structures of The Life-World*, Evanston: Northwestern University Press. 2 Vols.

Searle, John R. (1997 [1995]) *The Construction of Social Reality.* New York: The Free Press.

Silverman, David (1998) *Harvey Sacks. Social Theory and Conversational Analysis.* Oxford: Oxford University Press.

Sperber, Dan (1975) *Rethinking Symbolism.* Cambridge: Cambridge University Press.

Sperber, Dan (1996) *Explaining Culture. A Naturalistic Approach.* Oxford: Blackwell.

Stocking, George (1992) *The Ethnographer's Magic and Other Essays in the History of Anthropology.* Madison: The University of Wisconsin Press.

Stocking, George (1996) *Volksgeist as Method and Ethic. Essays on Boasian Ethnography and The German Anthropological Tradition.* Madison: The University of Wisconsin Press.

Stolcke, Verena (1995) 'Talking Culture. New Boundaries, New Rhetorics of Exclusion in Europe', *Current Anthropology*, 36(1): 1–24.

Strathern, Marilyn (1987) 'Out of Context. The Persuasive Fictions of Anthropology', *Current Anthropology*, 28(3): 251–281.

Strathern, Marilyn (1992) 'Parts and Wholes: Refiguring Relationships in A Post-Plural World', in Adam Kuper (ed.) *Conceptualizing Society*. London: Routledge. pp. 75–104.

Strathern, Marilyn (2004) *Partial Connections*. Oxford: Altamira Press.

Turner, Stephen (1994) *The Social Theory of Practices. Tradition, Tacit Knowledge and Presuppositions*. Oxford: Polity Press.

Tyler, Stephen A. (1986) 'Post-Modern Anthropology', in Phyllis P. Chock and June R. Wyman (eds) *Discourse and Social Life of Meaning*. Washington: Smithsonian. pp. 1–7.

Tyler, Stephen A. (1992) 'On Being Out of Words', in George E. Marcus (ed.) *Rereading Cultural Anthropology*. Durham: Duke University Press. pp. 23–50.

Tylor, Edward B. (1920 [1871]) *Primitive Culture*. Vol. 1. New York: J.P. Putnam's Sons.

Velasco, Honorio (1990) 'El folklore y sus paradojas', *revista española de investigaciones sociológicas*, 49: 123–144.

Velasco, Honorio and Ángel Díaz de Rada (1997) *La lógica de la investigación etnográfica*. Madrid: Trotta.

Weber, Max (1992 [1917]) 'Politik als Beruf', in *Max Weber Gesamtausgabe*, Band 17 edited by Wolfgang J. Mommsen, Wolfgang Schluchter and Birgitt Morgenbrod. Tübingen: J.C.B. Mohr. 17: 156–252.

Weiner, Annette B. (1995) 'Culture and Our Discontents', *American Anthropologist*, 97(1): 14–21.

Williams, Raymond (1976) *Keywords. A Vocabulary of Culture and Society*. New York: Oxford University Press.

Willis, Paul (1981a [1977]) *Learning to Labor: How Working Class Kids Get Working Class Jobs*. New York: Columbia University Press.

Willis, Paul (1981b) 'Cultural Production Is Different from Cultural Reproduction Is Different from Social Reproduction Is Different from Reproduction', *Interchange*, 12(2–3): 48–67.

12

Power and Social Class in the Twenty-first Century

Daniel Little

One might say that power and class are the two most important determinants of everyday life in the twenty-first century. Class relations – determined by the property system and the basic economic institutions within which we live – determine our opportunities, health, quality of life, and sometimes our basic freedoms. Power relations influence our careers, our speech, and very basic aspects of our behavior and choice in the workplace and the public square. It is reasonable to think that the systems of power and class within which we live constitute the basic framework within which our lives and purposes unfold.

Further, the two schemata of post-modern life are interrelated. The property system within which we live is a bit like a medieval cathedral – it cannot stand without the buttresses of power that retain its structure in the face of countervailing pressures. And the relations of power that exist in a society often derive much of their force from the structure of property that exists. Property holders need, want, and gain power; holders of power gain property.

But post-modern life is not so simple. There are multiple cross-cutting identities and positions that influence personal outcomes, not simply class or power. Race, ethnic group, and gender – these are social systems that have quite a bit in common with class, and they have relationships to power as well. Feminist scholars have sought to understand these linkages through the theory of intersectionality (Andersen and Collins, 1998); the fundamental insight is that there is no single "most fundamental" identity or position in society that essentially defines us. Like class; race, ethnicity, and gender are also social systems that contribute to determining the individual's outcome, behavior, and identity. One's status within the system of race or gender immediately influences one's opportunities, status, prestige, and power (Moya and Hames-Garcia, 2000; Wong, 1999). And one's position within these ascriptive systems also has implications for the class system; thus black workers faced a different working environment than white workers in the Detroit auto industry of the 1950s and 1960s (Sugrue, 1996), and female workers still often earn less than male counterparts in many businesses.

The theory of social class is a largely nineteenth-century theory (Babeuf et al.,

1977; Blanqui, 1885; Marx, 1974 [1852], 1977 [1867]; Marx and Engels, 1935), and its relevance in the twenty-first century has been questioned. The theory of power had even earlier origins in European thought (Hobbes, 1996 [1651]; Machiavelli, 1996 [1513]) – but there is no question that this construct is deeply relevant to the social world of the twenty-first century. What does social class have to do with power? The two concepts represent theories about how a modern society works, and there are some fundamental relationships between them. But at bottom they are separate social factors that allow for independent forms of social causation. The first is fundamentally concerned with the economic structure of a society, the systems through which wealth is created and distributed, and the positions that individuals occupy within these systems; while the second is concerned with the relations of subordination, domination, and control that exist within a society.

It is noteworthy that both class and power cross the traditional dichotomies of structure and agency. The class system sets some of the structural parameters within which individuals act, but it also creates some of the motivations and features of consciousness that constitute the agency of class actors. The forms of power present in a given society define some of the features of agency on the basis of which individuals and groups pursue their goals; but it is also fair to say that the institutions and social relations that define social power are also a part of the structured environment of action that is present in the social world. So both power and class are simultaneously features of structure and agency within a complex society; and the configurations created by class and power are causally inter-related without being isomorphic. Individuals wield power; but they only do so on the basis of resources and advantages that are conferred upon them by existing social relations. And these relations encompass the class relations of a society.

All social concepts need to be framed in such a way that it is feasible to provide them with *microfoundations* – detailed accounts of how these social properties are embodied in the actions, beliefs, and motives of socially situated individuals (Little, 2006, 1998). And this is true for the concepts of power and class. We need to know the mechanisms through which certain individuals wield power and influence, and we need to know the social processes through which individuals are assigned to classes and are led through a process of development corresponding to that class.

This article will examine some of the basic conceptual issues that serve to establish the social geometry of power and class. It will provide some basic ideas about the social mechanisms that underlie each of them. And it will attempt to assess the extent to which these venerable components of classical social theory are relevant to understanding social life and change in the twenty-first century.

POWER

Let us begin with power. The concept of "power" is a difficult one to place within our ontology of the social world. We have a pretty good idea of what we mean by institutions and structures – the relatively fixed social rules and constraints within which people engage in social activity; and we understand the ideas of agency and social action. But where does power come into this ontology? Is it a feature of institutions and structures? Does it attach to individuals and groups? Is it a feature of direct social relationships, or is it a structural feature conferring specific "powers" upon individuals? Does it depend on material aspects of society or is it equally a feature of mentality and subjectivity? There are aspects of all of these dimensions in the very ordinary statements we make about power, so it is difficult to offer a simple definition or analysis of the concept. And almost uniquely among social constructs, the concept of power attaches to both poles of structure and agency. (A good recent collection of sources on the social-science concept of power can be found in Haugaard (2002).)

We might define power in these terms: "access to social and material resources that permit an individual or group to control or influence social outcomes, including the behavior of other individuals and groups, the distribution of things, and the configuration of social institutions." And we can give a simple schematic description of the chief mechanisms and tactics through which control and influence are exercised in contemporary society: coercion, threat, manipulation of the agenda, manipulation of information and thought, and positional advantage. These are almost all relational characteristics – they have to do with the relationships of influence that exist among individuals and groups.

The exercise of power implies a conflict of wills; those exercising power are intending to secure actions and outcomes by others against their will, preferences, or interests. Power is needed to get 1.5 million people to leave their homes in Beijing to make way for Olympics developments. Power is needed to prevent striking miners from shutting down La Paz. Power is needed to protect the glittering shop windows of Johannesburg from disaffected young people. Power is exercised by states – through the military and police, through agencies and bureaucracies, through legislation; it is exercised by corporations and other large private organizations; and it is exercised by social movements and other groups within society.

It is evident that power is not a one-dimensional social characteristic like education level or financial panic. Instead, it is a compound social characteristic, a heterogeneous bundle of social facts that individuals and groups can deploy in order to compel the actions or inactions of other individuals or groups against their will or contrary to their interests, needs, and desires. One important cluster of items in this bundle has to do with the ability to impose coercion – truncheons, prisons, and punishment. Other elements derive from the ability of some agents within

society to set the agenda for future action – if we are forced to consider A or B, we don't get a chance to argue for C. And a third set of features has to do with the structures of decision making within social and political organizations – the fact that some people are given the authority to make the final decision in a way that affects other people. Power can be exercised through the use of violence; the threat of harm; promise of gain (bribes); shaping of beliefs and preferences; setting the rules and agendas of important social institutions; and the positional advantage of being in the chairman's seat. Power is sometimes wielded through simple force; but sometimes it is exercised through finesse, almost invisibly.

The exercise of power almost always has to do with *strategic* efforts by some people to gain advantage over other people, making the best use possible of the resources and options available to them. So power is "relational" – it always involves some degree of competitive struggle among rational agents vying for advantage. Powerful agencies in global society pursue their interests using the many forms of power available to them. Corporations, states, and powerful individuals exercise various kinds of power over ordinary people and groups. Coercion, deception, concealment, and intimidation rest in the portfolio of the powerful. But there are also power resources available to ordinary people against the misuse of power through mass mobilization, collective action, and other forms of popular politics.

Michel Foucault, along with Gramsci, is probably the most influential post-Marxist theorist of power in Europe or North America. Foucault identifies power as the fundamental concept for social theory in the twentieth century. And, unlike Hobbes or Machiavelli, his conception of power revolves around thought and knowledge as much as it does around coercion and violence. Pursuing such diverse topics as prisons and insane asylums, sexuality, and the university, Foucault attempts to work out the social relations and conceptual lineaments through which society exercises control over individuals; the forms of "discipline and punishment" through which the social order is enforced (Foucault, 1973, 1978, 1979). Here is one important formulation of his conception of power: "If we speak of the structures or the mechanisms of power, it is only insofar as we suppose that certain persons exercise power over others" (Foucault 1983: 217). This description highlights the point made above, that power is both structure and agency.

It is crucial to consider the specific micro-foundations that underlie the exercise of different forms of power – the social mechanisms through which some people, groups, and organizations are enabled to constrain or direct the behavior of others and the flow of resources in society. Hobbes and Machiavelli thought of this question in terms of coercion: the ability of individuals or states to threaten harm or death in order to compel behavior. But plainly the institutions that convey power to individuals and groups are more complex than this formula would allow. We need sociology of the mechanisms of power and influence as much as we need an inventory of the instruments of coercion.

Political and social power involves the exercise of social resources to compel various kinds of unwilling behavior by others. What creates power in society? What are the sorts of social and structural factors that permit individuals to exercise power? Consider a few examples that are relevant to the creation and exercise of power. For example, a privileged position within the property system – the possession of significant income and wealth – confers a resource advantage on people in that position. They can use their wealth to solicit powerful allies; they can purchase media outlets; they can influence politicians – all with an eye to achieving their goals in spite of the contrary wishes or interests of others. Likewise, a privileged position in the communications system – that of a television news producer or newspaper publisher, for example – can be used to alter the way in which stories are presented in so as to change the way the public thinks about the

issues, and these changes in thought can lead to changes in behavior. These resources allow some people to set the "cognitive" agenda and the interpretive frame through which other people view the world. And an elected official can exercise power by setting the agenda for others by including or excluding various options from consideration. Position determines one's capacity for power.

The mechanisms of power considered to this point are all ones that are utilized by the privileged groups. But of course there are mechanisms of power through which under-class groups can seek to influence social outcomes. Gramsci emphasizes the effectiveness of popular culture as a mechanism for building "anti-hegemonic" attitudes and loyalties thereby providing a basis for future mobilization (Gramsci, 1957, 1971). Group mobilization in class-based organizations – tenants' unions, labor and trade unions, environmental activists, and feminists – have an ability to coalesce a shared sense of group identity, a shared willingness to consider collective action, and an ability to apply pressure to the privileged and hegemonic forces. Mass mobilization is a substantial tool of power – consider general strikes in France and Italy, for example.

Power as influence

So far we have looked at power primarily as the socially embodied ability of some people to compel the behavior of others. But this is not the whole of what we would want to include within the scope of the uses of power. Other important aspects of power are more impersonal, having to do with influencing outcomes rather than controlling behavior. Powerful agents have the ability of some people to set the agenda; to influence the rules of the game (whatever game one is involved in, including the state); to influence the flow of resources; and to make decisions that will have important consequences for other people.

Numerous examples of "power as influence" can be given; and they all illustrate much of what C. Wright Mills hoped to capture in his theory of the "power elite" – a relatively compact group of people who are in a position to shape social outcomes to their liking by influencing the agenda, rules, or decisions (Domhoff, 1970; Mills, 1956). And it goes with this social empowerment of small groups, that the possibilities of self-serving and self-interest arise. When individuals are in a position to determine the way social outcomes will occur, we have to consider the likelihood that they will have favored outcomes that serve their own interests best. So power in this circumstance has a lot to do with distributive outcomes – who wins and who loses. And it had a lot to do with setting the rules of the game in ways that favor some and disfavor others.

These aspects of power are tremendously important in a complex society. People in positions to influence important decisions – private, corporate, or governmental – have a greatly amplified ability to shape outcomes to their own will. And this in turn permits elites to shape the social environment in ways that best serve their private interests. Stephen Lukes helped to develop this more articulated conception of the "three faces of power" in his important book, *Power: A Radical View* (Lukes, 1974). Lukes notes that power pertains to decision-making, agenda-setting, and preference-shaping, and that each of these activities involves substantially different sets of positional advantages.

In short, we can do a fairly good job of identifying some of the mechanisms, resources, and positions through which various individuals and groups are able to exercise power over others in a modern society. The sociology of power can be written. Let us now turn to a more detailed case: the exercise of power by an authoritarian regime.

Power: social movements

So what about popular power? What means exist for groups of disenfranchised people to exert power in defense of their interests,

against the machinations of elites? Social movements and community-based organizations represent potent resources for non-elites. And the sociology of popular politics and mobilization bears out this point. Social movements emerge from "under-class" groups who lack meaningful access to other official and institutionalized means of power. They are among the "weapons of the weak" (Scott, 1985, 1990), and their effectiveness usually turns on the ability of a sub-population to mobilize in collective action with determination and courage. Examples include the American Civil Rights movement, the use of strikes and boycotts by coal miners in the Ruhr after World War I, and the Solidarity Movement in Poland in the 1970s (Ackerman and Kruegler, 1994; McAdam, 1988).

The question here is, what are the scope, limits, and mechanisms of social power wielded through social movements? Is it possible for a social movement to cause change in basic structures, policies, and distributions of wealth and power in society? We can provide memorable examples of success. So the question is, how does this work? What positional advantages do the powerless have?

The first factor that provides an obvious source of potential power for the under-class group, is the size and functional role of the group in society. Several of the most obvious tactics for a social movement depend on this structural fact – the strike, boycott, and mass demonstration. By mobilizing, the group can interfere with the smooth workings of society, compelling other parties to negotiate. And it can demonstrate its broad, mass-based support. Besides mass mobilization, there is the tactic of broadening the movement through alliances. This strategy requires "changing consciousness" in the broader society by the actions of the under-class group. The group (primarily through its organizations and leaders) can strive to broaden the base of its movement through alliances with other like-minded groups and with the general public. And this depends upon successful communication – setting the terms of the struggle in such a way that it aligns with the moral values and material interests of other groups (Hardin, 1982, 1995).

So here we have several kinds of tactics for the social movement – direct mass mobilization, broadening of alliances, and a deliberate campaign to capture the moral discourse for the public. Social movements in democracies have a fighting chance of securing limited victories. But the obstacles to these mass-based tactics are severe – classic collective action problems, problems of coordination and communication, and the need for competent organizations and leaders. Once again, the tactical options and advantages residing with the powerful are substantial. The powerful control the media; they have an advantage in setting the agenda, and they have an extensive ability to co-opt potential allies of the popular movement (side deals, special accommodations, playing off divisions within the mass population). And the range of options available to the powerful (the state, police, mine owners) are imposing: repression and intimidation, divide and conquer, co-optation, control of the media, and a greater ability to wait out the struggle. (There is of course a huge literature on social movements. A few core sources are Tilly, 2004; Marx and McAdam, 1994; McAdam et al., 1996.)

Coercion: the power of the authoritarian state

If any collective entity possesses power, surely it is the state in a dictatorship, for example, the Burmese military dictatorship or the single-party states of Cuba or China. So how does an authoritarian state exercise power? It is common to equate power with the ability to coerce and threaten in order to compel behavior. And certainly force and repression play a crucial role in authoritarian politics. But even within a dictatorship the instruments of coercion are less than total. When the priests and young people of Burma went into the streets of Rangoon in 2008, the military rulers were able to use a mix of violence and threat that permitted them to prevail against a budding democracy movement in Burma. But in the past 20 years rulers in the Philippines, Czechoslovakia, and Tbilisi have found that their arsenals of water cannons, secret police, and truncheons have not sufficed to silence the streets. Plainly, then, control of the forces of repression is an important component of the power base of an authoritarian dictatorship; but its scope is not unlimited.

As is always true in thinking about power, we have to begin by asking about the relational situation of the relevant actors. What is the will of the state? What is the scope of behavior that the state wishes to control? Who are the agents who are subjects to the state's power? We might put the geometry of state power into a simple diagram:

goals and intentions => levers of influence (repression, persuasion, bribery, cooptation, horse trading) => varied actors (civil servants, military officers, community leaders, bandits, citizens) => behavior.

From the dictator's point of view, there are two sets of actors over whom power needs to be exerted: intra-state actors – persons charged within the government to carry out the dictator's will; and actors in civil society – the citizens and organizations who make up mass society. Intuitively, the power of a state is measured by its ability to constrain the behavior of both sets of actors in ways that permit it to achieve its goals.

Let's look first at the intra-state actors. A state is a bureaucratic entity with decision makers at a range of levels. Ministries and organs of the state – the police and military, for example – have their own sources of power and domains of influence that are not fully within the control of higher authority. So the highest authority – president or general – has only a limited ability to directly impose his will upon lower levels. In the extreme case the executive can discipline or remove the lower-level director. But this lever is imprecise; it leaves the agency director a certain amount of undetectable freedom of action. So we can readily envision the situation where the executive has announced a certain goal for his government, and where two important ministries come into conflict over what to do. And one or both may be motivated by local interests rather than the goals of the state. (This seems to be an important clue in explaining some current developments in China. Certain central policies enacted in Beijing are ignored or reconsidered in regional government offices.) In this instance we need to ask, what levers of power and influence does the executive have within the government itself through which it can compel compliance by both agencies?

At this level we find the familiar processes of co-optation, alliance, inducement – as well as threat – found in all organizations. Perhaps a singular difference is that the use of violence is closer to the surface in a dictatorship than in other political organizations. But the task facing the fascist dictator has much in common with that of the executive of other large organizations with multiple agendas. The twentieth century confronts us with some extreme cases – Stalin's terrorism extended within his government as well as towards Soviet society at large, and Stalin used purges and executions to compel bureaucratic compliance. But it is an important research question for organizational studies to assess the degree to which force and violence can effectively run a complex organization. And it seems likely that more ordinary mechanisms of persuasion and cooperation must usually be invoked.

So much for the problem of exercising power within the state. Now consider the larger and more interesting question of power used against civil society and ordinary citizens. The issue of power arises only when the state wants a certain kind of behavior and citizens do not want to behave in this way. Take the large issues over which states want to exercise their will over citizens: taxation, conscription, and delivery of agricultural products. There is, first, the use of the threat of punishment to compel conformance. Draft dodgers can be hunted down and punished,

villages can be threatened with violent retaliation if villagers avoid taxes, and food can be withheld from non-compliant regions (e.g., Stalin's war on the kulaks; see Viola, 2005). Moreover, if the state can establish a pervasive network of police and informants, it can make its threats credible – with the result that compliance with law and dictum is reasonably high. So the organs of repression are certainly an important element of power for the authoritarian state.

Beyond violence, beyond effective enforcement, what other levers of behavior modification exist for the state? Two come to mind immediately: propaganda and binding social institutions. States often have a substantial degree of control over the instruments of thought formation – schooling, media, and communications technology. And experience has made it clear that there is a substantial degree to which a population's behavior can be altered through these tools. Markets and other impersonal social mechanisms are another important mechanism for shaping behavior. China's one-child policy was successful in altering the reproductive behavior of hundreds of millions of Chinese people. And these policies turned on a combination of coercion, enforcement, and financial incentives.

So perhaps the question of how authoritarian states exercise power is somewhat straightforward to answer: through organized repression, through artful command of a bureaucracy capable of acting cohesively, through the development of alliances with actors inside and outside of government, through co-optation of some actors to the disadvantage of other actors, through management of large social structures such as the market, and through the ability to set the terms of political behavior through the media and schooling.

CLASS

Let us turn now to the topic of social class. Marx's theory of social class is founded on the idea of conflict of interest defined by the property system. Marx puts the point this way in the *Communist Manifesto*: "History is a history of class conflict." "Workers of the world, unite; you have nothing to lose but your chains" (Marx and Engels, 1974 [1848]). Individuals belong to classes depending on their position within the social property system. The social property system defines the access and use enjoyed by different groups of the resources available to a society at a given period of history. The primary resources are capital, land, and labor. (We might now want to add "knowledge" to this list of categorical resources.) Individuals belong to classes defined by the type of access and use they have to which kinds of resources.

This is a structural definition of the concept of class. A person's class is defined by their position within a system of property relations, defining one's location with a structure of domination, control, and exploitation. The group of people who share a similar position within the property relations of a society constitute a class. Their circumstances, resources, and opportunities are similar to those of others in the class, and they have common interests that are in opposition to members of some other classes. So class works as a social sorting process: individuals are tracked into one class or another through specific sociological mechanisms (schooling, parental attitudes, neighborhood). And it works to assign very different ranges of material outcomes to members of the various groups; working-class families are more poorly educated, less healthy, and more vulnerable to economic fluctuations than their counterparts in the landlord class, the financial elite class, or the capitalist class. Part of the challenge of developing a sociology of class involved identifying some of the concrete pathways of difference created by class with respect to specific opportunities – education, health, adequate nutrition, access to creative work, and other important social resources. (Harry Braverman's sociology of work makes an important contribution here; Braverman, 1975.)

Status and consciousness are also part of the sociology of class. And, of course, there is the concrete sociological task of better understanding the lived experience of people who wind up in the various segments of the class system (Sennett and Cobb, 1972; Ehrenreich, 2001). Individuals develop specific features of mentality out of the experience they have in the class environments of their parents, their schools, and their workplaces. These differences in turn give rise to differences in behavior – consumer behavior, political behavior, and inter-group behavior. Members of a class may acquire a common perspective on their situation – they may come to diagnose the social relations around them in a similar way, they may come to a common "class consciousness" that leads them to engage in collective action.

Evidently, the groups that own capital and land have access to material resources that owners of labor power do not; so capitalists and landlords have social advantages lacked by proletarians. Proletarians gain access to material goods by selling their labor power to the owners of capital and land; they become wage laborers. Class relations create substantial differences of material wellbeing and substantial inequalities of wealth and income. By controlling the wealth constituted by capital and land, these privileged classes are able to take a disproportionate share of society's wealth. The great modern social classes, in Marx's historical analysis, are the bourgeoisie (capital and land) and the proletariat (wage labor). In feudalism the great classes were the feudal aristocrats (owners of land and rights in the labor of serfs) and serfs (usufruct of small parcels of land, labor obligations to the lord).

Class and property are thus conceptually intertwined. An economic structure can be defined as a system for producing social wealth in which productive resources and the results of production are unevenly divided across different groups. Classes are the major social positions within an existing economic structure. Producers create wealth through their labor and creativity; property owners extract a part of this wealth through a system of social relations that privilege them. Another way of putting the point is to ask: where does the individual gain their income – from the sale of labor time, from the sale or rent of physical assets, or from the sale or rent of expertise? Workers derive their income from the sale of their labor time; capitalists, financiers, and landlords derive their income from their ownership of physical and financial resources, and professionals, experts, and intellectuals derive their income from their possession of scarce expert knowledge and skills.

In nineteenth-century France we might have classified the population into land owners, capital owners, wage laborers, artisans, professionals (accountants, architects), intellectuals, government officials, civil service workers, small merchants, smallholding farmers, tenant farmers, landless workers, and lumpenproletariat. And these groups can be roughly triangulated according to their ownership of three major elements: labor power, valuable skills and knowledge, and economic assets (land, property, wealth). Within any society there are groups that fall outside the primary classes – small traders, artisans, small farmers, intellectuals. It is central to Marx's theory of class, that there is a primary cleavage between owners of the means of production and the direct producers, and that this cleavage embodies a fundamental conflict of interest between the two groups.

Class, according to Marx, also constitutes a system of *exploitation*: a system in which a substantial share of the fruits of social production are transferred from one group to another, through the normal workings of the social-property system (Roemer, 1982, 1988). The producing class is exploited by the ascendant class: wealth is transferred from producers to owners. Serfs and lords, slaves and masters, workers and owners represent the primary classes of feudalism, ancient slavery, and nineteenth-century capitalism. The proletariat produces surplus value, and the bourgeoisie gains ownership of this surplus through the workings of the property system, in the form of profits, interest, and rents.

Finally, the theory of class suggests the need for a theory of *class consciousness*: the ways in which members of distinct classes understand their roles in society, and the social relationships that largely determine their fates (Lukács, 1971; Thompson, 1966). Marx's concept of *ideology* is intended to express the notion that large system of ideas serve a social function of concealing the conflictual nature of the property and class system in which people find themselves (Althusser, 1971; Colletti, 1972; Lichtheim, 1967; Mannheim, 1959 [1936]). The concept of *false* consciousness falls within this notion; members of a class possess false consciousness when they seriously misconstrue the nature of the social relations within which they live.

The sociology of class

The explanatory thrust of the theory of class goes along the lines of a sociological hypothesis: people who have a similar location within a system of property relations will also develop other important similarities: similarities of thought, values, style, behavior, and politics, for example. And so Marx believed that structurally-defined classes of people were likely to further develop a similar class consciousness – a similar framework of thought in terms of which they understand the social forces around them; and he expected that classes of people would come to share a signature framework of political motivation – a set of ideas, interpretations, and values that would motivate them to engage in collective action together. (Anthony Giddens is one of the scholars who has given close attention to Marx's theory of class as a sociological theory (Giddens, 1973).)

This is where the substantive sociology of class comes in; in order to provide credibility for this set of expectations about class consciousness and political motivation, we need to have some ideas about the concrete sociological mechanisms that might plausibly lead from "common position in the property relations" to "common forms of consciousness and political motivation." And here there are quite a few things that can be said – both by Marx in the 1850s and contemporary observers in the 2000s. First, a common position in the property relations often implies a number of concrete similarities of experience across individuals – common features of the workplace, common neighborhoods in cities, common experiences in the system of schooling that is in place. These kinds of shared social positions suggest two things: first, a common process of shaping through which perceptions and motivations develop in each individual; and second, a common reality that individuals who experience these environments are likely to be able to perceive. It is highly plausible that a group of men and women who have spent their lives in a nineteenth-century textile factory while living in a concentrated workers' slum, will have developed a similar consciousness and social style from the discipline and work processes of the factory and their shared social associations in their neighborhoods.

So miners in Wales or West Virginia are exposed to similar work environments; similar firms and styles of management; and similar life outcomes that might be expected to create a "miner's consciousness" and a miner's political mentality. Smallholding wine growers across the landscape of nineteenth-century France are exposed to similar natural, social, and economic circumstances that are likely to shape the development of their personalities and worldviews, that are in turn likely to create an ideal-typical "wine grower" who fairly accurately represents the worldview and behavior of wine growers.

Second, there is a fact that is more apparent today than it was to nineteenth-century sociological observers, that has to do with what we now understand about social networks and social capital (Lin et al., 2001). Common locations of work and residence make it highly likely that occupational groups (miners, architects, professors) will fall within sharply distinguished sets of social networks, and they will have access to different combinations of social capital (civic organizations, religious groups, secret societies). So the system of class relations also creates specific features in the social networks that exist in a society. A highly democratic and egalitarian society would be expected to have a social network graph that is widely and evenly distributed across the population. But in our society, it is likely that a social network map of Chicago would be highly differentiated along class lines: business people tend to know business people, manufacturing workers tend to know other manufacturing workers, and so forth. Pierre Bourdieu's analysis of class and distinction is relevant here (Bourdieu, 1985, 1989). French sociologist Didier Lapeyronnie makes use of some of these ideas in his analysis of social relations in the French *banlieue* and ghettos (Lapeyronnie and Courtois, 2008). This fact about class-based social networks in turn implies that there will be significant differences across classes with respect to social capital – the ability of people to call upon their social relationships and associations in pursuit of their goals and interests. And the consciousness and political behavior of an individual is surely influenced in profound ways by the networks and social organizations within which they fall. So the fact of similarities in these respects is likely to give rise to similarities in consciousness and action as well.

In addition, of course, there is the fact of the social reality of exploitation in each of these circumstances: miners and wine growers are subject to coercive social relations that succeed in separating them from a substantial portion of the fruits of their labors. Coal miners will identify the profit-driven mine owners as the source of their exploitation and wine growers may identify the wine jobbers who buy their product cheaply and sell it dearly in the cities as the source of their exploitation. But each group comes to recognize the social reality of the property relations through which their productive labor is "expropriated" by other powerful forces. Recognition of the fact of exploitation is a key component of the process of the formation of class consciousness.

So it seems plausible to suppose that there are identifiable social mechanisms through which occupational groups come to have shared worldviews and similar political behaviors. But the theory of class asserts more than this; it asserts that wage laborers in many occupations will come to recognize themselves as fundamentally similar to workers in other occupations. The theory of class postulates sociology of "escalation" of class identity, from the particular occupation, work group, and neighborhood to the larger (and more abstract) class that encompasses many occupations and work groups in widely separated locations. So, it is postulated, fast food workers, auto workers, and air traffic controllers will come to identify together, not simply as a set of occupational groups, but as an extended group of "persons who are forced to sell their labor to capital in order to satisfy life needs." And, further, the theory postulates that it will be possible for a strong form of group solidarity to emerge across this fairly heterogeneous and physically separated set of occupational groups.

It is not entirely clear what the sociological mechanisms are supposed to be that facilitate this escalation of class identity, however. Classical Marxism depends heavily on the idea of a party and a group of activists who do the "class education" that leads workers from a narrowly parochial view of their situation to one that encompasses the common situation of wage labor. But this depends on a fairly sizable historical coincidence – the emergence of a militant and disciplined class-based party. And it is very hard to see how non-planned forms of sociological change might lead to this escalation – hard to see, that is, how air traffic controllers, McDonald's workers, and steel workers might spontaneously come to regard each other as belonging to a single class subject to exploitation by another abstractly defined class.

Moreover, it is very apparent today that there are multiple axes around which collective identities can form. Kinship relations in southern China cut across structural class relations, and it is certainly possible that the Li clan will have a stronger sense of identity than the landless workers – even though the Li clan contains landlords, peasant farmers, and landless workers. Religious affinities may be mobilized as a source of collective identity – again, with the likelihood of creating groups that cut across class lines.

So this line of thought suggests that there is a fairly large gap in the theory of class in even its application to the nineteenth-century case: the problem of how to explain the postulated escalation of consciousness from the particular work group and occupation to the more general category, "working class."

Social class and the state

A central tenet of classical Marxism is the view that there is a close relationship between class interests, political power, and the state. Marx sometimes writes of the state as existing as a "superstructure" for the economic interests represented by the economic structure of society; or the idea that the state is nothing but the "managing committee for the bourgeoisie." Ralph Miliband was one of the most thoughtful scholars to try to work out the relations that existed between class and political power (Miliband, 1969, 1977) from a Marxist point of view. Miliband's treatment did not assert a mechanical or automatic relationship between class interests and the actions of the state; but it offered a detailed theoretical and historical account intended to demonstrate some of these linkages. This theory of the state became a central focus of debate within Marxist social thought in the 1970s, with thinkers such as Nicos Poulantzas and Perry Anderson arguing for the "relative autonomy" of the state from direct management by the dominant classes in society (Poulantzas, 1975, 1978; Anderson, 1974, 1976, 1978). On this view, the state apparatus was itself a source of a degree of power and autonomy in rule-making, and the state's policies are subject to contestation by various classes and parties within society. This perspective takes part of its lead from Marx's own analysis of the class struggles in France and the rise of Napoleon III (Marx, 1973 [1850]; Marx and Fernbach, 1973). However, there is always the view that the advantages created by ownership of property and wealth give an advantage to owners over producers.

This schematic representation of the interests associated with an unequal social-property system immediately provokes a struggle for power and for the instruments of power. Each group will attempt to gain influence or control over the institutions and organizations that can serve as mechanisms of influence and coercion. The state is chief among these. The use of the state and its police and military arms during the labor struggles of the United States from 1880 to 1930 are a clear instance; military coercion was used to suppress labor unions in their efforts to use strikes to gain recognition and favorable agreements (Lindsey, 1964).

Are there classes in America?

This leaves the most important question: to what extent is the theory of class relevant to twenty-first century society? To what extent can American political conflicts, perceptions, parties, and movements be explained on the basis of occupational and class identities? To what extent do the most important fissures in our society derive from economic conflicts that can be assimilated to the theory of class?

In order to answer the question in the affirmative, we would need to determine whether there are major social groups that are defined by their position within the economy, who share

- some degree of a common perspective on the social world;

- some degree of a common culture;
- a set of distinctive economic interests;
- the potential of engaging in collective political action in support of their interests.

Does American society possess groups with these characteristics? Or, in the negative, is the American population so homogeneous (or possibly, so heterogeneous) in values, interests, culture, and politics, that the concept of class has no bearing today?

There are certainly occupational groupings in the American workforce. The United States Department of Labor makes use of a hierarchical classification of jobs in the United States, with 23 major groups (Bureau of Labor Statistics, 2008). These include management occupations, business and financial operations, computer and mathematical operations, architecture and engineering operations, food preparation and serving occupations, community and social service occupations, legal occupations, education, training, and library occupations, healthcare support occupations, and, eventually, production occupations. Within production occupations there is a further differentiation of jobs among supervisors, production workers, assemblers, fabricators, food processing workers, and so on for dozens of other sub-categories. So there is certainly a very clear occupational structure to the American economy, and the sociological pathways that convey an individual into a particular location within this structure are well-defined and impactful on the future quality of life of the individual.

So we might consider classifying these occupations according to some higher-level categories and then constructing a theory of social classes around them: management, unskilled labor, skilled labor, professional labor, white collar, blue collar, pink collar, manufacturing, service, agriculture. And we might consider whether some of these groupings have the cohesion and sociological interconnectedness to constitute a "class." Are unionized, blue-collar, industrial workers a "class"? Are non-unionized service workers a class? Are accountants, architects, and engineers a social class? Are nurses and other healthcare workers a class? Are mid-sized family farmers a social class? And for that matter, are the owners and top managers of banks, investment companies, and financial firms a class? These are fruitful questions, and they begin in a recognition of the complex occupational structure of the US economy. Occupations have large impact on worldview, values, quality of life, and political behavior.

Second, there is certainly a great deal of persistent social stratification in the Unites States. The probability of a child remaining in the quintile of the income distribution where his parents found themselves is high; so the position of a family within the distributive system is fairly stable over time. And position within the income distribution has major consequences for a family's level of consumption and quality of life. Being persistently "near-poor" is a situation of deprivation and insecurity that is sharply different from the life situation of the moderately affluent. So we might consider several large social groups based on income – the extremely poor, the working poor, the middle-income, the rich, and the super-rich. Within each of these categories of society defined by income we are likely to find some characteristic features of lifestyle, values, and existential dilemmas. So the basic structure of stratification of social goods such as income, health status, and education might serve to define large social "classes."

Third, it would appear that there are clusters of values, styles, and mental frameworks that correspond to different economic segments of American society. This is the cultural dimension of the social reality of class. Patterns of use of leisure time, attitudes towards education, membership in different kinds of civic organizations, and attitudes towards other nations seem to distinguish social groups in America. So we might attempt to delineate social classes on the basis of clusters of values and mental frameworks. And this approach can certainly be approached empirically, through administration of instruments such as the World Values

Survey and domestic equivalents (*World Values Survey*, 2008). To what extent do studies like these demonstrate significant inter-group differences within the United States?

Fourth, it seems likely that there are differentiating patterns among various social groups based on the patterns of social relationships that exist within the group, that would be revealed by maps of social networks. And it seems probable that the distinct groups that emerge will have important economic relationships in common. Here is a hypothetical study that could not really be performed but may be interesting as a thought experiment. Suppose we ask everyone in an urban population for the names of five non-family members upon whom they could call in an emergency to perform an important favor. Now draw the network map that results from this survey. Are there "islands" of separate sub-populations that can be discovered, where the great majority of links fall within the island and only a small number extend across to another island? And are these islands related in some important way to economic situation and status of the individuals who are included? Would this study map out groups that could be identified as "social classes"? It seems likely that the answers to these questions are affirmative.

Each of these is a different starting place for a sociological analysis of social class in America. And if the theory of class is correct, we would expect that these different starting places would begin to converge around the same large social formations: occupations, incomes, cultures, and social networks may all call out the same large social groups.

Ultimately, the theory of class has to do with collective interests. We might say that the fundamental interests of a group involve income, job security, healthcare, opportunities, and pensions. A more intangible set of interests have to do with a demand for fair treatment in economic decision-making and a need for a sense of self-determination. And it is plain that there are business decisions and public policy decisions that are being made today that affect these interests very differently for different groups. This suggests that there are in fact large groups in American society whose members have shared interests with each other and who can be mobilized in political action in support of these interests. And this begins to suggest that class remains a social reality in America – and one that may become more politically salient rather than less in the coming decade or so.

What cannot be forgotten, though, is the fact that economic structures are only one aspect of the social mechanisms of distribution and control through which individuals' status is determined. The mechanisms of race, ethnicity, migration, and gender all affect individuals' core interests in ways that are somewhat independent from the structures of property and class we've been highlighting. And this has important consequences for political mobilization as well; it means that political affinities and action may be organized around race and ethnicity as readily as they are around wage labor and capital – witness the massive immigration rallies that took place in 2007.

CONCLUSION

So what does power have to do with class? The two social factors of class and power are intertwined in at least three ways.

First, a class system constitutes a set of social inequalities within which there are deep conflicts of interest. So a class system sets the stage for the exercise of power; various groups have an interest in wielding power over others within a class system. Ascendant groups have an interest in sustaining the productive economic activities of subordinates whom they exploit, and they have an interest in squelching acts of resistance. But likewise, subordinate groups have an interest in using instruments of power to reduce or overturn the exploitative social relations within which they function.

Second, a class system assigns resources and positions to different groups and individuals that greatly influence the nature and weight of the instruments and tactics of power available to them. Owners have economic assets, alliances, and the state in their column. Producers have their numbers and their key locations in the economic process. A strike of rail workers is a substantial exercise of power, given the centrality of transport in a complex economy. So the particulars of a class system provide key determinants of the distribution of power within society.

Finally, a class system also creates a subjectivity of power, powerlessness, and resistance that may iterate into new forms of the exercise of power. It may be an effective instrument of social control to cultivate a subjectivity of powerlessness in subordinate groups. And likewise, it may be materially empowering to subordinate groups to cultivate a culture of resistance – by making collective action and solidarity more attainable, for example.

REFERENCES

Ackerman, Peter and Christopher Kruegler (1994) *Strategic Nonviolent Conflict: The Dynamics of People Power in the Twentieth Century.* Westport, CT: Praeger.

Althusser, Louis (1971) *Lenin and Philosophy, and Other Essays.* London: New Left Books.

Andersen, Margaret L. and Patricia Hill Collins (eds) (1998) *Race, Class and Gender: An Anthology.* Belmont, CA: Wadsworth Pub. Co.

Anderson, Perry (1974) *Lineages of the Absolutist State.* London: New Left Books.

Anderson, Perry (1976) *Considerations on Western Marxism.* London: New Left Books.

Anderson, Perry (1978) *Passages from Antiquity to Feudalism.* London, New York: Verso, distributed in the USA by Schocken.

Babeuf, Gracchus, Viktor M. Dalin, Armando Saitta and Albert Soboul (1977) *Œuvres de Babeuf.* Paris: Bibliothèque nationale.

Blanqui, Auguste (1885) *Critique Sociale.* Paris: F. Alcan.

Bourdieu, Pierre (1985) 'The social space and the genesis of groups', *Theory and Society,* 7(1): 723–744.

Bourdieu, Pierre (1989) 'Social space and symbolic power', *Sociological Theory*, 7(1): 14–25.

Braverman, Harry (1975) *Labor and Monopoly Capital; The Degradation of Work in the Twentieth Century*. New York: Monthly Review Press.

Bureau of Labor Statistics (2008) US Department of Labor (cited December 20). http://www.bls.gov/soc/soc_majo.htm.

Colletti, Lucio (1972) *From Rousseau to Lenin; Studies in Ideology and Society*. New York: Monthly Review Press.

Domhoff, G. William (1970) *The Higher Circles; The Governing Class in America*. 1st ed. New York: Random House.

Ehrenreich, Barbara (2001) *Nickel and Dimed: On (Not) Getting by in America*. 1st ed. New York: Metropolitan Books.

Foucault, Michel (1973) *The Birth of the Clinic; An Archaeology of Medical Perception*. (1st American) ed., *World of Man*. New York: Pantheon Books.

Foucault, Michel (1978) *The History of Sexuality. Introduction*. New York: Pantheon.

Foucault, Michel (1979) *Discipline and Punish: The Birth of the Prison*. New York: Vintage Books.

Foucault, Michel (1983) 'Afterword: The subject and power', in H. Dreyfus and P. Rabinow (eds) *Michel Foucault: Beyond Structuralism and Hermeneutics*. Chicago: University of Chicago Press.

Giddens, Anthony (1973) *The Class Structure of the Advanced Societies*. London: Hutchinson.

Gramsci, Antonio (1957) *The Modern Prince, and Other Writings*. London: Lawrence and Wishart.

Gramsci, Antonio (1971) *Selections from the Prison Notebooks of Antonio Gramsci*. Trans. Q. Hoare and G. Nowell-Smith. New York: International.

Hardin, Russell (1982) *Collective Action*. Baltimore: The Johns Hopkins University Press.

Hardin, Russell (1995) *One for All: The Logic of Group Conflict*. Princeton: Princeton University Press.

Haugaard, Mark (2002) *Power: A Reader*. Manchester, UK; New York, NY: Manchester University Press. Distributed exclusively in the USA by Palgrave.

Hobbes, Thomas (1996 [1651]) *Leviathan*. Oxford, New York: Oxford University Press.

Lapeyronnie, Didier and Laurent Courtois (2008) *Ghetto Urbain: Ségrégation, Violence, Pauvreté en France Aujourd'hui*. Paris: Laffont.

Lichtheim, George (1967) *The Concept of Ideology, and Other Essays*. New York: Random House.

Lin, Nan, Karen S. Cook and Ronald S. Burt (2001) *Social Capital: Theory and Research, Sociology and Economics*. New York: Aldine de Gruyter.

Lindsey, Almont (1964) *The Pullman Strike: The Story of a Unique Experiment and of a Great Labor Upheaval*. Chicago: University of Chicago Press.

Little, Daniel (1998) *Microfoundations, Method and Causation: On the Philosophy of the Social Sciences*. New Brunswick, NJ: Transaction Publishers.

Little, Daniel (2006) 'Levels of the social', in S. Turner and M. Risjord (eds) *Handbook for Philosophy of Anthropology and Sociology*. Amsterdam, New York: Elsevier Publishing. pp. 343–371.

Lukács, Georg (1971) *History and Class Consciousness*. Cambridge: MIT Press.

Lukes, Steven (1974) *Power: A Radical View*. London; New York: Macmillan.

Machiavelli, Niccolò (1996 [1513]) *The Prince*. Trans. P. Sonnino. Atlantic Highlands, NJ: Humanities Press.

Mannheim, Karl (1959 [1936]) *Ideology and Utopia: An Introduction to the Sociology of Knowledge*. New York: Harcourt Brace.

Marx, Gary T. and Doug McAdam (1994) *Collective Behavior and Social Movements: Process and Structure*. Prentice Hall Foundations of Modern Sociology Series. Englewood Cliffs, NJ: Prentice Hall.

Marx, Karl (1973 [1850]) 'The class struggles in France', in D. Fernbach (ed.) *Surveys from Exile*. New York: Vintage.

Marx, Karl (1974 [1852]) 'The eighteenth brumaire of Louis Bonaparte', in D. Fernbach (ed.) *Surveys from Exile*. New York: Vintage. pp. 143–249.

Marx, Karl (1977 [1867]) *Capital*. Vol. 1. New York: Vintage.

Marx, Karl, and Frederick Engels (1974 [1848]) 'The Communist manifesto', in D. Fernbach (ed.) *The Revolutions of 1848: Political Writings,* 1: 62–98.

Marx, Karl and Friedrich Engels (1935) *Wage-Labour and Capital*. New rev. translation. ed. Moscow: Co-operative Publishing Society of Foreign Workers in the USSR.

Marx, Karl and David Fernbach (1973) *Surveys from Exile*. Harmondsworth, Baltimore: Penguin Books.

McAdam, Doug (1988) *Freedom Summer*. New York: Oxford University Press.

McAdam, Doug, John D. McCarthy and Mayer N. Zald (1996) *Comparative Perspectives on Social Movements: Political Opportunities, Mobilizing Structures, and Cultural Framings*. Cambridge Studies in Comparative Politics. Cambridge; New York: Cambridge University Press.

Miliband, Ralph (1969) *The State in Capitalist Society*. New York: Basic.

Miliband, Ralph (1977) *Marxism and Politics*. Oxford: Oxford University Press.

Mills, C. Wright (1956) *The Power Elite.* New York: Oxford University Press.

Moya, Paula M.L. and Michael Roy Hames-Garcia (eds) (2000) *Reclaiming Identity: Realist Theory and the Predicament of Postmodernism.* Berkeley, CA: University of California Press.

Poulantzas, Nicos Ar. (1975) *Classes in Contemporary Capitalism.* London: New Left Books.

Poulantzas, Nicos Ar. (1978) *Political Power and Social Classes.* London: Verso Editions.

Roemer, John (1982) *A General Theory of Exploitation and Class.* Cambridge: Harvard University Press.

Roemer, John E. (1988) *Free to Lose: An Introduction to Marxist Economic Philosophy.* Cambridge, MA: Harvard University Press.

Scott, James C. (1985) *Weapons of the Weak: Everyday Forms of Peasant Resistance.* New Haven: Yale University Press.

Scott, James C. (1990) *Domination and the Arts of Resistance: Hidden Transcripts.* New Haven: Yale University Press.

Sennett, Richard and Jonathan Cobb (1972) *The Hidden Injuries of Class.* 1st ed. New York: Knopf.

Sugrue, Thomas J. (1996) *The Origins of the Urban Crisis: Race and Inequality in Postwar Detroit, Princeton Studies in American Politics.* Princeton, NJ: Princeton University Press.

Thompson, Edward P. (1966) *The Making of the English Working Class.* New York: Vintage Books.

Tilly, Charles (2004) *Social Movements, 1768–2004.* Boulder: Paradigm Publishers.

Viola, Lynne (2005) *The War Against the Peasantry, 1927–1930: The Tragedy of the Soviet Countryside, Annals of Communism. Tragedy of the Soviet countryside, 1927–1939.* New Haven, CT: Yale University Press.

Wong, Paul (1999) *Race, Ethnicity, and Nationality in the United States: Toward the Twenty-First Century.* Boulder, CO: Westview Press.

World Values Survey (2008) http://www.worldvaluessurvey.org/.

13

Causality, Causal Models, and Social Mechanisms

Daniel Steel

INTRODUCTION

Causation is one of the most important and contentious issues in social science. Any aspirations for a better social world, whether they concern the alleviation of inequities or the promotion of wealth, must explicitly or implicitly rely on beliefs about the causes and effects of government policies, social institutions, norms, or other phenomena that fall within the purview of social science. Yet everyday exemplars of cause and effect relations are typically drawn from relatively simple physical setups and machines such as billiards and lawnmowers. Indeed, the expression "social mechanism" reflects this transfer of concepts from mechanical to social. Moreover, many important questions in social science concern social systems and phenomena – economies, racial segregation, etc. – whose extent and complexity make them difficult if not impossible to study in controlled laboratory settings. The result of all this is that causation is a central and perennial issue for the philosophy of social science. This chapter examines three general approaches to studying causation in

social science and the conceptual connections among them.

One commonly drawn distinction in social science research is between quantitative and qualitative approaches. Whereas quantitative research examines large sets of numerical data which are then analyzed by means of statistical techniques, qualitative research focuses in depth on a relatively small number of cases. A good representative of the mainstream view of the relationship between these two approaches can be found in the influential book, *Designing Social Inquiry: Inference in Qualitative Research* (King et al., 1994), which I will henceforth refer to as *DSI*. According to *DSI*, a shared logic underlies both quantitative and qualitative research and this logic is most clearly exhibited in quantitative research. Advocates of qualitative research, while mostly agreeing that there are important commonalities among the two approaches, reject what they perceive as *DSI*'s characterization of qualitative research as the poor relation to quantitative social science (McKeown, 2004; Ragin, 2004,). Charles Ragin also critiques the "quantitative versus qualitative" distinction, arguing that the intended contrast is better drawn in terms of variable-versus case-oriented research (Ragin, 1987). Ragin's formulation of this distinction associates the two approaches with distinct types of models: linear equations for variable-oriented and Boolean logic for case-oriented. I adopt the "variable versus case" version of the distinction mainly because I find the emphasis on types of causal model fruitful. Variable-oriented social science research is also contrasted with mechanism approaches (George and Bennet, 2005; Hedström and Swedberg, 1998,). Mechanism approaches study causal relationships by developing models, often represented by mathematical formula, of micro-processes that could generate a macro-sociological phenomenon of interest. Advocates of social mechanisms often claim that they can overcome difficulties associated with variable-oriented research, especially, the problem that a correlation found in the data may be explained by an omitted variable rather than a direct causal influence (Elster, 1983; Hedström and Swedberg, 1998; Little, 1991).

In this chapter, I explore the interrelationships among variable-, case-, and mechanism-oriented approaches to social science research. I agree that there is a common logic behind variable- and case-oriented approaches, but I suggest that this commonality is best formulated within an approach to causal inference that relies on Bayesian networks (Bayes nets, for short). More specifically, the types of causal models typically associated with the two approaches – linear equations for variable-oriented and Boolean logic for case-oriented approaches – are two types of parameterizations of Bayes nets. The Bayes nets framework, therefore, articulates model-general aspects of causal inference that pertain to these two as well as many other types of causal models and thereby can reasonably be taken to articulate the "underlying logic" of causal inference to which the authors of *DSI* refer. One useful consequence of this analysis is that it shows how challenges often associated with variable-oriented approaches – such as problems linked to omitted common causes – are also difficulties for case-oriented research. Finally, I consider the connection of mechanism-oriented research to variable- and case-oriented approaches to causal inference. Advocates of mechanisms in social science typically claim that mechanisms are valuable for explanation and for assisting causal inference. I focus on the second of these two claims here and suggest that the relationship between mechanism- and variable-oriented approaches is best understood by way of a distinction between what I call direct and indirect causal inference.[1]

VARIABLE- VS. CASE-ORIENTED APPROACHES

The contrast between quantitative and qualitative social science research naturally suggests a difference that has to do with numbers: quantitative researchers work with large samples of numerical data that they subject to statistical analysis, while qualitative researchers delve into non-quantifiable features of a relatively small number of cases. For example, this sort of distinction seems, at least to a first approximation, to capture central differences between such social science disciplines as econometrics and cultural anthropology. Those who pursue quantitative approaches to social sciences are more likely to see their methods as continuous with natural science, while a tendency to identify with research methods typical of the humanities is more common, though certainly not universal, among qualitative researchers. Thus, the quantitative versus qualitative distinction taps into an old and central debate about the nature of social science method and its relation to methods in the natural sciences. In this section, I focus on the positions taken on this issue in *DSI* and in reactions to it.

It is safe to say that *DSI* is the most widely discussed work on social science methodology published in the last 25 years (cf. Brady and Collier, 2004; George and Bennett, 2005). The central theme of *DSI* is that differences between quantitative and qualitative approaches to social research are primarily matters of style rather than substance and that both approaches rely on "the same underlying logic of inference" (p. 4). But while insisting that "neither quantitative nor qualitative research is superior to the other" (p. 5), *DSI* goes on to make clear that it regards good quantitative social research as a model for good social science in general.

> non-statistical research will produce more reliable results if researchers pay attention to the rules of scientific inference – rules that are sometimes more clearly stated in the style of quantitative research. … The very abstract, and even unrealistic, nature of statistical models is what makes the rules of inference shine through so clearly. (p. 6)

The central thesis of *DSI* and the arguments for it have stimulated a good deal of critical discussion among social scientists. One line of criticism stems from social scientists who identify as qualitative- or case-oriented researchers and who reject what they see as the lack of understanding or proper respect paid to their methods by *DSI*. The representative of this line of argument that I will focus on here is Charles Ragin, who is well known in the literature on social science methodology for developing an approach to the comparative method based on Boolean algebra (Ragin, 1987).

Ragin prefers to frame the "quantitative/ qualitative" distinction in terms of variable-versus case-oriented research (Ragin, 1987: Chapters 3 and 4). This way of drawing the distinction focuses attention on the type of research question asked and models used. I adopt Ragin's way of drawing the distinction since I think an emphasis on distinct types of causal models is more theoretically fruitful than stressing the presence or absence of numerical data. After all, seemingly qualitative ethnographic research in cultural anthropology often involves the collection of numerical data on such things as the number of individuals living in households or the time spent on various tasks according to age or gender. The "variable versus case" dis-

tinction is also more useful for a discussion of mechanism-oriented approaches, which are often quantitative in the sense of utilizing mathematical models but which usually do not involve statistical analyses of large data sets.

Variable-oriented research begins with a question about the impact of one or more variables on some outcome of interest, for example, the impact of gun control on crime or of budget deficits on economic growth. This type of question tends to treat the impact of a variable in abstraction from the variety of particular contexts and combinations of other causes in which it might occur. This point is closely related to an important feature of variable-oriented research as characterized by Ragin, namely, that it usually treats variables as acting independently of one another. This assumption is typically implicit in choosing to represent the influences of the causes upon the effect by means of a linear equation such as the following:

$$y = \alpha + \beta_1 x_1 + \beta_2 x_2 + \beta_3 x_3 + \varepsilon$$

Here y is the dependent variable (the effect), x_1 through x_3 are the independent variables (potential causes), α is the intercept, β_1 through β_3 are the coefficients, and ε is the error term which represents the effects of any omitted causes. For example, y might be a variable representing income, while x_1 through x_3, respectively, stand for educational attainment, IQ, and parents' income. The research question, then, might be: what impact do these three variables have on income? Possible answers correspond to distinct assignments of numbers to the coefficients. To assume that the correct answer fits the form of the above equation entails some assumptions about what the correct answer could be, for instance, that the independent variables act separately upon y (e.g., the impact of x_2 does not depend on the value of x_3).

In contrast, case-oriented research is motivated by an interest in one or a small number of cases. For example, a case-oriented researcher might be stimulated by an interest to explain the bursting of the "dot-com" bubble in the late 1990s, a question that would naturally invite comparisons with other stock-market busts. A key feature of case-oriented research as understood by Ragin is that it is deeply concerned with teasing apart complex interactions of causes found in particular cases. An interest in interpreting specific cases and in pinpointing the combinations of conditions, the causal complexes, that produce specific outcomes encourages investigators to view cases as wholes (Ragin, 1987: 52). Ragin's approach is intended for cases in which causes and effects can be represented as conditions or events that are present or absent. The goal, then, is to identify which combination of conditions (or absences) results in the outcome. Boolean logic, which will be familiar to anyone who has taken an introductory logic class, can be used to represent relationships among variables in such circumstances. This is best understood by way of an example. Consider the table in Figure 13.1, which is adapted from Ragin (1987: 96). This table is a hypothetical example of a study of three potential causes of a successful strike (S):

A	B	C	S	Number of cases
1	1	1	1	3
1	1	0	1	2
1	0	1	1	6
1	0	0	0	9
0	1	1	0	3
0	1	0	1	5
0	0	1	0	6
0	0	0	0	4

**Figure 13.1 A hypothetical example:
A = booming product market, B = threat of sympathy strikes, C = large strike fund, and S = successful strike.**

high demand for the product produced by the striking workers (A), threat that other workers will also go on strike out of sympathy or solidarity (B), and a large strike fund (C). In this figure, 1's indicates that the condition is present and 0's indicate that it is absent. For example, in the fourth row from the top, only A is present while B, C, and S are absent.

Given a table of this sort, Ragin describes some fairly simple procedures for identifying sets of minimal combinations of causes that generate the outcome. First, list the rows in the table for which the outcome S is present, which in Figure 13.1 are the first through third rows and the sixth row. This can be represented in the following Boolean equation:

$$S = ABC \oplus AB\bar{C} \oplus A\bar{B}C \oplus \bar{A}B\bar{C}$$

In this equation, a line over a letter indicates the absence of that characteristic, for instance, $\bar{C}$ indicates the absence of C. The $\oplus$ symbol is called "Boolean addition," which is equivalent to disjunction, that is, "or." Adjacent letters, such as ABC, represent "Boolean multiplication," which is equivalent to conjunction, that is, "and." Finally, the equals sign represents the biconditional, which can be expressed in English as "if and only if." Thus, the above equation is a compact representation of the rather cumbersome claim that S is present if, and only if, either A, B, and C are all present, or A and B are present while C is absent, or A and C are present while B is absent, or A and C are absent while B is present.

As Ragin explains, a Boolean equation like the one above can often be simplified to an equation containing fewer terms in two steps. The first step proceeds by finding what we can call *minimizing matches*. A minimizing match is a disjunction of two terms that are the same *except for one* letter which has line above in one term but not in the other. In the equation above, there are three minimizing matches: ($ABC \oplus AB\bar{C}$), ($ABC \oplus A\bar{B}C$), and ($AB\bar{C} \oplus \bar{A}B\bar{C}$). A minimizing match is logically equivalent to a single term that omits the letter that varies in the pair. For example, $(ABC \oplus AB\overline{C}) = AB$, $(ABC \oplus A\overline{B}C)$ $= AC$, and $(AB\overline{C} \oplus \overline{A}B\overline{C}) = B\overline{C}$.[2] Thus, the Boolean equation above simplifies to the following:

$$S = AB \oplus AC \oplus B\overline{C}$$

The next step consists of removing terms that are redundant in the sense that any way of making the term is true will also make one or more of the other terms true. For example, AB can be true in two ways: ABC or $AB\overline{C}$. Yet if it is ABC, then AC is true, and if it is $AB\overline{C}$, then $B\overline{C}$ is true. Notice that neither AC nor $B\overline{C}$ is redundant in this sense, for example, if $A\overline{B}C$, then AC is true and the other two terms are false. So after removing the redundant term AB, we are left with the following:

$$S = AC \oplus B\overline{C}$$

In this example, then, AC and $B\overline{C}$ are the "prime implicants" of S, that is to say, they are the minimal sets of conditions that are both necessary and sufficient for that outcome. Given a causal interpretation, this hypothetical example says that the two basic combinations of conditions that result in a successful strike are: (1) a booming product market and a large strike fund, and (2) threat of sympathy strikes and the absence of a large strike fund. Of course, real examples are unlikely to be as neat and clean as this hypothetical one. In real cases it often happens that there are some possible combinations of the potential causes that are not instantiated in any case, and it is also not rare that there are cases having the same values for the potential causes but differing outcomes.

Causal reasoning relying on Boolean logic forces one to pay careful attention to possible causal interactions among variables, which makes it an attractive approach for case-oriented research in which complexes of interacting causes are a central concern. In contrast, an approach to causal inference that relies on linear equations will tend to obscure such interactions. Instead, it will provide an overall estimate of the impact of each cause that depends on the frequency with which conditions necessary for the operation of that cause happen to be present in the population. Consequently, an estimate of this kind might provide very little information about what the impact of the cause would be in a distinct population wherein the frequency of those interacting causes are very different. However, the major downside of Boolean approaches to causal inference is that they are feasible only for cases involving a relatively small number of potential causes that can take on only a very limited number of possible values, since otherwise the table will be unmanageably huge. For instance, in the hypothetical example described above, there were only three potential causes and each potential cause had only two possible values (present or absent). In this case, the number of rows of the table is $2^3 = 8$. In general, then, the number of rows in a table will be n^m, where n is number of possible values per potential cause and m is the number of potential causes. It can be easily understood, then, why Boolean approaches would not be useful for research questions involving quantitative variables, such as income, whose range of possible values might be in the millions. Of course, it is possible to use statistical tests for interaction effects in conjunction with linear models like those considered above. But such tests typically focus on a few salient potential interactions, rather than considering every possible one as a Boolean analysis would.

Let us return, then, to the claim made in *DSI* that inferences in quantitative and qualitative social science are based on a common logic and differ mainly in matters of style. Provided that we interpret this claim by reference to Ragin's "variable versus case" rendering of the distinction, we can see that there is at least one difference that seems to be more than merely "stylistic," namely, the choice of which type of causal model to use. However, the authors of *DSI* would insist that the common logic to which they refer transcends differences in the type of causal model chosen (1994: 87–9). What, then, is this common logic? In part, the logic of scientific inference proposed in *DSI* consists of ideas about scientific method that are largely inspired by the writings of Karl Popper (1959). For example, *DSI* insists that hypotheses should be testable, and the more testable the better (1994: 19–20). In addition, *DSI* echoes Popper's strictures on the use of ad hoc modifications to save a hypothesis from apparent refutation by data: modifications that merely restrict the scope of application of a hypothesis, and hence reduce its testability, are undesirable (pp. 21–22). Some critics of *DSI*, especially Ragin, take issue with its stance on the use of ad hoc modifications in response to cases that contradict a theoretical prediction (2004: 126). Besides its insistence on some very general points about scientific method, *DSI* also gives more specific advice about appropriate methods for testing causal hypotheses. For example, *DSI* stresses that causal inference is possible only from data in which there is variation in the potential cause or causes (p. 108) as well as variation in the effect (p. 129) and that comparison groups that differ with respect to the potential cause or causes should be relevantly similar in other ways (pp. 91–95). Some critics take issue with the more specific recommendations about causal inference found in *DSI*, particularly, with regard to the role of mechanisms in causal inference and explanation (George and Bennett, 2005: 11).

The focus here will be on the aspects of a common logic that pertain specifically to causal inference rather than to scientific inference in general. In particular, I will propose that the Bayes nets approach to causation is a good candidate for a general framework that clearly articulates a common logic of causal inference. I explain how linear and Boolean models are simply two distinct kinds of parameterizations of Bayes nets. From this perspective, *DSI* is largely correct in its insistence that similar rules of causal inference apply to variable- and case-oriented research. For instance, I explain how the possibility of unmeasured common causes – often cited as major challenge for

variable-oriented research – arises for case-oriented approaches as well.

BAYES NETS AND CAUSAL MODELS

Bayesian networks (or Bayes nets, for short) are an increasingly commonly used framework for representing causal claims and, consequently, for causal inference from statistical data (cf. Pearl, 2000; Neopolitan, 2004; Spirtes et al., 2000). A Bayes net consists of two things: (1) a graph with arrows linking nodes that represent variables and (2) a probability distribution over the variables in the graph. Typically, Bayes nets approaches assume that graphs are *acyclic*.[3] A graph is acyclic if there is no chain of arrows aligned head-to-tail that begin and end with the same node. An acyclic graph consisting of nodes linked by arrows is called a directed acyclic graph, or DAG. An example of a DAG is provided in Figure 13.2. This DAG represents a hypothesis concerning the causal relationships among external threat (*ET*), external conflict (*EC*), domestic power inequalities (*DPI*), and democratization (*D*). When a DAG is used to represent causal relationships, an arrow between two variables represents an influence that is not mediated by any of the other variables in the DAG. However, the arrow does not specify the nature of that influence, for example, whether it makes the effect more likely or less likely to occur. Such information is provided by the probability distribution associated with the DAG rather than in DAG itself. Some terminology will be helpful for discussing the relationships represented in DAGs. In a DAG, a node X is said to be a *parent* of another Y if there is an arrow pointing directly from X to Y. For example in Figure 13.2, *ET* and *EC* are the parents of *D*. A directed path is a sequence of nodes $X_1, \ldots, X_n$ such that, for each pair X_i and X_{i+1} in the sequence, X_i is a parent of X_{i+1}. In Figure 13.2, $ET \rightarrow DPI \rightarrow EC$ and $DPI \rightarrow EC \rightarrow D$ are both directed paths. A node

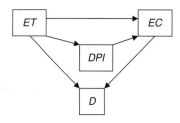

Figure 13.2   An example of a directed acyclic graph (Rasler and Thompson 2004: 885).

Y is said to be a descendant of X if there is a directed path from X to Y.[4] In Figure 13.2, for example, EC, DPI, and D are descendants of ET.

In a Bayes net, the probability distribution associated with a DAG is assumed to obey something known as the Markov condition, that is, each variable in the graph is probabilistically independent of its non-descendants conditional on its parents. In Figure 13.2, the parents of D are ET and EC, while DPI is the only nondescendant of D. Thus, the Markov condition requires that D is probabilistically independent of DPI conditional on ET and EC. Intuitively, that means that, once you know the values of ET and EC, learning the value of DPI doesn't tell you anything more about what the value of D is likely to be. A more precise understanding of what the Markov condition asserts requires introducing a bit of probability notation, especially the concept of conditional probability. A conditional probability is the probability of an event A among those cases in which B obtains. This is written as $P(A \mid B)$ and read "the probability of A given B." An example of a conditional probability is the rate of unemployment among those who have a college degree, which would presumably be lower than the rate of unemployment in the general population. In probability theory, it is a standard convention to use lower case letters to denote the particular values of a variable. For instance, if X is a variable representing height, then x might be a particular height (say, 6 feet). In the simplest case, variables have only two values. For example,

if D indicates democratization, then the two values of D might indicate the presence and absence of this feature, which might be denoted d_1 and d_2, respectively. Likewise, the values of ET (external threat) might be et_1 and et_2, indicating presence and absence of external threats, respectively. Given this set up, the claim that democratization is less likely among those states confronted by external threats would be expressed in probability symbols as follows: $P(D = d_1 \mid ET = et_1) < P(D = d_1 \mid ET = et_2)$. For convenience, the uppercase letters representing variables are often omitted, which in this example results in the following, more compact expression: $P(d_1 \mid et_1) < P(d_1 \mid et_2)$.

Given the notion of conditional probability, we can now provide a more precise definition of the notion of conditional probabilistic independence mentioned in the Markov condition: X is probabilistically independent of Y conditional on Z just in case, for every x, y, and z, $P(x \mid y, z) = P(x \mid z)$. As explained above, the lowercase letters are particular values of the variables represented by the corresponding uppercase letters. So this is saying that once you know the value Z, learning the value of Y provides no additional information about what the value of X is likely to be. The expression "$X \perp\!\!\!\perp Y \mid Z$" is often used as an abbreviation for "X and Y are probabilistically independent conditional on Z." For example, the Markov condition requires in Figure 13.2 that $D \perp\!\!\!\perp DPI \mid \{ET, EC\}$, which is a prediction that we may be able to test if we have a good sample of data for these variables. The expression $X \perp\!\!\!\perp Y$ indicates that X and Y are probabilistically independent, which means roughly that learning the value of X provides no information about the likely value of Y.

As this example suggests, the Markov condition facilitates causal inferences from statistical data. It will be helpful to list three of the most important consequences of the Markov condition in this regard. The simplest of these is that an absence of a causal connection between two variables entails an absence of probabilistic dependence between them. Let us say that there is a causal connection between X and Z if and only if X is a cause of Z, Z is a cause of X, or there is some third variable that is a common cause of both.

Consequence 1

If there is no causal connection between X and Y, then $X \perp\!\!\!\perp Y$.

This means that when data indicates that two variables are probabilistically dependent, we can infer that there is some causal connection between them, although we cannot infer from this alone whether that connection consists of one causing the other or a third variable that is a cause of both.

Consequence 2

In both $X \to Z \to Y$ and $X \leftarrow Z \to Y$, $X \perp\!\!\!\perp Y \mid Z$. In other words, intermediate causes screen-off upstream causes from their effects, and common causes screen-off their effects from one another.

The intuitive idea here is that, if X and Y are causally connected only through Z, then they no longer provide any additional information about one another once Z is known. For example, consider a sequence of messages passed among three friends, from Alice to Sue and then from Sue to Joe. In this situation, knowing Alice's message would provide information about the message that Joe received, provided that Sue is reasonably faithful in her transmission. But once we know the message that Sue sent, learning Alice's message provides no further information about Joe's message. This screening-off relation would also hold if, instead of a chain of messages, Sue had sent the message directly to both Joe and Alice. Similarly in Figure 13.2, D is linked to DPI both as an effect of a common cause, ET, and as an indirect effect through the path $DPI \to EC \to D$. Thus, the conditional independence $D \perp\!\!\!\perp DPI \mid \{ET, EC\}$ is an illustration

of consequence 2. Combining consequences 1 and 2 yields a common strategy for drawing causal inferences from statistical data. Suppose that two variables X and Y are correlated with one another and that we know that Y cannot be a cause of X, for instance, because X is prior in time to Y. Then we have evidence that X is a cause of Y if this correlation persists even when we condition on all of the possible common cause variables that we can think of. There are some shortcomings with this strategy – for example, some common causes might fail to be considered or a suspected common cause might actually be an intermediate cause. But the point here is merely to observe that this familiar strategy presupposes the Markov condition. A third and more surprising consequence of the Markov condition is also worthy of note.

Consequence 3

In $X \to Y \leftarrow Z$, it is not necessarily the case that $X \perp\!\!\!\perp Z \mid Y$. Since a node with two arrows pointing directly into it is known as a collider, this can be restated as: conditioning on a collider can create probabilistic dependence.

For example, recall the Vietnam era draft, in which men were issued draft numbers that were then randomly selected. Let X represent whether a person's draft number was called, Y service in Vietnam, and Z whether the person was patriotic. Both X and Z are causes of Y, but since draft numbers were selected at random, there is no causal connection between X and Z. Nevertheless, X and Z may be dependent *conditional* on Y. Consider a man Joe who served in Vietnam *despite the fact that his draft number was never called*. Plainly, the fact that Joe chose to go to Vietnam without being drafted will make us think it more likely that he was patriotic way back then. In other words, among those who are Vietnam veterans, we would expect a negative correlation between being drafted and (pre-draft) patriotism.

Let us return, then, to the variable- and case-oriented approaches to social research, which as we saw tended to be associated with distinct types of causal models: linear and Boolean equations, respectively. These two types of causal models are in fact distinct types of parameterizations of Bayes nets. To understand what this means, it is necessary to understand an important consequence of the Markov condition; namely, that it allows the joint probability distribution of a set of variables to be written as the product of the probability distribution of each variable conditional on its parents. Thus, the probability distribution for the DAG in Figure 13.2 can be broken down into $P(ET)$, $P(DPI | ET)$, $P(EC | ET, DPI)$, and $P(D| ET, EC)$. However, these conditional probabilities can be specified in a variety of distinct ways. For example, if each of the variables has only two possible values (present or absent), then the probabilities could be given simply by indicating the probability that the effect is present given each possible combination of values of its parents. For example, for $P(D | ET, EC)$, we might have $P(d_1 | et_1, ec_1) = .15$, $P(d_1 | et_1, ec_0) = .35$, $P(d_1 | et_0, ec_1) = .25$, and $P(d_1 | et_0, ec_0) = .75$.

The Boolean equation examined in the foregoing section is an example of just this sort of approach, except with the additional assumption that all of the probabilities are 1 or 0. However, as Ragin (1987) points out, in actual case-oriented research it often happens that cases having the same combination of values for the causes do not all exhibit the same outcome. In such circumstances, one could substitute a probability of the outcome for an absolute "yes" or "no," or perhaps code probabilities significantly less than .5 as 0 and those significantly higher than 0.5 as 1. So in a Boolean approach, a parameterization consists simply of specifying the probabilities of each variable given each combination of values of its parents. But as was explained in the previous section, Boolean models are infeasible for examples involving variables – such as gross domestic product or unemployment rate – that may take on any one

of a large number of possible values. Linear equations are a commonly used means for specifying probability distributions in such cases. For example, suppose that D, ET, and EC each have many possible values rather than only two. Then $P(D | ET, EC)$ might be specified with the aid of a linear equation like the following:

$$d = \alpha + \beta_1 et + \beta_2 ec + \varepsilon$$

In this case, a parameterization would consist of specifying numerical values for α, β_1, and β_2, and a probability distribution for the error term ε.[5] From a Bayes nets perspective, then, Boolean and linear models are simply distinct ways of specifying a probability distribution for a DAG.

Moreover, both approaches are consistent with the Markov condition, since the Markov condition is satisfied in any acyclic causal model in which the error terms are independent of one another (Steel, 2005). Independent error terms are typically regarded as an important facilitating condition for causal inference in variable-oriented research, since the failure of the condition may result from the presence of unmeasured common causes. When unmeasured common causes are present, a natural way to proceed is to suppose that the Markov condition holds true of a more extensive DAG in which the omitted common causes are included (cf. Spirtes et al., 2000: Chapter 6). For example, the method of instrumental variables used in econometrics (cf. Angrist et al., 1996; Lleras-Muney, 2005) can be understood in this way (Steel, 2008: 175–181). Furthermore, the minimization strategy used in Boolean models is a simple application of the Markov condition and of consequence 2 in particular. Recall that Ragin's approach to inferring causal relationships from a table like that in Figure 13.1 began by searching for minimizing matches. In a minimizing match, a change in the value of one variable makes no difference to the outcome, or probability of the outcome, so long as the values of the other variables remain the same.

ET	DPI	EC	D	$P(d_1)$ > .5
1	1	1	.15	No
1	1	0	.35	No
1	0	1	.15	No
1	0	0	.35	No
0	1	1	.25	No
0	1	0	.75	Yes
0	0	1	.25	No
0	0	0	.75	Yes

Figure 13.3 Boolean minimization and the Markov condition.

For example, consider the relationship between the *D*, *DPI*, *ET*, and *EC*. Suppose that each of these variables have only two possible values – present and absent denoted by 1 and 0, respectively – and let $P(D \mid ET, DPI, EC)$ be as represented by Figure 13.3.

In this figure, once the values of *ET* and *EC* are known, learning the value of *DPI* makes no difference to the probability that *D* is present, in other words, $D \perp\!\!\!\perp DPI \mid \{ET, EC\}$. Given the Markov condition, therefore, we can conclude that *DPI* is not a direct cause of *D*. We could also formulate this table as a Boolean equation like those considered in the foregoing section by coding the outcome as a "yes" or "no" depending on whether or not the probability that *D* is present is greater than .5. Then an application of Ragin's methods would yield the Boolean equation D = $\overline{ET}\,\overline{EC}$, that is, *D* is expected to be present when and only when both *ET* and *EC* are absent. Again, this yields the result that *DPI* does not directly impact *D*. In addition, interpreting Ragin's use of Boolean minimization in terms of Bayes nets has the significant advantage of clarifying just what causal inferences could be justified by such an analysis and under what circumstances. For example, one might be tempted to conclude from Figure 13.3 that *DPI* has no effect on *D* whatever. However, the table provides no basis for such an inference because it does not rule out the possibility that *DPI indirectly* impacts *D* through *ET* or *EC*. For example, the DAG in Figure 13.2 predicts that $D \perp\!\!\!\perp DPI \mid \{ET, EC\}$ but nevertheless says that $DPI \rightarrow EC \rightarrow D$. Thus, the most we can infer from Figure 13.3 is that *DPI* is not a *direct* cause of *D*; it might be an indirect cause or it might be no cause at all. Moreover, from Figure 13.3 alone, we cannot conclude that *ET* and *EC* are causes of *D*, since the data in that table could be explained by *D* causing *ET* and *EC* or by the existence of an unmeasured common cause. Thus, the procedures for case-based causal reasoning recommended by Ragin are trustworthy methods for identifying direct causes only when (1) the potential causes are not effects of the outcome variable, and (2) the outcome and potential causes are not common effects of unmeasured variables.[6] Of course, failures of (1) and (2) are challenges for causal inference generally, not only for case-oriented approaches. But that is merely an expectable consequence of the fact that these challenges can be explained in terms of the Markov condition and are independent of the particular choice of model.

The discussion in the previous paragraph relied on only consequences 1 and 2 of the Markov condition, but not consequence 3. Recall that consequence 3 asserted that conditioning on a collider may induce probabilistic dependence. This idea is closely related to something known as "selection bias." Consider the following example of selection bias provided in *DSI*.

Suppose we believe that American investment in third world countries is a prime cause of internal violence, and then we select a set of nations with major US investments in which there has been a good deal of internal violence and another set of nations in which there is neither investment nor violence. (1994: 128)

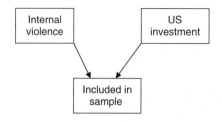

Figure 13.4   An example of selection bias.

In this example, there are three variables at play – internal violence, US investment, and inclusion in the sample – that are related as depicted in Figure 13.4. In Figure 13.4, inclusion in the sample is a collider, since it is an effect of both internal violence and US investment. That is, the researcher's decision about which nations to include in the sample is heavily impacted by the values of these two variables. And as nations not included in the sample are not considered, the researcher is effectively conditioning on a single value of that collider. Hence, from consequence 3, we can infer that there may be a correlation between internal violence and US investment in this sample even if there is no causal connection between them. Notice that if there were indeed no causal connection between internal violence and US investment, then the Markov condition would entail that these two variables would be probabilistically independent in a sample that was not subject to selection bias.

The upshot of the discussion in this section is that a number of central points of methodology of causal inference, such as those having to do with unmeasured common causes and selection bias, stem from very general considerations about the relationship between causality and probability articulated by the Markov condition. Such considerations, therefore, can be expected to be relatively insensitive to the researcher's choice of causal model, whether it is linear, Boolean or something else entirely. In contrast, some methodological considerations are closely tied to specific modeling assumptions. For example, the use of the method of instrumental variables to estimate a causal effect

depends crucially on the assumption that causal relationships are represented by linear equations. The main theme of this section is that Bayes nets constitute a good framework for understanding model-general aspects of causal inference and thereby can be reasonably regarded as an underlying logic of causal inference.

MECHANISMS AND CAUSAL INFERENCE

Like case-oriented researchers, advocates of social mechanisms also contrast their approach with "variable-centered" social science (Hëdstrom and Swedberg, 1998: 15–17). Proponents claim that mechanisms are a needed and effective means for addressing challenges that confront causal inference in social science, especially problems arising from unmeasured common causes (Elster, 1983: 47–8; Hedström and Swedberg, 1998: 9; Little, 1991: 24–5). Elsewhere I have argued that mechanism proponents have not adequately explained how attention to social mechanisms can alleviate these genuine challenges for causal inference (Steel, 2004). In this section, I discuss the concept of a social mechanism and then explain how, as I see it, attention to mechanisms can assist causal inference in social science.

Mechanisms in general are characterized as sets of entities and activities organized so as to produce a regular series of changes from a beginning state to an ending one (Machamer et al., 2000). Social mechanisms in particular are usually thought of as complexes of interactions among agents that underlie and account for macro-social regularities (cf. Little, 1991: 13; Schelling, 1998: 33; Stinchcombe, 1991: 367). The paradigm example of an agent is an individual person, but coordinated groups of individuals motivated by common objectives – such as a corporation, a government bureau, or a charitable organization – may also be treated as agents for certain purposes (cf. Mayntz, 2004: 248).

Social mechanisms typically involve some categorization of agents into relevantly similar groups defined by a salient position their members occupy with respect to others in the society (cf. Little, 1998: 17; Mayntz, 2004: 250–2). In the description of the mechanism, the relevant behavior of an agent is often assumed to be a function of the group into which he or she is classified. For example, consider the anthropologist Bronislaw Malinowski's (1935) account of how having more wives was a cause of increased wealth among Trobriand chiefs. Among the Trobrianders, men were required to make substantial annual contributions of yams to the households of their married sisters. Hence, the more wives a man had, the more yams he would receive. Yams, meanwhile, were the primary form of wealth in Trobriand society, and served to finance such chiefly endeavors as canoe building and warfare. Although individuals play a prominent role in this account, they do so as representatives of social categories: brothers-in-law, wives, and chiefs. The categorization of component entities into functionally defined types is not unique to social mechanisms. Biological mechanisms are often described using such terms as "enzyme" and "co-receptor". The terms "enzyme" and "co-receptor" resemble "chief" and "brother-in-law" in virtue of being functional: all of these terms provide some information about what role the designated thing plays in the larger system of which it is a part. In sum, social mechanisms can be characterized as follows. Social mechanisms are complexes of interacting agents – usually classified into specific social categories – that produce regularities among macro level variables.

This characterization of a social mechanism can be illustrated by another, more well known example. Consider Thomas Schelling's bounded-neighborhood model, which is intended to account for persistent patterns of segregated housing in spite of increased racial tolerance (Schelling, 1978: 155–166). In this model, the residents of a given neighborhood are divided into two

mutually exclusive groups (e.g. black and white). Each individual prefers to remain in the neighborhood, provided that the proportion of his or her own group does not drop below a given threshold, which may vary from person to person. Meanwhile, there is a set of individuals outside the neighborhood who may choose to move in if the proportions are to their liking. Clearly, this model divides individuals into groups with which characteristic preferences and subsequent behavioral patterns are associated, and by these means accounts for macro regularities.

Advocates of social mechanisms are motivated in large measure by concerns about the possibility that a correlation may be due to an unmeasured common cause rather than a direct causal influence, a difficulty sometimes referred to as 'spurious correlation' (cf Elster, 1983: 47). This was one of the general challenges for causal inference described in the foregoing section, and it is directly tied to the fact that the Markov condition allows that a probabilistic dependence between X and Y can be explained by X being a cause of Y, Y being a cause of X, or the presence of some third variable that is a cause of both (or any combination of these possibilities). Thus, in social science research it is often difficult to rule out the possibility that a correlation between variables is explained by a common cause that was not measured, and hence difficult to provide strong evidence of a genuine causal impact. An elucidation of underlying mechanisms – sometimes called *process tracing* – is suggested by mechanism advocates as a solution to this difficulty.

In order to properly understand process tracing, it is important to be clear about its intended contrast. It is sometimes said that process tracing is utterly distinct from methods that endeavor to draw causal inferences from statistical data. For example, Alexander George and Andrew Bennett write that, "Process-tracing is fundamentally different from methods based on covariance or comparisons across cases" (2005: 207). Yet it is difficult to see how this could be so if process-tracing is to enable one to establish claims about cause and effect (Steel, 2008: 185–7). That is because merely listing a sequence of contiguous events is not sufficient to demonstrate causation. After all, how are we to know that the events in the sequence are related as cause and effect rather than as mere coincidences? The most straightforward answer to this question is that we distinguish between causal and coincidental sequences of events on the basis of prior knowledge of what, in general, causes what. For example, I infer that being bitten by mosquitoes in Mali caused Joe's malaria because of my belief, in general, that mosquitoes in tropical climates are vectors of the *Plasmodium* protozoan that causes malaria. But if that is right, then it seems that process tracing already assumes a solution to very problem that mechanism advocates claim it can solve. That is, in order to use mechanisms to support causal inferences we already need to have a good deal of causal knowledge.

I suggest that a more adequate explanation of how process tracing is helpful for addressing challenges for causal inference depends on a better understanding of its proper contrast. The appropriate distinction is not between one method that relies on statistical data and another that can proceed independently of such information. Rather, the distinction is between what I call direct and indirect causal inference. Direct causal inference attempts to infer the causal relationships among a set of variables by examining the probabilistic relations among *those same* variables. By contrast, indirect causal inference attempts to learn the causal relationships among a set of variables by examining the causal relations among a *distinct yet related* set. In process tracing, the distinct yet related variables represent features of component parts of the larger system of interest.

The usefulness of process tracing, then, rests on the possibility that the causal relationships among the components are more directly accessible than those among the macro-features of the system. Let us consider this idea in more detail.

Suppose that one is interested in the causal relationships among a set of variables **V** that represent macro-features of a system S. The system might be an economy, an organism, or a machine. The variables in **V** might represent such things as inflation and unemployment if S is an economy or mosquito bites and malaria if S is a person. One strategy for learning about the causal relationships among the variables in **V** is by means of statistical data concerning those variables. I call this *direct causal inference* (or *direct inference* for short), since the strategy focuses directly on the variables of interest and the probabilistic relations among them. Direct inference can be represented schematically as follows depicted in Figure 13.5. For example, suppose that **V** contains variables representing federal deficits, inflation, economic growth, interest rates, and unemployment. Suppose, moreover, that the chief concern is to estimate the effect of federal deficits on economic growth. Then direct causal inference might proceed by comparing carefully matched periods that differ with respect to federal deficits. Attempting to infer the causal relationships among the variables in **V** from statistical data concerning them together with the Markov condition would also fall into the category of direct causal inference.

Process tracing does not focus directly upon the statistical relationships among the variables in **V**, but rather upon the components of S and their configuration. This can be depicted schematically as shown in

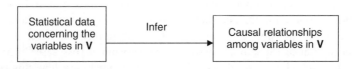

Figure 13.5   Direct causal inference.

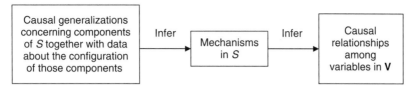

Figure 13.6   Process tracing as indirect causal inference.

Figure 13.6. Of course, direct inference and process tracing are not mutually exclusive: both could contribute to knowledge of the causal relationships among the variables in **V**.[7] Moreover, direct inference will almost certainly be an important source of knowledge of causal generalizations concerning the components. However, that inference would involve a set of variables distinct from **V**. Let **C** be a set of variables representing features of the components. Process tracing, then, exploits the possibility that the causal relationships among **C** may be more easily learned than those among **V**. One way this could be is if it is possible to perform experiments on the components, but not the system as a whole. For example, experimental economists can perform randomized experiments involving individuals or small groups but not entire economies. Similarly, ethical considerations prohibit an experiment in which humans are exposed to malarial mosquitoes, yet it is possible to experimentally study, say, the transmission and action of the *Plasmodium* protozoan in animal models or in vitro. Even when experiments cannot be performed on the component parts of the system, there may be better observational data with regard to the relevant features of the components than for the system as a whole, for instance, larger samples of more accurately measured data. Or it may be that the possible confounders have been more exhaustively listed and measured with regard to the components than for the macro-features of the system. In short, there may be a variety of practical reasons why the causal relationships among the variables in **C** can be more directly ascertained than among those in **V**. And when that happens,

indirect inference is a reasonable approach to pursue.

Process tracing is most easily noticed in research, such as Malinowski's study of the Trobriand Islanders, in which data necessary for direct inference is not available, but examples of process tracing can also be found in conjunction with direct inference. For example, consider John Donohue and Steven Levitt's (2001) essay, "The impact of legalized abortion on crime." Donohue and Levitt argue that the legalization of abortion in the United States following the 1973 *Roe v. Wade* decision is the most significant factor responsible for the decline in US crime rates in the 1990s. Although it may seem surprising that legalizing abortion could affect crime rates two decades later, Donohue and Levitt suggest a plausible mechanism linking the two (2001: 386–9). A woman chooses to have an abortion when the child would be unwanted, for example, because she would be unable to adequately care for and economically support a child or an additional child. Donohue and Levitt cite a variety of studies that report correlations between being raised in adverse family situations and criminality in early adulthood (2001: 388–9). Thus, Donohue and Levitt propose that the legalization of abortion in 1973 resulted in a birth cohort that, when entering its prime crime age 18 to 24 years later, contained a smaller proportion of individuals disposed to criminal behavior. Donohue and Levitt give several lines of statistical evidence for this hypothesis. For example, they show that the drop in crime rates occurred earlier in states that legalized abortion prior to *Roe v. Wade*, and that the initial decrease occurred in categories of crime disproportionately committed by those in the 18–24 age group (2001: 395–9). Not only does Donohue and Levitt's study illustrate the combination between process tracing and causal inference based on statistical data, it also illustrates the role of statistical data in process tracing itself. For example, the causal generalization that unwanted children are more likely to engage in criminal activity upon entering adulthood is obviously a proposition that must be tested by reference to statistical data.

Moreover, Donohue and Levitt's study illustrates how a closer approximation of experimental data might be attainable with regard to the mechanism than for the system as a whole. Some studies on the effects upon criminality of being an unwanted child focused on locations in which governmental approval was required before an abortion was allowed, as was once the case in some parts of Scandinavia and Eastern Europe (2001: 388). These studies found higher rates of criminal activity among children born to women who requested but were denied access to abortions than among the children of women of similar socioeconomic status who did not request abortions. These studies amount to a natural experiment involving an intervention directly on the proposed cause, namely, access to abortion among women who desire to have one. The closest thing to a quasi-experiment at the macro-level is Donohue and Levitt's comparison between earlier and later legalizing states, which found that the early legalizing states (Alaska, Hawaii, California, Washington, New York) experienced a correspondingly earlier drop in crime rates. However, as Donohue and Levitt point out, the early legalizing states also differed in some other potentially relevant respects such as the rate of abortions after *Roe v. Wade* (2001: 395–6). In addition, the small number of early legalizing states and the relatively small number of states altogether would make a statistical analysis more tentative. Thus, this example illustrates the point made above that, for a variety of reasons, data might allow for more firm conclusions concerning the causal

relationships at the level of mechanisms than at the level of the system as a whole. In such circumstances, indirect inference is a reasonable approach to pursue in attempting to establish a causal claim. Of course, it does not follow from this that process tracing is always necessary or even helpful for causal inference in social science. In some cases, the data may support a strong conclusion on the basis of direct inference alone and in some cases data needed for process tracing may be largely absent. But I think it is fair to say that process tracing, understood as indirect causal inference, is an important strategy for supporting causal conclusions in social science.

CONCLUSION

Learning about the causes and effects of social phenomena is an important but very difficult task. This chapter has described three approaches to studying causation that are found in social science: variable-, case-, and mechanism-oriented research. My aim has been to clarify the relationships among these three approaches. I suggested that variable- and case-oriented research can be fruitfully considered in terms of their association with distinct types of causal models – linear and Boolean equations, respectively – that nevertheless share some important features that are articulated in Bayes nets approaches to causation. The distinction between model-specific and model-general aspects of causal inference, I propose, is a useful basis for understanding the idea that a shared logic underlies these two approaches. Finally, I considered the claim that mechanisms play an essential role in overcoming challenges to causal inference in variable- and case-oriented research, such as the existence of unmeasured common causes. I suggested that this claim is best understood by reference to what I call indirect causal inference. Tracing mechanisms differs not in eschewing any reliance on statistical data; instead process tracing works by focusing attention on a distinct but related set of variables for which better data may be available.

NOTES

1. There are many interesting issues concerning causation and modeling in social science that I do not address in this essay. For instance, I will not consider the issue of whether models should be construed as definitions of complex predicates that may or may not be satisfied in particular cases (Hausman, 1992: 70–83), or as elucidations of the workings of a capacity in the ideal circumstance in which no interference is present (Cartwright, 1999), or as heuristics that indicate fruitful hypotheses to be tested (Alexandrova, 2008). Similarly, I will not discuss the foundations for principles connecting probability causality, such as the causal Markov condition, commonly assumed in Bayes nets (cf. Hausman, 1998; Steel, 2005).

2. Minimization is based on the fact that P is logically equivalent to the disjunction P and Q, or P and not-Q. For example, if Joe has red hair, then either he has red hair and green eyes, or he has red hair and does not have green eyes. And conversely, if we know that Joe either has red hair and green eyes or he has red hair and does not have green eyes, then we know that he has red hair.

3. Bayes nets approaches to causal systems that include cycles have also been developed (see Richardson and Spirtes, 1999).

4. Notice that the definition of directed path entails that any sequence containing only one node is a directed path, since in that case the requirement that each pair X_i and X_{i+1} is linked by an arrow pointing directly from X_i to X_{i+1} is trivially satisfied. Thus, every node in a DAG counts as a descendant of itself. This seemingly odd feature of the definitions is deliberate and facilitates the statement of the Markov condition.

5. In fact, structural equation modeling is an alternative format to DAGs for representing causal structures (Pearl, 2000; Hoover, 2001).

6. Conditions (1) and (2) are similar to Mackie's (1974) requirement of 'causal priority,' which he proposed as a qualification to his INUS theory of causation. As both Ragin's and Mackie's proposals are elaborations of Mill's (1851) methods of agreement and difference, it is not surprising that the two would be confronted by similar difficulties.

7. Danks (2005) gives an interesting normative proposal for how conclusions about the causal relationships among distinct yet related sets of variables can be integrated within a Bayes nets framework.

REFERENCES

Alexandrova, A. (2008) 'Making models count', *Philosophy of Science*, 75: 383–404.

Angrist, J., G. Imbens and D. Rubin (1996) 'Identification of causal effects using instrumental variables', *Journal of the American Statistical Association*, 91: 444–455.

Brady, H. and D. Collier (eds) (2004) *Rethinking Social Inquiry: Diverse Tools, Shared Standards*. New York, NY: Rowman and Littlefield Publishers, Inc.

Cartwright, N. (1999) *The Dappled World*. Cambridge: Cambridge University Press.

Danks, D. (2005) 'Scientific coherence and the fusion of experimental results', *British Journal for the Philosophy of Science*, 56: 791–808.

Donohue, J. and S. Levitt (2001) 'The impact of legalized abortion on crime', *Quarterly Journal of Economics*, 116: 379–420.

Elster, J. (1983) *Explaining Technological Change: A Case Study in the Philosophy of Science*. Cambridge: Cambridge University Press.

George, A. and A. Bennett (2005) *Case Studies and Theory Development in the Social Sciences*. Cambridge, MA: MIT Press.

Hausman, D. (1992) *The Inexact and Separate Science of Economics*. Cambridge: Cambridge University Press.

Hausman, D. (1998) *Causal Asymmetries*. Cambridge: Cambridge University Press.

Hedström, P. and R. Swedberg (eds) (1998) *Social Mechanisms: An Analytical Approach to Social Theory*. Cambridge: Cambridge University Press.

Hoover, K. (2001) *Causality in Macroeconomics*. Cambridge: Cambridge University Press.

King, G., R. Keohane and S. Verba (1994) *Designing Social Inquiry: Scientific Inference in Qualitative Research*. Princeton, NJ: Princeton University Press.

Lleras-Muney, A. (2005) 'The relationship between education and adult mortality in the United States', *Review of Economic Studies*, 72: 189–221.

Little, D. (1991) *Varieties of Social Explanation: An Introduction to the Philosophy of Social Science*. Boulder, CO: Westview Press.

Little, D. (1998) *Microfoundation, Method, and Causation*. New Brunswick, NJ: Transaction Publishers.

Machamer, P., L. Darden and C. Craver (2000) 'Thinking about mechanisms', *Philosophy of Science*, 67: 1–25.

Mackie, J.L. (1974) *The Cement of the Universe*. Oxford: Oxford University Press.

Malinowski, B. (1935) *Coral Gardens and Their Magic*. New York: American Book Co.

Mayntz, R. (2004) 'Mechanisms in the analysis of social macro-phenomena', *Philosophy of the Social Sciences*, 34: 237–259.

McKeown, T. (2004) 'Case studies and the limits of the quantitative worldview', in H. Brady and D. Collier (eds) *Rethinking Social Inquiry: Diverse Tools, Shared Standards*. New York, NY: Rowman and Littlefield Publishers, Inc. pp. 139–168.

Mill, J.S. (1851) *A System of Logic, Ratiocinative and Deductive: Being a Connected View of the Principles of Evidence and the Methods of Scientific Investigation*, 3rd edition. London: John W. Parker.

Neopolitan, R. (2004) *Learning Bayesian Networks*. Upper Saddle River, NJ: Prentice Hall.

Pearl, J. (2000) *Causality: Models, Reasoning, and Inference*. Cambridge: Cambridge University Press.

Popper, K. (1959) *The Logic of Scientific Discovery*. New York: Routledge.

Ragin, C. (1987) *The Comparative Method: Moving Beyond Qualitative and Quantitative Strategies*. Berkeley, CA: University of California Press.

Ragin, C. (2004) 'Turning the tables: How case-oriented research challenges variable-oriented research', in H. Brady and D. Collier (eds) *Rethinking Social Inquiry: Diverse Tools, Shared Standards*. New York, NY: Rowman and Littlefield Publishers, Inc. pp. 123–138.

Rasler, K. and W. Thompson (2004) 'The democratic peace and a sequential, reciprocal, causal arrow hypothesis', *Comparative Political Studies*, 37(8): 879–908.

Richardson, T. and P. Spirtes (1999) 'Automated discovery of linear feedback models', in Glymour C. and Cooper G. (eds), Computation, Causation, and Discovery. Cambridge, MA: MIT Press. pp. 253–302.

Roe v. Wade, (1973) 410 U.S. 113.

Schelling, T. (1978) *Micromotives and Macrobehavior*. New York: W. W. Norton and Co.

Schelling, T. (1998) 'Social mechanisms and social dynamics', in Hedström, P. and R. Swedberg (eds) *Social Mechanisms: An Analytical Approach to Social Theory*. Cambridge: Cambridge University Press. pp. 32–44.

Spirtes, P., C. Glymour and R. Scheines (2000) *Causation, Prediction, and Search*, 2nd edition. Cambridge, MA: MIT Press.

Steel, D. (2004) 'Causal inference and social mechanisms', *Philosophy of the Social Sciences*, 34(1): 55–78.

Steel, D. (2005) 'Indeterminism and the causal Markov condition', *British Journal for the Philosophy of Science*, 56: 3–26.

Steel, D. (2008) *Across the Boundaries: Extrapolation in Biology and Social Science*. New York: Oxford University Press.

Stinchcombe, A. (1991) 'The conditions of fruitfulness of theorizing about mechanisms in social science', *Philosophy of the Social Sciences*, 21: 367–388.

PART 3

A Philosopher's Guide to Social Science Paradigms

14

Rational Choice Theory

Cédric Paternotte

INTRODUCTION

An individual has to choose between different courses of action, the consequences of which she is uncertain about. How should she choose? We now observe her choice. How can we make sense of it? Those are the two questions that rational choice theory (RCT) aims to answer. They correspond to the traditional philosophical distinction between taking a normative or a descriptive stance. Ideally, any theory of rational choice should take both, that is, first, tell us what choices we should make in any given situation, and second, enable us to find out what behaviour can be called rational. The normative answer that RCT provides can be expressed by the following slogan: an agent should choose the course of action that leads to what she thinks are the best consequences. In other words, RCT relies on the fundamental tenet that agents should make *optimal* choices.[1] As for the descriptive part, RCT tells us that an agent's observed behaviour can be called rational as soon as we find out how she could see it as optimal.

A few preliminary remarks are in order. First, the RCT slogan makes it obvious that it is a consequentialist (or instrumental) theory. Courses of actions are evaluated solely in terms of the results they bring about. At first glance, this excludes cases where agents choose an action because they believe it is intrinsically good, for instance when it is prescribed by moral principles or when it has been ordered by someone the agent defers to.

Second, the explanations that RCT provides are predicated on only two types of mental states: beliefs and desires. An agent's needs to estimate the various consequences of her available actions, which correspond to her having beliefs about the state of the world. She also needs to evaluate and rank outcomes, which correspond to her having desires, or preferences, about every possible consequence of her actions.

Third, the agent's desires and beliefs are posited from the start and are not supposed to be open to discussion. Extremely idiosyncratic desires or erroneous beliefs should not be excluded; whether an agent is deemed rational or not depends on how she makes decisions on the basis of her desires and beliefs, not on how she came to entertain them in the first place.[2]

Fourth and consequently, that an agent is rational from RCT's point of view does not mean that the course of action she will choose is *objectively* optimal. Desires do not have to align with any objective measure of 'goodness': I may want to risk swimming in a crocodile-infested lake; I may desire to smoke or drink even though I know it harms me. Optimality is determined by the agent's desires, not the converse. Beliefs may be approximately true or even false; I may swim or smoke because I am simply ignorant of the danger. In a nutshell, objective optimality does not constrain choice at least because I may not desire the best option or fail to identify it.

Fifth, RCT does not presuppose that agents are self-interested or egoist, except in the sense that their choices are based on their own desires. This does not entail that an agent cannot desire what is good for someone else, or for a group. RCT does not exclude social or altruistic preferences. An agent can care about anything, from the extra payoff that he gets as compared to others, to the average gain of all.[3]

There is no such thing as a unique theory of rational choice, but rather one dominant paradigm with a host of refinements, variants and replacements or alternative paradigms. One basic distinction is to be made between decision theory and game theory. Decision theory deals with situations in which an isolated agent is uncertain of the consequences of her actions because she is uncertain of the state of the actual world. Suppose I am invited to a dinner and that I have to bring something to eat or drink and that I want to please my host. I may hesitate between bringing, say, starters, wine or dessert if I ignore what she has already taken care of herself.

Game theory deals with situations of *interaction*, where agents are uncertain of the consequences of their actions because those consequences also depend on the actions of others. Suppose I am invited to a dinner with several other unknown persons, that I know each of us has to bring something to eat or drink and that I want to bring something different from the others; I may hesitate between bringing starters, wine or dessert if I do not know what the others are bringing (knowing that others face a similar situation and have to make a choice too).

Why is this distinction fundamental? After all, from any given agent's point of view, others could be considered as part of a more general context in which she simply faces a decision problem. However, it is not the mere presence and actions of others that matters; it is the fact that everyone interacts, that is, that outcomes of *combinations* of actions now have to be considered. In a situation of interaction, the choices of all agents are intertwined and depend on each other. As a result, game theory must discover sets of choices that are *mutually* optimal.

Decision theory is a fascinating field to which an enormous amount of literature has been devoted. Understandably, this brief chapter can only scratch the surface and gesture towards its most flourishing regions. Our plan will be as follows. The next two sections will respectively introduce decision theory and game theory, as well as some specific problems each of them faces. The last section will then move on to the numerous philosophical issues raised by RCT in general.

DECISION THEORY

Formalism

As we have seen, decision theory is interested in choices an agent must make in situations of external uncertainty, that is, where the agent's choice has no causal effect on this uncertainty. Formally, decision theory studies situations defined in the following way. A decision problem faced by an agent consists of:

- A set of available courses of action, called *acts* or *alternatives*, among which the agent has to choose (e.g. to bring starters, wine or dessert).
- A set of *states of the world*, that express the different contexts or the way nature evolves (e.g. the host may prefer alcohol, sweets or salad). They are used to express the uncertainty of the agent; to be uncertain is to not know what the actual state of the world is.
- A set of *consequences*; a consequence is what happens when a specific alternative is chosen in a given state of the world. So a consequence can be simply understood as a pair (alternative, state

of the world) (e.g. to bring dessert when the host prefers alcohol).

- A *utility function* that assigns a numerical value to every possible consequence. It expresses the agent's desires, or preferences regarding what may happen. Utilities can usually be represented by matrices such as that in Table 14.1.

The above matrix can be interpreted like this: my utility is composed of one component corresponding to my personal taste (2 for wine, 1 for sweets, 0 for salad) and another corresponding to my caring that I bring what the host prefers (5 if I bring that, else 0).[4]A *probability measure* defined over the states of the world,[5] it expresses my degree of belief that each state may be the case (e.g. I believe with a degree 0.6 that the host prefers salad, 0.3 that she prefers sweets, 0.1 that she prefers alcohol).

How should an agent choose an optimal course of action when facing such a problem? Decision theory's answer is that she should choose the alternative that *maximises her expected utility*. The expected utility of an alternative is the weighted sum of the utilities of its possible consequences, where the weights are the probabilities pertaining to the relevant state of the worlds. For instance, the expected utility of my bringing starters is $0.6 \times 5 + 0.3 \times 0 + 0.1 \times = 3$; similarly, the expected utility for bringing dessert or wine is 2.5.[6] The maximisation of expected utility (MEU) principle thus says that it would be rational for me to bring starters.

Fundamental issues

The way RCT was introduced in the previous section makes clear why we need to take into account alternatives, states of the world and consequences. However, it may be puzzling that utility functions and probability measures, which seem to complicate the description of a decision problem, are necessary. Of course, they are needed for calculations of expected utilities, but the problem here is precisely to justify the MEU principle.

Utility functions

Let us start with the utility functions. The simplest way to represent an agent's desires or preferences does not seem to be to attribute numerical values to consequences but to rank them. This would amount to saying that the agent prefers above all to bring wine when the host prefers alcohol; that the next consequence he prefers is when she brings dessert and the host prefers sweets; and so on. It is indeed more economical; rankings can always be inferred from numerical values (as we just saw), but the converse is false. Moreover, attributing specific numbers to consequences seems artificial.

But first, most often mere rankings won't be enough. Say that action X can have consequences A or B with equal probability; that action Y can have consequences C or D with equal probability; and that I prefer A to C, but B to D. There is just no way to choose between A and B (it would not make sense to talk of expected preference). Secondly, it can be proved[7] that it is equivalent to assign a preference ranking over consequences or to assign them values through a utility function, as soon as the ranking possesses three elementary properties (the preferences are then said to be represented by the utility function). The two interesting properties among those three are *transitivity* (if I prefer A to B and B to C, then I must prefer A to C); and *completeness* (for any actions A and B, I have to prefer one of them to the other).[8] Respecting transitivity means that my choices are consistent, respecting completeness means that all the things I could have to choose between are commensurable.

Are those properties problematic? Transitivity will fail if I sometimes prefer

Table 14.1 Matrix of utilities

Acts	States		
	Host prefers salad	Host prefers sweets	Host prefers alcohol
Bring starters	5	0	0
Bring wine	1	6	1
Bring dessert	2	2	7

strawberries to apples, sometimes apples to oranges, and sometimes oranges to strawberries. But such cases often depend on the context (what I have eaten before, or my mood), that is, on the state of the world. Transitivity may also fail in cases of vagueness; I may prefer to have hair rather than to be bald, but not have any preference between having N or $N + 1$ hair (for any value of N). Completeness is slightly less compelling and will fail any time an agent cannot compare two consequences, for instance when they share no common aspect. But at least when consequences concern things of similar kinds, or even better, money, completeness is a reasonable assumption.

Another pair of objections targets the fact that utility functions assign precise numerical values to consequences. First, it seems psychologically implausible. But the fact that a preference ranking can be represented by a utility function does not mean that the latter is unique. The same theorem shows that if a utility function fits, multiplying it by any constant, or adding any constant to it, will result in another utility function that fits just as well. If I prefer A to B, I can respectively represent A and B by any values x and y as long as $x \geq y$. So the specific values are less important than the objection suggests. Second, it seems that on the contrary, in situations where the consequences only differ in terms of money for instance, only one utility function is acceptable, namely the one that coincides with the monetary values (or agent material payoffs). But the St Petersburg paradox shows that material payoffs are not always suitable. Consider a game in which a coin is repeatedly tossed until the result is heads; the payoff is $2 if the coin comes up heads on the first toss, $4 if it does on the second toss, $8 on the third, and so on. The expected *payoff* of this game is infinite, which means that if an agent's utility coincided with her payoff she should be ready to pay any finite amount of money in return for playing the game. This is particularly implausible. As a result, even if utility

functions and monetary payoffs are linked, they cannot be identical.

Beliefs

Let us now turn to beliefs. As in the case of utility functions, it may seem strange that beliefs admit precise numerical degrees and behave like probabilities. The idea that beliefs admit degrees is rather uncontroversial; when we do not know something, we can still be more or less certain that it is the case. But how can we measure those degrees? Ramsey (1926) offered a characterisation of such beliefs in terms of betting behaviour, which itself relies on the idea of expected utility. Consider the bet where you receive X if an event E happens, and have to pay Y if it does not. Ramsey's idea is that the degree of your belief that E will happen is the probability such that the bet is fair – that its expected value is 0.[9] It is debatable whether this is a reliable way to measure actual degrees of belief. But Ramsey's result went further. Call a Dutch Book a combination of bets where the better looses money whatever happens.[10] Ramsey established that one whose beliefs follow the axioms of probability[11] can never fall prey to a Dutch Book, and that for anyone whose beliefs do not follow those axioms there exists a Dutch Book to which she would fall prey. In short, (probabilistic) degrees of beliefs make sense in terms of (rational) betting behaviour.

One important assumption of decision theory is that states of the world are independent of alternatives; as a consequence, the probability measure corresponding to beliefs is defined over states of the world, not over consequences themselves. Consider the following decision problem. I can either choose to study or not before an exam (alternatives); I will either pass or fail the exam (states of the world). Whatever my choice is, I prefer to pass than to fail; but whatever the result is, I prefer to save the effort of studying. So I should choose not to study, regardless of the probabilities that I pass or fail. The answer is absurd because the decision problem is ill defined; the probabilities that I pass or fail depend on whether I study or not, so in this example beliefs were actually defined over outcomes. Beliefs should only be defined over states of the world, at least in order to avoid such ill-formed decision problems where actions causally influence states of the world.

Another assumption is that beliefs and desires are independent of each other. They are supposed to be unrelated and even complement one another in a sense. Beliefs have a mind-to-world direction of fit – what we believe should correspond to how the world is. Desires have a world-to-mind direction of fit – the world should become as they prescribe. Beliefs aim at being true; desires concern what one would like to be true. In theory, there is no reason why they should influence each other rather than being independent causal factors of human behaviour, however, several counter-examples jeopardise this assumption. Wishful thinking refers to cases where we tend to bend our beliefs to our desires, such as when we come to believe that something we desire is achievable whereas it is actually out of reach. In such cases, a fundamental desire constrains the set of beliefs we can adopt. In the sour grapes fable, the fox decides that it does not want the grapes after discovering it cannot reach them. Here, acquiring a new belief (the grapes are unreachable) seems to trigger a change of preference.

Representation theorems

The main objection regarding the MEU principle is that it is downright unrealistic. In most situations, people do not have the cognitive capacities or the time to actually compute the expected utility of every alternative. Even if they did, and even if belief admits degrees and preferences expressed by numerical values, it seems that we hardly ever accomplish those calculations consciously. How could the MEU principle then be justified?

Several technical results called *representation theorems* aim to quell this worry. They show that if an agent's choices (or preferences for *alternatives*) satisfy certain properties, there exists a probability measure and a utility function such that the agent behaves *as if* she was maximising expected utility.[12] So preferences with certain properties can be *represented* by expected utility.[13] Such results confer upon decision theory both normative strength and descriptive benefits; they justify expected utility by the particular properties it induces for preferences of alternatives, and they make possible its detection from observing agents' choices, rather than from measuring internal states.

There are two main representation theorems. The first one, due to von Neumann and Morgenstern (1944), concerns preferences about *lotteries*. Given a set of outcomes, a lottery is just a probability measure defined over a finite number of outcomes (for instance, gaining 10 with probability 0.4 and 3 with probability 0.6). Consider the set of all lotteries definable from a set of outcomes. There exists a utility function such that preferences over the set of lotteries can be represented by expected utility,[14] if and only if those preferences have the following properties: *completeness*, *transitivity*, *continuity* and *independence* (the first two have already been discussed).

Continuity is a technical axiom that we shall not discuss here. Independence, on the other hand, is simple and crucial. Independence states that my preference about a couple of lotteries is preserved if I combine both of them with some additional lottery. In other words, modifying every option of a decision problem by adding to them the possibility of another outcome should not lead me to modify my choice. If I have to choose between two things, adding something identical to both should not influence my choice.

The second theorem is due to Savage (1954). It is formulated in the vocabulary of outcomes, states of the world and acts (defined as functions that associate each state of the world to a consequence). It states that for every preference relation over acts that satisfy certain axioms, there exists both a probability measure and a utility function such that the preferences can be represented by the derived expected utility. The limited space of this chapter excludes a discussion of Savage's axioms, some of which are very technical. Let us just mention that they include completeness and transitivity again, as well as what is called the *sure-thing principle*. Roughly put, it states that if I prefer A to B given one state of the world S, and that both have one same consequence when S is not the case, then I should keep preferring A to B even if that common consequence changes. Whatever the consequences of A and B are when S is not the case, as long as they are identical, my choice between them should stay the same. My choice should be stable when new circumstances leave unchanged the crucial differences between my options. This formulation shows that the sure-thing principle and the independence axiom express the same intuition. This is why they are victims of the same counter-examples, to which we now turn.

Shortcomings

The main objections to decision theory are not so much conceptual as empirical, and cast doubt on the properties of preferences that are necessary for representation theorems to hold. Here, we will just focus on a few main results. The famous Allais paradox can be described as a set of two decision problems, each one asking to choose between two lotteries. It can be represented by Table 14.2.

Most people prefer C_1 to C_2, but also C_4 to C_3. However, It can be proved that whatever someone's utility function is, maximising expected utility should lead one to prefer either both C_1 and C_3, or both C_2 and C_4. These results can be interpreted as saying that people tend to overestimate small probabilities of losses, which makes them prefer C_1 to C_2 contrary to what MEU prescribes. However,

Table 14.2   The Allais paradox

	States		
acts	S_1 ($p^* = 0.89$)	S_2 ($p = 0.1$)	S_3 ($p = 0.01$)
C_1	$1000	$1000	$1000
C_2	$1000	$5000	$0
C_3	$0	$1000	$1000
C_4	$0	$5000	$0

* p = probability

notice that C_3 and C_4 can respectively be obtained from the first C_1 and C_2 in the same way, that is, by replacing one constant consequence[15] by another. Thus formally, agents who prefer both the first and fourth option violate the sure-thing principle.[16]

The Ellsberg paradox is more straightforward but just as destructive of classical decision theory. Imagine an urn containing 30 red balls and 60 black or yellow balls (in an unknown proportion). A ball is about to be randomly drawn. One decision problem asks you to choose between receiving $100 if the ball is red or receiving $100 if it is black. The second problem asks you to choose between receiving $100 if the ball is red or yellow or receiving $100 if it is black or yellow. Most people choose red in the first problem, black or yellow in the second. The interpretation consists in saying that people tend to prefer uncertainty (known probabilities) over risk (unknown probabilities). The probability of getting a red ball (1/3) and that of drawing a black or yellow ball (2/3) are inferred from known numbers, whereas the probability of drawing, say, a red or yellow ball, though it is 2/3 again, is inferred from our ignorance of the exact proportion; we have no reason to favour black over yellow balls. However, this double choice is underpinned by a violation of the sure-thing principle.[17] The Allais and Ellsberg paradoxes both show that one of the key axioms needed for representation theorems is false.

The sheer convincing strength of further counterexamples to decision theory led

Kahneman and Tversky (1979) to suggest an alternative theory, namely prospect theory.[18] Empirical evidence suggests that people routinely overestimate small probabilities (which contradicts the independence axiom) and estimate payoffs depending on reference points, like their current level of wealth, in comparison with which gains and losses of equal worth are valued differently.[19] In reaction to those findings, Kahneman and Tversky's model consists of the following.

- A specific utility function, which increases with payoffs, though more for losses than for gains (people are more sensitive to losses). Moreover, the function is concave (for gains), which expresses the fact that the subjective value of a given gain decreases with the level of wealth.
- A function that distorts probabilities in order to account for subjective biases.

The two functions are then combined in a formula similar to that of expected utility, if not for the fact that utilities are not weighted by probabilities anymore but by coefficients generated by probabilities. This last point is what makes the theory most radically depart from RCT; for as we have seen, any kind of utility function is consistent with RCT. The last part of the fourth section of the paper will go back over the general strategy of fiddling with utility functions to accommodate conflicting empirical data.

GAME THEORY

Compared to decision theory, game theory comes into the picture as soon as agents interact. Chapter 15 already provides a detailed, formal description of game theory, so this extremely short section will be content with mentioning its broad characteristics and one specific conceptual issue.

For the most part, game theory relies on the same set of concepts as decision theory. Agents must choose strategies (equivalent to courses of actions in simple cases) that can have various consequences depending on external conditions; consequences are valued according to utility functions, and agents have beliefs about every aspect of the situation. The external conditions may include states of the world again, but they always consist of (at least) other agents' strategies; the outcomes result from the combination of the strategies of every agent. Everyone's strategy depends on everyone else's. As a result, the solutions proposed by game theory are *equilibria*, and their main property is that of *stability*. At equilibrium, each agent's strategy is optimal given the equilibrium strategies of other agents – it is stable because no one has any incentive to adopt another strategy.

Game theory literature contains countless kinds of equilibrium concepts, depending on the kind of game agents play, the amount and sort of information they receive and various parameters that underlie a given situation. One of game theory's greatest qualities is that it can tackle an impressive variety of problems, many of which are of interest for other social scientists, such as collective action dilemmas. Game theory sheds light on the strategic aspects of threats, punishment, imperfect memories, reputations, incomplete information about agents' types, repeated interactions and so on.[20]

Though the fourth section will tackle several general worries raised by game theory, we will here focus on only one particular characteristic of game theoretic solutions that has been the target of criticisms. Game theoretic solutions are often accused of being far too idealised for any real individual to act accordingly. In particular, the conditions under which theorists can guarantee agents will act according to an equilibrium seem cognitively implausible.[21] The main problem seems to reside in the concept of common knowledge, that is, the epistemic state occurring when all agents know something, know that everyone knows this, know that everyone knows that everyone knows this, and so on. Most equilibria can only be guaranteed by the common knowledge of many things, among which the rationality of all agents. But how could such an epistemic condition ever be realised among a group? Not being able to answer this question would mean that there is no reason to give much credit to game theoretic solutions; individuals may reach them from time to time, but never reliably.

However, a deeper analysis of the concept of common knowledge shows that this is not the source of the problem. That it is formally defined by an infinite number of epistemic propositions does not mean that it can only be reached in this way. Actually, finite alternative definitions exist,[22] which show that common knowledge can arise from many realistic situations. Phenomena such as public announcements, highly salient perceptual cues (shrill sounds, blinding lights), widely watched advertisements, etc., are arguably possible sources of common knowledge. In a nutshell, if game theory solutions are to be criticised, it should not be because of their epistemic requirements, but probably more because of the strong rationality assumption they often necessitate.[23]

RCT THEORY AND SOCIAL SCIENCES

We now turn to the different issues pertaining to RCT and its role in social science. It is fair to say that, although it has proven useful and explanatory in a number of contexts, RCT is far from being accepted by default in most social sciences. The main objections to RCT are that it has too narrow a scope, that its explanatory power is rather limited (and its predictive power even more so), that it does not bring social sciences any closer to natural science and that it should at best be completed by other theories, at worst replaced by them. We now consider such objections in turn.

Structural issues

Many of RCT's issues stem from the limited number of situations it is actually able to deal with, even on its own terms. Boudon (1998) emphasises that the consequentialist side of RCT prevents it from dealing with non-instrumental actions, that is, actions motivated by reasons or principles rather than results. The main worry comes from the fact that actions cannot be straightforwardly separated into instrumental and non-instrumental ones. I may choose an act partly because of its consequences and partly because of what this act means, represents or symbolises. Worse, consider cases where those reasons are opposed, such as when my moral principles prescribe actions that can have harmful consequences for me. RCT provides no convincing way to arbitrate such motivational conflicts. Of course, one could always try to translate the effect of a normative principle by increasing the utility of all its possible consequences. However, most social scientists would question the very assumption that identifies a reason to act with a greater utility, arguing that these are conceptually different. On the other hand, the rational choice theorist could answer that utility only expresses motivation or incentives, and that any reason to act of any kind can be considered as an incentive or a deterrent.

RCT also fails to deliver a definite answer in very simple situations. When several actions have the same, highest expected utility, decision theory offers no further criterion of choice between them. When a game contains multiple equilibria of the same kind, one is as good as another. Usual solutions resort to non-formalised properties[24] such as salience[25] in order to distinguish one equilibrium from the others.

Another criticism stems from the theory itself, although it does not directly concern the MEU principle or game theory. Suppose that you have several preference rankings defined over a given set, corresponding to different criteria of choice or to the preferences of different agents, and that you want to aggregate them into a general preference ranking. In other words, suppose you want to produce one 'general' preference out of several 'individual' preferences. Arrow's theorem states that it will be impossible for this aggregation procedure to simultaneously have several intuitive properties. In other words, it may be impossible to satisfactorily combine preference rankings. The upshot is that even when we have several well defined criteria for rational choice, we may still be unable to reach an acceptable decision.[26]

Some attacks on RCT claim that its strong reliance on external parameters hinders its explanatory power. As we have seen, preferences, desires, beliefs and available information, are usually given from the start and thus left unanalysed; moreover, in game theory the fact that they are common knowledge among agents is presupposed as well, which points to the existence of mechanisms or phenomena that led to this commonality. On the other hand, trying to generate those parameters within the theory may drastically increase the complexity of a model or create unforeseen conceptual issues. For example, Elster (1986) notes that explaining information choice by appealing to some maximisation principles smacks of circularity; in order to choose whether she should get a piece of information, an agent must assess its value, which she cannot do if she does not already have it. Somewhat similarly, trying to explain coordination on one of many equilibria via external tools such as language only begs the question, since language itself is a convention and thus a solution to the coordination problem,[27] which itself demands explanation.

Empirical issues

One of the most common objections made to RCT concerns its alleged feeble empirical adequacy. In numerous situations, people do not act according to utility maximisation or to equilibrium requirements. We have already mentioned several counterexamples to decision theory. The main examples in game theory include the following.

- The prisoner's dilemma (and cooperative dilemmas in general) where the Nash equilibrium prescribes to not cooperate, whereas in experiments a significant proportion of people do indeed cooperate,[28] even in the case of non-repeated anonymous interactions.

- The ultimatum game, where one agent first chooses how to divide a sum of money (say 100 units) between herself and a second agent, who can then only accept or reject; both get nothing if the offer is turned down. Classical game theory says that the second agent should accept any offer that leaves him with 1 unit or more (if he rejected it, he would get only 0). But most individuals typically tend to reject offers under a certain limit.[29]

- The centipede game, where two agents play alternatively and have to share an increasing common sum. At each turn, one agent has to choose either to stop the game and share now, or to allow the sum to increase and to let the other agent decide. The shares are such that if an agent chooses to stop the game, the other one gains less than if he had chosen to stop on the previous turn. So each agent is tempted to let the other play and let the sum increase, unless he is sure enough that the game will stop at the following turn. Classical game theory says that the agent who plays first should stop immediately, which is implausible since she would gain strictly more two or more turns later. Moreover, experiments show that only a small proportion of players stop at the first turn.[30]

If game theory explanation fails even in those elementary cases, chances are slim that it will fare any better in more complex situations, where identifying Nash equilibria is far more demanding anyway. However, these are problems for only classical game theory and there are ways out of each of them, although these involve making the models more complex. Introducing the possibility that players be of different type, that is, they may reason on the basis of 'social' utility functions, can lead to resolutions of all of these problems.[31] The fact that they are still routinely introduced as problems for classical game theory is only meant to highlight the need for developments that came later.

Even then, some more realistic social phenomena seem to be left unexplained by game theory. Consider the classical game-theoretic model of voting behaviour.

Green and Shapiro (1994) notice that voters turnout appears to be a mystery, because costs (transportation, lost time) by far outweigh benefits (possibility that one's preferred candidate is elected, plus some potential psychic gratification from the act of voting). If the act of non-voting dominates voting, why do people bother to vote? Explaining it by positing social preferences only seems to beg the question: why would voters care about the community in the first place? Despite such attacks, it seems that RCT is actually more empirically successful than most would tend to think. Hechter (1997) mentions a host of studies that use a RCT framework to analyse various sociological mechanisms, ranging from influences of wives' opportunities for potential partners on divorce rates, to effects of strict religious views on the commitment of church members, including an analysis of Mafia characteristics as credible commitments that it offers reliable protection services. More generally, any study identifying incentives and deterrents that influence behaviour in a given context is usually consistent with RCT; for any incentive or deterrent can always be interpreted as an increase or a decrease of utility for the associated consequences. The first study of collective action, due to Olson,[32] already emphasised the importance of incentives for solving social dilemmas.

One last, deeper criticism threatens the belief-desire type of explanation itself by contending that there is no clear way to determine an agent's beliefs and desires from her observed behaviour. In other words, beliefs and desires would be underdetermined by observation. Say you observe someone taking their umbrella when it is raining outside: it may be that she does not want to get wet and believes that her umbrella will protect her; or it may be that she wants to get wet and that her umbrella will increase the amount of rain she receives. The person in the latter case appears to be irrational, but her case presents no logical impossibility. Recall Ramsey's measurement of beliefs by way of betting behaviour. What if an agent

is risk-seeking or risk-averse, that is, what if she has preferences regarding risk? She will then tend to accept bets that do not maximise her expected utility; bets will not be an adequate measure of her degrees of belief. Or suppose that we measure beliefs and desires by directly asking questions; to interpret their answers, we would have to suppose that they want to answer cooperate and believe that telling the truth is the best way to achieve this end. In other words, a desire-belief explanation could only be justified in a circular way.

RCT as a law?

As we have seen in the foregoing, RCT provides explanations based on two elementary kinds of mental states, beliefs and desires. The MEU principle, stating that an agent should choose the act that has the highest expected utility, can be considered as just another instance of a more general principle that can be expressed as follows: If an agent desires D and believes that he can fulfil D by doing the action A, then she will do A (DB). This may be a candidate for a law in social sciences. It is well known that though laws abound in natural science, they are rather scarce, not to say non-existent, in social sciences. This is one of the reasons why social sciences tend to be dismissed in comparison with 'real', fully fledged science. Getting our hands on a potential law bodes well for social sciences.

The problem is that DB does not seem to be a law. A law is supposed to be universally true, but we do not always observe that people's actions follow their desires and beliefs. People routinely make mistakes, slip, or are prevented to do what they wish by independent, external events. So it seems that we should reformulate DB by saying that an agent acts according to her desires and beliefs, when nothing else interferes (or all things being equal). Adding this caveat makes DB what is called a *ceteris paribus* law, which only holds in specific circumstances. The problem is that *ceteris paribus* laws seem to have little predictive power. Without being explicit about the circumstances in which the law holds, there is no way to infer any prediction from it in a given situation; if what is observed does not follow the law, it could always be said afterwards that the circumstances were not right to begin with.[33]

Note that *ceteris paribus* laws do not pertain to social sciences alone, and are not necessarily problems in themselves. Cartwright (1983) contends that even laws of natural science are *ceteris paribus*. For instance, the force between two bodies is never identical to what the law of gravitation stipulates – there will always be additional forces present – so we cannot say that the law is universally true. Nonetheless, this does not have to be a serious problem if we can identify the circumstances in which it holds. Cartwright argues that this is the case in natural science, where we can even sometimes build real experimental settings (by properly isolating them and suppressing interfering influences) that behave according to our theoretic laws. This would be impossible if we had no idea what those interferences are.

But in the case of the desire-belief law, we are actually unable to provide a list of all interfering factors. What should we do? We can simply give up the idea that there are laws at the psychological level, and either look for laws or mechanisms of a different kind, or at a different level, or even abandon the concept of laws in social sciences altogether. The first line is followed by advocates of functionalist accounts[34] or evolutionary approaches.[35] The second position is notably held by eliminativists[36] according to whom social science should ultimately get rid of any psychological concepts and focus on the search for neurological laws instead. The last option, which holds that social sciences do not need laws in the first place, is favoured be interpretivists, who think social science does not consist in predicting but in understanding and interpreting behaviours, or finding their meaning. This is not to deny

that there are causal effects in the social realm: Davidson (1980) for instance defends the idea that there can be causality without laws. Interpretivism typically attaches great importance to norms and rules, if not to laws. *DB* can then be salvaged, not as a law anymore, but as a rule that guides us when we interpret the behaviour of others. This echoes Davidson's principle of charity (or rational accommodation), according to which we should, so far as we can, cling to the presupposition that others hold true beliefs when we try to make sense of their actions.

RCT and methodological individualism

One common justification for RCT is that it provides explanations that are consistent with methodological individualism (MI). MI is the thesis that all predictions or explanations of human behaviour should be based on properties of individuals only, rather than resorting to entities or properties at the 'social' level (such as institutions, social norms, mortality rates, classes, etc.) – unless those can themselves be reduced to individual properties. Since RCT ultimately refers only to desires and beliefs, which are mental states of human beings, it can satisfy the methodological individualist.

This chapter cannot tackle the general issue of micro- and macro-level explanations.[37] Let us just notice that the relationship between MI and RCT is not as straightforward as it seems, and it would be a mistake to conflate them. One can have RCT without MI; the agents that face decision problems or games do not have to be human beings. Companies facing competition and market constraints must make rational decisions. At the other end, some theorists have built models in which intertemporal choice can be seen as resulting from the rational interaction of sub-agents,[38] for instance one representing the long-term interests and the other the short-term interests of the agents. RCT can thus be applied both at lower and higher levels than the individual's. As Don Ross (2008) emphasises, the economic agent does not have to coincide with the human individual.

One can also have MI without RCT. Phenomena of cultural transmission, learning, imitation, theory spread and change, innovation, etc. can arguably be understood by mentioning properties of individuals only, though they do not presuppose rational choice. In a nutshell, MI stipulates that our explanations of social phenomena should only mention individual properties, among which individual reasons to act; RCT is about a specific kind of reasons to act, that can be seen as motivating other entities as well.

Another more worrying criticism of RCT is that it *cannot* be consistent with MI, according to an argument already seen at the end of fourth section of the chapter. We have seen that RCT models are built from many external parameters, the origin of which is left unexplained. Desires and beliefs are formed in unknown ways. In particular, game-theoretic concepts such as common knowledge of utility functions and of available information have to originate from some prior social process or phenomena; else why do agents have similar beliefs about the world and each other? In Kincaid's words: 'Game theory explanations are parasitic upon prior social information at every turn.'[39] This is plausible at least, and if this is true, then no rational choice theorist can keep clinging to MI. Even theorists who are very committed to RCT are starting to acknowledge this point.[40]

However, this argument can be seen not as concerning the possibility of explanations compatible with MI, but as pertaining to the level of explanation we desire. That a model leaves some of its parameters unexplained does not mean that their origin could not be tackled by another explanation compatible with MI. It just indicates that such a model may be far too complex to retain any explanatory power. Models focus on specific phenomena while taking others for granted. It may be possible to build a general model that encompasses all social phenomena and

maybe even enjoys predictive success; but it probably would not provide intelligible explanations.[41]

Fiddling with utility functions

Previous sections showed that classical decision and game theory have encountered problems in trying to make sense of observed behaviours in several situations. The way theorists usually overcome those problems is by arguing that agents make choices on the basis of utility functions that are not uniquely determined by their material payoffs. Let us briefly review a few of them.

Regret theory[42] relaxes the assumption that an agent only cares about the consequences of her actions; what she could have obtained had she acted otherwise matters too. In other words, the utility of an outcome could depend on its payoff *and on the payoff of other outcome(s)*. To reflect this, a utility function is built as the difference between the payoff of an outcome and the maximum payoff that would have been obtained had another alternative been chosen. By this simple modification of utility functions, regret theory is able to successfully deal with several paradoxes of decision theory.

Fehr and Schmidt (1999) built a model where agents have *social preferences*, represented by utility functions that combine material payoffs and agents' distaste for inequality (understood in terms of differences between payoffs of different agents), whether advantageous or not; different agents may be more or less sensible to inequality. Such a model can explain why agents reject 'unfair' offers in the ultimatum game. Bicchieri (2006) presents a model that accounts for effects of social norms. She defines an agent's utility function for a consequence as the difference between her payoff and the maximum payoff loss created by all norm violations (modulated by her sensitivity to the norm). This model accounts for a host of phenomena, including cooperative behaviours in collective dilemmas.

In all those cases, problematic phenomena are accommodated by RCT at the expense of a modification of utility functions, which comes to depend not only on an agent's payoff, but also on payoffs corresponding to other consequences or other agents. Even when successful, such solutions can have several drawbacks. First, they seem to knock the wind out of RCT's sails; for most explanatory power they retain is located in the specific shape of a utility function and the new parameters it includes, themselves left unexplained. Second, we have seen that according to representations theorems, any preferences for actions that have certain properties can always be represented by a utility function. Consequently, finding a utility function that fits a given situation after tinkering with it for a while is not that surprising and hardly brings anything to the table. Theorists can answer both objections by arguing that it is predictive success that matters, rather than explanatory power. However, predictive success is hard to achieve when it depends on the precise values of so many parameters (such as those expressing 'sensitivities' to various effects). Moreover, the modifications brought to utility functions are clearly supposed to represent real effects. Fundamentally, those models still seem to be explanatory.

CONCLUSION: AN EVOLUTIONARY WAY OUT?

We have seen that rational choice theory is based on 'deceptively simple'[43] principles that nonetheless give rise to many issues, both conceptual and empirical. Overall, the more pervasive attacks have targeted its descriptive adequacy; empirical counterexamples to the basic tenets of both decision theory and game theory now abound.

By way of conclusion, let us sketch a possible way out of such problems. Systematic departures from RCT could be explained by evolutionary arguments.[44] The behaviours

we deem rational may not coincide with those that natural selection has selected. Recent literature has shown interest in such justifications of 'irrational' behaviours. We shall not describe it in detail here, but only mention two examples: Houston et al. (2007) argue that natural selection may favour the evolution of intransitive preferences; Robson and Samuelson (2009) make a similar statement, although for different reasons, regarding intertemporal preferences (the fact that we tend to prefer smaller rewards now to higher rewards later, which seems irrational). Such results suggest that some specific characteristics of past environments may have led to the evolution of behaviours and decision-making processes that our *normative* theories dismiss as irrational. However, providing such explanations allow one to consider such behaviours as optimal, though in an evolutionary sense. This may be the way to temper the derogatory attitude with which we tend to treat our 'irrational' tendencies.

NOTES

1 Note that this is a narrow conception of rationality. For alternative options, see Chapter 7.

2 There can be rational constraints on the way beliefs (or more controversially preferences) should evolve through time, for instance when evidence accumulates. But any constraint on the dynamics of belief does not prevent the initial one being arbitrary.

3 These points and others are discussed in Elster (1989).

4 The precise numerical values chosen here do not necessarily matter; more on this later.

5 Mathematically, a probability measure is not defined over a set but a sigma-algebra. Here, as in the rest of this chapter, I choose to favour simplicity and clarity over technicalities when it does not impinge on any major conceptual issues.

6 $0.6 \times 2 + 0.3 \times 2 + 0.1 \times 7 = 2.5$; $0.6 \times 1 + 0.3 \times 6 + 0.1 \times 1 = 2.5$

7 This result is due to Cantor (1915).

8 The third one, separability, is only of mathematical interest. It is also trivially satisfied when the set of consequences is finite so should not worry us here.

9 In this case, the belief that E happens would be $Y/(X + Y)$. This makes intuitive sense: the greater X is, the more I receive if E happens, so the weaker can be my belief that E will happen in order for me to accept the bet. To put it differently, a bigger reward offsets a weaker belief of being rewarded.

10 It may seem that nobody would ever enter a Dutch Book anyway. But there are ways to combine apparently innocuous bets in order to produce a Dutch Book situation.

11 Those axioms are: that the degrees of your beliefs should always range between 0 and 1; that you should believe what is certain with degree 1; and that if you believe something with degree p, you should believe the opposite with degree $1 - p$.

12 Less surprisingly, the theorems also state the converse, that is, that anyone who maximises expected utility will see her preferences for courses of actions have certain properties.

13 Note that this is not the same kind of representation that was discussed earlier. It was about knowing when preferences for *consequences* can be represented by a utility function (replaced by numerical values). Here, we discuss whether preferences for *acts* or *alternatives* (i.e. choices) can be represented by expected utility.

14 The relevant probability measures are given by the lotteries.

15 Corresponding to S_1 in the table. When restricted to S_2 and S_3, C_1 (resp. C_2) is identical to C_3 (resp. C_4).

16 The third and fourth option are equivalent to lotteries obtained by replacing the 89 per cent chance of winning 500000 in the first and second options by an 89 per cent chance of winning nothing, that is, by modifying a consequence that should have no influence on the choice if the sure-thing principle was respected.

17 In this case, it is straightforward to see that the second choice can be obtained from the second by adding a reward when a yellow ball is drawn in *both* options.

18 Cf. Kahneman and Tversky (1979).

19 In other words, you will value a good differently depending on whether you already possess it and consider losing it, or do not possess it and consider acquiring it.

20 Cf. Binmore (2007) or Osborne and Rubinstein (1994) for an introduction course to game theory.

21 Chapter 15 refers to such results as pertaining to the *epistemic foundation program* of game theory. A good example can be found in Aumann and Brandenburger (1995).

22 For example, fixed-point ones; this is not the place to engage such technicalities.

23 A possible move is to defend the use of equilibria that are cognitively less demanding. Gintis (2009), for instance, favours correlated equilibrium over Nash equilibrium.

24 Though some have tried to formalise them. Cf. Bacharach and Stahl (2000).

25 Cf. Schelling (1960).

26 Such situations are not limited to RCT but potentially to any field where multiple criteria for choice must be aggregated – even philosophy of science itself. See for instance Okasha (forthcoming) that locates a similar issue in Kuhn's account of theory change.

27 Cf. Lewis (1969).

28 Cf. Camerer (2003) or Rapoport and Chammah (1965).

29 A cross-cultural empirical study of behaviours in the Ultimatum game can be found in Henrich et al. (2005).

30 Camerer (2003).

31 Formally, this means shifting to an incomplete information framework.

32 Olson (1971).

33 For a general discussion of this issue, see Rosenberg (2008: Chapter 2).

34 See Chapter 21, and Kincaid (1996: Chapter 4) for a defence of functionalism.

35 See Chapter 20.

36 For example Churchland (1986).

37 On this topic, see Chapter 8.

38 See Fudenberg and Levine (2006) for example. Note that sub-agents do not have to be mere useful fictions; they may end up being identified with brain areas, for example.

39 Kincaid (1996: 160). Kincaid rejects MI because he deems another type of explanation, namely functionalism, more adapted to social sciences.

40 For a recent example, see Gintis (2009: Chapter 12).

41 This echoes Sober's (1999) answer to attacks on reductivism.

42 Cf. Loomes and Sugden (1986).

43 Elster (1989: 22).

44 For more on evolutionary explanations, see Chapter 20.

REFERENCES

Aumann, R.J. and Brandenburger, A. (1995) 'Epistemic conditions for Nash equilibrium', *Econometrica*, 64: 1161–1180.

Bacharach, M. and Stahl, O. (2000) 'Variable-frame level-*n* theory', *Games and Economic Behavior*, 32(2): 220–246.

Bicchieri, C. (2006) *The Grammar of Society: The Nature and Dynamics of Social Norms.* Cambridge: Cambridge University Press.

Binmore, K. (2007) *Playing for Real: A Text on Game Theory.* New York: Oxford University Press.

Boudon, R. (1998) 'The limitations of rational choice theory', *American Journal of Sociology*, 104(3): 817–828.

Camerer, C. (2003) *Behavioral Game Theory: Experiments on Strategic Interaction*. Princeton: Princeton University Press.

Cantor, G. (1915). *Contributions to the founding theory of transfinite numbers*. Chicago: Open Court.

Cartwright, N. (1983) *How the Laws of Physics Lie*. Oxford: Oxford University Press.

Churchland, P.S. (1986) *Neurophilosophy: Toward a Unified Science of the Mind/Brain*. Cambridge, MA: MIT Press.

Davidson, D. (1980) *Essays on Actions and Events*. Oxford: Clarendon Press.

Elster, J. (1986) 'Introduction', in J. Elster (ed.) *Rational Choice*. New York: New York University Press.

Elster, J. (1989) *Nuts and Bolts for the Social Sciences*. Cambridge, MA: Cambridge University Press.

Fehr, E. and Schmidt, K. (1999) 'A theory of fairness, competition and cooperation', *The Quarterly Journal of Economics*, 114(3): 817–868.

Fudenberg, D. and Levine, D. (2006) 'A dual self model of impulse control', *American Economic Review*, 96: 1449–1476.

Gintis, H. (2009) *The Bounds of Reason: Game Theory and the Unification of Behavioural Sciences*. Princeton: Princeton University Press.

Green, D.P. and Shapiro, I. (1994) *Pathologies of Rational Choice Theory: A Critique of Application in Political Science*. New Haven: Yale University Press.

Hechter, M. (1997) 'Sociological rational choice theory', *Annual Review of Sociology*, 23: 191–214.

Henrich, J., Boyd, R., Bowles, S., Camerer, C., Fehr, E., Gintis, H., McElreath, R., Alvard, M., Barr, A., Ensminger, J., Hill, K., Gil-White, Francisco., Gurven, M., Marlowe, F. W., Patton J. Q., Smith, N. and Tracer, D. (2005) '"Economic man" in cross-cultural perspective: Ethnography and experiments from 15 small-scale societies', *Behavioral and Brain Sciences*, 28: 795–855.

Houston, A.I., McNamara, J.M. and Steer, M.D. (2007) 'Violations of transitivity under fitness maximisation', *Biology Letters*, 3: 365–367.

Kahneman, D. and Tversky, A. (1979) 'Prospect theory: An analysis of decisions under risk', *Econometrica*, 47: 313–327.

Kincaid, H. (1996) *Philosophical Foundations of the Social Sciences: Analyzing Controversies in Social Research*. Cambridge, New York: Cambridge University Press.

Lewis, D. (1969) *Convention. A Philosophical Study*. Harvard, MA:Harvard University Press.

Loomes, G. and Sugden, R. (1986) 'Disappointment and dynamic consistency in choice under uncertainty', *The Review of Economic Studies*, 53(2): 271–282.

von Neumann, J. and Morgenstern, O. (1944) *Theory of Games and Economic Behavior*. Princeton: Princeton University Press.

Okasha, S. (forthcoming) 'Theory choice and social choice: Kuhn versus Arrow', *Mind*.

Olson, M. (1971) *The Logic of Collective Action: Public Goods and the Theory of Groups*. Harvard: Harvard University Press (revised edition).

Osborne, M.J. and Rubinstein, A. (1994) *A Course in Game Theory*. Cambridge, MA: MIT Press.

Ramsey, F. (1926) 'Truth and probability', in D.H. Mellor (ed.) *Philosophical Papers*. Cambridge, MA: Cambridge University Press. pp. 52–94

Rapoport, A. and Chammah, A. (1965) *Prisoner's Dilemma: A Study in Conflict and Cooperation*. New York: University of Michigan Press.

Robson, A.J. and Samuelson, L. (2009) 'The evolution of time preference with aggregate uncertainty', *American Economic Review*, 99(5): 1925–1953.

Rosenberg, A. (2008) *Philosophy of Social Science*. Boulder, CO: Westview Press.

Ross, D. (2008) 'The economic agent: Not human, but important', in U. Maki (ed.) *Handbook of the Philosophy of Science*, V.13. Amsterdam: Elsevier. pp. 627–671.

Savage, L.J. (1954) *Foundations of Statistics*. New York: John Wiley and Sons.

Schelling, T.C. (1960) *The Strategy of Conflict*. Cambridge, MA: Harvard University Press.

Sober, E. (1999) 'The multiple realizability argument against reductionism', *Philosophy of Science*, 66(4): 542–564.

15

Game Theory

Giacomo Bonanno

INTRODUCTION

Game theory is a branch of mathematics that deals with interactive decision-making, that is, with situations where two or more individuals (called *players*) make decisions that affect each other.[1] Since the final outcome depends on the actions taken by all the players, it becomes necessary for each player to try to predict the choices of his opponents, while realizing that they are simultaneously trying to put themselves in *his* shoes to figure out what *he* will do.

The birth of game theory is usually associated with the publication in 1944 of the book *Theory of Games and Economic Behavior* by the mathematician John von Neumann and the economist Oskar Morgenstern, although important results had been obtained earlier.[2] Applications of game theory can be found in many fields, most notably biology, computer science, economics,[3] military science, political science, and sociology.

Game theory has been traditionally divided into two branches: non-cooperative and cooperative. Cooperative game theory deals with situations where there are institutions that make agreements among the players binding. In such a setting the central question becomes one of agreeing on a best joint course of action, where 'best' could have different meanings, such as 'acceptable to all players and coalitions of players'[4] or 'satisfying some desirable properties'.[5] Non-cooperative game theory, on the other hand, deals with institutional settings where binding agreements are not possible, whether it is because communication is impossible or because agreements are illegal[6] or because there is no authority that can enforce compliance.[7]

Because of space limitations we shall deal exclusively with non-cooperative games. Our focus will be on the philosophical and epistemological issues that arise in non-cooperative games, in particular on the notion of rationality and mutual recognition of rationality. We shall begin with simultaneous or strategic-form games and then turn to games that have a sequential structure (extensive-form games).

STRATEGIC-FORM GAMES AND COMMON KNOWLEDGE OF RATIONALITY

A *game in strategic form with ordinal payoffs* consists of the following elements:

1 the set $N = \{1,...,n\}$ of *players*;
2 for every player $i \in N$, the set S_i of *strategies* (or choices) available to player i;

3   the set of possible *outcomes O*;
4   an *outcome function* $z : S \to O$ that associates, with every strategy profile (specifying a choice for each player) $(s_1, ..., s_n) \in S = S_1 \times ... \times S_n$, the resulting outcome;
5   for every player $i \in N$, a *weak total order* $\succsim_i$ on O representing player i's ranking of the outcomes.[8,9]

In order to simplify the representation of a game the last three elements are usually collapsed into a *payoff function* $\pi_i : S \to \mathbb{R}$, for every player *i*, which is a numerical function ($\mathbb{R}$ denotes the set of real numbers) satisfying the following property: the strategy profile *s* is assigned a number greater than or equal to the number assigned to the strategy profile *s′* if and only if player *i* considers the outcome resulting from *s* to be at least as good as the outcome resulting from *s′*. Formally, for every $s, s′ \in S$, $\pi_i(s) \geq \pi_i(s′)$ if and only if $z(s) \succsim_i z(s′)$.[10] Since $\succsim_i$ is a weak total order, if *O* is a finite set then such a payoff function always exists; furthermore, there is an infinite number of possible payoff functions that can be used to represent $\succsim_i$. It is important to note that the payoffs have no meaning beyond the ordinal ranking that they induce on the set of strategy profiles.

In the case of two players, a convenient way to represent a game is by means of a table where each row is labeled with a strategy of player 1 and each column with a strategy of player 2. Inside the cell that corresponds to the row labeled *x* and the column labeled *y* the pair of numbers $(\pi_1(x,y), \pi_2(x,y))$ is given, denoting the payoffs of player 1 and player 2, respectively. Table 15.1 represents a two-player game where $S_1 = \{a,b,c\}$ and $S_2 = \{d,e,f\}$. In this game, for example, player 1 is indifferent between $z(a,e)$ (the outcome associated with the strategy profile (a,e)) and $z(b,e)$; on the other hand, he prefers $z(a,e)$ to $z(c,e)$.

The *epistemic foundation program* in game theory aims to identify, for every game, the strategies that might be chosen by rational and intelligent players who know the structure of the game and the preferences of their opponents and who recognize each other's

Table 15.1   A strategic-form game with ordinal payoffs

		Player 2		
		d	*e*	*f*
	a	3, 2	3, 1	0, 1
Player 1	*b*	2, 3	3, 2	0, 1
	c	1, 2	1, 2	4, 1

rationality. The two central questions are thus: (1) under what circumstances is a player rational? and (2) what does 'mutual recognition of rationality' mean? The latter notion has been interpreted as *common knowledge* of rationality. Informally, something is common knowledge if everybody knows it, everybody knows that everybody knows it, ... and so on, *ad infinitum*.[11] A defining characteristic of knowledge is truth: if a player knows *E* then *E* must be true. A more general notion is that of *belief*, which allows for the possibility of mistakes: belief of *E* is compatible with *E* being false. Thus a more appealing notion is that of common belief of rationality; however, in order to simplify the exposition, we shall restrict attention to knowledge and refer the reader to Battigalli and Bonanno (1999) for the analysis of common belief. The state of interactive knowledge among a set of players can be modeled by means of a set of *states* Ω and, for every player $i \in N$, a partition $\mathbf{K}_i$ of Ω (thus $\mathbf{K}_i$ is a binary relation on Ω which is reflexive, transitive and symmetric, that is, an equivalence relation). Given a state $\omega \in \Omega$, we denote the cell of *i*'s partition that contains ω (that is, the equivalence class of ω) by $\mathbf{K}_i(\omega)$. The interpretation is that, at state ω, player *i* cannot distinguish between any two states in $\mathbf{K}_i(\omega)$, that is – as far as she knows – the true state could be any of the elements in $\mathbf{K}_i(\omega)$. The collection $\left\langle N, \Omega, \{\mathbf{K}_i\}_{i \in N} \right\rangle$ is called an *interactive knowledge structure*. A state $\omega \in \Omega$ is thought of as a complete description of the world and the subsets of Ω, which are called *events*, represent propositions about the world.

Knowledge pertains to propositions and a proposition is identified with the set of states where it is true. For every player i, we can define a *knowledge operator* $K_i : 2^\Omega \to 2^\Omega$ (where 2^Ω denotes the set of subsets of Ω) as follows: $K_i E = \{\omega \in \Omega : K_i(\omega) \subseteq E\}$. Thus at state ω player i knows (the proposition represented by) event E if E is true at every state that player i considers possible: $\omega \in K_i E$ (i knows E at ω) if and only if $\omega' \in E$ (E is true at ω') for every $\omega' \in K_i(\omega)$ (for every ω' that i considers possible at ω). This is illustrated in Figure 15.2 where $\Omega = \{\alpha, \beta, \gamma, \delta, \varepsilon\}$ and the cells of the partition of a player are denoted by rounded rectangles. Thus, for example, $K_1(\beta) = \{\beta, \gamma\}$, that is, at state β player 1 is uncertain as to whether the true state is β or γ. Consider the event $E = \{\alpha, \beta, \delta\}$. Then $K_1 E = \{\alpha, \delta\}$ and $K_2 E = \{\alpha, \beta\}$, so that $K_1(K_2 E) = \{\alpha\}$ while $K_2(K_1 E) = \varnothing$ ($\varnothing$ denotes the empty set).[12] Hence at state α both players know E ($\alpha \in K_1 E$ and $\alpha \in K_2 E$) and, while player 1 knows that player 2 knows E ($\alpha \in K_1 K_2 E$), it is not the case that player 2 knows that player 1 knows E ($\alpha \notin K_2 K_1 E$).

Given an interactive knowledge structure $\langle N, \Omega, \{K_i\}_{i \in N} \rangle$, in order to determine whether an event E is common knowledge at some state ω we construct a new partition, called the *common knowledge partition*, as follows. Let $\omega, \omega' \in \Omega$. We say that ω' is *reachable* from ω if there is a sequence $\langle \omega_1, \omega_2, ..., \omega_n \rangle$ in Ω and a sequence of players $\langle j_1, j_2, ..., j_{n-1} \rangle$ in N such that (1) $\omega_1 = \omega$, (2) $\omega_n = \omega'$, and (3) for every $i = 1, ..., n-1$,

$\omega_{i+1} \in K_{j_i}(\omega_i)$. Let $\mathbf{K}_*(\omega)$ denote the set of states reachable from ω. For example, in Figure 15.1, $\mathbf{K}_*(\alpha) = \{\alpha, \beta, \gamma\}$. The common knowledge partition is obtained by enclosing two states in the same cell if and only if one is reachable from the other. Figure 15.1 shows the common knowledge partition constructed from the partitions of player 1 and player 2. We can now define a *common knowledge operator* $CK : 2^\Omega \to 2^\Omega$ as follows: $CKE = \{\omega \in \Omega : \mathbf{K}_*(\omega) \subseteq E\}$.[13] In the example illustrated in Figure 15.1, $CK\{\alpha, \beta, \delta, \varepsilon\} = \{\delta, \varepsilon\}$ and $CK\{\alpha, \beta, \delta\} = \varnothing$. Thus, if $F = \{\alpha, \beta, \delta, \varepsilon\}$ then at state δ both players know F and both players know that both players know F, and so on; that is, at δ it is common knowledge that F has occurred. On the other hand, if $E = \{\alpha, \beta, \delta\}$ then, at state α both players know E but E is not common knowledge (indeed we saw above that at α it is not the case that player 2 knows that player 1 knows E).

Armed with a precise definition of common knowledge, we can now turn to the central question of what strategies can be chosen when there is common knowledge of rationality. In order to do this, we need to define what it means for a player to be rational. Intuitively, a player is rational if she chooses an action which is 'best' given what she believes or knows. In order to make this more precise we need to introduce the notion of model of a game. Given a game G and an interactive knowledge structure $\langle N, \Omega, \{K_i\}_{i \in N} \rangle$ we obtain a *model of G* by adding, for every player i, a function

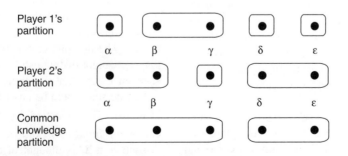

Player 1's partition

α β γ δ ε

Player 2's partition

α β γ δ ε

Common knowledge partition

Figure 15.1   An interactive knowledge structure with two players.

$\sigma_i : \Omega \to S_i$ that associates with every state a strategy of player i. The interpretation of $s_i = \sigma_i(\omega)$ is that, at state ω, player i plays (or chooses) strategy s_i. We impose the restriction that a player always knows what strategy he is choosing, that is, the function σ_i is constant on the cells of player i's partition: if $\omega' \in K_i(\omega)$ then $\sigma_i(\omega') = \sigma_i(\omega)$. The addition of the functions σ_i to an interactive knowledge structure yields an interpretation of events in terms of propositions about what actions the players take, thereby giving content to players' knowledge. Figure 15.2 shows a model of the game of Table 15.1, where $\sigma_1(\alpha) = a$, $\sigma_1(\beta) = \sigma_1(\gamma) = c$, $\sigma_2(\alpha) = \sigma_2(\beta) = e$ and $\sigma_2(\gamma) = f$.

The following is a very weak definition of rationality: at a state a player is *rational* if it is not the case that he knows that his payoff would be greater if he had chosen a different strategy than the one he is choosing at that state. This definition can be stated formally as follows. First we label a player as *irrational* at state ω if there exists a strategy $s_i' \in S_i$ such that (1) $s_i' \neq s_i$, where $s_i = \sigma_i(\omega)$, and (2) for every $\omega' \in K_i(\omega)$, $\pi_i(s_i', \sigma_{-i}(\omega')) > \pi_i(s_i, \sigma_{-i}(\omega'))$, where $\sigma_{-i}(\omega')$ denotes the strategy profile of players other than i at state ω': $\sigma_{-i}(\omega') = (\sigma_1(\omega'), ..., \sigma_{i-1}(\omega'), \sigma_{i+1}(\omega'), ..., \sigma_n(\omega'))$ [recall also that, by definition of

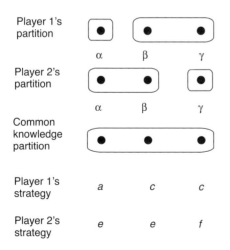

Figure 15.2 A model of the strategic-form game of Table 15.1.

model, $\sigma_i(\omega) = \sigma_i(\omega')$ for every $\omega' \in K_i(\omega)$]. Second, we define a player to be *rational* at state ω if and only if he is not irrational at ω. For example, in the model illustrated in Figure 15.2 (viewed as a model of the game of Table 15.1), player 1 is rational at state β despite the fact that a would be a better choice than c there (since player 2 is choosing e), because he does not know that player 2 is choosing e: he is uncertain as to whether player 2 is choosing e or f and c is a best reply to f. On the other hand, at state γ, player 2 is *not* rational because she knows that player 1 is choosing c and she would get a higher payoff by playing d. Let R_i denote the event that player i is rational. For example, in the model illustrated in Figure 15.2, $R_1 = \{\alpha, \beta, \gamma\}$ and $R_2 = \{\alpha, \beta\}$. Let R be the event that every player is rational: $R = \bigcap_{i \in N} R_i$.

In the model illustrated in Figure 15.2, $R = \{\alpha, \beta\}$ and there is no state where it is common knowledge that both players are rational: $CKR = \varnothing$. We are now in a position to express more precisely the question 'what strategy profiles are compatible with common knowledge or rationality?' as follows. Suppose that $\omega \in CKR$ (i.e. at ω it is common knowledge that all players are rational): what can we say about the strategy profile $\sigma(\omega) = (\sigma_1(\omega), ..., \sigma_n(\omega))$? To answer this question we need to introduce the following definition. Fix a game and let $s_i, s_i' \in S_i$ be two strategies of player i. We say that s_i' *strictly dominates* s_i if $\pi_i(s_i', s_{-i}) > \pi_i(s_i, s_{-i})$ for every $s_{-i} \in S_{-i} = S_1 \times ... \times S_{i-1} \times S_{i+1} \times ... \times S_n$, that is, if s_i' is strictly better than s_i for player i against every possible profile of strategies of the opponents. For example, in the game of Table 15.1, strategy d of player 2 strictly dominates strategy f. A strategy of player i is *strictly dominated* if there is another strategy of player i that strictly dominates it. In the game of Table 15.1, with the exception of strategy f of player 2, there are no other strategies of either player that are strictly dominated.

A rational player would not play a strictly dominated strategy s_i, since he can obtain a higher payoff by switching to a strategy that dominates it. If the other players know that he is rational, they know that they are in fact playing the smaller game obtained by ruling out strategy s_i. In this smaller game there might be a player who has a strictly dominated strategy and thus, if rational, she will not play it. Hence this strategy can also be ruled out and the game can be reduced further. This procedure of elimination of strategies is called the *iterated deletion of strictly dominated pure strategies*.[14] For example, in the game of Table 15.1 deletion of the strictly dominated strategy f of player 2 leads to a smaller game where strategy c of player 1 becomes strictly dominated by a; deletion of c leads to a yet smaller game where strategy e of player 2 becomes strictly dominated (by d); after deleting e, strategy b of player 1 becomes strictly dominated by a and deletion of b leaves only the strategy profile (a,d).

One of the first and most important results in the epistemic foundations of game theory is the following: *common knowledge of the rationality of all the players implies the play of a strategy profile that survives the iterated deletion of strictly dominated pure strategies*; furthermore, *every strategy profile that survives the iterated deletion of strictly dominated pure strategies is compatible with common knowledge of rationality*.[15] For example, in the game of Table 15.1, if there is common knowledge of rationality then player 1 will play a and player 2 will play d, since (a,d) is the only strategy profile that survives the iterated deletion of strictly dominated strategies.

NASH EQUILIBRIUM, CARDINAL PAYOFFS AND MIXED STRATEGIES

There are games where no strategy is strictly dominated and, therefore, common knowledge of rationality is compatible with *every* strategy profile. An example of such a game is given in Table 15.2.

Table 15.2   A strategic-form game with a unique pure-strategy Nash equilibrium

		Player 2	
		c	d
Player 1	a	3, 3	1, 0
	b	4, 1	1, 2

A stronger notion than the iterative deletion of strictly dominated strategies is that of *Nash equilibrium*. Given a game with ordinal payoffs $G = \left\langle N, \{S_i\}_{i \in N}, \{\pi_i\}_{i \in N} \right\rangle$, a strategy profile $s^* = \left(s_1^*, ..., s_n^*\right)$ is called a Nash equilibrium if no player could obtain a higher payoff by unilaterally changing his choice, that is, if, for every $i \in N$, $\pi_i(s^*) \geq \pi_i(s_1^*, ..., s_{i-1}^*, s_i, s_{i+1}^*, ..., s_n^*)$ for every $s_i \in S_i$. For example, in the game illustrated in Table 15.2, (b,d) is a Nash equilibrium, while none of the other strategy profiles is.[16] A possible interpretation of Nash equilibrium is in terms of a *self-enforcing agreement*. Recall that in non-cooperative games it is assumed that players cannot reach enforceable agreements and thus an agreement is viable only if nobody has an individual incentive to deviate from it, assuming that the other players will follow it. A Nash equilibrium is precisely such an agreement.

The Nash equilibrium (b,d) of the game of Table 15.2 has the following feature: there is another strategy profile, namely (a,c), that gives rise to an outcome that both players strictly prefer to the one associated with (b,d). When this is the case, we say that the Nash equilibrium is *Pareto dominated* or *Pareto inefficient*. This is a generic phenomenon: in 'almost all' games Nash equilibria are Pareto dominated (see Dubey, 1986). It is worth stressing that although in the game of Table 15.2 the strategy profile (a,c) yields a better outcome for both players than the Nash equilibrium, it is not a viable agreement: if player 1 expects player 2 to stick to the agreement by playing c, then he will gain by deviating from the agreement and playing b; realizing this, player 2 would want to play d, rather than the agreed-upon c. That is to say, (a,c) is not a Nash equilibrium.

There are games that have multiple Nash equilibria and games that have none. For example, if in the game of Table 15.2 one replaces the payoffs associated with (b,d) with $(0,2)$ then the resulting game has no Nash equilibria. Nash (1950, 1951) proved that every game with finite strategy stets has an equilibrium if one allows for mixed strategies. A *mixed strategy* for player i is a probability distribution over his set S_i of 'pure' strategies. The introduction of mixed strategies requires a theory of how players rank probabilistic outcomes or lotteries. For example, in the game of Table 15.2, suppose that player 2 uses the mixed strategy $\begin{pmatrix} c & d \\ \frac{1}{3} & \frac{2}{3} \end{pmatrix}$.[17]

Then if player 1 chooses the pure strategy a he faces the lottery $\begin{pmatrix} o_1 & o_2 \\ \frac{1}{3} & \frac{2}{3} \end{pmatrix}$, where o_1 is the outcome associated with (a,c) and o_2 is the outcome associated with (a,d), while choosing the pure strategy b means facing the lottery $\begin{pmatrix} o_3 & o_4 \\ \frac{1}{3} & \frac{2}{3} \end{pmatrix}$, where o_3 is the outcome associated with (b,c) and o_4 is the outcome associated with (b,d). The *Theory of Expected Utility*, developed by von Neumann and Morgenstern (1944), provides a list of consistency-of-preferences-over-lotteries axioms which yield the following representation theorem: there exists a numerical function U defined over the set of basic outcomes $O = \{o_1,...,o_m\}$ such that for any two lotteries $L = \begin{pmatrix} o_1 & o_2 & ... & o_m \\ p_1 & p_2 & ... & p_m \end{pmatrix}$ and $L' = \begin{pmatrix} o_1 & o_2 & ... & o_m \\ q_1 & q_2 & ... & q_m \end{pmatrix}$ the individual considers L at least as good as L' if and only if $EU(L) = p_1 U(o_1) + ... + p_m U(o_m) \geq EU(L') = q_1 U(o_1) + ... + q_m U(o_m)$. $EU(L)$ is called the *expected utility* of lottery L. Such a utility function is called a *von Neumann–Morgenstern utility function* or a *cardinal*

utility function. In the mixed-strategy extension of a game the payoff of player i associated with a mixed-strategy profile is the expected utility of the corresponding lottery over basic outcomes.

It is worth noting that the transition from games with ordinal payoffs to games with cardinal payoffs (when mixed strategies are considered) is not an innocuous one. In a given game, it is implicitly assumed that the game itself (that is, the sets of players, strategies, outcomes and the players' rankings of the outcomes) is common knowledge among the players. Assuming common knowledge of ordinal rankings of the basic outcomes is far less demanding than assuming common knowledge of von Neumann–Morgenstern payoffs. A player might be fully aware of his own attitude to risk (that is, his own preferences over lotteries), but will typically lack information about the attitude to risk of his opponents.

The epistemic foundations of Nash equilibrium are not as clear-cut as those for the iterated deletion of strictly dominated strategies; in particular, common knowledge of rationality does not imply the play of a Nash equilibrium.[18]

EXTENSIVE-FORM GAMES WITH PERFECT INFORMATION

While strategic-form games represent situations where the players act simultaneously (or, equivalently, in ignorance of each other's choices), extensive-form games represent situations where choices are made sequentially. An *extensive-form game with perfect information* consists of a finite rooted tree, an assignment of a player to each non-terminal node and a ranking of the set of terminal nodes for each player. The terminal nodes correspond to the possible outcomes and, as usual, we represent the rankings of the outcomes by using an ordinal payoff function for each player. Nodes that are not terminal are called decision nodes. The arrows that emanate from a decision node represent the possible choices for the player assigned to that node. Figure 15.3 represents a perfect-information game with two players (ignore, for the moment, the fact that some arrows have a double edge).

The solution concept most commonly used for this type of game is that of *backward induction*, which is the following algorithm. Start from a decision node whose immediate successors are all terminal nodes and select a choice at that node that maximizes the payoff of the player assigned to that node. Replace that decision node with the payoffs associated with the terminal node that follows the selected choice and repeat the procedure in the resulting smaller tree. When applied to the game illustrated in Figure 15.3, the backward induction procedure selects the choices highlighted by the double edges. The backward induction algorithm yields an actual play (in the game of Figure 15.3 the choice of *a* by player 1 followed by the choice of *c* by player 2) as well as hypothetical choices at nodes that are not reached by the actual play (for example, in the game of Figure 15.3, player 2's hypothetical choice of *e* at the unreached node *y*). A common interpretation of these hypothetical choices is in terms of *counterfactuals*. For example, in the game of

Figure 15.3, player 2's choice of *e* is interpreted as the counterfactual statement 'if player 2's node *y* were to be reached, player 2 would choose *e*'. Furthermore, the backward induction solution is often presented as capturing the notion of common knowledge of rationality. For example, in the game of Figure 15.3, the reasoning would be as follows: 'if node *z* is reached and player 1 is rational, then he will choose *h*; thus if node *y* is reached and player 2 knows that player 1 is rational, then player 2 knows that player 1 would follow with *h* if player 2 herself were to choose *f*; hence if player 2 is rational she will choose *e* at node *y*; etc'. There is an ongoing debate in the game theory literature as to whether this reasoning is sound [see, for example, Aumann (1995, 1996), Binmore (1987, 1996), Bonanno (1991), Brandenburger (2007), Halpern (2001), Reny (1992), Samet (1996), Stalnaker (1998)]. The reason for doubting the validity of this interpretation of the backward induction solution can be illustrated in the game of Figure 15.3. If the backward induction solution is implied by common knowledge of rationality, then common knowledge of rationality implies that node *y* will *not* be reached. Hence the hypothesis 'player 2 is rational and knows that player 1 is rational', which is used to conclude that player 2 would choose *e* at node *y*, will be false at node *y*. In particular, player 2 might conclude that player 1 is *not* rational and anticipate a choice of *g* by player 1 at node *z*, thus making *f* a better choice than *e* at *y*. In order to address these issues, once again one needs to have a precise definition of rationality as well as, possibly, a theory of counterfactuals.

A good starting point is the definition of rationality used above. That definition was formulated for strategic-form games and was based on the notion of model of a game, which associates with every state (in an interactive knowledge structure) a strategy profile. It is possible to associate with every perfect-information game a strategic-form game by using the following definition: a strategy for player *i* in a perfect-information

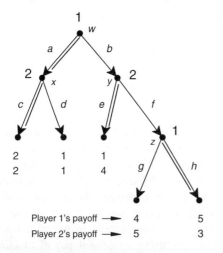

Player 1's payoff ⟶ 4   5
Player 2's payoff ⟶ 5   3

Figure 15.3   An extensive-form game with perfect information.

game is a list of choices, one for each node assigned to player *i*. For example, a possible strategy for player 1 in the game of Figure 15.3 is (*a,g*) and a possible strategy for player 2 is (*d,e*). A strategy profile determines a unique path from the root of the tree to a terminal node and thus one can associate with that strategy profile the payoffs of the corresponding terminal node. Figure 15.4 illustrates a perfect-information game (whose backward induction play is $a_1a_2a_3$), its corresponding strategic form and a model of the strategic form.

Using the definition of rationality introduced above, we have that both players are rational at every state (the only strictly dominated strategy is player 1's a_1d_3 and, after deleting it, there are no other strategies that are strictly dominated). It follows that at state α there is common knowledge of rationality, despite the fact that the associated strategy

profile is (d_1a_3, d_2), which is different from the backward induction solution. The issue is whether at state α we can validly label player 2 as rational. At that state player 2 *knows* that her node *y* is not reached and therefore her payoff is not affected by her choice. Hence, she is rational in a weak sense. However, a stronger notion of rationality would require us to evaluate her choice of d_2 as a plan of *what she would actually do if her decision node were to be reached*. This is a counterfactual statement at state α, since her node *y* is not reached there. Aumann (1996) proposes a notion of rationality, which he calls *substantive rationality*, and shows that common knowledge of substantive rationality implies the backward induction *play* (but not necessarily the backward induction strategy profile). While accepting the correctness of this result within the framework adopted by Aumann, Stalnaker (1998: 48) disputes its validity, arguing as follows:

> Player 2 has the following initial belief: player 1 would choose a_3 on her second move *if* she had a second move. This is a causal 'if' – an 'if' used to express 2's opinion about 1's *disposition to act* in a situation that they both know will not arise. Player 2 knows that since player 1 is rational, if she somehow found herself at her second node, she would choose a_3. But to ask what player 2 would believe about player 1 *if* he learned that he was wrong about 1's first choice is to ask a completely different question – this 'if' is epistemic; it concerns player 2's belief revision policies, and not player 1's disposition to be rational. No assumption about player 1's substantive rationality, or about player 2's knowledge of her substantive rationality, can imply that player 2 should be disposed to maintain his belief that player 1 will act rationally on her second move even were he to learn that she acted irrationally on her first.

In order to be able to carry out a rigorous analysis of the implications of common knowledge of rationality in perfect-information games, we need to move away from the type of models that we have considered so far. The reason for this is that the association of a strategy profile with every state gives rise (implicitly) to two types of counterfactuals: (1) an objective statement about

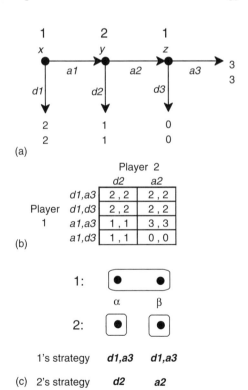

(a)

(b)

		Player 2	
		d2	a2
Player 1	d1,a3	2 , 2	2 , 2
	d1,d3	2 , 2	2 , 2
	a1,a3	1 , 1	3 , 3
	a1,d3	1 , 1	0 , 0

(c)

Figure 15.4 (a) A perfect-information game, (b) the corresponding strategic form and (c) a model of the strategic form.

what the relevant player would do at a node that is not reached and (2) (with the help of the partitions) a subjective statement about what a player believes would happen if he were to take a different action from the one he is actually taking. The two can be disentangled by (1) associating, with every state, not a strategy profile but a play and (2) adding a set of relations that can be used to obtain a formal interpretation of counterfactual statements. We start from the latter. For every state $\omega \in \Omega$ let P_ω be a 'proximity-to-ω' binary relation on Ω and, for every $\omega' \in \Omega$, let $P_\omega(\omega') = \{x \in \Omega : \omega' P_\omega x\}$. The interpretation of $\beta \in P_\omega(\alpha)$ or $\alpha P_\omega \beta$ is that state α is closer to state ω than β is, so that $P_\omega(\alpha)$ is the set of states that are not as close to ω as α is. We assume that the closest state to ω is ω itself and, for simplicity, that P_ω is a strict ordering of Ω.[19] The truth of the counterfactual 'if ϕ were the case then ψ would be the case' at state ω is then determined as follows: look for the closest state to ω at which ϕ is true, call it ω'; if ψ is true at ω' then the counterfactual is true at ω, otherwise it is false. Intuitively, closeness is interpreted as similarity: the closest state to ω where ϕ is true is interpreted as the most similar state to ω among the ones where ϕ is true. This theory of counterfactuals is due to Stalnaker (1968) and was later generalized by Lewis (1973).

We can use proximity orderings and counterfactuals to model strategies as well as hypothetical beliefs, by modifying our earlier definition of a model of a perfect information game as follows: (1) we replace the n functions $\sigma_i : \Omega \to S_i$ with a single function $d : \Omega \to P$, where P is the set of plays of the game, and (2) we add a set of proximity relations $\{P_\omega\}_{\omega \in \Omega}$, one for each state. Thus, with every state, we associate a play rather than a strategy profile and, for each state, we give a proximity ranking of the states, with the state itself being the closest of all. Figure 15.5 illustrates a model of the perfect information game of Figure 15.4.

In this model, at state α, node z of player 1 is not reached because his initial choice is d_1.

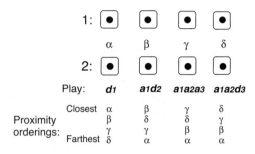

Figure 15.5   A model of the perfect-information game of Figure 15.4.

Is it true, however, at state α, that if node z were to be reached player 1 would play d_3? In order to answer this question we use the proximity ranking at α to find the closest state to α at which node z is reached. That state is γ. Then we check whether at γ player 1 plays d_3. Since at state γ player 1 plays a_3 rather than d_3, the answer is negative: it is not true at state α that if node z were to be reached player 1 would play d_3. The strategy profile implicitly associated with state α is thus $(d_1 a_3, d_2)$. In order to determine what a player would know or believe if a node which is not reached were to be reached, we proceed the same way: we look for the closest state where the node is reached and determine (using the cell of the information partition of this player that contains that node) the player's state of knowledge at that node. For example, at state α player 2 knows that player 1 is playing d_1 and therefore knows that her node y is not reached. What would player 2 know if her node were to be reached? The closest state to α at which node y is reached is β and at β player 2 terminates the game by playing d_2 and collecting a payoff of 1. Is this a rational choice for player 2? The answer depends on what player 2 believes would happen if she played a_2 (if node y were to be reached). To determine this we look for the closest state to β at which node z is reached. It is state δ. At state δ player 1 plays d_3, giving a payoff of 0 to player 2. Thus player 2's choice of d_2 is indeed rational at state β. This conclusion makes player 1's choice of d_1 at state

α rational. Furthermore, at state α player 2 is rational not only in a weak sense since she makes no choices at state α (because her node y is not reached) but also in the stronger sense that the choice that she would make if her node were to be reached (choice d_2 at state β) is rational, given her belief in that situation (that is, at state β). Since both players are rational at state α and the common knowledge partition coincides with the individual partitions, at state α there is common knowledge of rationality, despite the fact that the play at α is not the backward induction play. Thus, using this analysis based on a theory of counterfactuals one can conclude that common knowledge of rationality does not imply the backward induction play (let alone the backward induction solution, that is, the backward induction strategy profile).

In the model of Figure 15.5 at state α player 2 believes that if node z were reached then player 1 would choose a_3 (since the closest state to α where node z is reached is state γ and there player 1 chooses a_3); however, as we saw above, at state α it is also the case that player 2 would choose d_2 if her node y were to be reached (state β), based on the belief (at state β) that if she chose a_2 then player 1 would follow with d_3 (state δ). Hence what player 2 believes about player 1's behavior in the hypothetical world where node z is reached changes going from state α (where the game ends without node y being reached) to the closest state β where y is reached. Stalnaker (1998: 48, quoted above) argues that there is nothing wrong with such a change. Halpern (2001) shows that if one imposes the constraint that such changes in beliefs are not allowed, then Aumann's result that common knowledge of substantive rationality implies the backward-induction play holds.

Since the notion of subgame-perfect equilibrium (see next section) subsumes that of backward-induction solution (they coincide in the class of perfect-information games) and is a strengthening of Nash equilibrium, the epistemic foundations of subgame-perfect equilibrium involve a conceptual apparatus that is at least as complex as that required for those two notions.

EXTENSIVE-FORM GAMES WITH IMPERFECT INFORMATION

An extensive game is said to have *imperfect* information if at least one player is not fully informed about the choices made by other players in the past. To represent a player's uncertainty concerning past moves, we use *information sets* (which play the same role as the cells of the information partitions considered earlier). An information set of player i contains several nodes in the tree where player i has available the same choices and the interpretation is that the player cannot tell at which of these nodes her choice is being made. Figure 15.6 illustrates an extensive-form game with imperfect information. Player 2 has two information sets, one consisting of the two nodes v and w and the other consisting of the single node x.[20] The interpretation of information set $\{v, w\}$ of player 2 is that, when choosing between actions D and E, player 2 does not know whether player 1 chose A or B. Player 3 is in a similar situation at information set $\{y, z\}$ concerning the earlier choice of player 2 between F and G.

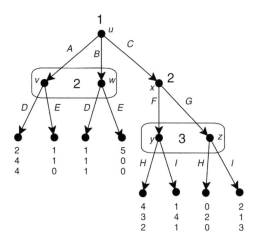

Figure 15.6 An extensive-form game with imperfect information.

As in the case of perfect-information games, we can associate with every extensive-form game with imperfect information a strategic form using the following definition: a *strategy* for player i is a list of choices, one for every information set of player i.[21] For example, the set of strategies of player 2 in the game of Figure 15.6 is $S_2 = \{DF, DG, EF, EG\}$. The solution concept most used in extensive games with imperfect information is that of *subgame-perfect equilibrium*, which is a generalisation of the notion of backward induction used in perfect-information games. A *subgame* is a portion of the entire game that (1) starts at a singleton information set $\{x\}$ and includes *all* the successors of node x and (2) if y is a successor of x that belongs to information set h (of some player) then every node in h is a successor of x. For example, in the game of Figure 15.6 the portion of the tree that starts at node x of player 2 is a subgame; the only other subgame is the entire game. A *subgame-perfect equilibrium* is a Nash equilibrium of the entire game that satisfies the following property: for every subgame, the restriction of the strategy profile to that subgame is a Nash equilibrium of the subgame. For example, in the game of Figure 15.6 (C, DF, H) is the unique subgame-perfect equilibrium: it is a Nash equilibrium of the entire game and, furthermore, the restriction of (C, DF, H) to the subgame that starts at node x, namely (F, H), is a Nash equilibrium of that subgame. It was proved by Selten (1975) that if one allows for von Neumann–Morgenstern payoffs and mixed strategies (see third section) then every finite extensive-form game with perfect recall[22] has at least one subgame-perfect equilibrium in mixed strategies.

GAMES WITH INCOMPLETE INFORMATION

An implicit assumption in game theory is that the game is common knowledge among the players. The expression 'incomplete information' refers to those situations where some of the elements of the game (e.g. the preferences of the players) are not common knowledge. In such situations the knowledge and beliefs of the players about the game need to be made an integral part of the model. Pioneering work in this direction was done by Harsanyi (1967, 1968). Harsanyi suggested a method for converting a situation of incomplete information into an extensive game with imperfect information (this is the so-called *Harsanyi transformation*). The theory of games of incomplete information has been developed for the case of von Neumann–Morgenstern payoffs (see third section) and the solution concept proposed by Harsanyi is *Bayes–Nash equilibrium* which is simply a Nash equilibrium of the imperfect information game so constructed. Although the traditional definition of games of incomplete information is in terms of types of players and of probability distributions over types,[23] we shall illustrate the Harsanyi transformation using the epistemic structures introduced above. States can be used to describe possible games and thus represent the uncertainty in a player's mind as to which game she is truly playing. Figure 15.7 illustrates a two-player situation of incomplete information using an interactive knowledge structure with the addition of a probability distribution for every cell of the information partition of each player.

Associated with every state is a strategic-form game. Let G be the game associated with states α and β (it is the same game) and G' the game associated with state γ. Fix a state, say, state α. Then state α describes the following situation.

1   Both player 1 and player 2 know that they are playing game G.
2   Player 1 knows that player 2 knows that they are playing game G.
3   Player 2 is uncertain as to whether player 1 knows that they are playing game G (which is the case if the actual state is α) or whether player 1 is uncertain (if the actual state is β) between the possibility that they are playing game G and the possibility that they are playing game G' and

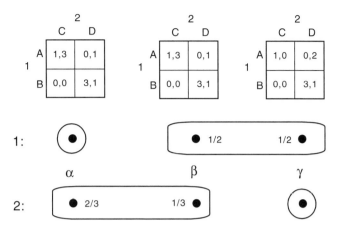

Figure 15.7   A two-player situation of incomplete information.

considers the two possibilities equally likely (that is, attaches probability $\frac{1}{2}$ to each); furthermore, player 2 attaches probability $\frac{2}{3}$ to the first case (where player 1 knows that they are playing game G) and probability $\frac{1}{3}$ to the second case (where player 1 is uncertain between game G and game G').

4   Player 1 knows the state of uncertainty of player 2 concerning player 1 (as described in sub (3) above).

5   It is common knowledge that each player knows his own payoffs and that player 2 also knows player 1's payoffs.

Harsanyi's suggestion was to represent a situation of incomplete information such as the one illustrated in Figure 15.7 as a game with imperfect information where the initial move is assigned to a fictitious player, called Nature, whose role is to choose the state with predetermined probabilities. No payoffs are assigned to Nature and it makes no further choices. Information sets are then used to capture the uncertainty of the players concerning both the actual state and the choices made by the other players. In order for such a representation to be possible, it is necessary that the probabilistic beliefs of the players at the cells of their information partitions be consistent in the following sense: there is a probability distribution μ over the set of states, called a *common prior*, which yields those probabilistic beliefs upon conditioning

on the information represented by a cell of an information partition. Conditional probabilities ought to be obtained from the common prior by using Bayes' rule. For example, in the situation illustrated in Figure 15.7 we want a function $\mu : \{\alpha, \beta, \gamma\} \rightarrow [0,1]$ such that

$$\mu(\beta \mid \{\beta, \gamma\}) = \frac{\mu(\beta)}{\mu(\beta) + \mu(\gamma)} = \frac{1}{2}$$

$$\mu(\alpha \mid \{\alpha, \beta\}) = \frac{\mu(\alpha)}{\mu(\alpha) + \mu(\beta)} = \frac{2}{3}$$

$$\mu(\alpha) + \mu(\beta) + \mu(\gamma) = 1$$

In this case a common prior exists and is given by $\mu(\alpha) = \frac{2}{4}$ and $\mu(\beta) = \mu(\gamma) = \frac{1}{4}$. Using this common prior to assign probabilities to Nature's choices we obtain the imperfect-information game shown in Figure 15.8.

A Nash equilibrium of this imperfect-information game is called a *Bayes-Nash equilibrium* of the corresponding incomplete-information situation. The following pure-strategy profile is a Nash equilibrium of the game of Figure 15.8: player 1's strategy is *AB* (that is, he plays *A* if informed that the state is α and plays *B* if informed that the state is either β or γ) and player 2's strategy is *CD* (that is, she plays *C* at her information set on the left and *D* at her information set on

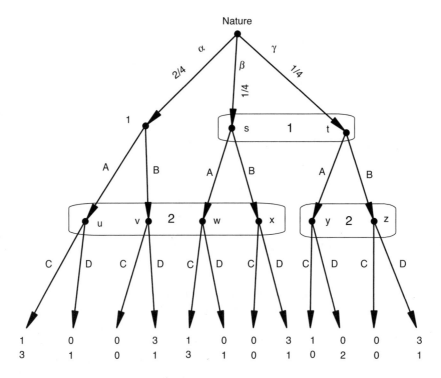

Figure 15.8   An extensive-form game with imperfect information that represents the incomplete-information situation of Figure 15.7.

the right). To verify that this is a Nash equilibrium, we need to check that no player can increase his expected payoff by unilaterally changing his strategy. We begin with player 1: (1) at the singleton information set on the left, A gives player 1 a payoff of 1 (given player 2's choice of C) while B would give him a payoff of 0 (hence A is the optimal choice); (2) at the information set on the right, by Bayes' rule player 1 must assign probability $\frac{1}{2}$ to node s and probability $\frac{1}{2}$ to node t; thus (given player 2's strategy CD) choosing A would give him an expected payoff of $\frac{1}{2}1+\frac{1}{2}0=\frac{1}{2}$ while B gives him an expected payoff of $\frac{1}{2}0+\frac{1}{2}3=\frac{3}{2}$ (hence B is the optimal choice). Similarly for player 2: (1) at the information set on the left, by Bayes' rule (given that player 1's strategy is AB) player 2 must assign probability $\frac{2}{3}$ to node u and $\frac{1}{3}$ to node x; thus choosing C gives her an expected payoff of $\frac{2}{3}3+\frac{1}{3}0=2$ while D would give her an expected payoff of

$\frac{2}{3}1+\frac{1}{3}1=1$ (hence C is the optimal choice); (2) at the information set on the right, by Bayes' rule (given that player 1's strategy is AB) player 2 must assign probability 1 to node z; thus choosing C would give her a payoff of 0 while D gives her a payoff of 1 (hence D is the optimal choice).

Besides the conceptual issues that arise with respect to the notion of Nash equilibrium, epistemic foundations for the notion of Bayes-Nash equilibrium would necessarily involve an epistemic justification or understanding of the notion of a common prior. Such a justification has been object of debate in the literature. [24]

CONCLUSION

The focus in this chapter has been on one of the central issues in philosophy, namely the notion of rationality of choice. Adopting the belief-desire framework for rationality (according to which an action is chosen rationally if – given the agent's beliefs – it yields an outcome which is at least as good as the outcome that can be obtained with a different choice) one encounters two difficulties in the context of multi-agent interactions. First of all, the description of the interactive situation encoded in a game provides the players' desires (their rankings of the outcomes) but not their beliefs. Thus one needs to augment that description by specifying the players' beliefs; this is done through the notion of a model of a game. The second difficulty arises from the fact that what counts as one player's best action (for her) depends on her beliefs about what the other players will do, and what counts as their best actions (for they too will want to choose optimally) similarly depends on their beliefs about her choice. Thus a rational player's beliefs about the actions of the other players need to reflect the realization that those actions must themselves be justified by appropriate beliefs; this mutual recognition of each other's rationality is captured by the notion of common knowledge of rationality. As a consequence, a theory of rational behavior in interactive situations touches on another central issue in philosophy, namely epistemology: the study of knowledge and how it relates to similar notions such as truth, belief, and justification.

We have reviewed the formal tools that make a precise analysis of the notion of common knowledge of rationality possible. For a less formal and wider-ranging introduction to game theory the reader is referred to Ross (2006). There are other important links between game theory and philosophy, in particular concerning issues of moral and political philosophy and ethics. For a discussion of these the reader is referred to Bicchieri (2006), Binmore (1994, 1998), de Bruin (2005) and Verbeek (2004).

In the social sciences, game theory has played a central role in economics[25] and political science[26]; however, its influence is spreading also to other fields such as sociology[27] and linguistics[28].

There are several branches and applications of game theory that we were not able to discuss because of space limitations.[29] Besides co-operative game theory,[30] which was mentioned in the introduction, we also left out evolutionary game theory,[31] the theory of repeated games[32] and bargaining theory.[33]

Finally it is also worth mentioning two new developments: experimental game theory and *neuroeconomics*. The former tries to test the predictions of game theory in controlled laboratory settings, while the latter aims to systematically classify and map the brain activity that correlates with (individual and interactive) decision-making.[34]

NOTES

1 An example is a sealed-bid first-price auction, where each participant submits a bid for an object, in ignorance of the bids chosen by his opponents, and the object is assigned to the highest bidder who pays his own bid, while the others pay nothing and receive nothing.

2 For a detailed historical account of the development of game theory see Aumann (1987).

3 The Nobel prize in economics was awarded to game theorists three times: in 1994 to John C. Harsanyi, John F. Nash Jr. and Reinhard Selten; in 2005 to Robert J. Aumann and Thomas C. Schelling and in 2007 to Leonid Hurwicz, Eric S. Maskin and Roger B. Myerson.

4 For example, the *core* of a co-operative game identifies a set of 'best' agreements in this sense.

5 For example, the *Shapley value* identifies the 'best' agreement in this sense.

6 For example, many countries have antitrust laws that forbid agreements among competing firms concerning prices or production.

7 As is the case in the international arena.

8 Thus $\succsim_i \subseteq O \times O$ is a binary relation on O which is connected (for all $o, o' \in O$, either $o \succsim_i o'$, or $o' \succsim_i o$, or both) and transitive (if $o_1 \succsim_i o_2$ and $o_2 \succsim_i o_3$ then $o_1 \succsim_i o_3$). The interpretation of $o \succsim_i o'$ is that player i considers outcome o to be *at least as good* as outcome o'. We denote that player i prefers outcome o to outcome o' by $o \succ_i o'$ and define it as $o \succsim_i o'$ and not $o' \succsim_i o$. Player i is *indifferent* between o and o', denoted by $o \sim_i o'$, if $o \succsim_i o'$ and $o' \succsim_i o$.

9 For example a sealed-bid first price auction with two bidders, two legal bids ($10 and $15), a tie-breaking rule that declares player 1 the winner and where each player values the object more than $15 and has selfish preferences corresponds to the following strategic-form game: $N = \{1,2\}$, $S_1 = S_2 = \{10, 15\}$, $O = \{a, b, c\}$ (where a is the outcome 'player 1 gets the object and pays $10', b is the outcome 'player 2 gets the object and pays $15' and c is the outcome 'player 1 gets the object and pays $15'), $z(10, 10) = a$, $z(10, 15) = b$, $z(15, 10) = z(15, 15) = c$, $a \succ_1 c \succ_1 b$ and $b \succ_2 a \sim_2 c$.

10 In the example of the previous footnote the following are possible payoff functions: $\pi_1(10,10) = 3$, $\pi_1(15,10) = \pi_1(15,15) = 2$, $\pi_1(10,15) = 1$ and $\pi_2(10,15) = 2$, $\pi_2(15,10) = \pi_2(15,15) = 1$.

11 The notion of common knowledge was introduced independently by Lewis (1969) and Aumann (1976).

12 From now on we shall write K_1K_2E instead of $K_1(K_2E)$.

13 It can be shown that, for every event E and for every state ω, $\omega \in CKE$ if and only if ω belongs to every event of the form $K_{i_1}K_{i_2}...K_{i_m}E$ (i_1 knows that i_2 knows that ... i_m knows E) where m is any positive integer and $i_1,i_2,...,i_m$ are any individuals.

14 The precise definition of this procedure is as follows. Given a game $G = \langle N, \{S_i\}_{i \in N}, \{\pi_i\}_{i \in N} \rangle$ (where $\pi_i : S \to \mathbb{R}$ is the ordinal payoff function of player i), for every player i let $S_i^0, S_i^1,...$ be the sequence of subsets of S_i defined recursively as follows: (1) let $S_i^0 = S_i$ and let $D_i^0 \subseteq S_i^0$ be the set of strategies of player i that are strictly dominated in G; (2) for $m \geq 1$ let $S_i^m = S_i^{m-1} \setminus D_i^{m-1}$, where $S_i^{m-1} \setminus D_i^{m-1}$ denotes the complement of D_i^{m-1} in S_i^{m-1} and D_i^{m-1} is the set of strategies of player i that are strictly dominated in the game whose strategy sets are given by $S_1^{m-1}, S_2^{m-1},...,S_n^{m-1}$. Define $S_i^\infty = \bigcap_{m \in \mathbb{N}} S_i^m$ (where $\mathbb{N}$ denotes the set of non-negative integers).

15 Formally, in an arbitrary model of a game G if $\omega \in CKR$ then $\sigma(\omega) \in S_1^\infty \times ... \times S_n^\infty$ (where the sets S_i^∞ are as defined in the previous footnote); conversely, if $s \in S_1^\infty \times ... \times S_n^\infty$ then there is a model of G and a state ω such that $\omega \in CKR$ and $s = \sigma(\omega)$. For more details on the history and various formulations of this result see Bonanno (2008). In particular, if one allows for cardinal – rather than ordinal – payoffs (see Section 3) and/or the notion of rationality is strengthened, then it may be possible to eliminate more strategy profiles.

16 For instance, (b,c) is not a Nash equilibrium because $\pi_2(b,c) = 1 < \pi_2(b,d) = 2$ and thus player 2 would be better off by unilaterally deviating from c to d.

17 For example, he rolls a die and if the outcome is 1 or 2 then he chooses c, otherwise he chooses d.

18 The epistemic conditions for Nash equilibrium are studied in Aumann and Brandenburger (1995).

19 That is, P_ω satisfies the following properties: (1) $\omega' \in P_\omega(\omega)$, for all $\omega' \in \Omega \setminus \{\omega\}$ (centeredness), (2) for every $\alpha, \beta \in \Omega$ with $\alpha \neq \beta$, either $\alpha \in P_\omega(\beta)$ or $\beta \in P_\omega(\alpha)$ (connectedness), (3) for every $\alpha, \beta \in \Omega$, if $\beta \in P_\omega(\alpha)$ then $\alpha \notin P_\omega(\beta)$ (asymmetry) and (4) for every $\alpha, \beta \in \Omega$, if $\beta \in P_\omega(\alpha)$ then $P_\omega(\beta) \subseteq P_\omega(\alpha)$ (transitivity).

20 When an information set is a singleton it is customary not to enclose it into a rectangle.

21 This definition coincides with the earlier one in games with perfect information since in the case of perfect information the information sets of a player are all singletons.

22 An extensive game has perfect recall if it satisfies the following property, for every player i: if h and g are two information sets of player i and there is a node in g which is a successor of a node in h, then every node in g comes after the same choice at h. Perfect recall implies that a player remembers his past choices as well as what he knew in the past (see Bonanno, 2004).

23 For an overview of the traditional approach see Battigalli and Bonanno (1999).

24 See, for example, Bonanno and Nehring (1999), Gul (1998) and Morris (1995).

25 For an overview see Aumann and Hart (2002).

26 Ordeshook (1986) is a classic reference. For a more recent account see McCarty and Meirowitz (2007).

27 See Swedberg (2001).

28 See Jaeger (2008).

29 An excellent source of information and resources for educators and students of game theory is the website www.gametheory.net.

30 For a recent overview of co-operative game theory see Peleg and Sudhölter (2007).

31 Evolutionary game theory was pioneered by the biologist John Maynard Smith (1982) and has been extensively applied not only in biology but also in the social sciences (see Samuelson, 1998; Weibull, 1995).

32 For a recent account of repeated games see Mailath and Samuelson (2006).

33 See, for example, Osborne and Rubinstein (1990).

34 A special issue of *Economics and Philosophy* (Volume 24, No. 3, November 2008) is devoted to a discussion of the philosophical and methodological issues and challenges that have been raised by neuroeconomics.

REFERENCES

Aumann, Robert (1976) 'Agreeing to disagree', *The Annals of Statistics*, 4: 1236–1239.

Aumann, Robert (1987) 'Game theory', in J. Eatwell, M. Milgate and P. Newman (eds) *The New Palgrave: A Dictionary of Economics*, London: Macmillan, 2: 460–482.

Aumann, Robert (1995) 'Backward induction and common knowledge of rationality', *Games and Economic Behavior*, 8: 6–19.

Aumann, Robert (1996) 'Reply to Binmore', *Games and Economic Behavior*, 17: 138–146.

Aumann, Robert and Sergiu Hart (2002) (eds), *Handbook of game theory with economic applications*. Volumes 1, 2 and 3. Elsevier, New York.

Battigalli, Pierpaolo and Giacomo Bonanno (1999) 'Recent results on belief, knowledge and the epistemic foundations of game theory', *Research in Economics*, 53: 149–225.

Bicchieri, Cristina (2006) *The Grammar of Society: the Nature and Dynamics of Social Norms*. Camridge: Cambridge University Press.

Binmore, Ken (1987) 'Modelling rational players I', *Economics and Philosophy*, 3: 179–214.

Binmore, Ken (1994) *Game Theory and the Social Contract*, Vol. 1: *Playing Fair*. Cambridge: MIT Press.

Binmore, Ken (1996) 'A note on backward induction', *Games and Economic Behavior*, 17: 135–137.

Binmore, Ken (1998) *Game Theory and the Social Contract*, vol. 2: *Just Playing*. Cambridge: MIT Press.

Bonanno, Giacomo (1991) 'The logic of rational play in games of perfect information', *Economics and Philosophy*, 7: 37–65.

Bonanno, Giacomo (2004) 'Memory and perfect recall in extensive games', *Games and Economic Behavior*, 47: 237–256.

Bonanno, Giacomo (2008) 'A syntactic approach to rationality in games with ordinal payoffs', in G. Bonanno, W. van der Hoek and M. Wooldridge (eds) *Logic and the Foundations of Game and Decision Theory*. Texts in Logic and Games, Amsterdam: Amsterdam University Press. pp. 59–86.

Bonanno, Giacomo and Klaus Nehring (1999) 'How to make sense of the common prior assumption under incomplete information', *International Journal of Game Theory*, 28: 409–434.

Brandenburger, Adam (2007) 'The power of paradox: Some recent developments in interactive epistemology', *International Journal of Game Theory*, 35: 465–492.

de Bruin, Boudewijn (2005) 'Game theory in philosophy', *Topoi*, 24: 197–208.

Dubey, Pradeep (1986) 'Inefficiency of Nash equilibria', *Mathematics of Operations Research*, 11: 1–8.

Gul, Faruk (1998) 'A comment on Aumann's Bayesian view', *Econometrica*, 66: 923–927.

Halpern Joseph (2001) 'Substantive rationality and backward induction', *Games and Economic Behavior*, 37: 425–435.

Harsanyi, John (1967) 'Games with incomplete information played by "Bayesian players", Part I', *Management Science*, 8: 159–182.

Harsanyi, John (1968) 'Games with incomplete information played by "Bayesian players", Part II', *Management Science*, 8: 320–334.

Harsanyi, John (1968) 'Games with incomplete information played by "Bayesian players", Part III', *Management Science*, 8: 486–502.

Jaeger, Gerhard (2008) 'Applications of Game Theory in Linguistics', *Language and Linguistics Compass* 2/3: 406–421.

Lewis, David (1969) *Convention*. Cambridge: Harvard University Press.

Lewis, David (1973) *Counterfactuals*. Cambridge: Harvard University Press.

Mailath, George J. and Larry Samuelson (2006) *Repeated Games and Reputations: Long-Run Relationships*. Oxford: Oxford University Press.

McCarty, Nolan and Adam Meirowitz (2007) *Political Game Theory: An Introduction*. Cambridge: Cambridge University Press.

Morris, Stephen (1995) 'The common prior assumption in economic theory', *Economics and Philosophy*, 11: 227–53.

Nash, John (1950) 'Equilibrium points in *n*-person games', *Proceedings of the National Academy of Sciences*, 36: 48–49.

Nash, John (1951) 'Non-cooperative games', *Annals of Mathematics*, 54: 286–295.

Ordeshook, Peter C. (1986) *Game Theory and Political Theory: An Introduction*. Cambridge: Cambridge University Press.

Osborne, Martin J. and Ariel Rubinstein (1990) *Bargaining and Markets*. New York: Academic Press.

Peleg, Bezalel and Peter Sudhölter (2007) *Introduction to the Theory of Cooperative Games*. New York: Springer.

Reny, Phil (1992) 'Rationality in extensive form games', *Journal of Economic Perspectives*, 6: 103–111.

Ross, Don (2006) 'Game theory', *Stanford encyclopedia of philosophy*. http://plato.stanford.edu/entries/game-theory/.

Samet, Dov (1996) 'Hypothetical knowledge and games with perfect information', *Games and Economic Behavior*, 17: 230–251.

Samuelson, Larry (1998) *Evolutionary Games and Equilibrium Selection*. Cambridge: MIT Press.

Selten, Reinhard (1975) 'Re-examination of the perfectness concept for equilibrium points in extensive games', *International Journal of Game Theory*, 4: 25–55.

Smith, John Maynard (1982) *Evolution and the Theory of Games*. Cambridge: Cambridge University Press.

Stalnaker, Robert (1968) 'A theory of conditionals', in N. Rescher (ed.) *Studies in Logical Theory*. London: Blackwell. pp. 98–112. Reprinted in E. Sosa (ed.) (1975) *Causation and Conditionals*. Oxford: Oxford University Press. pp. 165–179.

Stalnaker, Robert (1998) 'Belief revision in games: Forward and backward induction', *Mathematical Social Sciences*, 36: 31–56.

Swedberg, Richard (2001) 'Sociology and game theory: Contemporary and historical perspectives', *Theory and Society*, 30: 301–335.

Verbeek, Bruno (2004) 'Game theory and ethics', *Stanford encyclopedia of philosophy*. http://plato.stanford.edu/entries/game-ethics/.

von Neumann, John and Oscar Morgenstern (1944) *Theory of Games and Economic Behavior*. Princeton: Princeton University Press.

Weibull, Jörgen W. (1995) *Evolutionary Game Theory*. Cambridge: MIT Press.

16

Social Networks

Joan de Martí and Yves Zenou

INTRODUCTION

A large body of research, first in sociology, then in physics, and more recently in economics, has studied the importance of social networks in different activities. Social networks are indeed important in several facets of our lives. For example, the decision of an agent whether or not to buy a new product, attend a meeting, commit a crime, find a job is often influenced by the choices of their friends and acquaintances (be they social or professional). The emerging empirical evidence on these issues motivates the theoretical study of network effects. For example, job offers can be obtained from direct, and indirect, acquaintances through word-of-mouth communication. The spread of diseases, such as AIDS, also strongly depends on the geometry of social contacts. If the web of connections is dense, we can expect higher infection rates.

The study of social networks was indeed initiated by sociologists more than a century ago and has grown to be a central field of sociology over the past 50 years (see, for example, Wasserman and Faust, 1994). During that same period, a mathematical literature on the structure and properties of graphs has been developed and extensively studied (see Bollobás, 1998; Diestel, 2005).

A recent awakening of interest in social networks has occurred in the computer science and statistical physics literatures, mainly over the past five or six years (see Albert and Barabási, 2002; Newman, 2003, for an overview of these studies). While the importance of embeddedness of economic activity in social settings has been fundamental to sociologists (and to some extent to applied mathematicians) for some time, it was largely ignored by economists until the last decade. Indeed, studies of networks with economic perspectives and using game-theoretic modeling techniques have only emerged over the last decade (see Goyal, 2007; Jackson, 2007, 2008; Vega-Redondo, 2007).

A network is an abstract object that models these social interactions. In particular, a network is formed by *nodes* (or *vertices*) that represent the actors involved, and *edges* (or *links*) that express the linkage among these nodes. Networks provide a simplified geometrical representation of a complex magma of social relationships. However, if social interactions represent a first-order driving force for the problem under consideration, a detailed study of the characteristics of the network should reveal some relevant features of social structure that induce the resulting outcomes. In the job market example, it is of paramount importance to know the geometric characteristics of the network that induce job market outcomes and how different individuals end up in different situations due to their asymmetric positions in the network of personal relationships. Isolated individuals, or individuals with low-quality links with the rest of the community, have weaker positions in the network and are therefore more prone to be, and to stay, unemployed for a long period of time since they do not obtain (valuable) job information from their contacts.

Different fields have different approaches obviously. Most sociologists would explain (most) networks as an *unintended* outcome of other kinds of activities that individuals engage in. Individuals grow up in certain neighborhoods, they attend certain schools, they take jobs at certain workplaces, etc. and as a by-product of this, they get friends and acquaintances that become nodes in their networks. Their choice of friends and acquaintances is based rarely on their instrumental usefulness. On the contrary, economists would explain networks as an *intended* outcome stemming from strategic interactions. As Coleman (1988) puts it:

> There are two broad intellectual streams in the description and explanations of social action. One, characteristic of the work of most sociologists, sees the actor as socialized and action as governed by social norms, rules, and obligations. The principal virtues of this intellectual stream lie in its ability to describe action in social context and to explain the way action is shaped, constrained, and redirected by the social context. The other intellectual stream, characteristic of the work of most economists, sees the actor as having goals independently arrived at, as acting independently, as a whole self-interested. Its principal virtue lies in having a principle of action, that of maximizing utility. This principle of action, together with a single empirical generalization (declining marginal utility) has generated the extensive growth of neoclassical economic theory, as well as the growth of political philosophy of several varieties: utilitarianism, contractarianism, and natural rights.

The aim of this chapter is to survey the literature on social networks putting together the economics, sociological, and physics/applied mathematics approaches, showing their similarities and differences. In the next section, we will first present some measures of characteristics of social networks, mainly introduced by sociologists, which will be useful later on. Then we will expose and develop the two main ways of modeling network formation. While the physics/applied mathematics approach is capable of reproducing most observed networks, it does not explain why they emerge. On the contrary, the economics approach is very precise in explaining why networks emerge but does a poor job in matching real-world networks. The fourth section will analyze behaviors on networks, which take as given networks and study the impact of their structure on individuals' outcomes. We will use the game-theoretical framework, characteristic of economics, and will compare the results obtained to those in sociology. The last section will then conclude.

SOCIAL NETWORK ANALYSIS

Many techniques and concepts have been developed continuously over the years during the last century and there is right now a powerful machinery available under the corpus of social network analysis. It is not the aim of this survey to treat with full generality all relevant contributions in this field.[1] In particular, in this section, we are going to focus on a small subset of concepts, a set of *centrality measures*, that have been introduced in the literature to capture in a numerical form the prominence of actors inside a network.

Centrality measures aim at ranking individuals in terms of their relevance due to their position in the network. Social network analysis also introduces other characteristics of social structure such as the concept of *structural equivalence* (Lorrain and White, 1971) and *block modeling* techniques (White et al., 1976). The concept of structural equivalence tries to uncover similar roles and social positions shared by different actors in a network. The hypothesis behind structural equivalence is that actors who share a similar position inside a network are going to end up with similar outcomes. On the other hand, block modeling techniques aim at disentangling different roles in a network when considering social network data.

For convenience, in this section, we are going to interpret links as communication lines. This unifies the treatment and interpretation but has no technical implication on the concepts defined.

There are several ways of constructing numerical statistics that can give a measure of the relevance of an individual embedded in a complex web of social relationships. The simplest and a most natural way is simply to count the number of connections an agent has. This measure is called *degree centrality*. Under degree centrality, agents who have a higher degree enjoy a better position inside the network. This measure is associated to the idea that "the more connections one has, the better it is." For example, more connected individuals can have access to more information sources that can translate into better socioeconomic outcomes.

While degree distribution seems an appealing concept, it is only considering direct benefits derived from connections, abstracting from the potential contribution of indirect benefits derived from indirect connections. In that respect, degree centrality can be quite misleading in some situations.

Granovetter's (1973, 1983) seminal work extends this concept by distinguishing between strong and weak ties.[2] This taxonomy of social interactions determines different functions of different kinds of connections. Granovetter's thesis is that the strength of a tie among two different actors is proportional to the level of overlapping of their local social capital. Indeed, in a close network, everyone knows each other, information is shared and so potential sources of information are quickly shaken down, the network quickly becomes redundant in terms of access to new information. In contrast, Granovetter stresses the strength of weak ties involving a secondary ring of acquaintances

that have contacts with networks outside ego's network and therefore offer new sources of information on job opportunities. As Granovetter (1973) claims "whatever is to be diffused can reach a larger number of people, and traverse greater social distance (…), when passed through weak ties rather than strong ties" (p. 1366). In substance, weak ties foster widespread diffusion, while strong ties breed local sharing.

If as Granovetter suggests, increasing the number of informational sources can have some impact on outcomes, then direct links can be of different quality depending on whether they are providing access to new secondary sources of information or not. In the same way aggregating all kind of connections irrespective of their strength, as degree centrality does, can be quite misleading as a measure of influence and power inside the network. To understand this, let us look at *clustering* coefficients. An agent has a high level of clustering if most of the friends of his/her friends are also his/her friends. If this is the case, the local ego-centered network of an individual is weaker than that of another agent with the same number of connections but with a smaller clustering. This effect is, precisely, the redundancy of information associated to strong ties stressed by Granovetter.

It is in fact possible to incorporate indirect connections in a centrality measure in several ways. When considering direct and indirect benefits, it is natural to assume that the benefits of any connection dilute with the distance between agents involved in it. It is indeed not the same to receive information immediately from a direct connection (i.e., a close friend) and indirectly from individuals located several links away. The quality of information decays with distance. As a result, it seems quite natural to construct the following centrality measure. Give to any individual a particular numerical value for each of his/her direct connections. Then, give a smaller value to any connection at distance two and an even smaller value to any connection at distance three, etc.[3] When adding up all these values, we end up with a new numerical value that is now capturing both direct and indirect connections of any order. This is the idea behind Katz's (1953) and Bonacich's (1987) network centrality measure.[4] This is not at all an ad hoc construction. It arises naturally in the dynamic settings of social influence (Friedkin, 1991) or, as we will see below, as the equilibrium outcome of games with network complementarities (Ballester et al., 2006).

The degree and Katz–Bonacich centrality measures capture the power and influence of individuals as recipients of information. Although this can be the natural way to introduce power in a number of situations, there are other settings in which the power of an individual is induced by his/her position as an intermediate in the communication process. When an agent is relevant for most communication processes inside the network, he/she can exert an important role since he/she can deter or even prevent information transmission. Betweenness centrality, introduced by Freeman (1977, 1979), measures precisely this source of influence inside the network. Essentially, betweenness centrality calculates the relative number of indirect connections (or paths) in which the actor in consideration is involved in with respect to the total number of paths in the network. This strongly relates to the concept of *structural holes* due to Burt (1992). Holes in social structure emerge in situations in which there is a lack of connections between different subgroups. Burt claims that agents who bridge these structural holes can extract a disproportionate benefit compared to other individuals who share a similar social position but who are not linking holes. Betweenness centrality provides a mathematical way to characterize agents that are bridging structural holes. To illustrate the concepts presented in this section, consider the network shown in Figure 16.1.

In this network, the agent represented by a white circle is less relevant when considering degree centrality. He/she has a degree equal to two, while the rest of agents have a degree at least equal to 3. Instead, we can ensure that this same agent is the more central one

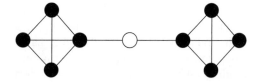

Figure 16.1   Bridge network and centrality measures.

when considering betweenness centrality. He/she is in a bottleneck position inside the network. All communication from one side to the other side of the network necessarily has to pass through him/her, and, if controlling information is important, he/she can extract large positive benefits. He/she is bridging a structural hole. If we now consider the Bonacich centrality measure, this individual can either be the less or the more central agent inside the network depending on the value of the discount factor. For small discount factors (i.e., indirect links give less benefits), the agent is the less central one while for high levels of discount (i.e., direct links are weighted less), this agent is the most central.

Hence, the three centrality measures rank agents differently. The adequacy of one measure over the other very much depends on the context and interpretation given to the network.

NETWORK FORMATION

One of the main goals of the analysis of social networks is to shed some light on the mechanisms explaining how and why networks form. If social networks are relevant, we need to understand how networks emerge and the forces determining their shape.

One possible reason why a link is formed is *pure chance*. Two individuals randomly meet and create a link between them, which can represent friendship or a stable working relationship. A set of different models have arisen based on this assumption. They are called *random models of network formation*.

Another possible reason for the formation of a link is strategic interactions. Individuals carefully decide with whom to interact and this decision entails some consent by both parts in a given relationship. *Strategic network formation models* are, precisely, grounded on this premise. We now discuss with some detail both domains of research.

Random models of network formation

The simplest useful model of a random network (and one of the oldest) is the *Bernoulli random graph*, often just called the *random graph* for short (Bollobás, 2001; Erdős and Rényi, 1959, 1960; Solomonoff and Rapoport, 1951). In this model, a certain number of vertices (or nodes) are taken and edges (or links) are created between them with independent probability p for each vertex pair. When p is small, there are only a few edges in the network and most vertices exist in isolation or in small groups of connected vertices. Conversely, for large p, almost every possible edge is present between the possible vertex pairs and all or almost all of the vertices join together in a single large connected group called a *giant component*.

Understanding when a network is going to be fully connected is important, for example, to characterize the possible dynamics of infection rates in a population. There are, in fact, several common characteristics shared by most social networks. While the random graph model illuminates our understanding about when a giant component emerges, it cannot correctly mimic other critical aspects of real-world networks. The recent physics/applied mathematics literature have proposed different models that solve these weaknesses of the Erdös–Rényi framework.

One of the main characteristics most networks have is that their *degree distribution* (i.e., the number of links each node has) is scale-free,[5] which in a mathematical form means that it follows a *power law*.[6] A power law implies that the probability that an agent is intensively connected to other agents in the society is non-negligible and strictly above zero. In particular, if a network is scale-free, we should expect that a small number of agents in the network show a high number of connections compared to the majority of agents who are involved in a small number of connections.

We can find empirical evidence of this pattern when analyzing, for example, the pattern of adult human sexual contacts. Liljeros et al. (2001) studied the 1996 Swedish survey of sexual behavior and provided neat evidence that the distribution of sexual partners follows a power law distribution, hence, validating the scale-free hypothesis. Figure 16.2 taken from Liljeros et al. (2001, Figure 2), plots the cumulative distribution of sexual connectivity.

More precisely, Figure 16.2a shows that, for male and female respondents, the cumulative distribution of the number of sexual partners over a period of 12 months before the survey while Figure 16.2b displays the same statistics for a much longer period, namely for the respondent's life up to the time of the survey. It is easy to see that, in both figures, the data closely follow a straight line in a double-logarithmic plot, which is consistent with power-law dependence and the fact that the degree distribution has fat tails. This means, in particular, that most of the people in the sample had very few sexual partners while a small group had a very high number of sexual partners over their lifetime (up to 600 for the most "active" ones!). Other networks such as the internet, the movie actor collaboration, or linkage due to scientific co-authorship (Albert and Barabási, 2002; Goyal et al., 2006) also display the same properties of scale-free networks and power laws.

It is interesting to compare the results of Liljeros et al. (2001) to those of Bearman et al. (2004). The latter is a thorough analysis of the structure of an adolescent romantic and sexual network in a population of over 800 adolescents residing in a mid-sized town in the midwestern United States.[7]

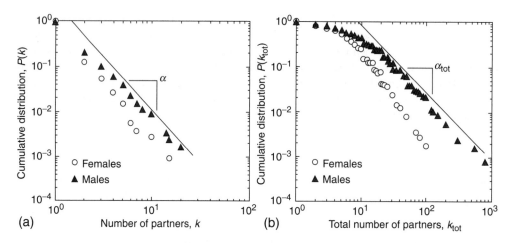

Figure 16.2   Network of sexual partners in Sweden. Scale-free distribution of the number of sexual partners for females and males. (a) Distribution of number of partners, k, in the previous 12 months. Note the larger average number of partners for male respondents: this difference may be due to 'measurement bias' – social expectations may lead males to inflate their reported number of sexual partners. Note that the distributions are both linear, indicating scale-free power-law behavior. Moreover, the two curves are roughly parallel, indicating similar scaling exponents. For females, $\alpha = 2.54 \pm 0.2$ in the range $k > 4$, and for males, $\alpha = 2.31 \pm 0.2$ in the range $k > 5$.
(b) Distribution of the total number of parners k_{tot} over respondents' entire lifetimes. For females, $\alpha_{tot} = 2.1 \pm 0.3$ in the range $k_{tot} > 20$, and for males, $\alpha_{tot} = 1.6 \pm 0.3$ in the range $20 < k_{tot} < 400$. Estimates for females and males agree within statistical uncertainty.

The authors analyzed reports of relationships of this adolescent network that occurred over a period of 18 months between 1993 and 1995. Interestingly, they found that the geometry of this network of adolescent sexual contacts was quite different from that of Liljeros et al. Most of its young members were included in a single giant component, which means that either directly or indirectly they were all connected to the majority of the students in the high-school. This, in particular, implies that the structure of this network looks very much like what the Erdös–Rényi model predicts: the degree distribution of each adolescent follows a gaussian (normal) distribution rather than a power law. These striking differences lead to distinct policy implications when trying to combat, for example, the spread of diseases related to sexual contacts. For adults, as suggested by Liljeros et al. (2001), it might be more productive to focus all efforts into targeting individuals in the upper tail of the degree distribution, that is,

the small number of people that have a high number of sexual contacts. This targeting would ensure that those nodes from which spread and contagion can be more harmful are controlled for or at least stimulated to take preventive measures. However, because of the results of Bearman et al. (2004), for adolescents, given that they are all essentially on equal footing within the network, a policy based on widespread education on healthy habits may be much more efficient.

The Erdös–Rényi model cannot rationalize scale-free degree distributions. In particular, it predicts that the probability that an individual has a large number of connections goes to zero as this number of connections increases. Barabási and Albert (1999) propose a model which is able to reproduce the scale-free nature of degree distributions and explain the fat-tailed degree distributions observed in some networks (like the sexual contact network described above). In the Barabási–Albert model, the population is increasing over time and agents show *preferential attachment*, meaning that new agents in the network are more likely to connect to agents that are already well connected. The authors show that the preferential attachment mechanism naturally induces the emergence of a power-law degree distribution. Although, other alternative mechanisms have been considered in both the theoretical and empirical literatures, preferential attachment has been frequently invoked as a probable source of scale-free properties in self organization of social, and other types of, networks.

Unfortunately, while the preferential-attachment model does a good job in trying to fit the empirical evidence on the scale-free nature of connectivity, it does not satisfy another widespread characteristic of many real-world networks: the *small-world* property.[8] A possible interpretation of this property is that agents in a network tend to show similar levels of connectivity and a high level of *clustering* (i.e., if John is friend with Patricia and if Patricia is friend with Patrick, then a high level of clustering means that John and Patrick are, most probably, also friends), and furthermore that the diameter of the network is quite small.

Watts and Strogatz (1998) provide a model that incorporates elements of both social structure and randomness to obtain networks that have the small-world properties. In this model, the "social structure" is represented by a uniform one-dimensional lattice (the circle), where each node is connected to its k nearest neighbors on the lattice, and "randomness" is characterized by a tunable parameter p, which specified the probability that a link in the lattice would be *randomly rewired* (see Figure 16.3 below). To be more precise, start with a strongly *regular* network in which nodes are located in a circular network and are also connected to the neighbors of their neighbors (in the panel at the extreme left of the figure, each node is connected to its two direct neighbors and to its two neighbors of length 2). Then, take randomly some of the existing links, just a small number of them, and rewire them across the network. This rewiring process leads to a new geometrical arrangement where the clustering level is still high, due to the initial topology of connections, and where the value of the diameter is reducing due to the rewiring process which randomly connects distant agents in the initial network. Figure 16.3, taken from Watts and Strogatz's work, provides a graphical intuition of the consequences of the rewiring mechanism.

The process starts with the network at the left of the picture. If no kind of rewiring and randomness are introduced, then the same regular network is sustained. When the level of rewiring/randomness starts to increase, we evolve to a situation in which only a small number of links are rearranged, leading to a characteristic small-world pattern, represented at the center of the picture. If there is too much rewiring/randomness (p close to 1), then, as can be seen from the right panel of

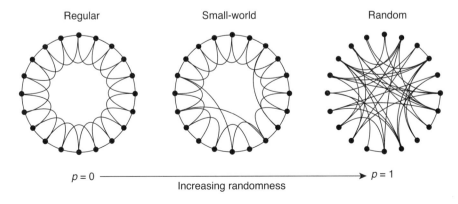

Figure 16.3 Networks with and without small world properties.

the figure, the process turns back to a purely random process à la Erdös–Rényi. However, because of the mechanism that governs this network formation process, Watts and Strogatz (1998) are not able to obtain the scale-free degree distribution property.

A recent paper by Jackson and Rogers (2007) overcomes this last problem by providing a hybrid model that has most of the properties shared by real-world networks, that is, low diameter, high clustering, small-world and scale-free properties. In this paper, Jackson and Rogers (2007) combine the pure random model of Erdös–Rényi with the preferential attachment model of Barabási and Albert (1999). More precisely, they develop a dynamic model of network formation where nodes find other nodes with which they form links in two ways: some are found uniformly at random (as in the Erdös–Rényi model) while others are found by searching locally through the current structure of the network, for example, meeting friends of friends (i.e., preferential attachment).

The authors then use their model to calibrate it with data from widely varied applications, in particular, the network of romantic relationships among high-school students exposed above (Bearman et al., 2004). They also find that the high-school romance networks are almost uniformly random. Interestingly, clustering is absent since the high-school romance network is predominately a heterosexual (bipartite) network.

Strategic network formation

We would like to expose now the economic approach of network formation where links are not formed at random or in a rather mechanical way (as in the preferential attachment model), but by a process for which agents form links that maximize their own well-being. Indeed, the main advantages of random graph models are that: (i) they generate large networks with well identified properties; (ii) they mimic real networks (at least in some characteristics); and (iii) they

tie a specific property to a specific process. However, as pointed out by Jackson (2007), they are unable to answer the *why* behind network formation. For example, in Watts and Strogatz (1998), the "social structure" is represented by a uniform one-dimensional lattice. This is an assumption and we do not know why and under which conditions this network structure prevails. Similarly, Barabási and Albert (1999) never justify why agents behave according to the preferential attachment rule. On the contrary, by focusing on the optimal behavior of agents in making links, we can understand why certain network structures emerge. The economics approach also has its limits since it is unable to derive "equilibrium" networks that have the properties of most real-world networks and, in particular, cannot tell which degree distribution should emerge.

The strategic component in network formation models relies on the fact that the utility function[9] of an agent depends on the activity undertaken by the rest of the agents with whom he/she is linked to. Hence, agents have to choose with whom they would like to form a link. At the same time other agents are considering the same kind of decision. Altogether, this specifies a game.

Game theory provides a set of rigorous and powerful tools to analyze such a situation (see, for example, Myerson, 1991). Strategic network formation analysis borrows from this literature and has also contributed to its recent enlargement. The Nash equilibrium is the key concept in game theory.[10]

Myerson (1977, 1991) provides an early formulation of a network formation game. The structure of the game is simple: agents have to decide about their potential partners and their strategies consist in naming those with whom they want to form a link with. For a link to be formed, it has to be that two individuals name each other, that is, there needs to be *mutual consent* in link creation. The Nash equilibrium concept can then be used to find out which strategy profiles are stable and, hence, which networks are the possible outcomes of the game.

The main problem of using the Nash equilibrium concept is that it exacerbates the coordination problems that arise when all agents are simultaneously deciding about friendship ties. In particular, the empty network (i.e., nobody forms a link) is always a Nash equilibrium of this game since no deviation is profitable. Indeed, deviating means here to name someone as a friend but this will not generate a link because of mutual consent. In general, with the Myerson game, there are many equilibria, which reduce the attractiveness of this approach.

A first solution to this problem has been proposed by Jackson and Wolinsky (1996). In their seminal paper, they introduce an alternative solution concept for network formation games, namely *pairwise stability*. To be pairwise stable, a network has to satisfy two conditions. First, no agent has incentives to severe any of the existing links, and, second, no pair of agents has incentives to create a non-existing link among them. Pairwise stability is a relatively weak solution concept that captures the essence of mutual consent. It still has limited prediction power, but introduces in network formation models the tendency to form mutually beneficial links and severing links that are counterproductive for at least one of the two parts of the relationship.

A second alternative to the Myerson game is to consider *directed* instead of *undirected* networks,[11] which solves the coordination problem of mutual consent. Bala and Goyal (2000) extend the Myerson model described above by only considering directed networks, that is, individuals form links *unilaterally* without requiring the consent of the other party to create a link.

Jackson and Wolinsky (1996) also introduce the so-called *connections model*, which uses a simple linear utility function aiming at capturing the usefulness of *direct* and *indirect* connections to gain access to a number of different resources (such as, for example, information on job openings) and the costs of establishing these connections. In particular, any connection, direct or indirect, is valuable, although more distant connections contribute less to an agent's well-being. Only direct links are, however, costly. Agents have to consider the costs and benefits of creating new links in a decentralized manner and, as a result, the set of possible outcomes can be characterized. Several network typologies can be pairwise stable and, quite naturally, the set of possible outcomes depends on the costs and benefits of forming a link.

One of the main virtues of using pairwise stability as a solution concept for network formation games is that it is relatively easy to check when a network is pairwise stable or not. For example, consider the star network in Figure 16.4, with a center (agent 1) connected to three peripheral agents (agents 2, 3, and 4).

In the connections model, connectivity rewards are computed through a discount factor $0 < \delta < 1$. A direct connection provides a reward equals to δ; a friend of a friend gives δ^2; a link with an indirect friend of length k gives δ^k; and so forth. Only the cost of forming direct friendships is considered and is denoted by $c > 0$. For the sake of exposition, let us consider the case in which $\delta = 0.5$ and $c = 0.6$. We can then see that the star network depicted above is not pairwise

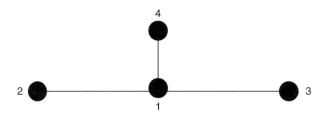

Figure 16.4 A star network with four agents.

stable because the central agent (agent 1) would improve his/her utility by cutting any of his/her existing links with agents 2, 3, and 4. Indeed, the reward of any of such connections is 0.5 while the cost is 0.6. This generates a disutility of –0.1. Therefore, for this particular parametric setup, given that the center has incentives to severe some of his/her existing links in the network, this star network is not pairwise stable.

Besides this pure positive analysis, a utilitarian perspective is introduced to conduct a *normative* analysis, trying to evaluate which networks are socially optimal. The tractability of the "connection model" offers a first reasonable benchmark to gain insight on this issue. Jackson and Wolinsky (1996) provide a characterization of the set of all efficient networks.[12] It is shown that the set of efficient networks usually does not equal, or only partially include, the set of pairwise stable networks.[13]

For example, coming back to the star network described above, it can be proved that this network is socially efficient when $\delta = 0.5$ and $c = 0.6$, while we have seen that it was not pairwise stable. Indeed, the central agent 1 is paying for three different connections, while the peripheral agents (2, 3, and 4) only pay for one, but they all benefit from indirect connections due to their direct link to the center (peripheral agents are all at a distance 2 from each other). It is the positive spreading of externalities from indirect neighbors that makes the star network efficient. However, this network is not pairwise stable because the cost the central agent is paying is too large compared to the benefit of maintaining links with peripheral agents. In that case, decentralized behavior cannot induce a socially optimal geometry of connections.

This analysis reveals that, in general, individual and social incentives are not compatible, and that decentralized behavior usually results in an inefficient arrangement of social ties.

This last result is particularly remarkable. This tension between individual incentives and social welfare leads quite naturally to the following question: is there any way this tension can be weakened? In other words, can we find welfare-enhancing policies that ensure that the resulting network of relationships is optimal, or closer to an optimum, for the society as a whole? For example, it is clear that identity issues shape friendship formation during childhood and adolescence (see, for example, Akerlof and Kranton, 2002; De Martí and Zenou, 2009). The assignment of students to classrooms can be then considered as a potential policy tool that impacts on the outcome of friendship formation mechanisms in school and schooling outcomes. Strategic network formation models can thus shed some light on these kinds of debates, in particular, in situations where individual decisions are driven by both private interests and social forces that can be incorporated into a utility function.

BEHAVIOR ON NETWORKS

In this section, we would like to take the network as given and study how its structure impacts on outcomes and individual decisions.

The theory of "games on networks" aims at determining the outcome of a game with n players or agents (that can be individuals, firms, regions, countries, etc.) who are all linked (directly or indirectly) together in a network and are choosing an action (that could be search effort, job market decisions, engagement in criminal activities, investment in R&D, etc.) that maximizes their utility. What is interesting in these games is that agents are utility maximizers that take into account the interdependencies generated by the social network structure. Social capital is incorporated in the utility function of each actor.

Most of this rather small and new literature has focused on *static* models (only what happens today prevails so that there is no time dimension) with *perfect information*, that is, all agents perfectly know the structure of the network and the actions taken, not only by their direct friends, but by all agents in the network. Even so, both premises can be relaxed to accommodate more realistic assumptions. For example, Galeotti et al. (2009) develop a general model of games played on networks, in which players have *private* and *incomplete information* about the network.[14] In this paper, agents do not know the whole network but are informed only of their own degree (i.e., number of links). Moreover, they assume that agents have beliefs about the rest of the network that depend on their own degree, which are summarized by a probability distribution over the degrees of their neighbors.

A networked model of peer effects

Consider an individual connected by a network of peer influences. In this network each agent reaps complementarities[15] from all his/her direct network peers. Ballester et al. (2006) computed the Nash equilibrium of this peer-effect game when agents choose their peer effort simultaneously. In their setup, restricted to linear-quadratic utility functions, they established that the peer-effect game described above has a unique Nash equilibrium[16] where each agent's strategy is proportional to his/her Katz–Bonacich centrality measure, already introduced above. This is the main theoretical result of Ballester et al. (2006), a good example of how the economic and sociological literature on networks can fruitfully borrow from each other. At equilibrium, individual decisions emanate from all the existing network chains of direct and indirect contacts stemming from each node, which is a feature characteristic of Katz–Bonacich centrality. Consider for example the network in Figure 16.5.

This network results from the overlap between two different dyads (dyad of agents 1 and 2 and dyad of agents 1 and 3) with a common partner, agent 1. Agent 2 reaps *direct* complementarities from agent 1 in one dyad who, in turn, reaps *direct* complementarities from agents 2 and 3 in both dyads. Thus, through the interaction with the central agent, peripheral agents end up reaping complementarities *indirectly* from each other. For this reason, the equilibrium decisions in each dyad cannot be analyzed independently of each other. Rather, each dyad exerts a strategic externality on the other one, and the equilibrium effort level of each agent reflects this externality.

What kinds of predictions can we learn from this model? Let us think of crime. It is well established that crime is, to some extent, a group phenomenon, and the source of crime and delinquency is located in the intimate social networks of individuals (see, for example, Sutherland, 1947; Sarnecki, 2001; Warr, 2002). Indeed, criminals often have friends who have themselves committed several offences, and social ties among criminals are seen as a means whereby individuals exert an influence over one another to commit crimes. In fact, not only friends but also the structure of social networks matters in explaining individuals' own criminal behavior.[17]

The model presented above predicts that a key determinant of one's criminal activities is the position in the network, that is, the more central (in terms of the Katz–Bonacich centrality index) a person is in a network, the higher his/her level of criminal activity is. In other words, it gives a causal relationship between network's location and criminal activities.[18,19]

But, in fact, the model can predict even more. It can propose new policies aimed

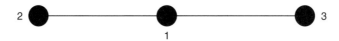

Figure 16.5 A star network with three agents.

at reducing crime. Indeed, in the standard economic literature on crime, where criminals decide to commit crime based on a cost–benefit analysis (see, for instance, the literature surveys by Garoupa, 1997, and Polinsky and Shavell, 2000), the standard policy tool to reduce aggregate crime relies on the deterrence effects of punishment, that is, the planner should increase uniformly punishment costs.

The model above, though, associates a distribution of delinquency efforts to the network connecting them. In particular, the variance of delinquency efforts reflects the variance of network centralities. In this case, a targeted policy that discriminates among delinquents depending on their relative network location, and removes a few suitably selected targets from this network, alters the whole distribution of delinquency efforts, not just shifting it. In practice, the planner may want to identify optimal network targets to concentrate (scarce) investigatory resources on some particular individuals, or to isolate them from the rest of the group, either through leniency programs, social assistance programs, or incarceration.

This type of discriminating policy has been studied in detail by Ballester et al. (2006, 2010). To characterize the network optimal targets, they propose a new measure of network centrality, the so-called *optimal inter-centrality measure*, which does not exist in the social network literature. This measure solves the planner's problem that consists in finding and getting rid of the key player, that is, the criminal who, once removed, leads to

the highest aggregate crime reduction. They show that the key player is, precisely, the individual with the highest optimal inter-centrality in the network.

The ranking of criminals according to their individual optimal inter-centrality measures, relevant for the selection of the optimal network target, need not always coincide with the ranking induced by individual equilibrium – Katz–Bonacich centralities. In other words, *the key player is not necessarily the most active criminal*. Indeed, removing a criminal from a network has both a direct and an indirect effect. First, fewer criminals contribute to the aggregate crime level. This is the direct effect. Second, the network topology is modified, and the remaining criminals adopt different crime efforts. This is the indirect effect. The key player is the one with the highest overall effect.

To illustrate this result, consider the network of 11 criminals in Figure 16.6. We can distinguish three different types of equivalent criminals in this network, which are shown in Table 16.1.

We can distinguish three different types of equivalent criminals in this network, which are the following:

We can identify the key player in this network of criminals.[20] If the choice of the key player were solely governed by the *direct* effect of criminal removal on aggregate crime, type-2 criminals would be the natural candidates. Indeed, these are the ones with the highest number of direct connections. But the choice of the key player needs also to take into account the *indirect* effect on

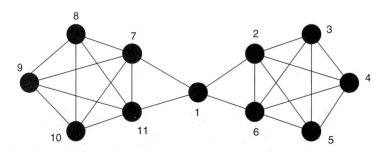

Figure 16.6   A bridge network with eleven criminals.

Table 16.1 Types of criminals in the bridge network

Type	Criminals
1	1
2	2, 6, 7, 11
3	3, 4, 5, 8, 9, 10

aggregate crime reduction induced by the network restructuring that follows the removal of one criminal from the original network. Because of his/her communities' bridging role, criminal 1 is also a possible candidate for the preferred policy target.

It can be showed that type-2 criminals always display the highest Katz–Bonacich centrality measure.[21] These criminals have the highest number of direct connections. Besides, they are directly connected to the bridge criminal 1, which gives them access to a very wide and diversified span of indirect connections. Altogether, they are the most central criminals and thus those who commit most crimes. However, the most active criminals are not the key players. Indeed, because indirect effects matter a lot, eliminating criminal 1 has the highest joint direct and indirect effect on aggregate crime reduction. Criminals counter the higher deterrence they face by spreading their know-how further away in the network and establishing synergies with criminals located in distant parts of the social setting. In that case, the optimal targeted policy is the one that maximally disrupts the crime network, thus harming the most its know-how transferring ability.[22]

Public good provision and innovation processes

Efforts can also be strategic substitutes[23] when we focus on a network model of public goods.[24] Examples of public goods abound. When a person plants a garden, his/her neighbors benefit. When a jurisdiction institutes a pollution abatement program, the benefits also accrue to nearby communities.

When individuals innovate – for example, experiment with new technology or generate new information – the results are often non-excludable in certain dimensions and thus others may benefit from the innovation. For example, in agriculture, one farmer's experience with a new crop can benefit other farmers, and the physical and social geography of the countryside can influence experimentation and learning. In industry, it has been long posited that research findings spill over to other firms.

The questions that these types of models seek to answer are the following: How does the social structure affect the level and pattern of public good provision? Do people exert effort themselves or rely on others? These are similar questions to the previous model in fourth section but the answers will be different because of the strategic substitutability assumption.

Bramoullé and Kranton (2007) develop a model along these lines. People who are linked directly or indirectly by a network of relationships desire a public good which is costly to produce. Individuals decide how much effort they want to exert to contribute to this good. The authors characterize the Nash equilibria of this game. Their analysis yields three main insights. First, networks can lead to *specialization*. Indeed, in any network there is a Nash equilibrium where some individuals contribute to the public good and others completely free ride (this was not possible in the case of strategic complementarities). In many networks, this extreme situation is the only equilibrium outcome. In all networks, such patterns are the only stable outcomes. Hence, agents' positions in a network can determine whether or not they contribute to the public good. Second, specialization can have welfare benefits. This outcome arises when contributors are linked, collectively, to many people in society. Finally, new links can reduce overall welfare. A new link increases access to the new information/public good, but also reduces individual incentives to contribute. Hence, overall welfare can be higher when there are *holes* in a network.

To illustrate some of these results, let us take an example. Consider the two *complete* networks with four individuals shown in Figure 16.7 (where the numbers are the effort levels provided by each individual).

Bramoullé and Kranton (2007) show that for complete networks, in any Nash equilibrium, the total aggregate effort is 1, and it can be split in any way among the agents. For example, as in the left panel, efforts could be equally distributed, so that each agent exerts 1/4, or, as in the right panel, one agent could be a specialist and provide an effort of 1 whereas all other individuals free ride by providing no effort. Consider then on the contrary star networks as shown in Figure 16.8.

In that case, only specialized profiles are equilibria. There are just two Nash equilibria: either the center is a specialist, or the three agents at the periphery are specialists. What do we learn from these simple examples? We learn that the structure of the network is the main determinants of the equilibria; denser networks can lead to less overall experimentation, and effort sharing is not always possible.

There is a growing field in economics studying innovation and diffusion of information, and there are many studies that suggest that social structures affect experimentation and spread of information. The present analysis suggests that individuals who have active social neighbors should have high benefits but exert little effort. Also, individuals who have prominent social positions are expected to bear less of the effort costs and instead rely more on others' efforts. This model indicates the importance of strategic and network efforts. For instance, in their study of the adoption of pineapple for export in Ghana, Conley and Udry (2001,

2010) find that, for a given farmer, (i) he/she is more likely to change his/her fertilizer use after his/her information neighbors who use similar amounts of fertilizer achieve lower than expected profits; and (ii) he/she increases (decreases) his/her use of fertilizer after his/her information neighbors achieve unexpectedly high profits when using more (less) fertilizer than he/she did.

Collective action, coordination, and social structure

Another important issue of games on networks is *collective action*. A group of people face a collective action problem in that an individual wants to participate only if joined by enough other individuals. We can therefore define a threshold for each individual as the number of people necessary for him/her to participate. However, a group's behavior can strongly depend on its internal configuration. Hence, when considering collective action problems, it is of paramount importance to understand how the arrangement of intra-group social ties is going to shape the decisions of their members.

Granovetter (1978) and Schelling (1978) provide dynamic models to analyze such issues, avoiding a clear linkage of outcomes to the social network structure in society. In particular, a snowball effect might be generated only if there are initially enough activists who are willing to participate, independently of others' decisions. Once these activists start the process, other agents will join as far as the number of people who have already joined is higher than their thresholds.

Chwe (1999, 2000) provides an alternative, static, formulation of the rising of such

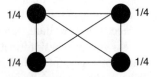 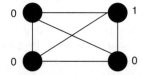

Figure 16.7   Two complete networks in a public-good model.

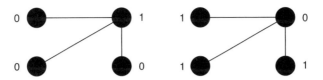

Figure 16.8   Two star networks in a public-good model.

processes rooted at the societal network geometry. He studies the internal structure of a group and analyzes how network configuration can lead to massive participation or to a failure in coordinating individual activity. Arguably, it does not contradict Granovetter's and Schelling's models but enriches the understanding of how coordination might be necessary to join the first *snowflakes*, which will then generate a snowball effect in collective action.

More precisely, in Chwe's model, agents in the network have to decide whether or not to participate in a common activity. They are only willing to participate in the activity if a minimum number of individuals also participate. There is a coordination problem since this information is not known in advance. Each person only knows the thresholds of his/her neighbors (i.e., direct links) in the social network ("local knowledge"). Individuals can communicate to their acquaintances the value of this minimum threshold on activists necessary for him/her to join the activity. The network, thus, shapes individual beliefs. To understand the mechanisms of the model, consider the two networks shown in Figure 16.9 and the situation in which any agent is willing to join the activity if and only if he/

she knows for sure that two more individuals are going to join it too.

In the first network, the circle, all agents share a symmetric situation. Agent 1 knows his/her own threshold and the threshold of his/her neighbours in the network, that is, individuals 2 and 4. Since all of them know the threshold of two other members of the network, it is immediate that all four agents are going to join the activity. Indeed, the three of them know that each one needs two other individuals to decide to join. Since this adds up to three, this suffices to confirm their engagement. Common knowledge emerges due to the configuration of the network geometry.

In the second network, the kite, the first three agents share a similar position inside the network while agent 4 is isolated with only one connection to agent 2. As in the circle, agents 1, 2, and 3 are going to join the activity because their respective thresholds are common knowledge to all of them. However, agent 4 is not going to join them. He/she knows that agent 2 needs two other agents to engage in the activity, but he/she does not know much about agents 1 and 3. Since agent 4 can not exclude the fact that agents 1 and 3 need four or more agents to join, he/she is not sure that either 1 or 3 is going to engage in the activity. Thus, agent 4 decides not to participate.

Observe that in both networks, the circle and the kite, there are four agents and four links. The different arrangement of these links, which differentiates both situations, are responsible for the fact that agent 4 has a different behavior in the two networks. Of course, more links are always going to increase the possibility that common knowledge emerges spontaneously.

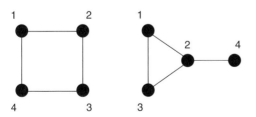

Figure 16.9   Collective action outcomes with different network structures.

Job market outcomes

So far, we have focused on static outcomes of agents who were connected by a network of relationships. Let us examine what happens in the long run when the network is assumed to be fixed and the same over time. We present the model by Calvó-Armengol and Jackson (2004) who discuss their framework in terms of the labor market, a natural application of dynamic processes since workers' employment status are not static but change over time.[25]

The authors study the evolution over time of the employment statuses of n workers connected by a network of relationships. They are able to determine how the network of relationships influences these outcomes. To be more precise, the network starts with some agents being employed and others not. Next, information about job openings is obtained. In particular, any given individual hears about a job opening with some probability. If the individual is unemployed, then he/she will take the job. However, if the individual is already employed, then he/she will pass the information along to a *direct* unemployed friend. Furthermore, when an employed worker hears about a job but all his/her friends (i.e., direct links) are already employed, then the job is lost for the period. It is also assumed that all unemployed neighbors are treated on an equal footing, meaning that the employed worker who has the job information does not favor any of his/her direct neighbors.

A network thus summarizes the links of all agents, where a direct link indicates that two individuals know each other, and share their knowledge about job information.

It is shown that, in steady-state, there is a *positive correlation in employment status between two path-connected workers*. This result is not trivial since, in the short run, the correlation is negative. Indeed, in a static model, if an employed worker is directly linked to two unemployed workers, then if he/she is aware of a job, he/she will share this job information with his/her two unemployed friends. These two individuals, who are path-connected (path of length two), are thus in competition with each other and only one of them (randomly chosen) will obtain the job and be employed while the other will remain unemployed. So their employment status will be negatively correlated (see Boorman, 1975; Calvó-Armengol, 2004; Calvó-Armengol and Zenou, 2005).

To get the main intuition on why this negative correlation result does not hold in a dynamic labor-market model, we focus on the case with three workers with a star-shaped network as shown in Figure 16.10.

In this figure, a black node represents an employed worker (individual 1), while unemployed workers (2 and 3) are represented by white nodes. In fact, even though in the short run, individuals 2 and 3 are "competitors" for the job information that is first heard by individual 1, this is not true in the long-run since individual 2 can benefit from individual 3's presence. Indeed, individual 3's presence helps improve individual 1's employment status. Moreover, when individual 3 is employed, individual 2 is more likely to hear about any job that individual 1 hears about. These aspects of the problem counter the local (conditional) negative correlation and help induce a positive correlation between the employment status of individuals 2 and 3.

To illustrate the fact that not only the network is of importance but also its structure, let us consider a network with four workers, that is, $n = 4$. Table 16.2 depicts the value of unemployment probabilities of worker 2, and the correlations between workers 1

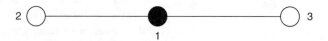

Figure 16.10   A star network with employed and unemployed workers.

and 2, and between workers 1 and 3, in the long-run steady state. These results are calculated using numerical simulations repeated for a sufficiently long period of time as shown in Table 16.2.

First, when there is no social network so that no information is exchanged between workers, the unemployment rate of each agent is just equal to its steady-state value. Thus, the probability of being unemployed for each worker is 13.2 percent, given that they cannot rely on other workers to get information about jobs and the only chance they can have of obtaining a job is by direct methods. Imagine now that only one link is added in this network so that workers 1 and 2 are directly linked to each other. Steady-state unemployment decreases substantially for workers 1 and 2, from 13.2 percent to 8.3 percent. When more links are added, the unemployment rate for each worker decreases even more from 13.2 percent when there are no links to 5 percent when the social network is complete. This table also shows the positive correlation between the employment statuses of different workers mentioned before.

This model provides a rationale, for example, of why ethnic minorities, who tend to have friends who are of the same ethnicity, have difficulties in finding a job. Since employment statuses between direct and indirect friends of the same network are correlated, then, like a disease, unemployment will spread among all individuals belonging to this network. Indeed, if at the beginning some individuals do not obtain a job (say because they are discriminated against), then they cannot help their friends to obtain a job, who themselves cannot help their own friends to obtain a job, etc.

This model is consistent with what research in sociology has found. First, its implications are similar to those from the *homophily* literature, that is, that links between similar people typically occur at a much higher rate than among dissimilar people (see McPherson et al., 2001, who provide an extensive review of this literature in sociology).[26] Furthermore, the result above that employment statuses between path-connected friends (i.e., weak ties) are correlated is consistent with Grannovetter's claim that weak ties are extremely important to provide information about jobs.[27]

The model goes even further in that it can give interesting policy predictions. As we have seen, *ex ante* identical individuals connected

Table 16.2 Workers' outcomes with different network structures

	Probability of being employed for individual 1	Correlations in employment statuses between 1 and 2	Correlations in employment statuses between 1 and 3
2 ● ● 3 1 ● ● 4	0.132	–	–
2 ● ● 3 1 ● ● 4	0.083	0.041	–
2 ● ● 3 1 ● ● 4	0.063	0.025	0.019
2 ● ● 3 1 ● ● 4	0.050	0.025	0.025

through a network can end up with very different outcomes. This *ex post* heterogeneity is mainly due to differences in geometry across local ego-centred networks. As a result, public policy needs to be tailored to the explicit role of the network. In particular, the planner can alter the allocation of network externalities across individuals and implement optimal redistributive schemes by suitably manipulating the network locally. Interventions to improve and sustain the employment status of a given agent also improve the outlook for the social acquaintances of the agents targeted by the intervention – a contagion effect in reverse. In a networked society, education subsidies and other labor market regulation policies display local increasing returns for the social topology. Targeted interventions magnify the initial effect of the policy, and the more so, the more the subsidies and programs are circumscribed to tightly clustered agents in a network. For this reason, targeting is more efficient than spreading resources more broadly, and the more concentrated the interventions, the higher the efficiency gains. This is similar to the targeted policies on crime (i.e., the key player policy) highlighted earlier.

analyzing the structure of social networks, which can be adopted in their modelling choices. Economists have contributed to the literature by enriching the behavior of actors inside the network. Utilitarianism has proved effective in incorporating individual incentives and social preferences that are, arguably, at the core of social network formation when agents act in a decentralized manner. Finally, physicists and applied mathematicians have tackled issue of complexity of webs with a large number of nodes. Their mathematical tools provide a systematic way of understanding the pattern of giant components in networks and give a neat picture of some of the relevant characteristics of these networks for applied works in other disparate areas such as, for example, medicine or criminology.[28]

We hope and expect that an increasing effort will be devoted in the coming years to build stronger connections between the different approaches. This can only enrich our view and understanding of social networks. It is only through this knowledge that we will be able to adopt more realistic policies and recommendations for practitioners.

CONCLUDING REMARKS

As we have seen, there are varied ways of approaching social networks. Our aim here has not been to cover exhaustively all possible contributions to this literature. Instead, we have tried to single out some of the representative works in each of the fields interested in understanding the shape and role of social networks. By doing so, we could pinpoint the main virtues of each approach and analyze how they can benefit from each other.

Some of the research presented in this chapter already merge concepts and techniques from different fields. For example, economists and physicists alike are increasingly being aware that sociologists have provided over the years a rich set of tools

ACKNOWLEDGMENTS

Joan de Marti gratefully acknowledges financial support from the Spanish Ministry of Education through the project SEJ2006-09993/ECON and a Juan de la Cierva fellowship, co-financed by the European Social Fund, and the support of Barcelona GSE and the Government of Catalonia.

NOTES

1 See Wasserman and Faust (1996) for an excellent and exhaustive survey of social network analysis.

2 Roughly speaking weak ties are indirect links such as acquaintances while strong ties are direct links such as close friends or family.

3 A simple way to construct these values is through a discount factor $0 < \delta < 1$. If a direct connection has value α, any indirect connection of order two then has a value equal to $\delta\alpha < \alpha$, an indirect connection of order three has a value of $\delta^2\alpha < \delta\alpha$, and so on.

4 These centrality measures are closely related to the so-called eigenvector centrality measures (see Bonacich and Lloyd, 2001) that lie at the core of ranking methods (see, for example, Palacios-Huerta and Volij, 2004), like Google's PageRank algorithm, or on recently developed segregation measures based on social interactions (Echenique and Fryer, 2007).

5 Of course, this is not a property of universal compliance in all kind of networks. There is empirical evidence against it (see, for example, the work of Amaral et al., 2000, on three different examples of social networks) and also some literature that partially corroborates this rule, with some inconsistency in the tails of the distribution (see Newman, 2001, for an example of a network that satisfies a kind of perturbed power law distribution when considering scientific collaborations).

6 A *power law* is any polynomial relationship that exhibits the property of scale invariance.

7 Data are drawn from the National Longitudinal Study of Adolescent Health (Add Health).

8 A network that displays small-world properties has the characteristic that most nodes can be reached from every other by a small number of steps. More precisely, a network displays a small-world property if the mean *geodesic distance* between vertex pairs (the geodesic distance between two vertices is the length of any shortest path between them) is small compared with the size of the network as a whole (often measured by its diameter, which is the length of the largest geodesic distance between any pair of vertices in the network). In a famous experiment conducted in the 1960s, the psychologist Stanley Milgram (1967) asked participants (located in the United States) to get a message to a specified target person elsewhere in the country by passing it from one acquaintance to another, stepwise through the population. Milgram's remarkable finding that the typical message passed though just six people on its journey between (roughly) randomly chosen. The research was groundbreaking in that it suggested that human society is a small-world type network characterized by short path lengths. The experiments are often associated with the phrase "six degrees of separation," although Milgram did not use this term himself.

9 A *utility function* is a mathematical expression that assigns real numbers (utils) to all possible choices.

10 Indeed, in game theory, the *Nash equilibrium* (named after John F. Nash) is a solution concept of a game involving two or more players, in which no player has anything to gain by changing only his or her own strategy (i.e., by changing unilaterally). If each player has chosen a strategy and no player can benefit by changing his or her strategy while the other players keep theirs unchanged, then the current set of strategy choices constitute a Nash equilibrium.

11 A network is *undirected* if links are reciprocal, that is if i is linked to j, then it has to be that j is linked to i. On the contrary, a network is *directed* if links are not reciprocal. In the latter case, a link has two distinct ends: a head (the end with an arrow) and a tail. Each end is counted separately. The sum of head endpoints count toward the *indegree* and the sum of tail endpoints count toward the *outdegree*. Friendships are usually modelled using undirected networks while, for the world wide web (i.e., a link is when someone clicks on a web page), directed networks are more appropriate.

12 Even if a utilitarian approach is considered valid, this is not necessarily the adequate one. We skip this debate here, and refer the interested reader to Moulin (2003).

13 See also Bala and Goyal (2000) for an analysis of the connections model in directed networks.

14 There are other studies of games with incomplete network knowledge in economics (see, in particular, Galeotti and Vega-Redondo, 2005; Sundararajan, 2006; Jackson and Yariv, 2007).

15 The efforts of two or more agents are called *strategic complements* if they mutually reinforce one another. For example, in a crime context, the effort decisions are strategic complements if an increase in the crime effort of one individual increases the marginal utility of the others, because, in that case, the others will have an incentive to provide more crime effort too.

16 Under the condition that network complementarities are smaller than the inverse of the largest eigenvalue of the graph (i.e., network).

17 See Glaeser et al. (1996) who model criminal activity through imitation in stylized social networks, and Calvó-Armengol and Zenou (2004) for an economic model of externalities in crime and social networks. For recent empirical studies on crime and social interactions, see, in particular, Patacchini and Zenou (2008, 2012), and Bayer et al. (2009).

18 The main obstacle to empirically identifying peer and social network effects is what Manski (1993) termed the *reflection problem*: absent further assumptions on the nature of peer influence, it is impossible to distinguish the causal impact of peers' behavior on an individual's behavior from the causal impact of peers' background characteristics on an individual's behavior. Manski refers to this type of causal influence as an *exogenous social effect*. It is also difficult to distinguish between peers' behavior and individual's behavior, independent of any other individual, peer, or contextual factors. This is referred to as an *endogenous social effect*. Consider, for example, a child's decision to initiate drug use. Is it because his/her next-door neighbor decided to initiate drug use (endogenous social effect)? Or is it due

to the fact that some peer background characteristic, such as a substance-abusing parent, caused both children to adopt the same behavior (exogenous social effect)? The distinction between these explanations is important for policy purposes. When true contagion effects operate, intervening to alter one child's behavior may have the net effect of changing several children's behavior. In other cases, such as when children initiate substance use because adults in their neighborhood provide opportunities to do so, these so-called *multiplier effects* do not exist (Brock and Durlauf, 2001). Correctly distinguishing endogenous from exogenous social effects is necessary for any effort to gauge the true net impact or social benefit of any behavioral intervention. Bramoullé et al. (2009) show how the simple existence of some asymmetry in a peer network can be a sufficient condition to ensure that endogenous and exogenous peer effects can be effectively identified. A nice literature survey on the empirics of social interactions can be found in Durlauf and Ioannides (2010).

19 Haynie (2001) tests the impact of the Bonacich centrality on delinquent behaviors using the AddHealth data (these data were already used by Bearman et al., 2004). Fixing arbitrarily the discount factor to 0.1 for all networks, she finds a positive and significant relationship. Using a more structural approach by estimating rather than fixing the discount factor (so that different networks have different discount factors), Calvó-Armengol et al. (2005, 2009) test the same relationship. They show that, after controlling for observable individual characteristics and unobservable network specific factors, a standard deviation increase in the Katz–Bonacich centrality increases the level of individual delinquency by 44 percent of one standard deviation.

20 Observe that, from a macro-structural perspective, type-1 and type-3 criminals are identical: they all have four direct links, while type-2 criminals have five direct links each. From a micro-structural perspective, though, criminal 1 plays a critical role by bridging together two closed-knit (fully intraconnected) communities of five criminals each. By removing criminal 1, the network is maximally disrupted as these two communities become totally disconnected, while by removing any of the type-2 criminals, the resulting network has the lowest aggregate number of network links.

21 See Ballester et al. (2006) for details.

22 A policy targeting a *group* of criminals rather than one criminal can also be implemented. See Ballester et al. (2010) for details.

23 Contrary to complementarities, effort decisions are substitutes if an increase in one individual's effort decreases the marginal utility of the others, giving them an incentive to provide less effort.

24 In economics, a *public good* is a good that is non-rivaled and non-excludable. This means, respectively, that consumption of the good by one individual does not reduce availability of the good for consumption by others; and that no one can be effectively excluded from using the good.

25 Sociologists and labor economists have produced a broad empirical literature on labor market networks. In fact, the pervasiveness of social networks and their relative effectiveness varies with the social group considered. For instance, Holzer (1987, 1988) documents that among 16–23 year old workers who reported job acceptance, 66 percent use informal search channels (30 percent direct application without referral and 36 percent friends/relatives), while only 11 percent use state agencies and 10 percent newspapers. See also Corcoran et al. (1980) and Granovetter (1995). More recently, Topa (2001) argues that the observed spatial distribution of unemployment in Chicago is consistent with a model of local interactions and information spillovers, and may thus be generated by an agent's reliance in informal methods of job search such as networks of personal contacts. Similarly, Bayer et al. (2008) document that people who live close to each other, defined as being in the same census block, tend to work together, that is, in the same census block. For a survey of the literature on social interactions and the labor market, see Ioannides and Loury (2004), and for other theoretical models, see Montgomery (1991, 1992, 1994), Calvó-Armengol (2004), Calvó-Armengol and Zenou (2005), Calvó-Armengol et al. (2007), Calvó-Armengol and Jackson (2007).

26 See also the recent paper by Currarini et al. (2009).

27 Interestingly, Patacchini and Zenou (2008) also find that weak ties matter in transmitting information about crime in adolescent networks.

28 A recent paper by König et al. (2009) combine the applied-mathematic and economic tools to tackle the issue of dynamic network formation with strategic interactions. Indeed, they combine the network game introduced by Ballester et al. (2006) where the Nash equilibrium action of each agent is proportional to his/her Bonacich centrality (see fourth section) with an endogenous network formation process where links are formed and severed on the basis of agents' centrality, reflecting strategic interactions between agents. A remarkable feature of their dynamic network formation process is that, at each period of time, the network is a *nested split graph*, a graph that has very nice mathematical properties. They show that there exists a unique stationary network (which is a nested split graph) whose topological properties completely match features exhibited by real-world networks (i.e., small world properties, that is, high clustering and low diameter, and power low distribution).

REFERENCES

Akerlof , G.A. and R. Kranton (2000) 'Identity and schooling: some lessons for the economics of education', *Journal of Economic Literature*, 40: 1167–1201.

Albert, R. and A.-L. Barabási (2002) 'Statistical mechanics of complex networks', *Reviews of Modern Physics*, 74: 47–97.

Amaral, L.A.N., A. Scala, M.Barthélémy and H.E. Stanley (2000) 'Classes of small world networks', *Proceedings of the National Academy of Sciences of the USA*, 97: 11149–11152.

Bala, V. and S. Goyal (2000) 'A non-cooperative model of network formation', *Econometrica*, 68: 1181–1229.

Ballester, C., A. Calvó-Armengol and Y. Zenou (2006) 'Who's who in networks. Wanted: the key player', *Econometrica*, 74: 1403–1417.

Ballester, C., A. Calvó-Armengol and Y. Zenou (2010) 'Delinquent networks', *Journal of the European Economic Association*, 8: 34–61.

Barabási, A-L. and R. Albert (1999) 'Emergence of scaling in random networks', *Science*, 286: 509–512.

Bayer, P., S.L. Ross and G. Topa (2008) 'Place of work and place of residence: Informal hiring networks and labor market outcomes', *Journal of Political Economy* 116: 1150–1196.

Bayer, P., R. Hjalmarsson and D. Pozen (2009) 'Building criminal capital behind bars: Peer effects in juvenile corrections', *Quarterly Journal of Economics*, 124: 105–147.

Bearman, P.S., J. Moody and K. Stovel (2004) 'Chains of affection: The structure of adolescent romantic and sexual networks', *American Journal of Sociology*, 110: 44–91.

Bollobás, B. (2001) *Random Graphs*. 2nd edition. New York: Academic Press.

Bonacich, P. (1987) 'Power and centrality: A family of measures', *American Journal of Sociology*, 92: 1170–1182.

Bonacich, P. and P. Lloyd (2001) 'Eigenvector-like measures of centrality for asymmetric relations', *Social Networks*, 23: 191–201.

Boorman, S. (1975) 'A combinatorial optimization model for transmission of job information through contact networks', *Bell Journal of Economics*, 6: 216–249.

Bramoullé, Y. and R.E. Kranton (2007) 'Public goods in networks', *Journal of Economic Theory*, 135: 478–494.

Bramoullé, Y., H. Djebbari and B. Fortin (2009) 'Identification of peer effects through social networks', *Journal of Econometrics*, 150: 41–55.

Brock, W. and S.E. Durlauf (2001) 'Discrete choice models with social interactions', *Review of Economic Studies*, 68: 235–260.

Burt, R.S. (1992) *Structural Holes*. Cambridge, MA: Harvard University Press.

Calvó-Armengol, A. (2004) 'Job contact networks', *Journal of Economic Theory*, 115: 191–206.

Calvó-Armengol, A.E. and M.O. Jackson (2004) 'The effects of social networks on employment and inequality', *American Economic Review*, 94: 426–454.

Calvó-Armengol, A.E. and Y. Zenou (2004) 'Social networks and crime decisions. The role of social structure in facilitating delinquent', *International Economic Review*, 45: 939–958.

Calvó-Armengol, A.E. and Y. Zenou (2005) 'Job matching, social network and word-of-mouth communication', *Journal of Urban Economics*, 57: 500–522.

Calvó-Armengol, A.E. and M.O. Jackson (2007) 'Social networks in labor markets: Wage and employment dynamics and inequality', *Journal of Economic Theory*, 132: 27–46.

Calvó-Armengol, A., E. Patacchini and Y. Zenou (2005) 'Peer effects and social networks in education and crime', CEPR Discussion Paper No. 5244.

Calvó-Armengol, A.E., Verdier, T. and Y. Zenou (2007) 'Strong ties and weak ties in employment and crime', *Journal of Public Economics*, 91: 203–233.

Calvó-Armengol, A., E. Patacchini and Y. Zenou (2009) 'Peer effects and social networks in education', *Review of Economic Studies*, 76: 1239–1267.

Chwe, M. (1999) 'Structure and strategy in collective action', *American Journal of Sociology*, 105: 128–156.

Chwe, M. (2000) 'Communication and coordination in social networks', *Review of Economic Studies*, 67: 1–16.

Coleman, J.S. (1988) 'Social capital in the creation of human capital', *American Journal of Sociology*, 94: S95–S120.

Conley, T.G. and C.R. Udry (2001) 'Social learning through networks: The adoption of new agricultural technologies in Ghana', *American Journal of Agricultural Economics*, 83: 668–673.

Conley, T.G. and C.R. Udry (2010) 'Learning about a new technology: Pineapple in Ghana', *American Economic Review*, 100: 35–69.

Corcoran, M., L. Datcher and G.J. Duncan (1980) 'Most workers find jobs through word of mouth', *Monthly Labor Review*, 103: 33–35.

Currarini, S., M.O. Jackson and P. Pin (2009) 'An economic model of friendship: Homophily, minorities, and segregation', *Econometrica*, 77: 1003–1045.

De Martí, J. and Y. Zenou (2009) 'Ethnic identity and social distance in friendship formation', CEPR Discussion Paper No. 7566.

Diestel, R. (2005) *Graph Theory*. Heidelberg: Springer-Verlag.

Durlauf, S.N. and Y.M. Ioannides (2010) 'Social interactions', *Annual Review of Economics* 2: 451–478.

Echenique, F. and R. Fryer (2007) 'A measure of segregation based on social interactions', *Quarterly Journal of Economics*, 122: 441–485.

Erdős, P. and A. Rényi (1959) 'On random graphs', *Publicationes Mathematicae*, 6: 290–297.

Erdős, P. and A. Rényi (1960) 'On the evolution of random graphs', *Publications of the Mathematical Institute of the Hungarian Academy of Sciences*, 5: 17–61.

Freeman, L.C. (1977) 'A set of measures of centrality based upon betweenness', *Sociometry*, 40: 35–41.

Freeman, L.C. (1979) 'Centrality in social networks: Conceptual clarification', *Social Networks*, 1: 215–239.

Friedkin, N. (1991) 'Theoretical foundations for centrality measures', *American Journal of Sociology*, 96: 1478–1504.

Galeotti, A. and F. Vega-Redondo (2005) 'Local externalities and complex networks,' Unpublished manuscript. University of Essex.

Galeotti, A., S. Goyal, M.O. Jackson, F. Vega-Redondo, and L. Yariv (2009) 'Network games', *Review of Economic Studies*, 77:218–244.

Garoupa, N. (1997) 'The theory of optimal law enforcement', *Journal of Economic Surveys*, 11: 267–295.

Glaeser, E., B. Sacerdote and J. Scheinkman (1996) 'Crime and social interactions', *Quarterly Journal of Economics*, 111: 507–548.

Goyal, S. (2007) *Connections: An Introduction to the Economics of Networks*. Princeton: Princeton University Press.

Goyal, S., M.J. van der Leij, and J.L. Moraga-Gonzalez (2006) 'Economics: An emerging small world', *Journal of Political Economy*, 114: 403–412.

Granovetter, M.S. (1973) 'The strength of weak ties', *American Journal of Sociology*, 78: 1360–1380.

Granovetter, M.S. (1978) 'Threshold models of collective behavior', *American Journal of Sociology*, 83: 1420–1443.

Granovetter, M.S. (1983) 'The strength of weak ties: A network theory revisited', *Sociological Theory*, 1: 201–233.

Granovetter, M.S. (1995) *Getting a Job: A Study of Contacts and Careers*. 2nd edition. Chicago: Chicago University Press.

Haynie, D.L. (2001) 'Delinquent peers revisited: Does network structure matter?', *American Journal of Sociology*, 106: 1013–1057.

Holzer, H.J. (1987) 'Informal job search and black youth unemployment', *American Economic Review*, 77: 446–452.

Holzer, H.J. (1988) 'Search method used by unemployed youth', *Journal of Labor Economics*, 6: 1–20.

Ioannides, Y.M. and D.L. Loury (2004) 'Job information networks, neighborhood effects, and inequality', *Journal of Economic Literature*, 42: 1056–1093.

Jackson, M.O. (2007) 'The economics of social networks', in R. Blundell, W.K. Newey, and T. Persson (eds) *Advances in Economics and Econometrics. Theory and Applications*, Ninth World Congress, Vol. I. Cambridge: Cambridge University Press. pp. 1–56.

Jackson, M.O. (2008) *Social and Economic Networks*. Princeton: Princeton University Press.

Jackson, M.O. and B.W. Rogers (2007) 'Meeting strangers and friends of friends: How random are socially networks?', *American Economic Review*, 97: 890–915.

Jackson, M.O. and A. Wolinsky (1996) 'A strategic model of social and economic networks', *Journal of Economic Theory*, 71; 44–74.

Jackson, M.O. and L. Yariv (2007) 'Diffusion of behavior and equilibrium properties in network games', *American Economic Review (Papers and Proceedings)*, 97: 92–98.

Katz, L. (1953) 'A new status index derived from sociometric analysis', *Psychometrika*, 18: 39–43.

König, M., C. Tessone and Y. Zenou (2009) 'A dynamic model of network formation with strategic interactions', CEPR Discussion Paper No. 7521.

Liljeros, F., C. Edling, L.A.N. Amaral, H.E. Stanley and Y. Åberg (2001) 'The web of human sexual contacts', *Nature*, 411: 908–909.

Lorrain, F. and H.C. White (1971) 'Structural equivalence of individuals in social networks', *Journal of Mathematical Sociology*, 1: 49–80.

Manski, C.F. (1993) 'Identification of endogenous effects: The reflection problem', *Review of Economic Studies*, 60: 531–542.

McPherson, M., L. Smith-Lovin and J.M. Cook (2001) 'Birds of a feather: Homophily in social networks', *Annual Review of Sociology*, 27: 415–444.

Milgram, S. (1967) 'The small world problem', *Psychology Today*, 2: 60–7.

Montgomery, J.D. (1991) 'Social networks and labor-market outcomes: Toward an economic analysis', *American Economic Review*, 81: 1408–1418.

Montgomery, J.D. (1992) 'Job search and network composition: Implications of the strength-of-weak-ties hypothesis', *American Sociological Review*, 57: 586–596.

Montgomery, J.D. (1994) 'Weak ties, employment, and inequality: An equilibrium analysis', *American Journal of Sociology*, 99: 1212–1236.

Moulin, H.J. (2003) *Fair Division and Collective Welfare*. Cambridge, MA: MIT Press.

Myerson, R. (1977) 'Graphs and cooperation in games', *Mathematics of Operations Research*, 2: 225–229.

Myerson, R. (1991) *Game Theory: Analysis of Conflict*. Cambridge, MA: Harvard University Press.

Newman, M.E.J. (2001) 'The structure of scientific collaboration networks', *Proceedings of the National Academy of Sciences of the USA*, 98: 404–409.

Newman, M.E.J. (2003) 'The structure and function of complex networks', *SIAM Review*, 45: 167–256.

Palacios-Huerta, I. and O. Volij (2004) 'The measurement of intellectual influence', *Econometrica*, 72: 963–977.

Patacchini, E. and Y. Zenou (2008) 'The strength of weak ties in crime', *European Economic Review*, 52: 209–236.

Patacchini, E. and Y. Zenou (forthcoming) 'Juvenile delinquency and conformism', *Journal of Law, Economics, and Organization*, forthcoming.

Polinsky, M.A. and S. Shavell (2000) 'The economic theory of public enforcement of law', *Journal of Economic Literature*, 38: 45–76.

Sarnecki, J. (2001) *Delinquent Networks: Youth Co-Offending in Stockholm*. Cambridge: Cambridge University Press.

Schelling, T.S. (1978) *Micromotives and Macrobehavior*. New York: Norton.

Solomonoff, R. and A. Rapoport (1951) 'Connectivity of random nets', *Bulletin of Mathematical Biophysics*, 13: 107–117.

Sundararajan, A. (2006) 'Local network effects and network structure,' Unpublished manuscript. New York University.

Sutherland, E.H. (1947) *Principles of Criminology*. 4th edition. Chicago: J.B. Lippincott.

Topa, G. (2001) 'Social interactions, local spillovers and unemployment', *Review of Economic Studies*, 68: 261–295.

Vega-Redondo, F. (2007) *Complex Social Networks*. Econometric Society Monograph Series. Cambridge: Cambridge University Press.

Warr, M. (2002) *Companions in Crime: The Social Aspects of Criminal Conduct*. Cambridge: Cambridge University Press.

Wasserman, S. and K. Faust (1994) *Social Network Analysis. Methods and Applications*. Cambridge: Cambridge University Press.

Watts, D.J. and S.H. Strogatz (1998) 'Collective dynamics of "small-world" networks', *Nature*, 393: 409–410.

White, H.C., S. Boorman and R. Breiger (1976) 'Social structure from multiple networks: I. Blockmodels of roles and positions', *American Journal of Sociology*, 81: 730–780.

17

Normative Criteria of Social Choice

Maurice Salles and Antoinette Baujard

INTRODUCTION

Social choice is concerned with the selection of options by a group of individuals. Equivalently, we can interpret social choice as individual choice in the presence of multiple criteria, each criterion corresponding to an individual of the group and the individual making the choice corresponding to the society. We study these selection procedures either from an abstract point of view (with the notions of aggregation functions, social choice functions, etc.) or from a practical point of view (for instance with the electoral procedures). This dichotomy has its origin in the historical sources of the theory of social choice. On the one hand, utilitarianism and welfare economics from Bentham to Bergson and Samuelson, on the other hand the analysis of voting procedures by Borda and Condorcet. In both cases, one can find precursors; for instance Hutcheson and Hume for the former, and Ramon Lull and Nicolas Cusanus for the latter.

The utilitarist motto generally attributed to Bentham, *the greatest happiness of the greatest number*, has been at the same time somewhat simplified and transformed by the economists in the maximization of the sum of individual utilities (i.e. the values taken by the individual – numerical – utility functions) over the set of options. This maximization obviously entailed that the values (real numbers) taken by these numerical functions had all the properties generally associated with real numbers. In fact, mathematically speaking, the economists wanted to use all the properties of the field of real numbers. This means that one can compare utilities for a given individual or for different individuals. For instance, if the utility of x for individual i is 4 and the utility of y for individual j is 2, one can assert that i with x has a utility twice as great as that the utility of j with y, and, furthermore, if utility is a kind of measure of satisfaction or happiness, one can assert that i is twice as happy with x than j is with y. One could also use the fact that 4 is the square of 2, that 4 minus 2 is 2, that 4 is greater than 2, etc. These multiple possibilities have been called into question from an individual perspective by what has been named *ordinalism* and from a collective perspective by what is probably the consequence of ordinalism viz. Paretian optimality. Ordinalism simply means that, for an individual, the only property of real numbers that can be taken into account is the ordering property. Then for individual i for two options x and y, it will be impossible to distinguish between utility 1000 associated to x and utility 1 associated to y, and utility 4 associated to x and utility 3 associated to y, since $1000 > 1$ and $4 > 3$. The option x is Pareto-optimal if there is no other option y that all the individuals prefer to x or, in its extended form, that all individuals consider at least as good as x and some individuals consider better than x, or in utility terms, that all the individual utilities associated to y are greater than or equal to the utilities associated to x and for some individuals these utilities are greater. These theoretical aspects in which the economist according to Robbins would not have the possibility (at least qua economist) to make value judgments mark the total victory of continental economic thought (Pareto) over the British thought (Marshall, Pigou). However, in the 1930s, inter-personal comparisons of utilities are reintroduced as (virtual) compensations by some of the most famous economists of the time, for instance Hicks, Kaldor, Harrod and Scitovsky (see the books edited by Arrow and Scitovsky (1969) and Baumol and Wilson (2001)). The basic principle of the compensations is the following. Suppose that we start with an option x and proceed to a new option y. Some individuals gain and some individuals lose in the change. Individuals are supposedly asked to evaluate their gains and losses in utilities. If the sum of utility gains exceeds the sum of utility losses, theoretically it would be possible to proceed to a redistribution to reach a situation which every individual would prefer (or in which every individual has a greater utility). The compensation theory is often associated to what has been called *new welfare economics*. However, this theory was using implicit utility comparisons but also was shown not to be immune to paradoxes. Bergson (see Arrow and Scitovsky, 1969) and Samuelson introduce the notion of *social welfare function* at the end of 1930s and beginning of the 1940s. What they are looking for is the possibility to go beyond the notion of Pareto optimality. This notion is obviously

insufficiently discriminating. In many circumstances, optimal situations are numerous. Consider for instance a simple distribution problem of a fixed amount of money (which can be assumed to be infinitely divisible) between egoist individuals (each individual prefers more to less; her utility function over the fixed amount is a strictly increasing function). Then there is an infinity (possibly uncountable depending on the considered infinite divisibility) of Pareto-optimal distributions. In Samuelson's version of the social welfare function (Samuelson, 1947), the social welfare function f associates a real number to a list of individual utilities $u_1, \ldots, u_n$ of individuals $1, \ldots, n$, each individual utility i being the value taken by the utility function i of individual i for some option in a fixed set. The individual utility functions i are fixed, for instance in the case of the positive part of a two-dimensional Euclidean space $\mathbb{R}^2_+$,[1] one could have $u_i(x) = (1/3)x_1^{1/2} x_2^{1/2}$ and the variables would be x_1 and x_2. This so-called Cobb–Douglas function with parameters 1/3, 1/2 and 1/2 would remain identical whatever the variables x_1 and x_2. The exclusion of Pareto-dominated options (non Pareto-optimal options) entails that the social welfare function be increasing in each i or, with appropriate assumptions on f and considering the local aspect of the property that $\dfrac{\partial f}{\partial u_i} > 0$.[2] We can establish some properties of the maximization of f in a rather abstract way. This is what is basically done by Bergson and Samuelson. It remains, however, to consider the practical selection among the Pareto-optimal options for public policy. For this to be done, one has to construct first a social welfare function f. But who will construct f? The answer to this question is rather vague in Samuelson's magisterial works.

At the end of the eighteenth century, two French members of the Royal Academy, Borda and Condorcet, studied electoral procedures, in particular the procedure in use at the Royal Academy of Sciences. Borda proposes a method based on scores. Each voter ranks k candidates according to her preference (with no ties). For a given ranking, the method attributes a score of $k - 1$ to the candidate ranked first, a score of $k - 2$ to the candidate ranked second etc., and a score of 0 to the candidate ranked last. The scores obtained by a candidate are then added, and the social (collective) ranking is based on the scores obtained by the candidates, the candidate socially ranked first being the candidate that has obtained the maximum in the summation and so on (note that ties are possible at the social level). Condorcet is in favor of a method that is nowadays called the majority decision rule. Given the rankings by voters, for two candidates x and y, if the number of times x is ranked before y is greater than the number of times y is ranked before x, then x is socially (collectively) ranked before y. Of course, Condorcet noticed that this method can lead to cycles at the social level. This is what we now call the Condorcet paradox. Consider three candidates a, b and c and three voters 1, 2 and 3. Suppose voter 1 ranks the three candidates as abc (a first, b second and c third), voter 2 ranked the candidates as bca, and voter 3 as cab. Then a is socially ranked before b who is socially ranked before c who is socially ranked before a, since two voters ranked a before b, two voters ranked b before c and two voters ranked c before a. In spite of this paradox, Condorcet considers that if a candidate is socially ranked before all the other candidates according to the majority rule, this candidate must be selected. Such a candidate is now called a Condorcet winner. Condorcet is critical of Borda's method as can be seen in the *Discours Préliminaire* to the *Essai sur l'Application de l'Analyse à la Probabilité des Décisions Rendues à la Pluralité des Voix* (Condorcet, 1785), because Borda's method can select a candidate who is not a Condorcet winner even though there exists such a Condorcet winner. He gives an example in page *clxxvij* and the following pages of the *Discours Préliminaire*. As an anecdotal remark, Borda is never mentioned. Condorcet only mentions a *Géomètre célèbre* (a famous geometer). In the nineteenth

century, the formal works on voting are rather rare, but one can mention some remarkable studies on proportional representation and apportionment methods and the articles by C.L. Dodgson (aka Lewis Carroll).

Before we present some of the main results of modern social choice, we will give some examples showing how, given a set of similar data, voting methods give rise to different results. These examples are based on examples given by Saari (2001). Incidentally, Saari (2008), although somewhat demanding for non-mathematically inclined social scientists, is highly recommended.

VOTING PROCEDURES: SOME EXAMPLES

In the first example we consider three candidates A, B and C, and 11 voters. Each voter ranks the candidates according to her preference $A \succ B \succ C$ meaning that A is ranked first, B second and C third. The integer before the ranking is the number of voters having this preference.

$$3\ A \succ B \succ C$$
$$2\ A \succ C \succ B$$
$$2\ B \succ C \succ A$$
$$4\ C \succ B \succ A$$

The three voting procedures applied to these data are (1) the plurality (one point is given to the candidate ranked first and 0 point to all others), (2) the anti-plurality (one point is given to each candidate except the candidate ranked last who gets 0 point) and (3) Borda's method described above. The obtained social rankings are:

$$(1)\ A \succ C \succ B$$
$$(2)\ B \succ C \succ A$$
$$(3)\ C \succ B \succ A$$

We now introduce vector scores for the candidates, the vector $(1,0,0)$ meaning that a candidate ranked first gets one point and the candidates ranked second and third get 0 point (this is the vector score associated to the plurality method). The vector $(1,1,0)$ is the vector score of the anti-plurality, and $(2,1,0)$ the vector score of Borda's rule. Considering various vector scores as given on the left below, one obtains the following results on the basis of the data of example 1. (We note $A \sim B$ when A and B get the same social score (they are tied).)

$$(1,0,0): A \succ C \succ B$$
$$(4,1,0): A \sim C \succ B$$
$$(7,2,0): C \succ A \succ B$$
$$(7,3,0): C \succ A \sim B$$
$$(2,1,0): C \succ B \succ A$$
$$(3,2,0): B \sim C \succ A$$
$$(1,1,0): B \succ C \succ A$$

In our second example, there are 5 candidates and 14 voters. As in the first example, the integer before the ranking is the number of voters having this preference.

$$3\ A \succ B \succ C \succ D \succ E$$
$$1\ A \succ C \succ E \succ D \succ B$$
$$2\ A \succ E \succ C \succ D \succ B$$
$$2\ C \succ B \succ D \succ E \succ A$$
$$2\ D \succ C \succ E \succ A \succ B$$
$$1\ E \succ A \succ C \succ D \succ B$$
$$3\ E \succ B \succ D \succ A \succ C$$

One can easily see that, according to whether voters vote for one, two, three, or four candidates, or whether Borda's rule is used that:

$(1,0,0,0,0)$: A is socially ranked first
$(1,1,0,0,0)$: B is socially ranked first
$(1,1,1,0,0)$: C is socially ranked first
$(1,1,1,1,0)$: D is socially ranked first
$(4,3,2,1,0)$: E is socially ranked first

Furthermore, if one uses the Condorcet method, one gets at the social level:

$$A \succ C, A \succ B, A \sim D, E \succ A, C \succ B$$
$$E \succ B, B \succ D, C \succ E, C \succ D, D \sim E$$

There is no Condorcet winner. Moreover, one can see:

$$C \succ E \succ A \succ C \text{ and}$$
$$C \succ E \succ A \succ C \succ B \succ D \sim E \succ B \succ D \sim A \succ B$$

These examples demonstrate the role played by the various methods in the social selection

and the necessity to have a deep knowledge of these methods. The next section is devoted to technical preliminaries.

BINARY RELATIONS, PREFERENCES, AGGREGATION

Let X be a set of options (social states whatever their precise meaning, candidates, allocations, etc.) and $\#X$ be the cardinal of this set (if X is finite, the cardinal of X is the number of its elements).

Definition 1

A *binary relation* $\succeq$ over X is a set of ordered pairs (x,y) with $x \in X$ and $y \in X$, or $\succeq$ is a subset of the Cartesian product $X \times X$.

We will denote $x \succeq y$ rather than $(x,y) \in \succeq$. The intuitive meaning of $x \succeq y$ is 'x is at least as good as y'. Then we implicitly assume that $\succeq$ is a reflexive relation.

Definition 2

The binary relation $\succeq$ is *reflexive* if for all $x \in X$, $x \succeq x$.

The asymmetric part, $\succ$, of $\succeq$ is defined by $x \succ y$ if $x \succeq y$ and $\neg y \succeq x$ ($\neg$ is the negation symbol). This will be read by 'x is better than y' or 'x is preferred to y'. The symmetric part, $\sim$, is defined by $x \sim y$ if $x \succeq y$ and $y \succeq x$. This will be read by 'there is an indifference between x and y'.

Definition 3

The binary relation $\succeq$ is *complete* if, for all $x, y \in X$, $x \succeq y$ or $y \succeq x$.

Completeness means that, whatever the options x and y, there is a relation 'at least as good as' between them. It is impossible to find two options a and b that would not be linked by this relation. If $\succeq$ is a complete binary relation, we have $x \succ y \Leftrightarrow \neg y \succeq x$.

Definition 4

The binary relation $\succeq$ is *transitive* if for all x, y, $z \in X$, $x \succeq y$ and $y \succeq z \Rightarrow x \succeq z$.

Definition 5

The binary relation $\succeq$ is *quasi-transitive* if for all x, y, $z \in X$, $x \succ y$ and $y \succ z \Rightarrow x \succ z$, that is, if $\succ$ is transitive.

Definition 6

The binary relation $\succ$ is *acyclic* if there is no finite subset of X, $\{x_1, \dots, x_k\}$ such that $x_1 \succ x_2$ and $x_2 \succ x_3$ and ... and $x_{k-1} \succ x_k$ and $x_k \succ x_1$.

It is easy to show that if the binary relation is transitive, it is also quasi-transitive and its asymmetric part is acyclic, the reverse implications being false.

Definition 7

A *preorder* over X is a reflexive and transitive binary relation.

We will assume in this chapter that all considered preorders are complete preorders. Since completeness entails reflexivity, we can say that a complete preorder is a complete and transitive binary relation. When X is finite, a complete preorder is nothing else than a ranking with possible ties. For instance for $X = \{a,b,c\}$, there are 13 complete preorders:

(1) $a \succ b \succ c$ (7) $a \succ b \sim c$ (13) $a \sim b \sim c$

(2) $a \succ c \succ b$ (8) $b \succ a \sim c$

(3) $b \succ a \succ c$ (9) $c \succ a \sim b$

(4) $b \succ c \succ a$ (10) $b \sim c \succ a$

(5) $c \succ a \succ b$ (11) $a \sim c \succ b$

(6) $c \succ b \succ a$ (12) $a \sim b \succ c$

Here, (1) means that a is preferred to b, b is preferred to c, and a is preferred to c. In relations (1)–(6), there are no ties, in relations (7)–(9), the options ranked second and third are tied and there is a unique option ranked first, in relations (10)–(12), two options are ranked first and there is a unique last option and in relation (13) the three options are 'equivalent'.

We can remark that for $X = \{a,b,c\}$ the relation where $a \succ b$ and $b \sim c$ and $a \sim c$ is not a complete preorder but, however, is a binary relation $\succeq$ complete and quasi-transitive and the relation where $a \succ b$ et $b \succ c$ et $a \sim c$ is a binary $\succeq$ relation $\succ$ complete with an acyclic asymmetric part.

Definition 8

The binary relation $\succeq$ is *anti-symmetric* if for all x, $y \in X$, $x \succeq y \succ y \succeq x \Rightarrow x = y$.

Definition 9

A *linear order* is a complete and anti-symmetric preorder.

For $X = \{a,b,c\}$, the set of linear orders consists of the relations (1)–(6). Given our definitions one can see that, for linear orders, indifference is reduced to equality.

We can then consider, in the finite case, that a linear order is a ranking without ties. In fact, one can also define a linear order as a binary relation $\succ$ which is transitive and satisfies a property of completeness that would be: for all x, $y \in X$, $x \neq y \Rightarrow x \succ y$ or $y \succ x$. Since the outcome of the social choice is the selection of options by a group of individuals, we have to introduce these individuals. We will consider a finite set N with cardinality n: $N = \{1, \dots, n\}$. We assume that each individual i has a preference over X given by a complete preorder $\succeq i$. The central question of social choice is the question of deriving a social preference, denoted $\succeq_S$ (not necessarily a complete preorder), or a chosen element in X, or, possibly, a chosen subset of elements from given individual preferences – one preference for each individual.

Let us denote the set of complete binary relations over X by **B**, the set of complete preorders over X by **P**, the set of linear orders over X by **L**, the set of complete and quasi-transitive binary relations over X by **Q** and the set of complete binary relations with an acyclic asymmetric part over X by **A**, and **P'**, **L'**, **Q'**, **A'** non-empty subsets of **P**, **L**, **Q**, and **A** respectively. An aggregation function is a function f which associates a social preference (a complete binary relation), $\succeq_S$, to a list of n individual preferences – a n-list of complete preorders – $(\succeq_1, \ldots, \succeq_n)$, that is: $f : (\succeq_1, \ldots, \succeq_n) \mapsto \succeq_S$. Formally we have the following definition.

Definition 10

An aggregation function is a function f: $\mathbf{P'}^n \to \mathbf{B}$.

An important notion (which plays a major rôle in several conditions and in many proofs) is the notion de decisiveness. We will call any non-empty subset of N a coalition (by misuse of language, this includes the case of a single individual).

Definition 11

A coalition C is *decisive for a against b* if, for all list $(\succeq_1, \ldots, \succeq_n) \in \mathbf{P'}^n$, $a \succ_i b$ for all $i \in C$ $\Rightarrow a \succ_S b$ where $\succ_S$ is the asymmetric part of $\succeq_S = f(\succeq_1, \ldots, \succeq_n)$. A coalition C is *decisive over* $\{a, b\}$ if it is decisive for a against b and decisive for b against a. An individual i is *decisive for a against b* if for all list $(\succeq_1, \ldots, \succeq_n) \in \mathbf{P'}^n$, $a \succ_i b \Rightarrow a \succ_S b$ where $\succ_S$ is the asymmetric part of $\succeq_S = f(\succeq_1, \ldots, \succeq_n)$. An individual i is *decisive over* $\{a, b\}$ if she is decisive for a againt b and decisive for b against a.

C is decisive for a against b if, whenever all the individuals in coalition C prefer a to b in the social preference, a is ranked before b. An individual i is decisive for a againsts b if whenever she prefers a to b, a is ranked before b at the social level. We must notice that with this definition the property is not reversible. If individual i prefers b to a, we cannot infer anything. However, this reversibility

is included in the definition of decisiveness over $\{a, b\}$.

We are now able to tackle the central themes of this chapter, starting by what is probably the most important result, Arrow's Theorem.

ARROW'S THEOREM

Arrow's Theorem (1950, 1951, 1963) concerns a particular class of aggregation functions called social welfare functions. However, the conditions that were introduced by Arrow can be applied to general aggregation functions since their definitions do not entail anything that is specific to social welfare functions.

Condition U (Universality)

An aggregation function f is *universal* if $\mathbf{P'=P}$.

From a mathematical standpoint this condition is extremely simple. It says that individuals can have any preference provided that this preference is given by a complete preorder. Individual rationality is defined by this hypothesis: individuals have preferences given by a complete preorder (any complete preorder). There is no super-rationality which could take the form of the exclusion of some complete preorders from the admissible list as will be done later. From a normative viewpoint, universality can appear as incorporating both rationality and some kind of freedom within the limits imposed by rationality. In the finite case, this means that each individual can rank the options with possible ties as she wishes. But rationality imposes that it is a ranking. The next condition is certainly the most complex.

Condition I (Independence)

Consider two (distinct) options a, $b \in X$ and two n-lists $(\succeq_1, \ldots, \succeq_n)$, $(\succeq'_1, \ldots, \succeq'_n) \in \mathbf{P'}^n$. If the restrictions to $\{a,b\}$ of the individual preferences are identical in the two lists, that is, if $\succeq_i |\{a,b\} = \succeq_i' |\{a,b\}$ for each $i \in N$, then $\succeq_S |\{a,b\} = \succeq_S' |\{a,b\}$ where $\succeq_S = f(\succeq_1, \ldots, \succeq_n)$ et $\succeq_S' = f(\succeq'_1, \ldots, \succeq'_n)$.

The underlying idea for independence (called independence of irrelevant alternatives by Arrow) is that if the preferences between a and b in the first and second list coincide for each individual, that is, if individual 1 has the same preference between a and b in both lists, if individual 2 has the same preference between a and b in both lists etc., then the social preference between a and b must be identical in both cases. Let us consider, for instance the case where $X = \{a,b,c,d,e\}$ and $N = \{1,2,3\}$ and we have two lists $(\succeq_1, \succeq_2, \succeq_3)$ and $(\succeq'_1, \succeq'_2, \succeq'_3)$ such that:

$(\succeq_1, \succeq_2, \succeq_3)$	$(\succeq'_1, \succeq'_2, \succeq'_3)$
$b \succ_1 c \sim_1 a \succ_1 d \sim_1 e$	$c \succ'_1 d \sim'_1 b \sim'_1 e \succ'_1 a$
$c \succ_2 d \succ_2 a \sim_2 b \sim_2 e$	$d \succ'_2 c \succ'_2 e \succ'_2 a \sim'_2 b$
$a \succ_3 c \succ_3 d \succ_3 e \succ_3 b$	$c \succ'_3 d \succ'_3 a \succ'_3 b \succ'_3 e$

Let us consider now uniquely the subset $\{a,b\}$, we have:

$(\succeq_1, \succeq_2, \succeq_3)$	$(\succeq'_1, \succeq'_2, \succeq'_3)$
$b \succ_1 - \sim_1 a \succ_1 - \sim_1 -$	$- \succ'_1 - \sim'_1 b \sim'_1 - \succ'_1 a$
$- \succ_2 - \succ_2 a \sim_2 b \sim_2 -$	$- \succ'_2 - \succ'_2 - \succ'_2 a \sim'_2 b$
$a \succ_3 - \succ_3 - \succ_3 - \succ_3 b$	$- \succ'_3 - \succ'_3 a \succ'_3 b \succ'_3 -$

Taking account only of the preferences over a and b, one gets:

$(\succeq_1, \succeq_2, \succeq_3)$	$(\succeq'_1, \succeq'_2, \succeq'_3)$
$b \succ_1 a$	$b \succ'_1 a$
$a \sim_2 b$	$a \sim'_2 b$
$a \succ_3 b$	$a \succ'_3 b$

The independence condition indicates that in this case the social preference between a and b must be the same in both cases. If, say, we have $a \succ_S b$, we must also have $a \succ'_S b$.

The majority decision rule described in the introduction satisfies this independence condition. In fact, any aggregation function where social preference between two options is uniquely defined from individual preferences over these two options will satisfy this condition. It is the case, for instance, for aggregation functions associated to a quota voting game. Consider the so-called majority game where the quota is fixed at $n/2$, we have $x \succ_S y$ if the number of individuals i for which $x \succ_i y$ is $>n/2$ and $y \succeq_S x$ otherwise. One can imagine other quotas or even a more general structure on voting games and keep the condition of independence.

In the proofs of various theorems, this condition of independence plays a major role in what has been called by Sen an epidemic outcome. As a matter of fact, if starting from a specific n-list $(\succeq=1,\ldots,\succeq=3)$, one obtains, say, $a \succeq_S b$ for two options a and $b \in X$, then, for all list $(\succeq'1, \succeq'2, \succeq'3)$ in which the individual preferences between a and b are identical to the individual preferences that were in the list $(\succeq1, \succeq2, \succeq3)$, we will obtain the same result: $a \succeq'_S b$.

This condition excludes Borda's rule as well as all rules that would take the intensity of preferences into account (even at the individual level not to mention rules using interpersonal comparisons of these intensities). For Borda's rule, let us consider the following example with $X = \{a,b,c,d\}$ and $N = \{1,2,3\}$, with the following lists $(\succeq_1, \succeq_2, \succeq_3)$ and $(\succeq'_1, \succeq'_2, \succeq'_3)$:

$(\succeq_1, \succeq_2, \succeq_3)$	$(\succeq'_1, \succeq'_2, \succeq'_3)$
$a \succ_1 b \succ_1 c \succ_1 d$	$a \succ'_1 c \succ'_1 d \succ'_1 b$
$b \succ_2 a \succ_2 d \succ_2 c$	$b \succ'_2 a \succ'_2 d \succ'_2 c$
$c \succ_3 b \succ_3 a \succ_3 d$	$c \succ'_3 b \succ'_3 a \succ'_3 d$

Each option ranked first gets three points, ranked second gets two points, ranked third gets one point and ranked last gets zero point. If we consider $\{a,b\}$, a obtains six points and b obtains seven points from the first list, and a obtains six points and b obtains only five points from the second list. However, one can check that the preferences of individuals 2 and 3 are entirely identical in both lists and for individual 1, we have $a \succ_1 b$ and $a \succ'_1 b$. The independence condition demands that in this situation we have the same outcome in both cases regarding a and b. But Borda's rule gives $b \succ_S a$ and $a \succ'_S b$. The fact that individual 1 ranks a first and b second in the first list and a first and b last in the second list must not have any consequence according to the independence condition. But we can easily imagine that the preference of 1 in favour of a compared to b is much stronger in $\succeq'_1$ than in $\succeq_1$. Using majority rule even if there is a Condorcet winner should not mask problems that could be solved by scoring rules such as Borda's rule. Suppose for instance that 101 individuals have to select an option among 15 options $\{x_1, \ldots, x_{15}\}$. Suppose further that 51 individuals rank the options from x_1 to x_{15} in the order of the indices: $x_1 \succ x_2 \succ x_3 \ldots \succ x_{15}$, and that 50 rank them in the following way: $x_2 \succ x_3 \succ x_4 \ldots \succ x_{15} \succ x_1$. Obviously, x_1 is a Condorcet winner, and, incidentally x_1 would be the winning option with many procedures (in particular with many voting procedures actually in use). However in this example x_1 is hated by nearly 50 per cent of the individuals and x_2 is the preferred option of nearly 50 per cent of the individuals and is ranked either first or second by all.

Some do not consider that independence is a normative condition. They think it is rather an epistemic solution to a difficult problem. It is already very difficult to make sense of intra-personal comparisons of intensity of preferences. One way to exclude these comparisons is to use a purely ordinal framework even in the aggregation. This is what the independence condition is meant to impose. Yet both the assertion and its justification are controversial. This condition basically rules out many necessary informations that could capture some normative views. For instance, it eschews any egalitarian ideas, so that eventually non-egalitarian views can only be captured. Be it by default, this is undoubtedly a strong normative commit-

ment. Formally, this condition is requesting some myopic notion, which even applies to ordinal preferences. When one has to derive a social preference between two options, then one discards all preference information that is not relevant to these two options, more precisely, discards all information that could lead to take intensity of preferences into consideration. Saari (1998, 2008) is critical of this locality type of assumption, essentially because individuals are assumed to rank the options and independence requires that the information included in the rankings is not used. Fleurbaey (2003) and Fleurbaey et al. (2005), among others, are indeed considering some weaker notions of independence than condition I which do restrict to ordinal non-comparable preferences, yet allow to use more of the relevant ordinal information. As we will see later, ordinal non-comparable preferences may be sufficient information for consistent and equitable social preferences as long as such modification is accepted.

The third condition is generally unreservedly accepted when it is presented to neophytes. This condition is generally associated to Pareto since it recalls the principle upon which Pareto optimality is based.

Condition P (Pareto principle)

Let a, $b \in X$ and $(\succeq_1, \ldots, \succeq_n) \in \mathbf{P'}^n$. If for all $i \in N$, $a \succ_i b$, then $a \succ_S b$, where $\succ_S$ is the asymmetric part of $\succeq_S = f(\succeq_1, \ldots, \succeq_n)$.

It is simply a unanimity principle. If all individuals prefer option a to option b, then, at the level of society, a must be ranked before b. Though this seems obvious, there is a consequence that is very often forgotten. If there are two options a and b such that individuals can either prefer a to b or b to a (so that there is at least a tiny diversity among the admissible lists), then, mathematically, the aggregation function cannot be constant. Such a constant function would associate the same social preference $\succeq_S$ to any n-list of complete preorders, that is, to any n-list of individual preferences. Are excluded social preferences which would be imposed by moral or religious codes. In the first edition of Arrow's book, there was an explicit condition of non-imposition. This explicit condition along with other conditions entails condition P.

According to Definition 11, the condition P amounts to state that the set N (of all individuals) is decisive over any $x,y \in X$. We now have to define the notion of dictatorship within the social choice theoretical framework.

Definition 12

A *dictator* is an individual i such that for all $x, y \in X$ and all n-list $(\succeq_1, \dots, \succeq_n) \in \mathbf{P}'^n$, $x \succ_i y$ $\Rightarrow x \succ_S y$ where $\succ_S$ is the asymmetric part of $\succeq_S = f(\succeq_1, \dots, \succeq_n)$.

We can remark that a dictator is an individual who is decisive over any $\{x,y\} \subseteq X$. It is often said that the asymmetric part of the social preference, $\succ_S$, coincide with the asymmetric part of the dictator's preference, $\succ_i$. This coincidence would require $\succ_S = \succ_i$. However, it is perfectly possible that for two options a and b, $a \succ_S b$ et $a \sim_i b$: the dictator imposes all his 'strict preferences,' he does not impose his 'indifferences'. Rather than $\succ_S = \succ_i$, we have $\succ_i \subseteq \succ_S$. Even if the dictator imposes only his 'strict preferences', it is rather difficult to imagine such a dictator in the 'real world'. Consequently, we can assert that the following fourth condition is a mild condition.

Condition D (No-dictatorship)

There is no dictator.

We will now define the class of aggregation functions studied by Arrow, viz. social welfare functions.

Definition 13

A *social welfare function* is an aggregation function $f: \mathbf{P}'^n \to \mathbf{P}$.

The social preference $\succeq_S$ is then a complete preorder. A remark: with three options we have 13 complete preorders. With three individuals, the domain of an aggregation function satisfying condition U consequently contains 13^3 elements (3-lists), that is 2197. With this same condition U, the number of possible social welfare functions is 13^{2197}, a really huge number (10^{2197} is 1 followed by more than 2000 zeros). Arrow's Theorem demonstrates that, given condition U, adding the three other conditions, we pull down this huge number to zero.

Theorem (Arrow)

If $n \geq 2$ and $\#X \geq 3$, there is no social welfare function satisfying conditions U, I, P and D.

A standard comment (but, to say the least, rather dishonest) amounts to assert that this theorem proves that democracy is impossible, or that democracy is only possible in two-party systems (X would then consist of only two elements). It is however clear that, from a mathematical standpoint, there exist various routes to get out of this negative result. One can challenge Condition U as will be seen later, or Condition I as has been done by Saari and his school by studying aggregation functions – à la Borda – based on scores, or also by reconsidering the type of aggregation functions. In this latter case, however, the results have been particularly discouraging. Gibbard replaces for social preferences **P** by **Q**. But he demonstrates that in this case, if the aggregation function satisfies Conditions U, I and P, there exists an oligarchy – a group of individuals decisive over all $\{x,y\} \subseteq X$ whose members (each member) have a veto power (each member of the oligarchy is able to prevent that a be ranked before b whenever this member prefers b to a). Mas-Colell and Sonnenschein demonstrate that replacing **Q** by **A** does not permit to obtain an interesting positive result either. The acyclicity of the asymmetric part $\succ$ of $\succeq$ is a very interesting property though. It has been proved by von

Neumann and Morgenstern that the acyclicity of the asymmetric part of a complete binary relation over X was a necessary and sufficient condition to have a maximum element (an element at least as good as all other elements) in all finite nonempty subsets of X. Finally, let us make a last remark on the finiteness of N. Does this assumption only make the proof easier or is it necessary for the theorem itself? The answer to this question was only given 20 years or so after Arrow's demonstration. This is a necessary assumption for the theorem itself. There exists indeed a social welfare function satisfying U, I , P and D when N is infinite (whatever the meaning attributed to this infinity).[3]

SEN'S THEOREM

The article published in the *Journal of Political Economy* by Sen (1970a) in which this theorem has been presented is only six pages long. These six pages, as well as Kolm's monograph (1972, 1997), had a fundamental importance in all posterior researches on the non-welfarist aspects in normative economics. Sen introduces the notion of rights (individual liberty) in the Arrovian social choice framework, viz. via aggregation functions. At about the same time, Kolm introduced the notions of fairness, equity and social justice within a formal construction and in a rather standard microeconomic model (using, for instance, so-called Edgeworth boxes).

If a social state is a description as detailed as we wish of a 'state of the world', it will be formally given as a list (as elsewhere in this chapter, we prefer the term list to the term vector, because, mathematically, a vector is an element of a vector space, space which has a structure defined in mathematics since many decades, though the set of social states is in general not endowed with this structure). This list can be considered as an element of a huge Cartesian product, element which includes features that are specific to individuals. One can have, consequently, two social states a and b that are entirely identical except that in a, in individual i's kitchen the oven is electrically powered and in b, i's oven is gas-powered. Sen suggests that, in this kind of situation, the social preference between a and b be determined by i's individual preference between a and b.

The type of aggregation function that Sen considers is more general than the social welfare functions. In Sen's terminology, they are called *social decision functions*.

Definition 14

A *social decision function* is an aggregation function f: $\mathbf{P'}^n \rightarrow \mathbf{A}$.

As we already indicated above, a result of von Neumann and Morgenstern (1953), rediscovered by Sen (1970b), shows that the acyclicity of a binary relation over X is a necessary and sufficient condition for the existence of a maximal element in all finite and nonempty subsets of X, and, therefore, to have a maximum (an element as good as all other elements) in all finite and nonempty subsets of X for a complete binary relation $\succeq$ with an asymmetric part $\succ$, it is necessary and sufficient that $\succ$ be acyclic. This justifies the term 'decision'. One can always find in any finite subset of the set of options an element that is 'acceptable'. The condition of liberalism can be easily formalized if we use the notion of decisiveness.

Condition L (Liberalism)

For each individual $i \in N$, there are two (distinct) options $a_i, b_i \in X$ such that i is decisive over $\{a_i, b_i\}$.

As a matter of fact, Sen obtains his negative result with a weaker condition saying that, rather than all individuals, at least two individuals enjoy liberalism as defined above.

Condition ML (Minimal Liberalism)

There exist two individuals i, $j \in N$ and for each of them two options a_i and $b_i \in X$ for i, and a_j and $b_j \in X$ for j, such that i is decisive over $\{a_i, b_i\}$ and j is decisive over $\{a_j, b_j\}$. The theorem is then very easy to state.

Theorem (Sen)

If $n \geq 2$ and if $\#X \geq 2$, there is no social decision function satisfying conditions U, P and ML.

This result can be easily proved. One can notice that there is no need of Condition I and that it is even true when there are only two options (in this case i and j are decisive over the same set $\{a,b\}$ and it suffices to consider a n-list in which we have $a \succ_i b$ and $b \succ_j a$; then one obtains $a \succ_S b$ and $b \succ_S a$, which is a cycle). Moreover, and contrary to Arrow's Theorem, Sen's Theorem remains true if N is infinite. It suffices then to replace n-lists by functions $\pi: N \rightarrow \mathbf{P}$, to replace $\mathbf{P}^n$ by the set Π of functions π and to replace $\mathbf{P'}^n$ by Π' with $\Pi' \subseteq \Pi$. An obvious corollary consists in replacing Condition ML by Condition L.

Many examples (some of which were crucial for the reputation of the theorem) show how the result is obtained or indicate the implications of assuming a Cartesian product over X. We are presenting first the classical example of *Lady Chatterley's Lover* that was originally given by Sen. Two individuals, one prude (denoted *pr*) the other lascivious (denoted *la*) have a unique copy of Lawrence's book. According to Sen, there are three options a, b and c: a is for '*pr* reads the novel', b is for '*la* reads it' and c for 'neither *pr* nor *la* read it'. The preferences of the two individuals are the following:

$$c \succ_{pr} a \succ_{pr} b$$
$$a \succ_{la} b \succ_{la} c$$

We assume that *pr* is decisive over $\{a,c\}$ and *la* is decisive over $\{b,c\}$. Consequently, one obtains:

$$c \succ_S a \text{ and } b \succ_S c$$

Since both individuals prefer a to b, Condition P entails $a \succ_S b$ and:

$$c \succ_S a \succ_S b \succ_S c$$

An important difficulty in this example is that it ignores the Cartesian product structure. If we assume now that there are two copies of the book, we can consider options with two components according to whether *pr* and *la* read or do not read the book. If we denote (*yes, no*) the option where *pr* reads the book and *la* does not read it (the first component is associated to *pr*, the second to *la*), we have a set of four options:

$$\{(yes,yes),(yes,no),(no,yes),(no,no)\}$$

The three last options correspond to a, b and c. Let us consider the following preferences:

$$(no,no) \succ_{pr} (yes,no) \succ_{pr} (no,yes)$$
$$\succ_{pr} (yes,yes)$$
$$(yes,yes) \succ_{la} (yes,no) \succ_{la} (no,yes) \succ_{la}$$
$$(no,no)$$

These preferences are said to be *non conditional* in Hammond's sense (some have named them separable preferences): for *pr*, $(no,..) \succ_{pr} (yes,.)$ whatever the second (same) component is. If we consider that each individual is decisive whenever the other's component is identical, *pr* is decisive over $\{(no,no), (yes,no)\}$ and over $\{(no,yes), (yes,yes)\}$, and *la* is decisive over $\{(no,no), (no,yes)\}$ and over $\{(yes,yes), (yes,no)\}$. It is easy to see that we obtain then two cycles, not only one:

$$(no,no) \succ_S (yes,no) \succ_S (no,yes) \succ_S (no,no)$$
$$(yes,yes) \succ_S (yes,no) \succ_S (no,yes) \succ_S$$
$$(yes,yes)$$

Theoretically it is even possible to obtain a cycle without using Condition P. Let us consider the four options constructed by ordered pairs of a and b, (a,a), (a,b), (b,a) and (b,b) and let us assume that we have the following two individual preferences for individual 1 (first component) and 2 (second component):

$$(b,a) \succ_1 (a,a) \succ_1 (a,b) \succ_1 (b,b)$$
$$(a,a) \succ_2 (a,b) \succ_2 (b,b) \succ_2 (b,a)$$

One obtains by applying the simple decisiveness of each individual:

$$(b,a) \succ_S (a,a) \succ_S (a,b) \succ_S (b,b) \succ_S (b,a)$$

The difficulties related to decisiveness, that is to liberalism in our context, can also conflict with individual decision making, for instance in the case of a prudent choice. Let us consider the following example due to Gibbard (1974) and thoroughly discussed by Gaertner et al. (1992), Sen (1992) and Pattanaik (1996). We still have two individuals 1 and 2 and we assume that, in the morning, each individual has the right to choose the shirt he is going to wear during the day. Each individual has two types of shirts in his wardrobe: grey shirts (g) and blue shirts (b). Similarly to the previous examples, we will define the options as ordered pairs so that, for a given day, there are four possibilities of forming ordered pairs of g and b. We can also imagine that these are social states that are identical except for the shirts worn by the two individuals. Let us consider individual 1 and let us suppose that he is decisive over $\{(b,g),(g,g)\}$ and that the preferences are given by:

$$(b,b) \succ_1 (g,g) \succ_1 (b,g) \succ_1 (g,b)$$
$$(b,g) \succ_2 (g,b) \succ_2 (g,g) \succ_2 (b,b)$$

We can see that individual 1 has a preference for uniformity and a preference for the blue, and that individual 2 has a preference for diversity and that he prefers grey shirts. Now let us assume that individuals are prudent and, accordingly, choose their shirts according to the maximin rule. Individual 1 will not choose a grey shirt that could lead to the option he ranks last. Then he will choose a blue shirt. Likewise, individual 2 will choose a grey shirt so that the determined option will be (b,g). But, individual 1, being decisive over $\{(b,g),(g,g)\}$, is assumed to be capable

to impose a social preference in favour of (g,g) that he prefers to (b,g). This example clearly shows that individual choices made with strong risk aversion are conflicting with the condition of liberalism.

As mentioned above Sen's Theorem marks the birth of works on the non-welfaristic aspects of normative economics. The term *welfarism* is associated to the idea that the goodness of social states is evaluated only on the basis of individual utilities attached to the social states. This leads to the following observation. If we have four social states a, b, c and d, and if each individual i attributes the same utility to, say, a and b, and the same utility to c and d, then the social ranking of a and c must be the same as the social ranking of b and d. This leads to various properties of neutrality for functions defined on lists of utility functions and this can be extended to lists of individual preferences in which case one obtains intra- and inter-lists neutrality. Intuitively, neutrality means that the names of social states do not matter (see section ninth for further commentaries). The liberalism condition obviously violates neutrality since specific social states are attached to specific individuals. Of course, anonymity, meaning that the names of the individuals do not matter, is also violated since specific individuals have a specific power over specific options.

In addition to the already cited papers, comments on Sen's theorem can be found in Brunel and Salles (1998), Li and Saari (2008), Saari (1998, 2001), Saari and Petron (2006) and Salles (2000, 2008, 2009). Apart from its intrinsic importance, taking individual rights and freedom into account within the theory of social choice is at the origin of developments on the analysis of rights in game theory (rights being constraints imposed on the space of individual strategies) and at the origin of researches about freedom of choice, researches based on the study of the sets over which individual choices are made (see Pattanaik and Xu (1990), Pattanaik et al. (2004) and Baujard (2007) for a survey of this literature).

GIBBARD-SATTERTHWAITE'S THEOREM

According to a gossip, most probably apocryphal, Borda would have responded to detractors (Condorcet?) saying that his method was easy to manipulate, that is, it was easy for an individual to reveal a non sincere ranking to obtain a better outcome than the outcome resulting from the revelation of the sincere ranking, that his method was devised for honest people. The notion of useful voting is frequent in election periods. A recent President of the French Republic always reminded voters when there were important elections. This means that some voters were invited not to vote for the candidate they ranked first because this would spoil their votes (in general, it is the case for voters choosing candidates of marginal political parties), but rather to vote for a candidate that has a good chance to win and would be for them a second best. In the 2000 US presidential election, George W. Bush won in Florida by a decision of the US Supreme Court, although Gore had approximately the same number of votes. Now there was another candidate, an ecologist, Nader, with a small but still significant percentage of votes. We must recall that according to who the winner is in each State (that is the plurality winner), this winner obtains the full set of the State presidential electors. One can easily imagine that most of those who voted for Nader ranked Gore before Bush. If these voters had thought of useful voting, they would have voted for Gore rather than for Nader, and Gore would have been President of the United States (and the world would have been totally different from what it became).

The general result on this topic was obtained independently by Gibbard (1973) and Satterthwaite (1975). However a fundamental contribution due to Dummett and Farquharson ten years before, in spite of being published in *Econometrica* got rather unnoticed.

We assume that X is finite and, for reasons of simplicity, that individual preferences are given by anti-symmetric complete preorders, that is, given by linear orders denoted by $\succ_i$. Rather than an aggregation function, the considered procedure is a selection: to a n-list $(\succ_1, \ldots , \succ_n)$ one associates an element $x \in X$. If $\mathbf{L'}^n$ is a subset of $\mathbf{L}^n$, we have the following definition.

Definition 15

A *social choice function* is a function $f: \mathbf{L'}^n \to X$.

We must now formally define the notion described above.

Definition 16

An individual $i \in N$ manipulates the social choice function f in $(\succ_1, \ldots , \succ_n) \in \mathbf{L'}^n$ if there exists $\succ'_i \in \mathbf{L'}$ such that: $f(\succ_1,\ldots,\succ_{i-1}, \succ'_i,\succ_{i+1},\ldots,\succ_n) \succ_i f(\succ_1,\ldots,\succ_i,\ldots,\succ_n)$.

If we assume that the n-list $(\succ_1, \ldots , \succ_n)$ is made of sincere individual preferences and that $\succ'_i$ is a 'lie', the definition means that individual i manipulates if, in revealing preference that is a 'lie' rather than her true preference, the result of the selection carried out by the social choice function is an option that this individual sincerely prefers to the option that would have been selected if she had revealed her true preference. Three conditions are going to be imposed on social choice functions.

Condition U^C (Universality)

The Condition U^C is satisfied if $\mathbf{L'} = \mathbf{L}$.

For comments on this condition, see our comments on Condition U in second section.

Condition NM (Non-manipulability)

There is no individual $i \in N$ and n-list $(\succ_1, \ldots , \succ_n) \in \mathbf{L'}^n$ for which i manipulates f in $(\succ_1, \ldots , \succ_n)$.

Condition S (Surjectivity)

The social choice function is surjective if $f(\mathbf{L}'^n) = X$.

Surjectivity means that, for all $x \in X$, there is a n-list $(\succ_1, \ldots, \succ_n)$ for which $f(\succ_1, \ldots, \succ_n) = x$. This condition is not entirely necessary. It suffices that there is a sufficient number of options in X that can be effectively selected. However, even though this condition might appear as purely mathematical, its intuitive content is far from being negligible. It excludes that the social choice function be a constant function. Again, the comments we made in the second section regarding Condition P can be applied here.

We now have to exclude dictatorship as we did for Arrow's Theorem. Since the framework is different we must first make precise what we consider to be a dictator in this social choice function setting. A dictator will be an individual who imposes that the function selects the option he ranks first.

Definition 17

An individual $i \in N$ is a *dictator for a social choice function f* if for all n-list $(\succ_1, \ldots, \succ_n) \in \mathbf{L}'^n$, $f(\succ_1, \ldots, \succ_n) \succ_i x$ for all $x \in X \_ \{f(\succ_1, \ldots, \succ_n)\}$.

Condition D^C

There is no dictator in the sense of Definition 17.

Theorem (Gibbard–Satterthwaite)

If $n \geq 2$ and $\#X \geq 3$, there does not exist a social choice function satisfying conditions U^C, NM, S and D^C.

We give a simple example of manipulation of Borda's rule where the selected option is the option who obtained the greatest score and, in case of ties, the first option according to the alphabetical order. Let us consider a

set of options $X = \{a,b,c,d\}$ and a set of individuals $N = \{1,2,3\}$ and let us assume:

$(\succ_1, \succ_2, \succ_3)$	$(\succ_1, \succ'_2, \succ_3)$
$a \succ_1 b \succ_1 c \succ_1 d$	$a \succ_1 b \succ_1 c \succ_1 d$
$c \succ_2 d \succ_2 b \succ_2 a$	$b \succ'_2 c \succ'_2 d \succ'_2 a$
$a \succ_3 b \succ_3 d \succ_3 c$	$a \succ_3 b \succ_3 d \succ_3 c$

It is clear that $f(\succ_1, \succ_2, \succ_3) = a$, $f(\succ_1, \succ'_2, \succ_3) = b$ and $b \succ_2 a$.

For plurality rule that is used in American and UK elections, it is obvious that a single individual cannot change the result by manipulation, since if an option a is selected, any change in favour of another option, say, b can only increase the total vote for b by one. Accordingly, at best, b can reach the level obtained by a. For the plurality rule to be a social choice function, one must add a tie-breaking mechanism. However various authors have shown that what was obtained for social choice functions was still essentially true if the social choice functions were replaced by social choice correspondences that select nonempty subsets of X.

Gibbard–Satterthwaite's Theorem was at the origin of a tremendous number of contributions in social choice theory, but also in public economics, in particular in the theory of implementation and the theory of games (see the remarkable surveys of Barbera (2001) and Jackson (2001)).

SINGLE-PEAKEDNESS AND MAJORITY RULE

At the end of the 1940s, that is approximately at the same time as Arrow, a British economist, Duncan Black, introduced the notion of single -peaked preference in a paper published in the *Journal of Political Economy*. He was studying the effects of this assumption of single-peaked preferences on the outcomes obtained by the procedure of majority decision rule and he demonstrated among other results what is now called the 'median voter' Theorem. He used a kind of geometric setting. Let us assume that the space of options is the closed interval $[a,b]$ of the real line $\mathbb{R}$ and that individual i's preference be given by a continuous function u_i defined over $[a,b]$. Furthermore, let us assume that u_i is increasing until it reaches a maximum in x_i, and then decreasing until it reaches b. In Figure 17.1, we have the curves of five functions representing five preferences.

In this figure, u_1 reaches its maximum for option a, u_2 for option x_2 and u_5 for option b. Individual 3 is the median individual and x_3 is the option selected by the majority decision rule. One can remark that here the functions u_i are what we generally called strictly quasi-concave functions (in the figure, the functions are in fact concave). We will now develop Black's analysis in a discrete setting, with a discrete version of single-peakedness that is essentially due to Arrow. Let us first formally define the majority decision rule.

Definition 18

The *majority decision rule* is an aggregation function such that for all $x,y \in X$ and all n-list $(\succeq_1, \dots, \succeq_n) \in P'^n$, $x \succ_S y \Leftrightarrow \#\{i : x \succ_i y\} > \#\{i : y \succ_i x\}$ and $y \succeq_S x$ otherwise.

We know since May (1952) that this method is characterized by conditions of symmetry as regards individuals (anonymity: if you permute the names of individuals, the outcome does not change), of neutrality regarding options (if we permute the options, the outcome is permuted likewise) and strict monotonicity (when there is an indifference between two options a and b at the social level for some n-list, the outcome of a new n-list in which option a increases preference-wise vis-à-vis option b in some individual preference and does not decrease preference-wise in any individual preference will be $a \succ_S b$). Clearly the condition of anonymity entails the condition D of nondictatorship.

The following version of the Arrovian version of single-peakedness is borrowed from Sen (1966). Let us consider three (distinct) options a, b and c.

Definition 19

A set of complete preorders over X satisfies the Condition of *single-peakedness over* $\{a,b,c\} \subseteq X$ if either $a \sim b$ and $b \sim c$, or there is an option among the three options, say, b, such that $b \succ a$ or $b \succ c$.

A set of complete preorders satisfies the Condition of *single-peakedness* if it satisfies the Condition of single-peakedness over all $\{x,y,z\} \subseteq X$.

We will denote by **BL** the set of complete preorders over X satisfying the Condition of single-peakedness. We can now state the Arrovian version of Black's Theorem.

Theorem (Black)

Let us assume that $n \geq 2$, $\#X \geq 3$ and $\mathbf{P'}=\mathbf{BL}$. Let us assume further that the number of individuals for whom $\neg(x \sim_i y$ and $y \sim_i z)$ is odd. Then the majority decision rule is a social welfare function satisfying Conditions I, P and D.

This simply means that the social preference $\succeq_S$ is transitive. The condition that the number of individuals who are not indifferent between the three options is odd can appear as problematic, but it is not so problematic. Indeed let us consider a new class of aggregation functions.

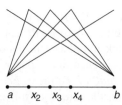

Figure 17.1 Black's single-peakedness.

Definition 20

A *social decision function of quasi-transitive-type* is an aggregation function $f: \mathbf{P'}^n \rightarrow \mathbf{Q}$.

We have then the following theorem due to Sen and Pattanaik (1969).

Theorem (Sen and Pattanaik)

Let us assume that $n \geq 2$, $\#X \geq 3$ and $\mathbf{P'}=\mathbf{BL}$. Then the majority decision rule is a social decision function of quasi-transitive-type.

This theorem indicates that the asymmetric component $\succ_S$ of the social preference is transitive.

With three options we know that there are 13 complete preorders. Single-peakedness is some kind of super-rationality. There are eight single-peaked complete preorders. One can represent these eight complete preorders. This representation (which was at the basis of the Arrovian version of single-peakedness) has a specific interest. If the three options a, b, and c are on a line with b between a and c, we have the eight possibilities shown in Figure 17.2.

When the options are on the same horizontal level, this means that there is an indifference, when an option x is above an option y, this means that $x \succ y$. The options a, b, and c are linearly ordered, with a on the left, b in the center and c on the right. It is then easy to give a political interpretation to the preferences, in particular if a, b, and c are candidates to an election. A major difficulty arises from the two preferences shown in Figure 17.3.

However, Dummett and Farquharson (1961) have shown that if we added these two preferences to the eight preferences of Black's single-peakedness we obtained a maximum element for the relation $\succeq_S$ when

the aggregation function was defined by: $x \succeq_S y \Leftrightarrow \#\{ i : x \succeq_i y \} > n/2$, or $\#\{ i : x \succeq_i y \} = n/2$, and $x \succeq_1 y$. This is what is now called majoritarian voting game with a casting vote given to individual 1.

The three complete preorders that are still missing are quite odd in a rational political world (Figure 17.4).

The 10 complete preorders of the extended version of single-peakedness remind us, in Black's geometric original setting, of a kind of quasi-concavity. 'Ordinary' quasi-concavity would then replace strict quasi-concavity. On this, we suggest that Nakamura (1975), Salles and Wendell (1977) and Salles (2007) be consulted.

In Figure 17.5, the curve on the left corresponds to a strictly quasi-concave function. It is not concave in contrast to the curves in Figure 17.1 because of the 'bend' in the decreasing part. The curve on the right represents a quasi-concave function. Then one can see that stationary parts (the horizontal parts of the curve) are possible in intermediary position and also at the maximum.

These variations about single-peakedness must not hide that there exist other conditions of the same type. However, they are in general, more difficult to interpret from an intuitive point of view. Papers by Inada (1969), Sen and Pattanaik (1969) and Gaertner and Salles (1981) demonstrate this fact and the book by Gaertner (2001) is the last word on this topic (at least at this time).

HARSANYI'S UTILITARIANISM THEOREM

John Harsanyi, in two papers (1953, 1955, 1976) considers welfare economics in risky

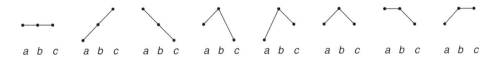

$a\ b\ c \qquad a\ b\ c \qquad a\ b\ c \qquad a\ b\ c \qquad a\ b\ c \qquad a\ b\ c \qquad a\ b\ c \qquad a\ b\ c$

Figure 17.2 Black's single-peakedness over {a,b,c}.

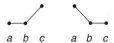

Figure 17.3 Extra complete preorders for an extended version of single-peakedness.

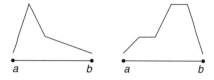

Figure 17.5 Strict quasi-concavity and quasi-concavity.

environments. In his famous 1955 paper, he proposes a major result that, in some sense, justifies utilitarianism from a technical perspective. Harsanyi's contribution has been at the origin of a large debate among the pros and cons of utilitarianism. If we adopt the view of post-Arrow–Debreu microeconomic theory that a utility function u is only a numerical representation of a preference, to be precise here, of a complete preorder, that is for options x and y in X, $u(x) \geq u(y) \Leftrightarrow x \succeq y$, utilitarianism in its most rudimentary form amounts to state that the social welfare associated to option x, $w(x)$, is the sum of the individual utilities (i.e. the values taken by the utility functions) associated to x:

$$w(x) = \sum\nolimits_{i=1}^{n} u_i(x)$$

where $u_i(x)$ is individual i's utility associated to x. This, of course, implies that the individual utilities are comparable.

Harsanyi's framework is borrowed from von Neumann and Morgenstern analysis of risks in game theory (1953). The set of options, L, is made of lotteries, that is probability distributions over a finite set of prizes. Given appropriate assumptions over the set of lotteries and the set of complete preorders $\succeq_i$ over L (some of these assumptions are continuity – topological – assumptions) it can be shown that there exists a utility function representing the complete preorder,

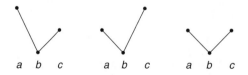

Figure 17.4 Excluded complete preorders.

utility function that further satisfies the so-called *expected utility property*.[4] If we assume that there are k prizes 1, ... , k and a probability distribution p_1, ... , $p_k - p_1$ being the probability of receiving prize x_1 etc.– the expected utility property states that for the lottery x defined by the k prizes x_1, ... , x_k and the probabilities p_1, ... , p_k, we have

$$u(x) = \sum\nolimits_{j=1}^{n} p_j u(x_j)$$

This means that the utility associated to the lottery x is the sum of the utilities associated to the prizes weighted by the probabilities of receiving these prizes. An important consequence of this property is that the utility function is not only unique up to an increasing transformation but to an increasing affine transformation.[5] Such utility functions are generally called von Neumann-Morgenstern utility functions. As a major consequence, differences of utilities are meaningful although they are not meaningful for 'ordinary' ordinal utility functions. Due to this extra information such functions are said to be *cardinal*.

Harsanyi assumes that both the social preference (a complete preorder) and the individuals' complete preorders are defined over L and satisfy the von Neumann–Morgenstern assumptions. Accordingly the complete preorders $\succeq_i$ can be represented by von Neumann-Morgenstern utility functions u_i.

We will introduce three assumptions. Since the prizes are fixed, we will denote the lotteries by the probability vectors so that $p = (p_1, \dots , p_k)$ is a probability distribution associated to $x_1, \dots , x_k$.

Condition P-I (Pareto indifference)

Let p, q be two lotteries. If for all $i \in N\ p \sim_i q$, then $p \sim_S q$.

If all individuals are indifferent between two lotteries, so is the society.

Condition S-P (Strong Pareto)

Let p, q be two lotteries. If for all $i \in N\ p \succeq_i q$ and for some $i \in N\ p \succ_i q$, then $p \succ_S q$.

This condition is the standard Pareto condition used in microeconomics to define Pareto optimality.

Condition I-Pros (Independent Prospects)

For each $i \in N$ there exist two lotteries p^i and $\in L$ such that $p^i \succ_i q^i$ and for all $j \neq i$ $p^i \sim_j q^i$.

This condition will be satisfied if for instance only individual i prefers some prize to another prize while all other individuals are indifferent between these two prizes.[6]

The following result, that can be considered as Harsanyi's utilitarianism Theorem, is basically due to Weymark (1991).

Theorem (Harsanyi–Weymark)

1 If Condition P-I is satisfied, then there exist real numbers a_i such that $\succeq_S$ is represented by w with $w = \sum_{i=1}^{n} a_i u_i$.

2 If Condition S-P is also satisfied, then there exist positive real numbers a_i such that $\succeq_S$ is represented by w with $w = \sum_{i=1}^{n} a_i u_i$.

3 If Condition I-Pros is also satisfied, the a_i are unique up to a positive factor of proportionality.

Although this very important result can be interpreted as a modern defense of utilitarianism, the philosophical and the technical justification of the use of the von Neumann–Morgenstern assumptions to give a thorough

founding of utilitarianism have been severely challenged. In his 1953 paper, Harsanyi justifies the use of the von Neumann–Morgenstern analysis by representing the decision of an impartial but sympathetic observer, considering what rational choice each individual would do when she ignores her own personal interests. This claim, soon reformulated as a 'veil-of-ignorance' argument, has been the source of a long-standing debate with John Rawls on the thickness of the veil, hence on the relevance of the assumptions of rationality under risky situations for justice issues. Besides, the hypothesis that $\succeq_S$ satisfies the von Neumann–Morgenstern assumptions has been challenged and shown to be unreasonable by Diamond (1967). Furthermore, a number of authors have criticized Harsanyi by arguing that his utilitarianism could not be associated to classical utilitarianism, mainly because of the von Neumann-Morgenstern necessary framework (see in particular Sen (1976), the discussion and references in Roemer (1996) and Fleurbaey et al. (2008)).

SOCIAL CHOICE, SOCIAL JUSTICE

As presented above, Arrow's theorem induces that no social choice may be derived from individual preferences for certain reasonable conditions. Little, Bergson or Samuelson among others, have argued that the Arrovian framework as such does not at all apply to welfare economics problems. Yet, Kemp and Ng (1976), Parks (1976), and others, have shown that a kind of Arrovian result would apply also for Bergson–Samuelson social welfare function (see first section of the chapter) after a suitable cosmetic modification of the basic framework. Let us here consider Parks's result. It applies to utilities rather than to preferences, and for a condition of neutrality rather than independence – but notice that, as explained in the introduction, for Bergson–Samuelson social welfare functions, the individual utility functions are fixed; the domain of a social welfare function is the set of social states, X, over which individual utility functions are also defined and there is a unique list of utility functions. Some authors speak of a *single-profile* type of problems. In this framework, the independence condition, Condition I, cannot be defined since we need two lists for its definition (the aggregation is over lists of individual preferences or individual utility functions). On the other hand, neutrality can be defined in both a single-profile framework and a multi-profile (Arrovian) framework. When defined for a multi-profile framework, there are important converse links between independence and neutrality as in Arrow's preliminary Lemma (see Sen, 1970b: 43). In a nutshell, neutrality amounts to say that the names of options should not count to derive the social ranking.

We need to introduce new notations. Each individual is assumed to have a complete preorder over X represented by a utility function $u_i(.)$. We let $u(x) = (u_1(x), \ldots, u_n(x))$. The Bergson–Samuelson social welfare function is a real-valued function f defined over the values taken by the individual utility functions, that is, one obtains a real number $f(u(.))$. Since a number is attached to each $x \in X$, this number being the social welfare in social state x, one can rank (if X is finite) the social states according to their welfare levels. The following conditions are meant to guarantee welfarism – that is, to rely only on individual utilities – and restrict attention to ordinal non-comparable utilities.

Condition PC (Pareto consistency)

For all x and y in X, if $u_i(x) > u_i(y)$ for all $i \in N$ then $f(u(x)) > f(u(y))$.

Condition DS (Diversity in Society)

Let $u_i(X)$ be the range of u_i on X, $S_i \subseteq u_i(X)$, and #S_i, be the cardinal number of the set S_i, and (a) For all i, #$u_i(X) \geq 3$, and (b) There

exist sets S_i, $i=1, \ldots, n$ with #$S_i = 3$ such that $\{\alpha \in \mathbb{R}^n : \alpha = (u_1(x), \ldots, u_n(x))\}$ for some x in $X\} \supseteq \prod_1^n S_i$.

Condition N (Neutrality)

If $[u_i(x) > u_i(y)$ iff $u_i(z) > u_i(w)$, and $u_i(x) = u_i(y)$ iff $u_i(z) = u_i(w)$, for all $i]$ then $f(u(x)) > f(u(y))$ iff $f(u(z)) > f(u(w))$.

Theorem (Parks)

If the social welfare function is Pareto consistent, neutral, and if there is diversity in society, then there is an individual i such that for all x, $y \in X$ if $u_i(x) > u_i(y)$ then $f(u(x)) > f(u(y))$.

Such an individual can be called a u-dictator after a suitable and easy adaptation of Definition 12.

Giving these disturbing results, solving the social choice problem in welfare economics amounts to answering the following questions: is it possible to obtain a non-dictatorial social welfare function from preferences represented by utility functions? Is it so even if these preferences are ordinal and non-comparable? Before concluding hurriedly that the Arrovian impossibility is taking welfare economics, hence any attempt to tackle justice issues, to a dead-end, a prior discussion is needed on the meaning of the conditions of independence and/or neutrality, and on the informational content of individual utility functions.

The condition of independence, as noted earlier in the fourth section, is ruling out any consideration of intensity of preferences, and any way to compare preferences from one person to another, relying exclusively on binary information. In other words, it excludes any inter or intra-comparisons of utility. Sen (1970b) has proposed some analyses of partial comparability of utility. Specific focus on the link between the informational content of utility functions and their invariance properties have been developed since then.

Assuming that comparisons of level of utilities are meaningful, there would hence exist an universal scale of utility – for instance on the set of real numbers – on which any person's utility can be measured. Any comparisons and calculations would be possible with the values of these utilities. This would be certainly convenient for social scientists – this was even the aim of Bentham at one time – but notice that hardly any value, be it physical, would respect these strong requirements. Temperature may indeed be measured on different scales, defined up to any increasing affine transformations, and yet convey the same information. Similarly, utilities will be said ordinal or cardinal, comparable or not, according to the invariance conditions. For instance, utilities are said to be ordinal non-comparable when $f(u) = f(u')$ if there exists a strictly increasing function ϕ_i for each $i \in N$ such that $\forall i$, $u'_i = \phi_i(u_i)$. They are said to be cardinal comparable (with meaningful differences of the utilities for any given individual) when $f(u) = f(u')$ if there exists $a > 0$, $b \in \mathbb{R}$ such that $u'_i = au_i + b$. Many intermediate informational contents may be captured through the invariance conditions. We suggest the reading of d'Aspremont and Gevers (2002) or Bossert and Weymark (2004) for an extended presentation of this literature. See also Blackorby et al. (2005) for an important application of such studies to population ethics.

At the technical level, deep critical comments of the Arrovian conditions underlay two distinct families of modifications of the Arrovian framework to go beyond the usual impossibilities in social choice theory. One of them challenges the condition of unrestricted domain, and proposes analyses in economic environments. The other one discusses the interpretation of individual preferences to make it consistent with a notion of justice and with the aim of implementing fair actual policies.

Some authors have considered the condition of unrestricted domain (Condition U) to be unadapted to welfare economics or even to economic problems in general: in these cases, preferences are characterized by certain usual structure, and they are well defined. On the one hand, restrictions of domains are now considered. Some narrower properties of preferences relations are taken into account, imposing to preferences for instance the conditions of continuity, monotonicity, convexity, etc. These conditions are standard in the economic literature, which justifies the label 'economic domains'. The single-peaked preferences presented above are one instance of the possible results that could be found with the other Arrovian conditions. The papers by Le Breton (1997) and Le Breton and Weymark (2010) provide a wide-ranging presentation of this literature. On the other hand, from the multi-profile setting which characterizes the Arrovian framework, one now considers a single profile setting – as in the Parks's result – more specific to allocations problems in actual contexts. Besides, the condition of independence (or neutrality) is ruling out too much information: in particular, it excludes some relevant ordinal information conveyed by the indifference curves. Fleurbaey (2003) provides a thorough analysis of the formulations, interpretations and stakes of these conditions. Let's summarize all these modifications. Considering one profile rather than several profiles meanwhile, restrictions of preferences to economic domains, and allowing to use all information from the indifference curves provide a renewed framework. Such a reformulation implies to focus on the distribution of allocation of commodities rather than on abstract social states, which allow to state whether such or such allocation is fair or not, according to specified equity criteria. Notice that the equity criteria are here explicitly given, and formulated independently of the individual preferences. Since the precursor paper by Pazner and Schmeidler (1978), possibilities now occur in the theory of fair allocations, on the basis of strictly ordinal non-comparable utilities, and their applications to distributive justice issues are uncontroversial. We strongly recommend the books written by Roemer (1996) or by Fleurbaey (1996, 2008), which provide extensive presentations of such results.

We will not go further in the presentation of the very fruitful theory of fair allocations because it would take us too far away from the scope of this paper, which should confine itself to social choice theory as such. The gap is twofold. Firstly, many of the conditions retained to restrict the domain of individual preferences prove controversial for justice issues. Let us consider any of the monotonicity conditions. The interpretation of such condition can be defended in problems implying consumer's choice as a collection habit – even though satiation proves to be a relevant fact for most goods and for most people. Now in justice issue, such a condition basically means that more is better than less putting aside the very controversial question of the relevance of distributional issues of fixed global (and bounded) endowments for people's welfare. Second, allocations are chosen on the basis of self-centered individual preferences defined on individual allocations while a social choice for justice issues would require to derive judgments from individual judgments on what is fair or not. Technically, this amounts to obtaining a ranking or a selection of vectors of individual allocations rather than individual allocations.

The other challenge concerns the interpretation and the properties for the preferences to be aggregated. A way to phrase this debate is to consider that the Arrovian framework is based on individual tastes, whereas the problem at stake in justice issues would rather be the aggregation of individual values. The stake of this discussion is not only philosophical but it is also technical, since the interpretation of individual preferences has some major consequences on their informational content, hence their properties, as we have seen above. The 'rehabilitation' of comparisons of utilities has been primarily defended by Sen in his 1970 book. His claims are now widely known as 'the comparative approach'.

One must remark that three basic conditions are necessary for the re-introduction of interpersonal comparisons and for recovering possibility results for justice issues. First, the interpretation of such comparisons is normative and should not be positive: it is meaningful to say that a transfer of $1000 to a poor household provides more welfare than a transfer of the same amount of money to Bill Gates's household, if this assertion is meant to capture the idea according to which the former situation is more fair than the latter, while it would be meaningless to say that it actually provides the former household more happiness. Whenever this approach is accepted, no use of a welfare concept should be accepted without a clarification of the corresponding conception of justice. Second, utility should be objective rather than subjective: it should be possible for the public decision maker to measure individual utility by observing facts or statistics. For these reasons, some would defend multi-dimensional accounts for individual welfare rather than the usual uni-dimensional utility. Such insights have opened a path to formal non-welfarism, in particular to the capability approach advocated by Amartya Sen. Third, as presented above, some analyses of Sen's paper on the impossibility of a Paretian Liberal have prompted researches to attach more importance to the value of freedom. Furthermore, aggregation of individual welfares are often generating impossibility results because of specific forms of external effects. Some works, though still in progress, consider cartesian products, that is, a more complex – and actually endogenously defined – structure of the domain of definition of preferences. Add to this that the reintroduction of comparisons allows possibilities even with partial orders.

A serious consideration of the role of the independence axiom on the informational content of utilities has proved necessary to adapt the Arrovian framework to social justice issues. This shift explains why value judgments have been reintroduced explicitly in the framework to be able to generate positive results, in equity criteria for the equity approach, within the individual welfare function for the comparative approach.

CONCLUSION

We have presented major results of social choice theory and we have tried to comment on the considered frameworks and conditions from a normative point of view. We wish to draw the attention on several important books. An excellent introduction to social choice theory is Gaertner (2006). Two volumes in the series of 'Handbook of Economics' – *Handbook of Social Choice and Welfare* edited by Arrow et al. (2002, 2010) are devoted to social choice and welfare economics. The books by Fleurbaey (1996, 2008) and Roemer (1996) are particularly recommended because economic theory and philosophy are considered on a par. Political science aspects are remarkably covered by the two volumes of Austen-Smith and Banks (1999, 2005).

NOTES

1 $\mathbb{R}$ is the set of real numbers.

2 This notation is the standard notation of partial derivatives. It is often intuitively interpreted (wrongly from a mathematical point of view) as the ratio of the increase – or decrease – of f, here the social welfare, to the increase – or decrease – of any u_i.

3 See Fishburn (1970).

4 We will not describe extensively these assumptions in this chapter. They are rather technically demanding and are excellently covered in advanced microeconomics or game theory textbooks. See the concluding section for some hints.

5 A utility function v is obtained from a utility function u by an increasing affine transformation if $v=\alpha u+\beta$, where α is a positive real number and β any real number.

6 As an example let x_1 be a piece of cheesecake and x_2 a piece of chocolate cake. Assume that $x_1 \succ_i x_2$ and for all $j \neq i$ $x_1 \sim_j x_2$. Then $p = (1, 0, \dots , 0)$ will be preferred by i to $q = (0, 1, 0, \dots, 0)$ or $p = (0.75, 0.25, 0, \dots , 0)$ will be preferred by i to $q = (0.5, 0.5,$ 0, ... , 0) and in both cases all the other individuals are going to be indifferent between p and q.

REFERENCES

Arrow, K.J. (1950) 'A difficulty in the concept of social welfare', *Journal of Political Economy*, 58: 328–346.

Arrow, K.J. (1951/1963) *Social Choice and Individual Values* . New York: Wiley.

Arrow, K.J. and Scitovsky, T. (eds) (1969) *Readings in Welfare Economics*. Homewood, IL: Irwin.

Arrow K.J., Sen A.K. and Suzumura K. (eds) (2002, 2010) *Handbook of Social Choice and Welfare*, vol 1. and vol. 2, Amsterdam: Elsevier.

d'Aspremont C. and Gevers L. (2002) 'Social welfare functionals and interpersonal comparability', in K.J. Arrow, A.K. Sen and K. Suzumura (eds), *Handbook of Social Choice and Welfare*, vol 1. Elsevier Science. pp. 459–541.

Austen-Smith, D. and Banks, J.S. (1999) *Positive Political Theory I. Collective Preference*. Ann Arbor, MI: University of Michigan Press.

Austen-Smith, D. and Banks, J.S. (2005) *Positive Political Theory II. Strategy and Structure*. Ann Arbor, MI: University of Michigan Press.

Barbera, S. (2001) 'An introduction to strategy-proof social choice functions', *Social Choice and Welfare*, 18: 619–653.

Baujard, A. (2007) 'Conceptions of freedom and ranking opportunity sets: A typology', *Homo Oeconomicus*, 24: 231–254.

Baumol, W.J. and Wilson, C.A. (eds) (2001) *Welfare Economics, Volume 1*. Cheltenham: Edward Elgar.

Black, D. (1948) 'On the rationale of group decision-making', *Journal of Political Economy*, 56: 23–34.

Black, D. (1958/1998) *The Theory of Committees and Elections*, second edition, I. McLean, A. McMillan and B. L. Munroe (eds). Boston, MA: Kluwer.

Blackorby, C., Bossert, W. and Donaldson, D. (2005) *Population Issues in Social Choice Theory, Welfare Economics, and Ethics*. Cambridge: Cambridge University Press.

Bossert, W. and Weymark, J. (2004) 'Utility in social choice', in S. Barberà, P. Hammond, and C. Seidl (eds) *Handbook of Utility Theory*, Kluwer. 2: 1099–1177.

Brunel, A. and Salles, M. (1998) 'Interpretative, semantic and formal difficulties of the social choice rule approach to rights', in J.-F. Laslier, M. Fleurbaey, N. Gravel and A. Trannoy (eds) *Freedom in Economics: New Perspectives in Normative Economics*. London: Routledge. pp. 101–111.

Condorcet, M. le Marquis de (1785) *Essai sur l'Application de l'Analyse à la Probabilité des Décisions Rendues à la Pluralité des Voix*. Paris: Imprimerie Royale. (Facsimile, New York: Chelsea, 1972).

Diamond, P. (1967) 'Cardinal welfare, individualistic ethics, and interpersonal comparisons of utility: Comment', *Journal of Political Economy*, 75: 765–766.

Dummett, M. and Farquharson, R. (1961) 'Stability in voting', *Econometrica*, 29: 33–43.

Fishburn, P.C. (1970) 'Arrow's Impossibility Theorem: Concise proof and infinite voters', *Journal of Economic Theory*, 2: 103–106.

Fleurbaey, M. (1996) *Théories Économiques de la Justice* . Paris: Economica.

Fleurbaey, M. (2003) 'On the informational basis of social choice', *Social Choice and Welfare*, 21: 347–384.

Fleurbaey, M. (2008) *Fairness, Responsibility, and Welfare*. Oxford: Oxford University Press.

Fleurbaey, M., Suzumura, K. and Tadenuma, K. (2005) 'The informational basis of the theory of fair allocation', *Social Choice and Welfare*, 24: 311–342.

Fleurbaey, M., Salles, M. and Weymark, J.A. (eds) (2008) *Justice, Political Liberalism, and Utilitarianism. Themes from Harsanyi and Rawls*. Cambridge: Cambridge University Press.

Gaertner, W. (2001) *Domain Conditions in Social Choice Theory*. Cambridge: Cambridge University Press.

Gaertner, W. (2006) *A Primer in Social Choice Theory*. Oxford: Oxford University Press.

Gaertner, W., Pattanaik, P.K. and Suzumura, K. (1992) 'Individual rights revisited', *Economica*, 59: 161–177.

Gaertner, W. and Salles, M. (1981) 'Procédures d'agrégation avec domaines restreints et théorèmes d'existence', in P. Batteau, E. Jacquet-Lagrèze and B. Monjardet (eds), *Analyse et Agrégation des Préférences*. Paris: Economica. pp. 75–115.

Gibbard, A. (1973) 'Manipulation of voting schemes: A general result', *Econometrica*, 41: 587–217.

Gibbard, A. (1974) 'A Pareto consistent claim', *Journal of Economic Theory*, 7: 388–410.

Harsanyi, J.C. (1953) 'Cardinal utility in welfare economics and in the theory of risk-taking', *Journal of Political Economy*, 61: 434–435.

Harsanyi, J.C. (1955) 'Cardinal utility, individualistic ethics, and interpersonal comparisons of utility', *Journal of Political Economy*, 63: 309–321.

Harsanyi, J.C. (1976) *Essays on Ethics, Social Behavior, and Scientific Explanation* Dordrecht: Reidel.

Inada, K.I. (1969) 'On the simple majority decision rule', *Econometrica*, 37: 490–506.

Jackson, M.O. (2001) 'A crash course in implementation theory', *Social Choice and Welfare*, 18: 655–708.

Kemp, M.C. and Ng, Y.-K. (1976) 'On the existence of social welfare functions, social orderings and social decision functions', *Economica*, 43: 59–66.

Kolm, S.-C. (1972) *Justice et Equité*, Editions du C.N.R.S., English translation with a new introduction, 1997, *Justice and Equity*. Cambridge, MA: MIT Press.

Le Breton, M. (1997) 'Arrovian social choice on economic domains', in K.J. Arrow, A.K. Sen and K. Suzumura (eds) *Social Choice Reexamined*, vol 1. Basingstoke: Macmillan. pp. 72–96.

Le Breton, M. and Weymark, J. (2010) 'Arrovian social choice theory on economic domains', in K.J. Arrow, A.K. Sen and K. Suzumura (eds) *Handbook of Social Choice and Welfare*, vol 2. Elsevier Science.

Li, L. and Saari, D. (2008) 'Sen's Theorem: Geometric proof, new interpretations', *Social Choice and Welfare*, 31: 393–413.

May, K.O. (1952) 'A set of independent, necessary and sufficient conditions for simple majority decision', *Econometrica*, 20: 680–684.

Nakamura, K. (1975) 'The core of a simple game with ordinal preferences', *International Journal of Game Theory*, 4: 95–104.

Nakamura, K. (1979) 'The vetoers in a simple game with ordinal preferences', *International Journal of Game Theory*, 8: 55–61.

Parks, R. (1976) 'An impossibility theorem for fixed preferences: A dictatorial Bergson–Samuelson welfare function', *Review of Economic Studies*, 43: 447–450.

Pattanaik, P.K. (1996) 'On modelling individual rights: Some conceptual issues', in K.J. Arrow, A.K. Sen and K. Suzumura (eds) *Social Choice Re-examined* vol 2, Basingstoke: Macmillan. pp. 100–128.

Pattanaik, P.K., Salles, M. and Suzumura, K. (eds) (2004) 'Special issue: Non-welfaristic issues in normative economics', *Social Choice and Welfare*, 22: 1–289.

Pattanaik, P.K. and Xu, Y. (1990) 'On ranking opportunity sets in terms of freedom of choice', *Recherches Economiques de Louvain*, 56: 383–390.

Pazner, E. and Schmeidler, D. (1978) 'Egalitarian equivalent allocations: A new concept of economic equity', *Quarterly Journal of Economics*, 92: 671–687.

Roemer, J. (1996) *Theories of Distributive Justice*. Cambridge, MA: Harvard University Press.

Saari, D. (1998) 'Connecting and resolving Sen's and Arrow's theorems', *Social Choice and Welfare*, 15: 239–261.

Saari, D. (2001) *Decisions and Elections. Explaining the Unexpected.* Cambridge: Cambridge University Press.

Saari, D. (2001a) *Chaotic Elections! A Mathematician Looks at Voting.* Providence, RI: American Mathematical Society.

Saari, D. (2008) *Disposing Dictators, Demystifying Voting Paradoxes.* Cambridge: Cambridge University Press.

Saari, D. and Pétron A. (2006) 'Negative externalities and Sen's liberalism theorem'. *Economic Theory*, 28: 265–281.

Salles, M. (2000) 'Amartya Sen. Droits et choix social', *Revue Economique*, 51: 445–457.

Salles, M. (2007) 'Michael Dummett on social choice and voting', in R.E. Auxier and L.E. Hahn (eds), *The Philosophy of Michael Dummett.* Chicago: Open Court. pp. 801–818.

Salles, M. (2008) 'Limited rights as partial veto and Sen's impossibility theorem', in P.K. Pattanaik et al. (eds) *Rational Choice and Social Welfare: Theory and Applications* . Berlin: Springer. pp. 11–23.

Salles, M. (2009) 'Limited rights and social choice rules', in K. Basu and R. Kanbur (eds) *Arguments for a Better World: Essays in Honor of Amartya Sen.* Oxford: Oxford University Press. pp. 250–261.

Salles, M. and Wendell, R. (1977) 'A further result on the core of voting games', *International Journal of Game Theory*, 6: 35–40.

Samuelson, P. (1947) *Foundations of Economic Analysis.* Cambridge, MA: Harvard University Press.

Satterthwaite, M.A. (1975) 'Strategy-proofness and Arrow's conditions: Existence and correspondence theorems for voting procedures and social welfare functions', *Journal of Economic Theory*, 10: 187–217.

Sen, A.K. (1966) 'A possibility theorem on majority decisions', *Econometrica*, 34: 491–499.

Sen, A.K. (1970a) 'The impossibility of a Paretian liberal', *Journal of Political Economy*, 78: 152–157.

Sen, A.K. (1970b) *Collective Choice and Social Welfare* San Francisco: Holden-Day.

Sen, A.K. (1976) 'Welfare inequalities and Rawlsian axiomatics', *Theory and Decision*, 7: 243–262.

Sen, A.K. (1992) 'Minimal liberty', *Economica*, 57: 139–159.

Sen, A.K. and Pattanaik, P.K. (1969) 'Necessary and sufficient conditions for rational choice under majority decision', *Journal of Economic Theory*, 1: 178–202.

Von Neumann, J. and Morgenstern, O. (1953) *Theory of Games and Economic Behavior.* Princeton: Princeton University Press.

Weymark, J.A. (1991) 'A reconsideration of the Harsanyi–Sen debate on utilitarianism' in J. Elster and J.E Roemer (eds) *Interpersonal Comparisons of Well-Being.* Cambridge: Cambridge University Press. pp. 255–320.

18

Analytical Sociology

Peter Hedström and Petri Ylikoski

INTRODUCTION

Analytical sociology is a reform movement within sociology and social theory. Its identity is not based on a common object of study, a shared historical tradition in sociological theory, or an empirical research method. Rather, it is founded on the idea that social sciences should do more than describe and classify social processes. According to analytical sociologists, the primary epistemic aim of the social sciences should be causal explanation of social phenomena. Sociological theory should aim to develop clear and precise accounts of the social mechanisms by which the intentional activities of social agents bring about social phenomena.

The emphasis on causal explanation distinguishes analytical sociology from the interpretive – cultural studies-influenced – sociology that shuns any explanatory ambitions or regards social scientific explanations as non-causal and non-continuous with the natural sciences. For analytical sociology, the same causal and explanatory ideals that motivate natural sciences should also drive the social sciences. The natural sciences are not an enemy, but a source of occasional inspiration and evidential support. The emphasis

on mechanisms separates analytical sociology from the quantitatively oriented and variable-based sociology that largely shuns the role of theory in social explanation and prefers to stay close to empirical data and to provide explanations mostly on an ad hoc basis. Analytical sociology does not oppose the use of quantitative data but it argues that social research should be more theory driven and that causal claims should be supported by a theoretical understanding of the causal mechanisms underlying the observed statistical regularities. Finally, the emphasis on precision and clarity and on the importance of tightly linking theory and empirical research contrasts analytical sociology with mainstream social theory. Analytical sociology advocates the idea that sociologists should focus on theories of middle range that can be tested and elaborated via empirical research.

The historical roots of analytical sociology can be traced back to the works of late nineteenth and early twentieth century sociologists such as Max Weber and Alexis de Tocqueville, and to prominent mid-twentieth century sociologists such as the early Talcott Parsons and Robert K. Merton. Among contemporary social scientists, Jon Elster, Raymond Boudon, Thomas Schelling, and

James Coleman have profoundly influenced the analytical approach. Although they are rather different types of scholars, they complement each other in important ways, and they all share a commitment to precise, abstract, and action-based explanations.

Beginning with his early work, that used modal logic to analyze social phenomena (Elster, 1978), and criticized the logic of functionalist explanations in the social sciences (Elster, 1983a, 1985), Jon Elster has demonstrated the relevance of the analytical philosophy tradition for the social sciences. Much of his work has been concerned with the logic of action-based explanations and the relationship between rationality, social norms, and emotions (Elster, 1979; 1983b; 1989a; 1989b; 1999). His writings have built important bridges between sociological theory, the philosophy of action, and behavioral economics. Elster has also been a consistent analytical realist. While arguing for the necessity of abstractions, he has expressed deep dissatisfaction with the instrumentalist attitude toward theories.

Also Raymond Boudon has insisted on the importance of action-based explanations and the dangers of instrumentalism. He has emphasized the importance of basing explanations on realistic theories of action that recognize the cognitive limitations of real individuals (e.g., Boudon, 1981; 1982; 1994; 2003). Much of his work has given close attention to the micro–macro link. Early on he used simulation models to analyze the link between the educational decisions of individuals and the social properties of the educational system at large (Boudon, 1974), and he argued for the general importance of "generative models" for explaining the social outcomes of action (Boudon, 1979).

From the vantage point of analytical sociology, Thomas Schelling's most important contributions are those dealing with the micro–macro link. *Micromotives and Macrobehavior* (1978) is one the most important contributions to sociology in recent decades. In it Schelling develops useful analytical tools and analyzes the social outcomes that groups of interacting individuals are likely to bring about. His study of patterns of racial segregation (Schelling, 1971) and related analyses show the apparent discontinuity between the macro and the micro levels. Aggregate or macro-level patterns usually say surprisingly little about why we observe particular aggregate patterns, and our explanations must therefore focus on the micro-level processes that brought them about.

The micro–macro link was a major focus of James Coleman's writings as well. Like most sociologists, he was primarily interested in social or macro-level phenomena, but unlike many sociologists he emphasized that changes in them must be explained by reference to the actions that brought them about. To account for a macro-level change it is not sufficient to simply relate macro-level phenomena to one another. To be explanatory a theory must specify the set of causal mechanisms that are likely to have brought about the change, and this requires one to demonstrate how macro states at one point in time influence individuals' actions, and how these actions bring about new macro-states at a later point in time. Another aspect of Coleman's work that is of considerable importance for analytical sociology is his view on how to link theory and quantitative research. While most quantitative sociologists use rather ad hoc statistical models in their research, Coleman insisted that statistical analyses are meaningful only in so far as they are based on plausible models of the processes through which the phenomena to be explained were brought about (Coleman, 1964; 1981; 1986; 1990). If this is not the case, the statistical estimates will have little bearing on the proposed sociological explanation.

The current generation of analytical sociologists are building upon the foundations laid by these authors aiming to develop an analytical middle-range approach to sociological theory that avoids the somewhat empiricist and eclectic tendencies of Merton's original middle-range approach (Merton, 1967). Examples of the recent work in this tradition can be found in anthologies edited by

Hedström and Swedberg (1998), Hedström and Bearman (2009), and in a monograph by Hedström (2005).

ANALYTICAL REALISM

The philosophy underlying analytical sociology could be characterized as realistic in a number of respects. First, in contrast to empiricist and instrumentalist views, it regards explanation as the principal epistemic aim of science. Sociological theories are not merely intellectual constructions that can be used for the purposes of prediction and control of social events. Their primary purpose is to represent causal processes that generate the observable phenomena. For the same reason, sociological theories that merely aim to classify social processes and institutions are regarded as misdirected and lacking proper ambition. Although the accurate description of social phenomena is an important part of the social sciences, it should not be the only one.

Second, in contrast to empiricist and behaviorist views, it does not regard the use of theoretical concepts to be illegitimate. As in the natural sciences, social scientists can employ theories that refer to unobservable entities and processes. There is no need to define them in terms of observational notions. According to analytical sociologists, it is not possible to represent general causal knowledge in the social sciences as invariant empirical regularities. The social scientific knowledge is based on understanding the causal mechanisms underlying observable regularities. Similarly, analytical sociologists employ the conceptual scheme of intentional psychology that refers to unobservable psychological states like beliefs and desires. Intentional explanation is regarded in analytical sociology as a species of causal explanation.

Third, contrary to the instrumentalist attitude common among many rational choice theorists, especially economists, analytical sociologists regard explanation as factive.

It is not enough that the theory or model "saves the phenomena," it should represent the essential features of the actual causal structure that produces the observed phenomena. Analytical sociology does not accept the "as if"-attitude displayed by many economists; it requires that ultimately the theoretical assumptions should be both empirically valid and compatible with the results of other disciplines.

Fourth, analytical sociology embodies the realistic spirit by not letting the considerations of elegance, simplicity, or tractability to override the aim of accurately describing the real causal mechanisms producing the observable phenomena. Contrary to a widespread practice among mathematically oriented economists and rational-choice sociologists, analytical sociologists do not accept the instrumentalist attitude according to which assumptions are instruments that can be freely tinkered with until one arrives at simple and elegant models. Parsimonious models with clear analytical solutions deserve praise only if they are not achieved at the cost of implausible theoretical assumptions.

Rather than seeking excessively precise fictions, social scientists should aim for theoretical assumptions known to be at least roughly correct in the real-world settings that they are analyzing. Such a modest and realist strategy characterizes some of the best theoretical work in sociology. A good example is Robert K. Merton's work on self-fulfilling prophecies (Merton, 1968). At the core of this elegant and highly influential piece of work, to be discussed in more detail below, is the assumption that the actions of others influence individuals' beliefs and subsequent actions, but Merton never specified any precise model of the decision calculus. Although such model would be possible, it would not add any insights to those found in Merton's analysis. Formalization often is required for explaining social phenomena but, if the model does not properly describe action principles observed in the real world, they are of little explanatory use. It is more important to base the analysis on clear and empirically plausible assumptions about the actions and interactions of individuals, as Merton did, and then on this basis develop theoretical models that allow us to get a handle on the social outcomes that the actors are likely to bring about. Such analyses either generate tendency statements about patterns likely to be observed or suggest plausible processes through which the phenomena to be explained could have been brought about. More precision might be desirable, but not excessive precision that simply amounts to precisely stating and assuming to be true what is known to be untrue.

Like most economists, but unlike some sociologists, analytical sociologists regard the method of isolation and abstraction as an indispensable part of theory-development: empirical reality is complex and it is futile to try to capture it as a whole. Building a complex model of a complex phenomenon does not provide much explanatory insight. For this reason, the strategy of intentional simplification is preferable: the scientist tries to capture the central features of the phenomenon first. The achievement of understanding is only possible by studying quite simplified but realistic theoretical models and gradually increasing the complexity of these models. The employment of this research strategy does not commit the scientist to the denial of the complexity of social life. To the contrary, the strategy of model building intends to avoid the hubris associated with one sweep attempts to capture complexity.

According to analytical sociology, an adequate sociological theory is abstract, realistic, and precise, and it seeks to explain specific social phenomena on the basis of explicitly formulated theories of action and interaction.

SOCIAL MECHANISMS

The core idea of analytical sociology is that sociological theory explains by specifying *causal mechanisms* by which social phenomena are brought about (Hedström

and Ylikoski 2010). The specifically social causal mechanisms are called social mechanisms. There is a number of different definitions of causal mechanism. A useful general characterization is provided by Machamer et al. (2000). According to it, mechanisms consist of *entities* (with their properties) and the *activities* that these entities engage in, either by themselves or in concert with other entities. These entities and activities, when organized spatially and temporally, produce regularities of change. If the relevant entities are intentional agents and the activities are social activities, we have a characterization of a social mechanism. A social mechanism describes a constellation of social entities and activities that produces regularly a particular type of outcome due to their organization. A mechanistic explanation provides understanding of *why* the observable empirical regularities happen as they do.

In the writings of analytical sociologists, a number of important ideas are associated with that of social mechanism. These ideas relate to explanation, causation and organization of social scientific knowledge.

First, analytical sociologists are dissatisfied with the traditional covering-law account of explanation. This fundamentally empiricist account of explanation has a number of shortcomings. Philosophers of science have shown that it is open to counter examples that suggest that it does not capture crucial elements of explanatory relationships. For example, the covering-law account does not seem to do justice to the role of causal considerations in explanation (Salmon, 1989). Another set of problems is associated with the concept of law of nature. The account was originally proposed with the hope that the notion of law could be given a satisfactory characterization, but not much philosophical progress has been made on this front. To the contrary, philosophers have started to doubt that laws have an important role in explanations outside fundamental physics. Empirical generalizations employed in the special sciences seem to lack many of the characteristics traditionally associated with laws (Woodward, 2003). Furthermore, as Cummins (2000) has observed, in the special sciences these empirical generalizations are usually the things to be explained, rather than things doing the explanation (see also Goldthorpe (2000) for a similar argument as far as the social sciences is concerned). All these observations support the idea that explanations should articulate causal mechanisms rather than simply subsume phenomena under empirical generalizations (Hedström and Ylikoski 2010). According to advocates of analytical sociology, the consequences of the covering-law account in the social sciences have been negative. It has provided justification for the use of "black-box" explanations in the social sciences as it does not require that the mechanism linking *explanans* and *explanandum* to be specified in order for an acceptable explanation to be at hand. This omission has given leeway for sloppy scholarship.

Second, the idea of causal mechanism is important in *justification* of causal claims. Distinguishing between real causal claims and spurious statistical associations is a major challenge in all special sciences. The real causal dependences are transmitted via causal processes and the search for causal mechanisms directs the attention to these processes. Apart from providing explanatory understanding as to why the dependency holds, the information about the causal mechanisms also provides justification for causal claims. Causal claims are much easier to accept if one can provide an account of the mechanisms by which the changes in the suggested *explanans* bring about the changes in the *explanandum*. Furthermore, the understanding of causal mechanisms provides information about the background conditions under which the empirical generalization holds. This information is crucial when making inductive inferences on the basis of empirical generalizations. So, in addition to providing explanatory understanding, the search for causal mechanisms also leads to more secure and fine-grained causal knowledge.

Third, the idea of mechanistic explanation brings sociology in line with the other special sciences. Recent philosophy of science has shown that biological sciences (molecular biology, developmental biology, evolutionary biology, and the neurosciences) are in the business on providing mechanistic explanations (rather than covering law explanations). The same observation holds for psychological and cognitive sciences (see Bechtel, 2005; 2008; Craver, 2007). There is no reason to assume that the social sciences should be different in this respect. Furthermore, having similar ideals of explanation makes interdisciplinary collaboration with these disciplines easier. Among the social sciences, economics has a long tradition of thinking in terms of mechanisms. As economics has provided much inspiration for analytical sociology, it is only natural that they emphasize this as an important bridge between the disciplines.

Finally, the idea of causal mechanisms is related to ideas about the growth and organization of social scientific knowledge. According to an old empiricist view, the general knowledge in the sciences consists of empirical generalizations and more abstract theoretical principles from which these generalizations can (ideally) be deduced. The mechanistic account of knowledge challenges this picture on two counts. First, the locus of generality (and explanatory power) in social scientific knowledge is considered to lie in the mechanism schemes. Social sciences do not have many valid empirical generalizations and those that they have are not particularly explanatory. The explanatory power – and general applicability – comes from knowledge of possible causal mechanisms. When social scientific knowledge expands, it does not expand by formulating empirical generalizations that have broader application, but by adding or improving items in its toolbox of possible causal mechanisms. Understanding of the social world accumulates as the knowledge of mechanisms gets more detailed and the number of known mechanisms increases in the theoretical toolbox of the social scientist (Hedström and Ylikoski 2010).

The accounts of mechanisms should be compatible with each other and with what is known in other disciplines, but like in the case of Merton's notion of middle-range theory, there is no attempt to unify all mechanisms under one general theory. This brings us to the second challenge to the traditional picture of social science knowledge: the ideal of general knowledge is no longer an axiomatic system, but a looser idea of an expanding theoretical toolbox. The expectation is that mature social science would be more like a textbook of modern cell biology than a treatise in elementary geometry.

The idea of a mechanistic toolbox is important in a highly specialized scientific discipline like sociology. Although empirical data, research methods, and substantial theories differ from one subfield of sociology to another, the general ideas about possible causal mechanisms are something these fields could share. In this view, sociological theory provides a set of explanatory tools that can be employed and adapted to particular situations and explanatory tasks. The mechanisms are (semi-)general in the sense that most of them are not limited to any particular application. For example, the same type of mechanism can be used for (partially) explaining residential segregation and success in cultural markets, and this generality has two important consequences. First, it allows for a novel type of integration of sociology which is important given the fact that sociology has become increasingly fragmented over the last few decades: various sub-fields of sociology can employ the same type of theoretical mechanisms and thereby benefit from each other's work. Second, the fact that the same mechanisms can be found in many different contexts provides a possibility to have more robust empirical support for them. This helps in fighting the danger of ad hoc-storytelling that is a constant challenge to explanatory social science.

THEORIES OF MIDDLE RANGE

Analytical sociology can be understood as a restatement of Robert K. Merton's call for sociological theories of the middle range

(Hedström and Udehn, 2009). According to Merton, theories of the middle range are

...theories that lie between the minor but necessary working hypotheses that evolve in abundance during day-to-day research and the all-inclusive systematic efforts to develop a unified theory that will explain all the observed uniformities of social behavior, social organization and social change. (Merton, 1968: 39)

A theory of middle range is a clear, precise, and simple type of theory which can be used for partially explaining a range of different phenomena, but which makes no pretense of being able to explain all social phenomena, and which is not founded upon any form of extreme reductionism in terms of its *explanans*. Middle-range theories isolate a few explanatory factors which explain important but delimited aspects of the outcomes to be explained. They do not bore the reader by trying to retell the causal story in minute detail; instead they seek to highlight the heart of the story.

Merton's account of self-fulfilling prophesies provides a clear example of a social mechanism. The basic idea behind the theory of the self-fulfilling prophecy is what Merton referred to as the Thomas Theorem: "If men define situations as real, they are real in their consequences" (Merton, 1968: 475). Merton focused on the process through which an initially false belief evokes behavior that eventually makes the false belief come true. His example was a run on a bank. Once a rumor of insolvency gets started, some depositors are likely to withdraw their savings, acting on the principle that it is better to be safe than sorry. These withdrawals strengthen others' beliefs that the bank is in financial difficulties, partly because the withdrawals may actually hurt the financial standing of the bank, but more importantly because the act of withdrawal in itself signals to others that something might be wrong with the bank. This causes even more withdrawals, which further strengthens the belief, and so on. By this mechanism, even an initially sound bank may go bankrupt if enough depositors withdraw their money in the (initially) false belief that the bank is insolvent. The theory of the self-fulfilling prophecy is a good example of a social mechanism as (1) it refers to a dynamic process; (2) the collective outcome is unintended by the individuals who bring it about; (3) the process is driven by social interactions between individuals; and (4) the process is endogenous and self-reinforcing. The mechanism is in principle quite general and it can be used to explain a range of different types of phenomena (Biggs, 2009).

However, there are some important differences between Merton and analytical sociology. First, analytical sociology is based on a more explicit philosophy of science. Second, it builds on the notion of social mechanism that is largely absent in Merton's work. Third, analytical sociology has a closer relationship to methodological individualism and rational choice theory than the sociological tradition represented by Merton has. Finally, the use of computer simulations is becoming an important tool for analytical sociology. We will next take a look at these latter three aspects of analytical sociology.

METHODOLOGICAL INDIVIDUALISM

The main focus of analytical sociology is on social (as distinct from psychological) *explananda*. One important characteristic of social *explananda* is that they are collective properties that are not definable by reference to any single member of the collectivity. Important examples of such properties include (Hedström, 2005):

- typical actions, beliefs, or desires among the members of a collectivity;
- distributions and aggregate patterns such as spatial distributions and inequalities;
- topologies of networks that describe relationships between members of a collectivity; informal rules or social norms that constrain the actions of the members of a collectivity.

Analytical sociologists account for these phenomena in terms of social mechanisms

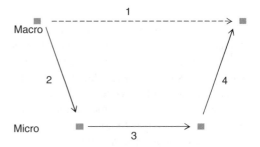

Figure 18.1   Coleman's micro-macro scheme.

that specify how these social patterns are produced by the actions of individual agents. The famous Coleman boat (Figure 18.1) illustrates both the idea of social mechanism and its relation to methodological individualism (see Coleman, 1990).

In this figure we have three types of mechanisms: *situational mechanisms* (arrow 2), *action-formation mechanisms* (arrow 3), and *transformational mechanisms* (arrow 4). The situational mechanisms describe how social structures constrain individuals' action and cultural environments shape their desires and beliefs, the action-formation mechanisms describe how individuals choose their preferred courses of action among the feasible alternatives, and the transformational mechanisms describe how individual actions produce various intended and unintended social outcomes.

The key insight of analytical sociology is that explanations that relate macro variables to each other (arrow 1) are unsatisfactory. They do not specify the causal mechanisms by which the changes in one macro variable can bring about changes in another. To acquire proper explanatory understanding we have to open the black box and find the causal mechanisms that make the observed regularity possible. That is, instead of analyzing relationships between phenomena exclusively on the macro level, one should always try to establish how macro-level events or conditions affect the individual (arrow 2), how the individual assimilates the impact of these macro-level events (arrow 3), and how a number of individuals, through their actions and interactions, generate macro-level outcomes (arrow 4). Only when we have understood the whole chain of situational, action-formation and transformational mechanisms, have we understood the causal relationship. This emphasis on mechanisms leads the focus to individuals and their interactions. For analytical sociologists, theories of individual action are essential as they form the core of the explanatory mechanisms.

The methodological individualism of analytical sociology is a consequence of its account of scientific explanation, not an independent metaphysical doctrine. For this reason, analytical sociology is only committed to a rather weak form of methodological individualism: *structural individualism* (see Udéhn, 2001). This is a methodological doctrine according to which all social facts, their structure and change, are in principle explicable in terms of individuals, their properties, actions, and relations to one another. It differs from traditional notions of methodological individualism (e.g., Elster, 1982) by emphasizing the explanatory importance of relations and relational structures. The mechanistic approach does not require that all explanatory facts are facts about individual agents in the strict sense: facts about topologies of social networks, about distributions of beliefs, resources or opportunities, and about institutional or informal rules and norms can play important roles in its explanations. Especially important is to recognize that transformational mechanisms (arrow 4) are not based on simple aggregation of individual actions, but depend on structural arrangements that cannot be defined in terms of atomistic attributes of individual agents. Although structural individualism is rather liberal when contrasted with more traditional characterizations of methodological individualism, it is not toothless. It is incompatible with radical holism or structuralism, since it requires that social explanations should specify how the pattern to be explained can be understood in terms of interactions of individual agents.

Mechanistic explanations of social phenomena aim to identify the micro foundations, or the social cogs and wheels through which the social facts to be explained are brought about. The central cogs and wheels of social life are actions and relations. Actions are important because everything of interest to sociologists is the intended or unintended outcomes of individuals' actions. Individuals' actions typically are oriented towards others and therefore relations to others are central when it comes to explaining why individuals do what they do. In addition, social relations are central for explaining why, acting as they do, individuals bring about the social outcomes they do. That relations are important for explaining outcomes does not mean that they are independent of individuals and their actions, however. Consider, for example, the case of vacancy chains as analyzed by White (1970). A retirement, motivated perhaps by a desire for a more leisurely life, creates an opportunity for others, that is, a job vacancy waiting to be filled by a new occupant. The vacancy generated by the retirement is filled by another individual whose reason for taking the job, perhaps, is to attain more status, or a higher salary, or just a change in venue, but this creates another vacancy in this persons old job, and in this way vacancy chains create social interdependencies which are important for explaining mobility. Individuals' desires – for retirement, for promotion, for status, or for a change in venue – motivate the system. Without such orientations, people may not move. However, the essential cogs and wheels are not exclusively found in the intentions of actors. Explanatory understanding is achieved by recognizing that action takes place in social structures that in this case channel mobility opportunities and thereby explain why we observe what we observe.

RATIONAL CHOICE THEORY AND THEORY OF ACTION

Historically analytical sociology has some of its roots in the tradition of rational choice sociology. However, current analytical sociology does not have any special commitment to the assumptions of rational choice theory. For this reason it is a mistake to take analytical sociology as rebranded rational choice sociology. For analytical sociologists, the appeal of rational choice theory and game theory is not based on its empirical or explanatory adequacy. Rather, analytical sociologists find rational choice theory interesting for methodological reasons. As rational choice theory is a formal theory, it advocates the same virtues of clarity and precision as analytical sociology does by forcing the theorist to make explicit her reasoning and by making it possible to see what follows from given assumptions. Similarly, rational choice theory allows for the same type of piecemeal theoretical development via model building that analytical sociology advocates.

Analytical sociology requires that the theory of action should satisfy the following basic desiderata: (1) it should explain action in meaningful intentional terms; (2) it should be as simple as possible; and (3) it should be psychologically and sociologically plausible (Hedström, 2005). The first requirement is based on the insight that social systems are composed of intentional agents. An adequate explanation of social processes should take into account the contents of the beliefs and desires of these agents. Naturally, the emphasis on intentional action does not imply that analytical sociology denies the relevance of habitual and unconscious psychological processes (Hedström and Ylikoski 2010).

Analytical sociology emphasizes the importance of intentional explanation, but it is not committed to *intentional fundamentalism* that attributes some special explanatory status to intentional explanations. Although intentional action provides a natural stopping-point for sociological explanations, there is no need to regard them as rock-bottom explanations. Analytical sociologists simply believe in a scientific division of labor: social scientists should trace causal mechanisms to the level of the individual agent and the other sciences will take over from there.

Psychological facts provide constraints for social theories, but social scientists do not have to go below them. Consequently, analytical sociology does not subscribe to a methodological separatism that claims that social sciences are somehow radically different from the natural sciences or psychology: intentional explanations are causal explanations.

The requirement that a theory of action should be as simple as possible is not based on any *a priori* aesthetic or epistemic principle. Its motivation is methodological. Analytical sociologists prefer clear and transparent theories that abstract away from all details that are inessential to the problem at hand. Sociological theories often face complex trade-offs between different components of a theory, and we can distinguish three types of components in sociological theories: (1) an individual-action component; (2) a component describing the structure of interaction; and (3) a component linking micro-actions to macro-outcomes. To allow greater complexity in the latter two components, which are typically of greater sociological interest, one must keep the action component as simple as possible by abstracting away all elements not considered crucial without thereby introducing fictional elements into the model.

The theory of action should be psychologically plausible because otherwise we would simply be telling an as-if story, not detailing the actual mechanisms at work. For example, billiard players may act as if they based their shots on highly complex mathematical calculations as observed by Milton Friedman (1953), although they obviously do not. Using a theory that assumes that billiard players make such calculations may allow us to predict what they will do, but it will not provide a correct explanation of why or how they do it.

The sociological plausibility requirement means that the theory should take into account the structure of social interaction. Accounts of action that treat agents as atoms outside a social context or as "over-socialized" dopes who mechanically follow predetermined scripts do not provide a satisfactory basis for understanding social interaction. Ignoring the structure of interaction would render the theory lacking for the very same reasons as psychologically implausible theories, namely, that we would then be giving an incorrect account of the mechanisms at work.

The appeal of rational choice theory is based on its simplicity, but it has clear problems with psychological and sociological plausibility. For this reason, to the extent that analytical sociologists make use of rational-choice theory, they tend to employ rather non-standard and informal forms of rational choice theory. For example, they emphasize the importance of taking into account various cognitive limitations of agents, and typically they are less interested in studying formal properties of game-theoretical models, and more interested in their applicability to empirical cases. Analytical sociology emphasizes the importance of action-based explanations, but this does not imply a commitment to any specific type of motive or intentional state that is assumed to explain why individuals act as they do.

In practice, many analytical sociologists employ a theory of action that could be described as desire-belief-opportunity theory (DBO theory) (Hedström, 2005). The simple DBO theory provides a building block for accounts of social mechanisms of interaction through which the actions of some actors may come to influence the beliefs, desires, opportunities, and actions of others.

COMPUTER SIMULATION

A recent development in analytical sociology has been the use of agent based computer simulations (Hedström, 2005; Macy and Willer, 2002; Macy and Flache, 2009). The adoption of this methodology is based on very similar motivations as the adoption of rational choice ideas. In fact, one could argue that simulation methodology is becoming a replacement for rational choice theory as analytical sociologists are finding the theoretical limitations of rational choice theory a hindrance for theoretical development and empirical application.

An important theme in analytical sociology is the emphasis on the importance of the transformational mechanisms (arrow 4 in Figure 18.1). As Coleman (1986) pointed out the link from the individual to the social has been the main intellectual obstacle to the development of explanatory theories of the social. We know a great deal about how individuals' desires, beliefs, opportunities, and so forth are influenced by the social contexts in which they are embedded (arrow 2), and we also know a great deal about how desires, beliefs, opportunities, and so forth influence actions (arrow 3), but when it comes to the link between individual actions and social outcomes we often resort to hand-waving. The way in which individual actions produce social patterns is rarely a simple process of aggregation and macro-level patterns are often difficult to predict from the individual level descriptions.

Studying these processes has been a major challenge, and only recently powerful computers and simulation software has changed the picture so much so that it is possible to have some confidence that agent-based computer simulations will transform important parts of sociological theory because they allow for rigorous theoretical analyses of large and complex social systems (see Macy and Flache, 2009). Although the dynamics observed at the social level typically are complex and hard to understand, the basic cogs and wheels of these social processes may be possible to describe with rather simple models. Thomas Schelling's (1978) famous segregation model is a good illustration of this. In this model, we have two kinds of individuals who are distributed on a lattice. Each individual decides where to live on the lattice, but the decision is influenced by the past decisions of others. Some constraints are present – most importantly, individuals only can move to vacant positions, and they prefer to live near at least some of their own kind. Schelling demonstrated that even if individuals have strong preferences for mixed neighborhoods, segregation often arises as an unintended consequence. He also showed that small and seemingly trivial differences at the micro-level can make huge differences at the macro-level.

Without the simulations, two fallacious inferences would have been probable. First, one would have inferred from the large differences in macro-level segregation that there has to be corresponding differences in the amount of prejudice among the individual agents. Second, one would not have expected significant differences at the macro level as the differences at the micro-level were not particularly pronounced. Both of these inferences are fallacious, as the simulations show that small changes at micro-level can bring about significant changes at the macro-level. Schelling's rather simple and stylized example demonstrates that macro-level outcomes and relationships tell us very little about why we observe the macro-level outcomes and relationships we observe. Trying to make causal inferences on the basis of macro-level data is highly error prone. Only by explicitly considering the individual-level attributes and the mechanisms of transformation can the tipping points and other explanations of macro-level outcomes be identified. The methodological lesson is this: In order to understand collective dynamics, we must study the collectivity as a whole, but we must not study it *as* a collective entity. Only by taking into account the individual entities, the relations between them and their activities, can we understand the macro-outcome we observe. For this reason, in order to explain macro-level dynamics, one of the most central goals of analytical sociology, one must focus on the actions and interactions of individual agents.

The agent-based simulations are not only a tool for theoretical exploration. Empirically calibrated agent-based models make it possible to integrate theoretical ideas with the results of empirical research. Another important feature of these models is that they do not impose any *a priori* constraints on the mechanisms assumed to be operating, except, of course, that the mechanism in some way or other must be action-related. Unlike rational-choice theory, agent-based modeling is not based on any specific theory of action or interaction. It is a methodology for deriving the social outcomes that groups of interacting actors are likely to bring about whatever the action logics or interaction structures may be.

Simulation studies that aim to account for empirical observations employ a *generative research strategy*. The basic structure of this strategy of research can be described as follows.

1. Start with a clearly delineated social fact that is to be explained.
2. Formulate different hypotheses about relevant micro-level mechanisms.
3. Translate the theoretical hypotheses into computational models.
4. Simulate the models to derive the type of social facts that each micro-level mechanism brings about.
5. Compare the social facts generated by each model with the actually observed outcomes.

A clear and simple example of this strategy is a study of the sexual and romantic networks of adolescents undertaken by Bearman et al. (2004). In this case the *explanandum* is the surprising discovery that the sexual and romantic network structure of students in the school resembles a spanning tree. The novelty of this study is the way in which the researchers use computer simulation to make inferences about the systematic influence of norms whose existence the individuals themselves would not have been able to articulate. It turned out that a crucial condition for the emergence of the spanning tree structure is the rarity of short cycles. In a heterosexual network the shortest possible cycle has a length of four. A cycle of this kind would mean, from a girl's point of view, that she formed a relationship with her prior boyfriend's current girlfriend's prior boyfriend. A spanning tree structure would follow if there were a norm prohibiting such partnerships. The high school students might not be able to articulate such a norm, but in the high school context a status loss would be associated with such relationships. The avoidance of this kind of status loss by the adolescents implies that they avoid four-cycle relationship partners. This micro-level account provides a likely explanation for the observed structure at the macro-level. The choices by the students are constrained by past actions of others and by their desire not to lose status in the eyes of their peers, and these constraints explain the spanning-tree structure of the network.

In the case of the adolescent sexual network, the generative research strategy produced rather clear-cut results. Of the various mechanisms, only one was able to generate the social fact to be explained. Obviously this is not always the case, but the generative methodology is generally applicable and it is a crucial part of the toolbox of analytical sociology.

CONCLUSION

Mechanism talk is becoming increasingly popular in the social sciences (Hedström and Ylikoski 2010). Although this could be interpreted as an indicator of the success of analytical sociology, it should also be taken as a source of concern. Many sociologists use the word "mechanism" in a loose sense without any commitment to the type of mechanism-based explanatory strategy focused upon here. This poses an important challenge for analytical sociology: it should be able to communicate its distinctive methodology and underlying philosophy of science more effectively. The key strategy should be the development of good exemplars of analytical sociology rather than, say, engaging in debates about the proper definition of mechanism. Contrary to a common stereotype, analytical sociology does reduce to the notion of social mechanism. This notion is more properly regarded as a vehicle for communicating ideas about aims and strategies of social scientific research.

REFERENCES

Bearman, P.S., J. Moody and K. Stovel (2004) 'Chains of affection: The structure of adolescent romantic and sexual networks', *American Journal of Sociology*, 110: 44–91.

Bechtel, W. (2005) *Discovering Cell Mechanisms. The Creation of Modern Cell Biology*. Cambridge: Cambridge University Press.

Bechtel, W. (2008) *Mental Mechanism. Philosophical Perspectives on Cognitive Neuroscience*. London: Routledge.

Biggs, M. (2009) 'Self-fullfilling prophesies', in P. Hedström and P. Bearman (eds) *The Oxford Handbook of Analytical Sociology*. Oxford: Oxford University Press. pp. 294–314.

Boudon, R. (1974) *Education, Opportunity, and Social Inequality: Changing Prospects in Western Society*. New York: Wiley.

Boudon, R. (1979) 'Generating models as a research strategy', in P.H. Rossi (eds) *Qualitative and Quantitative Social Research: Papers in Honor of Paul F. Lazarsfeld*. New York: The Free Press. pp. 51–64.

Boudon, R. (1981) *The Logic of Social Action: An Introduction to Sociological Analysis*. London: Routledge and Kegan Paul.

Boudon, R. (1982) *The Unintended Consequences of Social Action*. London: Macmillan.

Boudon, R. (1994) *The Art of Self-Persuasion: The Social Explanation of False Beliefs*. Oxford: Polity Press.

Boudon, R. (2003) 'Beyond rational choice theory', *Annual Review of Sociology*, 29: 1–21.

Coleman, J.S. (1964) *Introduction to Mathematical Sociology*. New York: Free Press of Glencoe.

Coleman, J.S. (1981) *Longitudinal Data Analysis*. New York: Basic Books.

Coleman, J.S. (1986) 'Social theory, social research, and a theory of action', *American Journal of Sociology*, 91: 1309–1335.

Coleman, J.S. (1990) *Foundations of Social Theory*. Cambridge, MA: The Belknap Press of the Harvard University Press.

Craver, Carl (2007) *Explaining the Brain: Mechanisms and the Mosaic Unity of Neuroscience*. Oxford: Clarendon Press.

Cummins, R. (2000) '"How does it work?" versus "what are the laws?": Two conceptions of psychological explanation', in F. Keil and R. Wilson (eds) *Explanation and Cognition*. Cambridge: MIT Press. pp. 117–144.

Elster, J. (1978) *Logic and Society: Contradictions and Possible Worlds*. Chichester: Wiley.

Elster, J. (1979) *Ulysses and the Sirens: Studies in Rationality and Irrationality*. Cambridge: Cambridge University Press.

Elster, J. (1982) 'Marxism, functionalism and game theory: The case for methodological individualism', *Theory and Society*, 11: 453–482.

Elster, J. (1983a) *Explaining Technical Change: A Case Study in the Philosophy of Science*. Cambridge: Cambridge University Press.

Elster, J. (1983b) *Sour Grapes: Studies in the Subversion of Rationality*. Cambridge: Cambridge University Press.

Elster, J. (1985) *Making Sense of Marx*. Cambridge: Cambridge University Press.

Elster, J. (1989a) *The Cement of Society: A Study of Social Order*. Cambridge: Cambridge University Press.

Elster, J. (1989b) *Nuts and Bolts for the Social Sciences*. Cambridge: Cambridge University Press.

Elster, J. (1999) *Alchemies of the Mind: Rationality and the Emotions*. Cambridge: Cambridge University Press.

Friedman, M. (1953) 'The methodology of positive economics', in M. Friedman (ed.) *Essays in Positive Economics*. Chicago: Chicago University Press. pp. 210–244.

Goldthorpe, J. (2000) *On Sociology: Numbers, Narratives, and the Integration of Research and Theory*. Oxford: Oxford University Press.

Hedström, P. (2005) *Dissecting the Social: On the Principles of Analytical Sociology*. Cambridge: Cambridge University Press.

Hedström, P. and R. Swedberg (eds) (1998) *Social Mechanisms: An Analytical Approach to Social Theory*. Cambridge: Cambridge University Press.

Hedström, P. and P. Bearman (eds) (2009) *The Oxford Handbook of Analytical Sociology*. Oxford: Oxford University Press.

Hedström, P. and L. Udéhn (2009) 'Analytical sociology and theories of the middle range', in P. Hedström and P. Bearman (eds) *The Oxford Handbook of Analytical Sociology*. Oxford: Oxford University Press. pp. 25–47.

Hedström, P. and P. Ylikoski (2010) 'Causal Mechanisms in the Social Sciences', *Annual Review of Sociology*, 36: 49–67.

Machamer, P., L. Darden and C.F. Craver (2000) 'Thinking about mechanisms', *Philosophy of Science*, 67: 1–25.

Macy, M.W. and R. Willer (2002) 'From factors to actors: Computational sociology and agent-based modelling', *Annual Review of Sociology*, 28: 143–166.

Macy, M.W. and A. Flache (2009) 'Population dynamics from the bottom up: Agent-based models of social interaction', in P. Hedström and P. Bearman (eds) *The Oxford Handbook of Analytical Sociology*. Oxford: Oxford University Press. pp. 245–268.

Merton, R.K. (1967) *On Theoretical Sociology*. New York: The Free Press.

Merton, R.K. (1968) *Social Theory and Social Structure*. New York: The Free Press.

Salmon, W. (1989) *Four Decades of Scientific Explanation*. Minneapolis: University of Minnesota Press.

Schelling, T.C. (1971) 'Dynamic models of segregation', *Journal of Mathematical Sociology*, 1: 143–186.

Schelling, T.C. (1978) *Micromotives and Macrobehavior*. New York: W.W. Norton.

Udéhn, L. (2001) *Methodological Individualism: Background, History and Meaning*. London: Routledge.

White, H.C. (1970) *Chains of Opportunity: System Models of Mobility in Organizations*. Cambridge: Harvard University Press.

Woodward, J. (2003) *Making Things Happen. A Theory of Causal Explanation*. Oxford: Oxford University Press.

19

Institutions

C. Mantzavinos

INTRODUCTION

Institutions keep society from falling apart, providing that there is something that keeps institutions from falling apart. (Elster, 1989: 147)

In this phrase of Jon Elster, the relevance of institutions for society comes successfully to the fore. It also pinpoints the reason institutions have been the object of inquiry for many scholars and philosophers from early one (Gemtos, 2001). The contemporary theory of institutions differs from earlier theories in two main ways: First, the very existence of institutions is no longer explained by the will of gods, the spirit of history, the decisions of a wise lawgiver, or by drawing on other simplistic causal patterns. Second, those explanatory schemes that have attempted to analyze the complex phenomenon of the emergence and change of institutions based on the tradition of methodological holism or functionalism seem to be of low credibility and on the retreat. There is instead, a great interest in most social sciences today in scientifically understanding institutional phenomena on the basis of methodological individualism,[1] that is, the meta-theoretical principle according to which all social phenomena, and thus also social institutions, must be explained as

the outcome of the interplay of individuals who are acting under different conditions.[2]

It is definitely compatible with developments in the different disciplines of the social sciences to claim that in the last decades we have been witnessing the development of a new research program, "The New Institutionalism in the Social Sciences." In Economics, for example, New Institutional Economics has become quite popular and widely accepted, mainly as it has been shaped by the works of Ronald Coase,[3] Douglass C. North,[4] and Oliver Williamson.[5] In Sociology there is also a discussion of New Institutionalism by Paul DiMaggio,[6] Walter Powell,[7] Victor Nee,[8] and others.[9] In Political Science New Institutionalism has been shaped by the work of a long series of authors such as Jim March,[10] Peter Hall,[11] Lin Ostrom,[12] Terry Moe,[13] etc. In Anthropology it is mainly the work of Jean Ensminger[14] that has had the greatest influence over the past few years. As is frequently the case when a research program is at its early stages, there are many problems that have not yet found a satisfactory solution. And as is frequently the case when different disciplines with different traditions and techniques of scientific research are to collaborate towards the solution of common problems, there are ambiguities, uncertainties, and difficulties in the communication of the results of the scientific research. This kind of weakness is even weightier in the case at hand, since the respective disciplines largely use theoretical patterns that lack an axiomatic basis, and the terms and concepts are therefore not always precisely defined.

In spite of these difficulties – and with a full awareness of the disagreement on a series of issues – I will start with an overview of the main principles and concepts of the theory of institutions. After explaining some basic concepts and principles of the contemporary theory of institutions, I will focus on the analysis of the mechanisms of the emergence and evolution of institutions. I will then proceed by providing the distinction between formal and informal institutions before discussing the problem of path dependence in the last part of the article and closing with a short epilogue.

BASIC CONCEPTS AND PRINCIPLES OF THE THEORY OF INSTITUTIONS

Institutions are normative social rules, that is the rules of the game in a society, enforced either through the coercive power of the state or other enforcement agencies that shape human interaction (Mantzavinos, 2001).[15] Institutions as normative patterns of behavior serve to (partially) solve the problem of cooperation in a society by providing a more or less permanent platform of conflict resolution. They define the rules of the socio-economic game, that is, the strategies which individuals are allowed to employ in order to pursue their goals and solve their problems. The existence of social institutions provides the first step towards overcoming the Hobbesian problem of social order, the second being the cooperation of individuals via exchange within the institutional framework.

It is quite common in the literature to employ the term "institution" in order to designate organizations of every kind. In order to avoid confusion, it is useful to distinguish between institutions and organizations. Institutions are the rules of the game; organizations are corporate actors, that is, groups of individuals bound by some rules designed to achieve a common objective (Coleman, 1990). They can be political organizations such as political parties, educational organizations such as universities, or economic organizations such as firms. Thus, organizations, when interacting with other organizations or individuals, submit to those general social rules that we have called institutions, that is, they are equally constrained by the general rules of the game.

Having now defined institutions and having provided the distinction between institutions and organizations, let us now proceed to the most fundamental problem of every theory of institutions: Why do institutions exist? There are two classes of reasons that can explain the existence of institutions on the basis of an individualistic approach. The first class of reasons refers to the motivational possibilities of *Homo sapiens* and the second class to the cognitive ones. Starting from the main assumption about motivation – namely, that every individual strives to increase his utility or, in other words, that every individual strives to better his condition by all means available to him – it becomes obvious that conflicts between individuals are bound to arise. Those settings in which the increase of one's utility presupposes the direct or indirect cooperation of other individuals can be defined as social problems. Such settings are to be termed "social" neither in the sense that the individuals involved are conscious of their involvement in such settings nor in the sense that they explicitly recognize their involvement in such settings. From the perspective of the observer, however, such social problems are clearly identifiable, and their basic characteristic is that the utility obtained by some kind of individual behavior depends in one way or another on the behavior of other individuals. Some stylized social problems have been worked out in game theory, such as the well known prisoner's dilemma, the coordination game, the game of trust, and so on.

Let us concentrate for a while on the prisoner's dilemma. The structure of this game is encountered very often in settings that constitute "social problems," defined as above. Let us think for a while of the setting that we are all involved very frequently in our everyday lives, on the sidewalks of some major cities in the world.

With reference to Table 19.1, each of us can increase his utility if he parks his car on the sidewalk (instead of incurring the costs of a parking lot) as long as others do not do so. The socially optimal and thus desirable situation is the one in which nobody parks on the sidewalk (1 + 1 = 2 units), whereas the worst situation is the one in which everybody parks on the sidewalk [(−1) + (−1) = −2 units]. Given the structure of the game and that we are all self interested, we end up parking on the sidewalk; that is, we end up with the worst possible solution.

Now, we can come back to institutions and to our central problem, namely why institutions exist: The first and most important reason for their existence has to do precisely with the fact that institutions are social rules constituting solutions to social problems and social conflicts that appear in the above mentioned form or some similar form. This is their most fundamental *raison d' être*: The life of man in a society without institutions would be, in the words of Hobbes (1651/1991), "solitary, poore, nasty, brutish and short" (Leviathan, ch. XIII: 89). This argument is presented by most social and political theorists, old and new, with the sole exception of the anarchists. But even the most optimistic among them, who doubt the necessity of the existence of a state, do not deny the necessity of informal institutions such as moral rules, social norms, and conventions for the existence of social order. Human egoism must be moulded by some form of social control in order for cooperation to emerge, and social institutions provide this mould.

But why do people agree to or accept institutions, that is, social normative *rules*, rather than deciding each time anew on particular norms or conventions to regulate a particular conflict every time one arises? Why not solve social problems ad hoc since, in a way, every problem situation – and thus also every *social* problem – is unique? The answer to this question lies in the cognitive structure of the human mind and provides the second class of reasons explaining the existence of social institutions. The human mind is far from being a perfect tool, able to perform all the difficult computations needed for solving problems that arise from interaction with other minds. Because of a restricted cognitive capacity, every individual mobilizes his energies only when a "new problem" arises, and follows routines when he classifies the problem situation as a familiar one. This distinction is rooted in the limited computational capacity of human beings and is a means to free up an individual's mind from unnecessary operations so that he can deal more adequately with the problem situations arising in his environment.

When we say that the environment of the individual is *complex*, we mean precisely this: His limited cognitive capacity makes his environment appear rather complicated to him and in need of simplification in order to be mastered. This refers to both the natural and the social environment of the individual, the latter being the focus here. Because of the perceived complexity of the social environment, people – consciously or unconsciously – adopt rules as solutions to social problems rather than deciding each time anew how to act and react to the settings where coordination with other individuals is needed.

Table 19.1 Prisoner's dilemma

		B	
		Does not park on the sidewalk	*Parks on the sidewalk*
A	Does not park on the sidewalk	(1, 1)	(−2, 2)
	Parks on the sidewalk	(2, −2)	(−1, −1)

Rules in general, as Hayek (1976/1982: 8) put it, "are a device for coping with our constitutional ignorance," they are the "device we have learned to use because our reason is insufficient to master the full detail of complex reality" (Hayek, 1960: 66). And social rules or institutions are our devices to deal with recurrent social problems arising in situations where self-interested individuals interact.[16]

The German anthropologist Arnold Gehlen made the same point when he stressed the role of institutions as a means of unburdening individuals from the need to constantly make decisions. Compared to animals, human behavior, according to Gehlen, is much more plastic and adaptable to varying environments. But this plasticity and openness regarding behavior, although beneficial on its own, causes uncertainty about the behavior of other individuals. Institutions serve to remove this difficulty.[17] By defining general normative patterns of behavior shared by the individuals, they serve individuals, unburdening them from having to decide each time anew. This relief provided by institutions is productive, according to Gehlen, because it makes it possible for an individual to concentrate his energies on other creative enterprises. Social rules make it possible for us to focus our energy on generating novel solutions to the *new* problems that emerge, a fact of obvious importance for social progress. This liberating function of institutions – their *Entlastung* (unburdening), according to Gehlen – is extremely important for a cognitively deficient being like man, because it provides him with the possibility to concentrate his limited cognitive resources on other activities and finally with the possibility to unfold all those activities that distinguish him from his fellows as a *unique personality*. As Gehlen splendidly puts it:

If the institutions provide us with a schema in certain respects, and if they shape our thoughts and feelings along with our behaviors and typify them, we can take advantage of these energy reserves in order to show within our particular set of circumstances the uniqueness which is bountiful, innovative, and fertile. He, who does not want to be a personality in *his own* circumstances but in *all* circumstances, can only fail. (Gehlen, 1961: 72; Translation by author)

There are thus also cognitive reasons for the existence of institutions (DiMaggio and Powell, 1991: 10f); they are a means of coping with the ignorance that individuals are facing when interacting with each other. The institutions, as the rules of the game, *stabilize expectations* and thus reduce the uncertainty of the agents.[18] They provide a preliminary structuring of their environment, a first more or less secure approximation of what will happen and what will not, and what might appear and what might not. But although the stabilizing *function* of institutions is very important, one should be careful to avoid the functionalist fallacy. It is therefore necessary to clearly distinguish between cause and effect. That institutions stabilize expectations is a mere effect of their existence. The *cause* of their existence lies – along with the motivational one – rather in the more general fact of the limits in the cognitive capacities of humans.

MECHANISMS OF EMERGENCE AND EVOLUTION OF SOCIAL INSTITUTIONS

Having presented, in as short an order as possible, some basic concepts and principles of the theory of institutions, I will now focus on the mechanisms at play in the emergence and evolution of social institutions. Institutions emerge either deliberately or spontaneously, that is, either as a product of collective action or as a product of a spontaneous process of social interaction. The institutions which emerge as a result of collective action, that is, the institutions that are designed deliberately, have been the object of inquiry of many scholars for centuries. The mechanisms of the emergence of spontaneous institutions, however, were first studied by the Scottish moral philosophers of the eighteenth century. David Hume, for example, envisioned a system of rules of justice which "is of course advantageous to the public; tho' it be not intended for that purpose by the inventors" (1740/1978: 529). Ferguson (1767/1966: 188) similarly observes that "[n]ations stumble upon establishments which are indeed the result of human action, but not the execution of any human design." And in Smith's famous metaphor, the merchant who intends only his own gain is "led by an invisible hand to promote an end which was no part of his intention" (1776/1976: 477).

This insight of the Scottish moral philosophers is relevant because, for the first time, the emergence of institutions is not explained exclusively by intentional action aimed at establishing them. Of the modern social scientists, the one that has offered the most profound analysis of the spontaneous emergence of institutions, integrating their evolution into a general theory of cultural evolution, is certainly Hayek. We shall therefore linger a while on his work. In Hayek's theory of cultural evolution, the growth of civilization is equated with the growth of knowledge, where the word "knowledge" is meant to "include all the human adaptations to environment in which past experience has been incorporated" (Hayek, 1960: 26). Hence, "knowledge" does not include "only the conscious, explicit knowledge of individuals, the knowledge which enables us to state that this or that is so and so. Still less can this knowledge be confined to scientific knowledge" (1960: 25). Moreover it includes "our habits and skills, our emotional attitudes, our tools, and our institutions – all [...] adaptations to past experience which have grown up by selective elimination of less suitable conduct." (1960: 26). Hayek contends, thus, that not only our scientific and practical knowledge is growing and is transmitted through time; so are our social rules and institutions.

But what does this mean more specifically? Hayek draws our attention to the analogy of social rules, used by individuals to solve the recurrent problems of social interaction, with tools, which in the same way serve to provide standard solutions to recurrent problems. His main argument is that "the various

institutions and habits, tools and methods of doing things, which [...] constitute our inherited civilization" (1960: 62) have been submitted to "the slow test of time" (1967: 111) in an evolutionary process of trial-and-error, (1976/1982: 135). "Those rules which have evolved in the process of growth of society embody the experience of many more trials and errors than any individual mind could acquire" (Hayek, 1967: 88).

According to Hayek, people, mostly in a subconscious manner, acquire and follow social rules that provide a solution to recurrent problems of social interaction in a quasi-automatic way. There are two main arguments against this view of cultural evolution. The first concerns the notion of group selection found in many parts of Hayek's work. Hayek, in explaining the evolution of culture, on the one hand, stresses the *innovation* of individuals experimenting with new rules, and, on the other hand, stresses the *competition* between old and new rules and the *selection* of the ones that led to the success of those groups which practiced them (Hayek, 1979/1982: 204, Note 48). The criterion of selection is, thus, group success; or, in other words, the "*transmission* of rules of conduct takes place *from individual to individual*, while what may be called the natural *selection* of rules will operate on the basis of greater or less efficiency on the resulting *order of the group*" (Hayek, 1967: 67, emphasis in original).

The argument against group selection is that it is incompatible with the postulate of methodological individualism and accordingly one has to show a relevant feedback mechanism relating how, in the end, individuals within groups are at least indirectly benefited by following certain cultural rules. It must be shown, in other words, that individuals in the group in the end adopt those rules that lead the group to success. If there is a free-riding problem, however, the argument is no longer sufficient.[19] On the contrary, in order for Hayek's theory to hold, one has to assume the altruistic behavior of every member of the group. This cannot safely be hypothesized, however, because the existence of even one free-rider, who enjoys the group advantage without sharing the group costs, would suffice to falsify the assumption.

The second argument against Hayek's theory of cultural evolution concerns the rules as tools analogy.[20] Although all *personal* rules followed by individuals can easily be understood as tools to solve personal problems, *social* rules cannot be always viewed with the aid of the rules-as-tools analogy. This analogy

> is less applicable the less the rules in question are susceptible to individual experimenting and selecting. [...] It is less plausible for rules that can only be tried out in collective experiments, in particular if the collective is a political community as opposed to, for instance, a private organization operating in a market environment. (Vanberg, 1994: 187f)

One has to distinguish, thus, between levels of experimenting with rules and levels of selection of rules, for example, between whether it is individual agents or collective entities, such as local authorities or national governments, who invent and imitate new social rules.[21] Accordingly only those social rules individually tried out and individually successfully imitated can safely be hypothesized as serving as a storage of experience for past generations, as Hayek contends.

It thus seems that although Hayek's theory of cultural evolution can be regarded largely as a very serious attempt to construct a general theory of institutional change, it nevertheless suffers in many parts. A more differentiated and systematic analysis of social institutions is thus necessary. In closing this section of the chapter, I would like to summarize by repeating that there are two basic mechanisms of the emergence and change of social institutions. They can either emerge deliberately as the outcome of collective action or as the unintended results of intentional human action. In the next section I will briefly show which mechanisms lead to the emergence of which kind of institutions.

FORMAL AND INFORMAL INSTITUTIONS

A very productive and very widely used distinction among types of institutions is based on the criterion of the enforcement agency of institutions. Institutions are commonly classified according to this criterion as shown in Table 19.2.

It is impossible to analyze in detail here how every type of institution emerges, the mechanism according to which it is enforced and how it is adopted. A short reference to each of these matters must suffice. The most important feature of conventions is their self-policing character. After they have emerged, nobody has an incentive to change rules that everybody else sticks to. In game theory, conventions are usually analyzed with the help of what are known as "coordination games." Examples of such rules are traffic rules, industrial standards, forms of economic contracts, language, etc. The moral rules (as empirical phenomena, not as a branch of normative ethics discussed in philosophy) are largely culture independent because they provide solutions to problems that are prevalent in every society, as Lawrence Kohlberg has shown in his famous empirical research (Kohlberg, 1984). The mechanisms for the enforcement of moral rules are entirely internal to the individual, and therefore no external enforcement agency for rule compliance is needed. Typical examples of moral rules are "keep promises," "respect other people's property," "tell the truth," etc. These have a universal character. However, their existence does not necessarily mean that they are also

Table 19.2   The classification of institutions

	Conventions	Self-policing
Informal institutions	Moral rules	First party
	Social norms	Third party: Social forces, i.e. individuals of the group
Formal institutions	Law	Third party: State

followed, and in fact many individuals break them. (Thus, the empirical phenomenon to be explained is the *existence* of moral rules in a society, which are followed by *part* of the population.) Social norms, on the contrary, are not of universal character, and they are enforced by an enforcement agency external to the agent, usually the other group members. The mechanism of enforcement refers to the approval or disapproval of specific kinds of behavior. Social norms provide solutions to problems of less importance than moral rules and regulate settings appearing mainly at specific times and places.

Although the enforcement agency of each different category of informal institution is different, as is the specific enforcement mechanism, a common element to each type of informal institution – and this is very important – is that they all emerge as the unintended outcome of human action. Their mechanism of emergence is thus an evolutionary process of the invisible hand type. This process starts as an individual perceives his situation as constituting a new problem because the environment has changed, and then in an act of creative choice, he tries a new solution to this problem. Both the problem and its solution are of a strictly personal nature, and the solution is attempted because the agent expects it to increase his utility. This novel response to a problem situation becomes an innovation as soon as other individuals decide to imitate it. In other words, innovation is a social phenomenon because it relates new solutions to new problems, and those solutions are also viewed as new by other individuals. (The case of an individual perceiving something as a new problem and trying out a solution that is novel to him but not to the other members of the social group thus, does not constitute an innovation.)

The reaction of other individuals and their imitation of the solution give rise to a cumulative process through which the new behavior or pattern of action becomes ever more widely adopted by those who expect to better their condition by doing so.[22] The diffusion of this innovative behavior among

many or all members of a community brings about the solution to a problem, which, from an external point of view, is social in nature. In other words, a social pattern or institution arises and the problem-solving individuals "do not have the overall pattern that is ultimately produced in mind, neither on the level of intentions nor even on the level of foresight or awareness" (Ullmann-Margalit, 1978: 271).

Whereas informal institutions emerge as the unintended results of human action in a process that no individual mind can consciously control, law or the sum of the social rules that I have called formal institutions, are products of collective decisions. The state as an organism[23] creates law, either by constructing, by the conscious decision of its organs new legal rules or by providing – by means of suitable adaptation – existing informal rules with sanctions (Gemtos, 2001: 36). Modern public choice theory tries to explain exactly how collective decisions lead to the emergence of institutions in the social arena.[24] The presupposition for them is the emergence of shared mental models (Denzau and North, 1994) with respect to the structure of the problems. In the end, the collective decisions that lead to the creation of legal rules are the result of the political process during which individuals and organizations succeed to a greater or lesser degree in using the power that they have in order to impose rules that further their interests. Since what we call "political power" is very difficult to theoretically identify, contemporary political theory frequently views "resources" as the decisive factor determining the behavior of the players in the political game. Those resources can be of three kinds – that is, economic, political, and ideological – and the degree of their availability to the players determines the extent of their bargaining power and thus how much they can influence the political process which in turn generates the formal institutions.[25]

Summarizing what we have said about the formal and informal institutions, we have to stress that the mechanisms for their emergence are distinct: Whereas the informal institutions are generated through an invisible-hand process – in a way endogenously from within the society – the formal institutions are the outcome of the political process which is imposed exogenously onto society from the collective decisions of agents who avail of resources, political, economic, and ideological. It is thus natural, if what I have said so far holds, that there is no necessity that informal and formal institutions complement each other in such a way that a workable social order is produced or in order for economic development to take place.

THE PROBLEM OF PATH DEPENDENCE

The theory of institutions still needs to grapple with the problem of the interaction between formal and informal institutions. In the philosophy of law, the respective discussion focuses on the relationship between law and the moral rules and on whether the moral rules must be viewed as an integral part of the concept of law or not. In New Institutionalism the problem is formulated in more general terms, mainly around the following two questions: (a) How do formal and informal rules interact to produce social order? (b) What institutional mix of formal and informal rules leads to a wealth-creating economic game (rather than to an unproductive game characterized by conflicts between groups for the distribution of wealth)?

I cannot refer to all the theoretical approaches that have been undertaken in an attempt to address these questions, and I will just mention that most of them have not been successful and we have only just begun to answer them. I will try to shed some light on one dimension of the problem since it has to do with the evolutionary change of institutions and is of fundamental importance. I thus will briefly deal with the evolutionary paths that societies follow and with the

phenomenon of path dependence. Let us approach the issue in a systematic way.

New Institutionalism differs from other theories of economic development precisely in systematically stressing the role of institutions for the development process of societies. The accumulation of physical and human capital and the technological progress, as they are stressed by neoclassical economic theory, are nothing but secondary factors of economic development. The problem of wealth creation is much more complex. New Institutionalism stresses the dominant role that institutions play as the rules of the economic game that define the incentives and more generally structure the behavior of economic agents, and thus channel their activities, lead to the accumulation of physical and human capital and to technological progress and, in the end, to economic growth and welfare.

It is important that neither the formal institutions nor the informal institutions alone are sufficient for economic development. The natural experiments that history has performed offer, I think, decisive support for this thesis. Germany, China and Korea were divided by the accidents of history and as a result came to live under different formal rules during most of the postwar period. The economic performance of West Germany, South Korea, Hong Kong and Taiwan has been incomparably greater than the respective performances of East Germany, North Korea, and Mainland China (Olson, 1996: 19). The informal rules that the populations in the divided nations shared did not reverse the different trajectories of growth. Societies with the same cultural heritage but different formal rules will exhibit different patterns of economic growth.

Societies that avail of the same formal institutional structure but whose populations have different informal rules are also bound to follow different economic paths. In other words, formal institutions alone are not sufficient to lead to economic growth. The experience with the transformation process of the ex-communist countries in Eastern

Europe seems to corroborate this thesis. The dogmatic transplantation of a set of formal institutions that have prevailed for decades or centuries in the countries of the West to those countries of the East did not automatically allow a good economic performance. Formal rules remain a piece of paper as long as they are not followed by the citizens.

It thus seems that a sufficient condition for economic growth is met only when both formal and informal institutions build an appropriate framework for a wealth-creating game. With regard to economic growth, the relationship between formal and informal rules is clearly a complementary one. Only when the whole network of institutions is mutually complementary in an appropriate way is it possible that a framework will be created that will lead economic subjects to undertake to productive activities and, thus, to the augmentation of the wealth of a society. Empirical research and the studies of economic history have shown that two kinds of formal institutions are sine qua non for economic development: (1) secure property rights and (2) those economic institutions that secure open markets. Since I cannot go into the details here, I just want to mention that this refers only to the *content* of the appropriate formal institutions, but there is of course the additional problem of the *credible commitments* on the part of the state that these institutions will in fact be provided and enforced.

The empirical research regarding the type of informal institutions that lead to economic development is still in its infancy.[26] The only thing that seems certain from a contemporary perspective is that only when the level of trust in a society is high – something that mainly informal institutions produce – can a wealth-creating game take place. More specifically, what is necessary is the existence of appropriate informal institutions that lead the citizens to protest every time that state actors do not respect their commitments to the rule of law.

I have tried to consistently argue in this article that the mechanisms behind the emergence of formal and informal rules are distinct. This enables me to reach two basic conclusions:

1 It seems to be rather rare that the spontaneous evolutionary process of the emergence of informal institutions and the conscious design of a polity coincide in an institutional mix which is appropriate for a wealth-creating economic game. Two distinct processes of a different nature and following a thoroughly different direction must coincidentally result in a framework suitable for economic growth to happen. The chances that this will happen do not seem to be that high, something that even a cursory glance at the world map can confirm which it reveals that only a few countries are on such a developmental path.
2 The complementary relationship between formal and informal institutions, plus the presence of learning, creates path dependence.

The recognition of the phenomenon of path dependence is in fact the recognition on part of the modern theory of institutions that history plays a decisive role in the further process of institutional change, or, to put it differently, that tradition shapes the further evolution of institutions. If, however, path dependence indicated nothing other than the rather commonsensical position that the choices of the present are dependent on the choices of the past, then nobody could seriously maintain that we have made serious progress vis-a-vis the older theories of institutions. "Institutional path dependence," however, refers more specifically to the fact that once an institutional mix has been established, then there are increasing returns[27] since agents adapt to their social environment according to the prevailing institutional framework at decreasing individual costs (adaptive efficiency). This phenomenon exists because two mechanisms are at work: On the one hand, the institutions that have been created lead to the emergence of organizations whose survival depends on the perseverance of these institutions, and these organizations therefore invest resources in order to block any change which could endanger their survival (North, 2005: 51).

On the other hand, the second and probably most important mechanism is of a cognitive nature. Setting up institutions requires collective learning on the part of the individuals during which individuals perceive, process and store in their memories the solutions to social problems. Since a considerable period of time lapses before this learning process is completed, the initial setup costs are very high. Once all or most individuals have internalized the rules of behavior, the institutional framework starts solving a variety of social problems in a specific way. One can speak of the "increasing returns of the institutional framework" in the sense that once the problem solutions have been learned by the agents, they are unconsciously applied each time the same or similar problems appear (Mantzavinos et al. 2004). The combination of those two mechanisms leads along paths which a society cannot easily abandon, firstly because of the organized interests that resist doing so, and second because cognitive mechanisms make it easy or automatic to follow the rules of the status quo. We end up being locked into a path that frequently nobody or very few wished for; and nobody has the incentive to start the enterprise of moving into a new one.

The issue of path dependence can be further clarified with the help of a simple example. Suppose that we are in front of an urn in which there are two balls, one white and the other red. If we put our hand into the urn without looking and randomly choose one ball, then the probability of the ball being white or red is 1/2. We proceed now according to the following rule: Each time that we choose a ball of a certain color out of the urn, we put that ball into the urn, as well as a new ball of the same color. If, in other words, we initially choose a white ball, the second time that we put our hand into the urn, there will be two white balls and one red one. The probability of choosing a white ball will now be 2/3, whereas the probability of choosing a red one will be 1/3. If we again choose a white ball, then the next time, three out of four balls in the urn will be white.

The probability that we will choose a white ball the next time will be 3/4 and so on.

The described procedure – Arthur et al. (1994: 36) call it the "Standard Polya Process" – is a path-dependent procedure, though of course it is of a simple nature: Each time that we choose a ball from the urn, the probability that we choose a ball of a specific color depends on the colors of the balls that were chosen in the past and the structure towards which this process tends to settle. In the case at hand, the specific analogy between white and red balls depends on the path that has been followed. The events that took place at the beginning of the process are especially important since the overall number of balls is still small and the proportion of one color decisively changes due to the addition of a ball of this color. After time lapses, however, the overall number of balls increases and the "perturbations" have only a very minor effect: The structure that has emerged no longer changes.

EPILOGUE

Let us summarize: New Institutionalism in the Social Sciences offers theoretical tools which facilitate the analysis of the complex phenomena of institutional change and provide some answers to the difficult questions which have been asked for centuries by social theorists. We are, however, only at the beginning. Many more questions remain open than have been satisfactorily answered. This is even truer with respect to the issue of the evaluation of institutions, which I could not touch upon here. Numerous problems remain to be addressed: What criteria are needed to evaluate institutions, what rational evaluative procedures can be used and, even more importantly, what are appropriate ways to move societies from the inefficient paths that they are often locked in? Only a theory of institutions that increases our information about the structure of social reality can provide us with the means of reorienting this reality in a direction that we find desirable. Some of the basic elements of such a theory and some of the problems involved with it have been discussed here.

NOTES

1 The first person to employ the term "methodological individualism" in order to describe this meta-theoretical principle was Joseph A. Schumpeter in his Habilitation-thesis "Das Wesen und der Hauptinhalt der theoretischen Nationalökonomie" (1908), drawing a clear boundary vis-a-vis "political individualism:" "Wir müssen scharf zwischen *politischem* und *methodologischem* Individualismus unterscheiden. Beide haben nicht das geringste miteinander gemein. Der erstere geht von allgemeinen Obersätzen aus, wie daß Freiheit zur Entwicklung des Menschen und zum Gesamtwohle mehr als alles andere beitrage und stellt eine Reihe von praktischen Behauptungen auf; der letztere tut nichts dergleichen, behauptet nichts und hat keine besonderen Voraussetzungen. Er bedeutet nur, dass man bei der Beschreibung gewisser Vorgänge von dem Handeln der Individuen ausgehe."(1908: 90f).

2 Albert (1998: 18): "[…] den *methodologischen Indiuidualismus*, das heißt: die Idee der Erklärung sozialer Tatbestände aus dem Zusammenspiel individueller Handlungen unter verschiedenen Bedingungen." See also Watkins (1953: 729): "[The principle of methodological individualism] states that social processes and events should be explained by being deduced from (a) principles governing the behavior of participating individuals and (b) descriptions of their situations." For a discussion of methodological individualism from a philosophical perspective, see the classic work of Popper *The Poverty of Historicism* (1957: 142f). (This discussion of Popper is unfortunately tied to a rather confused discussion of the so called "zero method." For a critique of this, see Mantzavinos (2005: Chapter 5).) For a discussion of methodological individualism from a sociological point of view, see Vanberg (1975: mainly ch. 8) and Bohnen (1975, 2000). For a discussion of the role of methodological individualism in economics, see Arrow (1994), Suchanek (1994: 125f), Kirchgässner (1991: 23f), and mainly Blaug (1992: 42f). Methodological individualism in political science was discussed in the 1990s with respect to the "rational choice controversy." See Green and Shapiro (1994: 15f), the collection of articles in Friedman (1996), but also Riker (1990) and Elster (1986). Obviously the issue of agency is more general than the postulate of methodological individualism which is far more specific; for a discussion of some

basic problems of agency see Mantzavinos (2009: Part I).

3 See Coase (1937, 1960).

4 See North (1981, 1990, 1994, 2005), North, Wallis and Weingast (2009).

5 See Williamson (1985, 1996).

6 See mainly DiMaggio (1998).

7 See mainly the edited volume by Powell and DiMaggio (1991).

8 See mainly Nee and Brinton (1998).

9 See for example Hasse and Krücken (2005).

10 See mainly March (1999).

11 See mainly the article by Hall and Taylor (1998), which gives an overview of the field, as well as the edited volume by Hall and Soskice (2001).

12 See especially Ostrom (1990, 2005).

13 See Moe (2005).

14 See especially the paper by Ensminger (1998) containing an overview of the field and her work on Orma in Kenya, Ensminger and Knight (1997).

15 This definition follows both North and Parsons. According to North's definition (1990: 3): "Institutions are the rules of the game in a society or, more formally, are the humanly devised constraints that shape human interaction. In consequence, they structure incentives in human exchange, whether political, social or economic." According to Parsons (1975: 97): "Institutions [......] are complexes of normative rules and principles which, either through law or other mechanism of social control, serve to regulate social action and relationships of course with varying degrees of success."

16 Whereas the traditional sociological analysis stressed mainly the normative dimension of institutions, new institutionalism puts a new emphasis on the cognitive dimension (Hall and Taylor, 1998: 25; DiMaggio and Powell, 1991: 15). See also Lindenberg (1998: 718): "In NIS [New Instiutional Sociology] the full internalization argument (which implied moral guidance of behavior) has been replaced by the idea of behavior guided by cognitive processes […]. The point is that institutionalization is linked to the establishment of cognitive habits which influence the very experience of reality (as a taken-for-granted reality) rather than just the response to reality."

17 See Gehlen (1961: 68): "Institutions like laws, marriage, property, etc. appear then to be supportive and formative stabilizers of those driving forces, which, thought of in isolation, appear to be plastic and lacking direction. Each culture 'stylizes' certain modes of behavior, making them obligatory and exemplary for all those who belong to it. For individuals, then, such institutions mean a release or relief from basic decisions and represent an accustomed security of important orientations, so that the behavior itself can occur free of reflection, consistently, and in mutual reciprocity." [Translation, by author]

18 This is a common argument of all institutionalists, old and new. See, for example, Commons

(1924/1968: 138) and Hayek (1973/1982: 102): "The task of rules of just conduct can thus only be to tell people which expectations they can count on and which not." See also Lachmann (1963: 63): "What is particularly required in order to successfully coordinate the transactions of millions of people is the existence of institutions. In these institutions, an objectification is achieved for us of the million actions of our fellow men, whose plans, objectives, and motives are impossible for us to know." [Translation by author]. See also Hall and Taylor (1998: 17f).

19 See the detailed discussion of this point in Vanberg (1994: 199).

20 See Hayek (1973/1982: 21): "Like all general purpose tools, rules serve because they have become adapted to the solution of recurring problem situations and thereby help to make the members of the society in which they prevail more effective in the pursuit of their aims. Like a knife or a hammer they have been shaped not with a particular purpose in view but because in this form rather than in some other form they have proved serviceable in a great variety of situations. They have not been constructed to meet foreseen particular needs but have been selected in a process of evolution. The knowledge which has given them their shape is not knowledge of particular future effects but knowledge of the recurrence of certain problem situations or tasks, of intermediate results regularly to be achieved in the service of a great variety of ultimate aims; and much of this knowledge exists not as an enumerable list of situations for which one has to be prepared, or of the importance of the kind of problems to be solved, or of the probability that they will arise, but as a propensity to act in certain types of situations in a certain manner."

21 On this issue, see Vanberg (1992: 114f), where he stresses: "The 'rules as tools' analogy [...] makes it appear as if the experimenting with and selecting among potential alternatives is essentially a matter of separate individual choices in both cases, for tools as well as for rules. [...] It seems obvious, however, that it is not generally applicable in the realm of rules and institutions. [...] To mention only two particular obvious examples: It is hardly possible for an individual driver to experiment with a 'left-driving rule' in a community where driving on the right side of the road is the rule; and it is simply unfeasible for an individual citizen to try out a new rule for electing a parliament – even if such individuals would firmly believe in the superiority of an alternative practice."

22 See Koppl (1992: 308).

23 See the famous definition of the modern state of Max Weber (1919/1994: 36): "The state is that human *Gemeinschaft*, which within a certain territory (this: the territory, belongs to the distinctive feature) successfully lays claim to the *monopoly of legitimate physical force* for itself." [Translation by author]

24 For an overview of the field, see Mueller (2003).

25 For a profound analysis of the role of political power in the emergence of formal institutions, see especially Knight (1992) and Moe (2005).

26 For an interesting and thought-provoking analysis of the connection between culture, institutions, and economic development see Greif (2006).

27 See North (1990: 95) and for a thorough study Ackermann (2001: Chapter 3).

REFERENCES

Ackermann, Rolf (2001) *Pfadabhängigkeit, Institutionen und Regelreform*. Tübingen: Mohr Siebeck.

Albert, Hans (1998) *Marktsoziologie und Entscheidungslogik*. Tübingen: Mohr Siebeck.

Arrow, Kenneth (1994) 'Methodological individualism and social knowledge', *American Economic Review*, 84: 1–9.

Arthur, Brian, Yu. M. Ermoliev and Yu. M. Kaniovski (1994) 'Path-dependent processes and the emergence of macro-structure', in Arthur, Brian (ed.) *Increasing Returns and Path Dependence in the Economy*. Ann Arbor: University of Michigan Press. pp. 33–48.

Blaug, Mark (1992) *The Methodology of Positive Economics*. Cambridge: Cambridge University Press.

Bohnen, Alfred (1975) *Individualismus und Gesellschaftstheorie*. Tübingen: Mohr Siebeck.

Bohnen, Alfred (2000) *Handlungsprinzipien oder Systemgesetze*. Tübingen: Mohr Siebeck.

Coase, Ronald (1937) 'The nature of the firm', *Economica*, 4: 386–405.

Coase, Ronald (1960) 'The problem of social cost', *Journal of Law and Economics*, 3: 1–44.

Coleman, James (1990) *Foundations of Social Theory*. Cambridge, MA: Harvard University Press.

Commons, John R. (1924/1968): *The Legal Foundations of Capitalism*, Madison: The University of Wisconsin Press.

Denzau Arthur and Douglass C. North (1994) 'Shared mental models: Ideologies and institutions', *Kyklos*, 47: 3–31.

DiMaggio, Paul (1998) 'The New Institutionalisms: Avenues of Collaboration', *Journal of Institutional and Theoretical Economics*, 154: 696–705.

DiMaggio, Paul and Walter Powell (1991) (eds) *The New Institutionalism in Organizational Analysis*. Chicago and London: Chicago University Press.

Elster, Jon (1986) 'Introduction', in Jon Elster (ed.) *Rational Choice*. Cambridge: Cambridge University Press. pp. 1–33.

Elster, Jon (1989) *Nuts and Bolts for the Social Sciences*. Cambridge: Cambridge University Press.

Ensminger, Jean (1998) 'Anthropology and the new institutionalism', *Journal of Institutional and Theoretical Economics*, 154: 774–789.

Ensminger, Jean and Jack Knight (1997) 'Changing social norms', *Current Anthropology*, 38: 1–24.

Ferguson, Adam (1767/1966) *An Essay on the History of Civil Society*. Edinburgh: Edinburgh University Press.

Friedman, Jeffrey (1996) *The Rational Choice Controversy*. New Haven and London: Yale University Press.

Gehlen, Arnold (1961) *Anthropologische Forschung*. Rowohlt: Reinbek bei Hamburg.

Gemtos, Petros (2001) Oikonomia kai Dikaio, vol. 2, Athens: Sakkoulas (in Greek).

Greif, Avner (2006) *Institutions and the Path to the Modern Economy. Lessons from Medieval Trade*. Cambridge: Cambridge University Press.

Green, Donald and Ian Shapiro (1994) *Pathologies of Rational Choice Theory*. New Haven and London: Yale University Press.

Hall, Peter and David Soskice (2001) (eds) *Varieties of Capitalism*. Oxford: Oxford University Press.

Hall, Peter and Rosemary Taylor (1998) 'Political science and the three new institutionalisms', in Karol Soltan, Eric M. Uslaner and Virginia Haufler (eds) *Institutions and Social Order*. Ann Arbor: University of Michigan Press. pp. 15–43.

Hasse, Rainmund and Georg Krücken (2005) *Neo-Institutionalismus*, 2nd rev. edition. Bielefeld: Transcript Verlag.

Hayek, Fridrich A. von (1960) *The Constitution of Liberty*. London and New York: Routledge.

Hayek, Fridrich A. von (1967) *Studies in Philosophy, Politics and Economics*. London: Routledge and Kegan Paul.

Hayek, Fridrich A. von (1973/1982) *Rules and Order*. Vol. I of Law, Legislation and Liberty. London: Routledge and Kegan Paul.

Hayek, Fridrich A. von (1976/1982) *The Mirage of Social Justice*. Vol. II of Law, Legislation and Liberty. London and New York: Routledge.

Hobbes, Thomas (1651/1991) *Leviathan*. Cambridge: Cambridge University Press.

Hume, David (1740/1978) *A Treatise of Human Nature*. Oxford: Oxford University Press.

Kirchgässner, Gebhard (1991) *Homo Oeconomicus*. Tübingen: Mohr Siebeck.

Knight, Jack (1992) *Institutions and Social Conflict*. Cambridge: Cambridge University Press.

Kohlberg, Lawrence (1984) *Essays on Moral Development*. Vol. II: The Psychology of Moral Development. The Nature and Validity of Moral Stages. New York: Harper & Row.

Koppl, Roger (1992) 'Invisible-hand explanations and neoclassical economics: Toward a post marginalist economics', *Journal of Institutional and Theoretical Economics*, 148: 292–313.

Lachmann, Ludwig (1963) 'Wirtschaftsordnung und Wirtschaftliche Institutionen', *ORDO*, 14: 63–72.

Lindenberg, Siegward (1998) 'The cognitive turn in institutional analysis? Beyond NIE and NIS?', *Journal of Institutional and Theoretical Economics*, 154: 716–727.

Mantzavinos, C. (2001) *Individuals, Institutions, and Markets*. Cambridge: Cambridge University Press.

Mantzavinos, C. (2005) *Naturalistic Hermeneutics*. Cambridge: Cambridge University Press.

Mantzavinos C. (2009) (ed.) 'Philosophy of the Social Sciences'. *Philosophical Theory and Scientific Practice*. Cambridge: Cambridge University Press.

Mantzavinos, C., Douglass North and Syed Shariq (2004) 'Learning, institutions and economic performance', *Perspectives on Politics*, 2: 75–84.

March, James (1999) *The Pursuit of Organizational Intelligence*. Oxford: Blackwell Publishers.

Moe, Terry (2005) 'Power and political institutions', *Perspectives on Politics*, 3: 215–233.

Mueller, Dennis (2003) *Public Choice III*. Cambridge: Cambridge University Press.

Nee, Victor and Mary Brinton (1998) (eds) *The New Institutionalism in Sociology*. New York: Russell Sage Foundation.

North, Douglass (1981) *Structure and Change in Economic History*. New York: W.W. Norton.

North, Douglass (1990) *Institutions, Institutional Change and Economic Performance*. Cambridge: Cambridge University Press.

North, Douglass (1994) 'Economic performance through time', *American Economic Review*, 84: 359–368.

North, Douglass (2005) *Understanding the Process of Economic Change*. Princeton: Princeton University Press.

North, Douglass, John Wallis and Barry Weingast (2009) *Violence and Social Orders*. Cambridge: Cambridge University Press.

Olson, Mancur (1996) 'Big bills left on the sidewalk: Why some nations are rich and other poor', *Journal of Economic Perspective*, 10: 3–24.

Ostrom, Elinor (1990) *Governing the Commons: The Evolution of Institutions for Collective Action.* Cambridge: Cambridge University Press.

Ostrom, Elinor (2005) *Understanding Institutional Diversity.* Princeton: Princeton University Press.

Parsons, Talcott (1975) 'Social structure and the symbolic media of exchange', in Peter M. Blau (ed.) *Approaches to the Study of Social Structure.* New York and London: Free Press. pp. 94–120.

Popper, Karl (1957) *The Poverty of Historicism.* London: Routledge.

Powell, Walter and DiMaggio Paul (1991) (eds): *The New Institutionalism in Organizational Analysis.* Chicago: The University of Chicago Press.

Riker, William (1990) 'Political science and rational choice', in James E. Alt and Kenneth A. Shepsle (eds) *Perspectives on Positive Political Economy.* Cambridge: Cambridge University Press. pp. 163–181.

Schumpeter, Joseph A. (1908) *Das Wesen und der Hauptinhalt der theoretischen Nationalökonomie.* Berlin: Duncker and Humblot.

Smith, Adam (1776/1976) *An Inquiry into the Nature and Causes of the Wealth of Nations.* Edwin Cannan (ed.). Chicago: Chicago University Press.

Suchanek, Andreas (1994) *Ökonomischer Ansatz und Theoretische Integration.* Tübingen: Mohr Siebeck.

Ullmann-Margalit, Edna (1978) 'Invisible-hand explanations', *Synthese*, 39: 263–291.

Vanberg, Viktor (1975) *Die Zwei Soziologien.* Tübingen: Mohr Siebeck.

Vanberg, Viktor (1992) 'Innovation, cultural evolution and economic growth', in Ulrich Witt (ed.) *Explaining Process and Change: Approaches to Evolutionary Economics.* Ann Arbor: Michigan University Press. pp. 105–121.

Vanberg, Viktor (1994) 'Cultural evaluation, collective learning and constitutional design', in David Reisman (ed.) *Economic Thought and Political Theory.* Boston, Dordrecht and London: Kluwer. pp. 171–204.

Watkins, John (1953) 'Ideal types and historical explanation', in Herbert Feigl and May Brodbeck (eds) *Readings in the Philosophy of Science.* New York: Appleton-Century-Crofts, Educational Division, Meredith Corporation. pp. 723–743.

Weber, Max (1919/1994) *Politik als Beruf.* Tübingen: Mohr Siebeck.

Williamson, Oliver (1985) *The Economic Institutions of Capitalism.* New York: Free Press.

Williamson, Oliver (1996) *The Mechanisms of Governance.* Oxford: Oxford University Press.

20

Evolutionary Approaches

Geoffrey Hodgson

A number of approaches in the social sciences claim to be evolutionary, and the use of such terms is growing rapidly. But words such as 'evolution' mean different things to different authors, even within the same discipline.

The aim of this article is to provide an overview of past and recent 'evolutionary' approaches in the social sciences. Although the term 'evolution' has multiple meanings, it raises the question of the relationship between biological and social evolution and the particular relevance of Darwinism to the social sciences. All these topics are addressed here.

AN EVOLVING AND CONTESTED TERM IN THE SOCIAL SCIENCES

Although explicit discussion of evolutionary approaches has been prominent at various times in the social sciences since the nineteenth century, the term 'evolution' and its derivatives have been used in a variety of different ways. Etymologically, the word derives from the Latin verb *evolvere* and refers to processes of unfolding or unrolling. It was first applied systematically to natural phenomena by the German biologist Albrecht von Haller in 1744. He used the word to characterise embryological development as the growth of a preformed miniature adult organism. Preformation – where the embryo is deemed to contain in microcosm the form of its future development – was a common idea in biology from the seventeenth to the nineteenth century.

It was Herbert Spencer, not Charles Darwin, who popularised the term 'evolution' in the nineteenth century. Darwin did not introduce the word until the sixth (1872) edition of the *Origin of Species*, and then he used it only sparingly. It was rarely applied to social phenomena until the 1870s, when writers began more commonly to refer to the evolution of language, law or society. Spencer's role in extending the usage of the term in the social sciences was crucial, particularly after the publication of the first edition of his *Study of Sociology* in 1873. By the end of the nineteenth century its usage was much more common.

A number of classic approaches in the social sciences have been described as 'evolutionary'. Among many others, diverse names such as Adam Smith, Karl Marx, Alfred Marshall, Carl Menger, Gustav Schmoller, Joseph Schumpeter, William Graham Sumner, Thorstein Veblen and Lester Frank Ward have been mentioned. Although their theoretical approaches were very different, they were all concerned with the phenomenon of social change.

For some 'evolution' connotes little more than change. Joseph Schumpeter (1942) used it more precisely but still very broadly to refer to processes of qualitative development. Others invest the term with questionable meanings of progress or predestination (which is one reason why Darwin was reluctant to use the word). Given this immense and disordered historical baggage, there is little point in pretending that 'evolution' has a precise and widely acceptable meaning.

This does not mean that we cannot identify some prominent themes in the 'evolutionary' literature in the social sciences. Many 'evolutionary' theorists express a discontent with static or equilibrium oriented theory, or theory that neglects vital driving forces such as technology and innovation (Dosi et al., 1988; Metcalfe, 1998; Nelson and Winter, 2002; Nelson, 2005; Witt, 2003). Another important theme in this literature is the recognition of the complexity of social phenomena and the fact that outcomes are often the result of an unpredictable process. Such laudable preoccupations are manifest, but they overlay a variety of contesting theoretical frameworks.

It is thus a mistake to use the term 'evolution' with the confidence and assurance that everyone knows and agrees what it means. Nothing is more guaranteed to generate confusion than to raise such a muddled term to the centrepiece of research, while simultaneously suggesting that a clear and well defined approach to scientific enquiry is implied. This does not mean that this term should be abandoned, but we should be aware of its looseness and inadequacy.

The immense diversity of views parading under the 'evolutionary' banner makes a detailed and comprehensive survey very difficult. In particular, there is no Darwinian copyright on the use of the term 'evolution'; instead social scientists typically invest it with a broader and looser set of connotations. But despite the lack of a clear definition of the term, its meaning tends to orbit two obvious although controversial attractors: (i) the more specific Darwinian conception of evolution, and (ii) the use of ideas from biology in helping to explain social phenomena.

After the First World War, and at least in the English-speaking world, there was a strong reaction against the use of biological ideas or terms in the social sciences (Degler, 1991). It took several decades for evolutionary terminology to reappear. Its first and most significant reappearances were in economics.

In economics after the Second World War there was a small but important flurry of debate between Armen Alchian (1950), Edith Penrose (1952) and others concerning the use of 'biological analogies' in explaining competition between firms. In America, the group of dissident economists inspired by Veblen and others founded the Association for Evolutionary Economics in 1966. Veblen (1899, 1919) had stressed both the evolution of social entities and their institutional character. But this 'old' version of institutional and evolutionary economics was then out of fashion.

It was not until after 1970 that a more influential current of 'evolutionary economics' emerged (Boulding, 1981; Dosi et al., 1988; Nelson and Winter, 1973, 1982). The *Journal of Evolutionary Economics* first appeared in 1991. By the 1990s, evolutionary ideas had also permeated mainstream economics – particularly in the form of evolutionary game theory. Evolutionary approaches in economics have proved particularly influential in business schools, especially when ideas are combined from multiple disciplines.

The development of evolutionary game theory is of particular interest. It originated as an extension of the theory of games in biological contexts (Maynard Smith, 1982). Key concepts such as an evolutionary stable strategy were transferred to economics (Sugden, 1986). Influential economic theorists adopted the approach in the 1990s, partly in an attempt to resolve the problem of multiple equilibria in previous theory and partly to relax the questionable assumption of hyper-rationality in preceding versions of game theory. In such models the frequency of strategies changes in the population through replication and selection (Friedman, 1991; Hofbauer and Sigmund, 1998; Samuelson, 1997; Weibull, 1995). Evolutionary game theory also has had a significant but lesser impact on sociology and anthropology.

Generally, however, evolutionary ideas in sociology have been met with stronger resistance. Earlier sociologists such as Franklin Giddings (1896), Lester Frank Ward (1903) and Edward Ross (1901) had discussed biological influences on human behaviour and incorporated Darwinian ideas. But Talcott Parsons (1937) followed Emile Durkheim (1895) and steered sociology in a very different direction, erecting a conceptual barrier between the social and the natural world. It became commonplace in sociology to deny the relevance of ideas from biology to the study of the social domain. Similar stances persist in sociology to this day.

Consequently, the publication by Edward O. Wilson of his *Sociobiology* (1975) and *On Human Nature* (1978) was met with huge controversy. Wilson argued that the constraints on human capacities can be explained in biological terms. His arguments were met by strong criticism, particularly by sociologists and others trained to believe that culture could explain human capacities. Nevertheless, some Chicago-style economists embraced the proposal that individual preferences could be explained in biological terms (Becker, 1976; Hirshleifer, 1977; Tullock, 1979). It was much later that some fringe sociologists began to argue that there were some significant biological determinants of human behaviour (Lopreato and Crippen, 1999). Peter Singer (1999) has attempted to turn the tide against the leftist critics, by arguing that biological influences and Darwinian ideas can sustain a reinvigorated politics of the left.

The sociobiology debate has continued for over thirty years, and taken many turns (Segerstråle, 2000). A prominent intermediate position has emerged in anthropology, with the idea of combining both cultural and genetic transmission in models of 'coevolution' or 'dual inheritance' (Boyd and Richerson, 1985; Durham, 1991).

The emergence of 'evolutionary psychology' in the 1990s introduced a new dimension to the controversy. Evolutionary psychology takes a diversity of forms (Barkow et al., 1992; Buss, 1999; Buller, 2005; Cosmides and John Tooby, 1994a, 1994b; Plotkin, 1997). Evolutionary psychologists argue that assumptions about the human psyche must be consistent with our understanding of the Darwinian evolution of the human species. Humans have existed for millions of years as groups of hunter-gatherers. Consequently, our mental capacities will largely reflect those relationships and that environment. These arguments have had some impact on the social sciences.

But the adoption of evolutionary ideas does not necessarily require the adoption of the view that human capacities are largely or entirely explicable in biological terms. As elaborated below, even the adoption of Darwinian ideas does not necessarily presuppose any particular degree of biological determination. Even if culture is much more important than biology in explaining human behaviour, there is the possibility, as Darwin himself suggested, that the Darwinian principles of variation, inheritance and selection apply directly to social as well as biological entities. This idea was originally suggested in politics by Walter Bagehot (1872), in epistemology by William James (1880), in ethics by Samuel Alexander (1892), in social theory by David Ritchie (1896), in economics by Thorstein Veblen (1899) and in sociology by Albert Keller (1915). But it lay underdeveloped until it was revived by the psychologist and polymath Donald T. Campbell (1965).

The idea of generalising Darwinian principles is present in key works in organisation science (Aldrich, 1999; Hannan and Freeman, 1989), in sociology (Blute, 1987, 1997; Runciman, 1998, 2001), in politics (John, 1999), and in economics (Hodgson and Knudsen, 2006a, 2010; Nightingale, 2000). The project to generalise Darwinian principles is discussed in more detail below.

Compared with economics, in sociology and politics the impact of evolutionary ideas and terminology has been relatively limited. This is partly because of the Durkheim–Parsons rejection of any explanation of social phenomena in biological terms. It is also because the ambiguous term 'evolution' is sometimes associated with untenable doctrines. For example Anthony Giddens (1979: 233) narrowly depicts evolutionary approaches as 'the progressive emergence of traits that a particular type of society is presumed to have within itself from its inception' and rejects them all for that reason. On the contrary, this unsophisticated preformationist view of evolution is on of several meanings of the term.

A FIRST CLASSIFICATION OF EVOLUTIONARY APPROACHES

There are a number of different ways of classifying different evolutionary approaches in the social sciences (Campbell, 1965; Hodgson, 1993, 1999, 2007). One relatively simple approach is to consider the difference between, first, the evolution (or development) of a single entity and, second, the evolution of a whole population of entities. In modern biology the former is referred to as development or ontogeny, and the latter as evolution or phylogeny. Accordingly, we may make the distinction between: (1) ontogenetic or developmental theories of social evolution that focus principally on a single entity or structure and consider its development through time; and (2) phylogenetic or population theories of social evolution that address the evolution of whole populations of entities.

For example, Hegel's and Marx's theories of history come into the category of ontogenetic or developmental theories of social evolution. In *Capital,* Karl Marx (1976: 90–92) focused on the development of the capitalism largely as a result of its own internal logic. Spencer (1862: 216) too was also primarily an ontogenetic theorist,

who defined evolution in terms of a single system and its 'change from an indefinite, incoherent homogeneity, to a definite, coherent heterogeneity through continuous differentiations'. Joseph Schumpeter was strongly influenced by Marx and focused principally on the development of singular systems. Like Marx, he saw evolution as a process of development of a system, largely 'from within' (Schumpeter, 1934: 63). A leading contemporary evolutionary economist who similarly emphasises endogenous change is Ulrich Witt (2003). Witt and others emphasise self-organisation as a spontaneous evolutionary process in society.

The idea of evolution 'from within' is a special type of ontogenetic theory. Crucially this stress on evolution 'from within', neglects interactions with the environment. In fact, many changes in society, the polity and the economy come about as a result of exogenous shocks. Developments from within are also important but it is a mistake to give them exclusive stress. The focus on self-organisation concentrates on the development of a single entity. It is inadequate to deal with cases of multiple entities. It provides no adequate explanation of how one entity rather than another adapts to survive in this environment.

Some versions of 'self-organisation' or 'self-transforming' evolution acknowledge the role of the environment. The emphasis is on the spontaneous generation of pattern in nature or institutional order in society. These phenomena are real and important. Nevertheless, the terminology can still be misleading and the ideas can be over-generalised. In biology neither individuals, species nor ecosystems are entirely 'self-transforming'. Evolution takes place within *open* systems involving *both* endogenous and exogenously stimulated change. Likewise, in social evolution, exogenously stimulated change is sometimes of great importance, partly because of the cultural mechanisms of imitation and conformism that tend to reduce internal variety and can lead to institutional ossification. Exogenous shocks sometimes overcome the rigidity of the system. On its own, self-organisation theory can adequately explain neither the current adaptedness nor the process of adaptation to the environment (Cziko, 1995: 323). Self-organisation is important in nature and society but it cannot offer a complete explanation of evolution in populations,

Concerning *phylogenetic or population theories of social evolution*, enlarging the scope of evolutionary theory from one entity to a population of entities introduces a number of additional and critical issues. First, there is the existence and possible regeneration of variety among this population. Second, there is the question of the differential survival of different members. As a result of either accident or differential fitness, some survive longer than others. Third, there is the possibility that some members of the population may pass on information concerning population solutions to others.

Immediately we are reminded of Darwin's (1859) famous trinity of principles of variation, selection and inheritance. Remarkably, however, as discussed later below, Darwinian ideas have been strongly resisted in the social sciences for most of the twentieth century. Some relatively recent and prominent works adopt the basic ideas of variation, selection and inheritance but play down (Hayek, 1979, 1988) or ignore (Nelson and Winter, 1982) their Darwinian pedigree.

Note that the difference between ontogenetic and phylogenetic theories of evolution stems from differences in the types of phenomena being addressed: ontogenetic theories address singular developing entities, while phylogenetic theories address populations. Matters are more complicated because phylogenetic evolution always involves the ontogenetic development of individual entities. Furthermore, ontogenetic development may involve phylogenetic selection of components, such as the selection of bacteria in the guts of animals, or the selection of routines within firms. These overlaps mean that ontogenetic and phylogenetic phenomena are sometimes confused, and a common mistake is to analyse phylogenetic phenomena in ontogenetic terms.

Problems and further taxonomic divisions arise when we consider what populations of entities are relevant in the social domain. While there was some early enthusiasm to apply Darwinian ideas to social evolution, particularly after the publication of Darwin's *Descent of Man* in 1871, this problem frustrated attempts to consider more precisely the mechanisms involved. Several early theorists of phylogenic social evolution regarded either human individuals or ideas as the relevant entities or units (Hodgson, 2004a: Chapter 5).

But the choice of individuals as the unit of selection in this context makes it difficult to distinguish the social and the biological levels among the evolutionary processes. A key question is this: what makes an entity social, rather than merely being a common attribute of a number of individuals?

The proposal to focus on populations of ideas – giving rise to what is described as 'cultural selection' – avoids the conflation of the biological and the cultural and for this reason it retains significant adherence among social scientists. But notwithstanding the success of modern theories of 'dual inheritance' (Boyd and Richerson, 1985; Durham, 1991) the detailed mechanisms involved in the transmission of ideas have been neglected. Part of the problem is that the status of ideas as mental rules or activities, recipes or behaviours, genotypes or phenotypes, still has not been resolved (Blackmore, 1999; Hull, 1982). Furthermore, it is doubtful whether the evolution of ideas captures all relevant essentials of social phenomena, particularly social structures, positions or institutions.

From this perspective, the early works of David Ritchie (1896), Thorstein Veblen (1899) and Albert Keller (1915) are extremely important because they were the first to consider explicitly the evolution of social institutions as elements of selection in a Darwinian process. However, despite these early important statements of the 'natural selection of institutions', the concept of social structure has yet to be adequately incorporated in a Darwinian evolutionary framework. And because of the unpopularity of this approach for much of the twentieth century, remarkably little progress to date has been made in following Ritchie, Veblen or Keller and establishing social institutions or structures as units of replication or selection. A pressing task is either to follow up these earlier hints in a rigorous way, or to show that such social units of replication or selection are unviable.

The case for following their lead is that in dealing with social phenomena we are addressing the phylogenetic evolution of populations of social entities, including firms, states and other institutions. A case has been made – but it remains controversial – that Darwinian principles apply in a generalised and abstract form to social evolution. The following sections address this issue and some of the controversies surrounding it.

DARWINISM AND THE EVOLUTION OF SOCIAL ENTITIES

Darwinism has revolutionised our understanding of the natural world. By contrast, it has had a limited impact in the social sciences. For much of the twentieth century, many social scientists upheld that biology is of little use in explaining social behaviour, and Darwinian principles are inapplicable to evolutionary processes in the social world. But since 1990 there has been increasing interest in the relevance of Darwinism for social science, both in terms of helping to explain underlying human dispositions, and providing general abstract principles to frame our investigations into evolutionary processes in society.

A host of misunderstandings surround the question of Darwinism and its relation with the social sciences. Contrary to widespread suppositions, Darwinism does *not* support any form of racism, sexism, nationalism or imperialism. Darwinism does *not* imply that

militant conflict is inevitable, that human inequalities or power or wealth are inevitable, that cooperation or altruism are unimportant or unnatural, that evolution always leads to optimisation or progress, that social phenomena can or should be explained in terms of biology alone, that organisms can or should be explained in terms of their genes alone, that human intention is unimportant, or that human agency is blind or mechanistic.

Very importantly, humans differ from plants and most animals, in that we have language and culture. We prefigure many actions and consequences in our minds, and act intentionally. The mechanisms of socio-economic evolution and biotic evolution are very different. In studying socio-economic evolution we are concerned with human welfare and well being, and not merely with survival or fecundity. All this is vitally important. But it does not diminish the importance or analytical value of Darwinism in the social domain.

As a basic tenet, Darwinism adopts the notion of *causal explanation*, where a cause is understood as necessarily involving transfers of matter or energy. Divine, spiritual, miraculous or uncaused causes are ruled out. Explanations of outcomes are in terms of connected causal sequences. Darwinism upholds that every event or phenomenon has a cause (Dennett, 1995; Hodgson, 2004b).

This applies to human intentionality as well as everything else. Contrary to widespread belief, causal explanation does not mean that intentions are ignored in Darwinism; it simply means that they are caused, and they have to be explained. Also contrary to widespread belief, the commitment to the idea that every event or phenomenon has a cause does not imply that every event is predictable, or event regularities are pervasive, or that the universe is a machine. The principle of causal determination is not the same as determinism, as it is often used. Although it is widely used by social scientists as a term of abuse, 'determinism' is an ambiguous and ill-defined term (Bunge, 1959; Hodgson, 2004a: 58–62).

The importance and enduring value of Darwinism is its elaboration of a causal mechanism of evolution involving the entwined triple concepts of variation, inheritance and selection. Darwinian evolution applies to populations of entities that face scarce resources and other difficulties, and can pass on adaptive solutions to these problems to their successors. In principle, these mechanisms could apply to any open and evolving system with a variety of units. Darwinian evolution occurs when there is some replicating entity that gives rise to imperfect copies of itself, and these copies do not have equal potential to survive.

The elucidation of these principles was nothing short of a scientific revolution. No other general systematic account of the evolution of such populations of complex entities has preceded or succeeded Darwinism.

The core ideas of Darwinism were not widely understood in the decades after 1859 (Bowler, 1988) and they are still widely misunderstood today. Darwin has been more widely associated with the proposition that humankind is descended from apes, rather than with his particular causal evolutionary mechanisms.

Despite the revival of 'evolutionary' ideas in the social sciences today, many devotees remain sceptical whether Darwinian ideas have any relevance to their field. Many retain 'evolutionary' claims for their theory but reject Darwinism as inappropriate. Some wrongly equate Darwinism with narrowly individualistic, selfish or anti-cooperative ideas that were not promoted by Darwin himself. Other critics address particular versions of 'Darwinism' that claim that evolution is always a progressive or optimising process. The critics then conclude that 'Darwinism' is inappropriate in the social domain. They seem unaware of Darwin's (1871: vol. 1, p. 166) own words that 'we are apt to look at progress as the normal rule in human society; but history refutes this'. However, in making this cautionary statement, Darwin did not refrain from applying his evolutionary principles to human society.

A pressing challenge for evolutionary thinkers in the social sciences today is to come to terms with Darwinism and its implications for the social as well as the biological world. A claim made by the present author and others is that Darwinism is the *only* general theoretical framework available to understand how evolution occurs among populations of entities – including firms and other organisations as well as biological organisms.

TWO WAYS IN WHICH DARWINISM MAY RELATE TO THE SOCIAL SCIENCES

In a highly prescient article of enduring significance, Campbell (1965) developed a taxonomy of different theories of the relationship between evolution in the natural and the social world. His primary and most important division was between theories that conceive of evolution that are (1) dependent on, or (2) independent of, changes in genetic characteristics. He then further subdivided each category according to the type of causal mechanism involved. The first category subdivided into (a) theories focusing on the influence of genes on social phenomena, (b) theories focusing on the influence of social phenomena on genes, and (c) theories focusing on the two-way interaction of genes with culture and other social phenomena. The third possibility was discussed at length by Campbell and has since been explored in further major contributions by Robert Boyd and Peter Richerson (1985), William Durham (1991) and others.

Campbell devised his taxonomy before the recent explosion of interest in evolutionary ideas in the social sciences. Debates since the 1990s over the relevance of Darwinism for economics have illuminated some important issues that are downplayed in Campbell's discussion. With the benefit of developments in recent decades, Campbell's original taxonomy can be revised (Hodgson, 2007).

There are two fundamental ways in which Darwinism has had, and can have, an impact on the social sciences. These two modes of application reflect a most fundamental distinction between ways in which theories may span the natural and the social world. These are as follows.

1 Theories of *interaction* – theories addressing the nature and extent of causal interaction between biological and social phenomena. Theories of this type consider causal mechanisms in either or both directions. There are also theories that deny significant causal influences from the natural to the social domain, or vice-versa. Within this set of theories there are those that consider the influence of biologically inherited characteristics on human dispositions and behaviour.
2 Theories of *communality* – theories addressing common laws or principles that apply to both biological and social phenomena. Such theories may or may not endorse an essential distinction between the biological and the social world. They focus on properties or processes, at some level of abstraction, that are shared by biological and social phenomena. There are also theories that deny significant communalities between biological and social phenomena.

Note that these two groups of theories both involve additional ontological claims, but of a different type. Theories of interaction focus specifically on causal connections, or the lack of them. By contrast, theories of communality concern the presence or absence of similarities or communalities at some level of abstraction, which may provide the foundations for concepts or theories shared by both domains.

Some recent theories of *interaction*, concern the influence of inherited biological characteristics on behaviour. Some earlier work in this area was influenced by sociobiology and retained notions of self-interested behaviour (Becker, 1976; Hirshleifer, 1977; Tullock, 1979). By contrast, the rigorous rehabilitation of the possibility of group selection in both the biological and the social world (Bergstrom, 2002; Henrich, 2004; Sober and Wilson, 1998) has opened up a broader debate concerning biological influences on human dispositions, including the idea that 'social' or 'other regarding' preferences have a biological as well as a cultural foundation. There is now a strong current of work in economics – formerly by contrast the exclusive province of self-interested 'economic man' – that argues that altruistic and cooperative behaviour has foundations in both social and biological evolution (Bowles and Gintis, 2005a, 2005b; Bowles, 2006; Field, 2001; Simon, 1990, 2005).

Among theories of *communality* there is an earlier wave of sociobiology-inspired theorists (Becker, 1976; Hirshleifer, 1977, 1985; Tullock, 1979) who propose that rational maximisation by and competition between individuals apply to both domains. This earlier wave was widely criticised by social scientists that denied such communality. This dismissal overlooked the possibility that there are such common principles, but they do not necessarily involve self-seeking behaviour and they may include altruism and cooperation in both domains. Darwin (1859, 1871) not only hinted that his ideas may apply to other evolving systems, including languages and social institutions, but also saw the evolutionary importance of altruism and cooperation in human society.

This idea of generalising the core Darwinian principles of variation, inheritance and selection was taken up by several authors after Darwin himself, and has recently enjoyed a revival in economics (Aldrich et al., 2008; Hodgson and Knudsen, 2006a, 2010; Nightingale, 2000), as well as being present in sociology (Runciman, 1997, 1998). Gary Cziko (1995) has described this as the 'second Darwinian revolution'. A generalised Darwinism does not claim that biological and social processes are similar at the level of detail, but that they share some common features at a high level of abstraction.

Generalising Darwinism is *not* about the use of biological analogies in the social sciences. It is about the existence of features and principles common to both the social and biological domain, at a high level of abstraction and not at the level of detail.

Note also that no particular theory of interaction flows logically from the idea of a generalised Darwinism. In particular, the proposal for a generalised Darwinism does not itself entail the proposition that human dispositions or behaviour are influenced by biological factors such as genes. Principles may be common to different sets of phenomena, independently of the degree of causal interaction between them.

Nevertheless, both theories of interaction and theories of communality have suffered from the long exclusion of biological ideas from the social sciences for much of the twentieth century. The taboo against biology is still highly significant in sociology and it even permeates some versions of 'evolutionary economics'. The fear of repetition of the horrific abuses of pseudo-biology in the twentieth century has curtailed much dialogue. Nevertheless, there has been such a conversation, in cycles of growing and then receding intensity over the last 150 years.

SOME PROBLEMS AND MISCONCEPTIONS

A number of objections, misconceptions and problems lie in the way of the project to generalise Darwinian principles so that they apply at an abstract level to both biological and social evolution. These include the proposals that Darwinism excludes or downplays human intentionality, that Darwinism is individualistic, and that social evolution is Lamarckian rather than Darwinian.

The commonplace objection that Darwinism downplays intentionality has been dealt with already. Darwin neither ignored nor underestimated the importance of intentionality, but he insisted that it must be subject to a causal and evolutionary explanation. For this reason Darwin (1859: 208; 1871: vol. 1, p. 46) saw the foreshadowing of human powers of reasoning and deliberation in some animals.

Darwin did not support rampant individualism. Referring explicitly to Smith's *Moral Sentiments*, Darwin (1871: vol. 1, pp. 81, 164) referred to 'the instinct of sympathy' and proposed that it 'was originally acquired, like all the other social instincts, through natural selection'. Darwin (1871: 162–163) also proposed that: 'Selfish and contentious people will not cohere, and without coherence nothing can be effected.' Altruism and cooperation with groups would also be promoted by natural selection. By contrast, the prevailing view of Darwin for much of the subsequent period was a champion of individualism and competition. This caricature was due more to his ideologically inclined admirers than Darwin himself. Nevertheless, it has dissuaded generations of social scientists from considering further the relevance of Darwinism for the understanding of human society (Degler, 1991; Hodgson, 2004a, 2004c).

Another prominent objection is that the processes of biological and socio-cultural evolution are so different that the generalisation of Darwinian principles to encompass them both is unwarranted or unhelpful (Fracchia and Lewontin, 1999; Nelson, 2006, 2007). The critique of Joseph Fracchia and Richard Lewontin (1999) rests on the claim that theories of cultural evolution lack an adequate concept of social structure, treating populations rather as aggregates. But they do not show that a Darwinian approach to social evolution would necessarily exclude an adequate treatment of social structures. By contrast, a multi-level Darwinian approach (including group selection) would require a notion of social structure to explain how groups or structured populations are maintained.

The argument that biological and social evolution are so different that the generalisation of Darwinian principles is unviable overlooks the fact that detailed mechanisms of evolution also differ greatly *within* the biological world. Biological organisms differ enormously in size, lifespan and reproductive fertility. Some species are social, others not. Haploid and diploid organisms have single and paired chromosomes respectively, and their mechanisms of reproduction differ in many ways. An even more fundamental difference is between prokaryotes (no cell nucleus) and eukaryotes (nucleated). The reproduction and selection of immunities and neural patterns involve very different processes, and these in turn are different from replication and selection of DNA, but all of these are subject to Darwinian principles (Darden and Cain, 1989; Edelman, 1987; Hull et al., 2001; Plotkin, 1994). As well as through seeds, some plants can reproduce by lateral root-sprouts or suckers, cloning a similar and independent plant with identical DNA. Generally, replication among invertebrates is very different from that among vertebrates. And so on.

The differences of mechanism *within* the biological world are as impressive in some ways as the differences between the biological and the social. Accordingly, the generalisation of the Darwinian principles within biology yields propositions of significance far beyond biology itself, encompassing the very different and itself intrinsically diverse world of social evolution. As David Hull (1988: 403) puts it, 'the amount of increased generality needed to accommodate the full range of biological phenomena turns out to be extensive enough to include social and conceptual evolution as well'.

As noted above, problems have arisen when the relevant units of selection have been addressed. Despite widespread and enduring enthusiasm for Richard Dawkins's (1976) concept of the 'meme' (Dennett, 1995; Blackmore, 1999), the new 'science of memetics' has not fulfilled its original promise. A major problem is that it is not clear what a meme is. The literature on memetics suffers from some confusion concerning the casual use of 'information' or 'ideas' as the analogue of the gene. Are memes (genotypic) instructions that drive behaviour, or (phenotypic) rationalisations of preceding actions or attitudes? Some meme enthusiasts wish to retain a broad definition of the meme, and

end up treating the meme as a genotype (or replicator) in one context, and a phenotype (or interactor) in another.

Resolution of these problems depends on adequate definitions of key concepts. In a manner similar to Kim Sterelny et al. (1996) and Peter Godfrey-Smith (2000), Dan Sperber (2000) refined a definition of the replicator. His argument was that entities described as memes could not universally qualify as replicators. One can respond by retreating from the idea that generalised Darwinian principles apply to social or cultural evolution. Alternatively one can move forward armed with more precise definitions to explore the potential of this project (Hodgson and Knudsen, 2006a, 2008, 2010). Only time will tell what response was the wiser.

But the project to generalise Darwinian principles does not depend on the concept of the meme and does not depend on the fate of memetics. Arguably it does depend on the identification of replicators and interactors in the social domain. Alternative and more precise candidates for social replicators are habits and routines, with organisations as interactors (Aldrich et al. 2008; Hodgson and Knudsen, 2004, 2006a, 2006b, 2006c, 2010).

The general importance of precise definitions – and the particular question of the meanings of replication or inheritance in the social domain – bears weightily on the issue of Lamarckism. A long list of eminent social scientists have described social evolution as 'Lamarckian' including Karl Popper (1972), Jack Hirshleifer (1977), Herbert Simon (1981), William McKelvey (1982), Richard Nelson and Sidney Winter (1982), John Gray (1984), Robert Boyd and Peter Richerson (1985), Friedrich Hayek (1988), Christopher Freeman (1992) and J. Stanley Metcalfe (1993). I have also been enticed by the label (Hodgson 1993).

A problem with this claim arises when Lamarckism and Darwinism are regarded as mutually exclusive alternatives. The proposition that social evolution is Lamarckian is wrongly taken to mean that it is not Darwinian. True enough, Lamarckian ideas have been marginalised in modern biology. But by contrast, Darwin (1859) himself openly embraced the idea of inheritance of acquired characters. Furthermore, the general Darwinian principles of variation, inheritance and selection logically do not rule out the possibility of acquired character inheritance. This point is generally overlooked in the organisation studies literature, where the important empirical dispute over whether populations of firms change predominantly through overall selection or individual adaptation is misinterpreted as a contest between 'Darwinian' and 'Lamarckian' theory (Hannan and Freeman, 1989; Usher and Evans, 1996; Van de Ven and Poole, 1995). In fact, in Darwin's own theory and all modern versions of Darwinism, *both* selection and individual adaptation are fully incorporated.

Dawkins (1983, 1986) argued powerfully that even if an evolutionary process is Lamarckian it would require Darwinism to complete its explanations. There must be some mechanism that minimises the inheritance of *injurious* characteristics. This mechanism is natural selection. Lamarckism, if valid in a particular domain, depends on Darwinian mechanisms of selection for evolutionary guidance. Even if social evolution was Lamarckian it would also *have to be* Darwinian.

Hull (1982) argued that memetic evolution cannot be Lamarckian, but it must be Darwinian. Hull denied that social learning could be treated as the inheritance of acquired characters – it is more like epidemiological infection or contagion. The inheritance of acquired ideas or memes is not an instance of the inheritance of acquired characters, because ideas and memes are analogous to genes, not characteristics. Hull thus underlined the importance of the genotype-phenotype distinction in the understanding of Lamarckism. Despite the popularity of the Lamarckian label in economics and other social sciences, it was a long time

before Dawkins's or Hull's arguments on Lamarckism had an impact.

GENERALISED DARWINISM AS A CHALLENGE FOR THE SOCIAL SCIENCES

Addressing theories of communality between the social and biological sphere, this section considers in more detail the possibility of generalising Darwinian principles to cover social evolution.

By the year 2000, biological theorists and philosophers of biology had made considerable progress in refining key Darwinian concepts such as selection (Hodgson and Knudsen, 2006c, 2010; Price, 1970, 1995) and replication (Godfrey-Smith, 2000; Sterelny et al., 1996; Sperber, 2000). This meant that it became possible to specify general Darwinian principles in more precise terms and their potential application to the social domain could be investigated with more rigour.

Despite the earlier precedents of Bagehot and Veblen, and the widespread interest in Darwinian ideas, until recently social scientists have been reluctant to consider the application of generalised Darwinian principles to their domain. Since 1990 the idea of a 'universal' or 'generalised' Darwinism has been taken up by some economists, sociologists, psychologists and organisation theorists with different degrees of reference to relevant preceding literature and with some variation of terminology (Herrmann-Pillath, 1991; Plotkin, 1994; Steele, 1996; Blute, 1997; Runciman, 1998; Aldrich, 1999; Nightingale, 2000; Pelikan, 2001; Hodgson, 2002; Stoelhorst, 2005; Hodgson and Knudsen, 2006a, 2010; Aldrich et al., 2008).

The idea of generalising Darwinism has been questioned and resisted, even by evolutionary economists (Cordes 2006, Nelson 2006, 2007, Witt 2006). A claim by the critics is that social and biological evolutionary are so different that common evolutionary principles cannot apply. By contrast, leading evolutionary economist Sidney Winter (1987: 617) argued that 'natural selection and evolution should not be viewed as concepts developed for the specific purposes of biology and possibly appropriable for the specific purposes of economics, but rather as elements of the framework of a new conceptual structure that biology, economics and other social sciences can comfortably share'.

Similarly, J. Stanley Metcalfe (1998: 21–22, 36) proposed that a common set of 'evolutionary ideas' apply to both social and biological phenomena: 'Evolutionary theory is a manner of reasoning in its own right quite independently of the use made of it by biologists. They simply got there first …'. But while upholding abstract principles that span both the biological and the social domain, Winter and Metcalfe refrained from describing them as Darwinian. According to the proponents of a generalised Darwinism, the only such general principles available in this broad context are those laid down by Darwin.

Despite the existence of the idea of a generalised Darwinism for 150 years since Darwin's *Origin,* we are entering an exciting new phase of theoretical development. It is too early to see where it will lead and what it will yield. The eventual challenge is to show that generalised Darwinism is more than definitional fine-tuning and abstract philosophising. Its proponents also have to show that it can have an important impact on the development of middle-range theory and serve as a useful guide for empirical enquiry.

CONCLUDING REMARKS

Despite the fact that 'evolution' is a broad and ill-defined term, many social scientists have energetically resisted such terminology, principally because it might serve as a Trojan Horse for biological ideas within the walls of the social sciences. These fears remain entrenched in some quarters, and debates about the possible contribution of biological ideas to the social sciences are ongoing.

Another group of social scientists have adopted 'evolutionary' terminology without any commitment to the possibility of explaining some human behaviour in biological terms. The fact that 'evolution' can have entirely different connotations in different scientific networks is testimony to its vagueness. Nevertheless, since the 1970s a number of important contributions have appeared in this genre, particularly in economics.

Since the 1990s a second front has been opened with debates about the possibility of generalising Darwinian ideas to processes in the social domain. Darwinism is a specific conception of evolution that applies to interacting entities in a population. The application of Darwinian principles is about generalisation rather than analogy, based on claims of ontological commonality at a highly abstract level. It is independent of whether some human behaviour can be explained in biological terms. This second front has already been opened within 'evolutionary economics' and organisation science. This debate is beginning to spread elsewhere.

For the foreseeable future these debates are likely to intensify rather than recede. Despite the huge variation of 'evolutionary' ideas in the social sciences the issues and debates involved are likely to have a major impact on the development of all the social sciences.

REFERENCES

Alchian, Armen A. (1950) 'Uncertainty, evolution, and economic theory', *Journal of Political Economy,* 58(2): 211–222.

Aldrich, Howard E. (1999) *Organizations Evolving.* London: Sage.

Aldrich, Howard E., Geoffrey M. Hodgson, David L. Hull, Thorbjørn Knudsen, Joel Mokyr and Viktor J. Vanberg (2008) 'In defence of generalized Darwinism', *Journal of Evolutionary Economics,* 18(5): 577–596.

Alexander, Samuel (1892) 'Natural selection in morals', *International Journal of Ethics,* 2(4): 409–439.

Bagehot, Walter (1872) *Physics and Politics, or, Thoughts on the Application of the Principles of 'Natural Selection' and 'Inheritance' to Political Society*. London: Henry King.

Barkow, Jerome H., Cosmides, Leda and Tooby, John (eds) (1992) *The Adapted Mind: Evolutionary Psychology and the Generation of Culture*. Oxford and New York: Oxford University Press.

Becker, Gary S. (1976) 'Altruism, egoism, and genetic fitness: Economics and sociobiology', *Journal of Economic Literature*, 14(2): 817–826.

Bergstrom, Theodore C. (2002) 'Evolution of social behavior: Individual and group selection', *Journal of Economic Perspectives*, 16(2): 67–88.

Blackmore, Susan (1999) *The Meme Machine*. Oxford: Oxford University Press.

Blute, Marion (1987) 'Biologists on sociocultural evolution: A critical analysis', *Sociological Theory*, 5: 185–193.

Blute, Marion (1997) 'History versus science: The evolutionary solution', *Canadian Journal of Sociology*, 22(3): 345–364.

Boulding, Kenneth E. (1981) *Evolutionary Economics*. Beverly Hills, CA: Sage.

Bowler, Peter J. (1988) *The Non-Darwinian Revolution: Reinterpreting a Historical Myth*. Baltimore: Johns Hopkins University Press.

Bowles, Samuel (2006) 'Group competition, reproductive leveling, and the evolution of human altruism', *Science*, 314(8): 1569–1572.

Bowles, Samuel and Gintis, Herbert (eds) (2005a) *Moral Sentiments and Material Interests: The Foundations of Cooperation in Economic Life*. Cambridge, MA: MIT Press.

Bowles, Samuel and Gintis, Herbert (2005b) 'Can self-interest explain cooperation?', *Evolutionary and Institutional Economics Review*, 2(1): 21–41.

Boyd, Robert and Richerson, Peter J. (1985) *Culture and the Evolutionary Process*. Chicago: University of Chicago Press.

Buller, David J. (2005) *Adapting Minds: Evolutionary Psychology and the Persistent Quest for Human Nature*. Cambridge, MA: MIT Press.

Bunge, Mario A. (1959) *Causality: The Place of the Causal Principle in Modern Science*. Cambridge, MA: Harvard University Press.

Buss, David M. (1999) *Evolutionary Psychology: The New Science of the Mind*. Needham Heights, MA: Allyn and Bacon.

Campbell, Donald T. (1965) 'Variation, selection and retention in sociocultural evolution', in H.R. Barringer, G.I. Blanksten and R.W. Mack (eds) (1965) *Social Change in Developing Areas: A Reinterpretation of Evolutionary Theory*. Cambridge, MA: Schenkman. pp. 19–49.

Cordes, Christian (2006) 'Darwinism in economics: From analogy to continuity', *Journal of Evolutionary Economics*, 16(5): 529–541.

Cosmides, Leda and Tooby, John (1994a) 'Beyond intuition and instinct blindness: Towards an evolutionary rigorous cognitive science', *Cognition*, 50(1–3): 41–77.

Cosmides, Leda and Tooby, John (1994b) 'Better than rational: Evolutionary psychology and the invisible hand', *American Economic Review (Papers and Proceedings)*, 84(2): 327–332.

Cziko, Gary (1995) *Without Miracles: Universal Selection Theory and the Second Darwinian Revolution*. Cambridge, MA: MIT Press.

Darden, Lindley and Cain, Joseph A. (1989) 'Selection type theories', *Philosophy of Science*, 56: 106–129.

Darwin, Charles R. (1859) *On the Origin of Species by Means of Natural Selection, or the Preservation of Favoured Races in the Struggle for Life*, 1st edition. London: Murray.

Darwin, Charles R. (1871) *The Descent of Man, and Selection in Relation to Sex*, 1st edition., 2 vols. London: Murray and New York: Hill.

Dawkins, Richard (1976) *The Selfish Gene*. Oxford: Oxford University Press.

Dawkins, Richard (1983) 'Universal Darwinism', in D.S. Bendall (ed.) *Evolution from Molecules to Man*. Cambridge: Cambridge University Press. pp. 403–425.

Dawkins, Richard (1986) *The Extended Phenotype: The Gene as the Unit of Selection*. Oxford: Oxford University Press.

Degler, Carl N. (1991) *In Search of Human Nature: The Decline and Revival of Darwinism in American Social Thought*. Oxford and New York: Oxford University Press.

Dennett, Daniel C. (1995) *Darwin's Dangerous Idea: Evolution and the Meanings of Life*. London and New York: Allen Lane, and Simon and Schuster.

Dosi, Giovanni, Freeman, Christopher, Nelson, Richard, Silverberg, Gerald and Soete, Luc L. G. (eds) (1988) *Technical Change and Economic Theory*. London: Pinter.

Durham, William H. (1991) *Coevolution: Genes, Culture, and Human Diversity*. Stanford: Stanford University Press.

Durkheim, Émile (1895) *Les Règles de la Méthode Sociologique*, 1st edition. Paris: Alcan.

Edelman, Gerald M. (1987) *Neural Darwinism: The Theory of Neuronal Group Selection*. New York: Basic Books.

Field, Alexander J. (2001) *Altruistically Inclined? The Behavioral Sciences, Evolutionary Theory, and the Origins of Reciprocity*. Ann Arbor: University of Michigan Press.

Fracchia, Joseph and Lewontin, Richard C. (1999) 'Does culture evolve?', *History and Theory*, 38(4): 52–78.

Freeman, Christopher (1992) *The Economics of Hope: Essays on Technical Change, Economic Growth and the Environment*. London and New York: Pinter.

Friedman, Daniel (1991) 'Evolutionary games in economics', *Econometrica*, 59: 637–666.

Giddens, Anthony (1979) *Central Problems in Social Theory*. Berkeley and Los Angeles: University of California Press.

Giddings, Franklin Henry (1896) *The Principles of Sociology: An Analysis of the Phenomena of Association and of Social Organization*. New York: Macmillan.

Godfrey-Smith, Peter (2000) 'The replicator in retrospect', *Biology and Philosophy*, 15: 403–423.

Gray, John (1984) *Hayek on Liberty*. Oxford: Basil Blackwell.

Hannan, Michael T. and Freeman, John (1989) *Organizational Ecology*. Cambridge, MA: Harvard University Press.

Hayek, Friedrich A. (1979) *Law, Legislation and Liberty; Volume 3: The Political Order of a Free People*. London: Routledge and Kegan Paul.

Hayek, Friedrich A. (1988) *The Fatal Conceit: The Errors of Socialism. The Collected Works of Friedrich August Hayek, Vol. I*, William W. Bartley III (ed.). London: Routledge.

Henrich, Joseph (2004) 'Cultural group selection, coevolutionary processes and large-scale cooperation', *Journal of Economic Behavior and Organization*, 53(1): 3–35.

Herrmann-Pillath, Carsten (1991) 'A Darwinian framework for the economic analysis of institutional change in history', *Journal of Social and Biological Structures*, 14(2): 127–148.

Hirshleifer, Jack (1977) 'Economics from a biological viewpoint', *Journal of Law and Economics*, 20(1): 1–52.

Hirshleifer, Jack (1985) 'The Expanding Domain of Economics', *American Economic Review*, 75(6): 53–68.

Hodgson, Geoffrey M. (1993) *Economics and Evolution: Bringing Life Back Into Economics*. Cambridge, UK and Ann Arbor, MI: Polity Press and University of Michigan Press.

Hodgson, Geoffrey M. (1999) *Evolution and Institutions: On Evolutionary Economics and the Evolution of Economics*. Cheltenham: Edward Elgar.

Hodgson, Geoffrey M. (2004a) *The Evolution of Institutional Economics: Agency, Structure and Darwinism in American Institutionalism*. London and New York: Routledge.

Hodgson, Geoffrey M. (2004b) 'Darwinism, causality and the social sciences', *Journal of Economic Methodology*, 11(2): 175–194.

Hodgson, Geoffrey M. (2004c) 'Social Darwinism in anglophone academic journals: A contribution to the history of the term', *Journal of Historical Sociology*, 17(4): 428–463.

Hodgson, Geoffrey M. (2007) 'Taxonomizing the relationship between biology and economics: A very long engagement', *Journal of Bioeconomics*, 9(2): 169–185.

Hodgson, Geoffrey M. and Knudsen, Thorbjørn (2004) 'The firm as an interactor: Firms as vehicles for habits and routines', *Journal of Evolutionary Economics*, 14(3): 281–307.

Hodgson, Geoffrey M. and Knudsen, Thorbjørn (2006a) 'Why we need a generalized Darwinism and why a generalized Darwinism is not enough', *Journal of Economic Behavior and Organization*, 61(1): 1–19.

Hodgson, Geoffrey M. and Knudsen, Thorbjørn (2006b) 'Dismantling Lamarckism: Why descriptions of socio-economic evolution as Lamarckian are misleading', *Journal of Evolutionary Economics*, 16(4): 343–366.

Hodgson, Geoffrey M. and Knudsen, Thorbjørn (2006c) 'The nature and units of social selection', *Journal of Evolutionary Economics*, 16(5): 477–489.

Hodgson, Geoffrey M. and Knudsen, Thorbjørn (2008) 'Information, complexity and generative replication', *Biology and Philosophy*, 43(1): 47–65.

Hodgson, Geoffrey M. and Knudsen, Thorbjørn (2010) *Darwin's Conjecture: The Search for General Principles of Social and Economic Evolution*. Chicago: University of Chicago Press.

Hofbauer, Josef and Sigmund, Karl (1998) *Evolutionary Games and Population Dynamics*. Cambridge: Cambridge University Press.

Hull, David L. (1982) 'The naked meme', in Henry C. Plotkin (ed.) *Learning, Development and Culture: Essays in Evolutionary Epistemology*. New York: Wiley. pp. 273–327.

Hull, David L. (1988) *Science as a Process: An Evolutionary Account of the Social and Conceptual Development of Science*. Chicago: University of Chicago Press.

Hull, David L., Langman, Rodney E., and Glenn, Sigrid S. (2001) 'A general account of selection: Biology, immunology and behavior', *Behavioral and Brain Sciences*, 24(3): 511–573.

James, William (1880) 'Great men, great thoughts, and the environment', *Atlantic Monthly*, 46: 441–459. Reprinted in James, William (1897) *The Will to Believe and Other Essays in Popular Philosophy*. New York and London: Longmans Green. pp. 216–254.

John, Peter (1999) 'Ideas and interests; agendas and implementation: An evolutionary explanation of policy change in British local government Finance', *British Journal of Politics and International Relations*, 1(1), April, pp. 39–62.

Keller, Albert Galloway (1915) *Societal Evolution: A Study of the Evolutionary Basis of the Science of Society*. New York: Macmillan.

Lopreato, Joseph and Crippen, Timothy (1999) *Crisis in Sociology: The Need for Darwin*. New Brunswick, NJ: Transaction.

Marx, Karl (1976) *Capital*, vol. 1, translated by Ben Fowkes from the fourth German edition of 1890. Harmondsworth: Pelican.

Maynard Smith, John (1982) *Evolutionary Game Theory*. Cambridge: Cambridge University Press.

McKelvey, William (1982) *Organizational Systematics: Taxonomy, Evolution, Classification*. Berkeley, CA: University of California Press.

Metcalfe, J. Stanley (1993) 'Some Lamarckian themes in the theory of growth and economic selection: A provisional analysis', *Revue Internationale De Systemique*, 7: 487–504.

Metcalfe, J. Stanley (1998) *Evolutionary Economics and Creative Destruction*. London and New York: Routledge.

Nelson, Richard R. (2005) *Technology, Institutions and Economic Growth*. Cambridge, MA: Harvard University Press.

Nelson, Richard R. (2006) 'Evolutionary social science and universal Darwinism', *Journal of Evolutionary Economics*, 16(5): 491–510.

Nelson, Richard R. (2007) 'Universal Darwinism and evolutionary social science', *Biology and Philosophy*, 22(1): 73–94.

Nelson, Richard R. and Winter, Sidney G. (1973) 'Towards an evolutionary theory of economic capabilities', *American Economic Review (Papers and Proceedings)*, 63(2): 440–449.

Nelson, Richard R. and Winter, Sidney G. (1982) *An Evolutionary Theory of Economic Change*. Cambridge, MA: Harvard University Press.

Nelson, Richard R. and Winter, Sidney G. (2002) 'Evolutionary theorizing in economics', *Journal of Economic Perspectives*, 16(2): 23–46.

Nightingale, John (2000) 'Universal Darwinism and social research: The case of economics', in William A. Barnett, Carl Chiarella, Steve Keen, Robert Marks and Hermann Schnabl (eds) (2000) *Commerce, Complexity, and Evolution*. Cambridge and New York: Cambridge University Press. pp. 21–36.

Parsons, Talcott (1937) *The Structure of Social Action*, 2 vols. New York: McGraw-Hill.

Pelikan, Pavel (2001) 'Self-organizing and Darwinian selection in economic and biological evolution: An enquiry into the sources of organizing information', in John Foster and J. Stanley Metcalfe (eds) *Frontiers of Evolutionary Economics: Competition, Self-Organization and Competition Policy*. Cheltenham: Edward Elgar: 121–151.

Penrose, Edith T. (1952) 'Biological analogies in the theory of the firm', *American Economic Review*, 42(4): 804–819.

Plotkin, Henry C. (1994) *Darwin Machines and the Nature of Knowledge: Concerning Adaptations, Instinct and the Evolution of Intelligence*. Harmondsworth: Penguin.

Plotkin, Henry C. (1997) *Evolution in Mind: An Introduction to Evolutionary Psychology*. Harmondsworth: Penguin.

Popper, Karl R. (1972) *Objective Knowledge: An Evolutionary Approach*. Oxford: Oxford University Press.

Price, George R. (1970) 'Selection and covariance', *Nature*, 227: 520–521.

Price, George R. (1995) 'The nature of selection', *Journal of Theoretical Biology*, 175: 389–396.

Ritchie, David G. (1896) 'Social evolution', *International Journal of Ethics*, 6(2): 165–181.

Ross, Edward Alsworth (1901) *Social Control: A Survey of the Foundations of Order*, 1st edition. New York: Macmillan.

Runciman, Walter Garry (1997) *A Treatise on Social Theory. Volume 3: Applied Social Theory*. Cambridge: Cambridge University Press.

Runciman, Walter Garry (1998) 'The selectionist paradigm and its implications for sociology', *Sociology*, 32(1): 163–188.

Runciman, Walter Garry (2001) 'From nature to culture, from culture to society', in Walter Garry Runciman (ed.) *The Origin of Human Social Institutions*. Oxford and New York: Oxford University Press. pp. 235–254.

Samuelson, Larry (1997) *Evolutionary Games and Equilibrium Selection*. Cambridge, MA: MIT Press.

Schumpeter, Joseph A. (1934) *The Theory of Economic Development: An Inquiry into Profits, Capital, Credit, Interest, and the Business Cycle*, translated by Redvers Opie from the second German edition of 1926, 1st edition, 1911. Cambridge, MA: Harvard University Press.

Schumpeter, Joseph A. (1942) *Capitalism, Socialism and Democracy*. London: George Allen and Unwin.

Segerstråle, Ullica (2000) *Defenders of the Truth: The Sociobiology Debate*. Oxford: Oxford University Press.

Simon, Herbert A. (1981) *The Sciences of the Artificial*, 2nd edition. Cambridge MA: MIT Press.

Simon, Herbert A. (1990) 'A mechanism for social selection and successful altruism', *Science*, 250: 1665–1668.

Simon, Herbert A. (2005) 'Darwinism, altruism and economics', in Kurt Dopfer (ed.) *Evolutionary Principles of Economics*. Cambridge and New York: Cambridge University Press. pp. 89–104.

Singer, Peter (1999) *A Darwinian Left: Politics, Evolution and Cooperation*. London, UK and New Haven, CT: Wiedenfeld and Nicholson and Yale University Press.

Sober, Elliott and Wilson, David Sloan (1998) *Unto Others: The Evolution and Psychology of Unselfish Behavior*. Cambridge, MA: Harvard University Press.

Spencer, Herbert (1862) *First Principles*, 1st edn. London: Williams and Norgate.

Spencer, Herbert (1873) *The Study of Sociology*, 1st edn. London: Williams and Norgate.

Sperber, Dan (2000) 'An objection to the memetic approach to culture', in Robert Aunger (ed.) (2000) *Darwinizing Culture: The Status of Memetics as a Science*. Oxford and New York: Oxford University Press. pp. 162–73.

Steele, Gerald Roy (1996) 'Universal Darwinism and the methodology of social science', *Journal of Social and Evolutionary Systems*, 19(4): 381–403.

Sterelny, Kim, Smith, Kelly C. and Dickison, Michael (1996) 'The extended replicator', *Biology and Philosophy*, 11: 377–403.

Stoelhorst, J. W. (2005) 'The naturalist view of universal Darwinism: An application to the evolutionary theory of the firm', in John Finch and Magali Orillard (eds) *Complexity and the Economy: Implications for Economic Policy*. Cheltenham, UK and Northamption, MA: Edward Elgar. pp. 127–147.

Sugden, Robert (1986) *The Economics of Rights, Co-operation and Welfare*. Oxford: Basil Blackwell.

Tullock, Gordon (1979) 'Sociobiology and economics', *Atlantic Economic Journal*, 7(1): 1–10.

Usher, John M. and Evans, Martin G. (1996) 'Life and death along gasoline alley: Darwinian and Lamarckian processes in a differentiating population', *Academy of Management Journal*, 39(5): 1428–1466.

Van de Ven, Andrew H. and Poole, Marshall Scott (1995) 'Explaining development and change in organizations', *Academy of Management Review*, 20(3): 510–540.

Veblen, Thorstein B. (1899) *The Theory of the Leisure Class: An Economic Study in the Evolution of Institutions*. New York: Macmillan.

Veblen, Thorstein B. (1919) *The Place of Science in Modern Civilization and Other Essays*. New York: Huebsch.

Ward, Lester Frank (1903) *Pure Sociology: A Treatise On the Origin and Spontaneous Development of Society*. New York and London: Macmillan.

Weibull, Jörgen W. (1995) *Evolutionary Game Theory*. Cambridge, MA: MIT Press.

Wilson, Edward O. (1975) *Sociobiology: The New Synthesis*. Cambridge, MA: Harvard University Press.

Wilson, Edward O. (1978) *On Human Nature*. Cambridge, MA: Harvard University Press.

Wilson, David Sloan and Wilson, Edward O. (2007) 'Rethinking the theoretical foundations of sociobiology', *Quarterly Review of Biology*, 82(4): 327–348.

Winter, Sidney G., Jr (1987) 'Natural selection and evolution', in John Eatwell, Murray Milgate and Peter Newman (eds) (1987) *The New Palgrave Dictionary of Economics*. London: Macmillan. Vol. 3, pp. 614–617.

Witt, Ulrich (2003) *The Evolving Economy: Essays on the Evolutionary Approach to Economics*. Cheltenham, UK and Northampton, MA: Edward Elgar.

Witt, Ulrich (2006) 'Evolutionary concepts in economics and biology', *Journal of Evolutionary Economics*, 16(5): 473–476.

21

Functionalism and Structuralism

Anthony King

INTRODUCTION

Although their relevance has receded today, functionalism and structuralism represented two of the most important intellectual strands especially in the middle decades of the twentieth century. Functionalism became the dominant intellectual framework for American sociology and in British social anthropology in this period, while structuralism became a central element in Continental social thought. This chapter explores the rise of functionalism and structuralism in twentieth century sociology and anthropology, considers briefly the criticisms of these approaches and describes the appearance of neo-functionalism in the 1990s in the work of Luhmann (1995; 1997) and Alexander (1998). It cannot, of course, claim to be comprehensive. Throughout the twentieth century, functionalism and structuralism assumed a multiplicity of forms across the disciplines in the social sciences, including psychology and politics. A major strand of European integration theory describes itself as functionalist (Haas, 1964), while structural Marxism developed into an important research programme especially in the 1970s (Althusser, 1977a, 1977b; Miliband, 1970; Poulantzas, 1975). Blau's 'exchange structuralism' (1964, 1975), as Turner (1978) called

it, is absent. It is impossible to discuss all the manifold varieties of functionalism and structuralism within this context. However, it is possible to delineate some of the main contributions to functionalism and structuralism in order to identify major strands of thought. The chapter concludes by suggesting that in the current historical conditions, social scientists may finally be moving beyond functionalism and structuralism, converging on an 'interactionist' position which genuinely transcends the twentieth century.

TWENTIETH CENTURY FUNCTIONALISM

British structural functionalism

In a typically ironic article, Ernest Gellner described, how Bronislaw Malinowski, the architect of British structural-functionalism, 'supplanted and killed' James Frazer's evolutionary anthropology, just as the Kings of the Woods at Nemi were themselves slain by their successors in Frazer's famous work, *The Golden Bough* (Gellner, 1988: 171; Jarvie, 1964: 43).[1] For Gellner, 1922, when Malinowski published *The Argonauts of the Western Pacific* (Malinowski, 1964), was the *annus mirabilis* of British social anthropology. This intellectual revolution comprised two elements; methodological and theoretical. First, in contrast to the dependence of Victorian anthropologists on archives of often dubious reliability, Malinowski invented anthropological fieldwork (Malinowski, 1964: 3–25). He turned his forced detention as a foreign national in the British Empire during the First World War into a research method, living with his subjects, the Trobriander Islanders, for extended periods to engage in participant observation with them. Although Malinowski could not be accorded total responsibility for this innovation, *The Argonauts* certainly demonstrated the fertility of ethnographic fieldwork as a method.

Second, *The Argonauts* also represented an important intellectual breach with Victorian evolutionism. *The Argonauts* was a richly empirical work and the theory of 'functionalism' was only ever implicit within it. However, it pointed forward to a new anthropological paradigm which would become known as functionalism. Malinowski later elaborated his functionalist theoretical position much more fully and it is this upon which Gellner has focused. In particular, as Gellner emphasised, Malinowski's functionalism was predicated on a rejection of the concept of survivals, so essential to *The Golden Bough* (Malinowski, 1944). Where Frazer maintained that exotic and apparently irrational practices should be seen a survivals from previous periods yet to be eliminated through a process of rational evolution, Malinowski insisted that all social practices, however apparently bizarre, were sustained only because they had social efficacy in the present. It was implausible to claim that humans would invest time and resources in a practice which had become entirely otiose. In a short essay on the topic, Malinowski used the example of London handsome cabs and fireplaces to illustrate the point. Both cabs and fireplaces were obsolete in the twentieth century as cars and gas heaters appeared

but neither could genuinely be described as mere survivals, retained because the native English were not yet rational enough to eliminate them. Cabs and fireplaces also had a clearly identifiable, rational function; they were deliberately 'used for retrospective sentiment', reflecting contemporary English attitudes on the 'sportive types of life and attachment to the domestic role' (Malinowski, 1944: 28–29). In short, past practices persisted only when they 'acquired new meanings'. Philosophically, survivals were impossible; they were, in fact, continually reinvested with new meaning and new purpose by living humans. They were given new functions and were not ultimately survivals at all.

From the rejection of survivals, Malinowski went on to develop an explicitly functionalist theory. British structural functionalism is typically described as conceiving society as an organic whole, the institutions in which function to sustain the whole. This kind of functionalism is very evident in the work of Radcliffe-Browne, where it was explicitly elaborated in terms of a complex of institutional roles which together sustained the society (Radcliffe-Browne, 1971: 11). Society was a self-referencing organism the institutions in which functioned to sustain the whole. By contrast, Malinowski's formal statement of functionalist theory differs somewhat from the standard organicist account. Malinowksi's functionalism is highly individualistic and, indeed, almost utilitarian. Malinowski maintained that society had to fulfil certain functions in order to sustain and reproduce itself. At base, these individual needs were biological. Malinowski was well aware of certain cultural needs, such as the requirement for meaning and association but he regarded the individual biological need to eat, shelter and procreate as primary. After all, without performing these acts, the individual would die and therefore society would not be sustained or reproduced. Society had to fulfill these biological imperatives. Malinowski's biological functionalism is not wholly crude. He recognised that humans had to co-operate with each other to provide for individual biological needs. Consequently, societies developed social and cultural institutions whose function was integrative; they organised individuals in order to fulfill collective functions. Although theoretically of second order, these institutions are finally essential to meeting fundamental biological needs. As Malinowski described, drives gave rise to co-operation and training groups, on the one hand, and techniques (including law, customs and ethics), on the other. These in turn produced 'artifacts' which ultimately led to 'integral satisfaction' (Malinowski, 1944: 141).

Malinowski may, in his theoretical writing, have proffered an individualistic and biological functionalism but, in his ethnographic work, he forwarded a more conventional institutional approach, which was typical of the work of other functionalists such as Radcliffe-Brown. This can be clearly seen in his analysis of Trobriand myth. Malinowski tried to demonstrate that these sacred stories were not irrational fantasies which obscured reality. Rather, myths functioned as sociological charters, justifying the social hierarchy and therefore inducing stability. Thus, the Trobriand origin myths describe the creation of the world. On this narrative, totemic animals emerged successively out of a hole in the ground, which Tobriands pointed out to Malinowski. The order in which the totemic animals appeared from the hole matched the hierarchy of the clans. The Dog, totem of the Lukuba clan came out first and, accordingly, was originally the senior clan. The pig of the Malasi clan came out next but, conveniently in the current myth, it saw the dog eating noku plant and cried; 'Thou eatest noku, thou eatest dirt: though art a low-bred, a commoner: the chief, the guya'u, shall be I' (Malinowski, 1974: 112). In this way, the highest subclan of Malasi clan justified their claim to the chiefdom. Malinowski recognised that the myth is an absurd story but, rather than an irrationality, it had a practical function in the present, whose function is identifiable. It affirmed the social hierarchy.

In reality, the ethnographies of British anthropologists in the middle decades of the twentieth century frequently exceeded their functionalist frameworks, to describe a more dynamic process of interaction and negotiation among native peoples than functionalism ever formally allowed. Malinowski's original work on the Trobriand's demonstrated not simply how the Kula exchange sustained by the social whole. Specifically, the work primarily sought to reject the economic 'utilitarian' paradigm, founded on the concept of the rational actor, which Malinowski regarded as the dominant philosophy in the social sciences at that time (Malinowski, 1964: 60). The work sought to demonstrate that the existence of the rational self-interested actor could not be assumed to be universal. Indeed, coherent economic practices could not be explained merely by reference to rational self-interest alone. On the contrary, economic exchange in fact presumed a common culture, shared understandings, on the basis of which participants could interact and exchange with each other. Consequently, Malinowski's analysis of the ceremonial exchange in the Trobriands demonstrated that economic activity was inextricable from the social contexts in which it took place. The Kula was a symbolic device to affirm but also to re-negotiate a complex political hierarchy. Similarly, Evans-Pritchard's (1950) analysis of Zande witchcraft describes the virtuosic local use of witchcraft to manipulate political and social relations in that society. Meyer Fortes' work on kinship (1949), perhaps, began to transcend functionalism most fully, noting that the reality of kinship relations did not match the formally described institution of marriage and affinity. Anticipating Bourdieu (1977), the model of kinship was a collective resource used to justify familial strategies rather than as representation of reality. Nevertheless, despite the potential dissonance between the theory and practice, in the middle decades of the twentieth century British social anthropology was oriented to a structural-functionalist paradigm in which institutions were understood to support the organic social whole. As such, it was a powerful and unified research programme.

Parsonian structural functionalism

British structural-functionalism is recognised as an important intellectual paradigm within anthropology. In fact, its influence was far greater. In particular, British structural-functionalism played a significant role in the development of one of the most famous forms of functionalism in the social sciences in the twentieth century – the work of Talcott Parsons. In the 1930s, Parsons had taken a master's degree at the LSE where he was lectured by Bronislaw Malinowski. As various commentators have noted, Parsons, especially in his early period, was deeply influenced by Malinowski (Gerhardt, 2005, 2002; Robertson and Turner, 1989, 1991). The nature and extent of this influence is often under-emphasised but it is pronounced. *The Argonauts* primarily sought to reject the economic 'utilitarian' paradigm, founded on the concept of the rational actor, which Malinowski regarded as the dominant philosophy in the social sciences at that time. The work sought to demonstrate that the existence of the rational self-interested actor could not be assumed to be universal. Indeed, coherent economic practices could not be explained merely by reference to rational self-interest alone. On the contrary, economic exchange in fact presumed a common culture, or shared understandings, on the basis of which participants could interact and exchange with each other. Consequently, Malinowski's analysis of the ceremonial exchange in the Trobriands demonstrated that economic activity presumed a shared culture which coordinated exchanges. Malinowski's critique of utilitarianism and his emphasis on shared culture as a basis of social action had a profound effect on Parsons. Indeed, *The Structure of Social Action* (1937/1966), Parsons' first major opus, might be read as a theoretical elaboration of Malinowski's ethnography.

Accordingly, *The Structure of Social Action* addressed the 'problem of social order'; Parsons sought to establish the fundamental basis of social action. He wanted to develop a theory which adequately explained how humans were able to co-ordinate their activities, co-operate and engage in regular social practice. Like Malinowski, the central purpose of the work was to reject utilitarian individualism which Parsons also regarded as the dominant philosophical paradigm at the time. Parsons famously demonstrated that on the individualist premises of utilitarianism,[2] social order was impossible. Parsons brilliantly noticed that the attempt to explain social order from the premise of rational, autonomous actors led to two unacceptable theoretical positions, which he called the 'utilitarian dilemma'.

> Either the active agency of the actor in the choice of ends is an independent factor in action, and the end element must be random; or the objectionable implication of randomness is denied, but then their independence disappears and they are assimilated to the conditions of the situation, that is to elements analyzable in terms of nonsubjective categories, principally heredity and environment. (Parsons, 1966: 64)

Utilitarianism must either assume that rational individuals are themselves determined by objective factors and, therefore, not independent or the autonomy of individuals was maintained, their choices were random and social order remained inexplicable. On a utilitarian account, social order could not be explained.

In addition to its critique of utilitarianism, *The Structure of Social Action*, sought to demonstrate a theoretical convergence between Marshall, Pareto, Weber and Durkheim (Camic, 1991). According to Parsons, all these scholars finally reached the same conclusion – against a utilitarian account – that social order can be explained only by reference to the existence of shared values and understandings. Here, his debt to Malinowski was once again very clear. 'A society can only be subject to a legitimate order, and therefore can be on a non-biological level something other than a balance of power of interests, only in so far as there are *common* value attitudes in the society' (Parsons, 1966: 670, 392).

Individuals are able to co-ordinate their actions because they share normative orientations; they commit themselves to common ends and means. They agree to unite themselves around common ends and bind each other to them. Consequently, they can engage in predictable and co-operative action. Precisely because participants must recognise and understand what these common values enjoin, Parsons avoids the second horn of the utilitarian dilemma. Social actors are not determined; they understand what they are doing and knowingly obligate themselves to shared ends. On Parsons' voluntaristic theory of action, they remain conscious, active participants in social action. However, common values involve compulsion unrecognised by utilitarianism. Individuals, on Parsons' model, are not rational, independent agents, free to do as they please. Shared values imply a moral obligation. Accordingly, participants enforce normative obligations on themselves and each other. The compulsion evident in social action exists but is created by the mutual interaction of the participants.

The Structure of Social Action is not explicitly a work of structural functionalism. It is a sociological critique of individualism. Parsons began to develop an explicitly structural-functionalist – or systems theory (Munch, 1982; Rocher, 1975) – approach only later in his 'middle period' usually dated to the early 1950s when he published a number of important works including *The Social System* (1952). From this time on, Parsons was concerned not so much with the problem of order but with how society with its major institutions coheres as a whole. As he addressed this question, he began to develop an approach which has been widely described as 'structural-functionalist'. There is considerable debate between scholars as to whether Parsons' middle 'structural-functionalist' period, constitutes a break from his early work. This cannot be determined

finally in this context; John Holmwood has argued for continuity (2006a, 2006b, 1996), while others (Martindale 1971; Gould, 1989, 1991; King, 2004; Schutz, 1978) maintain a divide in his work. It seems likely that at least the analytical focus minimally changed from the question of how participants co-ordinated their social action to a focus on the social system as a whole. As Parsons noted at the beginning of *The Social System*.

> The focus of this work, then, is within the action frame of reference as just outlined, on the theory of social systems. It is concerned both with personality and with culture, but not for their own sakes, rather in their bearing on *the structure and functioning* of the social system. (Parsons, 1952: 18–19, italics added)

Parsons understood the social system as a structure of roles and he saw the connection between roles, institutions and function in the following way:

> Roles are, from the point of view of the functioning social system, the primary mechanism through which the essential functional prerequisites of the system are met. There is the same order of relationship between roles and functions relative to the system in social systems, as there is between organs and functions in the organism. (Parsons, 1952: 115)[4]

Society is a system which consists of functionally necessary roles. Crucially, these roles can be fulfilled adequately only if individual role-takers internalise the appropriate norms. The concept of norms remained central to Parsons. However, in his middle period, Parsons no longer stressed that values are held in common as he did in *The Structure*. Individuals no longer agree to abide by shared norms which mutually obligated them to each other. Rather, they internalise institutional ones: 'It is only by virtue of internalisation of institutionalized values that a genuine motivational integration of behaviour in the social structure takes place, that the 'deeper' layers of motivation become harnessed to the fulfilment of role-expectations' (Parsons, 1952: 42). As the statement demonstrates, the key question for Parsons has become the issue of how individuals are integrated into their social roles. This is possible insofar as individuals internalise these institutional values. Significantly, Parsons maintains that this process of internalisation is Freudian. Indeed, Parsons' middle period and the development of his structural-functionalist theory could be substantially explained in terms of the influence of Freud's psycho-analysis. On this account, individuals absorb role norms privately. They create a superego for themselves which represses the ego and the id. In Parsons' mature functionalism, individuals now internalise autonomous norms and ensure their own adherence to these norms through private psychological processes of personal guilt and shame.

The internalisation of norms is central to Parson and he emphasises the point repeatedly. Thus he asks: 'will the personalities developed within a social system, at whatever stage in the life cycle, 'spontaneously' act in such ways as to fulfil the functional prerequisites of the social systems of which they are parts …?' (Parsons, 1952: 31). The answer for Parsons is predictably that such personalities will be developed so long as individuals internalise the appropriate institutional values for their role.

> The primary structure of the human personality *as a system of action* is organised about the internalization of *systems* of social objects which originate as the role-units of the successive series of social systems in which the individual has come to be integrated in the course of his life history. His personality structure is thus in sense a kind of 'mirror-image' of the social structures he has experienced. (Parsons and Bales, 1955: 54)

Unlike British functionalist anthropology, in *The Social System*, Parsons did not discuss empirically – or even theoretically – how the system was sustained by the fulfillment of institutional functions. Rather, having sketched out a theoretical outline of functionalism, Parsons developed an analytical scheme which he termed 'pattern variables'. The pattern variables consisted of four abstract categories, specificity or diffuseness,

neutrality or affectivity (Parsons, 1952: 84ff), which putatively enabled the sociologist to categorise every possible kind of norm and, therefore, every kind of role. Many commentators have been dismayed by Parsons' approach, noting that while Parsons claimed that the pattern variables represented were analytical, in fact they were no more than formal concepts which merely categorised roles, rather than provide a sociological explanation of them (Alexander, 1984).

In *Working Papers in the Theory of Action*, published less than a year after *The Social System*, Parsons committed himself to the so-called AGIL schema instead of the pattern variables.[5] Parsons was heavily influenced by Robert Bales' 'interchange' model which was designed to describe the structure of all small group interaction. Bales described the interchange model as involving adaptation to the environment (A), goal-attainment (G), group integration (I) and pattern-maintenance or latency (L). Through Bales' interchange model, which Parsons called the 'AGIL' model after the first letters of the four elements the model, Parsons believed he could create a general social theory which could be used at any analytical level from the institutional to the personal (Parsons et al., 1953: 63). Parsons argued that the social system consists of subordinate institutions (sub-systems) which can be understood as fulfilling four separate functions; adaptation, goal attainment, integration and latency. However, his application of this functional theory was formal. For instance, Parsons somewhat bizarrely applies the AGIL model to European society arguing that Renaissance Italy provided the latency function in this social system; it unified Europe culturally. Although the AGIL schema was intended to be analytical, it marks the apotheosis of Parsons' formalism. From the early 1950s onwards, this schema is employed to explain (but really only to formalise) everything (Wright Mills 1959).[6]

Although Parsons may have retreated into conceptual formalism, he was central to the functionalist paradigm in American sociology. There were some important contributions to functionalist analysis in the middle of the twentieth century. Undoubtedly the most celebrated of these contributions was Robert Merton's (1957) concept of manifest and latent function. In his discussion of the distinction, Merton draws a distinction 'between conscious motivations for social behavior and its objective consequences'. While social actors may prioritise their conscious motivations, it is essential that the social scientist recognises both unintended consequences of an action and indeed, the unrecognised pressures that might drive a group of actors into a particular course of action. Merton claimed that one of the most important benefits of the concept of manifest and latent functions as a heuristic device was that it allowed the social scientists to explain apparent irrationalities – the link with Malinowski's argument against survivals is close here. Merton cites the example of Hopi Rain ceremonies:

> to be sure, our meteorologists agree that the rain ceremonial does not produce rain; but this is hardly to the point ... Ceremonials may fulfill the latent function of reinforcing the group identity by providing a periodic occasion on which the scattered members of a group assemble to engage in a common activity.

The concept of latent and manifest function is, as Merton emphasises, potentially very fruitful for social scientists. It encourages sociologists to situate actions in a wider social context in order to explain their unrecognised origins and unintended consequences. As such, the concept of the latent function demonstrates the heuristic usefulness of the organic metaphor so often associated with functionalism.

During the middle decades of the twentieth century, functionalism became the dominant paradigm in British social anthropology and American sociology and important research was conducted in its name. The prominence of functionalism during this century has been connected to wider political economic conditions. Functionalism conceived of society as unified around common values, the institutions of which were united into a coherent self-supporting whole. In this way, the fundamental principle of functionalism seemed have an elective affinity with the Keynesian, statist regulatory regime which was dominant in Europe and America in this period. In particular, functionalism rejected utilitarianian individualism in favour of collectivism and, reflecting the international order of the twentieth century which consisted of more or less independent states, functionalism, presumed the existence of more or less autonomous societies. Parsons' functionalism in particular could be most easily characterised as an abstract sociology of American Fordism.

Perhaps inevitably, as that regulatory regime began to fragment, functionalism itself was increasingly called into question. From the 1960s, the critiques of functionalism began to appear, coinciding with the crisis of twentieth century capitalism. Critics rejected functionalism on three basic grounds. First, functionalism reduced agents to 'cultural dopes', explaining social activity independently of the understanding of participants. The revolution was begun by Talcott Parsons's own student, Harold Garfinkel and Erving Goffman, but by the early 1970s a doctrinal refutation of Parsons was almost a requirement to undertake postgraduate work in the Anglophone academy. Gouldner's famous work (1971) on the controversies of this period illustrates many of the tensions but is also an excellent example of the critique of Parsons from this period (Giddens, 1977). Secondly, since functionalism prioritised the maintenance of the social whole, it seemed to ignore the issues of power, contestation and exploitation, as well as individual strategy (Asad, 1973; Wrong, 1964). The conflict theorists of the 1960s, such as Ralf Dahrendorf or Lewis Coser, sought to replace apparently consensual functionalism with an approach which understood social reality in terms of the clash of interests. The Marxism and feminism which appeared in the 1970s might be aligned alongside Dahrendorf. These approaches also rejected Parsonian functionalism, understanding social reality in terms of fundamental divisions of interest. Third, ignoring history, functionalism seemed to be incapable of explaining social change (Jarvie, 1964). It was accused of being a theory of equilibrium not social change (Turner, 1978).

FRENCH STRUCTURALISM

In the United States and Britain, functionalism was the dominant research programme in the mid-twentieth century but, in France, an alternative approach was more evident: structuralism. Of course, Ferdinand de Saussure's *Course in General Linguistics* is widely regarded as the seminal work in twentieth century structuralism and was central to the development of a structural paradigm, not only in linguistics but across the social sciences much more widely. In that work, Saussure propounded an approach to the study of language which he hoped would germinate a radically new research programme in linguistics. In the *Course*, Saussure argued that words in a language did not gain their meaning from their objective reference as linguistics had widely assumed. On the contrary, with the minor exception of onomatopoeia, words were arbitrary 'sound-images' which became signifiers only in reference to the other words in a language. As a sound image (a phoneme), a word signified an object because it was differentiated from other sounds. A word's distinctiveness in the linguistic system allowed it to operate as a meaningful sign; 'Everything that has been said up to this point boils down to this; in language there are only differences' (Saussure, 1966: 120). Saussure gave the example of the Geneva-to-Paris train. Each train on this route gained its significance not from any intrinsic property (it was the same as any other train) but from its temporal distinction

from pluralise train; it was leaving at a different time to all other trains. Consequently, a linguistic system forms a synchronic unity on which speakers draw when they engage in diachronic speech. Linguistics identifies this hidden structure.

In the social sciences, the anthropology of Claude Levi-Strauss was one of the most important examples of French structuralism in the twentieth century.[3] Levi-Strauss was initially influenced by the Annales school and the work of Durkheim and Mauss, particularly *Primitive Classification* (1963) and *The Gift* (1967). While *Primitive Classification* opened up the question of cultural classifications, *The Gift* prioritised exchange and reciprocity as critical to social order. Both of these themes became central to Levi-Strauss's work. Indeed, in his first major work, *The Elementary Structures of Kinship* (1969), which describes the structure of different kinds of marriage patterns, he attempted to apply Mauss' concept of the gift to the question of the exchange of women. The work provided a quite different account of kinship structures than those typically found in British ethnographies of the period. Levi-Strauss was not so much concerned with how kinship structures functioned to sustain particular societies. Rather, he sought to elaborate the underlying logic connecting kinship forms and marriage patterns, identifying patterns of generalised and restricted exchange.

In the 1950s, the influence of structural linguistics and, especially, the work of Roman Jakobson and his concept of the binary opposition became increasingly central to Levi-Strauss' writing, although Levi-Strauss had originally attended a course of lectures by Jakobson in 1942–1943. He recognised a convergence between the methods developed by Prague phonology for reducing the diversity of phonological facts to a rational order and the method that he was himself developing in the analysis of kinship phenomena (Clarke, 1981: 157). As Levi-Strauss later noted: 'I can now, many year later, recognise more clearly than ever those themes in these lectures which most influenced me' (Levi-Strauss, 1978: xvii–iii; 1985: 142). Crucially, 'what I was to learn from structuralist linguistics was, on the contrary, that instead of losing one's way among the multitude of different terms the important thing is to consider simpler and more intelligible relations by which they are interconnected' (Levi-Strauss, 1978: xii; 1985: 139). The concept of the opposition was central to Levi-Strauss's discoveries. For instance,

> the meaning of marriage rules, which is incomprehensible when they are investigated in isolation, can only emerge by seeing them as mutual oppositions, in the same way that the true nature of the phoneme does not lie in its phonic individuality but in the oppositive and negative relations in which phonemes stand to one another. (Levi-Strauss, 1978: xviii; 1985: 142)

The importance of binary oppositions became particularly obvious with the publication of *The Savage Mind* (1966). In that work, Levi-Strauss described his approach as a reaction to functionalism. While functionalism adopted a commonsensical approach to the study of institutions and their operations, Levi-Strauss focused on what he regarded as more fundamental and obscure issues of cognition. He was interested in exposing the underlying cultural logics which patterned all human existence into coherent forms (e.g. 1973: 178–197). He shared some of functionalism's concerns, however. Against western ethnocentricism, he similarly rejected the notions that natives were stupid or childlike. Rather, he wanted to demonstrate that their thinking was 'rational' and, in fact, a form of science: not its poor cousin. He argued primitive thought was ordered not according to practical need but by the need to fit things into a classification system. *The Savage Mind* operated on a principle of *bricolage* where objects are stored not with a view to practical mastery but because they fit the existing into the classification system. For Levi-Strauss, the bricolage of the totemic savage mind was demonstrated by food taboos: 'It meets intellectual requirements rather than or instead of satisfying needs' (Levi-Strauss, 1966: 9). In short, food accords with the classification system. Thus, Levi-Strauss examined the way that among the Fang of Gabon, the eating of squirrel was banned to pregnant women. There is a clear cultural logic to this prescription. The Fang fear that the foetus will copy the squirrel and stay in its hole (Levi-Strauss, 1966: 61). Illustrating the universal operations of the human mind, Levi-Strauss noted similar cultural logics at work in other tribal groups. For instance, among the Hopi, burrowing animals are regarded favourably as food for pregnant women precisely because they get out of hole (Levi-Strauss, 1966: 61). For Levi-Strauss, these deep structural patterns recur across cultures, constituting the very nature of social reality. On the basis of these underlying cognitive templates, humans order their natural and social worlds, constituting what they in fact are. Paul Ricoeur (1992) perceptively described Levi-Strauss as a Kant without the categorical imperative. Levi-Strauss' binary structures were the equivalent of Kant's transcendental categories of apperception which made any experience possible.

The structural emphasis on enduring and underlying cognitive patterns is apparent in *The Savage Mind* and, during his subsequent work, the theme of binary oppositions becomes central to Levi-Strauss' analysis. Sometimes, this interest in binary oppositions reflects the empirically observable use of binaries in native cultures. Thus, in his brilliant discussion of north-west coast masks, Levi-Strauss notes the relationship between Kwakiutl Dzonokwa and the Salish Swaihwé masks; each is an inversion of the other. One is white, the other black, one has concave eyes, the other protruding eyes, one a lolling tongue, the other a pursed mouth (Levi-Strauss, 1983: 93): 'They are parts of a system with which they transform each other' (Levi-Strauss, 1983: 93). While the Kwakiutl Xwexwe mask embodied avarice, the Swaihwé (like the Dzonokwa mask) was seen as the propitious source of wealth with the power to transform 'real or virtual enemies into affines' (Levi-Strauss, 1983: 118). Accordingly, Levi-Strauss observed that the Swaihwé mask was structured around oppositions of water, land, up and down, human and animal. Levi-Strauss argued, therefore, that the Swaihwé mask represents the liminal realm between opposites; it signifies exchange between elements. It 'brings off the most improbably consents' (Levi-Strauss, 1983: 118). As such in a culture based on gift exchange, it is invested with great significance as a beneficent force. Yet, Levi-Strauss' structural analysis extended well beyond the interpretation of recognised binaries in native cultures. He sought to reveal the underlying, unconscious binary oppositions which structure human culture and therefore social reality, for the most part unknowingly (Levi-Strauss, 1966: 20–33). His analysis of the Oedipus myth is only one example of this interpretative licence where he imposed external meaning in accordance with his binary logics, independently of native understandings (Levi-Strauss, 1977: 206–231).

Levi-Strauss's structuralism has been very influential in the social sciences from the 1960s. Despite the evident divide between Anglophone functionalism and Francophone structuralism, the criticisms of each were closely compatible. In particular, like Parsons, he was accused of ignoring the meaning which actors attached to their culture, disinterest in politics and inattention to change (Clarke, 1981: 206–207). Indeed, Bourdieu's 'theory of practice' was substantially developed as a reaction to Levi-Strauss, as Bourdieu's critique of the structural analysis of gift-giving demonstrated (Bourdieu, 1977). From the late 1960s in France, structuralism began to be less attractive as a research paradigm. Levi-Strauss's structuralism was gradually superseded by the post-structuralism of Derrida, Lacan and Foucault. It is not always easy to define precisely the concept of post-structuralism since the work nominally defined as post-structuralist is diverse. Indeed, the work of Foucault later bore many resemblances to Levi-Strauss' work where

he identified underlying cultural codes (discourses) which structured diachronic historical eras. Other post-structuralists generally sought to question the unity and coherence of cultural categories, which Levi-Strauss presumed. Thus, Derrida maintained that all categories and concepts involved a 'difference', an absence, the implications of which gap the critical theorist had to explore.

NEO-FUNCTIONALISM: THE CONVERGENCE OF STRUCTURALISM AND FUNCTIONALISM

In the mid-twentieth century, functionalism and structuralism, concentrating respectively on institutions and cognition, were dominant – though never hegemonic – in the social sciences. By the end of the 1970s, however, structuralism and functionalism seemed to have become obsolete. Nevertheless, despite the fact that 'the protest against the hegemony of Parsons' theory essentially engendered by the social movements in the sixties curbed any serious reception [of his work]' (Joas, 1996: 7–8), the functionalist influences are still evident in social theory even today. Indeed, in the 1990s, neo-functionalism has reappeared in contemporary social theory, representing a fusion of institutional functionalism (systems theory) with cognitive structuralism.

Jeffrey Alexander's work on the multidimensional approach has been important in the appearance of neo-functionalism but the most mature work to date has been produced by Niklas Luhmann. Luhmann's neo-functionalism actively sought to fuse the functionalism and structuralism of the mid-twentieth century into a higher synthesis which addressed some of the enduring criticisms of these paradigms; above all, that they are incapable of dealing with change. As a synthesis, it marks the most developed statement of neo-functionalism at the end of the twentieth century. Luhmann accepts that any social system must be made up in the first instance of individuals and their actions (Luhmann, 1995: 215) but he rejects the argument that sociological analysis can limit itself merely to human social interaction (Luhmann, 1997: 47). 'Even the idea, initially attractive for sociologists, of an 'intersubjective' constitution of the world no longer helps; it is too self-evident and insufficiently theoretically productive. We employ the concept of a world as a concept for the *unity of the difference between system and environment*' (Luhmann, 1995: 208).

Luhmann is concerned ultimately with the dialectic between the social system and the environment in which that system exists. As the system transforms, the environment in which it operates also transforms producing a spiralling process of change. The environment is not an objective given which is independent of the system but the kind of environment which a system faces is partly a product of the character of the system itself. The world which confronts a system depends at least partly on what a system is trying to achieve. There is a dialectical relationship between system and environment. This immanent dialectic of system and environment is the central point of Luhmann's sociology and from it follows the other key arguments of Luhmann's system theory.

For Luhmann, the basis of all interaction within the system is communication. The system receives information about the environment through communication and therefore, communication determines the way in which the system can evolve. For Luhmann, the evolution of the system is a critical focus which distinguishes his systems theory from Parsons' structural-functionalism. While Parsons' structural-functionalism prioritises systemic equilibrium through the interrelation of whole and parts, Luhmann emphasises differentiation (Luhmann, 1995: 18). The system subdivides itself in the face of the environmental pressure created by its current relation to the environment. Yet, this differentiation necessitates further dialectic transformation because each differentiated subsystem is confronted by a new environment; the

environment of each new subsystem now consists of the other subsystems. Luhmann calls this immanent dialectic between systems their environments 'autopoiesis'; the term refers to the fact that the system makes itself. As the system receives new information about the difference between itself and the environment, it resonates with this new information stimulating self transformation. 'System resonance then is always in effect when the system is stimulated by its environment. The stimulation can be registered by the system if it possesses a corresponding capacity for information processing permitting it to infer the presence of an environment' (Luhmann, 1989: 16). When resonance reaches a certain pitch, the (sub)system is forced to adapt to the new situation, usually involving functional differentiation (Luhmann, 1989: 107–8).

According to Luhmann, the autopoietic process is structured by certain codes which underlie each (sub)system. Each subsystem is oriented around a binary code which mediates its relationship with its environment (Luhmann, 1989: 36; 1995: 231–4; Luhmann, 1997: 52). Thus, the legal system is structured by the code legal/illegal, the economic by the code possession/non-possession (Luhmann, 1989: 36) and every single system or subsystem is ultimately constituted by these transcendental binary codes; 'Codes are invariant for the system which identifies itself by them' (Luhmann, 1997: 52). Luhmann does not emphasise the point but the concept of binary codes seems to be drawn from Levi-Strauss' anthropology and they serve a similar purpose; pre-emptively orienting perception. Crucially, these codes determine the kinds of communication any system can receive or send and therefore the kind of autopoietic adaptations which can occur. These codes also structure the individuals operating in that system. The codes precede social action in any particular system, allowing the system to 'interpenetrate' the human subject. Luhmann uses the word 'interpenetrate' because he sees the social system and the human subject as a relationship between two systems and their respective environments. Both consequently influence or interpenetrate each other. However, although Luhmann might argue that the individual interpenetrates the social system, the latter is primary. The social system has determination over the individual whom it socialises by means of the imposition of these binary norms. Luhmann is explicit that interpenetration is the optimum concept because it 'avoids reference to the nature of human beings, recourse to the (supposedly foundational) subjectivity of consciousness, or formulating the problem as 'intersubjectivity' (which presupposes subjects)' (Luhmann, 1995: 216). Individuals are interpenetrated by binary codes in order that they can fulfil their roles. In modern societies with particular kinds of systems, these codes produce a specific kind of person; 'binary schematisms are the precondition for the emergence of a figure that in modern philosophy has gone by the name of the subject' (Luhmann, 1995: 233). Luhmann usefully summarises his discussion of the relationship between the individual and the system: 'All socialisation occurs as social interpenetration; all social interpenetration, as communication' (Luhmann, 1995: 243). The steering of any system is the automatic, self-transforming responses of the system to the communication it receives. In Luhmann's sociology, the self-equilibrating and self-transforming system is central.

Luhmann's neo-functionalist systems theory represents a fusion of sophisticated institutional functionalism with Levi-Straussian structuralism. Social institutions are mutually interdependent, each fulfilling a vital function which allows the other to operate. Moreover, subsystemic institutions are able to operate insofar as their members have internalised appropriate cognitive codes. They conduct themselves in a manner which is appropriate to the functioning of the particular subsystem in which they are located. In this way, Luhmann provides a more sophisticated picture of a dialectically dynamic system whose development is mediated by the codes established in its

different institutions. The codes ensure that the subsystems and therefore the individuals in them receive and act upon only the appropriate information to fulfil their functions.[4] Yet, while apparently more dynamic, it is very difficult to see how Luhmann's autopoetic system actually operates. He denies the importance of understanding and intersubjectivity. The interactions between participants and their shared understandings are subordinated to codes, interpenetration and the system. However, given the empty formality of his codes, where they prescribe only what is relevant to each subsystem, it is difficult to see how they could inform practice in particular institutional areas. Lawyers require a dense body of legal knowledge which is collectively re-affirmed by acting professionally in order to represent a client's case. Merely knowing whether something is legal or illegally is at best only a starting point. Indeed, one of the most important debates in the legal profession is precisely the definition of what is legal; the code which apparently defines this subsystem, in fact, has to be established recurrently by participants in it. In this context, it is difficult to see how subsystems would alter their patterns of interaction with each other if they were human activity was reduced merely to codes. Rather it would seem that once the codes are established in each sub-system, each would respond in the same way to external stimulus until the entire system and its environment stabilised.

CONCLUSION: BEYOND STRUCTURALISM AND FUNCTIONALISM

Functionalism, structuralism and neo-functionalism have been important research programmes for nearly a century. However, they have been recurrently criticised for their 'derogation of the lay actor' and for their inability to explain change; they prioritise the system before the actors. However, the structuralist tradition may itself provide a way out of the very difficulties of which it creates. In his celebrated novel, George Perec (2003) describes the inter-connected lives of the inhabitants of a Parisian apartment block, 11 Rue Simon-Crubellier. The novel reads as a highly entertaining series of short-stories where the diverse and often bizarre lives of the apartment dwellers are narrated. However, as the novel progresses the close but often unwitting interdependence of the characters emerges. Central to these interconnections is a wealthy Englishman, Bartlebooth who devises a plan that will both occupy the remainder of his life and spend his entire fortune. First, he spends 10 years learning to paint watercolors under the tutelage of Valene, who also becomes a resident of 11 Rue Simon-Crubellier. Then, he embarks on a 20-year trip around the world with his loyal servant Smautf (also a resident of 11 Rue Simon-Crubellier), painting 500 watercolours of different ports every two weeks. Bartlebooth then sends each painting back to France, where the paper is glued to a support board, and a carefully selected craftsman named Gaspard Winckler (also a resident of 11 Rue Simon-Crubellier) cuts it into a jigsaw puzzle. Upon his return, Bartlebooth spends his time solving each jigsaw, re-creating the scene. Each finished puzzle is treated to re-bind the paper with a special solution invented by Georges Morellet, another resident of 11 Rue Simon-Crubellier. After the solution is applied, the wooden support is removed, and the painting is sent to the port where it was painted. Exactly 20 years to the day after it was painted, the painting is placed in the seawater until the colors dissolve, and the paper, blank except for the faint marks where it was cut and re-joined, is returned to Bartlebooth. The plan is interrupted by events.

The central point of the novel is that the individual elements in life are irrelevant; individual existence is, *per se*, meaningless. It ends in the same circular oblivion of Bartlebooth's projected watercolours. However, while users of life should recognise that existence has no extrinsic meaning of itself, it generates its own internal meaning through the interdependence and interaction of actors. While the elements themselves are empty, together they form an internally coherent whole. The apartment block as a whole has a meaning which exceeds the lives of the individual inhabitants. Perec's novel is one of the most creative literary representations of structuralism. It is a manifestation of Saussurian linguistics in which the elements are arbitrary and meaningless but, in relation to each other, form a meaningful system. However, Perec's structuralism is not linguistic or cognitivist; it is a sociological structuralism grounded in the activities of living actions. In this way, it unwittingly echoes Malinowski's work on the Trobriand in which the eternal cycle of interlocking ceremonial exchanges sustained the social order. Indeed, although it presumes the existence of closed and stable systems, functionalism prioritises the interaction of institutions as its central focus. By emphasizing exchange and interrelations, Perec's work may be particularly useful in transcending the strictures of structuralism and functionalism, including Luhmann's neo-functionalism, by, ironically, identifying the fundamental insight of these paradigms: social life is about exchange or interchange.

Perec's novel is a structuralist work but, with its interactionist perspective, it is closest philosophically to Latour's Actor Network Theory. This approach seeks to understand institutions and social processes not in isolation but as manifestations of wide social networks consisting of actors utilising actants; a diversity of participants and things all comprise the network in which any particular activity has its meaning and even possibility. Latour eschews the distinction of structure or function. Instead, he seeks to analyse social practices within their historically specific configurations. He wants to situate social practice within a horizontal network of social relations. Crucially institutions themselves are seen not as monolithic entities which impose upon the individual but themselves merely human networks of people, utilising things, are they interact with each other. Latour in no way denies the manifest potency of large organizations but he understands their existence and reproduction in terms of the dense interaction of the multiplicity of agents both inside and outside who are essential to them: 'For ANT, if you stop making and remaking groups, you stop having groups. No reservoir of 'social forces' will help you' (Latour, 2005: 35). Although Latour has become extremely prominent, the kind of vision which his actor network model promotes can be identified more widely. Randall Collins' concept of the interaction ritual chain is very close to Latour's position (Collins, 2000, 2004). Like Latour, Collins sees society as a series of recurrent situations which must be actively created by participants in interaction. These situations are not determined by prior social facts but, situated in a configuration of past and simultaneous interactions, they have an independent internal dynamic which typically transcends expectation – for good or bad.

Against functionalist and structuralist perspectives, a new paradigm seems to be emerging in the philosophy of the social sciences today which may ironically return them to Saussure's original concept of structuralism in which the elements in a complex network are interdependent and mutually self-generating. Instead of explaining social reality in terms of institutional or cognitive structures which impose upon the individual from above, sociologists are increasingly explaining social action in terms of the wide horizontal networks in which it arises. Individual agency is a manifestation of the complex of social relations in which it is nested.

Of course, it is entirely possible to suggest a sociological explanation for the dominance of structuralism and functionalism in the twentieth century and its current supercession by an interactionist-network perspective. Functionalism and structuralism accorded with the social and political realities of the twentieth century when the nation state had more or less exclusive sovereignty over their citizens and territories. Globalisation,

by contrast, has involved the partial dissolution of this vertical international order with the acceleration of horizontal, transnational flows of people, goods, services and money around the world. Globalization seems to be characterised by greater horizontal interaction between once apparently discrete societies. As such, it seems likely that globalisation may have encouraged a network-centric imagination among sociologists. Indeed, Luhmann has tried effectively to capture the dynamism of this new social order with a revised, dialectical functionalism. However, the work of Latour and Collins seems to provide a more compelling, humanist (but not individualist) account of contemporary social action. Whether this vision is philosophically more sustainable than the now receding structuralist and functionalist paradigms cannot be ascertained here, but it would seem that in the early decades of the twenty-first century social scientists will operate within a quite different paradigm than their forebears in the twentieth century. Indeed, structuralism and functionalism may attain the historical status of Victorian evolutionism, which inspired Parsons to write in 1937, 'Who now reads Spencer?' In a globalising multi-polar world of transnational interaction, perhaps, the same may be said of the twentieth century proponents of functionalism and structuralism.

NOTES

1 Gellner's argument is substantially based the earlier work of Ian Jarvie, a close friend, who calls this rupture the 'revolution in anthropology' (Jarvie, 1964).

2 There has been extensive debate about Parsons' use of the term utilitarianism. The term does not refer to the philosophies of Bentham and Mill but rather to (rational) individualism which was central to economic theory.

3 His influence was marked even in the English-speaking academy (see Douglas, 1978; Leach, 1969, 1970, 1976).

4 Perhaps, surprisingly, the general contours of Luhmann's neofunctionalism is paralleled widely in

contemporary social theory. The work of Giddens, Habermas, Bhaskar, Foucault and Bourdieu all operate around a concept of an institutional system which individuals reproduce by the internalisation of codes, structures, discourses or habituses. These connections cannot be explored here.

REFERENCES

Alexander, J. (1984) *Theoretical Logic in Sociology, Volume 4: The Modern Reconstruction of Classical Thought: Talcott Parsons*, London: Routledge and Kegan Paul.

Alexander, J. (1998) *Neofunctionalism and After*. Oxford: Blackwell.

Althusser, L. (1977a) *For Marx*. London: New Left Books.

Althusser, L. (1977b) *Reading Capital*. London: New Left Books.

Asad, T. (ed.) (1973) *Anthropology and the Colonial Encounter*. London: Ithaca.

Bourdieu, P. (1977) *Outline of a Theory of Practice*. Cambridge: Cambridge University Press.

Camic. C. (1991) *Talcott Parsons: the Early Essays*. Chicago: Chicago University Press.

Clarke, S. (1981) *The Foundations of Structuralism*. Hassocks: Harvester.

Collins, R. (2000) *The Sociology of Philosophies*. London: Belknap Press.

Collins, R. (2004) *Interaction Ritual Chains*. Princeton: Princeton University Press.

Durkheim, E and Mauss, M. (1963) *Primitive Classification*. London: Cohen and West.

Fortes, M. (1949) *The Web of Kinship among the Tallensi*. London: Oxford University Press.

Frazer, J. (1906) *The Golden Bough*. Hertfordshire: Wentworth.

Gellner, E. (1988) 'The "Zeno of Cracow"; or 'Revolution at Nemi' or 'The Polish Revenge' in R. Ellen, E. Gellner, G. Kulica and J. Mucha (eds) *Malinowski between Two Worlds*. Cambridge: Cambridge University Press. pp.164–194.

Gerhardt, U. (2002) *Talcott Parsons: An Intellectual Biography*. Cambridge: Cambridge University Press. pp. 208–239

Giddens, A. (1977) 'Functionalism: apres la lutte', in *Studies in Social and Political Theory*. London: Hutchinson. pp. 96–129.

Gould, M. (1989) 'Voluntarism and utilitarianism; a critic of Camic's history of ideas', *Theory, Culture and Society*, 6(4): 637–654.

Gould, M. (1991) 'The structure of social action: at least sixty years ahead of its time', in R. Robertston and B. Turner (eds.) *Talcott Parsons: Theorist of Modernity*. London: Sage.

Gouldner, A. (1971) *The Coming Crisis in Western Sociology*. London: Heinemann.

Haas, E. (1964) *Beyond the Nation-State*. California: Stanford University Press.

Holmwood, J. (1996) *Founding Sociology? Talcott Parsons and the Idea of a General Theory*. London: Longman.

Holmwood, J. (2006a) 'Talcott Parsons: in his times and Ours' in J. Holmwood (ed.) *International Library of Essays in the History of Social and Political Thought*. Aldershot: Ashgate. pp. xiii-li.

Holmwood, J. (2006b) 'Economics, sociology and the "professional complex": Talcott Parsons and the critique of orthodox economics', *The American Journal of Economics and Sociology*, 65(1): 127–160.

Jarvie, I. (1964) *The Revolution in Anthropology*. London: Routledge and Kegan Paul.

Joas, H. (1996) *The Creativity of Action*, trans. by J. Gaines and P. Keast. Oxford: Polity.

King, A. (2004) *The Structure of Social Theory*. London: Routledge.

Latour. B. (2005) *Reassembling the Social*. Oxford: Oxford University Press.

Leach, E. (1969) *Genesis as Myth, and Other Essays*. London: Cape.

Leach, E. (1970) *Levi-Strauss*. London: Fontana.

Leach, E. (1976) *Culture & Communication*. Cambridge: Cambridge University Press.

Levi-Strauss, C. (1963) *Tristes tropiques* New York: Atheneum.

Levi-Strauss. C. (1966) *The Savage Mind*. Chicago: University of Chicago Press.

Levi-Strauss, C. (1969) *The Elementary Structures of Kinship*. London: Eyre and Spottiswoode.

Levi Strauss, C (1973) *Tristes Tropiques*. London: Jonathon Cape

Levi-Strauss, C. (1977) *Structural Anthropology, Vol 1*. London: Allen Lane.

Levi-Strauss, C. (1978) 'Preface' in R. Jakobson (ed.) *Six Lectures on Sound and Meaning*. Hassocks: Harvester. pp. xi-xxvi.

Levi-Strauss, C. (1983) *The Way of the Masks*. London: Cape.

Levi-Strauss, C. (1985) *The View From Afar*. Oxford: Blackwell.

Luhmann, N. (1989) Ecological Communication, trans. J.Bednarz. Cambridge: Polity.

Luhmann, N. (1995) *Social Systems*, trans. J. Bednarz with D. Baecker. Stanford: Stanford University Press.

Luhmann, N. (1997) 'The limits of steering', *Theory, Culture and Society*, 14(1): 41–57.

Malinowski, B. (1944) *A Scientific Theory of Culture and Other Essays*. Chapel Hill: University of North Carolina Press.

Malinowski, B. (1964) *Argonauts of the Western Pacific*. London: Routledge.

Malinowski, B. (1974) *Magic, Science and Religion*. London: Condor/Souvenir.

Martindale. D. (1971) 'Talcott Parsons' theoretical metamorphosis from social behaviourism to macro-functionalism', in H. Turk and R. Simpson (eds) *Institutions and Social Exchange: The Sociologies of Talcott Parsons and George Homans*. New York: Bobbs Merrill. pp. 165–74.

Mauss, M. (1967) *The Gift*. New York: Norton.

Merton, R. (1957) *Social Theory and Social Structure*. New York: Free Press.

Miliband, R. (1970) *The State in Capitalist Society*. London: Weidenfeld and Nicolson.

Munch, R. (1982) 'Talcott Parsons and the theory of action II: the continuity of development', *American Journal of Sociology*, 87(4): 771–826.

Parsons, T. (1952) *The Social System*. London: Tavistock.

Parsons, T. (1966) (first published 1937) *The Structure of Social Action*. New York: Free Press.

Parsons, T and Bales, R. (1955) *Family, Socialization and Interaction Process*, Glencoe, Ill.: Free Press.

Parsons, T, Bales, R and Shils, E. (1953) *Working Papers in the Theory of Action*, New York. Free Press.

Perec, G. (2003) *Life: A User's Manual*. London: Vintage.

Poulantzas, N. (1975) *Classes in Contemporary Capitalism*. London: New Left Books.

Radcliffe-Brown, A. (1971) *Structure and Function in Primitive Society*. London: Cohen & West.

Ricoeur, P. (1992) 'Structure and hermeneutics', in *The Conflict of Interpretation*. Evanston, Illinois: Northwestern University Press. pp. 27–60.

Robertson, R. and Turner, B. (1989) 'Talcott Parsons and modern social thought – an appreciation', *Theory Culture and Society*, 6(4): 539–558.

Robertston, R. and Turner, B. (1991) *Talcott Parsons: Theorist of Modernity*. London: Sage.

Rocher, G. (1975) *Talcott Parsons and American Sociology*. London: Nehon.

Saussure, de F. (1966) *Course in General Linguistics*. New York: McGraw-Hill

Schutz. A. (1978) 'Parsons' theory of social action', in E. Grathoff (ed.) *The Theory of Social Action: the correspondence of Alfred Schutz and Talcott Parsons*. Bloomington, IN: Indiana University Press. pp. 8–60.

Turner, J. (1978) *The Structure of Sociological Theory*. Homewood, Illinois: Dorsey.

Wright Mills, C (1959) The Sociological Imagination. New York: Oxford University Press.

Wrong, D. (1964) 'The oversocialized conception of man in modern sociology' in L. Coser and B. Rosenberg (eds) *Sociological Theory: A Book of Reading*. London: Macmillan. pp. 112–22.

22

Phenomenology, Hermeneutics, and Ethnomethodology

Hans-Herbert Kögler

This chapter presents some of the most systematic ideas that have been developed to ground an *interpretive social science*. By drawing on arguments and insights from phenomenology, hermeneutics, and ethnomethodology, we intend to offer an account of interpretive social understanding that is rich and robust enough to provide methodological guidance as well as theoretical support for qualitative empirical work. At the same time, our discussion is geared toward a reconstruction of the philosophical grounds that make the role of interpretation central to any endeavor of explaining human agency. Instead of going through the different phenomenological, hermeneutic, or ethnomethodological proposals historically, we reconstruct the methodological profile of the *phenomenological–hermeneutic approach* (PHA) towards understanding human agency.

Accordingly, our task will involve correlating diverse perspectives concerned with the interpretive understanding of human agency in the social sciences, including the psychological (Dilthey, 1959, 1982; Schleiermacher, 1957) and the ontological (Husserl, 1962; Heidegger, 1962) approaches in hermeneutics and phenomenology. A systematic integration of Gadamer's philosophical hermeneutics (Gadamer, 1989) in terms of dialogical realism will allow us to correlate these philosophical approaches with social phenomenology (Schutz, 1967) and ethnomethodology (Garfinkel, 1967). The core thesis of the ontological constitution of human agency as defined by a culturally and historically mediated self-understanding can thus be substantiated by grounding the philosophical theory in concrete phenomenological and ethnomethodological analyses.

We will draw on this ontological background to discuss core methodological aspects of a PHA to understanding human agency. The phenomenological–hermeneutic insights into the structure of understanding will be shown to lend themselves to a defense of explanatory aims in social science. The interpretive access to the domain of cultural meanings and practices enables the reconstruction of the intentional understanding of socially situated agents. The core task of our methodological discussion is to show that:

1 social-scientific understanding relates the perspective of the interpreter, which is based on his or her cultural pre-understanding, to the reconstruction of the agents' self-understanding, such that;

2 an explanatory and realist analysis of the other's actions based on intentional beliefs becomes possible.

THE PHENOMENOLOGICAL–HERMENEUTIC PROJECT OF UNDERSTANDING HUMAN AGENCY

Our first aim is to systematically introduce the core idea of the PHA to understanding human agency. Essential for PHA is the orientation at the understanding that agents themselves have vis-à-vis their world. The underlying claim is that an adequate account of what agents do requires taking into account what they themselves think they are doing. The need to give a methodological role to the *self-understanding of agents* was famously introduced by Max Weber in his assertion that the "subjective meaning" that human agents associate with their actions is to play a crucial role in explaining what these actions essentially are and why they happen (Weber, 1949, 1978). What is really at stake, to be sure, is a two-fold claim that entails (1) the requirement that an adequate description of the action must be based on an understanding of the agent's own comprehension of the situation, and (2) the implication that only an adequate description – adequate in the sense that it includes the reconstruction of the agent's self-understanding – will provide the social scientist with the tools to explain why the action occurred in the first place.

From a philosophical perspective, it becomes immediately clear that this methodological claim involves an ontological preassumption about the constitution of human agency. Claiming that only an adequate description of the agent's self-understanding is to lead to a causally correct explanation is implausible if the action's constitution is not to be intrinsically connected to the self-interpretation of agents. It is here that PHA provides a much needed – if not uncontested

– advance over purely methodological debates that only allow concrete research strategies (grouped under qualitative or quantitative, or otherwise differentiated) to be discussed. In PHA, the reconstruction of the interpretive nature of agency is itself considered an ontological aspect of agency as such.

According to a more traditional or, if you wish, empiricist or positivistic understanding of method, this amounts to a blurring of the essential distinction between the scientific subject and the object of science. In this view, the scientist is to analyze the tools for adequate understanding of the object domain prior to their application, so as to make sure that they constitute reliable and adequate venues of gaining explanatory insight. The scientific object is to be kept distinct from these methodological reflections to not infuse the theory with pre-assumptions about the object domain that would be detrimental to an unbiased understanding of the object's nature.

Yet while PHA is far from endorsing an uncontrolled infusion of subjective premises into the object's explanation, it questions the possibility of keeping subject and object apart in methodological reflections. For the subject's side, it is indeed questionable that the idea of a method's adequacy can be rendered plausible without a conception of the purpose it is supposed to serve, which in turn requires some understanding of the object at stake. A hammer's adequacy can be judged only by knowing its particular purpose, that is, the kind of objects and structures it is to handle, just as much as an epistemic method can be considered adequate only to the extent that it makes sense of an object's constitution (which thus has been known). To judge a method without knowing what object it is supposed to explain is like constructing a tool without knowing its purpose. With regard to the object, it is similarly implausible to assume that we can simply abstract from the object the method or approach that defines its understanding for us in order to approach its "pure being." To separate *our view of the object* from *the object itself* forgets that what we define as "the object itself" is still understood by us, and is thus necessarily based on an approach, however implicit, that delivers the object to us. In fact, the very claim that we can distinguish the method – understood as our subjective approach to the thing itself – and the object – understood as the pure entity that's at stake – would render the intent to do so mute, because the method's goal is to give us the object as it is, which is already presupposed in the distinction. It is implied that our understanding of the object is already based on the right method, as it gives us the object itself, which makes obsolete the whole attempt to distinguish the right approach from the object itself.

To be sure, the insight into the *intertwinedness of method and object* should not lead to a rejection of inquiring into the conditions and presuppositions of interpretive social-scientific understanding. On the contrary, what is at stake now is a *reflexive reconstruction of our own presuppositions of understanding*. We need to understand how our own pre-understanding of an object-domain shapes and influences the very understanding and explanation of its constitution. Indeed, PHA expands the concretely given pre-assumptions of our understanding into a general feature of human understanding per se. In other words, the fact that we always already pre-understand objects and events in our environment (which we can then turn into objects of controlled scientific analysis) indicates not just a methodological insight but rather presents us with an essential ontological fact about human agency itself (Heidegger, 1962). Humans are defined by understanding themselves and the world always already in a "pre-ontological," that is, substantively pre-defined way, according to which they define and structure their concrete thoughts, feelings, and intentions (Dreyfus, 1993; Gadamer, 1989). It is this general claim about the unavoidable and constitutive role of a thematically defined pre-understanding that grounds the phenomenological–hermeneutic approach to understanding human agency.

THE METHODOLOGICAL PROFILE OF THE PHENOMENOLOGICAL–HERMENEUTIC APPROACH

The ontological assumption that human agency is essentially structured by the agent's self-understanding concretely defines the methodological perspective of phenomenology and hermeneutics. This can be shown by taking up hermeneutics' most central claim about understanding, the "hermeneutic circle" (Grondin, 1994; Ormiston and Schrift, 1990). This term generally suggests that the interpretation of symbolic expressions and acts is to be distinguished from a subsumption of particular cases under a general law. Instead, in order to make sense of the intended meaning of a text, artwork, institution, cultural practice, etc., we need to be able to enter into a to-and-fro movement between the general thought, intent, or motivation of a human act or expression, and the particular expressions in which its basic thought or purpose is expressed. The claim that such a process is (in a productive way) "circular" proceeds from the assumption that the meaning of a symbolic expression or act (1) is only accessible through the articulated expressions or acts themselves, (2) constitutes the meaning of the object only in its full articulation, and (3) achieves an adequate understanding of meaning only once the whole text or context is understood.

Now, in order to begin to understand a written text or symbolic-cultural context, the interpreter has to be able to already understand its sentences or acts. In other words, while the whole meaning would only be accessible given the larger ramifications of a textual, discursive, or cultural setting, the reconstruction of these contexts is itself only possible by already assuming an understanding of the particular expressions. Entering into the process of reconstructing the context thus assumes an understanding of the particular elements which define, so to speak, the nodes in the network, while those nodal points are themselves only fully comprehensible given the holistic context. The context is only accessible by going step-by-step through the elements that make up its substance, while those elements receive their meaning – and thus full understanding – only once the context is understood. The interpretive understanding of such expressions or acts is thus defined by a constant back-and-forth adjudication of both the meaning of the parts and the whole. The interpretive process achieves a continuously refined comprehension of the meaning by exploring how the two dimensions of meaning are linked.

The methodological uniqueness of the hermeneutic circle can be brought out by drawing on the previously introduced ontological pre-assumption about human agency, namely that it is defined by self-understanding. We have seen that making such an assumption is not illegitimate; instead, it is rather unavoidable. According to this ontological premise, all human understanding is constituted by bringing into play a substantive pre-understanding about the issue at stake. But if it is indeed unavoidable for *any* human understanding to make some assumption about the object domain, the question arises why this should constitute a unique method or approach with regard to the human sciences, as the hermeneutic tradition has consistently claimed (Rorty, 1991; see also Taylor, 1985).[1]

The answer to this question can be found by looking at the resources the interpreter has to draw on to get the process started. Here, we find that the preliminary meaning that is needed to start making sense draws *on the interpreter's own comprehension* of the (meaningful) issues at stake. The interpreter obviously brings a lot to a symbolic text or social action before he or she can even begin with the construction of a scientifically elab-

orate account. Linguistic knowledge, topical knowledge, a certain pre-understanding of the context, a capacity to make sense of the references which are mentioned in the text or action – that is, thoughts, facts, institutions, feelings, etc. – are necessary to start an explanation. We already saw that such knowledge is considered preliminary because only the understanding of the text or act itself can enable an interpretation that can be considered valid. And yet, the thematico-linguistic pre-understanding is crucial if the access to the meaning – recall that the orientation here is at the *intended meaning of the text or act* – is to be possible at all. The interpreter has to be able to connect with the intended meaning, to access what the text or act is about, to understand what is at stake, what is thematically discussed or operationally intended, if any interpretation or explanation is to be possible at all. The question now becomes how exactly the relation between the pre-understanding of the social-scientific interpreter and the social-scientific object domain is to be understood.

With this formulation, we have reached the heart of the hermeneutic claim regarding human understanding. This is so because the relation between the interpreter and her "object" is considered unique due to the fact that both *are* human agents. Interpreter and "object" are able to uniquely "connect" due to the fact that both possess – as human agents – a unique form of self-understanding. *The methodological uniqueness of the human and social sciences is thus grounded in the ontological similarity between subject and object in this domain.* This ontological claim has an immediate methodological significance because the essential feature of human agency is defined as understanding. The fact that human agents are constituted by self-understanding lends itself to ground scientific analyses concerned with understanding human agency since what is at stake now is the social-scientific understanding of a social self-understanding. The object of understanding is thus itself understanding: it is an object that is essentially defined by being itself interpretive. Thus, capitalizing on the fact that humans understand themselves leads to a methodological perspective of how we should go about in analyzing meaning and action.[2]

THE PSYCHOLOGICAL APPROACH

We now need to inquire how particular preconceptions of human self-understanding have influenced and shaped PHA. In the early hermeneutic attempts to develop a general grounding for the human sciences, the reference to *the psychological origin of meaning* plays a crucial role. Friedrich Schleiermacher's *Lectures on General Hermeneutics* (1821) set out to provide the much needed methodological foundation for the newly emerged humanities (Schleiermacher, 1957). The interpreter requires a general understanding of how knowledge can be gained here. The common core of all humanistic disciplines is that thought is expressed in language (Herder and Rousseau, 1966; Humboldt, 1988). The formation of intentional thought in language is understood as a psychological process of meaning construction. Interpretation should therefore be understood as the reconstruction of such meaning—reversing, as it were, the initial productive process. But how is this reversal, this process of re-constructing meaning, precisely to be understood?

Schleiermacher's work gives rise to two answers. Both depend on the assumption that the process of meaning construction is a psychological event. In the romantic version, the interpreter transposes himself or herself into the other individual's mind in order to understand the objectified symbolic or cultural expressions. It is granted that such a full "empathetic" understanding is in need of a lot of preparatory steps, which are required to avoid an anachronistic assimilation of the other's background and context to the interpreter's own pre-understanding. Thus, substantive linguistic understanding

(grammatical interpretation) has to precede the psychological transposition into the other's inner thoughts and intentions ("psychological interpretation"). Yet the final objective of all interpretation, which consists of the full understanding of the other's thoughts, is only possible through a somewhat mysterious act of empathetic identification with the other. Needless to say, this is a unique "method" grounded in the psycho-ontological similarity between interpreter and author.

The second version maintains the orientation at the author's expressive thoughts and intentions. This approach equally illuminates the method of interpretation with reference to an account of the production of meaning. However, the process of the re-construction of meaning here does not culminate in the mysterious act of transposition. It is rather seen as the never fully completed process of projecting the intended meaning through a continuous (hermeneutic) circle between the comparative-contextual data and the textually expressed content. The object of interpretation is thus still the intended thought expressed in symbolic or cultural form (Kögler and Stueber 2000). Yet the romantic assumption of a "thought behind the text" is given up in favor of the "thought within the text." Since text and context mutually shape the determination of meaning, interpretation is less a rigorous science and more of an art; it is a practical skill that can never achieve absolute finality and certainty.[3]

This result did not sit well with Wilhelm Dilthey. At the end of the nineteenth century, the human sciences (now including humanities and social sciences) seem even more badly in need of a methodological grounding that could justify their claims to *scientific validity*. Dilthey aims for such a grounding, to provide both a synthesis between the splintering diverse disciplines and a practical orientation for their potential social impact (Dilthey, 1959). The envisioned approach, to be sure, was equally psychological. In the influential *Introduction to the Human Sciences* (1883), Dilthey attempts to ground the human sciences in the epistemico-ontological double-fact that both the understanding of the historical world as well as its production refers back to the human individual. Anticipated by Giambattista Vico's famous saying that in history *verum and factum convertuntur*, Dilthey aims to build the new methodology on two seemingly indisputable premises. Epistemically, he suggests, the "fact of consciousness" cannot be denied. Firmly on Cartesian–Kantian grounds here, Dilthey is convinced that all experience is to hark back to the phenomenological fact that it is an experience for me – that is, it refers back to my mind or consciousness. Ontologically, it seems equally clear that history and society are built up from individuals who produce higher-order entities like institutions and norms through their interactions. If the two assumptions are combined, a firm new foundation for knowledge in the human and social sciences can be erected. Due to the fact that consciousness understands itself – it is according to Descartes self-transparent – the "fact of consciousness" can be used to reconstruct the general laws and structures that are operative in society and culture at large. Since the individual mind has in its epistemic possession the very structure which constitutes the ontological Ur-element of history, its inner constitution and structures can thus be readily unpacked (Dilthey, 1959).

Dilthey's main idea is that the recourse to the mind will provide the needed foundation only if the human subject is considered in the fullness of its being. In contrast to the purely cognitive understanding of the mind in Kant and neo-Kantianism, he considers relevant all experiential dimensions, including cognition, emotion, and volition. This full-blooded grounding is needed since in the human sciences, the interpreter understands through re-experiencing (*Nacherleben*) what the agents intended, while in the natural sciences an "alien" (external) construction of laws is sufficient. Yet redefining the experiential basis as a threefold structure of cognitive-emotional-volitional aspects did

not prove most relevant in Dilthey's project. The crucial impact resulted from a productive dynamic in Dilthey's subsequent thought that led to the threshold of Heidegger's ontological redefinition of hermeneutics.

Dilthey sets out to develop the full-blown psychological foundation by means of a "descriptive psychology." The idea was to phenomenologically describe the essential features of our complex psychic life to ascertain a methodological foundation suited for the human sciences. But Dilthey now realized that *understanding the psychic life itself must involve taking into account the particular cultural, social, and historical circumstances that shape its expression.* Descriptive psychology must be aided by comparative psychology (1982). But this means that hermeneutic understanding is always already involved in developing its supposed foundation, just as the (inescapable) hermeneutic circle would suggest. This methodological insight becomes now, in a second radical move, understood as a feature of the object of understanding itself. The late Dilthey realizes in his path-breaking *The Construction of the Historical World in the Human Sciences* (1910) that the methodological triad of "Experience-Expression-Understanding" (*Erlebnis-Ausdruck-Verstehen*) is not merely the method of the interpreter, but defines how agents exist in the historical-social world (Dilthey, 2004). Agents always already understand themselves amidst the cultural expressions that pre-define their experience. They are "bathed," so to speak, in a culturally mediated sense that shapes their shared world through symbolic media of expression, and in light of which they experience and understand themselves.

THE ONTOLOGICAL APPROACH

Heidegger learns Dilthey's lesson through the lens of Husserl's phenomenology (Heidegger, 1962). This puts the concept of intentionality at the center of analysis (Husserl, 1970). Intentionality is considered to be the basic structure of consciousness and consists of the directedness of all thought toward something. Husserl's phenomenology sets out to capture what exactly is involved when subjects understand something as something. He devices the famous "phenomenological epoché" which consists in bracketing the assumption of reality with regard to any object of intentional thought (Husserl, 1962, 1991). The upshot of this move – bracketing say "house in front of me" in order to focus solely on how I perceive/conceive this house, regardless of its real existence – is to illuminate the intrinsic structure of consciousness and all it involves.

For Heidegger, Husserl's disciple, several aspects of this approach become pertinent (Heidegger, 1982). First, Husserl conceives of the analysis of intentionality in strictly logical terms, rejecting any kind of psychologism as devastating for philosophical truth claims. Heidegger shares with Husserl the departure from the psychologistic grounding of earlier hermeneutics. Second, Husserl remains a methodological Cartesian in that he understands consciousness to be accessible through self-consciousness alone, from which Heidegger's approach retains Husserl's orientation at an agent's self-understanding. Third, Heidegger takes over the foreground/background conception of intentionality, suggesting that whatever is apprehended as something can be so only against a more or less reflexive background understanding. Fourth, Heidegger understands the projection of something as something against an implicit horizon as a temporal process, just as Husserl. Finally, and perhaps most importantly, Heidegger shares Husserl's (early) approach toward a non-Cartesian form of intentional consciousness: the understanding of something as something, while prestructured, is not supposed to remain "inside" the mind. Rather, and in conjunction with the critique of psychologism, intentional thought goes out and refers to the object that it intends. It is supposed to be part of the world

that it discloses and not subject to a Cartesian encapsulation into some inner mental sphere of thought objects (Dreyfus, 1993).

To be sure, these important aspects of the phenomenological understanding of intentionality only become fruitful after Heidegger's pragmatic and holistic reconceptualization. What Heidegger takes issue with in Husserl is how the mind—or better: intentional acts that are experienced by self-consciousness—are thematized such that their true experiential nature is, once again, passed over instead of adequately articulated (Heidegger, 1962). Recall that phenomenology as a method attempts to capture what truly happens in conscious acts. It thus aims at a theoretically unbiased description of the facts of consciousness. Its ultimate objective is to fully reveal how intentional experience is structured. Yet, so Heidegger, in Husserl this crucial and legitimate aim gets paired with the intent to deliver a "rigorous science" of consciousness. Husserl aims to describe mental phenomena, but the description is carried out in the spirit of an *objective representation of mental objects* (Husserl, 1962, 1991). Hidden in this scientific-methodological perspective lies an ontological projection of intentional acts as separate and objectifiable phenomena. In the supposedly methodological neutral perspective of describing experiences of the mind purely and as such, we smuggle in the assumption that those phenomena exist as separate mental entities, which in turn grounds that they can be purely described as self-sufficient cognitive phenomena. Indeed, Husserl's *epoché* brackets reference to any other domain of reality in order to distill the mere facts of the mental realm. Gazing introspectively into that realm, pure mental phenomena now reveal themselves in their pure structure. In this methodologically created "laboratory of the mind" – just like in the psychological laboratories that separate agents from their usual everyday environments – the facts of intentionality are to be separated – distilled – from any context. It is a mental positivism of sorts.[4]

To start over, Heidegger's picks up the initial definition of the phenomenological attitude as an *unbiased description of experience* (Heidegger, 1962, 1985). The avoidance of bias is supposed to be accomplished by relating to experience as it presents itself without a theoretical framework. Yet we saw that the Cartesian methodology has indeed such a framework built into its method. How can we overcome this assumption and capture intentional understanding in its most basic and "immediate" form? Heidegger's answer: By observing intentional thought in its natural everyday environment. Instead of attempting to abstract pure mental facts, we have to reconstruct how the everyday self-understanding of agents proceeds. Heidegger labels this project "hermeneutics of facticity" because here, agents are considered in terms of their existence as full factual selves, as embodied, engaged, socially connected and practically situated subjects (Heidegger, 1999). Giving a phenomenologically true description of human experience in this manner transforms phenomenology into hermeneutics: Agents do not exist by exercising distinct cognitive functions, but rather as embedded intentionalities, as subjects that always already *understand themselves* in light of certain symbolic, practical, and situational beliefs and assumptions, and as agents who are always already directed towards some project or goal to which their actions are oriented.

To make clear that this analysis of human intentionality overcomes the Cartesian conception of a separate mental sphere, Heidegger calls the agent *Dasein* which indicates a general understanding of being towards which an agent is always oriented in some way. But Heidegger similarly introduces the complementary concept *Being-in-the World*, which defines *Dasein* as *embedded intentional orientation towards entities in an always already pre-understood world*. Heidegger's transformation of intentionality thus amounts to a pragmatic and holistic reconceptualization of its core grounding, since any intentional understanding emerges

from an engaged practical context. Equally important, this practical context is socially shared since the practical aims and referential contexts are socially typified, disclosed in socially shared ways, and refer to inter-subjective experiences with other agents. The horizon of intentional understanding thus becomes, in a reminiscence of Dilthey's shared sense of cultural pre-understanding, the socio-practical background understanding of a particular social context. It is this new grounding of the phenomenological concept of intentionality that enables the outline of the PHA perspective on social science.

An important mediating step is here provided by the philosophical hermeneutics of Hans-Georg Gadamer, and this for two reasons (Gadamer, 1989). First, Gadamer explicitly relates the insights of ontological hermeneutics back to the grounds of methodical human understanding. *Truth and Method* is widely accepted as having bridged and related the reconstruction of our interpretive nature as human beings to the project of human-scientific understanding and interpretation. Second, this reconnection of hermeneutics with the human sciences is developed in such a way that an enhanced role is granted to language. As Gadamer famously put it: "Being that can be understood is language." (Gadamer, 1989: 474). This formulation emphasizes both that reality for us is linguistically mediated, and that we have the capacity to understand the world through language.[5]

In Gadamer's view, the language-based interpretive process is structured like a *dialogue* where the interpreter, based on her own substantive pre-understanding of the subject matter, projects onto the text a question or issue *about which the text is to give an answer.* Interpretation is accordingly seen as a truth-oriented exchange involving different perspectives about a shared thematic issue (Gadamer, 1989). The subjective and methical control of the interpreting social scientist is thus put into question. Interpretation is precisely then successful and illuminating when the results have not been anticipated, when the interpreter is drawn into a productive self-examination of her previous views, when new insights about the subject matter become revealed. While Gadamer emphasizes that interpretation thus super-cedes methodological control, we must ask how this view of the interpretive process can be productively re-appropriated by interpretive social scientists.[6]

A METHODOLOGICAL MODEL FOR INTERPRETIVE SOCIAL SCIENCE

We now turn to the specific methodological impact of PHA for the social sciences. As we made clear at the outset, the issue consists in combining a plausible account of the meaningfulness of an intentional act with a causally convincing account that this meaning accounts for the motivation of the agent, that this is what actually triggered the act or expression. We will first focus on the methodological reasons that strongly suggest a need for the interpretive turn to develop afterwards evidence why this is also causally convincing.

The argument for an interpretive social science is suggested by the ontological definition that human agency is self-interpreting. Recall that we realized that the interpretive dimension is not only intrinsic to the social scientist's attempt to make sense of human agency, but rather inheres in its object domain, that is, is intrinsic to human agents themselves. In addition, the reconstruction of the grounds of this interpretive capacity of human agents revealed that it is always already culturally and historically mediated. We cannot simply unearth a basis for understanding human agency, but find the grounds of historical-cultural understanding itself *mediated* through historical and cultural contexts. This mediation matters because the contexts in which this interpretive capacity is exercised—and this applies both to the social-scientific interpreter as much as to the situated social agent—always differ.

In other words, we are faced with two assumptions, two well-grounded premises with regard to human actions. First, human actions are to an essential extent defined by the self-understanding of the agents. Second, the contexts in which agents interpret themselves are not identical, but differ in their internal organization. If we take both assumptions together, we cannot but acknowledge that in order to understand how actions are structured *in another context*, we have to get at the basis of *how the actions are understood in the other context*. If we could distill a basis that is unaffected by the contexts themselves, we might be able to reconstruct this ground without getting entangled in the understanding of the self-understanding of the agents. But we saw that this doesn't work. And if all contexts would be similar or identical, we also might be able to dispense with the labor of interpretation. We could then develop a golden key for one context and use it to disclose meanings in all others. Yet if meanings – and thus meaningful actions – are holistically structured, and if whole contexts differ from another, we need to develop an understanding of the different contexts if a respective action is to be understood (Gadamer, 1989; see also Davidson, 2001; Winch, 1991).

This argument draws the methodological consequence from the ontological claim that human agency is intrinsically defined by interpretive self-understanding, that is, culturally mediated meaning. If we could drop this assumption – that is, that understanding aims at the other's self-understanding – we might simply look how the phenomena that are available to an interpreter can be best grouped or organized according to a prevalent epistemico-interpretive scheme. The reference to the self-understanding would be bracketed or seen as entirely defined by the interpreter's schemes and their respective coherences. To be sure, if interpretive schemes are in competition as to how to understand a certain act (or action-sequence, practice, or institution), we cannot just leap over those competing frameworks to the facts themselves to decide which one is best suited. We must follow their interpretations internally, always with an eye towards the phenomenon which involves our own pre-understanding. We thus try to decide which framework best accounts for the act or expression at stake. Yet we can only try to do so, according to the hermeneutic conception of dialogical understanding, by *reconstructing the other's perspective and context in comparison and contrast to our own.* While we fully acknowledge the inescapability of our own standpoint, which indeed makes possible the beginning of the interpretive process, we necessarily remain oriented at the understanding of the other (i.e., at an interpretation of the other's self-understanding). Yet how are we to make methodological sense of the apparent paradox that we can only understand *the other's* self-understanding through *our own* interpretive lenses, which seems to reduce the other's meaning once more to our interpretation, to reduce the other's self-understanding to our conception of it?

The answer lies in taking a phenomenological look at how the interpretive understanding of meaningful social facts works. Indeed, the intentional reference at another intentional perspective or context is not merely smuggling in some objective reference that is in fact unattainable. Rather, one can see that the orientation at another's perspective whose "subjective meaning" (Weber, 1978, 1949) one aims to reconstruct plays a methodologically guiding role in understanding. The approach in which this view can best be articulated is the dialogical perspective. Here, we relate to another by means of our shared orientation at a certain subject matter (Gadamer, 1989; Kögler, 1999). To understand the other, we have to project, based on our view, what the other is saying, which we do all along when we are engaged in a conversation with someone. The subject matter and some more or less shared assumptions carry the understanding, while they equally enable the articulation of substantive differences in perspective,

value-orientation, outlook, etc. The extent to which shared beliefs and assumptions are in place might itself become questionable and revised within the interpretive process. The crucial point is that such an interpretive process, while necessarily relating back to one's own assumptions and practices, has a *disclosing power* with regard to another agent's beliefs and backgrounds. It does so because a certain orientation at the other's self-understanding in the encounter is implied, and is indeed unavoidable if understanding is to take place. We are forced, if we indeed are oriented at the understanding of the meaningful action of the other, to take the other's perspective – however mediated by our own – into account (Ricoeur, 1992).

Note that in the hermeneutic approach, the linguistically mediated interpretation of the other's (equally linguistically mediated) beliefs and assumptions is at stake. We are thus neither modeling interpretive understanding at a *first-person transposition*, or even self-transformation, into the other, nor are we endorsing a *third-person perspective* that is content with an external explanatory framework that aims at causal regularity and predictive power regardless of the agents' own understanding. Rather, the *dialogical or second-person approach* reconstructs the meanings and motivations which shape and guide another agent in his or her acts and expressions. We are thus looking, if you wish, at the "reasons" that another could and would mobilize if asked why this act, why that expression is the way it is. To be sure, the concrete form of those reasons and motives would differ widely. They look different if we ask for the motivation behind certain moves in a philosophical text, a novel's character, a choice of color and form in a painting, a riff in a blues song, the declaration of war in a state of political crisis. Yet what those meaning-oriented steps have in common is that they consider unearthing the rationale, the hermeneutic background context or "horizon of intelligibility" (Taylor 1989) that would give the act plausibility in the eyes of the interpreter, because it had plausibility in the eyes of the agent. If we are to understand at all, we have to be oriented at what would make the other's act meaningful for them.[7]

REASONS FOR THE INTERPRETIVE APPROACH

With this description of the dialogical process of understanding in hand, we can now present the main reasons for the need for an interpretive approach in social science. First, our object is defined as human action, which was shown to be meaningfully constituted. If we are to make good on the claim to understand and explain our object, we need to get at the meaning involved in agency. This requires an internal approach that draws on our own pre-understanding of concepts, values, and purposes, which are put into play to get at the other's perspective and context. Because human agency is intrinsically defined as meaningful, and because contexts of meaning differ, any approach aiming at understanding agency needs to make sense of the respective meaning-contexts at stake.

Second, the need for an interpretive approach becomes apparent when we try to identify our object of understanding as such (Hollies and Lukes, 1982; Krausz, 1989; Kögler, 2006; see also Roth, 2003). Recall that we accepted the premise that we need to reconstruct and understand the meaning-contexts at stake. This means that entering into the other's meaningful perspective requires a bridging act between our own pre-understanding of the intentional objects and the other's understanding of them. But this means that we can only identify the other's meaning if we approach the other dialogically. If we remain outside the intentional understanding of the issues at stake, we cannot even determine which acts and meanings of the other we are to explain. We need to understand what the other's actions and expressions entail, but this demands to take a second-person perspective by approaching

the other as someone who makes sense of things just as we do. Entering ever more deeply into the other's perspective means that we come to connect the other's symbolic expressions in a coherent manner. This new perspective emerges from a process in which we must involve ourselves in the articulated symbolic and cultural material. Understanding the other is thus a product of this encounter, based on the disclosing power of the dialogical process. Only by immersing ourselves into this dialogical process can the other's meaningful acts and expressions even be identified.

Third, the need for such an interpretation of the other's symbolic and cultural expressions is further grounded in the concrete interpretive challenges and obstacles that actions and expressions present to the interpreter. The possibility of unclear and problematic expressions refers back to the fact that the human social sciences emerged from a context in which unclear meanings should be clarified for an ongoing social and cultural life (Dilthey, 2004; Habermas, 1971, 1988). Paradigmatically, legal and theological texts require this kind of interpretation to make their meanings applicable to a current context of life. Equally, cultural expressions in the widest sense, ranging from artworks to literary texts to symbolic artefacts and social practices from different cultural contexts, require the work of interpretive understanding to connect them back to one's own intelligible context. They need to be interpreted so that they can speak to one's self and world. Accordingly, if the social sciences want to retain an internal connection to the reflexive self-understanding of agents, they need to build explanatory models that retain a relation to the agents' self-understanding. Without this connection, the reflexive infusion of social-scientific knowledge into the social life-world of situated agents would become impossible.

Fourth, the need for an interpretive connection to the agent's self-understanding is finally exemplified even by those approaches that critically challenge the situated perspective of the agents at stake (Horkheimer and Adorno, 1972; Hoy, 2004; Hoy and McCarthy, 1994). Indeed, much of social-scientific work consists in approaching the agent's own self-understanding as in some form limited, constrained, and uninformed by the background factors and social processes and structures that ultimately define a cultural context. Yet even if a symbolic perspective is defined as ideology or otherwise objectively structured, we still face the need to relate those structures to how agents see themselves and their world. For one, the sheer identification of the meaning of the ideological level requires that the agents' own conceptual and value-perspective be analyzed and reconstructed. And second, if ideology-critique is to have an impact on cultural and social life, the capacity for agents to critically reflect and adopt the social-scientific findings needs to be present. But this in turn implies that agents are able to exercise a bridging act between their own self-understanding and the social-scientific theories that unmask structural limits in their views. To enable this move, the social scientist cannot start from the agents' established understanding – however partial, limited, or systematically distorted – and relate it back to his or her own complex explanatory accounts.

SOCIAL-PHENOMENOLOGICAL AND ETHNOMETHODOLOGICAL INTERPRETATIONS OF AGENCY

PHA shows how the meaningful background of the interpreter plays a crucial role in understanding the self-understanding of authors and agents. We have seen how this process of understanding can be modeled as a dialogical encounter in which the interpreter relates to the intentional perspective of the other, always mediating her own preconceptions and practices with those that appear on the other side. This approach of a *dialogical realism* overcomes the unproductive dilemma between a totally subjectivist

conception of meaning attributions imposed onto the other and the naively objectivist claim to merely stating social facts. The real meaning of the other's beliefs, assumptions, and practices is shown to emerge from an engaged interpretation in which the other's voice and values profile themselves vis-à-vis the social scientist's own views and practices. Yet to fully work as a framework for social science, we need to see how the intentional attribution of the interpreter – that is, that our object of study is the other's intentional meaning – is justified when trying *to explain* human agency. In other words, we have to make good on the second shoe of PHA and show that the interpretive self-understanding is causally efficacious in shaping human action. It is here where the paradigms of social phenomenology (Schutz, 1967 and followers) and ethnomethodology (Garfinkel, 1967 and his school), with the probable addition of symbolic interactionism (Mead, 1934), prove essential.

To account for the causal role of intentional agency involves taking three aspects into account. First, agency must here be defined as self-conscious. Consciousness of something implies that one is conscious of being conscious of something. This does not mean that the subject is constantly reflecting on itself, nor that it can ever fully capture the "I" of the intentional act; yet it means that the self is *capable* of a reflexive relation to itself as an agent, allowing a wide range of answers how this reflexivity is displayed in concrete acts or practices. Second, agency has to be able to effect states in the world. It has to be causally efficacious in a real, non-vegetarian sense: it has to have causal bite with regard to its environment and situation. And third, both of these aspects have to be combined in a certain way, i.e., such that the agents' conscious understanding has to stand in a uniquely defined relationship to the effects caused by its own endeavors. This articulates the intuition about human agency that to act intentionally, that is, to act on the basis of rational motives, means that the effects to be had are themselves related to the reason and motives held such that the reasons and motives are themselves causally efficacious. Taken together, the view involves a conception of agency in which situated human selves are actively involved in constructing their selves (or self-identities) and environments by developing and articulating the reasons and norms that define their social worlds (Kögler, 2010).

The social-phenomenological project by Schutz and others exemplifies those aspects of human agency and sets out to show how on its basis an account of social life and order can be given (Lash, 1998; Schutz, 1967). Crucial here is the relation between the interpretive agency of situated selves and social norms. For social phenomenologists, *norms themselves are maintained through the interpretive activities of agents.* While it is granted that agents emerge as socially mature and autonomous selves only by means of being placed in normatively structured situations, the normative order itself depends for its symbolic and social reproduction on the collaborative activity of its agents. This view is emphasized against a Parsonian conception of action theory in which the normative structure is somewhat severed from the ongoing interpretive and reflexive activities of the situated agents (Heritage, 1984). For Parsons, the existence of norms is treated as a given in social theory. The explanation of human action becomes possible if an agent's acts and practices can be correlated with rational norms that are taken to prevail in a given context. The identified rational rules can then, if combined with a straightforward theory of socialization in which agents adopt the norms as part of their internalized psychic infrastructure, treated as social laws that will allow for the prediction and explanation of intentional acts. According to this model, the social scientist possesses an equivalent to laws in the natural sciences, only that the "laws" are here taken to be rational rules that are followed by agents due to early inculcation. Note that the social scientist has no need to further consult the agents' activities once the norms and the social situation is

known. The explanation becomes the result of the application of rational rules to a given context. In case that the observed behavior cannot be explained, that is, cannot be subsumed under those rules, additional factors explaining the irrational deviation from the norm must kick in.

For a hermeneutically informed social phenomenology, this view is unsatisfactory for the following reasons. To begin with, the methodological bifurcation regarding the explanation of rational and irrational behavior seems to rest on a problematic ontological assumption. In the case of rational actions, the internal reconstruction of plausible, sound, and valid grounds and motives is to suffice to account for an act. However, in cases deemed "irrational," the recourse to "empirical" or causal factors is recommended. This methodological split requires some account on the side of agency, which in turn must be seen as neatly divided into a rational part and one governed by external or empirical motives. Such an approach is at odds with the hermeneutic insights into the psychological and ontological mediations of situated agency, which strongly suggests a holistic approach towards how agents form reasons and motives. At the least it is in need of explicating the grounds upon which agents' reasons and motives can be assigned a rational and an irrational status, since so much hinges on which toolkit is to come to bear on their understanding and explanation.

A second concern directly relates to the rational standards. From whence is the interpreter, herself situated in a culturally and historically mediated context, to gain access to the allegedly pure and non-empirical sphere of rational reasons and motives? Given the context-dependency of the interpreter's access to the sphere of meaning, such claim to access seems far fetched, as the meaning is what counts as a reason or motive and therefore does transcend the entanglement of reason and cultural contexts. As we saw in the previous sections, what counts in the other agent's context as a reason and motive is itself an emergent product of the interpretive exchange based on previously held assumptions. Those assumptions stand the test of interpretive cogency and fruitfulness and cannot be treated as a prior standard of rational agency everywhere.

Finally, and perhaps most importantly, the norm-governed approach works with a view of rules that does not pass post-Wittgensteinian muster. The issue here concerns the idea of an internalized norm that functions as an internal law of action and is thus decipherable by an observing social scientist. However, this forgets that rules cannot determine their own application. As Wittgenstein and Kripke have shown, the definition of a rule does not itself provide sufficient conditions for applying it in a consistent manner (Kripke, 1982; Wittgenstein, 1953). Without a shared background context that suggests how a definition is to be understood, each particular rule-case opens itself to (almost) countless ways of being interpreted. This does not rule out a shared contextual understanding, but it does locate the source of common meaning one story down: in the shared background practices and skills that agents in concrete contexts acquire, possess, and display. Accordingly, the social-scientific interpreter cannot interpret the explicit rules as clear and transparent. This would mean to take the background assumptions of her own context and apply them, however inconspicuously, to the rules of the other. The scientist would thus miss the object of understanding. However, she is also prevented from somehow deducing how the other would apply and interpret her own rules, since these applications and interpretations are not pre-determined by the rules alone. What is needed instead is to get to the empirical level of agent-based rule application to see how the concepts and values are understood by the agents themselves. What is needed is access to rule-application in context, is to see how agents in concrete contexts are always already actively engaged in making sense of their broader beliefs and assumptions in the context of cultural practices and institutions.

Based on the rejection of a norm-governed conception, the alternative has to show *how agents construct the social world through their interpretive activities*. Alfred Schutz develops this approach by starting from the basic interactive situation of the face-to-face encounter between subjects (Heritage, 1984; Schutz, 1967). By analyzing how agents understand themselves and others in differing circles of proximity, he discovers the essential role of *interpretive schemes*. What emerges is that social order is maintained by agents' assumptions and expectations vis-à-vis other agents. Expectations are always already structured according to certain generalized type-assumptions, which nonetheless cannot be mistaken for some generalized rational algorithm. Rather, those schemes are open-ended and interpretively maintained frames of reference that guide and orient agents without determining their choices. Thus, the social order is built from the bottom up, it is ontologically created by means of interpretive acts, and it is based on the intersecting and networking acts and practices of situated subjects consciously oriented at others, themselves, and the world. The subsequent approach by Peter Berger and Thomas Luckmann can be seen as a further articulation of the "Social Construction of the World" (Berger and Luckmann, 1967; see also Hacking, 2000; Searle, 1995).[8]

While the role of *individual interpretive agency* is crucial for social phenomenologists, it is Harold Garfinkel's ethnomethodology that breaks the essential ground here (Garfinkel, 1967). Garfinkel drops an explicit interest in the big questions of social order, norms, and micro-macro-relations and focuses instead on the very activity of situated agents in concrete social situations. The aim is to bring out what truly *grounds* the interactive understanding of agents. In order to bring this "ground" to the fore, Garfinkel and his research team develop a wide array of "social experiments" in which agents are challenged in their "natural" expectations regarding the behavior of others. Taken together, these experiments show the importance of the agentive power of meaning construction with regard to creating an ordered social environment.

Agents approach other agents and situations with a strong *normative expectation* of what is permissible and what is prohibited. The slightest deviation from standardized responses or standardized scripts is greeted with deep hostility and rejection, displaying a strong normative infrastructure of expectations. These expectations are based on situational scripts which, while implicit and unarticulated, are nevertheless crucial for defining the situation. Garfinkel's research sparked the whole new field of conversation analysis, the object of which is the reconstruction of such underlying schemes. The normative expectation implies that agents are *individually held accountable* for maintaining the normative order of interaction. The agent is made responsible for any deviation, which displays the reflexive self-attribution of accountability within their own life world. Finally, the intersubjective construction of meaning involves a high level of *reflexivity,* as the order maintained by the script is developed through complex interactive steps. The interactively maintained script requires constant tracking how the other responded and how the other's response is to be understood. The ethnomethodological analyses show that agents fill in whatever is required to make the other's response or act appear meaningful, suggesting once more that as human agents, we are doomed to make sense.

CONCLUSION: LIMITS AND PROSPECTS OF A HERMENEUTIC SOCIAL SCIENCE

By arriving at ethnomethodology and social phenomenology, PHA has come full circle. We have now seen that interpretive social science has already developed conceptual tools to understand human agency as defined by interpretive practices. The need for an interpretive methodology to anchor itself in social reality such that interpretive intentional acts can have causal power has been answered by social phenomenological and ethnomethodological approaches. Their work shows that the interpretive approach is not restricted to the methodology of the social-scientific interpreter, but rather extends to the very (ethno)-methodology of the situated agents themselves. Yet the importance of the phenomenological and ethnomethodological emphasis on individual reflexive agency should not suggest that those approaches are not subject to legitimate criticism or further development.

First, the concern with "interpretive schemes" might not go far enough with regard to understanding the nature of skills and dispositions that make meaning possible. The critique of the norm-governed approach suggests that practical skills and competences are crucial, which cannot be captured fully by merely locating "schemes" within the practical background of the agents; rather, their constitution as embodied skills that apply schemes without being themselves articulated as such must be considered (Dreyfus, 1980; Stern, 2003).

Second, the acquisition of these skills and competences is a practical affair being actively initiated in the habitual use of schemes and rules. This means that the execution of individual agency is also less openly reflexive, if reflexivity means a self-conscious application of rules to situations. Rather, the real work of individual agency needs to be located on a pre-conscious and symbolic/practical level through which agents address their environment, while conscious reflexivity is introduced as a potential of situated agents (Wittgenstein, 1953; Bourdieu, 1977, 1990).

Third, the acquisition of the respective practical skills is intrinsically tied to the socially established schemes through which they are learned. Since these schemes are reflexive of larger cultural and social contexts, their relation to objective social situations and structures must be systematically considered.

While agents exercise creativity and reflexivity in each context, their embodied capacities nonetheless point back to larger settings that pre-structure what can possibly be said, thought, and experienced (Foucault, 1979; Bourdieu 1977, 1990).

Fourth, we must acknowledge that the individual's capacity to creatively and critically effect her environment encounters objective social, cultural, and political constraints. The bulk of social power will not be openly felt as such, due to prior inculcation in skills and schemes which are supportive of the status quo. The objective boundaries of discourses, fields, and social systems will limit what individual agency can possibly achieve in a given social context.

Phenomenological and ethnomethodological analyses ensure that such limits are never taken as a condition without escape, that social transformation based on individual reflexivity is always a built-in possibility of social situations. All the same, the future development of PHA needs to take into account those dimensions of the non-individual and non-reflexive background. It will have to integrate them into a conception of intentional human agency, one that does justice to the dialogical nature of interpretive understanding in the social sciences.

NOTES

1 We should recall that from the start we assume that the interpreter or social scientist is *oriented at understanding meaning*. We saw that in order to gain access to the meaning at stake, a to-and-fro movement between the part and the whole is unavoidable. The issue is now: How can this process get possibly off the ground, such that the other's real meaning becomes understandable? And, given the methodological uniqueness claim, why should the process of oscillating between the part and the whole be considered any different from what is happening in the adjudication of particular data and scientific generalizations in the natural or behavioral sciences?

2 Recall that the double thesis of the hermeneutic approach is (a) to deliver an adequate description of human understanding requires taking the self-understanding of agents into account, and (b) such an interpretive account must be causally explanatory. Taken together, it means that we have to show that agents are acting in ways causally related to their self-understanding. The grounding of social-scientific understanding in the ontological similarity between social scientist (the interpreter) and social agents (the interpreted) is to make good on this thesis.

3 Two points should be noted here. First, even though the romantic claim of a mysterious domain behind the thought is given up, the orientation of interpretation remains psychologically focused inasmuch as the object remains the intended thought as such. However, the process of re-constructing the thought is now seen as a discursive process undertaken by the interpreter to articulate the original intentions. Second, the fact that this reconstructive process is a quasi-infinite process means that the human sciences are methodologically different from their natural-scientific counterpart. Complete and final laws are not to be expected here.

4 To be sure, Husserl does not present consciousness in the Cartesian metaphors of a *res cogitans*, a mental substance, thus inviting the image of the mind as a container or box filled with ideas whose connection to external phenomena is problematic. Yet the methodological Cartesianism expressed in the scientific aims of his project implies the mind as a separate and self-sufficient sphere defined by its own structures.

5 Gadamer remains here influenced by the later Heidegger. In later Heidegger, language is understood as a transsubjective and holistic event that surpasses individual control while nonetheless framing all thought and experience, thus disempowering the role of the self-determined and reflexive subject (Heidegger, 1971, 1977).

6 By making the hermeneutic insights fruitful here, we might equally draw on early Heidegger's factual hermeneutics of agency since the target here is the understanding of intentional human actions, and not, like overwhelmingly in Gadamer, the interpretation of texts. To be sure, we might say that actions are themselves structured like texts inasmuch as they are symbolically mediated and always oriented at some purpose which defines their substantive subject matter. For further discussion on the concept of dialogue for interpretation, see Mandair and Zene 2005.

7 When we try to aim at the meaning of another text—most broadly construed—we cannot but take this approach if we are to make sense at all. If we want to get into the meaning, we need to draw on our pre-understanding, but we can only do this in the spirit of making sense of the other's linguistic, cultural, and symbolic expressions, which relates us to an external source that internally poses a resistance and a challenge to our own pre-conceptions

and assumptions. The experience of this challenge, with and against which we have to create a coherent picture of the other's intended thoughts and actions, defines the dialogical nature of interpretive understanding that overcomes hermeneutic idealism while retaining the strong relatedness of all understanding to the social-scientific interpreter's background.

8 The emergence of post-structuralism in social theory (Foucault, 1979, 1990, 1994; Bourdieu, 1977, 1990) allowed for further developments regarding the "social construction of reality." The latter approaches emerged from a structuralist position against which they emphasized the role of practices and agents' habitus. However, they never fully acknowledged the crucial role of individual creative and reflexive agency to the extent needed and developed by social phenomenologists and ethnomethodologists alike.

REFERENCES

Berger, Peter and Luckmann, Thomas (1966) *The Social Construction of the World*. Garden City, NY: Anchor Books.

Bourdieu, Pierre (1977) *Outline of a Theory of Practice*. Cambridge: Cambridge University Press.

Bourdieu, Pierre (1990) *The Logic of Practice*. Stanford: Stanford University Press.

Davidson, Donald (2001) *Inquiries into Truth and Interpretation*. Oxford: Oxford University Press.

Dilthey, Wilhelm ([1883] 1959) *Einleitung in die Geisteswissenschaften (Introduction to the Human Sciences)*. Ges. Schriften I. Stuttgart: Teubner.

Dilthey, Wilhelm (1982) *Die Geistige Welt (The World of the Mind)*. Stuttgart: Teubner.

Dilthey, Wilhelm ([1910] 2004) *The Construction of History in the Human Sciences*. Princeton: Princeton University Press.

Dreyfus, Hubert (1980) 'Holism and hermeneutics', *Review of Metaphysics*, 34(1): 3–24.

Dreyfus, Hubert (1993) *Being-in-the-World: A Commentary on Heidegger's Being and Time*. Cambridge MA: The MIT Press.

Foucault, Michel ([1975] 1979) *Discipline and Punish*. New York: Pantheon Books.

Foucault, Michel ([1966] 1990) *The Order of Things*. New York: Vintage Books.

Foucault, Michel ([1976] 1994) *History of Sexuality: An Introduction*. New York: Vintage Books.

Gadamer, Hans-Georg ([1960] 1989) *Truth and Method*. New York: Crossroads.

Garfinkel, Harold (1967) *Studies in Ethnomethodology*. Englewood Cliffs, NJ: Prentice-Hall.

Grondin, Jean (1994) *Introduction to Hermeneutics*. New Haven: Yale University Press.

Habermas, Jürgen (1971) *Knowledge and Human Interests*. Boston: Beacon Press.

Habermas, Jürgen (1988) *On the Logic of the Social Sciences*. Cambridge, MA: The MIT Press.

Hacking, Ian (2000) *The Social Construction of What?* Cambridge: Harvard University Press.

Heidegger, Martin ([1927] 1962) *Being and Time*. New York: Harper & Row.

Heidegger, Martin (1971) *On the Way to Language*. San Francisco: HarperCollins Publishers.

Heidegger, Martin (1977) *Basic Writings*. San Francisco: HarperCollins Publishers.

Heidegger, Martin (1982) *The Basic Problems of Phenomenology*. Bloomington: Indiana University Press.

Heidegger, Martin (1985) *History of the Concept of Time*. Bloomington: Indiana University Press.

Heidegger, Martin (1999) *Ontology: Hermeneutics of Facticity*. Bloomington: Indiana University Press.

Herder, Johann Gottfried and Jean-Jacque Rousseau (1966) *On the Origin of Language: Two Essays*. Chicago: University of Chicago Press.

Heritage, John (1984) *Garfinkel and Ethnomethodology*. Cambridge: Polity Press.

Hollies, Martin and Lukes, Stephen (1982) *Rationality and Relativism,* Cambridge, MA: The MIT Press.

Horkheimer, Max and Adorno, Theodor (1972) *Dialectic of Enlightenment*. New York: Herder and Herder.

Hoy, David (2004) *Critical Resistance*. Cambridge, MA: The MIT Press.

Hoy, David and McCarthy, Thomas (1994) *Critical Theory*. Oxford: Blackwell Publishers.

Humboldt, Wilhelm von (1988) *On Language: The Diversity of Human Language-Structure and its Influence on the Mental Development of Mankind*. Cambridge: Cambridge University Press.

Husserl, Edmund ([1913] 1962) *Ideas: General Introduction to Pure Phenomenology*. London: Collier MacMillan Publishers.

Husserl, Edmund (1970) *Logical Investigations*. London: Routledge.

Husserl, Edmund (1991) *Cartesian Meditations*. Dordrecht, Boston: Kluwer Academic Publishers.

Kögler, Hans-Herbert (1999) *The Power of Dialogue: Critical Hermeneutics after Gadamer and Foucault*. Cambridge: The MIT Press.

Kögler, Hans-Herbert (2006) 'Hermeneutics, phenomenology, and philosophical anthropology', in Gerard Delanty (ed.) *Handbook of Contemporary European Social Theory*. London: Routledge. pp. 202–217.

Kögler, Hans-Herbert (2010) 'Agency and the Other: On the intersubjective roots of self-identity'. Special issue: *New Ideas in Psychology*, B. Sokol and J. Sugarman, (eds), in press.

Kögler, Hans-Herbert and Stueber, Karsten (2000) (eds) *Empathy and Agency: The Problem of Understanding in the Human Sciences*. Boulder, CO: Westview Press.

Krausz, Michael (1989) (ed.) *Relativism: Interpretation and Confrontation*. Notre Dame, IN: University of Notre Dame Press.

Kripke, Saul (1982) *Wittgenstein on Rules and Private Language*. Cambridge, MA: Harvard University Press.

Lash, Scott (1998) *Another Modernity, A Different Rationality*. London: Blackwell Publishers.

Mandair, Arvind and Zene, Cosimo (2005) (eds) 'Dialogue as the inscription of "the West"', in: *Social Identities*, special issue 1, Vol 11, n 3, May 2005, London, New York: Routledge, 171–298

Mead, George Herbert (1934) *Mind, Self, and Society*. Chicago: University of Chicago Press.

Ormiston, Gayle and Schrift, Alan (1990) (eds) *The Hermeneutic Tradition: From Ast to Ricoeur*. Albany: SUNY.

Ricoeur, Paul (1992) *Oneself as Another*. Chicago, IL: Chicago University Press.

Rorty, Richard (1991) 'Inquiry as recontextualization: An anti-dualist account of interpretation', in *Objectivity, relativism, and truth, Phil. papers 1*. Cambridge: Cambridge University Press.

Roth, Paul (2003) 'Beyond understanding: The career of the concept of understanding in the human sciences', in Stephen Turner and Paul Roth (eds) *Philosophy of the Social Sciences*. Malden, MA, Oxford, UK: Blackwell. pp. 311–333.

Schleiermacher, Friedrich ([1819] 1957) *Hermeneutics: The Handwritten Manuscripts*. The American Academy of Religion, Atlanta, GE: Scholars Press

Schutz, Alfred (1967) *The Phenomenology of the Social World*. Evanston, IL: Northwestern University Press.

Searle, John (1995) *The Construction of Social Reality*. New York: The Free Press.

Stern, David (2003) 'The Practical turn', in Stephen Turner and Paul Roth (eds) *Philosophy of the Social Sciences*. Malden, MA, Oxford, UK: Blackwell. pp. 185–206.

Taylor, Charles (1985) *Human Agency and Language*. Cambridge: Cambridge University Press.

Taylor, Charles (1989) *Sources of the Self. The Making of the Modern Identity*, Cambridge, MA: Harvard University Press.

Weber, Max (1949) *Max Weber on the Methodology of the Social Sciences*. Edward Shils and Henry A. Finch (eds), Glencoe, Ill: The Free Press.

Weber, Max (1978) *Economy and Society*. Berkeley and Los Angeles: University of California Press.

Winch, Peter ([1959] 1991) *The Idea of a Social Science and its Relation to Philosophy*. London: Routledge.

Wittgenstein, Ludwig (1953) *Philosophical Investigations*. Cambridge: Cambridge University Press.

23

Pragmatism and Symbolic Interactionism

Alex Dennis

INTRODUCTION

Pragmatism and symbolic interactionism (SI) tend to be misrepresented in very similar ways. They are accused of being atheoretical, individualistic, incompatible with radical thought and merely competitors with, or responses to, more established philosophical and sociological approaches. Thus, for example, Lewis (1976: 347–348) argues that interactionism's 'subjectivist tendency' derives from the 'subjective nominalism' of William James and John Dewey. Huber (1973: 275) argues that SI 'shares with the philosophy of pragmatism, from which it originates, an epistemology which makes it reflect the social biases of the researcher and of the people whose behavior is observed'. Such subjective biases, she goes on to state, are 'sensitive to the forces of social control'. The 'subjectivity' of pragmatists and interactionists, then, renders them susceptible to ideological manipulation – as Garfinkel ([1964] 1967) puts it, they are 'judgmental dopes', irrationally reproducing as sociological fact aspects of the social world that are, viewed theoretically, the products of ideology.

These arguments are most bluntly articulated by da Silva (2008), who criticizes SI for its 'astructural bias' (see also Meltzer et al., 1975: 113). da Silva argues that symbolic interactionism introduced Mead's ideas to sociology in a distorted form:

In particular, Mead's contributions should not be reduced to an argument over the ownership of a sociological perspective which reverses Parsons' emphasis on social order and prioritizes, instead, *agency* over *structure*. On the contrary, Mead's seminal contribution is to suggest a completely different way of looking at the problem. (da Silva, 2008: 78)

According to da Silva, this is because, as others have argued, SI is a response to more conventional and mainstream sociological perspectives:

His [Blumer's] perspective has to be understood, from its very inception, as an alternative to Talcott Parsons' structural functionalism, the dominant perspective in American sociology until the end of the 1960s. As a consequence, Mead's inclusion in the sociological canon would be considered, for better or for worse, by this circumstance. (da Silva, 2008: 76)

As a consequence of its subjectivism and individualism, SI, da Silva argues, is incapable of dealing with the structural topics that define sociology. *Somehow* these phenomena emerge from the near-random coming together of individuals in interaction, but just how is unclear: 'Individual actors such as a manual laborer or the CEO of a large corporation contribute, through their "careers" as social actors, to the definition and development of large-scale phenomena of which they are only partially aware' (da Silva, 2008: 77). Such criticisms are unfounded. Neither pragmatism nor SI is inherently subjectivist; pragmatist and interactionist analyses are often both radical and critical; and neither perspective depends for its sense on better-established approaches.[1]

More problematic, however, is Fine's (1993) observation that many of SI's central ideas have become incorporated, often unacknowledged, into the sociological mainstream, rendering those ideas commonplace and weakening the perspective's distinctiveness and cohesion. Here, therefore, the distinction and cohesion of pragmatism and SI will be emphasized to try to show how some unexamined features of contemporary sociology can be more closely integrated as part of an original, and developing, theoretical and philosophical unity. For these purposes the works of the early pragmatists – Charles Sanders Peirce, William James, John Dewey and George Herbert Mead – and the 'Second Chicago School' of sociology – Herbert Blumer, Everett C. Hughes, Louis Wirth, William Lloyd Warner and their graduate students – will form the core of the discussion.

DEFINITIONS AND CONSEQUENCES

The most famous tenet of pragmatist thought is that the meaning of a phenomenon derives from its effects on the world rather than from any intrinsic properties it might have. This was originally articulated by Peirce in 1878 and elaborated by James in 1907: 'Consider

what effects, which might conceivably have practical bearings, we conceive the object of our conception to have. Then, our conception of these effects is the whole of our conception of the object' (Peirce, [1878] 1992: 132).

> What difference would it practically make to any one if this notion rather than that notion were true? If no practical difference whatever can be traced, then the alternatives mean practically the same thing, and all dispute is idle. Whenever a dispute is serious, we ought to be able to show some practical difference that must follow from one side or the other's being right. (James, [1907b] 1977: 377)

This has implications for sociology both ontologically and epistemologically. Ontologically it means that the practical uses to which something might be put determine what it 'is'. Anything – an object, social fact, economic indicator, film sequence, etc. – is only the thing it is because of the ways it is brought into human activities. Thus, the central problem for sociology must be the investigation of how things are defined and understood, because it is through such definition and understanding that the social world is constituted. We act on the basis of our understandings and our actions generate, animate, maintain and transform social reality. Thus, Hughes ([1962a] 1971) argues convincingly that all societies utilize a group of people to do the 'dirty work' of an in-group, namely to deal with the out-group seen as problematic, dirty, inferior, etc. By defining the work of dealing with that out-group as 'dirty' the in-group systematically avoids examining too closely just what that work might entail, making that work less constrained by social norms and more attractive to those of a cruel disposition. There is nothing necessarily cruel or vicious about, for instance, police officers, but if Hughes is right our definition of their work as 'dirty' – dealing with those we would rather not deal with ourselves, but who nevertheless require dealing with – is likely to make it more likely that they will bend the rules and attract bad apples. Dirty work becomes dirty in every sense and, as Thomas and Thomas

(1928: 572) famously asserted, '[i]f men define situations as real, they are real in their consequences'.

Epistemologically, the meaning of a phenomenon residing in its effects or consequences means sociology's topics of enquiry cannot be taken for granted. There is a permanent danger that sociologists will go native, treating the lay ideas of members of society as if they referred to objectively real things, or believing that there is a position external to the social world from which one can view its 'objective' features. Shalin (1986: 18) argues that pragmatist epistemology is founded on a recognition that rationalist approaches fail in five ways:

1 they posit 'objectivity' as requiring a vantage point external to the thing being examined;
2 they are based on a notion that bias, interest and partiality can be removed in observers;
3 they construe (some) facts as fixed entities instead of dynamic products of interaction;
4 they reduce complex cases to 'instances of' an overarching concept; and
5 they treat scientific and common sense knowledge as philosophically separate, rather than as variants of knowledge more generally.

In order to avoid such failings it is necessary to (try to) see the social world from the perspective(s) of those practically engaged in its production. This is what Dewey referred to as 'immediate empiricism':

> Immediate empiricism postulates that things – anything, everything, in the ordinary or non-technical use of the word 'thing' – are what they are experienced as. Hence, if one wishes to describe anything truly, his task is to tell what it is experienced as being. (Dewey, [1905] 1981)

Thus, for example, Lofland's (1966) ethnographic study of a millennial cult shows how their proselytizing activities make perfect sense given their beliefs, their backgrounds and the resources they have available, despite the fact that from any other point of view the same activities can only be understood as annoying, bizarre, inappropriate or even crazy – whether those 'points of view' are those of passers-by, members of other religious

groups, psychiatrists or politicians. No analytic privilege can be given to the 'academic' in this context: the understandings of philosophers or sociologists are no different to those of anyone else. This has radical implications for how pragmatists and interactionists understand empirical investigation.

EMPIRICAL INVESTIGATION

According to James, the 'cash-value' of truth depends on the difference it makes to experience:

> *True ideas are those that we can assimilate, validate, corroborate and verify. False ideas are those that we can not.* That is the practical difference it makes to us to have true ideas; that, therefore, is the meaning of truth, for it is all that truth is known-as. ... Truth *happens* to an idea. It *becomes* true, is *made* true by events. Its verity *is* in fact an event, a process; the process namely of its verifying itself, its veri*fication*. Its validity is the process of its valid*ation*. (James, [1907c] 1977: 430)

The emphasis for SI's research practice, then, is to generate statements that are capable of being validated: a 'finding' is something that can be checked and found to be the case. This requires a repeated and ongoing return to the empirical world as the source of sociological problems and the arbiter of sociological findings. Blumer (1969: 24–26) outlines how this analysis should proceed in a somewhat idealized step-by-step list of 'parts of scientific inquiry ... that are indispensable to inquiry in empirical science' (Blumer 1969: 24), founded on James' radical empiricism. Central to Blumer's account, however, is the assertion that we always have a 'picture' of the world being investigated prior to our investigations taking place. This is, as outlined above, inevitable: the world is always already interpreted and understood, and does not exist independently of our interpretations.[2] What *kinds* of 'pictures' we might have is, however, more problematic.

Pragmatists and interactionists alike are suspicious of preconceived theoretical accounts of the world. The pictures we might have of how things work should be tentative and open to empirical correction, and should not, on an a priori basis, restrict or presume what might be happening. They are 'guesses', to use Peirce's happy expression. Research, in short, should be driven by a desire to *describe accurately* rather than to explain or categorize prematurely. Sociological concepts should, therefore, emerge from investigations rather than drive them – and as such these are radically different in their constitution to the 'pictures' we (as lay members of society) will necessarily have of the settings we operate in.

SI is a *critical* sociology insofar as it questions the traditional sociological belief that concepts can be clear and distinct, that they could fit together logically and that they can be assembled to form a theoretically coherent picture of the world as a whole. As Hughes argued, '[e]veryone agrees that institutions should be the central object of sociological study, then promptly defines them in such a way that the most interesting and significant kinds of human collective enterprises are left out of account' (Hughes, 1971: 52). Blumer ([1956] 1969) took this further in his ferocious attack on variable analysis, in which he demonstrated the logical inconsistency of variable analytic sociology in its own terms, provoking 'one of the most telling 35-year silences in the recent history of academic life' (Watson, 1995: 317).[3]

The emphasis in SI research, then, is on fieldwork as the central form of sociological investigation (Becker and Geer, 1957), with other qualitative – and to a lesser degree quantitative – approaches relegated to substitute status. The field is typically approached with loose and open questions rather than a particular operationalized 'problem', and issues of 'cumulativity' are dissolved into comparative and formal sociological tropes (Becker, 2007). The classic statement of this approach is that of Glaser and Strauss (1967: 1):

> Most writing on sociological method has been concerned with how accurate facts can be obtained and how theory can thereby be more rigorously

tested. In this book we address ourselves to the equally important enterprise of *how the discovery of theory from data – systematically obtained and analyzed in social research – can be furthered*. We believe that the discovery of theory from data – which we call *grounded theory* – is a major task confronting sociology today, for, as we shall try to show, such a theory fits empirical situations, and is understandable to sociologists and laymen alike. Most important, it works – provides us with relevant predictions, explanations, interpretations and applications.

If the purpose of pragmatic investigations and symbolic interactionist research is to generate theory, then, how do these perspectives construe theoretical 'findings'?

THEORY

It should be remembered that in James' formulation (above) truth has a 'cash-value'. His point, in full, is as follows:

> 'God', 'Matter', 'Reason', 'the Absolute', 'Energy', are so many solving names. You can rest when you have them. You are at the end of your metaphysical quest.
>
> But if you follow the pragmatic method, you cannot look on any such word as closing your quest. You must bring out of each word its practical cash-value, set it at work within the stream of your experience. It appears less as a solution, then, than as a program for more work, and more particularly as an indication of the ways in which existing realities may be *changed*.
>
> *Theories thus become instruments, not answers to enigmas, in which we can rest.* We don't lie back upon them, we move forward, and, on occasion, make nature over again by their aid. (James, [1907b] 1977: 380)

Theory, for James, is not something that provides a finished picture of the world, an 'answer' to an 'enigma', but something which allows enquiry to move forward. Just as empiricism requires us to repeatedly return to the world to find things out, check the veracity of our ideas and develop new questions, theory provides us with a complementary moment in the process of enquiry: one in which we can consolidate what we have found and move forward to new investigations on the basis of that consolidation. The utility of a theory is the extent to which it *changes* our view of the world, and allows us to move forward with further investigations with a better-developed idea of what that world is and how our investigations might attain greater depth. The *process* of inquiry is just that: not something that will ultimately lead to a final answer, but an ongoing series of empirical and theoretical developments.

A similar orientation applies in SI:

> A great deal of time has, in my opinion, been wasted in taking the specific hypothesis of Durkheim on suicide, or some of those of Weber on protestantism or of Park on the marginal man or the race-relations cycle, and going through the exercise of proving those men wrong – as one obviously can. What one gets from such men, especially from those whose work was done before the more recent developments of empirical method, is a statement of general problems, a set of concepts, and sometimes some fruitful hypotheses and ideas with which to enrich one's own thinking and to suggest methods for solving the problems with which he is concerned. (Hughes, [1961] 1971: 565)

Interactionist practice tends towards the development of concepts and theories, but these are often very different to those in other sociological perspectives. Instead of a 'totality', SI theory seems to be 'about' discrete sets of activities and institutional workings, and where general statements are made they appear to be methodological rather than substantive. Thus, for example, Ball (1967: 301) makes the following modest, and slightly ironic, claim about his ethnographic study of an abortion clinic:

> Unfortunately, the confidential nature of this research does not allow one of the usual canons of science to be met, i.e., that regarding exact replication; and no claim regarding the typicality of the clinic described herein can be made. Hopefully, however, the materials have shed some light on a relatively little known area of social behavior. Given the incidence of abortion, it may be hoped that similar analyses can be conducted by others. Additionally, it may be suggested that the concept of rhetoric provides a useful tool for examining the dramas of social life, whether deviant or conventional, spontaneous or routine, unusual or mundane.

The irony here is that there is no inclination on the part of SI practitioners to adhere to these particular 'canons of science': reliability is something which is only relevant at the formal or methodological level, inasmuch as findings from one setting might provide useful tools for starting to examine another: the study of psychiatric hospitals as 'total institutions', for instance, provides a description of certain formal features of such institutions that might be relevant to the study of prisons, the military, ships and so on (Goffman, [1961] 1991); while, notoriously, Hughes ([1951] 1971: 316) argued that:

> The comparative student of man's work learns about doctors by studying plumbers; and about prostitutes by studying psychiatrists. This is not to suggest any degree of similarity greater than chance expectation between the members of these pairs, but simply to indicate that the student starts with the assumption that all kinds of work belong in the same series, regardless of their places in prestige or ethical ratings. In order to learn, however, one must find a frame of reference applicable to all cases without regard to such ratings. … Both the physician and the plumber do practice esoteric techniques for the benefit of people in distress. The psychiatrist and the prostitute must both take care not to become too personally involved with clients who come to them with rather intimate problems.

The emphasis on descriptive accuracy and generalization at the formal level, then, makes much SI work appear to be conceptually agnostic. As Blumer has it: What I would declare, then, is that to use concepts in science as natural ultimates instead of tentative convenient conceptions, or to be uncritical or unreflective as to their import, is not likely to lead to genuine understanding and control (Blumer, [1931] 1969: 170). Elsewhere, however, what counts for SI as theory can appear more methodological than substantive. It is to this form of interactionist theory I will now turn.

MEANING

Blumer's contribution to sociological 'theory', in particular, appears methodological – even epistemological – rather than substantive in form. Furthermore, it seems to be 'about' how actors understand the world, rather than 'about' how the 'social' is constituted. It takes the form of three 'premises' on the basis of which enquiries should be conducted:

> The first premise is that human beings act toward things on the basis of the meanings that the things have for them. … The second premise is that the meaning of such things is derived from, or arises out of, the social interaction that one has with one's fellows. The third premise is that these meanings are handled in, and modified through, an interpretative process used by the person in dealing with the things he encounters. (Blumer, 1969: 2)

This appears a strangely atheoretical (even unsociological) contribution to theory, until the radical pragmatist bases of these premises and their implications for practice are drawn out. First, it should be emphasized that 'meaning' here does not simply indicate, for example, a definition or name. SI's concern with meaning is not with a cognitive or philosophical concept, but rather with a *practical* term. Something is meaningful only to the extent it makes a practical difference to someone. Thus, for instance, Peirce ([1907] 1998) argues that it does not matter how we *experience* colors as long as we name and use them in the same ways in practical situations. If I 'see' a green traffic light in the same way you 'see' a red one – if different color-images appear to us – it makes no practical difference as long as we both give the name 'green' to our experience. The meaning of our terms-terms only comes under question if one of us starts mixing up different colors, by being unable to distinguish between red and green altogether for example.

Meaning is thus a fundamentally social phenomenon: we (broadly speaking) understand things the same way because we have to co-ordinate our activities around those things. Thus, our understandings of the world come from those activities: we do not have a meaningful world to start off with, and then do things in it – as, for instance, the logical positivists might assert – but rather the meaning of the world is constituted through the activities that make it up. Verbs precede nouns logically, as the 'things' around us emerge from, and are determined by, the 'doings' we undertake.

Meaning is not, however, fixed and determined. Each new activity we engage in requires us to put into practice again our previously-gathered understandings and experiences. This may be unproblematic, and may not even require conscious deliberation: driving the same route to work every day is something one can disconcertingly find one has done 'on automatic pilot', finding oneself arriving without any clear recollection of making the journey. Others, however, can be more difficult. Finding out that one established meaning does not hold in a new context forces one to revise either the understanding of that meaning or the sense the context might have. As Goffman ([1969] 1971) points out, the conclusion that someone may have mental health problems does not emerge unproblematically, but rather is a product of being unable to attach other meanings and understandings to that person's bizarre behavior. One can 'come to realize' something, 'view things differently', recontextualize a situation – in short, modify or change the meanings attached to things.

These concerns open up two related issues: the nature of the actor – the agent of this meaning-manipulation – and the relationship between the individual and the social.

THE SOCIAL ACTOR

SI's clearest debt to pragmatist thought can be found in the way interactionists understand the social actor and, in many respects, SI can be understood as a way of empirically studying the philosophical concerns with the nature of the individual initially raised by Dewey and Mead. The earliest pragmatist conception of the nature of the individual was advanced by Dewey in his 1896 paper

'The reflex arc concept in psychology' (Dewey, [1896] 1981). In this, Dewey systematically demolishes the idea that there can be such discrete phenomena as 'stimuli' that act on individuals and 'responses' those individuals make to them. The movement of an arm, for example, is always *both* response and stimulus: it is a response to the thing it is being moved to act on (whether to avoid it, hit it, grasp it, etc.) and also a stimulus for subsequent movement (its movement providing feedback which allows balance, other bodily adjustments, etc., to be made, particularly in conjunction with the operation of the eye and other senses). Dewey demonstrates that all stimuli are always also responses, and all responses always also stimuli, depending on the framework in which we understand them. This means that the terms only make sense in terms of greater co-ordinations: collections of stimuli and responses that make up meaningful human activities. The unit of psychological study, then, should not be physiological but semantic – because the 'meaning' of what we do, framed in terms of stimuli and responses, emerges from the *point* of what we are doing and not the other way around. We can not add up discrete physical phenomena – things which impinge on our sense organs, kinetic responses to those things, etc. – to 'make up' a meaningful world, but rather understand such physical 'things' through the meanings they have. As above, activity precedes the meaning of its component parts.

Dewey's problematic – how one can conceive of an embodied but always-social human actor – was the starting point of much of Mead's philosophy, as he sought to show how a self-conscious and semantically-aware individual could emerge. Mead ([1912] 1964) argued that is primarily through communication that the 'self' can develop. Just as social actors can make objects of things in the world (and thereby constitute them) they can also make objects of one another and, crucially, of themselves. Through language we are able to constitute objects in the world as part of our stream of experience

– manipulating and discarding them as an imagined plan of action prior to actually using them. This gives our actions a purposive character, where we do not merely react to external stimuli but transform the world in plans of action prior to, or in parallel with, our engagement with it. To do this, however, we must be able to imagine *ourselves* as objects: to think of ourselves as part of the field of activity, pursuing different hypothetical lines of action and choosing between them. This capacity to make ourselves objects of our own thought characterizes us as human (social) actors, and distinguishes us from other animals: it defines us as human, socialized, beings. Each of us is therefore both an 'I' and a 'me': the 'I' being the experiencing, acting agent in the world and the 'me' being our selves as made objects to the 'I' in thought.

This is a radically anti-Cartesian position. The 'self' is not a unified entity, experiencing an 'outer' world from an 'inner' space, but is rather populated by the contents of the world, including the self itself, in the form of the 'me'. Its radical nature can be made clearer if we consider two factors in Mead's account: the manner in which the self develops and the centrality of language and communication to its development and maintenance.

The self, for Mead (1934), develops through interactions between the human organism and its environment. At first, like animals, we experience the environment in terms of stimuli, which can be internal (e.g. hunger) or external (e.g. warmth). Like other higher animals, however, we also experience others like ourselves as part of our environment – and the behavior of other humans constitutes an important part of our world. These experiences are, initially, meaningless: just as the dominant posture of one dog will act as a stimulus for another to adopt a challenging or submissive posture, we experience others' behaviour as stimuli and respond unreflectively with behavior of our own. This 'conversation of gestures' is sufficient for very young infants to satisfy their basic bodily requirements: a scream in response to a sensation of hunger or discomfort will elicit an appropriate response from the baby's carer.

Through teaching language use, however, such gestures come to be replaced by meaningful interaction. As children are taught to speak a natural language, they learn to manipulate *significant symbols* – and thus to manipulate the world in imagination. This allows them to understand the perspective of others – to see how the world would look from another's point of view, and thus to interpret others' behavior not merely as a stimulus but as meaningfully produced to have desired effects. Other people become internalized as 'others' – producers of meaningful activity – rather than merely as objects. By playing, imagining him or herself as particular others, the child is able to adopt other roles: to pretend to be a father, mother, sibling, doctor, nurse, etc. Playing with others, where different roles are taken on and abandoned, provides the child with a wide range of possibilities in terms of what roles might be available for him or her to take in the social world he or she inhabits. More fundamentally, though, as play develops, each participant has to learn to subsume his or her play under the auspices of *rules*: to play a *game* means to share an orientation to a more impersonal and general set of imperatives (e.g. to play snakes and ladders requires one to accept the rule that the first dice throw made counts, however unfortunate the consequences of this might be). Abstract rules of this sort are internalized not as particular others, particular social roles, but as a *generalized* other: an internalization of the requirements of social proprieties taken as independent of the particular actors involved in any situation. Durkheim's 'moral order' appears here as a particular figure *within* the social actor.

THE PRIMACY OF THE SOCIAL

Just as in Durkheim's argument, for Mead – and Blumer – the social is primary and the individual secondary. The social world has

an 'obdurate reality', and – however inconvenient we might find it – no individual or group of individuals can decide to ignore or change it by will alone. What is important here, however, is the sense in which that social world is construed very differently to how other sociologists might conceive of it. Rather than there being social structures and individual agents operating at different 'levels' or requiring theoretical consolidation, the social world is made up *solely* of human actors, and each human actor is a 'self' composed of internalized representations of other individuals and roles, and of broader norms and rules to which all must orientate. There is no split between the social and the individual, as each logically implies the other – and both derive from the activities people engage in together. They are interactional products.

Just as Mead (1934) rejected Watsonian behaviorism for its assertion that there is nothing other than physiological behavior in human life, Blumer (1990) rejected the notion that 'social forces' like industrialization could shape or determine the social world. The concepts of both the behavioral bodily unit and the autonomous social fact are equally wrong: they give a misplaced concreteness to things that emerge from human activity, and treat products of such activities as if they were causes. As with James ([1907a] 1977), Mead's approach to the relationship between mind and society is to reject a dualistic approach in favor of one in which the terms of reference can be demonstrated to be aspects of the same thing: to dissolve a philosophical dilemma by demonstrating that it is a function of the way the problem is framed – by philosophers – rather than a feature of the 'real world'.

What does emerge from this account, however, is an understanding of social activity that is framed in very different terms: where meaning and possibility oscillate between determinacy and indeterminacy. The smaller the range of 'others' available the more restricted the sense of the world, as what sense(s) we can make of the world is shaped by the range of different roles we can imagine taking in that world. There must always be some slippage between what seems possible and what actually is, if only because some of our understandings have yet to be found wanting and others have yet to take their place as possibilities. The social world is constantly changing, and what requires accounting for sociologically is not how it changes but *how it is maintained as stable*. Its stability is an *achievement*, and we would be mistaken to believe otherwise – regardless of how much we might take that stability for granted (Shalin, 1986). As James points out:

> It seems *a priori* improbable that the truth should be so nicely adjusted to our needs and powers as that. In the great boarding-house of nature, the cakes and the butter and the syrup seldom come out so even and leave the plates so clean. Indeed, we should view them with scientific suspicion if they did. (James, [1896] 1977: 729)

Structure and agency, stability and change, agreement and dispute *all* emerge from the same social processes – our practical interactions in the social world – and it is the project of a pragmatist sociology to reveal how these, in particular circumstances and as formal features, operate. The ways in which people orientate to their internalized others, their reference groups, is a central plank of this project:

> Some people find, in this welter of 'others', some complex balance or compromise among several. Others let one or another tyrannize them. The nature of the combinations and balances is part of the organization of society itself. Judging the relative influence of various 'others' upon individuals is indeed one of the problems with which social surveys are most concerned. (Hughes, [1962b] 1971: 351)

One's activities and social position determine what 'others' are available and, by extension, what possible meanings one might be able to use as part of the flow of one's life. Having a wide range of others, and selecting creatively and ethically between them, defines the 'good citizen', and the importance of sociability (Simmel, [1911] 1949) as a way of lubricating social intercourse – in ways comparable to Mead's emphasis on play and

games – cannot be understated as a 'serious' matter. In these senses SI is a 'liberal' sociology, but these *liberatory* possibilities are important – as we shall see.

EXAMPLES

The 'classic' studies of symbolic interactionist sociology reflect and realize the demand for the empirical investigation of theoretical topics, and demonstrate that the referents of these topics are the products of practical activity in the social world rather than matters for disengaged consideration. The mutual dependence of the individual and the collective, mind and society, means these studies take a wide variety of forms, and cover a broad range of topics. A general rejection of *a priori* principles in favor of empirical investigation tailored to gaining the 'point of view of the actor' means that these can appear heterogeneous and disconnected, particularly in comparison to studies conducted in a framework of cumulativity and/or theoretical commitment. To demonstrate how such studies do relate to one another, and to the pragmatist foundations of SI more generally, I will outline the main points of two interactionist 'classics': Howard S. Becker's analysis of marijuana use, and Barney Glaser and Anselm L. Strauss' description of 'awareness contexts'.

Becker (1953) treats the smoking of marijuana as a matter requiring investigation because it is typically treated 'theoretically' and without respect to the meaning it has for those who engage in the practice. It is treated 'theoretically' insofar as it is assumed that particular personal characteristics determine who will smoke marijuana, and – as such – as something which can be 'explained' by establishing what personality variables correlate with the practice. Becker's objections to this approach are, firstly, that it cannot account for those people who smoke marijuana but do not have the 'appropriate' personality traits, and, second, that it is unable to handle variations in marijuana use over time.

Becker points out that learning how to smoke marijuana, learning how to recognize the sensations of being stoned, and learning how to experience those sensations as enjoyable are fundamentally *social* phenomena. The 'novice' user needs to be trained how to do all three, and this requires him or her to work out how to smoke marijuana for pleasure 'successfully' with reference to the experiences and explanations of more seasoned 'experts'. There is nothing intrinsic to the behavior of smoking marijuana, or to the physiological effects this practice has, that makes being stoned 'pleasant': to do it properly, and to experience it appropriately, are socially produced and learned activities. Becker here instantiates interactionist theory, by treating shared meanings as productive of social phenomena, and methods, by examining *how* an activity is learned and undertaken rather than assuming what that activity must 'be' from looking at its putative causes or effects. The 'others' to whom the novice smoker turns for advice or help will provide him or her with different ways of understanding what he or she is doing, and depending on who they are, and the circumstances of the novice's interaction with them, the social phenomenon of 'enjoying smoking marijuana' can be produced, modified, or even prevented from happening altogether – it is not amenable to theoretical or explanatory description separate to these circumstances.

Glaser and Strauss (1964), in their account of 'awareness contexts', provide an account of how what might appear to be the opposite can occur: the nature of a social context being shaped by the 'individual' understandings of parties to it. Taking their analysis from the different ways a terminally ill patient can be treated (in particular whether or not he or she is told he or she is dying) Glaser and Strauss are able to distinguish between different forms of 'awareness context', the 'total combination of what each interactant in a situation knows about the identity of the other and his own identity in the eyes of the other' (Glaser and Strauss, 1964: 670).

The number of parties to the interaction, whether they acknowledge one another's awareness of their identities, how aware they are of those identities ('aware', 'suspicious' or 'unaware') and what those identities are (one's own, the other's, and the other's view of one's own) can all vary. Glaser and Strauss are thus able to provide a formal framework, a 'paradigm', for understanding the character of different contexts in which interaction occurs, based on the understandings parties have of themselves and relevant others. This demonstrates a commitment to formal analysis, seeking to build upon Simmelian notions of social forms, modified through an understanding that identity emerges from interaction and the perceived or attributed identities of parties to a setting will shape and determine the nature of that setting. A 'theory' is developed which facilitates further study and, potentially, a new way of understanding alternative settings.

The individual and the social, in both these studies, are shown to be mutually implicative and structuring – and the sociological categories usually applied to such settings ('deviance', 'communication', etc.) revealed to elide as much as they reveal.

CRITICISMS AND DEVELOPMENTS

Several illegitimate criticisms have been leveled at symbolic interactionism and pragmatism, as outlined in the introduction. There are problems with both approaches, however, and to conclude I will outline some of these. First, as Fine (1993) points out, 'symbolic interactionism' has largely disappeared from the mainstream sociological vocabulary. There is little 'pure' SI research currently being undertaken, despite the strength of its scholarly society and journal, as the perspective's core concerns have broadened and, perhaps, been diluted through mixture with other sociological concerns and approaches. Equally, many of SI's concerns have been adopted and implemented by 'mainstream' sociologists: ethnographic research, an emphasis on meaning, a rejection of structural determinism, suspicion of variable analysis are now no longer marginal or subversive pursuits. This has meant that much of the integrity and distinctiveness of the pragmatist approach to sociological analysis has now been lost. Indeed, many of SI's concerns and features now seem commonplace, albeit stripped of their theoretical and philosophical bases. Sociologists, particularly qualitative researchers, may find themselves conducting symbolic interactionist work without recognizing that that is what they are doing – and, indeed, while disavowing the perspective for the kinds of reasons outlined in the introduction.

Second, both 'pragmatism' and 'symbolic interactionism' do not really exist in integrated forms. James and Blumer summarized existing bodies of philosophical and sociological work respectively, and brought them under the auspices of 'schools', but those bodies of work were *already present*, and many working within them disavowed their codification. Peirce, for instance, rejected James' version of pragmatism, and neither Becker nor Goffman felt comfortable with being described as symbolic interactionists. In some respects this is appropriate: philosophically and sociologically pragmatism rejects nominalism and codification, and it is appropriate that the labels 'pragmatism' and 'SI' were contentious among their own practitioners.

In recent years, however, both pragmatism and SI have been enjoying a resurgence. Philosophers such as Rorty (1999) have demonstrated the continuing relevance of pragmatist ideas to contemporary philosophical and ethical issues, and Louis Menand's bestselling *Metaphysical Club* (2001) illustrated the centrality of pragmatist ideas to America's development in the 20th century. Equally, contemporary ethnographers such as Duneier (2000) and Fine (2007) explicitly employ SI as a means of questioning the sociological mainstream and empirically investigating matters usually dealt with on a theoretical level.

NOTES

1 Indeed, Blumer's ([1931] 1969) earliest work predates Parsons' (1937) first major statement by some six years.

2 This does not, of course, mean that the world ceases to exist if we are not there to interpret it; merely that our interpretations make it the particular 'world' that it is.

3 This silence has yet to be broken.

REFERENCES

Ball, Donald W. (1967) 'An abortion clinic ethnography', *Social Problems*, 14(3): 293–301.

Becker, Howard S. (1953) 'Becoming a marijuana user', *American Journal of Sociology*, 59(3): 235–242.

Becker, Howard S. (2007) 'The art of comparison: Lessons from the master, Everett C. Hughes', Paper presented at the *Legacy of the Chicago School* conference, Manchester.

Becker, Howard S. and Blanche Geer (1957) 'Participant observation and interviewing: A comparison', *Human Organization*, 16(1): 28–32.

Blumer, Herbert ([1931] 1969) 'Science without concepts', in H. Blumer (ed.) *Symbolic Interactionism: Perspective and Method*. Englewood Cliffs: Prentice-Hall. pp. 153–170.

Blumer, Herbert ([1956] 1969) 'Sociological analysis and the "variable"', in H. Blumer (ed.) *Symbolic Interactionism: Perspective and Method*. Englewood Cliffs: Prentice-Hall. pp. 127–139.

Blumer, Herbert (1969) 'The methodological position of symbolic interactionism', in H.Blumer (ed.) *Symbolic Interactionism: Perspective and Method*. Englewood Cliffs: Prentice-Hall. pp. 1–60.

Blumer, Herbert (1990) *Industrialization as an Agent of Social Change: A Critical Analysis*. New York: Aldine de Gruyter.

da Silva, Filipe Carreira (2008) *G.H. Mead: A Critical Introduction*. Cambridge: Polity.

Dewey, John ([1896] 1981) 'The reflex arc concept in psychology', in J. J. McDermott (ed.) *The Philosophy of John Dewey*. Chicago: University of Chicago Press. pp. 136–148.

Dewey, John ([1905] 1981) 'The postulate of immediate empiricism', in J. J. McDermott (ed.) *The Philosophy of John Dewey*. Chicago: University of Chicago Press. pp. 240–248.

Duneier, Mitchell (2000) *Sidewalk*. New York: Farrar, Strauss and Giroux.

Fine, Gary Alan (1993) 'The sad demise, mysterious dis-appearance, and glorious triumph of symbolic interac-tionism', *Annual Review of Sociology*, 19: 61–87.

Fine, Gary Alan (2007) *Authors of the Storm: Meteorologists and the Culture of Prediction*. Chicago: University of Chicago Press.

Garfinkel, Harold ([1964] 1967) 'Studies of the routine grounds of everyday activities', in H. Garfinkel, *Studies in Ethnomethodology*. Englewood Cliffs: Prentice-Hall. pp. 35–75.

Glaser, Barney G. and Anselm L. Strauss (1964) 'Awareness contexts and social interaction', *American Sociological Review*, 29(5): 669–679.

Glaser, Barney G. and Anselm L. Strauss (1967) *The Discovery of Grounded Theory: Strategies For Qualitative Research*. New York: Aldine de Gruyter.

Goffman, Erving ([1961] 1991) *Asylums: Essays on the Social Situation of Mental Patients and Other Inmates*. Harmondsworth: Penguin.

Goffman, Erving ([1969] 1971) 'The insanity of place', in E. Goffman (ed.), *Relations in Public: Microstudies of the Public Order*. Harmondsworth: Penguin. pp. 335–390.

Huber, Joan (1973) 'Symbolic interaction as a prag-matic perspective: The bias of emergent theory', *American Sociological Review*, 38(2): 274–284.

Hughes, Everett C. ([1951] 1971) 'Mistakes at work', in Everett C. Hughes (ed.), *The Sociological Eye: Selected Papers*. Chicago: Aldine-Atherton. pp. 316–325.

Hughes, Everett C. ([1961] 1971) 'Tarde's *Psychologie economique*: An unknown classic by a forgotten sociologist', in E. C. Hughes (ed.), *The Sociological Eye: Selected Papers*. Chicago: Aldine-Atherton. pp. 557–565.

Hughes, Everett C. ([1962a] 1971) 'Good people and dirty work', in E. C. Hughes (ed.), *The Sociological Eye: Selected Papers*. Chicago: Aldine-Atherton. pp. 87–97.

Hughes, Everett C. ([1962b] 1971) 'What other?', in E. C. Hughes (ed.), *The Sociological Eye: Selected Papers*. Chicago: Aldine-Atherton. pp. 348–354.

Hughes, Everett C. (1971) 'Going concerns: The study of American institutions', in E. C. Hughes (ed.), *The Sociological Eye: Selected Papers*. Chicago: Aldine-Atherton. pp. 52–64.

James, William ([1896] 1977) 'The will to believe', in J. J. McDermott (ed.) *The Writings of William James: A Comprehensive Edition*. New York: Random House. pp. 717–735.

James, William ([1907a] 1977) 'The present dilemma in philosophy', in J. J. McDermott (ed.) *The Writings of William James: A Comprehensive Edition*. New York: Random House. pp. 362–376.

James, William ([1907b] 1977) 'What pragmatism means', in J. J. McDermott (ed.) *The Writings of William James: A Comprehensive Edition*. New York: Random House. pp. 376–390.

James, William ([1907c] 1977) 'Pragmatism's concep-tion of truth', in J. J. McDermott (ed.) *The Writings of William James: A Comprehensive Edition*. New York: Random House. pp. 429–443.

Lewis, J. David (1976) 'The classic American pragma-tists as forerunners to symbolic interactionism', *Sociological Quarterly*, 17(3): 347–359.

Lofland, John (1966) *Doomsday Cult: A Study of Conversion, Proselytization, and Maintenance of Faith*. Englewood Cliffs: Prentice-Hall.

Mead, George Herbert (1934) *Mind, Self and Society From the Standpoint of a Social Behaviorist*. Chicago: University of Chicago Press.

Mead, George Herbert ([1912] 1964) 'The mechanism of social consciousness', in A. J. Reck (ed.) *Selected Writings*. Chicago: University of Chicago Press. pp. 134–141.

Meltzer, Bernard N., John W. Petras and Larry T. Reynolds (1975) *Symbolic Interactionism: Genesis, Varieties, and Criticism*. London: Routledge and Kegan Paul.

Menand, Louis (2001) *The Metaphysical Club: A Story of Ideas in America*. New York: Farrar, Strauss and Giroux.

Parsons, Talcott (1937) *The Structure of Social Action*. New York: McGraw-Hill.

Peirce, Charles S. ([1878] 1992) 'How to make our ideas clear', in N. Houser and C. Kloesel (eds) *The Essential Peirce: Selected Philosophical Writings*. Vol. 1. Bloomington: Indiana University Press. pp. 124–141.

Peirce, Charles S. ([1907] 1998) 'Pragmatism', in The Peirce Edition Project (ed.) *The Essential Peirce: Selected Philosophical Writings*. Vol. 2. Bloomington: Indiana University Press. pp. 398–433.

Rorty, Richard (1999) *Philosophy and Social Hope*. Harmondsworth: Penguin.

Shalin, Dmitri N. (1986) 'Pragmatism and social interac-tionism', *American Sociological Review*, 51(1): 9–29.

Simmel, Georg ([1911] 1949) 'The sociology of sociabil-ity', *American Journal of Sociology*, 55(3): 254–261.

Thomas, William I. and Thomas, Dorothy Swaine (1928) *The Child in America: Behavior Problems and Programs*. New York: Alfred A. Knopf.

Watson, D.R. (1995) 'Some potentialities and pitfalls in the analysis of process and personal change in coun-seling and therapeutic intervention', in J. Siegfried (ed.) *Professional and Everyday Discourse as Behavior Change*. Norwood, NJ: Ablex. pp. 301–335.

24

Social Constructionism, Postmodernism and Deconstructionism

Patrick Baert, Darin Weinberg
and Véronique Mottier

INTRODUCTION

The structure and layout of handbooks reveals a lot about the state of an academic subject. First of all, it indicates the themes or perspectives that are regarded as important. Those that are left out also carry a message about priorities within the discipline. But sometimes it is books' organisation that exposes widespread preconceptions towards the particular perspectives that do receive coverage.

The fact that this chapter discusses social constructionism together with postmodernism and deconstruction might be taken as indicative of the extent to which interconnection is perceived between those three schools. They are widely regarded as sharing a distinct epistemological or theoretical outlook, similar to the way in which other chapters reflect the prevalent notion of a closeness between pragmatism and symbolic interactionism (Chapter 21) or an elective affinity between phenomenology, herme-neutics, and ethnomethodology (Chapter 22). The division of labour within the book implies that, at some fundamental level, social constructionism has more in common with postmodernism than with phenomenology or pragmatism.

In some respects, this is surprising. While postmodernism and deconstructionism have more or less a shared intellectual ancestry, we will demonstrate that some versions of social constructionism developed out of different theoretical traditions, and indeed a substantial number of social constructionists make quite different claims than the ones which are traditionally associated with the excesses of postmodernism. Nevertheless, the three intellectual traditions are frequently portrayed as presenting the same overall vision. All three are regularly portrayed as denying the existence of an external reality and, crucially, denying the possibility of scientific objectivity. All three are often seen as antithetical to the very idea of science.

We do not wish to argue that this view is completely wrong – rather that the overall picture is more complex and harder to map. It will become evident that most of the authors discussed in this chapter share an antifoundationalist stance, but it will become equally clear that there are substantial differences between the three perspectives and indeed considerable variety within each. This is indeed so true that the very prospect of parsing authors into each of the three camps in a way that avoids controversy seems to us a futile enterprise. Without presuming to have thereby avoided controversy, we have divided authors among the three camps on the following grounds. Those we associate with each of the three camps either self label as deconstructionists, postmodernists or social contructionists respectively or have been widely appropriated by scholars who so self label. So, for example, despite the fact that he never ascribed this label to himself, Michel Foucault is discussed under postmodernism because he has been widely ascribed an influential role in defining its arguments. Ludwig Wittgenstein is discussed under the auspices of social constructionism for the same reason. We will argue that the antifoundationalist writings that contribute most fruitfully to the social sciences are committed to forging alternatives to radical relativism and, more specifically, to defending the pragmatist emphasis on empirically driven intellectual debate.

DECONSTRUCTIONISM AND POSTMODERNISM

Deconstructionism

'Deconstruction' is a term most commonly associated with the writings of French philosopher Jacques Derrida and his followers. While there are a number of overlaps between postmodern and deconstructionist thought – in particular, its common rejection of foundationalist perspectives – deconstructionism goes much further in questioning the foundations or indeed the very possibility of social science. It is therefore hardly surprising that deconstructionism initially developed outside the realm of the social sciences. Its reception within the social sciences – as within philosophy – has been marked by a distinct amount of suspicion and, at times, open hostility, in contrast to its success within literary criticism.

The term deconstruction was first used by Derrida in his *Of Grammatology* (1978), published in the original French in 1967. Despite its centrality in Derridian perspectives, its originator, like a modern-day oracle, has limited himself to delphic pronouncements and scattered hints, refusing to provide a clear and concrete definition of what deconstruction actually means, and describing his own writings as a series of ongoing attempts to figure that out. As he put it himself: 'All my essays are attempts to have it out with this formidable question' (1988: 4). It has thus been left to his followers to try to provide conceptual clarification. While deconstruction generally refers to a particular mode of philosophical and literary analysis, its practitioners are at pains to point out that it does not constitute a method or a school. Rather, deconstructionist analyses refer to the myriad processes whereby readings of a text undercut authors' intentions and thereby defy authorial control.

In opposition to the Western philosophical tradition, deconstructionism seeks to reveal and contest the binary oppositions that structure texts which are widely regarded to have been highly influential in Western culture: for instance, male/female, white/ black, speech/writing, culture/nature, etc. However, for most of its proponents, the aim of deconstructionism is not just to provide new literary interpretations of texts. More fundamentally, deconstructionist readings aim to contribute to the critical dismantling of much of the Western philosophical canon, explaining why the most ferocious resistance to Derrida's ideas has come from philosophers. He develops a hermeneutics of suspicion towards categories of objectivity and absolute truth, which, he argues, mask the systematic hierarchical privileging of one term (e.g. male or white) over its opposite (female or black) in cultural, social and political life. The point is not to reverse the hierarchy of the binary opposition, but to question the hierarchy itself. For Derrida, there is no absolute truth outside of language which can act as a foundation for value judgments, knowledge or certainty. Echoing poststructuralist dissolutions of the human subject, individual consciousness is not the origin of all meaning, but is instead simply one more effect of signifying processes.

Consciousness, truth and knowledge are thus not built on the solid ground of empirical reality. They are construed only as textual effects whose meanings are necessarily, always, unstable and indeterminate. While the interpretation of texts may often involve what Derrida called an 'appeal to presence' – that is, a claim to have faithfully captured the author's true intentions – such efforts are always doomed to failure given the inherent openness of meaning. All theories of unequivocal knowledge are said to be founded on erroneous metaphysical appeals to the full presence of its referents. These cannot be substantiated by anything beyond the text and hence deconstructionists define knowledge and truth as inevitably nothing more than textual effects. There are no absolute foundations for truth or knowledge: interpretative analysis is instead an open-ended and never ending task. It is in that sense that, for Derrida, there is no determinate object or essence outside the text that might act as a guarantor of its validity.

Derrida's work has been influential in the anti-essentialist perspectives which flourished in the humanities and social sciences in the 1980s and 1990s. For example, authors such as Gayatri Spivak (1988) (who also translated *Of Grammatology*), Judith Butler (1999) and Homi Bhabha (1994) have drawn on Derrida to theorise gender, sexual and postcolonial identities not in terms of ontological essences but in terms of performance, parody and hybridity. The most valiant attempt to represent Derrida as a serious, systematic philosopher to date has been made by Rodolphe Gasché, whose work *The Tain in the Mirror: Derrida and the Philosophy of Reflection* (1986) aimed to rescue Derrida from literary criticism in order to bring him back into the home of philosophy. Neo-Marxists such as Ernesto Laclau (1996) and Chantal Mouffe (1996) have done much the same for political theory. Rejecting Habermas's attempts to found political values on universal conditions of speech, Laclau and Mouffe have instead drawn on deconstructionism to outline the contours of alternative, antifoundationalist models of radical democratic politics.

Derrida's critics have been numerous and loud. His idiosyncratic writings have been described as infuriatingly 'impenetrable' and 'obscure'; 'elitist' due to their privileging of high culture (a focus which is not shared by many of his followers whose analyses of many aspects of popular culture have in turn been accused of triviality); and 'nihilist' in their assault on Western thought and knowledge. Deconstruction has thus been used as a term of abuse by many critics, for whom it epitomises what they perceive as the excessive convolution and gratuitous complexity of continental, in particular French, philosophy. While we do not subscribe to this wholesale rejection of the value of deconstructionism, we do think that its radical disavowal of the very idea of empirical warrant significantly narrows its appeal for the social sciences. Moreover, its commitment to confining analysis to the play of signifiers occludes the fact that the opportunities and constraints of interpretation are often influenced not only by linguistic conventions but also by material arrangements of power. It is precisely the accomplishment of postmodernist authors to draw attention to and conceptualise the intricate relationship between discourses and power relations.

Postmodernism

The term 'postmodern' has been applied in different ways. For the sake of brevity, we are not exploring the use of 'postmodern' in the aesthetic or social realm, so we do not address the extensive discussions in the academic literature about the arrival of new aesthetic forms or the emergence of a postmodern, 'late capitalist' or 'hyper-real' society. We focus instead on the employment of the term specifically within the philosophy of social science and explore its consequences for the practice of social research.

Used by Jean-Francois Lyotard in *The Postmodern Condition* (Lyotard, 1984) to denote the emergence of a new socio-cultural phase, postmodernism quickly acquired a broader and often pejorative meaning. It has often been used to dismiss writings as pretentious, lightweight and anti-Enlightenment, similar to the way in which the term 'positivism' has been used to denigrate research for being unnecessarily unadventurous and dogmatically scientist. The term has been used increasingly in this pejorative sense ever since the outbreak of the so-called science wars in the 1990s and in particular since the 1996 Sokal affair, centred round Alan Sokal's publication in *Social Text*, which he simultaneously depicted as a hoax in *Lingua Franca* (Ashman and Baringer, 2001; Gross and Levitt, 1997; Sokal, 1996a, 1996b). Interestingly, while the term 'postmodernism' has been and remains to be, used on a regular basis to belittle the writings of others, there seem to be increasingly fewer self-proclaimed postmodernists.

As there is quite obviously no consensus as to what kinds of writings ought to be described as postmodernist, the question arises of what could be meant by 'postmodernism' in the philosophical context. If we consider the writings of Michel Foucault, Jean-François Lyotard and Gianni Vattimo, who in different ways epitomise the postmodern position, three analytically distinct features stand out. First, like many strands of social constructionism as well, 'postmodernism' denotes a general intellectual orientation according to which truth and knowledge claims are socially situated and socially constituted, and therefore variable and inevitably intertwined with ongoing power struggles. This view is diametrically opposed to various established intellectual positions: not only does it contradict the view that truth and knowledge reside within an extra-social realm, but it also undermines the notion that social science can or should play a role in emancipatory projects. This explains the discomfort of critical theorists like Jürgen Habermas towards postmodernism and their suspicion that it embodies at least a political quietism, if not a thinly disguised conservatism (Habermas, 1987). Postmodernists tend to rebut such charges with the counter-critique that so-called emancipatory projects generally tend to be less about liberation than the rise of various power-knowledge regimes (e.g. Foucault, 1975). Moreover, they insist that postmodernism is not incompatible with the idea of a critical social science so long as it does not entail providing unequivocal epistemological or normative guidelines.

Second, like deconstructionism and some strands of social constructionism, postmodernists want to move away from 'totalising theories' or overarching 'grand narratives' that artificially attribute continuity across time or conceive of history as a 'unitary process'. Nietzsche and Foucault's genealogical method of historical inquiry epitomises this philosophical position, focusing as it does on the role of contingency and discontinuity in history in contrast to notions of historical necessity and continuity. Echoing the sentiments of Nietzsche's rejection of 'antiquarianism', Foucault's genealogy operates as a 'history of the present' whereby historical analysis is not merely about acquainting ourselves with the past but is overtly construed as a device with which to challenge widespread presuppositions about the present (Foucault, 1977). Genealogy aims to show that various sets of practices and structures endemic to present constellations of power took different shapes in the past, and only developed into their current form as a result of a complex interplay of chance and power struggles. While there is a clear political dimension to genealogy in that it attempts to provide people with tools to redefine the present condition, it does so without commitment to a definite emancipatory project or an over-arching political agenda.

Third and most definitively, postmodern-ists take a self-consciously anti-modernist stance in that they wish to distance them-selves from a number of beliefs or aspira-tions associated with the so-called project of modernity. This anti-modernism mani-fests itself in the way in which postmodern authors position themselves against arche-typal figures of the Enlightenment era, in particular Kant, but also other thinkers, like Marx, who are sufficiently associated with this philosophical strand to be targeted. The postmodern critique of Enlightenment phi-losophy is basically twofold. It first of all criticises Enlightenment thinkers for drawing on an essentialist line of argument, which is seen as problematic because language and culture 'run all the way down'. This means that categories like the 'subject' or 'man' are no longer held to be absolutes, but must instead be historically situated. Postmodern feminists have, for example, been particularly hostile to essentialist conceptions of feminin-ity and masculinity. Thinking of gender in terms of innate, biological characteristics rather than historically constructed catego-ries is condemned as pernicious because it masks and reinforces existing power rela-tions between men and women (see, for instance, Flax, 1990).

The second component of the post-modern critique of Enlightenment thinking focuses on how it prioritises science, reason and technology, treating them as foundations for societal and human progress. Some ver-sions of the postmodern critique of the Enlightenment treatment of science and reason show affinities with neo-pragmatism in taking on an antifoundationalist stance, according to which there is no neutral algo-rithm that would ground cognitive (and indeed also aesthetic or ethical) claims (com-pare with Rorty, 1980. Other versions of this critique draw on Heidegger's rejection of the primacy of modern science and technology (Vattimo, 1988). Yet other versions draw on a more historical than philosophical argument according to which Enlightenment principles are no longer applicable because of major changes to Western society, in particular the transformations of the role of knowledge and science within it (Lyotard, 1984).

Note that while postmodernism is gener-ally derided, none of the three features men-tioned constitutes a particularly outlandish claim. Indeed, it could be argued that several other theoretical or philosophical strands take similar positions and that some of the postmodernist claims are now very much regarded as commonplace within academia. For instance, most liberal academics would agree with the rejection of totalising theories or grand narratives of history, and in this regard, postmodern thinkers have allies in unexpected quarters such as Popper-inspired critical rationalism and Giddens' structu-ration theory. This aspect of postmodern critiques seems particularly relevant in the light of Fukuyama's work and the revival of religious fundamentalism, presenting as they do totalising and historicist claims within the realm of political ideology.

SOCIAL CONSTRUCTIONISM

We have argued that a major source of motivation for linking deconstructionism, postmodernism, and social constructionism is their seemingly shared commitment to positing an impassable gulf between the objective identity of things and our experi-ences or representations of them. Whereas deconstructionists have insisted on the inescapability of the text, postmodernists have been apt to talk of the historically and culturally specific discourses that forever isolate us from the objective identity of things. Social constructionists, for their part, have too often been happy to forsake discussion of the real for discussion of our knowledge of it or the claims we make about it. In this section, we provide a brief genealogy of social constructionism that, while noting its historical tendency to separate the world of knowledge and experience from the world of objective structures and causes, is intended to demonstrate the movement of some social constructionist work towards bringing these worlds together. We thereby seek to highlight how some social constructionist contributions help us to provide more explicitly for the possibility of empirically grounded social scientific inquiry.

For the sake of exposition it is useful to divide the social constructionist literature into three broad categories: analytic, hermeneutic and critical.

Analytic constructionism

Among the analytic contributors to the social constructionist canon, we place authors like Ludwig Wittgenstein, Willard van Orman Quine, Nelson Goodman, Paul Feyerabend and Richard Rorty. These philosophers and a number of others have used the idiom of analytic philosophy to take issue with the premise that Western philosophy and science possess a rationality or access to reality that is not historically and culturally specific but unsurpassable in principle (Weinberg, 2008). Analytic constructionists have thereby helped to erode categorical distinctions between science and non-science – and, incidentally, between the philosophy of science and the philosophy of the social sciences – while legitimating a turn away from transcendental epistemology and toward social constructionism. Thus, for example, Wittgenstein trenchantly took issue with the notion that a concept's meaning could be decisively

established or verified by means of an 'ideal' logical language, arguing instead that the meaning of concepts can only be understood by learning how people actually use those concepts in their 'ordinary' or 'natural' languages (cf. Wittgenstein, 1953). Unsurprisingly, Wittgenstein's work on meaning and his linkage of the perceived coherence and compulsion of logic to the vicissitudes of social practice have pervasively influenced social constructionist thought.

In a justly famous critique of empiricism, Quine (1951) argued that linguistic propositions acquire meaning only in relation to other propositions. Hence empirical evidence can never decisively confirm or refute any particular proposition because by adjusting related propositions we can always change their meaning and, in turn, the theoretical consequences of the evidence. For Quine, then, empirical evidence cannot be set against propositions on a piecemeal basis but must be set against what he called conceptual schemes (sets of meaningfully related propositions) as wholes. Quine also suggested that different conceptual schemes might be equally capable of accounting for a given body of empirical evidence thus rendering theory choice 'under-determined' by empirical evidence (see also Goodman, 1978). Quine's arguments for meaning holism are equally fatal to the ambitions of both logical positivists and falsificationists to erect a philosophical partition between science and non-science on the foundation of brute experience, and for that reason lend powerful support to the social constructionist thesis that to understand the putative legitimacy of ideas we must look to their social contexts.

Feyerabend (1978) attacked both the views that science is conducted according to a unified 'method' that distinguishes it from non-science and that science ought to enjoy a categorically privileged position vis-à-vis the rest of culture. Kuhn (1970) did perhaps more than anyone else to promote a relativist and descriptive understanding of science in place of any kind of universalistic philosophical explanation or justification of it. Each of these philosophers argued effectively that science is neither methodologically uniform, discontinuous with the rest of culture, nor equipped to capture the empirical world in a manner untainted by theoretical preconceptions (see also Putnam, 1981; Rorty, 1991). Such claims have often been appropriated by social constructionists to philosophically strengthen their own claims to sociologically interpret or explain the production of knowledge or other types of hegemonic ideas, belief systems or practices.

Hermeneutic constructionism

The hermeneutic strain of social constructionist thought can be traced to the seminal arguments of Wilhelm Dilthey. Dilthey fiercely opposed the efforts of authors like John Stuart Mill, Herbert Spencer and Auguste Comte to produce mechanistic causal analyses of society. He insisted that because social life is purposeful, meaningful, and creative, it cannot be explained by natural laws but can only be grasped through *Verstehen*, or interpretive understanding. This emphasis on social actors' meaningful experiences is a staple of a great deal of social constructionist work. Dilthey advocated what he called a *Lebensphilosophie*, a 'philosophy of life', anchored neither in sense data nor in a grand philosophical cosmology, but in the variety and complexity of 'lived experience' itself. He argued that philosophy, like all meaningful activity, is inevitably motivated and informed by the socio-historical conditions under which it is accomplished (and from which it cannot be dislodged).

Max Weber adopted Dilthey's interpretative approach and did much to legitimate and popularise it throughout the human sciences. More specifically, his writings on ideal types, meaning, values and rationalisation exercised a variety of specific influences on other major contributors to the social constructionist canon including Alfred Schutz, Karl Mannheim and members of the Frankfurt School, including Jürgen Habermas. Whereas Weber had described ideal types as concepts of specific value to social scientific methodology, Schutz integrated it into a general phenomenology of the human *Lebenswelt*. Schutz argued that intersubjectivity is not preordained by logic, history or human nature but is actively achieved in ongoing social interaction through use of a vast catalogue of ideal types or 'typifications', compiled into a 'stock of knowledge' shared by social actors (Schutz, 1962). Because interaction requires people to interpret each other, Schutz criticised Weber and others for failing to ground adequately their own scientific typifications of social action in those used by social actors themselves. These ideas had an immense influence on constructionist studies primarily via their adoption by Berger and Luckmann (1967) and Garfinkel (1967). However, Schutz has also come in for a rather lengthy list of valid criticisms (cf. Lynch, 1993: 133–141). For the present, let us suffice to say that Schutz did not fully appreciate the importance of the facts that, first, perception and practical action are embodied; and, second, there is a deeply consequential continuity between the *Lebenswelt*, science and philosophy.

These ideas were better understood by another author influenced by Dilthey, Martin Heidegger. Heidegger argued that science did not, and could not attend to the phenomenological conditions of its own possibility. By its very nature, science must reify the distinction between theory and world, and hence can never explain how this distinction could itself emerge as a meaningful and useful picture of human life. In *Being and Time* (1962) he argued that to understand why humans distinguish theory from world, mind from body, and subject from object, it is necessary to draft a phenomenological ontology of human 'being-in-the-world'. This entailed acknowledging that prior to our conscious interpretation of it, we are always already variously engaged with, and immersed in, the world in ways that inevitably shape interpretation. This engagement is practical not theoretical, concerned not detached, inexplicit but sensually attentive, conceptually diffuse but skilled, and above all 'mindless' (Dreyfus, 1991). Coping is phenomenologically prior to theorising, and indeed prior to the conceptual identification of any 'thing' including our own 'self'. It is precisely this pre-theoretical coping that discloses aspects of the phenomenal world as relevant, meaningful, and either familiar or deserving of reflective consideration. Heidegger inspired unprecedented levels of concern for what Michael Polanyi (1967) has called 'tacit knowledge' and the priority of everyday coping, in all its diversity of skills, to theoretical or discursive knowledge (cf. Bourdieu, 1990). These ideas have been indispensable resources for many social constructionists who advocate a practice turn or a transition to understanding knowledge as competent performance rather than as beliefs or propositions that mirror things-in-themselves (cf. Chaiklin and Lave, 1993; Hutchins, 1995; Schatzki et al. 2001). It is also in his writings prioritising embodied social practice over theory that Heidegger comes closest to the critical and pragmatist strains of social constructionist research to which we now turn.

Critical constructionism

The critical strain of social constructionism owes most to Marx's writings on ideology. Marx developed this concept to suggest how people can suffer from a false consciousness that renders them complicit in their own oppression. This idea was developed by later Marxists like Georg Lukàcs and Antonio Gramsci whose elaborations on concepts like class consciousness, reification, and hegemony have exercised immense influences on social constructionist research by linking the putative legitimacy of ideas to the interests of actors sufficiently powerful to influence the standards by which their legitimacy is measured. This linkage of what societies regard as valid knowledge to the power structures comprising those societies has remained

a lively and fruitful enterprise. Beyond its Marxian roots, the linkage of power and knowledge can be seen in the social constructionist traditions stemming from the post-colonial writings of people like Edward Said, Stuart Hall and the Birmingham School of cultural studies, Michel Foucault's studies of power/knowledge, Pierre Bourdieu's studies of symbolic violence, the feminist standpoint theories of authors like Dorothy Smith and Howard Becker's studies of labelling.

Transforming the Marxian critical concept of ideology into a general and non-critical concept of knowledge as such, Karl Mannheim (1936) called for the sociological analysis of all knowledge (except natural science) as socially embedded and constructed. This was, of course, a monumental precedent for social constructionism but it tended to undermine the possibility of critiquing knowledge claims by levelling the epistemological ground between critic and the object of critique. Mannheim's sociology of knowledge was therefore looked upon by his Marxian contemporaries with considerable suspicion. Indeed, it has been precisely this difficulty of reconciling the sociology of knowledge (which seeks to explain ideas with reference to their social contexts) with epistemology (which seeks to establish procedures for validating ideas), that has, since Mannheim, continued to provoke the most passionate debate amongst social constructionists and their critics (cf. Hacking, 1999; Hollis and Lukes, 1982; Wilson, 1970). Mannheim (1936) sought to achieve this reconciliation by both exempting the natural sciences from his purview and by arguing that a 'socially unattached intelligentsia' (p. 155) might succeed in overcoming the biases inherent to their original class positions. However, he gave no real account of how they could do so and has been taken to task by critics for ducking the problem more than truly resolving it (cf. von Schelting, 1936; Merton, 1937).

Berger and Luckmann (1967) also exempted the natural sciences from their analysis and rather than seeking to resolve the tension with epistemology, simply declared it beyond the scope of the sociology of knowledge.

> To include epistemological questions concerning the validity of sociological knowledge in the sociology of knowledge is somewhat like trying to push a bus in which one is riding...Far be it from us to brush aside such questions. All we would contend here is that these questions are not themselves part of the empirical discipline of sociology. They properly belong to the methodology of the social sciences, an enterprise that belongs to philosophy and is by definition other than sociology. (Berger and Luckmann, 1967: 13)

Like Berger and Luckmann, most social constructionists have sought to avoid direct confrontations with either the natural sciences or epistemology. Hence, it has been common to distinguish between the natural and social dimensions of studied phenomena and confine attention to the social construction of the latter (as when feminist scholars distinguished between biologically determined 'sex' and socially constructed 'gender', or when medical sociologists distinguished between biologically determined 'disease' and socially constructed 'illness experience' or 'disability'). Likewise, most constructionists have passed the buck when it comes to dealing with the difficult question of distinguishing truth and falsity, or, for that matter, establishing any technique for arbitrating the intellectual value of competing claims, once the presumption to possess universal epistemological criteria has been abandoned. They instead rely implicitly on the epistemological standards of their own respective disciplines, or sub-disciplines, to assert the legitimate authority of their ideas and sociologically reductionist accounts of the ideas of those they study. The result is that most social constructionists have been forced to chose between an unsustainably parochial relativism and what Bloor (1991: 12) called the sociology of error. More precisely, they have had either to advocate a permanent suspension of questions concerning the comparative value of their own ideas and those they study, or dogmatically insist

that their own ideas are epistemologically sound and those they study amount to mere myths and illusions. In any case, most social constructionists have remained studiously silent on the question of how we might more reasonably, justly, compassionately or systematically arbitrate the intellectual value of competing claims. It is this silence that has most consistently infuriated critics. However, not all social constructionists have remained so silent, in particular not those constructionists allied with American pragmatist perspectives on antifoundationalism.

IS THERE A FUTURE FOR ANTIFOUNDATIONALIST SOCIAL SCIENCE?

Our answer to this question is an unequivocal yes. However, this future must be one that reflects the lessons of the past. In particular, it is our view that to contribute more fruitfully to the social sciences, antifoundationalists must provide alternatives to a self-refuting radical relativism and, relatedly, for the possibility of empirically grounded data driven debate. Throughout this chapter, it has emerged that the antifoundationalist claims associated with social constructionism, postmodernism and deconstructionism, have led to repeated accusations of epistemic or conceptual relativism. It is indisputable that many social constructionist, postmodernist and deconstructionist authors do eschew the notions of objectivity or empirical corroboration altogether on the grounds that these criteria are irretrievably corrupted by the influence of power or discourse. Accordingly, they argue that we are not merely conditioned by the forms of life into which we are socialised but irremediably confined by them. It must be noted, however, that their claim that the 'radical incommensurability' of different epistemic cultures wholly prevents meaningful communication across lines of cultural or intellectual differences is largely regarded amongst the most philosophically sophisticated antifoundationalists as an academic anachronism (cf. Habermas, 1987; Benhabib, 1992; Davidson, 2005). While there can be no doubting that the world certainly does remain divided by considerable differences of interest, perspective and communicative style that seriously interfere with our efforts to build social solidarities, cooperation and consensus, these differences are increasingly less often viewed as the fixed and insurmountable barriers to productive dialogue and mutual instruction that they once were.

Despite themselves, radical relativists remain bewitched by the spectre of what Dewey called the 'spectator theory of knowledge'. In other words, they accept the proposition that knowledge must be cast in terms of a correspondence between thought or language, on the one hand, and the essence of an independent reality on the other. If, as indeed they argue, such a correspondence cannot be achieved, then we are inevitably forced to accept the unhappy conclusion that any manner of faith in objective knowledge must be abandoned. But, like Dewey before them, antifoundationalists broadly allied with American pragmatism do not accept these terms of debate. Instead they argue that it is the spectator theory of knowledge – with its stark cleavage of the knower from the known – that must be abandoned. They construe knowledge not as an ethereal and otherworldly reflection of the world but as a constituent feature of it. The acquisition of knowledge thus consists not in transcending history to develop what Rorty (1980) called a mirror of nature but, less ethereally, in developing habits and practical skills that promote the good of the individual and society. Moreover, grounded as they are in the pursuits of actual communities, epistemic standards are best understood with reference to the interests and activities of those for whom they hold rather as abstract, universally valid principles. Pragmatists advise us to expect our epistemic terms of reference to be multiple and to change along with the changing conditions under which they are applied. The project of a comparative and, indeed, objective evaluation of knowledge claims is never forsaken but is nested deeply within the specific practical contexts within which it must inevitably be accomplished.

Very much in keeping with the pragmatist tradition, a growing contingent of antifoundationalist social theorists take seriously the idea that by reflexively interrogating the interests served by social scientific work we may succeed in making it a subtler and more valuable craft (cf. Baert, 2005; Bourdieu and Wacquant, 1992; Camic, 1996). To the extent we have lost faith in Berger and Luckmann's (1967: 13) foundationalist claim that devising 'the methodology of the social sciences ... belongs to philosophy and is by definition other than sociology', we must increasingly appreciate the need to naturalise our regard for our own epistemic bearings, locating them empirically in the historical legacy of our craft and in our worldly aspirations for that craft, rather than the otherworldly realm of a putatively transcendental analytic logic. Forsaking the false dream of achieving what Rorty (1991: 13) has called a 'God's eye point of view' of the world, means that we must assume responsibility for the mortality of our epistemic projects and the techniques by which we seek to see them through. This entails acquainting ourselves *empirically* with the worldly circumstances of our research, their attendant possibilities for learning and progress, and then devising the specific role(s) we would hope for our research to play in realising those possibilities. If we no longer countenance the claim that knowledge consists in articulating the sentences in which nature would, if it could, describe itself, then we must provide more justifiable statements of what it is we think our research is, and ought to be, doing. From this perspective, epistemic authority, and the legitimacy of the various epistemic standards upon which it rests, is not achieved unilaterally through textual tricks (as deconstructionists would have it), but *collectively*, as each of us engaged in a given domain of knowledge production proffer mutually critical assessments of the value of our own and each other's contributions to the work and worlds we share (Pels, 2000; Wacquant, 1992: 36–46; Weinberg, 2002, 2006). Empirically informed reflexive dialogue hones our research acumen by facilitating a more explicit regard for the specific nature of our collective work in all its myriad forms and the distinctive resources and constraints that attend the particular conditions under which it is accomplished. Indeed, this point can be generalised. Far from being threatened by the antifoundationalist gaze, all knowledge production stands to benefit considerably from a detailed regard for the myriad macro and micro social conditions that shape, facilitate, and constrain it.

REFERENCES

Ashman, K. and P. Baringer (eds) (2001) *After the Science Wars*. London: Routledge.

Baert, P. (2005) *Philosophy of the Social Sciences; Towards Pragmatism*. Cambridge: Polity Press.

Benhabib, S. (1992) *Situating the Self*. London: Routledge.

Berger, P. and T. Luckmann (1967) *The Social Construction of Reality*. New York: Anchor.

Bhabha, H. (1994) *The Location of Culture*. London: Routledge.

Bloor, D. (1991) *Knowledge and Social Imagery*, 2nd edition. Chicago: University of Chicago Press.

Bourdieu, P. (1990) *The Logic of Practice*. Stanford: Stanford University Press.

Bourdieu, P. and L. Wacquant (1992) *An Invitation to Reflexive Sociology*. Chicago: University of Chicago Press.

Butler, J. (1999) *Gender Trouble*. New York: Routledge.

Camic, C. (1996) 'Alexander's antisociology', *Sociological Theory*, 14(2): 172–186.

Chaiklen, S. and J. Lave, (eds) (1993) *Understanding Practice*. Cambridge: Cambridge University Press.

Davidson, D. (2005) *Truth, Language, and History*. Oxford: Oxford University Press.

Derrida, J. (1978) *Of Grammatology*. Baltimore: John Hopkins University Press.

Derrida, J. (1988) 'Letter to a Japanese friend', in D. Wood and R. Bernasconi (eds) *Derrida and Différance*. Evanston: Northwestern University Press. pp. 1–5.

Dreyfus, H. (1991) *Being-in-the-World*. Cambridge, MA: MIT Press.

Feyerabend, P. (1978) *Science in a Free Society*. London: New Left Books.

Flax, J. (1990) *Psychoanalysis, Feminism and Postmodernism in the Contemporary West*. Berkeley: University of California Press.

Foucault, M. (1975) *Discipline and Punish*. New York: Random House.

Foucault, M. (1977) 'Nietzsche, genealogy, history', in D. Bouchard (ed.) *Language, Counter-Memory, Practice; Selected Essays and Interviews*. Ithaca: Cornell University Press. pp. 139–164.

Garfinkel, H. (1967) *Studies in Ethnomethodology*. Englewood Cliffs, NJ: Prentice-Hall.

Gasché, R. (1986) *The Tain in the Mirror: Derrida and the Philosophy of Reflection*. Cambridge: Harvard University Press.

Goodman, N. (1978) *Ways of Worldmaking*. Indianapolis: Hackett.

Gross, G. and P. Levitt (1997) *The Flight from Science and Reason*. New York: New York Academy of Science.

Habermas, J. (1987) *The Philosophical Discourse of Modernity*. Cambridge: Polity Press.

Hacking, I. (1999) *The Social Construction of What?* Cambridge, MA: Harvard University Press.

Heidegger, M. (1962) *Being and Time*. New York: Harper & Row.

Hollis, M., and S. Lukes (eds) (1982) *Rationality and Relativism*. Oxford: Basil Blackwell.

Hutchins, E. (1995) *Cognition in the Wild*. Cambridge, MA: MIT Press.

Kuhn, T. (1970) *The Structure of Scientific Revolutions*. Chicago: University of Chicago Press.

Laclau, E. (1996) 'Deconstruction, pragmatism, hegemony', in S. Critchley and C. Mouffe (eds) *Deconstruction and Pragmatism*. London: Routledge. pp. 47–68.

Lyotard, J.P. (1984) *The Postmodern Condition: A Report on Knowledge*. Minneapolis: University of Minnesota Press.

Lynch, M. (1993) *Scientific Practice and Ordinary Action*. Cambridge: Cambridge University Press.

Mannheim, K. (1936) *Ideology and Utopia*. New York: Harvest.

Merton, R. (1937) 'The sociology of knowledge', *Isis*, 27(3): 493–503.

Mouffe, C. (1996) 'Deconstruciton, pragmatism, and the politics of democracy', S. Critchley and C. Mouffe (eds) *Deconstruction and Pragmatism*. London: Routledge. pp. 1–12.

Pels, D. (2000) 'Reflexivity: One step up', *Theory, Culture and Society*, 17(3): 1–25.

Polanyi, M. (1967) *The Tacit Dimension*, 2nd edition. New York: Anchor.

Putnam, H. (1981) *Reason, Truth, and History*. Cambridge: Cambridge University Press.

Quine, W. (1951) 'Two dogmas of empiricism', *Philosophical Review*, 60(1): 20–43.

Rorty, R. (1980) *Philosophy and the Mirror of Nature*. Princeton, NJ: Princeton University Press.

Rorty, R. (1991) *Objectivity, Relativism, and Truth*. Cambridge: Cambridge University Press.

Schatzki, T., K. Knorr-Cetina and E. von Savigny (eds) (2001) *The Practice Turn in Contemporary Theory*. London: Routledge.

Schutz, A. (1962) *Collected Papers, vol. 1*. The Hague: Nijhoff

Sokal, A. (1996a) 'Transgressing the boundaries: Towards a transformative hermeneutics of quantum gravity', *Social Text*, 14(1–2): 217–252.

Sokal, A. (1996b) 'A physicist experiments with cultural studies', *Lingua Franca*, May–June: 62–64.

Spivak, G. (1988) 'Practical politics of the open end', *Canadian Journal of Social and Political Theory*, 12(1–2): 104–111.

von Schelting, A. (1936). 'Review of *Ideologie und Utopie* by Karl Mannheim', *American Sociological Review*, 1(4): 664–674.

Vattimo, G. (1988) *The End of Modernity: Nihilism and Hermeneutics in Postmodern Culture*. Baltimore: Johns Hopkins University Press.

Wacquant, L. (1992) 'Toward a social praxeology: The structure and logic of Bourdieu's sociology', in P. Bourdieu and L. Wacquant (eds) *An Invitation to Reflexive Sociology*. Chicago: University of Chicago Press. pp. 2–59.

Weinberg, D. (2002) 'Qualitative research methods: An overview', in D. Weinberg (ed.) *Qualitative Research Methods*. Oxford: Blackwell. pp. 1–22

Weinberg, D. (2006) 'Language, dialogue, and ethnographic objectivity', in P. Drew, G. Raymond, and D. Weinberg (eds) *Talk and Interaction in Social Research Methods*. London: Sage. pp. 97–112.

Weinberg, D. (2008) 'The philosophical foundations of constructionist research', in J. Holstein and J. Gubrium (eds) *Handbook of Constructionist Reseach*. New York: Guilford Press. pp. 13–39.

Wilson, B. (1970) *Rationality*. Oxford: Basil Blackwell.

Wittgenstein, L. (1953) *Philosophical Investigations*. Oxford: Blackwell.

25

Theories of Culture, Cognition, and Action

Sun-Ki Chai

INTRODUCTION

The theoretical study of culture across the social science disciplines has long been hampered by a common malady: the tendency to view cultural theories and theories of action as disjoint, or even opposing, modes of analysis. This chapter investigates the nature and causes for this split, then surveys the growth in recent years of diverse attempts at theoretical synthesis. All these syntheses are to some extent interdisciplinary, but because of their origins in widely varying academic communities, they rest on fundamentally different bases. Nonetheless, it will be argued that they share something in common, something that holds promise of collaborative work in what up to now might have been seen as fundamentally incompatible paradigms. Not only has there been work in multiple, widely varying academic fields that tends to look at the (mutually) causal relationship between culture and action, but there has been a common recognition in all of these fields that in order to examine this, greater focus has to be placed on the cognitive and motivational activity of the mind as the process through which culture's effect on action is mediated.

There are so many theoretical and methodological approaches that appropriate the word "culture," conceiving of it in so many contradictory ways, that any attempt at survey of all major cultural paradigms in the social sciences is likely to be an exercise in futility. If anything, the number of working definitions of culture in the social sciences has multiplied since Kroeber and Kluckhohn compiled their grand review and critique of 164 definitions over half a century ago (1952). It is for that reason that, rather than attempting something so grand and ultimately impractical, I have chosen to focus on the particular subset of theoretical innovation that seeks to elucidate the relationship between cultural and action. One thing that past and current definitions share is the idea of culture as a collective phenomenon applied to a particular group or society, whether it describes consensually held attitudes, a distribution of such attitudes, or an emergent entity that cannot be described as an aggregation of individual attitudes.

The chapter examines three major lines of work: The first arises from criticisms, both external and internal, of general predictive theories of action, drawn largely from the rational choice tradition, which are applied primarily in economics, political science, and to some extent sociology. These criticisms have led to a call for a new version of these theories, one that views culture as a primary determinant of the preferences and beliefs upon which decision making rests. The second line of work comes from the interstices of anthropology, psychology, and sociology, particularly the development of mental typologies and models that are used to characterize societies and their cultures. Here, the key development has been moving beyond looking at culture as a set of taxonomies, and looking towards the way in which individual-level culture generates models of the world that impel action. The final line of work is the literature on epistemological "standpoints" that, developing from a base of feminist studies, examines the ways in which the structural positions of individuals affects their access to knowledge. This literature has had to deal with the tension between asserting the privileged knowledge of particular groups based on their common culture and recognizing significant differences in standpoints between members within such groups. It is moving towards a solution that recognizes analysis of individual self-construal as the way to sort out such similarities and differences.

Despite the wide differences between these three literatures (indeed, it would be difficult to think of three more disparate sources within the social sciences), the distinct characteristic shared by all is that analysis of the relationship between culture and individual action is seen as requiring the approaching of culture in a micro–macro fashion, not only as an attribute of a society as a whole, but in terms of individual qualities. The focus is thus not only on the causal implications of cognitions and motivations for action, but also the social process by which such cognitions and motivations are formed over time by culture, and sometimes on the feedback loop by which actions in turn affect culture. Hence it is possible to see common purposes and even possibilities for integration between

these literatures, even if they are typically seen as representing incompatible views on the philosophy of sciences. In this light, it is useful to look at the issues that divide contemporary syntheses, and discuss possibilities for reconciliation. It is not that the unification of all cultural theories of action is necessarily feasible or desirable, but that mutual critique and influence is preferable to parallel development.

Needless to say, even though I will only be surveying a small subset of theoretical work that purports to deal with culture, it is inevitable that huge swathes of literature will be covered in a small amount of space. It is hoped that what is written is not taken as some kind of general (or even partial) critique of these literatures, because it is not intended to be one. Instead, it is an attempt to identify certain trends that seem common to all of them. These trends in turn represent only parts of these literatures, and are often highly contested by older, "mainstream" versions. Nonetheless, the fact that there is significant theoretical movement in each literature towards roughly the same set of goals is notable and favorable to greater unification of the social science approaches to the relationships between culture, cognition, and action.

"CULTURAL CHOICE" APPROACHES

After a long imperialistic march that its most ardent supporters and detractors viewed as having the ultimate goal of becoming the dominant social science paradigm for modeling human action (Radnitzky and Bernholz, 1987; Radnitzky, 1992; Tommasi and Ierulli, 1995), the rational choice approach has tottered at its moment of seeming triumph, and has faced somewhat of an identity crisis in recent years (Lichbach, 2003; Van den Berg and Meadwell, 2004). Its basic assumptions have come under question, and critics, many of them internal, have begun to question its ability to perform with sufficient accuracy what has always been seen as its main methodological purpose, the general and testable prediction of behavior. As the scope of rational choice analysis has expanded, predictive anomalies and indeterminacies have multiplied. To deal with these problems, a number of "fixes" to the approach have been proposed, many revolving around bringing into analysis the concept of culture, which has traditionally been excluded from rational choice analysis, and indeed giving it pride of place.

Increasingly, it is being recognized that cultural analysis, rather than being the antithesis of rational choice (e.g., Barry, 1970), can coexist and even provide the solution to the paradigmatic crisis that the approach faces, while allowing rational choice to retain its existing theoretical strengths of generality and testability. To begin with however, some terminological issues must be clarified. The term *rational choice* can be defined into two different ways. A "thin" concept of rationality includes only the notion that an individual has a well ordered set of preferences, as well as logically and probabilistically consistent beliefs, and acts to maximize her preferences in light of those beliefs. This definition of rationality leaves open the question of what these preferences and beliefs are and how they are derived, thus rendering it incapable of making testable predictions. A "thick" concept of rationality makes prediction possible by including a model of preferences and beliefs (Elster, 1983; Taylor, 1989; Ferejohn, 1991). The problem with the thick concept that has been used in conventional rational choice is that it is based upon a simplistic model of self-regarding materialism and "information" (inference from observation) that is an anomaly-generator in environments that are not dominated by formalized, predictable, and purpose-specific institutions. Furthemore, such an approach can be accused of essentialism when certain preferences and beliefs are attributed to by assumption particularly ethnicities, classes, or genders (Ferber and Nelson, 1993).

Attention to cultural factors can fill in the thick concept of rational choice, yet do so in a way that is more realistic than the conventional model of preferences and beliefs. In this way, rational choice and culture, far from being at odds, are actually complementary modes of analysis (Chai, 1997). Culture allows for assumptions about preferences and beliefs that are not pulled out of the air, but rather based upon sustained empirical studies and inductive generalizations from those studies. However, this requires a way of measuring the cultural milieu. One way of doing this is taking physical and symbolic manifestations of culture, and converting them into internal motivations and cognitions. Another is modeling the generation of "internal" culture through endogenous models of preference and belief formation.

In economics, investigations of ways to modify the conventional assumptions of rational choice have not only reinvigorated the field of behavioral economics, but turned it into what is generally recognized as the cutting edge of the economic theory (Camerer et al., 2004; Diamond and Vartiainen, 2007; Fudenberg, 2006; Pesendorfer, 2006). While behavioral economics comprises a large number of theoretical threads, a major part of its focus has been on modeling the social forces that determine individual preferences, with a particular focus on other-regarding preferences, as well as those towards time discounting and risk.

The first type of preference in particular is the focus of a large literature that looks at the role of cross-national or cross-ethnic cultural differences in determining preferences. Much of this literature is tied into the equally quickly expanding field of experimental economics, which provides much of the empirical data to inform the theories being generated in behavioral economics. The field of "social preferences" (Fehr and Fischbacher, 2002; Rabin, 2006; Levitt and List, 2007) has focused on three major ways in which individual preferences can be other-regarding, each with distinct implications for behavior.

The first is perhaps the simplest: altruistic preferences, that is, the tendency to incorporate the welfare of others, whether all or a delimited group of others, into your own preferences over outcomes (Andreoni and Miller, 2002; Charness and Rabin, 2002). The implications for action are then fairly clear-cut – if one has the opportunity to contribute to a "public good," that is, one that benefits an entire group rather than just the actor alone, altruistic preferences towards that group will raise the incentives to make such a contribution, even when the private benefit of doing so will be exceeded by the costs. It has been long recognized that if such preferences exist, they can help to explain cases where individuals willingly contribute to public good even when there are opportunities to "free-ride" on the contributions of others (Olson, 1965), hence overcoming problems of collective action (Collard, 1978; Margolis, 1982; Phelps, 1975; Stark, 1995). However, only recently has altruism been widely incorporated into mainstream economic theory.

The second major way in which social preferences have been theorized is as embodying a desire for reciprocity (Dufwenberg and Kirchsteiger, 1998; Rabin, 1993), whereby individuals seek to reward those who have helped them in the past and punish those who have hurt them, even when the cost of administering reward or punishment exceeds any expected benefits from inducing greater cooperation in future interactions. This version of social preferences is more complex to model than altruism, since "history" in the form of one's partners' past actions must be built into an individual's preferences. It is also important to distinguish reciprocation as an action (Fehr et al., 2002) from reciprocity-desiring preferences. The latter tend to promote the former, but are not the same thing, and are neither necessary nor sufficient to cause reciprocating behavior. Reciprocating behavior may be distinguished between "strong reciprocity" (Gintis, 2000), motivated in part by an intrinsic desire to reciprocate and "weak reciprocity" motivated entirely by the expectation of benefits resulting from altering behavior of those with whom one is interacting. Likewise, since any

individual's preferences are multi-faceted, the reciprocity-desiring preferences may be outweighed by other preferences in determining actions, depending on the specific conditions.

The final major theorization of social preferences is difference/inequity aversion (Bolton and Ockenfels, 2000; Fehr and Schmidt, 1999). Such preferences seek to minimize the difference between one's own welfare and that of other members of the group, originally limited to the case where one's own welfare was lower than that of others in the group (Bolton and Ockenfels, 1991), but later expanded to include cases where one's welfare is higher, often referred to as "guilt" vs. "envy" (Fehr and Fischbacher, 2005). In either case, the "reference group" against which an individual compares herself must be defined as well. Inequity aversion will imply that an individual will be willing to suffer losses to her own welfare, if by doing so she will cause gains to those below her or losses to those above her. Hence they amount to a kind of effective negative altruism towards the "haves" and positive altruism towards the "have nots," each defined in relation to self.

Each of these investigations of social preferences allow for variations among individuals in the extent to which a particular social preference weighs against a preference for personal material welfare. Moreover, to extent that they theorize the origins of these variations, the implicit theory built into them is that the variations are caused by differences in individuals' cultural backgrounds. This in turn has triggered experimental investigation of social preferences that looks specifically at how people from different cultural backgrounds or identity groups vary in the strength of a particular social preference.

Questions about the role of culture and identity in determining action has generated literature examining variations in behavior across groups, typically national groups, in controlled experiments. The pioneering experiments of this kind transplanted common experimental treatments such as the "ultimatum game" to 15 relatively small-scale societies (Henrich et al., 2005; Henrich, 2004). The ultimatum game involves two players, one who proposes how to divide up a fixed amount of goods and one who either accepts or rejects (in which case neither players get anything). Observation indicates that there is a large amount of variation between societies in what is considered a fair distribution of goods, that patterns of norms do not contrast in any simple fashion with observed patterns in Western societies, and that there appear to be some relationship between norms of distribution and experiences within institutions, particularly market-style transactions. A later set of experiments looked primarily at 16 large, industrialized societies, and examined a different kind of game, the "voluntary contribution mechanism with punishment," in which individuals are given the opportunity to contribute an amount of their choosing to the provision of a collective good, and to later penalize those whose contributions are judged to be inappropriate (Herrman et al., 2008). Again, a wide variation in behavior between societies is noticed, as is a tendency in some societies to punish those whose contribution is too *high* as well as those whose is too low. Notably, the tendency to punish high contributions corresponds inversely to the strength of legal institutions and political stability.

CULTURE AND COGNITION APPROACHES

The examination of the relationship between culture and individual attitudes and actions has had a long history in American cultural anthropology, where the "culture and personality" paradigm was dominant from its early days until the 1970s. Its closest descendant, although naturally much different from its anscestor, is the field of psychological anthropology (Bock, 1994; Casey and Edgerton, 2007; Moore and Mathews, 2001). These differences are too numerous to list in

any detail, but include a much greater breadth and fragmentation in approaches (there is nothing approaching a dominant theory or methodology). The use of psychological literature is likewise much broader and more eclectic. Within psychological anthropology, the field of cognitive anthropology (D'Andrade, 1995; Garro, 2007; Holland et al., 1998; Quinn, 2005) focuses specifically on determining the internal worldviews of the individuals and groups being studied.

In psychology, the existence of subfields of social psychology called "cross-cultural" (Berry et al., 1997, 1997a, 1997b; Matsumoto, 2001; Smith, Bond, and Kagitcibasi, 2006) and "cultural" (Shweder, 2003; Lehman et al., 2004; Kitayama and Cohen, 2007) psychology is often confusing to the newcomer, something that is not helped by the presence of scholars who work in both fields and debate about what separates the two. Even to the expert, "the differences between cross-cultural and cultural psychology are small" (Triandis, 2007: 68). The most sweeping distinction that is made between the two is that cross-cultural psychology tends to study cultural differences at the aggregate, typically national, level while cultural psychology looks at cultural differences at the individual level, as mediated through structural constraints. Another is that cultural psychology often focuses on identifying mechanisms specific to particular cases, while cross-cultural psychology focuses primarily on identifying dimensions of culture that are transportable across cases.

Finally, in sociology, the emerging field of cognitive sociology (DiMaggio, 1997; Zerubavel, 1997; Cerulo, 2002) has attempted to inject cultural sociology with the methodological innovations associated with the cognitive revolution elsewhere in the social sciences. Classic cultural theories in sociology, influenced greatly by Talcott Parsons, began from the point of view that cultures determine an individual's decision-making process (cognition, cathexis, and evaluation) through the process of socialization (Parsons and Shils, 1951: 10–11). This tendency was caricatured rather succinctly many years ago by Wrong as "oversocialization" (1961; see also Barry, 1970), and while much has changed since the 1960s, cultural theories had previously not made much effort to bridge the micro–macro link, instead typically drawing a line directly from culture to institutional and structural outcomes.

The five academic fields just described, being inherently interdisciplinary, do not ignore work that is being done by similar researchers in other disciplines, and indeed the main research questions in psychological and cognitive anthropology overlap greatly with those in cross-cultural and cultural psychology (for a short discussion of their mutual origins, see Shore, 1996: 20). Furthermore, these fields each face a similar issue, which is how to model the impact of culture on cognition such that its implications for action are clear. As stated in an influential book in psychological and cognitive anthropology, an often-criticized problem with much individual-level theorizing in anthropology has been its origin in "ethnoscience," (Sturtevant, 1964) an approach that was devoted largely to taxonomies and "tended to squeeze the life out of culture by limiting cultural knowledge to abstract classificatory schemata divorced from human action" (Shore, 1996: 35). Whether or not one accepts this criticism wholeheartedly, one major distinguishing characteristic of recent work in psychological anthropology has been its attempt to build cultural models with clear implications for action.

The solution to this problem, proposed by a large number of scholars in these fields, but particularly in cognitive anthropology, is that representations of individual-level attitudes should supplement or replace abstract dimensions and taxonomies with cultural models, which are shared schemas representing empirical reality and its causal relationships, but which can also include values and motives (D'Andrade and Strauss, 1992; Strauss and Quinn, 1998). In cultural

psychology as well, the solution to problem of action is seen increasingly as the representation of individual-level attitudes as consisting of beliefs and values (Shweder, 1996: 20), the very same representation that is seen in the thin rational choice and "cultural choice" theories described in the previous section.

STANDPOINT THEORIES

Standpoint theories (Harding, 2004; Hartsock, 1998) can be distinguished from the previous two paradigms in that the assumption that cognition is determined by culture is taken further, and is used to challenge the very basis for conventional philosophies of science. Basically stated, a standpoint theory argues that an individual's structural position provides access to situated knowledge that is not accessible to those who do not share the same position, a position closely linked to postmodern views of self (Butler, 1995). A particular emphasis is placed on the privilegedness of social knowledge uniquely possessed by dominated and oppressed groups (Smith, 1974; Hartsock, 1983; Rose, 1987). It avoids the criticism of essentialism by arguing that the feminist standpoint is not genetically determined but acquired through common gender-determined experiences within a patriarchical society.

Based on Marx's notion of the standpoint of the proletariat from his *18th Brumaire* (Marx, 1852), the original formulation of feminist standpoint theory sought to use the concept of standpoint-situated knowledge as a force for resistance against those theorists who were seen as taking androcentric assumptions about humans and using them as universals in designing social theory. The dominance of feminist thought among contemporary standpoint theories is indicated by the fact that the terms "standpoint theory" and "feminist standpoint theory" are often taken as synonymous. This is understandable given the sheer breadth, depth, and insight of theory arising from the standpoint of outlook in feminist studies and its ties to feminist critiques of the scientific method (Keller and Longino, 1996; Kohlstedt and Longino, 1997; Mayberry et al., 2001).

Nonetheless, it can be argued that this type of perceived equation between "standpoint" and "feminist standpoint" tends to do harm by isolating feminist standpoint theories from other social science work comprising *de facto* standpoint theories that may be compatible with certain versions of standpoint feminism. This is to the mutual detriment of both, reducing opportunities for integration and contributing to the isolation of feminist standpoint theories from other theories of culture and action.

As noted in this paper, much of the current rational choice and psychological anthropology/cultural psychology literature's attributes a "privileged" set of beliefs and preferences to a particular group given its structural position. While these may or may not qualify as standpoint theories, depending on the definition, they share its concern with the relationship between structural position, belief, and values. Indeed, it is hard to conceptually separate a group's standpoint from its culture. As D'Andrade put it, culture is a "socially transmitted information pool" (1981: 181–182). Recognition of this commonality can help not only in providing theoretical integration, but in transforming anachronistic polemical debates between theorists into a search for common ground.It can be argued that the main benefit that standpoint theory can gain from engagement with other approaches to culture and action is its further development as a scientific paradigm rather than a meta-scientific theoretical discussion. While its contemporary incarnation was originally proposed as scientific paradigm and methodology to guide research (Harding, 2004: 1), in practice it has rarely moved beyond meta-theoretical analysis on the nature and extent of the feminist standpoint and how it relates to other potential standpoints, as well as discussion on how it could affect scientific

inquiry. As of yet, despite two decades of discussion, it has not developed its "normal science" component, and there is as of yet very little that can be called "applied standpoint theory" used to explain specific empirical phenomena in the social world.

Indeed, it would be difficult given the current state of the debate, to say what applied standpoint theory might look like. One direction, and perhaps the most consistent with mainstream social science, would be to posit groups of actors, each with its own structural position, and thus each with access to specific information that is not accessible to the other actors. A particular group of actors (oppressed minorities or women) may be said to have specific types of information or even solidarity that can arise only from their own shared experiences in collective action. A recent paper presented at the American Sociological Association conference indicates what this might look like (Harnois, 2008). In this paper, white and black women and men were surveyed regarding their attitudes towards oppression. The study found that the effect of ethnicity was substantially larger than that of gender.

Of course, many if not most feminist standpoint theorists might argue that this is not what they mean by the application of standpoint methodology, but such debates will prompt greater efforts to put forward a unified position on the rules for such a methodology, creating a line of scientific inquiry that would justify the term "paradigm." Engagement of standpoint theory with choice-theoretic and cognitive approaches can help to aid in this development, since these other approaches have been much more active in building an applied component to their meta-theorizing, generating explanations and predictions of actions that can be compared against real-world events.

On the other hand, what other approaches lack is the ability to internalize the cultural viewpoint of their subjects, a major focus of contemporary standpoint theories. Mainstream social science has often been criticized for clothing political viewpoints under the label of objective, disinterested assumptions, hence providing them with a spurious kind of separation from the real-world outlooks of their authors. This accusation is no doubt true – it is very difficult to think of a theoretical assumption, including that of self-regarding material welfare maximization or beliefs from "information," that does not in some way reflect the world view of its authors.

One way to address this is to provide the subject with the means to design the architecture of her own response, that is, to not impose arbitrary parameterizations on the subject's ideas, yet allow for responses that can be used to make comparisons across groups. Standpoint theories take seriously the provision that one should query the viewpoint of the subjects on their own terms, rather than impose some outside structure. In order to extend their influence to theories outside the standpoint approach, they need to proceed in developing a method for application that scholars can take into the field and use to conduct studies.

Perhaps the major internal critique of standpoint theory is that it typically fails to recognize the cultural diversity that exists among women, tending instead to assign them a single "female" standpoint. On the other hand, attempts to recognize the multiplicity of women's experiences leads to a kind of postmodernist relativism in which all standpoints are different and have equal validity, which dilutes the notion that women's standpoints are privileged compared to those of men (Hekman, 2004). However this problem is the very problem that is faced by the two other large bodies of work, which is to examine how group-level culture can be represented at the individual level, and how individual variation can be recognized without erasing the notion that groups share certain common values and beliefs. Moreover, it then segues into the problem of how that representation at the individual level can be used to predict action that has meaning at the aggregate level.

REFERENCES

Andreoni, J. and Miller, J. (2002) 'Giving according to garp: An experimental test of the consistency of preferences for altruism', *Econometrica*, 70(2): 737–753.

Barry, B. (1970) *Sociologists, Economists and Democracy*. London: Collier-MacMillan.

Berry, J.W., Poortinga, Y.H. and Pandey, J. (eds) (1997) *Theory and Method* (Vol. 1). Boston: Allyn and Bacon.

Berry, J.W., Dasen, P.R. and Saraswathi, T.S. (eds) (1997a) *Basic Processes and Human Development* (Vol. 2). Boston: Allyn and Bacon.

Berry, J.W., Segall, M.H. and Kagitc, C. (eds) (1997b) *Social Behavior and Applications* (Vol. 3). Boston: Allyn and Bacon.

Bock, P.K. (ed.) (1994) *Handbook of Psychological Anthropology*. Westport, CT: Greenwood Publishing.

Bolton, G. E. (1991) 'A Comparative Model of Bargaining: Theory and Evidence', *American Economic Review*, 81(December): 1096–1136.

Bolton, G.E. and Ockenfels, A. (2000) 'ERC: A theory of equity, reciprocity, and competition', *American Economic Review*, 90(1): 166–193.

Butler, J. (1995) 'Contingent foundations', in S. Benhabib (ed.) *Feminist Contentions: A Philosophical Exchange*. New York: Routledge. pp. 35–58.

Camerer, C., Loewenstein, G. and Rabin, M. (eds) (2004) *Advances in Behavioral Economics*. Princeton, NJ: Princeton University Press.

Casey, C. and Edgerton, R.B. (eds) (2007) *A Companion to Psychological Anthropology: Modernity and Psychocultural Change*. New York: Wiley-Blackwell.

Cerulo, K. A. (1997) 'Identity Construction: New Issues, New Directions', *Annual Review of Sociology* 23: 385–419.

Cerulo, K.A. (ed.) (2002) *Culture in Mind: Toward a Sociology of Culture and Cognition*. London: Routledge.

Chai, S. (1997) 'Rational Choice and Culture: Clashing Perspectives or Complementary Modes of Analysis?' in R. Ellis and M. Thompson (eds.), *Culture Matters: Essays in Honor of Aaron Wildavsky*. Boulder, CO: Westview Press, pp. 45–58

Charness, G. and Rabin, M. (2002) 'Understanding social preferences with simple tests', *Quarterly Journal of Economics*, 117(3): 817–869.

Collard, D. (1978) *Altruism and Economy: A Study in Non-Selfish Economics*. New York: Oxford University Press.

D'Andrade, R.G. (1981) 'The cultural part of cognition', *Cognitive Science*, 5: 179–195.

D'Andrade, R.G. (1995) *The Development of Cognitive Anthropology*. Cambridge: Cambridge University Press.

D'Andrade, R.G. and Strauss, C. (eds) (1992) *Human Motives and Cultural Models*. Cambridge: Cambridge University Press.

Diamond, P.A. and Vartiainen, H. (eds) (2007) *Behavioral Economics and Its Applications*. Princeton, NJ: Princeton University Press.

DiMaggio, P. (1997) 'Culture and cognition', *Annual Review of Sociology*, 23(1): 263–287.

Dufwenberg, M. and Kirchsteiger, G. (2004) 'A theory of sequential reciprocity', *Games and Economic Behavior*, 47: 268–298.

Elster, J. (1983) 'Rationality', in J. Elster (ed.) *Sour Grapes: Studies in the Subversion of Rationality*. Cambridge: Cambridge University Press. pp. 1–42.

Fehr, E. and Fischbacher, U. (2002) 'Why social preferences matter – the impact of non-selfish motives on competition, cooperation and incentives', *Economic Journal*, 112(478): C1–C33.

Fehr, E. and Fischbacher, U. (2005) 'Human Altruism – Proximate Patterns and Evolutionary Origins', *Analyse and Kritik* 27: 6–47.

Fehr, E. and Schmidt, K.M. (1999) 'A theory of fairness, competition, and cooperation', *Quarterly Journal of Economics*, 114(3): 817–868.

Fehr, E., Fischbacher, U. and Gachter, S. (2002) 'Strong reciprocity, human cooperation and the enforcement of social norms', *Human Nature*, 13: 1–25.

Ferber, M.A. and Nelson, J.A. (eds) (1993) *Beyond Economic Man: Feminist Theory and Economics*. Chicago: University of Chicago Press.

Ferejohn, J. (1991) 'Rationality and interpretation: Parliamentary elections in early Stuart England', in K.R. Monroe (ed.) *The Economic Approach to Politics: A Critical Reassessment of the Theory of Rational Action*. New York: Harper Collins. pp. 279–305.

Fudenberg, D. (2006) 'Advancing beyond advances in behavioral economics', *Journal of Economic Literature*, XLIV: 694–711.

Garro, L.C. (2007) '"Effort after meaning" in everyday life', in C. Casey and R.B. Edgerton (eds) *A Companion to Psychological Anthropology: Modernity and Psychocultural Change*. New York: Wiley-Blackwell, pp. 48–71.

Gintis, H. (2000) 'Strong Reciprocity and Human Sociality', *Journal of Theoretical Biology*, 206: 169–179.

Harding, S. (ed.) (2004) *The Feminist Standpoint Theory Reader: Intellectual and Political Controversies*. New York: Routledge.

Harnois, C. (2008) 'Race, gender and the black women's standpoint: An empirical investigation of standpoint theory', *Paper presented at the annual meeting of the American Sociological Association Annual Meeting, Sheraton Boston and the Boston Marriott Copley Place, Boston, MA*.

Hartsock, N.C.M. (1983) *The Feminist Standpoint: Developing the Ground for a Specifically Feminist Historical Materialism*. Boston: D. Reidel Publishing.

Hartsock, N.C.M. (1998) *The Feminist Standpoint Revisited and Other Essays*. Boulder, CO: Westview Press.

Hekman, S. (2004) 'Truth and method: Feminist standpoint theory revisited', in S. Harding (ed.), *The Feminist Standpoint Theory Reader: Intellectual and Political Controversies*. New York: Routledge, pp. 225–224.

Henrich, J.P. (ed.) (2004) *Foundations of Human Sociality: Economic Experiments and Ethnographic Evidence from Fifteen Small-Scale Societies*. Oxford New York: Oxford University Press.

Henrich, J., Boyd, R., Bowles, S., Camerer, C., Fehr, E., Gintis, H. et al. (2005) '"Economic man" in cross-cultural perspective: Behavioral experiments in 15 small-scale societies', *Behavioral and Brain Sciences*, 28(6): 795–855.

Herrmann, B., Thöni, C. and Gächter, S. (2008) 'Antisocial punishment across societies', *Science*, 319: 1362–1367.

Holland, D., Skinner, D., Lachiocotte Jr, W. and Cain, C. (eds) (1998) *Identity and Agency in Cultural Worlds*. Cambridge, MA: Harvard University Press.

Keller, E.F. and Longino, H.E. (eds) (1996) *Feminism and Science*. Oxford: Oxford University Press.

Kitayama, S. and Cohen, D. (eds) (2007) *Handbook of Cultural Psychology*. London: Guilford Press.

Kohlstedt, S.G. and Longino, H. (eds) (1997) *Women, Gender, and Science: New Directions*. Chicago: University of Chicago Press.

Kroeber, A.L. and Kluckhohn, C. (1952) *Culture: A Critical Review of Concepts and Definitions*. Cambridge, MA: Peabody Museum.

Lehman, D.R., Chiu, C.-y. and Schaller, M. (2004) 'Psychology and culture', *Annual Review of Psychology*, 55(1): 689–714.

Levitt, S. and List, J. (2007) 'What do laboratory experiments measuring social preferences reveal about the real world?', *Journal of Economic Perspectives*, 21(2): 153–174.

Lichbach, M.I. (2003) *Is Rational Choice Theory All of Social Science?* Ann Arbor, MI: University of Michigan Press.

Margolis, H. (1982) *Selfishness, Altruism and Rationality: A Theory of Social Choice.* Cambridge: Cambridge University Press.

Marx, K. (1852) 'The 18th Brumaire of Louis Bonaparte' *Die Revolution* 1. Translated (1937) Moscow: Progress Publishers.

Matsumoto, D. (ed) (2001) *Handbook of Culture and Psychology.* Oxford: Oxford University Press.

Mayberry, M., Subramaniam, B. and Weasel, L.H. (eds) (2001) *Feminist Science Studies.* New York: Routledge.

Moore, C.C. and Mathews, H.F. (eds) (2001) *The Psychology of Cultural Experience.* Cambridge: Cambridge University Press.

Olson, M. (1965) *The Logic of Collective Action.* Cambridge, MA: Harvard University Press.

Parsons, T. and E. Shils (eds.) (1951) *Towards a General Theory of Action.* Cambridge, MA: Harvard University Press.

Pesendorfer, W. (2006) 'Behavioral economics comes of age: A review essay on advances in behavioral economics', *Journal of Economic Literature,* XLIV: 712–721.

Phelps, E.S. (ed.) (1975) *Altruism, Morality and Economic Theory.* New York: Russell Sage Foundation.

Quinn, N. (ed.) (2005) *Finding Culture in Talk.* Houndsmills, Basingstoke, Hampshire: Palgrave MacMillan.

Rabin, M. (1993) 'Incorporating fairness into game theory and economics', *American Economic Review,* 83(5): 1281–1302.

Rabin, M. (2006) 'The experimental study of social preferences', *Social Research,* 73(2): 405–428.

Radnitzky, G. (ed.) (1992). *Universal Economics: Assessing the Achievements of the Economic Approach.* New York: Paragon House.

Radnitzky, G. and Bernholz, P. (eds) (1987) *Economic Imperialism: The Economic Approach Applied Outside the Field of Economics.* New York: Paragon House.

Rose, H. (1987) 'Hand, brain, and heart: A feminist epistemology for the natural sciences'. *Women and Religion* 9(1): 73–90.

Shore, B. (1996) *Culture in Mind: Cognition, Culture, and the Problem of Meaning.* Oxford: Oxford University Press.

Shweder, R.A. (2003) *Why Do Men Barbecue?: Recipes for Cultural Psychology.* Cambridge MA: Harvard University Press.

Smith, D. (1974) 'Women's perspective as a radical critique of sociology', *Sociological Inquiry,* 44: 7–13.

Smith, P.B., Bond, M.H. and Kagitcibasi, C. (eds) (2006) *Understanding Social Psychology Across Cultures: Living and Working in a Changing World.* Newbury Park, CA: Sage Publications.

Stark, O. (1995) *Altruism and Beyond: An Economic Analysis of Transfers and Exchanges within Families and Groups.* Cambridge: Cambridge University Press.

Strauss, C. and Quinn, N. (1998) *A Cognitive Theory of Cultural Meaning.* Cambridge: Cambridge University Press.

Sturtevant, W. C. (1964) 'Studies in Ethnoscience". *American Anthropologist* 66(3): 99–131.

Taylor, M. (1989) 'Structure culture and action in the explanation of social change', *Politics and Society,* 17: 116–161.

Tommasi, M. and Ierulli, K. (eds) (1995) *The New Economics of Human Behavior.* Cambridge: Cambridge University Press.

Triandis, H.C. (2007) 'Culture and psychology: A history of the study of their relationship', in S. Kitayama and D. Cohen (eds) *Handbook of Cultural Psychology.* London: Guildford. pp. 59–77.

Van den Berg, A. and Meadwell, H. (eds) (2004) *The Social Sciences and Rationality: Promise, Limits, and Problems.* New Brunswick, NJ: Transaction Publishers.

Wrong, D. (1961) 'The oversocialized conception of man in modern sociology', *American Sociological Review,* 26(2): 183–193.

Zerubaval, E. (1997) *Social Mindscapes: An Invitation to Cognitive Sociology.* Cambridge MA: Harvard University Press.

26

Communicative Action and Critical Theory

Martin Morris

INTRODUCTION: THE ORIGINS AND DEVELOPMENT OF CRITICAL THEORY

For much of the twentieth century the term Critical Theory referred to the work conducted by a group of scholars associated with the Institute for Social Research at the University of Frankfurt and the Institute's journal, *Zeitschrift für Sozialforschuung* (*Journal of Social Science*). These scholars were inspired most importantly by Marxist social critique, but during the early development of their work in the Germany of the 1930s, 'Critical Theory' was adopted as a prudent code word for such critique, since identifying with Marxism was politically dangerous. In exile in the United States after the rise of Nazi Germany, Critical Theory remained the key term for the Institute's unique approach (associating with Marxism was also politically dangerous in the United States), with outsiders later applying the name 'Frankfurt School' Critical Theory. The Frankfurt School is, however, perhaps better understood as a tradition of thought rather than a school, since there was no doctrine or set of propositions that guided its members.[1] Critical Theory was, from the beginning, an effort to radically rethink Marxist theory and

practice in light of historical developments in capitalist society and in actually existing socialism. Critical Theory's philosophy of social science is inherently oriented toward liberation from domination and oppression. But as such, it must be noted that the term can be appropriately applied to other contemporary theories whose interests also lie in liberation, such as critical race theory, certain feminism and gay liberation, and some post-colonial theories.[2] Those centrally associated with so-called 'first generation' Frankfurt School Critical Theory include Max Horkheimer, Theodor Adorno, Herbert Marcuse, Friedrich Pollock, Otto Kirchheimer, Erich Fromm, Franz Neumann and Leo Lowenthal, with Walter Benjamin the most important early fellow traveler. While an identifiable coherence to Frankfurt School Critical Theory really only applies to its early program of the 1930s, the strong continuities and affinities in the later work of its core figures has led to a recognizable tradition known as 'Critical Theory'.

Horkheimer, who took over as director of the Institute in 1929, used the term 'Critical Theory' in the 1930s in a series of programmatic essays on the difference between Critical Theory and what he called traditional theory. Traditional theory referred to political philosophy such as liberalism, Romantic spiritualism, *Lebensphilosophie* (a kind of biologically-biased metaphysics) and to the increasingly dominant positivism in philosophy of social science. Each form of traditional theory functioned in different ways to reconcile the individual to what was essentially a contradictory and alienating society. Instead, Horkheimer believed, it was *change* to this society that was vital and a new philosophy of science was required to show why. Positivism elevated such reconciliation to the level of scientific objectivity and respectability. For positivism, knowledge only concerns that which can be observed and which permits the discovery of laws, as is generally regarded to be the case in physics. Its method is founded on the observation of empirical behaviour and is unconcerned with what cannot be observed through scientifically verifiable data. For Horkheimer, this limits its approach to *appearances*, which entails that it is blind to the conditions and processes that *produce* the appearance of things. Reification, for example, could not be an object of knowledge, since how can one observe it either directly or empirically? A reified object can certainly present itself *as such* to thought, but for positivism, such appearance is simply the object's natural presentation to the senses. Scientific knowledge is the only actual knowledge possible on this approach – non-scientific knowledge is not knowledge at all but rather 'fancy' or 'non-sense' as those such as Carnap were fond of saying. 'Besides science there is art', for positivism (Horkheimer, 1989a: 139). As a result, questions concerning the proper or 'just' arrangement of social relations are excluded from consideration as philosophical or social scientific topics. Under positivism, individuals are encouraged to accept the social 'facts' of society as they are presented to empirical observation, as though historical social existence were akin to a universal natural existence. Fact is radically separated from value such that brutal dictatorship just as much as the struggles against such

tyranny are treated equally as abstract 'givens'. Powerful economic forces (namely, the capitalist class and its representatives) welcome such philosophy of science that eschews normative judgment and that reduces politics merely to contesting '"value judgments", private caprices, and uncontrollable feelings' (Horkheimer, 1989a: 178). As such, traditional theory supports and helps to perpetuate the status quo.

By contrast, Horkheimer regards Critical Theory as a mode of thinking and research oriented toward the concrete transformation of contemporary unfree and irrational society into the right kind of society' (Horkheimer, 1989b: 218). The *critical* nature of Critical Theory is hence found in its analysis of social injustice, oppression and domination, which does not treat such conditions as factual 'givens' but rather as circumstances to be abolished. A Critical Theory of 'society as it is', Horkheimer argues, is 'a theory dominated at every turn by a concern for reasonable conditions of life' (Horkheimer, 1989b: 198–199). Critical Theory he states:

> is motivated today by the effort really to transcend the tension and to abolish the opposition between the individual's purposefulness, spontaneity and rationality, and those work-process relationships on which society is built. Critical thought has a concept of man in conflict with himself until this opposition is removed. If activity governed by reason is proper to man, then existent social practice, which forms the individual's life right down to its least details, is inhuman, and this inhumanity affects everything that goes on in society. (Horkheimer, 1989b; 210)

Marcuse agreed, arguing that philosophy contained an inherent *interest* in freedom and happiness that could not be realized through philosophy itself but required socially transformative practice and 'the creation of a rational society' (Marcuse, 1968: 142). Marcuse was not talking of mere economic or bureaucratic rationality (he was one of the first on the Western scholarly Left to publicly criticize the Soviet Union), but rather the governance of society in the genuine interests of 'the freedom and happiness of the masses ...

of liberated mankind' (Marcuse, 1968: 144, 157). Critical Theory sets itself the task of developing a social science and philosophy that reveals the processes and conditions of domination and oppression, guided by the human interest in liberation. Consequently, Critical Theory must align itself with social movements of practical change, seeking, as Marx once said, to 'show the world what it is fighting for' (Marx, 1974: 15).

However, the failure of revolutionary movements in the West during the twentieth century, along with the rise of fascism in Europe, presented significant problems for Critical Theory: why did the working-class reject socialism and even embrace fascism during times of social crisis when anti-capitalist transformation is in its interests? Critical Theory sought to explain this by rethinking the concept of ideology through the analysis of the political dimensions of technology and mass society. The technology of industrial capitalism is not neutral, Critical Theory argues, but is revealed to be an expression of the relations of domination at the core of the system itself. No technology is, strictly speaking, a neutral instrument, just as the claims of science to be objective never escape the historical relations of domination for which its knowledge is mobilized. Technology, as the practical expression of knowledge and the control of nature, reflects the interests of enlightenment in the domination of nature, and by extension, the domination of human beings. This key critical idea of 'enlightenment' – of rational knowledge of the world progressively replacing myth, science overcoming superstition – is itself a reversal, another fateful form of myth, Horkheimer and Adorno write in what is arguably the most influential work of the Frankfurt School, *Dialectic of Enlightenment* (2002) [1944/47]. 'Enlightenment' (*Aufklärung*), it should be noted, has two distinct senses for Horkheimer and Adorno. First there is the particular historical Enlightenment of the European eighteenth century and its historical inheritance, which Horkheimer and Adorno identify with

the fully-fledged ideological realization of the scientific – or better, what would become the scientistic – approach to knowledge. Second, there is the more important sense of the historical process that governs conceptual power itself – the human capacity for overcoming or controlling that which the concept itself names, its material or its nature. That is, there is a domination that everyday language achieves weakly and that concepts entail strongly to control that which is named. Reason mediates such communication and hence tends toward unconsciously undermining its own good desire for knowledge. This is why enlightenment is always a *dialectic* of enlightenment. As Horkheimer and Adorno consistently point out, there is always a 'good' moment associated with enlightenment in this sense, even though the historical development of its dialectic has led to the most unspeakable horrors in the twentieth century and a late capitalist world in which self-preservation has 'gone wild'. It is precisely this consciousness of reason made aware of a needed and new justice of thinking – the 'justice of cognition' (Morris, 2001: 60–64) – that brings forth the ethical orientation of Critical Theory. It is this 'negative' critique of knowledge that gives Critical Theory its unique approach to social scientific endeavor.

Over the course of its development, the human species has increased its control over nature through the extension of instrumental reason, which receives its full release with the science of the European enlightenment and its application and institutionalization in industrial capitalism. Yet the progressive freedom from mythic fear that enlightenment is supposed to bring about redounds on its new modern subjects precisely in new myths that dominate them even more completely than the old ones did. The scientific reduction of nature to the stuff of technical manipulation and control is applied to the bodies and minds of humans themselves, such that increasing domination of nature corresponds to increasing domination of the nature of humans. The myth is that this is progress or enlightenment; it is instead regression. The inherent self-preservation requirement to adapt to nature is turned into the demand to adapt to the 'second' nature of mass industrial society, which produces and requires standardization and universal exchangeability. Sensuous perception and the cognitive life of individuals are debased and degraded by the demand for this adaptation.

> The more complex and sensitive the social, economic, and scientific mechanism, to the operation of which the system of production has long since attuned the body, the more impoverished are the experiences of which the body is capable ... The regression of the masses today lies in their inability to hear with their own ears what has not already been heard, to touch with their hands what has not previously been grasped; it is the new form of blindness which supercedes that of vanquished myth.

Hence, for Horkheimer and Adorno it is 'the concrete conditions of work in society which enforce conformism ... The powerlessness of the workers is not merely a ruse of the rulers but the logical consequence of industrial society' (2002: 28–29). Horkheimer and Adorno's concept of the 'culture industry' details this adaptation and shows how ideology (myth) is no longer 'superstructural' – that is, power is not maintained through a 'ruse'. The theory of the culture industry is not a theory of culture but of how industry has become culture and vice versa. The standardization of the assembly line required for mass production applies equally to cultural products, whose logic of design and production does not differ from any other industrial product. As a result, entertainment 'is the prolongation of work under late capitalism ... the off-duty worker can experience nothing but after images of the work process itself' (2002: 109). Mass entertainment debases and degrades the senses and the intellect in the same way the work process does, although, of course, the former must always offer an aesthetic or 'phantasmagoric' promise or 'bribe' in order to achieve this domination (Jameson, 1990: 29). Moreover, and most debilitating, the achievement of

this consumption of mass culture enacts a substitution for an authentic gratification and happiness that would otherwise correspond to freedom if such a social condition was permitted.

Yet Horkheimer and Adorno do not view this dialectic of enlightenment as conclusive or inevitable for social science or society. 'Enlightenment is more than enlightenment, it is nature made audible in its estrangement. The fateful contradiction in enlightenment's relation to power can be brought to awareness in the concept ... the self-reflection of thought ... which enables the distance which perpetuates injustice to be measured'. Enlightenment is opposed to domination in the 'remembrance of nature within the subject' (Horkheimer and Adorno, 2002: 29–32). Science could still help, as both Horkheimer's and Adorno's individual work and teaching in the ensuing decades showed. But philosophy must also always resist and criticize 'unreflective scientification' (Adorno, 1998a: 40) as well as phenomenology as 'eidetic intuition' (intuition of essences')[3] (Adorno, 1998b: 13) – including the latter's influential Heideggerian version, which Adorno attacks as the 'jargon of authenticity' (Adorno, 1973b).

Adorno's mature formulation of his Critical Theory as 'negative dialectics' – 'the ontology of the wrong state of affairs' (Adorno, 1973a: 11, trans. modified) – makes the 'primacy of the object' central to his philosophy of social science. The primacy or preponderance of the object is a key element of Adorno's philosophy of social science, although a complicated one, for it reiterates a *need* in thinking itself (see Burke, et. al., 2007). This is no easy task, since it requires thinking identity and nonidentity together, without resolving the contradiction in thought: 'An object can be conceived only by a subject but always remains something other than the subject, whereas a subject by its very nature is from the outset an object as well' (Adorno, 1973a: 183). It is a 'post-subjective' form of thought that nevertheless requires the objectivity of the subject – it is the 'second reflection [that] breaks the supremacy of thinking over its otherness, because it is otherness already, within itself' (Adorno, 1973a, 201).

This is one of the key philosophical reasons why Adorno develops an aesthetic theory in conjunction with negative dialectics. An *aesthetic* theory – literally – is one that is precisely sensitive to the primacy of the object, the repressed nature in the subject that nevertheless finds itself a mode of communication in aesthetic works and experiences. Philosophy requires the aesthetic, bodily, sensuous re-appropriation of that which has been dominated and mutilated by capitalism and the barbarism of reason. But art equally requires philosophy to show how it is no mere thing of contemplation but contains a necessary *truth-content*. For what 'is mediated in art, that through which the artwork becomes something other than its mere factuality, must be mediated a second time by reflection: through the medium of the concept' (1997: 358). An aesthetic *theory* is required (which is fundamentally different from a philosophical aesthetics, it should be emphasized) in order to bring to comprehension art objects, whose historical truth-content is not 'what they mean' nor a reflection of 'correct consciousness' (for this latter has 'not existed to this day'); instead, the truth content of artworks is 'the complete presentation of false consciousness' (1997: 129–130). Such presentation is always a dynamic process of critical thought – not merely some static representation of what is called 'false consciousness'. Thinking itself is always in motion and it is the interaction of art and theory that presents the possibility of overcoming 'false consciousness'. As such, this latter is perhaps better revised as 'unjust thinking'.

Marcuse builds upon Horkheimer and Adorno's analysis in his view of capitalism as a 'one dimensional society' of dissatisfying work compensated culturally (ideologically) by empty consumerism (Marcuse, 1964). Marcuse sought to show how ideology had finally become 'biological': the needs of the system no longer needed to be enforced or imposed on people externally since consumerism had transferred the needs of the system into their own felt human needs that were now indistinguishable from authentic need. The 'affluent society' did not advance freedom and happiness but instead introduced a new, more insidious form of domination. On the strength of such apposite social critique, Critical Theory became a guiding intellectual light for the New Left and the new social movements sparked in the 1960s and 1970s (e.g. the student movement, the peace movement, counterculture oppositions, environmentalism, feminism). Marcuse's work became especially resonant with these movements since, unlike Adorno's negative philosophical approach, with its emphasis on the truth-content of art as opposed to non-art and general practical disconnection from the ferment of the 1960s, Marcuse sought instead to theorize a 'biological foundation for socialism' in the 'new sensibility' of counterculture, protest, drugs, rebellious art, Third World liberation movements, and subcultural groups, which he saw as actively developing new ways of feeling, perceiving, and communicating. The new sensibility, Marcuse argues, 'emerges in the struggle against violence and exploitation', in the 'affirmation of the right to build a society in which the abolition of poverty and toil terminates in a universe where the sensuous, the playful, the calm, and the beautiful become forms of existence and thereby the *Form* of society itself' (Marcuse, 1969: 25). Marcuse, along with Horkheimer and Adorno, recognized that industrial capitalism had developed the technical means to abolish intellectual and material scarcity for all but the system prevented this due to the inherent imperative of capital accumulation and the embodiment of capital's social power in its technology. In order to recognize this, a new form of perception was required that was no longer beholden to the 'reality principle' (Marcuse, 1966) of accumulation-without-end and all that this requires. The new sensibility is an 'aesthetic ethos' of liberation, a 'culture of receptivity' sensitive to 'forms and modes of reality which thus far have been projected only by the aesthetic imagination. ...[Aesthetic needs] are the claims of the human organism, mind and body, for a dimension of fulfillment that can be created only in the struggle against institutions which ... deny and violate these claims'. For Marcuse, Critical Theory seeks to encourage the development of the new needs and new perceptions characteristic of a transformed society by showing how there might emerge in existing society a consciousness of and opposition to the mutilated experience of the human sensorium. Such liberation is required before anything like genuine freedom can be realized: 'the economic, political, and cultural features of a classless society must have become the basic needs of those who fight for it' before any real transformation can be successful (Marcuse, 1969: 25, 27, 89, 90).

This thoroughly practical-political philosophy of social science was taken up in a different way by Jürgen Habermas, who was Adorno's assistant and colleague in Frankfurt in the 1950s and 1960s. Adorno had continued his critique of positivism in the 1960s in what became known as the 'positivist dispute in German philosophy' (Adorno, 1976), and Habermas also contributed to this debate significantly. Beyond this, however, Habermas engaged in far-reaching critiques of social science and philosophy during this period including, most centrally, Marx's critical social thought. In his materialism, Habermas argued, Marx does not distinguish between the logical status of the natural sciences and of critique but instead tended to classify the science of man with natural science such that human self-constitution – 'the self-generative act of the human species' – was reduced to labour. The result of this was that Marx always saw work and social interaction as united in social practice, in social labour, and the dialectic of productive activity and the relations of production were consequently seen as 'different aspects of the same process'. To be sure, the critical nature of Marx's theory turned on

the transformation of the labour process into a scientific process that would bring man's 'material exchange' with nature under the control of a human species totally emancipated from necessary labour. Emancipation ... succeeds to the degree that institutions based on force are replaced by an organization of social relations that is bound only to communication free from domination. (Habermas, 1971: 44–53)

But Marx was unable to see the social scientific (and political) implications of this precisely because of his reduction of self-constitution to social labour. For Habermas, historical materialism must therefore be reconstructed in order to recognize social evolution as 'learning processes' along two key dimensions: that of 'technically useful knowledge decisive for the development of productive forces but also in the dimension of moral-practical consciousness decisive for the structures of interaction' (Habermas, 1979: 148). Each respective sphere – that of instrumental and strategic action and that of communicative action – has its specific mode of learning process and corresponding developmental logic. Politically, this distinction is important in order to recognize the need to develop the structures of communicative action independently of technical progress so that the possible future organization of 'communication free from domination' would not be assimilated to the 'administration of things', which, if realized, according to some – most notably Hannah Arendt (1958) – would result in the undesirable end of that which makes us fully human: political society itself.

In order to clarify the differentiation of knowledge in practical terms, Habermas linked cognition to quasi-transcendental universal human interests.

Whereas empirical-analytic methods aim at disclosing and comprehending reality under the transcendental viewpoint of possible technical control, hermeneutic methods aim at maintaining the intersubjectivity of mutual understanding in ordinary-language communication and in action according to common norms ... The methodological framework that determines the meaning of the validity of critical propositions ... is established by the concept of *self-reflection*. The latter releases the subject from dependence on hypostatized powers. Self-reflection is determined by an emancipatory cognitive interest. (Habermas, 1971: 176, 310)

There is consequently a technical, a practical and an emancipatory cognitive interest that constitute non-reducible corresponding scientific methods and 'establish the specific viewpoints from which we can apprehend reality as such in any way whatsoever' (1971: 311). The identification of freedom and autonomy with self-reflection in social science joined his view that what 'raises us out of nature is the only thing whose nature we can know: *language*. Through its structure, autonomy and responsibility are posited for us. Our first sentence expresses unequivocally the intention of universal and unconstrained consensus' (1971: 314). Habermas subsequently moves his critical theory into a thorough focus on language through the 1970s, which culminated in his magnum opus, *The Theory of Communicative Action* (1984, 1987b). In this text and others (1983, 1987a), Habermas articulates a fully-fledged reconstitution of the normative foundations of Critical Theory based on a paradigm shift to linguistic philosophy that explicitly breaks with the (negative) dialectics of Critical Theory and the so-called 'aporias' or dead-ends Habermas associates with earlier Critical Theory's alleged dependence on the paradigm of 'subject philosophy' or the 'philosophy of consciousness'.

There is, however, significant justification to question Habermas's claims regarding the connection between first generation Critical Theory and 'the exhaustion of the philosophy of consciousness' (Habermas, 1984: 386) as well as his paradigmatic criticisms of Critical Theory (see Morris, 2001). Indeed, Habermas makes the boldest of claims to have shifted paradigmatically the normative thrust of Critical Theory onto the linguistic plain and thereby saved its project from exhaustion. Notwithstanding such controversial claims, Habermas's research project dedicated to reconstituting the normative

foundations of Critical Theory has proved highly influential in the social sciences and humanities. Leaving Habermas's critique of first generation Critical Theory aside, let us turn now to a detailed examination of Habermas's key concepts of communicative action, communicative rationality and his reconstruction of a discourse ethics of communication at the core of his critical social science project.

COMMUNICATIVE ACTION, COMMUNICATIVE RATIONALITY AND THE PUBLIC SPHERE

In *The Theory of Communicative Action*, the three cognitive interests Habermas identified earlier are translated into a tripartite pragmatics of discursively mediated validity claims oriented toward three phenomenological worlds of experience. This is the result of his paradigm shift to linguistic philosophy. In human speech, Habermas argues, understanding the meaning of an utterance requires cognitive agreement between (at least two) communicating subjects in a special way. Communicating subjects reach understanding in language through a complex set of pragmatic presuppositions that involve three valences of understanding and agreement. 'Reaching understanding' (*Verständigung*) is a philosophical term that has a threefold meaning for Habermas. To reach an understanding with an utterance, speaker and hearer must assume that it is uttered in the *right* normative context of a legitimate intersubjective relationship between them, that the speaker makes a *true* statement that will be accepted as knowledge by the hearer, and that the speaker expresses his or her beliefs, intentions, feelings, and so on, *truthfully*, such that the hearer will give credence to what is said (Habermas, 1984: 307–308). Every utterance hence contains three distinct and irreducible claims to validity simultaneously: the claim to *normative rightness* that concerns the social world of intersubjective relations, a *truth claim* about the objective world, and a claim to the speaker's *truthfulness* or sincerity, which refers to his or her internal, subjective world. While these claims always appear together, one or other may tend to be the theme of the utterance. Yet any of these claims can be accepted, rejected, or left undecided by the hearer. Thus internal to every utterance is a pragmatic orientation toward seeking agreement and understanding from others that is necessary due to the demand for a response that claims to validity make. 'Reaching understanding is the inherent telos of human speech' (Habermas, 1984: 287).

This philosophical translation of Habermas's earlier phenomenology of knowledge-constitutive interests may be seen to blunt the thrust of the latter. This is especially so with the emancipatory interest that expresses Habermas's and Critical Theory's key concept of *self-reflection*, since this, in principle, refers to the kind of 'good' enlightenment that Horkheimer and Adorno identify and that Adorno and Marcuse link explicitly with the communicative power of the artwork and the potential of the aesthetic more generally. Habermas's emancipatory interest seems either to disappear into the aesthetic realm of new perception/expression or individual aesthetic creativity (see Habermas, 1988), or it morphs, as we shall see, into the linguistified critical reason of the 'better arguments' of rational discourse in the public sphere (an ideal of contemporary social democratic thought). Neither outcome would be satisfying to Adorno or Marcuse considering first generation Critical Theory's radical phenomenology.

The concept of the public sphere is the idea most commonly associated with Habermas, and one can begin to see how important it is for a theory that places reaching understanding and consensus at the center of its understanding of language. The public sphere is a 'realm of our social life in which something approaching public opinion can be formed. Access is guaranteed to all citizens. A portion of the public sphere comes into being in every conversation in which private individuals assemble to form a public body' (Habermas, 1989: 136). Following Habermas, needs are to be interpreted and public policy decided ideally in a democracy through intersubjective communicative processes of deliberation and decision-making carried out in the public sphere. The political public sphere (distinguished from other public spheres, such as the literary public sphere) is the social space between the power of the state and the citizens and groups of civil society. It is brought into existence every time matters of common concern are debated and discussed by groups of interested citizens. As such, the public sphere encompasses protest marches and public rallies as much as deliberation and discussion by groups of individuals or in the mass media. The public sphere is hence 'a network for communicating information and points of view' in which communication is filtered and synthesized into 'bundles of topically specified *public opinions*' (Habermas, 1996: 360). Ideally, the public sphere constitutes public opinion through free and open dialogue among equal citizens who, in expressing their concerns publicly, resolve them through rational discussion. Significant impediments to such a free and open public sphere exist in capitalist society, as first generation Frankfurt School critique shows. Early on Habermas theorized a weakening of the critical functions of the public sphere as a result of its 'structural transformation' in twentieth century welfare-state mass democracies. Large organizations 'strive for political compromises with the state and with one another, excluding the public sphere whenever possible' while still requiring electoral support and presenting the mere appearance of openness through the use of 'publicity' techniques (Habermas, 1989: 141). The ideal of deliberative democracy provides a normative critique of these conditions and shows why a transformation of the public sphere is required for democracy. Such political theory is closely related to Habermas's philosophy of social science, since the core concept of communicative rationality is decisive for both and the emancipatory cognitive interest must find expression in processes and institutions of public critique and argumentation.

According to Habermas, communicative rationality is of a different logical order from the rationalities of strategy or instrument, which are oriented toward egocentric success. Strategic-instrumental rationality is oriented toward success, which is 'the appearance in the world of a desired state, which can … be causally produced through goal-oriented action or omission'. Action oriented toward success is *instrumental* when following technical rules of action and *strategic* when following rules of rational choice that aim to influence the decisions of a rational opponent (Habermas, 1984: 285). One treats something instrumentally when a natural substance or a person (such as a worker following the company's orders) is controlled by the rationality of achieving a specific technical goal. In social interaction, A's strategic goals do not need to be shared by B who is subjected to A's strategy. The success of the strategy only requires B to respond in ways that accord with A's strategic goals. *Communicative* rationality, by contrast, is associated with the recognition of validity, which entails an orientation toward 'mutual understanding and agreement' (*Verständigung*) between speaking subjects. Habermas argues that one accepts or rejects a speaker's claim to validity on the basis of the 'warranty' implicit in the communicative offer, namely, that reasons can be given that would secure the claim to the satisfaction of speaker and hearer (1984: 302). A reciprocity of mutual orientation toward understanding is thus required for the recognition of validity that produces communicatively coordinated action. No such mutual understanding and agreement is required for the coordination of action mediated by strategic or instrumental rationality. Hence it is only in communicative interaction that the parties involved must each share the goal of mutual understanding. The achievement of a valid consensus is based upon the process of discussion and argument that establishes the motivation for

mutual recognition. Assent to validity is thus not based upon empirical motivations such as threat or reward and cannot be imposed by force or technical control precisely because the recognition of a validity claim requires understanding and acceptance of the reasons that back up the cognitive value of the claim (or the acceptance that reasons could be given if required). One cannot generate acceptance of a claim to validity by threatening or rewarding a hearer because in such cases the reasons for giving assent have to do with factors external to the cognitive content inherent in the claim.

The freedom to accept or reject claims to validity on the basis of criticizable reasons is thus a condition for such mutual understanding and agreement since only with the freedom to respond to a validity claim with 'yes' or 'no' (or leave it undecided) could we say that a consensus has been freely and rationally achieved and not imposed. The imposition of consensus is a product of unofficial (sometimes illegitimate) social power, as in the power of capitalist economic interest to exclude some topics from any public discussion or the effects of cultural hegemony or ideology that prevents certain kinds of discussion and certain identities from participating. Most consensus is, however, empirical consensus – *de facto* consensus that is 'unproblematic' in the sense that everyday social coordination requires a significant amount of background agreement in order to occur. Such background consensus may very well be the product of social power, so a democracy must permit critical challenges to society's self-understanding in the interests of freedom and equality. When consensus breaks down or is challenged, communicative interaction is required to restore agreement so that social coordination can resume. A consensus that is produced by discussion and deliberation under conditions of freedom and reciprocity may then be called a rational consensus and a legitimate expression of democratic power because, in principle, it can be justified to all whose interests it affects.

Instead of a correspondence theory of truth that regards a true statement as that which corresponds to an equivalent state of affairs in the world (and which is thereby independent of what people may think of it – such as that which positivism espouses), Habermas adopts a consensus theory of truth that emphasizes the historical contingency of truth that is established by agreement within an existent communication community. Yet unlike contemporary postmodernist emphases on the historical contingency of truth, this contingency is mitigated for Habermas by the everyday operation of communicative action and the possibility of the democratic production of consensus following the universal norms and conditions of discourse ethics. Any consensus, even a rational consensus, is fallible and potentially revisable if new information or interests emerge within the communication community. The restoration of consensus concerning the truth of the matter (what is the case) then ought to depend on appropriate communicative processes. So Habermas does not need utilitarianism to justify an orientation toward truth seeking, since the moral motivation is not instrumental or consequential, but a result of an orientation toward seeking mutual understanding and agreement inherent in the truth-seeking nature of speech communication itself.

COMMUNICATIVE ACTION AND DISCOURSE ETHICS

Habermas's discourse ethics hence seeks to reconstruct the normative conditions and discursive processes through which legitimate consensus on questions of common concern can be generated. Those engaging in argumentative speech, Habermas believes, are oriented toward reaching a rationally motivated agreement and must rule out 'all external or internal coercion other than the force of the better argument and thereby also [neutralize] all motives other than that of the cooperative search for truth' (Habermas, 1990: 90–91).

For people to be willing to argue, they must presuppose something approximating an 'ideal speech situation' – a general symmetry and reciprocity between them such that a hearer is convinced by a speaker's argument only on the basis of its rational acceptability (and not because of some inducement or coercion). While these conditions are a counter-factual idealization (they rarely, if ever, occur in real life), they are nevertheless inescapable pragmatic presuppositions in order for argumentation itself to make sense to participants. How, the Habermasian wonders, could protagonists in argument (as opposed to those engaged in manipulation or force) *not* be oriented toward a mutual recognition of the better argument? These pragmatic presuppositions are necessary and unavoidable in the sense that denying them would not only involve us in performative self-contradiction, but would show that we did not have the relevant know-how to participate in argumentation itself (Benhabib, 1986: 305; Habermas, 1990: 89–90, 95–96). As soon as one engages in argumentation, one enters into a relationship of symmetrical reciprocity with the other; each participant presupposes that the claims he or she makes will either be freely accepted or rejected on the basis of reasons, for otherwise one would not be engaging in argumentation at all but in something else. For example, the manipulation of speech in which A suppresses relevant facts from B or lies to B is a case of strategic communication not communicative action – A's goal is not shared by B. If A's claims cannot be questioned by B, then this lack of reciprocity and equality indicates the one-way communication of instrumental or technical control not communicative action. If A's claims are not meant as arguments, then the social context suspends the pragmatic presuppositions in favor of language's function of 'world disclosure' (as in literature or art in general) (see Habermas, 1987a: 185–210) or entertainment, as in the 'arguments' of stand-up comedians, for example.

From this analysis of the presuppositions of argumentation, Habermas derives a principle of universalization ('U') as a rule of argumentation concerning social norms:

> a contested norm cannot meet with the consent of the participants in a practical discourse … [u]nless all affected can *freely* accept the consequences and side effects that the *general* observance of a controversial norm can be expected to have for the satisfaction of the interests of *each individual*. (Habermas, 1990: 93[original emphasis])

The principle of discourse ethics ('D') then states that 'only those norms can claim to be valid that meet (or could meet) with the approval of all affected in their capacity as participants in a practical discourse' (Habermas, 1990). The principle of universalizability asks us to put ourselves in the place of the other and imagine our conversation with those potentially affected by a particular norm. As such, 'U' is a principle that guides argumentation – no concrete moral norms can be derived from it. Critics have consequently complained that "U" is 'either too indeterminate or too complex or too counterfactual' to serve as a test of procedure for what is intersubjectively permissible. Benhabib (1992: 36–37) suggests 'that 'U' is actually redundant in Habermas's theory and that it adds little but consequentialist confusion to "D" – the basic premise of discourse ethics'. It does seem too indeterminate since the 'interests' of each individual could fall on either side of any number of norms and too consequentialist since it requires consensus as the outcome. Instead, Benhabib (1992: 31), who has followed Habermas along the discourse ethics path, argues that the test of universalizability is sufficiently met with the principles of universal moral respect (we ought to respect each other as beings whose standpoint is worthy of equal consideration) and egalitarian reciprocity (we ought to treat each other as concrete human beings whose capacity to express this standpoint should be enhanced by social practices embodying the discursive ideal). Such principles are readily available to modern subjects as aspects of the political culture of 'equal dignity' that accompanies modernity (see Taylor, 1994). The principle 'U' functions to

guarantee consensus for Habermas, but, following Benhabib, consensus emphasizes the *result* of the process of moral judgment, whereas what is more important is the *process* for the attainment of such judgment. Consensus is often difficult to expect in complex moral conflicts. Better, according to Benhabib (1992: 38), is to place less emphasis on rational agreement and more on 'sustaining those normative practices and moral relationships within which reasoned agreement *as a way of life* can flourish and continue'. Discourse ethics' normative thrust of rational argument oriented toward mutual understanding and agreement is thus preserved without the requirement that a specific result emerge.

At its most elemental, discourse ethics requires actual intersubjective participation in discourse and deliberation that is free and equal. As Bohman (1997) argues, such participation requires 'effective social freedom' if the 'political poverty' of certain groups of citizens – their inability to initiate the joint activity of public deliberation – is to be avoided. Powerful economic groups in society have greater social freedom through their use of unofficial power by excluding many topics from public debate – threats of capital flight block discussion of redistributive measures, for example – which limits everyone's political equality (Bohman, 1997: 338–339). Political equality would require improving the resources as well as the capabilities of such disadvantaged citizens and groups. Hence Sen (1992) argues that the liberal distributive justice of ensuring a basic level of primary goods is not enough since it cannot respond adequately to the human diversity of condition, ends, means, and opportunities that require qualitatively different forms and levels of primary goods. Instead, Sen contends that human diversity requires 'capability equality' such that the 'beings and doings' of persons are considered constitutive of well-being: 'Capability reflects freedom to pursue these constitutive elements, and may even have … a direct role in well-being itself, insofar as deciding and choosing are also parts of living' (Sen, 1992: 39, 42). In other words, like J.S. Mill's advocacy of positive liberty, one must have equal 'effective freedom' to successfully pursue and attain social goods – something that is not guaranteed by conventional welfare redistribution. Yet, as Bohman (1997: 334) argues, Sen's emphasis on individual capability freedom cannot capture what is important for effective social freedom in deliberative democracy, for the latter is measured not merely by 'the capacity to convert resources and other objective conditions into achievements of the agent's goals [but] by effective participation in a public process of decision-making'. Such effective participation is measured instead by the uptake or recognition by others of my reasons – not by my achieving my particular goal – and this success 'only shapes and influences the process of deliberation itself, so that I can at least recognize my reasons as having shaped and influenced the outcome favorably' (Bohman, 1997: 335). When one argues, when one participates in public deliberation, one must be motivated by 'the cooperative search for truth' (Habermas, 1990: 91), since strategic or instrumental 'argument' is not really argument at all due to the latter's manipulations, deceits and/or exclusions that disqualify any orientation toward mutual understanding and agreement. One of the key goals of deliberation is thus free cooperation itself, which is an intersubjective, social goal incapable of being measured instrumentally or economically. Effective *communicative* freedom through the enhancement of communicative resources and capacities is hence required for the realization of political equality against the undue influence of unofficial social power.

It is at this point that we may make a connection between communicative action and social bonding. Communicative action constitutes sociality through the binding and bonding effect that raising and redeeming validity claims accomplishes. The motivation that binds speakers and hearers is a rational force yet, as we have seen, it is not an empirical force like that of threats or rewards.

The communicative speaker is bound to the hearer through the validity claiming action inherent in his or her utterance, since every validity claim is always accompanied by the 'warranty' that, if necessary, it can be secured with reasons. The communicative coordination of their social action together expresses this social bond between speakers and hearers and embodies a relation of free and equal interaction centered on the maintenance of mutual understanding and agreement.

Although individual autonomy is required to raise and redeem validity claims, this autonomy would not be possible without the mutual recognition of intersubjectively conceived identity. Persons become individualized only through a process of socialization that involves gradually taking on an identity in a particular life context. Intellectual autonomy is achieved through symbolic communication with others, as George Herbert Mead made clear (Habermas, 1992). Thus the system of rights and morality that protects individual identity 'cannot safeguard the integrity of individual persons without at the same time safeguarding the vitally necessary web of relationships of mutual recognition in which individuals can stabilize their fragile identities only mutually and simultaneously with the identity of the group' (Habermas, 1993: 98). This means that, in the 'post-metaphysical' context of modernity (i.e. societies not oriented by a religious or a cosmological worldview), individual autonomy is internally related to group solidarity – the reproduction of collective cultural identity depends on the exercise of autonomous communication by individual members and the autonomy of individual communication requires 'a politics of recognition that protects the integrity of the individual in the life contexts in which his or her identity is formed' (Habermas, 1998: 208). Solidarity is no longer limited to the embodiment of a particular collectivity – the concrete lifeworld of family, tribe, city, class or nation – but is extended and universalized through discourse into 'an ideal communication community ... that includes all subjects capable of speech and action' (Habermas, 1993: 99). The tension between individual autonomy and the solidarity of group membership is potentially resolved not through any new identity but through the protection and enhancement of the processes of communication that allow the raising of validity claims and the communicative contexts of mutual recognition in which persons of equal dignity appear.

CONCLUSION

What each version of Critical Theory discussed here demands – first generation Critical Theory as well as Habermas and his followers – is that any analysis of social 'facts' is subject to normative and practical constraints or, perhaps better, dimensions (to invoke a spatial metaphor that seems so crucial for many of the problems faced today). Philosophy of social science cannot advance without critical intellectual and practical progress. This philosophy of social science is, in a definitive sense, *political* – but it is not political in this sense of mere competing theoretical or ideological interests or even in the Kuhnian sense of an essentially political clash of scientific paradigms. This is because Critical Theory embodies a meta-theory of cognition and social practice that cannot be reduced to a Kuhnian paradigm (or, for that matter, a Foucaultian 'episteme'). Such a theory is methodologically self-reflective at its core – it contains recognition of its own conditions of possibility as an internal moment of its theorizing. Hence, in acknowledging the inherent 'politics of theory' entwined with any historical intellectual project, Critical Theory theorizes social science always as a distinct practical-political project. It is one of the key continuities throughout the tradition of Critical Theory that critical social science (or, for that matter, any social science) cannot be conducted as epistemology. Critical Theory, in this sense, is more akin to the ancient 'political science'

articulated by Aristotle: namely, that philosophical endeavor should be guided by an orientation toward the good of the whole, the community of beings, but, of course, without any implications or requirements for institutionalized class and gendered social relations, slavery, or the automatic domination of nature that were present in the ancient art.

Each version of Critical Theory discussed here clearly articulates a normative vision that is intended to overcome distortions and manipulations in the dynamic of knowledge acquisition that occur for individuals and the mass public. In this way, Critical Theory maintains its interest in the liberation of the dominated, even if its addressees continue to suffer from an 'inability to hear with their own ears what has not already been heard, to touch with their hands what has not previously been grasped'.

NOTES

1 Although, on the other hand, much of its constitution – in the ancient sense – would equal a school of thought for all intents and purposes, see Heller (2002).

2 The term 'critical theory' is used as a description of theory across disciplines in the social sciences and humanities. Most commonly, these theories are today inspired by postmodernist or poststructuralist sources, which complicate the concept of 'critical' – for example, poststructuralism's anti-humanism may be critical in an emancipatory sense, but if there is no longer a goal of liberation, what is the point of being 'critical' (see, for example, Hardt and Negri, 2000)? There are clearly certain affinities between poststructuralist critical theory and Frankfurt School Critical Theory, although the details are quite controversial and, indeed, have been further complicated by the Habermasian turn in Frankfurt School Critical Theory that I discuss below. Since Critical Theory inspired by the Frankfurt School tradition nevertheless remains a vital and on-going project today across the social sciences and humanities – sometimes in competition with poststructuralist critiques, at others in league with and complementary of such critiques – I limit myself to the discussion of this tradition and capitalize the term in order to indicate this.

3 'Wesenschau', which refers to Husserl's method of phenomenological reduction to intuit the forms of consciousness underlying perceptual cognition (Adorno, 1998b: n. 19, p. 319).

REFERENCES

Adorno, T.W. (1973a) *Negative Dialectics* (E.B. Ashton, Trans.). New York: Seabury Press.

Adorno, T.W. (1973b) *The Jargon of Authenticity.* Evanston, IL: Northwestern University Press.

Adorno, T.W. (1976) *The Positivist Dispute in German Sociology.* London: Heinemann.

Adorno, T.W. (1997) *Aesthetic Theory* (R. Hullot-Kentor, Trans.). Minneapolis, MN: University of Minnesota Press.

Adorno, T.W. (1998a) 'A note on human science and culture' (H.W. Pickford, Trans.), in *Critical Models: Interventions and Catchwords.* New York: Columbia University Press. pp. 37–40.

Adorno, T.W. (1998b) 'Why still philosophy' (H. W. Pickford, Trans.), in *Critical Models: Interventions and Catchwords.* New York: Columbia University Press. pp. 5–18.

Arendt, H. (1958) *The Human Condition.* Chicago: University of Chicago Press.

Benhabib, S. (1986) *Critique, Norm, and Utopia.* New York: Columbia University Press.

Benhabib, S. (1992) *Situating the Self.* New York: Routledge.

Bohman, J. (1997) 'Deliberative democracy and effective social freedom: Capabilities, resources, and opportunities', in J. Bohman and W. Rehg (eds), *Deliberative Democracy: Essays on Reason and Politics.* Cambridge, MA: MIT Press. pp. 321–348.

Burke, D. A., Campbell, C. J. Kiloh, K., Palamarek, M. K. and Short, J. (eds.) (2007), Adorno and the Need in Thinking: New Critical Essays. Toronto: University of Toronto Press.

Habermas, J. (1971) *Knowledge and Human Interests* (J.J. Shapiro, Trans.). Boston: Beacon Press.

Habermas, J. (1979) *Communication and the Evolution of Society* (T. McCarthy, Trans.). Boston: Beacon Press.

Habermas, J. (1983) *Philosophical-Political Profiles.* Cambridge, MA: MIT Press.

Habermas, J. (1984) *The Theory of Communicative Action* (T. McCarthy, Trans. Vol. 1). Boston: Beacon Press.

Habermas, J. (1987a) *The Philosophical Discourse of Modernity* (F.G. Lawrence, Trans.). Cambridge, MA: MIT Press.

Habermas, J. (1987b) *The Theory of Communicative Action* (T. McCarthy, Trans. Vol. 2). Boston: Beacon Press.

Habermas, J. (1988) 'Questions and counterquestions', in R.J. Bernstein (ed.) *Habermas and Modernity.* Cambridge, MA.: MIT Press. pp. 192–216.

Habermas, J. (1989) 'The public sphere: An encyclopedia article', in S.E. Bronner and D. Kellner (eds), *Critical Theory and Society: A Reader.* New York: Routledge. pp. 136–142.

Habermas, J. (1990) *Moral Consciousness and Communicative Action* (C. Lenhardt and S.W. Nicholsen, Trans.). Cambridge, MA: MIT Press.

Habermas, J. (1992) 'Individuation through socialization: On George Herbert Mead's theory of subjectivity', in *Postmetaphysical Thinking: Philosophical Essays.* Cambridge, MA: MIT Press. pp. 149–204.

Habermas, J. (1993) 'Justice and solidarity', in M. Fisk (ed.), *Justice: Key Concepts in Critical Theory.* Atlantic Highlands, NJ: Humanities Press. pp. 89–100.

Habermas, J. (1996) *Between Facts and Norms* (W. Rehg, Trans.). Cambridge, MA: MIT Press.

Habermas, J. (1998) *The Inclusion of the Other* (C. Cronin, Trans.). Cambridge, MA: MIT Press.

Hardt, M. and Negri, A. (2000) *Empire.* Cambridge, MA: Harvard University Press.

Heller, A. (2002) 'The Frankfurt School', in J.T. Nealon and C. Irr (eds) *Rethinking the Frankfurt School: Alternative Legacies of Cultural Critique.* Albany: State University of New York Press. pp. 207–221.

Horkheimer, M. (1989a) 'The latest attack on metaphysics', in M. Horkheimer, *Critical Theory: Selected Essays.* New York: Continuum. pp. 132–187.

Horkheimer, M. (1989b) 'Traditional theory and critical theory', in M. Horkheimer, *Critical Theory: Selected Essays.* New York: Continuum. pp. 188–252.

Horkheimer, M. and Adorno, T.W. (2002). *Dialectic of Enlightenment* (E. Jephcott, Trans.). Stanford: Stanford University Press.

Jameson, F. (1990) *Signatures of the Visible.* New York: Routledge.

Marcuse, H. (1964) *One Dimensional Man.* Boston: Beacon Press.

Marcuse, H. (1966) *Eros and Civilization.* Boston: Beacon Press.

Marcuse, H. (1968) *Philosophy and Critical Theory.* Boston: Beacon Press.

Marcuse, H. (1969) *An Essay on Liberation.* Boston: Beacon Press.

Marx, K. (1974) 'The civil war in France', in D. Fernbach (ed.) *The First International and After: Political Writings.* Harmondsworth: Penguin. p. 417.

Morris, M. (2001) *Rethinking the Communicative Turn.* Albany: State University of New York Press.

Sen, A.K. (1992) *Inequality Reexamined.* Cambridge, MA: Harvard University Press.

Taylor, C. (1994) *Multiculturalism and 'The Politics of Recognition'.* Princeton: Princeton University Press.

PART 4

Methodology: Assessing and Using Social Theories

27

Facts, Values, and Objectivity

Heather Douglas

Although concern over values in social science spans a century, no serious commentator has argued that values have no relevance for social science. Even Max Weber, the figure most associated with the ideal of value-neutrality for social science, is quite clear that social science cannot proceed without values. However, how the values do and should play a role in social science has been a central issue. Questions at the forefront of discussion include: When are values legitimate in social science? When are they necessary? When are they a threat to objectivity? How should objectivity as an ideal for science be understood? And does social science face greater problems concerning values and objectivity than natural science?

In this chapter, I will first review the key positions on values in social science from the twentieth century. With this background in place, it will be clearer both how to parse the various roles for values in social science and what these roles mean for the objectivity of social science. Using recent work, I will map the terrain of values in social science and then turn to a discussion of objectivity in light of this terrain. Objectivity turns out to be a complex concept, with multiple facets which can bolster our confidence in social science work. Perhaps most intriguing,

I will discuss arguments that the objectivity of science itself is underwritten by the social. Rather than suggesting that the social undermines the possibilities for objectivity, as was often presumed by commentators from the first part of the twentieth century, such an understanding places the social at the center of scientific objectivity.

VALUES AND SOCIAL SCIENCE: A LOOK BACK

The central questions on values in social science were addressed repeatedly over the course of the twentieth century. Although there is much agreement on how best to understand values in science, there are also points of disagreement. In particular, there have been major shifts over whether the social sciences face unique challenges with respect to values and objectivity. Max Weber, for example, thought that the complexities that social scientists attempted to study meant that social science had unique difficulties in achieving the proper stance with respect to values, placing objectivity further from reach. In contrast, mid-twentieth century philosophers influenced by the unity of science movement argued that social sciences faced no special challenges, that the natural sciences had similar kinds of difficulties with respect to values. At the same time, the mid-century saw the formation of a much more definitive and clear value-free ideal. Debate over that ideal helped to map the terrain for values in science.

Weber on values in science

Max Weber had a more complex view of the relationship between values and science than is often recognized, as can be seen in his 1904 essay, " 'Objectivity' in Social Science and Social Policy." It was an editorial essay, describing his vision for the scope and nature of the journal *Archiv für Sozialwissenschaft und Sozialpolitik*, of which he was assuming editorship (along with Werner Sombart and Edgar Jaffé) (Weber, 1949: iv). The essay was to clear the ground for the kind of forum he thought should exist for the journal and for social science in general. A methodological essay of the great subtlety, he argues in it that although there is a clear *conceptual* distinction between is and ought, and social science is interested in the development of descriptive "is" claims, social science cannot proceed without value judgments. Despite the dependency of social science on values, he also argues that social science, as an empirical science, must maintain some boundaries between science and values, in order to protect the value of empirical science.

Foundational to Weber's understanding of the necessity of values in social science is his awareness that the complexity of human social life is simply too overwhelming and variable for us to ever completely capture all social facts. Because of this, the social scientist must proceed with some sense of what is significant. What is significant requires some kind of value judgment, Weber argues. Where we choose to look in gathering data and what kind of data it seems worthwhile to gather requires values. We must value something to find it significant enough to measure,

to pluck it from the complexity of human social life, and to see it as a set of phenomena worthy of study. " 'Culture' is a finite segment of the meaningless infinity of the world process, a segment on which *human beings* confer meaning and significance" (Weber, 1949: 81). Because we must decide what is important enough to study, "the significance of cultural events presupposes a *value-orientation* towards those events" (p. 76). The conferring of significance on social phenomena begins the process of structuring social science research."The very recognition of the existence of a scientific problem coincides, personally, with the possession of specifically oriented motives and values" (p. 61). Social science cannot have clearly defined problems without values to indicate what is significant. Weber emphasizes this point in refuting economics' claim of being a wholly objective and value-free approach to social science, writing: "There is no absolutely 'objective' scientific analysis of culture ... or 'social phenomena' independent of special and 'one-sided' viewpoints according to which ... they are selected, analyzed, and organized for expository purposes" (p. 72). Social science requires values as presuppositions to direct our attention and structure our basic concepts. Thus, when Weber argues for value-neutral social science, he does not mean social science proceeding without values altogether. Indeed, he eschews any sort of naïve inductive positivism (p. 78).

In addition, social science itself, indeed all science, is dependent upon being valued by society. Weber suggests that this need not be the case, that we could live in a culture that did not value the pursuit of empirical truths: "It should be remembered that the belief in the value of scientific truth is the product of certain cultures and is not a product of man's original nature" (p. 110). The very fact that empirical truths, and the social science that produces them, is valued at all is based on a particular cultural value.

Not only are values essential to the conduct of social science, but also social science has several ways in which it can usefully comment on values, according to Weber. First, it can tell us whether, given our ends, a particular means would be effective in achieving those ends (pp. 52–53). Thus, we can use social science to critique the ends based on their viability as ends. Indeed, the assessment of the means could help us to see how problematic our ends are, by unveiling other possible consequences of the means which we might use to achieve those ends (pp. 52–53). Although this is a crucial service social science can offer social policymaking, Weber thought social science cannot ultimately answer the question of whether "the attainment of a desired end" would cost too much "in terms of the predictable loss of other values" (pp. 52–53). How to make such tradeoffs in practice is beyond the bounds of social science, even as the discovery of the necessity of such tradeoffs lies well within its purview.

Second, social science can help to clarify the values we do have by "making explicit and developing in a logically consistent manner the 'ideas' which actually do or which can underlie the concrete end" (p. 53). Social science, in clarifying what we believe our ends to be, can help provide a "rational understanding" of those ends (p. 54). In addition, social science can judge the internal consistency of one's ideals and ends (p. 54). By providing a more precise description of values, and clarification on the historical development of our values, social science can make our values open to clearer analysis and understanding, even if it cannot *determine* those values. In addition to providing helpful assistance to society, such clarity about the nature of values ultimately aids the objectivity of the social scientist, helping to prevent confusion between the scientist's values and the way reality is.

Thus, according to Weber, there are multiple ways in which values are crucial to social science, and social science can be useful for understanding values. Yet he was at pains to make clear that he thought there were important boundaries between values and science as well. Maintaining these

conceptual boundaries was central to scientific objectivity.

Given all these interrelationships between science and values, in what does scientific objectivity consist according to Weber? Weber rejects some easy answers: "An *attitude of moral indifference* has no connection with *scientific* 'objectivity'" (p. 60). Social scientists are not to pretend to have no moral response to the phenomena they study. Weber does not believe in the cold-hearted scientist. Nor is a middle path among moral extremes to be taken as objective: "To mediate between antagonistic points of view … has nothing whatsoever to do with scientific 'objectivity.' *Scientifically the middle course is not truer even by a hair's breadth*, than the most extreme party ideals of the right or left" (p. 57). Finding the moderate position within one's culture may have political, but not scientific advantages. Thus, moral indifference or artificial neutrality are not laudatory goals for the social scientist.

More central to Weber's understanding of objectivity is his warning against the social scientist blurring their moral responses with their empirical work. Weber calls on social scientists to be clear about the values and ideals that structure their conceptual approach:

> it should be constantly made clear to the reader (… and above all to one's self!) exactly at which point the scientific investigator becomes silent and the evaluating and acting person begins to speak. In other words, it should be made explicit just where the arguments are addressed to the analytical understanding and where to the sentiments. (Weber, 1949: 60)

Weber stresses that "is" claims should still be kept distinct from "ought" claims in the conduct and discussion of empirical social science, even if one understands that values structure the starting points and the ideas with which one begins any social scientific investigation.

Weber admonishes that such clarity should also be maintained in the use of ideal types that structure our understanding of complex social phenomena. Weber argues that these ideal types (e.g., the ideal type of medieval Christianity) are essential to gaining any traction with the concrete reality of social life, but we are never to confuse the ideal type with the complex reality from which the ideal type is abstracted. Further, we should not conflate the use of an ideal type in social science with an endorsement of it as an appropriate ideal. Doing social science properly "requires a sharp, precise distinction between the logically *comparative* analysis of reality by ideal-*types* in the logical sense and the *value-judgment* of reality *on the basis of ideals*" (Weber, 1949: 98). The social scientist was not to decide which ideals were the correct ideals nor whether a society should meet certain ideals, but rather the social scientist should focus on what ideals helped to best understand a culture and how descriptively close that society is to an ideal. Weber makes clear that he thinks science can confer no legitimacy upon the ultimate ends or core values one holds. "As to whether the person expressing these value-judgments *should* adhere to these ultimate standards is his personal affair; it involves will and conscience, not empirical knowledge" (p. 54). Thus, social science cannot and should not tell us what our ideals should be. It can only inform our understanding of our ideals in the ways sketched above.

With these separations of science and value, Weber can understand science as producing universal truths, albeit in a constrained sense. "A social science journal … to the extent that it is *scientific* should be a place where those truths are sought, which … can claim even for a Chinese, the validity appropriate to an analysis of empirical reality" (Weber, 1949: 59). While noting that variations in what is significant will occur among both cultures and individuals within cultures, he explicitly rejects a science subjective to the individual: "It obviously does not follow from this that research in the cultural sciences can only have results which are 'subjective' in the sense that they are *valid* for one person and not for others. … For scientific truth is precisely what is valid for all who *seek* the truth"

(p. 84). Presumably, even if one disagreed with the starting choices of significance or basic ideas, one could see the difference between a properly and an improperly done analysis following from those starting ideas. For Weber, scientific objectivity is to be found in analysis that all who examined it would find acceptable. He does not claim that the social sciences could discover eternal truths about human social life – in fact he is explicitly skeptical about this possibility (pp. 104–105). But within a given framework, there should be broad agreement about the results of science. Once one is working with a set of ideals and categories (shaped by what one thinks is significant), objective, empirical truths are available:

> The *objective* validity of all empirical knowledge rests exclusively upon the ordering of the given reality according to categories which are *subjective* in a specific sense, namely, in that they present the *presuppositions* of our knowledge and are based on the presupposition of the *value* of those *truths* which empirical knowledge alone is able to give us. (Weber, 1949: 110)

Given the starting points of valuing empirical science and a particular set of ideas about what is significant in social life, objective truths are possible as long as one does not confuse the normative and the descriptive as one's scientific work goes forward.

Values and social science in the mid-twentieth century

Two different lines of inquiry into the relationship between social science and values sprouted from Weber's work. One, which we shall not pursue here, centered on the need for a science of ethics. Critics of Weber, such as Leo Strauss, argued that Weber's views necessarily lead to nihilism, as each person is forced back to their own subjective value choices, with no scientific or universal framework for comparing their morals (Strauss, 1953). In order to avoid such nihilism, a science of ethics was needed. This science would presumably demonstrate the universal and scientific validity of the correct framework of ethics. Discussion of a social science of ethics, which could determine universally valid ends, was a serious endeavor in the 1950s. Authors such as Strauss (1953), Gottshalk (1952), and Hartmann (1950) pursued such a science with vigor, but their efforts were relegated to the academic backwaters by 1960. The problem of drawing a normative justification from a descriptive account remained unmet.

A second line of inquiry was to have greater traction. This line concerned itself with the question of how different social science really was from natural science, and whether there were qualitative differences in how important values were for the two types of science and for the objectivity of each. For Weber, the complexity of social phenomenon and the need for some sense of significance marked social science as having distinctive methodological issues when it came to values and objectivity. Other thinkers disputed these conclusions, most notably George Lundberg and Ernest Nagel.

That social science was qualitatively distinct from natural science, facing unique methodological problems, seemed to explain the development of social science for some observers. As the social sciences developed in the twentieth century and carved out a place for themselves in the academy, the question arose of why social science did not seem to be producing *results* as quickly or effectively as the natural sciences. In many of these discussions, it was argued that social science was more inextricably tied with values than natural science, and thus was unable to produce the same kind of reliable objective results. For example, Julian Huxley argued in 1940 that while "values are deliberately excluded from the purview of natural science," social science could not avoid serious and problematic entanglements with values. He believed that "to understand and describe a system involving values [as any human social system does] is impossible without some judgment of values" (quoted in Lundberg, 1941: 350).

In response to this line of thought, others defended social science as not being importantly distinct from natural science with respect to the role of values in science. Arguments that there were no sharp differences between the natural and social sciences were part of the logical empiricist effort to unify the sciences, an effort originally motivated by the need to roll back the fascist impulses separating the natural and social sciences (Uebel, 2007: 254). In the postwar context, both George Lundberg and Ernest Nagel argued that social science had no special problems in relation to values and that whatever challenges existed were present for natural as well as social science. (Rudner (1966) argues for a similar position concerning objectivity in social science. Unfortunately he seriously misconstrues Weber in that discussion.) Unpacking these arguments allows for insight into their views on the role of values in social science. For the sake of brevity, I will focus on Nagel's arguments here, as they provide one of the clearest and most thorough expositions on this point.

In the final three chapters of *The Structure of Science* (1961), Nagel undertakes a careful examination of social science. The chapter of most relevance for our purposes, "Methodological problems of the social sciences," focuses on the question of whether there are distinctive and insuperable challenges faced by the social sciences, challenges which might prevent it from ever achieving the kind of powerful and overarching explanatory laws Nagel thought characterized the physical sciences (Nagel, 1961: 450). He argues that there are no such special challenges – that although social science might not yet have achieved such laws, there is nothing inherent in its subject matter or methodologies that meant it would be kept from such achievement. In addition to addressing such potential methodological pitfalls as limited opportunity for controlled experimentation (pp. 450–459), the historical and cultural contingency of social phenomena (pp. 459–466), and the potential for a study to influence the particular behavior under study (pp. 466–473), Nagel tackles the subjective nature of social science's subject matter (pp. 473–485), and the role of values in social science (pp. 485–502). For each of these, Nagel argues that the problem can be adequately addressed or that the natural sciences face a similar problem (or both). Thus, Nagel systematically undermines the idea that there is something distinctive about the social sciences that creates difficulties for their objectivity.

For example, a key objection to the potential objectivity of social science had been the fact that the subject matter of the social sciences often centers on subjective human states, such as internal emotions. Although social science inquiry often concerns the internal states of human actors, Nagel sees this as no insurmountable obstacle to objective evidence in social science. Objective observational evidence is needed, according to Nagel, to check our imputation of internal states to human actors, but we can gather such evidence by examining behavior, and it is no more mysterious than imputing "internal states" to matter that we cannot see (such as electrical current), yet still have evidence for (p. 484). Empathy with other humans can assist the social scientists in developing hypotheses about human behavior, but evidence concerning observable behaviors serves to test those hypotheses (pp. 484–485).

More central to our concerns here, Nagel's examination of values in social science continues his theme of similarity between natural and social science. He discusses four different locations where values may have a role in social science (legitimately or not) and finds little difference between social and natural sciences. Examining these roles will show both where Nagel thought values posed a methodological problem for science and where values played acceptable roles.

First, Nagel notes the importance of values in selecting what one will study, a similar role to what Weber called the value-laden choice of what seems "significant." While Weber saw this as a particular problem for

social science, for any delineation of culture automatically contained value judgments on what is significant, Nagel sees parallels with the selection of research problems in natural science: "There is no difference between any of the sciences with respect to the fact that the interests of the scientist determine what he selects for investigation" (p. 486). That such a selection necessarily occurs in social (or natural) science is no obstacle to scientific objectivity. Values can (and should!) direct a scientist's attention without threatening scientific objectivity.

Nagel next addresses the problem of one's values influencing the conclusions one draws, purportedly a particularly acute problem for social science because so many social scientists are hoping to reform society in view of some ideal they hold, an ideal that reflects their own values. Nagel argues that solving this problem depends on the conceptual distinction between facts and values, and that if this distinction holds (and he defends it in the following section), then it should be possible to work on keeping values from unduly influencing social science results (p. 489). He notes that one way to counteract the potential undue influence of values is to have "social scientists abandon the pretense that they are free from all bias, and that instead they state their value assumptions as explicitly and fully as they can" (p. 489). This is not to be done with an eye towards gaining agreement among all social scientists on the correct values, nor so that social science can settle the question of the correct values. Rather it is so that questions of fact and value can be more readily disentangled. Here we see echoes of Weber's approach to the problem, calling on social scientists to be explicit in their values and to work to keep the normative and the descriptive conceptually distinct.

Nagel, however, cautions against expecting value explicitness from providing too much:

> Although the recommendation that social scientists make fully explicit their value commitments is undoubtedly salutary, and can produce excellent

fruit, it verges on being a counsel of perfection. For the most part we are unaware of many assumptions that enter into our analyses and actions, so that despite resolute efforts to make our preconceptions explicit some decisive ones may not even occur to us. But in any event, the difficulties generated for scientific inquiry by unconscious bias and tacit value orientations are rarely overcome by devout resolutions to eliminate bias. They are overcome, often only gradually, through the self-corrective mechanisms of science as a social enterprise. (Nagel, 1961: 489)

It is this suggestion – that the social aspects of scientific practice are the appropriate remedy for bias, and thus a key location for the objectivity of science – that will be taken up by feminist critics of science, as we will see below. At any rate, the problem of potentially pernicious bias is a problem that runs throughout science, and so it is no special problem for social science.

Nagel then tackles the issue of whether values are actually distinguishable from facts (p. 490). He argues that a key distinction in the nature of value judgments is needed to clarify the matter. There are value judgments that express approval or disapproval, that is, "appraising value judgments," and there are value judgments that assess whether some entity has a property and how much of the property it has, that is, "characterizing value judgments" (pp. 490–491). The former express the ought-claims that must be kept conceptually distinct from factual claims, whereas the latter are part of making factual claims. Nagel notes that sometimes our language can embed the appraisal in the characterization – it is hard to not hear disapproval in terms like deceitful or mercenary (p. 494). (More recent commentators have noted these difficulties, as I will discuss below.) Yet Nagel thought it possible to distinguish the disapproval from the description. Nagel argues that "there are no good reasons for thinking that it is inherently impossible to *distinguish* between the characterizing and appraising judgments implicit in many statements, whether the statements are asserted by students of human affairs or natural scientists" (p. 494). The distinction

between normative and descriptive statements, while potentially tricky in practice, is not conceptually undermined. In addition, this is not a problem unique to social science. This problem also occurs in natural science, with terms like anemic (when applied to organisms) or inefficient (when applied to a pumping system). Thus, there is again no special problem for social science.

Finally, Nagel addresses the concern over the use of values in assessing available evidence (a variant on the arguments of Rudner (1953), discussed in more detail below). He notes that in deciding whether statistical evidence is sufficient for supporting or rejecting a hypothesis, one must make a choice between risking two types of error: rejecting a true hypothesis and accepting a false one (Nagel, 1961: 496). As no inference rule can minimize both errors simultaneously, the scientist makes the choice based on which errors are to be more assiduously avoided, and that choice can be based on the scientist's valuation of the consequences that may follow from the two kinds of error (p. 497). Nagel does not think that the specific consequences of error, and thus valuations of those specific consequences, are always involved in this choice. Instead, the choice may be guided solely by more general commitments to the development of scientific knowledge, such as "to conduct his inquiries with probity and responsibility" (p. 498). As we will see below, Nagel is mirroring a key aspect of the value-free ideal which is developing at this time. Regardless of how it is handled, the need for such a choice is found in both natural and social science, so again no special problem of values in social science presents itself.

Thus, for each of the four challenges values pose for social science, none are insurmountable (indeed the first is no problem but an acceptable aspect of the scientific enterprise), and none are distinctive to the social sciences. For Nagel, there is no special problem for social science concerning values. The problem of values in science was a general one, resolved by most philosophers of science with the value-free ideal.

The value-free ideal for science

While the preponderance of argument was shifting away from considering social science as distinct from natural science in methodological challenges concerning values, philosophers of science were settling on a new ideal for values in science generally. Discussions over values in science gained greater precision, and forced a reconsideration of legitimate and illegitimate roles for values in science.

The new ideal emerged from debates begun over arguments made by C. West Churchman and Richard Rudner about the indispensability of value judgments in scientific practice (Churchman, 1948; Rudner, 1953). Rudner's 1953 essay, "The scientist *qua* scientist makes value judgments," most clearly laid out the argument. In that essay, Rudner acknowledges the importance of values for both deciding to do science and for the selection of projects one is to pursue (Rudner, 1953: 1). This role for values, however, he calls "extra-scientific" or "pre-scientific" and thus it has "not been shown to be any part of the *procedures* of science" (pp. 1–2). In order to show that values are an essential aspect of doing science properly, Rudner focuses on the need for scientists to accept or reject hypotheses. Because no hypotheses is ever completely proven by inductive evidence, "in accepting a hypothesis the scientist must make the decision that the evidence is *sufficiently* strong or that the probability is *sufficiently* high to warrant the acceptance of the hypothesis" (p. 2). In making this assessment, Rudner argues that it is "the *importance*, in the typically ethical sense, of making a mistake in accepting or rejecting the hypothesis" that must be considered by the scientist (p. 2). Because values are needed to decide whether the available evidence is sufficient to warrant accepting or rejecting

a hypothesis, values are essential to all scientific reasoning.

Rudner's argument was well publicized at the time (he gave a talk based on the paper at the joint Philosophy of Science Association/American Association for the Advancement of Science meeting in December 1953 and a shortened version of the paper was published in *Scientific Monthly* in 1954). It drew several critical responses. For example, Richard Jeffrey critiqued one of Rudner's key presumptions, arguing that scientists properly speaking never accept or reject hypotheses (Jeffrey, 1956). Instead, Jeffrey suggested that they merely assign probabilities to them. However, Rudner had already considered this line of argument, and countered it by noting that one still had to accept or reject the probability, which required the same kind of value judgment (Rudner, 1953: 4).

A response that gained more traction among philosophers of science was put forth by Isaac Levi (Levi, 1960, 1962). Levi argued that Rudner was correct in noting the need for a value judgment, but that scientists should be constrained in the values used to make such a judgment, constrained to consider only the "canons of scientific inference" (Levi, 1960: 355). As philosophers of science developed this idea, the canons became the set of epistemic or cognitive values, such as simplicity, scope, explanatory power, consistency and predictive accuracy (Kuhn, 1977). Thus the value-free ideal for science became codified as the cognitive-values-only rule when assessing the strength of evidence for a hypothesis. Cognitive values were to fill the gap between the set of available evidence and the hypothesis under scrutiny, not social or ethical values. Philosophers of science from Ernan McMullin (1983) to Hugh Lacey (1999) and Sandra Mitchell (2004) have defended this ideal.

Although disputed by Leach (1968) and Scriven (1974), this view remained the standard ideal for science through the rest of the twentieth century. What philosophers of science usually mean when they say science should be value-free is that when assessing the sufficiency of a body of evidence with respect to a theory, only cognitive values should be used. Thus, the value-free ideal should not be taken literally to mean no values in science – instead it should be taken to mean cognitive values only in science, once a research project is underway.

It must be noted, however, that most cognitive values have little direct epistemic import. Whether a theory is simple, has broad scope, or has explanatory power provides no clear indication that it is true (Laudan, 2004; Wylie and Nelson, 2007). The history of science is littered with explanatory theories (caloric, ether), broadly scoped theories (mechanical theories of matter), simple theories (Newton's space–time), and even precise theories (Kepler's spacing of the planets with platonic solids) that have gone by the wayside. If cognitive values do not indicate that a theory is more likely to be true, why are they held up as canonical in science? The justification has usually been a descriptive one – scientists just *do* value theories of scope, simplicity, explanatory power, and precision (Kuhn, 1977). These values are internal to science and part of its historical functioning. If one examines the scientific community as a closed community driven by its own internal dynamics, then cognitive values are indeed the only justifiable values to be utilized.

Upon reflection, such a view of the functioning of science, natural or social, should be suspect. As many have noted, particularly for the social sciences, the social relevance of the work cannot be ignored. Social science does not function as a closed community divorced from the society that it studies, nor should we want such complete separation that the value-free ideal seems to demand. As this author (Douglas, 2003a, 2009: Chapter 4) and others (Forge, 2008) have argued, scientists have unavoidable moral responsibilities to consider the consequences of their work, particularly the consequences of error. If so, the value-free ideal must be rejected. A new map of values in science is needed.

MAPPING THE TERRAIN OF VALUES IN SOCIAL SCIENCE

The entanglement between science and values remains as complex, or more so, than in Weber's account. In agreement with Weber, it is widely acknowledged that science can assist our investigation of human values both through descriptive accounts of values and by clarifying the means required to meet various ends we might hold. As Hempel noted in the mid-1960s, science can tell us little about what our categorical values should be, but can greatly inform our instrumental values (Hempel, 1965). If we have certain goals (e.g., smaller recidivism rates for released prisoners), social science can help inform how to reach those goals (e.g., which kinds of social interventions reduce recidivism rates). The science informs our instrumental values, and may even assist us in assessing our goals, if the means of achieving them appear too costly. But a direct assessment of the worthiness of our goals is outside the bounds of social science.

More central for the philosophy of social science are the ways that values play important and legitimate roles in the scientific process. Key locations for the influence of values include: (1) the value placed on science by society, exemplified by the social support given to science; (2) the decision to pursue a particular research project because of the value placed on the knowledge likely to be produced, whether it is a value to society as a whole, a value to the particular field's internal questions, or the quirky interest of the investigator; and (3) the ethical restrictions on methodological means to pursue a research project, particularly when working with human subjects. The importance of values for these decisions is not disputed, nor is the need for values at these locations seen as a threat to the legitimacy or objectivity of science produced, despite the strong and direct role values must play in shaping the decisions.

Despite the acceptability of values in selecting research projects and restricting methodological options, values must not direct the scientist to construct a methodology that will most certainly confirm their favorite theory. As feminist critics of science have noted, failure to gather and examine the full range of possible evidence can assure that the results of a study conform to researcher (and societal) expectations (e.g., Wylie, 2002: 186). This is a pernicious and problematic role for values, as it undermines our confidence in the empirical reliability of the results. If evidence that could contravene a theory is systematically left ungathered or ignored, because it presents an undesirable challenge to the theory, then values are playing a determinative role in shaping the outcome of the results. This gets to the heart of concerns over values in science, that we could confuse our desire that the world be a particular way with evidence that it actually is. If values blind us to unpleasant evidence, the value of the empirical enterprise is undermined.

This same concern arises in the use of values to assess the sufficiency of evidence to support a theory. The value-free ideal holds that in the interpretation of results, only cognitive values should have any influence. It was hoped that this would maintain the needed objectivity in theory assessment. However, as scientists have taken on a more prominent public role as authorities whose guidance for policy issues is sought, the cognitive values only ideal has looked increasingly suspect. First, in the weighing of the importance of uncertainty – the key role for values in science by Rudner's argument – it is doubtful that cognitive values will provide an appropriate weighing. As noted above, cognitive values are poor indicators of epistemic reliability. The presence of a cognitive value like scope or simplicity may give one hope that uncertainty can be diminished as research moves forward, as theories exemplifying cognitive values are easier to work with, easier to draw additional testable implications, and thus more fruitful in general. With the ease of further testing, discovery of error and epistemic refinement becomes more likely. But policymakers and

the general public need to use the research now. Policymaking does not have the luxury of the long view. Thus, some appropriate weighing of uncertainty with respect to current use is needed.

Jeffrey's proposal that scientists only report the probabilities they attach to hypotheses might seem an attractive option. And many scientists do report their work with such probabilities. Nevertheless, they still need to bridge an inductive gap, assessing whether the reported probabilities are the correct ones to use. In addition, there are decisions of interpretation prior to the final assessment of the strength of the initial hypothesis in the face of the new evidence that will remain hidden. The scientists have to decide whether a characterization of data is sufficiently reliable before they can decide whether that data sufficiently supports the evidence. Thus, the uncertainties to be assessed in a piece of scientific research can run deep. It is the significance of those uncertainties, particularly with respect to the consequences if the science proves inaccurate, that are of heightened concern to policymakers and the public.

It is for these reasons that some (including myself) have argued that, given the importance of scientists as public experts, social and ethical values are essential in the internal reasoning of science. Social scientists need the values to weigh the significance of error in their work, evaluating the probable consequences if their claims prove incorrect (see Douglas, 2003b for an example). However, in using values to assess the sufficiency of evidence, one must be careful not to confuse the values with the evidence. In order to do this, it is crucial that the values assess the importance of uncertainty only. Thus, the less uncertainty is present, the less the values will shape the choice of theory. In this way, both cognitive and social values play the same role – as hedges against the uncertainty and the consequences of error (Douglas, 2009: Chapter 5). If values are used to direct choices in a stronger way, if values serve as the reason in themselves for a theory choice, we have confused the normative and the descriptive in precisely the ways that Weber and Nagel warned us against. Our values are not a good indication, in themselves, of the way the world is.

LANGUAGE AND VALUES IN SOCIAL SCIENCE

So far I have discussed the role of values in explicit social science reasoning. However, as both Weber and Nagel noted, our language can make a clear distinction between the normative and descriptive difficult. Values can become embedded in our ideas and ideal types, and carry with them connotations of approval and disapproval. They can also become embedded in the ways that we define key concepts. Thus, we need to consider how the language we use to describe social phenomena and how we define social concepts encode values into our accounts, for better or for worse.

Some terms used by social scientists unnecessarily carry with them evaluative connotations, and in doing so can obscure the nature of social phenomena. The danger of this is seen in John Dupré's discussion of scientific explanations of rape (Dupré, 2007: 32–35). Some sociobiologists draw parallels between the human phenomena of rape and what they see as similar behavior in animals, which they also call "rape." In utilizing the term "rape" for both animal and human forced copulation, they seek to explain rape in terms of a reproductive strategy employed by those who cannot otherwise attract mates. While such naturalized explanations of rape are not meant to justify rape, they have problematic effects on our normative take on rape, altering our understanding of the crime, making it appear "natural" even if still morally wrong. More problematically, the explanations ignore crucial evidence about rape in humans. Much human rape is reproductively futile, targeting women who are not fertile. In addition, it is phenomenologically far more about violence and control than reproduction. Thus, to seek an explanation for the behavior along naturalistic lines, and to include animal behaviors in the construct of "rape" obscures key evidence about the nature of rape among humans. Here concerns over the role of values in overly shaping both hypotheses and the methodological approach utilized come to the fore. In attempting to naturalize rape, the scientists ignore the evidence that goes against their account, and in doing so, devalue the experience of the victims of the crime. It would be both normatively preferable and descriptively more accurate to use a less fraught term for the animal behaviors, dismantling the explanatory parallels.

In other cases, the normative connotations embedded in language choice and conceptual construction are helpful in revealing phenomena. Social scientists construct categories, such as "spousal abuse" or "alcoholism," and in doing so they are seeing certain behaviors as having similar enough characteristics to be able to be grouped together (Root, 2007). Unlike in the "rape" case discussed above, the parallels among phenomena drawn here reveal further aspects of the phenomena, rather than obscuring key evidence about it. Placing disparate events under the same label and then studying them collectively can then generate awareness about a new social problem and potential remedies. The act of categorization allows the problem, such as "spousal abuse," to be seen, even if social actors did not see the behaviors as problematic or even similar prior to the work of the social scientist. Here values directing the attention of the social scientist produce new insights, just as the use of the value-laden term "abuse" helps to properly reveal the nature of the phenomena. The social scientist sees and cares about a particular potential problem, generates the study that codifies the problem, gathers important evidence about it, and places it before the public's eye, ultimately shifting normative judgments about that problem.

Yet many cases of normatively laden language in social science are more difficult to assess. Consider an example drawn from economics, a field riddled with value judgments at its foundations, recounted in Hausman and McPherson (2006) concerning "involuntary unemployment." This term is supposed to capture the situation where one is out of work and cannot find employment. But economists debate whether this situation ever actually exists – that is, whether or not the failure to find a job is simply a reflection of one's unwillingness to take a lower-paying or more menial job, and thus the unemployment is in some sense voluntary. Hausman and McPherson note that economists in this debate draw upon too different senses of "involuntary": whether one has choices for employment but all the jobs are so poor the situation feels coercive versus whether one has literally no choices (which very rarely, if ever, occurs). If one defines involuntary in the second sense, almost no unemployment is involuntary. If one defines it in the first sense, it can occur at substantial rates. Hausman and McPherson point out that ethicists usually do not consider choices under duress "voluntary." Thus, they argue that because the term "voluntariness is at root a moral notion," economists should use the term voluntary in a way informed by ethical theories of freedom and choice (pp. 37–38). But the problem runs deeper than being clear about what "voluntary" should mean. In the case of unemployment, whether or not the person facing choices about jobs is in a coercive situation will be a matter of dispute. Does the person have reasonable alternatives or not? Answering this question will depend on what one considers to be reasonable expectations, another morally fraught decision (pp. 275–277).

This example can be used to illustrate two points. First, there is a deep potential inconsistency in the skepticism about involuntary unemployment. Economists who doubt the existence of involuntary unemployment but consider the marketplace the best protection for individual autonomy are imposing their view of what should count as reasonable alternatives on the workforce. If autonomy is a value to be defended, we should each be able to define for ourselves what would be a reasonable employment option, and thus "involuntary unemployment" is a robust phenomena. Second, the example shows how deep and complex the normative judgments embedded in the language of social science can be. In this case, the normative judgments are rather inaccessible, and they are at the heart of the definition of the concept. As Nagel noted, it can be difficult to fully explicate the value commitments embedded in social science methodologies. And this might mean social science does have a special problem with respect to values – not a difference in kind with natural science, but a sufficient difference in degree that social scientists need to pay special attention, as Weber suggested.

With the potential for such deeply embedded normative commitments that they are difficult to explicate, social scientists need to be especially careful to examine and clarify the normative commitments driving their work and to make sure such commitments are not causing them to ignore evidence. Even with attention to these methodological concerns, it seems that there is no place in scientific practice where values do not have some role to play. Values shape the projects to be pursued, the methodologies employed, the characterization and interpretation of evidence, and the assessment of hypotheses. Given this, what are we to make of objectivity?

OBJECTIVITY IN SOCIAL SCIENCE

With the entanglements between science and values discussed above, it seems we may have breached the normative/descriptive divide, and opened science to rampant relativism. Is there anything left of objectivity? If we construe objectivity as a basis for the trust and endorsement of a result, various aspects of objectivity can bolster our confidence in social science.

First, as should be clear from all of the above discussion, there is always a need for some restraint on values in science. In this restraint we find a key aspect of objectivity. Social science must be protected from the conflation between a desire that the world be a certain way and evidence that it is so. This can be accomplished by distinguishing between two different roles for values in science, a direct role and an indirect role. A direct role occurs when values are a reason for a particular choice, when the value directs that choice on its own. This is a legitimate role for values in social science when one is selecting a particular project – the scientist chooses the project *because* of the value s/he places in that project. It is also a legitimate role when values dictate that a methodological approach is ethically unacceptable, such as the use of human subjects without their consent. However, it is an illegitimate role when values dictate a particular result, one the scientist wants. This can happen through a pernicious shaping of methodology (so that only desired evidence is produced) or through a problematic assessment of evidence (so that only desired evidence is noticed). Values should not direct the *results* of research in this strong way. To do so undermines the very value we place in science, that it can capture aspects of the world that may be surprising (even if unwelcome) to us.

The importance of values in the assessment of evidence and hypotheses is better captured by the indirect role for values. In this role, the values are not assessing the desirability of the hypothesis or theory per se, but rather the uncertainty around the hypothesis. As noted above, cognitive, ethical, and social values all have a role to play here. Keeping values to their proper roles requires some *detachment*, or *disinterestedness*, a traditional aspect of objectivity (Douglas, 2004; Merton, 1973).

There is more to objectivity, though, than a stance taken with respect to values in scientific reasoning about evidence. As much recent work on objectivity has noted (Daston and Gallison, 1992; Lloyd, 1995), objectivity is a complex concept carrying with it multiple meanings. Following Fine (1998), one can characterize these meanings as all providing a key epistemic function, of indicating bases for trustworthiness. Indeed, it is a particularly strong kind of trustworthiness of interest to us, that of "I trust this and you should too." With a pluralistic understanding of objectivity, we can have multiple bases for evaluating the trustworthiness of social science claims. There are several kinds of things we can look at when deciding whether a claim should be considered objective. We can examine the evidential basis; we can examine the thought processes of the scientists (the role of values in the reasoning, discussed above); we can examine the social processes scientists utilized to produce the claim (Douglas, 2004).

One key basis for assessments of objectivity rests on multiple lines of independent evidence. As Alison Wylie describes, when different evidential sources, none of which is causally dependent on the others, point towards the same hypothesis, our confidence in the objectivity of that hypothesis is substantially increased (Wylie, 2002: 191–198). For example, Wylie describes how isotopic analysis of skeletal remains, paleobotanical analysis of the remains of plants found in households, and other lines of evidence point towards an account of how the development of the Inka state changed the lives of people in the Andes, particularly in a gender differential way (p. 193). Without the independence of these lines of evidence, we would have substantially less confidence in the theory. Utilizing different lines of evidence to date historical artifacts (chemical composition, isotopic analysis, stylistic considerations, provenance discussions) also exemplifies this aspect of objectivity. When the evidence from independent lines of inquiry converges, the claim supported by the evidence appears substantially more objective, although assessments of independence must be made carefully (pp. 206–209).

Another aspect of objectivity in social science is the ability to utilize the claim to consistently and reliably perform tasks in the world. The scientific claim becomes a tool, ready to intervene in processes in a regular and predictable way (Hacking, 1983). An example of this sort of manipulable objectivity might be found in behavioral economics: the utilization of "inertia" or a "status quo bias" in structuring programs to increase savings rate (Thaler and Benartzi, 2004). Because we are consistently loathe to make changes to the status quo once a pattern is in place, behavioral economists were able to structure a savings program that sets increases in contributions in the future when employees get raises. Such programs proved wildly popular and greatly increased the savings rates of participants, as intended. Scientists were able to use the status quo effect as a tool to get increased retirement contributions. Further uses of this effect would increase the sense of manipulable objectivity. As with any tool, there can arise moral concerns over its use, particularly when used to manipulate human behavior. In the savings case, all participation was fully informed, voluntary, and the goal was generally paternalistic. Less benign goals could raise more serious worries. In addition, some tools may lose effectiveness if the humans on which it is used become aware of the knowledge underlying the tool – a problem of negative reflexivity. However, some results are likely to be robust even with full awareness of the human actors. Finally, no ability to use a tool to manipulate events guarantees that one has captured one rather than several phenomena (or vice versa) under one's categories. The ready manipulability gives the theory underlying one's interventions its objectivity, but whether one has characterized the phenonema fully and correctly can still be an open question.

Another aspect of objectivity focuses on practices that reduce the need for individual judgment. It can be useful to have agreed upon processes for working through data such that the same data set will always produce the same outcome, regardless of the practitioner. Developing this kind of "mechanical" or "procedural" objectivity

was crucial to the rise of social statistical measures (such as the census or crime rates) in the nineteenth century (Porter, 1995). Yet we should keep in mind that such procedural objectivity does not eliminate biasing factors; instead it merely makes sure that the biases (or values) are encoded into the procedure, thus eliminating the need for individual judgment among the users of the procedure. The procedure itself becomes the location for contestation. For example, utilizing market values to assess the worth of aesthetic experiences may provide a procedurally objective way to assess aesthetic worth, but then whether the market values can properly capture the aesthetic value becomes the locus of dispute.

Just as crucial for social science are the aspects of objectivity that arise from group efforts to vet scientific claims. It can be helpful to distinguish here between simple agreement among multiple observers (all the observers of a particular event record the same description – what I have called concordant objectivity) and agreement that arises from the social discourse of science (what I have called interactive objectivity) (Douglas, 2004). Both senses of objectivity depend upon some diversity of participants to strengthen the claim to objectivity – that is the more diverse the observers or discussants who come to agree, the more confidence we have that the claim is objective. An example of concordant objectivity can be found in the phenomenon of preference reversals. Both the social scientists who first theorized the existence of preference reversal behavior and skeptics who doubted the robustness of the phenomenon found the same behavior (Angner, 2002: 289). If all who look see the same thing, we have some basis for claiming an objective result.

However, in facing the pervasive challenges of values in social science discussed above, it is the discursive, interactive aspect that has come to the fore. Indeed, increasing the diversity among scientists has had a profound and positive influence on social science. For example, as feminist critics of science have noted, the introduction of large numbers of women has helped to reveal problematic blinders and biases in science. Women have helped to develop alternative hypotheses, to problematize unquestioned presuppositions, and to point out where inferences were based on shoddy work. Longino (1990) discusses how women critiqued the traditional centrality of "man-the-hunter" stories for human evolution theories by introducing an equally plausible alternative story centered on "woman-the-gatherer." In developing an alternative account, the obviousness of the original account, shaped in part by the sexist presuppositions of male anthropologists, was undermined, the presence of their presuppositions exposed (Longino, 1990: 106–111). Or consider Wylie and Nelson's account of how an increasing number of women in archaeology altered the kinds of evidence gathered and the kinds of hypotheses explored, thus greatly enriching accounts developed by archaeologists (Wylie and Nelson, 2007: 64–70). The same is suggested for the increase of diversity by class (p. 63). By increasing the diversity of participants in science, the scientists are forced to consider a wider array of plausible theories, to argue for their claims under greater scrutiny, and thus to work harder to convince their fellow scientists. In this process of vetting, our confidence in the claims ultimately produced is bolstered. The social process of science is central to the objectivity of its results.

Indeed, in Longino's account, science is objective precisely because it is an interactive social process (Longino, 1990: 76–80, Longino, 2002: 128–135). It must be properly structured to maximize its objectivity, but it is in its interactive social nature that its objectivity lies. By properly structured, Longino is concerned not just with the diversity of the participants, but also with the nature of the discourse. For example, is intellectual authority properly distributed, that is as equally as possible? Are there recognized avenues for critique and response, and are participants responsive to critique? Are there shared standards for argument and are these also subject to reflection and critique? It is in the shared epistemic efforts of a diverse group of people that we can have the most confidence problematic bias will be revealed and excised.

CONCLUSION

With the development of the social at the core of scientific objectivity, the trajectory for the objectivity of social science has come full circle. At the beginning of the twentieth century, Weber argued that social science's focus on the social presented unique problems for its objectivity. Philosophers of science at the middle of the twentieth century argued that there were no qualitatively different challenges for social science compared to natural science with respect to objectivity and values. At the beginning of the twenty-first century, it is the social that provides a key resource in assessing and achieving objectivity for all science, social, or natural.

We should perhaps not be surprised by this conceptual turn. As noted above, Nagel wrote in the early 1960s that the social processes of science were essential to grappling with problematic roles for values in science. And even before Nagel, in 1935 Ludwig Fleck suggested that the notion of a fact, an objective claim that required no further contestation, depended on the social aspects of science – that it was first and foremost a reflection of the group consensus on a topic, even if it shifted its form and content over time (Fleck, 1979). If the very nature of the fact depends on the social, it should not surprise us that the social has become a focal point for understanding objectivity in both natural and social science. Objectivity is to be found in epistemically useful detachment, disunity, diversity, disagreement, and discourse.

Thus, despite the entanglements between values and social science catalogued above, there are still plenty of resources with which to assess the objectivity of a scientific claim.

The entanglements between the normative and the descriptive cast doubt on the possibility for any truly value-free statement of fact, but that need not mean we can have no objective statements. Central to such objectivity is the maintenance of at least a conceptual distinction between the descriptive and the normative. Even as values shape the projects pursued, the acceptability of methodologies, the concepts employed, and the sufficiency of evidence, we must refrain from conflating values and evidence, or from allowing values to determine the results of our studies. No particular descriptive claim can be cut free from the value judgments needed to do science, but we can still maintain the boundary that keeps the normative from dictating the descriptive, the core concern at the discussion of science and values.

ACKNOWLEDGEMENTS

I would like to thank Anna Alexandrova, Ted Richards, and Eric Schliesser for comments on this chapter, and Erik Angner, Paul Roth, and Alison Wylie for help with examples. Deficiencies remaining are wholly my own.

REFERENCES

Angner, Erik (2002) 'Levi's account of preference reversals,' *Economics and Philosophy*, 18: 287–302.

Churchman, C. West (1948) 'Statistics, pragmatics, induction', *Philosophy of Science*, 15: 249–268.

Daston, Lorraine and Peter Gallison (1992) 'The image of objectivity', *Representations*, 40: 81–128.

Douglas, Heather (2003a) 'The moral responsibilities of scientists: Tensions between autonomy and responsibility', *American Philosophical Quarterly*, 40(1): 59–68.

Douglas, Heather (2003b) 'Hempelian insights for feminism', in Sharyn Clough (ed.) *Siblings Under the Skin: Feminism, Social Justice, and Analytic Philosophy*. Aurora, CO: Davies Publishing. pp. 283–306.

Douglas, Heather (2004) 'The irreducible complexity of objectivity', *Synthese*, 138(3): 453–473.

Douglas, Heather (2009) *Science, Policy, and the Value-Free Ideal*. Pittsburgh: University of Pittsburgh Press.

Dupré, John (2007) 'Fact and value', in Harold Kincaid, John Dupré, and Alison Wylie (eds) *Value-Free Science?: Ideals and Illusions*. New York: Oxford University Press. pp. 27–41.

Fine, Arthur (1998) 'The viewpoint of no-one in particular', *Proceedings and Addresses of the APA*, 72: 9–20.

Fleck, Ludwig (1979) *Genesis and Development of a Scientific Fact*. Chicago: University of Chicago Press. (First published in 1935.)

Forge, John (2008) *The Responsible Scientist*. Pittsburgh: University of Pittsburgh Press.

Gotshalk, D.W. (1952) 'Value science', *Philosophy of Science*, 19: 183–192.

Hacking, Ian (1983) *Representing and Intervening*. New York: Cambridge University Press.

Hartman, Robert (1950) 'Is a science of ethics possible', *Philosophy of Science*, 17: 238–246.

Hausman, Daniel and Michael McPherson (2006) *Economic Analysis, Moral Philosophy, and Public Policy*. New York: Cambridge University Press.

Hempel, Carl G. (1965) 'Science and human values', in *Aspects of Scientific Explanation*. New York: The Free Press. pp. 81–96.

Jeffrey, Richard (1956) 'Valuation and acceptance of scientific hypotheses', *Philosophy of Science*, 22: 237–246.

Kuhn, Thomas (1977) 'Objectivity, value, and theory choice', in *The Essential Tension*. Chicago: University of Chicago Press. pp. 320–339.

Lacey, Hugh (1999) *Is Science Value-Free? Values and Scientific Understanding*. New York: Routledge.

Laudan, Larry (2004) 'The epistemic, the cognitive, and the social', in Peter Machamer and Gereon Wolters (eds) *Science, Values, and Objectivity*. Pittsburgh: University of Pittsburgh Press. pp. 14–23.

Leach, James (1968) 'Explanation and value neutrality', *British Journal for the Philosophy of Science*, 19: 93–108.

Levi, Isaac (1960) 'Must the scientist make value judgments?', *Journal of Philosophy*, 57: 345–357.

Levi, Isaac (1962) 'On the seriousness of mistakes', *Philosophy of Science*, 29: 47–65.

Lloyd, Elizabeth (1995) 'Objectivity and the double standard for feminist epistemologies', *Synthese*, 104: 351–381.

Longino, Helen (1990) *Science as Social Knowledge*. Princeton, NJ: Princeton University Press.

Longino, Helen (2002) *The Fate of Knowledge*. Princeton, NJ: Princeton University Press.

Lundberg, George (1941) 'The future of the social sciences', *The Scientific Monthly*, 53: 346–359.

McMullin, Ernan (1983) 'Values in science', in Peter D. Asquith and Thomas Nickles (eds) *Proceedings of the 1982 Biennial Meeting of the Philosophy of Science Association, Volume 1*. East Lansing: Philosophy of Science Association, 2: 3–28.

Merton, Robert (1973) 'The normative structure of science', in Norman W. Storer (ed.) *The Sociology of Science*. Chicago: University of Chicago Press. pp. 267–278.

Mitchell, Sandra (2004) 'The prescribed and proscribed values in science policy', in Peter Machamer and Gereon Wolters (eds) *Science, Values, and Objectivity*. Pittsburgh: University of Pittsburgh Press. pp. 245–255.

Nagel, Ernest (1961) *The Structure of Science: Problems in the Logic of Scientific Explanation*. New York: Harcourt, Brace & World, Inc.

Porter, Theodore (1995) *Trust in Numbers: The Pursuit of Objectivity in Science and Public Life*. Princeton, NJ: Princeton University Press.

Root, Michael (2007) 'Social problems', in Harold Kincaid, John Dupré, and Alison Wylie (eds) *Value-Free Science? Ideals and Illusions*. New York: Oxford University Press. pp. 42–57.

Rudner, Richard (1953) 'The scientist *qua* ascientist makes value judgments', *Philosophy of Science*, 20: 1–6.

Rudner, Richard (1966) *Philosophy of Social Science*. Englewood Cliffs, NJ: Prentice-Hall.

Scriven, Michael (1974) 'The exact role of value judgments in science', in K.F. Shaffner and R.S. Cohen (eds) *PSA 1972*. Dordrecht, Holland: D. Reidel Publishing. pp. 219–247.

Strauss, Leo (1953) *Natural Right and History*. Chicago: University of Chicago Press.

Thaler, Richard and Shlomo Benartzi (2004) 'Save more tomorrow: Using behavioral economics to increase employee savings', *Journal of Political Economy*, 112: S164–S187.

Uebel, Thomas (2007) 'Philosophy of social science in early logical empiricism: The case of radical physicalism', in Alan Richardson and Thomas Uebel (eds) *The Cambridge Companion to Logical Empiricism*. New York: Cambridge University Press. pp. 250–277.

Weber, Max (1949) *The Methodology of the Social Sciences* (Edward A. Shils and Henry A. Finch, trans.). Glencoe, IL: Free Press.

Wylie, Alison (2002) *Thinking from Things: Essays in the Philosophy of Archaeology*. Berkeley: University of California Press.

Wylie, Alison and Lynn Hankinson Nelson (2007) 'Coming to terms with the values of science: Insights from feminist science studies scholarship', in Harold Kincaid, John Dupré and Alison Wylie (eds) *Value-Free Science? Ideals and Illusions*. New York: Oxford University Press. pp. 58–86.

28

Idealised Representations, Inferential Devices and Cross-Disciplinary Tools: Theoretical Models in Social Sciences

Tarja Knuuttila and Jaakko Kuorikoski

INTRODUCTION

The term 'model' is in wide use nowadays across the sciences, and this is increasingly so in the social sciences. This proliferation of the things called models in sciences reflects the increasing mathematisation of diverse disciplines as well as the increasing importance of computational techniques. Although modelling may be regarded as a specific theoretical strategy bearing 'a historical signature' (Godfrey-Smith, 2006), it is equally clear that such things that we would now conceptualise as models have existed throughout the history of science and technology. However, the importance of models grew in the nineteenth century largely as a result of the need to postulate and reason about unobserved theoretical entities in a tractable but rigorous manner (Hesse, 2000). The word model usually referred to concrete objects, like mechanical

models, composed of, for example, movable bars, cords, wheels and rollers or to moulds made of wax as well as physiological (anatomical) models made of plastic. Indeed, in his famous encyclopedia entry on models, Ludwig Boltzmann precludes maps, charts, musical notes or figures from being models, since models 'always involve a concrete spatial analogy in three dimensions' (1911). Boltzmann did not require, however, that models should physically exist for they could also be mentally conceived. In Boltzmann's essay scientific models still retain a close relationship to many other things denoted by the word 'model', such as exemplars, moulds, or even people functioning as models for the artist or the medical student. Yet at the same time models are couched in more modern terms as representations, standing to objects in the same kind of relationship as 'thoughts stand to things' (Boltzmann, 1911).

If the word model was polysemous in Boltzmann's days, this certainly applies to our present understanding of models. The kinds of things called models in science include for instance physical three-dimensional things, diagrams, mathematical equations, computer programmes, organisms and even laboratory populations. To this heterogeneous ensemble the social sciences add their own characteristic understanding of models: In social sciences often an analytically useful conceptualisation of phenomena represented in a 2–2 field or a hypothesis represented by a boxes and arrows diagram can be called a model. In the face of this plurality we limit our focus to what we call theoretical models, sometimes called formal models (Hesse, 2000; Morton, 1999). By theoretical models we mean devices that are used to infer non-trivial consequences from prior, usually theoretical, assumptions. By non-triviality we mean that the inference is not transparent to the unaided theorist, but instead essentially involves some kind of manipulation of the model, usually syntactic manipulation of symbols according to well-defined rules. Thus such models are often indeed 'formal' in the sense that they express 'the form or structure of physical entities or processes without any semantic referring to specific objects or properties' (Hesse, 2000). Obvious candidates for theoretical models in the sense intended here are mathematical models, but also chemical formulas (such as H_2O for water), simulations, iconic presentations like diagrams, and purely physical devices, such as the hydraulic economy of A.W. Phillips, qualify (see Morgan and Boumans, 2004). The focus on theoretical models also means that we are not addressing statistical models of either a descriptive or causal kind. Although statistical models always involve prior theoretical assumptions, they are still essentially data-driven in the sense that the conclusions of interest are about *estimates* of some parameter or other. Especially causal models involve completely different philosophical issues from those of theoretical modelling and would thus deserve a separate entry.

When it comes to constructing and using theoretical models economists have undoubtedly been pioneers among the social scientists: since the Second World War model-building has become the main theoretical practice of economists (e.g. Solow, 1997). Subsequently, the modelling methods adopted and developed by economists have been disseminated to other social sciences. The political scientists have been inspired especially by the rational choice style of modelling and the associated mathematical techniques used by the economists (see Morton, 1999) whereas sociologists have preferred statistical modelling being rather sceptical towards modelling social phenomena in abstract mathematical terms (Edling, 2002). However, the situation is changing rapidly as various kinds of modelling methods, studied below, have increasingly crossed the borders of different social sciences.

In the following section, we will first study the nature of models, reviewing general philosophical perspectives to models with a special emphasis on their relationship to theories on one hand, and to the world, on the other. In later sections, we consider more specifically some important topics pertaining to modelling: representation, idealisation, and the different uses models are put to in science. Then we study some modelling methods and associated practices that are most widely used across social sciences. The modelling practices covered include rational choice methods, evolutionary game theory, network models and agent-based simulations (for a more thorough treatment of agent-based simulations the reader is referred to Chapter 32 on artificial worlds and agent-based simulation in this book). Our account is grounded on the general philosophy of science and largely inspired by the relatively encompassing philosophical and methodological discussions on economics, which are due to the more pervasive role of modelling in economics than in other social sciences. However, we expect our discussion to apply also to the other social sciences to the extent that they use theoretical models.

GENERAL PHILOSOPHICAL PERSPECTIVES ON MODELS

The discussion of models in the philosophy of science has heterogeneous beginnings, testifying to a variety of theoretical, formal and practical aspirations that have different and even conflicting goals (see, for example, Bailer-Jones, 1999). The current philosophical interest in models may be seen as arising from two historical trends. First, the problems facing the received syntactic view of the structure of scientific knowledge have given rise to general philosophical accounts of theories construed around the concept of model. Second, the focus has shifted from the use of formal logical machinery and the so-called general philosophy of science to cover also the philosophies of the special sciences, which address problems closer to the actual scientific practice. And that praxis is usually highly model-centred. Because of these divergent backgrounds and motivations, philosophical accounts of modelling have tended to concentrate on different questions. What has been common is the interest in representation, although what is at stake differs with respect to what questions are asked. Finally, whereas models have traditionally been conceived through their relationship to the theories on one hand and to the world, on the other hand, in the recent discussion models have been relegated to an independent cognitive or epistemic status. This has served to underline what is specific to modelling as a theoretical strategy of its own.

Models and theories: the syntactic and the semantic approach

Philosophy of science provides us with two attempts to formalise the general structure of scientific knowledge: the syntactic view of theories, once called the 'received view', and the more recent model-theoretic semantic approach. According to the syntactic view, a model is designed to give an interpretation of an uninterpreted formalism or calculus. For the proponents of the syntactic view, a scientific theory was such an uninterpreted or partially interpreted formalism, a syntactic structure consisting of a set of axioms. Thus, for instance Ernest Nagel, defined a model as an interpretation of 'the abstract calculus which supplies some flesh for the skeletal structure in terms of more or less familiar conceptual or visualizable materials' (1961: 90). To interpret a theory was to specify a model for it, which makes all the axioms of the theory true (or false). Consequently, a model for a theory T could be defined as a set of true propositions with the same formal structure or calculus as T (p. 96).

The semantic conception contested this 'linguistic' view of theories by replacing the syntactic formulation of the theory with the theory's models, which are non-linguistic entities. In this view, theories are not assemblages of propositions or statements, but 'extralinguistic entities, which may be described or characterised by a number of different linguistic formulations' (Suppe, 1977: 221). These extralinguistic entities – models – were taken to be structures that are defined either by the use of set-theoretical predicates (e.g. Suppes, 1961; da Costa and French, 1990) or by the use of any suitable mathematical language (e.g. van Fraassen, 1980), such as a set of trajectories in some state-space (Giere, 1988). The emergence of the semantic conception dates back to the 1960s with impulses both from mathematics and computer science (see Suppe, 1989: Prologue) as well as from the intrinsic problems of the syntactic approach arising from its linguistic orientation.

Of the semantic approaches to models (and theories) perhaps the best known are those of Bas van Fraassen (1980) and Ronald Giere (1988). According to both of them a theory can be identified more or less with a family of models, although their approaches differ from each other in the degree of their abstractness and in the ways they utilise aspects of the semantic approach to accommodate their divergent standpoints to the empiricism-realism debate (French and Ladyman, 1999: 104). For van Fraassen, the 'new picture of theories' is thoroughly empiricist with only the empirical substructures having a role in theory evaluation (they should be isomorphic to the structure of appearances consisting of experimental and observational reports).

In contrast, Giere, a (constructive) realist, denies that the relation between a model and a real system should be isomorphic. Giere (1988) develops his account of models on the basis of classical mechanics as presented in standard textbooks proposing that the 'linear oscillator', for example, is not a single model with different specific versions but a cluster of models of varying degrees of specificity (p. 80). Consequently Giere finds in physics textbooks 'a population of models consisting of related families of models' (p. 82). The models as such are not true or false with respect to the world; the role of the theory is rather to claim a 'good fit' between the models and some important types of real systems. Consequently, Giere suggests that a theory is comprised of two elements: (1) a population of models, and (2) various hypotheses linking those models with systems in the real world (p. 85). Another important strand of the semantic approach consists of the German structuralists (see, for example, Balzer et al., 1987), who are mostly concerned with the architectonics of scientific research programmes than with individual models.

Although both syntactic and semantic accounts were originally presented in the context of physics, echoes of these general ways of thinking can be found in the methodological writings of economists and philosophers of economics. The standard microeconomic principles are often presented in an axiomatic form and the intuition that axiomatisation in itself has some obvious intrinsic epistemic virtues leads quickly to the idea that the function of the models is to relate the theory to observations. Thus, for instance, Tjalling Koopmans defined in his famous *Three Essays on The State of Economic Science* (1957) economic theory as a set of postulates. Since the implications of these postulates are neither self-evident, nor 'readily tested by observation' one has to resort to modelling:

> In this situation, it is desirable that we arrange and record our logical deductions in such a manner that any particular conclusion or observationally refutable implication can be traced to the postulates on which it rests [...]. Considerations of this order suggest that we look upon economic theory as a sequence of conceptional *models* that seek to express in simplified form different aspects of an always more complicated reality. (Koopmans, 1957: 142)

Here the idea of the economic theory as a set of axioms from which logical consequences can be deduced is close to the syntactic approach to scientific theories. Indeed, the axiomatic ideal of science has long roots in economics: already in the nineteenth century the so-called Marginalist economists attempted to axiomatise demand functions as logical consequences of more fundamental properties of individual behaviours. Their aim was to provide an axiomatic foundation for the model of market equilibrium (see Brown and Deaton, 1972). This way of proceeding has been coined by Weintraub (1985) as 'a neo-Walrasian research program'.

However, Koopmans's idea of economic theory as a sequence of models seems also to anticipate the semantic conception. Somewhat more recently, Daniel Hausman has also argued for a semantic interpretation of economic models along the lines of the German structuralists. Hausman conceives what he calls the core equilibrium *theory* to be a set of law-like sentences which can be used to construct more or less demanding definitions (predicates) of kinds of systems. These definitions are the models that economists work with and their primary usage, being definitions, is conceptual exploration. According to Hausman, it does not make sense to ask whether definitions are true or not – the empirical content lies in theoretical hypotheses, which are putative applications of these predicates to real systems in the world (Hausman, 1992: Chapter 5). Chao (2002) in turn argues that the semantic conception of models provides also a fruitful vantage point from which to approach econometric modelling.

Practice-oriented approaches

Whereas the syntactic and semantic approaches focus on defining models and situating them vis-à-vis to theories, the more practice-oriented approaches to models have targeted the pragmatic and cognitive role of models in scientific enterprise. This usually involves detailed investigation of specific models and taking into account different aspects of the actual *production* of scientific knowledge. For instance in the turn of 1960s, when the discussion on models was beginning to flourish, various writers including Achinstein (1968), Black (1962), Hesse (1966) and Hutten (1954) likened models to analogies and metaphors in their attempt to understand how models function in scientific reasoning. Moreover, both Max Black and Peter Achinstein created typologies of models in an effort to give a more complete account of the variety of models used in science.

It is of interest that both Black and Achinstein still started their discussion of models by considering scale models, three-dimensional physical objects, which Black thought were the 'standard cases' of models in the literal sense of the word. The purpose of making scale models is to reproduce selected features of the 'original' in a relatively manipulable or accessible embodiment.

> We try to bring the remote and the unknown to our own level of middle-sized existence. There is, however something self-defeating in this aim, since ... we are forced to replace a living tissue by some inadequate substitute, and a sheer change of size may upset the balance of factors in the original. (Black, 1962: 221)

Thus, 'inferences from a scale model to an original are intrinsically precarious and in need of supplementary validation and correction' (Black, 1962). Achinstein, too, paid attention to the manipulability or 'workability' of physical models (which he called representational models). According to him 'representational models, although used in all the sciences, are particularly central in engineering. Instead of investigating an object directly, the engineer may construct a representation of it, which can be studied more readily' (1968: 209).

The idea of models as stand-ins that enable surrogate reasoning was later formulated by Swoyer (1991) and has now been taken up by many other authors writing about models. What characterises theoretical modelling is a certain epistemic dynamic making use of surrogate reasoning: one first builds something or sets something up, then investigates the properties of that constructed thing, and then ponders how the discovered properties of the constructed thing relate to the real world. Weisberg (2007) and Godfrey-Smith (2006) have characterised this specifically model-based reasoning as *indirect representation*. They claim that instead of directly abstracting some salient aspects of data or a target system into a workable and more systematic scientific representation (direct representation), modellers seek to understand the real world through the procedure of constructing and analysing hypothetical systems – in other words, models. A modeller begins to attack a problem by coming up with a set of simple theoretical principles that, when combined, might be expected to solve the problem (such as providing an explanation for a puzzling phenomenon). This account of models takes them close to fiction in that instead of directly representing actual systems, modellers examine 'tightly constrained' possible systems (for fiction in science see Suárez, 2008). Reasoning with models is thus essentially learning about *hypothetical* surrogate systems (since any representation, whether direct or indirect, can, in a sense, be considered a surrogate with respect to the real systems).

Margaret Morrison and Mary Morgan's conception of *models as mediators*, as investigative instruments between theory and data, also stresses the epistemic importance of building models and inferring or learning from models. Additionally, they extend the idea of manipulating a mathematical model to be, to some extent, analogous to experimentation (see also Mäki, 1992, 2005). The mediating role of models between theory and data was inspired by Morgan's earlier work on econometric modelling (Morgan, 1990) and also builds on the work of Nancy Cartwright (1983). In arguing that the fundamental laws of physics do not describe the occurrent regularities that exist in nature, Cartwright turned her focus to models. There is a gap between the general theoretical principles of physics and the messiness and complexity of data which phenomenological laws in turn strive to capture. It is the task of models to bridge this gap: 'The route from the theory to reality is from theory to model, and then from model to the phenomenological law. The phenomenological laws are indeed true of the objects of reality — or might be; but the fundamental laws are true only of objects in the model' (p. 4). For a model to function as a bridge between theory and data, a model has to include some genuine properties of the objects modelled. But in addition to that, models contain properties of convenience and fiction (p. 15). These features are needed to bring the objects modelled into the confines of the theory. Thus model-building is a pragmatic activity in which 'adjustments are made where literal correctness does not matter very much in order to get correct effects where we want to get them; and very often ... one distortion is put right by another' (p. 140). In both Cartwright's account of models as bridges and that of Morrison and Morgan's as mediators models occupy the middle space between the theory and the world (or data), thus linking them.

In their account on models as mediating instruments Morrison and Morgan stress, too, how 'additional "outside" elements' are brought into models (1999: 11). With this they mean that models cannot entirely be derived from either theory or data, which, apart from making them 'at least' partly *autonomous*, also enables them to connect the different realms. Marcel Boumans (1999) moves even further away from the simple theory-data-framework by showing how heterogeneous kinds of ingredients seemingly simple mathematical models can be made of. The business cycle models Boumans studied contained analogies, metaphors, theoretical notions, mathematical concepts, mathematical techniques, stylised facts, empirical data and, finally, relevant policy views. The role of the model is not only to mediate, but also to provide a common forum in which all these considerations can be jointly handled.

The idea of models as mediators resonates interestingly with Robert Merton's appeal for theories of the middle range, theories that would mediate between grand sociological theories and empirical research. Merton famously accused sociological theorising as being too abstract and general for being any use in understanding specific empirical phenomena. Grand theories á la Talcott Parsons serve only to conceptualise empirical social phenomena and do not actually exclude any possibilities. Thus grand theories do not offer any grounds for making inferences to what might happen or might have happened and are for this reason non-explanatory. On the other hand, banal empiricism, either in the guise of simply running regressions or cataloguing the qualitative interpretations or meanings that the subjects attach to their social context, is purely descriptive and thus also non-explanatory (Merton, 1957: 5). Model building can indeed be seen as a promising methodology for providing such mediating theories (e.g. Hedström, 2005).

Models and the world: representation

The philosophical discussion on models has spawned a discussion on scientific representation. The hope has been that the notion of (adequate) representation might capture the epistemic value of models better than the concept of truth (see however, Mäki, 2009b). Despite the differences in their approaches, philosophers of science have tended to be nearly unanimous in saying that models have to be representative in order to give us knowledge (Bailer-Jones, 2003; da Costa and French, 1990; French and Ladyman, 1999; Frigg, 2002; Morrison and Morgan, 1999; Giere, 2004b). Often, representation has been made *the* crucial property of models (see for example Hughes, 1997; Suárez, 1999; Contessa, 2007; Mäki, 2009b). A characteristic statement of this linkage is given by Paul Teller (2001: 397):

> I take the stand that, in principle, anything can be a model, and that what makes a thing into a model is the fact that it is regarded or used as a representation of something by the model users. Thus in saying what a model is the weight is shifted to the problem of understanding the nature of representation.

However, here the agreement between philosophers tends to end as their preferred accounts of representation differ widely from each other. In the discussion on models and scientific representation three different kinds of approaches can be discerned depending on whether representation is analysed in terms of a two-place or (at least) a three-place relation, or as a combination of the two.

The semantic accounts conceive of representation as a two-place relation between the model and a target system. This representational relationship between models and their target systems is usually analysed in terms of isomorphism or a partial isomorphism: a given structure represents its target system if both are structurally isomorphic or partially isomorphic to each other, that is, there is a relation-preserving mapping between the model and its target (van Fraassen, 1980; Suppe, 1977; French, 2003; French and Ladyman, 1999). Another candidate relation offered for the analysis of representation by the proponents of the semantic view is similarity (Giere, 1988). However, as similarity

seems to be an observer and purpose relative notion, the recent formulations of similarity account of representation tend to be pragmatic (Giere, 2004, 2010).

Although perhaps intuitively appealing, the accounts of representation that are formulated in terms of a two-place relation of either isomorphism or similarity are ridden with numerous problems. Firstly, as such they do not have the formal and other properties that a satisfactory account of representation is expected to possess (see for example Suárez, 2003 and Frigg, 2006). For instance, both isomorphism and similarity denote a symmetric relation whereas representation does not: we want a model to represent its target system but not vice versa (this critique goes back to Nelson Goodman, 1972). Secondly, isomorphism is a relationship between two structures, whereas scientific representation assumes a relationship between a structure and a real world target system. Roman Frigg (2006) argues that structural isomorphism is not sufficient to pin down a representational relationship between a model and a target since the same structure can be instantiated by different target systems. On the other hand, a given target system does not exemplify a single unique structure since it can be sliced up in multiple different ways, depending on the perspective adopted (Frigg, 2006: 56–59). Isomorphism alone is thus not able to fix the extension of representation.

Eventually, the structuralist account on representation turns out not to be an account of how models link to the world, but an account of how models link to each other. Since real world systems are not 'structures' in any obvious way, any isomorphic relationship between them and the real world target systems involves that these parts of the empirical world are already modelled (or represented) somehow. This has, of course, been noticed by the proponents of the semantic theory: Patrick Suppes (1962) invoked 'models of data' as the empirical benchmark against which theoretical models are compared. Thus the isomorphism required by the structuralist account concerns actually the relationship between a theoretical model and an empirical model. Indeed, in their attempt to rehabilitate the semantic conception via the notion of partial isomorphism, French and Ladyman remark (in a footnote) that they are not claiming that the

> gap between a theory or model and reality can be closed simply by a formal relation between model-theoretic structures. The gap is more fundamental than that ... What is required is an understanding of the relationship between one category of things, 'the world', 'reality', whatever, and another category, namely, that which represents the world. (1999: 119)

The pragmatic approaches to representation deny that the representational relationship could be regarded as a two-place relation of correspondence between the representative vehicle and its target (Suárez, 2004, 2010; Giere, 2004, 2010; Frigg, 2006). This way of conceiving representation, the pragmatists claim, tends to reduce the intentional judgements of representation-users to the respective properties of the representative vehicle and its target object (see especially Suárez, 2004: 768). Since from the pragmatist perspective representation presumes always an intentional activity from the part of representation users, the representational relation is at least a three-place relation including also the users of representation (Bailer-Jones, 2003; Giere, 2010). Depending on the analysis in question, also other factors, such as the purposes of the representers and the possible audiences are taken into account (Giere, 2004, Mäki 2009a).

The hybrid accounts of representation in turn try to steer a middle course between the structural and pragmatic conceptions by combining a two-place relation between a model and a target with the pragmatic aspects of representation. Andreas Bartels (2006) suggests that representation can be grounded on a weaker notion of homomorphism which dispenses with a one-to-one bijective mapping required by isomorphism. Homomorphism provides thus an explication for the 'representational content' of a model. Yet, for a model to be able to refer

to any target an intentional or causal representational mechanism is also needed. Mäki (2009b), in turn, combines the pragmatic representative aspect of models with the resemblance aspect (understood in largely semantic terms). The idea is that the intended goals, audiences and several other factors specify the pragmatic constraints in the context of which resemblance aspect highlights the ontological constraints imposed on representation by the world.

One might interpret the hybrid accounts as attempts to overcome the deflationary nature of pragmatic accounts while still admitting the inherently pragmatic nature of representation. Namely, the thoroughly pragmatic approaches to representation (dis)solve some of the problems of the semantic notion of representation mentioned above, either by avoiding them, or by the introduction of the intended uses which create the directionality needed to establish a representational relationship. But this comes at a price. When representation is grounded primarily on the specific goals and representing activity of humans as opposed to the facts about the representative vehicle and the target object, as a result nothing very substantive can be said about the relationship of representation in general. This seems not to be a problem for the proponents of the pragmatic approach (see Giere, 2004; Suárez, 2004), of whom Mauricio Suárez has gone farthest in arguing for a minimalist account of representation which resists saying anything substantive about the supposed basis on which the representational power of representative vehicles rests (that is, whether it rests, for instance, on isomorphism, similarity or denotation). Instead, Suárez builds his inferential account of representation directly on the idea of surrogate reasoning: that is, the model represents something in virtue of its capacity to lead a 'competent and informed user to a consideration of the target', and it has to have the right kind of constitution to allow agents to correctly draw inferences from it (Suárez, 2004). While the aforementioned representational capacity of a model is created and maintained by the inferential activity of representation-users, the stipulation concerning the right kind of constitution saves the intuition that the properties of the model objects should have something to do with their intrinsic qualities – which accounts for the objectivity that is expected from scientific representation. Suárez's account on scientific representation is thus in line with Robert Brandom's view of representation in general: it is the inferential properties of objects that constitute their representational properties and appealing to any primitive representational concepts to explain inferential properties would therefore put the cart before the horse (Brandom, 1994).

If the semantic properties of a model do not determine its pragmatic dimensions but rather vice versa, then the epistemic value of models need not be tied to their putative success in representing their target systems *accurately*. As de Donato and Zamora (2009) point out, this opens up a fresh perspective on the acceptability of models: what makes a model 'enlightening' apart from its predictive success is the amount and successfulness of the inferential links it forges to our existing corpus of commitments. Also, the model should reduce the cognitive or computational cost of the activity of drawing consequences, which requirement is closely bound to its inferential enablings. Thus Donato and Zamora ask, rather provocatively from the traditional perspective, whether there are 'any other criteria to judge a model *right* (or *probably true*, or *approximately true,* or *probably approximately true*) besides the fact that it leads us to adopt conclusions which are corroborated by different means?' (2009: 107).

Taken together the above mentioned pragmatically inclined accounts imply a larger unit of analysis than the earlier interest in the relations between models and theory or models and their real world systems. Conceiving models as independent entities and construing their representational capacity on the basis of their inferential enablings

paves the way for considering modelling simply as a form of extended cognition, as extended inference in which the relevant cognitive unit of analysis is the user-model pair. Kuorikoski and Lehtinen (2009) deny that any philosophical account of representation (or other semantic notion for that matter) can explain the epistemic value of models, since there is nothing to be explained: modelling is simply inference or argumentation using external cognitive aids (such as a formal language or a diagram).

Paying attention to the inferential nature of models leads us to approach models from a novel perspective: Knuuttila (2005, 2009a) argues that the traditional emphasis on representation places excessive limitations on our view on what kind of entities models are and how they function in scientific practice. She suggests that models should be thought of as epistemic artefacts through which we gain knowledge in diverse ways. Focusing on scientific models as multi-functional artefacts releases them from any pre-established and fixed representational relationships and stresses their intentional construction that allows for various kinds of inferences. From this naturalist perspective, informed importantly by the idea of distributed cognition, models simplify and modify the complex problems facing the scientists turning them into a workable and perceptual form by making use of various representational media (see also Knuuttila and Voutilainen, 2003; Vorms, 2009).

UNREALISTIC ASSUMPTIONS AND IDEALISATION IN SOCIAL SCIENTIFIC MODELS

One common property of the models in social sciences is their highly simplified and idealised nature, which might seem more problematical in the context of social sciences than in natural sciences. A usual complaint levelled against theoretical models in social sciences is the apparent unrealisticness of the assumptions they make concerning the behaviour of social actors. There are indeed three basic properties of social phenomena that prompt the question whether modelling them requires special modelling strategies or even whether modelling should be considered as a plausible epistemic strategy to begin with. First, social systems are heterogeneously constituted, open and constantly changing, which means that models have to rely heavily on abstraction and idealisation. Second, social systems are constituted by human action and, in contrast to the natural sciences, social sciences need to take into account the reflexive dimension of both their subject matter (intentionality of the subjects) and the nature of their theorising (performativity, see MacKenzie, 2006). Third, the special status of intentional action also means that, as social actors, we judge ourselves already to have a reasonably good pre-understanding of social phenomena, and this pre-understanding seems to contradict the usual idealisations made in theoretical modelling.

There are numerous ways to justify the idealisations, approximations and simplifications that are characteristic of modelling. A good overall view on this problematic is provided by the so called 'realism of the assumptions' issue in economics, which dates back to the beginning of mathematisation of economics in the nineteenth century. While the classical economists often interpreted the basic assumptions of economics realistically as subjectively available self-evident truths concerning human nature (see, for example, Caldwell, 1982), especially later in the twentieth century the attitudes of economists and the general public alike became more critical towards the basic behavioural assumptions of economics. Thus the question became how to save them as the significant part of economic theory was based on them.

Several economists have, in their attempts to save economic theory, taken the seeming falsity of the basic postulates of economics at face value. Thus Milton Friedman famously defended economic theory on instrumentalist grounds, claiming that the 'unrealism' of the assumptions did not matter since the goal of science was to develop hypotheses that gave 'valid and meaningful' predictions about the phenomena (Friedman, 1953). Although Friedman's classic statement has created a more extensive secondary literature than any other piece on economic methodology, in the recent discussion, economic models are considered to be valuable because of their explanatory function rather than due to their predictive success. This applies to other models in social sciences as well: although unrealistic, they are nevertheless considered to give us some understanding on social processes.

The main defences of the unrealistic assumptions used in social scientific models proceed through two lines. On the one hand economic models have been conceived of as surrogate systems through which we can obtain knowledge if they succeed in *isolating* or abstracting some causal mechanisms, factors or tendencies correctly (Cartwright, 1989; Mäki, 1992; 2009a), while on the other hand it has been suggested that they are rather like pure constructions or fictional entities that nevertheless license different kinds of inferences (Sudgen, 2002, 2009; see also Knuuttila, 2009b). Of course, there are overlaps between these two alternatives, but for the sake of exposition we keep them separate in what follows.

The main exponents of the isolation account, Nancy Cartwright and Uskali Mäki, both have derived from J.S. Mill the idea that models abstract causally relevant capacities, factors or mechanisms of the real world for the purpose of working out deductively what effects those few isolated capacities or factors have in particular controlled model environments. Cartwright focuses on causal capacities, which are the ontologically primary causes of the regular associations between events. Regularities are produced when causal factors work together in particular configurations isolated from other disturbing factors. In models we study the behaviour of the causal capacities of interest by idealising (or abstracting) away the workings of the other factors (Cartwright, 1999a). While Cartwright writes variably and sometimes more or less interchangeably about abstraction, isolation and idealisation, Mäki (2005) makes isolation the central concept of his account of modelling.

According to Mäki, theoretical models in economics are outcomes of the method of isolation, in which a set of elements is theoretically removed from the influence of other elements in a given situation (Mäki, 1992: 318, see also Mäki, 1994). For Mäki, abstraction is a subspecies of isolation: the isolation of the universal from its particular exemplifications. Idealisations and omissions, in turn, are techniques for generating isolations: idealisations being deliberate falsehoods, which either understate or exaggerate to the absolute extremes (Mäki, 1992). The idea of isolation shows that unrealistic assumptions can even be the very means of striving for the truth, which Mäki puts as boldly as stating that 'an isolating theory or statement is true if it correctly represents the isolated essence of the object' (1992: 344, see also Mäki in this handbook).

However, the idea of isolation is beset with a couple of major problems: Firstly, the problem is that the 'causal structure' of the real world is often such that the causes are not separable and thus may not vary independently as the method of isolation assumes (Boumans and Morgan, 2001: 16; Alexandrova, 2008). More likely, rather than 'sealing off' the disturbing factors, models assume simpler relations than the actual ones for causal interactions. In econometric work it is often found that the causes are not separable and so they should not be treated as independent of other previously included and omitted factors (see Morgan and Knuuttila, 2011).

Secondly, idealisations in economic models are often driven by the requirements of tractability (see Hindriks, 2006). This is why Cartwright has lately asked whether economic models are, in fact, 'over-' constrained' to facilitate the study of the

isolated processes of interest (e.g. Cartwright, 1999b). The specific problem with economic models is that many of their idealisations are not meant to shield the operation of the causal factor or tendency of interest from the effects of other disturbing forces. Rather, the model economy is often attributed very special characteristics so as to allow mathematical representation from which, given some minimal economic principles such as utility maximisation, one could derive deductive consequences (Cartwright, 1999b; see also Alexandrova, 2006 for 'derivation facilitators'). Thus the model assumptions do not merely neutralise the effect of the other causal factors. They do much more: they construct the modelled situation in such a way that it can be conveniently mathematically modelled making the results derived model-dependent. In an attempt to overcome this problem Kuorikoski and Lehtinen (2009) advocate robustness analysis, the use of multiple models with different and independent tractability assumptions to derive the same conclusions, as a tool for assessing the model-dependence of modelling results. They claim that much of modelling practice can be interpreted as kind of robustness analysis (see also Kuorikoski et al., 2010).

As opposed to the idea of modes as isolating entities, economic and other social models have been also defended on fictionalist grounds. An early fictionalist interpretation of economic theorising was presented by Fritz Machlup who suggested that *homo oeconomicus* should be regarded as a Weberian *ideal type* (Weber, 1904). As an ideal type *homo oeconomicus* is to be distinguished from real types. Thus economic theory should be understood as a heuristic device for tracing the predicted actions of imagined agents to the imagined changes they face in their environment. According to Machlup, economists are not interested in all kinds of human behaviour related to business, finance and production: they are only interested in certain reactions to specified changes in certain situations: 'For this task a *homunculus oeconomicus*, that is, a postulated (constructed, ideal) universal type of human reactor to stated stimuli, is an indispensable device' (Machlup, 1978: 300). Yet Machlup reminds us that regardless of the artificiality of the ideal type-construct, the motivational assumptions attributed to it should be 'understandable' in the sense that we could imagine reasonable people acting according to them at least on some occasions.

In his account on modelling Robert Sugden (2002) also reverts to fiction, although instead of 'understandability' he invokes 'credibility'. He contests the idea that modellers proceed by first isolating causally relevant factors of the real world and then studying their consequences. In his view economic models should rather be regarded as fictional constructions, which instead of being abstractions from reality are *parallel realities*. A good example towards that end, according to Sugden, is Thomas Schelling's famous 'checkerboard model', which he uses to explain segregation by colour and by sex in various social settings (Schelling, 1978). The model consists of a grid populated by dimes and pennies that either migrate or stay put depending on the number of immediate neighbours that are of the other type. The migration of dimes and pennies continues until all the coins are content. As a result, strongly segregated distributions of dimes and pennies tend to appear – even if the number of neighbouring 'others' tolerated were quite high.

According to Sugden, it seems rather dubious to assume that a model like the checkerboard model is built by presenting some key features of the real world and sealing them off from the potential influence of other factors at work: 'Just what do we have to seal off to make a real city – say Norwich – become a checkerboard?' he asks (2002: 127). Thus, 'the model world is not constructed by starting from the real world and stripping out complicating factors: although the model world is *simpler* than the real world, the one is not a simplification of the other' (p. 131). Sugden treats model-world inferences as a

species of simple induction, which is legitimate when the model describes a state of affairs that is *credible* given our knowledge of the real world, and in doing so it could be considered realistic in much the same fashion as a novel can. Even though the characters and the places in the novel might be imaginary, we could consider them credible in the sense that we take it to be possible that there are events that are outcomes of people behaving as they do in the novel.

THE USES AND TYPES OF MODELS IN THE SOCIAL SCIENCES

Although economic modelling is the biggest game in town, it is not the whole story about formal modelling in the social sciences. The boundaries between the different social sciences have traditionally been drawn according to the scale and nature of the entities they study. Sociology studies the non-market driven societal or macro phenomenon in industrial and post-industrial societies, economics (arguably) phenomena governed by markets, social psychology interaction in relatively small groups etc. These traditional ways of defining the division of labour in the social sciences do correspond to some extent to the differences in their modelling practices. Economists' theoretical practices consist nowadays nearly entirely of modelling, with only a relatively limited set of modelling methodologies, whereas few sociologists rely on modelling, but those who do, use a more heterogenous set of model templates (Edling, 2002).

However, modelling frameworks cross disciplinary boundaries and an argument could be made that the traditional way of dividing the disciplines should be, and is actually in the process of being, replaced by a division of labour according to the use of different modelling tools (Humphreys, 2004: 71). Most models in social sciences are indeed more or less of the off-the-shelf type, that is, abstract structures that can be applied with varying degrees of adjustment to systems with intuitively very different causal make-up – the principles of stochastic processes, network models or constrained optimisation are similar regardless of who or what (individuals, groups, countries, ideas …) is doing the random walking, networking or maximising. Therefore the following brief survey on modelling practices in use in social sciences is organised around different model templates, rather than according to traditional disciplinary boundaries. However, as will become apparent later, this does not mean that there would be no important discipline related differences in the ways in which these templates are applied. For example, sociologists and economists conceptualise, use and interpret network models in importantly different ways, which reflect the deep methodological and substantial differences in their approaches to social phenomena.

We do not treat computer simulation as a distinct modelling format, since computational methods can and are used in connection with each of the following modelling practices. We acknowledge that not all uses of computational methods are simulations in any interesting sense (Hartmann, 1996; Lehtinen and Kuorikoski, 2007a), and that computational methods in general, and computer simulations in particular, involve important philosophical issues. But these issues cannot be adequately addressed here. Many model-types can also be, and are in fact, solved by manipulating diagrammatic graphical representations rather than symbolic mathematics, but this difference in the way of solving the model does not (usually) entail differences in the types of inferences that the model makes possible.

What kind of model template is considered appropriate depends on the goals of modelling: some types of models are obviously better suited to some specific purposes than others. Social scientific models can be used to suggest explanations for certain specific or general phenomena; to carry out virtual experiments; to specify and even help to execute policies based on a model; to design new institutions; to make predictions; to conduct thought experiments using a model; to derive solutions to theoretical problems; to explore the limits and range of possible outcomes consistent with questions that can be answered using a model; to develop concepts and classificatory systems; or simply as a pedagogical aid.

Simple and analytically tractable models are usually taken to be good at conceptual elaboration, theory development and explanation. Among others, Boyd and Richerson (1987) argue that replacing unintelligible phenomena with unintelligible models does not increase our understanding and that simple models are thus appropriate for explanation. However, their uses can be limited: for example, Grüne-Yanoff (2009) argues that extremely simple or 'minimal' models can only be used to disprove pre-theoretic impossibility intuitions (such as surely racial segregation cannot arise from non-racist preferences). Simple models (such as the famous IS-LM model in macroeconomics) are also usually well suited for pedagogical purposes, although complex simulations can also be used to provide illustrative examples. Relatively simple atheoretical associational models are often superior to more complex theoretical models in pure prediction tasks. On the other hand, policy analysis is often conducted with the aid of extremely complicated and data-rich computer simulations that are used to predict the consequences of possible interventions (e.g. epidemiological models and computational models used by central banks).

One common misconception about modelling is that modelling automatically entails a preference for quantitative data or quantifiable issues over a more qualitative approach. Much of theoretical modelling in the social sciences is about qualitative features of the social systems modelled and need not involve any explicit statistics. The function of the mathematics is not to relate numbers, but to facilitate secure derivations from theoretical principles and thus to enable reasoning about matters that are too complex for natural language (Simon, 1957: Chapter 6).

What follows is a simple typology of commonly used model-templates in the social sciences – rational choice, dynamical systems, network models and agent-based models – and some examples of how they are used. Our typology mirrors Cristofer Edling's (2002) classification of sociological models into models of process, structure and purposive agent, with the crucial difference that ours is based on the model-structure rather than on the intended interpretation.

Rational choice and traditional game theory (purposive agent–models)

Although rational choice ideas are now widespread in many social sciences, many applications of rational choice are little more than applications of economic concepts such as incentives, commodities and prices to domains of social phenomena without explicit market institutions or immediately obvious common currency (such as rational choice theories of religion, see essays in Young, 1997). Much of this reconceptualisation is not (and need not be) backed up by substantial formal models. Perhaps the field with the longest tradition of true model-building is political science, in which rational choice models have been used to explore the properties of different kinds of voting rules and political institutions (see, for example, Morton, 1999).

In conceptual terms, rational choice modelling begins with a postulation of a set of agents with preference orderings over a set of alternative outcomes and a postulation of a condition under which the simultaneous satisfaction of these preferences would be in some sense mutually consistent (the solution concept). In practice, the mathematical apparatus needed to build and solve this general analytic problem may vary, even quite radically. What is common is the importance of the solution concept or equilibrium, which allows the modeller to abstract away much of

the fine detail of the modelled situation, most importantly the dynamics, that is, an account of how and why the social system ends up in the final state.

If the social situation can be modelled as if it exemplified a competitive market, that is, the outcomes concern what commodities the agents posses after the interaction, there is a common currency in which the commodities can be valued and the actions of any given individual are not significant enough so as to affect the market prices, the models can be formulated and solved using simple principles of constrained optimisation and the corresponding solution concept is the market equilibrium. If the strategic element in the joint choice situation cannot be ignored, game theoretical methods have to be used: preference orderings and the possible outcomes are jointly defined as the payoffs and some appropriate solution concept chosen (most often the Nash equilibrium), which is then used to derive a solution.

Much of the philosophical discussion concerning rational choice modelling is about the extent to which it is sensible to treat humans as rational agents. This discussion is often connected to conceptual issues in action theory or normative issues concerning the concept of rationality. Some rational-choice theorists themselves defend their approach by appealing to the alleged intrinsic intelligibility of rational action and that rational choice is therefore a 'rock-bottom' explanatory theory (e.g. Boudon, 1998; see also Ylikoski and Kuorikoski, 2008). The question of the legitimacy of rationality assumptions can also be tackled by simply treating it as an instance of the general problem of idealisation, that is, under which conditions literally false idealising assumptions about agent-behaviour are fatal for the interpretation of the model or for the external validity of the model result. Approaching the issue from an action-theoretic viewpoint might also make one miss the fact that not all rational choice models rely on attributions of intentional states to the agents for their explanatory value. In some rational choice models the structural constraints of the choice situation carry the main explanatory weight, and sometimes even the behavioural assumptions (i.e. that individual agents act as if maximising some quantity) may be largely a matter of modelling convenience (Satz and Ferejohn, 1994). It is thus misleading to talk about a single theory of rational choice, since what is assumed by any given model, in other words the actual empirical content of the model, varies according to how the model is construed and used (Lehtinen and Kuorikoski, 2007b).

However, this very flexibility of the conceptual and mathematical frameworks have subjected rational choice models to charges of triviality in that they can only deal with features of social situations in such an abstract level that such models only serve to reformulate things that were already well understood or that the results are of little practical or theoretical interest. For example models of voting behaviour demonstrating the prevalence of preference cycles have been used to argue that democratic institutions are somehow inherently in disequilibrium. These extremely abstract models have been met with scepticism regarding whether they say anything empirically interpretable in the first place (Green and Shapiro, 1994).

Evolutionary game theory and dynamical systems (models of process)

Evolutionary game theory can be seen as an attempt to answer two central problems facing the traditional game theory. First, the requirement of formulating explicit dynamics can be seen as an attempt to answer the problem of equilibrium selection arising from the fact that most games have multiple Nash equilibria and that the consequent equilibrium refinement literature failed to pick a clear favourite replacement out of the multiplicity of intuitively reasonable stronger solution concepts. That the fact that game theory could not always make a definite

point-prediction was seen as a fatal problem perhaps indicates that game theory was indeed seen more as a substantial predictive or explanatory theory, rather than as a modelling framework. Second, specifically evolutionary dynamics can be seen as an answer to the accusation that traditional game theory attributes wildly unrealistic psychological capacities to the agents: since sets of evolutionary stable strategies are also Nash equilibria, evolutionary game theory is sometimes interpreted as showing how selection eventually drives a population into a state in which the units of the population exhibit strategic best-response behaviour, regardless of whether the units actually carry out any strategic deliberation.

Models of evolutionary dynamics are a special case of dynamical systems. Mathematically, dynamical systems are usually defined as systems of differential or difference equations, but we can also throw in stochastic processes for good measure. For example, game theory becomes evolutionary when the payoffs are interpreted as fitness, which is in turn operationalised as (or analytically linked to) the relative frequency of a given strategy in the next generation (replicator dynamics). This allows the model to be built as a simple system of difference equations, which can be solved for equilibrium. The equilibrium is thus still an essential concept, now defined as a fixed point of a dynamical system, that is, as a point in a trajectory in which the rate of change of the system in any direction is zero. In evolutionary game theory, a further constraint is usually imposed, according to which the equilibrium should also be stable under the introduction of invading alternative strategies. However, point equilibria are not the only outcomes of interest in dynamical systems, since many interesting social dynamics involve oscillations or other kinds of stable orbits. With certain assumptions, the stability properties of fixed points and orbits of relatively simple dynamical systems can be explored analytically (usually through the use of linearisation). Since in most cases of theoretical modelling, empirical grounds for favouring particular functional forms over alternatives are hard to come by, rough estimates about the qualitative behaviour of a loosely defined dynamic systems can usually be obtained by graphically reasoning with a phase diagram. Not surprisingly, using computational methods to explore the properties of dynamic systems has become the norm rather than the exception.

Dynamic systems are most prevalent in economics: many macroeconomic models are explicitly dynamic and are fitted to data using complex statistical models built from stochastic processes. Theoretical uses of stochastic processes in sociology mostly derive from the models presented by James Coleman in his textbook on mathematical sociology (1964). Many philosophers have also encountered dynamical systems as a vehicle for studying the possible evolutionary scenarios leading to the emergence of altruistic behaviour. One of the earliest sociological applications is the famous dynamic model of interaction in social groups by Herbert Simon (1952). Simon builds a simple system of differential equations to explore the comparative statics implications of George Homans' three postulates concerning the relationships between aggregate interaction, friendliness, activity and externally imposed activity within a social group and then discusses their further extensions to clique-formation and regulatory enforcement. The model is a good illustration of how a formal model can reveal implications of theoretical postulates that would have been hard or impossible to reach by using only natural language as the medium of argumentation.

A well known approach to using ecological model templates in the social sciences is Hannan and Freeman's tract on organisation ecology (1989), in which dynamical population models are used to analyse field-level effects of organisations competing for scarce resources in a niche-space. Evolutionary models and other dynamic systems are also often used to model population-level effects of social or evolutionary learning and even

gene-culture co-evolution. For example, Richard McElreath (2004) uses a simple analytic dynamic model to discuss how a level of between-group cultural diversity is sustained under imitation and migration due to the way individuals have to strike a balance between costs and benefits of individual learning (trial and error) versus social learning (imitation) in a changing environment. The value of the model is in the formulation of hypotheses concerning dependencies between different kinds of learning problems and cultural variation. These hypotheses were then checked against interview data gathered from East African tribes with intra-ethnic cultural variation between pastoralists and farmers. The model thus provides a general (functional) possible explanation of the preservation of cultural variation in the face of immigration and imitation and implies hypotheses about responses to different kinds of learning tasks.

Network models (models of structure)

Social life is largely constituted by the relationships people have with each other. Not surprisingly, then, different kinds of network models form a large part of formal modelling in the social sciences (see, for example, Wasserman and Faust, 1994). Much of this network modelling is data-driven. The point is often to collect or use existing data to statistically measure the number and strength of connections and interactions between agents (people, firms, countries, etc.) or social positions. The beginnings of network modelling can indeed be traced to the idea of sociometrics, the measurement of interpersonal relations. However, there are also theoretical uses for network models. First, a theoretical network model can show that a given network structure can give rise to a certain phenomenon. Thus network models can be used to show how the social structure can give rise to some surprising social regularities. Second, a network model can be supplemented with additional theoretical content providing an account of how micro-mechanisms give rise to networks with certain structural properties.

Network models can be seen as applications of graph-theory, a mathematical theory linking diagrams to joint distributions of random variables. The models consist of nodes and vertices. The nodes represent units, usually individuals or social positions, and the vertices some relation(s) of interest that may obtain between the units. What is distinctive about most network models is that they employ essentially structural variables over and above variables representing properties of the units. For example, social connectivity can be treated as an attribute of an individual (as a predictor of occupational achievement, for example) or as a structural attribute of the whole network. The vertices are often conceptualised as resource flows or resource asymmetries between the units. This approach can be used, for example, to model structures of social power by defining power as a resource asymmetry between social positions (not individual people holding the positions).

Network models can be used to explain societal patterns by showing how the structure of the network constrains the joint distribution of the attributes of the nodes. For example the speed and shape of diffusion processes depend on the general structure of the network in which the diffusion takes place. Accordingly, network models can be used to explain certain characteristics of the spread of diseases, practices, ideas or party affiliation. Network models can thus be seen as a clear operationalisation of what might sometimes be meant by the notoriously vague term 'structural property'. Moreover, social structure is also sometimes identified through the *absence* of social ties in a network and the strategy of focusing on 'structural holes' to make inferences about the structural properties of social systems is an important part of theoretical network modelling.

Network models can also be supplemented with explicit models of unit-level behaviour or decision making. Thus the network structure can function as an *explanandum* as well as an *explanans*. Often this means adding a game-theoretical element to the model, but this is not necessary. For example Bearman et al. (2004) found out that the network-structure of romantic affiliations of adolescents in a US high-school did not obey the assumptions of standard disease transmission models. Using simulation techniques, Bearman et al. concluded that the observed network structure could arise from a norm prohibiting chains of length four (thou shall not date your old partner's current partner's old partner). Bearman et al. theorised that this 'norm' is the result of a common aversion to possible status loss amongst peers, which overrides any other preferences in partner choice.

Agent-based models

Social sciences are about phenomena that arise out of the interaction of a number of people. Because of the demands of analytic tractability, most mathematical models are ill-equipped to do justice to the differences between people and instead have to directly relate aggregate or macro variables, or resort to using representative agent -constructs. However, aggregation, brute macro constructs and representative agent constructs are all subject to well known problems and biases (see, for example, Kirman, 1989). Since the individual agent is in many ways the most natural ontological building block of social phenomena, models that are built directly upon these agents, models that show how simple decision rules governing the behaviour of heterogenous agents give rise to social phenomena, would seem an attractive methodological option. In such agent-based models, solving the model does not mean that an external consistency condition is imposed on the action of the agents (such as a solution concept) in order to derive a solution, but the agents are instead left to interact 'by themselves' and the modeller simply observers how the system behaves.

Since computational methods can overcome the constraints of analytic tractability that would quickly become overwhelming for any truly agent-based model (which, in principle, should include a separate set of equations of behaviour for each individual), most agent based models are computer simulations (the chapter on artificial worlds and agent-based simulation in this book addresses in more detail this rapidly growing field of social modelling). In principle, however, the idea of agent-based modelling is independent of the technology of computer simulation. One of the first and most famous agent-based models is Schelling's checkerboard model of urban segregation (although the checkerboard may alternatively be considered to be a non-computerised simulation).

Agent-based models cope well with two issues that are difficult to model analytically: heterogeneity and configuration of agents. By heterogeneity we mean that the agents not only have different preferences, but also behave according to (possibly qualitatively) different decision rules. Since the model is built from individual agents, the model builder can, in principle, freely postulate different kinds of agents. The ability to take agent heterogeneity into account also means that agent-based models can investigate distributional effects. By configuration, we mean properties or behaviour of agents that is dependent on an agent's relative distance to other agents according to some metric. This distance can often, but not necessarily, be interpreted as a spatial distance. Many agent-based models (such as cellular automata, of which the checkerboard is an example) are based on a grid, in which the agents' behaviour is dependent only on the behaviour of their immediate neighbours.

CONCLUSION

In this chapter we have discussed the general philosophical perspectives on modelling, which we have then related to the special problems of social sciences and the distinctive modelling practices that are in use in the social sciences. Whereas the philosophical discussion on modelling used to be about the general structure of all scientific knowledge, a general trend towards more practice-oriented accounts taking seriously the various uses of models in specific sciences can be discerned in the prevailing philosophical discussion on modelling. Models are seen as mediating between theory and observations, but this mediating role requires models to incorporate content that is not directly derivable from the theory making models autonomous. Model-based reasoning is also surrogative in that it essentially involves manipulation of the model, thus making modelling to some extent analogous to experimentation. Since models are not linguistic entities, the concept of truth has been largely replaced by the concept of representation as the criterion of epistemic achievement. However, it is not clear whether the concept of representation could be used to *explain* this epistemic value.

To this philosophical discussion modelling in the social sciences provides an interesting and challenging problematic of its own. It does not presuppose quantitative orientation to the modelled phenomena or adherence to any kind of nomothetic ideal of science in general. The value of theoretical modelling lies in keeping our reasoning about complex phenomena tractable and open to rigorous scrutiny. Theoretical modelling comes on its own in situations in which natural language and informal reasoning lose their traction, and many social phenomena are undoubtedly of such kind. Models of social phenomena face difficulties arising from openness and heterogeneity of social systems, the lack of experimental controls and paucity of data. However, all models are idealised and a model is good or bad only with respect to a particular modelling goal. Social sciences employ a number of different formal model templates and there are no reasons to suspect that the nature of social phenomena would make such modelling frameworks infertile, quite the contrary.

ACKNOWLEDGEMENT

The authors would like to thank the Academy of Finland for the support of this research.

REFERENCES

Achinstein, Peter (1968) *Concepts of Science. A Philosophical Analysis.* Baltimore: Johns Hopkins Press.

Alexandrova, Anna (2006) 'Connecting economic models to the real world: Game theory and the FCC spectrum auctions', *Philosophy of the Social Sciences*, 36(2): 173–192.

Alexandrova, Anna (2008) 'Making models count', *Philosophy of Science*, 75(3): 383–404.

Bailer-Jones, Daniela (2003) 'When scientific models represent', *International Studies in the Philosophy of Science*, 17(1): 59–74.

Balzer, Wolfgang, C., Ulises Moulines and Joseph D. Sneed (1987) *An Architectonic for Science. The Structuralist Program.* Dordrecht: Riedel.

Bartels, Andreas (2006) 'Defending the structural concept of representation', *Theoría*, 21(1): 7–19.

Bearman, Peter S, James Moody and Katherine Stovel (2004) 'Chains of affection: The structure of adolescent romantic and sexual networks', *American Journal of Sociology*, 110(1): 44–91.

Black, Max (1962) *Models and Metaphors. Studies in Language and Philosophy.* Ithaca, NY: Cornell University Press.

Boltzmann, Ludwig (1911) 'Models', in *Encyclopaedia Britannica* (11th edition). Cambridge: Cambridge University Press. pp. 638–640.

Boudon, Raymond (1998) 'Social mechanisms without black boxes', in Hedström, Peter and Swedberg, Richard (eds), *Social Mechanisms: An Analytical Approach to Social Theory.* Cambridge: Cambridge University Press.

Boumans, Marcel (1999) 'Built-in justification', in Mary S. Morgan and Margaret Morrison (eds) *Models as Mediators. Perspectives on Natural and Social Science.* Cambridge: Cambridge University Press. pp. 66–96.

Boumans, Marcel and Mary S. Morgan (2001) 'Ceteris paribus conditions: Materiality and the application of economic theories', *Journal of Economic Methodology*, 8(1): 11–26.

Boyd, Robert and Peter Richerson (1987) 'Simple models of complex phenomena', in J. Dupre (ed.) *The Latest of the Best.* Cambridge, MA: The MIT Press. pp. 27–52.

Brandom, Robert (1994) *Making It Explicit: Reasoning, Representation and Discursive Commitment.* Cambridge, MA: Harvard University Press.

Brown, Alan and Deaton, Angus (1972) 'Surveys in applied economics: Models of consumer behaviour', *Economic Journal*, 82: 1145–1236.

Caldwell, Bruce J. (1982) *Beyond Positivism: Economic Methodology in the Twentieth Century.* London: Allen & Unwin.

Cartwright, Nancy (1983) *How the Laws of Physics Lie.* Oxford: Oxford University Press.

Cartwright, Nancy (1989) *Nature's Capacities and their Measurement.* Oxford: Clarendon Press.

Cartwright, Nancy (1999a) *The Dappled World. A Study of the Boundaries of Science.* Cambridge: Cambridge University Press.

Cartwright, Nancy (1999b) *The Vanity of Rigour in Economics: Theoretical Models and Galilean Experiments.* London: Centre for Philosophy of Natural and Social Science. Discussion paper series 43/99.

Chao, Hsiang-Ke (2002) *Representation and Structure. The Methodology of Econometric Models of Consumption.* Tinbergen Institute Research Series no. 289. Amsterdam: University of Amsterdam.

Coleman, James (1964) *An Introduction to Mathematical Sociology.* Glencoe, IL: Free Press

Contessa, Gabriele (2007) 'Representation, interpretation, and surrogate reasoning', *Philosophy of Science*, 71: 48–68.

da Costa, Newton C.A. and Steven French (1990) 'The model-theoretic approach in the philosophy of science', *Philosophy of Science*, 57: 248–265.

de Donato Rodríguez, Xavier and Jesús Zamora-Bonilla (2009) 'Credibility, idealisation, and model building: An inferential approach', *Erkenntnis*, 70: 101–118.

Edling, Cristofer R. (2002) 'Mathematics in sociology', *Annual Review of Sociology*, 28: 197–220.

French, Steven (2003) 'A model-theoretic account of representation (or, I don't know much about art… but I know it involves isomorphism)', *Philosophy of Science*, 70: 1472–1483.

French, Steven and Ladyman, James (1999) 'Reinflating the semantic approach', *International Studies in Philosophy of Science*, 13: 99–117.

Friedman, Milton (1953) *Essays in Positive Economics.* Chicago: Chicago University Press.

Frigg, Roman (2002) *Models and Representation: Why Structures Are Not Enough. Measurement in Physics and Economics Discussion Paper Series.* London: London School of Economics.

Frigg, Roman (2006) 'Scientific representation and the semantic view of theories', *Theoria*, 55: 49–65.

Giere, Ronald N. (1988) *Explaining Science: A Cognitive Approach.* Chicago: University of Chicago Press.

Giere, Ronald N. (2004) 'How models are used to represent reality', *Philosophy of Science*, 71: S742–S752.

Giere, Ronald N. (2010) 'An agent-based conception of models and scientific representation', *Synthese* 172: 269–281.

Godfrey-Smith, Peter (2006) 'The strategy of model-based science', *Biology and Philosophy*, 21: 725–740.

Goodman, Nelson (1972) 'Seven strictures on similarity', in N. Goodman (ed.) *Problems and Projects*. Indianapolis, IN: Bobs-Merrill. pp. 437–447.

Green, Donald and Ian Shapiro (1994) *Pathologies of Rational Choice Theory: A Critique of Applications in Political Science*. New Haven: Yale University Press.

Grüne-Yanoff, Till (2009) 'Learning from minimal economic models', *Erkenntnis*, 70: 81–99.

Hannan, Michael T. and John Freeman (1989) *Organizational Ecology*. Cambridge, MA: Harvard University Press.

Hartmann, Stephan (1996) 'The world as a process. Simulations in the natural and social sciences', in Hegselmann, Rainer, Ulrich Müller and Klaus Troitzsch (eds) *Modelling and Simulation in the Social Sciences from the Philosophy of Science Point of View*. Theory and Decision Library. Dordrecht: Kluwer. pp. 77–100.

Hausman, Daniel (1992) *The Inexact and Separate Science of Economics*. Cambridge, UK: Cambridge University Press.

Hedström, Peter (2005) *Dissecting the Social: On the Principles of Analytic Sociology*. Cambridge, UK: Cambridge University Press.

Hesse, Mary (1966) *Models and Analogies in Science*. Milwaukee: University of Notre Dame Press.

Hesse, Mary (2000) 'Models and analogies', in W.H. Newton-Smith (ed.) *A Companion to the Philosophy of Science*. Bodmin: Blackwell. pp. 299–307.

Hindriks, Frank A. (2006) 'Tractability assumptions and the Musgrave-Mäki-typology', *Journal of Economic Methodology*, 13: 401–423.

Hughes, R.I.G. (1997) 'Models and representation', *Philosophy of Science*, 64: S325–S336.

Humphreys, Paul (2004) *Extending Ourselves: Computational Science, Empiricism, and Scientific Method*. Oxford: Oxford University Press.

Hutten, Ernest H. (1954) 'The role of models in physics', *British Journal for the Philosophy of Science*, 4: 284–301.

Kirman, Alan (1989) 'The intrinsic limits of modern economic theory: The emperor has no clothes', *Economic Journal*, 99: 126–139.

Koopmans, Tjalling (1957) *Three Essays on The State of Economic Science*. New York: McGraw Hill.

Knuuttila, Tarja (2005) 'Models, representation, and mediation', *Philosophy of Science*, 72: 1260–1271.

Knuuttila, Tarja (2009a) 'Representation, idealization, and fiction in economics: From the assumptions issue to the epistemology of modeling', in Mauricio Suárez (ed.) *Fictions in Science: Philosophical Essays on Modeling and Idealization*. New York & London: Routledge. pp. 205–231.

Knuuttila, Tarja (2009b) 'Isolating representations versus credible constructions? Economic modeling in theory and practice', *Erkenntnis*, 70: 59–80.

Knuuttila, Tarja and Atro Voutilainen (2003) 'A Parser as an epistemic artefact: A material view on models', *Philosophy of Science*, 70: 1484–1495.

Kuorikoski, Jaakko and Aki Lehtinen (2009) 'Incredible worlds, credible results', *Erkenntnis*, 70: 119–131.

Lehtinen, Aki and Jaakko Kuorikoski (2007a) 'Unrealistic assumptions in rational choice theory', *Philosophy of the Social Sciences*, 37: 115–138.

Lehtinen, Aki and Jaakko Kuorikoski (2007b) 'Computing the perfect model: Why do economists shun simulation?', *Philosophy of Science*, 74: 304–329.

Kuorikoski Jaakko, Aki Lehtinen and Caterina Marchionni (2010) 'Economic modeling as robustness analysis', *British Journal for Philosophy of Science*, 61: 541–567.

Machlup, Fritz (1978) *Methodology of Economics and Other Social Sciences*. New York: Academic.

MacKenzie, Donald (2006) *An Engine, Not a Camera: How Financial Models Shape Markets*. Cambridge, MA: The MIT Press.

Mäki, Uskali (1992) 'On the method of isolation in economics', *Poznań Studies in the Philosophy of Science and Humanities*, 26: 316–351. Amsterdam: Rodopi.

Mäki, Uskali (1994), 'Isolation, Idealization and Truth in Economics', *Poznan Studies in the Philosophy of the Sciences and the Humanities*, 38: 147–168. Amsterdam: Rodopi.

Mäki, Uskali (2005) 'Models are experiments, experiments are models', *Journal of Economic Methodology*, 12: 303–315.

Mäki, Uskali (2009a) 'MISSing the world: Models as isolations and credible surrogate systems', *Erkenntnis*, 70: 29–43.

Mäki, Uskali (2009b) 'Models and truth: The functional decomposition approach', in M. Dorato, M. Rèdei and M. Suárez (eds) *EPSA Launch of the European Philosophy of Science Association*, Vol I: Epistemology and Methodology of Science. Dordrecht: Springer, pp. 177–189.

McElreath, Richard (2004) 'Social learning and the maintenance of cultural variation: An evolutionary model and data from East Africa', *American Anthropologist*, 106: 308–321.

Merton, Robert K. (1957) *On Theoretical Sociology*. New York: The Free Press.

Morgan, Mary S. (1990) *The History of Econometric Ideas.* Cambridge, UK: Cambridge University Press.

Morgan, Mary S. and Marcel Boumans (2004) 'Secrets hidden by two-dimensionality: The economy as a hydraulic machine' in S. de Chadarevian and N. Hopwood (eds) *Models: The Third Dimension of Science.* Stanford University Press. pp 369–401.

Morgan, Mary S. and Tarja Knuuttila (2011), 'Models and modelling in economics', in Uskali Mäki (ed.) *The Handbook of the Philosophy of Economics*, Elsevier.

Morgan, Mary and Margaret Morrison (1999) *Models as Mediators. Perspectives on Natural and Social Science.* Cambridge: Cambridge University Press.

Morrison, Margaret and Mary S. Morgan (1999) 'Models as mediating instruments', in Mary S. Morgan and Margaret Morrison (eds), *Models as Mediators. Perspectives on Natural and Social Science.* Cambridge: Cambridge University Press. pp. 10–37.

Morton, Rebecca M. (1999) *Methods & Models: A Guide to the Empirical Analysis of Formal Models in Political Science.* Cambridge: University of Cambridge Press.

Nagel, Ernest (1961) *The Structure of Science.* New York: Harcourt, Brace & World.

Satz, Debra and Ferejohn, John (1994) 'Rational choice and social theory', *Journal of Philosophy*, 91: 71–87.

Schelling, Thomas C. (1978) *Micromotives and Macrobehavior.* New York: Norton.

Simon, Herbert (1952) 'A formal theory of interaction in social groups', *American Sociological Review*, 17: 202–212.

Simon, Herbert (1957) *Models of Man: Social and Rational; Mathematical Essays on Rational Human Behavior in a Social Setting.* New York: Wiley.

Solow, Robert M. (1997) 'How did economics get that way and what way did it get?', *Daedalus*, 126: 39–58.

Suárez, Mauricio (1999) 'Theories, models, and representations', in Lorenzo Magnani, Nancy J. Nersessian and Paul Thagard (eds), *Model-Based Reasoning in Scientific Discovery.* New York: Kluwer. pp. 75–83.

Suárez, Mauricio (2003) 'Scientific representation: Against similarity and isomorphism', *International Studies in the Philosophy of Science*, 17: 225–244.

Suárez, Mauricio (2004) 'An inferential conception of scientific representation', *Philosophy of Science* (Symposia), 71: 767–779.

Suárez, Mauricio (ed.) (2008) *Fictions in Science: Philosophical Essays on Modeling and Idealization.* New York and London: Routledge.

Suárez, Mauricio (2010) Scientific Representation. *Blackwell's Philosophy Compass*, 5: 91–101.

Sugden, Robert (2002) 'Credible worlds: The status of the theoretical models in economics', in Uskali Mäki (ed.) *Fact and Fiction in Economics: Models, Realism, and Social Construction.* Cambridge: Cambridge University Press. pp. 107–136.

Sugden, Robert (2009) 'Credible worlds, capacities and mechanisms', *Erkenntnis*, 70: 3–27.

Suppe, Frederick (1977) *The Structure of Scientific Theories*, 2nd edn [1st edn, 1974]. Urbana: University of Illinois Press.

Suppe, Frederick (1989) *The Semantic Conception of Theories and Scientific Realism.* Urbana: University of Illinois Press.

Suppes, Patrick (1961) 'A comparison of the meaning and uses of models in mathematics and the empirical sciences', in H. Freudenthal (ed.) *The Concept and the Role of the Model in Mathematics and the Natural and Social Sciences.* Dordrecht: Reidel. pp. 163–177.

Suppes, Patrick (1962) 'Models of data', in E. Nagel, P. Suppes and A. Tarski (eds) *Logic, Methodology and Philosophy of Science: Proceedings of the 1960 International Congress.* Stanford: Stanford University Press. pp. 252–261.

Swoyer, Chris (1991) 'Structural representation and surrogative reasoning', *Synthese*, 87: 449–508.

Teller, Paul (2001) 'Twilight of the perfect model', *Erkenntnis*, 55: 393–415.

van Fraassen, Bas C. (1980) *The Scientific Image.* Oxford: Oxford University Press.

Vorms, Marion (2009) 'Formats of representation in scientific theorising', *in PhilSci Archive: [2009] Models and Simulations 3* (Charlottesville, VA; March 5–7, 2009). http://philsci-archive.pitt.edu/archive/00003901/.

Wasserman, Stanley and Katherine Faust (1994) *Social Network Analysis: Methods and Applications.* Cambridge and New York: Cambridge University Press.

Weber, Max (1904) '"Objectivity" in social science and social policy' in Edward A. Shils and Henry A. Finch (trans. and eds (1949)) *The Methodology of the Social Sciences.* New York: Free Press.

Weintraub, E. Roy (1985) *General Equilibrium Analysis: Studies in Appraisal.* Cambridge: Cambridge University Press.

Weisberg, Michael (2007) 'Who is a modeler', *British Journal for the Philosophy of Science*, 58: 207–233.

Ylikoski, Petri and Jaakko Kuorikoski (2008) 'Intentional fundamentalism', in A. Hieke and H. Leitgeb (eds) *Reduction and Elimination in Philosophy and the Sciences – Papers of the 31st International Wittgenstein Symposium*, Vol XVI, Kirchberg am Wechsel, Austria: Austrian Ludwig Wittgenstein Society. pp. 405–407.

Young, Laurence A. (ed.) (1997) *Rational Choice Theory and Religion – Summary and Assessment.* New York: Routledge.

29

Empirical Evidence:
Its Nature and Sources

Julian Reiss

INTRODUCTION

With the rise of evidence-based movements in medicine and social policy, the topic of evidence has come to the forefront of research in the philosophy and methodology of science. But the issue is far from new. Observation, experiment, induction and confirmation – all practices very closely related to evidence – have been central concerns of philosophers ever since the birth of Western philosophy. The primary aim of this article is to provide an introduction to and illumination of these topics in so far as they are relevant to the social sciences.

Empirical evidence in the social sciences is extraordinarily varied. It is produced by methods including the collection of physical artefacts in archaeology, conducting censuses in demography, mathematical modelling in economics, thought experimentation in history, expert judgement in political science, laboratory experimentation in psychology and causal modelling in sociology, among many others. Even within one and the same science, evidence can have a variety of sources. To take economic policy as an example, the traditional way to substantiate economic policy claims is to first build a

structural model, which is based on economic theory, then to operationalise its terms and test the fit of the model against data. This structural equation modelling approach was developed by members of the Cowles Commission in the 1930s and 1940s and has since been supplemented by a variety of other techniques in econometrics such as the analysis of natural experiments, but also laboratory experiments, simulation and various forms of conceptual or thought experimentation.

This article has two parts. In the first part, I will survey philosophical theories of evidence and in so doing attempt to answer questions regarding the nature of evidence and the nature of the inference from evidence to hypotheses. The second part will give a necessarily incomplete overview of the different sources of evidence in the social sciences and asks how to combine their products.

Before diving into the various philosophical proposals for theories of evidence and inference, a few terminological clarifications are in order. First, the notion of scientific evidence has at least three connotations that are relevant here. According to *Webster's New World Dictionary* (Second College edition), 'evidence' refers to: (1) the condition of being evident; (2) something that makes another thing evident; indication; sign; and (3) something that tends to prove; ground for belief. Accordingly, *scientific* evidence means, first, the more or less observable outcomes of scientific tests such as experiments, statistical analyses and surveys. Used in this way, the notion is more or less synonymous with 'data' or 'scientific result'. According to the second entry, scientific evidence means hint, sign, indication of or a reason to believe (the negation of) a scientific hypothesis. According to the third, the word means (something that furnishes) proof of or good or cogent reason to believe (the negation of) a hypothesis. The ambiguity between the latter two meanings is illustrated by a passage from Wesley Salmon (Salmon, 1975: 6):

> As Carnap pointed out in *Logical Foundations of Probability*, the concept of confirmation is radically ambiguous. If we say, for example, that the special theory of relativity has been confirmed by experimental evidence, we may have either of two quite distinct meanings in mind. On the one hand, we may intend to say that the special theory has become an accepted part of scientific knowledge and that it is very nearly certain in light of its supporting evidence. If we admit that scientific hypotheses can have numerical degrees of confirmation, the sentence, on this construal, says that the degree of confirmation of the special theory of relativity on the available evidence is high. On the other hand, the same sentence might be used to make a very different statement. It might be taken to mean that some particular evidence – for example, observations on the lifetimes of mesons – renders the special theory more acceptable or better founded than it was in the absence of this evidence. If numerical degrees of confirmation are again admitted, this latter construal of the sentence amounts to the claim that the special theory has a higher degree of confirmation on the basis of the new evidence than it had on the basis of the previous evidence alone.

In what follows I will use 'evidence' almost always in sense 2, indication or sign, the only exception being Peter Achinstein's theory of evidence, which is a theory of a good or cogent reason to believe. Evidence in sense 1 will play an important role but I will say

'data' or 'test result' or something similar for it.

Second, as the passage from Salmon illustrates, the notion of evidence is closely related to those of confirmation and induction. Hypotheses are confirmed by evidence, and most theories of evidence that will be discussed below have been introduced as theories of confirmation. Induction refers to the mode of reasoning or inference from evidence to hypothesis. As the hypothesis contains more, or at least different, information than the evidence, this mode of reasoning is ampliative – enlarging what is already known. It contrasts with deductive reasoning, which proceeds in reverse order from a more general claim to a more specific claim. Unlike deductive reasoning, which is truth preserving, reasoning from evidence is fallible.

TAKING THE CON OUT OF CONFIRMATION

Some preliminary remarks

Philosophers of science often treat theories of evidence and of induction (or confirmation) as if they were of the same kind. But this would be a mistake. Theories of evidence are supposed to answer questions regarding the nature of evidence and the kinds of observations or tests a researcher needs to make in order to have evidence in favour of the hypothesis at stake. Theories of induction, by contrast, begin with an antecedently understood notion of evidence and ask what the kinds of inferences are that one is justified to make given one has evidence of the required type at hand.

Bayesianism, for example, is often described as a theory of evidence (as in Achinstein, 2001) but it is completely silent on the issue of the nature of evidence. Rather, it tells us what a rational agent should do in a situation where she comes to believe an evidential statement (*viz.*, to update her degree of belief in the hypothesis according to a specific rule). Colin Howson and Peter Urbach describe the matter as follows:

> The Bayesian theory we are proposing is a theory of inference from data; we say nothing about whether it is correct to accept the data ... The Bayesian theory of support is a theory of how the acceptance as true of some evidential statement affects your belief in some hypothesis. How you came to accept the truth of the evidence, and whether you are correct in accepting it as true, are matter which, from the point of view of the theory, are simply irrelevant. (Howson and Urbach, 1993: 272)

By contrast, Mill's methods, though often described as a theory of induction (as in Norton, 2003) are in fact at best informative about the types of observations one must make in order to support a (in this case, causal) hypothesis. For instance, the method of difference tells us evidence in favour of a causal hypothesis can be provided by two situations that are exactly identical except with respect to the phenomenon of interest. The method, by itself, is not informative about the kinds of inferences warranted by the observation of two such situations. It does not say, for example, whether, after having made the observation, we should accept the causal hypothesis as true or raise our degree of confidence in the hypothesis or rather assess the probability of accepting a false hypothesis if the test were run again and again.[1]

That inference to the best explanation and Bayesianism are compatible has been noticed before (see for instance Lipton, 2004: Chapter 7; Okasha, 2000). According to the position defended here, this is no accident. The two theories belong to different categories members of which play complementary roles. Inference to the best explanation is, despite its name, a theory of *evidence* that tells us what are the kinds of observations we should make, what are the kinds of tests we need to run in order to confirm or disconfirm a hypothesis. (As theory of evidence I will therefore refer to it as 'explanationism'.) It is silent about the types of inferences to be drawn from the evidence. Bayesianism is a

theory of *induction* that tells us what inferences are warranted after the evidence has come to be believed. This theory is silent about what evidence is. A full account of learning from evidence requires both. Here I will look at theories of evidence first, then at theories of induction and finally at a number of hybrid theories.

Theories of Evidence

In this section I will look at two families of theories of evidence, instance theories and hypothetico-deductive theories. The former regards an instance of a hypothesis evidence for it, the latter, its entailments.

Instance Theories

According to the first family of theories of evidence, a state of affairs provides evidence for a general hypothesis if and only if it is an instance of the hypothesis. Here I will look at theories of evidence regarding two kinds of general hypotheses: simple subject-predicate hypotheses and causal hypotheses.

Simple natural laws

By 'simple natural laws' I refer to universally quantified statements that ascribe a property to a kind or substance such as 'All ravens are black' (Hempel, 1945) or 'All samples of the element bismuth melt at 271°C' (Norton, 2003). According to this first theory, evidence for such a generalisation is constituted by the instances of the generalisation.

Formulated in first-order logic, the account is subject to the famous 'ravens paradox'. The hypothesis 'All ravens are black' is logically equivalent to the hypothesis 'All non-black things are non-ravens'. Now, an instance of the latter hypothesis is a red shoe, and therefore observing a red shoe provides evidence for it. On the plausible assumption that if a state of affairs is evidence for one hypothesis, then it is evidence for a logically equivalent hypothesis, observing a red shoe provides evidence for the hypothesis 'All ravens are black', which is absurd (Hempel, 1945).

What is more important in the present context is that few interesting hypotheses in the social sciences have the form of a simple natural law. First, because of the high degree of biological, psychological and social variability, few claims are true of all tokens of a given type. Second, the theory restricts evidence to what is describable by 'phenomenal', that is, observable (such as 'black') or measurable (such as 'melts at 271°C'), predicates. To the extent that social science hypotheses have some generality, they tend to stem from explanatory theories, which involve theoretical predicates and require a different kind of evidence (see below).

Causal hypotheses

Despite these limitations, the idea that an instance provides evidence for its generalisation is behind a very influential set of principles for causal inference. There is a fundamental and critical distinction between sequences that are genuinely causal and those that are 'merely' accidental. To use a philosopher's stock example, smoking is said to *cause* cancer. On the other hand, many people who have nicotine-stained fingers will later develop cancer but having yellow fingers isn't a cause of cancer. The difference between the two is as important for explanation as it is for planning and policy. John's smoking may explain his cancer; stained fingers don't. And if John wants to avoid certain kinds of cancer, to stop smoking would be a good idea; avoiding yellow stains by wearing gloves wouldn't.

Building on the seminal work of Francis Bacon, John Stuart Mill developed five principles to distinguish between causal and accidental sequences: the methods of agreement, of difference, the joint method (of agreement and difference), of residues and of concomitant variation (Mill, 1843 [1874]: Book III, Chapter 3). Exemplarily, let us look at the first two in more detail.

The method of agreement seeks two sequences of situations in which the phenomenon of interest occurs such that they differ in every respect but one. Then, the factor

that is followed by (or follows) is the cause (or the effect) of the phenomenon. Call ϕ the phenomenon of interest; f a factor and $\mathbf{X}$, $\mathbf{x}$, $\mathbf{Y}$, and $\mathbf{y}$ vectors of 'other circumstances' (where $X_i \neq Y_j$ and $x_i \neq y_j$ for all i, j and $X_i \in \mathbf{X}$, $Y_j \in \mathbf{Y}$, $x_i \in \mathbf{X}$, $y_j \in \mathbf{Y}$), then we can say schematically:

1 Method of agreement

> $f\mathbf{X}$ is followed by $\phi\mathbf{x}$
> $f\mathbf{Y}$ is followed by $\phi\mathbf{y}$
> Therefore, f is a cause of ϕ.[2]

The method of difference, by contrast, seeks two sequences of situations, one in which the phenomenon of interest occurs and one in which it doesn't, that are exactly identical with respect to every factor save one, then that factor is the cause (or the effect) of the phenomenon. Schematically:

2 Method of difference

> $f\mathbf{X}$ is followed by $\phi\mathbf{X}$
> $\mathbf{X}$ is followed by $\mathbf{X}$
> Therefore, f causes ϕ.[3]

The method of difference is the method of the controlled experiment. Both Mill's methods and the simpler instance theory constitute accounts of evidence because they tell us what the kinds of observations or tests are that one must take in order to support a hypothesis. It is true that both are associated with a rule of inference according to which the evidence warrants accepting the truth of the hypothesis – an inference rule I call 'categorical induction' (for Mill's case, see Mill, 1843). Norton (2003) therefore classifies the simple instance theory and Mill's methods under accounts of induction of the type 'inductive generalisation'.

However, the accounts are only accidentally wedded to this specific inference rule. There is nothing in the principles themselves that prevent using other rules such as probability updating or error correction (for a discussion of these rules of inference, see below).

Hypothetico-deductivism

The feature that unites the second family is: what makes a statement a statement about evidence is its being entailed by a hypothesis and suitable auxiliary assumptions. The advantages of these theories over instance theories are immediate: any theory, using both predicates that refer to observables and those that refer to unobservables, can in principle be supported by evidence, not just generalisations. But there is also an immediate problem: few evidential statements are entailed by only one hypothesis. The usual case is that there are many mutually incompatible hypotheses, all of which entail the evidential statement. The main question for these theories of evidence is consequently how to discriminate between the different evidence-entailing hypotheses. I discuss two ways here, which I call eliminativism and explanationism, respectively.

Eliminativism

The most straightforward way to discriminate among evidence-entailing hypotheses is to devise tests or series of tests that eliminate all but one of the alternatives. This idea too goes back to Francis Bacon (see for instance Klein, 2003). The evidence relevant to a hypothesis is therefore constituted by the testable implications of the hypothesis at stake as well as those of its alternatives.

A large randomised controlled trial can serve as the paradigm because it eliminates many alternative hypotheses in one fell swoop. A hypothesis about the effectiveness of a new training programme, say, can be tested by dividing subjects at random into a treatment group (which receives the new training) and a control group (which receives the standard training) such that the distribution of other factors influencing performance is identical in the two groups. Then, if performance is on average higher in the treatment group than in the control group, it must be due to the new programme.

But it is not necessary that alternative hypotheses be eliminated by one and the same test such as a randomised trial. Michael Scriven proposes the following form of inference in the context of causal analysis in history (Scriven, 1966: 249–50; emphasis original):

> For in order to establish a causal claim on behalf of a factor what does the historian need? Merely evidence that his candidate was present, that it has on other occasions clearly demonstrated its capacity to produce an effect of the sort here under study (or there might be theoretical grounds for thinking it a possible cause rather than previous direct experience of its actual efficacy), and the *absence* of evidence (despite a thorough search) (a) that its *modus operandi* was inoperative here, and/or (b) that any of the other possible causes was present. If the event studied had a cause at all (which the historian assumes it did), then he may confidently assert that the residual condition is elected. This argument *proves* his claim – and it requires nothing the historian does not possess. The only general proposition that might be involved would be a list of the known possible causes of the kind of effect in question. Explanation proceeds by the elimination of possible causes …

The principal worry about elimination of alternative hypotheses in the social sciences is that it is frequently the case that methods such as the randomised trial are not applicable or applicable only in an attenuated form, and that there are too many possible alternatives not all of which can be ruled out. In medical research, a randomised trial is a powerful blinding device: neither patient nor doctor knows whether which of a number of treatments (including a placebo) is administered. Blinding in this sense is often not an option when a treatment is a training programme or some other social policy (Scriven, 2008).

Explanationism

If several theories or hypotheses entail the evidential statement, then that which best explains the evidence is confirmed according to this theory. Additional evidence is therefore provided by a fact about the theory: its relative degree of explanatoriness or explanatory quality.

One might argue that calling such a fact 'evidence' would be misleading. This is correct, but only on the first reading of the term 'evidence' as 'data' or 'test result'. On the second reading of 'evidence' as 'hint', 'sign' or 'indication' (or even on the third reading as 'proof'), there is nothing unusual about calling facts about a theoretical hypothesis evidence. At any rate, these facts are taken as evidence by proponents of explanationism.

A connection between evidence and explanation was already present in Hempel's (1965) account because according to his deductive-nomological theory of explanation, a hypothesis, if it is true, fulfils some additional criteria and, together with other statements entails the evidential statement, it *explains* the evidential statement. Turned around, one can say that according to this account, a statement is evidence for a hypothesis if and only if the hypothesis, if true, explains it. Explanationism adds a criterion to discriminate between competing potential theoretical accounts. In Gilbert Harman's words (Harman, 1965: 89):

> In making this inference one infers, from the fact that a certain hypothesis would explain the evidence, to the truth of that hypothesis. In general, there will be several hypotheses which might explain the evidence, so one must be able to reject all such alternative hypotheses before one is warranted in making the inference. Thus one infers, from the premise that a given hypothesis would provide a "better" explanation for the evidence than would any other hypothesis, to the conclusion that the given hypothesis is true.

This raises the question how to determine which of a given set of alternative hypotheses is 'best'. Many suggestions have been made: the simplest, the most unifying, the most detailed, that which confers most understanding on its user. This mode of reasoning is fairly common in theory-driven branches of the social sciences such as in parts of economics and sociology. In economics, for instance, a model is accepted as explanatory – or as more explanatory than an alternative – if it portrays a world that is *credible* (Sugden, 2000) or if it makes assumptions about structural features that can be found in a great range of economic phenomena; in other words, if the model is *unifying* (see Reiss, 2008: Chapter 6).

Explanationism is subject to an important objection sometimes called 'Hungerford's objection' (Lipton, 2004: Chapters 4 and 9) is that the various explanatory virtues such as credibility, simplicity, unifying power or mechanism are too subjective and varied to provide an acceptable ground for inductive reasoning.

An important role evidence plays in scientific and other controversies is that of an objective arbiter. If, say, one political party holds that minimum wages are an effective tool to provide a living wage for everyone and another that minimum wages are counterproductive because they destroy jobs, then such disagreements about apparently purely factual matters ('is X an effective strategy to promote Y?' when it is agreed that Y is a desirable state of affairs) should, in principle, be solvable on the basis of evidence. Inference to the best explanation reintroduces subjectivity through the back door because (a) there is no one generally accepted explanatory virtue; (b) there is no generally accepted schema that ranks or weighs the different explanatory virtues; (c) there are no objective criteria that determine whether and to what extent any given virtue applies to a given case – what's simpler (or more unifying or …) to one person isn't to another (on this latter point, see Norton 2003).

Contextualism

As can be seen, all theories of evidence that have been discussed so far have limited applicability. They work, to the extent that they do, only for a specific type of hypothesis and under favourable epistemic conditions. According to a position one may call evidential contextualism, this is to be expected (see for instance Reiss, 2008: Chapter 1; cf. Kincaid, 2007). Scientists' epistemic interests and their domains of investigation are too heterogeneous to subsume all kinds of clues that may indicate a hypothesis under one universal scheme or even a small finite set of schemes of limited generality.

According to evidential contextualism, it is context-specific background knowledge that informs scientists what kinds of techniques work in what domains and under what conditions. At the general level no more can be said than that evidence is an observation or test result about which background knowledge entails that it is relevant to the assessment of a hypothesis of the given type and for the purpose at hand. There are numerous examples of the kinds of considerations that lead a (social) scientist to accept an observation or test result as evidence for different kinds of hypotheses and in the light of different kinds of purposes in the third section of this article.

Theories of Induction

Once we have evidence, what can we infer from it? This is the question addressed by theories of induction. In this section I will discuss three types of theory: categorical induction, two probabilistic theories and Norton's 'material theory of induction'.

Categorical Induction

What I call 'categorical induction' is the rule to infer the truth of the hypothesis from the evidence. Conjoined with the instance theory of evidence, we get enumerative induction or the 'more of the same' rule of inference. Conjoined with the first form of hypothetico-deductivism, we get eliminative induction and conjoined with its second form, inference to the best explanation or abduction.

Enumerative induction

This rule prescribes to infer from a finite set of observed instances to the corresponding generalisation. For example,

Raven 1 is black
Raven 2 is black
...
Raven n is black
Therefore, all ravens are black.

One problem is that the account is vague: it does not say how many instances must be observed in order to warrant inferring the truth of the generalisation. Another problem is that the rule itself is underspecified unless

supplemented with an account of natural kinds that provides limits for the types of predicate that are admissible for being quantified over. Nelson Goodman's famous 'grue paradox' illustrates the problem.

Goodman's paradox, in short, is as follows. The evidential statement 'All emeralds that have been observed so far have been green' confirms the generalisation 'All emeralds are green'. Now, we can define a new predicate, 'grue' as 'green if examined before t or blue otherwise'. Thus, before time t, we have exactly parallel evidence that all emeralds are green and that all emeralds are grue. But obviously only one of the two hypotheses can be true. The question, then, is which one we are warranted to infer. Some (e.g. Quine, 1969) have argued that 'green emerald' represents a natural kind while 'grue emerald' doesn't – and therefore that we are warranted to infer the former hypothesis but not the latter.

And it is not necessary to introduce artificial predicates such as 'grue' to make that point. A more scientific example due to John Norton can be used similarly. Consider the following inferences (Norton, 2003: 649):

Some samples of the element bismuth melt at 271°C.
Some samples of wax melt at 91°C.
Therefore, all samples of the element bismuth melt at 271°C.
Therefore, all samples of wax melt at 91°C.

The obvious difference between the two arguments is that 'bismuth' refers to a chemical element – a type of natural kind – whereas 'wax' names a variety of different mixtures of substances. Using simple enumerative induction as an inference rule is successful in the former case because of a known fact about chemical elements: elements are generally uniform in their physical properties. No such fact is true of the different mixtures of hydrocarbons that are jointly referred to as 'wax'.

Of course, restricting the inference rule to hypotheses regarding natural kinds is epistemically not helpful. Natural kinds are just those kinds certain properties of which are uniform across all instances, knowing that already presupposes that the inferential problem has been solved.

Eliminative induction

Alexander Bird calls this rule inference to the only explanation (in contrast to inference to the best explanation, see below) and describes it thus (Bird, 2007: 424–432):

> By Inference to the Only Explanation (IEO) I intend something quite specific, that at the end of inquiry we can be in the position to infer the truth of some hypothesis since it is the only possible hypothesis left unrefuted by the evidence. It is the form of inference advocated by Sherlock Holmes in his famous dictum 'Eliminate the impossible, and whatever remains, however improbable, must be the truth'.

There are three main worries that beset this form of induction. First and foremost is the idea that theoretical hypotheses are always underdetermined by the evidence available at a certain point in time. This is the Duhem–Quine underdetermination thesis. There are good reasons to believe that the thesis in its most general form – any theoretical hypothesis is always underdetermined by all available evidence – is false (see for instance Norton, 2008). In many actual scientific cases, all *plausible* hypotheses but one could be eliminated. The just mentioned article by Bird reconstructs Semmelweis' discovery of the cause of puerperal fever along these lines. But in the social sciences we often face situations in which the available evidence *de facto* underdetermines the choice of theoretical hypotheses. The list of possible and even plausible alternatives can be very long indeed, potentially open ended. Thus, the 'problem of confounders' (Steel, 2004) is a real obstacle to social-science research.

There are two further problems but they are less specific to social science. One is the question whether the list of plausible alternatives contains the true hypothesis. Eliminative categorical induction is only guaranteed to result in the true theory if it does. But, as Bas van Fraassen reminds us, the rule 'infer the

truth of the hypothesis that is the only one to be consistent with the evidence' (1985: 143), '… is a rule that selects the best [supported] among the historically given hypotheses. We can watch no contest of the theories we have so painfully struggled to formulate, with those no one has proposed. So our selection may well be the best of a bad lot'. The final criticism is whether the evidence requires an explanatory hypothesis at all. Perhaps some facts are just brute.

Inference to the best explanation

The proponent of inference to the best explanation or abductive reasoning infers the truth of a hypothesis from two considerations: (a) the hypothesis *explains* the evidence; (b) among the evidence-explaining alternative hypotheses it is the one that scores best on some scale of explanatory merit. For Peter Lipton, for example, the 'loveliness' of an explanation is the relevant criterion. Hence, the loveliest explanatory hypothesis is inferred to be true, according to this rule.

This inductive schema is subject to what has been called 'Voltaire's objection' (Lipton, 2004: Chapters 4 and 9). The objection denies the connection between goodness and truth. It asks, why should the world be simple or intelligible or lovely? In the context of the social sciences the link between explanatory 'loveliness' and truth often seems particularly tenuous. In economics, for example, a 'lovely' explanatory model portrays agents as perfectly rational, uses equilibrium concepts to solve equations and is mathematical in nature. There is little plausibility in the idea that considerations such as these should be a reliable guide to truth (see Reiss, 2008: Chapter 6).

Probabilistic Theories

Probabilistic theories ascribe a probability to the hypothesis and understand evidential support in terms of probabilistic relations.

Bayesianism

Standard Bayesianism combines an interpretation of probability as subjective degrees of belief with Bayes' rule – itself a theorem of probability theory – and an interpretation of belief-updating as confirmation to yield a schema for making inductive inferences.

Aside: Five interpretations of probability

The five major interpretations of probability are: classical, logical, subjective, frequency and propensity. The *classical* theory holds that probability is the ratio of the favourable cases to the total number of equally possible cases. For instance, the probability of the event 'rolling a number larger than three with a fair die' is $(1 + 1 + 1)/6 = 1/2$. According to the *logical* interpretation, too, all possible states of affairs are assigned probabilities but it relaxes the requirement of equal weights. A probability measure assigns numbers to so-called state descriptions, which describe all individuals in a universe in maximum detail.[4] According to *subjectivists* such as Bayesians, probabilities are constraints a rational agent lays upon the degrees to which he holds a belief. Probability expresses the confidence with which an agent holds a belief. *Frequentism* identifies probability with the frequency of favourable outcomes in a (finite or infinite) reference class (e.g. the frequency of 'heads' in a finite series of tosses of a coin or a hypothetical infinite series). Finally, according to *propensity* theorists, probability is a physical disposition of a chance set up to generate outcomes (such as the tendency of an atom to decay within a certain amount of time).

Bayes' theorem has numerous forms (see Howson and Urbach, 1993: Chapter 2); for an arbitrary hypothesis h, its negation $\sim h$ and evidential statement e, it can be expressed as follows:

$$P(h \mid e) = P(h)/[P(h) + (P(e \mid \sim h)/P(e \mid h))$$
$$P(\sim h)] \qquad (29.1)$$

where the expression $P(e \mid \sim h)/P(e \mid h)$ is called the 'likelihood ratio'. Since $P(\sim h) = 1 - P(h)$, $P(h \mid e)$, the posterior probability of the hypothesis given the evidence, is a function of its prior probability $P(h)$ and the likelihood ratio.

Together with the interpretation of probability as subjective degree of confidence or belief in a hypothesis and the idea that updating entails confirmation, Bayes' theorem entails an inference rule: upon coming to believe the evidential statement, update your degree of belief in the hypothesis in accordance with (29.1). Evidence in favour of (against) a hypothesis increases (decreases) the degree of belief in the hypothesis.

To illustrate how Bayes' theorem works as an inference rule, consider a medical example. Suppose that a diagnostic test is 99 per cent accurate; that is, it gives a correct test result in 99 per cent of cases, both positive (when the disease is present) and negative (when the disease is absent). If the test gives a positive result, what is the probability that the person actually has the disease? Let h = 'person has disease' and e = 'test result is positive'. The quantity we would like to infer is the posterior probability $P(h \mid e)$, the probability that the person has the disease *given* that the test result is positive. The likelihood ratio is $P(e \mid \sim h)/P(e \mid h) = 1\%/99\%$. Let the h's prior probability, in cases such as this called the base-rate, be 1/10,000 (i.e. one person in ten thousand has the disease). Then, by (29.1):

$$P(h \mid h) = .0001/[.0001+$$
$$(.01/.99)*.999] \approx .00981$$

Because of the low base-rate, the probability that the person taking the test has the disease, despite the positive test result, is below 1 per cent. Nevertheless, a positive test result provides evidence for the hypothesis because $P(h \mid e) \approx 1\% > .01\% = P(h)$.

Several criticisms have been levied against the Bayesian inductive rule, two of which I want to discuss here. According to the Bayesian, a hypothesis' probability assessment after coming to believe the evidence depends, as we have seen, on two factors: the hypothesis' prior probability and the likelihood ratio. The first criticism finds fault with prior probabilities; the second is suspicious that evidence enters the inference *only* via the likelihood.

In ordinary probability theory, probabilities are defined over events or outcomes or a sample space. Making probability statements entails that things could be different than the way they actually are. For instance, saying that the probability of rain today is 90 per cent means that it might either rain or not (and that it should rain on 90 per cent of days like today). Scientific hypotheses, by contrast, are either true or false (or, if one prefers, empirically adequate or not or reliable or not), they are not 'probable' in the sense that rain is. If there were probabilities, this would imply that there are many worlds, in which case the probability of a hypothesis could measure the frequency of worlds in which the hypothesis is true. But there is only one world – and thus, there are no priors (Mayo, 1996: Chapter 3).

The other criticism can be illustrated by the debate regarding stopping rules. A stopping rule specifies when to stop collecting new data. To test whether a coin is fair, for instance, one might toss it 20 times, record the number of heads and tails (say, 8 and 12) and then assess whether the specific outcome was more likely if the coin was fair or if it was unfair. Alternatively, one might continue tossing the coin until one has recorded eight heads or a ratio of two heads to three tails. Intuitively, it should matter a great deal how the test is set up. For instance, it should matter whether a specific outcome was likely or not given how the procedure was designed. Bayesianism entails that to the assessment of the fairness of the coin these considerations should not play a role. Another way of putting it is that Bayesianism is only sensitive to the actual outcome (the actual series of 8 heads and 12 tails) not also to the outcomes the test could have produced but did not.

Likelihoodism

The likelihood view is essentially Bayesianism without the priors. An attractive feature of it is that it regards evidence always as relevant to a hypothesis relative to an alternative. The law of likelihood states that evidence *e* supports hypothesis h_1 over hypothesis h_2 if and only if $P(e \mid h_1) > P(e \mid h_2)$ (see Hacking, 1965).

As in Bayesianism, a positive test result is evidence for the hypothesis that a person has the disease, even if the posterior probability might be low. Using the same numbers as above and defining h_1 as the hypothesis 'John has the disease' and h_2 as its negation, the evidence 'positive test result' supports h_1 as:

$$P(e \mid h_1) = .99 \gg .01 = P(e \mid h_2)$$

Likelihoodism is an account of evidence that addresses the question, 'Which of two hypotheses is better supported by the evidence?' That this can lead to counterintuitive results is illustrated with example due to Ian Hacking (Hacking, 1972: 136): 'We capture enemy tanks at random and note the serial numbers on their engines. We know the serial numbers start at 0001. We capture a tank number 2176. How many tanks did the enemy make? On the likelihood analysis, the best supported guess is: 2176'. That is, after capturing that one tank with the number 2176, the hypothesis that the number of tanks the enemy made is just that number is better supported than any other hypothesis. As likelihoods are the only way evidence enters reasoning, this account is subject to the criticism regarding stopping rules in the same way as Bayesianism is.

Naturalism

Naturalism asserts that the best place to look for insights regarding inductive rules is science itself. It is suspicious of substantive philosophical claims of great generality that are made independent of the details of specific scientific practices. Here I will look at two examples: Norton's 'material' theory of induction and the error correction perspective.

Norton's 'Material' theory of induction

All above mentioned families of theories of induction purport to have universal range, that is, they are thought to apply to every domain of inquiry, independently of the more specific facts true within the different domains. In a recent paper John Norton has challenged the feasibility of the general project behind these 'formal' theories of induction as he calls them (Norton, 2003). Unlike deductive schemata of inference such as modus ponens or universal instantiation, which do enjoy universal validity, there is no inductive schema that has not been subject to criticism and counterexample. All examples of inductive rules discussed above are cases in point.

Hence, according to Norton, what licenses the inference is not the *form* of the inductive schema – as that is the same in instances where it works and where it doesn't – but rather particular material facts true of the situation in which the inference is made. Norton shows that all formal inductive schemata work where they do because of such material facts. Thus, inductive inferences derive (Norton, 2003: 648):

> their license from facts. These facts are the material of the inductions; hence it is a 'material theory of induction'. Particular facts in each domain license the inductive inferences admissible in that domain – hence the slogan: 'All induction is local'. My purpose is not to advocate any particular system of inductive inference. Indeed I will suggest that the competition between the well established system is futile. Each can be used along with their attendant maxims on the best use of evidence, as long as we restrict their use to domains in which they are licensed by prevailing facts.

Material facts, according to this theory, license not only that inductive inferences are made from evidence but also what specific types of inferences can be made.

Error correction

Inferences from evidence to a hypothesis are subject to a variety of errors able to invalidate conclusions. As an example that is highly relevant in the context of the social sciences, consider a correlation between two variables X and Y as evidence for a causal hypothesis. That correlation does not entail causation is

well known. If a correlation is nevertheless taken as evidence for a causal claim – and it certainly provides a clue that two variables may be causally related – other sources of correlation must be controlled for if the hypothesis is to be inferred reliably. If the hypothesis of interest is 'X causes Y', one first wants to rule out reverse causation from Y to X as well as common factors that influence both variables. In addition there are numerous non-causal sources of correlation: sampling error, measurement error, nonstationarity and other statistical properties of the variables, mixing, variables that are conditioned on common effects and so on. A hypothesis can be inferred reliably to the extent that these sources of error have been controlled successfully (Reiss, 2008: Chapter 1; cf. Schickore, 2005; Hon, 1989, 1995).

There is no general account of error that is independent of the type of hypothesis, specific domains of science and the purposes to which the hypothesis is put. This is the main difference between this account and eliminative induction. There is no requirement that either the hypothesis of interest or a potential inferential error explain the evidence. A hypothesis about the future value of a variable, for instance, does not explain whatever evidence one might have in its favour, nor does a descriptive hypothesis about, say, the inflation rate, explain why an index number has such and such a value (see sections on Index Numbers and Expert Political Judgement, respectively). The source of information about potential errors in inference lies, rather, in context-specific background knowledge about the domain of investigation.

There are two main problems with naturalism. First, it is hardly a *theory* of induction. Theories in the philosophy of science do not only aim to show what is the common logic behind a scientific practice such as scientific explanation, inference, measurement or experimentation but also to *explain the rationale* behind these practices. Norton's account does neither. He denies that there is a universal logic of induction. The second naturalistic account appeals to vague 'logic of controlling for known errors' but neither account provides a justifying rationale for why a given inferential practice can be expected to work or why it is rational to draw inferences in the way described. These accounts therefore lack normative power. If one asks, say, why a certain methodology such as that of the randomised trial is as successful as it is and one hears that this is due to specific facts about the 'physical probabilities of the randomizer' (Norton, 2003: 655), one hasn't been answered.

Second, the different formal theories differ dramatically in both their informational requirements or inputs as well as their outputs. Bayesianism, say, requires a prior probability and likelihoods and yields a posterior probability. By contrast, the error-statistical approach denies that prior probabilities attach to hypotheses. Naturalism has no resources to inform us about where and when either inference rule can and should be used. This is important as the different rules yield different results *even in cases where the material facts are undisputed* (Steel, 2005a). An appeal to scientific practice isn't informative when scientists themselves are divided about what inferences are licenced by a situation.

Hybrid Theories

Hybrid theories provide resources that not only allow us to classify a piece of information such as an observation or test result as evidence, they also contain rules of inference. These accounts do not simply conjoin a theory of evidence with an inference rule. Rather, the two aspects are parts of an integrated whole. In this section I discuss two such theories, the error-statistical account and Achinstein's theory.

Error Statistics

The error statistical account develops classical statistical testing of Neyman and Pearson into a full-fledged philosophical theory of evidence and induction. As a theory of evidence, it regards an observation as evidence for a hypothesis to the extent that it has been produced by a test procedure that would have made it very unlikely that the observation would have been produced if the hypothesis were false. More precisely (Mayo, 2000: S198; emphasis original): 'Data *e* produced by procedure *T* provides good evidence for hypothesis *H* to the extent that test *T severely passes H* with *e*'.[5] Hypothesis *H* passes a *severe test* with *e* if (i) *e* fits *H* (for a suitable notion of fit or 'distance') and (ii) the test procedure *T* has a very low probability of producing a result that fits *H* as well as (or better than) *e* does, if *H* were false or incorrect.

Thus, the approach requires that hypotheses be subject to a test that is as stringent as a randomised controlled trial (for a detailed discussion, see section on Evidence-Based Policy). A randomised trial eliminates all sources of error in one fell swoop. Hence, it will 'pass' the hypothesis if it is false only for statistical reasons, because of sampling error. This error can, however, be controlled by the procedure's 'error-probabilities'.

There are two error probabilities. Type-I errors consist in rejecting the null hypothesis (usually the hypothesis that there is no treatment effect) when it is in fact true. It is controlled by choosing the significance level of the test. Type-II errors consist in not rejecting the null when it is in fact false. It is controlled by designing the test such that it has high power, which is one minus the probability of a type-II error. Significance level and power aren't entirely independent, however. If sample and effect size are given, fixing the significance level determines power and vice versa. Thus, at a chosen level of significance (and assuming that the effect size cannot be manipulated), the power of the test can only be increased by increasing the sample size.

Error statisticians Deborah Mayo and Aris Spanos add a third error probability to these, that of 'attained power' or 'severity' (Mayo and Spanos, 2006). It is a post-data measure and therefore sensitive to the sample realisation (whereas significance and power are pre-data and independent of the realisation). To measure severity, one must define a value for discrepancy from the null one deems as substantially significant (for instance, a treatment effect size). Severity is then defined as one minus the probability that a test result like the one obtained occurs if the discrepancy is in fact larger.

What we infer from a test about the hypothesis therefore depends on what we deem as scientifically significant. Suppose that a new training programme is under scrutiny. The null hypothesis says that it is ineffective (relative to the current best programme, say). Testing the proposition by statistical means does not by itself allow us to draw an inference. If the test yields an insignificant result (let us say), we cannot simply infer that there is no treatment effect. In addition we have to specify the type of inference we wish to draw in terms of a distance from the null. Then, once the data is in, we can calculate the probability of the test producing data like these if the distance is in fact greater, that is, if there is in fact a (greater) treatment effect.

Intuitively, this makes a lot of sense. If a certain result is produced that is statistically insignificant, it is one thing to conclude 'there is (probably) no effect' and quite another 'there is (probably) no *large* effect'. Accordingly, the severity with which the test passes these two hypotheses differs. The same is of course true when the result is significant. Then, given the result, the larger the discrepancy (i.e. the treatment effect) one wishes to infer from this result, the lower the severity.

Finally, the inference we draw is about the frequency of achieving a certain test result were the test repeated many times, just as in classical statistics. Thus, we do not infer a hypothesis (as in categorical induction) or a degree of belief in a hypothesis (as in Bayesianism) but rather a claim about a probability of a certain test result. That is, the probability claims of the error-statistical approach attach to test procedures, not to the

hypothesis of interest. The confirmation of hypotheses is therefore of a purely qualitative nature.

Construed as a theory of evidence, the error-statistical approach is exceedingly narrow as it can only be used to test statistical hypotheses. To be sure, statistical inference is an important part of research in all areas awash in data. But it is just one part. To infer a causal claim from an experiment we do want to know whether the observed correlation is real or due to chance. But there are many other sources of error that we want to control – measurement error, confounding, non-causal sources of correlations and what have you. The error-statistical approach has no answer to these.[6]

Achinstein's Theory

Peter Achinstein combines a form of explanationism as theory of evidence with a form of Bayesianism as inductive rule. He first distinguishes various concepts of evidence: subjective, ES-, potential and veridical (Achinstein, 2001: Chapter 2). Essentially, an agent has *subjective* evidence *e* for *h* if she believes *e* and takes it as a reason to believe *h*. ES refers to an agent's 'epistemic situation'. In a specific epistemic situation *C*, *e* is *ES-evidence* that *h* if, in *C*, *e* is a good reason to believe *h*. *e* is potential evidence in *h* if it is a good reason to believe *h* simpliciter and *e* is veridical evidence that *h* if *e* is potential evidence that *h* and *h* is true.

Achinstein thinks that veridical and potential evidence are the concepts most relevant for scientific practice, and most of his work is dedicated to explicating those concepts. He defines (Achinstein, 2001: 170):

PE. *e* is potential evidence that *h*, given *b*, [if and[7]] only if

1 P (there is an explanatory connection between *h* and *e* | *e*&*b*) > 1/2
2 *e* and *b* are true
3 *e* does not entail *h*

where *b* signifies background knowledge. By 'explanatory connection' Achinstein means that it is either the cases that the hypothesis explains the evidence, that the evidence explains the hypothesis or that a common factor explains both. This condition is supposed to rule out classical counterexamples to 'high probability' accounts of evidence and confirmation. Achinstein's example (p. 149):

> *h*: Michael Jordan will not become pregnant.
> *e*: Michael Jordan eats Wheaties.
> *b*: Michael Jordan is a male basketball star.

On a simple high probability account, *e* is evidence *h* because the probability that *h* gives *e* is high. Achinstein assumes that in this case *e* and *h* are not explanatorily connected: neither does his eating Wheaties explain that he won't become pregnant nor vice versa, nor is there a common factor that explains both.[8] Eating Wheaties is explanatorily irrelevant for not becoming pregnant.

Achinstein uses the general requirement that *h* and *e* must be explanatorily connected rather than that, say, *h* explain *e*, because causes can provide evidence for effects, effects for causes and joint effects of common causes for each other. Thus, taking a potent medicine can be evidence for relief, relief for taking medicine and the drop in the barometer reading can be evidence for the storm.

To require that there be an explanatory connection between evidence and hypothesis is plausible but too strong. If evidence is to be a mark or a symptom of the truth of a hypothesis it is enough that there be a correlation between the states of affairs hypothesis and evidential statement express, there need not be causal or explanatory relation. A widely discussed case involving a 'spurious correlation' demonstrates this. Elliott Sober describes his case thus (Sober, 1987[1994]: 161–162 [quoted from Sober, 2001: 332]):

> Consider the fact that the sea level in Venice and the cost of bread in Britain have both been on the rise in the past two centuries. Both, let us suppose, have monotonically increased. Imagine that we put this data in the form of a chronological list; for each date, we list the Venetian sea level and the going price of British bread. Because both quantities have increased steadily with time, it is true that higher than average sea levels tend to be associated with higher than average bread prices. The two quantities are very strongly positively correlated.

Now, if there is a strong correlation between the two quantities, we can use, say, the fact that one quantity is very high as evidence for the hypothesis that the other is high as well. But there isn't any explanatory connection between the two. High bread prices do not explain high sea levels, nor do high sea levels explain high bread prices and nor is there a common factor that explains both. Time can be used to predict whether the quantity is high or low but it does not explain why this is so. Or, to take a case due to Jossi Berkovitz (as described by Dan Steel, 2005b: 19): '… imagine two slot machines constructed entirely independently of one another but which, coincidentally enough, have precisely the same initial conditions and internal mechanics'. Here we are facing a brute correlation (or a set of such correlations) that once more has no explanation. And again, we can use the state of one machine to predict – provide evidence for – the state of the other.

That correlations rather than explanations are required as evidentiary relationship is also shown by the reverse case, where two quantities have an explanatory connection without a correlation being induced. A philosophers' stock example regarding the connection between correlation and causation concerns the relation between birth control pills and thrombosis (originally due to Hesslow, 1976). Birth control pills cause thrombosis via one route but they also prevent thrombosis by preventing pregnancies, as pregnancies are themselves a cause of thrombosis. Depending on the actual frequencies, the probability raising and lowering channels might just cancel each other out so that the probability of developing thrombosis is the same whether or not a given woman takes the pill. Knowing that, we should not take facts about oral contraceptives as evidence for hypotheses about the likelihood of contracting thrombosis. Nevertheless, there is an explanatory connection. For instance, the reason for a given occurrence of thrombosis might lie in the woman having taken the pill.

The seemingly arbitrary requirement that the probability of there being an explanatory connection be greater than .5 stems from Achinstein's absolutist concept of evidence. A good reason to believe *h* cannot also be a good reason to believe not-*h*. Hence the probability given the evidence and background knowledge must at least be .5. Further, Achinstein includes the third condition because he does not want evidence and hypothesis to be too 'close' to each other. The drop in the barometer reading is not evidence for the change of the barometer reading.

As inferential rule, Achinstein uses Bayesian updating, which makes him a Bayesian of sorts. The main difference between his account and standard Bayesian is his 'objective epistemic' interpretation of probability (Achinstein, 2001: Chapter 5). Standard Bayesianism interprets probability as degree of belief. Apart from adhering to the axioms of probability theory, there are no constraints on what a subject ought to believe.[9] Achinstein defines probability as 'degree of reasonableness of belief'. It is therefore not a measure of how strongly a person believes in a proposition but rather one of the quality of the reasons for holding a belief. Further, it is not subjective in the sense of being relative to a particular agent. The degree of reasonableness of a certain drug producing relief may be .8 even though no single agent holds this belief.

Apart from this difference in interpreting probability, Achinstein is a Bayesian. In particular, he must assume hypotheses (and evidence) to have prior probabilities, which makes his account vulnerable to the same objection regarding priors as standard Bayesianism.

SOURCES OF EVIDENCE

As indicated in the Introduction, there is an enormous variety of evidence-generating methods or 'sources' of evidence, both across all sciences as well as within a single science. It is impossible to review all the methods used in the social sciences here, or even all those one can find in a single social science. In what follows, I will therefore present a highly selective partial overview. The selection is guided partly by considerations of scientific importance and philosophical interest but partly also by my expertise. I group the methods into three categories: sources of evidence for (a) descriptive claims; (b) explanatory claims; and (c) policy claims.

Descriptive Inference

This type of inference and the associated methods are frequently ignored by philosophers but they are all the more important in social science. Hardly any property that is of interest from a social science point of view is immediately observable. In order to establish facts, even purely descriptive facts about a society, the investigator has to make inferences on the basis of new immediate observations, already established facts and background knowledge. I focus on two examples here: participant observation (used, for instance, in anthropology, communication studies, criminology, social psychology and sociology) and index numbers (used mostly in economics). In a sense, participant observation and index numbers represent the two extremes of the same spectrum. The participant observer is an actor who, by immersing herself in the culture she researches, becomes an expert in that culture and as such makes informed *judgements* about whether this or that fact obtains. When establishing facts by means of index numbers, the aim is to reduce expert judgement to a minimum by standardising procedures. To be sure, measuring quantities such as inflation or unemployment also requires judgements at various points, even when procedures are standardised. For example, a government statistician must judge whether the goods he finds in a chosen supermarket are indeed comparable to the goods chosen previously, and if not, what type of adjustment procedure to use. Similarly, Bureau of Labor surveyors must interpret the responses of households when measuring unemployment.

Participant Observation

A key idea of participant observation is that the researcher occupies a role within the group she observes and its aim, at least when done in cultural anthropology, is to produce an ethnography. Typically, participant observation involves (DeWalt and DeWalt, 2002: 4):

- living in the context for an extended period of time;
- learning and using local language and dialect;
- actively participating in a wide range of daily, routine, and extraordinary activities with people who are full participants in that context;
- using everyday conversation as an interview technique;
- informally observing during leisure activities (hanging out);
- recording observations in field notes (usually organized chronologically); and
- using both tacit and explicit information in analysis and writing.

There are two main forms of the technique: overt and covert participant observation. In the former case, the observed group both knows and permits the researcher to participate and conduct her investigation, which has advantages and disadvantages. Advantages include easier access to the group as a whole and subgroups (if one is allowed to participate!) as well as easier recording of the observations made; the main disadvantage is that as a result of knowing to be observed the group may change its behavioural patterns (the so-called 'observer effect'). Covert participant observation is carried out secretly, without the group's knowledge and permission. Apart from obvious ethical worries, disadvantages include the danger of losing objectivity on the researcher's part and greater difficulties in recording data. The advantages are that access to groups that would not normally allow it can be gained and that there are greater chances of avoiding the observer effect.

A similar trade-off obtains at the level of the degree of involvement of the individual participant observer. One end of the spectrum is occupied by the researcher who 'goes native' never to return from the field. His immersion is complete but just as complete is his loss of objectivity and detachment, and he obviously relinquishes the aim of producing a scientific outcome. At the other extreme are researchers who aim to keep active involvement at a minimum but thereby also forfeit the goal of gaining entry to inside knowledge. One important source of ethical conflict in this area is the question to what extent a researcher should intervene if she finds an observed practice objectionable.

Another problem is that involved research can be intrusive, which raises concerns about the privacy of the observed groups; but there is often no other way to access information of this kind.

A further trade-off besets the description of the observed social practices. Traditionally, social 'facts' used to be reported as if valid for all (places and) times: 'Social group G engages in practice ψ'. After the 'reflective turn', however, reports resembled more what in philosophy is called a protocol sentence: a statement about the observation of a concrete event, along with details about when, where and how the observation was made. This mode of recording facts has been criticised as subjective and even as overly indulgent in personal details of the researcher. On the other hand, it reduces the risk of hasty generalisation and unwarranted inference.

Index Numbers

Index numbers are widely used in economics in order to estimate quantities of interest such as the price level, inequality or wellbeing. Suppose for example we would like to assess whether the price level in the following two-by-two toy economy has increased, decreased or stayed put as illustrated in Table 29.1.

Only if all prices change at the same rate, an unequivocal answer can be given. If not, as in the example, some weighted average must be drawn, and different methods of averaging or

Table 29.1   A two-by-two toy economy

	Price cocoa	Quantity cocoa	Price cloves	Quantity cloves
Year 1	100	3	50	2
Year 2	50	2	100	3

Source: Reiss, 2008: 68

aggregating the raw data give different, sometimes widely disparate, results. Table 29.2 shows five different indices, computed for the above data.

Index numbers are a particularly clear case showing that philosophical theories of evidence have few resources to help with concrete scientific problems concerning evidence. Suppose our index number, say, a Laspeyres index, computes the inflation rate in a region and period to be 3 per cent. Call this our evidence e. Then suppose our hypothesis is that the inflation rate in that region and period is indeed 3 per cent. There is no explanatory connection between the evidence and the hypothesis. The evidence is a mathematical construct, and there is no good sense in which it is caused by (even less so, causes) the quantity of interest. Nor is there a good sense in which observing the evidence should lead us to revise our belief in the hypothesis – unless further assumptions are made (and then it is these further assumptions that justify the inference). There is also no good sense in which the 'test' (computing the index number) passes the hypothesis 'severely'. What is the probability that the index yields this result if 'true' inflation were different from 3 per cent?

Rather, whether or not the datum '3 per cent' is evidence for our hypothesis depends on considerations of the following kind. A Laspeyres index – a *price* index – gives exact

Table 29.2   Different indices

	Arithmetic	Geometric	Harmonic	Laspeyres	Paasche
Rate of change	25%	0%	−20%	−13%	14%

Source: Reiss, 2008: 68

results only if nothing but prices change in the economy. If other things change, for instance traded quantities, the answer is ambiguous unless further assumptions are made. If we assume that consumers respond to price changes by adjusting expenditures (relatively more expensive goods are substituted by relatively cheaper goods), it can be shown that the Laspeyres index *over*states inflation. To get rid of this 'substitution effect' one can compute a so-called 'superlative index', of which the geometric mean between Laspeyres and Paasche index is an example.

Price and quantity changes are not, however, the only changes between two periods. Tastes, environments, the quality of the exchanged goods as well as the range of available goods may change too. In each of these cases decisions must be made about how to adequately incorporate a source of change into the index. The index-number purpose will guide these decisions. For instance, to measure consumers' cost-of-living, it makes sense to include mortgage payments in the budget. By contrast, if the purpose is to test monetary theory, mortgage payments should be excluded as they are directly proportional to interest rates, which play an important explanatory role in that theory.

Explanatory Inference

Accurate descriptive inference is an important goal of social science in its own right. It also plays a preparatory role for further inferences regarding the explanation of social phenomena. There are numerous models of explanation in the social sciences but the causal model is currently the dominant, and I will focus on causal inference here.

Qualitative Comparative Analysis
Above, we have already looked at Mill's methods of causal inference. Squarely in the Humean tradition, Mill understood causation to be a kind of complex regularity. To him, a cause was an insufficient but non-redundant

part of an unnecessary but sufficient, short INUS, condition (this analysis is due to John Mackie, see Mackie, 1974). To define a cause as INUS condition says three things.

1   Any cause is followed by its effect only if certain enabling conditions are present and disturbing factors absent.
2   For any effect, there are many alternative sets of causes that may precede it.
3   The relationship between cause and effect is invariant; that is, when the right causal conditions are in place, the effect must follow and vice versa.

Qualitative comparative analysis (QCA), developed by the sociologist Charles Ragin (see for instance Ragin, 1998) builds on the understanding of cause as INUS condition and makes use of it in drawing causal conclusions from comparing a small number of cases. It has been applied to fields as wide-ranging as sociology, political science, economics and criminology (for a full list of applications, see the bibliographical database at www.compasss.org). QCA aims to overcome the problem of small sample sizes by making the maximum possible number of comparisons among the sampled units.

The method identifies causes of phenomena of interest (e.g. ethnic political mobilisation among Western European minorities) by first arranging the all observed instances (in this case, minorities) in a table and determining whether or not the phenomenon is present. Then a list of factors (in this case, size, linguistic ability, wealth relative to core region and population growth) is constructed and it is noted whether each factor is present or absent. A factor is judged to be a cause whenever it is a member of a group such that that group of factors is always associated with the phenomenon of interest and no subgroup is always associated with the phenomenon – in other words, if it is an INUS condition.

The analysis of causation in terms of INUS conditions is deficient, as Mackie himself understood. In his famous example it is the sounding of the Manchester hooters at 5.00 p.m. that is shown to be an INUS condition for the Londoners to leave work shortly thereafter, but of course the Londoners do not leave the factory *because* of the sound of the Manchester hooters (see Mackie, 1974: 81–84). Nevertheless, Ragin's account demonstrates how regularities of a certain kind can constitute – defeasible – evidence for causal hypotheses. The most likely source of deficiency is the omission of common causes. As Mackie's hooters example shows, omitting a common cause – in his case, it being 5.00 p.m. – leads one to misinterpret what is in fact joint effect as a cause. When causes operate indeterministically – in the social sciences a possibility one should not exclude *a priori* – the full set of causal conditions does not have to be sufficient for its effect, which also makes the application difficult in this area.

Causal Modelling

Whereas QCA is based on (or can be explicated with) the Mill-Mackie analysis of 'cause' as an INUS condition, the various approaches to causal modelling relate to the probabilistic theory of causation, according to which causation is a specific form of correlation or probabilistic dependence.[10] The most popular form of causal modelling is currently that of the so-called Bayesian networks or short Bayes' nets.

A Bayes' net is a directed acyclic graph or DAG with an associated probability distribution. A graph is a set of vertices (representing *variables*) and a set of edges connecting the vertices (representing *relations* among the variables). A graph is directed when all its edges are directed and acyclic when there are no directed cycles. There is assumed to be a joint probability distribution over the variables. If the graph is Markov, it can be used to represent certain kinds of probabilistic independencies among the variables. For instance, in both DAG1 X1 and X3 are independent conditional on X2 and in DAG2 X2 and X3 are independent conditional on X1 as shown in Figure 29.1.

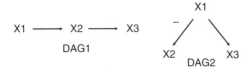

Figure 29.1 Two directed acyclic graphs (DAGs).

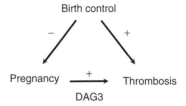

Figure 29.2 A potential counterexample to FC.

By themselves, DAGs are abstract mathematical objects that could be used to merely store probabilistic information efficiently. From the point of view of causal inference, they become interesting when vertices are interpreted as causal factors and edges as causal relations. DAG1, for instance, can be used to represent the causal chain 'obesity causes diabetes causes heart attacks', and DAG2 the common-cause structure 'drop in atmospheric pressure causes change in barometer reading and storm'.

A causal Bayes' net is assumed to satisfy the causal Markov condition (CMC), according to which CMC is a variable X is independent of all other variables in a graph except its effects, conditional on its direct causes.

Thus, we expect heart attacks to be independent of obesity conditional on diabetes and the change in the barometer reading to be independent of storm conditional on atmospheric pressure. The CMC is a generalisation of the screening-off condition found in various probabilistic theories of causation. It provides the link from correlation to causation: if there is a correlation, then it must have a causal explanation.

For causal inference, another condition is essential, *viz.* the Faithfulness condition (FC), according to which FC is a causal graph has only those probabilistic independencies that are entailed by the CMC.

FC says that all variables that are causally related are also correlated. It thus provides the link between correlation and causation in the reverse direction, from causation to correlation: if two variables are causally related, they are also correlated. That this does not always have to be the case is illustrated by

Figure 29.2 (this is the above mentioned example due to Hesslow, 1976).

In the example birth control affects thrombosis via two independent routes: directly and indirectly through pregnancy. If the causal strength of the two routes is identical and therefore the positive direct influence is exactly cancelled by the negative indirect influence, Birth control can be causally related, albeit not correlated with thrombosis.

The CMC, too, is subject to counterexamples. Not all correlations have a causal explanation, especially correlations among social science variables. In many cases, correlations can be induced by certain statistical properties of the time series describing variables, for instance when they are non-stationary (Sober, 1987, 2001; Hoover, 2003; Reiss, 2007). Moreover, common causes do not always screen off their joint effects – for example when causes operate genuinely indeterministically (Cartwright, 1999).

If both CMC and FC can be assumed to hold, simple algorithms can be applied to infer causal relations from statistics. According to the FC, causation entails correlation so all variables that are found to be correlated must be causally connected in one way or another. The CMC can then be used to distinguish direct, indirect and common causal relations. The theory of Bayes' nets provides a variety of algorithms that do precisely that. However, the basic idea is the foundation for all causal inference from statistics.

Process Tracing
Statistical methods of causal inference work only under fairly stringent conditions.

To begin with, they assume a tight link between causation and correlation, an assumption that is not always well warranted in social science research. But even if this very fundamental assumption can be made, statistical methods often fail for purely practical reasons. For example, one can infer causation from correlation – at best – when all common causes of the variables considered are measured. The complexity of the social world often makes this an insurmountable hurdle. Further, the statistical inference from observed frequencies to probabilities is only reliable when the samples are relatively large, and large sample size isn't always guaranteed in social research.

In such cases process tracing may be a viable alternative method of causal inference. Frequently, when a macro social variable causes another, its action is mediated by a more or less continuous process or mechanism. If this is so, there is uncertainty as to whether two specific variables are indeed causally related and social mechanisms are epistemically more readily accessible than relations between macro variables, knowledge about the mediating mechanism can be used for causal inference. In these cases, information about mechanisms provides evidence for hypotheses about causal relations among macro social variables of interest.

Sometimes the stronger claim that *only* knowledge about mechanisms provides sufficient evidence to provide a good reason to believe a causal hypothesis is made (Friedman and Schwartz, 1963: 59):

> However consistent may be the relation between monetary change and economic change, and however strong the evidence for the autonomy of the monetary changes, we shall not be persuaded that the monetary changes are the source of the economic changes unless we can specify in some detail the mechanism that connects the one with the other.

Necessary for successful causal inference or not, there is no doubt that if the mechanism is epistemically more readily accessible than the macro causal relation, learning about a

mechanism connecting two social variables can be a powerful source of evidence for causal claims.

Sociologists call this method of inference 'process tracing'. Daniel Steel describes the method as follows (Steel, 2004: 67): 'Process tracing consists in presenting evidence for the existence of several prevalent social practices that, when linked together produce a chain of causation from one variable to another'. In the example discussed by Steel, the hypothesis at stake is Malinowski's (1935) claim that the possession of many wives was a cause of wealth and influence among Trobriand chiefs. The social practices that constitute evidence for the hypothesis are (a) the custom whereby brothers contribute substantial gifts of yams to the households of their married sisters; and (b) the fact that political endeavours and public projects undertaken by chiefs are financed primarily with yams.

While certainly a useful alternative method of causal inference, process tracing too has serious limitations. And obvious one is that the 'facts' used for process tracing such as those reported in (a) and (b) above have to be substantiated with evidence themselves. Together they are supposed to form a causal chain, so each link is itself causal in nature and must be substantiated with adequate methods. While often at this level other tools are available – for instance, participant observation as in the Malinowski case – there is no guarantee that the problem of inferring causal relations from observations is more easily solvable than at the aggregate or social level. And even in the best case, the results of process tracing are pretty modest. The method can only be used to establish a purely qualitative claim about the causal connection between two variables. It may well be the case that there are other mechanisms that undermine the effect of the process studied. For instance, the correctness of Malinowski's reasoning is not inconsistent with the possession of many wives actually being a prohibitor of wealth and influence because of other mechanisms that are quantitatively stronger than the one established. Moreover, many disagreements in the social sciences are about the quantitative strength of a cause, not whether or not one variable is linked to another 'in one way or another'.

Policy Inference

Whereas descriptive and explanatory inferences are past- and present-regarding, policy inferences concern the future. Social scientists do not only aim to describe and explain: they also try to anticipate future events to facilitate planning, and to prepare policy decisions. In this final section of the overview of methods of evidence generation, I will look at two instances of sources of evidence for policy: expert political judgement and evidence-based policy.

Expert Political Judgement

Every day, countless 'experts' make predictions about political events that may or may not occur some time in the future. The ability to foresee such events, be they the outcome of a national election, the outbreak of a war or the end of a political era, with a reasonable degree of accuracy would be enormously useful for political decision makers, investors and society at large, if it could be achieved.

But sceptics argue that successful prediction is unattainable. There are two types of sceptics: those who deny that the world is predictable and those who deny that humans have the cognitive capacities to make successful predictions. Economic historian and methodologist Deirdre McCloskey belongs to the former group. She argues essentially that successful predictions are self-defeating because people would try to capitalise on and thereby undermine them (McCloskey, 1998: 150–151). Philosophers Michael Bishop and J.D. Trout belong to the latter group. They argue that cognitive limitations such as memory and computing deficiencies as well as psychological phenomena such as overconfidence prevent us from achieving predictive success to the extent that the

nature of the world would allow it (Bishop and Trout, 2005).

A recently published report of over 20 years of research on political experts by Philip Tetlock strikes a balance between these sceptics and meliorists – those who maintain that 'the quest for predictors of good judgment, and ways to improve ourselves, is not quixotic and that there are better and worse ways of thinking that translate into better and worse judgements [regarding future political events]' (Tetlock, 2006: 19). Many of his results confirm the sceptic (Tetlock, 2006: Chapter 2). For example, human experts' subjective probability judgements of outcomes are no better calibrated to the frequencies of these outcomes than those of a dart-throwing (randomising) chimpanzee who assigns an equal probability to all outcomes.[11] Whether the forecaster was an expert in the relevant field made hardly any difference to overall predictive accuracy, nor did education, experience, gender or political orientation. Moreover, statistical models of various degrees of sophistication beat even the best expert.

On the other hand, certain factors did make a difference to some outcomes and relative to some baselines. For instance, while randomising achieves a higher score on calibration, humans beat chimps with respect to discriminating between high and low probability events.[12] Experts perform better than undergraduates on both calibration as well as discrimination scores. Short-term forecasts are more accurate than long-term forecasts.

By far the most informative factor about an expert's judgement is his cognitive style. Tetlock uses Isaiah Berlin's metaphor of hedgehogs and foxes to characterise experts' cognitive style. Hedgehogs are thinkers who know one big thing and try to systematise every fact within the explanatory schema of that one big thing. Foxes know many little things, are sceptical of grand schemes and excel in 'ad hocery'. Foxes outperform hedgehogs on both calibration as well as discrimination and the best come close to some statistical models. Controlling for cognitive style also changes the interpretation of other effects. Thus, while expertise has no across-the-board effect, it is beneficial for foxes and outright harmful for hedgehogs. Foxes also score higher in the long-term than in the short-term while the opposite is true of hedgehogs (Tetlock, 2006: Chapter 3).

The important lesson from Tetlock's study is that there are better and worse experts, and there are ways to tell who is what. Tetlock's results confirm those reported by Bishop and Trout in that even the foxiest experts are outperformed by statistical models. But to the extent that political expertise is likely to maintain an important role in society, we had better know who to trust, how far and with respect to what claims.

Evidence-Based Policy

The evidence-based practice[13] movement can be understood as a reaction to what was perceived as over-reliance on expertise and related sources of knowledge such as folk-lore and tradition. These, in the eyes of proponents of the movement, unreliable guides to practise should be substituted by rigorously established scientific evidence, and many regard the randomised controlled trial (RCT) as the 'gold standard' of evidence. The movement became prominent first in medicine and other fields of health care and policy but is now gaining popularity in social and public policy in the United States and many other countries. RCTs have been conducted to study questions as diverse as the effect of CCTV surveillance on crime, class size on academic achievement, cognitive-behavioural treatment on anti-social behaviour, correctional boot camps on offending and many more.

In a RCT eligible subjects are divided into two groups using a random number generator. The aim of randomisation is to create two groups that are 'exchangeable' from a statistical point of view; that is, identical in all respects relevant for the assessment of the treatment effect. One group is assigned a treatment while the other figures as control group (and either remains untreated, receives

an alternative treatment or a placebo). In a double-blind trial neither the participating subjects nor the treatment administrators know which is the treatment and which the control group. There are also multiple-blind trials in which also the statistician who analyses the data and other researchers are blinded.

RCTs are regarded as the gold standard of evidence in evidence-based practice because they are, if implemented successfully, a highly reliable sources of evidence for causal claims. But there are two catches. The first is indicated by the qualification 'if implemented successfully': RCT results are certain only under highly stringent, and indeed unrealistic conditions. These conditions include that the set of all other factors that affect the outcome are distributed identically between the two groups and that correlations always have a causal explanation (see for instance Cartwright, 2007a). However, randomisation in no way guarantees that treatment and control group are identical with respect to all confounders (see for instance Worrall, 2002), and especially in social-science applications, correlations have a variety of non-causal sources (Reiss, 2007).

The second catch is that the result of a RCT, even if it was implemented successfully, while known with certainty, is of very limited use. What a RCT at best proves is that a treatment has a causal effect *on average* and *in the population studied*. If there is an average causal effect, then the treatment must be effective in at least some individuals but we don't know which. In particular, it is not inconsistent that a treatment should be beneficial on average and yet harmful for some individuals. Further, the RCT result is valid only with respect to the particular arrangement of confounders present in the experiment. It is not informative about the effectiveness of the treatment in populations with a different arrangement of confounding factors.

The latter difficulty has come to be called the 'problem of external validity': if a test result is valid for an experimental population, how do we apply it outside the experiment, 'in the field'? This issue has been taken up in recent philosophy of science and now there exist a variety of approaches to deal with it: based on knowledge of mechanisms (Steel, 2008), on analogy (Guala, forthcoming, 2005) and on causal capacities (Cartwright, 2009). But none of these have the logical stringency of the ideal RCT. Therefore, the certainty associated with testing a policy proposition using RCTs is at least to some extent illusory.

Integrating, Weighing and Aggregating Evidence

A serious problem arises when pieces of evidence tell different stories about the hypothesis at stake. This can happen when, for instance, estimated correlations vary greatly between different studies or when different sources of evidence (e.g. statistical versus mechanistic evidence) give incompatible results. How do we combine such conflicting items of evidence in a way such as to draw reliable inferences regarding a hypothesis? Peter Achinstein discusses the following strategies (Achinstein, 2001: 124):

1 Write a review article that summarises the different studies and results, without attempting to resolve the issue.
2 Choose a single, favourite study from the set and agree with its conclusions.
3 Compute overall averages for relevant statistics across the entire set of studies, independently of the sizes of the sample in each study or the conditions under which the samples were taken.
4 Take a vote. If a majority of the studies favour one conclusion, then that is the conclusion supported by the studies.
5 Employ meta-analysis, which its proponents regard as a much more sophisticated and reliable set of methods than 3 and 4 above.

(1) Obviously doesn't solve the problem. (2) seems arbitrary unless the chosen study is the only one without clearly identifiable methodological flaws. If either several studies are not subject to methodological problems or all studies have some flaws, the question simply reappears. (3) is a less sophisticated version of (5), which will be dealt with in more detail below. (4) again seems arbitrary. What if the best studies support a conclusion different from the majority? This strategy also works at best for simple yes/no results such as whether or not a treatment is effective. Many disagreements, however, are about the size of the effect, not its presence or absence.

Meta-analyses combine research results from a range of studies in a quantitative way. Many meta-analyses identify a common metric of effect size and model it using some form of regression in which the results of the individual studies figure as inputs. Meta-analyses have a variety of advantages over alternatives, including an increase in statistical power (over individual studies) and the ability to control a variety of sources of error (see Hunter and Schmidt, 2004: Chapter 2). But they also come with serious drawbacks and limitations.

There are two obvious limitations. The first is that meta-analyses can only combine *statistical* evidence. The important problem of integrating evidence from different sources is not addressed. Second, the method requires that the individual studies deal with the same hypothesis. It is frequently not clear, however, what that amounts to.

But even if one restricts coverage to statistical evidence and is able to formulate reasonable inclusion criteria, meta-analysis is subject to criticisms. The most important of these is that the method assumes that differences between the studies are due to statistical error alone whereas in fact they often arise systematically. If, say, one study shows a positive treatment effect and another shows a negative effect or none, this may be due to differences in the causal structures characterising the two populations. Averaging over the two studies masks these differences and treats the samples as if drawn from one underlying population. This way important information is lost. Similar considerations apply to the choice of measurements used and other aspects of the study design.

In sum, to the extent that individual studies are biased for statistical reasons (for instance, because of sampling error), meta-analyses are a powerful tool to reduce these types of bias. They do not, however, eliminate the need for context-sensitive judgements about the quality of the individual studies entering the analysis.

EVIDENCE FOR USE

All scientific methods are associated with specific types of hypotheses the researcher is entitled to infer by the evidence generated by them. Often, there is a kind of trade-off: the more reliable the method (that is, the more secure the inference based on the evidence produced by it), the narrower the range of hypotheses that can be supported by that method. Some methods, such as the RCT, 'clinch' their results: under a suitable set of background assumptions, the evidence deductively entails the hypothesis. But the epistemic certainty is bought at a cost: the situations of which the assumptions are likely to be true are very rare. Other methods, such as participant observation only 'vouch' for their results: the evidence makes the hypothesis more likely without proving it. These methods tend to be more broadly applicable but there always remain reasons to believe that the conclusion is false (for the clincher/voucher dichotomy, see Cartwright, 2007b).

The value of knowing a hypothesis is constrained by the certainty with which it is known but also by the value of the ways in which it can be put to use. Philosophers in the analytic tradition have tended to be impressed by the paradigm of 'exact science' and consequently focused on the former at the expense of the latter. But for many important applications, there simply are no techniques that produce evidence of the desired quality.

Cartwright (2006) argues that philosophers, rather than develop methods with certain epistemologically desirable characteristics, should instead start from scientifically – and politically – desired uses and work on methods designed to target hypotheses knowledge of which is advantageous in their light. At the core of her project is a kind of contextualism regarding evidence (Cartwright, 2006: 983): 'What justifies a claim depends on what we are going to do with that claim, and evidence for one use may provide no support for others'. 'Evidence for use' is a research project that urges philosophers and methodologists to pay closer attention to the demands of scientific practice and social utility. Arguably, the foundational debates in the social sciences can profit from such a reorientation too. Much philosophical effort is spent, perhaps needlessly, on debating whether social science is real science, whether one should or shouldn't study the social world with essentially the same methods as the natural world, how to effectively separate 'facts' and 'values', whether there is such a thing as society or rather a mere heap of individuals – while significant social issues remain unnoticed by the philosophers claiming to be experts in these debates.

NOTES

1 These three inferences allude to enumerative induction, Bayesianism and the error-statistical approach, respectively. See below for detailed descriptions.

2 If f and φ are exchanged, the same method is used to argue that f is an effect of φ.

3 Once more, if f and φ are exchanged, the same method is used to argue that f is an effect of φ.

4 This interpretation was at the heart of Carnap's 1950 influential theory of evidence.

5 Mayo inserts a footnote here saying that she prefers to phrase this in terms of data e being a 'good indication' of H.

6 See also Hon (1998) and Carrier (2001) for similar criticisms. It should be noted, however, that error statisticians *claim* to have a philosophy of evidence and induction of entirely general scope: see Mayo (1997, 2000, 2004); Mayo and Spanos (2004, 2006).

7 Achinstein first defines only a necessary condition but later qualifies: 'the conditions in (PE) are proposed as both necessary and sufficient' (2001).

8 'Being male' might explain Wheaties eating behaviour in the same sense that gender explains other preferences. Achinstein assumes that this isn't the case here.

9 Though many Bayesians require satisfaction of the so-called 'principal principle', which says that if an agent knows the physical probability of an outcome, his degree of belief should be the same. The term is due to David Lewis (1980).

10 Some authors, in the methodological literature most notably Kevin Hoover (2003) distinguish the two notions. With most other philosophers I will glance over the differences here (for a discussion, see Reiss, 2007).

11 What is meant by 'calibrated' here is that the subjective probability judgements reflect the objective frequencies of those types of events. For example, those events assigned a probability of 10 per cent should actually happen in 10 per cent of the cases.

12 Perfect discrimination is achieved when all those events that obtain are predicted as 'certain' and all those that do not obtain as 'impossible'.

13 With 'evidence-based practice' I refer to evidence-based movements in all branches of knowledge creation and policy such as medicine, health care and policy as well as management, social and public policy. 'Evidence-based policy' is narrower, covering only the latter two fields. To my knowledge, there is no standardised terminology in this area.

REFERENCES

Achinstein, P. (2001) *The Book of Evidence*. Oxford: Oxford University Press.

Bird, A. (2007) 'Inference to the only explanation', *Philosophy and Phenomenological Research*, 74(2): 424–432.

Bishop, M. and J.D. Trout (2005) *Epistemology and the Psychology of Human Judgment*. Oxford: Oxford University Press.

Carnap, R. (1950) *Logical Foundations of Probability*. Chicago, IL: University of Chicago Press.

Carrier, M. (2001) 'Critical notice: Error and the growth of experimental knowledge', *International Studies in the Philosophy of Science*, 15(1): 93–98.

Cartwright, N. (1999) *The Dappled World*. Cambridge: Cambridge University Press.

Cartwright, N. (2007a) 'Are RCTs the gold standard?', *BioSocieties*, 2(2): 11–20.

Cartwright, N. (2007b) *Hunting Causes and Using Them*. Cambridge: Cambridge University Press.

Cartwright, N. (2009) 'Evidence-based policy: What's to be done about relevance', *Philosophical Studies*, 143(1): 127–136.

DeWalt, K. and B. DeWalt (2002) *Participant Observation: A Guide for Fieldworkers*. Walnut Creek, CA: AltaMira Press.

Friedman, M. and A. Schwartz (1963) 'Money and business cycles', *Review of Economics and Statistics*, 45(1, Part 2, Supplement): 32–64.

Guala, F. (2005) *The Methodology of Experimental Economics*. Cambridge: Cambridge University Press.

Guala, F. (forthcoming) 'Extrapolation Without Process Tracing', *Philosophy of Science*, PSA 2008.

Hacking, I. (1965) *The Logic of Statistical Inference*. Cambridge: Cambridge University Press.

Hacking, I. (1972) 'Likelihood', *British Journal for the Philosophy of Science*, 23: 132–137.

Harman, G. (1965) 'Inference to the best explanation', *Philosophical Review*, 74(1): 88–95.

Hempel, C. (1945) 'Studies in the logic of confirmation (I)', *Mind*, 54(213): 1–26.

Hempel, C. (1965) *Aspects of Scientific Explanation and Other Essays in the Philosophy of Science*. New York, NY: Free Press.

Hesslow, G. (1976) 'Discussion: Two notes on the probabilistic approach to causality', *Philosophy of Science*, 43: 290–292.

Hon, G. (1989) 'Towards a typology of experimental errors: An epistemological view', *Studies in History and Philosophy of Science*, 20: 469–504.

Hon, G. (1995) 'Is the identiciation of experimental error contextually dependent? The case of Kaufmann's experiment and its varied reception', in J. Buchwald (ed.) *Scientific Practice: Theories and Stories of Doing Physics*. Chicago, IL: University of Chicago Press. pp. 170–223.

Hon, G. (1998) 'Exploiting errors', *International Studies in the Philosophy of Science*, 29(3): 465–479.

Hoover, K. (2003) 'Nonstationary time-series, cointegration, and the principle of the common cause', *British Journal for the Philosophy of Science*, 54: 527–551.

Howson, C. and P. Urbach (1993) *Scientific Reasoning: The Bayesian Approach*. 2nd edn. Chicago, IL: Open Court.

Hunter, J. and F. Schmidt (2004) *Methods of Meta-Analysis: Correcting Error and Bias in Research Findings*. Thousand Oaks, CA: Sage.

Kincaid, H. (2007) 'Contextualist morals and science', in H. Kincaid, J. Dupré and A. Wylie (eds) *Value-Free Science? Ideals and Illusions*. Oxford: Oxford University Press. pp. 218–238.

Klein, J. (2003) 'Francis Bacon', *Stanford Encyclopedia of Philosophy (Spring 2009)* E. Zalta (ed.), URL = < http://plato.stanford.edu/archives/spr2009/entries/francis-bacon/> (accessed 23 November 2009) .

Lewis, D. (1980) 'A subjectivist's guide to objective chance', R. Jeffrey (ed.) *Studies in Inductive Logic and Probability*. Berkeley and Los Angeles: University of California Press. pp. II.

Lipton, P. (2004) *Inference to the Best Explanation*. 2nd edn. London: Routledge.

Mackie, J. (1974) *The Cement of the Universe: A Study of Causation*. Oxford: Oxford University Press.

Malinowski, B. (1935) *Coral Gardens and Their Magic*. New York, NY: American Book Co.

Mayo, D. (1996) *Error and the Growth of Experimental Knowledge*. Chicago: University of Chicago Press.

Mayo, D. (1997) 'Error statistics and learning from error: Making a virtue of necessity', *Philosophy of Science*, 64(PSA 1996): S195–212.

Mayo, D. (2000) 'Experimental practice and an error statistical account of evidence', *Philosophy of Science*, 67(Proceedings): S193–207.

Mayo, D. (2004) 'An error-statistical philosophy of evidence', in M. Taper and S. Lele (eds) *The Nature of Scientific Evidence*. Chicago, IL: University of Chicago Press. pp. 79–96.

Mayo, D. and A. Spanos (2004) 'Methodology in practice: Statistical misspecification testing', *Philosophy of Science*, 71: 1007–1025.

Mayo, D. and A. Spanos (2006) 'Severe testing as a basic concept in a Neyman–Pearson philosophy of induction', *British Journal for the Philosophy of Science*, 57: 323–357.

McCloskey, D. (1998) *The Rhetoric of Economics*. 2nd edn. Madison, WN: University of Wisconsin Press.

Mill, J. S. (1843 [1874]) *A System of Logic*. New York, NY: Harper.

Norton, J. (2003) 'A material theory of induction', *Philosophy of Science*, 70(4): 647–670.

Norton, J. (2008) 'Must evidence underdetermine theory?', in M. Carrier, D. Howard and J. Kourany (eds) *The Challenge of the Social and the Pressure of Practice*. Pittsburgh, PA: Pittsburgh University Press. pp. 17–44.

Okasha, S. (2000) 'Van Fraassen's critique of inference to the best explanation', *Studies in the History and Philosophy of Science*, 34(4): 691–710.

Quine, W.v.O. (1969) 'Natural kinds', in W.v.O. Quine (ed.) *Ontological Relativity and Other Essays*. New York, NY: Columbia University Press. pp. 114–138.

Ragin, C. (1998) 'The logic of quality comparative analysis', *International Review of Social History*, 43(Supplement): 105–124.

Reiss, J. (2007) 'Time series, nonsense correlations and the principle of the common cause', in F. Russo and J. Williamson (eds) *Causality and Probability in the Sciences*. London: College Publications. pp. 179–196.

Reiss, J. (2008) *Error in Economics: Towards a More Evidence-Based Methodology*. London: Routledge.

Salmon, W. (1975) 'Confirmation and relevance', G. Maxwell and R. Anderson (eds) *Induction, Probability, and Confirmation*. Don Mills, ON: Burns & Maceachern. VI: 3–36.

Schickore, J. (2005) '"Through thousands of errors we reach the truth" – but how? On the epistemic roles of error in scientific practice', *Studies in History and Philosophy of Science*, 36: 539–556.

Scriven, M. (1966) 'Causes, connections and conditions in history', in W. Dray (ed.) *Philosophical Analysis and History*. New York, NY: Harper and Row. pp. 238–264.

Scriven, M. (2008) 'A summative evaluation of RCT methodology and an alternative approach to causal research', *Journal of MultiDisciplinary Evaluation*, 5(9): 11–24.

Sober, E. (1987[1994]) 'The principle of the common cause', in *From a Biological Point of View*. Cambridge: Cambridge University Press. pp. 158–174.

Sober, E. (2001) 'Venetian sea levels, British bread prices, and the principle of the common cause', *British Journal for the Philosophy of Science*, 52: 331–346.

Steel, D. (2004) 'Social mechanisms and causal inference', *Philosophy of the Social Sciences*, 34(1): 55–78.

Steel, D. (2005a) 'The facts of the matter: A discussion of Norton's material theory of induction', *Philosophy of Science*, 72: 188–197.

Steel, D. (2005b) 'Indeterminism and the causal Markov condition', *British Journal for the Philosophy of Science*, 56: 3–26.

Steel, D. (2008) *Across the Boundaries: Extrapolation in Biology and Social Science*. Oxford: Oxford University Press.

Sugden, R. (2000) 'Credible worlds: The status of theoretical models in economics', *Journal of Economic Methodology*, 7(1): 1–31.

Tetlock, P. (2006) *Expert Political Judgment: How Good Is It? How Can We Know?* Princeton: Princeton University Press.

van Fraassen, B. (1985) *Laws and Symmetry*. Oxford: Oxford University Press.

Worrall, J. (2002) 'What evidence in evidence-based medicine', *Philosophy of Science*, 69: S316–330.

30

Experiments

Francesco Guala

INTRODUCTION

While laboratory experiments are widely considered a powerful method of investigation in the natural sciences, the social sciences seem to be stuck at a pre-Galilean stage of development, where the epistemic advantages and limitations of the experimental method are still controversial. The landscape, to be sure, is variegated: whereas in some disciplines, like economics, experimentation has made a breakthrough, in others, like political science, it is gaining a foothold with difficulty.[1] Meanwhile, laboratory research is still considered marginal and is used only rarely by sociologists and anthropologists.

Accounting for these differences would require an inquiry into the history of the various branches of the social sciences that goes well beyond the scope of this chapter. One claim, however, is true pretty much across the board: in spite of its controversial status within the social science, experimentation has always exerted an influence from the *outside*, that is, from those disciplines that use it regularly for the generation of scientific knowledge. The most important influence has not come from the natural sciences, though, but from *psychology*.

From a methodological point of view, experimental psychology had reached a high level of stability by the middle of the twentieth century, and had developed a set of tools that could be easily exported and applied in neighbour disciplines.[2] Given the affinity of their subject matter, it was more natural for social scientists to borrow methodological tools from psychologists than from, say, nuclear physicists. For the same reason it was easier for single experimental results to cross the disciplinary boundaries and be transferred from psychology to the social sciences. So quite paradoxically many social scientists have relied in their work on psychological findings produced using a methodology that was not highly regarded in their discipline.

The examples that will be discussed in this chapter are quite typical, in this respect. The first one, the obedience experiments designed and conducted by Stanley Milgram in the early 1970s, is a study of social psychology that has exerted a huge influence on sociological debates and theorising. The second example, the Ultimatum Game experiments that are now routinely used throughout the social sciences, is a direct offspring of the contamination between economic theory and the psychology of decision making that took place in the 1970s and 1980s.

These examples have been selected mainly for illustrative purposes, to highlight the remarkable uniformity, at the methodological level, that holds across the experimental branches of the various social sciences. In spite of different goals and theoretical motivations, laboratory experiments share a hard core of design principles aimed at supporting a special kind of inferences and securing a particular sort of scientific knowledge. A large part of this chapter will be devoted to illustrating what this knowledge and inferences are, and how the design principles can help in achieving these goals. Finally, I shall outline the most pressing methodological challenges faced by experimental scientists, and discuss some solutions that have been proposed in the philosophical and scientific literature.

A proviso is required before I start: I will devote this chapter entirely to laboratory experiments performed in controlled conditions. These are not the only experiments performed by social scientists. So-called 'quasi-experiments', 'field experiments', 'natural experiments' and 'policy experiments' are widely used and – space permitting – would deserve an equally detailed methodological examination. However, to cope with the limits of space I have decided to focus on controlled experiments for two main reasons: understanding controlled experimentation is the necessary preliminary step for understanding the other forms of less tightly controlled experimentation. The very concepts of 'quasi-experiment', 'field experiment' and so forth, are defined in relation to the perfectly controlled experiment. Once the latter is understood, the virtues and limitations of other forms of investigation are relatively easy to articulate. Second, while quasi- and natural experiments have a long history and are relatively uncontroversial in social science, the rise of laboratory science has been fraught with many obstacles and was opposed by sceptical challenges of various kinds. These challenges provide a particularly interesting arena for philosophers and methodologists interested in the improvement of social scientific research.

Philosophical critiques of laboratory experimentation tend to follow a standard argumentative pattern. Typically some features of social reality are highlighted that distinguish it sharply from natural reality. Thus, for example, Roy Bhaskar in a well known essay states that 'the objects of social inquiry [...] only ever manifest themselves in open systems' (1979: 45). According to an editorial in *The Economist*, the difference is that 'economics yields no natural laws or universal constants' (Economics Focus, 1999: 96) – and so on and so forth. The second step consists in claiming that such features impede a fruitful application of the experimental method for the production of social scientific knowledge: the experimental method requires full control of disturbing factors ('closed systems', in critical realist jargon), or the existence of laws of nature that hold both within and outside the laboratory walls. The argument then concludes by stating the futility – or even the impossibility – of laboratory experimentation in the social sciences.

Such arguments are unimpressive, for a number of reasons. To begin with, they usually betray an outdated and unrealistic conception of the methodology of the natural sciences. It is by now widely accepted, for example, that so-called laws of nature play a marginal role in many disciplines, such as biology, where the experimental method is routinely and fruitfully used. Second, these arguments often rely on ontological assumptions (about human intentionality and free will, for example) that are as controversial as the conclusions they are meant to support. But finally, and most importantly, philosophical sceptics often turn out to be refuted by the development of science itself. For example it has become extremely difficult to keep arguing that economic experiments are impossible or futile, now that experimenters have received a Nobel Prize. As in other historical cases (e.g. the debates on the possibility of pure void, or on the interpretation of the infinitesimal calculus) scientific progress makes philosophers look in retrospect like conservative complainers who fail to see what new methodological tools can deliver. To avoid that fate, we should better start from science itself, and simply see how far it can take us. The next two sections will be entirely devoted to that.

MILGRAM'S OBEDIENCE EXPERIMENTS

How does a laboratory experiment look in the social sciences? Although the stereotype of the physicist or biologist in a white coat is well entrenched in the public perception of science, most people have difficulties imagining a laboratory experiment in sociology or economic science. For this reason, it is useful to describe a couple of examples that will inform our methodological discussion in later sections of the chapter. The first example is an undisputed classic of experimental social science, and perhaps one of the greatest scientific experiments of all times.

In *Obedience to Authority*, Stanley Milgram (1974) reports a series of studies of people's propensity to follow orders that violate core moral principles. The structure of Milgram's experiments is quite simple. Experimental subjects were recruited by means of an advert requesting volunteers for an 'experiment on learning'. Upon arrival at the laboratory, each volunteer was paired with an actor pretending to be a subject, and briefed by the experimenter. Both the naïve subject and the confederate were told that they were to participate in a scientific study of the effect of negative incentives on learning. One of them was selected randomly to be the 'learner', and the other the 'teacher' in the experiment. The selection procedure, however, was rigged so that the naïve subject would always end up in the teacher's role.

The actor/learner was tied to a chair and connected to an electric circuit, while the subject/teacher would sit in front of a control panel. The naïve subject was instructed to read a series of pairs of words; then, he/she would read the first word from one of these pairs, followed by a list of four other words, which included the one that was originally matched with it. For example, the subject would read:

blue box, nice day, wild duck, (etc.)

Followed by

blue:
sky, ink, box, lamp.

The learner at this point was asked to choose the word that was originally matched with 'blue' ('box', in this case). If the learner made a mistake the subject was instructed to punish using an electric shock. The charges were initially supposed to be quite mild (15 volt, labelled on the control panel as 'slight shock') but increased step by step as the learner made more mistakes, until they reached the maximum level of 450 volt (labelled as 'danger: severe shock'). The actor in fact did not receive the shocks, but nevertheless displayed increasing signs of discomfort and pain. If the experiment reached the highest shock levels for example he would scream, asked to be released, and refused to cooperate with the experiment.

The reactions of the subject/teacher were the main experimental variable under study. Whenever the naïve subject asked to interrupt the experiment, the experimenter would reply with a series of standardised sentences, such as 'Please continue the experiment', 'It is absolutely essential that the experiment is carried on', and the like. At the fifth consecutive refusal to continue, the experiment would terminate, and the subject would be fully debriefed about the true nature and aim of the study.

In his baseline condition, where teacher and learner sat in different rooms, Milgram observed that the majority of participants went all the way to administering the maximum shock level. Many subjects did so in spite of internal conflict and psychological distress, while others seemed to follow the experimental procedures rather unproblematically. Because of the psychological strain inflicted on some of the participants, it would be impossible today to run experiments of this kind. Milgram's footage of the experimental sessions, however, is one of the most vivid documents of the power of social scientific research, and is still widely used for teaching purposes.

THE ULTIMATUM GAME

My second specimen comes from a rather different area of research – a subfield of experimental economics devoted to the investigation of bargaining behaviour. Imagine you have just been given $10. The sum will have to be shared with an anonymous, invisible partner, and you will have to agree with her on how to divide it. The room for discussion is almost inexistent: you (the 'Proposer') will only be able to offer one division of the cake and your partner (the 'Responder') will only be able to accept or reject it. If she rejects it, you will both lose the opportunity of sharing the $10; if she accepts, you will both walk out with your share, as determined by the proposed division.

This is essentially the strategic situation known as the Ultimatum Game. The Ultimatum Game was first designed and run by a group of German experimental economists led by Werner Güth in the early 1980s (Güth et al., 1982). Güth and colleagues intended to investigate sequential bargaining, and chose the Ultimatum Game because it is the simplest possible sequential bargaining problem that one can conceive of. Bargaining is customarily represented in economic theory as a sharing problem, where the surplus from exchanging two goods has to be allocated among the parties. The $10 in the Ultimatum Game stands for this surplus. Simplicity was sought to minimise the cognitive costs of computation. It is well known in fact that people struggle when they have to analyse complex dynamic games. In the Ultimatum Game no one can fail to realise that the game will be over after the Responder's move, so the noise in the data due to misunderstandings of the decision situation should be minimal.

According to standard game theory, Proposers should offer close to nothing and Responders should accept.[3] The idea is that Responders face a seemingly trivial decision problem: either get nothing or get whatever Proposers have offered. Let us suppose that the minimum amount that can be offered is $1. One dollar is better than nothing, so Responders should accept. Proposers know this, and thus should offer $1. Under common knowledge of the game and of rationality, the $1/9 split is the only equilibrium of the Ultimatum Game.[4]

In their first study, Güth et al. found that Proposers offer on average 35 per cent of the cake. There was a substantial mode at 50 per cent and very few rejections by Responders (about 10 per cent). When the game was repeated a week later ('experienced players' condition) the average offer went down to 31 per cent. The mode at 50 per cent disappeared, with most offers lying in the range of 20 to 30 per cent. There were also more rejections with repetition (about 30 per cent). These results have since been replicated several times, and constitute what is sometimes called the 'Ultimatum Game anomaly'.

THE POLITICS OF EXPERIMENTATION

Over the last two decades Ultimatum Games have stirred a heated debate. Ultimatum data, to begin with, seem to refute one of the few solid planks of theoretical social science: the model of selfish rationality that is at the core of much economics, political science and even theoretical biology and anthropology. Against standard rational choice theory, experimental data seem to vindicate the folk intuition that human behaviour is heavily influenced by social factors and often driven by other-regarding motives.[5] For this reason, the Ultimatum Game has become an important investigative tool in the die-hard, trans-disciplinary debate on human morality (Gintis et al., 2005).

Milgram's obedience experiments raised a huge controversy too. They were called 'obnoxious' and 'nasty' (Harré, 1979: 109), and the results 'quite simply a delusion' (Mixon, 1989: 40).[6] At the heart of the debate were issues of individual responsibility and determinism that call into question the experimental method itself, for Milgram's work illustrated in a vivid fashion how absolutely normal people can easily be induced to engage in utterly immoral actions. The experimental method itself is based on the assumption that such manipulation of behaviour is possible. Laboratory science aims at *control*, and the control of human beings is obviously a politically charged issue.

At the level of metaphysics, the experimental method seems to clash with widely held beliefs in free will and individual agency. According to folk ontology human beings differ from atoms and molecules in that their behaviour does not obey strict laws of nature. And yet, as any experimenter knows, *human behaviour is highly predictable*. Of course the behaviour of a single, specific individual may be hard to predict exactly. But the behaviour of aggregates (even relatively small groups) follows very systematic patterns, in some circumstances. The circumstances are important: predictability often depends on the creation of rather precise choice situations, and much experimental work is aimed at discovering what these situations are.

None of these qualifications, however, constitutes a major difference with respect to experimentation in the natural sciences. The average behaviour of an aggregate (of, say, particles) is always easier to predict than the behaviour of each constituent. And outside well specified initial and boundary conditions, the behaviour of physical particles may be as unpredictable as the choices of human beings. Since folk ontology in this case (as in many others) is misleading, we had better set it aside and concentrate on the actual practices of experimental scientists. As we shall see later, there are much better explanations of the greater success of experimental scientists in the natural, compared to the social

sciences. These explanations have little to do with the ontology, and much more with the *politics* of social scientific research. To put it briefly, there are things that we do not *want to do* with human beings, which prevent us from exploiting the full power of the method of experimental control.

THE GOALS OF EXPERIMENT

But what is this method, exactly? Philosophical studies of experimental science have been surprisingly sparse until recently. Philosophers of science have for a long time endorsed a theory-centred view of scientific knowledge, according to which what we know is mostly encapsulated in our (best) theories. Under the influence of logical positivism in the twentieth century they came to represent even experimental data as sets of *linguistic reports* of perceptual experience. As Karl Popper puts it in an often-quoted passage, 'theory dominates the experimental work from its initial planning up to its finishing touches in the laboratory' (1934: 107).

During the 1980s, however, a new generation of studies of experimental practice have challenged the theory-dominated approach.[7] One of the novel insights provided by this literature concerned the relative independence between theoretical and experimental knowledge. Historians and philosophers noticed that a major goal of laboratory science is the discovery, replication, and measurement of *experimental phenomena*. A 'phenomenon' in scientific jargon is an interesting regularity observed either in the field or in a controlled setting. It usually cannot be directly observed, but rather requires some inference from 'noisy' data (Bogen and Woodward, 1988). Finally, and importantly, it displays a remarkable stability across changes in theoretical paradigms.

Experimental phenomena are often surprising. Sometimes they violate the predictions of an established scientific theory, as in the case of the Ultimatum Game. Sometimes they contradict our commonsensical intuitions about how people should behave in situations of a certain kind. Milgram for instance expected that the majority of his subjects would quit the experiment relatively early on. But this is not what he observed. In his baseline condition, where teacher and learner sat in different rooms, 65 per cent of subjects administered the maximum level of punishment (450 volt). Milgram was so surprised that he came to question his own intuitions. In order to test them, he acquired the habit of surveying the audiences of his lectures and seminars by asking them to predict when *they* would interrupt the experiment, if they were in the role of the teacher. Everyone – including professional psychologists – predicted that they would never reach the level of 450 volt, contrary to what the evidence clearly showed. Most people indicated break-off points that were widely unrealistic, compared to the behaviour observed in the laboratory.

The observation of a surprising phenomenon, however, is just the beginning of an experimental programme. Most experimental work is devoted to investigating the *robustness* and *replicability* of phenomena in laboratory conditions. And eventually, social scientists hope that the phenomenon observed in the lab will teach them something about social behaviour and institutions *outside* the laboratory walls. To understand how this long journey takes place, and how laboratory experiments can contribute to our knowledge of the social world, we need to dig deeper in their methodological and logical structure. The logic of Milgram's experiment is summarised in an important passage of his book:

> This laboratory situation gives us a framework in which to study the subject's reactions to the principal conflict of the experiment. [...] this conflict is between the experimenter's demands that he continue to administer the electric shock and the learner's demands, which become increasingly insistent, that the experiment be stopped. The crux of the study is to vary systematically the factors believed to alter the degree of obedience to the experimental commands and to learn under what

condition submission to authority is most probable and under what conditions defiance is brought to the fore.

> What the experimental situation does is to condense the elements present when obedience occurs in the larger world such that the essential ingredients are brought into a relatively narrow arena where they are open to scientific scrutiny. The power of the situation derives from the fact that we are able to see, and the subject can experience, the concurrent operation of antagonistic forces that in the larger world rarely impinge on him at the identical instant. (Milgram, 1974: 27)

Let us begin from the end of this long quotation. Milgram intended to investigate a psychological mechanism that is of great importance for the functioning of our societies. Prima facie, he took the existence of obedience in the 'real world' for granted. Like many social psychologists and social scientists of his generation, Milgram was particularly concerned about the abhorrent aspects of obedience – in particular how it can lead one to commit crimes against harmless individuals. The background of the experiments, as Milgram makes clear in his book, are the debates on the 'banality of evil' sparked by Hannah Arendt's (1963) essay on Eichmann, and the then budding research on the social organisation of the Holocaust. As a scientist, Milgram could not be satisfied by explanations that appealed to the abnormal personalities of Nazi leaders. The discovery of the My Lai massacre in 1972 cast even more serious doubts on this type of explanation, suggesting that absolutely ordinary people can engage in appalling crimes if put in the 'appropriate' social conditions (cf. Milgram, 1974: 180–189).[8]

The method of controlled experimentation allows pursuing this line of investigation in especially favourable conditions. In the quoted paragraphs Milgram highlights two important advantages: (1) in the laboratory the experimenter can create a situation of conflict, where individuals are pulled in opposite directions by contrasting motives; and (2) the conditions can be varied systematically so as to discover which factors promote or hinder obedience to authority. The first point is crucial for *measurement*, while the latter is functional to the discovery of *causal relations* among variables.

MEASUREMENT

Milgram's measurement exploits a conflict that has been artificially set up by the experimenter, 'between the experimenter's demands that he [the subject] continue to administer the electric shock and the learner's demands, which become increasingly insistent, that the experiment be stopped' (1974: 27). This sort of conflict is crucial for measurement. Intuitively, we want to avoid situations in which subjects have a unique incentive to behave in a certain manner, for in this case we shall always observe the same behaviour no matter what (plus or minus random error). We want instead to create a situation where two opposite forces are set against each other, and where it is possible to manipulate the strength of each one independently.

The logic of the Ultimatum Game is very similar. Although it was first devised for testing a theory, since the early 1990s the Ultimatum Game has been used primarily as a measurement device. The Ultimatum Game belongs to the broad class of 'mixed motives' games, in which players face two seemingly conflicting incentives. In the Prisoner's Dilemma, for example (probably the most famous game of this kind) each player knows that it is in his/her narrow interest to defect, but also that it is in everybody's interest to cooperate. In the Ultimatum Game, the Responder has an incentive to take whatever is offered, but also experiences an impulse to punish unfair offers; similarly, the Proposer must take into account both fairness and self-interest in formulating the 'best' offer. It is in virtue of this conflict that the Ultimatum Game can be used as an effective measurement device.

The first application of this sort can be found in an important article by an international group of game theorists led by Alvin Roth. Roth and colleagues (1991) ran Ultimatum experiments in four different countries (USA, Japan, Yugoslavia and Israel). They found significant differences in behaviour: Japanese and Israeli Proposers tend to make lower offers (mode at 40 per cent) than Americans and Slovenians but, interestingly, unfair offers in Tokyo and Jerusalem are as likely to be accepted as the 50/50 splits offered in Pittsburgh and Lubljana.[9]

For an analogy, consider the working of a thermometer: unless the expansion of mercury encounters some resistance, it will simply fill all the volume in the glass tube. It is by keeping the resistance fixed and by varying the level of heat that a useful measure of the temperature is obtained. In Milgram's case, the main measure of obedience is given by the level of (fake) electric shocks administered during each session. The Ultimatum Game, similarly, can provide a measure of fairness only insofar as the latter is counterbalanced by individuals' tendency towards self-interest.

CAUSAL INFERENCE

Measurement in social science is rarely aimed at the determination of constants of nature that hold universally across different contexts, but rather at the discovery and quantitative testing of causal hypotheses. In *Obedience to Authority*, Milgram reports measurements made in a 'baseline' condition together with those made in eighteen other conditions or *treatments*, in which various elements of the design have been varied one at a time. The variations operated by Milgram include: distance between teacher and learner, voice feedback, physical touch, personality and identity of the experimenter, gender, learner's contract, institutional context, freedom to choose shock level, effect of contradictory commands, putting the experimenter in the role of victim, rebellion of peer teachers, among others. Similarly, many variations have been tried on the basic version of the Ultimatum Game: levels of anonymity, information about others' payoffs, physical proximity, group identity, property rights, effort and several other variables have been manipulated to identify the factors that may hinder or foster egalitarian splits in the Ultimatum Game.

In a competently performed experiment each treatment or condition is designed so as to introduce variation in one (and only one) potential causal factor. The method of variation is a characteristic hallmark of experimental science, which is, in turn, the most powerful method for the discovery of causal relations among variables. These statements may seem surprising, for the notion of causation has suffered from a lot of bad press during the last hundred years. The twentieth century was dominated by anti-metaphysical philosophies, and social scientists under the influence of logical positivism, in particular, have argued for decades that 'cause' and 'effect' are dubious metaphysical notions that scientists should (and can) do without.[10]

Despite several valiant attempts to reduce causality to more 'respectable' concepts (such as constant conjunction or statistical association), however, it is now generally agreed that causal relations have intrinsic features – like asymmetry, counterfactual dependence, invariance to intervention – that cannot be explained away by means of a reductive analysis. There are now several non-reductive theories of causation in the philosophical and scientific literature, which are reviewed by Daniel Steel in another chapter of this handbook. Luckily we do not have to get into this issue in great depth here, for in spite of continuing disagreement over the metaphysics of causation (what it means and what it is), there is broad agreement that the method of the controlled experiment is a powerful tool for causal discovery. The reason is that controlled experimentation allows underlying causal relations to become manifest at the level of empirical regularities. In a competently performed experiment,

single causal connections can be 'read off' directly from statistical associations.

A homely example illustrates this type of inference nicely. Imagine we want to discover whether flipping the switch is an effective means for turning the light on (or whether 'flipping the switch causes the light to turn on'). The flipping of course will have such effect only if other enabling background conditions are in place, for example if the electricity supply is in good working order. Thus we shall first have to design an experimental situation where the 'right' circumstances are instantiated. Then, we shall have to make sure that no other extraneous variation is disturbing the experiment. Finally, we will check whether by flipping the switch on and off we are producing a regular association between the position of the switch (say, up/down) and the light (on/off). If such an association is observed, and if we are confident that every plausible source of error has been controlled for, we will conclude that flipping the switch is causally connected with turning the light on.

Causal discovery, in a nutshell, requires *variation, but not too much variation, and of the right kind*. In general, you want variation in one factor while keeping all the other putative causes fixed 'in the background'. This logic is exemplified in the *model of the perfectly controlled experiment* (see Table 30.1).

The K_i are the background factors, or the other causes that are kept fixed across the experimental conditions. The conditions must differ with respect to just one factor (X, the treatment) so that any significant difference in the observed values of Y ($Y_1 - Y_2$) can be attributed to the presence (or absence)

Table 30.1 The perfectly controlled experimental design

	Treatment (putative cause)	Putative effect	Other factors (K)
Experimental group	X	Y_1	Constant
Control group	--	Y_2	Constant

of *X*. A good experimenter thus is able to discover *why* one kind of event is associated regularly with another kind of event, and not just that it does. In the model of the perfectly controlled experiment one does not simply observe that 'if *X* happens then *Y* happens', nor even that '*X* if and only if *Y*'. Both conditionals are material implications, and their truth conditions depend on what happens to be the case, regardless of *why* it is so. In science in contrast – and especially in those disciplines that regularly inform policy making, like the social sciences – one is also interested in 'what would be the case if' such and such a variable was manipulated. Scientific intervention and policy-making must rely on counterfactual reasoning. A great advantage of experimentation is that it allows checking what would happen if *X* was *not* the case, while keeping all the other relevant conditions fixed.

We can now draw a first important contrast between the experimental method and traditional statistical inferences from field data. Using statistical techniques one can establish the strength of various correlations between economic variables. But other than in some special happy conditions, the spontaneous variations found in the data do not warrant the drawing of specific causal inferences. Typically, field data display either too little or too much concomitant variation (sometimes both). Some variations of course can be artificially reconstructed post-hoc by looking at partial correlations, but the ideal conditions instantiated in a laboratory are rarely found in the wild (except in so-called 'natural experiments', that is).

This does not mean that total experimental control is always achieved in the laboratory. The perfectly controlled experiment is an idealisation, and in reality there are always going to be uncontrolled background factors, errors of measurement, and so forth. To neutralise these imperfections, experimenters use various techniques, like for example *randomisation*.[11] In a randomised experiment subjects are assigned to the various experimental conditions by a chance device,

so that in the long run the potential errors and deviations are evenly distributed across them. This introduces an important element in the inference from data, that is, *probabilities*. A well designed randomised experiment makes it *highly likely* that the effect of the treatment is reflected in the data, but does not guarantee that this is going to be the case. Assuming for simplicity that we are dealing with bivariate variables (*X* and ~*X*; *Y* and ~*Y*), in a randomised experiment if (1) the 'right' background conditions are in place, and (2) *X* causes *Y*, then $P(Y|X) > P(Y|{\sim}X)$. In plain words: if (1) and (2) are satisfied, *X* and *Y* are very likely to be statistically correlated.

Some authors (notably Cartwright, 1983) have used this relation or some close variant thereof to define the very notion of causation. Such a definition is essentially a probabilistic equivalent of Mackie's (1974) famous INUS account, with the important addition of a 'screening off' condition.[12] The latter is encapsulated in the requirement that all other causal factors in the background are kept fixed, so as to avoid problems of spurious correlation. Several interesting philosophical implications follow from such a definition of causation, which however would take us too far away from our present concerns. Since the main focus of this chapter is methodological, I shall skip these metaphysical issues here (and refer the interested reader to Dan Steel's chapter).

EXTERNAL VALIDITY

Experiments in the social sciences are rarely aimed at investigating phenomena that take place within laboratory walls only. Milgram, as we have seen, was interested in the extreme manifestations of a phenomenon (obedience to authority) that he took to be ubiquitous in modern societies. Nevertheless, it is not obvious that his experiment teaches anything useful about, say, the Holocaust. The social structure of Nazi Germany, its hierarchies of power and the social mechanisms devised to implement the Final Solution were vastly more complex than the simple experiments designed by Milgram at Yale. The Ultimatum Game, similarly, was devised to shed light on some aspects of two-person bargaining, in particular the role played by fairness norms · in determining the allocation of surplus. And yet, bargaining comes in a variety of forms, and is regulated by different institutions in different social contexts. It is far from obvious that any general claim can be derived from the highly stylised set-up known as the Ultimatum Game.

Qualms of this kind are very familiar to experimental social scientists. Scientists are aware that the successful discovery and testing of causal claims does not automatically ensure that these claims can be generalised to non-experimental circumstances. For this reason they draw a crucial distinction between *internal* and *external validity* of experimental results. Problems of internal validity have to do with the drawing of inferences from experimental data to causal mechanisms in a given laboratory set-up. Typical internal validity questions are: Do we understand what goes on in *this* particular experimental situation? Are we drawing correct inferences *within* the experiment? External validity problems instead have to do with the drawing of inferences from experimental data to what happens in other (typically, non-laboratory) situations of interest. They involve asking questions like: Can we use experimental knowledge to understand what goes on in the 'real world'? Are we drawing correct inferences *from* the experiment?

The method of the perfectly controlled experiment is maximally useful to tackle internal validity problem – when the issue is to find out what is going on within a given experimental set-up or laboratory system. Since the method relies on the control of background and boundary conditions, there is usually a trade-off between internal and external validity. A simple experiment such as the Ultimatum Game for example, which reproduces many idealisations of a theoretical model, is easier to control in the laboratory.

But it also constitutes a weaker starting point for extending experimental knowledge to other situations where these idealisations do not hold.

According to an old tradition in experimental psychology, the problem of external validity should be framed in terms of *representativeness* (Hogarth, 2005). There are, more precisely, at least *two* dimensions of representativeness in an experiment: *subjects sample* and *design*. Whereas statistical techniques and random sampling can be used to tackle subject representativeness, however, they do not help with issues of design. The designs of social and psychological experiments are idiosyncratic if compared to real-world situations, and are certainly not randomly picked from the target population (e.g. the set of real-life choice-situations or real social decisions). For this reason, the 'representativeness' framework, while helpful to highlight the nature of the problem, does not do much in terms of pointing to its solution.

Why do experimenters not sample randomly from a set of real-life situations? Sampling makes sense if you are trying to capture a central tendency in a population of individuals with varying traits. But there may be no such central tendency in a set of, say, market exchanges. Take bargaining for example: different details of the situation, such as repeated interaction or anonymity, can influence the outcome drastically. If this is true, then an average description of different bargaining outcomes is likely to be uninformative, and hide most of the interesting variations in the data. What we want is instead to understand how different factors or causal mechanisms interact to generate different outcomes. This is why experimenters sometimes privilege simple designs that capture the working of just one mechanism in isolation, where somewhat 'extreme' results are vividly instantiated.

Following an established terminology in the philosophy of science, let us call such designs 'Galilean experiments' (McMullin, 1985; Cartwright, 2006). A Galilean experiment displays the influence of one factor or set of factors acting in isolation on a dependent variable. However, it does not guarantee that such an influence persists when other factors or mechanisms interfere. When it does, we will say that the experiment has succeeded in identifying a *tendency law*. Following John Stuart Mill (1836), '$A \rightarrow B$' is a tendency law not only if A has the capacity of making B happen in the 'right' set of circumstances, but also if it *tends* to make it happen when the conditions are not right. Or, to put it slightly differently, if A *contributes* to the instantiation of B even when other 'disturbing' or 'counteracting' factors are at work.[13] An important dimension of external validity, thus, is the problem of discovering social tendencies in the experimental lab.

It is important to realise that the existence of tendency laws is an empirical issue. There is no a priori guarantee that the (numerous) factors that are kept fixed in the background during an experiment combine additively. If they do not – if they *interact* with the main experimental variables – then the experimental result will not be valid outside the narrow domain of its instantiation. To put it differently: an effective method of causal discovery is not necessarily effective for the discovery of tendencies. Experiments are very useful to establish causal laws that are valid in a given domain, but unless they are also tendency laws robust to changes in the boundary conditions, this knowledge will be of rather limited use outside that domain.

If the external validity of social experiments is an empirical issue, it is also unlikely to afford a general yes/no, black/white answer. There may be areas of the social (as well as the physical) realm dominated by factors whose effects are relatively stable across contexts. Other areas might be characterised by less orderly interactions and more 'chaotic' behaviour. Finally it may be impossible to reproduce and study some real-world phenomena in the experimental laboratory (Bardsley, 2005). But how can we find out? To answer this question, we need to explicate the logic of external validity inferences in more detail.

INFERENCES FROM THE EXPERIMENT

External validity inferences rely on the effective combination of field and experimental data. Before we examine some solutions to the problem of external validity, it is important to be clear about the nature of the problem, and to outline the desiderata that a solution must meet. Minimally, a satisfactory account must be able to answer a challenge that Daniel Steel (2007) has called the 'extrapolator's circle':

> Additional information about the similarity between the model and the target – for instance, that the relevant [causal] mechanisms are the same in both – is needed to justify the extrapolation. The extrapolator's circle is the challenge of explaining how we could acquire this additional information, given the limitations of what we can know about the target. In other words, it needs to be explained how we could know that the models and the target are similar in causally relevant respects without already knowing the causal relationship in the target. (2007: 78–79).

Steel's answer to the extrapolator's circle is based on a methodology articulated by Darden and Craver (2002) and Glennan (2005), and variously called 'forward-chaining', 'backtracking', or 'process tracing'. Let us call a set of inter-connected, regularly operating causal relationships that generate one or more regularities between (observable or unobservable) events, a *mechanism*. Clearly much scientific research in the natural and social sciences is devoted to the discovery and theoretical description of such mechanisms. In order to discover the fine-grained structure of a mechanism, one can start from one of its endpoints (one of the initial causes, or one of the final effects) and then step by step reconstruct the path that connects them with the other elements of the mechanism via the intermediate nodes.

Notice that in this case process tracing is used to uncover the structure of a *single* mechanism. In the case of external validity the scientist is facing a different problem: how to infer from knowledge of a causal mechanism in A, to the existence of a similar mechanism in B. *Comparative process tracing* can be articulated in two preliminary steps and an inductive inference:

1 First, learn the mechanism in the model organism (or experimental system), by means of process tracing or other experimental means.
2 Second, compare stages of the mechanism in which the two (the experimental and the target systems) are most likely to differ significantly.
3 In general, the greater the similarity of configuration and behaviour of entities involved in the mechanism at these key stages, the stronger the basis for the extrapolation. (Steel, 2007: 89)

How does comparative process tracing answer the challenge of external validity? The extrapolator's circle is broken by pointing out that comparisons are required *only* at those nodes where the two mechanisms are most likely to differ. The more nodes are available for inspection, the stronger the inference is. So full knowledge of the target mechanism, while desirable, is not required in principle. Moreover, large portions of the mechanisms can be safely ignored, in some circumstances. Suppose that one of the initial causal factors is likely to leave a mark that is transmitted in the causal chain. In such happy circumstances, it will be sufficient to check for *downstream* differences in the two mechanisms (Steel, 2007: 95). Again, full knowledge of the target is not required for the external validity inference to take off.

What kind of inference is warranted by comparative process tracing? Several philosophers have noticed that external validity inferences display some characteristic features of analogical reasoning (La Follette and Shanks, 1995; Thagard, 1999; Guala, 2005). They have argued that external validity inferences can be reconstructed as analogical arguments of the following kind.

1 The target system has property *Y*.
2 The experimental system has property *Y*.
3 In the laboratory, property *Y* is caused by *X*.
4 In the target *Y* is therefore also caused by *X*.

Since analogical inferences are fallible and vary in strength, an analogical account must

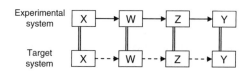

Figure 30.1   Analogical reasoning and chain graphs.

explicate the conditions that make external validity inferences reliable (or not). Steel (2010) shows how to do it using a modelling technique known as 'chain graphs'. In the chain graph of Figure 30.1, the arrows (directed edges) represent causal relations and the double lines (undirected edges) represent similarity relations. The dotted lines stand for the fallible conclusion reached by the external validity inference.

The double lines cannot be simply postulated, but ought to be based on empirical information. They constitute the *base* of the analogy, and can in principle be assigned quantitative (probabilistic) values. A key feature of analogical reasoning is that two similar entities or causal mechanisms provide information about each other. Thus, if the base of the analogy is strong, the fact that *X* causes *Y* in the laboratory tells us that *X* is also likely to be at work in the target. Chain graphs allow to represent formally this sort of inference and, potentially, to compute the relevant probabilistic dependences quantitatively (Steel, 2008).

EXPERIMENTING AS ENGINEERING

Steel's chain graph method unifies the two main approaches to external validity inference (the analogical approach and comparative process tracing) that have been proposed in the philosophical literature. This theoretical achievement, however, should not make us forget how difficult it often is, in practice, to construct an adequate base in support of external validity inferences. A crucial condition for drawing an undirected edge between two components of different mechanisms, to begin with, is that the similarity at the level of the effects is not merely a coincidence or a spurious effect of some undetected causal factor. This is equivalent to the familiar requirement in causal reasoning that no background variation (in the K_i) is confounding the inference one is making. Consider the case of internal validity: a correlation between two variables is too weak a basis to infer that a causal relation exists between the two. Similarly, the fact that X causes Y in A does not guarantee that X causes Y in B. We must make sure that no other causal factor is confounding the inference.

Unsurprisingly, social scientists are most confident in drawing external validity inferences when they have *made sure* that no relevant causal disanalogies confound the inference. A celebrated example comes from the field of auction theory. Following governmental instructions, in 1993 the Federal Communication Commission (an agency of the US government, FCC from now on) faced the problem of devising a new system to sell licences for Personal Communication Systems (airwave frequencies for portable faxes and mobile phones, etc.).[14] The FCC consultants were faced with a typical problem of 'mechanism design': given a set of goals to be achieved in regulating this market, what institution could be reasonably expected to do the job?

The economists involved in this project tackled the problem in a piecemeal way, by modelling particular aspects of the auction game rather than aiming at a unique, general theoretical analysis. They came up with the abstract design of an institution called 'simultaneous ascending auction',[15] that had never been put to use before. To complement the theory, therefore, the FCC consultants made use of laboratory experiments, devised by a team led by the prominent experimental economist Charles Plott. By the summer of 1994, the FCC were convinced that a satisfactory set of rules for the continuous

ascending auctions had been specified. The resulting mechanism had been working well in the laboratory, delivering allocations that satisfied the FCC *desiderata*.[16] A real auction took place in Washington, DC, in October 1994. Laboratory tests with similar parameters to those expected for the real auction were run beforehand so that the results could be compared after the event. The experimental auctions had been constructed so as to have the same number of players, the same number of auctioned items, complementarities such as those presumably existing in the real market, a similar number of rounds, similar values, and so forth. Then, a large amount of data collected both in the lab and in the real auction was systematically compared. This data included bidding patterns, pricing trajectories, the rise of 'bubbles', and several other phenomena of interest.

The data patterns in the real auctions turned out to be remarkably similar to those observed in the experiments. The prices in the two markets evolved in a similar way, and the experimenters, being highly confident that the laboratory auctions delivered approximately efficient outcomes, concluded that an efficient allocation had been achieved in the Washington auction as well. 'If indeed the same principles were operating in the FCC environment then the FCC auction converged to near the competitive equilibrium and exhibited high efficiency' (Plott, 1997: 637).

All analogical inferences face problems of underdetermination: similar phenomena may be generated by different causal mechanisms. This is a ubiquitous issue in science, and from this respect there is nothing special with external validity inferences. So what made *this* particular inference a reliable one? Plott and the other economists who constructed the FCC auction tried to make sure that the same processes took place in reality as those that they had seen at work in their laboratory. The transportation of the mechanism outside the laboratory was as smooth, gradual, and carefully monitored as possible. The same causes were supposed to operate because experimenters built the two systems so as to be as structurally similar to one another as possible.

THE POLICY AND POLITICS OF EXPERIMENTAL SCIENCE

The FCC case is a rare example of external validity inference drawn in favourable conditions for the experimenter. Social scientists often do not possess enough background knowledge to support inferences to what happens when the initial and boundary conditions in the wild are very different from those in the laboratory. This is not surprising, considering that experimental social science is a relatively young area of research. The stunning technological applications of physics and molecular biology are built on an enormous body of experimental knowledge that sometimes has been waiting for years in search of a concrete application. And in some cases experimental results never step outside the laboratory walls. As I have argued elsewhere (Guala, 2005: 229–230), most experimental research contributes to building a huge 'library of phenomena' – a list of mechanisms, effects that are potentially relevant in concrete applications. In order to apply this knowledge to real-world situations, it is then necessary to examine the specific characteristics of the target domain, and on the basis of this local information, evaluate the relevance of the phenomena found in the 'library', case by case.

Another important lesson is that the application of experimental knowledge often involves intervention on target systems. Students of natural science experiments have pointed out that successful science is often a matter of manipulating the world so as to make it look like our laboratories, rather than the other way around (e.g. Latour, 1984; Gooding, 1990). Disturbing factors must be shielded to prevent interference with the causal mechanism of interest, as in

the TV boxes that adorn our living rooms. But in many cases the very mechanisms must be crafted to create effects that would have not existed independently of human intervention and manipulation (Hacking, 1983, 1992; Cartwright, 1999). The FCC case demonstrates that pockets of order can be created by more or less deliberate intervention in the social world too. In many ways this is not big news: the history of social science provides several examples of mechanisms created and preserved by human design. Unemployment measures, to take a well known example, never reflected a given, spontaneous phenomenon. Rather, they always presupposed a heavy institutional setting of incentives and punishments (administered by Trade Unions, National Insurance schemes, etc.), devised to manage people by changing their strategic incentives.[17]

What sort of mechanisms are at work (and their narrow or wider scope) depends at least partly on what we, as a society, decide to set up. Accounting for the difference between the success of natural and social science by postulating deep metaphysical divides is therefore both unnecessary and defeatist. That difference can be equally well explained by practical and political differences, between what we think is appropriate to do in the natural and in the social realm.[18] We feel there are things that can be done to inanimate objects (and animals) that would be unacceptable for human beings. (This demarcation line has changed through time, of course, and is fundamentally historical in character.)

The question of the implementation of social science thus is partly the issue of *how much* control we want to impose on human behaviour. Some phenomena are 'local' simply because a social arrangement that we find appropriate in a certain context is deemed unacceptable in another domain. We might not want the whole of society to be managed as a mental asylum, nor perhaps as a perfectly competitive free market inhabited by one-dimensional greedy economic men and women – despite the fact that both institutions perform egregiously well certain specific tasks in specific contexts. The gap between the natural and the social sciences may well be political and moral, rather than ontological, in character.

NOTES

1 The work of reference for experimental economics is Kagel and Roth (1995, On experiments in political science, see Morton and Williams (2008).

2 Danziger (1994) and Mandler (2007) are excellent sources on the history of experimentation in psychology.

3 This 'standard prediction' is actually derived from a fairly complex machinery: roughly, from a theory of strategic play (the 'core' of game theory), plus a set of assumptions about people's preferences and beliefs. Without such assumptions, game theory does not issue any specific prediction about behaviour. A more detailed discussion of this issue can be found in Guala (2006, 2008).

4 More precisely: it is the only 'sub-game perfect equilibrium' of the game. Here and in the course of this chapter I gloss over the most technical aspects of game theory, except when it is required by the discussion. In another chapter of this handbook Giacomo Bonanno provides an introduction to the literature on game theoretic models in the social sciences.

5 A critical survey of the main interpretations of Ultimatum data can be found in Bicchieri (2006: Chapter 3). See also Woodward (2009).

6 Surveys and analyses of the Milgram controversy can be found in Miller (1986) and Blass (2000). For a critique of Milgram's critics, see Pleasants (1999: Chapter 7).

7 Hacking (1983) is widely recognised as the pioneer of this 'new experimentalism'. Useful surveys of the literature can be found in Franklin (1998) and Morrison (1998).

8 Moral philosophers have recently rediscovered this strand of social psychology experiments. Doris (2002) is a good example of how empirical evidence can be used to question virtue ethics and other moral doctrines based on the notion of individual 'character'.

9 The Ultimatum Game is now used as a measurement tool, not only in economics, but in the social sciences at large. In 2000 the anthropologist Joe Henrich reported a series of 'surprising' observations collected using the Ultimatum Game among the Machiguenga, a group of Peruvian slash-and-burn horticulturalists. The Machiguenga proposed *more*

unequal splits of the cake, and rejected unfair offers *less* often than Western subjects. In other words: they behaved more (but not entirely) like *homi oeconomici*. Henrich concluded that different peoples have different cultural expectations and norms of fairness, and that we need to know more about how these norms are created and sustained in each social context. With this idea in mind, a group of economists and anthropologists set out to compare behaviour in some classic experimental designs across 15 'small-scale societies' in South America, Africa, and Asia. This project, funded by the MacArthur Foundation, is the most ambitious and exciting attempt to use experiments for heuristics and measurement purposes ever attempted in the social sciences so far (see Henrich et al., 2004).

10 Russell (1912) is a seminal and influential example.

11 Other techniques are used when the model of the perfectly controlled experiment cannot be applied for some reason, but I shall not examine them in detail here (they are illustrated in most textbooks and handbooks of experimental methodology, cf. e.g. Christensen, 2001).

12 INUS stands for an Insufficient Non-redundant condition within a set of jointly Unnecessary but Sufficient conditions for an effect to take place. There are several problems with such an approach, some of which are discussed by Mackie himself. The 'screening-off' condition fixes some of the most obvious flaws of the INUS account.

13 Modern formulations of Mill's theory of tendency laws can be found in Cartwright (1989) and Hausman (1992).

14 A detailed discussion of this case is provided in Guala (2005). Alexandrova (2008) relies on the FCC case to outline a novel account of the use of theoretical models in applied social science.

15 In an 'ascending' auction, bidders drop out one after the other as the price rises, until only the winner is left; in a 'simultaneous' auction several markets are open at the same time and each potential buyer can be active on all of them at once. Simultaneity helps the bidders to compose the preferred package of items, whereas the ascending system allows for keeping an eye on what the other bidders are doing and avoiding problems of overpricing.

16 Mirowski and Nik-Khah (2006) provide a detailed reconstruction of how the desiderata were shaped by the economic consultants themselves, which in some respect conflicts with my account (Guala, 2005).

17 Topalov (1994) reconstructs the social 'construction' of unemployment (the concept *and* the empirical phenomenon) along these lines. For other examples (mostly from economics) see the case studies in McKenzie et al. (2006).

18 See Latour and Woolgar (1979: 256–257) for a seminal discussion of this important point.

REFERENCES

Alexandrova, A. (2008) 'Making models count', *Philosophy of Science*, 75: 383–404.

Arendt, H. (1963) *Eichmann in Jerusalem: A Report on the Banality of Evil*. London: Faber & Faber.

Bardsley (2005) 'Experimental economics and the artificiality of alteration', *Journal of Economic Methodology*, 12: 239–251.

Bicchieri, C. (2006) *The Grammar of Society*. New York: Cambridge University Press.

Blass, T. (ed.) (2000) *Obedience to Authority: Current Perspectives on the Milgram Paradigm*. Lawrence Erlbaum

Bogen, J. and J. Woodward (1988) 'Saving the phenomena', *Philosophical Review*, 97: 303–352.

Cartwright, N. (1983) *How the Laws of Physics Lie*. Oxford: Clarendon Press.

Cartwright, N. (1989) *Nature's Capacities and Their Measurement*. Oxford: Oxford University Press.

Cartwright, N. (1999) *The Dappled World: A Study of the Boundaries of Science*. Cambridge: Cambridge University Press.

Cartwright, N. (2006) 'The vanity of rigour in economics: Theoretical models and Galilean experiments', in *Hunting Causes and Using Them*. Cambridge: Cambridge University Press.

Christensen, L.B. (2001) *Experimental Methodology* (8th edition). Needham Heights, MA: Allyn & Bacon.

Danziger, K. (1994) *Constructing the Subject: Historical Origins of Psychological Research*. Cambridge: Cambridge University Press.

Darden, L. and Craver, C. (2002) 'Strategies in the interfield discovery of the mechanism of protein synthesis', *Studies in History and Philosophy of Biological and Biomedical Sciences*, 33: 1–28.

Doris, J. (2002) *Lack of Character: Personality and Moral Behavior*. New York: Cambridge University Press.

Economics Focus (1999) 'News from the lab', *The Economist*, May 8th: 96.

Franklin, A. (1998) 'Experiment in physics', in E.N. Zalta (ed.) *The Stanford Encyclopaedia of Philosophy*. http://plato.stanford.edu/entries/physics-experiment.

Gintis, H., Bowles, S., Boyd, R. and Fehr, E. (eds) (2005) *Moral Sentiments and Material Interests*. Cambridge, MA: MIT Press.

Glennan, Stuart (2005) 'Modeling mechanisms', *Studies in History and Philosophy of Biological and Biomedical Sciences*, 36: 443–464.

Gooding, D. (1989) *Experiment and the Making of Meaning*. Dordrecht: Kluwer.

Guala, F. (2005) *The Methodology of Experimental Economics*. New York: Cambridge University Press.

Guala, F. (2006) 'Has game theory been refuted?', *Journal of Philosophy*, 103: 239–263.

Guala, F. (2008) 'Paradigmatic experiments: The ultimatum game from testing to measurement device', *Philosophy of Science*, 75: 658–669.

Güth, Werner, Rolf Schmittberger and Bernd Schwarz (1982) 'An experimental analysis of ultimatum bargaining', *Journal of Economic Behavior and Organization*, 3: 367–388.

Hacking, I. (1983) *Representing and Intervening*. Cambridge: Cambridge University Press.

Hacking, I. (1992) 'The self-vindication of the laboratory sciences', in A. Pickering (ed.) *Science as Practice and Culture*. Chicago: University of Chicago Press, pp. 29–64.,

Harré, R. (1979) *Social Being: A Theory for a Social Psychology*. Oxford: Blackwell.

Hausman, D.M. (1992) *The Inexact and Separate Science of Economics*. Cambridge: Cambridge University Press.

Henrich, J., Boyd, R., Bowles, S., Camerer, C., Fehr, E., and Gintis, H. (eds.) (2004) *Foundations of Human Sociality: Economic Experiments and Ethnographic Evidence from Fifteen Small-Scale Societies*. Oxford: Oxford University Press.

Hogarth, R.M. (2005) 'The challenge of representative design in psychology and economics,' *Journal of Economic Methodology*, 12: 253–263.

Kagel, J.H. and A.E. Roth (eds) (1995) *The Handbook of Experimental Economics*. Princeton: Princeton University Press.

La Follette, H. and N. Shanks (1995) 'Two models of models in biomedical research', *Philosophical Quarterly*, 45: 141–160.

Latour, B. (1984) *Les Microbes: Guerre et Paix*. Paris: Métailié; Engl. trans. *The Pasteurisation of France*. Cambridge, MA: Harvard University Press, 1988.

Latour, B. and S. Woolgar (1979) *Laboratory Life: The Construction of Scientific Facts*. Princeton: Princeton University Press. (2nd edition, 1986.)

MacKenzie, F. Muniesa and L. Siu (eds.) (2006) *Do Economists Make Markets? On the Performativity of Economics*. Princeton: Princeton University Press.

Mackie, J.L. (1974) *The Cement of the Universe*. Oxford: Clarendon Press.

McMullin, E. (1985) 'Galilean Idealization', *Studies in History and Philosophy of Science* 16: 247–273.

Mandler, G. (2007) *A History of Modern Experimental Psychology*. Cambridge, MA: MIT Press.

Milgram, S. (1974) *Obedience to Authority*. London: Pinter & Martin.

Mill, J.S. (1836) 'On the definition of political economy and the method of investigation proper to it', in *Collected Works of John Stuart Mill*, Vol. 4. Toronto: University of Toronto Press, 1967.

Miller, A.G. (1986) *The Obedience Experiments: A Case Study of Controversy in Social Science*. New York: Praeger

Mirowski, P. and Nik-Khah, E. (2006) 'Markets made flesh: Callon, performativity, and a crisis in science studies, augmented with consideration of the FCC auctions', in D. McKenzie, F. Muniesa, and L. Siu, (eds) *Do Economists Make Markets? On the Performativity of Economics*. Princeton: Princeton University Press.

Mixon, D. (1989) *Obedience and Civilization: Authorized Crime and the Normality of Evil*. London: Pluto Press.

Morrison, M.C. (1998) 'Experiment', in E. Craig (ed.) *The Routledge Encyclopaedia of Philosophy*. London: Routledge, pp. 514–518.

Morton, R. and Williams, K. (2008) 'Experimentation in political science', in J. Box-Steffensmeier, H. Brady and D. Collier (eds) *The Oxford Handbook of Political Science*. New York: Oxford University Press, pp. 339–356.

Pleasants, N. (1999) *Wittgenstein and the Idea of a Critical Social Theory*. London: Routledge.

Plott, C.R. (1997) 'Laboratory experimental testbeds: Application to the PCS auction', *Journal of Economics and Management Strategy*, 6: 605–638.

Popper, K.R. (1934) *Logik der Forschung*. Vienna: Springer; Engl. transl. *Logic of Scientific Discovery*. London: Hutchinson, 1959.

Roth, Alvin, Vesna Prasnikar, Masahiro Okuno-Fujiwara and Shmuel Zamir (1991) 'Bargaining and market behavior in Jerusalem, Lubljana, Pittsburgh and Tokyo: An experimental study', *American Economic Review*, 81: 1068–1095.

Russell, B. (1912) 'On the notion of cause', *Proceedings of the Aristotelian Society*, 13: 1–26.

Steel, D. (2007) *Across the Boundaries: Extrapolation in Biology and Social Science*. New York: Oxford University Press.

Steel, D. (2010) 'A new approach to argument by analogy: Extrapolation and chain graphs'. *Philosophy of Science*, in press.

Thagard, P. (1999) *How Scientists Explain Disease*. Princeton: Princeton University Press.

Topalov, C. (1994) *Naissance du Chômeur: 1880–1910*. Paris: Albin Michel.

Woodward, J. (2009) 'Experimental investigations of social preferences', in H. Kincaid and D. Ross (eds) *The Oxford Handbook of the Philosophy of Economics*. New York: Oxford University Press.

31

Mathematics and Statistics in the Social Sciences

Stephan Hartmann and Jan Sprenger

Over the years, mathematics and statistics have become increasingly important in the social sciences.[1] A look at history quickly confirms this claim. At the beginning of the 20th century most theories in the social sciences were formulated in qualitative terms while quantitative methods did not play a substantial role in their formulation and establishment. Moreover, many practitioners considered mathematical methods to be inappropriate and simply unsuited to foster our understanding of the social domain. Notably, the famous *Methodenstreit* also concerned the role of mathematics in the social sciences. Here, mathematics was considered to be the method of the natural sciences from which the social sciences had to be separated during the period of maturation of these disciplines.

All this changed by the end of the century. By then, mathematical, and especially statistical, methods were used as standard, and their value in the social sciences came relatively uncontested (see, for example, Fogel (1975)). The use of mathematical and statistical methods is now ubiquitous: Almost all social sciences rely on statistical methods to analyze data and form hypotheses, and almost all of them use (to a greater or lesser extent) a range of mathematical methods to help us understand the social world.

Additional indication for the increasing importance of mathematical and statistical methods in the social sciences is the formation of new subdisciplines, and the establishment of specialized journals and societies. Indeed, subdisciplines such as Mathematical Psychology and Mathematical Sociology emerged, and corresponding journals such as *The Journal of Mathematical Psychology* (since 1964), *The Journal of Mathematical Sociology* (since 1976), *Mathematical Social Sciences* (since 1980) as well as the online journals *Journal of Artificial Societies and Social Simulation* (since 1998) and *Mathematical Anthropology and Cultural Theory* (since 2000) were established. What is more, societies such as the Society for Mathematical Psychology (since 1976) and the Mathematical Sociology Section of the American Sociological Association (since 1996) were founded. Similar developments can be observed in other countries.

The mathematization of economics set in somewhat earlier (Backhouse, 1995; Beed and Kane, 1991; Rosenberg, 1992; Vazquez,

1995; Weintraub, 2002, 2008). However, the use of mathematical methods in economics started booming only in the second half of the last century (Debreu, 1991). Contemporary economics is dominated by the mathematical approach, although a certain *style* of doing economics became more and more under attack in the last decade or so. Recent developments in behavioral economics and experimental economics can also be understood as a reaction against the dominance (and limitations) of an overly mathematical approach to economics. There are similar debates in other social sciences. It is, however, important to stress that problems of one method (such as axiomatization or the use of set theory) can hardly be taken as a sign of bankruptcy of mathematical methods in the social sciences *tout court*.

This chapter surveys mathematical and statistical methods used in the social sciences and discusses some of the philosophical questions they raise. It is divided into two parts. The first two sections are devoted to mathematical methods, and the third to seventh section to statistical methods. As several other chapters in this handbook provide detailed accounts of various mathematical methods, our remarks about the latter will be rather short and general. Statistical methods, on the other hand, will be discussed in-depth.

A PLURALITY OF MATHEMATICAL METHODS

Social scientists use a wide variety of mathematical methods.[2] Given the space constraints of the present chapter, it is impossible to list them all, give examples, examine their domain of applicability, and discuss their methodological problems. Instead, we broadly distinguish between three different kinds of methods: (1) methods imported from the formal sciences, (2) methods imported from the natural sciences, and (3) social scientific methods *sui generis*. We review them in turn.

Methods imported from the formal sciences

These include (linear) algebra, calculus (including differential equations), the axiomatic method, logic and set theory, probability theory (including Markov chains), linear programming, topology, graph theory, and complexity theory. All these methods have important applications in the social sciences.[3] The axiomatic method nicely illustrates what one can call *the mathematician's approach* to the social sciences. Here, a set of general principles is formulated, which enable the study of the formal aspects of the system under investigation. The tradition of proving impossibility theorems in social choice theory is a good example for this approach.

In recent years, we have seen the importation of various methods from computer science into the social sciences. There is also a strong trend within computer science to address problems from the social sciences. An example is the recent establishment of the new interdisciplinary field *computational social choice* which is dominated by computer scientists.[4] Interestingly, much work in computational social choice uses analytical and logical methods. There is, however, also a strong trend in the social sciences to use powerful numerical and simulation methods to explore complex and (typically) dynamical social phenomena (Gilbert and Troitzsch, 2005; Hartmann, 1996; Hegselmann et al., 1996; Marchi, 2005). The reason for this is, of course, the availability of high-powered computers. But not all social scientists follow this trend. Especially many economists are reluctant to employ simulation methods and do not consider them appropriate tools for the study of economic systems.[5]

Methods imported from the natural sciences

These methods are becoming increasingly popular in the social sciences. These methods are more specific than the formal methods mentioned above. They involve substantial assumptions that happen – or so it is claimed – to be fulfilled in the social domain. These methods comprise tools for the study of multi-agent systems, the theory of complex systems, non-linear dynamics, methods developed in synergetics (Weidlich, 2006) and, more recently, in econophysics (Gallegatti et al., 2006, Mantegna and Stanley, 1999). The applicability of these methods follows from the 'observation' that societies are nothing but many-body systems (like a gas is a many-body system composed of molecules) that exhibit certain features such as the emergence of ordering phenomena. Hence, these features can be accounted for in terms of a statistical description, just like the behavior of gases and other many-body systems which are studied in the natural sciences. Such methods are also used in new interdisciplinary fields such as environmental economics.

Besides providing various methods for the study of social phenomena, the natural sciences also inspired a certain way of addressing a problem. Meanwhile, model building is considered to be the core activity in the social sciences.[6] The developed models contain idealized assumptions, and their consequences are often obtained with the help of simulations. Due to its striking similarity with physics, we call this approach the *physicist's approach* to social science, and contrast it with the mathematician's approach to social science, described above.

Mathematical methods that emerged from problems in the social sciences

Finally, these methods include powerful instruments such as decision theory,[7] utility theory, game theory,[8] measurement theory (Krantz et al., 1971), social choice theory (Arrow et al., 1960; Gaertner, 2006), and judgment aggregation (List and Puppe, 2009). The latter were invented by social scientists for social scientists, with a specific social-science

application in mind. They help addressing specific problems that arise in the context of the social sciences that did not have an analogue in the natural sciences when they were invented. Only later some of these theories also turned out to be useful in the natural sciences or have been combined with insights from the natural sciences. Evolutionary game theory is a case in point.[9] Other interesting examples include the study of quantum games (Piotrowski and Sladkowski, 2003) and the application of decision theory in fundamental physics (Wallace, 2010). Many of the methods that emerged from problems in the social sciences are in line with the mathematician's approach, although the physicist's approach is increasingly gaining ground.

Interestingly, there are other methods that cannot be attached to one specific science. Network theory is a case in point: As networks are studied in almost all sciences, parallel developments took place, and much can be learned by exploring achievements in other fields (Jackson, 2008).[10]

Having listed a large number of methods, the question arises which method is appropriate for a certain problem. This question can only be answered on a case by case basis, and it is part of the ingenuity of the scientist to pick the best method. But let us stress the following: While some scientists ask themselves which problems they can address with their favorite method, the starting point should always be a specific problem. Once a problem is chosen, the scientist picks the best method that helps solve it. To have some choice, it is important that scientists are acquainted with a variety of different methods. Mathematics and related disciplines provide the scientist with a *toolbox* (to use a popular metaphor) out of which they have to pick an appropriate tool.

WHY MATHEMATIZE THE SOCIAL SCIENCES?

A historically important reason for the mathematization of the social sciences was that mathematics is associated with precision and objectivity. These are (arguably) two requirements any science should satisfy, and so the mathematization of the social sciences was considered a crucial step for the transformation of the social sciences into real science. Some such view has been defended by many authors. Luce and Suppes (1968), for example, provide a similar argument for the importance of theoretical axiomatization in the social sciences. Here, mathematics is used to precisely formulate a theory. By doing so, the latter's structure becomes transparent, and the relationships that hold between the various variables can be clearly specified or inferred. Above all, mathematics provides clarity, generality, and rigor.

There are many ways to represent a theory. For a long time, philosophers have championed the syntactic view, requiring theories to be represented in first-order logic; or the semantic view in its various forms, identifying a theory with the collection of its models (Balzer et al., 1987; Suppes, 2001). While such reconstructions may be helpful for devising a consistent version of a theory, it usually suffices for all practical purposes to state a set of equations that constitute the mathematical part of the theory.

The pioneers of the mathematization in the social sciences also developed measurement theory (Krantz et al., 1971), that takes as its starting point the idea that science is crucially about measurement.[11] Contrary to this tradition, it has been argued that the subject matter of the social sciences does not require the level of precision demanded by the natural sciences, and that the social sciences are, and should, rather be inexact (cf. Hausman, 1992). After all, what works in the natural sciences may well not work in the social sciences.

While Sir Karl Popper, one of the towering figures in the methodology of social science, did not promote the mathematization of the social sciences in the first place, it is clear that it nevertheless plays an enormous role in his philosophy. Given his focus on prediction and falsifiability (Hands, 2008), it makes sense to prefer a theory that is mathematized to a theory that is not. This is due to the fact that it is generally much easier to obtain falsifiable conclusions from clearly stated propositions than from vague and informal claims.

It is a mistake, however, to overestimate the role of mathematics in the social sciences. In the end, mathematics provides the social scientist only with tools, and the result of using these tools will crucially depend on explicit or implicit assumptions. This is a variant of the well known GIGO principle from computer science ('garbage in, garbage out'). All assumptions are informally motivated. Formulating them in the language of mathematics just helps to put them more precisely. Once the assumptions are formulated mathematically, the machinery of mathematics helps to draw inferences in an automated way. This holds for analytical calculations as well as for numerical studies, including computer simulations (Frigg and Reiss, 2009; Hartmann, 1996).

This brings us to another advantage of mathematical methods in the social sciences. While non-formal theories often remain rather simplistic and highly idealized, formal theories can be made increasingly complicated and realistic, reflecting the messiness of our world. The mathematical machinery then helps to draw inferences which could not be obtained without them (Humphreys, 2004). Often, different assumptions of a theory or model pull in opposite directions, and it is not clear which one will be 'stronger' in a specific situation. However, when implemented in a mathematical model, what happens in which part of the parameter space can be calculated. And so the availability of powerful computers allows the systematic study of more realistic models.

There is, however, also a danger associated with this apparent advantage. Given the availability of powerful computers, scientists may be tempted to construct very complex models. But while these models may do well in terms of empirical adequacy, it is not so clear that they also provide *understanding*.

This is often provided by rather simple models (sometimes called 'toy models'), that is, models that pick only one crucial aspect of a system and help us get a feel for its implications.[12]

There are several other reasons for mathematization in the social sciences:

1. Theory Exploration: Once a theory is represented in mathematical terms, the mathematical machinery can be employed to derive its qualitative and quantitative consequences. This helps to better understand what the theory is all about and what it entails about the world. The deductive consequences of the theory (and additional assumptions that have to be made) can be divided into retrodictions or predictions. For retrodictions, the question arises which additional assumptions have to be made to obtain a certain (already measured) value of a variable.

2. Theory Testing: The predictions of a mathematically formulated theory can then be used to test the theory by confronting its consequences with relevant data. In the end, the theory will be confirmed or disconfirmed, or to put in Popperian terms, 'corroborated' or 'falsified'.

3. Heuristics: Once the mathematical structure of a theory is apparent, a look at it may reveal analogies to other phenomena. This may inspire additional investigations, and lead to a better understanding of the class of phenomena under investigation. Also, a numerical study of a theory may suggest new patterns that can be incorporated into the assumptions of another theory.

4. Explanation: While it is controversial what a scientific explanation is, it is clear that – once the theory is mathematically formulated – a phenomenon can be fitted into a larger theoretical framework (as the unification account demands) or a causal story can be read off from it (Kitcher, 1989; Strevens, 2009; Woodward, 2003).

This list suggests the existence of interesting parallels between the use of mathematics in the natural and the social sciences. Indeed, mathematization has similar functions in both kinds of sciences. There are further parallels: In both kinds of sciences, we find a variety of methods ranging from the axiomatic method to the use of computer simulations. Moreover, the models that are constructed range, in both kinds of sciences,

from toy models to models that fit large amounts of data (e.g. in econometrics). The latter is achieved with the help of statistical methods, which we will discuss in the following sections.

The similarities (and dissimilarities!) between the use of mathematics in the natural and social sciences are in need of further philosophical exploration. We hope that future research will shed more light on these questions.

THE DEVELOPMENT OF STATISTICAL REASONING

Statistical reasoning is nowadays a central method of the social sciences. First, it is indispensable for *evaluating experimental data*, for example, in behavioral economics or experimental psychology. For instance, psychologists might want to find out whether men act, in a certain situation, differently from women, or whether there are causal relationships between violent video games and aggressive behavior. Second, the social sciences heavily use statistical models as a *modeling tool* for analyzing empirical data and predicting future events, especially in econometrics and operational research, but recently also in the mathematical branches of psychology, sociology, and the like. For example, time series and regression models relate a number of input (potential predictor) variables to output (predicted) variables. Sophisticated model comparison procedures try to elicit the structure of the data-generating process, eliminate some variables from the model, select a 'best' model and, finally, fit the parameter values to the data.

Still, the conception of statistics as an *inferential tool* is quite young: Throughout the 19th century, statistics was mainly used as a *descriptive tool* to summarize data and fit models. While, in inferential statistics, the focus lies on testing scientific hypotheses against each other, or quantifying evidence for or against a certain hypothesis, descriptive statistics focuses on summarizing data and fitting the parameters of a given model to a set of data. The most famous example is maybe Gauß' method of the least squares, a procedure to center a data set (x_n, y_n) around a straight line. Other important descriptive statistics are contingency tables, effect sizes, and tendency and dispersion measures.

Descriptive statistics were, however, 'statistics without probability' (Morgan, 1987), or as one might also say, statistics without uncertainty. In the late-nineteenth and early-twentieth century, science was believed to be concerned with *certainty*, with the discovery of invariable, universal laws. This left no place for uncertain reasoning. Recall that, at that time, stochastic theories in the natural sciences, such as statistical mechanics, quantum physics, or laws of inheritance, were still quite new, or not yet invented. Furthermore, there was a hope of reducing them to more fundamental, deterministic regularities, for example, to take the stochastic nature of statistical mechanics as an expression of our imperfect knowledge, uncertainty, and not as the fundamental regularities that govern the motion of molecules. Thus, statistical modeling contradicted the *nomothetic ideal* (Gigerenzer, 1987), inspired by Newtonian and Laplacean physics, of establishing universal laws. Therefore, statistics was considered a mere auxiliary, imperfect device, a mere surrogate for proof by deduction or experiment. For instance, the famous analysis of variance (ANOVA) obtained its justification in the nomothetic view through its role in causal inference and elucidating causal laws.

Interestingly, these views were held even in the social sciences, although the latter dealt with a reality that was usually too complex to isolate causal factors in laboratory experiments. Controlling for external impacts and confounders poses special problems to the social sciences, whose domain is not inanimate objects, but humans. The search for deterministic, universal laws in the social sciences might thus seem futile – and

this is probably the received view today. Yet, in the first half of the 20th century, many social scientists thought differently. Statistics was needed to account for measurement errors and omitted causal influences in a model. But it was thought to play a merely provisional role:

> statistical devices are to be valued according to their efficacy in enabling us to lay bare the true relationship between the phenomena under consideration. An ideal method would eliminate all of the disturbing factors (Schultz, 1928: 33).

Thus, the view of statistics was *eliminativist*: As soon as it has done the job and elucidated the laws at which we aim, we can dismiss it. In other words, the research project consisted in eliminating probabilistic elements, instead of discovering statistical laws and regularities or modeling physical quantities as probabilistic variables with a certain distribution. This methodological presumption, taken from 19th century physics, continued to haunt social sciences far into the first half of the twentieth century. Economics, as the 'physics of social sciences', was particularly affected by that conception (Morgan, 2002).

In total, there are three main reasons for inferential statistics' recognition as a central method of the social sciences:

1. The advances in mathematical probability, as summarized in the seminal work of Kolmogorov (1933/56).
2. The inferential character of many scientific questions, for example, about the existence of a causal relationship between variables X and Y. There was a need for techniques of data analysis that ended up with an inference or decision, rather than with a description of a correlation.
3. The groundbreaking works by particularly pioneering minds, such as Tinbergen and Haavelmo in economics (Morgan, 1987).

The following sections investigate the different ways in which inferential statistics has been spelled out, with a focus on the most prominent school in modern social science: Fisher's method of significance testing.

SIGNIFICANCE TESTS AND STATISTICAL DECISION RULES

One of the great conceptual inventions of the founding fathers of inferential statistics was the *sampling distribution* (e.g. Fisher, 1935). In the traditional approach (e.g. classical regression), there was no need for the concept of a sample drawn from a larger population. Instead, the modeling process directly linked the observed data to a probabilistic model. In the modern understanding, the actual data are just a sample drawn out of a much larger, hypothetical population about which we want to make an inference. The rationale for this view consists in the idea that scientific results need to be *replicable*. Therefore, we have to make an inference about the comprehensive population (or the data-generating process, for that matter) instead of making an 'in sample'-inference, whose validity is restricted to the particular data we observed. This idea of a sampling distribution proved crucial for what is known today as frequentist statistics. That approach strongly relies on the idea of the sampling distribution, outlined in the seminal works of Fisher (1925, 1935, 1956) and Neyman and Pearson (1933, 1967), parting ways with the classical accounts of Bayes, Laplace, Venn and others.

In frequentist statistics, there is a sharp division between approaches that focus on inductive *behavior*, such as the Neyman–Pearson school, and those that focus on inductive *inference*, such as Fisherian statistics. To elucidate the difference, we will present both approaches in a nutshell. Neyman and Pearson (1933) developed a behavioral framework for deciding between two competing hypotheses. For instance, take the hypothesis H_0 that a certain learning device does not improve the students' performance, and compare it to the hypothesis H_1 that there is such an effect. The outcome of the test is interpreted as a judgment on the hypothesis, or the prescription to take a certain action ('accept/reject H_0'). They contrast two hypotheses H_0 and H_1 and develop testing procedures such that the probability of erroneously rejecting H_0 in favor of H_1 is bounded at a certain level α, and that the probability of erroneously rejecting H_1 in favor of H_0 is, given that constraint, as low as possible. In other words, Neyman and Pearson aim at maximizing the *power* of a test (i.e., the chance of a correct decision for H_1) under the condition that the *level* of the test (the chance of an incorrect decision for H_1) is bounded at a real number α. Thus, they developed a more or less symmetric framework for making a decision between competing hypotheses, with the aim of minimizing the chance of a wrong decision.

While such testing procedures apply well to issues of quality control in industrial manufacturing and the like, the famous biologist and statistician Ronald A. Fisher (1935, 1956) argued that they are not suitable for the use in science. First, a proper behaviorist, or decision-theoretic, approach has to determine costs for faulty decisions (and Neyman–Pearson do this implicitly, by choosing the level α of a test). This involves, however, reference to the purposes to which we want to put our newly acquired knowledge. For Fisher, this is not compatible with the idea of science as pursuit of truth. Statistical inference has to be 'convincing to all freely reasoning minds, entirely independent of any intentions that might be furthered by utilizing the knowledge inferred' (Fisher, 1956: 103).

Second, in science, a judgment on the truth of a hypothesis is usually not made on the basis of a single experiment. Instead, we obtain some provisional result which is refined through further analysis. By their behavioral rationale and by making a 'decision' between two hypotheses, Neyman and Pearson insinuate that the actual data justify a judgment on whether H_0 or H_1 is true. Such judgments have, according to Fisher, to be suspended until further experiments confirm the hypothesis, ideally using varying auxiliary assumptions and experimental designs. Third, Neyman and Pearson test a statistical hypothesis against a definite alternative. This leads to some seemingly paradoxical results.

Take, for instance, the example of a normal distribution with known variance $\sigma^2 = 1$ where the hypothesis about the mean H_0: $\mu = 0$ is tested against the hypothesis H_1: $\mu = 1$. If the average of the observations centers, say, around -5, it appears that neither H_0 or H_1 should be 'accepted'. Nevertheless, the Neyman–Pearson rationale contends that, in such a situation, we have to accept H_0 because the discrepancy to the actual data is less striking than with H_1. In such a situation, when H_0 offers a poor fit to the data, such a decision is arguably weird.

Summing up, Fisher disqualifies Neyman and Pearson's decision-theoretic approach as a mathematical 'reinterpretation' of his own significant tests, that is utterly inappropriate for use in the sciences. In fact, he suspects that Neyman and Pearson would not have come up with their approach, had they had 'any real familiarity with work in the natural sciences' (Fisher, 1956: 76). Therefore, he developed a methodology of his own which proved extremely influential in the natural as well as the social sciences. His first two books, *Statistical Methods for Research Workers* (1925) and *The Design of Experiments* (1935) quickly went through many reprints and shaped the applications of statistics in the sciences for decades. The core of his method is the *test of a point null hypothesis*, or *significance test*. The objective here is to tell chance effects from real effects. To this end, we check whether a null (default, chance) hypothesis is good enough to fit the data. For instance, we want to test the effects of a new learning device on students' performance, and we start with the default assumption that the new device yields no improvement. If that hypothesis is apparently incompatible with the data (if the results are 'significant'), we conclude that there is some effect in the treatment. The core of the argument consists in *Fisher's Disjunction*:

'Either an exceptionally rare chance has occurred, or the theory [= the null hypothesis] is not true'. (Fisher, 1956: 39)

In other words, the occurrence of a result that is very unlikely to be a product of mere chance (students using the device scoring much better than the rest) strongly speaks against the null hypothesis that there is no effect. Significant findings under the null suggest that there is more than pure chance involved, that there is some kind of systematic effect going on. As we will see below, this disjunction should be regarded with great caution, and it has been the source of many confusions and misunderstandings.

Figure 31.1 illustrates the difference between Neyman–Pearsonian and Fisherian tests for the case of testing hypotheses on the mean value of a normal distribution. The probability

$$p(\text{x}): = P\,(T > T(\text{x}) \mid H_0)$$

gives the *significance level* which the observed value x achieves under H_0, with respect to a function T that measures distance from the null hypothesis H_0. The probability $p(\text{x})$ is also often called the *p-value* induced by x, and is supposed to give a rough idea of the tenability of the null. The higher the discrepancy, the more significant the result.

The rationale underlying Fisher's Disjunction displays a striking similarity to Karl Popper's falsificationist philosophy of science: A hypothesis H_0, which should be as precise and ambiguity-free as possible, is tested by checking its observational implications. If our observations contradict H_0, we reject it and replace it by another hypothesis. However, this understanding of falsificationism only applies to testing deterministic hypotheses. Observations are never incompatible with probabilistic hypotheses; they are just very unlikely. Therefore, Popper (1959: 191) expanded the falsificationist rationale by saying that we regard a hypothesis H_0 as false when the observed results are improbable enough. This is exactly the rationale of Fisher's Disjunction. Notably, Fisher formulated these ideas as early as Popper, and independently of him.

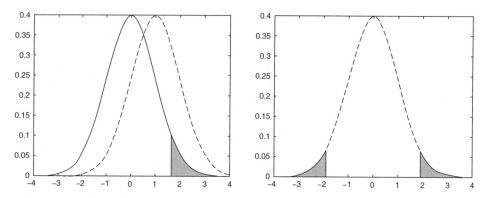

Figure 31.1   Left figure: The null hypothesis H0: N(0,1) (full line) is tested at the 5%-level against the alternative H1: N(1,1) (dashed line). Right figure: a Fisherian significance test of H_0 against an unspecified alternative. The shaded areas represent the set of results where H_0 is rejected in favor of H_1, respectively where the results speak 'significantly' against H_0.

The methodological similarity between Popper and Fisher's views becomes even more evident in the following quote:

> [...] it should be noted that the null hypothesis is never proved or established, but is possibly disproved, in the course of experimentation. Every experiment may be said to exist only in order to give the facts a chance of disproving the null hypothesis. (Fisher, 1935: 19)

This denial of positive confirmation of the null by non-significant results fits well not only with Popper's view on confirmation and corroboration, but also with a more modern textbook citation:

> Although a significant departure [from the null] provides some degree of evidence against a null hypothesis, it is important to realize that a 'nonsignificant' departure does not provide positive evidence in favor of that hypothesis. The situation is rather that we have failed to find strong evidence against the null hypothesis. (Armitage and Berry, 1987: 96)

Thus, the symmetry of the Neyman–Pearsonian approach is broken: While Neyman–Pearson tests end up 'accepting' either hypothesis (and building action on the basis of this decision), Fisherian significance tests understand a significant result as strong evidence against the null hypothesis, an insignificant result does not mean evidence for the null.

The attentive reader might have noticed that Fisher's Disjunction is actually inconsistent with his own criticism of the Neyman–Pearson approach. Recall that Fisher argued that significant outcomes do not deliver final verdicts on the feasibility of the null hypothesis. Rather, they state provisional evidence against the null. But how is this compatible with the idea of 'disproving the null' by means of significance tests? To reconcile both positions, Fisher has to admit some abuse of language:

> [...] if we use the term rejection for our attitude to such a [null] hypothesis, it should be clearly understood that no irreversible decision has been taken; that as rational beings, we are prepared to be convinced by future evidence that [...] in fact a very remarkable and exceptional coincidence had taken place. (Fisher, 1959: 35)

In light of these ambiguities, it does not surprise that Fisher's writings have been the source of many misunderstandings, and that scientists sometimes use fallacious practices or interpretations while believing that these practices have been authorized by a great statistician. Before describing the problems of significance tests, however, we would like to shed light on the contrast between frequentist statistics, which comprise Fisher's approach as well as the Neyman–Pearson paradigm, and the rivaling school of Bayesian statistics.

FISHER VERSUS BAYES

Bayesian inference is a school of statistics with great significance for some theoretical branches of the social sciences, such as decision theory, game theory, and the psychology of human reasoning. Since the principles of Bayesian inference are explained in the chapter on decision theory, we restrict ourselves to a brief outline of the basic idea. Bayesian statistics is, essentially, a theory of belief revision: Prior beliefs on the credibility of a hypothesis H are represented by mathematical probabilities, modified in the light of incoming evidence E and transformed into posterior beliefs (represented by a conditional probability, $P(H|E)$). The relevant formula that expresses how these beliefs are changed is Bayes's Theorem:

$$P(H \mid E) = \frac{P(H)\,P(E \mid H)}{P(E)}$$

$$= \frac{P(H)\,P(E|H)}{P(E \mid H)\,P(H) + P(E| \neg H)\,P(\neg H)}$$

$$= \left(1 + \frac{P(\neg H)}{P(H)} \cdot \frac{P(E| \neg H)}{P(E|H)}\right)^{-1}$$

Thus, the sampling distributions of E under H and ~H are combined with the prior probability of H in order to arrive at a comprehensive verdict on the credibility of H in the light of evidence E.

Modern philosophers of statistics – but also scientists themselves – have stressed the contrast between frequentist and Bayesian inference, depicting them as mutually exclusive schools of statistics (Howson and Urbach, 2006; Mayo, 1996). The polemics which both Bayesians and frequentists use to mock their respective opponents adds to the image of statistics as a deeply divided discipline where two enemy camps are quarreling about the right foundations of inductive inference. In particular, Bayesians have been eager to point out the limitations and shortcomings of frequentist inference for scientific applications, such as in the seminal paper of Edwards et al. (1963). Notably, this influential methodological contribution appeared not in a statistics journal, but in *Psychological Review*! On the other hand, frequentist criticisms of Bayesian inference read equally harshly.

These heated debates do not do justice to the intentions of the founding fathers, who were often more pragmatic than one might retrospectively be inclined to think. Take the case of Ronald A. Fisher. Although Fisher is correctly perceived as one of the founding fathers of frequentist inference, it is wrong to see him as an anti-Bayesian. True, Fisher objects to the use of prior probabilities in scientific inference. But it is important to see why and under which circumstances. In principle, he says, there is nothing wrong with using Bayes' formula to revise one's belief. It is just *practically* impossible to base a sound scientific judgment on them. For how shall we defend a specific assignment of prior beliefs vis-à-vis our fellow scientists if they are nothing more than psychological tendencies? Most often, there is no knowledge available on which we could base specific prior beliefs (1935: 6–7; 1956: 17). That said, Fisher speaks very respectfully about Bayes and his framework: Bayesian inference may be appropriate in science if genuine prior knowledge is available (1935: 13), and he admits the rationality of the subjective probability interpretation in spite of his own inclination to view probabilities as relative frequencies.

It is therefore important to note that the debate between frequentist (here: Fisherian) and Bayesian statistics is not in the first place a debate about the principles of inductive inference in general, but a debate about which kind of inference is more appropriate for the purposes of *science*. The following section will cast some doubts on the appropriateness of pure, unaided significance testing in the social sciences.

THE PITFALLS OF SIGNIFICANCE TESTING

The practice of significance tests has been dominating experiments in the social sciences for more than half a century. Journal editors and referees ask for significance tests and p-values (quantities describing the level of significance), standardizing experimental reports in a wide variety of branches of science (econometrics, experimental psychology, behavioral economics, etc.). Alternative approaches, for example, the application of Bayesian or likelihoodist statistics to the evaluation of experiments, have little chance of being published.

These publication practices in the last decades are at odds with the existence of a long methodological debate on significance testing in the social sciences (e.g. Rozeboom, 1960). In that debate, statisticians and social scientists – mostly mathematically educated psychologists – have repeatedly criticized the misuse of significance tests in the evaluation and interpretation of scientific experiments. Before going into the details of that debate, we briefly list some apparent advantages of significance testing.

1 Objectivity: Significance tests avoid the subjective probabilities of Bayesian statistics. Thereby, the observed levels of significance seem to be an objective standard for evaluating the experiment, for example, for telling a chance effect from a real one.
2 No Alternative Hypotheses: Significance tests are a means of testing a single, exact hypothesis, without specifying a certain direction of departure (i.e., an alternative hypothesis). Therefore, significance tests detect more kinds of deviation from that hypothesis than Neyman–Pearson tests do.
3 Replicability: Significance tests address the issue of replicability – namely the significance level can be understood as the relative frequency of observing a more extreme result if (i) the null hypothesis were true and (ii) the trial were repeated very often.
4 Practicality. Significance tests are easy to implement, and significance levels are easy to compute.

However, it is not clear whether these advantages of significance tests are really convincing. We discuss some objections.

Fisher's Disjunction revisited

The original example which Fisher used to motivate his famous disjunction was the hypothesis that the stars are evenly distributed in the sky, that is, the chance that a star is in a particular area of the sky is proportional to the size of that area. Thus, if there are a lot of stars next to a particular star, such an event is unlikely to happen due to chance. Indeed, clusters of stars are frequently observed. According to Fisher's Disjunction, we may rule out the hypothesis of uniform distributions and conclude that stars tend to cluster.

However, Hacking (1965: 81–82) has convincingly argued that such an application of Fisher's Disjunction is fallacious. Under the hypothesis of uniform distribution, every constellation of stars is extremely unlikely, and there are no likely versus unlikely chances, but *only* 'exceptionally rare chances'. If Fishers Disjunction were correct, we would, independent of the outcome, always have to reject the hypothesis of uniform distribution. This amounts to a *reductio* of significance testing, since, clearly, hypotheses that postulate a uniform distribution are testable, and they often occur in scientific practice.

To circumvent Hacking's objection, we might interpret Fisher's Disjunction in a different way. For instance, we could read the 'exceptionally rare chance' as a chance that is exceptionally rare *compared to other possible events*, instead of 'a probability lower than a fixed value p'. Still, this does not help us in the present problem, because the uniform distribution postulates that all star constellations are equally likely or unlikely. Thus, the notion of a relatively rare chance ceases to apply (Royall, 1997: 65–68).

One might concede Hacking's objection for this special case and try to rescue significance tests in general by introducing a parameter of interest, μ. This is a standard situation in statistical practice. For instance, let us take a coin flip model which has 'heads' and 'tails' as possible outcomes, and where the parameter μ denotes the propensity of the coin to come up heads. Under the null hypothesis H_0: $\mu = 0.5$, all sequences of heads and tails are equally likely, but still, it is ostensibly meaningful to say that 'HHHHHTTTTT' or 'THTHTHTHTH' provides less evidence against H_0 than 'HHHHHHHIIHH' does. The technical concept for implementing this intuition consists in calculating the chance of a transformation of the data that is a *minimally sufficient statistic* with respect to the parameter of interest μ, such as the number of heads or tails. Then we get the desired result that ten heads, but not five heads versus five tails (in whatever order) constitute a significant finding against H_0. Thus, there is no exceptionally rare chance as such – any such chance is relative to the choice of a parameter that determines *the way in which the data are exceptional*.

This line of reasoning fits well with the above example, but it introduces implicit alternative hypotheses. When relativizing unexpectedness to a parameter of interest, we are committing ourselves to a specific class of potential alternative hypotheses – namely those hypotheses that correspond to the other parameter values. When applying Fisher's Disjunction, we do not judge the tenability of H_0 'in general', without recourse to a specific parameter of interest or a class of alternatives. We always examine a certain way the data could deviate from the null. Thus, we are not testing the probability model H_0 as such, but a particular aspect thereof, such as 'why that value of μ rather than another one'? The choice of a parameter reveals a class of intended alternatives.[13]

This has some general morals: What makes an observation evidence against a hypothesis is not its low probability under this hypothesis, but its low probability compared to an alternative hypothesis. An improbable event is not evidence against a hypothesis *per se*, but

> [...] what it does show is that if there is any alternative hypothesis which will explain the occurrence of the sample with a more reasonable probability [...] you will be very much more inclined to consider that the original hypothesis is not true. (William S. Gosset ('Student') in private communication to Egon Pearson, quoted in Royall, 1997: 68)

Thus, Fisher's Disjunction and the inference from relatively unlikely results to substantial evidence is caught in a dilemma: Either we run into the inconsistencies described above, or the choice of the test statistics reveals implicit alternatives to which the hypothesis is compared. Then, the falsificationist heuristics of Fisher's Disjunction has to be replaced by an account of contrastive testing. Then, it is unclear to what extent the Fisherian framework of significance testing can claim any advantage vis-à-vis Neyman and Pearson's tests of two competing hypotheses.

The base rate fallacy

Gigerenzer (1993) famously characterized the inner life of a scientist who uses statistical methods by means of an analogy from psychoanalysis: There is a Neyman–Pearsonian Super-Ego, a Fisherian Ego and a Bayesian Id. The Neyman–Pearsonian Super-Ego preserves a couple of unintuitive insights, for example, that we cannot test a theory without specifying alternatives, that significance tests only give us the probability of data given a hypothesis instead of an assessment of the hypothesis' credibility. The Bayesian Id is located at the other end of the spectrum, incorporating the researcher's desire for posterior probabilities of a hypothesis, as a measure of its tenability or credibility. The Ego is caught in the conflict between these extremes, and acts as the scientist's guide through reality. It adopts a Fisherian position where both extremes are kept in balance: Significance tests neither give behavioral prescription, nor posterior probabilities. Rather, they yield 'a rational and well-defined measure of reluctance to the acceptance of the hypotheses they test' (Fisher, 1956: 44).

However, the Bayesian Id sometimes breaks through. As pointed out by Oakes (1986) and Gigerenzer (1993), most active researchers in the social sciences – even those with statistical education – tend to interpret significance levels (e.g. p = 0.01) as posterior probabilities of the null hypothesis, or at least as overwhelming evidence against the null. Why is this inference wrong?

Assume we want to test a certain null hypothesis against a very implausible alternative, for example, that the person under test has a very rare disease. So, the null denotes absence of the disease. Now, a highly sensitive test, that is right about 99.9 percent of the time, indicates presence of the disease, yielding a very low p-value. Many people would now be tempted to conclude that the person probably has the disease. But since that disease is rare, the posterior probability of the null hypothesis can still be very large. In other words, *evidence* that speaks to a large degree against the null is not sufficient to support a *judgment* against the null. It would only do so if the null and the alternative were about equally likely at the outset. Such a failure to recognize the dependency between the *base rate* of the null hypothesis and the strength of the final evidential judgment is called the *base rate fallacy*.

Although that fallacy is severe and widespread (and similar misinterpretations of significance tests abound, see Gigerenzer, 2008), those fallacies might speak more against the practice of significance testing than against significance tests themselves. In any case, they invite misinterpretations, especially because p-values (significance levels) are hard to relate to scientifically meaningful conclusions.[14]

The replicability fallacy

This fallacy is more subtle than the base rate fallacy. It does not interpret p-values as posterior probabilities, but understands a p-value of, say, 0.05 as saying that if the experiment were repeated, a result that was at least as significant as the present observations would occur at 95 per cent of the time. Thus, the outcome is believed to have implications for the recurrence of a significant result and for the replicability of the present observations. And replicability is, needless to say, one of the main quality brands of good experiments.

In principle, there is nothing wrong with connecting replicability to significance testing. But a crucial premise is left out – namely that the replication frequency holds only *under the assumption that the null hypothesis is true*. Since the power of many significance tests is low, implying that nonsignificant results often occur when the null is actually false, the kind of replicability that significance tests ensure is much more narrow than desired (Schmidt and Hunter, 1997). A solution to this problem that has gained more and more followers in the last decades is to replace significance levels by confidence intervals that address the issue of replicability regardless of whether the null hypothesis is actually true.

The Jeffrey–Lindley paradox

This problem sheds light on the importance of sample size in statistical testing, and applies to both Fisher's and Neyman and Pearson's frameworks. For a large enough sample, a point null hypothesis can be rejected at a significant level, while the posterior probability of the null approaches one (Lindley, 1957). Take, for instance, a normal model $N(0,1)$ where we test the value of the mean, $H_0: \mu = 0$, against an alternative, $H_1: \mu = 1$. Since the sampling distribution of the mean of n samples approaches $N(0, 1/n)$, any slight deviation of the mean from the null hypothesis will suffice to make the result statistically significant. Even more, if we decide to sample on until we get significant results against the null hypothesis, we will finally get them (Mayo and Kruse, 2001).

At the same time, the posterior of the null hypothesis also converges to 1 with increasing n, as long as the divergence remains rather small. Thus, for large samples, significance levels do not reliably indicate whether or not a certain effect is present, and can grossly deviate from the hypothesis' posterior credibility. Significance tests may tell us whether there is evidence against a point null hypothesis, but they do not tell us whether that effect is large enough to be of scientific interest.

Statistical versus practical significance

Typically, the null hypothesis denotes an idealized hypothesis, such as 'there is no difference between the effects of A and B'. In practice, no one believes such a hypothesis to be literally true. Rather, everyone expects there to be differences, but perhaps just at a minute degree: 'The effects of A and B are always different – in some decimal place – for some A and B. Thus asking 'Are the effects different?' is foolish' (Tukey, 1991: 100).

However, even experienced scientists often read tables in an article by looking out for asterisks: One asterisk denotes 'significant' findings ($p < 0.05$), two asterisks denote 'highly significant' ($p < 0.01$) findings. It is almost impossible to resist the psychological drive to forget about the subtle differences between statistical and scientific significance, and many writers exploit that fact: 'All psychologists know that statistically significant does not mean plain-English significant, but if one reads the literature, one often discovers that a finding reported in the Results sections studded with asterisks becomes in the Discussion section highly significant or very

highly significant, important, big!' (Cohen, 1994: 1001).

Instead, statistical significance should at best mean that evidence speaks against our idealized hypothesis while we are still unable to give the direction of departure or the size of the observed effect (Kirk, 1996). This provisional interpretation is in line with Fisher's own scepticism regarding the interpretation of significance tests, and Keuzenkamp and Magnus' (1995) observation that significance testing in econometrics rarely leads to the dismissal of an economic theory, and its subsequent replacement.

Finally, under the assumption that null hypotheses are strictly spoken wrong, it is noteworthy that significance tests bound the probability of erroneously rejecting the null while putting no constraints on the probability of erroneously *accepting* the null, that is, the power of a test. Considerations of power, sample size and effect size that are fundamental in Neyman and Pearson's approach fall out of the simplified Fisherian picture of significance testing. This is not to say that these tests are worthless: For instance, in econometrics, a series of significance tests can be very useful to detect whether a model of a certain process has been *misspecified*. Significance tests look for directions in different departures (autocorrelation, moving average, etc.), and significant results provide us with reasons to believe that our model has been misspecified, and make us think harder about the right form of the model that we want to use in future research (Mayo and Spanos, 2004; Spanos, 1986).

In that spirit, it should be stressed once more that Fisher considered significance tests to be a preliminary, exploratory form of statistical analysis that gives rise to further investigation, not to final decisions on a hypothesis. But reading social science journals, it is not always clear that the practicing researchers are aware of the problem. The penultimate section briefly sketches how this problem was addressed in the last decades.

RECENT TRENDS

The criticisms of significance testing have led many authors to conclude that significance tests do not help to address scientifically relevant questions. Using them in spite of their inability to address the relevant questions only invites misuse and confusion (Cohen, 1994; Schmidt, 1996). Since the problem and its discussion were especially pronounced in experimental psychology, we focus on the reactions in that field.

Recognizing that those criticisms were justified, the American Psychological Association (APA) appointed a Task Force on Statistical Interference (TFSI) whose task consisted in investigating controversial methodological issues in inferential statistics, including significance testing and its alternatives (Harlow et al., 1997; Thompson, 1999a; Wilkinson et al., 1999). After long deliberation, the Task Force issued some recommendations that made the APA change their publication guidelines, and this affected major journals affiliated to the APA, such as *Psychological Review*. The commission stated, for instance, that p-values do not reflect the significance or magnitude of an observed effect, and 'encouraged' authors to provide information on effect size, either by means of directly reporting an effect size measure (e.g. Pearson's correlation coefficient r or Cohen's effect size measure d), or power and sample size of the test.

However, as predicted by Sedlmeier and Gigerenzer (1989), and observed by a large body of empirical studies on research practice (e.g. Keselman et al., 1998), the admonitions and encouragements of the APA publication manual proved to be futile. First, psychologists were not trained at computing and working with effect sizes. Second, 'there is only one force that can effect a change, namely the editors of the major journals' (Sedlmeier and Gigerenzer, 1989: 315). Encouragement was likely to be ignored when compared to the compulsory requirements when submitting a manuscript and abiding by formatting

guidelines: 'To present an "encouragement" in the context of strict absolute [manuscript] standards [...] is to send the message "these myriad requirements count, this encouragement doesn't"' (Thompson, 1999b: 162).

However, the extensive methodological debate finally seems to bear fruit. As pointed out by Vacha-Haase et al. (2000), several editors changed their policy, requiring the inclusion of effect size measures, where unwillingness to comply with that guideline had to be justified in a special note. This development, though far from overturning and eliminating all fallacious practices, shows that sensitivity for the issue has increased, and raises hope for the future.

Also, Bayesian methods (and other approaches, such as Royall's (1997) likelihoodism) gain increasing acceptance beyond purely technical journals. Such inferential methods can now, to an increasing extent, also be found in major psychology journals. Finally, there is an increasing amount of journals that address a readership that is interested in mathematical and statistical modeling in the social sciences, as well as in methodological foundations. Although the presentation and interpretation of statistical findings in the social sciences is still wanting, there is some reason for optimism: The problems have been discovered and addressed, and we are now in the phase where a change towards a more reliable methodology is about to be effectuated. As stated by Cohen (1994), this change is slowed down by the conservativeness of many scientists, and their desire for automated inferential mechanisms. But such 'cooking recipes' do, as the drawbacks of significance tests teach us, not exist.

SUMMARY

Let us conclude the present chapter. In this contribution, we have surveyed and classified a variety of mathematical methods that are used in the social sciences. We have argued that such techniques, in spite of several methodological objections, can add extra value to social scientific research. Then, we have focused on methodological issues in statistics, that is, the part of mathematics that is most frequently used in the social sciences, in particular in the design and interpretation of experiments. We have represented the emergence of and rationale behind the ubiquitous significance tests, and explained the pitfalls to which many researches fall prey when using them. Finally, after comparing significance testing to rival schools of statistical inference, we have discussed recent trends in the methodology of the social sciences, argued that there is reason for optimism, and that awareness of methodological problems, as well as interest for mathematical and statistical techniques is growing.

ACKNOWLEDGMENTS

Thanks to Paul Humphreys and Alex Rosenberg for helpful comments on an earlier draft of this chapter.

NOTES

1 In our usage, 'social science' includes disciplines such as anthropology, political science, and sociology, but also economics and parts of linguistics and psychology.

2 Throughout this chapter, we use the word 'method' in a rather broad sense, including specific methods such as the axiomatic method as well as more specific tools like utility theory. The latter is a method in the sense that it is used to address certain questions that arise in the social sciences.

3 For a lucid exposition of many of these methods, and interesting though somewhat outdated examples from the social sciences, see Luce and Suppes (1968).

4 See http://www.illc.uva.nl/COMSOC/

5 For a discussion of computer simulations in the social sciences, see Hegselmann et al. (1996). In this context it is interesting to study the influence of the

work done at the Santa Fe Institute on mainstream economics. See for example, Anderson et al. (1988). See also Waldrop (1992).

6 For a more detailed discussion of modeling in the social sciences, see Chapter 28 ('Idealized representations, inferential devices and cross-disciplinary tools: Theoretical models in social sciences') of this handbook. For a general review of models in science, see Frigg and Hartmann (2006). See also Sugden (2008).

7 See Chapter 14 ('Rational choice theory') of this handbook. See also Bermúdez (2009).

8 See Chapter 15 ('Game theory') of this handbook. See also Morrow (1994).

9 See Chapter 17 (Normative Criteria of social choice) of this handbook.

10 See also Chapter 16 (Social networks) of this handbook.

11 This view can be traced back to *Kelvin's dictum* '... when you can measure what you are speaking about and can express it in numbers, you know something about it; but when you cannot measure it, when you cannot express it in numbers, your knowledge is of a meagre and unsatisfactory kind'. See Merton et al. (1984). It gave rise to much controversy in the philosophy of social science, reflecting deeper issues in the philosophy of mind and metaphysics.

12 For more doubts about some of the uses of simulations in the social sciences, see Humphreys (2004).

13 There is no canonical class of alternatives: we could plausibly suspect that the coin has an in-built mechanism that makes it come up with alternating results, and then, 'THTHTHTHTH' would not be an insignificant finding, but speak to a high degree against the chance hypothesis.

14 See Casella and Berger (1987) and Berger and Sellke (1987) for more detailed discussions of the evidential value of p-values in different testing problems.

REFERENCES

Anderson, P., K. Arrow and D. Pines (eds) (1988): *The Economy As An Evolving Complex System*. Redwood City: Addison-Wesley.

Armitage, P. and G. Berry (1987) *Statistical Methods in Medical Research*. 2nd edn. New York: Springer.

Arrow, K. et al. (eds) (1960) *Mathematical Methods in the Social Sciences*. Stanford: Stanford University Press.

Backhouse, R. (1995) *A History of Modern Economic Analysis*. Oxford: Blackwell.

Balzer, W., C.U. Moulines and J. Sneed (1987) *An Architectonic for Science: The Structuralist Program.* Dordrecht: Reidel.

Beed, C. and O. Kane (1991) 'What is the critique of the mathematization of economics? *Kyklos*, 44(4): 581–612.

Berger, J.O. and T. Sellke (1987) 'Testing a point null hypotheses: The irreconciliability of p-values and evidence (with discussion)', *Journal of the American Statistical Association*, 82: 112–122.

Bermúdez, J.L. (2009) *Decision Theory and Rationality.* Oxford: Oxford University Press.

Casella, G. and R.L. Berger (1987) 'Reconciling Bayesian and frequentist evidence in the one-sided testing problem', *Journal of the American Statistical Association*, 82: 106–111.

Cohen, J. (1994) 'The earth is round (p < .05)', *American Psychologist*, 49: 997–1001.

Debreu, G. (1991) 'The mathematization of economic theory', *American Economic Review*, 81(1): 1–7.

Edwards, W., H. Lindman and L.J. Savage (1963) 'Bayesian statistical inference for psychological research', *Psychological Review*, 70: 450–499.

Fisher, R.A. (1925) *Statistical Methods for Research Workers.* Edinburgh: Oliver and Boyd.

Fisher, R.A. (1935) *The Design of Experiments.* Edinburgh: Oliver and Boyd.

Fisher, R.A. (1956) *Statistical Methods and Scientific Inference.* New York: Hafner.

Fogel, R.W. (1975) 'The limits of quantitative methods in history', *American Historical Review*, 80(2): 329–50.

Frigg, R. and S. Hartmann (2006) 'Models in science' in *The Stanford Encyclopedia of Philosophy*, (Spring 2006 Edition).

Frigg, R. and J. Reiss (2010) 'The philosophy of simulation: Hot new issues or same old stew?', *Synthese*, 169(3): 593–613.

Gaertner, W. (2006) *A Primer in Social Choice Theory.* New York: Oxford University Press.

Gallegatti, M., S. Keen, T. Lux and P. Ormerod (2006) 'Worrying trends in econophysics', *Physica A*, 370: 1–6.

Gilbert, N. and K. Troitzsch (2005) *Simulation for the Social Scientist.* New York: McGraw-Hill.

Gigerenzer, G. (1987) 'Probabilistic thinking and the fight against subjectivity', in L. Krüger, G. Gigerenzer and M. Morgan (eds) *The Probabilistic Revolution, Vol. 2: Ideas in the Sciences.* Cambridge, MA: MIT Press. pp. 11–33.

Gigerenzer, G. (1993) 'The superego, the ego, and the id in statistical reasoning', in G. Keren and C. Lewis (eds) *A Handbook for Data Analysis in the Behavioral Sciences: Methodological Issues.* Hillsdale, NJ: Erlbaum. pp. 311–339.

Gigerenzer, G. (2008):*Rationality for Mortals: How Humans Cope with Uncertainty.* Oxford: Oxford University Press.

Hacking, I. (1965) *Logic of Statistical Inference.* Cambridge: Cambridge University Press.

Hands, W. (2008) 'Popper and Lakatos in economic methodology', in D. Hausman (ed.) *The Philosophy of Economics: An Anthology.* Cambridge: Cambridge University Press. pp. 188–203.

Harlow, L., S. Mulaik and J. Steiger (eds) (1997) *What If there Were No Significance Tests?* Mahwah, NJ: Erlbaum.

Hartmann, S. (1996) 'The world as a process: Simulations in the natural and social sciences', in R. Hegselmann et al. (eds) *Modelling and Simulation in the Social Sciences from the Philosophy of Science Point of View.* Dordrecht: Kluwer. pp. 77–100.

Hausman, D. (1992) *The Inexact and Separate Science of Economics.* Cambridge: Cambridge University Press.

Hegselmann, R. et al. (eds) (1996) *Modelling and Simulation in the Social Sciences from the Philosophy of Science Point of View.* Dordrecht: Kluwer.

Howson, C. and P. Urbach (2006) *Scientific Reasoning: The Bayesian Approach.* 3rd edn. Open Court, La Salle.

Humphreys, P. (2004) *Extending Ourselves: Computational Science, Empiricism, and Scientific Method.* Oxford: Oxford University Press.

Jackson, M. (2008) *Social and Economic Networks.* Princeton: Princeton University Press.

Keselman, H.J. et al. (1998) 'Statistical practices of educational researchers: An analysis of their ANOVA, MANOVA and ANCOVA analyses', *Review of Educational Research*, 68: 350–386.

Keuzenkamp, H. and J. Magnus (1995) 'On tests and significance in econometrics', *Journal of Econometrics*, 67: 5–24.

Kirk, R. (1996) 'Practical significance: A concept whose time has come', *Educational and Psychological Measurement*, 56: 746–759.

Kitcher, P. (1989) 'Explanatory unification and the causal structure of the world', in P. Kitcher and W. Salmon (eds) *Scientific Explanation, vol. XIII of Minnesota Studies in the Philosophy of Science.* Minneapolis: University of Minnesota Press. pp. 410–505.

Kolmogorov, A.N. (1933/56) *Foundations of the Theory of Probability.* New York: Chelsea. Original work published in German in 1933.

Krantz, D.H., R.D. Luce, P. Suppes and A. Tversky (1971) *Foundations of Measurement. Vol. I. Additive and Polynomial Representations.* New York: Academic Press.

Lindley, D. (1957) 'A statistical paradox', *Biometrika*, 44: 187–192.

List, C. and C. Puppe (2009) 'Judgment aggregation: A survey', in P. Anand, C. Puppe and P. Pattaniak (eds) *Oxford Handbook of Rational and Social Choice*. Oxford: Oxford University Press. pp. 457–482.

Luce, R.D. and P. Suppes (1968) 'Mathematics', in *International Encyclopedia of the Social Sciences, Vol. 10*. New York: Macmillan and Free Press. pp. 65–76.

Mantegna, R. and H. Stanley (1999) *An Introduction to Econophysics: Correlations and Complexity in Finance*. Cambridge: Cambridge University Press.

Marchi, S. de (2005) *Computational and Mathematical Modeling in the Social Sciences*. Cambridge: Cambridge University Press.

Mayo, D. (1996) *Error and the Growth of Experimental Knowledge*. Chicago: Chicago University Press.

Mayo, D. and M. Kruse (2001) 'Principles of inference and their consequences', in D. Corfield and J. Williamson (eds) *Foundations of Bayesianism*. Dordrecht: Kluwer. pp. 381–403.

Mayo, D. and A. Spanos (2004) 'Methodology in practice: Statistical misspecification testing', *Philosophy of Science*, 71: 1007–1025.

Merton, R., D. Sills and S. Stigler (1984) 'The Kelvin dictum and social science: An excursion into the history of an idea', *Journal of the History of the Behavioral Sciences*, 20: 319–331.

Morgan, M. (1987) 'Statistics without probability and Haavelmo's revolution in econometrics', in L. Krüger, G. Gigerenzer and M. Morgan (eds) *The Probabilistic Revolution, Vol. 2: Ideas in the Sciences*. Cambridge, MA: MIT Press. pp. 171–197.

Morgan, M. (2002) *The History of Econometric Ideas*. Cambridge: Cambridge University Press.

Morrow, J. (1994) *Game Theory for Political Scientists*. Princeton: Princeton University Press.

Neyman, J. and E. Pearson (1933) 'On the problem of the most efficient tests of statistical hypotheses', *Philosophical Transactions of the Royal Society A*, 231: 289–337.

Neyman, J. and E. Pearson (1967) *Joint Statistical Papers*. Cambridge: Cambridge University Press.

Oakes, M. (1986) *Statistical Inference. A Commentary for the Social and Behavioral Sciences*. New York: Wiley.

Piotrowski, E. and J. Sladkowski (2003) 'An invitation to quantum game theory', *International Journal of Theoretical Physics*, 42: 1089–1099.

Popper, K.R. (1959) *The Logic of Scientific Discovery*. London: Routledge.

Royall, R. (1997) *Statistical Evidence – A Likelihood Paradigm*. London: Chapman & Hall.

Rozeboom, W.W. (1960) 'The fallacy of the null hypothesis significance test', *Psychological Bulletin*, 57: 416–428.

Schmidt, F.L. (1996) 'Statistical significance testing and cumulative knowledge in psychology: Implications for training of researchers', *Psychological Methods*, 1: 115–129.

Schmidt, F.L. and J.E. Hunter (1997) 'Eight common but false objections to the discontinuation of significance testing in the analysis of research data', in Harlow et al. (eds) *What if There Were No Significance Tests?* Mahwah, NJ: Erlbaum. pp. 37–64.

Schultz, H. (1928) *Statistical Laws of Demand and Supply with Special Application to Sugar*. Chicago: University of Chicago Press.

Sedlmeier, P. and G. Gigerenzer (1989) 'Do studies of statistical power have an effect on the power of studies? *Psychological Bulletin*, 105: 309–316.

Spanos, A. (1986) *Statistical Foundations of Econometric Modelling*. Cambridge: Cambridge University Press.

Strevens, M. (2009) *Depth: An Account of Scientific Explanation*. Cambridge MA: Harvard University Press.

Sugden, R. (2008) 'Credible Worlds: The Status of Theoretical Models in Economics', in D. Hausman (ed.) *The Philosophy of Economics: An Anthology*. Cambridge: Cambridge University Press, pp. 476–509.

Suppes, P. (2001) *Representation and Invariance of Scientific Structures*. Chicago: University of Chicago Press.

Thompson, B. (1999a) 'If statistical significance tests are broken/misused, what practice should supplement or replace them?', *Theory & Psychology*, 9: 167–183.

Thompson, B. (1999b) 'Journal editorial policies regarding statistical significance tests: Heat is to fire as P is to importance', *Educational Psychology Review*, 11: 151–169.

Tukey, J.W. (1991) 'The philosophy of multiple comparisons', *Statistical Science*, 6: 100–116.

Vacha-Haase, T., J.E. Nilsson and D.R. Reetz (2000) 'Reporting practices and APA editorial policies regarding statistical significance and effect size', *Theory & Psychology*, 10: 413–425.

Vazquez, A. (1995) 'Marshall and the mathematization of economics', *Journal of the History of Economic Thought*, 17: 247–265.

Waldrop, M. (1992) *Complexity: The Emerging Science at the Edge of Order and Chaos*. New York: Simon & Schuster.

Wallace, D. (2010) 'How to proof of the Born Rule', in S. Saunders et al. (eds), *Many Worlds? Everett, Quantum Theory, and Reality*. Oxford: Oxford University Press, 227–263.

Weidlich, W. (2006) *Sociodynamics: A Systemic Approach to Mathematical Modelling in the Social Sciences.* New York: Dover Publications.

Weintraub, R. (2002) *How Economics Became a Mathematical Science.* Durham: Duke University Press.

Weintraub, R. (2008) 'Mathematics and economics', in S. Durlauf and L. Blume (eds) *The New Palgrave Dictionary of Economics.* New York: Macmillan.

Wilkinson, L. and Task Force on Statistical Inference (1999) 'Statistical methods in psychology journals: Guidelines and explanations', *American Psychologist*, 54: 594–604.

Woodward, J. (2003) *Making things happen.* Oxford: Oxford University Press.

32

Artificial Worlds and Agent-Based Simulation

Till Grüne-Yanoff

INTRODUCTION

Agent-based simulations (ABS) are often hailed as a new way of doing social science. By generating 'artificial societies' on the computer, social scientists may generate a new object of study, or a new tool for scientific study. This article investigates these claims by examining in detail the methods of ABS and its uses in the social sciences. It starts out by illustrating the different uses of ABS, and giving a short historical overview of its emergence. ABS is then contrasted with related practices in the social sciences and other disciplines. A brief philosophical discussion of some of its basic concepts follows.

After this overview, the article addresses the novelty claim head on, and discusses it in relation to existing scientific practices. The general position here will be cautious: the author's view is that ABS does not so much constitute a novel scientific practice, but is closely linked to the existing modelling practices in the social sciences. Thus the view of ABS *as* experiments or *as* theory will be treated critically, while the interactions between these practices will be

shown to be fruitful. The view of ABS as models, in contrast, will be presented in a more favourable light, but important differences that concern the way of construction, the validation and link to the target system are pointed out. Finally, potential reasons for the notable difference with which different disciplines have adopted ABS will be discussed.

Based on these results, the uses of ABS in the social sciences are investigated and appraised. This discussion will clarify the differences between the various ABS models. In particular, it is shown that uses determine many characteristics of ABS models, in terms of their level of abstraction, their necessary validation and their need for replication. Again, the position presented here will be cautious: against the many enthusiastic claims made about ABS, this article points out the various deficits that many contemporary simulation studies exhibit, particularly when in the business of explanation or forecasting. Instead, the articles points out uses with somewhat lesser profiles, like deliberation support and heuristic application, as important areas where ABS can be fruitfully employed.

USES OF ARTIFICIAL SOCIETIES

To generate a pattern or regularity with the tools of agent-based simulation is to 'situate an initial population of autonomous heterogeneous agents in a relevant special environment; allow them to interact according to simple local rules, and thereby generate – or "grow" – the macroscopic regularity from the bottom up' (Epstein, 1999: 41). The 'agents' referred to are structural entities of the simulation model. They are 'heterogeneous', because the model can specify different attributes for different agents. The simulation updates these attributes solely on the basis of the agents' interaction with each other and their environment. Agents are 'autonomous', because their interactions are determined by individual behavioural rules. 'Macroscopic regularities' concern the regular behaviour of many or all agents in certain environments. Because the simulation only computes the updating of individual agents' attributes, and the macroscopic events are only summaries of the individual changes, the simulation is said to 'grow' the regularities 'from the bottom up'. The tool of agent-based simulation has found many applications in the sciences. For illustrative purposes, a few will be described here.

Uses in the Social Sciences

ABS are used in the social sciences to generate regularities akin to social phenomena. For this reason, ABS employed in the social sciences are often called *artificial societies*. Epstein and Axtell (1996) present a general recipe for their construction in the book *Growing Artificial Societies: Social Science from the Bottom Up*. Their simulation programme *Sugarscape* is a kind of simulation laboratory. Agents move over a two-dimensional rectangular grid. Their existence, their movement and their interaction is conditional on certain agent attributes and regulated by certain rules. By manipulating the initial number and position of agents, and their

attributes and rules, different patterns arise on parts or the whole of the grid. Epstein and Axtell interpret these patterns as similar to certain social phenomena. They claim that their artificial society experiences migration, population developments, cultural identities, markets, wealth inequalities, wars and epidemics. Crucially, they claim that they can *generate* such (representations of) social phenomena by the manipulation of agent attributes and rules alone. The social thus *emerges* from the interaction of individuals in their agent-based simulations.

Many social scientists have adopted ABS as useful tools or as interesting objects of study. Today, one finds agent-based simulations of crowd dynamics (Pan et al., 2007), epidemics (Eubank et al., 2004), consumer markets (Moss, 2002), electricity markets (Bunn and Oliveira, 2003), stock markets (LeBaron, 2001; Samanidou et al., 2007), geopolitical change (Cederman, 2002) and even ancient societies (Dean et al., 2000; Axtell et al., 2002). As will be discussed later, the application of ABS in these fields follows a variety of objectives. Sometimes the goal is to be explained what is simulated, as for example, in the case of the ancient society simulation. In some other cases, the goal is to predict outcomes, for example, of strategic withholding behaviour in the electricity market. Finally, in many cases simulations are used to assess the outcomes of different policy interventions, as for example through crowed control or vaccination programmes.

Uses in Other Sciences

ABS have been widely used in disciplines outside the social sciences. First and foremost is ecology, which has produced as many agent-based models as all other disciplines together over the last 30 years (Grimm et al., 2005). Ecological applications range from modelling the spatiotemporal dynamics of beech forests of central Europe (Wissel, 1992; Rademacher, 2005), spatial distribution of animals (Catling and Coops, 2002) to agricultural change (Happe et al., 2006). Another important application is found in behavioural ecology, which studies the behaviour of animal groups, swarm and flocks. The most famous of these is Reynolds 'boid' model (Reynolds, 1987)

Other Artificial Systems

Computer simulations do not only aim at constructing artificial societies (AS), but are also, and perhaps better, known to be used for the construction of artificial intelligence (AI) and artificial life (ALife). It is clear that all these attempts have the same roots (see section on other simulation approaches), however, the branches have developed important differences.

AI is the attempt to build or construct computers to do the sort of things minds can do. Major textbooks define the field as 'the study and design of intelligent agents' where an intelligent agent is a system that perceives its environment and takes actions that maximise its chances of success (Poole et al., 1998: 1; cf. also Nilsson, 1998; Russell and Norvig 2003). Classical AI differs from AS in its focus on top-down processing. In top-down processing, a high-level description of the task (e.g. a goal or a grammar) is employed to start, supervise or guide detailed actions. In bottom-up processing, in contrast, it is the detailed input of the system that determines what will happen next. In classical AI, the top-down approach dominates, while AS exclusively operates on bottom-up processing.

Although connectionist AI works bottom up, it still differs from AS because it cannot alter its fundamental organisation. The behaviour of a connectionist model depends on the local interactions of the individual units, none of which have an overall view of the task. In that respect, it resembles AS. But all a connectionist system can do is to change the weights of different connections; while the fundamental organisation of the connections remains unchanged (Boden, 1996: 4).

AS, in contrast, can completely reorganise its own social structure – in fact, it can even cease to exist as a consequence of its own actions.

ALife employs computer simulation to study systems of life, its processes and its evolution. Although the concept of life has no universally agreed definition, certain properties are often associated with it, including autonomy, reproduction and metabolism (Boden, 1996: 1). These concepts give a first distinction of ALife from AS: while ALife studies systems that are autonomous, are reproducing and have a metabolism, none of that can be said of systems studied by AS. Although agents in AS may be autonomous, and may reproduce, artificial societies are not assumed to do so – and of course, they do not metabolise either. Further, ALife is beset with the question of *strong ALife*: whether the entities created in the computer could be genuinely said to be Alife (Ray, 1996; Sober, 1996). A similar question does not exist for AS, which generally is left burdened with less metaphysical baggage.

Other Simulation Approaches

Many different computer simulation techniques are used in the social sciences. ABS must be distinguished from equation-based and micro-simulations. Sometimes, ABS are also distinguished from Cellular Automata (CA), although the difference is not so clear-cut.

Equation-based simulations describe the dynamics of a target system with the help of equations that capture the deterministic features of the whole system. Typical examples of such equation-based simulations are system dynamics simulations, which use a set of difference or differential equation that derive the future state of the target system from its present state. System dynamics simulations are restricted to the macro level: they model the target system as an undifferentiated whole. The target system's properties are then described with a set of attributes in the form of 'level' and 'rate' variables representing the state of the whole system and its dynamics. ABS, in contrast, lack an overall description of the system's macro-properties. Instead of simulating the system's dynamics by numerically calculating the equations that describe the system's dynamics, ABS *generate* the system's dynamics by calculating the dynamics of the system's constituent parts, and aggregating these dynamics into the system dynamics.

Micro-simulations predict the effect of aggregate changes (e.g. taxation changes) on aggregate results (e.g. tax revenue) by calculating the effect of the aggregate change on sub-groups or individuals and then aggregating the individual results. No interaction between groups or individuals is taken into account here; rather, the effect on each group is determined by equations pertaining to this group. Thus, despite its focus on the micro-level, and the subsequent constitution of the macro-result as an aggregate of the micro-level, micro-simulations belong in the equation-based category. What sets ABS apart from such micro-level equation-based simulations is that they model interactions between autonomous agents, thus including a level of *complexity* not existent in equation-based models.

Cellular automata (CA) share this complexity with ABS. CAs consist of cells in a regular grid with one to three dimensions. Every cell has a number of states, which change in discreet time. The states of a cell at a given time period are determined by the states of that same cell and of neighbouring cells at earlier times. The specific kind of these influences is laid down in behavioural rules, which are identical for all cells. A famous example of a CA is Conway's Game of Life (Berlekamp et al., 1982), in which each cell is either 'dead' or 'alive'. 'Dead' cells with exactly three neighbours become 'alive', and 'alive' cells with fewer than two or more than three neighbours die. Conway's Game of Life has attracted much interest because of the surprising ways in which patterns can evolve. It illustrates the

way that complex patterns can emerge from the implementation of very simple rules.

When the internal processing abilities of automata are sufficiently high, one speaks about 'agents', and agent-based simulations, not cellular automata. Agents share with CA their autonomy from others' direct control, their ability to interact with others, react to environmental changes and actively shape the environment for themselves and others. In contrast to CA, agents are not fixed on a grid, can change their neighbours, may have multiple relations with different agents and can change on multiple levels. Because the agents' processing abilities are a matter of degree, it is difficult to draw a clear line between CA and ABS.

History

While the history of CA begins in the late 1940s with von Neumann's construction of a self-replicating machine on a paper grid, the beginnings of agent-based models lie with Thomas Schelling's model of segregation (Schelling, 1969, 1971).[1] Schelling originally used coins and graph paper rather than computers, but his models embody the basic concept of agent-based models as autonomous agents interacting in a shared environment with an observed aggregate, emergent outcome. Shortly afterwards, and apparently completely independent of Schelling, the British biologist Maynard Smith and the American chemist George R. Price devised a simulation technique for their novel solution concept of an 'evolutionary stable strategy' (Maynard Smith and Price, 1973; cf. also Sigmund, 2005). This method was very much at odds with the analytic methods used by game theorists at the time, and now stands as one of the earliest examples of an agent-based model. ABS thus had close links with evolutionary game theory and the study of adaptive systems early on and has retained them since (see Chapter 20).

ABS gained serious attraction with the advent of more powerful computers, and the development of agent-based simulation packages like SWARM and Sugarscape in the 1990s. It is noteworthy that the majority of applications in the social sciences can be found in sociology (cf. Chapter 18), while economics has been rather slow in adopting these computational methods (for an overview of the development in economics, see Tesfatsion, 2006).

CONCEPTUAL FOUNDATIONS

In this brief overview of ABS and its related fields, a number of concepts were used to characterise and differentiate ABS. However, these notions are often philosophically problematic. In the following, some of these problems are addressed.

Agents and Agency

The central difference between CA and ABS is the presence of autonomous agents in the latter (see also Chapters 8 and 14). However, cells in a CA are also often said to enjoy a degree of autonomy, so that the central difference must lie in the agency of ABS elements. But what does that mean?

Agency and action are related to the intuitive distinction between the things that merely happen to people — the events they suffer — and the various things they genuinely do. These latter doings are the actions of the agent. Philosophers have discussed at length about the nature of action, in particular, what distinguishes an action from a mere happening or occurrence. Yet most of these discussions are too fine-tuned for the current purpose. Here, it is sufficient to point out that an often used criterion for agency is goal-directedness: In artificial intelligence, for example, an *intelligent agent* is a unit which observes and acts upon an environment and directs its actions towards achieving certain goals (e.g. Russell and Norvig, 2003). Such agents may be very simple: a thermostat

is an intelligent agent, for example, which measures the environment and interferes in the heating mechanisms, with the goal of maintaining a constant temperature in the room. Further, the purposeful behaviour of animals constitutes a low-level type of purposive action. When a spider walks across the table, the spider directly controls the movements of his legs, and they are *directed at* taking him from one location to another. Those very movements have an aim or purpose for the spider, and hence they are subject to a kind of teleological explanation (Frankfurt, 1978).

Most ABS, in contrast, fail to endow their agents with a purpose. Agents in ABS commonly behave according to homogenous behavioural rules. They may differ in their attributes (e.g. age, sex, home address, occupation) and may exhibit different behaviour to the same situation due to these differences in attributes, yet these attributes are not distinguished into purposive and non-purposive ones. In the Anasazi simulation (Dean et al., 2000), for example, there is no difference when an agent moves place of settlement to when an agent dies of old age. Both are direct functions of environmental variables, and the settlement decision is – contrary to one's intuitive identification as a purposeful action – not mediated by any kind of utility function of the agent. Similarly in the small-pox simulation (Eubank et al., 2004): there is no difference between the agents' going to work and them getting infected. Although many would say that the first is a purposeful action, and the second is not, the ABS does not make a difference between them. This lacking attribution of any goal or utility function to the ABS agents makes it difficult to subject them to any teleological explanation; and hence the agency of ABS agents is somewhat insecure.

Artificiality

The results of ABS in the social sciences are often called 'artificial societies'. The nature of these societies' artificiality is ambiguous. Depending on its interpretation, not all ABS in the social sciences may be artificial societies, or artificial societies may be the results not only of ABS. At least three different interpretations can be distinguished: artificiality as (1) non-realisticness, (2) constructedness or (3) computer-generated.

Artificial societies may refer to the classes of unrealistic simulations. In some sense, all ABS-generated societies are artificial in this sense: they are codes on a computer platform and not societies in the world. Yet some of these ABS yield societies realistic at least in some respects, in that they closely resemble *aspects* of human societies. The Anasazi ABS (Dean et al., 2000), for example, is claimed to resemble the housekeeping, reproductive and migration behaviour of actual ancient people on the micro-level, and it is also claimed to resemble its population and settlement dynamics on the macro-level. In contrast to this, other ABS are not intended as simulations of human societies at all. Doran (1998), for example, simulates a society in which agents have perfect foresight (i.e. they know what will befall them in the future). Such a society may be called artificial in the sense that it is largely based on assumptions known to be false in the real world. While such a distinction would have certain merits, it would exclude many ABS, despite the fact that these ABS are commonly called artificial societies.

It may therefore be more adequate to interpret 'artificial' as 'constructed' or 'man-made'. Artificial societies are the result of modelling and programming efforts, while real societies have evolved without the intentional input of a designer or constructor. Such a distinction, however, would include under the term artificial societies social phenomena created in the laboratory, as for example produced by experimental economists. This does not seem to comply with standard usage of the term.

One may therefore be forced to narrow the interpretation further to computer simulations. Artificial society refers to processes *in silico*, which model social phenomena, as opposed to material exemplars of these processes themselves. However, the material basis of social phenomena could be challenged. While this issue has not arisen in the context of artificial societies so far, a lively debate exists with respect to artificial life. The strong Alife position claims that life is a process that can be abstracted away from any particular medium. Defenders of such a position avoid the term artificial and instead prefer 'synthetic biology' (Ray, 1996). In a similar vein, it could be argued that sociality is a process independent of its material basis, and that computer-generated interactions between agents constitute social phenomena in the same way as interactions of real-world agents.

Emergence

ABS generate macroscopic patterns from 'the bottom up' – from the interactions of many microscopic agents. It is often said that these macroscopic patterns or properties *emerge* from the microscopic ones. The term 'emergence' has a long history, which unfortunately makes its use more difficult. Some conceptual clarification is necessary.

In early twentieth century philosophy, emergence came to denote a metaphysical position on higher-level properties. Emergent properties, it was claimed, 'arise' from some lower-level properties and yet are 'irreducible' to them. The positions varied in the way properties arose and were said to be irreducible. Although different in detail, both Mill (1843) and Broad (1925) claimed that these properties are associated with irreducible higher-level causal powers; while Alexander (1920) claimed that although the emergent properties were primitive, their causal powers do not supersede more fundamental interactions. It is controversial whether Alexander's proposal is coherent as an ontological position, while Mill's and Broad's imply *downward causation*, which sits uncomfortable with many. According to downward causation, the emergent property's causal influence is irreducible to the micro-properties from which it emerges; it bears its influence in a *direct* downward fashion, *not* through the aggregation of its micro-level powers (for a defence, see O'Connor, 1994).

One way to avoid downward causation is to re-interpret emergence as an epistemic, not an ontological notion. Emergent properties then are characterised in terms of limits on human knowledge of complex systems. A property is thought of as emergent, accordingly, if it could not have been predicted from knowledge of features of its parts. More specifically, it could not have been predicted without the help of simulation (Bedau, 1997: 378). Such a concept of *weak emergence* is conceptually unproblematic, but does not capture the metaphysical spirit of previous notions.

ABS IN THE CONTEXT OF SCIENTIFIC PRACTICE

Simulation, Models and Theory

Simulations rest on models (see Chapter 28). Without models of the networks through which epidemics spread, or the landscape on which the Anasazi settle, the examples of the previous section could not have simulated anything. But while it is uncontroversial that models are important and possibly constitutive elements of simulations, it is less clear whether simulations themselves can be treated as models. Of course, in a colloquial sense, models and simulations are not properly delineated. For example, most economists think of Schelling's (1971) checkerboard model as a model, while it is also considered to be one of the earliest examples of an agent-based simulation. However, a number of differences can be identified.

One difference is the temporal dimension of simulations. Scientists often speak about a model 'underlying' the simulation. The recent smallpox infection simulation of Eubank et al. (2004), for example, is based on a model of Portland, OR, consisting of around 181,000 locations, each associated with a specific activity, like work, shopping, school and maximal occupancies. Additionally, each model inhabitant is characterised by a list of the entrance and exit times into and from a location for all locations that person visited during the day. This huge database was developed by the traffic simulation tool TRANSIMS, which in turn is based on US census data. When speaking about the model underlying the simulation, people often have such a static model in mind. The simulation itself proceeds by introducing a hypothetical 'shock' into the system (in this case, a number of infected inhabitants) and then observing how the infection spreads through the population. This dynamic aspect is often not included when people speak about the underlying model. This may be a sensible distinction, as the dynamic aspect of the simulation makes various diachronic stability assumptions that were not included in the static model (Grüne-Yanoff, 2010). Of course, the dynamic aspects may be referred to as the 'dynamic model' which includes the 'static model', yet common practice in such cases seems to be that the 'static model' is referred to as the 'underlying model'.

A second difference lies in the methods by which models can be analysed. The common way that mathematical models in the natural science or in economics are analysed is to find a solution to the set of equations that make up the model. For this purpose, calculus, trigonometry and other mathematical techniques are employed. Being able to write down the solution this way makes one absolutely sure how the model will behave under any circumstances. This is called the *analytic solution*, because of the use of analysis. It is also referred to as a closed-form solution.

However, analytic solutions work only for simple models. For more complex models, the maths becomes much too complicated. Instead, the model can be 'solved' by simulation. For, say, a differential equation that describes behaviour over time, the numerical method starts with the initial values of the variables, and then uses the equations to figure out the changes in these variables over a very brief time period. A computer must be used to perform the thousands of repetitive calculations involved. The result is a long list of numbers, not an equation. Appropriately presented, numerical simulation is often considered a 'solution' of the model.

Some proponents of simulation have argued that for every computation, there is a corresponding logical deduction (Epstein, 1999), hence from a technical standpoint, deductive modelling is but a special case of simulative modelling. However, this claim neglects important epistemic and psychological differences. As Lehtinen and Kuorikoski (2007) point out, economists largely shun simulations for epistemic and understanding-related reasons. They explain this observation by arguing that economists place a high value on the *derivation* of an analytical result, based on their belief that the cognitive process of solving a model constitutes the understanding of the model. In most simulations, the computer is a necessary tool: humans could not, even if they wanted to, perform the computations needed. The derivation of results in these simulations is outside of the reach of human agents. They leave the solution process, in the words of Paul Humphreys, 'epistemically opaque'. This opaqueness makes economists shun simulation when they seek understanding from the analytic solution process itself. It also constitutes an important difference between standard (analytically solvable) models and simulations.

To summarise, simulations differ from models mainly in their temporal expansion (and sometimes also in their representation of a temporal process) as well as in their epistemic opacity.

Simulations versus Experiments

Another perspective on simulations links them to experiments (see Chapter 30; see also Dowling, 1999; Rohrlich, 1991: 507).

Because simulations are typically based on calculations that are intractable, the results of a simulation cannot be predicted at the time when the simulation is constructed or manipulated. This allows seeing the simulation as an unpredictable and opaque entity, with which one can interact in an experimental manner. However, the legitimacy of a computer simulation still relies on the analytic understanding of at least the underlying mathematical equations, if not the computation process itself. Thus the experimental approach to simulations consists in a strategic move to 'black-box' (Dowling, 1999: 265) the known programme, and to interact 'experimentally' with the surface of the simulation.

Whether this observation suffices to subsume simulations under experiments, remains an open question. Most scientists agree that simulations have experimental moment, but hasten to add a qualifier, for example, that simulations are 'computer experiments'. Along these lines, many philosophers of science have pointed out that despite their experimental moment simulations differ from experiments in important ways.

The first argument for such a difference points to a perceived difference in the similarity relations of experiments and simulations to their targets. Gilbert and Troitzsch (1999: 13), for example, argue that in a real experiment, one controls for the actual object of interest – while in a simulation one is experimenting with a model rather than the object itself. Following a thought of Herbert Simon (1969), Guala (2005: 215) addresses a similar issue, arguing that in a real experiment, the same material causes are at work as those in the target system; while in simulations, not the same material causes are at work, and the correspondence between the simulation and its target is only abstract and formal.

Parker (2009) contradicts these claims. She points out that the use of simulations in what she calls 'computer simulation studies' involves intervention, just as laboratory experiments do. Computer simulation studies intervene on a material system, namely the programmed computer. Such studies are thus material experiments in a straightforward sense.

The second argument for the difference between experiments and simulations points out the different epistemological challenges that experiments and models face. Morgan (2003: 231) argues that they differ in their 'degree of materiality', and that this makes experiments epistemically privileged compared to simulations. One can argue for the external validity of laboratory experiments by pointing out that they share 'the same stuff' with their targets. Simulations, however, only have a formal relation to their targets, which makes establishing their external validity that much harder. Note that this argument draws on the ontological difference identified above; yet Morgan stresses the epistemological implications of these differences, and does not claim that simulations are otherwise fundamentally different from experiments.

Winsberg (2009) offers another version of this epistemological argument. Instead of drawing on the make-up of simulations, he argues that the justification for the claim that a simulation stands for a target rests on something completely different from a similar justification for experiments. The justification for simulation rests on our trust in the background knowledge that supports the construction of the simulation, in particular principles deemed reliable for model construction. The justification for experiments, in contrast, relies on a variety of factors, the most prominent maybe being that experimental object and target are of the same kind. Thus, Winsberg denies, *pace* Morgan, that experiments are epistemically privileged, but insists that the knowledge needed for a good simulation is different from the knowledge needed for a good experiment.

The Novelty Claim

Related to the above discussions is the question whether and to what extent simulation poses a novelty for philosophy of science. While it is obvious that simulation has brought many innovations to science, it is more controversial whether simulation poses new problems for the philosophy of science. Schweber and Wächter (2000) for example, suggest that the widespread use of simulation in the sciences constitutes a 'Hacking-type revolution'. By this they mean that modelling and simulation have achieved a qualitatively new level of effectiveness, ubiquity and authority. Consequently, new problems arise for philosophy of science. Rohrlich (1991: 507) argues that computer simulations require a new and different methodology for the physical sciences. Humphreys (1991: 497) agrees that computer simulations require 'a new conception of the relation between theoretical models and their application'. He advances similar arguments in his 2004 book. Finally, Winsberg (2001: 447) claims that 'computer simulations have a distinct epistemology'.

Against these novelty claims, others have argued that simulations are very similar to traditional tools of science, and do not constitute a revolution in the principles of methodology (Stöckler, 2000). To understand these arguments better, it is helpful to analyse in which way simulations are supposed to pose new problems for the philosophy of science. Frigg and Reiss (2009: 595) present the following list of purportedly novel problems:

1 *Metaphysical:* Simulations create some kind of parallel world in which experiments can be conducted under more favourable conditions than in the 'real world'.
2 *Epistemic:* Simulations demand a new epistemology.
3 *Semantic:* Simulations demand a new analysis of how models/theories relate to concrete phenomena.
4 *Methodological:* Simulating is a sui generis activity that lies 'in between' theorising and experimentation.

Against (1) Frigg and Reiss argue that the parallel world claim already has been made with respect to standard deductive models (cf. Sugden, 2000). Against (2) they argue that the issues with simulation are part of the larger problem from where (complex) models get their epistemic credentials. Against (3) they argue that first, simulations do not clash with either the semantic or the syntactic view, and second, that the dynamic aspect of simulation is not new. Against (4) they argue, first, that simulation does not have an 'in-between status' with respect to its reliability, but that, second, other interpretations of simulations being 'in-between' – like being a hybrid or a mediator – are not new and have been claimed for models already.

Against this sceptical position, Humphreys (2009) argues for the truth of at least (2) and (3). He argues that the epistemic opacity of simulations and their dynamic aspects are new features that are not sufficiently captured by existing accounts of philosophy of science. In addition, he claims that the application process of the simulation to the real world requires a new conceptual framework, and that the limitations of what is computable and hence simulatable in a given time have important implications for the philosophical debate as well.

In this debate, a lot obviously depends on how simulation is defined (cf. section on Uses in the Social Sciences). Frigg and Reiss prefer a more abstract account of simulation that is not strongly differentiated from models, while Humphreys prefers an account that is clearly embedded in the programming and computer implementation of simulation. We feel that both positions have their merits. The sceptical position helps one not get too distracted when trying to explain how modern science works: it avoids the abandonment of central but enduring problems for novel but possibly superficial problems of current practice. The novelty position takes the actual practices of scientists very seriously, as have previous philosophers of science (e.g. Kuhn or Hacking). We believe that the debate between these two factions will not be resolved soon. Many of the problems of more traditional practices of science, which the sceptics claim can account for simulation as well, have not been given a satisfactory solution so far. Whether there are special problems of simulation remaining may only come into high relief once these more general issues have been adequately addressed, and the relevance of their answers for simulations explored.

THE SCIENTIFIC USES OF SIMULATIONS

The sciences use simulations for multiple purposes. In this section, we first explicate how scientists pursue their aims with the help of simulations, and secondly point out the conditions necessary to justifiably pursue these uses with simulations.

PREDICTION

A prediction is a claim that a particular event will occur (with certain probability) in the future (see also Chapter 34). A simulation may predict a phenomenon without explaining it. For example, a model bridge may show that a design will work without explaining why it will work. A model car's performance in a wind tunnel simulation may indicate the car's wind resistance without explaining its wind resistance. However, such cases might be restricted to material simulations: one may be able to successfully exploit the material causes operating in such a simulation for predictive purposes, without being able to identify these causes, and hence without being able to explain why the system operates in the way it does. In non-material simulations, in particular in computer simulations, one has to explicitly construct the principles governing the simulation. Claiming that such a simulation could predict without explaining would then raise the 'no miracles' argument: predictive success would be miraculous if the simulation and its underlying principles did not identify the actual causes at work in the real system. Full *structural validity* of the model – that is, the model not only reproduces the observed system behaviour, but truly reflects the way in which the real system operates to produce this behaviour – vouches for both predictive and explanatory success.

Yet there are different ways in which simulations are based on 'underlying principles'. The simplest is the case in which the simulation is based on natural laws. Take for example vehicle crash simulations. A typical 'first principle' crash simulation takes as input the structural geometry of a vehicle and the material properties of its components. The vehicle body structure is analysed using spatial discretisation: the continuous movement of the body in real time is broken up into smaller changes in position over small, discrete time steps. The *equations of motion* hold at all times during a crash simulation. The simulation solves the system of equations for acceleration, velocities and the displacements of nodes at each discrete point in time, and thus generates the deformation of the vehicle body (cf. Haug, 1981).

Such 'first principle' simulations were built to predict effects of changes in vehicle composition on the vehicle's crash safety. They analyse a vehicle 'system' into its components and calculate the behaviour of these components according to kinematic laws (partly expressed in the equations of motion). Because the computational generation of the behaviour strictly adheres to the causal laws that govern the behaviour in reality, the generation also causally *explains* it.

The builders of crash simulations are in the lucky position that the generated events match the findings of empirical crash tests very precisely, while their models are fully based on laws of nature. This is often not the case. One reason may be the absence of true generalisable statements about the domain of interest. Take for example Coops and Catling's (2002) ecological simulation. Their aim is to predict the spatial distribution and relative abundance of mammal species across

an area in New South Wales, Australia. They proceed in the following steps. First, they construct a detailed map of the area indicating for each pixel the 'habitat complexity score' (HCS), which measures the structural complexity and biomass of forested vegetation. This map is estimated from the relationship between HCS observed from selected plots and aerial photographs taken of the whole area. Second, they estimate a frequency distribution of HCS for each selected plot. From this they predict the HCS of each pixel at any time period. This prediction in effect constitutes a simulation of the HCS dynamics for the whole area. Finally, they estimate a linear regression model that links HCS to spatial distribution and relative abundance of the relevant mammal species. Based on this model, they simulate the dynamics of the mammal population throughout the area.

Clearly, Coops and Catling cannot base their simulation on natural laws, because there aren't any for the domain of phenomena there are interested in. Instead, their research paper has to fulfil the double task of estimating general principles from empirical data, and then running the simulation on these principles. Understanding this also makes clear that the main predictive work lies in the statistical operations, i.e. the estimations of the HCS frequency distributions and the linear regression model. The simulation of the HCS dynamics is a *result* of the HCS frequency estimations. It then helps provide the data for the linear regression model; but it can only do so (and one would accept the data it provides as evidence only) if the HCS frequency distributions were estimated correctly. The predictive power of the simulation thus clearly depends on the principles used in it, and the validity of these principles seems not very secure in this case.

Another reason for failing to incorporate independently validated principles is that many simulations do not successfully match the target events or history when relying solely on laws, even if those laws are available. Take for example the following case from climate research (described in Küppers and Lenhard, 2005). In 1955, Norman Phillips succeeded in reproducing the patterns of wind and pressure of the entire atmosphere in a computer model. Phillips used only six basic equations in his model. They express well-accepted laws of hydrodynamics, which are generally conceived of as the physical basis of climatology.

Phillips' model was a great success, because it imitated the actually observed meteorological flow patterns well. But the model also exhibited an important failure: the dynamics of the atmosphere were stable only for a few weeks. After about four weeks, the internal energy blew up, and the system 'exploded' — the stable flow patterns dissolved into chaos.

Subsequent research searched for adequate smoothing procedures to cancel out the errors before they could blow up. This strategy was oriented at the ideal of modelling the true process by deriving the model from the relevant laws in the correct fashion. Instabilities were seen as resulting from errors – inaccurate deviations of the discrete model from the true solution of the continuous system.

The decisive breakthrough, however, was achieved through the very different approach of Akio Arakawa. It involved giving up on modelling the true process, and instead focused on imitating the dynamics. To guarantee the stability of the simulation procedure, Arakawa introduced further assumptions, partly contradicting experience and physical theory. For example, he assumed that the kinetic energy in the atmosphere would be preserved. This is definitely not the case in reality, where part of this energy is transformed into heat by friction. Moreover, dissipation is presumably an important factor for the stability of the real atmosphere. So, in assuming the preservation of kinetic energy, Arakawa 'artificially' limited the blow-up of instabilities. This assumption was not derived from the theoretical basis, and was justified only by the results of simulation runs that matched the actually observed meteorological flow patterns over a much longer period than Phillips' model.

This last example requires us to be more precise when talking about the validity of a model. Structural validity we encountered before: it requires that the model both reproduces the observed system behaviour and also truly reflects the way in which the real system operates to produce this behaviour. But Phillips' model obviously violates structural validity, and still seems to be successful at predicting global weather. In that case, we must speak of *predictive validity*, in which the simulation matches data that was not used in its construction. (One may add that Coops and Catling's 2002 simulation may not be predictively but *replicatively valid*: it matches data already acquired from the real system). By distinguishing structural and replicative validity, we admit that some simulations may predict but do not explain.

Explanation

Agent-based simulations are often claimed to be explanatory (Axtell et al., 2002; Cedermann, 2005; Dean et al., 2000; Epstein, 1999; Sawyer, 2004; Tesfatsion, 2006). Often these claims are ambiguous about how agent-based simulations are explanatory, and what they explain. In the following, we discuss three possible accounts of what kind of explanations ABS may provide (see also Chapters 13 and 33).

Full Explanations

Some simulations are claimed to explain concrete phenomena. Such singular explanations purport to explain why a certain fact occurred at a certain time in a certain way, either by providing its causal history, or by identifying the causal relations that produced it. For example, Dean et al. (2000) claim that by simulating actual population dynamics and settlement densities of the Anasazi, they manage to explain these population dynamics.

Although the simulation matches data during most of the period studied, it does not match data at the period's end. Dean et al.

conclude that some factor outside the simulation influenced population and its distribution at that time. They conjecture that some households left the valley because of social ties to other households leaving the valley and not because potential maize production was not enough to sustain them.

Thus, by the author's own account, the simulation fails as a full explanation of the particular Anasazi history. It omits, besides social pull, social institutions and property rights. It may nonetheless yield a partial explanation that treats some explanatory factors, such as maize production, and controls for other explanatory factors, such as social pull. It may control for an explanatory factor by, say, treating a period during which that factor does not operate. Elaboration of the simulation may add explanatory factors, such as social pull, to extend the simulation's range and make its explanation more thorough. The next section further explores simulations' power as partial explanations of particular phenomena.

However, as Grüne-Yanoff (2009 argues, it is unlikely that this history could ever be explained via simulation, as it is unlikely that the underlying model could ever be sufficiently validated. Instead of providing full or partial explanations of particulars, simulation may only provide *possible explanations*. Such possible explanations, which will be discussed in 4.3.3, may help in the construction of actual explanations, but do not constitute actual explanations themselves.

Partial Explanation

A partial explanation describes the operation of some factors behind a phenomenon's occurrence. This requires the model to successfully *isolate* these explanatory factors (Mäki, 1994). For a partial explanation, each assumption must control for an explanatory factor, or else the theorem's results must be *robust* with respect to variation in the assumption. Yet it turns out that many ABS fail to be robust.

Lacking robustness is a widespread problem for the success of partial explanations

with simulation studies. Take for example Huberman and Glance (1993), who examine simulations of generations of players in Prisoner's Dilemmas. The simulations use cellular automata, with cells located in a square. One simulation treats time as discreet and has all cells update at the same time to produce the next generation. Another simulation, more realistically, treats time as continuous so that at a moment at most one cell updates to produce an offspring. Suppose that both the synchronous and the asynchronous simulations begin with the same initial conditions: a single defector surrounded by cooperators. The synchronous simulation maintains widespread cooperation even after 200 rounds, whereas the asynchronous simulation has no cooperation after about 100 rounds. Cooperation is not robust with respect to the updating's timing in these simulations. So unless timing is an explanatory factor in the world and not just an artifact of the simulation, a simulation that generates cooperation using synchronous updating does not yield a partial explanation of cooperation.

Consequently, proponents of the explanatory value of a simulation show that the simulation robustly generates the target phenomenon's representation. That is, the simulation generates the phenomenon's representation over a wide range of variation in the simulation's unrealistic assumptions. The robustness may be with respect to variation in initial conditions, dynamical laws, or values of the simulation's parameters. Justin D'Arms et al. (1998: 89–92), for example, use robustness as a guideline for assessment of simulations and models of adaptive behaviour. They say that a result is robust if it is achieved across a variety of different starting conditions and/or parameters. They take robustness as necessary but not sufficient for a successful simulation.

However, a model's robustness with respect to all assumptions is neither necessary nor sufficient for a phenomenon's partial explanation. A partial explanation requires robustness with respect to variation in assumptions that introduce features irrelevant to the model's target phenomenon. Altering those assumptions should not make a difference to the model's results. In contrast, robustness need not hold with respect to assumptions that control for explanatory factors. In fact, a good model, as it becomes more realistic by incorporating more explanatory factors, does not robustly yield the same results. When it is completely realistic, it exhibits a limited type of robustness. It steadfastly yields its target phenomenon as the model's parameters vary in ways that replicate the phenomenon's natural range of occurrence. Thus, a partial explanation requires only limited robustness, namely, robustness with respect to variation in assumptions that do not control for explanatory factors.

Potential Explanation

We have argued that many simulations often do neither fully nor partially explain any particular phenomenon. Nevertheless, many authors of simulation studies claim that their simulations are in some way explanatory. It may therefore make sense to expand the notion of explanatoriness to include not only full or partial explanations, but also potential explanations. A model or theory may be considered a potential explanation if it shares certain properties with actual explanations, but where the *explanans* is not true (cf. Hempel, 1965: 338). In that sense, simulations may be potential explanations, or as some simulation authors prefer, 'candidate explanations' (Epstein, 1999: 43), and hence may be considered explanatory.

Emrah Aydinonat (2008) offers a good example of such reasoning. He argues that Menger's theory of the origin of money, and more recent simulations building on Menger's work, are partial potential explanations.

Carl Menger (1982) investigated the question how money arose as a medium of exchange. His question was theoretical in that it asked for the general underlying causes for the origin of money, and not for the causal history of any particular instance of money. Envisioning a world of direct exchange,

Menger postulated that some goods are more saleable than others, depending on properties like their durability, transportability, etc. Self-interested economic agents, he then argued, would tend to purchase the most saleable good, even if they do not need it, in cases where they cannot directly exchange their goods for goods that they do need. Because everyone would gravitate towards the most saleable good in the marketplace in such situations, it is that good that emerges as the medium of exchange – as the unintended consequences of economising agents.

Aydinonat admits that Menger's model neglects many institutional particularities, and in general is not able to verify its assumptions. It thus cannot offer a full or partial explanation. However, he argues that 'Menger's conjecture alerts us to certain explanatory factors that *may have been* important in the development of a medium of exchange' (Aydinonat, 2008: 48, my emphasis). In particular, Menger's model identifies *some* factors, not all; hence his model offers only a partial explanation. Furthermore, the model identifies only possible factors, not actual ones; hence it offers only a potential explanation.

Many authors have since tried to develop Menger's model further. As an example, take the simulation study by Marimon et al. (1990); they model the trade interactions of three types of agents in the population. Each type consumes a different good, which she does not produce herself. To be able to consume, the agents have to exchange with others. Yet each agent can only store one kind of good, and storage costs for a specific kind of good depends on the type of agent who stores it. In the simulation, agents are matched pairwise at random, offer their goods simultaneously, and decide whether to accept the trade offer. Offers of an agent's consumption goods are always accepted. But if they are not offered their consumption goods, they have to decide whether to accept a good they cannot consume. Agents know a menu of behavioural rules (including 'accept if storage costs are low', 'accept if other agents accept', etc.) and attach strength to each rule. This strength index determines how probable it is that an agent chooses a certain rule. After each round, agents update the strength index according to the success of the rule used.

Marimon et al. find that under specific conditions, the population converges on an equilibrium where every agent prefers a lower-storage-cost commodity to a higher-cost-commodity, unless the latter is their own consumption good. Thus, they show that under these conditions, a medium of exchange emerges as an unintended consequence of the agents' economising behaviour. However, they also find that this convergence is rather sensitive to the initial conditions. Aydinonat therefore concludes that the simulation 'teaches us what we may consider as possible under certain conditions. Yet they do not tell us whether these conditions were present in history or whether there are plausible mechanisms that may bring about this possibility' (Aydinonat, 2008: 112). The simulation offers neither a full nor a partial explanation of the origin of money. But it makes more precise the possible worlds in which Menger's conjecture holds; it specifies in precise detail some environments, and some sets of causal relations under which a medium of exchange emerges. In this sense, the simulation may be considered progress with the possible explanation offered by Menger.

In a similar vein, one may consider the Anasazi simulation progress with possible explanation of the population dynamics. Yet what does the progress consist in? What distinguishes serious contenders for such possible explanations from mere fantastic constructs? Hempel had the formal rigor of the Deductive-Nomological account to fall back onto when referring to the 'other characteristics' of an explanation. But in the age of simulation, indefinite numbers of potential explanations can be produced. With so many possible causes identified, simulation may confuse instead of clarify, and reduce understanding instead of improving it.

One problem, Grüne-Yanoff (2009) argues, may lie in the focus on causes and mechanisms. Aydinonat, for example, claims that simulations 'try to explicate how certain mechanisms … may work together' (2008: 115). Yet these simulations operate with thousands of agents, and indefinitely many possible mechanisms. Identifying a single set of possible mechanisms that produce the explanandum therefore does not, *pace* Aydinonat improve the *chances* of identifying the actual mechanisms. The numbers of possible mechanisms is just too large to significantly improve these chances.

Instead, Grüne-Yanoff suggests that a simulation run offers an instance of the simulated system's *functional capacities* and its functional organisation. Functional analysis shows how lower-level capacities *constitute* higher-level capacities. The capacity of the Anasazi population to disperse in times of draught, for example, is constituted by the capacities of the household agents to optimise under constraints, and their capacity to move. The dispersion *is* nothing but the individual movings. Yet there are many different household capacities that constitute the same higher level capacity. The role of simulation studies, Grüne-Yanoff (2009) argues, is not to enumerate possible household capacities (or mechanisms), but to explore the system's possible functional organisations under which different sets of household capacities constitute higher-level capacities, and hence the 'working' of the whole system. This is in line with current practice. Reports of simulations do not offer comprehensive lists of possible mechanisms that produce the explanandum. Rather, they offer one or a few selected settings, and interpret these as instances of how the system may be functionally organised in order to yield the explanandum. Occasionally, they also conclude from such singular simulation settings that the simulation is not correctly organised and that additional functional components are needed. In the Anasazi case, for example, the authors conclude that additionally push and pull factors are needed. For this reason, it may be preferable to think of simulations as providing potential *functional* instead of potential *causal* explanations.

Policy Formulation

Simulations have long been used to support policy formulation. Drawing on economic theory, Jan Tinbergen constructed a macroeconomic model of the Dutch economy. It led to simulations of six policies for alleviating the Great Depression. Because of the results of the simulations, Tinbergen recommended that the Dutch government abandon the gold standard, which it did.

Today, agent-based models are widely used to simulate the impact of external shocks on complex social phenomena. For example, a number of recent papers have investigated how a smallpox epidemic would spread through a population, and how different vaccination policies would affect this spread. Some of these simulations stay on a relatively abstract level, while others become incredibly detailed and in fact purport to simulate the population behaviour of a whole city (Eubank et al., 2004, who simulate Portland, OR) and even a whole country (Brouwers et al., 2006, who simulate Sweden). Authors of such simulations, in particular from the latter category, often give policy advice based on the simulation results alone.

What kind of policy decisions can be made of course depends on the validity of the simulation (Grüne-Yanoff, 2010). If correct predictions can be made on the basis of the simulation, a straightforward utility maximisation or cost–benefit analysis can be performed. But with most ABS, such point-predictions are out of reach. Instead, ABS at best offer possible scenarios, and allow weeding out certain scenarios as inherently inconsistent or not co-tenable (Cederman, 2005). The goal of simulation studies then is *exploratory modelling*, in which researchers run a number of computational experiments that reveal how the world would behave if the

various conjectures about environments and mechanisms were correct.

The results of exploratory modelling are sets or ensembles of possible worlds. This leads to the question how such resulting sets of scenarios can be used as the basis of policy decisions. If the parties to the decision do not know the probabilities of the models in the ensemble, situations of 'deep uncertainty' arise (Lempert, 2002: 7309–7313). Under deep uncertainty, models of uncertain standing produce outcomes with uncertain relevance. Instead of predicting *the* future of the system with one model or with a set of probabilistically weighted models, simulations only yield a 'landscape of plausible futures' (Bankes et al., 2001: 73).

How can the policy maker base her decisions on such a set? Two different strategies have been discussed. The first focuses on worst-case scenarios, against which policies should be hedged. This approach is similar to the maximin decision rule: the policy maker chooses that policy that maximises the minimal (worst) outcome. The second approach pays equal attention to all models, and chooses that policy which performs relatively well, compared with the alternatives, across the range of plausible futures. If 'performs relatively well' is interpreted as performing well against a set minimal threshold, then this approach is similar to the satisficing decision rule: the policy maker sets a threshold in the light of the specific policy goals, and then evaluates the different policy alternatives by their performance in a sufficiently large number of simulation runs.

Both maximin and satisficing are very sensitive to the number of models considered. The wider the scope, the more likely the inclusion of some outlandish terrible future, which will affect maximin choice. Similarly, the wider the scope, the more likely the inclusion of some outlier below the threshold, which will affect satisficing choice. Given the uncertain status of many model specifications, exploratory modelling is prone to such misspecifications. This leads to the question how the scope of the model ensemble can be constrained.

Grüne-Yanoff (2010) argues that neither references to the actual world, nor references to intuitions are sufficient to appropriately restrict the scope of model ensembles. Only through integrating the simulation ensemble under a theory does exploratory modelling gain sufficient systematicity. In such a setting, simulations would unpack the implications of their theoretical hypotheses. If implications are found untenable, the authors can go back to the theory, which provides constraints on how alternative hypotheses can be constructed. Yet current modelling practice rarely follows this approach. For this reason, the usefulness of exploratory modelling for policy formation is not entirely clear.

CONCLUSION

In this article, we argued that agent-based simulation is an important new tool for the social scientist. Although it shares many features with both models and experiments, its dynamic aspects, its ability to compute vast amounts of data, and its epistemic opacity are novel features that set it apart from other scientific tools. This novelty leads to a number of potentially new uses in the sciences. Yet the conceptual foundations for these new employments are still shaky. In particular, we pointed out the potential, but also the difficulties of explaining with simulations, and of supporting policy advice. We hope that this article helps sharpen the understanding of these problems, which may eventually lead to their solution.

ACKNOWLEDGEMENT

I thank Mette Sundblad for bibliographic research and help in formatting this article.

NOTE

1 A possible connection is James M. Sakoda, who apparently was the first person to develop a CA-based model in the social sciences. He published his model in Sakoda 1971, but the basic design of the model was already present in his unpublished dissertation of 1949 (Hegselmann and Flache, 1998: 3.2). However, Schelling has stated to never have heard of Sakoda (Aydinonat, 2005: 5).

REFERENCES

Alexander, S. (1920) *Space, Time, and Deity*. 2 vols. London: Macmillan.

Axtell, R.L., Epstein, J.M., Dean, J.S., Gumerman, G.J., Swedlund, A. C., Harburger, J., Chakravarty, S., Hammond, R., Parker, J. and Parker, M. (2002) 'Population growth and collapse in a multiagent model of the Kayenta Anasazi in Long House Valley', *Proceedings of the National Academy of Sciences*, 99(3): 7275–7279.

Aydinonat, N.E. (2005) 'An interview with Thomas C. Schelling: Interpretation of game theory and the checkerboard model', *Economics Bulletin*, 2(2): 1–7.

Aydinonat, N.E. (2008) *The Invisible Hand in Economics: How Economists Explain Unintended Social Consequences*, INEM Advances in Economic Methodology. London: Routledge.

Bankes, S.C., Lempert, R.J. and Popper, S.W. (2001) 'Computer-assisted reasoning', *Computing in Science and Engineering*, 3(2): 71–77.

Bedau, M. (1997) 'Weak emergence', *Philosophical Perspectives*, 11: 375–399.

Berlekamp, E.R., Conway, J.H. and Guy, R.K. (1982) Winning *Ways for your Mathematical Plays*. Volume 2: *Games in Particular*. London: Academic Press.

Boden, M.A. (ed.) (1996) *The Philosophy of Artificial Life. Oxford Readings in Philosophy*. New York: Oxford University Press.

Brouwers, L., Mäkilä, K. and Camitz, M. (2006) 'Spridning av smittkoppor – simuleringsexperiment', *SMI-Rapport*, 5.

Broad, C.D. (1925) *The Mind and Its Place in Nature*. London: Routledge & Kegan Paul.

Bunn, D.W. and Oliveira, F.S. (2003) 'Evaluating individual market power in electricity markets via agent-based simulation', *Annals of Operations Research*, 121: 57–77.

Cederman, L.-E. (2002) 'Endogenizing geopolitical boundaries with agent-based modelling', *Proceedings of the National Academy*, 99(suppl. 3): 7796–7303.

Cederman, L.-E. (2005) 'Computational models of social forms: Advancing generative process theory', *American Journal of Sociology*, 110(4): 864–893.

Coops, N.C. and Catling, P.C. (2002) '*Prediction* of the spatial distribution and relative abundance of ground-dwelling mammals using remote sensing imagery and *simulation* models', *Landscape Ecology*, 17(2): 173–188.

D'Arms, J., Batterman, R. and Górny, K. (1998) 'Game theoretic explanations and the evolution of justice', *Philosophy of Science*, 65: 76–102.

Dean, J., Gumerman, G., Epstein, J., Axtell, R., Swedlund, A., Parker, M. and McCarroll, S. (2000) 'Understanding anasazi cultural change through agent-based modelling', in T. Kohler and G. Gumerman (eds) *Dynamics in Human and Primate Societies: Agent-Based Modelling of Social and Spatial Processes*. Santa Fe Institute Studies in the Science of Complexity. New York: Oxford University Press. pp. (179–205)

Doran J.E. (1998) 'Simulating collective misbelief', *Journal of Artificial Societies and Social Simulation*, 1(1): http://www.soc.surrey.ac.uk/JASSS/1/1/3.html.

Dowling, D. (1999) 'Experimenting on theories', *Science in Context*, 12(2): 261–273.

Epstein, J.M. (1999) 'Agent-based computational models and generative social science', *Complexity*, 4(5): 41–57.

Epstein, J. and Axtell, R. (1996) *Growing Artificial Societies: Social Science from the Bottom-Up.* Cambridge, MA: MIT Press.

Eubank, S., Guclu, H., Kumar, V.S.A., Marathe, M., Srinivasan, A., Toroczcai, Z. and Wang, N. (2004) 'Modelling disease outbreaks in realistic urban social networks', *Nature*, 429: 180–184.

Frankfurt, H. (1978) 'The problem of action', *American Philosophical Quarterly*, 15: 157–162.

Frigg, R. and Reiss, J. (2009) 'The philosophy of simulation: Hot new issues or same old stew?', *Synthese*, 169(3): 593–613.

Gilbert, N. and Troitzsch, K.G. (1999) *Simulation for the Social Scientist.* Milton Keynes: Open University Press.

Gilbert, N. (2004) 'Agent-based social simulation: Dealing with complexity', *Centre for Research on Social Simulation Mimeo.* Guildford: University of Surrey.

Grimm, V., Revilla, E., Berger, U., Jeltsch, F., Mooij, W. M., Railsback, S.F., Thulke, H.-H., Weiner, J., Wiegand, T. and DeAngelis, D.L. (2005) 'Pattern-oriented modelling of agent-based complex systems: Lessons from ecology', *Science*, 310: 987–991.

Grüne-Yanoff, T. (2009) 'The explanatory potential of artificial societies', *Synthese*, 169(3): 539–555.

Grüne-Yanoff, T. (2010) 'Agent-based models as policy decision tools: The case of smallpox vaccination', *Simulation and Gaming.* Published online 7 September 2010. DOI: 10.1177/1046878110377484.

Guala, F. (2005) *The Methodology of Experimental Economics.* Cambridge: Cambridge University Press.

Happe, K., Kellermann, K. and Balmann, A. (2006) 'Agent-based analysis of agricultural policies: An illustration of the agricultural policy simulator AgriPoliS, its adaptation and behaviour', *Ecology and Society*, 11(1): 49.

Haug, E. (1981) 'Engineering safety analysis via destructive numerical experiments', *EUROMECH 12, Polish Academy of Sciences, Engineering Transactions*, 29(1): 39–49.

Hegselmann, R. and Flache, A. (1998) 'Understanding complex social dynamics: A plea for cellular automata based modelling', *Journal of Artificial Societies and Social Simulation*, 1(3): http://www.soc.surrey.ac.uk/JASSS/1/3/1.html.

Hempel, C.G. (1965) *Aspects of Scientific Explanation.* New York: The Free Press.

Huberman, B. and Glance, N. (1993) 'Evolutionary games and computer simulations', *Proceedings of the National Academy of Science*, 90: 7716–7718.

Humphreys, P. (1991) 'Computer simulations', in A. Fine, M. Forbes and L. Wessels (eds) *PSA 1990, 2.* East Lansing: Philosophy of Science Association. pp. 497–506.

Humphreys, P. (2004) *Extending Ourselves: Computational Science, Empiricism, and Scientific Method.* New York: Oxford University Press.

Humphreys, P. (2009) 'The philosophical novelty of computer simulation methods', *Synthese*, 169(3): 615–626.

Küppers, G. and Lenhard, J. (2005) 'Validation of simulation: Patterns in the social and natural sciences', *Journal of Artificial Societies and Social Simulation*, 8(4): http://jasss.soc.surrey.ac.uk/8/4/3.html.

LeBaron, B. (2001) 'Empirical regularities from interacting long and short memory investors in an agent-based financial market', *IEEE Transactions on Evolutionary Computation*, 5: 442–455.

Lehtinen, A. and Kuorikoski, J. (2007) 'Computing the perfect model: Why do economists shun simulation?', *Philosophy of Science*, 74(3): 304–329.

Lempert, R.J. (2002) 'New decision sciences for complex systems', *Proceedings of the National Academy of Sciences*, 99(supplement 3): 7309–7313.

Mäki, U. (1994) 'Isolation, idealization and truth in economics', in B. Hamminga and N. De Marchi (eds) *Idealization-VI: Idealization in Economics. Poznan Studies in the Philosophy of the Sciences and the Humanities*, 38: 7–68. Dordrecht: Kluwer.

Marimon, R., McGrattan, E. and Sargent, T.J. (1990) 'Money as a medium of exchange in an economy with artificially intelligent agents', *Journal of Economic Dynamics and Control*, 14(2): 329–373.

Maynard Smith, J. and Price, G. (1973) 'The logic of animal conflict', *Nature*, 146: 15–18.

Menger, C. (1982) 'On the origin of money', *Economic Journal*, 2: 239–255.

Mill, J.S. (1843) *System of Logic*. London: Longmans, Green, Reader, and Dyer. [8th edn, 1872].

Morgan, M.S. (2003) 'Experiments without material intervention: Model experiments, virtual experiments and virtually experiments', in H. Radder *(ed.) The Philosophy of Scientific Experimentation*. University of Pittsburgh Press. pp. 217–235.

Moss, S. (2002) 'Policy analysis from first principles', *Proceedings of the US National Academy of Sciences*, 99(Suppl. 3): 7267–7274.

Nilsson, N. *(1998) Artificial Intelligence: A New Synthesis*. Morgan Kaufmann Publishers.

O'Connor, T. (1994) 'Emergent properties', *American Philosophical Quarterly*, 31: 91–104.

Pan, X., Han, C.S., Dauber, K.and Law, K.H. (2007) 'A multi-agent based framework for the simulation of human and social behaviors during emergency evacuations', *AI & Society*, 22(2): 113–132.

Parker, W. (2009) 'Does matter really matter? Computer simulations, experiments and materiality', *Synthese*, 169(3): 483–496.

Poole, D., Mackworth, A. and Goebel, R. (1998) *Computational Intelligence: A Logical Approach. New York: Oxford University Press.*

Rademacher, C., Neuert, C., Grundmann, V., Wissel, C. and Grimm, V. (2004) 'Reconstructing spatiotemporal dynamics of Central European natural beech forests: The rule-based forest model BEFORE', *Forest Ecology and Management*, 194: 349–368.

Ray, T.S. (1996) 'An approach to the synthesis of life', in Margaret A. Boden (ed.) *The Philosophy of Artificial Life. Oxford Readings in Philosophy.* New York: Oxford University Press. pp. 111–145.

Reynolds, C. (1987) *'Flocks, herds and schools: A distributed behavioural model', SIGGRAPH '87: Proceedings of the 14th Annual Conference on Computer Graphics and Interactive Techniques (Association for Computing Machinery). pp. 25–34.*

Rohrlich, F. (1991) 'Computer simulation in the physical sciences', *Philosophy of Science Association*, 2: 507–518.

Russell, S.J. and Norvig, P. (2003) *Artificial Intelligence: A Modern Approach.* 2nd edn. Upper Saddle River, NJ: Prentice Hall.

Sakoda, J. M. (1971) The checkerboard model of social interaction, *Journal of Mathematical Sociology*, 1: 119–132.

Samanidou, R., Zschischang, E., Stauffer, D. and Lux, T. (2007) 'Agent-based models of financial markets', *Reports on Progress in Physics*, 70: 409–450.

Sawyer, R.K. (2004) 'Social explanation and computational simulation', *Philosophical Explorations*, 7(3): 219–231.

Schelling, T. (1969) 'Models of segregation', *The American Economic Review*, 59(2): 488–493.

Schelling, T. (1971) 'Dynamic models of segregation', *Journal of Mathematical Sociology*, 1: 143–86.

Schweber, S. and Wächter, M. (2000) 'Complex systems, modelling and simulation', *Studies in the History and Philosophy of Modern Physics*, 31(4): 583–609.

Simon, H.A. (1969) *The Sciences of the Artificial.* Cambridge, MA: MIT Press.

Sigmund, K. (2005) 'John Maynard Smith and evolutionary game theory', *Theoretical Population Biology*, 68: 7–10.

Sober, E. (1996) 'Learning from functionalism – Prospects for strong artificial life', in Margaret A. Boden (ed.) *The Philosophy of Artificial Life. Oxford Readings in Philosophy.* New York: Oxford University Press. pp. 361–378.

Stöckler, M. (2000) 'On modelling and simulations as instruments for the study of complex systems', in M. Carrier, G. Massey and L. Ruetsche (eds) *Science at Century's End: Philosophical Questions on the Progress and Limits of Science.* Pittsburgh: University of Pittsburgh Press. pp. 355–373.

Sugden, R. (2000) 'Credible worlds: The status of theoretical models in economics', *Journal of Economic Methodology*, 7(1): 1–31.

Tesfatsion, L. (2006) 'Agent-based computational economics: A constructive approach to economic theory', in L. Tesfatsion and K. Judd (eds) *Handbook of Computational Economics* Vol. 2. North Holland: Elsevier. pp. 1–50.

Winsberg, E. (2001) 'Simulations, models, and theories: Complex physical systems and their representations', *Philosophy of Science*, 68(supplement): S442–S454.

Winsberg, E. (2009) 'A tale of two methods', *Synthese*, 169(3): 575–592.

Wissel, C. (1992) 'Modelling the mosaic-cycle of a Middle European beech forest', *Ecological Modelling*, 63: 29–43.

33

Explanation in the Social Sciences

Jeroen Van Bouwel and Erik Weber[1]

INTRODUCTION

In his introduction to the third edition of *Philosophy of Economics*, Daniel Hausman divides the central issues in philosophy of science into five groups (Hausman, 2008: 5).

1 Goals – what are the goals of science; scientific realists versus antirealists?
2 Explanation – what is a scientific explanation?
3 Theories – what are scientific theories, laws, models?
4 Testing, induction and demarcation – how to test, confirm or disconfirm scientific theories?
5 Are the answers to these four questions the same for all sciences at all times? Can human actions and institutions be studied in the same way that one studies nature?

Each of these issues can be explored within one discipline, for example, physics, biology, sociology or they might be analysed for science in general. While the *philosophies of the special sciences*, for example, philosophy of physics, of biology, of cognitive sciences, of social science, etc. aim at the clarification of subject specific theories, forms of explanation, methods, concepts and principles, etc., the *general philosophy of science* considers

these issues in the sciences as a whole. Typical topics of the latter are realism, the unity of science, the structure of scientific explanations, reduction, causation, objectivity, science versus non-science, etc.

This chapter will explore the exchanges between general philosophy of science and the philosophy of social science. Discussing the interaction between the philosophy of social science and general philosophy of science on all the topics mentioned above would be too ambitious a project for this chapter, therein we limit ourselves to debates on scientific explanation and causation. First, in order to clarify how philosophers of social science can learn from general philosophy of science, we explore the debate on scientific explanation: we give an overview of the general philosophy of science literature on scientific explanation, then ask whether the results of this literature have been sufficiently used in the philosophy of social science and, subsequently, show that a more extensive use of this literature would be very helpful. Second, to show how general philosophy of science can learn from philosophy of social science, we explore some debates on causation. Again, we will also remark that there was not enough interaction between general philosophy of science and philosophy of social science in the past, and argue that more exchange would be useful.

GENERAL PHILOSOPHY OF SCIENCE AND THE NATURE OF SCIENTIFIC EXPLANATION

Introduction

Controversies on scientific explanation have been going on for decades within the philosophy of science community (cf. Salmon, 1989). Central questions are: What qualifies as a scientific explanation? What is the role of laws in explanation? What is the role of mechanisms in explanation? Are real explanations inevitably causal? Is explanation achieved through (or only through) unification? What is the role of pragmatics in explanation? Closely related to these questions is the issue of reductionism, as there is a prevailing intuition that we explain occurrences at a certain level by reducing them to something more fundamental. What is reduction? Does reduction really explain? Are some theories more fundamental than others? Can some theories be reduced to others?

In this section, we first summarise the ideas of Carl Hempel, the godfather of this subdomain of philosophy of science. Then we present the problems that other philosophers have raised in connection with Hempel's theory of explanation and clarify how the major research traditions in the field that have emerged after Hempel, can be seen as different reactions to these problems.

The Hempelian models

The first very influential contribution to the debate on the nature of scientific explanations was from Carl Hempel (1965). He developed two main models of scientific explanation, the deductive-nomological (DN) and the inductive-statistical (IS) models.

According to the deductive-nomological model of scientific explanation, the *explanandum*, the phenomenon to be explained, is deduced from a set of true statements, the *explanans*, of which at least one is a *law*. Let's consider an example (inspired by Hempel and Oppenheim, 1948: 246).

> C_1: This thermometer consists of a glass tube which is partly filled with mercury.
> C_2: This thermometer was rapidly immersed in hot water.
> L: In glass tubes which are partly filled with mercury and are rapidly immersed in hot water, the mercury level first drops and then rises.
> E: Immersing this thermometer rapidly in hot water, we observe a temporary drop of the mercury column, followed by a swift rise.

If all these claims are true, we have a *true* explanation.

For Hempel, explanations are the instruments by which understanding of the world is achieved. So understanding the world is the intellectual benefit we expect to acquire by constructing explanations. What does this understanding of the world consist in? Hempel's answer is the following:

> Thus a D-N Explanation answers the question '*Why did the explanandum-phenomenon occur?*' by showing that the phenomenon resulted from certain particular circumstances, specified in $C_1, C_2, \ldots, C_k$, in accordance with the laws $L_1, L_2, \ldots, L_r$. By pointing this out, the argument shows that, given the particular circumstances and the laws in question, the occurrence of the phenomenon *was to be expected*; and it is in this sense that the explanation enables us to *understand why* the phenomenon occurred. (Hempel, 1965: 337, italics in original)

In other words: *understanding* must be identified with *expectability*, and expectability is the one and only intellectual benefit we can acquire by constructing explanations.

Hempel has extended the DN model to probabilistic explanations in what is called the IS (Inductive-Statistical) model. Let us begin with a characterisation given by Hempel.

> Explanations of particular facts or events by means of statistical laws thus present themselves as arguments that are inductive or probabilistic in the sense that the explanans confers upon the

explanandum a more or less high degree of inductive support or of logical (inductive) probability; they will therefore be called inductive-statistical explanations; or I-S explanations. (1965: 385–386)

Explanation is still linked with expectability, but in this case expectability comes in degrees. The idea of law-like sentences thus has to be extended to account for *statistical laws* that have the conditional form $Prob(G|F) = r$, where r denotes the probability that an object of the set F is also a member of the set G. A simple example of an I-S explanation would be the explanation of why John Jones (j) recovered (R) from a streptococcus infection (S), when our knowledge system also contains the information that John was administered penicillin (P), and the probability (r, which is close enough to 1) of recovery from an infection given that penicillin is administered:

C$_1$: Sj
C$_2$: Pj
L: $Prob(R \mid S \& P)=r$
================= [r]
E: Rj

Hempel, after introducing this example, immediately remarks that an important problem remains to be solved. Not all streptococcal infections can be cured by administrating penicillin and some streptococcus strains are even resistant to penicillin. The probability of recovery among the people who are treated with penicillin *and* are infected by a resistant strain is a number s very close to 0 (equivalently, we could say that the probability of not recovering among these people is a number $1 - s$ very close to 1).

Some problems with Hempelian models

Philosophers have pointed at several problems in these Hempelian models, the most salient ones being *accidental generalisations*, *irrelevant premises* and *asymmetry*.

Accidental generalisations

Hempel realised that he needed to distinguish between genuine laws and accidental generalisations. Consider the following two statements, apparently equivalent as far as their logical form goes (see Salmon, 1989: 15):

1   No gold sphere has a mass greater than 100,000 kg.
2   No enriched uranium sphere has a mass greater than 100,000 kg.

Whereas the second statement seems to be the expression of a lawful fact (since the critical mass for enriched uranium is just a few kilograms), the truth of the first statement seems to be a contingent matter of fact (it just happens to be the case that no one did produce such a sphere as yet).

Hempel's example is this: if we derive that Horace is bald from the premises (1) that Horace is a member of the Greenbury School Board, and (2) that all members of the Greenbury School Board are bald, this is not an explanation because we have used an accidental generalisation. Hempel's problem is that he has no viable account of how to distinguish between laws and accidental generalisation (he admits this).

Irrelevant premises

Other counterexamples to Hempel's models are inspired by the fact that the relation of logical deduction is monotonous: if you add premises to a deductive argument, the result is still a deductive argument. This is not the case for explanations: most people will not regard arguments with superfluous premises (that otherwise satisfy Hempel's conditions) as explanations. Well known examples are as follows.

1   This sample of table salt dissolves in water because I have hexed it, and all samples of hexed salt dissolve in water.

The problem is that non-hexed salt also dissolves in water.

2   John Jones did not get pregnant during the last year because he took birth control pills, and men who take birth control pills don't get pregnant.

Here the premise about the birth control pills is superfluous.

Asymmetry

Several people have argued that explanation is asymmetrical. Because arguments can be reversed, this asymmetry is a problem for Hempel's models. Consider the following questions and answers.

> *Question 1*: Why does this flagpole have a shadow of 10 m long?
> *Answer 1*: The flagpole is 10 m high. The sun is at 45° above the horizon. Because light moves in a straight line, we can derive (by means of the Pythagorean Theorem) that the flagpole has a shadow of 10 m in length.
> *Question 2*: Why is this flagpole 10 m long?
> *Answer 2*: The flagpole has a shadow of 10 m long. The sun is at 45° above the horizon. Because light moves in a straight line, we can derive (by means of the Pythagorean Theorem) that the flagpole is 10 m high.

The problem is that only the first argument is an intuitively acceptable explanation, while both answers are DN explanations in Hempel's sense.

Before we go to the strategies for solving these problems, it must be noted that Hempel did not regard asymmetry as a problem: for him the examples show that we have bad intuitions about explanations. Once we realise that understanding equals expectability, we can get rid of the bad intuitions (because we realise that explanations are symmetrical).

A range of solutions

Faced with these problems of the Hempelian models, a range of solutions has been developed within general philosophy of science. We will discuss *a neo-Hempelian solution*, *unificationism*, *causal derivations* and *causes without derivations*.

A neo-Hempelian solution

A first strategy to deal with these problems consists of three parts:

a Hold on to the idea of 'understanding = expectability' and thus reject that explanations are asymmetrical.
b Add a condition to the models, that explanations should not contain irrelevant premises.
c Develop an adequate account of laws, in which laws are symmetrical.

Part (b) is trivial. Part (c) is not trivial but feasible (see below). The reason why hardly anyone has defended such a neo-Hempelian account is that the first part (a) is unacceptable for most people. An elaborated neo-Hempelian account can be found in Wilson (1985: 86–105, where he argues that explanation is symmetrical).

Sandra Mitchell (2000) has developed an account of laws in terms of a continuum of contingency. She claims that we should not try to make a dichotomic distinction between on the one hand laws (supposedly universal, necessary truths), and on the other hand all that is not a law (not universal, contingent). We should rather allow for a continuum of generalisations of the form '$(x)(Px{\rightarrow}Qx)$' to count as 'laws'. Some of them will be more contingent, and others more universal, but as long as they play a particular functional role, they deserve to be called 'law'. The function is that they *describe some stable relationship between different facts/events*. And the ranking on the continuum will be by the stability of the conditions on which the relations are contingent. Consider the generalisations about the golden and uranium spheres. It is clear on what conditions the first generalisation (1) is contingent: the availability of gold, the enormous amounts of effort and money that would have to be put in the production of such a sphere, etc.

> What conditions would have to be different to undermine the alleged law about uranium spheres? If the ways in which the particles of uranium interact were changed a sphere of [100,000 kg] would be possible. Note that this discussion is not about the conditions stated in the antecedent of the law statement. That is to say, it is not the Px in (x) (P$x{\rightarrow}$Qx). Rather I am referring to the conditions which underwrite the truth of the *relation* between P and Q described by the law. (Mitchell, 2000: 253–254)

Indeed, the state of the world as described by Mitchell is certainly possible (although it is not the actual one), and so the truth of the supposedly law-like statement is still contingent on certain factual conditions that have to hold. But, as everyone would agree, these conditions are much more stable than the conditions in the case of the golden sphere.

> The conditions that allow the gold law to be true are also stable, but less so – if we had "played the tape" of the origin and evolution of the universe again it might have been the case that more of this element would have amalgamated naturally on the earth. Indeed, it may well be that such a configuration of gold may be found elsewhere in the universe. (Mitchell, 2000: 254)

Mitchell's account entails no asymmetry, because stability is purely spatio-temporal: some correlations between events are limited to small regions of space and time, while others have greater spatio-temporal stability. Therefore her account is adequate for the neo-Hempelian. The account of laws we find in Woodward (2001, 2003) is not suited for the neo-Hempelian. Like Mitchell, Woodward claims that lawlikeness is a matter of degree. However, according to his *invariance view* all laws are necessarily causal. Using Woodward's account of laws in a model of explanation entails that explanation becomes asymmetrical.

Unificationism

The second strategy is to develop a unificationist account of explanation. The idea is that scientific explanation is a matter of 'exhibiting the phenomena as manifestations of common underlying structures and processes that conform to specific, testable basic principles' (Hempel, 1966: 83). Kitcher ascribes to Hempel the view that, besides expectability, explanations can confer a second intellectual benefit upon us: unification. Whether or not this ascription is correct does not matter; the important thing is that Kitcher (1981) regards *unification* as the one and only benefit that explanations may produce; according to Kitcher, we don't evaluate explanations one by one, but we judge sets

of explanations by reference to the extent to which they *unify* data under a systematic world view. (Note that, in Section 7 of his paper, Kitcher claims that he can solve the problems mentioned here above.) An earlier formulation of the unificationist idea can be found in Michael Friedman (1974), where the basic motivational idea behind unification is that 'science increases our understanding of the world by reducing the total number of independent phenomena that we have to accept as ultimate or given' (p.15).

Causal derivations

After describing the counterexamples mentioned above, Daniel Hausman writes: 'The most plausible diagnosis of these cases of DN arguments that are not explanations is that the premises in these arguments fail to focus on the *causes* of the phenomena described in their conclusions' (1998: 157). Hausman's solution is straightforward: only derivations from causes (causal derivations) are explanatory, derivations from effects are not explanatory. Referring to our example above, the length of the shadow is an effect of the position of the sun and the length of the flagpole, so the derivation which uses the length of the shadow as premise is not explanatory. Note that Hausman holds on to the idea that all explanations are arguments. He simply adds a criterion which ensures that the factors in the explanans are causes of the fact to be explained.

Causes without derivations

Causalists like Nancy Cartwright, Wesley Salmon, James Woodward and Paul Humphreys share Hausman's diagnosis. However, they consider his solution inadequate because they believe that explanations are not arguments. If explanations are not arguments, one cannot require that the derivation must be causal since there is no derivation.

A typical example used by these causalists is this: one can explain why the mayor contracted paresis by invoking that he had untreated latent syphilis. Only 7 per cent of people with latent untreated syphilis get paresis, so there is no inductive argument: the probability of the explanandum given the explanans is low. Nevertheless, this is a good explanation because syphilis is a positive causal factor: without latent syphilis, one cannot contract paresis.

We can distinguish two different approaches within the group of 'non-derivationist' causalists: (a) the non-contrastive approach, and (b) the contrastive one.

Causalists: the non-contrastive approach

According to Salmon, explaining '[...] involves the placing of the explanandum in a causal network consisting of relevant causal interactions that occurred previously and suitable causal processes that connect them to the fact-to-be-explained' (1984: 269). The explanation should provide us with the causal history of an event in a spatio-temporal continuous way.

According to Humphreys (1989a, 1989b) singular explanations have the following canonical form: 'Y in S at t (occurred, was present) because of ϕ, despite ψ'. Here ϕ is a (non-empty) list of terms referring to contributing causes of Y, ψ a (possibly empty) list of terms referring to counteracting causes of Y. Furthermore, Humphreys argues against the idea that all explanatory requests are implicitly contrastive or that non-contrastive explanatory requests are essentially ambiguous or illegitimate; the potential ambiguity is

> often the result of allowing the question to fix the format of the explanandum description through the use of some particular why-question. This is a dangerous practice, for it fails to make allowance for the important fact that the explainee ordinarily knows less about the explanandum event than does the explainer. (1989a: 137)

Causalists: the contrastive approach

Critics of the non-contrastive approach point out that the causal history of an event often includes a vast number of elements that are not explanatory relevant. Explanatory relevance is determined by the particular (implicit or explicit) explanation-seeking why-questions we are addressing; questions which are (often) contrastive. This is nicely illustrated in the following example.

> Suppose that my car is belching thick, black smoke. Wishing to correct the situation, I naturally ask why it is happening. Now imagine that God (or perhaps an evil genius) presents me with a full Deductive-Nomological explanation of the smoke. This may not be much help. The problem is that many of the causes of the smoke are also causes of the car's normal operation. Were I to eliminate one of these, I might only succeed in making the engine inoperable. By contrast, an explanation of why the car is smoking rather than running normally is far more likely to meet my diagnostic needs. Of course diagnosis and repair is only one of the motives for asking why-questions, but an investigation of the others would reveal still further reasons why we so often make our questions contrastive. (Lipton, 1993: 53)

Making explanation-seeking questions contrastive often helps to resolve vagueness and make our explanatory interests explicit. As Lipton's example shows, asking why something happens is often inquiring why things are different than we expect or want them to be. A similar contrastive approach to explanation has been developed by van Fraassen (1980), where the contrast specifies what the *explainee* wants to know.

Let us now specify how this range of views on scientific explanation can inspire philosophers of social science.

VARIETIES OF EXPLANATION IN THE SOCIAL SCIENCES

Introduction

There are a lot of debates on explanation in the social sciences. To mention just a few classical ones: the debate on the level of explanation, that is, whether the best explanations are found on the individual (lower) level or on the social (higher) level, the debate on the possibility and value of functional explanations, and the debate on using remote or proximate causes in explanations. These debates are often intertwined with ontological debates, but that is an issue we will not elaborate on in this chapter (see Van Bouwel, 2004). In the following subsections we show how the aforementioned contributions to general philosophy of science can help us in clarifying the debates on explanation in the social sciences and advance philosophy of social science.

In the past, the general literature on scientific explanations has not always been sufficiently exploited neither by social scientists (even those with an interest in theoretical issues) nor by most philosophers of social science. If some of the literature was mentioned, it concerned nearly always Hempel's DN model; later developments were omitted, or, the consequences for the actual debates in social science were not pondered. One of the reasons this was the case, might be that a lot of energy has been dedicated to *methodological individualism* and explanation, a discussion which was to a very large extent hijacked by ontological issues, rather than by issues concerning the forms and logic of explanation. Spending more attention to the latter issues might be fruitful, as we will argue in what follows.

Explicating the positive influence which general philosophy of science can have on philosophy of the social science requires a few *meta-decisions*, decisions on how to study the topic of explanation.

1   We have to choose a *naturalistic* approach to explanation. Naturalistic philosophers of explanation do not make claims about 'the nature of explanation' or 'the nature of understanding'. Instead they scrutinise how the different models of explanation developed in general philosophy of science have been used in scientific practice, and use these philosophical accounts of models as a toolbox for analysing debates on explanation in various disciplines, including the social sciences.
2   We have to take a *pragmatic* approach to explanation. There is a variation in the aims that scientists want to achieve by formulating explanations. In other words: there is a variety of types of understanding (this might, for instance, depend on the knowledge-context and epistemic interests of the explainee). We call an approach to explanation pragmatic if it acknowledges this

variation and investigates how this variation in types of understanding leads to variation in types of explanation and variation in criteria for evaluating the explanations.

These starting points can be systematised in a framework which we use to compare different forms of explanation applied by social scientists. In order to evaluate competing explanations, we need some philosophical instruments to *make the explananda as explicit as possible*, and to reveal the variation of *underlying epistemic interests*. Explicit explanation-seeking why-questions are a good candidate to help us; the explanations are considered as answers to why-questions (Hempel, 1965, supra).

Looking at social scientific explanatory practice, we can distinguish at least four types of explanatory questions that are omnipresent.

1   Why does object *a* have property P?
2   Why does object *a* have property P, rather than the (ideal) property P'?[2]
3   Why does object *a* have property P, while object *b* has property P'?
4   Why does object *a* have property P at time t, but property P' at time t'?

This shows how different explanation-seeking questions about one social fact can be formulated, motivated by different epistemic interests and needs – the different benefits of explanation mentioned above are, for instance, *expectability* (Hempel), *unification* (Kitcher, Friedman), *opening a black box* (Salmon), *diagnosis* and *repair* (Lipton). First, non-contrastive, explanation-seeking questions – of the form (1) – can have different motivations. One possible motivation is sheer intellectual curiosity, the desire to know how the fact 'fits into the causal structure of the world'. A more pragmatic motivation is the desire to have information that enables us to predict whether and in which circumstances similar events will occur in the future (or the anticipation of actions of persons/groups). Another possible motivation concerns causally connecting object *a* having property P to events with which we are more familiar.

Second, explanation-seeking questions – of the forms (2–4) – can require the explanation of a contrast; these explanations can have a therapeutic function, or are motivated by 'unexpectedness'. They isolate causes that help us to reach the ideal, comparing the actual fact with the one we would like to be the case. Or they could be intended to help us to remove the observed difference between objects, or they could be meant to tell us why things have been otherwise than we expected them to be.

Equipped with this framework, we will present two examples to illustrate how the general philosophy of science can help to clarify debates in (the philosophy of) social science.[3] The first example illustrates how the debate between adherents of a unificationist account of explanation and non-unificationists can shed light on the debate in (the philosophy of) social science concerning the preferred level of explanation, and on the desirability of unification in the social sciences. The second example elucidates how the debate between contrastive and non-contrastive approaches to explanation can put several controversies concerning the best explanatory model for social science in a different light.

Unification and social explanations

As an example, we will use an article by Michael Taylor (1988) on revolutionary collective action in which he tries to develop a reformulation of the thesis in Theda Skocpol's classic *States and Social Revolutions* (1979). What interests us here is how Taylor defends an explanation using rational choice theory in historical sociology against higher-level or macro-explanations of the non-voluntarist sort provided by Skocpol.

Before we discuss Taylor's critique of Skocpol's work, we should define the terms that we will use. By an *intentional* explanation we mean an explanation of a social fact in terms of the intentional states (desires, opinions, perceived opportunities) and actions of one or more individuals. In our conceptual scheme, intentional explanations are always *lower-level* or *micro-explanations*. We define *structural* explanations as *higher-level* or *macro-level* explanations that are *causal*. Structural explanations come in different varieties: sometimes they invoke proximate causes, sometimes remote causes. They can also differ with respect to the kind of social event they invoke as *explanans*: it can be of a materialistic nature or be an idealistic factor. Intentional explanations differ from idealistic structural explanations in that the latter use properties of *groups* rather than intentional states of *individuals*. Examples of such group properties are: 'A majority in this group believes X', 'Everyone in this group wants Y', 'Some people in this group possess personality trait Z (lazy, aggressive, stubborn, …)' and so on.

Let us now analyse Taylor's arguments concerning the explanation of social revolutions. Taylor defends the thesis that the higher-level phenomenon or entity (the revolution) is nothing more than a set of intentional actions; in this way the higher level is ontologically dependent on the lower level. What are the consequences of this for explaining revolutions? Taylor states that micro-foundations should be provided, but that this does not necessarily lead to an incompatibility between the higher-level and lower-level account.

In order to provide micro-foundations, Taylor shows how the participation of vast numbers of peasants in collective action could be explained by using *the logic of collective action* advanced by Mancur Olson. Taylor invokes the use of economic incentives and selective social incentives, especially those supporting conditional cooperation. Taylor calls this a thin theory of collective action. According to his thin theory, the collective action of peasants in revolutions was based on communal norms and sanctions (as many historians have argued), and this is mainly why the large numbers of peasants were able to overcome the free-rider problem familiar to students of collective action.

Starting from the idea of micro-foundations, Taylor draws some conclusions about which explanations are preferable. He advocates 'that good explanation should be, amongst other things, as *fine-grained* as possible: causal links connecting events distant in space-time should be replaced wherever possible by chains of "shorter" causal links'.[4] So, ontological dependence leads, according to Taylor, to a preference for fine-grain micro-explanations. (Taylor tolerates higher-level, structural explanations, but thinks they must ultimately be cashed out in terms of intentional explanations that explain by means of the instrumental rationality of the agents involved.)

Let us now consider three explanation-seeking questions related to Taylor's reformulation of Skocpol's explanation of social revolutions.

1 Why did the French revolution start in 1789, rather than in 1750?
2 Why was there a revolution in Bourbon France, Manchu China and Romanov Russia?
3 Why did the French revolution occur in 1789?

Question (1), which is a contrastive question, can be answered by Skocpol's theory. By using comparative methods, Skocpol formulated a structural explanation for three successful modern social revolutions in agrarian-bureaucratic monarchies (the French, Russian and Chinese revolutions). The structural conditions that, in her view, make a revolution possible (that is, the revolutions can be successfully mounted only if these structural preconditions are met) relate to the incapacity of the central state's machinery, especially the weakening of the state's repressive capacity. This weakening is caused by external military (and economic) pressure: because of the backward agrarian economy and the power of the landed upper class in the agrarian-bureaucratic monarchy, any attempt to increase military power leads to a fiscal crisis. Escalating international competition and humiliations particularly symbolised by unexpected defeats in wars (which inspired autocratic authorities to attempt reforms)

trigger social revolutions. These macroscopic causal relations can explain contrasts (in the most efficient way). The foreign military pressure that triggered the respective social revolutions, were: Bourbon France (1787–1789): financially exhausted after the War for American Independence and because of the competition with England in general; Romanov Russia (1917): massive defeats in World War I; Manchu China (1911–1916): Sino–Japanese War (1895) and the Boxer debacle (1899–1901). The point here is that a Skocpol-type macro-explanation can explain why the French Revolution occurred in 1789 rather than 1750: at the earlier time the conditions necessary for a successful revolution were not yet in place.

Question (2), which is a question for the explanation of a set of similar facts, might appear to be better addressed by Taylor: 'When the peasant community was sufficiently strong, then, it provided a social basis for collective action, including revolutionary collective action and rebellions and other popular mobilizations' (1988: 68). The explanation Taylor provides refers to a property of a group or community. Basically, it claims that if the coherence within groups or communities is strong, a revolution can occur, and that is exactly the case in Bourbon France, Manchu China, and Romanov Russia. But parsed in this way, it ought to be clear that Taylor's is not in fact a micro-level explanation: it is a macro-level idealistic explanation. The important thing is that questions like (2), which are about similar facts, can only be answered by means of a macro-explanation. If we ask questions like this, the underlying aim is *unification*: we want to know what is common in the causal ancestry of the different phenomena. In our example, we want to know what the causal mechanisms that led to these three revolutions have in common. This question cannot be answered by giving three stories at the micro-level: we need an account that points at their similarities.

Finally, answering question (3) requires a micro-level explanation: we have to know who did what in order to make the revolution occur. That is, even if the macro-structural conditions were in place by 1789 in France, it still took the activities of particular agents with their particular beliefs and desires to respond to these conditions at the particular time they did. This can only be done by means of a fine-grained intentional explanation of the sort Taylor trumpets.

Some questions, like (3), can be answered only by a micro-explanation; other questions, like (2), need a macro-explanation. This is due to the inherent relevance relation: in (2) the 'why' means 'what are the common aspects of the causal ancestry of', while in question (3) the 'why' stands for 'what are the intentional acts that served as the causal mechanism that led to'. And unless we discard one of them as an illegitimate question that should not be asked, such questions constitute good reasons for questioning the unificationist project of replacing macro-explanations of the non-voluntarist sort provided by Skocpol by a rational choice theory account.

Taylor's attempt to replace Skocpol's account can be considered an instance of one of the most successful unificationist projects in the social sciences, namely the so-called *economics takeover* or *economics imperialism.* The central idea of the economics takeover is that economists (and other social scientists) improve knowledge in the social sciences by applying the dominant or orthodox theory and method in economics far beyond its original home in territories inhabited by other disciplines. As such the degree of unification can be increased applying rational choice theory to new kinds of *explananda* outside economics.

Following some general philosophers of science, we would achieve increased understanding through such a unification, an incorporation of Skocpol's account within a single overarching framework (cf. Friedman, 1974); 'Science advances our understanding of nature by showing us how to derive descriptions of many phenomena, using the same patterns of derivation again and again, and, in demonstrating this, it teaches us

how to reduce the number of types of facts we have to accept as ultimate (or brute)' (Kitcher, 1989: 432). Hence, advocates of the *economics takeover* might find philosophical arguments to substantiate their project.

More recent contributions to general philosophy of science (e.g. De Regt, 2004), as well as our discussion of Taylor's contribution, do however qualify this unificationist drive; even if unification conveys increased understanding for some people (relative to their interests at a given time), it will always obstruct understanding for others (with different interests). Recognising the plurality of possible epistemic interests helps us to move on from the *winner-takes-all-approach* to explanation, and to stop regarding the plurality of theoretical perspectives and forms of explanation as a problem. On the contrary, this plurality is a strength in achieving understanding. All of which puts the eternal debate on the level of explanation in the social sciences, that is, are the best explanations found on the individual (lower) level or on the social (higher) level, in a very different light.

Contrastive and non-contrastive explanations in the social sciences

Bringing in the general philosophy of science dispute between the contrastive and non-contrastive approach, discussed above, opens up new perspectives on the debates on social scientific explanations as well, as we illustrate in this section with an example derived from Robert Axelrod's analysis of unofficial truces.[5] In World War I, there were unofficial truces by units on both sides: each side continued to fire its weapons but without intending to inflict much damage. Axelrod explains these truces as rational behaviour based on a strategy of conditional cooperation in a repeated prisoner's dilemma situation (this strategy amounts to: start with cooperation, and keep on cooperating as long as the opponent cooperates). Trench warfare, which guarantees a relatively stable, clearly identifiable enemy (units are not replaced overnight) whose reactions can be easily observed, presents an excellent situation for conditional cooperation to emerge. In different types of warfare (Blitzkrieg, guerrilla) similar truces are impossible because there is no stable enemy and no clearly identifiable reaction and response. Axelrod's question is non-contrastive:

4   Why were there informal truces in World War I?

But we can also formulate some interesting contrastive questions about these truces, for instance:

5   Why did unit A have informal truces, while unit B kept on fighting?
6   Why were there informal truces in World War I, but not in World War II?

Axelrod's original question is about a 'stylised fact', not about a specific, concrete fact. This question can be answered (as it is by Axelrod) by providing a possible belief-desire constellation that leads to an informal truce. Axelrod's explanation is an intentional explanation, highlighting the rational behaviour of individuals.

A possible motivation for questions (5) and (6) would be the desire to prevent similar truces (a military strategist might be interested in this). The best answers (but not the only possible ones) to these questions are structural ones. In the case of question (5), the answer should refer to a difference in 'corporate culture' between units A and B: unit B is a very docile or a very heroic one, such that its members obey orders without questioning them, or they really like fighting; unit A has a different culture: it is a critical unit that does not like fighting at all. (Note that this explanation is situated at the macro level, because it refers to shared values and attitudes [group culture] rather than to individual thoughts and actions). In the case of question (6), the answer should refer to material circumstances: in World War II, there was no trench warfare, units did not have

stable enemies, so conditional cooperation could not emerge.[6]

These structural explanations are not the only possible answers to questions (5) and (6). Intentional explanations are possible, too, but the structural explanations are much more *efficient*, because the information about individual soldiers in the units is not essential for understanding the difference between A and B, or between units in World War I and in World War II. Efficiency refers to the amount of (research) work that needs to be done in order to construct the explanation and to show that it is correct. The intentional explanations of (5) and (6) require a lot of information about individual agents, while structural explanations do not contain that kind of information. So, *ceteris paribus*, structural explanations are to be preferred in this case for pragmatic reasons, because they require less work. (We acknowledge that the structural explanations presuppose certain intentionality on the part of the soldiers – they are instrumentally rational, and it is only because they are so that the structural conditions cited as explanations for their behaviour can be the causes they are. But this intentionality is of a perfectly general sort that applies to agents as such, not to particular agents and their specific beliefs and desires. As a result, the structural explanations continue to be far more efficient than possible particular intentional explanations.)

With respect to the informal truces we can also ask non-contrastive questions that are more specific than question (4), for instance:

7   Why did unit A have an informal truce in period *t*?

This question seems to require a micro-explanation: in order to answer this question, we have to refer to the actual desires, beliefs, and decisions of members of this unit. A general rational-choice explanation, as in Axelrod's answer to (4), original question will not do, because what we have to explain is why something that actually occurred did so, not how some stylised fact was possible.

What we want to illustrate with this example is that not all explananda in social science are (implicitly or explicitly) contrastive; non-contrastive explananda are rife in social science and require a detailed causal history in a non-interrupted causal chain across time ending with the explanandum or an explanation that follows a covering law model. Such an account of the actual causal history is not required when we deal with contrastive explananda. In the latter case the explanations should enable us to obtain information about the features that differentiate the actual causal history from its (un)actualised alternative, by isolating the causes that make the difference.

The discussion in general philosophy of science taught us to make the explananda as explicit as possible – to find out whether they are contrastive or non-contrastive (reflecting different underlying epistemic interests). Furthermore, we learnt that the form of explanation required, differs depending on whether a contrastive or a non-contrastive explanation-seeking question has to be answered – as was illustrated by the different questions we raised about the phenomenon of unofficial truces.

CAUSATION: WHAT CAN GENERAL PHILOSOPHY OF SCIENCE LEARN FROM THE PHILOSOPHY OF SOCIAL SCIENCE?

Probabilistic causation has been studied by general philosophers of science and by philosophers and methodologists of the social sciences. Till recently, there was hardly any interaction between the two groups. The absence of interaction has led to completely different theories, as we will show below. We will also show how general philosophy of science could have benefited from input from the philosophy of the social sciences on this topic.

Let us start with the philosophers and methodologists of social science. In Morgan

and Winship (2007: 5–6 and 31–37), the authors present their *counterfactual model of causal analysis*, also known as the *potential outcome model*. This approach has a long history, including important work by Donald Rubin and James Heckman (see Morgan and Winship, 2007: 4 for detailed references). To get a grip on this approach, we use one of their favourite examples dealing with the question: 'Are Catholic schools more effective than public schools in teaching mathematics to equivalent students?' Suppose that each individual in the population of interest (the class of all students) can be exposed to two alternative states of the presumed cause (either she attends a Catholic school or a public school). These states are referred to as treatment and control, respectively. Each state potentially affects the outcome of interest (a mathematics test score). The key assumption of the counterfactual model is that each student has a potential outcome under each state of the cause, even though each individual can be observed in only one state at any time. For example, students in Catholic schools have observable test scores under the treatment state *and* theoretical what-if (i.e., counterfactual) scores under the control state. (The converse holds for students in public schools: they have observable test scores under the control state *and* counterfactual scores under the treatment state.) Technically, two potential outcome random variables are defined over all individuals in the population of interest: Y^1 and Y^0 measure the actual and counterfactual potential outcomes in the treatment state and in the control state respectively.

For each student i, the *individual-level causal effect* of Catholic schooling δ_i may be defined as the difference between her observable/counterfactual test score under the treatment state (y_i^1) and her counterfactual/observable test score under the control state (y_i^0): $\delta_i = y_i^1 - y_i^0$. It is the what-if difference in test score that could be calculated if we would simultaneously educate her in both a Catholic school and a public school. By definition, these individual-level causal effects cannot be observed or directly calculated. By consequence, attention is focused on estimating various average (population-level) causal effects, such as the *average treatment effect* $E[\delta] = E[Y^1 - Y^0]$.

The first theory of probabilistic causation in general philosophy of science was that of Patrick Suppes. In his view, genuine (probabilistic) causes are prima facie causes that are not spurious (1970: 24). The definition of a prima facie cause is as follows:

The event $B_{t'N}$ is a prima facie cause of the event A_t if and only if:

(i) $t' < t$,
(ii) $P(B_{t'}) > 0$,
(iii) $P(A_t \mid B_{t'}) > P(A_t)$. (p. 12)

Spurious causes are defined as follows:

An event $B_{t'N}$ is a spurious cause in sense one[7] of A_t, if and only if, $B_{t'N}$ is a prima facie cause of A_t and there is a $tO < tN$ and an event C_{tO} such that:

(i) $P(B_{t'} \cdot C_{t''}) > 0$,
(ii) $P(A_t \mid B_{t'} \cdot C_{t''}) = P(A_t \mid C_{t''})$,
(iii) $P(A_t \mid B_{t'} \cdot C_{t''}) \geq P(A_t \mid B_{t'})$. (p. 23)

These definitions are Suppes' answer to the question 'What do probabilistic causal claims mean?' The crucial differences between the potential outcome model and Suppes', is that the latter refers to the presence and absence of positive statistical relevance relations in the *real* world, and causation is a relation among *events*.

What is wrong with Suppes' theory? In her recent book *Hunting Causes and Using Them* (2007), Nancy Cartwright says that in the philosophical study of causation '[m]etaphysics, methods and use must march hand in hand' (2007: 1). By this she means that philosophers of causation should try to develop an integrated account, which answers three interrelated questions about causation: What do causal claims mean? How do we confirm them? What use can we make of them? In the work of Morgan and Winship and their predecessors on the tradition of the potential outcome model, Cartwright's ideal is realised. Suppes, on the other hand, clearly does

not manage to forge a link between his definition and use. Why should policy makers want causal knowledge? If we adopt Suppes, the answer is not clear, because it refers to the real world, not to a hypothetical world that policy makers can create. Policy makers need answers to what-if questions (what if everyone went to a Catholic school? What if no one would smoke?). In Suppes' definition, there is no connection between causal knowledge and what-if questions. Moreover, it refers to singular relation among events, while policy makers deal with populations: policy makers need relations between *types* of events, not between singular events.

Ellery Eells (1991) has developed a so-called context unanimity theory of probabilistic causation. Here is a crucial passage:

Then we say that *X* is a *positive causal factor* for *Y* if and only if, *for each i*, $Pr(Y/K_i \& X) > Pr(Y/K_i \& {-}{\cdot}X)$. *Negative causal factorhood* and *causal neutrality* are defined by changing the "always rises" (>) idea to "always lowers" (<) and "always leaves unchanged" (=), respectively. The idea that the inequality or equality must hold for each of the background contexts K_i is sometimes called the condition of contextual unanimity, or context unanimity. ... Note that these three relations of positive, negative and neutral causal factorhood are not exhaustive of the possible causal significance that a factor X can have for a factor Y: There remains the possibility of various kinds of mixed causal relevance, corresponding to various ways in which unanimity can fail. (pp. 86–87)

Like Suppes, Eells defines causation in terms of positive statistical relevance relations in the real world. The advantage is that he uses populations and variables, rather than singular events. However, the policy relevance of causal claims in the sense of Eells is not clear, because – like in Suppes' definition – the counterfactual element is absent. On top of that, it can be argued that the context unanimity requirement is problematic.

The characteristic property of causes in the sense of the context unanimity theory is that the causal tendency cannot be reversed (from positive to negative) or annihilated (from positive or negative to causally neutral) in a subpopulation. Eells gives the following example:

> [I]ngesting an acid poison (X) is causally positive for death (Y) when no alkali poison has been ingested (~F), but when an alkali poison has been ingested (F), the ingestion of an acid poison is causally negative for death. I will argue that in a case like this it is best to deny that X is a positive causal factor for Y, even if, overall (for the population as a whole), the probability of death when an acid poison has been ingested (that is, even if $Pr(Y/X) > Pr(Y/\sim X)$). I will argue that it is best in this case to say that X is causally *mixed* for Y, and despite the *overall* or *average* probability increase, X is nevertheless not a positive causal factor for Y in the population as a whole. (p. 58)

Policy makers need average effects; context unanimity is not required for a rational policy. Furthermore, the context unanimity theory entails that scientific inquiry cannot support probabilistic causal claims (see Weber, 2007 for these issues).

Finally, let us look at the definition of Paul Humphreys (1989a: 74):

> B is a *direct contributing cause* of A just in case
> (i) A occurs;
> (ii) B occurs;
> (iii) B increases the chance of A in all circumstances Z that are physically compatible with A and B, and with A and B_0, where B_0 is the neutral state of B, i.e., $P(A|BZ) > P(A|B_0Z)$ for all such Z; and
> (iv) BZ and A are logically independent.
> Similarly, B is a *direct counteracting cause* of A just in case (i), (ii), (iii), and (iv) hold, with 'increases' replaced by 'decreases' and with the inequality reversed.

This definition also includes a context unanimity requirement. And like the definitions of Suppes and Eells, it refers to the real world. Like Suppes, it refers to singular events. So this definition faces all the problems mentioned before, if we want to link it to policy.

To sum up, we think the typical theories of probabilistic causation developed by general philosophers of science are quite unworldly, while the models developed by philosophers and methodologists of social science are better, in the sense that they integrate the three aspects mentioned by Cartwright. Hence, general philosophy of science could have benefited from more interaction with the philosophy of social science.

GENERAL CONCLUSION

Discussing the debates on scientific explanation and causation in general philosophy of science and philosophy of social science has shown that they have a lot to learn from each other, more so than realised up to now. General philosophy of science discussions have an obvious (philosophy of) social science relevance and the very precisely articulated instruments developed through those discussions have improved the (analysis of) the social sciences – but more can be made out of it. The philosophy of social science, on the other hand, has generated a lot of insights of how to make use of theories and how to deal with a plurality of epistemic interests – aspects often neglected by general philosophy of science.

NOTES

1 The authors would like to thank Merel Lefevere and Jan De Winter for their comments on earlier versions of this chapter.

2 P and P' are supposed to be mutually exclusive.

3 For more examples, see Van Bouwel and Weber (2008a, 2008b).

4 Taylor (1988: 96), where he refers to Jon Elster's (1983: 24, 28–29).

5 This example is elaborated by Robert Axelrod (1984), and discussed in Daniel Little (1991: 58).

6 In this particular case, there is no correct 'idealistic' answer to the second question, because there is no factor of this nature that 'makes a difference'; and there is no correct 'materialistic' answer to the first question, because the material factors are identical. But there is no reason to generalise this: it is possible that in some cases we may have a correct idealistic and a correct materialistic answer to the same question.

7 Suppes distinguishes a second sense of spurious cause, but that type is not important here.

REFERENCES

Axelrod, Robert (1984) *The Evolution of Cooperation*. New York: Basic Books.

Cartwright, Nancy (2007) *Hunting Causes and Using Them. Approaches in Philosophy and Economics*. Cambridge: Cambridge University Press.

De Regt, Henk (2004) 'Discussion note: Making sense of understanding', *Philosophy of Science*, 71: 98–109.

Eells, Ellery (1991) *Probabilistic Causality*. Cambridge: Cambridge University Press.

Elster, Jon (1983) *Explaining Technical Change: A Case Study in the Philosophy of Science*. Cambridge: Cambridge University Press.

Friedman, Michael (1974) 'Explanation and scientific understanding', *Journal of Philosophy*, 71: 5–19.

Hausman, Daniel (1998) *Causal Asymmetries*. Cambridge: Cambridge University Press.

Hausman, Daniel (2008) *The Philosophy of Economics* (3rd edition). Cambridge: Cambridge University Press.

Hempel, Carl and Oppenheim Paul (1948) 'Studies in the logic of explanation', in Carl Hempel, Carl (1965) *Aspects of Scientific Explanation and other Essays in the Philosophy of Science*. New York: Free Press. pp. 245–290. (Originally in: *Philosophy of Science*, 15).

Hempel, Carl (1965) *Aspects of Scientific Explanation and other Essays in the Philosophy of Science*. New York: Free Press.

Hempel, Carl (1966) *Philosophy of Natural Science*. Englewood Cliffs: Prentice-Hall.

Humphreys, Paul (1989a) *The Chances of Explanation*. Princeton, NY: Princeton University Press.

Humphreys, Paul (1989b) 'Scientific explanation: the causes, some of the causes, and nothing but the causes', in Philip Kitcher and Wesley Salmon (eds) *Scientific Explanation*. Minneapolis: University of Minnesota Press. pp. 282–306.

Kitcher, Philip (1981) 'Explanatory unification', *Philosophy of Science*, 48: 507–531.

Kitcher, Philip (1989) 'Explanatory unification and the causal structure of the world', in Philip Kitcher and Wesley Salmon (eds) *Scientific Explanation*. Minneapolis: University of Minnesota Press. pp. 410–505.

Lipton, Peter (1993) 'Making a difference'. *Philosophica*, 51(1): 39–54.

Little, Daniel (1991) *Varieties of Social Explanation*. Boulder: Westview Press.

Mitchell, Sandra (2000) 'Dimensions of scientific law', *Philosophy of Science*, 67: 242–265.

Morgan, Stephen and Christopher Winship (2007) *Counterfactuals and Causal Inference. Methods and Principles for Social Research*. Cambridge: Cambridge University Press.

Salmon, Wesley (1984) *Scientific Explanation and the Causal Structure of the World*. Princeton, NY: Princeton University Press.

Salmon, Wesley (1989) 'Four decades of scientific explanation', in Philip Kitcher and Wesley Salmon (eds) *Scientific Explanation*. Minneapolis: University of Minnesota Press. pp. 3–219.

Salmon, Wesley (1998) *Causality and Explanation*. Oxford: Oxford University Press.

Skocpol, Theda (1979) *States and Social Revolutions*. Cambridge: Cambridge University Press.

Suppes, Patrick (1970) *A Probabilistic Theory of Causality*. Amsterdam: North-Holland Publishing Company.

Taylor, Michael (1988) 'Rationality and revolutionary collective action', in Michael Taylor (ed.) *Rationality and Revolution*. Cambridge: Cambridge University Press. pp. 63–97.

Van Bouwel, Jeroen (2004) 'Individualism and holism, reduction and pluralism', *Philosophy of the Social Sciences*, 34: 527–535.

Van Bouwel Jeroen and Erik Weber (2008a) 'A pragmatist defense of non-relativistic explanatory pluralism in history and social science', *History and Theory*, 47: 168–182.

Van Bouwel Jeroen and Erik Weber (2008b) 'De-ontologizing the debate on social explanations: a pragmatic approach based on epistemic interests', *Human Studies*, 31: 423–442.

Van Fraassen, Bas (1980) *The Scientific Image*. Oxford: Oxford University Press.

Weber, Erik (2007) 'Conceptual tools for causal analysis in the social sciences', in Federica Russo and Jon Williamson (eds) *Causality and Probability in the Sciences*. London: College Publications. pp. 197–213.

Wilson Fred (1985) *Explanation, Causation and Deduction*. Dordrecht: D. Reidel Publishing Company.

Woodward James (2001) 'Law and explanation in biology: Invariance is the kind of stability that matters', *Philosophy of Science*, 68: 1–20.

Woodward James (2003) *Making Things Happen. A Theory of Causal Explanation*. Oxford: Oxford University Press.

34

Prediction

Gregor Betz

PREDICTIVE SUCCESS AS AN AIM OF SCIENCE

We shall start with the question whether successful prediction is an aim of science at all. And if so, why? There are two ways in which a positive answer to this question can be justified. First, one might stress the practical importance of predictions for policy making in particular, and decision making in general. Second, and independently of that first point, the aim of predictive success might be defended by claiming that reliable forecasting is a universal litmus test for scientific knowledge and that, as a consequence, any science, qua being a science, aims at improving its predictive performance. Let us consider these two answers in turn.

That prediction is (possibly among other things) a pragmatic goal which stems from its relevance for rational decision-making is widely agreed upon.[1] It is noteworthy that according to this characterisation prediction is not an intrinsic epistemic aim (of science) but rather an extrinsic one, a goal whose appeal stems from our practical interests.

Besides being a pragmatic, extrinsic aim of science, predictive success is sometimes considered an intrinsic epistemic aim of science, too. We shall discuss this suggestion in the remainder of this section. Friedman (1953),

for instance, would clearly subscribe to this view. He starts his reflections on the methodology of positive economics with the following sentence: 'The ultimate goal of a positive science is the development of a "theory" or "hypothesis" that yields valid and meaningful (i.e. not truistic) predictions about phenomena not yet observed' (p. 183). This, however, is a basic premise of his reasoning for which no further arguments are given.

Rosenberg, in a series of texts, has consistently defended prediction as an intrinsic epistemic aim of science (Rosenberg, 1988, 1992, 1993). Epistemic aims, though, might be of different strength. A strong aim formulates a necessary condition for a body of statements to count as knowledge at all (e.g. consistency, as most philosophers would say); a weak aim expresses a desirable feature which, if not satisfied, does not imply that the respective set of statements does not represent knowledge (mathematical simplicity, for instance). Taking this qualification into account, Rosenberg seems to claim that prediction is a central, a strong epistemic aim of science (Rosenberg, 1992: 18f.).

Before having a closer look at some arguments which can be put forward to warrant the thesis that predictive success is a central, intrinsic epistemic aim of science, we should briefly note that Rosenberg himself is cautious regarding the status of this aim. In spite of defending it as a necessary condition of scientific knowledge and in spite of questioning the cognitive status of economics on the grounds of its systematic predictive failure, he acknowledges that it is impossible to strictly demonstrate why prediction is a central aim of science[2] and warns us not to interpret that condition as a 'litmus test-like demarcation principle' (Rosenberg, 1993: 163).

We can distinguish three arguments which seek to show that prediction is an intrinsic epistemic aim. I label them: 'The argument from confirmation', 'the argument from explanation', and 'the pragmatic argument'.

The argument of confirmation (cf. Rosenberg, 1992: 13) can be reconstructed as, argument A:

1   Empirical confirmation (of beliefs) is a central epistemic aim of science.
2   Without predictive success, no beliefs would be empirically confirmed.
3   If X is a central aim of some enterprise and X won't be achieved without Y, then Y is a central aim of that enterprise, too.
4   *Thus*: Predictive success is a central epistemic aim of science.

This argument is valid, but hardly sound. The problematic premise is (A.2).[3] Prediction is not necessary for empirical confirmation. Successful explanations, for instance, might confirm hypotheses as well (via inference to the best explanation). The argument from confirmation crucially hinges on the premise that prediction is the only or at least the best way for confirming hypotheses and theories.

The argument from explanation can be considered as a response to the critical remark regarding the previous argument. We have noted that explanation might empirically confirm a hypothesis, too. But, Rosenberg (1993: 161f.) claims, explaining e implies predicting e, argument B:

1   If one acquires knowledge, one has either successfully predicted or successfully explained.
2   Successful explanation incorporates successful prediction.

3   *Thus:* If one acquires knowledge, one has successfully predicted.
4   Acquiring knowledge is a central epistemic aim of science.
5   If X is a central aim of some enterprise and X won't be achieved without Y, then Y is a central aim of that enterprise, too.
6   *Thus*: Predictive success is a central epistemic aim of science.

The crucial premise of this valid argument seems to be premise (B.2). Does explanation, as Rosenberg, referring to Hempel, claims, always require prediction? What about historical sciences which merely aim at making past events intelligible, for instance by embedding them in our web of beliefs? And doesn't the theory of evolution represent a counter example to premise (B.2)? What is the nature of scientific explanation at all? It is obvious that the controversy regarding the role of predictive success in evaluating science has to turn on these issues (as it has, see for example McCloskey, 1986; Rosenberg, 1988).

The pragmatic argument, finally, derives that predictive success is a necessary condition any science must meet from the aim of policy relevance. We should note that, although the conclusion of this argument is identical with the previous argument's conclusions, it cannot be said anymore that it shows prediction to be an *intrinsic* epistemic aim. At the core of this argument is Rosenberg's strong claim that science without prediction is irrelevant for public and private policy (Rosenberg, 1992: 20). Taking that for granted, it seems to follow, given that science should be practically relevant, that it should also aim at predictive success. However, is science without prediction really irrelevant? What's the argument for this claim? Does it follow from the undeniable statement that foreknowledge is required for rational policy? Argument C:

1   Successful prediction is required for rational (private and public) decision making.
2   *Thus*: If science does not yield successful predictions, it is irrelevant for (private and public) decision making.

3 Whatever is required for science to be relevant for (private and public) decision making is a central epistemic aim of science.
4 *Thus*: Predictive success is a central epistemic aim of science.

The problem with this argument is the inference from (C.1) to (C.2). That inference is not valid. Consider

1 Salt and pepper are required for good tomato soup.
2 *Thus*: If tomatoes don't yield salt and pepper, they are irrelevant for good tomato soup.

Coming back to the policy relevance of social sciences, what do these sciences have to offer – besides prediction – which is of relevance for policy making? I don't think this is a very difficult question: Accurate descriptions of past and present social phenomena are of crucial importance for an adequate normative judgement regarding the current state of affairs. How are income and wealth distributed in a society? Is there racial discrimination regarding the access to higher education? Understanding and explaining complex social relationships, or identifying causal relationships, too, might help us to better evaluate the effectiveness of policy measures. Has urban poverty been reduced in the last three years due to the reform of the health system? Did the promotion events and advertising campaigns incite more undergraduate students to study mathematics? Science has more to give than prediction, and justification of scientific results, the critical appraisal of the previous arguments suggests, doesn't necessarily rely on prediction. That is why prediction-free science is not inevitably irrelevant for policy making.

ON THE VERY POSSIBILITY OF PREDICTION IN THE SOCIAL SCIENCES

Is prediction in the social sciences possible at all? We shall have a closer look at the positions of some philosophers who denied this question for more or less fundamental, even a priori, reasons. These predictive sceptics include Oskar Morgenstern, Otto Neurath, Karl R. Popper and Friedrich von Hayek.

In an elaborated philosophical study on economic forecasting, likely the first of its kind, Oskar Morgenstern claimed to show that macroeconomic forecasting is impossible once and forever for a priori reasons (Morgenstern, 1928). His argument can be divided into three major parts. In its first part, he tries to show that there is a causal relation between the publication of a macroeconomic forecast and the predicted event. Taking this as a starting point for the second part, he then deduces that macroeconomic forecasts generally fail. The third part finally excludes the possibility that they are corrected.

Morgenstern argues as follows, argument D:

1 A published macroeconomic forecast has a causal influence on the economic agents' expectations.
2 The economic agents' expectations causally influence their behaviour.
3 The aggregated behaviour of economic agents is the object of a macroeconomic forecast.
4 The causal relation is transitive.
5 *Thus*: There is a causal relationship between the publication of a macroeconomic forecast and its object.
6 Unless a forecast considers all causally relevant factors ex ante, it will not become true.
7 Macroeconomic forecasts cannot anticipate the effects of their dissemination.
8 *Thus*: Macroeconomic forecasts will not become true.
9 A revision of a macroeconomic forecast is a macroeconomic forecast.
10 If there is no correct revision (or revision of a revision or …) of a macroeconomic forecast, the forecast cannot be corrected.
11 *Thus*: Macroeconomic forecasts don't become true and cannot be corrected.
12 If a forecast of a certain object neither becomes true nor can it be corrected, forecasting in this domain is not possible.
13 *Thus*: Macroeconomic forecasting is not possible.

Given the reconstructed reasoning, we see that premise (D.6) is obviously too strong an assumption. It is absolutely possible that forecasts based on time-series methods which do not take into account all causally relevant factors are correct. The falsity of this premise is the major reason why Morgenstern's ambitious project – to prove the impossibility of macroeconomic forecasting a priori – is doomed to failure. Note that this principle figures in other arguments, too (E.4, I.10, J.6), which are discredited as a priori arguments for the same reason.[4]

Otto Neurath has been concerned with the methodology of the social sciences throughout his academic life and was highly pessimistic regarding the predictive powers of social sciences. In *Foundations of Social Sciences* (1944: 28f.), he briefly states two main reasons for social unpredictability. The first reason consists in the 'instability' of some social situations. Neurath observes that minor changes in the initial conditions might have 'tremendous' effects on the outcome of social processes. Joined with the fact that social scientists will always have limited data and information about initial states, instability gives rise to unpredictability. As a second reason, Neurath cites, without going into details, the reflexivity of social predictions, that is, the very reason Morgenstern considered crucial. But how fundamental are these problems? Do they really represent a priori *limits* of social forecasting? Hardly so; they seem to rely on empirical facts about the structure of social systems and our contingent cognitive capacities.[5]

Karl R. Popper is another admitting skeptic regarding the predictability of social processes.[6] In the preface to *The Poverty of Historicism*, he boldly claims: 'I have shown that, for strictly logical reasons, it is impossible for us to predict the future course of history' (Popper, 1957: ix). The core of his argument can be reconstructed as follows, argument E:

1 The growth of scientific knowledge cannot be predicted.
2 What cannot be predicted, cannot be considered by a forecast *ex ante*.
3 *Thus*: The growth of scientific knowledge cannot be considered by a forecast ex ante.
4 Unless a forecast considers all causally relevant factors ex ante, it is not reliable.

5 *Thus*: Unless a forecast of a social phenomenon which causally depends on scientific innovation considers the development of scientific knowledge ex ante, it is not reliable.
6 *Thus*: Predictions of social phenomena which causally depend on scientific innovation are not reliable.

But does Popper's argument, thus understood, also show that *any kind of* social prediction is impossible? Hardly so. Social sciences try to predict many phenomena which are not significantly influenced by the growth of scientific knowledge: For example, the outcomes of auctions, the short-term effects on unemployment rates of introducing minimum wages, the likelihood of successfully negotiating an international treaty on climate change. Popper was fully aware of this limitation and stressed explicitly that his argument does not exclude all sorts of social predictions (Popper, 1957: x).

The crucial and characteristic ingredient of Popper's argument is obviously premise (E.1). Why does Popper think scientific innovation is unpredictable? He develops an argument around the following idea: No scientific predictor can predict, by scientific methods, its own, future scientific results (Popper, 1957: x). In Popper (1982: 62), the argument starts to appear more clearly, and is stated as a reductio ad absurdum: We cannot predict scientifically, and hence know today, what we will only know tomorrow. The line of thought Popper (1982: 66f.) unfolds is composed of two major steps. In a first step, Popper argues that the prediction of scientific knowledge that will be acquired in the future requires the co-prediction of currently unavailable evidence which backs the future theory (F.1–F.4). In a second step, this is shown to be impossible (F.5–F.12). Argument F:

1 One reliably predicts, by scientific methods, scientific knowledge which will be acquired in the future if one reliably predicts the acceptance of a theory under the influence of new (currently available or unavailable) evidence.
2 If the new evidence under the influence of which one reliably predicts the acceptance of a theory

is currently available, one merely shows that the respective theory is part of our current scientific knowledge.

3 If one merely shows that a theory is part of our scientific knowledge now, one does not predict, by scientific methods, scientific knowledge which will be acquired in the future.

4 *Thus*: One reliably predicts, by scientific methods, scientific knowledge which will be acquired in the future if one reliably predicts the acceptance of a theory under the influence of new, *currently unavailable* evidence.

5 *One can reliably predict, by scientific methods, scientific knowledge which will be acquired in the future.*

6 *Thus*: One can reliably predict the acceptance of a theory under the influence of new, currently unavailable evidence.

7 To reliably predict the acceptance of a theory under the influence of new, currently unavailable evidence requires that there are events not yet observed which one predicts on the basis of now accepted theories *T* and which will lead to the acceptance of some not yet accepted theory *T**.

8 *Thus*: There are, possibly, events not yet observed which one predicts on the basis of now accepted theories *T* and which will lead to the acceptance of some not yet accepted theory *T**.

9 Events not yet observed and predicted on the basis of now accepted theories *T* would represent evidence in favour of the accepted theories *T* and not in favour of the not yet accepted theories *T**.

10 Events which represent evidence in favour of accepted theories *T* instead of not yet accepted theories *T** will not lead to the acceptance of *T**.

11 *Thus*: There are, possibly, events not yet observed which will not lead to the acceptance of some not yet accepted theory *T** and which will lead to the acceptance of some not yet accepted theory *T**.

12 *Thus*: One cannot reliably predict, by scientific methods, scientific knowledge which will be acquired in the future. [By reduction of (5) given the logical falsity of (11).]

Is Popper's reasoning sound? The following distinction warns us not to accept his argument too quickly. A prediction of the growth of scientific knowledge might consist in forecasting

1 *that* a certain scientific question will be answered, a certain problem will be solved, or

2 *how* a certain scientific question will be answered, a certain problem will be solved.[7]

The first kind of prediction is weaker than the second insofar as a forecast of how a scientific puzzle is solved implies the forecast that it will be solved, but not vice versa. In the light of this conceptual differentiation, Popper's entire reasoning might turn out to be based on an equivocation. Premise (F.1) is plausible insofar as predictions of the second type are concerned. However, the conclusion (F.12) of that very argument, understood in this way, is not able to fuel Popper's core argument: Premise (E.2) becomes false, if one identifies prediction with detailed prediction, since a generic prediction *that* some scientific question will be answered is frequently sufficient for considering the predicted innovation when making a social forecast. A prediction, for example, of the global energy markets in the mid-21st century would, among other things, merely require to forecast *that* solar cells will become more efficient and *that* one will be able to produce them at much lower costs. Such a forecast does not demand a detailed co-prediction of the technological and scientific innovation which brings about these changes in efficiency and production costs. Yet, if one reads Popper's argument F as referring to generic predictions of scientific innovation, premise (F.1) becomes probably false inasmuch as it is likely (and in any case not logically impossible) that there are some stable patterns of technological change and innovation (like Moore's Law) which provide a robust basis for extrapolation and reliable prediction. Popper's arguments fail as an a priori reason for social unpredictability.

The economist Friedrich A. von Hayek was highly sceptical vis-à-vis the possibility of social prediction, too. In von Hayek (1972), he names complexity of social systems as the main reason for his scepticism, where complexity leads both to factual and fundamental limits of forecasting. The factual limit of social prediction, according to von Hayek, consists in the difficulty to collect all data necessary to forecast an individual event. We shall discuss this in more detail later. The fundamental problem complexity gives rise to, however, is the seemingly contradictory concept of a system which predicts itself. Before having a closer look at why this problem establishes an a priori limit of prediction, we briefly note that, according to von Hayek, the factual, not the logical, problems ultimately determine the boundaries of social prediction.

In *The Sensory Order*, von Hayek (1976) argues that a system P can only predict a system O if P's degree of complexity is higher than O's. His argument can be summarised as follows. Prediction of a system O requires classification of the system's states. If these states can differ in n different aspects, that is, they can be subsumed under n different predicates, there are 2^n different types of states a classificatory system P must be able to distinguish. As the number of aspects with regard to which states might differ is an indicator of O's complexity and as the degree of complexity of a classificatory system P is at least as large as the number of different types of states it must be able to distinguish, P is more complex than O. Argument G:

1   *System P can predict system O.*
2   A system P can predict a system O only if P can classify the states of O (O-states).
3   P can classify the O-states if P can represent all types of O-states.
4   *Thus*: P can represent all types of O-states.
5   The number of types of O-states is of a higher magnitude than the degree of complexity of O.
6   If P can represent all types of states of O and the number of types of O-states is of a higher magnitude than the degree of complexity of O, then the number of O-states P can represent is of a higher magnitude than the degree of complexity of O.
7   *Thus*: The number of O-states P can represent is of a higher magnitude than the degree of complexity of O.
8   The degree of complexity of a system P is at least as high as the number of states it can represent.
9   *Thus*: P is more complex than O.
10 *Thus*: If a system P can predict a system O, then P is more complex than O. [By elimination of assumption (1).]

Where (5) is warranted as follows, argument H:

1   The number of types of O-states (2^n) is of a higher magnitude than the number of aspects in which two O-states can differ (n).
2   The degree of complexity of some system is identical with the number of aspects in which its states can differ.
3   *Thus*: The number of types of O-states is of a higher magnitude than the degree of complexity of O.

One of the main problems this line of reasoning faces is that complexity does not seem to be an objective property of systems, that is, a property a system exhibits independently of how we describe and conceive it. Quite the contrary, as von Hayek (1976: 186) notices, it is not the system itself, but the conceptual framework we apply to describe the system which determines the number of aspects in which two system states may differ. But this has far reaching consequences. A system's degree of complexity might be high under one, yet relatively low under another description. This said, can one still hold on to premise (G.8)? If one describes a glass of water in terms of molecular velocities, it can represent very many different states (in terms of cybernetic complexity: The minimum amount of information needed to describe the system is relatively large). However, the very same system might be characterised by simply stating its temperature; and in that case, it is of very low complexity. Taking this idea a bit further, it seems to be consistent with von Hayek's main ideas that a predicting system can be described in a way according to which it is less complex than the system it predicts. But let us put this criticism aside and see whether social prediction really would be impossible if the argument's conclusion were true.

As no system is more complex than itself, von Hayek's thesis implies that no system can predict itself. In particular, a human brain can't predict itself. Doesn't this establish a fundamental limit of social prediction since we seem to be unable, for a priori reasons, to predict human behaviour? A corresponding argument might look like this, argument I:

1   A system P can predict a system O only if P is more complex than O.

2 No system is more complex than itself.

3 *Thus*: No system can predict itself or any other system of (roughly) the same degree of complexity. (No self-referential prediction)

4 All human brains are (roughly) of the same degree of complexity.

5 *Thus*: Human brains cannot predict human brains.

6 Our brains are the only predicting systems at our disposal (i.e. if we cannot predict a phenomenon with our brains, it is, for us, unpredictable).

7 *Thus*: Human brains are unpredictable, for us.

8 What is unpredictable, for us, cannot be considered by a forecast ex ante.

9 A person's brain exhibits significant causal influence on the person's behaviour.

10 Unless a forecast considers all causally relevant factors ex ante, it is not reliable.

11 *Thus*: Human behaviour is unpredictable.

Von Hayek, however, sees that this is a fallacious deduction. The fact that no brain can predict itself does by no means imply that scientists cannot, for example, with the help of other systems (such as computers which run neural simulations), predict their own or other person's brains, or behaviour in general. Premise (6) is wrong. This said, even if the self-referential argument were defensible against its criticism, it would not give rise to a priori limits of social prediction.

This section has discussed different arguments which sought to establish a priori limits of social forecasting. Summing up, these attempts can be refuted as ill-founded. Social prediction is hampered – not by a priori, for example, logical, metaphysical, conceptual, but – by contingent and empirical problems. Thence, the remainder of this article shall investigate the nature of social prediction, in particular: assess and explain its performance, while taking empirical facts into account.

EMPIRICAL FACTS ABOUT SOCIAL PREDICTION – ITS MODE, OBJECT AND PERFORMANCE

We turn to the question how well social, and in particular economic forecasts actually perform. Macroeconomic business-cycle forecasts, that is, predictions of GDP growth and inflation, clearly count as some of the most prominent economic predictions. Quite a considerable econometric and statistical literature has developed within the last decades that is dedicated to an empirical assessment of such forecasts. I will briefly report the main conclusion which can be drawn from that literature. These conclusions are based on the studies recorded in Table 34.1.

Most business-cycle predictions are, and, in particular have been, deterministic point forecasts of GDP or inflation. The following observations report the literature's findings regarding these forecasts, while, unless stated otherwise, the respective predictions have a one-year forecast horizon.

1 Observation 1 (Absolute forecast error): The mean absolute forecast error (root mean square error) of macroeconomic growth forecasts is typically slightly greater (largely greater) than 1 per cent and thence of the same order of magnitude as the predicted variable itself. Inflation forecasts are characterised by smaller errors.

2 Observation 2 (Naïve benchmark): Macroeconomic forecasts closely outperform naïve benchmarks such as the no-change forecast or a random walk. This is in general not the case for financial forecasts.

3 Observation 3 (Directional forecasts): Directional macroeconomic forecasts do not perform any better than point forecasts. This holds in particular because of the complete failure to predict turning-points.

4 Observation 4 (Forecast horizon): Forecast performance decreases in absolute and relative terms with forecast horizon. The economic future beyond a two-year horizon (at most) has to be considered as unpredictable.

5 Observation 5 (Forecasters): No single professional forecasting institution consistently outperforms all the rest of the forecasting institutions (including private sector, government, academics).

6 Observation 6 (Methods): There are no significant differences between the different forecasting methods with regard to their predictive performance. Complex methods perform as well as less sophisticated ones. 'Theory-free' methods are as accurate and precise as methods based on economic theory.

Table 34.1 Empirical studies of macroeconomic forecast performance. Countries other than those explicitly mentioned include mainly OECD-countries except 9. A 'primary evaluation' is a statistical evaluation of a forecast's performance while 'secondary evaluation' denotes a survey of such primary evaluations. Studies marked with a '*' discuss so called forecasting-competitions. The epistemic mode of the forecasts evaluated is either deterministic ('D') or probabilistic ('P').

	Evaluated forecast				Evaluation		
	GDP/CPI	Period	Country	Mode	prim.	sec.	Reference
1	+/+	1960-75	US, UK	D	-	+	(Armstrong 1984)
2	+/+	1953-90	US	D	+	+	(Zarnowitz 1992)
3	+/+	1968-90	US	D	+	+	(Zarnowitz and Braun 1992)
4	+/+	1971-91	US	D	+	+	(McNees 1992)
5	+/+	1965-89	US	D	+	-	(Joutz and Stekler 2000)
6	+/+	1971-98	13	D	+	-	(Öller and Barot 2000)
7	+/+	-	-	D	+	+	(Makridakis and Hibon 2000)
8	+/+	1991-2000	5	D	+	-	(Blix et al., 2001)
9	+/+	1989-98	63	D	+	-	(Loungani 2001)
10	+/+	1970-2000	US, UK	D	-	+	(Burns 2001)
11	+/-	1970-2000	UK	D	+	+	(Osborn et al., 2001)
12	+/+	1990-2000	UK	D	-	+	(Coyle 2001)
13	+/+	-	-	D	-	+	(Fildes and Ord 2002) *
14	+/-	1990-98	4	D	+	-	(Camba-Mendez et al., 2002)
15	+/-	1966-2001	G	D	+	-	(Dicke and Glismann 2002b)
16	+/-	1964-2001	G	D	+	-	(Dicke and Glismann 2002a)
17	-/+	1997-2002	UK	P	+	-	(Clements 2004)
18	-/+	1993-2003	UK	P	+	-	(Mitchell and Hall 2005)
	16/14	1950-2003			14	9	Total: 18

7 Observation 7 (Problem of dimensionality): Forecast evaluations have to be judged with care as they are tainted with problems that stem from the tension between the high number of factors forecast performance actually depends on and the comparatively small forecast record.

This last caveat holds even more so for probabilistic macroeconomic forecasts because only very few institutions set up probability density forecasts at all;[8] and those who do have started to do so only recently. Thence, forecast records are virtually unavailable. Yet, the first studies which have evaluated the pioneering density forecasts of the Bank of England (items 16 and 17 in Table 34.1), have come to the following result.

8 Observation 8 (Probability forecasts): The few probability forecasts available fare poorly however evaluated. They are rejected by different statistical tests as inadequate.

The previous observations conclude that today's predictive performance is poor, yet they disregard the evolution of predictive performance in time. So the question arises: Has the accuracy and precision of macroeconomic forecasts at least increased within the last decades and centuries? Is there any predictive progress? The empirical assessments of macroeconomic forecasts back the following results.[9]

9 Observation 9 (Forecasting boom): The forecasting literature and industry have been growing constantly since the end of World War II.
10 Observation 10 (Lack of improvement): The quality of macroeconomic forecasts hasn't improved in the post-war period, in any case not in the last 40 years.
11 Observation 11 (Role of econometrics): Although not being a predominant method, econometric models have become more and more important for the production of macroeconomic forecasts.
12 Observation 12 (Methods' performance): It may be inferred from the evidence that there has been no significant improvement in any macroeconomic forecasting method either.

The previous paragraphs focused on GDP and inflation forecasts. In spite of the pitfalls any evaluation of such forecasts faces, assessing the performance of these quantitative forecasts which deal with a relatively well-defined phenomenon is still a much simpler task than evaluating the predictive performance of economic theory in general. Yet, this seems to be at least desirable if one wants to make a statement about whether economics is a predictively progressive science or not. Assessing the predictive performance of economic theory in general can be a daunting challenge: First of all, does it make sense to talk about economic theory as a homogeneous body of knowledge given the plurality of diverse questions, domains of applications, models, and theories economic science is composed of? Second, what is the benchmark against which predictions derived from theory should be assessed? A natural answer to this second problem is to assess the predictive performance relative to previous economic theories and models. But then, what if the respective theories and models also differ with respect to which phenomenon they predict; how could entirely different predictions be compared?

Given these intrinsic difficulties, it is not surprising that the issue of economics' predictive performance is debated rather controversially among philosophers of social science. I shall briefly sketch the main arguments of both sides.

Alexander Rosenberg accuses economic theory of complete predictive failure, claiming that the predictive performance of economic theory has not improved in the last 100–150 years (Rosenberg, 1992). He gives two reasons for this claim: One is that the methodological controversy about unrealistic assumptions underlying economic models would not have taken place if the predictive performance of economic theory were satisfying. Second, Rosenberg points to, while referring to Wassily Leontief's diagnosis, the apparent disinterest of economists in testing their theoretical models against data as a further indicator of poor predictive performance. It is noteworthy that Rosenberg does not carry out a direct assessment of economic forecasts; his reasons represent merely inferences to the best explanation. However, historical case studies which find that economic theories were not rejected in spite of empirically falsified predictions (de Marchi, 1970) might lend some additional support to Rosenberg's case.

A first line of defence against these charges consists in distinguishing two types of predictions: detailed forecasts of specific events on the one hand and generic predictions of tendencies, relationships or patterns on the other hand. While the failure of detailed economic forecasts is admitted, generic predictions are claimed to be feasible (cf. de Marchi, 1970; Hoover, 2002). This defence, however, can be rebutted by questioning whether generic predictions are sufficient to establish predictive success or progress. Rosenberg (1992), for instance, does not think so because theoretical controversies in economics are still prevailing and not resolvable with recourse to contrary (generic) predictions of the alternative theories.

A second line of defence consists in citing particular counter examples to the general claim that all predictions of economic theory fare poorly. Sutton (2002) who paints a nuanced picture of the performance of economic theory identifies pricing and predicting stock options as well as auctions as two economic phenomena which theory describes and predicts rather successfully. Hausman (2008), too, names stock options as a counter-example to Rosenberg's claim (see also Clarida et al., 2001; Mariano, 2002; Mills, 2002). These examples suggest that a further distinction might be helpful to accurately describe the predictive performance of economic theory, since both stock options and auctions might be considered as 'nomological machines' (Cartwright, 1999; Guala, 2001), that is, economic set ups which fulfil a certain function or give rise to regular behaviour by virtue of their construction. More generally, the predictive performance of economic theory seems to be rather good as long as experimentally-controlled, well-shielded phenomena are concerned (Roth, 1995; Guala, 2005). In other words, predictability breaks down to the extent that shielding and control of the predicted phenomenon vanishes. Rosenberg's claim seems to be in need of a further qualification: The performance of detailed economic predictions has not progressed insofar as uncontrolled economic phenomena, for example, macroeconomic phenomena relating to the economy as a whole, are concerned.

UNDERSTANDING POOR FORECAST PERFORMANCE

The outstanding result of the empirical assessment of detailed social predictions, in particular macroeconomic forecasts, is their complete failure. Understanding economic forecasts, hence, predominantly implies understanding their failure and limits. This section discusses different factual – in contrast to a priori – explanations for the poor predictive performance.

Limits of accurate description

If we are not in a position to accurately describe what is the case, we are even less able to forecast what is going to be the case. This is one explanation for macroeconomic forecast failure some philosophers and economists put forward. Thus, Rosenberg (1992: 64), referring to Wassily Leontief, stresses that economic prediction is hampered by a poor data basis which, in addition, cannot be augmented. Moreover, Rosenberg identifies a systematic problem since economic data is not only, in a possibly unproblematic way, theory laden (gained with econometric methods) but based on unverified assumptions.

Similarly, von Hayek (1972, 1992) argues that a factual reason for the predictive limits of social sciences is that they deal with complex phenomena. More specifically, this factual limit brings about the difficulty to establish all data required for an individual forecast. The sheer abundance of relevant individual causal factors and events makes accurate forecasts of individual events, according to von Hayek, impossible.

These rather abstract fears about limits of accurate description can be verified by having a closer look at how GDP data is actually generated.[10] Four relevant issues are: that GDP data is successively revised and corrected (Young, 1995; Fixler and Grimm, 2002; Weidmann, 2002), that the theory underlying GDP measurement changes continuously (Essig and Hartmann, 1999), that different methods for measuring GDP come to different results (Young, 1995: 444), and that, finally, GDP data relies on problematic assumptions (Levin, 1995; Young, 1995).

The role of unrealistic assumptions

Economic theory involves unrealistic, contrary-to-fact assumptions (e.g. Ochs, 1995; Roth, 1995; Sheffrin, 1996; Krugman, 1998). Does this observation, however, furnish an explanation of forecast failure? Although it is tempting to blame predictive failure on false assumptions, the entire issue is more complicated than it might appear at first glance, and it touches the more general methodological debate about unrealistic assumptions. To start with, Friedman's methodological point of view seems to imply that the mere use of unrealistic assumptions is not sufficient to explain why some theory or model fails predictively. More specifically, Friedman argues that models necessarily involve unrealistic assumptions in order to attain their epistemic aims (Friedman, 1953: 188): A good model, Friedman claims, is capable of explaining or predicting many different phenomena *with reference to a few central relationships or facts*. In order to do so, a model is necessarily highly abstract and disregards many individual or detailed facts. It would be wrong, Friedman concludes, to refute a model on the grounds of the idealisation it involves. In sum, epistemically successful models involve unrealistic assumptions, too, so this cannot be the reason for predictive failure. Friedman's central point, namely that all models involve idealisations, can hardly be contested (Frigg and Hartmann, 2008) and seems to block the simple false-assumptions-explanation. It is independently backed by Laudan's catalogue of counterexamples against the so-called no-miracle argument for scientific realism (Laudan, 1981). In order to undercut the inference to the best explanation from predictive success to truth, Laudan lists historical examples of predictively successful theories that involved false assumptions. Recent studies on the methodology of simulation, too, show that unrealistic assumptions do not always lead to false prediction – quite the contrary, they might be necessary to improve predictive performance (Winsberg, 2006).[11]

To explain forecast failure, it is not sufficient to simply pinpoint false assumptions. But this, in turn, does not mean that unrealistic assumptions do not figure in any explanation of predictive failure whatsoever. A convincing false-assumption-explanation would causally attribute the detected forecast error to the unrealistic assumptions in an explicit way. This could be done by (i) replacing the unrealistic assumptions with more realistic ones and (ii) demonstrating that the rectified model outperforms the original one. In that case, the unrealistic assumptions would, indeed, have been shown to be responsible for forecast failure. This is, by the way, how the predictive failure of the ideal gas law can be explained by reference to the unrealistic assumptions (such as zero volume of molecules) employed in its molecular kinetic deduction (Betz, 2006: 169–174).

External effects

Does poor predictive performance stem from the fact that forecasts are interpreted as categorical rather than conditional (Barrell, 2001; Turner, 2001)? In other words: Are unpredictable external effects hampering (unconditional) social predictions?

Two types of this particular problem can be distinguished: Unpredictable external effects and artificial external effects. In the first case, some phenomenon, the external effect, causally influences the predicted event which, in turn, does not affect the external factor. The external factor really is causally independent of the predicted phenomenon. A model which correctly represents this causal structure might nevertheless fail to yield accurate predictions because the evolution of the external factor, entering as a boundary condition in the forecast derivation, is itself unpredictable. Consider this example: National income in some countries whose economies mainly consist in agricultural production significantly depends on natural climate variation (such as monsoons), which is itself independent of economic activity. Despite a correct representation of this causal relationship, economic output of these countries will be unpredictable if climate variation is so.

The second problem, artificial external factors, arises because there is no model of everything and because, in order not to grow too big, models of complex social systems do have to treat factors, incorrectly, as external. In such a case, the model misrepresents the causal structure of the predicted system by assuming that a certain factor is causally independent of the predicted phenomenon (i.e. is external) although it isn't. That contrary-to-fact assumption provides an explanation of forecast failure insofar as the detected error is explicitly attributed to the false presupposition. Technological progress, for instance, is an important determinant of long-term growth. Moreover, it depends itself on the size of the economy. Yet, the predictive failure of growth models which misrepresent this causal structure by assuming that technological change is an external factor would only be explained if one showed that predictive performance improved by modelling technology as an internal variable.

Non-linear behaviour

If social systems were not only complex but also chaotic, the inability to accurately predict them would be even more comprehensible. For a chaotic system exhibits a feature which provides a straight forward explanation of forecast failure: sensitive dependence on initial conditions (SDIC). This is what Neurath had in mind when referring to unstable social situations. If minor changes in the initial state of a system yielded entirely different outcomes and if the initial measurement error grew exponentially when projecting the system's future development, the respective system would be inherently unpredictable – because even the smallest measurement errors would significantly affect the predicted outcome.

So, do social systems in general, and the economy in particular, display SDIC? There exist at least two alternative means for diagnosing SDIC, the conceptual 'routes to chaos' approach (Nicolis and Prigogine, 1998) and statistical data-analysis. The latter makes use of the fact that data records of non-linear systems exhibit characteristic features which can be detected statistically. It has primarily been applied to analyse financial markets (Frank and Stengos, 1988; Gao and Wang, 1999; Tsay, 2002). For a non-economic application see Musselwhite and Herath (2007). The general idea of the conceptual approach is this: There are certain minimal, paradigmatic (mathematical) models such as coupled oscillators (Seydel, 1994) or cellular automata (Wolfram, 1986; Chopard and Droz, 1998; Katerelos and Koulouris, 2004) which exhibit SDIC. Each such model gives rise to another 'route to chaos': By showing that central features of the complex predicted system constitute a structure which is adequately modelled by the minimal model, one has shown that any model of the predicted system which does not disregard these central features exhibits SDIC.

Regarding the economy, a first route to chaos emerges because the economy as a whole is characterised by multiple causal feedback processes which operate simultaneously. These give rise to a structure that is modelled by coupled oscillators (Lorenz, 1993). So every economic model which represents these feedbacks exhibits SDIC.

A second route to chaos arises since the economy consists of economic agents which interact with each other. This basic feature allows for modelling the economy by cellular automata as Ormerod (2000) demonstrates, but compare also Keynes' 'castle in the air theory' of financial markets (Malkiel, 1999: 31f).

Predicting people

The previous explanations of forecast failure apply to social sciences as well as extra-laboratory natural sciences (such as geology or climatology). Yet are there particular features of social sciences that obstruct accurate prediction? Instead of predicting natural phenomena, social sciences predict human behaviour. Is this particularly difficult and does it explain poor predictive performance?

Rosenberg (1992, 1995) thinks so: He partially blames unreliable folk psychology for poor performance of social predictions. Besides, he thinks that one fails to explain predictive failure fully if one disregards this particularity because other explanations offered (such as non-linear behaviour, external effects) are insufficient (Rosenberg, 1993: 164).

Rosenberg's main explanatory argument against detailed economic prediction goes as follows, argument J:

1 Beliefs and desires cannot be adequately described by a quantitative, mathematical model (such as rational choice theory).
2 What cannot be adequately described by a quantitative, mathematical model, cannot be predicted in a precise and detailed way.
3 What is unpredictable (in a precise and detailed way), for us, cannot be considered by a forecast ex ante (in a precise and detailed way).
4 *Thus*: Beliefs and desires cannot be considered by a forecast ex ante (in a precise and detailed way).
5 Beliefs and desires causally influence human behaviour.
6 Unless a (detailed) forecast considers all causally relevant factors ex ante (in a precise and detailed way), it is not reliable.
7 *Thus*: Human behaviour is unpredictable (in a precise and detailed way).

Rosenberg (1992: 146) gives two reasons for the crucial premise (J.1).

First, beliefs and desires cannot be measured, for this would require to establish an identity statement between beliefs and desires on the one side and neural states or observable behaviour on the other side. Such an identity, though, does not hold, because descriptions of beliefs and desires are *intensional*, whereas descriptions of brain states and behaviour aren't.

Second, beliefs and desires are holistic. What a certain belief or desire means depends on the other beliefs and desires of the respective person. It is therefore empirically inadequate to divide up mental states and consider single desires and beliefs in isolation like a quantitative model of human behaviour (such as rational choice theory) does.

These arguments carry us directly into the philosophy of mind and I shall leave them without comment here. Rather, I'd like to pinpoint that Rosenberg's argument explains at most the predictive failure of economic theories which try to forecast the behaviour of individual (possibly representative) economic agents. Thus, only theories that implement the methodological ideal of microfoundations are concerned here (as Rosenberg (1992: 150) notices, too). Rosenberg's reasoning does not spell out why macroeconomic forecasts which are not based on the prediction of individual behaviour but rather describe the economy in more aggregated terms consistently fail. In other words, as unpredictable individual behaviour might nevertheless give rise to stable aggregated regularities, Rosenberg's explanation does not rule out the possibility of macroeconomic prediction in general. Its failure remains unexplained. Or so it seems. At this point, however, the so-called Lucas critique (Lucas, 1976) enters the scene. In a certain way, it seems to supplement Rosenberg's reasoning by filling its explanatory gap: Lucas argued that any attempt to model the economy while disregarding economic behaviour of individual agents and, in particular, their expectations, will ultimately fail to find stable macroeconomic regularities because these supervene on individual behaviour and thence will alter with changing expectations of the economic agents.

Reflexivity

A further special feature of social prediction is its reflexivity (though Buck (1963) and Grünbaum (1963) discuss whether natural science can be reflexive, too). The problem of self-fulfilling or -vindicating forecasts arises as a result of publication- and dissemination-feedbacks and has been discussed by Morgenstern (1928), Grunberg and Modigliani (1954), Simon (1954), Grunberg (1986); reflexivity is also pivotal in Luhmann's theory of social systems (Luhmann, 1984; 1990).

As Morgenstern's argument – which is a poor a priori argument but not necessarily a bad explanation of forecast failure – shows, the problem of reflexivity is a special case of explaining forecast failure by identifying a misrepresentation of the causal structure of the predicted system. That is what premise (D.7) in Morgenstern's argument does. But is it just because we lack appropriate models and theories that a forecast cannot anticipate the effects of its dissemination? At first glance, there seems to be more to it: Some forecasts, such as the prediction that a severe recession will catch many families unprepared, are self-vindicating. But by the same token, some are self-fulfilling. Keynes' 'castle in the air theory' of financial markets which has been mentioned above is a case in point. Actually, as Grunberg and Modigliani (1954) have shown, an empirically adequate model of the publication- and dissemination-effect of predictions would allow to construct self-fulfilling forecasts. So, reflexivity does not necessarily prevent accurate prediction, rather, it is our lacking knowledge about the specific causal processes (triggered by forecast publication) that represents an obstacle to correct forecasting.

Finally, the rational expectations hypothesis (REH) originally proposed by Muth (1961) can be applied to the problem of reflexivity. It gives rise to a further critique of Morgenstern's argument. According to REH, the publication of a forecast is, contrary to premise (1), neutral since the forecast had already been anticipated by the rational economic agents. REH, however, yields an alternative explanation of forecast failure, because macroeconomic models which implement REH imply that macroeconomic variables follow unpredictable random walks (Hall, 1978; Malkiel, 1999).

CONCLUSION

What can be concluded from the reported results with regard to (i) the future development of social sciences' predictive performance, (ii) the aims and methods of social sciences, and (iii) the role of social sciences in democratic policy making?

1 For the sake of self-referential consistency, this chapter won't conclude with a forecast of the future development of social sciences' predictive performance. It is hard to tell whether predictive progress – in scope (forecasting more types of phenomena) or in depth (increased forecast precision) – will be achieved. What is clear is that, for this to happen, major obstacles that prevent reliable prediction and that explain current forecast failure would have to be overcome. This said, an optimistic outlook (e.g. Butz and Tory, 2006) seems to be difficult to defend.

2 The observed forecast failure is no reason to dismiss social sciences as a scientific enterprise. For one, prediction is not the only meaningful epistemic aim of scientific enterprises, and science is already policy relevant if it yields accurate descriptions or insightful explanations. Moreover, a closer look at forecast performance has revealed that some social phenomena might be predictable. It would be unwise to ban predictions from social scientists' agenda.

3 Scientists, policy makers, the media alike should acknowledge that the social consequences of many policy measures are not predictable. Claiming to have accurate foreknowledge where prediction is (factually) impossible means misleading the public and undermining a rational discourse about alternative policy options. The limits of social prediction call for shifting the mode of our public discourse: the complexities and uncertainties surrounding the most important decisions we face, and our attitudes towards these risks, are not yet fully taken into account.

NOTES

1 See Friedman (1953: 181), Theil (1961: 2), Rosenberg (1988: 147) and Rescher (1998: 12). Note that page numbers of Friedman (1953) refer to its reprint in Hausman (1994a).

2 Cf. Rosenberg (1992: 19). Although being an epistemological pluralist on a metalevel, Rosenberg forcefully defends and applies his personal epistemological convictions when it comes to judging scientific enterprises.

3 Abbreviation for: premise (2) of argument A.

4 In contrast to Morgenstern's own intention, one might, however, interpret his argument as an a posteriori explanation of macroeconomic forecast failure and, in such a context, the assumption seems to be quite acceptable. For if we observe that a forecast has failed and discover that a relevant causal factor has been omitted, this generally counts as an explanation. This line of reasoning gives rise to the reflexivity explanation of forecast failure which will be discussed later.

5 Neurath's remark that these problems do not touch our language or our scientific procedures is a hint that he, himself, did not think that these obstacles represent a priori limits of social prediction (Neurath, 1944: 30).

6 Popper's scepticism has been developed in a series of texts (Popper, 1957, 1963, 1982).

7 With the terminology of Rosenberg (1993: 171), this distinction might also be described as *generic* versus *detailed* prediction of scientific innovation.

8 The Bank of England, with its fan charts, is an early adopter of this technique (Bank of England, 2003). Compare for this new field Ericsson (2001, 2002), Tay and Wallis (2002), Hall and Mitchell (2007).

9 Compare, besides the empirical assessments cited in Table 34.1, also Wallis (1989) and Burns (2001).

10 Compare also Betz (2006: 99–108).

11 Note that these claims do not contradict Hausman's comment on Friedman (Hausman, 1994b). For Hausman merely stresses that predictive success is not the only test of a theory: false assumptions can *indicate* that something is wrong with a theory and that a previously predictively successful model might fail to deliver accurate forecasts in the future. That is the reason why it is important, heuristically, to 'look under the hood' and to check assumptions for realism.

REFERENCES

Armstrong, J.S. (1984) 'Forecasting with econometric methods: Folklore versus fact', in S.G. Makridakis (ed.) *The Forecasting Accuracy of Major Time Series Models*. Chichester: John Wiley. pp. 19–34.

Bank of England (2003) *Inflation Report*.

Barrell, R. (2001) 'Forecasting the world economy', in D.F. Hendry and N.R. Ericsson (eds) *Understanding Economic Forecasts*. Cambridge, MA: MIT Press. pp. 149–169.

Betz, G. (2006) *Prediction or Prophecy? The Boundaries of Economic Foreknowledge and Their Socio-Political Consequences*. Wiesbaden: DUV.

Blix, M., J. Wadefjord, U. Wienicke and M. Adahl (2001) 'How good is the forecasting performance of major institutions?', *Sveriges Riksbank Economic Review*, 2001(3): 38–68.

Buck, R.C. (1963) 'Reflexive predictions', *Philosophy of Science*, 30: 359–369.

Burns, T. (2001) 'The cost of forecast errors', in D.F. Hendry and N.R. Ericsson (eds) *Understanding Economic Forecasts*. Cambridge, MA: MIT Press. pp. 170–184.

Butz, W.P. and B.B. Tory (2006) 'Some frontiers in social science', *Science*, 312: 1898–1900.

Camba-Mendez, G., G. Kapetanios, et al. (2002) 'The forecasting performance of the OECD composite leading indicators for France, Germany, Italy, and the UK', in M.P. Clements and D.F. Hendry (eds) *A Companion to Economic Forecasting*. Malden, MA: Blackwell. pp. 386–408.

Cartwright, N. (1999) *The Dappled World: A Study of the Boundaries of Science*. Cambridge: Cambridge University Press.

Chopard, B. and M. Droz (1998) *Cellular Automata Modeling of Physical Systems*. Cambridge: Cambridge University Press.

Clarida, R.H., L. Sarno, M.P. Taylor and G. Valente (2001) 'The out-of-sample success of term structure models as exchange rate predictors: a step beyond', NBER Working Paper, No. 8601 2001(8601).

Clements, M.P. (2004) 'Evaluating the Bank of England density forecasts of inflation', *Economic Journal*, 114: 844–866.

Coyle, D. (2001) 'Making sense of published economic forecasts', in D.F. Hendry and N.R. Ericsson (eds) *Understanding Economic Forecasts*. Cambridge, MA: MIT Press. pp. 54–67.

de Marchi, N. (1970) 'The empirical content and longevity of Ricardian economics', *Economica*, 37(147): 239–276.

Dicke, H. and H.H. Glismann (2002a) 'Haben sich die Konjunkturprognosen des Sachverstandigenrates verbessert?', *Wirtschaftsdienst Zeitschrift für Wirtschaftspolitik of the HWWA*, 82(12): 736–740.

Dicke, H. and H.H. Glismann (2002b) 'Konjunkturprognosen und wissenschaftlich-technischer Fortschritt', *Wirtschaftsdienst Zeitschrift für Wirtschaftspolitik of the HWWA*, 82(3): 167–169.

Ericsson, N.R. (2001) 'Forecast uncertainty in economic modeling', in D.F. Hendry and N. R. Ericsson (eds) *Understanding Economic Forecasts*. Cambridge, MA: MIT Press. pp. 68–92.

Ericsson, N.R. (2002) 'Predictable uncertainty in economic forecasting', in M.P. Clements and D.F. Hendry (eds) *A Companion to Economic Forecasting*. Malden, MA: Blackwell. 19–44.

Essig, H. and N. Hartmann (1999) 'Revision der Volkswirtschaftlichen Gesamtrechnungen 1991–1998', *Wirtschaft und Statistik*, 99(6): 449–478.

Fildes, R. and K. Ord (2002) 'Forecasting competitions: Their role in improving forecasting practice and research', in M.P. Clements and D.F. Hendry (eds) *A Companion to Economic Forecasting*. Malden, MA: Blackwell. pp. 322–353.

Fixler, D.J. and B.T. Grimm (2002) 'Reliability of GDP and related NIPA estimates', *Survey of Current Business*, (January): 9–27.

Frank, M.Z. and T. Stengos (1988) 'Chaotic dynamics in economic time-series', *Journal of Economic Surveys*, 2(2): 103–133.

Friedman, M. (1953) 'The methodology of positive economics', in M. Friedman (ed.) *Essays in Positive Economics*. Chicago: University of Chicago Press. pp. 3–43.

Frigg, R. and S. Hartmann (2008) 'Models in science', E.N. Zalta (ed.) *The Stanford Encyclopedia of Philosophy*, http://plato.stanford.edu/archives/fall2008/entries/models-science/.

Gao, A.H. and G.H.K. Wang (1999) 'Modeling nonlinear dynamics of daily futures price changes', *Journal of Futures Markets*, 19(3): 325–351.

Grünbaum, A. (1963) 'Comments on Professor Roger Buck's paper "Reflexive Predictions"', *Philosophy of Science*, 30: 370–372.

Grunberg, E. (1986) 'Predictability and reflexivity', *American Journal of Economics and Sociology*, 45: 475–488.

Grunberg, E. and F. Modigliani (1954) 'The predictability of social events', *Journal of Political Economy*, 62(6): 465–478.

Guala, F. (2001) 'Building economic machines: The FCC auctions', *Studies in History and Philosophy of Science*, 32: 453–477.

Guala, F. (2005) *The Methodology of Experimental Economics*. Cambridge: Cambridge University Press.

Hall, R.E. (1978) 'Stochastic implications of the life cycle-permanent income hypothesis: Theory and evidence', *Journal of Political Economy*, 86(6): 971–987.

Hall, S.G. and J. Mitchell (2007) 'Combining density forecasts', *International Journal of Forecasting*, 23: 1–13.

Hausman, D. (ed.) (1994a) *The Philosophy of Economics: An Anthology*. Cambridge: Cambridge University Press.

Hausman, D. (1994b) 'Why Look Under the Hood?', in D. Hausman (ed.) *The Philosophy of Economics: An Anthology*. Cambridge: Cambridge University Press. pp. 183–187.

Hausman, D.M. (2008) 'Philosophy of economics', in E.N. Zalta (ed.) *The Stanford Encyclopedia of Philosophy*, http://plato.stanford.edu/archives/fall2008/entries/economics/.

Hoover, K. (2002) 'Symposium on Marshall's tendencies: 5 Sutton's critique of econometrics', *Economics and Philosophy*, 18: 45–54.

Joutz, F. and H.O. Stekler (2000) 'An evaluation of the predictions of the federal reserve', *International Journal of Forecasting*, 16: 17–38.

Katerelos, I.D. and A.G. Koulouris (2004) 'Is prediction possible? Chaotic behavior of multiple equilibria regulation model in cellular automata topology', *Complexity*, 10: 23–36.

Krugman, P. (1998) 'How I work', in M. Szenberg (ed.) *Passion and craft: Economists at work*. Ann Arbor: University of Michigan Press. pp. 143–154.

Laudan, L. (1981) 'A confutation of convergent realism', *Philosophy of Science*, 48: 19–48.

Levin, J. (1995) 'Government' in the 1993 System of National Accounts'. In J.W. Kendrick (ed.) *The New System of National Accounts*. Dordrecht: Kluwer. pp. 1–24.

Lorenz, H.-W. (1993) *Nonlinear Dynamical Economics and Chaotic Motion*. Berlin: Springer.

Loungani, P. (2001) 'How accurate are private sector forecasts? Cross-country evidence from consensus forecasts of output growth', *International Journal of Forecasting*, 17: 419–432.

Lucas, R.E. (1976) 'Econometric policy evaluation: A critique', *Carnegie-Rochester Conference Series on Public Policy*, 1: 19–46.

Luhmann, N. (1984) *Soziale Systeme: Grundriß einer allgemeinen Theorie*. Frankfurt A.M.: Suhrkamp.

Luhmann, N. (1990) *Die Wissenschaft der Gesellschaft*. Frankfurt a.M.: Suhrkamp.

Makridakis, S.G. and M. Hibon (2000) 'The M3-competition: Results, conclusions and implications', *International Journal of Forecasting*, 16: 451–476.

Malkiel, B.G. (1999) *A Random Walk down Wall Street*. New York: W.W. Norton.

Mariano, R.S. (2002) 'Testing forecast accuracy', in M.P. Clements and D.F. Hendry (eds) *A Companion to Economic Forecasting*. Malden, MA: Blackwell. pp. 284–298.

McCloskey, D. (1986) *The Rhetoric of Economics*. Madison: University of Wisconsin Press.

McNees, S.K. (1992) 'How large are economic forecast errors?', *New England Economic Review*, 1992 (July/August): 25–42.

Mills, T.C. (2002) 'Forecasting financial variables', in M.P. Clements and D.F. Hendry (eds) *A Companion to Economic Forecasting*. Malden, MA: Blackwell. pp. 510–538.

Mitchell, J. and S.G. Hall (2005) 'Evaluating, comparing and combining density forecasts using the KLIC with an application to the Bank of England and NIESR "Fan" charts of inflation', *Oxford Bulletin of Economics and Statistics*, 67: 995–1033.

Morgenstern, O. (1928) *Wirtschaftsprognose: Eine Untersuchung ihrer Voraussetzungen und Moglichkeiten*. Wien: Springer.

Musselwhite, G. and G. Herath (2007) 'Chaos theory and assessment of forest stakeholder attitudes towards Australian forest policy', *Forest Policy and Economics*, 9: 947–964.

Muth, J.F. (1961) 'Rational expectations and theory of price movements', *Econometrica*, 29(3): 315–335.

Neurath, O. (1944) *Foundations of Social Sciences*. Chicago: University of Chicago Press.

Nicolis, G. and I. Prigogine (1998) *Exploring Complexity. An Introduction*. New York: W. H. Freeman.

Ochs, J. (1995) 'Coordination problems', in J.H. Kagel and A.E. Roth (eds) *Handbook of Experimental Economics*. Princeton: Princeton University Press. pp. 195–252.

Öller, L.-E. and B. Barot (2000) 'The accuracy of European growth and inflation forecasts', *International Journal of Forecasting*, 16: 293–315.

Ormerod, P. (2000) *Butterfly Economics: A New General Theory of Social and Economic Behavior*. New York: Pantheon Books.

Osborn, D.R., M. Sensier and P.W. Simpson (2001) 'Forecasting and the UK Business Cycle', in D.F. Hendry and N.R. Ericsson (eds) *Understanding Economic Forecasts*. Cambridge, MA: MIT Press. pp. 104–123.

Popper, K.R. (1957) *The Poverty of Historicism*. London: Routledge and Paul Kegan.

Popper, K.R. (1963) 'Prediction and Prophecy in the Social Sciences' in K.R. Popper (ed.) *Conjectures and Refutations*. London: Routledge and Paul Kegan. pp. 336–346.

Popper, K.R. (1982) *The Open Universe*. Totowa: Rowan and Littlefield.

Rescher, N. (1998) *Predicting the Future. An Introduction to the Theory of Forecasting*. Albany: State University of New York Press.

Rosenberg, A. (1988) 'Economics is too important to be left to the rhetoricians', *Economics and Philosophy*, 4: 129–149.

Rosenberg, A. (1992) *Economics–Mathematical Politics or Science of Diminishing Returns?* Chicago: University of Chicago Press.

Rosenberg, A. (1993) 'Scientific innovation and the limits of social scientific prediction', *Synthese*, 97: 161–182.

Rosenberg, A. (1995) *Philosophy of Social Science*. Boulder, CO.: Westview Press.

Roth, A.E. (1995) 'Introduction', in J.H. Kagel and A. E. Roth (eds) *Handbook of Experimental Economics*. Princeton: Princeton University Press. pp. 3–109.

Seydel, R. (1994) *Practical Bifurcation and Stability Analysis*. New York: Springer.

Sheffrin, S.M. (1996) *Rational Expectations*. Cambridge: Cambridge University Press.

Simon, H.A. (1954) 'Bandwagon and underdog effect and the possibility of election prediction', *Public Opinion Quarterly*, 18: 245–253.

Sutton, J. (2002) *Marshall's Tendencies: What Can Economists Know?* Cambridge, MA: MIT Press.

Tay, A.S. and K.F. Wallis (2002) 'Density forecasting: A survey', in M.P. Clements and D.F. Hendry (eds) *A Companion to Economic Forecasting*. Malden, MA: Blackwell. pp. 45–67.

Theil, H. (1961) *Economic Forecasts and Policy*. Amsterdam: North-Holland.

Tsay, R.S. (2002) 'Nonlinear models and forecasting', in M.P. Clements and D.F. Hendry, *A Companion to Economic Forecasting*. Malden, MA: Blackwell. pp. 453–484.

Turner, P. (2001) 'Economic modeling for fun and profit', D.F. Hendry and N.R. Ericsson (eds) *Understanding Economic Forecasts*. Cambridge, MA: MIT Press. pp. 42–53.

von Hayek, F.A. (1972) *Die Theorie komplexer Phänomene*, J.C.B Mohr: Tübingen.

von Hayek, F.A. (1976) *The Sensory Order*. London: Routledge.

von Hayek, F.A. (1992) 'The Pretence of Knowledge', in A. Lindbeck (ed.) *Nobel Lectures in Economic Sciences 1969–1980*. Singapore: World Scientific Publishing. pp. 179–189.

Wallis, K.F. (1989) 'Macroeconomic forecasting – a survey', *Economic Journal*, 99: 28–61.

Weidmann, J. (2002) 'Hat sich die Prognosetreffsicherheit des Sachverständigenrates systematisch verändert?'

Wirtschaftsdienst Zeitschrift für Wirtschaftspolitik of the HWWA, 82(12): 741–748.

Winsberg, E. (2006) 'Models of success vs. the success of models: Reliability without truth', *Synthese*, 152: 1–19.

Wolfram, S. (1986) *Theory and Applications of Cellular Automata*. Singapore: World Scientific Publishing.

Young, A.H. (1995) 'Reliability and Accuracy of Quarterly GDP Estimates: A Review', in J. W. Kendrick (ed.)

The New System of National Accounts. Dordrecht: Kluwer. pp. 423–456.

Zarnowitz, V. (1992) *Business Cycles: Theory, History, Indicators and Forecasting*. Chicago: University of Chicago Press.

Zarnowitz, V. and P. Braun (1992) 'Twenty-two years of the NBER-ASA quarterly economic outlook surveys: Aspects and comparisons of forecasting performance', NBER Working Paper, No. 3965 1992(3965).

35

Science and Technology Studies and Social Epistemology: The Struggle for Normativity in Social Theories of Knowledge

Steve Fuller

Science and technology studies (STS) and social epistemology are types of social theories of knowledge that claim to be both 'naturalistic' in method and 'normative' in orientation. What they mean by the two quoted terms can vary significantly. 'Naturalistic' may range over historical, social scientific and perhaps natural scientific (e.g. neo-Darwinian) studies of epistemic activities. 'Normative' may cover ultimate and auxiliary values that knowledge producers uphold in their own practice, refer to long-term tendencies of beneficiaries and victims or project ideals that are informed by history but may suggest a future that radically breaks from it. While I shall allude to my own views in what follows, drawing on work coming out of Fuller (1988), the chapter proceeds by critically examining two general trends in STS and social epistemology that have resulted in 'normative recession' – that is, a retreat from the classical philosophical

aspiration of charting the growth of knowledge understood as 'science' in the robust sense of systematically organised knowledge made universally available (Fuller, 2007). The first is the reduction of science to expertise, which is the principal focus of the first three sections. The second is the self-understanding of social epistemology and STS as themselves 'expertises' in this reduced sense, which is the main concern of the fourth and fifth sections. In particular, the fifth section presents the cautionary tale of Bernalism, the well-intentioned but ill-fated attempt to found social epistemology on Marxism understood as a form of expertise.

SCIENCE AND EXPERTISE: NATURAL BEDFELLOWS OR MORTAL ENEMIES?

Although science and expertise appear identical in today's postmodern world, not least in the literatures associated with Science and Technology Studies (or 'STS') and social epistemology, at least as practised by analytic philosophers (Kusch and Lipton, 2002), they have been regarded as antithetical forms of knowledge in both the ancient and the modern world. The ancient Athenians associated science (*epistemé*) with the contemplative life afforded to those who lived from inherited wealth. Expertise (*techné*) was for those lacking property, and hence citizenship. Such people were regularly forced to justify their usefulness to Athenian society. Some foreign merchants, collectively demonised in Plato's *Dialogues* as 'sophists', appeared so insulting to citizen Socrates because they dared to alienate aspects of this leisured existence (e.g. the capacity for articulate reasoning) and repackage them as techniques that might be purchased on demand from an expert – that is, a sophist. In effect, the sophists cleverly tried to universalise their own alien status, taking full advantage of the strong analogy that Athenians saw between the governance of the self and the polis. Unfortunately, Plato, the original spin doctor, immortalised Socrates' laboured and hyperbolic rearguard response to these sly and partially successful attempts at dislodging hereditary privilege.

In any case, science and expertise led a more harmonious existence in the pre-modern Christian era, as everyone was expected to live by the sweat of their brow, an aspect of the labour theory of value that joined Thomas Aquinas to Karl Marx. Medieval monasteries were the original communes, in which the monks alternated between contemplating God and taking turns at the scriptorium and/or the vineyard. A privatised version of this ethic came to be known as the 'Renaissance Man', as exemplified by the careers of Leonardo da Vinci and especially Galileo. In this context, the boundary separating science and expertise became more porous, specifically enabling technical arts of instrumentation and experimentation to become constitutive of scientific inquiry itself. The Royal Society

of London famously institutionalised that attitude.

However, the unprecedented achievement of Newtonian mechanics led many Enlightenment thinkers to conclude that science had nearly reached the limits of human comprehension, such that our ingenuity is best spent on making the most of this knowledge through applications that ameliorate the human condition and extend our dominion over the earth. The Greek attitude had been turned on its head: instead of science being the luxury of those who did not need to live by their expertise, expertise came to be seen as a political imperative to make the most of the virtually completed body of scientific knowledge. This shift in attitude was perhaps clearest in the case of mathematics, as championed by Diderot's co-editor of *L'Encyclopédie*, Jean D'Alembert, who regarded his discipline as an adjunct of engineering and political economy, a statistically driven search for tolerable error in socially relevant contexts – not a Cartesian quest for superhuman certainty. The uncertainty of statistics was tolerable precisely because science, at least to the *philosophes'* satisfaction, had replaced theology as the foundation of knowledge.

This view of science persists in the legal incentives that modern states provide for inventors to turn the 'laws of nature' to their advantage – not least in the Enlightenment's most enduring political legacy, the US Constitution, which names patenting as a civil right. A society that took seriously how wrong we might turn out to be about the laws of nature – that science is, in Karl Popper's phrase, an 'unended quest' – would never have created a special category of 'patents' that confers a privilege on invention beyond what can be fetched on the open market. Instead an invention would be treated as an ordinary good possessing only exchange value, not some deeper value from one's having worked over a parcel of common reality, also known as 'intellectual property'. It follows that the sales registered for the invention prior to its market replacement would be sufficient reward, with no further need to grant the inventor some additional legal protection simply because he brought the idea to market first (Fuller, 2002: Chapters 1–2).

The nineteenth century witnessed the reinvention of the university as the institutional seat of science and the guarantor of expertise, under the aegis of nation-states with world-historic aspirations. This development followed a 'secular' and a 'sacred' course, the former traceable through Wilhelm von Humboldt's promotion of philosophy as the synthetic discipline of citizen education in Prussia, the latter through William Whewell's promotion of Newtonian mechanics as the Anglican Church's scientific face, which justified all other theoretical and practical pursuits. Where Humboldt wanted a curriculum that would shift student allegiance from the church to the state, Whewell aimed to ensure that the church remained relevant to a rapidly secularising economy. In both cases, the university would 'internalise the externalities' of a society that encouraged innovation without having anticipated its long-term consequences: expertise could not be based simply on the personal testimony of either the producers or the consumers of a purveyed good or technique. Rather, expertise must be underwritten by scientific principles, which the reinvented universities would be in the business of nominating, organising, testing and promulgating.

In the final quarter of the twentieth century, Jean-François Lyotard (1983) fashioned the phrase 'the postmodern condition' to capture the 'always already' doomed character of the university's mission. Here Lyotard made an invidious but persuasive comparison with the mythically 'progressive' status that socialism had acquired, albeit sometimes by violent means, over roughly the same two centuries. For Lyotard 'science' (understood as a unified body of knowledge instantiated in the university) and 'society' (understood as a unified body of action instantiated in the state) were fictions that had outlived whatever usefulness they ever had in bounding developments whose very nature exceeded all attempts at bounding. Lyotard argued the point in largely empirical terms, observing just how much intellectual innovation in the recent past (e.g. computer science, molecular biology) occurred off-campus in heterogeneous research teams lacking any obvious disciplinary home. He concluded that what universities continue to mystify as 'science' – understood as a version of what states continued to mystify as 'society' or better still, 'welfare' – is really the product of locally developed expertises, which universities – again as extensions of states – only later exploited to their own advantage.

Lyotard drove a stake into the heart of any project that drew sustenance from the Enlightenment legacy, a main beneficiary of which has been STS, notwithstanding Latour (1993), which 'doth protest too much' in trying to distance STS's self-professed 'non-modernism' from Lyotard's postmodernism. At a general level, STS adopts the standard postmodernist line of denying the canonical historical narratives of scientific knowledge production, not merely because they do not assign epistemic credit properly (as a Marxist might argue) but on the more principled ground that there is no privileged standpoint from which to tell the history of science, due to a lack of normative closure on the ends of science (Fuller, 2000b: 365–378). More specifically, the anti-university vision shared by Lyotard and STS may be contrasted with my own pro-university vision in terms of an analogy drawn from political economy. On the one hand, Lyotard sees the university as the appropriator of surplus value from the truly creative researchers and inventors who work in places kept apart – both conceptually and physically – from the university's inner sanctum, the classroom and the curriculum committee. On the other hand, I see the university as a vehicle of 'epistemic justice', precisely through its educational function, which effectively redistributes knowledge-based advantage from the elite clients who are the primary beneficiaries of innovation to a student audience that has historically encompassed a broader range of backgrounds and interests. Thus, whereas Lyotard saw universities as commissioning expertise by granting it epistemic authority, I see them as decommissioning it by spreading that authority widely (Fuller, 2009b).

EXPERTISE AS SITE FOR NORMATIVE RECESSION IN ANALYTIC SOCIAL EPISTEMOLOGY

Over the past quarter century, analytic philosophy, perhaps *malgré lui*, has moved in a postmodern direction, though largely without acknowledging the corresponding world-historic trends. Indeed, analytic philosophy's two main conceptions of expertise are rarely distinguished, let alone perceived in mutual tension. One is Hilary Putnam's (1979) 'linguistic division of labour', the other Philip Kitcher's (1993) 'division of cognitive labour'. While trading on the sociological idea of 'division of labour', they nevertheless divide the relevant labour rather differently. Putnam's point is that speakers normally know what they mean from the context of usage, except for 'hard cases' that require experts to spend their time studying what distinguishes p from $\sim p$. Implied here is a theory of expertise that would tell us to seek a physician only when we cannot manage our bodies by the usual means. In contrast, Kitcher's point is that reality is carved up into discrete expertises, such that our claims to know something are always already accountable to those who spend their time studying it. Implied here is a theory of expertise that would tell us to seek a physician on a regular basis, since *prima facie* the physician knows our body better than we do. Of course, in most cases, our own and our physician's judgement might converge – but the convergence matters, at least epistemologically.

What distinguishes Putnam's and Kitcher's positions? The difference here clearly matters for those who worry that things are done for the right reasons. However, if all that concerns us is that the right things are done, regardless

of reasons, then Putnam and Kitcher merely chart alternative routes to destinations that will coincide in the vast majority of cases. The sociology of knowledge gives us some initial insight into this matter, since Putnam (born 1926) and Kitcher (born 1947) belong to different generational cohorts. Putnam writes when Marxism was most respectable in Anglo–American academia (and Putnam himself would drop quotes from Mao and Althusser), while Kitcher writes in a post-Marxist, neo-liberal world (which does not think twice about using neo-classical economics to model the science system). Putnam's view presumes that we are epistemic equals unless shown otherwise, while Kitcher's presumes the exact opposite. Behind these presumptions are opposed social-epistemological worldviews that provide alternative answers to the question: does our status as competent members of society *ipso facto* underwrite our epistemic authority? Putnam says yes, Kitcher no.

For his part, Putnam takes seriously that everyone enjoys equal access to reality. When people disagree, it is simply because they have different evidence at their disposal or weigh the same evidence differently, all of which is tractable to negotiations with other people who are in the same epistemic state. Call this the 'primitive communist' approach to social epistemology. It implies that the need for expertise is limited to 'technical matters', where an unusually prolonged focus on a specific topic serves to resolve uncertainty and disagreement. Although the Athenians held a notoriously elite view of citizenship, their attitude towards expertise was very much in this vein: mere *techné*. Thus, Plato and Aristotle praised expert craftsmanship for its capacity to realise in matter an idea that would otherwise remain inchoate in the client's mind. But there is no sense that the craftsman is either the source of the idea or the ultimate arbiter of its realisation.

The conversion of *techné* to bureaucracy – from commercial trade to civil service – is a signature theme in modern German philosophy, starting with Humboldt, Fichte and

Hegel. It is how the Athenian attitude came to be democratised. The German idea was to incorporate more people as epistemic equals through a proactive state-based educational system, with expertise relegated to increasingly detailed and potentially routinised administrative tasks. When Marx and Engels spoke about the 'withering away of the state' under Communism, they were refashioning a phrase Fichte had used to chart this trajectory. Indeed, Marx and Engels saw the party carrying on the work of the university as expedited by the industrial development of labour-saving technology provided that the social relations of production were wrested from capitalist control. In the resulting communist utopia, expertise would be on tap (in a black box?) to remove the drudgery as we explore the multifarious aspects of our humanity.

Before turning to Kitcher's rather different attitude towards expertise, two remarks are in order about Putnam's social-epistemological vision. First, I believe that, despite its empirical failure and unfashionable status, this vision takes seriously the fullness of our humanity. Its revival will not be easy, however, and the tenor of STS research goes largely against it. But 'utopian' here should be interpreted to mean 'difficult' or 'against the grain' not 'impossible', let alone 'wrong'. Second, seen as a historically unfolding idea, this vision reveals the underrated appeal of an 'instrumentalist' philosophy of science and even the 'instrumentalisation' of scientific practice. These notions presuppose that humans supply the ends on whose behalf those 'instruments' would be deployed. By not building ends into the instruments themselves – that is, by denying that science as such or its constitutive practices have ends of their own – we as humans are given a potentially free hand to fashion the ends for ourselves. I say 'potentially', of course, because the question of the 'ends of science' gets shifted from something about how science intrinsically works, to who has the right and power to deploy the relevant instruments without interruption. To be sure, the question of

who 'we' are remains subject to contestation but no less so than the question of what it is about a practice that makes it scientific. However, the same question posed in political terms focuses the mind – and action – in a way that it does not when posed in metaphysical terms: the former is about what it takes to be free, the latter about what it takes to be determined.

For his part, Kitcher's conception of expertise is proprietarian, an extension of John Locke's version of the labour theory of value. No one can lay authoritative claim over a domain of reality, even the reality of one's own body, until they have worked it over with intensive study. For Locke, this position constituted, on the one hand, a criticism of the casual instrumentalisation of persons allowed by the law of slavery and, on the other, an endorsement of the Protestant idea that persons are obliged to undergo the self-study associated with the cultivation of conscience and the adoption of discipline. The former removed an arbitrary royal privilege, while the latter constituted modes of inquiry that the Protestants had wrenched back from the pastoral mission of the Catholic clergy and, to a lesser extent, secular medicine. Locke, a physician notoriously intolerant towards Catholics, took the 'empiric' – that is, sceptical – view that allopathic intervention should be permitted under extreme circumstances after several physicians had been consulted. Such was the model for Locke's legislative prerogative over either royal edict or personal judgement in a just society (Romanell, 1984).

There was a period from, say, 1700 to 1900, when the religious and scientific senses of 'discipline' vis-à-vis the human body were largely the same. This period coincides with the secularisation of conscience as consciousness, and the ascendancy of 'introspection' as a putatively reliable mode of epistemic access. However, the route from Locke to Kitcher starts to get paved in the second half of the nineteenth century, when a scientifically reinvigorated medical profession, including psychiatry, provided new secular grounds for claims to expertise over personal space previously held (and by then largely abandoned) by the pastoral clergy. As a result, we now routinely defer to the advice of physicians without equating it with the fear of God or the demands of slave masters. This is because we naturally approach our own bodies less as seats of agency, let alone sovereign power, than as sites of investigation that are *terra incognita* until staked out by those who have undergone proper training, which typically involves restricting, if not undoing, the lessons of personal life experience. In that respect, we are all already 'patients'. This is the epistemic version of the social contract to which lay people and experts agree in Kitcher's division of cognitive labour. It results in the familiar image of the history of science as the colonisation of what the later Husserl called the 'life-world'. In our times, the lawyer Peter Drahos (1995) has observed the emergence of a second-order version of the same tendency in cyberspace under the rubric of 'information feudalism'.

EXPERTISE AS SITE FOR NORMATIVE RECESSION IN STS

Kitcher's social-epistemological vision is also one with which STS is largely – and regrettably – comfortable. The origins of this attitude lie in issues associated with the most influential school of sociology in early STS research: ethnomethodology. Over 30 years ago, ethnomethodologists had raised the question of knowledge 'ownership', partly in response to a perennial problem in the politics of ethnography that had come to a head in the heightened academic consciousness of the 1960s: to what extent is the analyst accountable to the analysed? This problem arises because an ethnographer's subjects are potentially subject to the designs of her clients in government or business who have a vested interest in understanding the movements of natives, deviants and other key target groups. Does a good ethnographer in the name of 'giving voice' to these groups end up betraying whatever secrets had enabled them to elude more powerful forces in society? The fact that even today cooperative subjects are called 'informants' suggests that the problem has not been fully solved. In a heated debate with Howard Becker at the US Society for the Study of Social Problems in the 1960s, Alvin Gouldner accused ethnographers of illicitly appropriating the knowledge of vulnerable groups, effectively placing them at risk, while presenting themselves as champions of dispossessed countercultures (Fuller, 2000b: 363). (Were Gouldner alive today, he would probably make a similar argument against medical anthropologists who work for pharmaceutical industries on bioprospecting projects.)

Against this critical backdrop, ethnomethodologists provided a self-protective scholastic response (e.g. Sharrock, 1974). They identified the possession of knowledge with the production of accounts of knowledge. Insofar as the accounts of the analyst and the analysed are produced in different contexts, in different words and for different ends (which may or may not be achieved), they are different pieces of knowledge, each owned by their respective producer, as a labour theory of value would have it. Ethnomethodologists were especially well-placed epistemologically to make this argument. They broke with traditional ethnography on two crucial points relating to their radical social constructivism. First, ethnomethodologists upheld a minimalist view of knowledge as whatever passes for knowledge in a particular social context, without presuming, say, the prior existence of cognitive traditions, unless they are conjured up (discursively) in that context. Second, ethnomethodologists were notorious for their strategic interventions in ongoing social practices, very much in the spirit of experimentation, which deliberately undermined any notion that their accounts 'mirrored' or even 'represented' the subjects analysed.

At first STS seemed to adopt the ethnomethodologist's pose towards knowledge production unproblematically. The field made a persuasive case that it had staked out its own distinct domain of knowledge that drew on agents' first-order experiences but presented them in a fashion that was at once alien from yet illuminating to those agents. The exemplar of this moment is Jonas Salk's preface to Latour and Woolgar (1979), whose laboratory in San Diego provided the site for what remains *the* classic STS ethnography. While the language of *Laboratory Life* was hardly obscurantist by the standards of the late 1970s – the period when Foucault and Derrida were translated into English – it was nevertheless sufficiently indebted to discourses unfamiliar to either their subjects or those who might be interested in their subjects' activities to carry a strong sense of autonomy and integrity.

At the same time, however, the excitement surrounding early STS fed off the frisson of radical critique associated with the rhetoric of 'alienation', which tapped into the rediscovery of the 'young' or 'humanist' Karl Marx, whose unpublished manuscripts were translated into English in the 1960s. This Marx tended to treat social, including economic, structures as alienated ideological formations – 'reifications', to recall Gyorgy Lukacs' term – abstracted from concrete practices, or 'praxes'. The bellwether text was Berger and Luckmann's *The Social Construction of Reality* (1966), which continues to be fondly cited by STSers of the 1968 generation regardless of their current politics. For a fleeting moment, the cunning of reason greeted the invisible hand: cold War polarities appeared to self-deconstruct once Marx was revealed to have been an avid reader of Adam Smith before the latter became a capitalist icon.

However, this early flirtation with Marxism came back to haunt STS after the collapse of Communism and the onset of the Science Wars. These two events are connected by science's loss of default generous national funding, once the Soviet Union was no longer seen as a substantial high-tech security threat. In this shifted context, talk of 'material practices' appeared to turn science into an activity whose own practitioners were its primary and perhaps sole beneficiaries. Here STS suggested that work done outside the laboratories was required for work done inside them to acquire scientific status. If so, shouldn't scientists themselves – rather than an already overloaded state – bear the burden of recruiting allies to advance any research programmes? Intentionally or not, STS promoted the idea that science had to be justified not in some general, long-term, collective sense but in terms of specific, short-term, constituency-based horizons: a shift from a state to a market vision of science.

For STS to evolve into a kind of 'metascientfic' expertise, an increasing proportion of those competent in the field should enter 'science policy', broadly defined, to orchestrate this transition in the mode of science's societal justification. In fact, this has probably already happened. However, in practice, such people have effectively abandoned STS's research arena to an academically based community that has moved in the exact opposite direction. For those steeped in STS, this schism is exemplified in the contrasting trajectories of Bruno Latour (who articulates the ideology of policy-making STS) and Harry Collins (who articulates the ideology of academic STS), neither of which from my own standpoint is satisfactory.

Suppose we ask the pointed question: who won the 'Science Wars', the phrase that *Social Text* editor Andrew Ross (1996) coined for the increasingly visible clashes between scientists and STS practitioners and fellow travellers in cultural studies that took place in the 1990s over the character and disposition of science in a post-Cold War multicultural world: 'them' (the scientists) or 'us' (the STSers)? From the standpoint of the normative criteria used in contemporary science policymaking, 'we' seem to have emerged victorious. Whenever a funding agency evaluates a grant proposal in terms of the 'users and beneficiaries' from outside the peer scientific reference group, STS expertise is vindicated. Yet at the same time academic STS has increasingly cast its own expertise as simulating, if not approximating, the expertise of first-order science. Thus, Collins and Evans (2002) plot the history of STS as progressing through three stages: no expertise, interactional expertise and contributory expertise. Accordingly, STS charts its success by how much its researchers can contribute substantively to the projects of the scientists they study.

Yet this narrative comes close to saying that the task for STS researchers is to reinvent by exclusively sociological means the sorts of skills that science pedagogy normally – and more efficiently – provides. But why should sociologists interested in acquiring 'contributory expertise' in a science not simply acquire a degree in the science instead? It would certainly be quicker than picking up the relevant knowledge by osmosis over many years by hanging around the relevant scientists. Indeed, for a field like the study of gravitational waves, it would probably result in a more streamlined presentation than the 864 pages of Collins (2004). Under the circumstances, the take-home lesson of 'contributory expertise' for *STS* as an autonomous body of knowledge remains obscure if it is not denied altogether. 'Contributory expertise' is an unequivocally *progressive* moment in the history of STS only if the final court of appeal for the value of STS research are the scientists whom STS studies. In that respect, 'they' won the Science Wars.

And while Collins may have the most developed record of research in the STS study of expertise, his general orientation to expertise is implicit in how STS judges its own work. I belong to the first generation of people trained in the STS fields who were told that our intellectual credibility would be enhanced by mastering the science of which one would do the history, philosophy or sociology. Whatever one now makes of this advice (which I didn't take), it strongly suggested that STS research could only be as good as the mastery of the studied science that it displayed. Whatever distinctive slant or perspective STS provided was in addition to,

and presumably detachable from, the show of scientific competence. Consequently, the least controversially excellent work in STS is by people – say, Donald MacKenzie and Peter Galison – whose intellectual calling card is technical virtuosity presented with a light theoretical touch. As it turns out, MacKenzie, Professor of Sociology at Edinburgh, is the heir of the Strong Programme in the Sociology of Scientific Knowledge that began the philosophical career of STS, while Galison, Professor of History of Science at Harvard, is the heir of the department that through its house journal *Isis* established the field as the humanist face of science in American academia through figures like Gerald Holton and I.B. Cohen.

Given MacKenzie's succession of research topics – statistical controversies in genetics, accuracy in military weapons, the computerisation of mathematical proofs and the modelling of financial markets – it probably comes as no surprise that he began his academic career with a first class honours degree in applied mathematics from the University of Edinburgh. Indeed, if an overall pedagogical lesson is to be gleaned from MacKenzie's career, it is that very little sociology goes a very long way, if the STS researcher already possesses a first-hand understanding of the science she studies. For his part, Galison bypassed the circumambulations of Collins' 'contributory expertise' by going native and acquiring a physics PhD alongside his doctorate in the history of science. He sees 'theory' as providing shade and nuance to locally constrained practices, much in the manner of an artist whose technique compensates for potential deficiencies in the observer's perspective on an object (Galison, 2004). What theory does *not* do is to place the object in a radically different light, potentially subjecting it to criticism.

Here it is worth recalling that the prehistory of STS consisted of people who approached matters from quite the other way around: they were already expert in the natural sciences and mathematics but they wanted to distance the nobler concerns of their disciplines from their secular entanglements in World War I, World War II and the Cold War. (I mean here to cover everyone from Rudolf Carnap to Barry Barnes.) That aim forced them to move into history, philosophy and sociology, disciplines that still allowed the expression of rapidly disappearing, if not entirely lost, normative ideals. To be sure the ideals promoted by, say, Carnap and Popper, Kuhn and Lakatos, Barnes and Bloor varied in detail. Nevertheless, they had a shared sense of the task – namely, to justify science by 'natural philosophical' standards that Newton would have recognised as his own. However, these were not necessarily the standards to which most scientists in the twentieth century have aspired, let alone realised. Indeed, the prehistory of STS can be read as an invocation of the past to criticise contemporary science for being too fragmented, instrumentalised and otherwise fallen.

All of this stands in striking contrast with the decidedly 'anti-critical' stance of STS vis-à-vis science in the wake of *both* Latour and Collins. For example, when MacKenzie (2006) writes of the 'performative' character of economic models of financial markets, he is more concerned with how models succeed in shaping markets than with whatever power the models exert as critical forces, especially when they *fail* to shape markets. Yet the epistemic authority of economics, like that of medicine, is evidenced more in the guilt that society feels for failing to live up to its normative ideals than in the ease with which it can make society conform to its explanatory ideals. (Consider attitudes towards inflation and obesity: rarely managed but always regretted.) To be sure, in both cases the same models are at play but they are seen in rather different lights – specifically, in terms of what might be called the 'vector of accountability': are economists ultimately accountable to the markets they help bring into being, or are markets accountable to economists, whose criticism renders markets problematic in ways that demand a concerted social response? Economists in both cases

may get their way, but it is only in the latter case that their expertise counts as an independent force countermanding other, locally based and typically elite, expertises.

Let us take stock by drawing together the various strands of the argument. Science and expertise are historically opposed ideas: the former evokes a universalistic ideal meant to be pursued in leisure, while the latter consists of particular practices pursued to earn a living. However, expertise can serve the universalistic ideal of science by undermining the authority of other expertises that would cast doubt on the viability of this ideal. Put bluntly, expertise is 'progressive' only when it serves as the second moment of a Hegelian dialectic. *Contra* Lyotard and most STS treatments of science, I see the modern university – specifically through its teaching function – as the place where this moment most often happens. STS has failed to recognise that the project of 'democratising knowledge' ultimately means that expertise is not to be conserved but actively decommissioned. It follows that what is still often valorised in STS circles as the 'tacit' or 'craft' character of expertise should be critiqued as a mystified version of what economists call 'path dependency' – that is, in philosophical terms, an attempt by those who originated a robust body of knowledge to conflate the contexts of discovery and justification to maintain their initial advantage.

The challenge here to STS can be posed as an explicit research imperative: if we remain committed to the democratisation of knowledge, we should always try to find some less costly alternative path to the modes of thought and action currently licensed by a given expertise – and then ask why that cheaper route is not already dominant. This drive towards intellectual efficiency includes rendering esoteric research pedagogically tractable, transferring skills from humans to machines, converting virtuosity into routine and reassigning the significance of the division of labour from its role in Kitcher to that in Putnam. It also means restoring *breadth* to its rightful place ahead of *depth* as a value in knowledge. We shall see in the next section that philosophers of science have been all too willing to abide by their own expert-centred epistemology, which in turn renders them uncertain allies in the research challenge I have posed to STS.

THE SELF-IMPOSED NORMATIVE LIMITS OF ANALYTIC PHILOSOPHY OF SCIENCE

For better or worse, Thomas Kuhn was the most influential theorist of science in the second half of the twentieth century. For 'worse', if one takes straight Kuhn's account of science as a succession of paradigms punctuated by revolutions, which is in fact how Kuhn has been largely taken. Assisted by the Science Citation Index and other science indicators (themselves Cold War cousins of Kuhn's account of science), many fledgling fields, especially in the social sciences (not least STS), have tried to refashion themselves as sciences in the image and likeness of *The Structure of Scientific Revolutions* (Kuhn, 1970).

Luckily there is some evidence – albeit from a surprising quarter – that this use of Kuhn's 'do-it-yourself' model of science is now waning. The brand of neo-creationism known as 'intelligent design theory', which I have defended in court and in public, typically draws on a more Popperian metascientific sensibility that takes the neo-Darwinian paradigm in biology as an appropriate target for criticism, simply because its institutional dominance blocks alternative lines of inquiry into the origins and nature of life that in the past have proved fruitful and that could well make sense of issues left unexplained and sometimes even untouched by neo-Darwinism (Fuller, 2008).

Unlike the Kuhnian strategy, the Popperian one does not require that challengers to the dominant paradigm have an up-and-running alternative, since Popperians do not recognise particular groups of scientists as exercising ownership over the collection or interpretation of data. After all, much if not most of the data currently subsumed under neo-Darwinian explanations were not originally gathered by scientists who (would have) supported neo-Darwinism, and were the neo-Darwinists given (as some would wish to have) absolute authority over the licensing of how data is collected and interpreted, science would renege on its commitment to the 'open society'. The precedent for this line of thought is Ernst Mach's *Science of Mechanics* (1960), whose historico-critical argument against the Newtonian paradigm in physics inspired Einstein and Heisenberg.

But Kuhn's influence has not been all bad, though his 'better' side tends to be overlooked by his more wishful readers. I refer here to Kuhn's thesis that the succession of paradigms punctuated by revolutions is ultimately a historiographic fiction constructed by defenders of the current paradigm to make its ascendancy appear to be a logical necessity. Thus, in retrospect the prior history of science appears as a series of episodes in which the wheat of truth is sifted from the chaff of error and then passed along for empirical consolidation and theoretical projection, eventuating in the current state of the discipline. Kuhn himself shrewdly described this process as an 'Orwellian' contrivance, since the account will need to be rewritten with each new scientific revolution, in accordance with, so to speak, the shift in the epistemic polestar that is now used to guide all prior and subsequent research. Such systematically applied self-deception, common to both textbooks and popular science works, is designed to motivate the latest generation of paradigm contributors, whose own work is most likely to make only marginal improvements on the paradigm's knowledge base. In that case, it is essential that they stay focused on the task at hand – also known as normal science – and not be encouraged to have second thoughts, let alone regrets, about how the future might have turned out, had an anomalous result been taken as the prompt for a new research direction rather than reworked as a consequence of the dominant paradigm.

In *Thomas Kuhn: A Philosophical History for Our Times* (Fuller, 2000b), I observed that Kuhn's achievement was paradoxical in that, on the one hand, he clearly recognised that the promotion of scientific progress depends on scientists recognising the peculiar relationship in which they stand to their history; yet on the other hand, it never occurred to Kuhn to apply this insight to his own case, namely, someone who was trained in the dominant paradigm of his day but left it in order to pursue a career in the history and philosophy of science. What Kuhn failed to appreciate, or at least not properly acknowledge, is that scientists in his position might not so much be discarded by the dominant paradigm – as if they were the detritus of Hegel's world-historic spirit – as voluntarily abandon it because of what they perceive as an illegitimate turn in the paradigm's development. Kuhn clearly saw his departure from physics shortly after being awarded a doctorate from Harvard as an active rejection of the field's 'Big Science' metamorphosis that he had experienced first-hand in World War II (Fuller, 2000b: 395–396). Nevertheless, he treated the decision as being no more than of biographical interest – not an opportunity to theorise the distinction between corporate rejection and individual dissent in science.[1]

The distinction between corporate rejection and individual dissent in science is subtle, entailing different styles of historiographic rationalisation. The same situation may be equally characterised as science as a system casting off a dysfunctional part or science as a project losing sense of its mission and hence some of its original followers. The subtlety of this distinction needs to be kept in mind when trying to understand the relationship between the first-order sciences and the second-order 'metascientific' disciplines like the history, philosophy and sociology of science. In effect, for all the lip service that continues to be paid to Kuhn, we have merely picked up his bad habits and none of his good ones.

By way of example, consider the following, which appears as the opening paragraph of a recent article that calls for the philosophy of science to become a genuinely 'social epistemology' that might usefully inform public debate about science. I single it out because it captures very well a certain 'post-Kuhnian' consensus in the philosophy of science that fancies itself alive to the social and historical contexts of science:

> There is no more interesting nor sobering chapter in the history of 20th-century philosophy of science than that which tells the story of the discipline's disengagement at mid-century from the social and political concerns that shaped its earlier years. In Europe, near the century's start, conservative Catholics like Pierre Duhem, social democrats like Ernst Mach, and revisionist Marxists like Otto Neurath all understood that science was central to the modernist outlook then asserting its cultural authority and that a philosophy of science must, therefore, among other tasks, theorize the manner in which science is embedded in a social, cultural, and political context and the manner in which it contributes to the transformation of the world. (Howard, 2009: 199)

What's wrong with this picture? Briefly put, Don Howard damns with faint praise. It is only in hindsight that Duhem, Mach and Neurath can be so easily lumped together as 'philosophers of science' who were engaged with the sciences of their day in order to make them more socially relevant. This characterisation presupposes a sharp distinction between what is 'internal' and 'external' to science that they themselves were loath to admit. All three were trained as – and saw themselves as – practitioners of first-order natural and (in Neurath's case) social sciences, who were 'philosophical' mainly in the sense of asking fundamental questions about the *modus operandi* of their disciplines, which in practice meant challenging institutionalised dogmas. As it turns out, each lost his battle and, in this respect, the identity of 'philosopher' amounts to a consolation prize bestowed by later generations who implicitly concede that Duhem, Mach and Neurath were indeed wrong about strictly scientific matters but said some interesting things of a general nature nonetheless.

My historiographic squabble with Howard bears on the grounds on which philosophy of science can launch (or re-launch?) itself as a full-fledged social epistemology. Drawing on Reisch (2005), Howard bemoans how the logical positivists were driven to increasingly formal and technical pursuits in the foundations of the sciences once they moved to the United States, through a combination of Communist paranoia and collegial spinelessness. (Interestingly, Howard underplays the rather more proactive suspicions of some pragmatist philosophers like John Dewey and especially his student Sidney Hook, who found the positivists' 'unified science' agenda potentially subversive of liberal democracy.) He believes that this traumatic transatlantic adjustment set the tone for philosophy of science's politically quiescent attitude towards science in the second half of the twentieth century, out of which the field is now only emerging, thanks in part to the post-Kuhnian influence of history and sociology of science. Again, what is wrong with this picture?

The problem here lies in identifying the exact source of philosophy's legitimacy to make normative pronouncements about science, especially ones involving criticisms of science's social entanglements: what gives the philosopher the right to pass such judgements in the first place? The answer typically given by analytic philosophers who practice social epistemology is that philosophy is so authorised by virtue of the sort of discipline that it is. It is an answer that only a philosopher could both devise and believe. Moreover, analytic philosophers have a peculiar way of interpreting their charge. Because they adopt a *primus inter pares* approach to the other disciplines, they quite happily cede authority to the scientific establishment on strictly scientific matters – indeed, 'scientific underlabourer' is a badge of honour worn by analytic philosophers (Fuller, 2000b: Chapter 6). Thus, they confine their critical comments to areas where they can speak in a uniquely 'philosophical' voice. This can

leave someone who reads across disciplinary boundaries with a distinct sense of the enterprise's artificiality. This point can be illustrated by considering two exchanges relating to social epistemology that were published in the journal *Philosophy of Science* in the past few years.

The first exchange transpired at the 2001 Pacific Division meeting of the American Philosophical Association. There Janet Kourany (2003) argued that philosophy of science needs to recover its sense of social responsibility, which the logical positivists lost when they emigrated to the United States. Moreover, feminism is well poised to redress this normative deficit, not only due to its free-standing political commitment to social justice but also the sheer empirical fact that women constitute most of the human population and an increasing percentage of the scientific workforce and pool of research subjects. On closer inspection, however, Kourany's understanding of the matter turns out to be quite narrow. For example, the entire Marxist tradition – ranging from rather orthodox Bernalists (about whom more below) to such heterodox followers of the Frankfurt School as the early Habermasians of the 'finalisationist' school (Schaefer, 1984) – is omitted. Also missing is what might be called the 'left' wing of the Popperian (e.g. Agassi, 1985; Feyerabend, 1979) and Kuhnian (e.g. Ravetz, 1971; Rouse, 1987) schools. Indeed, even within feminism itself, Kourany omits mention of fellow philosopher Sandra Harding (1986), let alone a philosophically inclined historian of science like Donna Haraway (1991).

Common to these excluded sources – and here I might add my own work – is their relatively liberal appeal to substantive claims about the overall trajectory of the history of science. These in turn provide the pretext for a critique of contemporary science. To be sure, many of the claims, which turn on alleged power relations, are empirically contestable. But that fact simply underscores the extent to which these missing sources routinely blurred the boundary between philosophy and the special sciences. But Kourany is not one to blur boundaries. Instead she follows Helen Longino – more about whom below – in grounding her sense of critique in the bare logical point of the so-called Duhem–Quine thesis of the underdetermination of theory choice by data, namely, that a given body of evidence can be deduced from any number of mutually incompatible theories. Armed only with that philosophical premise, Kourany concludes that we can and should promote forms of scientific inquiry that comport with our own values, especially her primary value, egalitarianism. But the underdetermination thesis at most necessitates a role for values in scientific theory choice but not which values they are. This does not disturb Kourany because she presumes that values by their very nature are subjective, which she glosses as 'political'. Kourany is not one to make ontological inquiries into whether things are valuable because we desire them or we desire things because they possess value.

Nevertheless, whatever ultimate value science might have aside from its immediate practical value is arguably what the metaphysical dispute between realists and instrumentalists has always been about (Laudan, 1984, Proctor, 1991). For her part, Kourany simply takes instrumentalism as read, revealing the philosophical weakness of her argument, a point politely but firmly made in response by Ronald Giere (2003), one of earliest and most consistent supporters of science and technology studies among analytic philosophers of science. Giere insists on holding Kourany to their shared analytic-philosophical scruples, which in this case requires strict agnosticism with regard to what might count as 'politically correct' inquiry, absent a philosophically grounded argument about the ends of science. And here Pierre Duhem can be counted to testify for the prosecution. After all, when Duhem first proposed the underdetermination thesis roughly a century ago, he did not use it to try to convert his colleagues to his own Roman Catholicism. Rather, Duhem's polemical intent was to rebuff French Third Republic secularists who had claimed that science rendered nugatory the knowledge claims of theology.

The second exchange over social epistemology occurred in mutual reviews of two contemporaneous books by leaders in the field, Helen Longino (2002a) and Philip Kitcher (2001), both analytic philosophers of centre-left persuasion. Longino's strongest words of praise for Kitcher is indicative of the entire exchange: '… one of the great merits of this book is that it shows how much scope for social and political considerations can be established on the basis of relatively canonical epistemological stances' (Longino, 2002b: 568). Well, yes, and that is the *problem*. It seems that the main difference between Longino's and Kitcher's social epistemology of science turns on how the relevant social interests are identified so as to constitute what Kitcher calls a 'well-ordered science'. Kitcher (2002) is more concerned that all the relevant interests are adequately represented – by as many or few people as it takes – whereas Longino (2002b) is more concerned that people are capable of representing themselves in research that may impact on their lives. If Kitcher's social epistemology suggests that a benevolent philosopher-bureaucrat might design a well-ordered science all by himself, Longino's raises the spectre of direct democratic approval for each research proposal. These alternatives are reminiscent of the working conditions under which, respectively, the US and the French national constitution were drafted (Fuller, 2000a: Chapter 8).

Strikingly common to both accounts is a static conception of politics, as if interests were fixed, either objectively (*a la* Kitcher) or subjectively (*a la* Longino). Yet, the stuff of politics is the organisation of interests for purposes of collective decision-making. Greater attention to institutional design – a topic now widely studied by sociologists, political economists and economists – would have made this clear. Two examples suffice. First, the identification of units of representation with geographical regions inhabited by roughly the same number of people, rather than fixed interest groups, continually forces both the represented and the representatives to think about their interests in terms of those of others. This staple of modern democracies has tended to encourage greater openness to change. While not an unmitigated good, it serves to minimise what under philosophical analysis might appear as irreconcilable value differences. A second example is the constitution of juries by parties relatively disinterested to the issue under deliberation who nevertheless must reach a binding agreement, as in so-called consensus conferences (Fuller, 2006a: Chapter 6).

CONCLUSION: THE PROMISE AND PERILS OF A NORMATIVELY 'FULLER' SOCIAL EPISTEMOLOGY – THE FATE OF BERNALISM

The historiographically soundest answer to philosophy's normative legitimacy over science is not one that the analytic philosophy community normally countenances – namely, that philosophers of science adopt the normative standpoint of dissenting scientists. I mean specifically that they purport to uphold the same norms as those of the scientific community, but they accuse the community of having taken one or more wrong turns in the application of those norms over the course of history. The orthodoxy that defines who is in and out of the community merely masks the original error, which if anything has only intensified over time. On this view, philosophers of science, far from being supercilious outsiders, see themselves as directly implicated and affected by whatever mistakes that they feel that the majority of their colleagues have made. Were Pierre Duhem, Ernst Mach or Otto Neurath resurrected now, this is the standpoint from which they would make their case.

Needless to say, it would be a controversial position because it dispenses with the usual relativistic pretence that philosophers and scientists are bound to understand science differently because of their different disciplinary perspectives. Instead philosophers and scientists are placed in explicit opposition as rival heirs to the same intellectual lineage. Philosophers are simply dispossessed scientists and scientists no more than philosophers suffering from tunnel vision. In that case, one would expect philosophers and scientists to avail themselves of the same mix of conceptual, empirical and methodological arguments. Philosophers would not be limited – as they are today – to providing rival justifications for the same canonical historiography of science. (Here I allude to the various schools of 'realists' and 'instrumentalists' who disagree over everything except the exemplary episodes in the history of science that they need to justify.) Rather philosophers would continue to contest the research choices originally taken by scientists, since the presumptive correctness of those decisions underwrites the legitimacy of the dominant paradigm (Fuller, 2003: Chapters 8–10).

To be sure, there are many styles in which this contestation might occur, most of which are in evidence in Popper and his followers. For example, at various points in his career, Popper was notorious in scientific circles for contesting the Copenhagen Interpretation of quantum mechanics and Darwin's theory of evolution by natural selection. Here was a clear case of a philosopher issuing a first-order challenge to scientific authority by contesting whether scientists had applied their own norms correctly as they rallied around particular theories. Although the hardening of disciplinary boundaries in the twentieth century cast Popper from the outset as a 'philosopher', he was operating in the spirit of Duhem and Mach, and perhaps a generation or two earlier would have been treated as they were, a dissenter from within the scientific ranks. Perhaps unsurprisingly then, while Popper was admirably forthright in his criticism, he did not succeed in changing many scientific minds.

His students approached the matter more indirectly. In particular, Imre Lakatos' (1970) self-styled 'rational reconstructions' of the history of science aimed to show that, even if we grant that science is now where it ought to be, it could have arrived much sooner had it made more epistemologically perspicuous decisions along the way. Lakatos aimed to divest the history of science not of its content but of its necessity. In other words, scientists have managed to advance knowledge almost in spite of themselves, given their hit-and-miss ways. Ever the Hegelian, Lakatos believed that philosophy added modal ballast ('necessity') to a pursuit that might otherwise appear desultory. However, he shied away from claiming anything more than wisdom in hindsight – the Owl of Minerva taking flight at dusk – for his rational reconstructions. Paul Feyerabend (1975) pressed home this point by specifically tracing the haphazard character of the history of science not to scientists violating methodological rules but to their taking the rules too seriously, thereby overlooking that the balance of evidence vis-à-vis competing theories is bound to change over time with the introduction of new methods and instruments of inquiry.

However, more ambitious Hegelians like the left wing British science activist John Desmond Bernal (1901–1971) wanted to do more than simply use a philosophically informed understanding of history to highlight the limitations of scientists' current paradigmatic assumptions. Bernal explicitly followed Marx in believing that something like a Lakatosian rational reconstruction of the history of science could provide guidance on science's future trajectory, what nowadays is called 'foresight' in science policy circles to suggest an epistemic symmetry with 'hindsight'. His *Social Function of Science* (1939) written at the peak of Western enthusiasm for the scientific promise of the Soviet Union, followed by the most comprehensive Marxist history of science ever written, the four-volume *Science in History* (1971), are worthy precursors of social epistemology and are among the earliest works in the

sociology and social history of science. So before considering the nature of Bernalism's ultimate failure, the exact nature of the argument for what Bernal was happy to call the 'science of science' is worth recalling:

1 The history of science displays an overall trajectory of progress, in that, on the whole, we deem it better than not that science has become increasingly prominent in world culture.
2 However, it is equally clear that the history of science could have proceeded more efficiently, which would have resulted in more benefits and less harms for more people.
3 By understanding the various retardant forces that have operated in science's past, we can plan so that neither they nor anything like them are operative in science's future.

This argument contains a hidden premise:

4 The difference between 'necessary' and 'contingent' features in the historical development of science corresponds to the distinction between its normatively 'progressive' and 'regressive' features.

The premise is recognisably Hegelian but not exclusively. It reflects the confidence of a whole host of professedly non-ideological historians, philosophers and (Mertonian) sociologists of science who distinguished 'internalist' and 'externalist' approaches to science prior to the rise of science studies (Shapin, 1992). For them an idealised account of science is *ipso facto* one that identifies what 'really' makes science works. For most other human endeavours, this assumption would appear empirically ill-founded if not naïve. When does steadfastness of purpose guarantee desired outcomes? The answer of course is when there is an unlimited power behind the purpose, such that the end always justifies the means. Only spiritually driven projects in the Abrahamic tradition, and mainly in Christianity and Islam, have consistently had this 'progress as purification' character, which in the twentieth century was secularised and technologically enhanced in the totalitarian projects of Communism and Nazism (Löwith, 1949). Such projects do not countenance the prospect that, so to speak, any attempt to remove the dirt from one's dirty hands always acquires new dirt in the process.

Thus, Bernal held that scientists could free themselves from the corruption of priests and capitalists without falling into the arms of some other 'external' force, as long as they constituted themselves as a high-skilled version of the universal proletariat who collectively set the terms by which science might be steered for the betterment if not perfection of humanity: in short, an updated version of the power for good that naturally flows from a community of true believers. This sentiment is already in clear display in Bernal's youthful science fiction work, *The World, The Flesh and the Devil* (1929), which anticipated the recent science policy turn towards 'transhumanism', with its promised convergence of nano-, bio-, info- and cogno-technosciences as a strategy for 'enhancing' human evolution in ways that will address long-term problems of economic productivity and national security (Freeman, 1999: 126–131; Roco and Bainbridge, 2002; Fuller, 2009a). The properly scientific society will not only cast aside atavistic institutions like the church and the market but will also increasingly turn away from the human body itself, at least in its natural state.

Of course, to Darwinian ears, 'enhancing evolution' sounds less like utopian futurism than a Lamarckian throwback, as it privileges humans with the capacity to provide direction to a process that – at least according to Darwin – is fundamentally purposeless, given the high element of chance that has been always at play in species survival. While such Darwinian scepticism is likely to become less compelling in the twenty-first century as we become more expert in reversing millions of years of evolution through biotech interventions (no doubt with unintended consequences), Bernal himself was accused of high-tech wishful thinking with his staunch support of the Soviet agricultural minister Trofim Lysenko, whose Lamarckian approach to agronomy was given free rein

on ideological grounds, resulting in many decades of failed farm policies.

Without wishing to excuse Bernal's behaviour, I would draw attention to two aspects of the logic of his situation that show his clear grasp of the meta-level issues involved in social epistemology, despite his faulty first-order judgements.

1   Bernal in his scientific capacity ran one of the laboratories devoted to X-ray crystallography that contributed technical expertise to the quest to crack the genetic code. Like many involved in the early history of molecular biology, he was a physical scientist by training who moved into biology to tackle the ultimate questions surrounding the nature of life that Darwinists, due to their background in more ecological approaches to biology and geology, were inclined to leave shrouded in rather mysterious chance-based historical processes, which in turn gave the impression that artificial selection could never trump natural selection, and hence life could never be, strictly speaking, 'manufactured'. From this standpoint, Bernal may have seen in Lysenko's neo-Lamarckianism a very premature version of what is now increasingly possible in biotechnology.

2   Bernal in his philosophical capacity believed that science was a vehicle for the self-realisation of the humanity, in which Abrahamic talk of 'spirit' was to be understood as a metaphorical rough draft for a project that would be brought to completion by dialectical materialism. In his own day, especially in the aftermath of the First World War, Bernal detected a fragmentation of scientific effort from this universalist aspiration that was largely driven by nationalist and capitalist concerns, the results of which increasingly destabilised the world order, measured in both military or financial terms. In this respect, Bernal regarded science as being in a 'fallen' state pitted against society, and both suffering as a result. This perspective led Bernal back to visions of unified science put forward by the likes of Friedrich Engels and ultimately Lamarck (whose views Engels did not distinguish clearly from Darwin's) that were designed to redress various wrong turns taken in science's recent history.

The attractive feature of Bernal's perspective is that his construal of the problem of theory choice in science was not dictated primarily by either orthodox scientific opinion or, for that matter, a strong sense of evidential warrant. At first glance, this seems strange, since most versions of social epistemology practiced by analytic philosophers fall back on some combination of authoritative expertise and evidential warrant to support normative conclusions about the direction that scientific inquiry should take. Bernal's rejection of these two epistemic staples reflects his realisation that the value of evidence is relative to which authorities one takes seriously, which in turn rests on the reasons one has for pursuing science in the first place. After all, evidence that directly addresses a long-standing problem within a particular scientific field is clearly of high value only if that field is worth pursuing. Otherwise, one might be prepared to downplay or ignore such evidence in pursuit of other ends. In short, both expertise and evidence can be reasonably weighted on many different scales, but in any case the judgements involved are simultaneously scientific and philosophical.

Bernal often looks bad nowadays because he is inserted into a historiography of science that presupposes an axiological horizon quite opposed to his own. That horizon, influenced by Kuhn, takes the purposeless diversification of the sciences as an irreversible long-term tendency. Thus, Bernal's endorsement of Lysenko is typically faulted as an instance of ideological commitment clouding one's vision to unfavourable evidence, as if Bernal's project of unifying science to emancipate humanity were itself to blame. In contrast, I believe that merely Bernal's dogmatic attitude towards the pursuit of his project proved to be his Achilles heel. After all, Bernal could have declared Lysenko a false prophet of human emancipation after enough crop failures and moved on to seek new exemplars, instead of tying his project so closely to Lysenko's fate, or perhaps more generally the fate of the Soviet Union as the vanguard world-historic state. In any case, as the 'cunning of reason' would have it, Bernal's legacy lived longest where it was most actively opposed, namely, in the scientific establishment norm of

'communitarianism', Robert Merton's sublimated version of Bernal's original call for the formation of class consciousness amongst scientists (Mendelsohn, 1989).

For a larger perspective on the implications of Bernal's normative failure for the history of science and technology studies, Gary Werskey (2007) offers a canny diagnosis that respects the intellectual brilliance and political efforts by Bernal and his colleagues on the scientific left. The Cold War division of the Allies into 'Liberals' and 'Communists' produced two competing scientific lefts with universalist aspirations that spent the second half of the last century squandering enormous financial and intellectual capital on campaigns of mutual suspicion that verged on 'mutually assured destruction', when they should have been focussing on where they agreed to relieve global misery. The result, to which we bear witness today, is an overall shift to the right in the centre of political gravity that casts aspersions on much of what both sides of the Cold War stood for, not least the idea of science as an emancipatory force. Werskey astutely observes that much of our 'postmodern condition', including the ideological cast of science and technology studies, can be understood in these terms. I also agree that the 'subaltern' forms of knowledge championed by postmodernists may complement, but not replace, historically 'Western' science in addressing global problems.

Nevertheless, Werskey skirts a very important blindspot of the Bernalists: they were not 'democrats', in the civic republican sense of trusting ordinary people to decide matters of public import through the ballot box. This point is crucial to grasp today because characteristic of our postmodern condition, especially the actor-network theory that dominates contemporary science and technology studies, is the tendency to conflate democratic decision-making and consumer choice. To put the matter in terms of the 'state/market' binary popularised by welfare economics in the Cold War (i.e. the failure of one elicits the need for the other), democracy is now normally found on the 'market' side of the binary (Fuller, 2006a: 63–67). The Bernalists unwittingly helped the postmodernists make this point by exemplifying the stereotype to which the equation 'democracy = market' seems like a reasonable response. In particular, the Bernalists operationalised the scientific planning of society in terms of the cooptation of right-minded elite scientists to state ministries and select committees. They gave little thought to chains of accountability to the people themselves.

In terms of 'democracy', my concern here is less that scientists constituting the planning board would not be statistically representative of all qualified scientists, let alone the society targeted by their policies, than that the Bernalists failed to see the need for the planning board to subject its judgement to regular public checks, as per elections. This does not deny the Bernalists' democratic credentials by more meritocratic criteria. They clearly believed that talent was equally distributed across social classes, which led them to campaign for 'equality of opportunity' to enable the talented to rise up the ranks quickly (Werskey, 1988: 243). However, such a policy amounted to a technocratically updated version of Plato's cultivation of philosopher-kings in *The Republic*. Plato also realised that those fit to rule might be of inferior birth and therefore must be given the opportunity to prove themselves (e.g. through examinations). But none of this – in either its Platonic or Bernalist form – challenged the overall vision that the best should be given absolute political authority over the rest.

Here it is worth recalling that the use of 'proletarian' to modify 'standpoint' or 'science' by Marxist theorists after the First World War reflected a general distancing from – and disappointment with – the activities of the actual working classes who were supposed to have led the communist revolution. Consequently, 'proletarian' came to refer to the relationship that the working class stands 'objectively' (i.e. according to Marxist theory) to the means of production *regardless* of whatever beliefs or desires the

workers themselves expressed. This soon generated a 'vanguardist' mentality, now associated with high modernism, whereby a more enlightened non-working-class group might be better placed to provide subjective expression of the proletarian standpoint. The history of so-called Western or 'critical' Marxism, which increasingly became the preserve of academic intellectuals, captures this transition, of which Bernalism was an important part. Thus, the Bernalists with their Oxbridge pedigrees believed that they might articulate a 'proletarian science' better than a working class that had been seduced by a capitalist aspirationist ideology.

In fairness to the Bernalists, however, it must be said that the adoption of the proletarian standpoint suits the scientific class in one sense, given the increasing relevance of scientific training to managing the means of production. Nevertheless, very often the science behind this training is of little more than symbolic value (i.e. a screening mechanism for employers in an overpopulated labour market), since the actual skills employed (e.g. in computer-based work) are just as mindless as anything previously required under industrial capitalism. Thus, the identification of science-based workers with the proletariat turns out to be literally correct – but with an ironic twist unforeseen by the Bernalists, namely, that they are the functional equivalent of the old industrial workers, their superior training notwithstanding. In that respect, the task of raising class consciousness has returned to where Marx and Engels started over 150 years ago.

An interesting symptom of Bernal's obliviousness to the fallibility of scientifically based political judgement appeared in his review of the second edition of Karl Popper's *The Open Society and Its Enemies* for *The British Journal for the Philosophy of Science* (Bernal, 1955). He characterised Popper as a *philagnoist*, a neologism literally meaning 'lover of ignorance'. It is telling that Bernal took Popper's doubts about the certitude of scientific knowledge to be an embrace of ignorance rather than recognition of fallibility.

It is as if Bernal could imagine only two positions: acceptance of the (Bernalist) truth and its denial – but not its outright falsification. At the very least, this reveals Bernal's instinctive commitment to a positivistic, rather than a dialectical, conception of science, a point that even his admirers have been forced to concede (Rose and Rose, 1999: 143–144).

More seriously, in terms of the various ways knowledge and power might be interrelated, Bernal seemed to conflate the magnitude and the irreversibility of science-based change to infer the inevitability of social progress. Thus, Bernal accused Popper's piecemeal social engineering approach of 'obscurantism' for ignoring the palpably revolutionary difference that modern science has made to our technical mastery of nature. Yet, for Popper, no public policy, however strongly backed by scientific developments, should ever propose social changes that cannot be reversed later, in light of the consequences. What a consensus of right-minded scientific elites gains in power, it does not necessarily also gain in knowledge. My point here is that Bernal's attempt to cast Popper as an anti-scientific thinker reveals Bernal's own limited conception of science's democratic accountability.

Bernal's fate is interestingly contrasted with that of Barry Commoner, who figures as an icon of 'critical science' in Ravetz (1971). Commoner was inspired by Bernal's *The Social Function of Science* to join the Bernalist American Association of Scientific Workers (AASW) as a student at Harvard (Egan, 2007: 19–20). Then Harvard president and soon-to-be Kuhn mentor, James Bryant Conant, saw the AASW was seen as a Communist threat (Fuller, 2000b: 162–164). However, Commoner's subsequent career can be read – from anti-nuclear to pro-ecological activism – as a call for scientists to shift their political base from the state to the populace. Armed with information supplied by activist scientists, the people could then become more directly involved in science-based decision-making. The result would be a scientific version of what the Protestant reformers urged vis-à-vis the Roman Catholic Church, in light of the Church's own internal problems, the general spread of literacy and the printing of personal bibles. Mindful of this precedent, I have used the phrases *secularisation of science* (Fuller, 1997: Chapter 4; Fuller, 2006b: Chapter 6) and *Protscience* (Fuller, 2010: Chapter 4) to characterise approaches like Commoner's.

Commoner realised that the logical conclusion of his position was to allow the people a free vote on the role that science plays in their life. While this attitude displayed a patience and trust in the wisdom of the crowds, something that Bernal's vanguard elitism – more than any taste for totalitarianism – rendered him incapable of appreciating, it was not without its own faults. Commoner's fifth-place finish as the Citizens Party's candidate for US president in 1980 arguably played a spoiler role vis-à-vis Jimmy Carter comparable to Ralph Nader's role vis-à-vis Al Gore twenty years later. The former resulted in eight years of Ronald Reagan, the latter in eight years of George W. Bush.

NOTE

1 Kuhn's use of history and philosophy of science as an 'exit strategy' contrasts interestingly with that of another scientist-turned-metascientist of his generation, Freeman Dyson (2007), whose involvement in World War II did not result in his feeling the same sense of betrayal of physics' world-historic mission. Dyson began life as the most promising protégé of J. Robert Oppenheimer and Richard Feynman on the Manhattan Project, sharing their faith in the efficiency-based arguments for nuclear arms as a deterrent to conventional warfare. Without ever quite renouncing that faith, Dyson has spent the bulk of his career on just the right side of respectability while challenging orthodoxies in physics and biology about life's origins and prospects, typically by fuelling various contra-Darwinian currents, most notably the idea that human life could thrive indefinitely in completely artificial environments in outer space. It would be easy to read such a career ironically as apt atonement for having worked on the project that did the most to underscore the transience of the human condition on Earth. For Dyson's evil twin, imagine a compound counterfactual in which the Nazis triumphed, or at

least survived, and Albert Speer then out of a vague sense of guilt decided to devote his life to the support of indigenous peoples in 'separate but equal' environments.

REFERENCES

Agassi, J. (1985) *Technology: Philosophical and Social Aspects.* Dordrecht: Kluwer.

Berger, P. and T. Luckmann (1966) *The Social Construction of Reality.* Garden City, NY: Doubleday.

Bernal, J.D. (1929) *The World, the Flesh and the Devil.* London: Kegan Paul.

Bernal, J.D. (1939) *The Social Function of Science.* London: Macmillan.

Bernal, J.D. (1955) 'Has history a meaning?', *British Journal for the Philosophy of Science,* 6: 164–169.

Bernal, J.D. (1971) *Science in History.* 4 vols. Cambridge MA: MIT Press.

Collins, H. (2004) *Gravity's Shadow.* Chicago: University of Chicago Press.

Collins, H. and R. Evans (2002) 'The third wave of science studies: Studies of expertise and experience', *Social Studies of Science,* 32(2): 235–296.

Drahos, P. (1995) 'Information feudalism in the information society', *The Information Society,* 11: 209–222.

Dyson, F. (2007) *The Scientist as Rebel.* New York: New York Review of Books.

Egan, M. (2007) *Barry Commoner and the Science of Survival.* Cambridge, MA: MIT Press.

Feyerabend, P. (1975) *Against Method.* London: Verso.

Feyerabend, P. (1979) *Science in a Free Society.* London: Verso.

Freeman, C. (1999) 'The social function of science', in B. Swann and F. Aprahamian (eds) *J.D. Bernal: A Life in Science and Politics.* London: Verso. pp. 101–31.

Fuller, S. (1988) *Social Epistemology.* Bloomington, IN: Indiana University Press.

Fuller, S. (1997) *Science.* Milton Keynes, UK: Open University Press.

Fuller, S. (2000a) *The Governance of Science.* Milton Keynes, UK: Open University Press.

Fuller, S. (2000b) *Thomas Kuhn: A Philosophical History for Our Times.* Chicago: University of Chicago Press.

Fuller, S. (2002) *Knowledge Management Foundations.* Woburn MA: Butterworth-Heinemann.

Fuller, S. (2003) *Kuhn vs Popper: The Struggle for the Soul of Science.* Cambridge, UK: Icon.

Fuller, S. (2006a) *The Philosophy of Science and Technology Studies.* London: Routledge.

Fuller, S. (2010) *Science: The Art of Living.* Montreal: McGill-Queens University Press.

Fuller, S. (2007) *New Frontiers in Science and Technology Studies.* Cambridge, UK: Polity Press.

Fuller, S. (2008) *Dissent over Descent: Intelligent Design's Challenge to Darwinism.* Cambridge, UK: Icon.

Fuller, S. (2009a) 'Knowledge politics and new converging technologies: A social epistemological perspective', *Innovation,* 22: 7–34.

Fuller, S. (2009b) *The Sociology of Intellectual Life: The Career of the Mind In and Around the Academy.* London: Sage.

Galison, P. (2004) 'Specific theory' *Critical Inquiry,* 30: 379–383.

Giere, R. (2003) 'A new program for philosophy of science?', *Philosophy of Science,* 70: 15–21.

Haraway, D. (1991) *Simians, Cyborgs and Women.* London: Free Association Books.

Harding, S. (1986) *The Science Question in Feminism.* Ithaca, NY: Cornell University Press.

Howard, D. (2009) 'Better red than dead – putting an end to the social irrelevance of postwar philosophy of science', *Science and Education,* 18: 199–220.

Kitcher, P. (1993) *The Advancement of Science.* Oxford: Oxford University Press.

Kitcher, P. (2001) *Science, Truth and Democracy.* Oxford: Oxford University Press.

Kitcher, P. (2002) 'The third way: Reflections on Longino's *The Fate of Knowledge*', *Philosophy of Science,* 69: 549–559.

Kourany, J. (2003) 'A philosophy of science for the 21st century', *Philosophy of Science,* 70: 1–14.

Kuhn, T.S. (1970) *The Structure of Scientific Revolutions.* 2nd edn. [Orig. 1962]. Chicago: University of Chicago Press.

Kusch, M. and Lipton, P. (eds) (2002) 'Special issue on testimony', *Studies in History and Philosophy of Science,* 33: 209–423.

Lakatos, I. (1970) 'Falsification and the methodology of scientific research programmes', in I. Lakatos and A. Musgrave (eds) *Criticism and the Growth of Knowledge.* Cambridge, UK: Cambridge University Press. pp. 91–196.

Latour, B. (1993) *We Have Never Been Modern.* [Orig. 1991.] Cambridge, MA: Harvard University Press.

Latour, B. and S. Woolgar (1979) *Laboratory Life: The Social Construction of Scientific Facts.* London: Sage.

Laudan, L. (1984) *Science and Values.* Berkeley: University of California Press.

Longino, H. (2002a) *The Fate of Knowledge*. Princeton: Princeton University Press.

Longino, H. (2002b) 'Science and the common good: Reflections on Kitcher's *Science, Truth and Democracy*', *Philosophy of Science*, 69: 560–568.

Löwith, K. (1949) *Meaning in History*. Chicago: University of Chicago Press.

Lyotard, J.-F. (1983) *The Postmodern Condition*. [Orig. 1979.] Minneapolis: University of Minnesota Press.

Mach, E. (1960) *The Science of Mechanics: A Critical and Historical Account of its Development,* 6th US edn. [based on 9th German edn. of 1933 (Orig. 1883)] La Salle, IL: Open Court Press.

MacKenzie, D. (2006) *An Engine, Not a Camera: How Financial Models Shape Markets*. Cambridge, MA: MIT Press.

Mendelsohn, E. (1989) 'Robert K. Merton: The celebration and defense of science', *Science in Context*, 3: 269–299.

Proctor, R. (1991) *Value-Free Science?* Cambridge, MA: Harvard University Press.

Putnam, H. (1979) *Mind, Language and Reality*. Cambridge, UK: Cambridge University Press.

Ravetz, J. (1971) *Scientific Knowledge and Its Social Problems*. Oxford: Oxford University Press.

Reisch, G. (2005) *How the Cold War Transformed the Philosophy of Science*. Cambridge, UK: Cambridge University Press.

Roco, M. and W.S. Bainbridge (eds.) (2002) *Converging Technologies for Improving Human Performance: Nanotechnology, Biotechnology, Information Technology, and Cognitive Science*. Arlington, VA: US National Science Foundation.

Romanell, P. (1984) *John Locke and Medicine*. Buffalo, NY: Prometheus.

Rose, H. and S. Rose (1999) 'The red scientist', in B. Swann and F. Aprahamian (eds) *J.D. Bernal: A Life in Science and Politics*. London: Verso. pp. 132–159.

Ross, A., ed. (1996) *Science Wars*. Durham, NC: Duke University Press.

Rouse, J. (1987) *Knowledge and Power*. Ithaca, NY: Cornell University Press.

Schaefer, W. (ed.) (1984) *Finalization in Science*. Dordrecht: Kluwer.

Shapin, S. (1992) 'Discipline and bounding: The history and sociology of science as seen through the externalism-internalism debate', *History of Science*, 30: 333–369.

Sharrock, W. (1974) 'On owning knowledge', in R. Turner (ed.) *Ethnomethodology*. Harmondsworth, UK: Penguin. pp. 45–53.

Wers**ey, G. (1988) *The Visible College: Scientists and Socialists in the 1930s*. 2nd edn. [Orig. 1978]. London: Free Association Press.

Wersky, G. (2007) 'The Marxist critique of capitalist science: A history in three movements?', *Science as Culture*, 16: 397–461.

36

Expert Judgement

María Jiménez-Buedo and
Jesús Zamora-Bonilla

INTRODUCTION

In recent times, we have witnessed a revived interest in the question of expertise, which has traditionally been a relatively underexplored topic in all but a few philosophical and social scientific subfields. In the case of the philosophy of science, this renewal of attention is linked to the discussion around the broadening and revision of the notion of evidence and the problems that surround the consideration of expert judgement as one of its sources. Expertise has also become key to the concept of tacit knowledge and important to the debates related to the distinction between fact and value in science and in particular, in relation to social scientific knowledge.

In turn, and in the case of sociology of knowledge, the increasing importance of the study of expertise is to be explained by the realisation of the centrality of the notion to policy-making processes. The determinants of the specialist's status and the criteria on who counts as expert are necessarily at the heart of the tension between scientifically informed policy on the one hand and participatory and democratically informed collective decisions on the other. Meanwhile, careful empirical recompilations of the predictive record of publicly recognised experts have opened the debate regarding the conditions of political accountability of certified specialists.

In addition, the enhanced interest in expertise on the part of epistemologists stems from the centrality of testimony to rising approaches in social epistemology, where many of the questions of interest revolve around the conditions that make the layperson or novice justified in his or her acceptance of the expert's declarations. Finally, the developments in formal approaches to the study of expertise in economics and social epistemology testify to the growing significance of the notion.

In this chapter, we review and analyse these and kindred approaches and research programmes dealing with important social scientific or philosophical aspects as they relate to the notion of expertise. We first review a recent attempt at conceptualising the problem of choosing between contradictory expert opinions and then introduce the main current philosophical and social scientific debates regarding the role of experts with an emphasis on their role in policy making processes. The chapter ends with a brief review of formal social epistemology analyses of expertise.

THE EPISTEMOLOGY OF EXPERTISE AND THE EXPERT/EXPERT PROBLEM

Much of the emerging debate around the epistemology of expertise draws, quite naturally, on the concept and epistemology of testimony, and the discussion is thus crucially interested in the conditions that justify the novice, or the layperson, in accepting a particular expert's testimony. Alvin Goldman's position on the matter has become a crucial point of reference (2001) since it constitutes an important opening exercise in the social epistemological literature in that it seeks to establish a set of empirical criteria that can make the novice's choice to accept expert's advice a justified one.

Goldman has explicitly departed from earlier attempts in the epistemology of testimony and the question of trust since he thinks that these approaches, in their fleeing from full-fledged scepticism about testimony, end up falling into arguments that rely on what Goldman classifies as *blind* confidence in the expert's claims. Departing from the positions of Hardwig (1985) or Foley (1994), Goldman's aim is to avoid the kind of prima facie justification of testimony that these authors defend, whereby a novice cannot be *rationally justified* in trusting an expert. In particular Goldman is interested in a specific sub-problem within the array of relations between laypeople and experts, that is, the case in which the novice is confronted with two or more putative experts making conflicting claims about a given subject, or as he calls it, the expert/expert problem. As he argues, the kind of default principles about prima facie trust in testimony are necessarily at a loss when it comes to trusting conflicting propositions from different sources: in the presence of two experts claiming contending theses: in those cases, the novice simply cannot blindly trust both experts simultaneously, and so she will need to rely on certain criteria that will lead her to a choice between the two.

The kind of criteria that Goldman sets for discriminating among conflicting sources of expertise are based on the kind of secondary evidence that the novice can gather without acquiring any knowledge in the domain of expertise, that is, without him or herself becoming an expert. These criteria are:

a Arguments presented by the contending experts to support their own views and criticise their rivals' views.
b Agreement from additional putative experts on one side or other of the subject in question.
c Appraisals by 'meta-experts' of the experts' knowledge (including appraisals reflected in formal credentials earned by the experts).
d Evidence of the experts' interests and biases vis-à-vis the question at issue.
e Evidence of the experts' past records.

Source (A) relies on what Goldman labels 'indirect argumentative justification'. The author concedes that whilst a novice lacks the expert's reasons for believing a certain conclusion, the novice may still have reasons for believing that one expert has better grounds for believing her conclusion than her opponent has for hers. In other words, the novice may be justified in taking the dialectical superiority of one expert over another as evidence for superior knowledge of the domain at stake.

Source (B) stems from the weight of numbers: with the adequate provisos about the mutual independence of experts,[1] Goldman claims that the bigger the number of experts supporting a given claim, the more justified will be the novice in believing it, despite the presence of dissenting voices. Source (C) requires the same provisos as (B), but the novice has to focus on the support other experts give to a particular expert (rather than to her particular claims). This support can come in various forms; credentials provide a good example: academic degrees, professional accreditations, etc. In sum, the more support an expert receives from other experts, the more the novice should rely on her advice, contends Goldman.

Source (D) helps the novice to calibrate the experts' credibility. If comparative evidence about the experts' potential partiality is available, the novice can reasonably assign less credibility to those experts who may have a vested interest (material or otherwise) in defending one particular position. Finally, the experts' track records in a given domain constitute source (E). The novice should verify how successful each expert has been in the past and choose whoever has a better record.

In sum, Goldman claims that this list, though by no means exhaustive, provides criteria on the justification of our choice of expert, with ultimately both theoretical and practical implications. While Goldman does not go into the issue of how the criteria above should be aggregated, the basic intuition seems to point to the straightforward strategy: a novice would be justified in accepting an expert's claim if this expert scores highly in A, B, C and E and there is no evidence of him or her being biased.

TACIT KNOWLEDGE, OBJECTIVITY AND EXPERT BIAS AND PREDICTION

Goldman's criteria presuppose at least to a certain extent that experts' performance can be assessed relative to some objective standard. Yet, and as Reiss (2007) discusses in his analysis of the Boskin commission (an expert panel in charge of revising the official calculation of the US inflation rate during the 1990s), very often, there is just no objective standard against which expert judgement can be assessed. In his example, inflation must inevitably be defined in terms of the measurement procedure that a given group of experts may agree upon. In fact, it is very often the case that collectively binding expert judgement is called upon precisely, due to a lack of standardised procedures or protocols for the generation of atomised, personal judgement. This in turn connects with a central tenet around the notion of expertise, the idea of the expert as one possessing a kind of information that is not easily transferred, nor verified, and that links expertise

to the notion of *tacit knowledge*. The classic examples ranging in exoticness (think of the expert that can tell the difference between the copy and an original painting, the experienced doctor that can diagnose by reading signals in an X-ray plate that would escape other medics, or the wine connoisseur), the idea is that an essential component of expertise lies in the fact that expert knowledge is difficult to transfer or to systematise in ways that can de-link it from the expert individual possessing it.[2] This sets up the scene for the expert's privileged status, but also for its curse: the specialist in this sense has almost monopolistic access to a parcel of knowledge yet he also lacks the means of standard proof against the doubts of the skeptic.

Whether or not, and under which conditions expert advice can be rendered objective and by which means it may be so rendered is part of the subject of Theodore Porter's *Trust in Numbers* (1996). Porter's main thesis is that contrary to the commonly held view, the developments towards quantitative and standardised measures in the modern state and the social science are, rather than a spin-off from similar processes in the natural sciences, a reaction of some professional groups that saw how this quantification could appease external social demands for accountability that would otherwise be in the way of securing these groups' positioning within the state's decision-making apparatus (Hagendijk, 1999). Porter has depicted this process of quantification of public life as implying the replacement of human judgement (including thus some types of expert judgement) with systematic rules, a point that has been found to be insufficiently nuanced, since quantified science also implies many sorts of subtle expert judgement (see Levy, 2001).

Through various case studies centred in Britain, France and the United States during the nineteenth and twentieth centuries, Porter illustrates how some groups of professionals – actuaries, accountants, civil engineers and scientists – had to resort to the quantification and standardisation of the rules and calculations of their procedures as a way to increase their credibility in the eyes of the state and the general public. Against the background of an increasing de-personalisation of the relations between the expert professional and its client, a general trust in the elite was no longer sufficient to avert the spectre of bias and personal preference in the eyes of an emerging public that was then beginning to demand new styles of (at least formally) democratic governance, and so the quantification of expertise filled this gap. In Porter's interpretation, the drive to substitute personal judgement by quantitative rules must be decoded as a sign of weakness and exposure on the part of the professional guilds of experts, rather than as a sign of force: those who cannot make their own expert claims suffice as a warrant, must then resort to impersonal quantitative measures in an appeal to scientific knowledge based on 'mechanical objectivity'. In sum, the impetus behind the quantification of expertise can and must be explained politically: expert decisions made by appeal to numbers and mechanical procedures may or may not be more correct than those made on the basis of intuition or tacit knowledge, but they are publicly acceptable in virtue of *at least* having the appearance of objectivity.

Regarding the systematic study of expert judgement and advice in the social sciences, it is social psychologists and decision-making theorists who have devoted themselves to the revising of expert's output seemingly most prone to objectification and quantification, that is, their issuing of predictions. In this kind of literature, experts' predictive output and expert's cognitive processes in arriving at that output are normally contrasted with those of novices, those of statistical models and also, those of uninformed, stochastically produced guesses.

Although the psychological literature that pioneered the systematic study of expert performance started out analysing the behaviour and cognitive processes of individuals that excelled in their fields (as in, for example

De Groot's early studies of chess masters' cognition (Ericsson and Lehman, 1996)), in a majority of the works in social psychology and decision theory experts are defined just by their mere professional status, or all those that have the qualifications and/or the experience, in their respective field, to be considered an authority. Encompassing reviews across many different fields like, medical diagnosis, criminal recidivism, incidence of violence or financial investment, tend to point in the same direction: experts' predictive record is no better than that of superficially trained novices and it tends to be worse than those of simple statistical models in virtually all domains.

Camerer and Johnson (1991) have summarised the characteristics of the experts' predictive processes that can explain their poor performance relative to simple statistical models and lightly trained novices. Compared with novices or laypeople, experts seem to use their superior background knowledge in ways that end up being detrimental to the quality of their predictions: they search for less information in view of a problem relative to laypeople and they are more likely to display a contingent rather than systematic pattern in their search for evidence to corroborate their hypotheses.[3]

Moreover, experts have been found to use configural rules (where a decision about, say, a diagnosis is made on the basis of a certain protocol in which the impact of one variable depends on the values of other variables, so for example: 'diagnose Z if the patient has symptoms X *and* Y *or* if levels of variable U are below a critical threshold'). Whereas the use of configural rules is appealing (they are easy to use and often provide plausible causal narratives), they often are based on illusory correlations and frequently lead to overgeneralisations. Moreover, the evidence suggests that confirmation biases will often cause experts to refine configural rules rather than discard them, even in the presence of prompt and systematic feedback clearly suggesting that the rules are wrong (Kahneman and Tversky, 1973).

THE PREDICTIVE PERFORMANCE OF SOCIAL SCIENTIFIC EXPERTS

Philip Tetlock's work on expert political judgement is the most encompassing, systematic attempt to date to document the predictive capacities of professional specialists in the social sciences, in particular in the fields of international politics and political economy. Tetlock, a political psychologist previously interested in the role of cognitive biases in political thinking, has been constructing along a number of years, roughly from the end of the 1980s to the mid 1990s, a series of databases recording the answers of a stable group of experts followed through time. The experts were asked to make predictions on the potential developments of standard political variables like the relative success of certain political parties, or economic variables such as government spending and interest rates. In addition, he also demanded experts to make predictions on variables coinvolved in significant historical events such as potential developments regarding the outbreak of wars, or the evolution of the European Union.

Tetlock (2005) measures the predictive performance of experts on two dimensions that are often conjectured to stand in a trade-off relationship. *Calibration* refers to the degree to which a forecaster's assignment of probabilities to an event actually matches the actual frequency with which the event takes place (so that an expert shows a high calibration score if outcomes assigned a 50 per cent likelihood happen more or less 50 per cent of the time). *Discrimination* instead refers to the ability of forecasters to do better than the strategy that would simply predict the base rate probability of an event (so an expert gets a high discrimination score when she assigns probabilities close to one to events that do end up happening and probabilities close to zero to events that do not take place).

According to Tetlock's analysis, political and economic experts tend to do better on both of these dimensions than undergraduate students, but they do not outperform what the author classifies as 'dilettantes', that is, people who regularly consult the mildly specialised media, reading sources such as the *New York Times* or *The Economist*. On the discrimination score both experts and dilettantes outperform the random-guessing strategy, but both of these groups do a poorer predictive job in their calibration of probabilities than a mere random assignment. In congruence with previous accounts of predictive success in the social and medical sciences, simple statistical models seem to do better than experts on all accounts. These results would seem to give us reasons to side with what the author has depicted as 'the radical sceptic view' regarding prediction, embodied by either those who think the world is too complex to be guessed out, or by those who consider that our limited epistemic capacities as humans make this guessing impossible.

Tetlock's best defence against this radical sceptic view, that he opposes, lies in the fact that even though the results of expert forecasters seem indeed rather poor, there appear to be systematic differences between the performances of experts dependent on their cognitive styles of reasoning. He gathers the experts' styles of reasoning into two groups, resonating of the categories employed by a classic Isaiah Berlin essay, that is, the hedgehog and the fox. Hedgehogs, defined as those experts/thinkers who view the world through the lens of a single defining idea, seem on average to be outperformed in their predictive capacities by foxes, defined by the miscellaneous sources of their beliefs. Hedgehogs know one big theory, while foxes draw their inferences from many eclectic models. Foxes predict better, but in turn, hedgehogs seem to be valued by demanders of expertise because of their other capacities, like the ability to come up with innovative prognoses departing from common knowledge. In this sense, both types of experts, foxes and hedgehogs, often used in combination, have a place in the media and in the forecasting business in general. Surprisingly enough, though, Tetlock also reports the finding that the more well known and sought after an expert is, the worse his or her predictions tend to be.

Part of the explanation for this can be sought in a factor underlined by Angner (2006):[4] overconfident subjects (i.e. agents who believe that they have a predictive success rate higher than their real one) will naturally self-select themselves into advisory posts more often than well calibrated subjects, precisely, because they will tend to overestimate their predictive capacities, and so it could well be that the more overconfident amongst these experts tend also to be the louder ones. In his work, Erik Angner reports an extensive literature documenting the phenomenon of overconfidence in prediction, that is, the extent to which the measure of confidence in one's predictions is higher than one's success rate.

A wide psychological and decision-making research tradition experimentally illustrates persistent overconfidence in judgement, whether subjects are students and laypeople, doctors, market analysts or experts in a wide range of topics. These laboratory studies also show an interesting list of related phenomena, like for example, that overconfidence seems to increase with the difficulty of the judgement task, with the motivation or incentives attached to getting an accurate judgement or with the confidence of the subjects, that is, the higher the confidence of a subject in his or her judgement, the higher the probability this confidence is ungranted.

In sum, this kind of work, drawing on previous literature on decision making and cognitive biases (Kahneman et al., 1982) provides reasons why both lay people and experts do not revise their predictions in a way that makes them realise the systematicity of their overconfidence in order to improve their calibration scores and illustrates the well known phenomena of hindsight and confirmation biases and the self-interested use of suspect counterfactuals. Experts in these and related fields tend therefore to explain their own correct predictions as a result of their deep understanding of underlying processes yet, they hardly ever explicate their predictive fiascos as a result of their ignorance.[5]

In view of this dismal picture of the predictive performance of economic and political specialists, one cannot but agree to the fact that experts (even those that are requested as forecasters) are very often called upon for reasons other than their predictive capabilities. Yet, in the relevant literature, the reaction to the expert's bad record often results in a normatively driven plea for the increase in accountability of experts (whether media experts or those working for private and public organisations), including the need to collectively sanction those experts giving ambiguous or vague predictions that can be ex post facto accommodated with almost any kind of evidence. This recommendation, for all its desirability, strikes us as hardly implementable. As Angner's case study itself shows, reputed western economists were not called upon by the Russian government in the 1990s so that they could give predictions on the rate at which the Russian GDP would first fall and then recover as a result of shock therapy. For all the vagueness with which these experts would formulate their predictions (saying, for example, that gross domestic product would initially fall by *at least* 20 per cent), a more precise forecast could not either save nor condemn them as advisors, for their function as experts was not mainly that of issuing predictions, but to provide general guidance in an unprecedented process with mostly unknown outcomes. Prediction is indeed a sound place from which to start assessing experts' performance, but it is by no means the only relevant aspect of expertise, and only very arguably, the most important one. As historical political economy shows, and as we will see in the next section, experts are often most relevant to policy outcomes when uncertainty sets in. Their influence and power turns out to be amplified in times of crises, where the windows of opportunity for change in policy are most open. It is during turbulent and unpredictable times that politicians or demanders of expertise in general seek the guidance from experts that may give advice beyond routinely-defined formulae.

EXPERTS AND POLICY CHANGE

Contemporary social science analysis of say, policy making processes (an obvious field in which the role of expert advisors could be considered, at least a priori, crucially important) has not traditionally displayed a great deal of interest on the role of experts in these social or political outcomes. The fact is that current political and social science is normally more concerned with variables amenable to systematic scrutiny, and expertise and its influence on policy outcomes does not bring itself easily to methodical analysis. For this reason, in the field of comparative politics and international political economy, the role of experts in policy outcomes has been studied only indirectly, insofar as it is mediated by the ideas that experts embody or the institutions and government positions that those experts occupy. The work of Peter Hall (1989) on the impact of Keynesian ideas in post-World War II Western economies constitutes a particularly relevant example of ideational approaches in which experts played the mere role of carriers of policy advice and policy innovation.[6,7]

Though close to ideational approaches in scope and topics of interest, an exception in the field of international political economy, in the sense of having dealt more directly with the role and influence of experts on policy outcomes is to be found on the work of Peter Haas and those authors who have dwelled upon the notion of the *epistemic communities* and their role on policy making processes (Haas, 1992; Adler and Haas, 1992). An epistemic community in this sense is 'a network of professionals with recognised expertise and competence in a particular domain and an authoritative claim to policy-relevant knowledge within that domain or issue-area' (Haas, 1992: 3).

Through the historical analysis of several case-studies, like those linked to the existence of multilateral agreements on a progressive banning on the use of chlorofluorocarbon gases in the late 1980s, the managing of nuclear arms deployment or banking regulation agreements, the research programme linked to the concept of epistemic communities claims that the existence of networks of experts sharing common ideas and normative stands can have an independent influence on policy outcomes and thus can help explain several policy outcomes in a comparison between countries where epistemic communities were effective and those where not. Proponents of the epistemic community approach have cautiously distinguished these epistemic communities from other potentially influencing collectives like interest groups, social movements or professional associations including those formed by legislators or bureaucrats by arguing that, unlike other collectives, it can be uncontroversially said of epistemic communities that they share not only a set of common beliefs about the workings of a given policy domain (e.g. what Haas calls 'causal beliefs') but also a common set of 'principled beliefs', that is, the same normative stand vis-à-vis a particular issue, and a set of common criteria for evaluating the validity of evidence in the domain of their expertise. In this vein, Keynesian economists and their influence in the building of western welfare states would constitute a classical example of what proponents of this line of research have in mind.

The main point of this research programme would be that of affirming that in times of crises or political situations in which uncertainty over outcomes is great, the existence of a close-knit group of experts can crucially shape policy outcomes not only through their technical advice, but also by helping to define the interests of policy makers or politicians, that is, the ultimate decision-making actors. The whole project linked both to the epistemic communities research programme and to ideational approaches is that of attacking the idea that all policy outcomes are the mere result of system-level variables and that political results can be guessed out from a close look at pre-determined, unambiguously defined material interests of the actors involved. In this sense, these approaches to studying the role of experts in the determination of political outcomes tend to oppose experts and their views to the concept of structural power and material interests and insist on the role that experts can have in the shaping or realisation of those interests. Moreover, these analyses (together with more recent work by, for example, Blyth, 2002 and Lindvall, 2006, 2009), have proven useful in underlining the centrality of *uncertainty* (as related to moments of institutional crises) to the causal impact on policy outcome of 'expert ideas'. In this way, and according to Blyth, expert ideas shape the way in which crucial policy actors interpret these institutional crises and help in the building of new coalitions of interests and in the easing of collective action problems.

Critics of these approaches have hinted that this kind of research posits, in the end, more questions than it answers: Haas explains that the policy ideas advocated by members of an epistemic community become influential when decision makers solicit their information and delegate responsibility to them, however, as, for example, Yee points out (1996) acknowledging that such things as epistemic communities exist and that they do play a role in the policy-making processes leaves unanswered the question on why some epistemic communities gain influence over others, and which characteristics of those communities and of the ideas they defend make them more influential. In this respect, we can hypothesise whether some criteria along the lines of Goldman's principles or Tetlock's cognitive styles may have a role in determining which epistemic communities become influential, though in sweeping process of institutional crises and change, many other things may matter rather more. In any case, experts composing Haas' influential epistemic communities are not, unlike Goldman's experts, expected to be neutral, and are instead sought and valued, precisely, for their militancy and political compromise around certain topics.

Furthermore, Hall, Haas and Blyth's emphasis in the *appeasing* dimension of expertise in times of uncertainty provides a sharp contrast with the traditional stress on the predictive functions of experts, that after all can be seen as leaving us puzzling over the fact that experts are still sought even when they fail to provide accurate prognoses. In line with Porter's theses, the underlying values and epistemic norms embedded in the experts' practices are possibly more important in the public's acceptance of their influence.

RECENT SOCIOLOGICAL APPROACHES: STUDIES OF EXPERTISE AND EXPERIENCE

In recent years, Harry Collins, an essential contributor to the Sociology of Scientific Knowledge and father of the 'empirical programme of relativism', together with his co-author Robert Evans, has revived the debate around the sociology of expertise. Their efforts have given rise to a new research programme that they have suggested be called Studies of Expertise and Experience (SEE) (Collins and Evans, 2007). Their starting point comes from their perception that there is the need to set off a third wave of Science Studies that could serve as a corrective to the relativist excesses of its recent past. A first wave, tainted by positivism, in which the privileged social and epistemological status of science made the question of the determinants of expertise redundant, was followed by a second one, in which under the influence of an unrestrained social constructivism, Science Studies made both implicit and explicit calls for the reform of science and scientific institutions that would be participatory and inclusive of the whole of the citizenry. This, according to Collins and Evans, led to a watering down of the role of the expert, and of the notion itself, via for example, the coining of terms like the 'lay expert' and other such theoretical attempts normatively inspired by the need to democratise science.

Their project can thus be understood as a corrective to several research programmes in the SST literature emerging during the

1990s. These research programmes described the evolution of Science and Technology Systems in the richest nations as driven by a rise in the demands for greater accountability of the scientists towards the citizenry. With important parallels in their aims and scope, these approaches have helped disseminate the idea of a profound transformation of science towards a greater permeability for societal demands and preferences. This transformation has been referred to as 'Mode 2 of scientific production', or 'post-normal science', in contrast to a classic period of Science dominated by the interests and preferences of scientists themselves (Gibbons et al., 1994; Functovicz and Ravetz, 1993; Nowotny et al., 2001, 2003). Though the main aim of these contributions was descriptive, these approaches share, among other things, a strong normative leaning towards greater participation from the citizen in the science and technology policy-making processes. Subsequent related theoretical developments further pressing for more citizen participation in science managed to reach the policy-making sphere and have now permeated the parlance of policy makers and official documents in science policy organs (Jasanoff, 2003).

Collins and Evans see these developments, stemming from a general call towards the democratisation of expertise, as suffering from two problems, one epistemological, and one of a pragmatic, technical, nature. The first of these problems comes from viewing, as it has been traditional of the sociological constructivist SST literature, expertise as a merely relational and attributional phenonenon, whereby the determination of who is an expert is entirely defined socially. For Collins and Evans, there is then little or no room to assess normatively, and ex-ante, what exactly constitutes optimal expertise. That is, there is no way to discriminate among better or worse types of expertise or to discriminate among alternative procedures for arriving at demanding or choosing amongst competing pieces of expert advice. The second, technical problem comes directly from this one: if expertise is attributional and relational only,

and existing prescriptive analyses advocate for an extension of the concept to include the citizens at large, collective decision making in which universal inclusion of all those concerned is carried out becomes unfeasible, unless citizen participation is to be retained at a very shallow, even superficial level.

For these reasons Collins and Evans want to put a bridle on the constructivist view of expertise by affirming that though the status of expertise is attributed and relational, expertise is also a *real* capacity. For the authors, expertise is acquired through experience and comes as a result of successful socialisation within a relevant community linked to a particular domain of knowledge, be this scientific or technical. Given this emphasis on the importance of experience in the acquiring of expertise their notion of the expert relies heavily on the idea of tacit knowledge (Evans, 2008). Expertise is thus a real capacity that is gradually acquired through contact with the relevant community and that is exerted and deployed by displaying the competence to interact, communicate and possibly contribute to the knowledge of that community: becoming an expert or acquiring expertise is a gradual process that depends on the acquisition of knowledge that is then sanctioned within a network of actors.

According to the proponents of SEE, the classifying of types of experts is the central tenet to any project aimed at understanding the phenomenon of expertise and can be crucial in contributing to setting the adequate boundaries to citizens' participation in science policy. To this end, they propose what they call a Periodic Table of Expertise, in which they present an exhaustive, ordered categorisation of expert knowledge. Though their classificatory attempts have evolved from their first works to the more recent ones, partly as a result of the theoretical and empirical contributions of other scholars sympathetic to the approach, the core of their classification has remained the same.

The basic tenet in their classification is the distinction between interactional expertise and contributory expertise. In this way, and in continuity with some of Collins' previous projects, Collins and Evans emphasise that having the skills and aptitudes to communicate scientific knowledge and interact with scientists does not imply having the capacity to generate this very knowledge, though both sets of aptitudes are relevant and important. The other, less central types of expertise coined by Collins and Evans ('ubiquitous' and 'referred' or *meta-expertise*) complete the picture. We briefly review their classification in turn.

According to Collins and Evans's classification, *ubiquitous expertise* is embodied in those skills shared by all members of a community, such as a normal mastering of a natural language. Arguably, the authors contend that though counterintuitive, this type of knowledge needs to be included in their 'periodic table' because it is the kind of ability that serves as a prerequisite for all the other types of expertise. This is so because it allows for the socialisation of an individual in the relevant community in which expertise is either acquired or displayed.

More central to their classification is the distinction between interactional and contributory expertise. *Interactional expertise* is the kind of ability displayed by which an agent that can engage in active conversation with a specialist in given field without displaying the kind of formal knowledge that would allow him or her to contribute substantively to the field. The example that Collins and Evans tend to favour in this respect is that of a sociologist who immerses in a laboratory long enough to understand the practices and the object of the scientists that she studies (and is thus capable of discussing capable to discuss intricate and technical questions on the matter), but is nevertheless unable to contribute with her knowledge to the laboratory activity. In contrast, *contributory expertise* would be the kind of experience that allows a person to contribute to a given body of knowledge.

Finally, *referred expertise* is the kind of expertise that is created in one field and then referred to, or transferred into another one, and it is typical of the managers of large scientific projects, where typically one manager moves from one project to the next applying knowledge acquired in yet another field. Referred expertise is one type, if the most important one, among what Collins and Evans define as *meta-expertise*: the capacity to judge on the expertises of others without possessing their knowledge.

SEE has received wide attention and Collins and Evans's classification of types of expertise has now been applied to a wide array of phenomena. To name just a few examples: the analysis of the type of expertise that the South African president relied upon in order to decide whether antiretrovirals destined to treat HIV mothers were to be state-financed, the studies on the interaction of the different expertises belonging to fishermen and scientists in their joint attempts to find solutions to the issue of collateral damages to dolphins whilst fishing tuna, or the examination of the expertise pertaining to those translators occupied with helping technological transfer from Japan to Brazil in the steel-making sector (Collins, 2007).

In part, this very broad variety of subjects may be symptomatic of the problems behind the notion of expertise embedded in their periodic table. Other than the more conceptually suspect types (like the almost oxymoronic notion of *ubiquitous expertise*), the overall authors' insistence on putting the emphasis on the aspects of expertise that are linked to experience and knowledge to the detriment of the relational, attributional aspects of the phenomenon seem to end up being excessive. In this way, Collins and Evans' efforts to depart from constructionist theses lead them up to a noxious stretching of the concept of expertise to the point where it becomes indistinguishable from the notion of knowledge.

Collins and Evans thus seem to fall into a unnecessary opposition between the constructed and the real: contra what they suggest, underlining the social character of expertise or even asserting the constitutively social character of expertise (Fuller, 2006), does not imply having to forego the search for criteria that discriminate between good and bad expertise.

One can willingly grant Collins and Evans that the constructivist leaning of much sociological work on expertise has often led to conclusions suggesting that there were no reasons to deny expert status to snake oil salesmen or TV evangelists, (Mieg, 2001) provokingly quotes several of those examples. Some of the sociological analyses of expertise have indeed assumed that once we sustain that expertise is mainly a social role, a minimum criterion for assessing whether a given individual is an expert is the existence of a constituency that perceives him or her as an expert, or put in other words, that attributes to him or her an expert status. This however, does not necessarily imply that nothing can be said either about the empirical conditions under which that attribution is made or about the criteria of adequateness of the ascription of the role of expert.

In the remainder of this chapter, we analyse recent contributions to the literature on the economics of information and the problem of judgement aggregation that can provide answers to the question around the adequacy and optimality of relying on expert judgement and advice.

FORMAL APPROACHES TO MODELLING EXPERTISE

As we have seen, expertise understood as a social phenomenon and as a relevant factor in the political process, has been an important object of study in the social sciences (though perhaps not as centrally as could be expected). In this section we shall turn to formal, rational-choice-based approaches in the social sciences, in order to look for what they can contribute to our understanding of expertise as a social epistemic phenomenon. We shall refer a couple of those approaches: economics of information and judgement aggregation, of which we shall limit ourselves to give a very concise description of

the main questions that can be illuminated with their help.

Information economics

Traditional economic theories were based on the assumption of 'perfect knowledge', that is, it was assumed that the economic agents (e.g. demanders and suppliers of an economic good) had all the information that was relevant and needed for the problem situation they were facing, and perhaps more importantly, these theories assumed that the distribution of that information was *symmetric*, in the sense of equally shared by all the agents. Information economics started its development in the 1970s mainly as an attempt to understand the influence that the non-fulfilment of this latter assumption had on the equilibrium the agents' interactions led to. So, for example George Akerlof's epoch making paper on 'The market for lemons' (1970) discussed how the different distribution of knowledge between sellers and buyers about the quality of used goods may conduce to market prices that do not reflect real differences in quality, or can even push some types of goods out of the market. More relevant to the question of expertise was Michael Spence's 1973 paper on 'Job market signalling': workers know usually much better how productive they are than do their potential employers, and so there in an incentive for the former to 'signal' their real productivity; this last situation refers, obviously, to all possible types of 'workers' and of 'employers': the former might be, for example, a medical doctor, a macro economist, or a top executive, and the latter a patient, a politician, or a group of stockholders, respectively, looking for the former's advice. The problem consists, then, for the 'workers' in finding out how to make the 'employers' aware of the quality of the products they are able to 'sell', or, at least, of the differences between the quality of competing 'workers'.

The economics of information can be considered as an attempt to respond to the 'new' mathematical development of economics that had been put in the 1940s by Friedrich Hayek, who, in his paper 'The use of knowledge in society', wrote:

> What is the problem we wish to solve when we try to construct a rational economic order? (...) If we possess all the relevant information, if we can start out from a given system of preferences, and if we command complete knowledge of available means, the problem which remains is purely one of logic (...) This, however, is emphatically not the economic problem which society faces. (...) The reason for this is that the "data" from which the economic calculus starts are never for the whole society "given" to a single mind which could work out the implications and can never be so given. The economic problem of society (...), to put it briefly, is a problem of the utilization of knowledge which is not given to anyone in its totality. (Hayek, 1945: 219–220)

Without, of course, trying to solve this critical 'informational problem of society', scholars in the new field of information economics have tried to take advantage of the sophisticated mathematical tools of game theory which allow them to model the effects in the interaction between actors characterised by differences in the information they possess. These tools have allowed these scholars to undertake the particular problems that these informational asymmetries can generate. One of the essential instruments with which this has been done is known as the *principal-agent model*. The basic version of this model represents an individual or a group, the 'principals', who is or are unable to perform a certain task as efficiently as other individuals or groups, the 'agents', so that the former 'hires' the latter to carry out the job; the agents, however, are assumed to be *not directly* interested in the fulfilment of the task, that is, they may put too little effort on it, or at least, less effort than what the principal would consider appropriate. The literature distinguishes between 'signalling models' (in which the contract is proposed by the agent) and 'screening models' (in which it is proposed by the principal). The 'principal-agent *problem*', consists, then, in determining a *contract*, or an incentive scheme, that

both parts are interested in signing, and that warrants to the principal that the agent will perform her task in a satisfactory way. This line of research has led to the development of a successful branch of game theory, known as *mechanism design*, which can be considered the reverse of classical game theory: whereas in the latter the problem was to predict the choices made by the players of a game whose rules were given, the former can be seen as the attempt to design a game (i.e., a set of formal rules) that leads players to choose the outcome that 'we' (which usually personalises the principal) desire. Two of the main concepts developed by this research line are those of 'pooling equilibrium' and 'separating equilibrium'. The former exists when the contract (or the situation) is not capable of distinguishing (or 'separating') the different agents according to their quality; efficient contracts (or institutional rules, be they consciously designed or 'evolved') are, hence, those that lead to a separating equilibrium (see Gerardi and Yariv, 2008: esp 193).

Another example of the application of economics of information to the peculiarities of expertise, in particular *scientific* expertise, is presented by Zamora Bonilla (2006). The article describes the game between the reader of a scientific paper (in this case, the 'principal') and its author (the 'agent'), who after coming up with a certain scientific result based on an experiment or observation faces the choice between several different ways of describing these results; in the model, there is a trade off between the interest or relevance of the experiment, according to the chosen interpretation, and the degree of empirical support of that interpretation. The essential aspects of this situation are two: first, naked data must be given some interpretation without which they are scientifically useless, but they do not compel us by themselves to a particular one; the talent of a good scientist is, in large part, that of devising *interesting* interpretations. Second, the author of the paper and the reader may have different *preferences* about what is the 'best' interpretation of the data; so, which one will be finally proposed is necessarily the result of a kind of negotiation between both agents. Zamora Bonilla's paper shows that, in the absence of institutions constraining the choice made by the author, the latter will tend to propose the most interesting possible interpretation, at the cost of having the minimal degree of empirical support which is compatible with the reader accepting the result, a choice which is too far from the optimal combination of relevance and support according to the reader's preferences. This justifies the creation of institutions that force authors to propose interpretations of their results more consistent with the interests of the 'principal', that is, of those that are going to *use* those results.[8]

Lastly, an important formal result in mechanism-design theory is known as the 'revelation principle', which states that, for every Nash equilibrium of a game with asymmetric information, there exists some mechanism leading to the same result and in which the dominant strategy for the players is to truthfully reveal the information they have (Dasgupta et al., 1979); of course, this does not entail that finding out the appropriate revelation mechanism is a trivial task. Through the lens of mechanism design and of the revelation principle, the economics of information merged with another branch of formal economics: social choice, the study of the formal principles limiting the aggregation of individual preferences and the implementability of collective decisions. This leads us to the second formal approach to expertise we shall present in this section.

Judgement aggregation

As we have already seen, an important problem in the analysis of expert opinion emerges when the views of different experts are at odds with each other (or what Goldman has called the expert/expert problem). The problem for the layperson, or the 'principal', can be not only to identify who the experts are, but to 'translate' the diversity of opinions

that they express into a single recommendation of action or statement of facts. This is obviously also a problem for collective bodies composed by several experts (or, for that matter, of experts and non-experts), who want to communicate a single, coherent piece of information as the result of their deliberations. Economic theory had made an extensive analysis of the problems of aggregation of preferences, since the seminal work by Kenneth Arrow in the mid-twentieth century, a work that led to the constitution of the field of social choice theory. Perhaps the most important result within this field was the demonstration that, in most cases, there is no consistent way of constructing something like 'the preferences of a group' out of the preferences of its individual members, or at least, that it is not possible that this construction satisfies simultaneously several conditions that are, each of them, independently desirable; this is the well known 'Arrow impossibility theorem' (Arrow, 1951). This constitutes in itself, of course, a problem for decision making in groups of experts; but when what is to be aggregated are not preferences, but *judgements*, there is still an additional complication: we not only want that the judgements of the group are consistent in the sense which we say that somebody's *preferences* are 'consistent' (i.e. that they are, at least, transitive), but we would like as well that they can be arranged in the form of an *argument* (i.e. that those judgements are consistent with the rules of logic). This corresponds with what Philip Pettit has called the requisite of *contestability*: collective agents, in order to be recognisable as agents, have to act in a 'contestable' way, that is, it must be possible for the individuals interacting with the collective agent (not only *within* it) to do this interaction by means of a series of arguments, through something having the nature of a 'conversation' or a 'deliberation' (Pettit, 2001). In practice, this means that, when a collective body presents a certain proposition or propositions as the result of putting together the informed opinions of its members (say, its 'conclusions'), it must be capable of presenting as well a *justification* of these propositions, that is, some argument having as premises other sentences that the collective body also accepts, and leading logically to the group's conclusions.

The problem is that there is no way in which this *desideratum* can be systematically satisfied, that is, there is no way of aggregating the opinions of each member of the group (which are assumed to be logically coherent), in such a way that the 'collective opinions' are *necessarily* coherent. As first proved by List and Petit (2002), if a group has more than two members, there is no algorithm for aggregating consistent individual opinions that leads necessarily to consistent collective judgements and satisfies also the following reasonable conditions: first, the algorithm must be applicable to any possible profiles of individual judgements; second, it must not give different weights to different individuals; and third, the same algorithm must be applied to every proposition. The practical consequences of such an impossibility theorem are easily understood by reference to what is known as the 'discursive dilemma' (Kornhauser and Sager, 1986): imagine that there is a committee of three editors of a mathematical journal, deciding whether to accept a paper; this paper contains a 'proof' of a theorem, derived from a set of premises; each member of the committee agrees that the theorem is valid (the committee's conclusion: *T*, or not *T*) if and only if those premises are true (*P*) and the deduction is correct (*D*). The Table 36.1 gives, in each row, the opinion of each editor about the truth value of each of these three propositions, while

Table 36.1 An example of collective judgement

	P	D	T
x	yes	yes	yes
y	yes	no	no
z	no	yes	no
K	yes	yes	no

K represents the 'collective opinion' of the editorial board, as the result of merely applying majority voting over the opinions of the board's members.

As it is clear from this example, each editor has a *consistent* opinion, that is, she can justify her decision of accepting or rejecting the paper on the basis of her opinions about the validity of the premises and the deduction process. But what about the *board's* judgement?: the conclusion seems to be that the board will reject the paper 'because' it thinks that *both* the premises and the deductions are right! Petit and List suggest that this leaves two fundamental alternatives regarding the constitution of collective judgements: either groups are concentrated in voting the conclusions (i.e. the theses they are basically discussing), and do not try to offer a consistent justification of the collective judgement; or they concentrate in voting first the premises (i.e. the propositions from which the truth of the conclusions might be inferred), and, instead of voting the conclusion, they simply 'let logic decide' (i.e. they collectively accept the logical conclusions that happen to follow from the premises they have agreed about). Both procedures have severe shortcomings, however: the conclusion-based procedure makes the group judgement non-contestable, whereas the premise-based procedure respects this principle, but it often leads most of the members of the group to accept a conclusion they do not agree with. A possible way to escape this dilemma is by taking into consideration the aggregation mechanism that would be preferred by the members of the group *themselves*. This strategy, however, will not solve all the possible problems (for some of these problems will be more important for the group members than others), and therefore an account of the *practical* consequences of the adoption of each algorithm over others is needed (Zamora Bonilla, 2007). Of course, this also entails that there is not an exclusively formal solution to this problem, given that the preferability of an aggregation mechanism will depend on the peculiarities of each group. So, the aggregation mechanism chosen by the members of the group (and on behalf of the 'principal', for whom the group is serving as an 'agent') should be understood as a kind of 'constitution', or at least as part of the 'epistemic constitution' according to which the group regulates the production of 'knowledge'. An important aspect of this constitution, particularly when chosen by the members of the group themselves, is that it must not be understood as producing a kind of 'knowledge' which is *epistemically better* than the opinions expressed by the individual members. After all, the aggregation of judgements is supposed to be made *after* all relevant deliberation has taken place: if a member of the group were to change her opinion after observing the result of the aggregation procedure, then we could say that it should have been this *new* individual opinion (rather than the old one), that should have been taken into account as input into the aggregation mechanism. So, as long as differences of opinion remain after all deliberation and aggregation has taken place, the members of the group *will not think* that the group judgement represents the *truth* about the matter (since almost all members will disagree with the collective judgement in at least some aspects). They nevertheless, will agree with the fact that group expresses the resulting proposition as the group's judgement.[9] From this point of view, judgement aggregation must not be seen, hence, as a way of producing a kind of knowledge which is better than individual opinions, but as a way in which individuals may still live together in spite of their epistemic diversity.

CONCLUSION: EXPERTISE AND THE SOCIAL SCIENCES

In recent years, and partly as a by-product of a collective search for criteria that can tell us what is the optimal degree of citizen engagement in public policy and collective decisions, we have witnessed a revitalisation of the interest in the phenomenon of expertise.

In this chapter we have reviewed and analysed some approaches and research programmes dealing with important social scientific or philosophical aspects as they relate to the notion of expertise. In view of a proximal foreseeable increase in the number of works devoted to the topic of expert judgement in the philosophy of the social sciences and related fields, our aim throughout this piece is to contribute to the discussion on the conditions for a viable research agenda devoted to the study of expertise and equally, conditions for its failure or for interest in it becoming a mere short-lived fad.

It is possible that after years of a certain dominance of some constructivist currents in the study of expertise and expert advice it may have become pertinent to remind ourselves of the importance of taking into account the concrete and real capacities of experts and to study from a normative point of view the suitability of certain practices regarding the social role of the specialist. It is important, however, to not forget that for the social scientist and the philosopher of the social sciences the crucial aspect regarding expertise still lies in its attributional character, that is, the fact that some agents (collectively or individually) attribute epistemic authority to other agents, either rationally, or driven by social considerations that make the decision to ascribe expertise a suboptimal one. Otherwise, we risk revisiting, under the rubric of expertise, a series of epistemological debates that have been long sustained about the various aspects of knowledge; be this tacit, explicit, institutionally recognised as scientific or traditionally dismissed by the scientific establishment.

NOTES

1 For a thorough examination and critique of Goldman's assumptions regarding independence, see Coady (2006).

2 Bechmann and Hronszky refer to the distinction tacit/explicit distinction as experiential versus codified knowledge (2003).

3 A more recent tradition also documents problems in the experts' dealing with probabilities in their diagnostic inferences (Hoffrage and Gigerenzer, 2004).

4 Angner offers an in-depth case study based on the experience of Anders Aslund, a reputed Swedish economist who offered advice to the Russian government in the years between 1991 and 1994. Aslund, who also stood out in the media as a prominent public figure in support for his ideas, was a firm defender of the convenience of 'shock therapy' for countries in the area of influence of the ex-USSR, or the rapid deregulation of the existing economic and productive institutions in order to transform the country into a market-based economy.

5 A reason why they may not be held accountable by their potential public is provided by Posner (2003), according to whom the typical consumer of the public intellectual's output is not necessarily in search for 'information', but rather, for confirmation of their own political prejudices.

6 See also Weir and Skocpol (1985).

7 Blyth has more recently addressed the more problematic aspects of traditional ideational approaches, in particular, with respect to the conceptual distinction between ideas and interests and between ideas and institutions (2002). Lindvall (2006, 2009) has recently coined the term 'expert ideas' to refer to 'shared beliefs about cause-and-effect relationships, developed and disseminated by actors who are widely recognised as having special knowledge about a certain policy's target area'. Some of their theses are spelled out further in the section.

8 See Zamora Bonilla (forthcoming) for a survey of other contributions to this 'economics of scientific knowledge'.

9 Some models, in particular those inspired by Lehrer and Wagner (1981), lead necessarily to the group forming a consensus, in a similar way as in Bayesian game theory it is assumed that in the long run all agents' subjective probability functions will converge. See Bradley (2007) for a comparison of these two approaches.

REFERENCES

Adler, E. and P. M. Haas (1992) 'Conclusion: Epistemic communities, world order, and the creation of a reflective research program', *International Organization*, 46(1): 367–390.

Angner, E. (2006) 'Economists as experts: Overconfidence in theory and practice', *Journal of Economic Methodology*, 13(1): 1–24.

Akerlof, G.A. (1970) 'The market for "lemons": Quality uncertainty and the market mechanism', *The Quarterly Journal of Economics*, 84(3): 488–500.

Arrow, K. (1951) *Social Choice and Individual Values*. New York: Wiley.

Bechmann, G. and I. Hronszky (2003) *Expertise and its Interfaces. The Tense Relation of Science and Politics*. Berlin: Sigma.

Blyth, M. (2002) *Great Transformations: Economic Ideas and Institutional Change in the Twentieth Century*. Cambridge: Cambridge University Press.

Bradley, R. (2007) 'Reaching a consensus', *Social Choice and Welfare*, 29: 609–632.

Coady, D. (2006) 'When experts disagree', *Episteme*, 3: 68–79.

Camerer, C.F. and E.J. Johnson (1991). 'The process-performance paradox in expert judgment: How can experts know so much and predict so badly?', in K.A. Ericsson and J. Smith (eds), *Towards a General Theory of Expertise: Prospects and Limits*. New York: Cambridge University Press. pp. 195–217.

Collins, H. (ed.) (2007) 'Case studies in expertise and experience', Special issue of *Studies in History and Philosophy of Science*, 38(4): 615–760.

Collins H. and R. Evans (2007) *Rethinking Expertise*. Chicago: Chicago University Press.

Dasgupta, P., P. Hammond and E. Maskin (1979) 'The implementation of social choice rules: Some results on incentive compatibility', *Review of Economic Studies*, 46: 185–216.

Ericsson, K.A. and Lehman A.C. (1996) 'Expert and exceptional performance: Evidence of maximal adaptation to task constraints', *Annual Review of Psychology*, 47: 273–305.

Evans, R. (2008) 'The sociology of expertise: The distribution of social fluency', *Sociology Compass*, 2(1): 281–298.

Foley, R. (1994) 'Egoism in epistemology', in F. Schmitt (ed.) *Socializing Epistemology*. Lanham, MD: Rowman & Littlefield. pp. 53–74.

Fuller, S. (2006) 'The constitutively social character of expertise', in E. Selinger and R. Crease (eds) *The Philosophy of Expertise*. New York: Columbia University Press. pp. 342–57.

Funtowicz, S. and J. Ravetz (1993) 'Science for the post-normal age', *Futures*, 25(7): 739–755.

Gerardi, D. and L. Yariv, (2008) 'Costly Expertise', *The American Economic Review*, 98: 187–193.

Gibbons, M., C. Limoges, H. Nowotny, S. Schwartzman, P. Scott and M. Trow (1994) *The New Production of Knowledge: The Dynamics of Science and Research in Contemporary Societies*. London: Sage.

Goldman, A. (2001) 'Experts: Which ones should you trust?', *Philosophy and Phenomenological Research*, 53(1): 85–110.

Haas, P. (1992) 'Knowledge, power and international policy coordination', Special issue of *International Organization*, 46(1): 1–35.

Hagendijk, R. (1999) 'An agenda for STS: Porter on trust and quantification in science, politics and society', *Social Studies of Science*, 29(4): 629–637.

Hall, P. (1989) *Keynesianism Across Nations: The Political Power of Economic Ideas*. Princeton, NJ: Princeton University Press.

Hardwig, J. (1985) 'Epistemic dependence', *Journal of Philosophy*, 82: 335–349.

Hoffrage, U. and G. Gigerenzer (2004) 'How to improve the diagnostic inferences of medical experts', in E. Kurz-Milcke and G. Gigerenzer (eds) *Experts in Science and Society*. New York: Kluwer.

Jasanoff, S. (2003) 'Breaking the waves in science studies: Comment on H. M. Collins and R. Evans, "The third wave of science studies"', *Social Studies of Science*, 33(3): 389–400.

Kahneman, D. and A. Tversky (1973) 'On the psychology of prediction', *Psychological Review*, 80: 237–251.

Kahneman, D., P. Slovic and A. Tversky (eds) (1982) *Judgment Under Uncertainty: Heuristics and Biases*. New York: Cambridge University Press.

Kornhauser, L.A. and L.G. Sager (1986) 'Unpacking the court', *Yale Law Journal*, 96: 82–117.

Lehrer, K. and C. Wagner (1981) *Rational Consensus in Science and Society*. Reidel: Dordrecht.

Levy, E. (2001) Quantification, Mandated Science and Judgment. *Studies In History and Philosophy of Science* Part A. 32(4): 723–737.

Lindvall, J. (2006) 'The politics of purpose: Swedish economic policy after the Golden Age', *Comparative Politics*, 38(3): 253–272.

Lindvall, J. (2009) 'The real but limited influence of expert ideas', *World Politics*, 61(4): 703–730.

List, C. and P. Pettit (2002) 'Aggregating sets of judgments. An impossibility result', *Economics and Philosophy*, 18: 89–110.

Mieg, H. (2001) *The Social Psychology of Expertise: Case Studies in Research, Professional Domains and Expert Roles*. London: Lawrence Erlbaum.

Nowotny, H., P. Scott and M. Gibbons (2001) *Re-Thinking Science: Knowledge and the Public in an Age of Uncertainty*. Cambridge: Polity Press.

Nowotny, H., P. Scott and M. Gibbons (2003) 'Introduction. "Mode 2" revisited: The new production of knowledge', *Minerva*, 41: 179–194.

Pettit, P. (2001) 'Deliberative democracy and the discursive dilemma', *Philosophical Issues*, 11: 268–299.

Porter, T.M. (1996) *Trust in Numbers. The Pursuit of Objectivity in Science and Public Life*. Princeton: Princeton University Press.

Posner, R. A. (2003) *Public Intellectuals: A Study of Decline*. Cambridge, MA: Harvard University Press.

Reiss, J. (2007) *Error in Economics: Towards a More Evidence-Based Methodology*. London: Routledge.

Spence, M. (1973) "Job Market Signalling". *The Quarterly Journal of Economics*. 87(3): 355–374.

Tetlock, P. (2005) *Expert Judgment. How Good is it? How Can we Know?* NJ: Princeton University Press.

Weir, M. and Skocpol, T. (1985) 'State structures and the possibilities for Keynesian Responses to the Great depression in Sweden, Britain and the United States', pp. 107–165 in P. Evans, P., Rueschemeyer, D. and Skocpol, T. (eds) *Bringing the State Back In*. Cambridge: Cambridge University Press.

Yee, A.S. (1996) 'The causal effects of ideas on policies', *International Organization*, 50(1): 69–108.

Zamora Bonilla, J.P. (2006) 'Rhetoric, induction, and the free speech dilemma', *Philosophy of Science*, 73: 175–193.

Zamora Bonilla, J. (2007) 'Optimal judgment aggregation', *Philosophy of Science*, 74: 813–824.

Zamora Bonilla, J.P. (forthcoming) 'The economics of scientific knowledge' in Uskali Mäki (ed.) *Handbook of the Philosophy of Science, Vol. 13, Philosophy of Economics*. Elsevier.

37

Social Technology

Maarten Derksen and Anne Beaulieu

INTRODUCTION

The term 'social technology' has little currency in reflections on society and the social sciences. It appears to assume distinctions that have become increasingly problematic: between social and material technology, society and nature, human and non-human. It has become common to emphasize the extent to which the two sides of such dichotomies are interwoven, the difficulty in teasing them apart, or the outright impossibility of making the distinction. Hybridity, heterogeneity and cyborgs are the current catchwords in social theory. If the term 'social technology' is used at all, it is as a heuristic, accompanied by an explicit disavowal that it refers to a separate category. Thus, Shapin and Schaffer distinguish three technologies of fact-making in their study of Robert Boyle's experimental physics – material, literary and social – but add that 'each embedded the others' (Shapin and Schaffer, 1985: 25). Pinch et al. (1992) are equally ambivalent. They first define as 'social' any technology that, although it may incorporate material artifacts, 'has its origins in the social sciences' (1992: 266) and is intended to change human behaviour. However, they go on to reassure the reader that they do not want to resurrect 'old fashioned' distinctions, and that

the issues raised by their analysis may apply to all sorts of technology (Pinch et al, 1992).

Nevertheless, we believe the term 'social technology' can be used to probe key philosophical, political and empirical issues that are papered over when it is avoided. We want to reintroduce the question of the distinctiveness of the social, not as an a priori category, but as an empirical phenomenon that is articulated in certain technological assemblages. We accept the common dictum that 'all technology is social', but add that technologies can be differently social. In other words, we propose the term 'social technology' as an invitation to study differences, rather than as a category of technologies defined by an essential 'humanness'. We further motivate our use of 'social technology' in relation to the work of Michel Foucault, Bruno Latour and the scholars they have inspired.

THE DISSOLUTION OF THE SOCIAL

Reflection on the practical role of social science has been dominated since the 1970s by Michel Foucault and authors drawing on his work, such as Paul Rabinow, Nikolas Rose and Ian Hacking. Without pretending to do justice to this large and growing corpus, we select a few themes that are particularly prominent. First, Foucault emphasized the intimate bond between social science and modern forms of government, phrased most succinctly as 'governmentality'. Political power is exercised through knowledge of the human mind in general – its mechanisms, strengths and weaknesses – of the distribution of individual capabilities, shortcomings (including mental illness and deviance), preferences, opinions and attitudes in a population. This knowledge is obtained and deployed through techniques that act on the mentality and behaviour of individuals, groups and populations. This is the entwinement of 'power/knowledge'. Second, this mode of governing, of 'the conduct of conduct', is not confined to politics, but has spread from the state into every domain of social life, including notably the management of the self by the self. Neoliberal societies in particular require citizens to be autonomous and regulate themselves (Dunn, 2004). The techniques of the self that the social sciences offer – tests, therapies, training programs etc. – help to fulfill this 'duty to be free'. Third, discipline and self-discipline take place to an important extent through a 'microphysics of power': the meticulous manipulation and distribution of bodies, creating lines of sight, directing the gaze, separating or grouping individuals, restricting or guiding their movements. Fourth, power is productive. It does not primarily constrain or suppress subjectivity, it produces subjects. Its disciplinary techniques demand or suggest ways of being, and make them possible, mandatory, or desirable.

In recent years, the attention of scholars in the Foucauldian mold has increasingly turned to 'bio-power'. Paul Rabinow for instance has argued that through the new genetics, a 'truly new type of autoproduction' (Rabinow, 1992: 241) will emerge, a form of self-fashioning he calls 'biosociality'. Increasingly, group and individual identities and practices will focus on knowledge of genetic risks and the medical interventions to alleviate or overcome them. As a result, both the catego-

ries of 'nature' and 'the social' (and 'culture') will be dissolved. The dichotomy of nature – as that which simply is – and culture – that which stands outside nature – is rendered unstable. 'Nature is no longer behind us as a necessity. Nature is ahead of us with a horizon of new and immense possibilities' (Bertilsson, 2003: 125). The result is a 'politics of life itself' (Rose, 2001). Thus, the category of the social seems to dissolve, and technologies that stem from the psy-complex (Rose, 1985) are fast becoming irrelevant, as the self comes to be defined in biomedical terms.

According to Bruno Latour, the dichotomy of social and natural (and related conceptual pairs) was always misleading. He and other scholars around Actor-Network Theory (ANT) have called for recognition of the social nature of things/the natural world. Distinctions made between the social and the natural are always post-hoc, and best considered accomplishments rather than matters of fact. This approach has been labeled non-dualist, and seeks to problematize the role attributed to this dualism in the formation of modern society – Latour's quip, we have never been modern, is a familiar summation of this approach. The notion of 'social technology' seems problematic in the light of ANT. Any technology is 'social', according to ANT. To understand our present societies, we must recognize them as 'collectives' made up of humans and non-humans, as 'sociotechnical imbroglios' (Latour, 1994). Societies are the result of heterogeneous engineering, tying together artifacts, people, texts, plants, animals, substances and other kinds of actants into networks. Moreover, typical of technology is the redistribution of roles and functions among the actants in a network. There is thus no essentially human role or function that people perform in society, nor is there a corresponding non-human contribution of artifacts. There is no non-social technology.

A famous example of this approach to technology is the door-closer analyzed by Latour (1992). Onto this mundane artifact is delegated the task of closing the door after one has entered through it, thus providing a more dependable, mechanical solution to a problem that before was solved morally. A human skill and obligation (to close the door) has been delegated to a non-human. However, mechanical door-closers prescribe certain competences on the part of their users, such as the strength needed to operate them, that are often beyond the capability of children, people carrying heavy objects or elderly people. Thus, door-closers and their users (and non-users) are part of a collective in which the roles of humans and non-humans have been redistributed, and it is impossible to define a priori the 'material' and 'social' aspects of this technology.

'SOCIAL TECHNOLOGY'

Rethinking the dichotomy of nature and culture has been of tremendous importance in reflecting on our current ways of living, as evidenced by the many studies of biopower inspired by Foucault and the studies of technology revitalized by ANT. An unfortunate consequence, however, has been a relative neglect of technologies that are not built around devices. Foucauldians increasingly focus on biotechnology; in ANT, 'technology' refers to objects (see, for example, Michael, 2000; Latour, 2005). The importance of material technology is clear, but many roles and functions are fulfilled by primarily human means. The door problem, for example, is sometimes solved by employing a doorman, because they have qualities specific to people.[1] In other words, we use different kinds of technology in different circumstances. Similarly, that the self is increasingly defined in biological terms, and acted upon with biomedical techniques, is undeniable, as are the implications for social theory. The 'fascination and alarm' (Brown, 2003: 185) evoked by the life sciences, however, should not obscure the continued importance of technologies stemming from the social sciences. Practices such as genetic counseling can be considered a social technology that sustains the further geneticization of health, through its social function in

sustaining forms that emerge from the life sciences. (Rose, 2001; Brunger and Lippman, 1995).

Second, the ascent of the life sciences and associated technologies may not render all dualism obsolete. Whereas Rabinow sees 'the dissolution of the category of "the social"' (Rabinow, 1992: 242; see also Bertilsson, 2003; Haraway, 1991) as the likely result of the recent developments in biotechnology, Ian Hacking (2005) has recently argued that the manipulability of the body that is on offer creates an everyday Cartesian dualism. Our bodies appear as objects the more we can intervene in them. Hacking is quick to emphasize that he does not promote a 'material' dualism of mind and body, nor does he think that Descartes himself intended to do so. The duality is of two increasingly different sets of practices, two ways of talking and of representing with respect to ourselves. Hacking's analysis of the revival of Cartesianism is similar to our approach of 'social technology': an interest in distinctions that appear in our experiences and practices as both resource and constraint, without according them a transcendental status.

Our focus on the distinctiveness of the social as an empirical phenomenon is not fundamentally at odds with ANT. We do not intend to contribute to the modern project of purification (Latour, 1993), of dividing the world into humans and their relations on the one hand, and nature on the other. On the contrary, we will show that versions of humanness and sociality, sometimes distinctly unnatural, are produced in heterogeneous practices. We call such practices 'social technology', not because they involve a specific category of techniques, but because they raise the issue of the specificity of the social. We look for such technologies along three vectors that seem especially promising.

1 Technologies from the social sciences. Faculties of social science turn out large numbers of graduates each year, schooled in a panoply of techniques for investigating and manipulating the mind and behaviour of other people. This is first of all an intriguing aspect of the social sciences to explore because hardly any analyses of such technology

as technology have been done using the concepts and theories of technology studies. Second, traditional issues in the philosophy of the social sciences, such as reflexivity or the double hermeneutic, appear in a new light when approached as technological challenges or affordances.

2 Technologies that consist entirely or predominantly of human action. Without assuming that there is anything essentially different about human action, it is worth investigating its particular qualities as a component of technology. Human action, for one thing, often ties a technology to its context in culturally specific ways. This invites a comparison with the role of predominantly material technologies in building and stabilizing 'collectives'.

3 Technologies that depend on social interaction for their constitution. A web-based chatroom, for example, only functions if there are people chatting in it. An election only works if there are voters turning up. Open source software only gets developed if there is a community of programmers engaging with it. This matters at all kinds of levels, and not just in terms of their 'use' by individuals.[2] While the point might again be raised that all technologies modulate social behaviour in some form, considering technology that *is intended* to do that raises interesting points that tend to disappear when we lazily cling to the 'everything is social' idea. To take but one example, social software platforms are interesting because they exploit and enhance the human capacity for, and interest in assigning meaning, for classifying, for recognizing and evaluating patterns, which in turn enriches the possibilities of these platforms to deliver interesting material to the users, etc. Thus, the concept of 'social technology' allows a study of human qualities, without assuming a priori a human essence.

In the following, we offer three case studies that illustrate the concept of 'social technology': priming and automaticity research; surveys, polling and focus groups; and social software platforms.

PRIMING: PEOPLE AS MACHINES

Paradoxically, attempts to treat people as machines are among the most revealing social technologies, in that they tend to raise the issue of the specificity of the social. In 1748, Julien Offray de La Mettrie published *L'Homme Machine*, in which he extended Descartes 'thesis that animals are soulless automatons to human beings. (La Mettrie, 1748) The idea that people are machines has subsequently inspired many grand schemes of social engineering. The Scottish businessman Robert Owen, for example, turned the concept of *L'Homme Machine* into a Utopian engineered community for the workers in his cotton mills. These 'living machines' (Owen, 1972: 74), as he called them, could be delivered from vice and poverty, if provided with proper care and education, based on accurate knowledge of their nature. Children in particular – 'passive and wonderfully contrived compounds' (1972: 34) – were to be the target of rationally designed education that would mould their character.

Utopian social engineering, as Popper (1966) called it, has fallen out of favour, with the demise of the Soviet Union often referred to as proof that it doesn't work and should not be tried again. Yet *L'Homme Machine* has survived and still provides the philosophical backdrop of many technologies in social science. A recent example is priming and automaticity research. 'Priming' concerns the way recent or current experience influences people's perceptions and behaviour, although they are not aware of it. In an experiment that the field considers classic, participants are first shown a series of strings of words, and asked to construct grammatical sentences out of each. They are told this is a 'language proficiency experiment'. When the participant leaves the laboratory after completing the task, a confederate of the experimenter records the time it takes him or her to walk the corridor to the elevator. In the experimental condition, the garbled sentences contain a number of words that are related to old age, such as 'worried', 'Florida' and 'knitting'. They are, in the words of the researchers, part of 'the elderly stereotype' (Bargh et al., 1996: 236). Participants in the experimental condition, unaware that they had been primed, walked slower than those in the control group. Similarly, priming with a briefcase instead of a rucksack makes participants work harder, and priming with rudeness makes participants more prone to interrupt someone.

Priming is the central technology in a psychological paradigm called 'automaticity theory'. Its proponents regularly engage in philosophical reflection, putting the results of priming studies to use in arguments concerning consciousness and free will (Bargh, 2008). Although usually stopping short of claiming that we are nothing but automatons, priming is used to show that we are much less in control of our actions than we like to think. Automaticity research is a social technology in that it raises fundamental questions regarding humanness: how and to what extent can human behaviour be controlled, and who does the controlling? If people are machines, who or what operates them? Its primary answer is that substantial control lies outside the subject. The automaticity paradigm stands in a long tradition when it equates automaticity with passivity. Robert Owen wrote that children have 'that plastic quality' that can be moulded 'to have any human character' (Owen, 1972: 34). A century later his claim was echoed by the behaviourist John Watson, who boasted he was able to turn 'healthy infants' into any kind of professional he chose ('even beggarman and thief') if he was given 'his own specified world to bring them up in' (Watson, 1930: 82). The power that the situation has over human behaviour was also the basis of Skinner's Utopian scheme, Walden Two, which matched Owen's in its optimism and grandeur (Skinner, 1976). Education and behaviour modification have long been the technologies most associated with *L'Homme Machine*. The automaticity paradigm appears to go in a different direction: it has been criticized as a return to behaviorism (Kihlstrom, 2004), but its version of passivity is different. Like behaviourism, it takes aim at consciousness and free will, but it is not committed to educability. With cognitivism, 'living machines' have become too complex

to be molded. Instead, they can be played by modifying the situation.

To fully appreciate the philosophical relevance of priming research, however, it pays to examine more closely the technology itself. The priming effect requires a careful distribution of information and misinformation. As in most social-psychological research, participants must not be told what the experiment is about, or what hypothesis is being tested. Instead they are told a cover story, the 'language proficiency experiment' in the example I described earlier, or the description is kept so vague as to be uninformative. Alternatively, priming researchers may use subliminal presentation, where the priming stimulus is presented very briefly, so that the participant remains unaware of its identity or meaning. Additional measures may be necessary: in the example above, participants were given a false debriefing after the 'language proficiency experiment', and the confederate who subsequently timed their walk to the elevator (using a concealed stopwatch) was positioned so that he appeared to be waiting to talk to someone in another office.

To produce automatic behaviour, in other words, requires carefully controlling the participant's awareness. This control itself cannot be applied automatically: like most experiments, priming studies require a lot of tinkering to be made to work. Even when control is effected by means of devices, such as the computers that produce the subliminal stimuli, it is advisable to include 'awareness checks' in the set up, to make sure participants are not 'tipped off' (Bargh and Chartrand, 2000). These are in effect moments of interaction with the aware agent, where reliance on awareness is essential in order to establish its limitations, and this resource has been used in some of the more reflexive studies in this area (Jack and Roepstorff, 2002; Sip et al., 2008). Thus, priming research is framed by procedures and concepts – deception, awareness and so on – that are at odds with the idea that people are automatons at the mercy of the situation. Automaticity in priming research is accompanied by the shadows of autonomous, aware and obstinate individuals.

Resistance is also evoked when automaticity theory is applied. One such application is the Implicit Association Test (IAT), a technique that probes people's implicit, unconscious association between categories of concepts, and is used mainly as a research tool for assessing individual differences. The IAT is a sorting task, in which participants have to sort stimuli by pressing keys on a keyboard. In a typical example (Nosek et al., 2006) the items are male or female faces, and words with a 'good' or 'bad' meaning. In the critical phase of the test, stimuli from both dimensions are presented simultaneously. Response latency and number of errors are taken to be an indication of the strength of association between categories: if participants for example manage to correctly sort male faces combined with positive words quicker than they do contrasting presentations, they are thought to implicitly associate men with good things, regardless of their explicitly stated attitudes.

Like every psychological test, the IAT requires that it is designed and administered in precisely circumscribed ways that take into account what is known about the capabilities and proclivities of participants. Among the more urgent issues is 'faking'. The IAT is explicitly intended to counter the participant's capacity to resist measurement. Indirect measures such as the IAT 'reduce the likelihood of deliberate faking by obscuring what is being measured, how it is being measured, or limiting the ability to control the response content' (Nosek et al., 2006: 275). A number of studies have attempted to measure to what extent, and under which circumstances, the IAT is 'fakeable', and have found that it holds up well in this regard, provided participants are not too experienced with the test, and are not told how they can control their scores. However, researchers also realize that attempts[3] to fake may actually be a sincere effort to control one's automatic associations: an authentic wish not to be misogynist, for instance (Nosek

et al., 2006: 276). An artifact has become a subject in its own right. This appears to be a growing trend: resistance and control, which were actively marginalized before, are now moving into the centre of automaticity researchers' attention. (*Social Psychology and the Unconscious*, 2006) The object is more and more to study the 'mixtures of automatic and controlled features' of behaviour (Bargh, 2007: 3). Doing so is also seen as a route to the application of automaticity theory outside research contexts. Specifying exactly what role awareness plays in consumer behavior, for instance, is a first step towards aiding 'consumers in controlling and improving their decisions' (Chartrand, 2005: 209). Likewise, the insight gained into 'the interplay of automaticity and control in close relationships' must now be put to work in answering the question how and when control can be exerted over relationship processes (Chen et al., 2007: 164).

Thus, lurking behind *L'Homme Machine* of automaticity theory, there is a different, more controlling and aware kind of subject, that has been brought out into the open as the paradigm develops and finds application outside the lab. This shift from mechanical objects to controlling subjects has also occurred in behaviourism. Karen Baistow has argued that the period between 1960 and 1990 saw the emergence of an 'autonomous, self-managing behavioural subject' (Baistow, 2001: 311), as techniques of behaviour modification found widespread use in therapies, training courses and other efforts to help people manage themselves and be 'in control' (2001: 324). The spread of behavioural techniques was accompanied by a transition in theory. Skinner's fully mechanical, environmentally determined human being was gradually replaced by a subject that was aware of its reinforcers and exerted some control over the contingencies of its behaviour (Bandura, 1974). At the same time, behaviourists scaled down their view of social technology, endorsing the application of behaviourist principles in the form of black-boxed 'pure techniques' that could be employed without any specialist knowledge. In this way, behaviour modification became compatible with 'neo-liberal political rationalities concerning regulated autonomy' (Baistow, 2001: 325).

Priming is an example of the way technology can create, enable, and even depend on resistance to it.[4] In their efforts to produce objective, mechanical behaviour, automaticity researchers simultaneously create the opposite: an autonomous subject with free will. The priming effect comes paired with awareness, the automatic processes occur in tandem with control processes, automaticity gives rise to discussions of 'free will' (demarcated but not entirely obliterated), and as the theories and technologies of priming and automaticity research move further from the laboratory, they turn into techniques, tools to be deployed by people in control of themselves, of their relationships, or of others.

SURVEYS, POLLING AND FOCUS GROUPS

Whereas priming and automaticity research is interesting because of the resistance that it reveals, our second case shows among other things the paradoxical effects of cooperation and adoption. It concerns a set of techniques and procedures to gather information about people's behaviour, opinions, preferences and so on, that date back at least to Francis Galton, among whose many inventions is the self-report questionnaire. Trying to support his theory of hereditary genius, Galton sent an extensive list of questions to 192 distinguished Fellows of the Royal Society, and received 104 in return (Galton, 1874). The respondents answered questions on their psychological qualities – memory, energy, intelligence – and those of their relatives. From the answers Galton drew the conclusion that his thesis, that genius is hereditary, a matter of 'nature' rather than 'nurture', was largely correct.

Galton implicitly ascribed to his respondents the ability to accurately gauge their own and others' memory and intelligence. The social sciences, psychology in particular, have tended to be very skeptical in this regard. The demarcation of expert, social scientific methods and knowledge from those of lay people – including other scientists – has been a constant in their history (Coon, 1992). Yet the questionnaire has found widespread use as an instrument to elicit all kinds of information from people, preferably about matters they *can* be considered experts on: their own opinions, views and preferences. Similar technologies include focus groups, and various types of interview. They illustrate the three vectors that we have introduced earlier: they often originate in the work of social scientists, they partly depend on human action, and they work to constitute the social.

History

In her history of American survey research, Sarah Igo asks the question: 'In what ways is a society changed by the very tools employed to represent it?' (Igo, 2007: 4). Three developments that characterize the rise of mass surveys in the twentieth century make this question especially pertinent. First, this rise involved a shift in focus. Whereas nineteenth century social studies had focused on criminals, degenerates, the urban poor, and other deviant and marginal groups, in the twentieth century attention shifted to normal, typical or 'average' Americans. A mass public became visible. Second, social studies were increasingly dominated by social scientists and their methods and vocabularies, rather than by the bureaucrats and reformers that had surveyed society in the nineteenth century. A crucial technique was the representative sample, 'as important to the social sciences in the twentieth century as the telescope was in the sixteenth', according to Thomas Osborne and Nikolas Rose (1999: 383), who traced some of its genealogy. Third, surveys did not only make the American public visible to social scientists, marketers, and politicians. Through the mass media the results of opinion polls and market research also reached the people whose opinions and preferences had been measured. Mass surveys seemed to offer the public a mirror in which it could see itself. Each could measure their opinions and behaviours against those of others, and know how average or unusual one was with regard to them. Thus, these surveys, and the media attention they attracted, created a self-conscious mass public.

Looping

Surveys blur the demarcation between expert and lay knowledge that is otherwise so important to the social sciences. In surveys, Igo notes, 'the public is simultaneously object, participant and audience' (2007: 4). Rather than a hierarchical relation between object and representation, surveys create a circular relation between them. The result is what Ian Hacking has termed a 'looping effect': the object and its representation, the class and the classification, 'emerge hand in hand' (Hacking, 1986: 228). Mass surveys created a mass public in and by the process of measuring it. The average American that the surveys presented became available as a role to be adopted or rejected, thus feeding back into new surveys. Similarly, Osborne and Rose argue that the opinion poll was instrumental in creating the phenomenon of a public opinion. '(T)he existence of questionnaires and surveys themselves promote the idea that there is a public opinion "out there" to be had and measured' (1999: 387). As a consequence, people come to feel the need to have 'opinions',[1] learn to formulate them in the appropriate way, and use the results of earlier polls to do so. Polling constitutes sociality as much as it describes it.

The looping effect and other reflexive phenomena raise the question whether they are particular to the social sciences and their 'objects' (people).[6] In Hacking's formulation, looping arises because people may care about the way they are classified, whereas natural kinds are insensitive to what is said about them.[7] Osborne and Rose on the other hand emphasize that the creation of new phenomena (such as public opinion) makes the social sciences more similar to the natural sciences. What is different is the speed at which this happens: creating new kinds of humans is a slow process compared to production of phenomena in the laboratories of the natural sciences. The question has recently been taken up by Roger Smith (2005). His thorough review of the reflexivity literature is relevant to our purposes because it advocates a pragmatic, technological view of the issue. Smith too argues that reflexivity does not point to a fundamental ontological difference between humans and other objects of science. After all, 'knowledge understood as practice, as technology, manifestly changes the world' (2005: 13). Knowledge is part of the world, and science in particular has wrought enormous changes in the world, including in the objects it studies. Attempts to distinguish the social and natural sciences on the basis of reflexivity moreover fall prey themselves to reflexive thinking: Foucault for instance turned reflexivity on itself and placed the attempt to use it to ground human uniqueness in a historically specific 'regime of truth'. Instead of ontologizing reflexivity, Smith proposes a pragmatic approach. 'What separates the natural sciences and the human sciences is not the claim that human beings have language or soul, or that only they change with knowledge, but that it is part of the human sciences (and humanities) *to make the reflexive process self-conscious*' (2005: 17; emphasis in original).

We agree with Smith that the search for ontological foundations of human uniqueness serves little purpose, and that looping processes are interesting in themselves, whatever science they involve. But we also believe that it is misleading to speak of 'the reflexive process', as Smith does. Yes, all knowledge changes the world, but reflexive processes may involve very different technologies. Our term 'social technology' tries to capture some of these differences, without fixing them in ontology. Some of the techniques involved in harvesting opinions illustrate this point.

Techniques, skills and craft

According to Deborah Coon (1993), late-nineteenth and early-tweentieth century introspectionist psychology held a 'techno-scientific ideal'. Psychologists trained themselves to become machine-like parts of their experiments, so as to form one mechanical whole with their wood-and-brass instruments.[8] But at the same time, being a good subject was a craft that could not be learned from a book. 'Craft' and related concepts regularly crop up in social scientific handbooks and manuals to point to skills, ways of doing or being, that cannot be formulated in rules and thus can only be vaguely indicated by the books and manuals themselves. Conducting an interview for example is an activity that can be standardized and regulated to a large extent, but always requires skills on the part of the interviewer that escape formulation.

One of the most important skills may be termed the management of spontaneity. In his study of the epistemology of focus groups, Javier Lezaun (2007) notes the conflicting demands placed on the moderator. Moderators must resolve a tension inherent in the focus group method: they must encourage a lively conversation that allows each member to express authentic, individual opinions, but must prevent the formation of a collective. Doing so requires the moderator to balance control with empathy, artificiality with naturalness. The training manuals and handbooks that Lezaun studied emphasize that moderating is an art, embodied in the person of the moderator, but not fully transferable as standard routines and techniques.

Among the most important objectives of the moderator's art is the 'proper management – the incitement, orientation and taming

– of [the members'] reflexivity' (Lezaun, 2007: 136). When participants become too aware of the artificial nature of the group, of the experimental setting, of the moderator or of the presence of other observers behind a one-way mirror, they may start to sabotage the process. In their efforts to prevent this from happening, however, moderators must take care not to seem directive, or to draw too much attention to themselves. '(N)on-direction needs to be actively engineered into the behaviour of the moderator and into the responses he elicits from the research subjects' (2007: 138). The focus group, in other words, must be managed to spontaneously produce individual opinions. This requirement is not restricted to focus groups, but is part of many social scientific technologies. Administrating psychological tests (Derksen, 2001) and conducting interviews also require unobtrusive directivity, in order to encourage a spontaneous and authentic show of subjectivity. Crucial is the development and maintenance of good 'rapport', a 'comfortable, cooperative relationship' (Keats, 2001: 23) between researcher and respondent.

Polling, surveys, focus groups and interviews illustrate the value of the three vectors we formulated in the Introduction. Their development owes much, though certainly not everything, to social scientists; human behaviour is an intrinsic part of their functioning; and, third, they modulate sociality. Regarding this last aspect, it is noteworthy that each of these technologies depends on a conception of what social relations are or should be. Lezaun for example argues that focus groups are typically meant to produce what he calls 'an isegoric situation' (Lezaun, 2007: 140): one in which each individual member is allowed and encouraged to express opinions in equal measure, but hierarchy, coalitions and in particular the formation of group opinion are prevented as much as possible. In other words, the focus group embodies a particular kind of social order, one that privileges the individual and considers the group as a tool that must not become an end in itself. Our last case study illustrates a similar version of sociality, produced in a novel way.

SOCIAL SOFTWARE PLATFORMS

Our third case study addresses a set of emerging social and cultural forms. We examine a social networking technology, namely the photo-sharing platform Flickr. This case is especially interesting because it highlights how digitally-mediated interactions have become significant as a social phenomenon, one which is addressed in the social sciences as object, context and tool of study.

A key feature of social networking technologies is the built-in functionality that enables users to represent themselves and to articulate links to other users. Ongoing sociability is a key feature of social software (Fuller, 2003). The self and one's relations to others – two core concerns of social science – are therefore inscribed and foregrounded in these settings. This can be done through filling in a personal profile (name, hobbies, photo and witty self-description) that appears on a webpage, and by designating other users of the system as friends or acquaintances, thereby linking one's own profile to that of others. Another defining element is that besides personal profiles, Flickr also supports the provision of content created by users. While Flickr focuses on photography (and more recently on video), similar systems also exist for sharing music, texts, videos, scientific articles, etc. These systems furthermore make use of traces that are generated by the use of the system and of its content – whether this be tagging of material by users, download statistics, user preferences or ratings. In other words, 'content' is also used as a resource for sociality in these settings (not just user profiles) (Lange, 2007). Social software platforms are therefore highly iterative: representations of users, contents, and use are made visible in these platforms, and are all used to further structure the functioning of the sites. In Flickr, for example, the platform's most interesting photos are selected based on the preferences of users, while the preferences of some users weigh more heavily because of the particular place they occupy within the networks elaborated between users, photos, comments and number of 'views' for certain photos.[9] While the specific configurations vary across platforms, the elements of user profiles, of 'user-generated content' and the use of self-referential traces are defining features of the so-called 'Web 2.0' applications. These constitute important sites of sociality that draw on and feed the social sciences in significant and complex ways.

The web as field and lab

The use of online social networks and social software for social scientific research is still in development. While no definitive archeology of this approach to social science can yet be written, a number of trends are nevertheless visible. Among these is a significant reconfiguration of how the social sciences make their object. Namely, the web as a setting is being configured in a way that draws attention to and problematizes an important distinction in the social sciences: the field versus the lab (Gieryn, 2006). A growing body of work conceptualizes platforms such as Flickr, YouTube, Digg or Facebook as settings that combine features that have traditionally been attributed in a mutually exclusive way to either the lab or the field. These web-based settings are considered to be a place to observe naturally occurring, bottom-up types of behaviour of interest to social science. The web as a setting is therefore contrasted to artificial settings for social science research such as interviews, focus groups or surveys. This approach assumes that the platforms constitute a setting in which various social behaviours take place, be they identity construction, or the constitution of social forms like communities, cliques, friendships, celebrity, gift-giving.

These settings are also examined as sites of politics, commerce, citizenship and culture (Bruns, 2008; Jenkins, 2006; Kim and Yun, 2007; Surowiecki, 2005).

Yet, the platforms are not only valued as sites where social behaviour occurs, but they are also considered valuable because of the way in which users and their activities are mediated. Because user profiles, interaction and many other kinds of activity on these sites leave traces, the mediated aspects of these settings align them with a 'laboratory' approach, where behaviours could traditionally best be recorded or measured. These sites therefore also have features of the 'lab', where phenomena produce traces (Knorr Cetina, 1999; Rheinberger, 1997), which can then be 'harvested' for analysis. These sites are therefore valued as sources of 'naturalistic behavioral data' (boyd and Ellison, 2007). As research contexts such parts of the web are therefore, somewhat paradoxically, ideally natural and ideally available for scrutiny. This paradox is sustained by a view of digital media as transparent and of social software as self-contained spaces, in which the whole of a social form can be apprehended.

The sheer numbers of participants and the impressive volume of content on these platforms are potent arguments for the social sciences to pay attention to these sites. This strong presence makes it all the more important to examine what makes them such good sites of study. The seeming paradox in what makes these sites attractive is also telling of assumptions in the creation of social science objects. These sites bring together what were traditionally seen as mutually exclusive features of knowing about the social: behaviours were either spontaneous and natural, or amenable to measurement through mediation. Whereas these were generally mutually exclusive aspects, social software brings them together. In this light, it becomes crucial to see what new configurations of objects this will bring to the social sciences, and what kinds of new knowledge claims will follow (Beaulieu, 2004; VKS, 2008).

One emerging trend that sustains this characterization of social software as a site for the study of the social, is a strong tendency to see digital media as transparent and discrete:

'Flickr is transparent: every username, every group name, every descriptive tag is a hyperlink that can be used to navigate the site, and unless it has been designated private, all content is publicly viewable and in some cases modifiable' (Lerman and Jones, 2007).

The materiality and structuring effects of social software as technologies therefore risk being underestimated, if they are only ever leveraged as a source of empirical data about human behaviour. Furthermore, by taking these platforms as self-contained sites, other practices and behaviours that take place around these sites may be missed, though they can be an important component of the social forms of interest – for example, meet-ups at photogenic spots of photographers who know each other through Flickr groups play an important role in shaping their interactions in the Flickr platform. In developing these approaches to the study of social software, social scientists would do well to draw on the ample tradition of reflexive critical work that interrogates methodological assumptions. Finally, these traces can themselves become resources for users (rather than only traces), who assign particular meanings to them. By taking into account how the traces of sociality are shaped by infrastructure and media, and by understanding practices (whether through or around infrastructures), social science research may be able to explore new social forms constituted around these platforms. With reference to our earlier discussion of Foucault and Latour, we see this entwinement of the social and the material as requiring a very precise analysis of how these aspects mutually shape each other, rather than a celebration of 'pure sociality'. It is on the basis of such careful characterization that we can best approach these settings, which are both field and lab in the traditional sense.

Human-technology oppositions

One of the important elements in characterizing these platforms is therefore the distinctive sociality they produce. We noted earlier that a social technology approach could be valuable in making visible how human attributes are constituted, in cases where the technological and the human are opposed. Around platforms such as Flickr, an intricate distribution and entwinement of human and non-human abilities takes place. Masses of information have to be organized on these platforms and there is a strong tendency to identify and embed specifically human abilities in the technological. Sometimes termed 'social browsing' or 'social information filtering', the exercise of human abilities is retrieved from these contexts. They then become resources in building technologies:

> 'Social browsing is a natural step in the evolution of technologies that exploit independent activities of many users to recommend or rate for a specific user' (Lehman and Jones, 2007).

A very mundane, pioneering form of this is embedded in a function at Amazon, where further books are presented with the phrase: 'people who bought this book also looked at *x, y, z*.' Another form of this practice is the tagging of material by users. This is something at which humans are considered to excel, whereas tasks such as tagging photos, as happens on Flickr, are considered a huge challenge for machines. This assumes particular qualities for humans in relation to what technology can do.

Research in this vein then tries to capture not only the tags, but also to relate them to other kinds of 'meta-data' that are produced by human users. The information gathered is then put to use in the functioning of technology, for example, to build better search engines. To illustrate this, if a user were to type beetle in the Flickr search engine, the results might include photos of bugs and of Volkswagen cars. But if the users' contacts are taken into account, this search process can be 'improved'. If the user has marked

as 'friends' other users whose accounts contain mostly photos of cars, then the search engine can take this into account as a form of meta-data that will shape the search towards photos of VW beetles.[10] The social is here defined as shared interests, which in turn is used as input to determine which 'meanings' should be favoured in filtering information.

Aggregation and Individuals

It is therefore important to analyze and make visible the kind of sociality that is being built by and into these information tools. In the case of much work done on Flickr, it is a view of the social that is highly individualistic, based on a notion of 'preferences' that are articulated according to templates and functions built into the platforms. Some forms of sociality may also be filtered out in these applications; because friends were 'digging' (recommending) each other's stories (and therefore getting them to the front page), the platform Digg started trying to 'remove' this sociality – a 'group' or 'clique' effect – and to measure the 'diversity of the individuals digging the story' (Lerman, 2007). (Like in the case of focus groups discussed earlier, group dynamics are undesirable because they pollute the desired form of aggregation.) In this case, the capacity of a human to judge whether a story is interesting is considered valuable. But, the model of sociality being used here rejects that judgment should be entwined with social ties, that one might judge a friend's story to be better. This is a 'bottom-up' view of how the social should be expressed, retrieved and fed back into these platforms, and one which is widely distributed across information and library science, and computer science (Kolbitsh and Maurer, 2006). This work seeks to isolate the single human, the individual, and to remove the biasing effect of social ties on pure cognition. Other work, however, tends to see mediated networks as an integral part of the context of social relations. This work articulates a more complex view of the social, where not only content and rating, but also the 'social meta-data (e.g. relationships, indications of other-orientedness and reciprocal patterns)' (Skågeby, 2008: 293) are considered as basis for shaping interests and concerns in these settings. The links that are created between users and contents and various sites are also objects of concern: links, tagging and comments become ties to manage, rather than bias to be removed (Ito et al., 2008). Social meta-data and traceable socio-technical relations are taken as human behaviours and part and parcel of 'the social.

Another way in which the social is being configured in these settings is through the use of tagging practices as representative of shared cultural meanings, a phenomenon sometimes labeled 'folksonomies' (Davies, 2006: 223). These can in turn be used to filter information and to address 'information overload' (Lehman and Jones, 2007).[11] But they can also be interesting elements to interrogate practices that may be arising in these contexts, for example, how users may begin to use tags that are popular, in order to increase interest in their photos (Davies, 2006), or how tagging and commenting can be forms of acknowledgment, reward or gift-giving.

While such use of social information can seem trivial, the degree to which these approaches are deployed and the impact they have in shaping the information we retrieve should not be underestimated. These social technologies combine aspects of what is considered to be uniquely human insight (such as assigning meaning to an image) and combine these with some of the strengths of computing technologies (handling huge amounts of data and correlating bits of information and visualizing them) to support all kinds of activities around databases.

This work suggests that social sciences can have an important contribution to make, as to the soundness of the social models being deployed. Participant observation research in this area has shown that in mediated settings (whether social networks, virtual worlds or gaming environments), interactions and settings are strongly shaped by collectivities, groups, guilds or subcultures. Rather than an aggregation of individual users, complex social dynamics can be observed (Jakobsson and Taylor, 2003; Boellstorff, 2008). Furthermore, since this kind of sociality is being 'built into' these kinds of services, interrogation of these forms is a crucial component of contemporary politics of knowledge (Mackenzie, 2006). The notion of individual may also be in need of further attention.

The human subject being configured in these settings is that of a cognitively competent, individual user.[12] Social software also fosters a particular kind of behaviour that exacerbates and possibly transforms aspects of the traditional view of the liberal, capitalist self. The user, who creates and produces in these settings, partakes in new labour relations. These platforms provide the possibility of creative freedom for users, and purport to support this uniquely human creativity. At the same time, these settings also harness and valorize this creativity through particular forms of sociality (Boellstroff, 2008; Hayles, 2005).

The challenge for social science is to understand mediation and feedback loops, networked social relations and the dynamics emergent from such systems. Besides being directed at the body or operationalised in face-to-face settings, our third case shows that social technologies also mediate the social, leading to a particular version of the informationalised self and of networked sociality.

CONCLUSION

Many other technologies could be analyzed as social technologies: the lie detector, behavior modification through operant conditioning, the 'sleeping policeman' (Callon and Latour, 1992), laws, constitutions, house rules, genetic counseling (Brunger and Lippman, 1995), military drill (McNeill, 1995), standards (Edwards, 2004), etc. We hope to have shown how an interrogation of these as social technologies can be a fruitful way to raise the issue of the distinctiveness of the social. Rather than attempt to discuss many examples of social technology, a strategy that might end up reifying these as a category, we have focused on showing how a particular set of dynamics ensure the constitution, use and efficacy of social technologies. We have also stressed how these technologies, as they become widespread, can convey particular versions of the social. Perhaps most importantly for the readers of this volume, we have pointed out that social technologies matter a great deal both across society and in the knowledge-making practices of the social sciences.

We have shown how social technologies can be used to produce a proper relation to an object, and lead to successful interactions, for example in the case of the social scientist leading a focus group. This form also exists outside the lab, for example, in the self-discipline that traders must exercise in order to deal successfully with the market (Zaitloom, 2004) or in the way 'friendship' is factored out of online recommendation systems. Social technologies are therefore not only extensions or applications of social scientific knowledge, but integral to them. The cases discussed in this chapter highlight the importance of reflecting on the relations that are necessary for making knowledge, and how these relations configure objects, subjects and experiments in the social sciences.

By showing that we can understand the social sciences by considering how they build and use social technologies, we also distinguish this approach from a view of social technologies as the ideologically-driven 'application' of social science knowledge, such as that of Pickel (2001):

'Unlike social science, social technology is based on political norms and moral standards that determine what constitutes an unsatisfactory state of affairs, a desirable goal, and acceptable means' (Pickel, 2001: 466).

Pickel draws a sharp contrast between knowledge and technology, on the basis of the latter's value-ladenness. Such distinctions between technology and knowledge are highly problematic, as our case studies have shown. This line of work could be further developed by elaborating on work done in studies of science and technology. Rheinberger's work on epistemic and technical objects has served to analyze experimental systems in biology. To be adapted to the social sciences, the interrelation between the two components, noted by Rheinberger, would need to be further examined and adjusted. Various efforts in this direction are ongoing: we note the analysis of the dynamics of teamwork and collaboration in the social sciences in terms of the creation of objects and their interrogation (Collier et al., 2006); examinations of the use of case studies in the social sciences as both objects and experimental systems (Beaulieu et al., 2007), analyses of the constitution of particular 'objects' that are claimed to unify the social sciences, from the bottom up (Derksen, 2005), and critiques of the ontological power exercised by the social sciences (Law and Urry, 2003).

While we wish to stress the importance of social technology for the operation of the social sciences in their practices of knowledge production, we also want to note that there is an instrumental connotation to the notion of technology. Black-boxing, packaging, can be an extremely useful strategy to have knowledge claims circulate, to establish agreement, or to extend networks. But the creation and circulation of a technology can also be a liability for the social sciences. When social scientific expertise becomes packaged, it can seem suspect. Instrumentalisation implies a loss of the complex subject-object relation we discussed earlier, at the level of specific techniques. For example, much self-help consists on a practical level of techniques very similar to orthodox psychology. Psychologists would probably say that the advice is not quite scientifically correct, and that anyway therapy is best done person-to-person, because 'rapport' is essential to success. Instrumentalization also has implications for the legitimacy of the social sciences.

Finally, this work also contributes to further problematisation of the notion of 'technology'. Specifically, a reflection on technology in the social sciences provides an interesting contrast to the work being done in 'technology studies', an important area of science and technology studies (STS). The object of technology studies tends to be material devices, either in everyday life (bicycles, water pumps, computers) or in the natural and life sciences (vaccines, DNA techniques, MRI scanners) – though more recent work has also considered information and communication technology (electronic patient record, telephones, databases). In contrast, the topic of social technology enables a focus on fields of knowledge production (such as education science, psychology, anthropology, marketing, criminology) that are relatively neglected in the study of technology. Two related circumstances have shaped this relative neglect. First, science and technology studies have focused on the traditional sciences, and on engineering and medicine. The reasons for this are multiple, but include the relative high status of these areas, their perceived weightiness and consequences for Western society, and the availability of funding. A second issue is the importance of the device in shaping the object of technology studies. While several critiques of the conceptualization of technologies have been pursued, stressing the changeability and multiplicity of technologies (De Laet and Mol, 2000; Newman, 1998), technologies have overwhelmingly been defined as material objects – mass produced and widely deployed by users and consumers. While drawing on insights from this body of work, our chapter contributes to a reorientation of the study of technology, towards the consideration of technologies arising from the social sciences that are not primarily devices.

technological artifacts capable of fulfilling the same function ' (Michael, 2000: 23).

2 The social construction of technology approach has documented a large number of cases where the development of institutions, corporations and infrastructures were shaped by the sociality associated with particular technologies. The early years of the telephone were marked by strong debates in the part of the US served by Bell, about what was the proper sociality for it to support (i.e. business telephoning, between head office and factory, versus gossiping women) (Fischer, 1992: 78–79).

3 It is easier to change IAT scores by manipulating the environment, than by giving instructions to fake; they are malleable, but not fakeable. (Nosek et al., 2006: 280).

4 See also Akrich (1992), Michael (2000: 36).

5 Most of them, at least. 'I don 't think Syd has opinions as such', said David Gilmour when asked what Syd Barrett, the former frontman of Pink Floyd, thought about the fact that he had been replaced by Gilmour. http://www.sydbarrett.net/subpages/articles/new_musical_express_april_13.htm

6 The literature on this question is extensive. We mention only Danziger (1997) and Richards (2002) for psychology, and Ashmore (1989) for science in general.

7 See also Macintyre (1985).

8 See also Benschop and Draaisma (2000).

9 Users ' positions are themselves defined on the basis of the popularity of their own photos and the number and type of relations they entertain with other users. The fact that the exact functioning of such weighing formulas is considered a company secret is in itself highly interesting: measurement of expertise, influence and sociality become highly valuable commodities in these settings. This extends the practices around audience measurement, political polling, etc.

10 This example, used by Lerman in explaining her lab 's work, assumes that ambiguity is undesirable.

11 So the reasoning is that sociality will be the basis for better tools, which will be necessary because human abilities to sustain sociality (in its current form) will not be able to deal with the volume of ties, relations and meanings on these platforms.

12 The cases of multiple users of single accounts and of multiple accounts for single users are too often brushed over as a minor confounding issue, and would be deserving of much more scrutiny.

NOTES

1 Also noted by Michael: 'Under the appropriate economic and cultural network conditions, forms of human servitude are "more efficient and convenient" than the development and application of

REFERENCES

Akrich, M. (1992) 'The de-scription of technical objects', in W. Bijker and J. Law (eds), *Shaping Technology/ Building Society: Studies in Sociotechnical Change.* Cambridge, USA: MIT Press. pp. 205–224.

Ashmore, M. (1989) *The Reflexive Thesis: Wrighting Sociology of Scientific Knowledge.* Chicago, USA: University of Chicago Press.

Baistow, K. (2001) 'Behavioural approaches and the cultivation of competence', in G.C. Bunn, G. Richards and A.D. Lovie (eds) *Psychology in Britain.* London UK: Science Museum (Great Britain), British Psychological Society. pp. 309–329.

Bandura, A. (1974) 'Behavior theory and the models of man' *American Psychologist,* 29(12): 859–869.

Bargh, J.A. (2007) 'Introduction', in J.A. Bargh (ed.) *Social Psychology and the Unconscious: The Automaticity of Higher Mental Processes.* New York: Psychology Press. pp. 1–9.

Bargh, J.A. (2008) 'Free will is un-natural', in J. Baer, J. Kaufman, and R.E. Baumeister (eds) *Are we Free? Psychology and Free Will.* New York: Oxford University Press. pp. 128–154.

Bargh, J.A. and Chartrand, T.L. (2000) 'The mind in the middle: A practical guide to priming and automaticity research', in H.T. Reis and C.M. Judd (eds) *Handbook of Research Methods in Social and Personality Psychology.* New York: Cambridge University Press. pp. 253–285.

Bargh, J.A., Chen, M. and Burrows, L. (1996) 'Automaticity of social behavior: Direct effect of trait construct and sterotype activation on action', *Journal of Personality and Social Psychology,* 71: 230–244.

Beaulieu, A. (2004) 'Meditating ethnography: Objectivity and the making of ethnographies of the internet', *Social Epistemology,* 18(2–3): 139–164.

Beaulieu, A., Scharnhorst, A. and Wouters, P. (2007) 'Not another case study: A middle-range interrogation of ethnographic case studies in the exploration of e-science', *Science, Technology & Human Values,* 32: 672–692.

Benschop, R.J. and Draaisma, D. (2000) 'In pursuit of precision. The calibration of minds and machines in late 19th-century psychology', *Annals of Science,* 57: 1–25.

Bertilsson, T.M. (2003) 'The social as trans-genic: On bio-power and its implications for the social', *Acta Sociologica,* 46(2): 118–131.

Boellstorff, T. (2008) *Coming of Age in Second Life: An Anthropologist Explores the Virtually Human.* Princeton: Princeton University Press.

boyd, d.m. and Ellison, N.B. (2007) 'Social network sites: Definition, history, and scholarship', *Journal of Computer-Mediated Communication,* 13(1), article 11. http://jcmc.indiana.edu/vol13/issue1/boyd.ellison.html (accessed18 November 2008). Brown, S. (2003) Natural writing: The case of Serres. *Interdisciplinary Science Reviews,* 28(3), 184–192.

Brunger, F. and Lippman, A. (1995) 'Resistance and adherence to the norms of genetic counselling', *Journal of Genetic Counseling,* 4(3): 151–167.

Bruns, A. (2008) Blogs, Wikipedia, Second Life, and Beyond: From Production to Produsage. New York: Peter Lang.

Callon, M. and Latour, B. (1992) 'Don't throw the baby out with the bath school! A reply to Collins and Yearley', in A. Pickering (ed.) *Science as Practice and Culture.* Chicago: University of Chicago Press. pp. 343–368.

Chartrand, T.L. (2005) 'The role of conscious awareness in consumer behavior', *Journal of Consumer Psychology,* 15(3): 203–210.

Chen, S., Fitzsimmons, G. and Andersen, S. (2007) 'Automaticity in close relationships', in J. Bargh (ed.) *Social Psychology and the Unconscious. The Automaticity of Higher Mental Processes,* Frontiers of social psychology. New York: Psychology Press. pp. 133–172.

Collier, S., Lakoff, A. and Rabinow, P. (2006) 'What is a laboratory in the human sciences?', *ARC Working Paper,* No 1. http: //www.anthropos-*lab*.net/workingpapers/no1.pdf (accessed October 2 2008)

Coon, D.J. (1992) 'Testing the limits of sense and science. American experimental psychologists combat spiritualism, 1880–1920', *American Psychologist,* 47(2): 143–151.

Coon, D. (1993) 'Standardizing the subject – experimental psychologists, introspection, and the quest for a technoscientific ideal', *Technology and Culture,* 34(4): 757–783.

Danziger, K. (1997) *Naming the Mind: How Psychology Found its Language.* London: Sage.

Davies, J. (2006) 'Affinities and beyond! Developing ways of seeing in online spaces', *E-Learning,* 3(2): 217–234.

De Laet, M. and Mol, A. (2000) 'The Zimbabwe bush pump: Mechanics of a fluid technology', *Social Studies of Science,* 30(2): 225–263.

Derksen, M. (2001) 'Discipline, subjectivity and personality. An analysis of the manuals of four psychological tests', *History of the Human Sciences,* 14(1): 25–47.

Derksen, M. (2005) 'Against integration. Why evolution cannot unify the social sciences', *Theory & Psychology,* 15(2): 139–162.

Dunn, E.C. (2004) 'Standards and person-making in east central Europe', in A. Ong and S. Collier (eds) *Global Assemblages:Technology, Politics and Ethics as Anthropological Problems.* London: Blackwell Publishing. pp. 173–193.

Edwards, P.N. (2004) 'A vast machine: Standards as social technology', *Science,* 304(5672): 827–828.

Fischer, C. (1992) *America Calling: A Social History of the Telephone to 1940*. Berkeley: University of California Press.

Fuller, M. (2003) *Behind the Blip: Essays on the Culture of Software*. Brooklyn, USA: Autonomedia.

Galton, F. (1874) *English Men of Science: Their Nature and Nurture*. London: Frank Cass Publishers.

Gieryn, T.F. (2006) 'City as truth-spot: Laboratories and field-sites in urban studies', *Social Studies of Science*, 36: 5–38.

Hacking, I. (1986) 'Making up people', in T.C. Heller, M. Sosna and D.E. Wellerby. (eds) *Reconstructing Individualism*. Stanford, USA: Stanford University Press. pp. 222–236.

Hacking, I. (2005) 'The Cartesian vision fulfilled: analogue bodies and digital minds', *Interdisciplinary Science Reviews*, 30(2): 153–166.

Haraway, D.J. (1991) *Simians, Cyborgs and Women: The Reinvention of Nature*. London: Free Association Books.

Hayles, N.K. (2005) *My Mother was a Computer: Digital Subjects and Literary Texts*. Chicago: University of Chicago Press.

Igo, S. (2007) *The Averaged American: Surveys, Citizens, and the Making of a Mass Public*. Cambridge, MA: Harvard University Press.

Ito, M., Baumer, S., Bittanti, M., boyd, d., Cody, R., Herr, B., Horst, H. A., Lange, P. G., Mahendran, D., Martinez, K., Pascoe, C.J., Perkel, D., Robinson, L., Sims, C. and Tripp, L. (Forthcoming) *Hanging Out, Messing Around, Geeking Out: Living and Learning with New Media*. Cambridge, MA: MIT Press.

Jack, A.I. and Roepstorff, A. (2002) 'Introspection and cognitive brain mapping: from stimulus-response to script-report', *Trends in Cognitive Sciences*, 6(8): 333–339.

Jakobsson, M. and Taylor, T.L. (2003) 'The Sopranos meets EverQuest: Social networking in massively multiplayer online games', *Ezine*, 17(18). http://www.mediacritica.net/courses/711/jakobsson.pdf (accessed March 9, 2008).

Jenkins, H. (2006) *Convergence Culture: Where Old and New Media Collide*. New York: New York University Press.

Keats, D.M. (2001) *Interviewing: A Practical Guide for Students and Professionals*. Buckingham: Open University Press.

Kim, K.-H. and Yun, H. (2007) 'Cying for me, cying for us: Relational dialectics in a Korean social network site', *Journal of Computer-Mediated Communication*, 13(1), article 15. http://jcmc.indiana.edu/vol13/issue1/kim.yun.html (accessed 15 October 2008).

Kihlstrom, J.F. (2004) 'Availability, accessibility, and subliminal perception', *Consciousness and Cognition*, 13(1): 92–100

Knorr Cetina, K. (1999) *Epistemic cultures*. Cambridge, MA.: Harvard University Press.

Kolbitsch, J. and Maurer, H. (2006) 'The transformation of the Web: How emerging communities shape the information we consume', *Journal of Universal Computer Science*, 12(2): 187–213.

Mettrie, J.O. de La (1748) *L'Homme Machine*. Leyden: Elie Luzac.

Lange, P.G. (2007) 'Publicly private and privately public: Social networking on YouTube. *Journal of Computer-Mediated Communication*, 13(1). http://jcmc.indiana.edu/vol13/issue1/lange.html (accessed 30 October 2008).

Latour, B. (1992) 'Where are the missing masses? The sociology of a few mundane artifacts', in W.E. Bijker and J. Law (eds) *Shaping Technology/Building Society: Studies in Sociotechnical Change*. Cambridge, MA: MIT Press. pp. 225–258.

Latour, B. (1993) *We Have Never Been Modern* (trans. Catherine Porter). Cambridge, MA: Harvard University Press.

Latour, B. (1994) 'Pragmatogonies – a mythical account of how humans and nonhumans swap properties', *American Behavioral Scientist*, 37(6): 791–808.

Latour, B. (2005) *Reassembling the social: An introduction to Actor-Network-Theory*. Oxford: Oxford University Press.

Law J. and Urry J. (2003) 'Enacting the social', published by the Department of Sociology, and the Centre for Science Studies, Lancaster University, Lancaster. www.lancs.ac.uk/fass/sociology/papers/law-urry-enacting-the-social.pdf (accessed 18 November 2008).

Lerman, K. and Jones, L. (2007) 'Social browsing on Flickr', *Proceedings of International Conference on Weblogs and Social Media*, Boulder, CO, USA. Extended version available on arXiv (cs.HC/0612047).

Lerman, K. (2007) 'Social networks and social information filtering on Digg', *Proceedings of Int. Conf. on Weblogs and Social Media*, Boulder, CO, USA (poster). Extended version available on arXiv (cs.HC/0612046).

Lezaun, J. (2007) 'A market of opinions: The political epistemology of focus groups', *The Sociological Review*, 55: 130–151.

Mackenzie, A. (2006) *Cutting Code: Software and Sociality*. New York: Peter Lang.

MacIntyre, A. (1985) 'How psychology makes itself true – or false', in S. Koch and D.E. Leary (eds) *A Century of Psychology as a Science*. New York: McGraw Hill. pp. 897–903.

Michael, M. (2000) *Reconnecting Culture, Technology and Nature: From Society to Heterogeneity*. London: Routledge.

McNeill, W. (1995) *Keeping Together in Time: Dance and Drill in Human History*. Cambridge, MA: Harvard University Press.

Newman, S. (1998) 'Here, there, and nowhere at all: Distribution, negotiation and virtuality in postmodern ethnography and engineering', *Knowledge and Society*, (11): 235–267.

Nosek, B.A., Greenwald, A.G. and Banaji, M.R. (2006) 'The implicit association test at age 7: a methodological and conceptual review', in J.A. Bargh (ed.) *Social Psychology and the Unconscious: The Automaticity of Higher Mental Processes*. New York: Psychology Press. pp. 265–292.

Osborne, T. and Rose. N. (1999) 'Do the social sciences create phenomena: The case of public opinion research', *British Journal of Sociology*, 50(3): 367–396.

Owen, R. (1972) *A New View of Society: Or, Essays on the Formation of the Human Character, Preparatory to the Development of a Plan for Gradually Ameliorating the Condition of Mankind* (2nd edition). Clifton, NJ: A. M. Kelley. (Original work published 1816.)

Pickel, A. (2001) 'Between social sciences and social technology: towards a philosophical foundation for post-communist transformational studies', *Philosophy of the Social Sciences*, 31(4): 459–487.

Pinch, T.J., Ashmore, M. and Mulkay, M. (1992) 'Technology, testing, text: Clinical budgeting in the U.K. National Health Service', in W.E. Bijker and J. Law (eds), *Shaping Technology/Building Society: Studies in Sociotechnical Change*. Cambridge, MA: MIT Press. pp. 265–289.

Popper, K.R. (1966) *The Open Society and Its Enemies* (5th edn). London: Routledge & K. Paul.

Rabinow, P. (1992) 'Artificiality and Enlightenment: From sociobiology to biosociality', in J. Crary and S. Kwinter (eds) *Incorporations*. New York: Zone. pp. 234–257.

Rheinberger, H.-J. (1997) *Toward a History of Epistemic Things: Synthesizing Proteins in the Test Tube*. Stanford, USA: Stanford University Press.

Richards, G. (2002) 'The psychology of psychology', *Theory & Psychology*, 12: 7–36.

Rose, N. (1985) *The psychological complex : psychology, politics and society in England, 1869–1939*. London: Routledge & Kegan Paul.

Rose, N. (2001) 'The politics of life itself', *Theory, Culture & Society*, 18(6): 1–30.

Shapin, S. and Schaffer, S. (1989) *Leviathan and the Air-Pump: Hobbes, Boyle, and the Experimental Life*. Princeton, USA: Princeton University Press.

Sip, K.E., Roepstorff, A., McGregor, W. and Frith, C. (2008) 'Detecting deception: the scope and limits', *Trends in Cognitive Sciences*, 12(2): 48–53.

Skågeby, J. (2008) 'Semi-public end-user content contributions - A case-study of concerns and intentions in online photo-sharing', *International Journal of Human Computer Studies*, 66(4): 287–300.

Skinner, B.F. (1976) *Walden Two*. New York: Macmillan.

Smith, R. (2005) 'Does reflexivity separate the human sciences from the natural sciences?', *History of the Human Sciences*, 18(4): 1–25.

Surowiecki, J. (2005) *The Wisdom of Crowds*. New York: Anchor.

VKS (2008) 'Messy shapes of knowledge: STS explores informatization, new media, and academic work', in E.J. Hackett, O. Amsterdamska, M. Lynch and J. Wajcman (eds) *The Handbook of Science and Technology Studies*. Cambridge, MA: MIT Press. pp. 319–352.

Watson, J.B. (1930) *Behaviorism*. New York: W.W. Norton & Company.

Zaitloom, C. (2004) 'The disciplines of speculators', in A. Ong and S. Collier (eds) *Global Assemblages: Technology, Politics and Ethics as Anthropological Problems*. London: Blackwell Publishing. pp. 253–269.

Epilogue

Rationality in the Social Sciences: Bridging the Gap

Jesús Zamora-Bonilla

THE GREAT DIVIDE

Traditionally, there has been a 'great divide' in the social sciences between those theories based on a 'rational choice' approach to human behaviour, and those based on some kind of 'hermeneutic' approach.[1] The first side of the divide started in economic theory, as a formalisation of the idea of the 'economic man' of the Classical economists from the eighteenth and nineteenth centuries, though it has been 'colonising' other branches of the social sciences, particularly from the 1960s; one of its main features when seen at a distance, that is, when we don't enter too much into its details, is just its tendency to produce formal models: social outputs are computed as the result of individual choices, in such a way that both the individual choices and their possible interconnections are assumed to be subjected to some mathematical constraints (the 'assumptions' of the models). Hermeneutic approaches, on the other hand, don't like the 'scientism' that all this modelling transpires, and pretend to be (more) faithful to the qualitatively and essentially subjective essence of the human realities that constitute the social practices they study;

these approaches tend to see their intellectual products more as a part of the 'humanities', than as a part of 'science' (in the Anglo-Saxon, straight sense of 'science' as either 'natural science', or research conducted according to the methods of natural science). Of course, there are other relevant differences, and, more importantly, there are other significant 'divides'; for example, there is the essential question of to what extent the social context or situation determines individual choices, and there are different answers to this last question in each part of the rational-choice vs. non-rational-choice debate. My aim in this final chapter is not, however, to map all these distinctions, but to concentrate on a very specific, but also very general and fundamental question, which is the conception of *rationality* that underlies the 'rational choice' and 'hermeneutic' approaches, for I think it is the one that has created the worst misunderstandings in the philosophy of social sciences, and it can serve better than other concepts to gather some ideas that have appeared in the preceding chapters. Still more specifically, my claim is that the main difference between both conceptions is connected to the attitude they have towards the concept of *normativity*;[2] in a nutshell, rational choice theories have too few analytic resources to deal with the richness of the implications that this notion has in the social realm, but hermeneutic theories are too stuck to the prejudice that their interpretation of normativity capture it 'as it really is', that is, they ignore that 'normativity' (as 'rationality', 'interpretation', etc.), is just a 'theoretical term' in the social sciences, that can be logically analysed and refined; stated differently, hermeneutic approaches ignore that what they are producing is just *scientific models*. My goal is, then, to devise a strategy that can 'translate' the hermeneutic analysis of normative action into a 'formal model', in such a way that the relations between both paradigms are easier to see, and their virtues and drawbacks can more easily be compared.

NORMATIVITY AND REASONING

Rational choice theory (cf. Chapters 7 and 14) has often been criticised for purporting to treat human agents as 'mechanical', mere 'automata' programmed to maximise a function ('expected utility') on which those agents just have no say at all. I think this criticism is not fair, for rational choice theory is based on the assumption that it is not its own goal to *discover* what are the real 'utility function' (nor the 'probability function') behind real people's choices. The theory puts simply some limits to what an 'admissible' function is, a limit that reduces to logical consistency and the internal coherence of the preferences. What are the *real* expected utility functions of people is not a theoretical, but an *empirical* question, though our common-sense knowledge of how people are often allows us to introduce some additional assumptions (like diminishing marginal utility, a preference for more income instead of less, and the like).[3] So, rational choice approaches' eluding of the question of 'what do people really think and how do they really take their decisions' does not presume that human agents

are automata, or something like that, but is the expression of the fact that, in general, those models simply take for granted that agents *have* 'rationally' thought and decided 'already', and analyse what *follows* from the assumption that those decisions are rational and mutually consistent.

Another usual criticism is that rational choice theory describes people as 'egoistic', only interested in the maximisation of their own welfare and as unresponsive to moral or ethical considerations. I also think this criticism is not fair, for, although it is true that in most rational choice models it is assumed that the agents' utility functions only depend on each individual's well being, this is not a *necessary* assumption of the theory, but a reflection of the idea that, in most 'economic' circumstances, people simply look out for their own welfare and that of their close relatives. But nothing precludes that, among the variables in the utility function's domain, one can include the 'moral sense of duty' the agent attaches to each possible action or each possible outcome.[4] The fact that economists and other rational choice social scientists do not usually include them is not a matter of principle (cf. Chapter 9), but it is probably because they consider that the hypothesis that 'people tend to do what they must do' has a little flavour of 'ad hocness'. Of course, a hypothesis being ad hoc does not entail that it is false, but scientists tend to prefer more parsimonious explanations (see Chapter 33); in this case, explaining people's complying with social and moral norms as an outcome of the interdependence of many individuals' self-interest (e.g. under the form of a network – Chapter 16) is clearly more parsimonious, because the self-interest assumption also explains many other facts about social life.

Nevertheless, there is indeed a grain of truth (or two) in these criticisms, but they are a little bit hidden. Regarding the first one, it is true that rational choice theory only attempts to identify the action or decision that is the *outcome* of the agent's reasoning process, and not the reasoning process itself (it simply assumes it is 'rational', that is, that the process leads to the same outcome – or 'solution'– the rational choice model identifies, no matter how the agent manages to find it). But one can point to the fact that *reasoning is itself an action*, particularly (but not only) when it takes the form of *public deliberation* (see especialy Chapters 26 and 36). Hence, if we ask 'how does one reason *rationally?*', the theory has just *no* hint to give us; it seems to assume that people have some 'magical' capacity to discover the 'solution' of the equations that represent their choice problem, but it is obvious that, in general, people frame these problems in a way that is completely different from the representation of them that we find in microeconomic textbooks.[5] Frequent references to 'procedural rationality' (see Chapter 7) point to the fact that reasoning and deliberation is a real and costly activity, but these 'heterodox' approaches have concentrated in the investigation of 'non-fully-rational' thought processes (i.e. how do people think when they can not find out the 'rational' – that is optimal–solution), and my question is that rational choice theory has no resources even to describe the functioning of *rational* reasoning processes, because it does not even consider 'mental' processes as actions that are to be explained by the application of rational choice theory. After all, if the reasoning process leading to a 'rational' choice were an action whose *own* right outcomes (each of the *steps* of reasoning) came from the application of something like a rational choice model, this would lead us to an infinite regress, for we should also claim that the rational choice process leading us to the determination of the *steps* of the first reasoning is itself 'rational', and so on.

Regarding the problem of normativity, though it is true that rational choice theory is agnostic about the content of the individual's preferences, and this makes perfect room for the agent's having some *moral* preferences (amongst others), it is still true that the theory, which is based on the empiricist interpretation of preferences as mere *dispositions* to choose, or *revealed* preferences

(i.e. $u(A) > u(B)$ if and only if the agent *would not choose B* if A were an available option), has no conceptual means at all to specify the difference between the *kinds of reasons* one may have to prefer an option to another one: it cannot tell whether you decide not to steal a jewel because a policeman is walking around (and you prefer to remain free instead of going to jail), or just because you think you *mustn't* do it. This might be regarded as a weak criticism, because, after all, rational choice theory does not also distinguish between *other* types of preferences (e.g. whether you prefer to study in order to get a job, or because you enjoy it, or in order not to upset your parents), and this is not taken as a problem, in general. But in this case there is a significant difference, because to say that you *must* do something is to say that you must do it *no matter what your preferences are*. A normative reason *being* a reason, hence, seems to consist in something different from being 'just' a preference. Actually, we can generalise this idea and apply it not only to *moral* reasons, but to all those cases in which we can say that one *has a reason* to perform an action, even if she chooses not to perform it, or vice versa. Hence, what rational choice theory fails to explain is what it is exactly *to be a reason*: the model assumes that the agent has a coherent repertoire of *dispositions* to choose, but it cannot answer the question about the nature of the *motivations* to choose, in particular, it fails to understand motivations *as* reasons, that is, it cannot answer the question about the connection between these motivations and the *reasoning* process we discussed in the previous paragraph.[6]

Normativity, intentionality, rule following, reasoning (at least in the sense of the interweaving of meanings that connects an agent's situation with her appropriate behaviour) and hence, meaning, are, instead, basic concepts in most of the non rational choice approaches in the philosophy of social sciences (cf., for example Chapters 6, 9 and 21–26). Many of these approaches have been based on the idea that the most fundamental human capacity, and that on which society and culture are constructed, is *language*, an idea that has received a lot of conceptual support and analytical machinery from contemporary philosophy of language, mainly from the stream that flows from the 'second' Wittgenstein and the theory of 'speech acts' (see Chapter 5). I will take issue with this tradition in the following sections, by presenting a *model* of rational action which is based on the analysis of 'language games', and which, if successful, will allow us to show the mutual *consistency* of the hermeneutic and the rational choice options, by showing that the latter can be described as a *particular case* of the former. In particular, I want also to show that, though the hermeneutic approach is usually contrasted with rational choice theory on the basis of the latter's exemplification of a *nomological* kind of explanation of social facts, opposed to the idea of explanation as *understanding* proper of the former (see Chapters 1, 2 and 3), this is actually a mistake, for we can understand 'understanding' in a perfectly 'nomological' sense once the connections between meaning, normativity, and action are described in a 'scientific' model; a model, furthermore that allows us to connect in a 'natural' way the insights of hermeneutics with a *naturalistic* view of the human mind. So, one of the morals would be that hermeneutics is capable of absorbing the rational choice approach as a special case, to the 'cost' of recognising that there is only one basic form of scientific explanation, that is, nomological explanation, and one way of being 'scientific', that is, naturalism (see Chapter 4).

MEANING, ACTION AND DEONTIC SCOREKEEPING

In order to perform this task, I shall make use of one recent and powerful trend in the study of language and action. It consists in viewing linguistic actions, and particularly argumentation and persuasion dialogues, as governed by the submission to each speaker to certain *norms* that govern the connections between the *commitments* implicit or explicit in her past speech acts. There are several authors that have developed a normative approach of argumentation and language on similar lines (Stephen Toulmin, 1958; Chaim Perelman and L. Olbrechts-Tyteca, 1958; Jürgen Habermas, 1981; Douglas Walton, 2007; Frans van Eemeren and R. Grootendorst, 2004; Philip Pettit, 2001; and others), but I shall refer to the exposition by Robert Brandom (1994), which I think is particularly suitable for philosophical discussion on the theory of rational action. My point of departure is a naïve psychological view of the ontology of mind and action presupposed in many social and philosophical theories: the mind contains *beliefs* and *desires*, which are somehow combined in more complex entities called *intentions*, and which in turn produce the agent's *actions*. Actions and other events induce changes in the world that may have the effect (amongst others) of bringing out new beliefs and desires. In this naïve view, the four referred types of entities are 'natural', in the sense that they are conceived as things (really, as 'natural kinds') that exist in human brains as an outcome of their natural functioning. Rational choice theory adds to this description three *theoretical assumptions*, intended both to capture the rationality of the agents, and also to give predictive and empirical content to the theory; these assumptions are, of course, that preferences are complete and transitive, that beliefs respect the axioms of probability, and that the performed action is the one that maximises expected utility (a mathematical combination of beliefs and desires). Although rational choice theory is often associated to an empiricist, nomological view of social science, the truth is that this view *is difficult to* 'naturalise', in part because of what we have seen in the previous section: how a 'natural' brain is able to implement the algorithms allowing it to systematically produce an outcome consistent with optimisation theory (while most often doing no calculations at all!) is indeed a difficult question to answer. As we will see, a heuristic approach is, in fact, considerably *easier* to integrate within a naturalistic framework.

Robert Brandom, however, rejects this 'belief-desire-intention' furniture of the world (as well as its *prima facie* naturalism), and substitutes it for the conception that the elements and basic structure of human action are *fundamentally normative*, not 'natural'.[7] Brandom's description is, instead, something like the following: the basic units of our rational activity (which includes not only speech acts, but all kinds of intentional behaviour)[8] are *commitments*, which can be of two types: doxastic (commitments to maintain the truth of a claim) or practical (commitments to perform, or not to perform, some particular action). These commitments (and entitlements)[9] can be subjected to two fundamental *normative attitudes*: they can be *undertaken* (by oneself), and they can be *attributed* (to oneself or, more often, to others). The combination of all the commitments and entitlements undertaken by, or attributed to an agent at a given moment, is the agent's *normative status*. The most interesting aspect of Brandom's theory is that these statuses are essentially *inferential*, that is, they do not 'mean' anything in isolation, actually they are *nothing* in isolation (just a bunch of meaningless psychological humours or unintelligible noises, so to say), for their normative force is constituted by their being subjected to *inferential norms*. This means that undertaking a commitment consists in accepting *other* commitments, that is, those that 'follow' from the former commitment and the application of the relevant inferential norms (e.g. if I assert that my car has been stolen, I become committed to justifying my claim, to accept all the other claims that follow from the former, and to remove the inconsistencies with other commitments I have accepted before and that happen to be incompatible with the new one). Inferential norms are 'conceptual' norms in

the sense that they are what gives content and meaning to the *concepts* employed in my claims: *meaning* something by some words consists in accepting what follows from the use of them. Of these inferential norms, some are 'intralinguistic', in the sense that they connect claims with claims (or doxastic commitments with doxastic commitments), but others connect language with other facts; basically, there are 'entry' rules, that confer a new normative status to an agent thanks to the happening of some physical event (paradigmatically, in the case of *perception*), and there are also 'exit' rules, that have practical commitments as their output (and, in the end, *actions*).[10] Lastly, interaction between rational agents basically takes place by what Brandom calls 'deontic scorekeeping', that is, each agent's taking into account the commitments and entitlements she is attributing to the others, and vice versa.

So, in a nutshell, as compared to the naïve psychology of the theory of action, now we have within the Brandomian framework doxastic commitments (and entitlements) instead of beliefs, and practical commitments (and entitlements) instead of desires, preferences or intentions. And, as compared to rational choice theory, *instead* of the assumption of logical coherence and mathematical optimisation, what we have now is the assumption that all the commitments of an agent *are inferentially articulated* according to the conceptual norms the agent is subjected to. As a representative of the hermeneutic approach, we see that the immense variety of inferential norms makes human action, as explained by Brandom's theory, much richer and more complex than what the 'toy' models of rational choice theory allow (an easy way of visualising this difference is to think of the fact that the actors habitating rational choice models hardly *talk* at all, they seem to live, so to say, in the times of silent movies);[11] but, of course, the cost of this richness is that a theory of action like Brandom's is nearly incapable of providing models that can be simple and manageable enough to be empirically testable through definite predictions something that Brandom's theory is, on the other hand, surely not intending to do, of course.

SOME DIFFICULTIES FOR AN INFERENTIALIST MODEL OF ACTION

There are actually other things in Brandom's theory that impede its direct transformation into a 'fully fledged' theory of social action. The most important one is that there is no *explicit connection* between practical commitments (i.e. commitments to act) and actions themselves. One doesn't know, after reading what Brandom says about practical commitments, if the agent will *actually* do what she is committed to do, or will not; also one doesn't know what happens when the agent has incurred several mutually incompatible practical commitments (by the way, Brandom's theory also does not tell what happens when what are incompatible are doxastic commitments: the agent has there the *responsibility* to remove the inconsistency, but the theory does not say how to do it),[12] neither when the agent is simply 'entitled' to perform several incompatible actions (i.e. how does she *choose* in this case?; is it just by good-old-fashion utility maximisation?). Stated differently, in order to be employed as a template for social science models, we need to add to Brandom's theory some assumptions about the *causal efficacy* of commitments, or at least, we need some *empirical* criterion to determine what behaviours constitute the fulfilment of a commitment and which do not. In a sense, what we need is something analogous to what Paul Samuelson in the 1930s did about the concept of preference when replacing it by 'revealed preference', but for the case of 'commitment' or 'duty'; hence, we would need something like a concept of 'revealed duty'.

Another related problem comes from what is actually a philosophical virtue of Brandom's theory: in order to explain how 'objectivity' is achieved by a system based on the attribution of normative statuses, he claims[13] that we must look to the perspectival difference between undertaking and attributing a commitment: it is not that there exists a 'privileged' perspective (e.g. that of 'the' community) that serves to define the objective truth (which commitments are true and which ones are false), but that *every* 'subjective' perspective includes within its linguistic machinery the mechanisms for expressing the *conceptual* distinction between the commitments an agent really *has*, on the one hand, and, on the other hand, the commitments somebody *attributes* to that agent; analogously, these mechanisms allow the expression of the conceptual distinction between the fact that an agent is *committed* to some claim, on the one hand, and, on the other hand, the *correctness* of that claim. Basically, this means that, in order to attribute a doxastic commitment to somebody, you have to be able to distinguish the fact that she is committed to the claim, from the fact that the claim is true or not; hence, although you necessarily accept as true those doxastic commitments that you believe, you can also apply that perspectival mechanism to *yourself*, so recognising the *conceptual possibility* of your being *mistaken* in accepting that claim. This perspectival approach to commitments is, however, difficult to insert into an empirical model of action, because it creates a gap between the commitments one agent *actually undertakes* and the commitments the same agent 'really' has (not to talk of the commitments other agents actually attribute to her); the question is, what of these set of commitments are the ones we (as social scientists) must take into account as *causally* leading to action? A natural answer is that only *undertaken* commitments have *causal* efficacy, but if this is so, then, what is the role of 'real' commitments in the model?

A different way of expressing this problem is the following: when somebody accepts ('undertakes') a set of propositions (*P*), then she is 'committed' to accept *anything* (*F*) that follows from those propositions by the application of the inferential rules she abides by. The question is that some of the elements of *F* will be *actually* recognised by the agent as being so, but many others will not, and hence probably she will not *undertake* consciously the latter, nor even implicitly (i.e. she may, mistakenly, even believe and express the negation of some elements of *F*). Hence, if we want to model the *dymanics* of normative scores, the problem is that we face a choice between including in an agent's score *all* the consequences of the claims she undertakes, or only those that she consciously recognises. The first option has the problem that it is obscure how an unrecognised commitment can have a causal effect on behaviour, whereas the second option ignores the fact that, after all, the agent *is* committed to those claims even if she does not notice it in any way, and we are left without any hint about how is it possible that the actual concatenations of arguments and reasons by an agent can be said to be *subjected* to inferential rules.

As a matter of fact, the two problems I have mentioned so far (what are the connection between commitments and actual behaviour, and what are the different explanatory roles of 'undertaken' vs. 'attributed' or 'real' commitments) are part of a single difficulty, that of understanding the connection between the 'normative' aspects of commitments and the 'descriptive' aspects of behaviour (see Chapter 22). But there is also a third important problem, which refers to *the nature of inferential rules*. From my point of view, the most severe shortcoming in Brandom's theory is that it gives no hint about where the conceptual rules come from. This is true both from the ontogenetic point of view (i.e. how does an individual *learn* what are the conceptual rules that regulate her use of words and the connection of words to perception and action, and in such a way that what he learns is not only an empirical correlation, but a 'necessary' – in the normative sense – semantic relation), and from the phylogenetic point of view (i.e. how have the actual rules that govern the 'right' use of

words come to be exactly the ones they are). Furthermore, it is not clear whether Brandom equates all inferential norms with conceptual norms (i.e. rules that determine the *appropriate* use of concepts), or if there can be some inferential norms that are not 'conceptual' (e.g. *moral* norms, as 'you must not lie', can be interpreted as norms about practical inferences, as 'if you are asked something, then you must tell the truth').

HOMO DELIBERATOR: TOWARDS AN INFERENTIALIST MODEL OF ACTION

I think that all the difficulties pointed out in the previous section have to do with Brandom's insistence in keeping his theory as an analysis of a merely *normative* reality, and from his assumptions that the normative cannot be naturalised, and that norms are not reducible to regularities.[14] So, in order to transform inferentialism into the template of an empirical model for the social sciences, the following moves are suggested:[15]

1 The first thing to do is to become agnostic about a realm of norms that cannot be 'objects in the causal order',[16] and keep our attention *only* on the normative *attitudes* that transform a 'mere' psychological event into an attribution or an undertaking of deontic scores. That is, the idea is not to substitute 'purely' normative statuses for 'merely' psychological states, but to recognise *that some psychological states can consist in the recognition of a normative status*. In a more sophisticated way, we can also include *degrees* of commitment, for an agent can be more or less strongly committed to either a claim or an action. These degrees of commitment are, of course, psychological properties.

2 Given some actual commitments made by an agent (including the commitment to follow certain *norms*), we have to introduce some hypotheses about the *probabilities* of the actions the agent can perform. I will call these hypotheses 'behavioural laws'. The simplest assumption is that the agent *will* perform that action she is most strongly committed to, but other assumptions are possible (e.g. that the stronger a

commitment is, the higher is the probability of fulfilling it).[17] Actually, we can define 'rational' *action* as that which obeys some of these alternative assumptions; other types of behaviour, instead (i.e. when you do not tend to do what you are committed to do), would be 'irrational'. It remains an empirical question to what extent some people act 'rationally' or 'irrationally' in this sense. However, it is also true that, if we find that somebody seems to act against the commitments *we* attribute to her (or that we think she attributes to herself), we have to decide whether to revise our hypothesis about what behavioural law she is following, or our hypotheses about what are the commitments she is undertaking.

3 Commitments are inferentially articulated, which means that acknowledging some of them will lead you to undertaking others, according to the inferential norms you are accepting; since undertaking a commitment is an action, it will be taken according to some 'behavioural law'. Some inferential norms (those referred to as 'entry rules' above) command one to undertake certain commitments, given not (or not only) some previous commitments, but also certain circumstances as they are perceived by the agent. All this process of reaching some commitments from other ones, or from other things, is what *reasoning*, in a broad sense, consists of. Reasoning being 'rational' means, hence, that it follows a 'behavioural-law-for-the-undertaking-of-doxastic-commitments' which is 'rational' according to the sense explained in the previous point. This is coherent with recent 'dual-system theories' of cognition,[18] according to which, human reasoning works at two different levels: first, inferential jumps which are basically subconscious and 'intuitive'; second, 'reflective' inferential steps which are reducible to combinations of first-level jumps, but that consist in the conscious following of a rule. The capacity of being both *subjected* and capable of *mastering* the inferential links of your commitments, is the basic feature that makes of you, as a human being, an *homo deliberator*.

4 Psychological events, like having a belief or a desire, are also part of the 'circumstances' experienced by an agent. It is also possible, hence, that some 'entry rules' allow her to undertake a certain doxastic or practical commitment (with a higher or lower strength), under the assumption that she experiences certain psychological states that can be interpreted as beliefs or desires.

5 When the situation includes *more than one agent*, then the actions of each agent are part of the 'circumstances' of the others, and have to be taken into account according as how the inferential rules accepted by the agents command them to react to those circumstances.

In a nutshell, the basic elements of an inferentialist model of action are:

1 a description of the inferential (doxastic or practical) rules each agent accepts;
2 a description of the 'initial' commitments of the agents;
3 a description of their relevant circumstances;
4 behavioural laws indicating the probability that certain actions (including the undertaking of further commitments) are performed by the agents, given their previous commitments and their circumstances.[19]

The main problem with a model like this is, of course, that we have to introduce so many pieces of information that they can be adjusted ad hoc so to reach any conclusion we want (which is, obviously, a problem widely spread in the social sciences; cf. Chapter 34); so, the more constraints we are able to introduce into the elements *a* to *d*, the better for increasing the empirical content of the model. Rational choice models have an analogous problem (e.g. the utility and subjective probability functions can be manipulated ad hoc), though the number of independent variables in the case of inferential models can be much bigger (think, for example, of all the norms governing the meanings of each word, and all the practical rules regulating different circumstances). In some way, this difference is the core of the distinction between rational choice and hermeneutic theories: the former tend to *simplify* the social situations so that the modeller can draw some definite conclusions, whereas the latter tend to *replicate* the richness of the inferential articulation of reasoning processes. But my point is that this is only a difference of *degree*, not of kind: utility functions can in principle be made as complex and 'rich' as one wants (losing with that their predictive power), but inferential models can also be made less and less complex (losing with that the 'sense of closeness' they give us).

To conclude this section, I will discuss briefly what can be the *logical* connections between inferentialist and rational choice models. The most important difference between them is that inferentialist models do not (or not necessarily) employ the concepts of utility and subjective probability, which were the result of *applying the hypothesis of logical coherence* to the more 'naturalist' concepts of desires and beliefs; instead, inferentialist models apply to the latter concepts the assumption that they are *inferentially articulated* by means of a network of practical and epistemic norms. The two models represent, hence, *two different theoretisations of the rationality assumption*, and it is hard to see whether both are mutually translatable. Nevertheless, once the psychological operations within an agent's mind or within a collective deliberation process have led the agents to some commitments, the link between the strength of the commitments and the actual choices could be described as a kind of maximisation (though I doubt this is necessarily so; see Note 17). Also, the process of reasoning can be modelled according to some Bayesian principles (though doxastic commitments are difficult to interpret systematically in terms of subjective probabilities). So, in principle, it is an open question whether we can replicate any inferentialist model by means of a rational choice model, or vice versa. If this were the case, however, I do not think it should be taken as a triumph of any of the approaches: it would only show that in both cases what we have are not the *real facts* themselves, but simply a couple of *abstract models* of the facts, and their mutual substitutability would entail that the 'great divide' is only an artifact of the history of thought.

More interestingly, and less speculatively, is the following: we can expect that there are cases in which agents *can* calculate (explicitly or implicitly) probabilities and utilities, and in these cases, it is possible

that the *norm* of maximising expected utility is included within the inferential commitments of agents. Or there can also be cases where the actual inferential norms are mathematically equivalent (or very approximate) to some maximisation decision criterion. So, the inferentialist models allow that, in some cases, that *homini deliberatores* behave according to rational choice theory, or in a way that can be replicated by a rational choice model. This can be particularly the case when the inferential norms lead subjects to situations in which there is no action to which they are very strongly committed, but have, instead, several incompatible actions they are *entitled* to perform.

WHERE DO INFERENTIAL NORMS COME FROM?

In the previous section I have assumed that a social situation is defined, among other things, through the inferential rules accepted by the agents included in it. In order to build a scientific model of that situation, this is the appropriate strategy, of course, for we will be trying to analyse what actually happens in it. But this is open to a couple of questions. In the first place, it can be the case that 'we', as social scientists or philosophers studying that empirical situation, do not *share* exactly the same inferential norms (this can be obvious for practical norms, but it can also be the case for conceptual or epistemic ones). I don't think this can be taken as a problem; after all, it can happen that not all the agents *within* the same situation accept the same norms, and our model must take this possibility into account; so, why are the agents going to share exactly *our* norms? Of course, what is important is that the modeller is conscious of this possibility, and does not unjustifiedly project her own conceptual and practical norms upon her subjects.

In the second place, and more importantly, it is a scientifically relevant question *why* the rules admitted within a social situation are the ones they are. It is unlikely that the agents have a systematic power to decide what will be the rules (in some cases –for example, the study of legislation – it can be the case, but this is rare), so they cannot 'change' them. But, on the other hand, it is also a fact that in different situations and places the rules are different, so rules *actually do change*. The naturalistic model sketched in the previous section gives us some hints to explain how this can happen. First, rules have to be learned, and are actually abstracted and conjectured from concrete circumstances; so, it is not necessary that in all circumstances the same rules arise, nor that all the agents learn exact 'replicas' of the same rules. Second, and perhaps more interestingly: our model recognises the existence of beliefs and desires *besides* that of doxastic and practical commitments; only the latter are inferentially articulated, that is, only from them we reach other commitments by applying or following the inferential norms we accept; but our, so to say, more 'basic' beliefs and desires, that arise in our minds as a result of merely *causal* processes (some internal, some linked to the external world),[20] are not necessarily *consistent* with the conclusions of our deliberations; actually, having certain rules (instead of others) will lead social groups to reach certain results (instead of others), for example, given the same 'external' circumstances, two communities with different conceptual and epistemic rules will end undertaking different doxastic commitments; it is, then, possible that one of these communities experiments with a higher degree of *cognitive dissonance*, in the sense that there are more and more severe inconsistencies between the doxastic commitments they have actually undertaken and the actual beliefs they have formed (because the latter do not arise *only* from those doxastic commitments, but also from other psychological mechanisms relating to perception, for example), and one community can also experiment with a higher degree of *dissatisfaction*, in the sense that the actions to which its members are committed don't actually lead to very

pleasurable outcomes as often as in the case of the other community. My hypothesis is that those conceptual or practical norms leading to more severe cases of cognitive dissonance and dissatisfaction will tend to be replaced by others, perhaps in some 'Darwinian' way (see Chapter 20). Formal models for the evolution of norms within this framework (in which both deontic scores and psychological properties have a causal role) can be highly interesting to develop.

INNOCUOUS INDIVIDUALISM; HARMLESS COLLECTIVISM

The naturalist approach to inferentialism depicted in the previous sections allows us to understand in a very simple way one of the most enduring debates within the philosophy of social sciences: the individualism/collectivism question (see Chapter 8). In this debate, there is an undeniable bit of truth in the thesis that all social systems are constituted 'just' (or, 'in the end') by individuals; inferentialist models recognise this in accepting that 'original' attributions and undertakings of commitments are always psychological events, and hence, are the product of an individual's mind. This does not mean that there cannot be *collective* commitments: the inferential rules the agents abide by can perfectly allow the creation of this type of commitments, for the difference between an individual commitment and a collective one resides only in the different allocation of duties and entitlements characteristic of each case; as long as a particular commitment is necessarily 'linked' to more than one agent (in the sense that it can only be created or destroyed if it is created or destroyed for all the members of the group simultaneously), it will be a *collective* commitment, which can very well be different from the commitments of individual members.[21] Neither the social scientists nor the philosopher can legitimately establish a priori that inferential norms allowing the allocation of deontic scores in such a way are not valid, that is, it is an empirical question whether those norms exist or not. It is also the case that the inferential rules can allow the creation of *collective agents* (like firms, clubs, armies, states and so on), which have *their own* deontic scores, not reducible to the duties and rights of particular individuals. Of course, the *undertakings* of entitlements and commitments by a collective agent can only take place *through* the actions of some individuals (for collectives have no 'original' psychological states), according to the relevant inferential norms, but this does not entail that those commitments and entitlements are *not* those of the collective agent (e.g. if a firm has the duty of paying a bill in a year's time, this is not equivalent to a list of duties of their employees or their owners, for all these people can be replaced by others in the next twelve months; the duty to pay is a duty *of the firm*).

Furthermore, inferentialist models also recognise, in a way that rational choice models do not, another usual claim of the critiques of individualism in the social sciences, namely, that the way in which the social situation is *normatively structured* is a determinant of the situation's outcome (cf. Chapter 22). According to rational choice models, only individuals' beliefs and preferences, together with the 'real' constraints faced by them (costs, resources and so on), determine the solution of the model; at most, some norms are recognised to have a causal role in the sense that some physically possible actions are prohibited by social or legal norms, though, in the 'deepest' applications of the rational choice model, these prohibitions are also explained as endogenous outcomes of the equilibria in the game between agents. In inferentialist models, however, rules are double-faced; on the one hand, they are constitutively normative, irreducible to combinations of individual strategies, and pre-existing to individuals (who have to learn them in many cases before they become fully capable of *rational* reasoning and action); on the other hand, they only work when they are *learned* by the individuals, who have to

have a previous mastery of very complex cognitive abilities to be able even to interpret the behaviour of others as examples of rules. So, in this case as in the topic discussed in the previous paragraph, acknowledging that our models allow us to handle collective agents, collective commitments, transindividual norms and the like, does not force us to reject, nor to put within brackets, the *naturalist* stance on which the inferentialist models are built. I think the concept of 'institution' can represent in a more neutral way what inferentialism allows us to say about the natural realty of individuals and collectives. By an *institution* I mean a particular set of interrelated inferential norms connecting the normative scores of a group of agents (see Chapter 19). Some authors have defended a *communitarian* view according to which epistemic practices only make sense within groups or communities.[22] The schema depicted in the last paragraph is coherent to some extent with this communitarian view, but it also recognises that humans can only master a rich and meaningful system of inferential rules by learning it from others, and this is only possible thanks to the individual's ability to interpret the *behaviour* she is observing in others according to some patterns of thinking she must already have 'in her brain' (although the process of learning can substitute those patterns for others). The behaviour of other agents is always an 'external event' for you, and you cannot *see* the inferential norms your neighbours are following: the only thing you can do about it is to *guess* which norms they are, but in order to make sense of the others' behaviour as governed by some norms, you must first be able to discern whether your predictions about others' behaviour are fulfilled or not (e.g. how do you learn that 'no' means *no*?), and this ability is basically the same one that allows you to find out *physical* regularities in your environment and become angry or surprised when your predictions fail.[23] Your guessing the rules followed by others proceeds by trial and error, not necessarily until the actual inferential norms you master happen to be *identical* with those of your neighbours, but only until the moment when you have *no further reason to revise them*, and this can happen in a social state in which each individual has some *different* interpretation of the inferential norms from the one other members of the group may have. This view of inferential norms as more or less variable is consistent with the observation that communities do not constitute completely homogeneous clusters with immense differences with other communities, but more or less diffuse sets with gradual differences (cf. Chapter 11). Hence, institutions, societies or cultures are more an idealised description of clusters of interconnected social practices, than some monolithic collective entities which exist independently of individuals. Nevertheless, our schema does not only allow us to describe institutions as constituted by the interrelated norms of single individuals, but, as I said in the previous paragraph, it also permits us to describe some institutions as collective agents which have their *own* deontic scores and inferential norms. Institutions in the first sense are *collective practices*, whereas in the second sense they are *collective bodies*.

PLAYING GAMES WITH HERMENEUTIC AGENTS[24]

How would a couple (or more) of *homini deliberatores* behave when confronted with a situation that can be depicted in game-theoretic terms? In principle, it seems that the strategic rationality assumed in game theory and the hermeneutic rationality described in this paper are very different: the former is about choices determined by payoffs, whereas the latter is about doing what one has to do. But I shall try to show that, though there are differences, they are not too large, and the ones that exist, are worth being exploited. Much confusion on the philosophical (and technical) implications of game theory has derived from the fact

that, due perhaps to an excessive desire of simplification, or just to intellectual sleaziness, the usual description of a game (with the players and their possible strategies, on the one hand, and, on the other hand, the 'payoffs' got by the players depending on what combination of strategies is chosen) hides *three* different things behind the apparently simple concept of 'payoff'. First, there is the *outcome* (or expected outcome) of each player's choosing one particular strategy; this outcome is the, so to say, 'physical' or 'natural' *consequence*, or consequences, of the players' *actions*. Usually, simplified games just state how much money each player gets in that case; in general, it is a description of how the gains and losses from the game are *distributed*. Second, there is the *valuation* each player makes of those outcomes or distributions, or the *wellbeing* she would get in each case, or, in general, the *psychological* description of the situation.[25] And third, there is the (usually counterfactual) *description of the choices* each agent would make on the basis of those valuations, that is, her *behavioural* dispositions (in rational choice theory, this corresponds to the maximisation assumption: the option with the greatest payoff *will* be chosen). The first two elements are usually also mixed under the single concept of 'utility function' (they correspond to the elements (3) and (5) in the definition of a 'strategic-form game', in Chapter 15): in fact, the concept of utility function, as it is technically employed in rational choice theory and much of social science, exclusively represents 'revealed preferences'; that is, the fact that $u(A) > u(B)$ means only that the player *would choose* A if she were offered a choice between A and B (if utilities are in *numbers*, these only reflect how this choice would depend on the numerical probabilities of getting the consequences of the actions A and B, if these consequences are uncertain). The utility function does not reflect per se any kind of psychological degree of satisfaction which might be greater if the agent chooses A instead of B.

The prisoner's dilemma		Player B	
		Left	Right
Player A	Up	3 3	4 1
	Down	1 4	2 2

Figure 1   The prisoner's dilemma.

For example, when we examine the description of a game, like the prisoner's dilemma in Figure 1, and see that in one cell an agent gets a payoff of 3, and in another cell she gets 4, this *means* that, in describing the game in such a way, we are *assuming* that the agent would make a choice leading to the second cell if she had to opt between both. The question is, is that assumption *true*? If numbers are *also* assumed to represent thousands of euros, for example, then our hypothesis about the choice can obviously be true or false, depending on the player's valuations: if player B *actually* prefers the *distribution* of money given in the UL cell to the distribution in the UR cell, then she would not choose 'right', but 'left', if player A chose 'up', and this entails that the numbers reflecting the choice disposition of player B are *not* the ones given in the figure. As we saw in the second section, it can be the case that the real preferences of an agent include a concern for what *others* get, and so, we must understand the utilities or payoffs given in a game form as choices that agents would make *all-things-considered*, that is, as choices that take into account the player's total valuation of the *distributions* of gains and losses associated to each cell. We should give, in fact, two different tables in Figure 1: one representing the distribution of money associated to each cell, and another one representing the agents' valuations (that do not necessarily take only into account what an agent gets for herself) and their dispositions to choose (just if these dispositions are automatically identical to what follows from their wellbeing levels, what might not be: in case it is not, we would

need an additional table, one representing the chances of behaving in one way or another taking into account the valuations depicted in the second table). Figure 2 shows the valuations of the outcomes described in Figure 1, corresponding to agents having something like a Kantian moral sense (numbers represent here the valuation each agent makes of the distribution depicted in the same cell in Figure 1; the higher the number, the more valued a distribution is; different valuation would have emerged if, for example, each agent's utility function comprises as arguments, with different weights, the outcome got by each player).

If the player is a *homo deliberator*, whose reasoning and decision processes are subjected to inferential norms, then this just means that it is those reasoning processes what we must take into account for deciding what numbers to write in the second (or third) table describing the game. In the same way as there is no universal law giving, for each possible set of outcomes, a definite utility function, we cannot either offer a general hypothesis about what inferential norms (doxastic and practical) each person will obey. But in both cases (choice models based on utility functions, or on deontic scores) we can make reasonably simplified assumptions, based on limited generalisations about what we empirically know about real people. For example, common descriptions of games assume that people would simply prefer more money to less (what is true in many cases, and false in many other cases); and,

The prisoner's dilemma for 'Kantian' beings		Player B	
		Left	Right
Player A	Up	3 3	2 2
	Down	2 2	1 1

Figure 2   The prisoner's dilemma seen by players abiding by Kant's categorical imperative.

in the same way, we can assume that people examine many of the situations in which they participate, by trying to find out 'what they must do'. Usually, the task of finding out such a 'solution' to the game is carried out in a collective way, that is, by collective deliberation or 'communicative action' (cf. Chapter 26): each party offers reasons, and discusses or accepts the reasons offered by the others, till the point when the players agree in what is the 'cell' of the game that *must* be chosen, or find no further reasons to move each other's claim about what must be done. The practical inference for each player is, then, 'choose the option leading to that cell'. Technically, when there is an agreement on which is the 'best' cell, this usually transforms a non-cooperative game into a cooperative one.[26]

Naturally, two complications arise here. The first is that there is no guarantee that the collective process of deliberation leads to such an agreement, *even* if players are led by merely 'normative' considerations (e.g. they may have conflicting ethical values); in this case, in a game of more than two players it can be the case that some of them form coalitions that behave cooperatively within themselves, but non-cooperatively with the other coalitions. The second complication is that, as game theorists know well, a player's 'word' (or public commitment) is not always trustworthy, or, as we saw in above, the probability that an agent does what she is committed to do is not necessarily equal to one; so, the players have to take into account that, for each other agent, there is some probability that she fulfils her commitments and the inverse probability of her behaving in a merely strategic way.[27] So, what the inferentialist approach to rationality would suggest regarding the application of game theory to social situations is that these situations must be modelled in such a way that, in the first place, the *inferential norms* that allow the players to determine the values of each outcome must be made as explicit as possible. And second, a certain probability should be given to the hypothesis that players

will behave according to deliberational principles, and the inverse probability that they will behave in a merely strategic way;[28] this entails that the game must be decomposed not only into a description of the outcomes and a description of the valuations, but in the latter case we must also give *more than one* description of the valuations: one that follows from the collective application of inferential norms, and another which follows from the individual application of these norms, in order to take into account the cases in which no agreement is reached, or cooperative behaviour does not take place from the beginning. The analysis of the game must take into account all these possibilities, but this is not an insurmountable difficulty for game theory, nor something really uncommon in it.

INFERENTIALISM AS SOCIAL EPISTEMOLOGY

To end this proposal, I will mention that the inferentialist approach can also be useful to illuminate some problems in epistemology, and particularly in social epistemology. I shall just point here to a couple of examples.[29] First, the model allows us to understand the concept of 'knowledge' in a way that is not affected by the problems of its traditional definition as 'justified true belief'. Similar to the strategy of Craig (1990) of asking how the need for a concept like 'knowing' might have evolved in prehistoric times (instead of asking what 'knowledge' is), we may ask what is the inferential role that calling something 'knowledge' plays within deontic scorekeeping games. My hint is that 'knowledge' is basically a term of praise: we say (as agents *within* a game, not as philosophers examining the epistemic game from the *outside*) that somebody knows something when we are doxastically committed to the truth of what she says she knows (under circumstances that make us accept she is truthful, of course), and hence, to say that someone 'knows' is just a way of undertaking a commitment, or acknowledging a systematic way of inferring a commitment *for us* from a commitment *of her*. In a parallel way, you say that you *know* something when you think that you are *entitled* to 'pass' to the audience your own doxastic commitment to that statement, for example, because the evidence on which you base your opinion could be publicly displayed if necessary (and, *mutatis mutandis*, you say that you *believe* something when you don't think you are entitled to transfer your commitment in such a way to others, either because your commitment is not very strong, or because you are not capable of presenting the appropriate evidence).[30] So, saying that a commitment is a piece of knowledge means simply something about the *quality of the warrants* (according to what the inferential norms say that warrants *are*) that the speakers are able to display between them in the game of transferring commitments from agent to agent.[31]

The former is an explanation of what counts for an agent or a community to *take* something *as* knowledge. Another obvious epistemological question is how to *assess* this knowledge and the epistemic practices allowing us to attain it. An epistemic institution (i.e. a collection of interrelated inferential norms leading mainly to doxastic commitments) will objectively tend (under given circumstances) to produce commitments with some properties rather than ones lacking those properties; we can call *implicit epistemic values* those goals that an epistemic institution seems to be promoting (see Chapter 35 for an examination of the normativity issue within social epistemology). Of course, the agents can also have themselves an *explicit* view of which ones are the goals they are promoting through the application of their inferential norms. From a more or less simplistic perspective, we could say that, for the individual or the group considered, those claims are just the ones they think they *must* make, and so they don't need any *further* assessment than the one which is implicit in the constitution of that stock

of knowledge (i.e. the assessment implicit in *their* inferential norms). This view, however, would be simplistic because agents can reach a *defective* situation even according to their *own* standards (e.g. they can have misapplied the inferential norms, according to their own interpretation of them). A normative assessment of the set of claims attained by those agents could consist, then, in showing what other claims *would have been better* according to *their own* standards. But there is still a further step we can take, for we can make an assessment of the inferential norms themselves; after all, some norms can conflict with others, pulling into different directions, so to say, and we can try to identify in the set of criteria employed by the agents some 'metanorms' that help to solve this tension; or we can find out some argument showing that some goals the agents actually endorse would be promoted much more efficiently with a different set of inferential norms. Naturally, all this applies as well to the assessment of *our own* epistemic practices. So, epistemology, when it touches the basic philosophical question of what is it that a statement has to have in order to *deserve* to be taken as a doxastic commitment, reduces basically to the question of what are the 'best' epistemic practices, or inferential rules, *we* could have.

This idea is also helpful when applied to another old dispute in epistemology, that between rationalists and relativists. For it opens a new bridge between the position according to which all knowledge claims are biased by interests and prejudices and the position according to which there are objective and absolute standards of truth and certainty. This bridge consists in recognising both that knowledge claims always derive from *contingent* epistemic practices and rules, that might in principle be different for different groups or contexts *and* that the social scientists (and the philosophers as well) are themselves agents *committed* to certain epistemic norms. Hence, the fundamental role of deliberation in the pursuit of knowledge would consist in asking the other agents what would they *take* as 'knowledge', what ways of establishing a claim would they take as *appropriate*, what do they think would be persuasive for *them*, and afterwards engage in an epistemic practice that accords those standards. So, the goal of knowledge production is by no means that of establishing truths according to 'absolute' criteria, but to do it according to the criteria that *real* contenders would accept. One might object that this is too base a goal for science and philosophy, but this objection would be contested by simply demanding the standards to which the objector would defer.

The survey of approaches, theories and methods included in this handbook reflects, I think, how social sciences and their philosophical understanding are moving towards something similar to this deliberative paradigm. People working in different 'schools' are progressively more willing to use ways of reasoning that (at least according to their own understanding) approach those of 'rival' traditions, not least because of the flexibility allowed by new mathematical technologies (cf. Chapters 31 and 37), a flexibility that has contributed to blocking the old identification of certain schools with the application – or presumed impossibility of application – of a given corpus of maths. If this is just an optimistic illusion produced by the recent wealth of new software, or something that is going to change radically the way that social sciences are practised, is something that only time will tell.

NOTES

1 I am using the term 'hermeneutic' here in a rather wide sense; I admit that not every non-rational-choice approach in the social science is, literally speaking, a 'hermeneutic' one, but I think that the 'hermeneutics' label represents, particularly for philosophers, a quick way to concentrate on those few features that most non-rational-choice approaches share.

2 The divide between rational choice and hermeneutic approaches is more often perceived as referring to different 'decision mechanisms' each presupposes:

maximisation and rule-following, respectively. In a sense, I accept most of that line of thought in what follows (some classical criticisms to rational choice theory for not being able to deal with rule-following behaviour are Simon (1957), Sen (1970) and Vanberg (1994); see Lahno (2007) for a review; but I think that maximisation is not a deliberational mechanism that rational choice assumes people really use, it only assumes that the behaviour of the *agents* leads to the same outcome that the *social scientists* find as a solution to a maximisation problem, and is agnostic about the real cognitive process taking place in the 'heads' of the agents. By the way, it might perfectly well be the case that a set of psychological steps, each one consisting in a piece of rule following, might lead to the maximising solution (after all, what the social scientist does when solving the problem is to follow the rules of calculus). My suggestion is that the connection of each approach with the concept of normativity is a more essential difference between them.

3 What is more strange (to say the least), is how *little* empirical research to discover 'real' utility functions has been carried out, as compared to the effort put in building models based on 'convenient' assumptions on those functions. It is as if, in chemistry, after noting that the atomic and molecular weights of substances are essential data to be used in our formulae, almost no effort had been put into measuring the weights of *real* substances. I think the explanation of this apparent anomaly is that rational choice model builders assume that real utility functions vary a lot (not only from subject to subject, but from time to time), and they are trying to build their models with as few assumptions as possible, in order to give their models the *maximum applicability*, at the cost of a *reduced precision*.

4 Cf. for example, Gintis (2008).

5 This has some weird consequences in some branches of economics (e.g. rational expectation macroeconomics, and its derived approaches), where the assumption is often made that the agents already know the 'model' that the modeller is attempting to find! If this assumption is true, one can ask what is the added value of the modeller's work.

6 In psychology there is a parallel debate about the alternative models to the 'rationality-as-optimisation' paradigm derived from rational choice theory. Cf. Sahlin et al. (2010).

7 See, for example, Brandom (1994: 15).

8 Cf. op. cit., pp. 229 and ff.

9 Brandom's theory also demands the introduction of a different and parallel normative entity: *entitlements*, that according to him are *not* reducible to commitments by double negation (like in 'you are entitled to X if you are not committed to not doing X'), but the argument is complicated and is not necessary for the thesis I am proposing here. See Brandom (1994: 159 ff).

10 Op. cit., Chapter 4. A commitment to act is, hence, a 'reason for action' in the sense of Searle (2001).

11 Cf. Zamora Bonilla and del Corral (2008).

12 For some theories intending to do this, see, for example, Gärdenfors (1988) or Hansson (1999). For the connections between belief revision theory and economics, see Rott (2003).

13 Brandom (1994: 599 ff).

14 Brandom (1994: 26 ff).

15 For the applicability of these concepts (or some close to them) to formal models, and in particular to computer multi-agent models, see for example, Conte and Castelfranchi (2001) or Boella et al. (2008).

16 Op. cit., p. 626.

17 According to rational choice theory, it is irrational to choose actions probabilistically in such a way that, the higher the utility of an option, the higher the probability with which it is chosen; rather on the contrary, the only rational choice is deterministically identified with the option that gives the highest expected utility (because an aleatory choice will always have less utility on average than this option). But our case is completely different, for our notion of 'strength of commitment' must not be identified with 'utility' or 'expected utility'.

By the way, this notion of a probabilistic connection between an agent's degree of commitment with action X and her actually performing action X serves to illuminate John Searle's notion of 'the *gap*' (Searle, 2001: 61 and ff): the intuition that one's reasons for an action are not experienced as sufficient causes of the action itself; from the point of view defended here, the gap arises simply because the conscious process of deliberation modifies the agent's deontic score, but the action itself (including its phenomenological feeling of voluntariness) emerges out of a neural process of which the deontic score (i.e. one's degrees of commitment with this and with alternative actions) constitutes only a *partial* causal factor, the *rest* of the process being completely *unconscious* for the agent. This interpretation allows to account for the phenomenological description Searle offers of rational action, without the need of introducing metaphysical elements such as a 'substantial self' (whose own way of influencing the chain of physical processes leading to material actions remains obscure) or real gaps within the causal structure of the world (apart from the merely probabilistic indeterminacies that might depend on quantum events), and without concluding that consciousness is an epiphenomenon (since conscious deliberation has a real causal influence in modifying one's deontic score, which in turn affects unconsciously the probabilities of one's choosing an action or another).

18 Cf., Carruthers (2006), Evans (2008).

19 The combination of these elements within a model will usually have the form of a *Markov chain* (cf. Chapter 13): for each possible ordered pair of 'states of the world' (as described by the commitments each agent undertakes in them, and the rest of the relevant circumstances), we will have a certain probability of passing from the former to the latter. This allows us to calculate the probability of certain outcomes (subsets of states), given any initial situation. This technique is particularly appropriate for computer modelling.

20 Of course, I don't claim that deliberation according to inferential rules is not a causal process; only that it is just a *subclass* of the whole of psychological mechanisms underlying the dynamics of our cognitive states.

21 A paradigmatic explanation of joint commitments is in Gilbert (1996).

22 See for example, Kusch (2002).

23 More literally understood, this is not exactly true, for there are cognitive mechanism that are *specific* for the interpretation of some sensory evidence as a human being, as human action, or as a social situation; but these mechanisms enter into the same cognitive equipment we have been biologically – not socially – endowed to cope with our physical and social environment.

24 I thank José Luis Ferreira for comments and criticisms on a previous version of this section.

25 Of course, an agent's valuation of a situation is not the same thing as her wellbeing in that situation (she might value other things, apart from wellbeing).

26 Cf. Osborne and Rubinstein (1994: esp. Chapters 14 and 15).

27 Actually, this is also a simplification: we should add, at the least, the probability of the player not behaving 'rationally' neither in the hermeneutic nor in the strategic sense.

28 I am conscious of the fact that 'thinking strategically' is no less 'thinking' than engaging in a collective deliberation; so, we have to take into account that the reasoning process that one player adopts when she does not expect to find out a collective agreement about what is the best option, or when she does not want to cooperate in its achievement, can nevertheless be represented as an *inferential* process, as depicted in part II, save that in this case the 'active' commitments, those more probably leading to actual behaviour, will be those based on her personal *desires*.

29 See Zamora Bonilla (2006, 2010) for the application of the model to the philosophy of science.

30 By the way, these two *different* reasons why a doxastic commitment can not be transferable to other agents allow us to explain a curious paradox in the common use of the term 'belief': on the one hand, by saying that one believes something we can mean that she *is sure* of it (it is in this sense that we talk of knowledge as a *species* of belief, for example, as justified true belief); on the other hand, we can

also mean that one *is not sure* of what she believes (as when we speak of 'degrees of belief'). The first sense of 'belief' is the one preferred in analytical epistemology, and the second one in Bayesian epistemology. It is a curious fact that almost no philosophical research has been devoted to the question of why the term 'belief' can be used to mean two *contradictory* concepts.

31 The norms governing this transfer of commitments can relate to moves from individual to individual (as in testimony), or from the members of a group to the group itself as a collective agent (as in judgement aggregation or collective belief), or vice versa.

REFERENCES

Boella, G., L. van der Torre and H. Verhagen (eds) (2008) Special Issue on Normative Multiagent Systems, *Autonomous Agents and Multi-Agent Systems*, 17(1).

Brandom, R. (1994) *Making It Explicit*. Cambridge, MA: Harvard University Press.

Carruthers, P. (2006) *The Architecture of the Mind*. Oxford: Oxford University Press.

Conte, R. and C. Castelfranchi (2001) 'From conventions to prescriptions: Towards an integrated view of norms', *Artificial Intelligence and Law*, 7: 323–340.

Craig, E. (1990) *Knowledge and the State of Nature*. Oxford: Oxford University Press.

van Eemeren, F. and R. Grootendorst (2004) *A Systematic Theory of Argumentation: The Pragma-Dialectical Approach*. Cambridge: Cambridge University Press.

Evans, J.S.B.T. (2008) 'Dual processing accounts of reasoning', *Annual Review of Psychology*, 59: 255–278.

Gärdenfors, P. (1988) *Knowlede in Flux: Modeling the Dynamics of Epistemic States*. Cambridge, MA: The MIT Press.

Gilbert, M. (1996) *Living Together: Rationality, Sociality, and Obligation*. Lanham, MD: Rowman and Littlefield.

Gintis, H. (2008) *The Bound of Reason: Game Theory and the Unification of Behavioural Science*. Princeton: Princeton University Press.

Habermas, J. (1981) *Theorie des kommunikativen Handelns*. Frankfrut am Mein: Suhrkamp.

Hansson, S.O. (1999) *A Textbook of Belief Dynamics: Theory Change and Database Updating*. Dordrecht: Kluwer.

Kusch, M. (2002) *Knowledge by Agreement: The Programme of Communitarian Epistemology*. Oxford: Oxford University Press.

Lahno, B. (2007) 'Rational choice and rule following behaviour', *Rationality and Society*, 19(4): 425–450.

Osborne, M.J. and A. Rubinstein (1994) *A Course in Game Theory*. Cambridge, MA: The MIT Press.

Perelman, Ch. and L. Olbrechts-Tyteca (1958) *Traité de l'Argumentation: La Nouvelle Rhétorique*. Paris: Presses Universitaries de France.

Pettit, P. (2001) *A Theory of Freedom: From the Psychology to the Politics of Agency*. Oxford: Polity Press.

Rott, H. (2003) 'Economics and economy in the theory of belief revision', in Vincent F. Hendricks, Klaus F. Jørgensen und Stig A. Pedersen (eds) *Knowledge Contributor*. Dordrecht: Kluwer. pp. 57–86.

Sahlin, N.E., A. Wallin and J. Persson (2010) 'Decision science: From Ramsey to dual process theories', *Synthese*, 172: 129–143.

Searle, J.R. (2001) *Rationality in Action*. Cambridge, MA: The MIT Press.

Sen, A. (1970) *Collective Choice and Social Welfare*. San Francisco: Holden Day.

Simon, H.A. (1957) *Models of Man*. New York: John Wiley and Sons.

Toulmin, S. (1958) *The Uses of Argument*. Cambridge: Cambridge University Press.

Vanberg, V. (1994) *Rules and Choice in Economics*. New York: Routledge.

Walton, D. (2007) *Dialog Theory for Critical Argumentation*. Amsterdam: John Benjamins Publishers.

Zamora Bonilla, J.P. (2006) 'Science as a persuasion game: An inferentialist approach', *Episteme*, 2: 189–201.

Zamora Bonilla, J.P. (2010) 'Science: The rules of the game', *The Logic Journal of the IGPL*, 18: 294–307.

Zamora Bonilla, J.P. and M. del Corral (2008) 'Also sprach der homo oeconomicus', *Journal of Economic Methodology*, 15(3): 241–244.

Index

f denotes figure and ff denotes following pages.